BANKRUPTCY AND DEBTOR–CREDITOR LAW

CASES AND MATERIALS

SECOND EDITION

By

THEODORE EISENBERG
Professor of Law
Cornell University

Westbury, New York
THE FOUNDATION PRESS, INC.
1988

COPYRIGHT © 1984 THE FOUNDATION PRESS, INC.
COPYRIGHT © 1988 By THE FOUNDATION PRESS, INC.
                    615 Merrick Ave.
                    Westbury, N.Y. 11590

Library of Congress Cataloging-in-Publication Data

Eisenberg, Theodore.
  Bankruptcy and debtor-creditor law: cases and materials / by Theodore Eisenberg.—2nd ed.
    p. cm.—(University casebook series)
  Includes index.
  ISBN 0–88277–643–6
  1. Bankruptcy—United States—Cases. 2. Security (Law)—United States—Cases. 3. Debtor and creditor—
United States—Cases.

I. Title. II. Series.

KF1501.A7E36 1988
346.73'078—dc19
[347.30678]

                                                                    88–6938
                                                                       CIP

 TEXT IS PRINTED ON 10% POST
CONSUMER RECYCLED PAPER    Printed with Printwise
Environmentally Advanced Water Washable Ink

  Eisenberg—Bankr. & Debt.—Cred.Law 2nd Ed. U.C.B.
  2nd Reprint—1995

To
Lisa, Kate, and Annie

*

PREFACE

These materials attempt to probe general and unifying themes of debtor-creditor law. In covering Article 9 and state debt collection doctrine, they highlight and develop the connections between the two areas. The bankruptcy materials emphasize the relationship between bankruptcy law and state debtor-creditor law systems. In addition to the emphasis on basic themes of debtor-creditor law, I have tried to expand and upgrade the secondary materials relied upon to teach the subject. Existing debtor-creditor texts seem reluctant to deal in detail with scholarly ideas at the forefront of the field. Throughout the materials I have included excerpts from provocative or definitive works of recent scholarship.

The materials begin with Article 9 and Chapters 1–4 include the basic materials for an introduction to secured transactions. But the treatment of Article 9 also includes some interesting and challenging aspects of the subject that are not traditionally included in debtor-creditor teaching materials. *Leasing Consultants* (p. 200) combines questions about multistate transactions, the nature of leasing, and the nature of chattel paper. *Michelin Tires (Canada) Ltd.* (p. 156) explores the rights of the assignee of security. Despite the late Professor Gilmore's important article—"The Assignee of Contract Rights and His Precarious Security"—and the importance of assignee transactions in modern financings, one rarely finds this topic treated in basic Article 9 materials. *Miller v. Wells Fargo Bank International Corp.* (p. 217) helps to place the Article 9 apparatus in perspective both by addressing an important modern area in which Article 9 does not operate and by showing how courts must struggle when there are no Article 9-like rules to govern the details of a secured transaction.

The question of how to teach state law remedies is a difficult one. The issues depend heavily on state law, yet no law school course can efficiently explore all the important nuances that arise in various state provisions. Both from the standpoint of "learning the rules" and from the standpoint of assessing how those rules operate as part of the debtor-creditor system, it is useful to teach a particular state's system of creditors' remedies. The notes therefore emphasize the treatment of debt collection in two states, New York and California. In addition to their commercial importance, these states present contrasting approaches to the codification of creditors' remedies. New York employs relatively few provisions to deal with questions that now occupy hundreds of pages of the California Code of Civil Procedure.

Some instructors may wish to replace or supplement the coverage of New York and California law in Chapters 6 and 7 by concentrating on the law of another state. The notes and questions should remain useful in exploring the laws of any state but some supplementary statutory materials may be necessary. Other instructors may not wish to systematically study the laws of a particular state. The principal cases have been selected for their general interest and emphasis on the issues they raise should enable an instructor to highlight the central issues of debt collection without having to develop in depth any particular state's law.

Those who teach Article 9 as part of the debtor-creditor course (or whose students have knowledge of Article 9), may use Article 9 as a pedagogical foundation for the debt collection part of the course. One need not treat prejudgment attachment and post-judgment enforcement as subjects totally distinct from Article 9. Many, even most, attachment and enforcement problems correspond to problems that arise under Article 9. How does one create an interest in the debtor's property? May a creditor reach after-acquired property? May the creditor's interest be made secure as against third parties? Each of these inquiries, well known under Article 9, arises in the study of state law remedies.

The choice of California law as one vehicle for teaching state law remedies gives rise to further interaction between the Article 9 material and the material on state remedies. In many respects, California law now treats attachment and enforcement-of-judgments as variants of Article 9 security interests. New provisions in the California Code of Civil Procedure expressly adopt most of the key terms employed by Article 9. Article 9's system of classifying property is completely adopted. The California provisions also rely on Article 9 concepts to resolve priority battles, and contain an Article 9-like filing system. In sum, much of California's remedial system now presents an express unifying theme between Article 9 and creditors' remedies.

Chapter 6, entitled "Limitations on Debtors' Avoidance Efforts," has further goals. It tries to establish a theme, suggested by the title, that links several doctrinal areas within creditors' remedies. This theme is used later in Chapter 12 to explore the relationship between fraudulent conveyance doctrine and equitable subordination. See Clark, "The Duties of the Corporate Debtor to Its Creditors," 90 Harv.L.Rev. 505 (1977). The bulk transfer provisions contained in Article 6 of the U.C.C. also fit comfortably within the theme of protecting creditors against misbehavior by debtors.

I also believe that materials on fraudulent conveyance law may be reoriented towards modern problems that affect a wide range of corporate transactions. For example, most existing materials do not cover the validity of intercorporate guaranties, a fraudulent conveyance problem faced by every major (and many minor) law firms. *Zellerbach Paper Co. v. Valley National Bank* and *In re Ollag Construction Equip. Corp.* are included in Chapter 6 as vehicles through which the intercorporate guaranty problem may be explored.

Chapters 9–17 cover bankruptcy. If oftens seems forgotten that bankruptcy law is not a totally independent system of substantive federal law through which claims of creditors are handled. At bottom, bankruptcy is little more than a federal procedure through which to vindicate state-created rights. The bankruptcy portions of the book are designed to constantly probe this theme. Beginning with issues dealt with early in the bankruptcy chapters (for example, involuntary bankruptcy proceedings in Chapter 10) the materials introduce and pursue the central theme of the relationship between federal and state law in bankruptcy. As the federal-state theme has important implications for questions of jurisdiction and forum, I have included in Chapter 17 materials on bankruptcy court jurisdiction.

There is, of course, more to bankruptcy than a single theme. If creditors view it in part as a mechanism for adjusting state law rights, debtors enjoy the benefits of discharge that only federal bankruptcy law provides. In probing the discharge theme (Chapter 13), I have tried, through the Weistart excerpt, to encourage teachers and students to place the bankruptcy discharge against the larger background of contract law to which it is so fundamentally related.

Passage of the new Bankruptcy Act presents the opportunity to explore at least one new theme—the extent to which the new act in fact improves upon the old one. As the materials in Chapter 10 on involuntary bankruptcy proceedings and the assets of the estate suggest (see also the materials covering the new preference exceptions in Chapter 14), it is not clear that the new act always captures the spirit of what a bankruptcy law should be better than the old act did.

The new act strengthens one theme that is both practically important and theoretically interesting. To what extent should a creditor be able to choose a form of transaction that avoids potential entanglements with the debtor's trustee in bankruptcy? Many provisions of the new act operate to keep non-bankrupt parties unwillingly locked into deals with bankrupts (see §§ 541, 362, 365—Chapters 10 and 11). Yet other provisions and decisions leave creditors some room to plan to avoid dealing with the debtor in the event of bankruptcy. The weapons employed to assist creditors in avoiding the trustee include letters of credit, state trust law, escrow deposits, and other devices. Despite the common goal of all these devices, one usually finds little specific treatment of them and no unifying notes on the general theme of avoiding dealings with the trustee. See Chapter 11D.

In assembling these materials I have benefitted from the works of many authors. In addition to those listed in the "Acknowledgments" section, I would like to note my debt to the following authors and works: V. Countryman, Cases and Materials on Debtor and Creditor (2d ed. 1974), D. Epstein & J. Landers, Debtors and Creditors (2d ed. 1982), S. Riesenfeld, Creditors' Remedies and Debtors' Protection (2d ed. 1979), and W. Warren & W. Hogan, Cases on Debtor-Creditor Law (2d ed.

1981). A different sort of debt is owed to L. Eisenberg & K. Hall, Chicken Jokes and Puzzles (1978).

I also would like to thank Brian Gaj, Cornell Law School Class of 1984, and James McShane, Cornell Law School Class of 1985, for their able research assistance. Generous financial support was provided by Dean Peter Martin and the Cornell Law School. My deepest thanks must go to Karen Wilson for her cheerful, efficient, and skillful preparation of the manuscript.

Course Coverage. These materials were developed while teaching a four semester-hour debtor-creditor law course. In recent years I have omitted the material covered by Chapters 5 and 8 and have excluded selected other topics. I have not taught the materials in Chapter 17. In addition, some of the materials may be more suitable for background reading than for extensive class coverage. I usually assign Chapter 1 prior to the first class and cover it only on that day. I assign most of Chapter 9 as background reading. In the years that I have reached the material in Chapter 16, I assign the Bonbright excerpt as background reading and do not cover it in class. In some recent years, I have done the same with the Schwartz excerpt at the beginning of Chapter 12.

For those who do not cover Article 9 in a debtor-creditor course, Chapters 5–17 provide more than enough material for a three semester-hour course on other aspects of debtor-creditor law. For those who teach a course on secured transactions, there is enough material for a two semester-hour course and, with selected additions from the bankruptcy provisions that most affect secured creditors, there may be enough material for a three hour course.

Statutory Supplement. I recommend that instructors assign The Foundation Press statutory supplement entitled, "Commercial and Debtor-Creditor Law: Selected Statutes" (available spring 1984). The supplement has been designed to take account of this book's coverage and includes the U.C.C., the Bankruptcy Act, and all relevant state laws covered in Chapters 6 and 7. The supplement also includes all statutory provisions needed in teaching most courses on commercial law. Therefore, students who purchase it should not find it necessary to purchase a second statutory supplement for other commercial law courses.

THEODORE EISENBERG

Ithaca, New York
November, 1983

PREFACE TO THE SECOND EDITION

This edition employs the same organization as the first edition. Only minor changes have been made in Part I (Secured Transactions). More substantial updating occurs in Part II (Debt Collection). Especially noteworthy is the development of fraudulent conveyance case law in complex corporate transactions. The potential applicability of fraudulent conveyance doctrine to leveraged buyouts has attracted much interest. These matters are pursued through new cases in Chapter 6.

Bankruptcy law under the 1978 Act continues to develop rapidly. A growing number of Supreme Court and Courts of Appeals decisions resolve old issues and raise new ones. The Supreme Court's decision in *Timbers of Inwood Forest* (in Chapter 11) answers important questions about the scope of adequate protection that secured creditors enjoy. Where possible, the case law in Part III has been significantly reworked to provide leading cases that discuss the 1978 Act.

The Foundation Press's statutory supplement, "Commercial and Debtor-Creditor Law: Selected Statutes", which is periodically updated, continues to supply all statutory materials needed in courses based on this book.

Users are invited to send comments to the author.

THEODORE EISENBERG

Ithaca, New York
March 1988

*

EDITING CONVENTIONS AND ABBREVIATIONS

Unless otherwise indicated, footnotes contained in quoted material, including cases, retain their original numbers. Footnotes added by the author are designated by letters of the alphabet. Footnotes and citations in quoted materials have been deleted without indication. Citation forms sometimes have been modified, also without indication. Ellipses indicate the deletion of textual material.

To conserve space and enhance readability, the following abbreviations are employed:

Commission Report—Report of the Commission on the Bankruptcy Laws of the United States, H.R.Doc. No. 93–137, pts. I & II, 93d Cong., 1st Sess. (1973)

Gilmore—G. Gilmore, Security Interests in Personal Property (1965) (2 vols.)

House Report—H.R.Rep. No. 95–595, 95th Cong., 1st Sess. (1977)

Senate Report—Sen.Rep. No. 95–589, 95th Cong., 2d Sess. (1978)

*

ACKNOWLEDGMENTS

I gratefully acknowledge the permission extended by the following authors and publishers to reprint excerpts from the works indicated:

Baird & Jackson, Fraudulent Conveyance Law and Its Proper Domain, 38 Vand.L.Rev. 829, 832–36, 850–54 (1985), copyright 1985 Vanderbilt Law Review.

J. Bonbright, The Valuation of Property 233–66 (1937), McGraw-Hill, Inc.

Clark, Abstract Rights Versus Paper Rights Under Article 9 of the Uniform Commercial Code, 84 Yale L.J. 445–47, 473–79 (1975), reprinted by permission of the Yale Law Journal Company and Fred B. Rothman & Company from *The Yale Law Journal*, Vol. 84, pp. 445–47, 473–79.

Clark, The Duties of the Corporate Debtor to Its Creditors, 90 Harv.L.Rev. 505, 506–13, 519–20, 530–31 (1977), copyright © 1977 by the Harvard Law Review Association.

Clark, The Interdisciplinary Study of Legal Evolution, 90 Yale L.J. 1238, 1250–54 (1981), reprinted by permission of the Yale Law Journal Company and Fred B. Rothman & Company from *The Yale Law Journal*, Vol. 90, pp. 1238, 1250–54.

Coogan, Article 9—An Agenda for the Next Decade, 87 Yale L.J. 1012, 1014–16, 1030–36 (1978), reprinted by permission of the Yale Law Journal Company and Fred B. Rothman & Company from *The Yale Law Journal*, Vol. 87, pp. 1012, 1014–16, 1030–36.

Coogan, The New UCC Article 9, 86 Harv.L.Rev. 477, 544–50 (1973), copyright © 1973 by The Harvard Law Review Association.

Coogan, Is There A Difference Between A Long-Term Lease and An Installment Sale of Personal Property?, 56 N.Y.U.L.Rev. 1036, 1045–49, 1055 (1981), copyright 1983 by Matthew Bender & Co., Inc., and reprinted with permission from UCC Secured Transactions.

Countryman, Executory Contracts in Bankruptcy: Part I, 57 Minn.L.Rev. 439, 450–52, 458–61 (1973).

Countryman, The Use of State Law in Bankruptcy Cases, Part I, 37 N.Y.U.L.Rev. 407, 473–74 (1972).

W. Davenport & D. Murray, Secured Transactions (1978) 22–23, 23–30, 198–99, 401–07, copyright 1978 by the American Law Institute. Reprinted with the permission of the American Law Institute-American Bar Association Committee on Continuing Professional Education.

Eisenberg, Bankruptcy Law in Perspective, 28 UCLA L.Rev. 953, 972–73, 963–66, 996 (1981).

G. Gilmore, Security Interests in Personal Property (1965) 6, 7, 288–93, 1286–89, 1290, 1298, Little, Brown and Company.

Gilmore, The Purchase Money Priority, 76 Harv.L.Rev. 1333, 1337–38 (1963), copyright © 1963 by The Harvard Law Review Association.

G. Glenn, Fraudulent Conveyances and Preferences §§ 37, 39 (rev.ed.1940), The Lawyers Co-operative Publishing Co.

T. Jackson, The Logic and Limits of Bankruptcy Law 47–49, 154–55, 228–37, 243, 255–57 (1986). Harvard University Press.

Jackson, Bankruptcy, Non-Bankruptcy Entitlements, and the Creditors' Bargain, 91 Yale L.J. 857, 864, 866, 872–75, 902–06, 893–96, 896–97 (1982), reprinted by permission of The Yale Law Journal Company and Fred B. Rothman & Company from *The Yale Law Journal*, Vol. 91, pp. 857, 864, 866, 872–75, 902–06, 893–96, 896–97.

Kennedy, Automatic Stays Under the New Bankruptcy Law, 12 U.Mich.J.L.Ref. 3, 10 (1978), copyright © 1978 by the University of Michigan Law School, reprinted by permission of the University of Michigan Journal of Law Reform.

Kronman, The Treatment of Security Interests in After-Acquired Property Under the Proposed Bankruptcy Act, 124 U.Pa.L.Rev. 110, 144–47 (1975).

Landers, A Unified Approach to Parent, Subsidiary, and Affiliate Questions in Bankruptcy, 42 U.Chi.L.Rev. 589, 599 (1976), © 1976 by the University of Chicago. Reprinted by permission from 42 U.Chi.L.Rev. 589 (1976).

Landers, Another Word on Parents, Subsidiaries and Affiliates in Bankruptcy, 43 U.Chi.L.Rev. 527, 536–38 (1976), © 1976 by the University of Chicago. Reprinted by permission from 43 U.Chi.L.Rev. 527 (1976).

Phillips, Flawed Perfection: From Possession to Filing Under Article 9—Part I, 59 B.U.L.Rev. 1, 47 (1979).

Plumb, The Federal Priority in Insolvency: Proposals for Reform, 70 Mich.L.Rev. 12–14 (1971).

Posner, The Rights of Creditors of Affiliated Corporations, 43 U.Chi.L.Rev. 499, 518, 523–24 (1976), © 1976 by the University of Chicago. Reprinted by permission from 43 U.Chi.L.Rev. 499 (1976).

Riesenfeld, Collection of Money Judgments in American Laws—A Historical Inventory and A Prospectus, 42 Iowa L.Rev. 155, 156–63 (1957), copyright 1957, University of Iowa (Iowa Law Review).

ACKNOWLEDGMENTS

Schwartz, Security Interests and Bankruptcy Priorities: A Review of Current Theories, 10 J.Leg.St. 1, 2, 7–13, 22–25, 27–28, 30–31 (1981), © 1981 by the University of Chicago.

Shimm, The Impact of State Law on Bankruptcy, 1971 Duke L.J. 879, 881–94, copyright 1971, Duke University School of Law.

Treister, Bankruptcy Jurisdiction: Is It Too Summary?, 39 S.Cal.L.Rev. 78, 78–81.

R. Trost, G. Treister, L. Forman, K. Klee & R. Levin, The New Federal Bankruptcy Code (1979), pp. 237, 239, 241, 243, copyright 1979 by The American Law Institute. Reprinted with the permission of the American Law Institute-American Bar Association Committee on Continuing Professional Education.

Weistart, The Costs of Bankruptcy, 41 L. & Contemp.Prob. 107, 108–12 (1977), copyright 1977, Duke University School of Law.

Whitford, Structuring Consumer Protection Legislation to Maximize Effectiveness, 1981 Wis.L.Rev. 1018–19, 1022–24, © 1981 Wisconsin Law Review.

Discussion, 41 L. & Contemp.Prob. 123, 169–70 (1977), copyright 1977, Duke University School of Law.

Note, Security Interests in Notes and Mortgages: Determining the Applicable Law, 79 Colum.L.Rev. 1414, 1415 (1979), copyright © 1983 by the Directors of the Columbia Law Review Association, Inc. All rights reserved. This article originally appeared at 79 Colum.L.Rev. 1414, 1415 (1979). Reprinted by permission.

*

SUMMARY OF CONTENTS

*

TABLE OF CONTENTS

TABLE OF CONTENTS

Page

TABLE OF CONTENTS

Page

*

TABLE OF CASES

Principal cases are in italic type. Cases cited or discussed are in roman type. References are to Pages.

TABLE OF STATUTES

TABLE OF STATUTES

TABLE OF STATUTES

xli

BANKRUPTCY AND DEBTOR–CREDITOR LAW

CASES AND MATERIALS

*

Part I

SECURED TRANSACTIONS

Chapter 1

INTRODUCTION

A. Introduction to Debtor–Creditor Law

Given a choice, most people prefer being repaid to not being repaid. Fortunately, most debtors repay their debts without involving the legal process or requiring creditors to resort to contractual remedies. Much of this book is about steps creditors may take to limit the risks of nonrepayment and to coerce repayment.

A creditor wishing to reduce the risk of a debtor's default may require the debtor to furnish collateral (also called security) to reinforce the repayment obligation. If the debtor does not repay, the creditor applies the collateral against the defaulted loan obligation. A creditor who obtains such collateral or security is a secured creditor and the contractual right to take collateral in the event of default is a security interest. A bank that holds a mortgage on a home is a form of secured creditor. (When the collateral consists of real property, however, different terminology is used. Lenders with loans secured by real property receive "mortgages" or "deeds of trust," not "security interests.") Part I of this book covers the creation, perfection and enforcement of security interests in personal property.

Most extensions of credit are not secured by collateral and those that initially are secured may become unsecured because of loss or diminution in value of the collateral. The unsecured creditor who is owed money may try informal methods of persuasion to induce a debtor to repay, including a lawyer's letter or employment of a debt collection agency. If informal pressure fails to induce repayment, the creditor may abandon its claim or resort to formal enforcement mechanisms, such as the filing of a lawsuit. Part II of this book focuses on creditors' efforts to collect amounts allegedly owed them. Loosely stated, it deals with two questions: (1) what steps may a creditor take to assure that any judgment ultimately recovered will in fact be satisfied? (2) once a judgment is obtained, what steps must and may the judgment creditor take to enforce the judgment?

The creditors emphasized in Parts I and II share many characteristics. When a judgment creditor obtains a specific interest in a debtor's property, the judgment creditor becomes a close cousin of the secured creditor. They both have interests in specific property of the debtor to

1

enforce monetary claims against the debtor. The origins of their claims, however, are significantly different. [The secured creditor obtains an interest in the debtor's property through a consensual contractual arrangement with the debtor. The judgment creditor obtains its interest in the debtor's property as the result of successful prosecution of a lawsuit and enforcement of the resulting judgment.]

There are other ways in which creditors obtain interests in debtors' property. An interest in property granted by a statute (often called a "lien") is the most important other way. By operation of law (in this case a federal statute), the United States has a lien on all the property of taxpayers who fail to pay their taxes. See Chapter 8. States grant themselves similar rights to secure payment of state taxes. Garagemen and construction workers usually have liens against property to secure payment for work done on property. See Chapter 14D. Attorneys may have liens on their clients' papers to secure payment of attorneys' fees.

The statement that secured creditors, judgment creditors, and statutory lienholders have rights in specific property (sometimes each of these interests may be called a lien) is vague. What does it mean to have an interest in property or a lien on that property? The statement may mean different things in different contexts. Often it means that the person having the lien may seize the property (or have the sheriff seize it on his behalf) and apply it to satisfaction of his debt. It also may mean that a transfer of the property by the debtor will be made subject to the creditor's interest. One cannot sell one's mortgaged home without paying off the bank or making some other arrangement to satisfy the bank. Otherwise, a buyer's interest is subject to that of the bank. Sometimes the lien will take priority over the rights of one group of transferees and be subordinate to the rights of another group of transferees. These matters are explored throughout the book.

As the above suggests, there are many ways in which creditors may obtain interests in specific property of debtors. Given the ease with which some such interests arise (mere agreement is all that is needed to create a consensual lien or security interest), and the variety of such interests, many situations arise in which more than one creditor asserts a lien or interest in a single piece of the debtor's property. Much of debtor-creditor law is devoted to ranking competing creditor interests in the same property. See, e.g., Chapter 3. There is a need for ranking whether the competing interests arise from the same source (as when the debtor grants a security interest in the same collateral to two different creditors) or from different sources, as when one creditor obtains an interest in property through one branch of debtor-creditor law (for example, by virtue of a statutory lien), and the other creditor obtains an interest in the same property through a different branch of debtor-creditor law (for example, by enforcing a judgment).

Part III of the book deals with collective proceedings affecting debtors and creditors. Federal bankruptcy law dominates this area and provides the exclusive mechanism through which a debtor may be relieved permanently of debts. Bankruptcy law also tries to provide an orderly setting in which competing claims to the debtor's limited pool of assets may be fairly ranked and satisfied. Chapter 9 contains a more detailed introduction to bankruptcy law.

B. Introduction to Secured Transactions

1. Early Security Devices

IN RE GERMAN PUBLICATION SOCIETY

United States District Court, Southern District of New York, 1922.
289 F. 509, affirmed 289 F. 510.

In Bankruptcy. In the matter of the German Publication Society, bankrupt. On petition to review decision of referee adverse to Crombie & La Mothe, Inc. Petition dismissed.

LEARNED HAND, DISTRICT JUDGE. It is everywhere agreed that the significant distinction between a pledge and a mortgage is that in the first the creditor gets no title, but what is vaguely called a "special property," while in the second he does. Although no pledge is good without the pledgee's possession, the converse is not true of chattel mortgages, under which the goods sometimes do, and always may, pass at once into the mortgagee's possession. If only the forms of the transaction were observed by the courts, it would be easy to distinguish a pledge from a mortgage, because any absolute grant must be a mortgage, and any other agreement for security must be a pledge.

No such convenient rule can be drawn from the books. In the case of choses in action like shares of stock it was early held that a transfer, though absolute in form, might be a pledge. Wilson v. Little, 2 N.Y. 443, 51 Am.Dec. 307, a case recently followed in White River Bank v. Capital Bank, 77 Vt. 123, 59 Atl. 197, 107 Am.St.Rep. 754. This was explained on the theory that, as there could be no delivery of possession unless the title had also passed, absolute formal title did not necessarily mark the transaction as a mortgage.

However, when the same question came up as to chattels in cases where the writing contained an absolute transfer, some courts ruled that that transaction also was a pledge. Walker v. Staples, 5 Allen (Mass.) 34; Thompson v. Dolliver, 132 Mass. 103; Copeland v. Barnes, 147 Mass. 388, 18 N.E. 65; Petition of Chattanooga Savings Bank (C.C.A. 6th) 261 Fed. 116. In Wright v. Ross, 36 Cal. 414, the court even went so far as to hold an assignment a pledge which had a defeasance in the body of it. In Gandy v. Collins, 214 N.Y. 293, 108 N.E. 415, the assignment appears to have been absolute and was held to be a mortgage, but that may well have been, and probably was, because the creditor had not taken possession.

It seems to me very difficult to find any rule which the cases will bear out, and the whole matter floats nebulously in that fog, "the intent of the parties," out of which courts are so apt to evoke what they most want. Still I suppose that we may use only the words of the parties themselves, and in the case at bar I find it pretty difficult to see how they could have been more definite in making this a mortgage. It is true the language is inartificial, but the defeasance clause is present as clearly as though it had been drawn by a conveyancer. It is, of course, possible always to say that, when possession is delivered at the time of execution, the transaction is a pledge. That would be a clear rule, but it would not be true. Unless one is prepared to go so far, I cannot see anything but the hardship of the result, which should move me to ignore the form in which these parties chose to express their purposes.

. . .

Order affirmed; petition to review dismissed.

1 GILMORE, SECURITY INTERESTS IN PERSONAL PROPERTY 6–7 (1965)

The distinction between mortgage and pledge was of considerable importance in determining the rights of the parties to the security transaction or of third parties affected by it. The pledgor's right to redeem the collateral from the pledgee after default and before foreclosure was firmly established at law at a time when the mortgagor's comparable right was available only in equity. Thus, if the action to recover the property were brought at law, the creditor could win at least a temporary victory (and perhaps a permanent one if laches barred the equity action) by proving himself a mortgagee. Contrariwise, in equity, the creditor's strategy would be to prove himself a pledgee so that, since there was an adequate remedy at law, the action would not lie. It may also be true that the degree of possession required of a mortgagee who elected to perfect his mortgage by taking possession was less than the possession required to perfect a pledge. In most states either a pledge or a mortgage could be perfected subsequently to the creation of the security interest, but even within the same state the effect of such late perfection might be one thing for pledge and quite a different thing for mortgage. Thus in New York a late perfecting mortgagee was vulnerable to the claims of general creditors which accrued before perfection; such creditors could levy on the mortgaged property after perfection and despite knowledge of it. The New York pledge rule, on the other hand, was that a late perfecting pledgee could be defeated only by good faith purchasers or by creditors who procured a lien on the property before the pledgee took possession. In other states a mortgage had to be perfected, if at all, within a certain period after execution while there was no comparable time limitation for the pledge. Finally in many jurisdictions the rules for foreclosure of mortgages differed from the rules for foreclosure of pledges; thus if a creditor had disposed of the property under the pledge rules, it might be possible to hold him (perhaps, for conversion) on the theory that the transaction had been a mortgage, or vice versa.

The courts never devised a workable rule for making the distinction between pledge and mortgage on which so many important issues turned. Perhaps a workable rule was the last thing that was wanted; so long as the grounds on which the distinction was made remained impenetrably obscure, there was room for judicial maneuver which may have led to doing rough justice between the parties at, to be sure, some harm to the idea of commercial certainty.

HUGHBANKS, INC. v. GOURLEY
Supreme Court of Washington, 1941,
12 Wn.2d 44, 120 P.2d 523.

STEINERT, JUSTICE.

Plaintiff Hughbanks Incorporated, claiming to be the owner and entitled to the immediate possession of certain automotive machinery, instituted a claim and delivery proceeding under Rem.Rev.Stat. § 573, to procure the surrender thereof from defendant W.B. Severyns, sheriff of King county, who had theretofore taken the machinery from one Elmer W. Findley pursuant to a writ of attachment previously issued in a civil action for debt brought by defendant R.C. Gourley against Findley. Defendant Gourley appeared in opposition to plaintiff's claim. Upon a summary trial by the court without a jury, findings and conclusions were rendered, pursuant to which the court entered a judgment declaring plaintiff to be the legal owner and entitled to the possession of the machinery, free and clear of any right, title, interest, lien, or claim of defendants, or either of them. Both defendants have appealed, although the contest is actually between plaintiff Hughbanks Incorporated, hereinafter designated respondent, and defendant R.C. Gourley, to whom we shall henceforward refer as though he were the sole appellant.

The present controversy between these parties is the outgrowth of a transaction originally had between respondent and Elmer W. Findley concerning a Cletrac tractor and an hydraulic "bulldozer" attachment which together comprise the property here involved. The legal effect of that transaction constitutes the basic dispute between the contesting parties. Respondent's position herein is that the transaction was in fact, as well as in form, a conditional sale of the property by it to Findley. Appellant's contention, on the other hand, is that the transaction, though in form a conditional sale, was in legal effect a chattel mortgage to secure a loan from respondent to Findley of funds with which to purchase the tractor and attachment from a third party.

At all times pertinent to this case respondent has been engaged in a general finance and investment business. Prior to April 26, 1940, Findley, who was engaged in a business involving the moving of earth, had purchased from respondent, under a conditional sale contract, a tractor equipped with a "bulldozer" attachment. Findley desired, however, to get a newer and better tractor thus equipped, although he had not yet completed his payments on the old one. After some inquiry and investigation he located a suitable tractor and attachment then owned by one Claude Williams, who had purchased the machine from Pacific

Hoist & Derrick Co. Findley inspected the entire equipment and discussed the price with Williams, but he did not have the money with which to purchase it. He therefore sought the assistance of respondent and succeeded in effecting an arrangement with the latter's vice-president whereby respondent agreed to purchase the Williams' machine and immediately sell it to Findley on conditional sale contract. Findley was to turn in his old tractor and attachment and receive credit in the sum of five hundred dollars on the contract. In furtherance of this arrangement, respondent agreed to pay Williams thirteen hundred dollars in cash for his machine and to deliver to him Findley's old tractor and attachment valued at five hundred dollars. At the same time, Williams arranged to purchase another new machine from Pacific Hoist & Derrick Co. to replace the one which he was selling to respondent.

In accordance with the arrangements agreed upon, Findley surrendered his old machine to respondent, whose officers in turn had him deliver it to Pacific Hoist & Derrick Co. At approximately the same time, Williams executed to respondent a bill of sale of his tractor and attachment and delivered the machinery at a vacant lot, owned by respondent or an affiliated company, on the outskirts of Seattle, where Findley was directed by respondent to take possession of it. Respondent issued its check for thirteen hundred dollars to Williams, who immediately indorsed it over to Pacific Hoist & Derrick Co. to apply on his purchase of a new tractor. On the same day, and as part of the arrangements effected, respondent and Findley executed a written agreement, in form a conditional sale contract, whereby respondent agreed to sell and Findley agreed to purchase the tractor and attachment which Williams had purportedly sold and delivered to respondent at its premises. The purchase price designated in the contract was $2,030, against which Findley was given a credit of five hundred dollars for his old tractor and attachment, leaving a balance of $1,530 to be paid by Findley in monthly installments of one hundred dollars. The contract did not call for any interest on the deferred installments. It will be observed that the total amount which Findley was to pay respondent under the alleged conditional sale contract was two hundred thirty dollars more than the amount which respondent had paid Williams for the same tractor and attachment.

The purported conditional sale contract contained the usual provision with reference to retention of title by the seller until the full purchase price should be paid, with authorization to respondent to retake possession of the tractor at any time or place if Findley should fail to make any of the agreed monthly payments and, in such event, to retain all payments theretofore made by Findley, as rental for the use of the property and as liquidated damages. Upon these terms and conditions, Findley was allowed to take the Williams tractor and attachment from the premises where Williams had made delivery to respondent.

At the time the property was seized by the sheriff under appellant's writ of attachment, Findley was not in arrears in any of his installment payments. Having posted a bond, pursuant to the statute, and taken possession of the machine from the sheriff, respondent sold the property to a party not involved in this action.

At the trial, appellant, on cross-examination of respondent's officers, elicited the information that respondent was primarily engaged in the investment business and had only occasionally acted as a broker or distributor of personal property. He established, furthermore, that respondent's officers did not even know from whom they had purported to purchase the tractor and attachment which they contend they later sold to Findley. The two officers both asserted that they had acquired the machine from Pacific Hoist & Derrick Co., and neither of them was clear as to the position of Williams, who was in fact the true owner of the equipment in question. It was also made clear in the course of such cross-examination that no one connected with respondent had ever seen the tractor and attachment prior to the alleged purchase thereof from Williams, and, further, that the machine had been resold to Findley even before it had been delivered to respondent as mentioned above. Respondent's officers and Findley himself, however, testified that the agreement between them was exactly as evidenced by the conditional sale contract itself, and that Findley had agreed to purchase the tractor and equipment from respondent on a monthly installment basis because he was financially unable to purchase the same property direct from Williams for cash. Under his arrangement with respondent, the difference between the price at which respondent bought the property and the price at which it sold to Findley was claimed by respondent to represent its profit on the transaction. The trial court found in accordance with respondent's contentions and rendered judgment accordingly.

This court has held that it is not the office of a conditional bill of sale to secure a loan of money. Its purpose, rather, is only to permit an owner of personal property to make a bona fide sale on credit, reserving title in himself, for security, until the purchase price is fully paid. Lyon v. Nourse, 104 Wash. 309, 176 P. 359. This particular security device, with its severe remedial incidents, is not favored in the law and its use has been restricted to situations where persons standing in the actual relation of vendor and vendee have desired to effect a credit sale. It is in such cases that it finds its only legitimate use.

Where, on the other hand, one who is the owner of a particular chattel wishes to borrow money and is willing to let the chattel stand as security for his debt, a chattel mortgage is the appropriate means for affording such protection to the creditor. And this is as true where the property mortgaged is purchased with the borrowed funds as where it has long been in the borrower's possession.

Cases have arisen in this state in which attempts have been made to employ a conditional bill of sale to secure the interest of one who, though purporting to sell the chattel involved, merely lends money to facilitate its purchase from a third person. But this court has uniformly refused to sanction such a misuse of the conditional bill of sale. Thus in Lyon v. Nourse, supra, one who lent money to take up the draft attached to the bill of lading for a car consigned to his borrower tried to secure his loan by giving the latter a conditional bill of sale covering the car. This court held that the lender could not in this way secure the payment of his debt without the formalities required by the statutes governing the execution of chattel mortgages. See, also, Mahon v. Nelson, 148 Wash. 110, 268 P. 144, where a similar attempt to make a conditional bill of sale perform the function of securing the repayment of money was also held improper. . . .

rule

The cases above discussed or cited establish the rule that any attempt to employ a conditional bill of sale for the purpose of securing money lent will not receive judicial sanction, regardless of the intention of the parties so to use it. The problem is not one of determining whether the parties intended to mould their transaction into the form of a conditional sale rather than that of a chattel mortgage, but of deciding whether in a pure financing arrangement the conditional sale can ever be adopted as a means of securing a loan. And the answer is that the contract of conditional sale may be used only by an actual vendor in the economic sense, and not by one who in a particular transaction occupies the status of a financier or lender of money, even though the latter may go through the form of taking title and possession of the chattel which he purports to sell, as respondent has done in this case. To permit the use of the conditional sale by mere lenders of money would enable them not ony to avail themselves of the extraordinary remedies of the conditional vendor but also to evade the provisions of the usury laws by marking up the "price" charged to the borrower so as to include, in the guise of a "profit," a return in excess of that permitted by law.

In the light of these rules the conclusion is inevitable that, as to the tractor and attachment here involved, respondent does not come within the class of those entitled to employ a conditional bill of sale as a means of security. This conclusion does not rest solely on the fact that respondent is primarily engaged in the finance and investment business, although that fact may raise an initial question as to the validity of its resort to a conditional sale in any case. The use of the conditional sale contract is not restricted to merchants; it may be employed by anyone who actually makes a sale and assumes the risks incident to the business of selling goods. In the course of its regular business respondent might on occasion be forced to take over property in order to protect its equity therein, and in such cases, having assumed the risks of ownership, it would be entitled to sell such property under contracts of conditional sale. But that is not the case here. Findley located the tractor and attachment, discussed terms with the owner thereof, and then called on respondent for the necessary financial assistance. Despite the care exercised in routing title through itself and in taking technical possession of the tractor, respondent was a mere moneylender in a financing arrangement incident to a sale of the tractor and attachment by Williams to Findley. We therefore hold that despite the intention of the parties to cast their transaction in the form of a conditional sale, their purpose cannot be recognized and given effect.

In consequence of the foregoing conclusion, it follows that, as between respondent and Findley, the attempted conditional sale gives rise to a chattel mortgage, the validity of which, as to third persons, is dependent upon the statutes governing the execution and filing of such mortgages. . . .

Notes & Questions

1. *The Importance of the Proper Security Device.* In *Hughbanks,* why did it matter whether the transaction was viewed as a conditional sale or as a chattel mortgage? One of the goals of Article 9 is to eliminate the numerous, sometimes overlapping, preexisting security devices. How does Article 9 address the problem posed by *German Publication Society* and *Hughbanks?* See §§ 1–201(37), 9–102(2).

2. *Goals of the Law.* What should be the other goals of a personal property security law?

2. The Background to Article 9

1 GILMORE, SECURITY INTERESTS IN PERSONAL PROPERTY 288–93 (1965)

§ 9.1. **The background.** In the growth of the law there are periods of relative stability and periods of rapid change. The introduction of some radically new element into a stable situation leads to a pendulum-like swing from simplicity to complexity and then, as the new element becomes assimilated, back towards simplicity. In the field of personal property security law the new element, which became apparent in the course of the nineteenth century, was the demand that all types of personal property be made available as security even though, because of the nature of the property or because of its intended use, it was not possible or feasible for the lender to take it in pledge. This demand ran counter to long-established rules of law which had, like all rules of law, made sense against the background out of which they had evolved. These rules had restricted the assignability of choses in action outside the narrow limits of negotiable instruments law and had required a visible change of possession as a condition of an effective security interest in chattels. It is not surprising that the process of replacing these rules with their opposites caused a disturbance in the law which has been working itself out for more than a hundred years. Nor is it surprising that the rules were whittled away, sliver by sliver, instead of being all at once disposed of. The whittling-away process led, as exceptions grew and new devices flourished, to a state of law of extraordinary complexity in which a transaction relatively simple in itself had become fragmented into bits and pieces. It was predictable that the long period of disintegration would be succeeded by a movement toward synthesis, a putting back together of the scattered pieces.

Article 9 of the Commercial Code is an attempt at such a synthesis. However, revolutions, in law as in politics, merely record what has, imperceptibly, already taken place. If, for convenience, 1950 is taken as the date of Article 9, it can be fairly said that the movement toward a synthesis had been in process for fifty years. By 1900 or thereabouts most types of personal property had become available as security, with or without a pledge. The old rules had stood up longest in the fields of inventory and intangibles. Their breakdown in inventory—under the trust receipt, under field warehousing, under the factor's lien—had been followed by a corresponding breakdown in intangibles as accounts receivable financing became established and as long-term receivables followed short-term accounts into the security pattern. As the old rules lost their vitality, the unity which underlay the apparent diversity of the system of independent security devices imposed its own logic. The first and most striking evidence of an inarticulate awareness of the essential similarity of all personal property security transactions was the statutory fusion of the conditional sale and the chattel mortgage—preserved as separate devices under separate statutes but now fitted into the same pattern and made for most purposes indistinguishable. The similarity of pattern became even more marked as the inventory devices, and, somewhat later, assignments of accounts receivable, reached their statutory maturity. In a sense the unified structure of personal property security law had already been built: all that remained was to knock down the scaffolding which had been a temporary necessity during construction. Article 9 is not so much a new start or a fresh approach as it is a reflection of work long since accomplished.

§ 9.2. **Some drafting history.** In the course of drafting, Article 9 went through a process not unlike that which has just been outlined in connection with the history of personal property security law. The idea which the draftsmen started with was that the system of independent security devices had served its time; that the formal differences which separated one device from another should be scrapped and replaced with the simple concept of a security interest in personal property; that all types of personal property, whether held for use or for sale, should be recognized as available for security. Their initial analysis, however, assumed that various types of financing transactions were so diverse that each would have to be dealt with in a separate statute: the principal difference between the Secured Transactions Article and pre-Code law was conceived to be that the distinctions assumed to be necessary would be made along "functional" rather than "formal" lines. That is, instead of a chattel mortgage statute, a conditional sales statute, a trust receipt statute, and so on, there would be a statute devoted to each major type of financing. The traditional differentiation between possessory (pledge) and nonpossessory interests was accepted without question. The nonpossessory interest was thought to be divisible into five major categories, according to the type of property used as collateral or the use which the collateral served. The five categories were: (1) inventory and accounts receivable financing; (2) financing on the security of long-term intangibles or "contract rights;" (3) industrial or business equipment financing; (4) agricultural financing; (5) consumer goods financing. The category of equipment financing was thought of as a residual catch-all; any transaction which did not fall under one of the other categories would be treated as if it involved industrial equipment. In the light of this analysis, the draftsmen set out to prepare six interrelated but essentially separate statutes—one on pledge and one on each of the nonpossessory categories; the earliest drafts set out these statutes as "Parts" of the Article.

Everything has to start somewhere; only in myth does Minerva spring fully armed from Jove's brow. [One defect of the drafting approach just outlined was that it required an exceedingly elaborate classification of the types of collateral which would fall into one or another of the slots of the six-fold division.] Goods alone had to be subdivided four ways, according to whether they were "inventory" (the basic idea was goods held for sale, although other types of use came in to complicate the definition), "equipment" (goods held for use by a business, plus anything not covered by some other definition), "farm products (crops, livestock and so on in the possession of a farmer) or "consumer goods" (goods held for use by an individual primarily for personal, family or household purposes). The idea of treating short-term receivables financing and long-term receivables financing in separate Parts led to definitions of the short-term "account" and the long-term "contract right." Acceptance of the distinction between the possessory and nonpossessory interest further required definitions of intangibles which could be pledged: these were "instruments" (very broadly defined in language inspired by the Uniform Trust Receipts Act), "documents" (bills of lading, warehouse receipts and the like) and "chattel paper" (for example, a conditional sale contract—a writing which evidences both a money obligation and an interest in specific goods). Even this five-fold subdivision of intangibles was found to be inadequate. A sixth, or catch-all, category was eventually added under the name of "general intangibles" (any intangible personal property not covered by one of the other definitions). The introduction of "general intangibles" was evidently an improvement over the simple-minded idea that all unclassifiable intangibles should be treated as equipment.

As the drafts of the planned series of separate statutes took shape, it became apparent that the differences in the several types of financing were by no means as great as the initial analysis had assumed. Each statute or "Part" tended to become substantially a repetition of the others. Eventually the idea of six separate statutes was abandoned and the Article was redrafted as one statute, in a series of Parts devoted to such major subdivisions as the Validity of Security Agreements, the Perfection of Security Interests, the Rights of Third Parties, Filing, and Default. This reorganization made largely irrelevant the painstakingly precise definitions which had been a necessary feature of the earlier scheme. Unfortunately, however, the draftsmen and their advisers had by this time lived with the definitions so long and had become so accustomed to picking their way through the definitional jungle that it never occurred to anyone to see whether the classifying definitions could not usefully be consigned to oblivion. The Article in its final form clung grimly to its four-fold classification of goods and its six-fold classification of intangibles. Anyone who approaches the Article for the first time will do well to bear in mind that the forbidding string of definitions in Part 1 of the Article can for most purposes be disregarded. The classification plays its principal role in the Parts which deal with perfection of the security interest and with the mechanics of filing, comes in to some extent in the priority sections, and makes a final appearance in the Part on Default.

3. The Vocabulary of Article 9

Article 9 unifies several systems of personal property security law. In so doing, it establishes its own vocabulary for identifying and discussing secured transactions. An early effort to master Article 9's vocabulary will facilitate understanding modern secured transactions.

Every secured transaction shares certain features. There always will be: (1) a *debtor* (§ 9–105(1)(d)), the person who borrows money and grants an interest in property to secure repayment; (2) a *secured party* (§ 9–105(1)(m)), the person who extends credit and who is granted a security interest; (3) a *security interest* (§ 1–201(37)), the interest in property that the borrower (debtor) grants to the extender of credit (secured party) to secure repayment; and (4) *collateral* (§ 9–105(1)(c)), the property subject to the security interest. As the Gilmore excerpt indicates, Article 9 divides collateral into several subcategories. See Comment 3 to § 9–105. A secured transaction also usually requires a *security agreement* (§ 9–105(1)(*l*)), the agreement in which the debtor grants the secured party a security interest in the collateral.

Section 9–105(1) contains most of Article 9's definitions. Section 9–105(2) contains a useful index of definitions covering terms defined elsewhere in Article 9. Other important definitions may be found in the U.C.C.'s general definition provision, § 1–201.

Chapter 2

THE SECURITY INTEREST

A. Creating the Security Interest

1. The Security Agreement

IN RE BOLLINGER CORP.

United States Court of Appeals, Third Circuit, 1980.
614 F.2d 924.

ROSENN, CIRCUIT JUDGE.

This appeal from a district court review of an order in bankruptcy presents a question that has troubled courts since the enactment of Article Nine of the Uniform Commercial Code (U.C.C.) governing secured transactions. Can a creditor assert a secured claim against the debtor when no formal security agreement was ever signed, but where various documents executed in connection with a loan evince an intent to create a security interest? The district court answered this question in the affirmative and permitted the creditor, Zimmerman & Jansen, to assert a secured claim against the debtor, bankrupt Bollinger Corporation in the amount of $150,000. We affirm.

I.

The facts of this case are not in dispute. Industrial Credit Company (ICC) made a loan to Bollinger Corporation (Bollinger) on January 13, 1972, in the amount of $150,000. As evidence of the loan, Bollinger executed a promissory note in the sum of $150,000 and signed a security agreement with ICC giving it a security interest in certain machinery and equipment. ICC in due course perfected its security interest in the collateral by filing a financing statement in accordance with Pennsylvania's enactment of Article Nine of the U.C.C.

Bollinger faithfully met its obligations under the note and by December 4, 1974, had repaid $85,000 of the loan leaving $65,000 in unpaid principal. Bollinger, however, required additional capital and on December 5, 1974, entered into a loan agreement with Zimmerman & Jansen, Inc. (Z&J), by which Z&J agreed to lend Bollinger $150,000. Z&J undertook as part of this transaction to pay off the $65,000 still owed to ICC in return for an assignment by ICC to Z&J of the original note and security agreement between Bollinger and ICC. Bollinger executed a promissory note to Z&J, evidencing the agreement containing the following provision:

Security. This Promissory Note is secured by security interests in a certain Security Agreement between Bollinger and Industrial Credit Company . . . and in a Financing Statement filed by [ICC]

13

. . ., and is further secured by security interests in a certain security agreement to be delivered by Bollinger to Z and J with this Promissory Note covering the identical machinery and equipment as identified in the ICC Agreement and with identical schedule attached in the principal amount of Eighty-Five Thousand Dollars. ($85,000).

No formal security agreement was ever executed between Bollinger and Z&J. Z&J did, however, in connection with the promissory note, record a new financing statement signed by Bollinger containing a detailed list of the machinery and equipment originally taken as collateral by ICC for its loan to Bollinger.

Bollinger filed a petition for an arrangement under Chapter XI of the Bankruptcy Act in March, 1975 and was adjudicated bankrupt one year later. In administrating the bankrupt's estate, the receiver sold some of Bollinger's equipment but agreed that Z&J would receive a $10,000 credit on its secured claim.

Z&J asserted a secured claim against the bankrupt in the amount of $150,000, arguing that although it never signed a security agreement with Bollinger, the parties had intended that a security interest in the sum of $150,000 be created to protect the loan. The trustee in bankruptcy conceded that the assignment to Z&J of ICC's original security agreement with Bollinger gave Z&J a secured claim in the amount of $65,000, the balance owed by Bollinger to ICC at the time of the assignment. The trustee, however, refused to recognize Z&J's asserted claim of an additional secured claim of $85,000 because of the absence of a security agreement between Bollinger and Z&J. The bankruptcy court agreed and entered judgment for Z&J in the amount of $55,000, representing a secured claim in the amount of $65,000 less $10,000 credit received by Z&J.

Z&J appealed to the United States District Court for the Western District of Pennsylvania, which reversed the bankruptcy court and entered judgment for Z&J in the full amount of the asserted $150,000 secured claim. The trustee in bankruptcy appeals.

II.

Under Article Nine of the U.C.C., two documents are generally required to create a perfected security interest in a debtor's collateral. First, there must be a "security agreement" giving the creditor an interest in the collateral. Section 9–203(1)(b) contains minimal requirements for the creation of a security agreement. In order to create a security agreement, there must be: (1) a writing (2) signed by the debtor (3) containing a description of the collateral or the types of collateral. Section 9–203, Comment 1. The requirements of section 9–203(1)(b) further two basic policies. First, an evidentiary function is served by requiring a signed security agreement and second, a written agreement also obviates any Statute of Frauds problems with the debtor-creditor relationship. Id. Comments 3, 5. The second document generally required is a "financing statement," which is a document signed by both parties and filed for public record. The financing statement serves the purpose of giving public notice to other creditors that a security interest is claimed in the debtor's collateral.

Despite the minimal formal requirements set forth in section 9–203 for the creation of a security agreement, the commercial world has frequently neglected to comply with this simple Code provision. Soon after Article Nine's enactment, creditors who had failed to obtain formal security agreements, but who nevertheless had obtained and filed financing statements, sought to enforce secured claims. Under section 9–402, a security agreement may serve as a financing statement if it is signed by both parties. The question arises whether the converse is true: Can a signed financing statement operate as a security agreement? The earliest case to consider this question was American Card Co. v. H.M.H. Co., 97 R.I. 59, 196 A.2d 150, 152 (1963) which held that a financing statement could *not* operate as a security agreement because there was no language *granting* a security interest to a creditor. Although section 9–203(1)(b) makes no mention of such a grant language requirement, the court in *American Card* thought that implicit in the definition of "security agreement" under section 9–105(1)(h) was such a requirement; some grant language was necessary to "create or provide security." This view also was adopted by the Tenth Circuit in Shelton v. Erwin, 472 F.2d 1118, 1120 (10th Cir. 1973). Thus, under the holdings of these cases, the creditor's assertion of a secured claim must fall in the absence of language connoting a grant of a security interest.

The Ninth Circuit in In re Amex-Protein Development Corp., 504 F.2d 1056 (9th Cir. 1974), echoed criticism by commentators of the *American Card* rule. The court wrote: "There is no support in legislative history or grammatical logic for the substitution of the word 'grant' for the phrase 'creates or provides for'." Id. at 1059–60. It concluded that as long as the financing statement contains a description of the collateral signed by the debtor, the financing statement may serve as the security agreement and the formal requirements of section 9–203(1)(b) are met. The tack pursued by the Ninth Circuit is supported by legal commentary on the issue. See G. Gilmore, Security Interests in Personal Property, § 11.4 at 347–48 (1965).

Some courts have declined to follow the Ninth Circuit's liberal rule allowing the financing statement alone to stand as the security agreement, but have permitted the financing statement, when read in conjunction with other documents executed by the parties, to satisfy the requirements of section 9–203(1)(b). The court in In re Numeric Corp., 485 F.2d 1328 (1st Cir. 1973) held that a financing statement coupled with a board of directors' resolution revealing an intent to create a security interest were sufficient to act as a security agreement. The court concluded from its reading of the Code that there appears no need to insist upon a separate document entitled "security agreement" as a prerequisite for an otherwise valid security interest.

> A writing or writings, regardless of label, which adequately describes the collateral, carries the signature of the debtor, and establishes that in fact a security interest was agreed upon, would satisfy both the formal requirements of the statute and the policies behind it.

Id. at 1331. The court went on to hold that "although a standard form financing statement by itself cannot be considered a security agreement, an adequate agreement can be found when a financing statement is considered together with other documents." Id. at 1332.

In the case before us, the district court went a step further and held that the promissory note executed by Bollinger in favor of Z&J, standing alone, was sufficient to act as the security agreement between the parties. In so doing, the court implicitly rejected the *American Card* rule requiring grant language before a security agreement arises under section 9–203(1)(b). The parties have not referred to any Pennsylvania state cases on the question and our independent research has failed to uncover any. But although we agree that no formal grant of a security interest need exist before a security agreement arises, we do not think that the promissory note standing alone would be sufficient under Pennsylvania law to act as the security agreement. We believe, however, that the promissory note, read in conjunction with the financing statement duly filed and supported, as it is here, by correspondence during the course of the transaction between the parties, would be sufficient under Pennsylvania law to establish a valid security agreement.

III.

We think Pennsylvania courts would accept the logic behind the First and Ninth Circuit rule and reject the *American Card* rule imposing the requirement of a formal grant of a security interest before a security agreement may exist. When the parties have neglected to sign a separate security agreement, it would appear that the better and more practical view is to look at the transaction as a whole in order to determine if there is a writing, or writings, signed by the debtor describing the collateral which demonstrates an intent to create a security interest in the collateral. In connection with Z&J's loan of $150,000 to Bollinger, the relevant writings to be considered are: (1) the promissory note; (2) the financing statement; (3) a group of letters constituting the course of dealing between the parties. The district court focused solely on the promissory note finding it sufficient to constitute the security agreement. Reference, however, to the language in the note reveals that the note standing alone cannot serve as the security agreement. The note recites that along with the assigned 1972 security agreement between Bollinger and ICC, the Z&J loan is "further secured by security interests in a certain Security Agreement

to be delivered by Bollinger to Z&J with this Promissory Note, ...
(Emphasis added.) The bankruptcy judge correctly reasoned that "[t]he
intention to create a separate security agreement negates any inference
that the debtor intended that the promissory note constitute the security agreement."   At best, the note is some evidence that a security
agreement was contemplated by the parties, but by its own terms,
plainly indicates that it is not the security agreement.

Looking beyond the promissory note, Z&J did file a financing
statement signed by Bollinger containing a detailed list of all the
collateral intended to secure the $150,000 loan to Bollinger.   The
financing statement alone meets the basic section 9–203(1)(b) requirements of a writing, signed by the debtor, describing the collateral.
However, the financing statement provides only an inferential basis for
concluding that the parties intended a security agreement. There
would be little reason to file such a detailed financing statement unless
the parties intended to create a security interest. The intention of the
parties to create a security interest may be gleaned from the expression
of future intent to create one in the promissory note and the intention
of the parties as expressed in letters constituting their course of
dealing.

The promissory note was executed by Bollinger in favor of Z&J in
December 1974. Prior to the consummation of the loan, Z&J sent a
letter to Bollinger on May 30, 1974, indicating that the loan would be
made "provided" Bollinger secured the loan by a mortgage on its
machinery and equipment. Bollinger sent a letter to Z&J on September 19, 1974, indicating:

> With your [Z&J's] stated desire to obtain security for material
> and funds advanced, it would appear that the use of the note would
> answer both our problems. Since the draft forwarded to you offers
> full collateralization for the funds to be advanced under it and bears
> normal interest during its term, it should offer you maximum
> security.

Subsequent to the execution of the promissory note, Bollinger sent to
Z&J a list of the equipment and machinery intended as collateral under
the security agreement which was to be, but never was, delivered to
Z&J. In November 1975, the parties exchanged letters clarifying
whether Bollinger could substitute or replace equipment in the ordinary course of business without Z&J's consent. Such a clarification would
not have been necessary had a security interest not been intended by
the parties. Finally, a letter of November 18, 1975, from Bollinger to
Z&J indicated that "any attempted impairment of the collateral would
constitute an event of default."

From the course of dealing between Z&J and Bollinger, we conclude
there is sufficient evidence that the parties intended a security agreement to be created separate from the assigned ICC agreement with
Bollinger. All the evidence points towards the intended creation of
such an agreement and since the financing statement contains a

detailed list of the collateral, signed by Bollinger, we hold that a valid Article Nine security agreement existed under Pennsylvania law between the parties which secured Z&J in the full amount of the loan to Bollinger.

. . . The judgment of the district court recognizing Z&J's secured claim in the amount of $150,000 will be affirmed. . . .

Notes & Questions

1. *Basic Statutory Structure.* The discussion in *Bollinger,* upholding the validity of the asserted security interest, masks the underlying statutory structure that makes the existence of the security interest important. Assuming that Article 9 settles the matter, what is it in Article 9 that makes the outcome in *Bollinger* turn on whether there is a security agreement? The court alludes to § 9–203(1)'s requirement of a security agreement. Does § 9–203 say that, in the absence of a security agreement, a lender loses to the trustee in bankruptcy? See §§ 9–201, 9–301 to 9–305.

2. *Security Agreement and Financing Statement.* Note that even though Z & J, the lender in *Bollinger,* did not require a new security agreement, it did file a financing statement. Why? What is the role of the financing statement and how does it differ from the security agreement? See § 9–302.

3. *Security Agreement Alone.* If Z & J had received a proper security agreement but had not filed a financing statement how would it have fared in its battle with Bollinger's trustee in bankruptcy? Please read §§ 9–201 and 9–301 to 9–303 and try to be able to trace the statutory steps that support the following assertion: "If Z & J had not filed a financing statement, it would have lost its battle with the bankruptcy trustee."

4. *Formality.* Section 9–203 sets forth the formalities required to create an enforceable security interest. As between the debtor and the secured party, should any greater formality be required than is required in other contracts?

5. *The Context of Priority Battles.* Note the context in which the dispute in *Bollinger* arose. The case does *not* involve a dispute between the debtor and a lender over whether a security interest existed. Nor does it involve a dispute between some actual lender and Zimmerman & Jansen over who is entitled to priority in Bollinger's assets. Instead, the dispute is between Zimmerman & Jansen and Bollinger's trustee in bankruptcy. In fact, disputes with bankruptcy trustees are probably the most common context in which the validity of security interests is tested. As you will see in Chapter 14, the trustee in bankruptcy is endowed with the rights of a lien creditor on the date of bankruptcy. Bankruptcy Act § 544(a). Article 9 endows the trustee with a similar status in § 9–301(3).

Should courts' attitudes towards technical flaws in security interests (particularly those courts that do not allow informal substitutes for security agreements) vary depending upon the context in which a security interest is challenged? Should the U.C.C.'s approach to the problem vary according to context?

. . .

Most secured lenders do obtain security agreements. From time to time it may be helpful to have one in front of you. The following agreement is taken from W. Davenport & D. Murray, Secured Transactions (1978).

Security Agreement

This Agreement is entered into this 1st day of June 1977, between No-Fault Discount, Inc. ("Debtor"), whose address is set forth below, and Last Chance Bank, Any Town, Illinois ("Secured Party").

1. *Definitions.* When used herein, the following terms shall have the following meanings:

a. "Account Receivable" shall include any and all accounts, notes, drafts, and general intangibles consisting of rights to payment, whether now existing or hereafter arising or acquired, all as defined in the Illinois Uniform Commercial Code.

b. "Account Debtor" shall mean any party who is obligated on any Account Receivable.

c. "Eligible Account Receivable" shall mean an Account Receivable that meets each of the following requirements: (i) it arises from the sale or lease of goods or performance of services and such goods have been shipped or delivered or such services have been rendered to the Account Debtor; (ii) it is a legally enforceable obligation of that Account Debtor, without setoff or counterclaim; (iii) it is not subject to any lien or security interest whatsoever, other than the security interest hereunder; (iv) it is evidenced by an invoice rendered to that Account Debtor; (v) that Account Debtor is not one whose obligations Secured Party, in its sole discretion, shall have previously notified Debtor in writing are not deemed to constitute Eligible Accounts Receivable; and (vi) any payment due hereunder is not in arrears for more than ninety (90) days from the date which the invoice bears. An Account Receivable that is at any time an Eligible Account Receivable shall cease to be an Eligible Account Receivable whenever it ceases to meet any one of the foregoing requirements.

d. "Inventory" shall mean all goods, merchandise, and other personal property, now owned or hereafter acquired by Debtor, held for sale or lease, or furnished or to be furnished under any contract of service, or held as raw materials, work in process, or materials used or consumed, or to be used or consumed, in business.

e. "Invoice" shall mean a bill submitted to an Account Debtor for goods sold or services rendered on or before the date which it bears. Each invoice shall indicate the time when and location where such goods were shipped or delivered or services were performed and the amount due therefor, and shall, on its face, be due not more than 30 days after the date which it bears.

2. *Grant of Security Interest: Collateral.* To secure the Obligations described in paragraph 3 Debtor hereby assigns to Secured Party all of Debtor's

rights in connection with, and grants to Secured Party a security interest in the following personal property ("Collateral"):

a. All Inventory of Debtor now owned or hereafter acquired;

b. All returned, rejected or repossessed goods, whether now owned or hereafter acquired, which were Inventory before sale;

c. All Accounts Receivable of Debtor now existing or hereafter arising or acquired;

d. All proceeds of the foregoing, including all proceeds of any insurance covering the Inventory; and

e. Any other property of Debtor in the possession of Secured Party at the time of any default by Debtor.

3. *Obligations.* The obligations secured by this Agreement ("Obligations") are the following:

a. Any and all sums due to Secured Party, pursuant to the terms of any Schedule now attached or hereafter identified to this Agreement;

b. Any and all sums advanced by Secured Party in order to preserve the Collateral or to perfect its security interest in the Collateral;

c. In the event of any proceeding to enforce the collection of the Obligations, or any of them, after default, the reasonable expenses of retaking, holding, preparing for sale or lease, selling or otherwise disposing of or realizing on the Collateral, or of any exercise by Secured Party of its rights in the event of default, together with reasonable attorneys' fees and court costs; and

d. Any other indebtedness or liability of Debtor to Secured Party, whether direct or indirect, joint or several, absolute or contingent, now or hereafter existing while this Agreement is in effect, however created or arising and however evidenced.

4. *Representations, Warranties, and Promises.* Debtor further represents, warrants and agrees:

a. The Debtor is the owner of the Collateral and grants the security interest herein in consideration of Secured Party's loan, the proceeds of which Debtor hereby acknowledges receipt.

b. Debtor will not hereafter grant a security interest in, or sell the Collateral to, any other person, firm or corporation.

c. Debtor will at all times defend the Collateral against any and all claim[s] of any person adverse to the claims of Secured Party.

d. Debtor will take such action and execute such documents as Secured Party may from time to time request to maintain a perfected security interest on the part of Secured Party in the Collateral (free of all other liens and claims whatsoever) to secure payment of the Obligations.

e. Debtor will use the Collateral in conformity with all applicable laws and will pay all taxes and assessments on it or its use when due.

f. Debtor has full power and authority to enter into this Agreement.

g. Debtor will furnish to Secured Party within ninety (90) days after each fiscal year of Debtor (which ends June 30, 1977) a copy of the annual audit report and audited statements (balance sheet and profit and loss statement) of Debtor prepared in conformity with generally accepted accounting principles applied on a basis consistent with that of the preceding fiscal year. Debtor will also furnish to Secured Party within ninety (90) days after the close of each fiscal quarter, a copy, similarly prepared, of its unaudited financial statement for such quarter, signed by a proper accounting officer of Debtor.

h. In case of failure by Debtor to procure or maintain insurance, or to maintain the Collateral, or to pay any fees, assessments, charges or taxes arising with respect to the Collateral, all as herein specified, the Secured Party shall have the right, but shall not be obligated to effect such insurance, or cause the Collateral to be maintained, or pay such fees, assessments, charges or taxes, as the case may be, and, in that event, the cost thereof shall be payable by Debtor to the Secured Party immediately upon demand together with interest at the rate of 8 per cent from the date of disbursement by the Secured Party to the date of payment by the Debtor.

i. Except for the security interest granted hereby, the Collateral is free from any lien, security interest, encumbrance, or other right, title, or interest of any other person, firm or corporation.

j. Debtor shall keep the Inventory insured against loss or damage by fire (with extended coverage), theft, physical damage, and against such other risks, including without limitation public liability, in such amounts, in such companies and upon such terms as Secured Party may reasonably require. Debtor will obtain loss payable indorsements on applicable insurance policies in favor of Debtor and Secured Party as their interests may appear and will deposit the insurance policies with the Secured Party. Debtor shall cause each insurer to agree, by indorsement on the policy or policies or certificates of insurance issued by it or by independent instrument furnished to Secured Party, that such insurer will give thirty (30) days written notice to Secured Party before such policy will be altered or cancelled. The proceeds of any insurance from loss, theft, or damage to the Inventory shall be held, disbursed and applied as Secured Party may see fit, either in reduction of the Obligations or applied toward the repair, restoration or replacement of the Inventory. Debtor irrevocably appoints Secured Party as Debtor's attorney in fact to make any claim for, to negotiate settlement of claims, to receive payment for and to execute and indorse any documents, checks or other instruments in payment for loss, theft, or damage under any insurance policy.

k. Debtor's business is the selling of merchandise. The Inventory Collateral consists of appliances, furniture and clothing.

l. All Inventory Collateral covered by this Agreement is and will be kept at the following location only: 330 North Wabash Street, Chicago, Illinois. All records concerning Accounts Receivable Collateral are, and will be, kept at the following location only: 330 North Wabash Street, Chicago, Illinois. Debtor's chief executive office is located at 330 North Wabash Street, Chicago, Illinois. Inventory Collateral or records concerning Accounts Receivable Collateral shall not be removed to, or kept at, any another place without the prior written consent of Secured Party. If Collateral is at any time kept or located at locations other than those above listed, Secured Party's security interest therein shall continue.

m. All records concerning the Accounts Receivable are, and will be, kept at the following location only: 330 North Wabash Street, Chicago, Illinois. Records concerning the Accounts Receivable shall not be removed to, or kept at, any other place without the prior written consent of Secured Party. Debtor's chief executive office is located at 330 North Wabash Street, Chicago, Illinois.

n. At the time an Account Receivable becomes Collateral under this Agreement the Account Receivable will be a valid, undisputed, *bona fide* indebtedness incurred by the Account Debtor for merchandise sold to or services performed for the Account Debtor by Debtor. There will be no setoffs or counterclaims against any such Account Receivable. No agreement under which deduction or discount (other than a trade discount for prompt payment) may be claimed will be made with an Account Debtor except with the prior written consent of Secured Party.

o. Debtor will permit Secured Party to inspect the Collateral and any books and records of Debtor relating thereto at any time during regular business hours and to verify Accounts Receivable, or any of them, by any method satisfactory to Secured Party.

p. Debtor will prepare and furnish schedules of Accounts Receivable on a form, and at regular intervals, satisfactory to Secured Party.

q. Debtor will, if the amount of unpaid indebtedness under this Agreement exceeds 80 per cent of the combined amount of Inventory and Eligible Accounts Receivable, provide Secured Party upon its request at any time, within 30 days after such request, with additional collateral satisfactory to Secured Party or reduce the Obligations by payment in cash of the excess.

r. Debtor will, from time to time as Secured Party may request, furnish Secured Party with a certificate in the form attached hereto as Exhibit A and with such other information relevant to this Agreement and Debtor's performance thereunder as Secured Party may request.

5. *Right of Secured Party To Collect Accounts Receivable.* Debtor authorizes Secured Party to notify any and all Account Debtors (whether or not Debtor is in default) to make payment directly to Secured Party. Debtor agrees to deliver to Secured Party promptly upon receipt thereof, in the form in which received (together with all necessary indorsements), all payments received by Debtor on account of any Account Receivable. Secured Party may apply all such payments against Debtor's Obligations or at Secured Party's option to Debtor's checking account.

6. *Authorization To Sell Inventory.* As long as Debtor is not in default hereunder, Debtor may sell its Inventory in the ordinary course of its business.

7. *Events of Default.* Debtor shall be in default under this Agreement upon the occurrence of any one or more of the following events or conditions:

a. Nonpayment of any of the Obligations when due, whether by acceleration or otherwise, or nonperformance of any promise made by Debtor in this Agreement;

b. Breach of any warranty made by Debtor in this Agreement;

c. Any misrepresentation made by Debtor in this Agreement or in any document furnished by Debtor, or in Debtor's behalf, to Secured Party in connection with this Agreement or the Collateral;

d. Use of the Collateral in violation of any statute or ordinance;

e. Any event which results in the acceleration of any indebtedness of Debtor to any party or parties under any undertaking by Debtor of any kind;

f. The creation of any encumbrance upon the Collateral or the making of any levy, judicial seizure, or attachment thereof or thereon;

g. Any uninsured loss, theft, damage to, or destruction of any of the Collateral;

h. Dissolution, termination of existence, or insolvency of Debtor; or

i. The appointment of a receiver for any part of the property of Debtor, the making by Debtor of an assignment for the benefit of creditors, or the initiation by or against Debtor of any proceeding under the Federal Bankruptcy Act or any state insolvency law.

8. *Rights of Parties upon Default.* In the event of a default by Debtor, in addition to all the rights and remedies provided in Article 9 of the Illinois Uniform Commercial Code and any other applicable law, Secured Party may (but is under no obligation to Debtor so to do):

a. Take physical possession of Inventory Collateral and of Debtor's records pertaining to the Collateral (whether Inventory or Accounts Receivable) which are necessary to administer properly and control the Collateral or the handling and collection of Accounts Receivable Collateral and sell, lease or otherwise dispose of the Collateral in whole or in part, at public or private sale, on or off the premises of Debtor;

b. Require Debtor to assemble the Collateral to which Debtor has or is entitled to possession at a place designated by Secured Party, which is reasonably convenient to both parties;

c. Collect any and all money due or to become due and enforce in Debtor's name all rights with respect to the Collateral;

d. After notice to Debtor, settle, adjust or compromise any dispute with respect to any Account Receivable;

e. Receive and open mail addressed to Debtor; or

f. On behalf of Debtor, indorse checks, notes, drafts, money orders, instruments or other evidence of payment.

9. *Notice.* Any notice of any sale, lease, other disposition, or other intended action by Secured Party shall be deemed reasonable if it is in writing and deposited in the United States mails ten (10) days in advance of the intended disposition or other intended action, first class postage prepaid, and addressed to Debtor at its address set forth below, or any other address designated in a written notice by Debtor previously received by Secured Party.

10. *Waiver.* Waiver by Secured Party of any Event of Default hereunder, or of any breach of the provisions of this Agreement by Debtor, or any right of Secured Party hereunder, shall not constitute a waiver of any other Event of Default or breach or right, nor of the same Event of Default or breach or right on a future occasion.

11. *Law Governing.* This Agreement and the rights and obligations of the parties hereunder shall be construed and interpreted in accordance with the law of the State of Illinois applicable to agreements made and to be wholly performed in such state.

12. *Duration.* This Agreement shall remain in effect from the date first above mentioned until all of the Obligations have been fully satisfied.

13. *Assigns.* This Agreement and all rights and liabilities hereunder and in and to any and all Collateral shall inure to the benefit of the Secured Party and its successors and assigns, and shall be binding on the Debtor and Debtor's heirs, executors, administrators, successors and assigns.

Debtor acknowledges that this Agreement is and shall be effective upon execution by the Debtor and delivery to and acceptance hereof by the Secured Party, and it shall not be necessary for the Secured Party to execute any acceptance hereof or otherwise to signify or express its acceptance hereof to Debtor.

NO–FAULT DISCOUNT, INC.
By
Its President
Address of Debtor:
330 North Wabash Street
Chicago, Illinois 60611

2. Describing and Classifying the Collateral

Problem

You represent a lender who has agreed to lend debtor $20 million, and the lender is to receive a security interest in all of the personal property in debtor's food processing plant. The plant includes 20,000 separate items of personal property. How do you satisfy the requirements of §§ 9–203 and 9–110 that the security agreement reasonably identify the collateral?

IN RE LAMINATED VENEERS CO., INC.

United States Court of Appeals, Second Circuit, 1973.
471 F.2d 1124.

OAKES, CIRCUIT JUDGE:

Appellant made a secured loan to the bankrupt, Laminated Veneers Co., Inc., which was validly executed on December 20, 1968. The covering security agreement specifically pledged items (including a truck) described in its Schedule A and generally pledged other items through an "omnibus clause" set out in the margin below.[1] The omnibus clause gave the appellant a valid secured interest in accounts receivable, inventory, fixtures, machinery, equipment, and tools of the bankrupt. The question here is whether Commercial's secured interest in "equipment" gave it a lien on two Oldsmobile automobiles owned by the bankrupt. We hold that it did not.

The appellant relies upon the broad language of New York Uniform Commercial Code § 9–109(2) (McKinney 1964) (hereinafter cited as "U.C.C.") to show that the "equipment" term of the omnibus clause included the two automobiles. Section 9–109(2) defines "equipment" for present purposes as a residual category which includes all goods not

---

1. In addition to all the above enumerated items, it is the intention that this mortgage shall cover all chattels, machinery, equipment, tables, chairs, work benches, factory chairs, stools, shelving, cabinets, power lines, switch boxes, control panels, machine parts, motors, pumps, electrical equipment, measuring and calibrating instruments, office supplies, sundries, office furniture, fixtures, and all other items of equipment and fixtures belonging to the mortgagor, whether herein enumerated or not, now at the plant of Laminated Veneers Co., Inc. located at 115–02 15th Ave. College Point, New York, and all chattels, machinery, fixtures, or equipment that may hereafter be brought in or installed in said premises or any new premises of the mortgagor, to replace, substitute for, or in addition to the above mentioned chattels and equipment with the exception of stock in trade.

included in the definitions of inventory, farm products or consumer goods. Thus automobiles would fall within this broad category if the definition of Section 9–109 governed for purposes of the security agreement. The classifications of Section 9–109, however, are intended primarily for the purposes of determining which set of filing requirements is proper.

We look rather to U.C.C. § 9–110 which requires that the description of personal property "reasonably identif[y]" what is described. The conclusion that greater specificity is required finds additional support in U.C.C. § 9–203(1)(b), which provides that the security agreement must contain a "description" of the collateral. Certainly the word "equipment" does not constitute a "description" of the Oldsmobiles. Unlike a financing statement (U.C.C. § 9–402) which is designed merely to put creditors on notice that further inquiry is prudent, see In re Leichter, 471 F.2d 785 (2d Cir. 1972), the security agreement embodies the intentions of the parties. It is the primary source to which a creditor's or potential creditor's inquiry is directed and must be reasonably specific.

What would a potential creditor find upon examination of the security agreement in this case? The only mention of vehicles of any kind in the agreement is the listing of an International truck in Schedule A. Beyond that there is only the "omnibus clause" and the generic "equipment" therein. Any examining creditor would conclude that the truck as the only vehicle mentioned was the only one intended to be covered. . . .

For the reasons stated above we affirm the decision of the court below.

LUMBARD, CIRCUIT JUDGE (dissenting):

The majority correctly states the question here as "whether Commercial's secured interest in 'equipment' gave it a lien on two Oldsmobile automobiles owned by the bankrupt." Essentially, this question resolves itself into two very distinct issues: 1) was it the intent of the parties, as expressed in the security agreement, that Commercial could look to these Oldsmobiles as collateral for its loan to the bankrupt; 2) if such was the expressed intent, is the term, "equipment," a sufficient description of the collateral under §§ 9–110 and 9–203 of the New York Uniform Commercial Code to create a valid security interest in this collateral? The majority appears to answer both of these questions in the negative, as did the referee and the district judge. From this holding, I must dissent.

Initially, I would hold the referee's and the district judge's finding that the parties did not intend the security interest to extend to the two automobiles in issue to be clearly erroneous. It seems to me that the very breadth of the omnibus clause of the security agreement is indicative of an intent to cover all personal property owned by the bankrupt, with the exception of stock in trade. The trustee presented no evidence to indicate that this omnibus clause was not intended to mean exactly what it says. Therefore, I feel that the question of intent should have been resolved in appellant's favor.

There is no argument that the Oldsmobiles would not be included under the Uniform Commercial Code's definition of "equipment" in § 9–109(2).[1] The question is whether the use of such a generic term is a sufficient "description of the collateral" for purposes of § 9–203(1)(b).[2] The cross reference for this description requirement is to § 9–110, which provides that

> For purposes of this Article any description of personal property . . . is sufficient whether or not it is specific if it reasonably identifies what is described.

The official comments to § 9–110 elaborate on the nature of the description requirement:

> The requirement of description of collateral (see Section 9–203 and Comment thereto) is evidentiary. The test of sufficiency of a description laid down by this Section is that the description do the job assigned to it—that it make possible the identification of the thing described. Under this rule courts should refuse to follow the holdings, often found in the older chattel mortgage cases, that descriptions are insufficient unless they are the most exact and detailed nature, the so-called "serial number" test.

The precise issue here seems to have been considered only once before. In Goodall Rubber Co. v. News Ready Mix Corp., 7 U.C.C. 1358 (Wisc.Cir.Ct., 1970), the court held that this generic term was sufficient to satisfy §§ 9–110 and 9–203. In addition, there have been a number of cases that have considered, in the context of both security agreements and financing statements, the sufficiency of descriptions phrased in other generic terms. The decisions have not been uniform. Compare In Re Trumble, 5 U.C.C. 543 (U.S.D.C., W.D., Mich., 1968) ("con-

---

1. Goods are . . . (2) "equipment" if they are used or bought for use primarily in business (including farming or a profession) or by a debtor who is a nonprofit organization or a governmental subdivision or agency or if the goods are not included in the definitions of inventory, farm products or consumer goods . . ..

From this quotation, it is apparent that the majority is not entirely correct when it states that "[s]ection 9–109(2) defines 'equipment' for present purposes as a residual category which includes all goods not included in the definitions of inventory, farm products or consumer goods." Such a statement ignores the standards enunciated in the first half of the definition for determining when goods are "equipment." Similarly incorrect is the majority's unsupported statement that "[t]he classifications of Section 9–109

. . . are intended primarily for the purposes of determining which set of filing requirements is proper." The official comments to § 9–109 state:

The classification is important in many situations: it is relevant, for example, in determining the rights of persons who buy from a debtor goods subject to a security interest (Section 9–307), in certain questions of priority (Section 9–312), in determining the place of filing (Section 9–401) and in working out rights after default (Part 5). Comment 5 to Section 9–102 contains an index of the special rules applicable to different classes of collateral.

2. . . . [A] security interest is not enforceable against the debtor or third parties unless . . . (b) the debtor has signed a security agreement which contains a description of the collateral . . ..

sumer goods" held to be sufficient), Thomson v. O.M. Scott Credit Corp., 1 U.C.C. 555 (Pa.Ct. of Common Pleas, 1962) ("inventory" sufficient), In Re Goodfriend, 2 U.C.C. 160 (U.S.D.C., E.D., Pa., 1964) ("inventory" sufficient), and Security Tire and Rubber Co., Inc. v. Hlass, 441 S.W.2d 91 (Ark.S.Ct., 1969) ("inventory" sufficient) with In Re Bell, 6 U.C.C. 740 (U.S.D.C., Colo., 1969) ("consumer goods" insufficient), Household Finance Corp. v. Kopel, 303 F.Supp. 317 (U.S.D.C., Colo., 1969) ("consumer goods" insufficient), and Mammoth Cave Production Credit Association v. York, 429 S.W.2d 26 (Ky.Ct. of App., 1968) ("farm equipment" insufficient). The two Colorado cases holding "consumer goods" to be insufficient were decided under the Colorado version of § 9–110, which in terms requires much more specificity in a description of consumer goods than does the New York version.[3] It appears that the majority of courts that have considered the sufficiency of descriptions stated in terms of § 9–109 definitions, when § 9–110 was phrased as it is in New York, have held such descriptions to have been sufficient. In this regard, it should be noted that borrowing by businesses in return for security interests in their "inventory," another generic term defined in § 9–109, has become a common financing device under Article 9 of the Uniform Commercial Code.

I do not mean to suggest that the court should hold that all descriptions in terms of "equipment" will necessarily satisfy §§ 9–110 and 9–203. Arguably, any such *per se* rule would be inconsistent with the mandate of § 9–110 that the description "reasonably identif[y] what is described." This language, as well as the official comments, would seem to indicate a more *ad hoc,* factual analysis. In this case, we have two Oldsmobile automobiles that were owned by a corporation in the retail lumber business. The most logical conclusion for any reasonable subsequent lender was that these automobiles were being used by the corporation in its business and were thus equipment, with respect to which he was charged with notice of a prior security interest. At the very least, a subsequent lender should be put on inquiry by these circumstances and should seek to learn from the borrower and the prior lender the nature of the use of this property. Therefore, I would reverse the district court's holding that the description was insufficient under the Uniform Commercial Code, and I would hold that the description in terms of "equipment" was, on the facts of this case, sufficient to "reasonably identify" the automobiles and to bring them under the security agreement. . . .

I would reverse.

3. CRS 1963, § 155–9–110 provides:

For purposes of this article, any description of personal property is sufficient if it specifically identifies and itemizes in the security agreement what is described as to consumer goods, and whether or not it is specific if it reasonably identifies what is described as to all other personal property.

Notes & Questions

1. *The Parties' Intent.* As between the debtor and the secured party, was there any doubt that they intended to create a security interest in the automobiles? See the description of the collateral in the security agreement reproduced in note 1 of the court's opinion. Could one have interpreted the word "equipment" to encompass the cars? See § 9–109.

2. *Where Third Parties Look.* The court's opinion does not contain any express doubts about what the parties meant to do. Rather, it seeks to protect the interests of third parties who may be misled by the description of the collateral in the security agreement. Do third parties usually see what is contained in the security agreement? May they find out about its contents? See § 9–208.

3. *Describing Collateral.* Does the description in *Laminated Veneers* suffice for purposes of the financing statement? Assume that you represent a lender contemplating a loan to Laminated Veneers. You dutifully search the U.C.C. filings and find Commercial's financing statement. If your lender were looking to the Oldsmobiles as collateral would you advise your lender to make the loan? Would any sane attorney (or nonattorney)? Should the trustee in bankruptcy prevail when no reasonable lender would have relied on whatever flaws exist in Commercial's description of the collateral?

Would Commercial have been better off to describe the collateral in one word: "everything"?

Notes on Classifying Collateral

By focusing attention on the term "equipment," *Laminated Veneers* introduces another important Code concept—classification of collateral. In *Laminated Veneers,* the class of collateral referred to as "equipment" was sought to be used for descriptive purposes as a short-hand for many specific items of collateral. But the classification of collateral has many other consequences under Article 9. The particular class into which collateral falls influences priority battles, § 9–312(3), filing requirements, § 9–401, perfection requirements, § 9–302, and rights on default, § 9–505. See generally Comment 1 to § 9–109 (list of provisions in which classification of collateral matters); 1 Gilmore §§ 12.1 to 12.6. To familiarize yourself with the Code's classification scheme work through the following problem.

Problem

Data Haven sells and leases computers. When Data Haven sells or leases a computer, it agrees to make available to the purchaser or lessee significant technological advances in the equipment and to supply prompt maintenance and repair services. Data Haven often sells computers on a credit basis, and reserves a security interest in all leased and credit sale computers. Classify under Article 9 the following items of collateral (See §§ 9–109, 9–105, 9–106):

(a) The computers while they are in Data Haven's possession prior to sale.

(b) The computers after they are sold to Data Haven's business customers.

(c) Data Haven's promise to make available technological advances and to service the computers it sells and leases.

(d) The rights Data Haven acquires from customers who lease computers or purchase them on credit.

In each case be sure you understand who will be using the potential items of collateral to obtain a secured loan.

3. Rights in the Collateral

FIRST NATIONAL BANK OF ELKHART COUNTY v. SMOKER

Court of Appeals of Indiana, Third District, 1972.
153 Ind.App. 71, 286 N.E.2d 203.

SHARP, JUDGE.

This action, initiated by Dwight Smoker (Smoker), plaintiff-appellee, against the First National Bank of Elkhart County (Bank), defendant-appellant, is for an alleged conversion by the Bank of sides of beef and hides from 85 head of cattle and for misappropriation of the proceeds from the sale of said cattle. The conversion allegedly occurred when the Bank exerted dominion and control over the cattle when they were in the hands of its debtor, J.L. Whisler and Sons, Inc. (Whisler) but when title to said cattle remained with Smoker. Trial was had before the court without the intervention of a jury and resulted in a judgment for Smoker in the sum of $17,576.40. The Bank duly filed its motion to correct errors, which was overruled, and this appeal was then taken.

. . .

The trial court, upon request, made special Findings of Fact and Conclusions of Law, which read as follows:

"FINDINGS OF FACT

I

The Plaintiff, Dwight Smoker, is now and was prior to April 19, 1967, a producer of fat cattle, who, beginning in September 1966 and continuing until April 19, 1967, sold to J.L. Whisler and Sons, Inc., over fifteen hundred (1500) head of said cattle on a grade-and-weight basis.

II

Throughout the course of dealing between the Plaintiff and the said J.L. Whisler and Sons, Inc., the transactions between the parties had been in accordance with the recognized custom and usage in the trade, to-wit: cattle were delivered live by the Plaintiff, slaughtered by the packer; shrouded and hung to chill and then approximately twenty-four (24) hours later were graded by the Government grader and, at that time, the United States Department of Agriculture price list for the day of delivery, which was published the day after deliver[y], was applied to the grade and weight of Plaintiff's cattle in order to determine the price to be paid Plaintiff and then a check was issued in payment thereof.

III

On April 19, 1967, pursuant to a telephone request of the previous day, the Plaintiff delivered to J.L. Whisler and Sons, Inc., eighty-five (85) head of cattle to be sold on a grade-and-weight basis in keeping with the course of dealing between the parties and the custom and usage of the trade.

IV

It was the intention of the Plaintiff and J.L. Whisler and Sons, Inc., to be bound by their course of dealing and the custom and usage in the trade as to the shipment delivered April 19, 1967.

V

After delivery on the morning of April 19, 1967, the cattle were slaughtered, shrouded and placed in the cooler at J.L. Whisler and Sons, Inc., but were not graded or priced.

VI

On the 19th of April 1967, the Defendant, First National Bank of Elkhart County, who had in full force and effect, security agreements and financing statements on the inventory of J.L. Whisler and Sons, Inc., which was, according to the terms of said instruments, owned by J.L. Whisler and Sons, Inc., made a demand for the payment of all sums due it from J.L. Whisler and Sons, Inc. Upon failure of the said J.L. Whisler and Sons, Inc. to meet the demand, the First National Bank of Elkhart County, by and through its agent, Clayton Emmert, offset all corporate bank accounts of J.L. Whisler and Sons, Inc. against said indebtedness and instructed J.L. Whisler and Sons, Inc. to proceed to liquidate all meat held by said packer on said date in the normal course of business, but to surrender all sums received to the Defendant.

VII

Thereafter, pursuant to the direction and orders of the Defendant, the carcasses of the eighty-five (85) head of cattle delivered by the Plaintiff on April 19th were sold and the proceeds therefrom placed under the control of the Defendant who applied these sums and all others received to the payment of certain administrative expenses; payment for certain other cattle received the 19th day of April, after the shipment delivered by the Plaintiff; and, to the liquidation of the debt of J.L.Whisler and Sons, Inc., to the Defendant.

VIII

The Plaintiff never received any payment for the eighty-five (85) head of cattle delivered April 19, 1967.

IX

At the time the Defendant made its demand of J.L. Whisler and Sons, Inc., the eighty-five (85) carcasses, representing the cattle delivered by the Plaintiff, had neither been graded nor priced.

X

The title to and ownership of the eighty-five (85) carcasses delivered by the Plaintiff on April 19, 1967 to J.L. Whisler and Sons, Inc., remained at all times in the Plaintiff.

XI

The Defendant converted the property of the Plaintiff to its own use and benefit.

XII

At the time of said conversion by Defendant the value of said cattle was $20,679.80.

XIII

Plaintiff recovered from a bond of J.R. Whisler and Sons, Inc., because of their failure to pay for said cattle, $3,103.40 and the damage to Plaintiff is thus mitigated by that amount.

Upon the foregoing findings of fact, the Court states the following:

CONCLUSIONS OF LAW

I

The law is with the Plaintiff, Dwight Smoker, and against the Defendant, First National Bank (formerly known as First National Bank of Elkhart County).

II

Ownership of and title to the eighty-five (85) head of cattle delivered April 19, 1867 by the Plaintiff to J.L. Whisler and Sons, Inc., remained at all times in the Plaintiff.

III

The Defendant, First National Bank of Elkhart County, converted to its own use and benefit the proceeds from the sale of Plaintiff's cattle.

IT IS THEREFORE ORDERED, ADJUDGED AND DECREED, That the Defendant is indebted to the Plaintiff in the sum of Seventeen Thousand Five Hundred Seventy-six Dollars and Forty cents ($17,576.40), and that judgment is hereby entered against the defendant First National Bank (formerly known as First National Bank of Elkhart County) for said amount.

Costs of this action are charged to the Defendant."   . . .

There are two separate and distinct transactions which precipitated this action. The first involves the perfected security agreement between the bank and Whisler creating a security interest in all the inventory, accounts receivable, after acquired property and proceeds of Whisler. The second transaction is the oral contract for sale of eighty-five head of cattle to Whisler by Smoker, said oral contract being based upon custom and usage in the trade and the course of dealing between the immediate parties. We are concerned with the interrelation of these two separate transactions and the legal efficacy of each vis-a-vis the interests of third parties. The issue is one of priority of interests between a secured party with a "floating lien" and a supplier of raw materials to the debtor. The fundamental issue is whether an oral agreement between a buyer and seller, relying heavily on custom and usage in the trade, can delay the passage of title to goods already delivered to the buyer so as to defeat the rights of third party secured creditors of the buyer and transform such a creditor into a convertor of goods in the possession of the buyer. To put it another way, will a secured party holding a perfected security interest in a buyer's inventory, accounts receivable, after-acquired property and proceeds, when liquidating the buyer's inventory upon default, be deemed to have converted the property of a subsequent unperfected seller who delivers goods to the buyer before default but who reserved title until a specified time after delivery?   . . .

The argument advanced by Smoker in favor of the judgment below is essentially that the parties to the contract for the sale of the cattle intended title to pass only after the cattle had been graded on the day following delivery. Smoker contends that the law prior to the passage of the Uniform Commercial Code was that passage of title depended upon the intentions of the parties to the contract, and that custom and usage in the trade and course of dealing, when applicable, were to be given effect in determining the intentions of the parties. Allegedly, the Code left this prior law unchanged and thus title remained in Smoker at the time the Bank made demand for payment of its note. The subsequent exercise of dominion or control by the Bank over the cattle was a conversion by the Bank.

Smoker's argument, bereft of glossing and reduced to essentials, is that custom and usage in the trade plus the course of dealing between Smoker and Whisler amounted to an express agreement as to when title to the goods was to pass. This explicit agreement, because it is based on the above ingredients, negates and prevents the application of I.C.1971, 26–1–2–401; Ind.Ann.Stat. § 19–2–401 (Burns 1964), and the applicable sections of the Article on Secured Transactions (Article 9). An ancillary argument is that the cattle, although in the possession of Whisler, were not identified to the contract prior to grading. Since goods must be identified to the contract before the buyer can obtain a special property in the goods and before title passes, Whisler did not have an interest in the cattle at the time of demand so as to allow the security interest to attach under I.C.1971, 26–1–9–204; Ind.Ann.Stat. § 19–9–204 (Burns 1964).

On February 16, 1966, Whisler executed a Security Agreement in favor of the Bank whereby Whisler granted to the Bank a security interest in all inventory then owned and thereafter acquired and all accounts receivable, then existing and thereafter arising, other collateral and proceeds and products of the foregoing categories of collateral. The Bank duly perfected its security interests by filing a Financing Statement with the Secretary of State of Indiana on February 18, 1966, in accordance with I.C.1971, 26–1–9–401; Ind.Ann.Stat. § 19–9–401 (Burns 1965). The Bank, thereafter made a series of working capital loans to Whisler based on its secured position as evidenced by a promissory note dated March 31, 1966 which was secured by the above-mentioned security agreement.

Under I.C.1971, 26–1–9–204; Ind.Ann.Stat. § 19–9–204 (Burns 1964), a security interest cannot attach to specific goods or collateral until there is an agreement that it attach and value is given and the debtor acquires rights in the collateral. It is uncontroverted that the first two requirements were met by the bank in this case. Nor does Smoker specifically and directly argue that Whisler did not have such rights in the cattle as to allow the Bank's security interest to attach thereto. Thus, although not specifically mentioned by either party, we deem it necessary to determine what rights Whisler had in the cattle and whether the rights were sufficient to allow the Bank's security interest to attach to the same.

Several courts have considered the question in the context of whether absolute ownership in and title to collateral was the requisite right necessary to permit the attachment of the secured creditor's interest. They uniformly have held that the location of the nebulous concept "title" was immaterial in ascertaining whether a debtor had sufficient rights in specific collateral. In James Talcott, Inc. v. Franklin Nat. Bank, Minn., 194 N.W.2d 775 (1972), the court stated:

"Thus, the draftsmen of the code intended that its provisions should not be circumvented by manipulation of the locus of title. For this reason, consignment sales, conditional sales, and other arrangements or devices whereby title is retained in the seller for a period following possession by the debtor are all treated under Art. 9 as though title had been transferred to the debtor and the creditor-seller had retained only a security interest in the goods. See, Sussen Rubber Co. v. Hertz, 19 Ohio App.2d 1, 249 N.E.2d 65 (1969), involving a consignment sale. For the purposes of analyzing rights of ownership under Art. 9, we hold, based upon the stipulated facts of this case, that defendant had only a security interest in the equipment despite a purported reservation of title and that debtor 'owned' the equipment at the time that the extension agreement was executed."

Also, in Cain v. Country Club Delicatessen of Saybrook, Inc., 25 Conn.Sup. 327, 203 A.2d 441 (1964), the court, in attempting to ascertain when a buyer obtained rights in the collateral, observed that mere possession was insufficient to constitute such rights in the collateral. The court held that it was only when the conditional sales contract was executed some time after possession that the debtor acquired rights in the collateral so as to allow the security interest to attach.

Thus, it would follow that when a debtor acquires possession of collateral under a contract, he has acquired such rights in the collateral as to allow the security interest of his creditor to attach to the collateral, and this is true regardless of who may be deemed to have title to and ownership of such collateral.

This line of reasoning is further supported by the fact that once the cattle come into the possession of Whisler, they cease to be classified as "farm products" and become "inventory." The official comments to I.C.1971, 26–1–9–109; Ind.Ann.Stat. § 19–9–109, while not binding, are persuasive and read in pertinent part as follows:

"Goods are 'farm products' only if they are in the possession of a debtor engaged in farming operations.

. . .

"When crops or livestock or their products come into the possession of a person not engaged in farming operations they cease to be 'farm products.' If they come into possession of a marketing agency for sale or distribution or a manufacturer or processor as raw materials, they become inventory."

Thus, regardless of whether Whisler had obtained title to the cattle, they became part of his inventory upon their coming into his possession pursuant to a contract for sale. As inventory, Whisler acquired such rights in and to the cattle so that the security interest of the Bank attached.

Having determined that the Bank had a perfected security interest in the eighty-five head of cattle as part of the inventory of Whisler, it remains to be determined if the oral agreement between Smoker and Whisler, in conjunction with the provisions of Article 2, in any way negate or vitiate the security interest of the bank. We must determine the legal efficacy of the retention of title by a seller after delivery of goods upon a prior perfected security interest.

In this regard, we must look to I.C.1971, 26–1–2–401, Ind.Ann.Stat. § 19–2–401 (Burns 1964), which reads as follows:

"Each provision of this Article [Chapter] with regard to the rights, obligations and remedies of the seller, the buyer, purchasers or other third parties applies irrespective of title to the goods except where the provision refers to such title. Insofar as situations are not covered by the other provisions of this Article [Chapter] and matters concerning title become material the following rules apply:

(1) Title to goods cannot pass under a contract for sale prior to their identification to the contract (section [19–]2–501, and unless otherwise explicitly agreed the buyer acquires by their identification a special property as limited by this Act [Chapters 1 to 9 of this title]. Any retention or reservation by the seller of the title (property) in goods shipped or delivered to the buyer is limited in effect to a reservation of a security interest. Subject to these provisions and to the provisions of the Article [Chapter] on Secured Transactions (Article 9 [§§ 19–9–101—19–9–507]), title to goods passes from the seller to the buyer in any manner and on any conditions explicitly agreed on by the parties.

(2) Unless otherwise explicitly agreed title passes to the buyer at the time and place at which the seller completes his performance with reference to the physical delivery of the goods, despite any reservation of a security interest and even though a document of title is to be delivered at a different time or place; and in particular despite any reservation of a security interest by the bill of lading

(a) if the contract requires or authorizes the seller to send the goods to the buyer but does not require him to deliver them at destination, title passes to the buyer at the time and place of shipment; but

(b) if the contract requires delivery at destination, title passes on tender there.

(3) Unless otherwise explicitly agreed where delivery is to be made without moving the goods

(a) if the seller is to deliver a document of title, title passes at the time when and the place where he delivers such documents; or

(b) if the goods are at the time of contracting already identified and no documents are to be delivered, title passes at the time and place of contracting.

(4) A rejection or other refusal by the buyer to receive or retain the goods, whether or not justified, or a justified revocation of acceptance revests title to the goods in the seller. Such revesting occurs by operation of law and is not a 'sale.' " . . .

Absent an explicit agreement, title to goods under § 19–2–401(2), supra, passes to the buyer at the time and place at which the seller completes his performance with reference to physical delivery of the goods. Thus, if Smoker and Whisler had not entered into an explicit agreement concerning when title was to pass, said title would have passed upon the physical delivery of the goods and Smoker would have had, at most, a purchase money security interest, I.C.1971, 26–1–9–107; Ind.Ann.Stat. § 19–9–107 (Burns 1964). But, as was pointed out earlier, Smoker argues that there was an explicit agreement based on custom and usage in the trade and the course of dealing between the parties, and that this explicit agreement prevents the application of § 19–2–401(2) supra, and allows title to remain in Smoker after delivery. . . .

. . . [E]ven assuming that the evidence of custom and usage and the course of dealing between the parties was sufficient to establish an explicit agreement, it is of no avail to Smoker. The argument of Smoker ignores the sentences in § 19–2–401(1), supra, regarding explicit agreements concerning retention of title to the effect that "any retention or reservation by the seller of the title (property) in goods shipped or delivered to the buyer is limited in effect to a reservation of a security interest." . . . Thus, the legal effect of retention of title by a seller is only the reservation of a security interest and therefore, the seller must comply with the provisions of Article 9, wherein § 19–9–202 specifically states that each provision of the article apply whether title to the collateral is in the secured party or the debtor.

The final question to be answered concerns the definition and scope of the term "identification," and whether the cattle in question were identified to the contract prior to grading. I.C.1971, 26–1–2–501, Ind. Ann.Stat. § 19–2–501 (Burns 1964), reading as follows:

"(1) The buyer obtains a special property and an insurable interest in goods by identification of existing goods as goods to which the contract refers even though the goods so identified are nonconforming and he has an option to return or reject them. Such identification can be made at any time and in any manner explicitly agreed to by the parties. In the absence of explicit agreement identification occurs

(a) when the contract is made if it is for the sale of goods already existing and identified;

(b) if the contract is for the sale of future goods other than those described in paragraph (c), when goods are shipped, marked or otherwise designated by the seller as goods to which the contract refers; . . .

(2) The seller retains an insurable interest in goods so long as title to or any security interest in the goods remains in him and where the identification is by the seller alone he may until default or insolvency or notification to the buyer that the identification is final substitute other goods for those identified. . . .

Title cannot pass before identification but the two are not synonymous. Identification is of limited importance under the Code although it does determine the earliest point at which title may pass. While § 19–2–501 does provide that identification may be made at any time and in any manner explicitly agreed to by the parties; this does not mean that the parties may delay the passage of title by the simple expedient of agreeing that the goods are not yet identified to the contract when, in fact, they have already been delivered to the buyer. Identification refers to when the goods are still in the possession of the seller. Thus, by explicit agreement, the parties may decide that the goods are identified at a point in time earlier than those enunciated in § 19–2–501, but in no event can they delay such identification after the goods are in the possession of the buyer. This case does not deal with identification but rather with I.C.1971, 26–1–2–305; Ind.Ann.Stat. 19–2–305 (Burns 1964) concerning open price terms. Our view is supported by other sections of the Code dealing with the remedies of the seller upon default by the buyer.

Pursuant to the above cited provisions, we hold, as a matter of law, that Smoker retained only a purchase money security interest in the eighty-five head of cattle upon the delivery of such cattle to Whisler under an oral contract for sale. To have effectively reserved his rights, Smoker would have had to proceed under Article 9, § 19–9–101 et seq., concerning secured transactions, specifically I.C.1971, 26–1–9–312(3); Ind.Ann.Stat. § 19–9–312(3). Since Smoker failed to perfect his security interest in the inventory of Whisler, his rights in the eighty-five head of cattle or the proceeds thereof are subordinated to the rights of the Bank, which had a prior perfected security interest, § 19–9–312(5), and this is true regardless of whether Smoker, by explicit agreement, retained title to the goods. . . .

Notes & Questions

1. *Undelivered Goods.* In *Smoker,* the collateral had been delivered to the debtor, which obviously facilitates a finding that the debtor has rights in the collateral. Suppose the cattle had not yet been delivered to debtor. Or, outside the farm context, suppose an order of manufactured goods has not yet been delivered to a buyer. At what point may the buyer's secured party (or the bank in *Smoker*) look to the goods as collateral for its loan? May the debtor ever have rights in collateral before possessing them? See §§ 2–509, 2–319. May a debtor *not* have rights in collateral even if the collateral is in his possession? See Cain v. Country Club Delicatessen (noted in *Smoker*); Manger v.

Davis, 619 P.2d 687 (Utah 1980) (consignee lacked authority to pledge ring in his possession to secure personal loan).

2. *Identification.* Consider *Smoker's* discussion of the Article 2 concept of identification. If goods in a seller's possession (or in transit) have been identified to a contract, is the occurrence of identification sufficient to confer upon the debtor rights in the collateral within the meaning of § 9–203(1)(c)? How firm a process is identification under Article 2? See §§ 2–501, 2–502.

The court indicates that the parties to a contract are free to agree upon a time of identification that precedes the time when title normally would pass. Does this suggest a possible course of action for lenders lending to buyers that may maximize the amount of collateral subject to a security interest?

May a buyer have rights in collateral prior to identification under a sales contract? See §§ 2–716, 2–722, 2–105(2).

3. For present purposes, it is less important that you grasp why the secured party won or lost in *Smoker* than that you try to grasp the "rights-in-the-collateral" concept. Contests between secured parties and unpaid sellers will be studied in Chapter 3C.

STATE BANK OF YOUNG AMERICA v. VIDMAR IRON WORKS, INC.

Supreme Court of Minnesota, 1980.
292 N.W.2d 244.

YETKA, JUSTICE.

The appellant State Bank of Young America brought this action against Vidmar Iron Works, Inc., to recover under security interests it held securing the unpaid debts of Adaptable Industries, Inc. Trial was held before the Carver County District Court, and the court entered findings and conclusions against the appellant. The appellant then moved for a new trial or, in the alternative, for amended findings and conclusions. The court denied that motion, and the appellant has appealed the order denying the motion. We reverse and remand.

This case presents the following issues for decision:

I. Did the State Bank of Young America have a valid security interest which would entitle it to collect the debts owed by Vidmar Iron Works, Inc., to Adaptable Industries, Inc.? . . .

B. Did the bank's security interest in the inventory of Adaptable Industries cover raw materials owned by Vidmar Iron Works which Adaptable was converting into finished products to the extent of the value added by Adaptable? . . .

There is no dispute as to the material facts. Adaptable Industries, Inc., ("Adaptable") is a metal goods fabricating shop of which Norman and Diane Briggs are the sole shareholders, directors and officers. On December 10, 1973, the appellant, State Bank of Young America ("the bank"), loaned Adaptable $1,000. The loan was secured by a security agreement covering all accounts receivable of Adaptable. The agreement secured all present and future debts of Adaptable to the bank.

On January 11, 1974, the bank loaned Adaptable an additional $500. On January 30, the original $1,000 loan was paid off and the $500 note was renewed. Subsequently, the bank continued to make additional loans to Adaptable. One note executed on June 30, 1975, indicates on its face that it is secured by an existing security agreement covering "receivables."

On March 4, 1975, in conjunction with another loan, Adaptable gave the bank a security interest in both its inventory and its machinery, tools and equipment. The security agreement included the proceeds of such items and secured all present and future debts. A second security interest in both inventory and equipment securing present and future debts was executed on September 2, 1975. All three security agreements referred to were duly filed in the appropriate offices.

The bank ultimately loaned Adaptable approximately $165,000 from time to time, the bulk of which was paid in due course. The outstanding balance on the debts at any one time ranged from $500 to $30,000.

Adaptable had apparently made a number of purchases from a steel supply company, Paper Calmenson & Company ("PACAL"), and was in debt to PACAL. In the hope that Adaptable would be able to pay its debt, a representative of PACAL introduced Norman Briggs of Adaptable to the respondent, Vidmar Iron Works, Inc. ("Vidmar"). Vidmar is a larger metal shop which was looking for help with some of its overflow work. The record clearly shows that an agreement was entered into between PACAL and Vidmar that payments made to Adaptable by Vidmar would include PACAL's name on the checks in order to repay the debt Adaptable owed PACAL.

On August 7, 1975, Vidmar placed its first order with Adaptable at a price of $15,250. It later placed two smaller orders with Adaptable. The contracts involved paying Adaptable to do fabricating work on raw materials supplied by Vidmar. In early September 1975, the bank telephoned Mr. Vidmar, president of Vidmar Iron Works, and notified him of its security interest in Adaptable's accounts receivable. There was some question as to whether the call was received before or after Vidmar's first payment to Adaptable on September 11. However, Mr. Vidmar's testimony that they had intended to put the bank's name on the first check shows that the call came first. At that time, Mr. Vidmar said he would consult the company's attorney. . . .

Ultimately, however, the bank called in all of its notes and liquidated the assets of Adaptable. After deducting the proceeds of the liquidation sale, the bank claims a deficiency of principal and accrued interest of approximately $23,000. The bank further claims that payments made by Vidmar to Adaptable total approximately $31,000, all of which were made after the bank's first phone call to Mr. Vidmar.

The basis of the bank's right of action against Vidmar rather than Adaptable is found in the security agreements. The agreements provide that the bank may, at any time, make direct collection of the accounts or proceeds of goods secured. Cf. Minn.Stat. §§ 336.9–318(3), –502(1), (1978). The agreements also authorize the bank to consider the debtor in default if it deems its security impaired or its risk materially increased. Cf. Minn.Stat. § 336.1–208 (1978). Vidmar does not deny that it is liable to the bank if the issues discussed below are resolved against it. . . .

I.B. Vidmar next argues that since it owned the steel which was processed by Adaptable, the bank's inventory security interest could not attach to it. The U.C.C. states that goods taken as collateral are classified as "inventory:"

> if they are held by a person who holds them for sale or lease or to be furnished under contracts of service or if he has so furnished them, or if they are raw materials, work in process or materials used or consumed in a business.

Minn.Stat. § 336.9–109(4) (1978).

The U.C.C. does not require that collateral be owned by the debtor. In at least two instances, the U.C.C. specifically refers to situations in which the debtor is not the owner of the collateral. In defining the term "debtor," section 336.9–105(1)(d) states "[w]here the debtor and the owner of the collateral are not the same person, the term 'debtor' means the owner of the collateral . . .." Section 336.9–112 is entitled "Where Collateral is Not Owned by Debtor" and specifies certain rights of the owner which are not relevant here. The lack of a requirement of ownership of the collateral is consistent with the U.C.C.'s general non-reliance on the use of "title" to determine rights. See sections 336.2–401, 336.9–202.

Rather than requiring title, the U.C.C. only requires that the debtor have "rights in the collateral." Section 336.9–203(1). Professor Gilmore has written:

> The Article [Article 9] does not specify the quantum of "rights" which a debtor must have in collateral to support a security interest: evidently less than full "legal title" will do and the secured party will get whatever rights the debtor had . . ..

1 G. Gilmore, Security Interests in Personal Property § 11.5 at 353 (1965).

Vidmar's argument that Adaptable had no rights in the steel is erroneous. Adaptable had contract rights in the goods to the extent of the amount due for its work and had a statutory lien in the goods to secure it. The lien would have been one granted for "personalty in possession" under Minn.Stat. §§ 514.18–.22 (1978). Section 514.19(4) allows such a lien for anyone "[m] aking, altering or repairing any article, or expending any labor, skill or material thereon." Such a lien would even have had a priority over any perfected security interest in the steel held by Vidmar or its creditors. Section 336.9–310 (1978) states:

> When a person in the ordinary course of his business furnishes services or materials with respect to goods subject to a security interest, a lien upon goods in the possession of such person given by statute or rule of law for such materials or services takes priority over a perfected security interest unless the lien is statutory and the statute expressly provides otherwise.

This court has never considered whether the rights of one in Adaptable's position are sufficient to allow a security interest to attach. However, in James Talcott, Inc. v. Franklin National Bank, 292 Minn. 277, 194 N.W.2d 775 (1972), this court held that a security interest could attach to property purportedly leased by the debtor. Looking to the substance of the transaction, the court held that ownership for Article 9 purposes was not dependent upon formal title. The court stated:

> [T]he draftsmen of the code intended that its provisions should not be circumvented by manipulation of the locus of title. For this reason, consignment sales, conditional sales, and other arrangements or devices whereby title is retained in the seller for a period following possession by the debtor are all treated under Art. 9 as though title had been transferred to the debtor and the creditor-seller had retained only a security interest in the goods.

292 Minn. at 285, 194 N.W.2d at 781. . . .

We hold that Adaptable had sufficient "rights in the collateral" under section 336.9–203(1) to allow the bank's inventory security interest to attach. However, as Professor Gilmore stated, supra, the secured party only gets rights in the goods to the extent of the debtor's rights in them. Adaptable's rights in the goods were based on the payments due under the contracts from Vidmar. In this case, the bank properly seeks only to recoup those payments and is not claiming the value of the raw materials as supplied by Vidmar. The payments made are more than sufficient to cover the remaining unpaid debt of Adaptable.

. . .

Notes & Questions

1. *Debtor's Rights as Limit on Secured Party's Rights.* The court states that "the secured party only gets rights in the goods to the extent of the debtor's rights in them." Is *Smoker* consistent with this statement? In *Vidmar Iron*, the payments due under the contracts from Vidmar Iron were sufficient to pay Adaptable's debt to the bank and the parties therefore did not really join issue over the value of the raw materials supplied by Vidmar Iron. Could the bank successfully have asserted a security interest in the materials supplied by Vidmar Iron to Adaptable? If a secured party only acquires an interest in collateral to the extent that the debtor has "rights in the collateral," does the

"rights in the collateral" requirement have any substantive content? See and compare § 2–403(1).

2. *Bases for Deciding When "Rights-in-the-Collateral" Exist.* If rights in collateral (sufficient to allow a secured party to enforce a security interest upon the debtor's default) arise at a relatively early time (e.g., upon formation of a contract), there is an increase in the seller's risk of losing goods despite no full performance by the buyer-debtor. Will this force sellers to pay greater heed to Article 9 filings against their buyers? If rights in the collateral do not arise until near the end of the contractual process (e.g., upon delivery), there is an increase in the buyer's secured party's risk of losing the benefit of collateral he might be relying upon. Who is in a better position to protect himself? What steps can be taken to protect these interests?

These considerations may be relevant to a *Smoker*-type situation. How do they pertain to a case such as *Vidmar Iron* where the debtor possesses the potentially disputed collateral under something other than a purchase contract? What should Vidmar Iron do to protect itself from Adaptable's creditors?

B. The Scope of the Security Interest

C.O. FUNK & SONS, INC. v. SULLIVAN EQUIPMENT, INC.

Supreme Court of Illinois, 1982.
89 Ill.2d 27, 59 Ill.Dec. 85, 431 N.E.2d 370.

UNDERWOOD, JUSTICE:

This case involves a Uniform Commercial Code issue not heretofore considered by this court.

In March 1978 plaintiff C.O. Funk & Sons, Inc. (Funk) sold its farm implement business to defendant, Sullivan Equipment, Inc. (Sullivan). The unpaid balance of the purchase price was secured by a security agreement covering specified inventory, equipment and the proceeds. That agreement with Sullivan authorized the sale of certain inventory, but required that Sullivan deposit 90% of the sale price in an escrow account from which Funk would receive installment payments. Sullivan financed its inventory purchases in part with a loan from the intervenor, First National Bank and Trust Company of Tuscola (bank). This loan was secured by a security agreement covering inventory, equipment, after-acquired property, and accounts receivable. Both security agreements were perfected by the filing of financing statements pursuant to Code sections 9–401 and 9–402, with Funk's the first filed. (Ill.Rev.Stat.1977, ch. 26, pars. 9–401, 9–402.) Between June 1978 and December 1979 Sullivan was in arrears in its payments to the escrow account; a total of $29,673.73 which should have been deposited in it was instead deposited in its general business account. From the latter account Sullivan purchased inventory during this same period which far exceeded in value the amount of arrearage.

By December 1979 Sullivan was experiencing financial difficulty and planned an auction of some of its inventory. Funk then sought and obtained a temporary restraining order requiring that the net proceeds of the auction be deposited with the court, and amended its complaint to include an action for breach of contract, demanding damages in the amount of the arrearage. The bank sought and received leave to intervene to protect its interests. At that time Sullivan owed the bank $425,596.78, which was secured in part by the inventory sold at auction.

The auction produced some $115,000. Of this, the portion resulting from the sale of specific items described in the Funk-Sullivan sales agreement is concededly Funk's. Funk claims in addition only the $29,673.73 arrearage, and the circuit court of Piatt County held it was entitled to the funds. The appellate court reversed and remanded with directions to distribute the funds to the bank. (92 Ill.App.3d 659, 48 Ill. Dec. 24, 415 N.E.2d 1308.) We granted leave to appeal. The controlling issue before us is whether the proceeds of the collateral sold by Sullivan were sufficiently identified to subject them to Funk's security interest when the proof of identity consists only of a showing that the account into which they were deposited was also used for the purchase of new inventory.

Funk claims that under sections 9–306 and 9–312 of the Uniform Commercial Code (Ill.Rev.Stat.1977, ch. 26, pars. 9–306, 9–312) it has a prior perfected security interest in certain inventory sold at auction because that inventory represents proceeds of the sale of inventory which was the subject of its initial security interest. Section 9–306, in pertinent part, provides:

"(1) 'Proceeds' includes whatever is received upon the sale, exchange, collection or other disposition of collateral or proceeds. Insurance payable by reason of loss or damage to the collateral is proceeds, except to the extent that it is payable to a person other than a party to the security agreement. Money, checks, deposit accounts, and the like are 'cash proceeds.' All other proceeds are 'non-cash proceeds.'

(2) Except where this Article otherwise provides, a security interest continues in collateral notwithstanding sale, exchange or other disposition thereof unless the disposition was authorized by the secured party in the security agreement or otherwise, and also continues in any identifiable proceeds including collections received by the debtor." Ill.Rev.Stat.1977, ch. 26, pars. 9–306(1), (2).

Section 9–306(2) clearly provides that Funk's security interest would continue in proceeds of the sale of the original inventory, if Funk could identify those proceeds. Once identified, Funk's claim to the proceeds, in whatever form, would be superior to the bank's, because Funk held a purchase money security interest in the original inventory (Ill.Rev.Stat. 1977, ch. 26, par. 9–312(3)) and was also the first to file (Ill.Rev.Stat. 1977, ch. 26, pars. 9–312(5), (6)). That security interest, however, continues only in "identifiable proceeds." Should Funk fail to identify those proceeds, the bank's security interest in inventory and after-acquired property entitles it to the balance of the auction proceeds.

Although the Code provides no guidance as to how proceeds might be identified, section 1–103 directs that the Code be supplemented by "principles of law and equity," and this provision has been construed to permit application of a tracing theory known in the law of trusts as the "lowest intermediate balance" rule. As Professor Skilton notes (1977 So.Ill.U.L.J. 120, 133 n. 21), the argument that a proceeds security interest terminates when those proceeds are deposited in a bank account since they can no longer be identified has found little favor with the courts.

The rule, which operates on a common-sense view that dollars are fungible and cannot practically be earmarked in an account, provides a presumption that proceeds remain in the account as long as the account balance is equal to or greater than the amount of the proceeds deposited. The proceeds are "identified" by presuming that they remain in the account even if other funds are paid out of the account. If Sullivan is likened to the trustee of a constructive trust imposed because he commingled funds, then the lowest-intermediate-balance rule directs that Funk's proceeds in Sullivan's account are preserved to the greatest extent possible as the account is depleted. Under the rule, however, if the balance of the account dips below the amount of deposited proceeds, Funk's security interest in the identifiable proceeds abates accordingly. This lower balance is not increased if, later, other funds of the debtor are deposited in the account, i.e., the added amounts are not subject to an equitable lien, unless the latter deposits are made in restitution. (Restatement of Restitution sec. 212 (1937).) Thus the claimant has no priority over other creditors to any amount in excess of the lowest intermediate balance. In this case, Funk cannot assert a security interest in proceeds superior to that asserted by the bank unless Funk can show that those proceeds were preserved in Sullivan's commingled account or that other inventory was purchased with those proceeds at a time, and to the extent, that those proceeds were identified in the account. The identification of the funds, as stated, is subject to the lowest intermediate balance of the account.

Funk offered no evidence of the balance of Sullivan's account during the 18 months Sullivan was in arrears in payments to the escrow account. As a consequence, the lowest intermediate balance remains unknown, and the proceeds to which Funk was entitled have not been identified as remaining in the account.

Funk argues that it established a *prima facie* case by showing that secured property was sold, that the proceeds were deposited into an account, and that other items of inventory were purchased from that account, and that upon such showing the burden should shift to another to segregate the wrongfully commingled funds. Were we concerned here with the rights of Funk against Sullivan this argument would have considerable merit. The bank, however, was neither responsible for Funk's position nor for the commingling and is at least as innocent as Funk. We find no principles in law or equity which dictate that the innocent third party must suffer the consequences of Funk's predicament. Section 9–306 says that the security interest attaches to identified proceeds. Since Funk is claiming a prior security interest in property which is otherwise identified as collateral belonging to the bank under its after-acquired property clause, the burden of identifying the proceeds is properly upon Funk. . . . Funk failed to offer the proof required to identify the claimed proceeds and is not now entitled to a second opportunity to do so. . . .

Judgment affirmed.

Notes & Questions

1. *Trust Tracing in the Code.* Consider the trust tracing theory approved by the court. Suppose a debtor in possession of collateral subject to a security interest has a bank account with $8,000 in it. On February 20 debtor deposits in the account $6,000 consisting of proceeds of the collateral. On February 21, debtor withdraws $7,000, leaving a balance in the account of $7,000. What is the extent of the secured party's interest in the bank account? Does Article 9 dictate a particular answer to this question?

To what extent is the secured party's security interest perfected? See § 9–306(3).

2. *The Suitability of Trust Tracing Principles.* Note the trust law roots of what the court calls the "lowest intermediate balance" rule. In contests between a trustee and a trust beneficiary, who does the rule seem to favor? Why? Many courts, including the *Funk* court, adopted the trust tracing rule for Article 9 contests over proceeds. Do the same considerations that underlie adoption of the rule in the trust context apply in the Article 9 context? Can you suggest an alternative rule?

Should the tracing rule be phrased in terms of the existence or nonexistence of a security interest? Or should it be phrased in terms of the relative priority of the parties to a bank account? In a dispute between the debtor and the secured party, would it make sense to apply the dominant Article 9 tracing rules?

3. *Choosing a Tracing Rule.* Can one arrive at a rational tracing rule for cases like *Funk* by focusing on the party best able to protect itself? In *Funk*, was Funk or the bank better able to protect itself? What could the bank do in future cases?

4. *Attenuated Connection.* Contrast Funk's effort to connect proceeds of bill of sale items to later acquired inventory with the secured party's effort in Chemical Bank v. Miller Yacht Sales, 173 N.J.Super. 90, 413 A.2d 619 (1980). There the debtor purchased a 32-foot boat with a loan from Chemical Bank and granted the bank a security interest. The debtor (using a different name) later used the boat as a trade-in to

help purchase a 36-foot boat. A different bank helped finance the purchase of the second boat and took a security interest in it. Does Chemical Bank's security interest reach the 36-foot boat? The court suggested that it did not. "In the rather extraordinary circumstances here," the new boat's relationship to the old boat "was so attenuated and remote" that it should not be considered as "proceeds" of the old boat.

5. *Should a Security Interest Continue in Transferred Goods?* Should a security interest in goods continue notwithstanding their sale or other disposition? What factors should bear on this issue? The issue is likely to arise when a debtor, in violation of a security agreement, transfers collateral. As between an innocent purchaser and a secured party, who should prevail in a dispute over the collateral? Is the secured party or the purchaser likely to be better able to protect itself against such debtor behavior? Which party is likely to be able to obtain reasonable insurance against such occurrences?

A few states have adopted a rather drastic approach to this problem. For example, Illinois Code ch. 26, ¶ 9–306.01 makes it a felony to wrongfully dispose of collateral or not to account to a secured party for the proceeds of the sale of collateral.

6. *Section 9–306(3)(a).* What does the last clause of § 9–306(3)(a) mean? Who does it seek to protect? Does it apply in *Funk?* For a case construing the provision, see In re Swafford Furniture Co. of College Park, Inc., 10 B.R. 293 (Bkrtcy.N.D.Ga.1981).

Note on After-Acquired Property and Future Advances

Notice that the omnibus clause quoted in footnote 1 in *Laminated Veneers,* supra, granted the secured party a security interest in property that the debtor might acquire after the execution of the security agreement. "After-acquired property" clauses of this kind are common in security agreements and are expressly authorized by § 9–204(1), as qualified by § 9–204(2). These declarations are part of a complex struggle for acceptance of after-acquired property clauses. The history of that struggle is summarized in 1 Gilmore §§ 2.3, 2.4. Comment 2 to § 9–204 alludes to the past controversy.

This Article accepts the principle of a 'continuing general lien'. It rejects the doctrine—of which the judicial attitude toward after-acquired property interests was one expression—that there is reason to invalidate as a matter of law what has been variously called the floating charge, the free-handed mortgage and the lien on a shifting stock. . . .

The widespread nineteenth century prejudice against the floating charge was based on a feeling, often inarticulate in the opinions, that a commercial borrower should not be allowed to encumber all his assets present and future, and that for the protection not only of the borrower but of his other creditors a cushion of free assets should be preserved. That inarticulate premise has much to recommend it. This Article decisively rejects it not on the ground that it was wrong in policy but on the ground that it was not effective. In pre-Code law there was a multiplication of security devices designed to avoid the policy: field warehousing, trust receipts, factor's lien acts and so on. The cushion of free assets was not preserved. . . . This Article, in expressly validating the floating charge, merely recognizes an existing state of things. . . .

Section 9–204(3) provides that a security agreement may secure future advances or other value. Lenders thus may make a series of loans to a borrower under the umbrella of a single security agreement. The ability to secure future advances has led to some interesting priority problems that are pursued in Chapter 3.

C. Perfecting a Security Interest

1. When Filing Is Required

As you will already have gathered, the concept of a "perfected" security interest is central to the structure of Article 9. Only secured parties with perfected security interests have substantial rights against third parties. Only perfected security interests can survive attacks by bankruptcy trustees. Section 9–303 tells when a security interest is perfected and refers to §§ 9–302, 9–304, 9–305, and 9–306 for the specific steps necessary for perfection. As with many other Article 9 issues, one cannot begin to apply the perfection provisions without some ability to classify collateral.

What forms would you expect perfection to take? As in so many areas, possession of property plays a significant role in the Article 9 perfection scheme. Benedict v. Ratner, 268 U.S. 353, 45 S.Ct. 566, 69 L.Ed. 991 (1925), was a milestone in the dominance of possession as a means of perfecting security interests in personal property. In *Benedict*, a bankruptcy case, Justice Brandeis construed New York law to invalidate a security interest in accounts where the debtor exercised continuing control over the collections on the accounts. New York law did not stand alone in condemning security arrangements that left the debtor in control of the collateral. Section 9–205 expressly rejects the *Benedict* rule. Much of Article 9 is designed to facilitate perfection through nonpossessory means.

**COOGAN, ARTICLE 9—AN AGENDA FOR THE
NEXT DECADE, 87 Yale L.J. 1012 (1978)**

. . .

I. An Historical Preface

The idea that paramount significance attends the possession of property is the oldest concept of chattel security law. Until the early nineteenth century, the only way to create a valid security interest in personal property was by physical pledge—the transfer of possession of the property (collateral) by the debtor (the pledgor) to the creditor or secured party (the pledgee). An attempt to transfer a security interest in property that remained in the debtor's possession was considered fraudulent and invalid against third parties. This historic antipathy to nonpossessory security interests has two aspects crucial to my thesis. The first is the rationale for holding such interests fraudulent. It was assumed that potential creditors and purchasers would rely on a debtor's apparent ownership of assets physically in his possession; this was part of the basic common law doctrine of protecting creditors against undisclosed interests in property. In other words, it was a requirement that there be public notice of the creation of a security interest; physical pledge, presumably, gave that public notice. The second important aspect was the especial hostility reserved for a particular kind of nonpossessory security interest—the interest in after-acquired property, particularly in the form of inventory and accounts receivable. This hostility resulted less directly from the status attributed to possession but nonetheless may be traced to that source.

During the late nineteenth and early twentieth centuries, there developed an increasingly pressing need for credit secured by collateral that remained in the debtor's possession, especially after-acquired collateral and especially in the form of inventory and receivables. Slowly, debtors and creditors devised ways to overcome the obstacles posed by the two aspects of the possession idea noted above. The history of this struggle, manifested by a proliferation of security devices, is a fascinating story well told by Professor Gilmore; it need not be repeated here. The outcome, on the eve of the drafting of the U.C.C., was that nonpossessory interests could usually be successfully created; in the process, however, "the law of personal property security transactions [had come] to resemble the obscure wood in which Dante once discovered the gates of hell."

Article 9 brought this "labyrinthine" mélange of personal property security law under one roof. It legitimized the status of nonpossessory interests and provided a workable mechanism—filing in a public office—for satisfying the requirement that potential creditors be put on notice that certain assets of the debtor might be subject to claims by others. The draftsmen, however, did not abandon established doctrine; indeed, they accepted "without question" the distinction between possessory and nonpossessory security interests. Article 9 retains a category of exclusively possessory security interests: certain types of collateral must be pledged, essentially in the old fashion. It likewise designates a category of exclusively nonpossessory security interests: for certain types of collateral, one cannot use the pledge. For most types of collateral, however, either method is permissible. On its face, then, Article 9 only slightly reduces the role of possession. But commercial developments in the years since its drafting suggest that its nonpossessory interests are of major importance and that its retention of exclusively possessory interests is of questionable utility and, indeed, sometimes proves to be little more than a stumbling block. . . .

III. Possession and Public Notice: The Challenge for Article 9

. . . One of the most striking developments in commercial practices in recent years has been the effort to eliminate in a variety of contexts the need for "paper" evidences of interests or claims. The trend creates severe problems for Article 9, for the representative piece of paper usually falls within the category of exclusively pledgeable collateral, and the consequence of eliminating it is that the collateral becomes exclusively nonpledgeable. And then one must file to perfect one's security interest, an alternative that would appear, at first blush, to be unsatisfactory for a number of reasons—although, as I will suggest, we may have to change some notions here. . . .

Public notice is required to perfect virtually all security interests under Article 9. The requirement can be satisfied in one of two basic ways. "Notice filing" in a public office—a central Article 9 concept and in most respects a significant improvement over pre-Code systems—is a permissible means of notice for security interests in most types of collateral;[76] it is the only permissible method for "accounts" and "general intangibles."[77] Article 9 also recognizes the old-fashioned pledge as a public notice mechanism; filing, with the two exceptions noted above, is excused when the collateral is in the possession of the secured party.[78] The pledge is the exclusive method of notice for "instruments" and money.[79] The upshot is that one *must file* as to accounts and general intangibles; one *must take possession* of instruments and money; and one may do either in most other cases.[80] . . .

---

76. The general provision is § 9–302, which is phrased in terms of when filing is *not* required. . . . Numerically, filing (under the U.C.C. or some other system) is probably the most important method of public notice; notation on automobile title certificates would probably be next.

77. By virtue of omission from § 9–305 ("When Possession by Secured Party Perfects Security Interest Without Filing") and from the other exceptions to § 9–302, filing is required to perfect security interests in accounts and general intangibles. But cf. § 9–306(2), (3) (temporary automatic perfection of security interest in proceeds).

78. Section 9–302(1)(a) (filing not required when collateral is in possession of secured party under § 9–305); § 9–305 (possession by secured party perfects security interest in letters of credit, advices of credit, goods, instruments, money, negotiable documents, or chattel paper).

79. Section 9–304(1). This too must be qualified in light of §§ 9–304(4), (5) (tempo-

rary automatic perfection of security interests in instruments, negotiable documents, and goods in possession of bailee), 9–306(2), (3) (temporary automatic perfection of security interest in proceeds). If an instrument forms a part of chattel paper, perfection as to the whole (i.e., as to the chattel paper along with its accompanying instrument) may be by filing. Sections 9–105(1)(b), 9–304(1).

80. The overgeneralization in the text must be read in light of the exceptions and qualifications listed in notes . . . 76–79 supra. The most significant exception, in terms of sheer numbers, is the provision for notation on vehicles' certificates of title, § 9–302(3)(c), (4). Such security interests are so common that this mechanism might even be considered a third "basic way" of satisfying Article 9's public notice requirement. In addition, it bears repetition to emphasize that neither filing nor taking possession alone suffices to "perfect": the security interest must also attach under § 9–203(1).

A. Does the Pledge Really Give Public Notice?

The assumption behind the pledge is that, if a debtor retains possession of property he does not own "free and clear," he may use these apparently unencumbered assets to deceive potential creditors or purchasers. Hence, if such fraud is to be prevented, encumbered assets must be removed from the debtor's control. Article 9 implements the pledge through three basic provisions. Section 9–302(1)(a) excuses filing, and no other form of public notice is required. Section 9–203(1) (a) excuses the requirement of a writing signed by the debtor that describes the collateral when "the collateral is in the possession of the secured party pursuant to agreement." Thus the transfer of possession satisfies the statute of frauds provision as well as the public notice requirement. Finally, section 9–305 deems a secured party to be in possession if any bailee has possession and is notified of the secured party's interest in the collateral. The text does not require that the bailee in any way act for the secured party, but the official comment contemplates that the bailee will function as the secured party's "agent," or at least be free of the debtor's control. It then adds that the bailee need not transfer the property to the secured party or even acknowledge that he now holds the property on the secured party's behalf.

The 1988 Committee to Review Article 9 should thoroughly reconsider each aspect of this mode of "perfection" through possession. Its most fundamental function—providing public notice—seems of questionable utility, even if the secured party himself takes possession. Without possession, of course, the debtor could not obtain false credit through another physical pledge, nor could he deceive a potential creditor into relying on his possession and apparent ownership of the collateral. Many items of pledgeable collateral, however, would never be seen by inquiring creditors. A second security interest could be created through filing in certain cases, and in any event the debtor could sell the collateral despite his nonpossession. Often, it would only be by pure accident that a prospective creditor would learn that certain of the debtor's property was unavailable because now in the possession of someone else. Whatever significance there is in the pledge idea lies not in the secured party's possession but in the debtor's nonpossession, and nonpossession no longer gives much warning that the property is subject to a security interest. . . .

Public filing or recording systems were originally considered "merely as a less desirable alternative to possession." Perhaps the question of whether public filing suffices to replace a physical change of possession should now be reversed: is the surrender of possession really the equivalent of some kind of public record of the existence of a security interest? It is obvious that creditors usually bottom their credit judgments on examinations of their debtor's financial statements, not on his possession or nonpossession of particular items of property. The notion of public notice through filing may also be overplayed, but, on the whole, placing even a sketchy warning on the public record seems a much more effective way to protect the rights of all affected parties. The unfortunate dilemma is that neither the *existing* Article 9 filing system nor the physical pledge seems quite adequate or appropriate for the types of security transactions that are emerging from new developments in commercial practices.　.　.　.

See also Phillips, Flawed Perfection: From Possession to Filing Under Article 9—Part I, 59 B.U.L.Rev. 1 (1979).

The Financing Statement

To achieve public notice of a security interest by filing, one usually files a financing statement. The financing statement is a simple document, the required contents of which are set forth in § 9–402. A sample of the form of financing statement commonly used in California follows.

This FINANCING STATEMENT is presented for filing pursuant to the California Uniform Commercial Code.

1. DEBTOR (LAST NAME FIRST—IF AN INDIVIDUAL)	1A. SOCIAL SECURITY OR FEDERAL TAX NO.
1B. MAILING ADDRESS — 1C. CITY, STATE	1D. ZIP CODE
2. ADDITIONAL DEBTOR (IF ANY) (LAST NAME FIRST—IF AN INDIVIDUAL)	2A. SOCIAL SECURITY OR FEDERAL TAX NO.
2B. MAILING ADDRESS — 2C. CITY, STATE	2D. ZIP CODE
3. DEBTOR'S TRADE NAMES OR STYLES (IF ANY)	3A. FEDERAL TAX NUMBER
4. SECURED PARTY NAME / MAILING ADDRESS / CITY / STATE / ZIP CODE	4A. SOCIAL SECURITY NO., FEDERAL TAX NO. OR BANK TRANSIT AND A.B.A. NO.
5. ASSIGNEE OF SECURED PARTY (IF ANY) NAME / MAILING ADDRESS / CITY / STATE / ZIP CODE	5A. SOCIAL SECURITY NO., FEDERAL TAX NO. OR BANK TRANSIT AND A.B.A. NO.

6. This FINANCING STATEMENT covers the following types or items of property **(include description of real property on which located and owner of record when required by instruction 4).**

7. CHECK IF APPLICABLE [X]   7A. [ ] PRODUCTS OF COLLATERAL ARE ALSO COVERED   7B. DEBTOR(S) SIGNATURE NOT REQUIRED IN ACCORDANCE WITH INSTRUCTION 5(a) ITEM: [ ](1) [ ](2) [ ](3) [ ](4)

8. CHECK IF APPLICABLE [X]   [ ] DEBTOR IS A "TRANSMITTING UTILITY" IN ACCORDANCE WITH UCC § 9105 (1) (n)

9. ► SIGNATURE(S) OF DEBTOR(S)   DATE:

TYPE OR PRINT NAME(S) OF DEBTOR(S)

► SIGNATURE(S) OF SECURED PARTY(IES)

TYPE OR PRINT NAME(S) OF SECURED PARTY(IES)

10. THIS SPACE FOR USE OF FILING OFFICER (DATE, TIME, FILE NUMBER AND FILING OFFICER)

11. Return copy to:
NAME
ADDRESS
CITY
STATE
ZIP CODE

(1) FILING OFFICER COPY   FORM UCC-1—FILING FEE $3.00 Approved by the Secretary of State

[C7749]

Problem

Recall, from an earlier problem, Data Haven, a store that sells and leases computers. Data Haven carries a full line of computers, from some inexpensive Texas Instruments programmable models that sell for under $200 to relatively large models that can cost up to $50,000. When Data Haven sells on credit, it reserves a security interest in the computers to secure full payment. Data Haven is located in a small college community. Many of its small computers are sold to students for school use. Its small and middle size models are sold to consumers for home use and to college scientists for use in their work. Many of the computers sold are used for both home entertainment (video games) and for serious scientific work. The largest computers are sold mostly to college departments for research functions. What routine should Data Haven follow to perfect its security interests in the products it sells? See Part 3 of Article 9 and § 9–107.

What should Data Haven do to protect its interest in the case of the law professor who starts out playing video games on the computer he purchased and later uses it for grading exams and other professional tasks? See Cal. Commercial Code § 9–303(4).

Note on Field Warehousing

Possessing collateral obviously gives lenders a greater degree of protection than filing a financing statement. In the case of inventory to be used as collateral, it would be awkward for the debtor to give the secured party possession because the debtor would not have anything left to sell. The field warehouse, whereby a "warehouse" is set up on the debtor's premises, offers the secured party some of the protection afforded by more classic forms of possession while allowing the debtor to conduct normal sales operations. Article 7 of the U.C.C. covers the rights and duties of a warehouseman. The main benefits of a field warehouse, described below, are to protect against debtor misbehavior. Although a properly run field warehouse should qualify as perfecting a security interest by possession, there seems to be little reason for a secured party employing a field warehouse not to also obtain a security agreement and file a financing statement.

. . . Many lenders are unwilling to take the moral risk of a debtor's integrity in the conduct of his business operations. Accordingly, if the presence of the inventory collateral on the debtor's premises is a matter of economic necessity, the secured party obtains possession of it through the use of a "field" (or "on location") warehouse. The warehouse consists of all or a portion of the debtor's premises, screened off or blocked off, or a designated area on the debtor's premises to which access is exclusively controlled by the field warehouseman, leased to the warehouseman for a nominal sum. Warehouse receipts, generally nonnegotiable, are then issued by the field warehouseman in the name of the secured party. Withdrawals are permitted by the field warehouseman upon the request of the secured party in the form of a release. Usually the field warehouseman's representative on the debtor's premises is an employee of the debtor placed on the payroll of the field warehouseman. When not performing warehouse duties, the warehouse employee performs his customary duties for the debtor. The debtor pays the field warehouseman the full amount of the employee's salary plus a service charge. Signs are posted in conspicuous places on the premises indicating the maintenance of a field warehouse operation.

This has been the traditional theory of a field warehouse. A more recent variation is a procedure known as "certified inventory control," which is equivalent to a field warehouse operation with the exception that no signs are required. A minimum hold figure on the inventory of the debtor is established in the tripartite agreement among the secured party, the debtor, and the field warehouseman. The consent of the secured party to further withdrawals of inventory after the hold figure has been reached is necessary.

The advantage of a field warehouse arrangement is that a secured party can obtain a valid security interest in inventory through a pledge of documents or documents issued in his name. The disadvantage of such an arrangement is that its requirements impose restrictions that are sometimes, mildly stated, inconvenient to the debtor. On the other hand, some field warehouse arrangements are conducted very loosely, in that signs may not be posted and employees of the debtor (i.e., someone other than the field warehouseman's employee) may have access to the premises. A cautious secured party may prefer to file notwithstanding the field warehouse arrangement, since he has nothing to lose and possibly much to gain. He must file if "certified inventory control" is employed.

W. Davenport & D. Murray, Secured Transactions 198–99 (1978).

IN RE B. HOLLIS KNIGHT CO.

United States Court of Appeals, Eighth Circuit, 1979.
605 F.2d 397.

HEANEY, CIRCUIT JUDGE.

The trustee in bankruptcy appeals from a decision of the District Court directing him to pay Union National Bank of Little Rock $8,444.69, the amount owed to Union National by the debtor, B. Hollis Knight Company, Inc. (BHK), on the date BHK filed its petition in bankruptcy. The sole issue on appeal is whether Union National has a security interest in an account receivable of BHK that was perfected prior to the lien of the trustee. We conclude that the District Court applied an incorrect legal standard and, therefore, reverse and remand for further proceedings.

BHK, a mechanical contractor, received a $12,000 loan from Union National on November 26, 1976. The loan was evidenced by a promissory note and secured by various accounts receivable and other collateral. The security interest was supposedly perfected by means of financing statements that Union National had filed on all accounts receivable and contract rights owned or thereafter acquired by BHK. These financing statements had been prepared in connection with another loan to BHK and were filed on August 29, 1974, at the Pulaski County Circuit Clerk's office and at the office of the Arkansas Secretary of State. The filing in the office of the Secretary of State designated Ben

H. Knight [1] and BHK as debtors. The filing in the Circuit Clerk's office, however, designated only Ben H. Knight as the debtor. Thus, as of November 26, 1976, Union National did not have a perfected security interest in BHK's accounts receivable since it failed to list BHK as a debtor on the filing in the Circuit Clerk's office as required by Arkansas law. See Ark.Stat.Ann. §§ 85–9–401, 85–9–402.

On January 11, 1977, BHK received another loan from Union National in the amount of $6,800. The loan was evidenced by a promissory note and secured by an assignment of an account receivable from a general contractor who owed $9,720 to BHK for work on a construction job completed on January 3, 1977. The assignment stated that it was intended

> as security for the repayment of indebtedness owing by the under-signed [BHK] to the said Union National Bank of Little Rock now in the sum of Six Thousand Eight Hundred & No/100—($6,800.00) and of any other indebtedness that may become due to the said Bank by the undersigned so long as any of the debt mentioned herein remains unpaid[.]

The assignment was signed by the president of BHK and a notice of the assignment was acknowledged by an authorized representative of the general contractor on January 11, 1977. This assignment was the only assignment to Union National from BHK. No financing statements were filed in connection with the transaction. On January 11, 1977, BHK's accounts receivable totaled $68,374.58.

On January 19, 1977, BHK filed a voluntary petition in bankruptcy. On that date, it owed Union National $6,814.90 on the January 11, 1977, note and $1,629.79 on the November 26, 1976, note for a total indebtedness of $8,444.69. The schedules filed with the petition listed accounts receivable of $68,364.68. The trustee, however, was unable to collect any accounts receivable other than the account which had been assigned to Union National. The trustee collected $8,919.72 of this account and placed this sum in a special bank account by agreement of the parties pending the outcome of this action.

In his complaint, the trustee alleged that Union National's security interest in the account receivable was unperfected and subordinate to the trustee's lien which came into existence on the date of bankruptcy. The Bankruptcy Court disagreed. It determined that Union National's security interest in the account receivable was perfected on January 11, 1977, prior to the trustee's lien. The court reasoned that the assignment of the account receivable was not a "significant part" of BHK's outstanding accounts receivable within the meaning of Ark.Stat.Ann. § 85–9–302(1)(e) and, thus, Union National was not required to file a financing statement. Consequently, Union National's security interest was perfected without filing under Ark.Stat.Ann. § 85–9–303(1). The

---

1. Ben H. Knight was the owner of BHK prior to July 1, 1976.

court directed the trustee to pay Union National $8,444.69. The District Court affirmed the Bankruptcy Court.

The parties agree that for Union National to prevail, it must show that it has a perfected security interest in the account receivable under Arkansas law. The answer to this question turns on an interpretation of Ark.Stat.Ann. § 85–9–302(1)(e) which provides:

(1) A financing statement must be filed to perfect all security interests except the following:

. . .

(e) an assignment of accounts which does not alone or in conjunction with other assignments to the same assignee transfer a significant part of the outstanding accounts of the assignor[.] . . .

The District Court . . . reasoned that the account receivable assigned to Union National represented roughly fourteen percent of the outstanding accounts and, thus, was not a "significant part" within the meaning of Ark.Stat.Ann. § 85–9–302(1)(e).

The trustee argues, initially, that the District Court erred in considering the bulk of BHK's accounts receivable as outstanding accounts, since most of the accounts were unearned by performance at the time of the assignment and, thus, were uncollectible by the trustee after bankruptcy intervened. The evidence established that out of the $68,374.58 listed by BHK as accounts receivable, approximately fifty percent of this amount constituted retainage on construction contracts. The retained amounts were listed on BHK's balance sheet as accounts receivable, although successful completion of the job was a condition precedent to receiving payment. Since BHK did not complete its work on any projects after it filed bankruptcy, the retainage proved to be uncollectible due to various counterclaims and setoffs.

In our view, the District Court correctly included the retainage in the total outstanding accounts of BHK. Ark.Stat.Ann. § 85–9–106 defines "account" as "any right to payment for goods sold or leased or for services rendered . . . whether or not it has been earned by performance." Since an account need not be earned by performance, the retainage was properly classified as part of BHK's outstanding accounts although it would not be paid until the job was satisfactorily completed. Moreover, the mere fact that the trustee was unable to collect certain accounts after bankruptcy would not remove these accounts from inclusion as BHK's outstanding accounts. The determination of whether an assignment constitutes a significant part of the assignor's outstanding accounts must be made on the basis of the facts available at the time of the assignment.

The trustee . . . contends that the court should have examined all of the circumstances surrounding the transaction in deciding whether the assignment was a significant part of the outstanding accounts.

The term "significant part" is not defined in the U.C.C. Although most courts have not undertaken a careful analysis of this term, see In re Munro Builders, Inc., 20 U.C.C.Rep. 739 (W.D.Mich.1976), two tests appear to have emerged as aids in its interpretation, the "casual or isolated" test and the "percentage" test.

The casual or isolated test is suggested by the language of Comment 5 to U.C.C. § 9–302 which provides that

> [t]he purpose of the subsection (1)(e) exemptions is to save from *ex post facto* invalidation casual or isolated assignments: some accounts receivable statutes have been so broadly drafted that all assignments, whatever their character or purpose, fall within their filing provisions. Under such statutes many assignments which no one would think of filing may be subject to invalidation. The subsection (1)(e) exemptions go to that type of assignment. Any person who regularly takes assignments of any debtor's accounts should file.

The test requires a court to examine the circumstances surrounding the transaction, including the status of the assignee, to determine whether the assignment was casual or isolated. If a court finds that the transaction was not part of a regular course of commercial financing, it will not require filing. The underlying rationale behind the test appears to be the conclusion that it would not be unreasonable to require a secured creditor to file if he regularly takes assignments of a debtor's accounts, but it would be unreasonable if this was not a usual practice.

The percentage test, in contrast, focuses on the size of the assignment in relation to the size of the outstanding accounts.[2] . . . The test attempts to define the term "significant part" in a manner that is consistent with the statute and that promotes certainty in application. J. White and R. Summers, Uniform Commercial Code § 23–8 at 808–809.

Some courts have taken the approach that a proper interpretation of the section requires application of both tests. See, e.g., City of Vermillion, S.D. v. Stan Houston Equipment Co., 341 F.Supp. 707, 712 (D.S.D.1972). We are in substantial agreement with the courts that take this eclectic approach.

Both of the policies underlying the two tests appear to be valid limitations on the scope of U.C.C. § 9–302(1)(e). The language of the section would not permit an assignee to escape the filing requirement if he received a large proportion of an assignor's accounts whether or not the transaction was an isolated one. See In Re Boughner, supra. On the other hand, it is not unfair to require a secured party who regularly takes such assignments to file, since the comments to U.C.C. § 9–302(1)(e) indicate that the section was designed as a narrow exception to the filing requirement—not applicable if the transaction was in the general course of commercial financing.

2. Of course, the language of Ark.Stat. Ann. § 85–9–302(1)(e) requires a court to examine the total of all assignments to the secured party whether or not they took place in a single transaction.

We note, moreover, that Standard Lumber Company v. Chamber Frames, Inc., supra, is not inconsistent with this position. In *Standard,* the secured party, Standard Lumber Company, did not regularly take assignments from its suppliers. There was no question that the assignment was an isolated one and, thus, there was no reason for the District Court to consider the issue.

Thus, in the absence of any Arkansas law to the contrary, we hold that in determining what is a significant part of the outstanding accounts of the assignor, a court must examine all of the facts and circumstances surrounding the transaction, including the relative size of the assignment and whether it was casual or isolated.

The trustee contends that we should not consider the assignment an isolated or casual one simply because Union National is a national banking institution that regularly lends money and has, on previous occasions, made loans to BHK. We disagree with the trustee's analysis. The relevant question is whether Union National regularly took assignments of accounts receivable. There is no evidence in the record that they did. The Bankruptcy Court found that BHK had not assigned any other account receivable to Union National and the trustee does not dispute this finding. The record does not indicate that Union National ever received another assignment of accounts receivable from any other person. While Union National may do so as a matter of fact, the assignment of accounts receivable is a specialized method of securing loans, and we are not willing to assume that it was a regular practice.

The trustee also contends that, under the circumstances of this case, it was inappropriate for the District Court to have applied an arbitrary percentage. We agree. The District Court improperly limited its inquiry since its analysis ignores the qualitative differences in accounts receivable.

The ultimate uncollectibility of an account receivable standing by itself would not remove the account from consideration as one of the assignee's outstanding accounts. If, however, the assignee knew when an assignment was made that certain accounts were uncollectible, he would also recognize that their value as outstanding accounts is minute. The reasoning is similar when there are significant limitations on the collectibility of some accounts.

An assignee would have to discount their value as outstanding accounts to determine whether his assigned account constituted a significant part of the total.

This analysis merely recognizes that the liquidity of an account receivable is one of the primary considerations of a lender who is secured by a lien on the account. An assignee who receives accounts that are not subject to any limitations is usually in a better position than one who receives accounts that are subject to some limitations, although each may hold the same dollar amount of accounts. Thus, the account assigned to Union National may be a significant part of BHK's outstanding accounts although it represented only fourteen percent of the total amount since it was the only account that was not subject to significant limitations on collectibility.

Although the District Court did not make a specific factual finding in this regard, there is sufficient evidence in the record to support a finding that Union National knew there were significant limitations on the collectibility of BHK's accounts receivable.[3] The president of BHK testified that he knew the only account he could collect within thirty days was the account assigned to Union National. It is reasonable to infer that he communicated this knowledge to Union National when he applied for the $6,800 loan, since Union National specifically requested the assignment of that particular account. Moreover, Union National had some familiarity with BHK's business practices and its assets insofar as it had loaned money to BHK on prior occasions. We infer from this that Union National may have known of BHK's precarious financial position and that there was a substantial risk that the remaining accounts would not be collected because the jobs would not be completed.

Since additional factual findings must be made prior to a determination of whether the account assigned to Union National constituted a significant part of BHK's outstanding accounts, we remand the cause to the District Court. . . .

Notes & Questions

Article 9 singles out accounts (and chattel paper) for special treatment in at least one other way. Section 9–102(1)(b) provides that Article 9 covers any *sale* of accounts or chattel paper. This is qualified by § 9–104(f) which states that Article 9 does not apply to a sale of accounts or chattel paper "as part of a sale of the business out of which they arose, or an assignment of accounts or chattel paper which is for the purpose of collection only . . . or a transfer of a single account to an assignee in whole or partial satisfaction of a preexisting indebtedness . . . ." One commentary explains the above provisions as follows:

. . . [A]ssignments of accounts receivable evolved into two forms: (1) factoring, when the financer assumes the credit risk of the account debtor without recourse against the seller and notifies the account debtor to pay him directly; and (2) accounts receivable financing, when the account debtor is not notified of the assignment and the borrower retains the credit risk with respect to the account debtor. The former closely resembles an outright sale of the account; the latter, a typical secured transaction in which a security interest is taken. The two are not always easily distinguished, nor is there any need to classify a given transaction as being within one of the two forms, since both kinds of transactions constitute methods

---

3. Union National knew of this fact because it had actual knowledge of it. See Ark.Stat.Ann. § 85–1–201(25).

of commercial financing. A similar situation exists with respect to . . . chattel paper. As a result, Article 9 applies to sales as well as to security transfers of accounts . . . and chattel paper.

If all sales of accounts . . . and chattel paper are to be subject to Article 9, a problem obviously arises, since some such sales clearly do not serve as a form of commercial financing. Intermediate drafts of the 1952 Text of Article 9 extended its application "to any financing sale of accounts, contract rights, or chattel paper." By inclusion of financing sales only, the draftsmen sought to exclude all sales that did not have commercial financing as their purpose. That delineation was thought to be so vague that it would prove unworkable. As a result, the draftsmen prepared specific categories of exclusions of transactions not generally thought to serve a financing function, in place of a blanket exclusion of nonfinancing transactions.

W. Davenport & D. Murray, Secured Transactions 22–23 (1978).

2. The Effectiveness of a Particular Filing

In most secured transactions there is little difficulty in deciding, within a given state, where to file a financing statement. The ground rules for the initial filing are set forth in § 9–401(1).

CITIZENS SAVINGS BANK v. SAC CITY STATE BANK

Supreme Court of Iowa, 1982.
315 N.W.2d 20.

REYNOLDSON, C.J. In this appeal we are required to examine, as a matter of first impresssion, several provisions of our Uniform Commercial Code (UCC), chapter 554, The Code, in order to determine which of two Sac City banks, as a prior secured lienholder, is entitled to the liquidated assets of a defunct auto dealership.

Following a bench trial on a petition for declaratory judgment filed by plaintiff Citizens Savings Bank (Citizens), the court held defendant Sac City State Bank (Sac City), as prior lienholder, was entitled to $146,746.99, constituting the sale proceeds of the dealership assets. This amount currently is held by a third bank stakeholder. Trial court denied Sac City's counterclaim against Citizens for $72,582.51. This sum represented General Motors Corporation (GM) "holdbacks" paid to Citizens on the dealership's assignment. We affirm in part, reverse in part, and remand with directions.

This dispute centers around the validity of certain security agreements, their perfection, and the collateral to which the security agreements, if valid, extend.

Trial court's decree carefully distilled from the record the following relevant facts:

April 7, 1969: Sac City, which had previously been loaning money to Thomas Johnson, on this date receives a security agreement from him for a "loan" covering inventory and accounts receivable and proceeds therefrom. Inventory is defined as including but not limited to, all goods, merchandise, raw materials, goods in process, and finished goods. Accounts receivable includes, but is not limited to all accounts, notes, drafts, instruments, chattel paper and documents. The security agreement contains an after-acquired property clause.

Two provisions of said agreement, relating to all collateral secured, are pertinent to the case at bar:

"5. Debtor will not sell, lease or otherwise dispose of any Collateral Inventory other than in the ordinary course of its business at prices constituting the then fair market value thereof, without written consent of Secured Party.

"17. . . . All rights of Secured Party hereunder shall inure to the benefit of the heirs, executors, administrators, successors and assigns of Secured Party; and all obligations of Debtor shall bind the heirs, executors, administrators, successors and assigns of Debtor."

November 17, 1970: Sac City files a financing statement numbered G–65180 covering the same collateral as the security agreement and listing the debtor as "Thomas S. Johnson d/b/a Tommy Johnson Chev. Co."

May 1st, 1972: The auto dealership is incorporated as "Tommy Johnson Chevrolet, Inc." [TJC, Inc.] All assets of the operating proprietorship of Thomas S. Johnson are transferred to the corporation. The corporation retains the same address, employees, telephone number and business. Evidence reveals that Sac City knew of the incorporation at least in the early part of May, if not before. Thomas S. Johnson executes a personal guaranty to Sac City on this date guaranteeing payment of indebtedness of "Tommy Johnson Chev., Johnson Motors, Tommy Johnson Chev. Inc. and Tommy Johnson" to Sac City.

May 1972 through November 1972: Payments made on two notes from Thomas S. Johnson which were executed on January 5, 1970 and February 19, 1971 and [drawn] on the dealership's corporate account in Citizens.

May 3, 1972: A resolution of the corporate board authorizing the corporation to procure loans from Sac City is executed by Corinne M. Johnson and Thomas S. Johnson, secretary and president of the corporation respectively.

October 24, 1972: Citizens files a financing statement covering inventory, some real estate and proceeds of said collateral and lists debtor as "Tommy Johnson Chevrolet, Inc. formally (sic) d/b/a Tommy Johnson Chevrolet Co., a/k/a Thomas S. Johnson, Sac City, Iowa 50583."

November 9, 1972: Thomas S. Johnson and his wife filed for a real property arrangement under Chapter XII of the Bankruptcy Act.

December 12, 1972: Sac City filed a claim in the Johnson bankruptcy for the amount of notes claimed here.

1972–1977: Sac City purchased consumer paper with full recourse from the corporation. Payments were made on the corporate account in Citizens. Approximately $88,000.00 of consumer paper remains unpaid.

January 3, 1973: Thomas S. Johnson and his wife filed a proposed plan with the bankruptcy court. Sac City accepted the plan.

January 23, 1973: Citizens requested a UCC lien search on the following: (1) Johnson, Thomas Stratford and Corinne Johnson, Husband and Wife d/b/a Tommy Johnson Chev., Inc., Sac City, Iowa; and (2) Tommy Johnson Chevrolet, Inc., formally (sic) d/b/a Tommy Johnson Chevrolet Co., a/k/a Thomas S. Johnson, Sac City, Iowa. The search revealed only Plaintiff's financing statement.

On the same date Citizens requested a UCC search on "Tommy Johnson Chevrolet Co., Sac City, Iowa 50583." Said search revealed the Sac City financing statement, G–65180, and General Motors Acceptance Corporation's financing statement.

February 1, 1973: Citizens assist [TJC, Inc.] in filing an SBA Loan application. The application acknowledges Sac City's first lien.

July 24, 1973: [TJC, Inc.] executes a security agreement with Citizens. A security interest is granted in: accounts receivable, dealer holdbacks, warranties, dealer reserves and credits for parts returned to Chrysler Motors Corporation, Chevrolet Motor Division and GMAC.

November 11, 1975: Sac City files a continuation statement with the Secretary of State on items covered by the November 17, 1970 statement, G–65180.

March 7, 1977: Citizens again assists [TJC, Inc.] with an SBA loan application on which Sac City's first lien is noted.

September 12, 1977: Evidence shows Citizens received a security agreement from the corporation covering: accounts, contract rights, general intangibles, furniture, fixtures, inventory, machinery equipment and after-acquired property and proceeds therefrom. . . .

September 13, 1977: Financing Statement covering the above-described items is filed with the Secretary of State.

November, 1977: The corporation ceases doing business and assets are sold.

November 24, 1977: Sac City begins listing debtor as "Tommy Johnson Chev. Inc.," in its ledger.

September 13, 1977: Citizens requests a UCC lien search on, inter alia: (1) "Tommy Johnson Chev. Inc.," and (2) "Tommy Johnson Chev. Inc." The search reveals the Sac City financing statement G–65180 and its timely continuance.

April 28, 1978: Sac City withdraws its claims in the Thomas S. Johnson bankruptcy.

June 12, 1978: Supplemental bankruptcy court order stating Sac City's claim was withdrawn by reason of claim satisfaction from sale of secured property.

September 25, 1978: The instant action is filed.

January 29, 1979: Thomas S. Johnson's bankruptcy plan was confirmed by the bankruptcy court.

. . .

IV. Does Sac City Have Priority in the Proceeds of the Collateral Transferred to TJC, Inc.?

Trial court's recital of relevant facts (which, except as hereafter noted, we find in our de novo review to be fully supported in the record) reflects that when Thomas S. Johnson's dealership assets were transferred to TJC, Inc., the inventory and accounts receivable were subject to a first perfected security interest held by Sac City. This is not contested by Citizens. The latter bank contends Sac City lost its security interest in these assets because it authorized this disposition of the collateral.

This transfer of the collateral occurred in May 1972, therefore the pertinent statute is section 554.9306(2), The Code 1971:

"Except where this Article otherwise provides, a security interest continues in collateral notwithstanding sale, exchange or other disposition thereof by the debtor *unless his action was authorized by the secured party in the security agreement or otherwise,* and also continues in any identifiable proceeds including collections received by the debtor." (Emphasis added.)

This section has been amended slightly since 1971, but not substantively changed.

There was no written authorization for this specific sale or disposition. Citizens places some reliance on paragraph 17 of Sac City's security agreement (set out in trial court's findings, above) that provides the "obligations of the Debtor shall bind the . . . successors and assigns of Debtor." To interpret this as an authorization for a subsequent transfer free of the security interest would violate the overall intent and purpose of the agreement, and require us to nullify paragraph 5 (quoted above) that forbids this type of disposition without the written consent of the secured party.

We agree with trial court that no conduct of Sac City could be interpreted as a section 554.9306(2) authorization. Although the testimony is conflicting, we find Sac City did not know of the incorporation and transfer of assets until shortly after the event. We have held a *prior* course of dealing may overcome express terms in the security agreement and translate into an authorization for sale free of lien. But here there was no prior course of dealing to support a finding that Sac City authorized a bulk conveyance of business assets. . . .

Because we find Sac City did not authorize the transfer from Johnson to the corporation, Sac City's security interest continued in its collateral transferred to TJC, Inc., and in any "identifiable proceeds" from the disposition of that collateral. See § 554.9306(2), The Code. Sac City's subsequent knowledge of the transfer does not change this result.

The third sentence of subsection 554.9402(7), The Code, provides:

"A filed financing statement remains effective with respect to collateral transferred by the debtor even though the secured party knows of the transfer."

This third sentence, unlike the first sentence in subsection 554.9402(7), The Code 1977, is not deemed a change in the law but declaratory of the meaning of the law at the time these events occurred. See § 554.11108, The Code. Therefore, a new financing statement was not required to preserve Sac City's priority for this collateral.

V. Did Sac City have a Security Interest in Assets Later Acquired by TJC, Inc.?

The record discloses the money held by the stakeholder bank resulted from the sale of assets of TJC, Inc. Some of these assets were acquired from Tommy Johnson and subject to the perfected security interest of Sac City. The corporation acquired other assets after it took over the dealership. Citizens insists Sac City had no security interest in the corporation's after-acquired personal property because Sac City did not have possession of this personalty or a security agreement signed by the corporation, citing subsection 554.9203(1), The Code, and Kaiser Aluminum & Chemical Sales, Inc. v. Hurst, 176 N.W.2d 166, 168 [7 UCC Rep 730] (Iowa 1970).

Sac City seeks to cloak the corporation's after-acquired property with its security interest in Tommy Johnson's transferred assets, placing reliance on the second sentence of subsection 554.9402(7), The Code:

"A financing statement sufficiently shows the name of the debtor if it gives the individual, partnership or corporate name of the debtor, whether or not it adds other trade names or the names of the partners. *Where the debtor so changes his name or in the case of an organization its name, identity or corporate structure that a filed financing statement becomes seriously misleading, the filing is not effective to perfect a security interest in collateral acquired by the debtor more than four months after the change, unless a new appropriate financing statement is filed before the expiration of that time.*

A filed financing statement remains effective with respect to collateral transferred by the debtor even though the secured party knows of the transfer."

(Emphasis added.) We have carefully analyzed the second sentence of this section. It distinguishes between debtor and organization in the first clause. However, the UCC definitions of debtor and organization may overlap. See §§ 554.9105(1)(d) (debtor), .1201(30) (person), .1201(28) (organization), The Code. Consequently, we conclude the first reference to debtor refers to individual debtors. See id. §§ 554.9105(1)(d), .1201(30). The second reference to debtor includes both individuals and organizations. See id. §§ 554.9105(1)(d), .1201(30), .1201(28).

Sac City analyzes the situation before us as one of a mere "name change" that was not seriously misleading, hence its security interest covered after-acquired personalty of the corporation. There are at least three fatal flaws in this analysis.

First, this was not a name change situation. The dealership had been operated as a sole proprietorship. Thomas S. Johnson did not change his name. A corporation was formed with four stockholders: Thomas Johnson, Corinne Johnson, Gerald Bunker, and Bob Johnson. Although the address, employees, phone number, and business remained the same after incorporation, the business structure, documentation, employer's identification numbers, tax forms, checking accounts, and advertising did change. Sac City made no effort to establish those factors to be considered in "piercing the corporate veil." See Northwestern National Bank v. Metro Center, Inc., 303 N.W.2d 395, 398–99 (Iowa 1981). On this record we cannot view the corporation as the alter ego of Johnson. We must treat it as a distinct and different legal entity.

This leads us to the second flaw. The corporation cannot be viewed as "the debtor" as that reference appears for the second time in the second sentence in subsection 554.9402(7). Following the context of the sentence as applied to the facts of this case, the debtor acquiring collateral must be the same debtor whose name, identity, or corporate structure has been changed. But TJC, Inc., did not undergo any of these changes.

Finally, Sac City's financing statement was insufficient to perfect a security interest in after-acquired property of the corporation. Subsection 554.9402(1), The Code 1971, required that the financing statement be signed by the debtor. Further, section 554.9402(3), The Code 1971, makes it clear that the name of the debtor should be on the financing statement. See also § 554.9403(4), The Code. Sac City's financing statement does not carry the name of TJC, Inc. Thus even if Sac City had a security interest in the corporation's after-acquired property, it was never perfected.

Many of the conflicting authorities relied on by the respective parties are exhaustively analyzed by William M. Burke, Chairman of the Committee on Uniform Commercial Code of the American Bar

Association Section on Corporation, Banking and Business Law, in The Duty to Refile Under Section 9–402(7) of the Revised Article 9, 35 Bus. Law. 1083 (1980). Burke thus distills the rule that in varying factual situations will best withstand rigid scrutiny under applicable UCC provisions:

> "With respect to new property acquired by the transferee, the secured creditor must establish both the existence of security interest in the property and perfection of the security interest. Assuming that the secured creditor can establish the existence of a security interest in the property acquired by the transferee, the last sentence of section [554.9402(7), The Code] clearly does not operate to perfect the security interest. The new property acquired by the transferee is by definition not 'collateral transferred by the debtor,' within the meaning of the last sentence of section [554.9402(7), The Code]; and a financing statement filed in the name of the transferor can not perfect a security interest in property acquired by the transferee. *As to new property acquired by the transferee after the transfer, the secured creditor should obtain a new security agreement signed by the transferee and file a new financing statement signed by the transferee.*"

Burke, 35 Bus.Law. at 1100 (emphasis added and footnotes omitted). In this case Sac City did not demand a new security agreement and financing statement from the corporation, although it knew of the incorporation before Citizens filed its financing statement.

Because Sac City's financing statement was inadequate to perfect a security interest in the corporation's after-acquired personalty, Citizen's security interest prevails as to this property or its proceeds. See §§ 554.9301, .9312, The Code. . . .

Notes & Questions

1. *Change of Name.* Bank A lends money to ABC Corp. and receives and perfects a security interest in ABC's equipment. A few weeks later ABC changes its name to XYZ Corp. XYZ seeks a loan from Bank B, offering a security interest in the same equipment and not disclosing Bank A's interest. Bank B consults you about prior interests in the equipment. You conduct a U.C.C. search (see § 9–407(2)) and find no filings against XYZ Corp. Bank B makes the loan and files against XYZ. If XYZ Corp. defaults on both loans who has the prior perfected security interest in the equipment?

2. *Misfiling.* Suppose the filing officer misfiles or fails to file a proper financing statement. A subsequent lender lends on the basis of the same collateral as is covered by the misplaced financing statement and properly perfects its security interest. Does the initial lender have a perfected security interest? See § 9–403(1). Which party is in a better position to protect itself? Suppose the first lender knows that the second lender is erroneously relying on the absence of filings against the debtor?

3. *Section 9–306(2) & § 9–402(7).* What is the relationship between § 9–306(2) and § 9–402(7)? The last sentence of § 9–402(7) states that a filed financing statement remains effective notwithstanding transfer of the collateral, even though the secured party knows of or consents to the transfer. If a secured party consents to a disposition of collateral, does he even have a security interest to which a financing statement might pertain? Does *Citizens Savings Bank* provide a factual situation to which § 9–402(7) applies but to which § 9–306(2) does not? Is there any other way to reconcile the sections?

4. *Multistate Transactions.* Questions attending the effectiveness of a filing in a secured transaction involving only a single state should be separated from the question of the proper state in which to file in a secured transaction involving more than one state. The proper place of filing in multistate transactions is explored in Chapter 4A.

D. Rights Upon Default

LIBERTY NATIONAL BANK OF FREMONT v. GREINER

Court of Appeals of Ohio, Sandusky County, 1978.
62 Ohio App.2d 125, 405 N.E.2d 317.

POTTER, PRESIDING JUDGE.

On September 7, 1973, defendants-appellants executed and delivered to plaintiff-appellee their promissory note in the amount of $56,419.56. The note was a consolidation of several business loans made by appellee to appellants and was secured by security agreements covering thirteen used trucks. Appellants defaulted on payments of both principal and interest and, with the knowledge and consent of appellant Gary Greiner, appellee took possession of eleven of the used trucks in September of 1974. Appellee sold seven of the trucks at an auction and the remaining four vehicles were sold upon written bids. The amount received from the sale less certain expenses was applied to reduce appellants' indebtedness. Subsequently, appellee sought a deficiency judgment for the remaining balance of the promissory note and was granted said judgment in the amount of $39,515.20 by the Sandusky County Common Pleas Court. Prior to the entry of the judgment, the court, pursuant to Civ.R. 52, made findings of fact and conclusions of law. The conclusions of law pertinent to this appeal are:

"1. Plaintiff gave the defendants proper notice of its intended disposition of the collateral under [U.C.C. § 9–504(3)].

"2. Plaintiff's disposition of the collateral was commercially reasonable under Section [9–504(3)]. . . .

"4. Plaintiff would be entitled to this deficiency judgment if it had failed to give defendants proper notice of its intended disposition of the collateral and/or failed to dispose of the collateral in a commercially reasonable manner because the deficiency represented the difference in the value of the collateral and the defendants' obligation to plaintiff."

Appellants now appeal to this court and file the following assignments of error:

"1. The trial court erred in finding that the plaintiff gave proper notice of its intended disposition of the collateral under Section [9–504(3)] of the Ohio Revised Code.

"1–A. The trial court erred in finding that any notice was given to defendant, Shirley Greiner.

"2. The trial court erred in finding that the disposition of the collateral was commercially reasonable under Section [9–504(3)] of the Ohio Revised Code.

"3. The trial court erred in finding that the plaintiff was entitled to a deficiency judgment."

Upon taking possession of the trucks, appellee was bound by [§ 9–504(3)], which provides:

"Disposition of the collateral may be by public or private proceedings and may be made by way of one or more contracts. Sale or other disposition may be as a unit or in parcels and at any time and place and on any terms but every aspect of the disposition including the method, manner, time, place, and terms must be commercially reasonable. Unless collateral is perishable or threatens to decline speedily in value or is of a type customarily sold on a recognized market, reasonable notification of the time and place of any public sale or reasonable notification of the time after which any private sale or other intended disposition is to be made shall be sent by the secured party to the debtor, and except in the case of consumer goods to any other person who has a security interest in the collateral and who has duly filed a financing statement indexed in the name of the debtor in this state or who is known by the secured party to have a security interest in the collateral. The secured party may buy at any public sale and if the collateral is of a type customarily sold in a recognized market or is of a type which is the subject of widely distributed standard price quotations he may buy at private sale."

Appellee concedes that the collateral involved herein was not such as to exempt appellee from the reasonable notice requirements of [§ 9–504(3)]. Appellee also concedes that no notice of the intended sale was given by it to appellant Shirley Greiner, wife of appellant Gary Greiner and a co-signer on the promissory note, who was entitled to separate notice. Cf. Modern Finance Co. v. Enmen (1970), 25 Ohio Misc. 216, 267 N.E.2d 450, a decision under R.C. 1319.07, now repealed.

Appellant Gary Greiner did receive some notice of the intended disposition of the collateral when appellee repossessed the trucks and again when appellee sent a formal notice to Gary Greiner by certified mail. Appellants contend, however, that the notice given by appellee was inadequate and failed to comply with the notice requirements in [§ 9–504(3)]. Only the notice which was hand delivered to Gary Greiner when the trucks were repossessed, on or about September 9,

1974, was made part of the record. There is no contention that the notice sent by certified mail and received on October 7, 1974, differed in any respect from that which was hand delivered to appellant. In pertinent part, the notice read as follows:

"You are hereby given notice that the property secured by the financing statement or security agreement bearing the file number shown above will be sold on the tenth (10) day after receipt of this letter at Fremont, Ohio, and the minimum price for which the secured property may be sold is $4,000."

The notice also described the property, informed appellant that he would be held liable for any deficiency, and notified appellant on the last line of the notice letter that, "Any person may appear at the time and place of sale and bid on said property."

A reading of the first quoted portion of the notice would indicate that the vehicles were to be sold through a private sale. The information therein conveyed, i.e., the date after which the property would be sold, would satisfy the notice requirements of [§ 9–504(3)] for a private sale. The last line of the notice letter, however, indicates that a public sale with competitive bidding would be held. Thus, aside from any other deficiency, the notice was patently ambiguous as to what type of sale would be held. In fact, two different methods of sale were utilized by appellee. Seven of the vehicles were sold by auction on October 23, 1976. Appellee advertised this sale in several area newspapers under the caption "Public Auction." The remaining vehicles were not at the place where the auction was held and were sold upon written bids. The date of that sale was not established.

Appellee argues that although the methods of sale differed, both the auction and the sale upon written bids were private sales. Appellee contends that despite the fact that the auction was advertised as public and the public did appear, the auction was a private sale because the auction was "with reserve."

We do not agree. [U.C.C. § 2–328] provides that auctions are with reserve unless otherwise explicitly specified and the drafters' comments to that section state that an auction with reserve is the normal procedure. The term "public sale" is not defined in the code. Cases interpreting that term generally, and as used in the Uniform Commercial Code, have held that several conditions, such as publicity, competitive bidding and invitation to the public must be met before a sale can be classified as a public sale. The case law does not indicate that the distinction between auctions with reserve and auctions without reserve is relevant to the determination of the public or private character of the sale. See Annotation, 4 A.L.R.2d 575. The sale held by appellee on October 23, 1976, was advertised as open to the general public, the public did attend and competitive bidding was held. We find, therefore, that this auction was a public sale as the term is used in [§ 9–504(3)].

[U.C.C. § 9–504(3)] requires that the secured party send the debtor reasonable notification of the time and place of the public sale. Clearly, the written notice received by appellant did not fulfill this requirement. The notice did not specify the time of the sale and the designation of Fremont, Ohio, as the place of the sale is too broad to constitute effective notice of the location. The notice of the location of the sale provided for in [§ 9–504] contemplates a reasonably precise designation of the place where the sale is to be held. . . . We find, therefore, that the written notice received by appellant Gary Greiner was insufficient to comply with the mandate of [§ 9–504]. We also find that the general advertisements of the sale placed by appellee in the classified sections of area newspapers did not constitute notice to appellants of the time, place and date of sale.

As previously noted, in the case of a private sale [§ 9–504] requires only that the debtor be informed of the date after which the property will be sold. Appellee's sale of the four trucks upon written bids was a private sale. While the written notice received by appellant did contain the necessary information, when read as a whole the notice indicated that a public sale would be held. We find that the combination of the form notice for private sale with the language indicating a public sale would be held is inherently misleading and, as such, does not constitute proper notice of a private sale, pursuant to [§ 9–504(3)]. We find that assignments of error 1 and 1–A are well taken.

Our holding that appellee failed to comply with the notice requirements of [§ 9–504(3)] effects both the second and third assignments of error. We find that these remaining assignments of error are so related that our determination of the third assignment of error must precede our consideration of the second assignment of error. In their third assignment of error, appellants contend that a creditor who fails to comply with the notice requirements of [§ 9–504(3)] cannot obtain a deficiency judgment. The Uniform Commercial Code does not specifically address this issue and the question is one of first impression in Ohio. Decisions from other jurisdictions based on basically the same statute have not been uniform. See Annotation, 59 A.L.R.3d 401. Many courts have held that compliance with the code requirements on disposition of collateral is a condition precedent to recovery of a deficiency judgment and that the creditor's failure to give the required notice is an absolute bar to recovery of a deficiency judgment.

In its fourth conclusion of law, the trial court in the case *sub judice* apparently adopted a different approach which has also been accepted in other jurisdictions. Under this approach the creditor's failure to comply with the notice provisions of [§ 9–504(3)] does not automatically bar the recovery of a deficiency judgment; however, the creditor's failure to prove compliance with code requirements raises the presumption that the value of the collateral was equal to the amount of the debt and places the burden on the creditor to prove the fair market value of the collateral by evidence other than the price obtained upon resale. If the creditor fails to overcome the presumption, no deficiency judgment is allowed. A related line of cases allows the creditor who failed to give proper notice to recover the deficiency subject to a credit or setoff for the loss caused by the creditor's noncompliance. The amount of damages is presumed equal to the amount of the deficiency unless the creditor proves otherwise.

While there is respectable authority which supports the trial court's finding, we hold that the better and more reasonable construction of [§ 9–504(3)] requires us to adopt the view that a creditor's full compliance with the statutory notice requirements is a condition precedent to the recovery of a deficiency judgment. We hold, therefore, that the creditor's failure to prove that a proper notice of disposition was sent to the debtor operates as a complete defense in a deficiency action brought by the creditor. While [§ 9–507] does provide certain remedies for the debtor whose creditor has not proceeded in accordance with code rules on the disposition of collateral, that provision clearly contemplates affirmative relief and has no application to defenses. Therefore, the courts' traditional equitable power to deny deficiency judgments may be implemented pursuant to [§ 1–103].

The notice provisions of [§ 9–504(3)] were intended to afford the debtor an opportunity to bid on the collateral and to solicit any available bidders in order to insure a full and fair price and minimize the possibility of a deficiency. The code's notice provisions are minimal; requiring compliance with them before any deficiency judgment can be obtained will not impose an undue burden on creditors. See II Gilmore, Security Interests in Personal Property 1261, Section 44.9.4 (1965). We find the reasoning in Skeels v. Universal C.I.T. Credit Corp., supra persuasive. It states, in part, at 702:

"It seems to this Court, however, that to permit recovery by the security holder of a loss in disposing of collateral when no notice has been given, permits a continuation of the evil which the Commercial Code sought to correct. The owner should have an opportunity to bid at the sale. It was the secret disposition of collateral by chattel mortgage owners and others which was an evil which the Code sought to correct. It is important to note in the instant case that there was no waiver of the right to notice on disposition of collateral. A security holder who disposes of collateral without notice denies to the debtor his right of redemption which is provided him in Section 9–506."

We find that appellee failed to prove that proper notice was sent to the debtors in accordance with the mandate of [§ 9–504(3)] and because proof of compliance with such notice requirements is a condition precedent to the recovery of a deficiency judgment, we hold that the trial court committed prejudicial error in granting appellee the deficiency judgment. Appellants' third assignment of error is, therefore, well taken.

Appellants' second assignment of error concerns the determination of the commercial reasonableness of the disposition of the collateral and raises the issue of the relationship between that determination and a finding that the creditor failed to comply with the notice provision of

[§ 9–504(3)]. [U.C.C. § 9–504(3)] requires that "every aspect of the disposition including the method, manner, time, place, and terms must be commercially reasonable." The term "commercially reasonable" is not clearly defined in the code, although [§ 9–507] does provide some basic rules to assist in the determination of commercial reasonableness. In pertinent part, that section provides:

"The fact that a better price could have been obtained by a sale at a different time or in a different method from that selected by the secured party is not of itself sufficient to establish that the sale was not made in a commercially reasonable manner. If the secured party either sells the collateral in the usual manner in any recognized market therefor or if he sells at the price current in such market at the time of his sale or if he has otherwise sold in conformity with reasonable commercial practices among dealers in the type of property sold, he has sold in a commercially reasonable manner."

Further, the creditor's conduct in disposing of the collateral should be evaluated in light of the obligation to act in good faith imposed by [§ 1–203].

The code does not specifically define the relationship between the notice provisions of [§ 9–504(3)] and the requirement that the disposition of the collateral be made in a commercially reasonable manner. Some courts have held that the "commercially reasonable" requirement is general in scope and effect and is not mutually exclusive of the notice requirement. These courts consider compliance with the notice requirement as one of several elements bearing on the question of commercial reasonableness. See e.g. Mallicoat v. Volunteer Finance & Loan Corp. (1966), 57 Tenn.App. 106, 415 S.W.2d 347. Other courts have treated the issues of notice and commercial reasonableness as related but independent requirements. See e.g. Beneficial Finance Co. v. Reed (Iowa 1973), 212 N.W.2d 454. We find that the latter view best reflects the language employed by the drafters and best effectuates the purposes and policies behind the two requirements. While the issue of notice to the debtor should be considered in the determination of commercial reasonableness, that factor alone is not controlling.

In the case *sub judice,* appellee hired a qualified appraiser, sufficiently advertised the sale to the public, properly attempted to obtain the highest possible bids for the collateral, and selected an auctioneer who conducted the sale fairly. Therefore, we find that except for the failure to give the debtors proper notice, appellee otherwise complied with its obligations of good faith and commercial reasonableness. To that extent, the second assignment of error is not well taken. However, because we have found that proper notice is an independent requirement, our determination that the sale was otherwise conducted in a commercially reasonable manner does not alter the effect of appellee's failure to send the debtors proper notice of the disposition. Where, as in the case *sub judice,* the creditor fails to comply with the notice provisions of [§ 9–504(3)] the creditor cannot establish a condition precedent to recovery and, therefore, cannot obtain a deficiency judgment even if the requirement of commercial reasonableness has otherwise been met.

On consideration whereof, the court finds substantial justice has not been done the parties complaining, and the judgment of the Sandusky County Common Pleas Court is reversed.

Judgment reversed.

Notes & Questions

1. *Defining Default.* What triggers the availability of the remedies set forth in Part 5 of Article 9? What is a "default" under Article 9? See the security agreement reproduced supra.

2. *Repossession.* In *Greiner,* the secured party obtained possession of the collateral with the debtor's consent. Even without such consent, and independent of the remedies mentioned in § 9–501(1), a secured party has on default the right to take possession of the collateral. § 9–503. The secured party may do so without judicial process if this can be done without "breach of the peace," a term that encompasses something more than physical encounters.

Supreme Court due process decisions in the 1960s and 1970s raised questions about the constitutionality of § 9–503's self-help repossession remedy. Those courts facing the issue upheld the section against constitutional attack.[a] In Flagg Brothers, Inc. v. Brooks, 436 U.S. 149, 98 S.Ct. 1729, 56 L.Ed.2d 185 (1978), the Supreme Court held that self-enforcement of a warehouseman's lien under U.C.C. § 7–210 did not involve state action and, therefore, did not violate due process.

In Sharrock v. Dell Buick-Cadillac, Inc., 45 N.Y.2d 152, 408 N.Y.S.2d 39, 379 N.E.2d 1169 (1978), the New York Court of Appeals invalidated, as violative of the state constitution's due process clause, provisions of the Lien Law which authorized garagemen to foreclose possessory liens for repairs and storage charges. In Crouse v. First Trust Union Bank, 109 Misc.2d 89, 438 N.Y.S.2d 438 (1981), a New York supreme court relied on *Sharrock* to invalidate under the state constitution § 9–503 and portions of § 9–504. The Appellate Division reversed, 86 A.D.2d 978, 448 N.Y.S.2d 329 (4th Dept. 1982), stating:

> [In *Sharrock*], the Court [of Appeals] found [state] action or involvement from the fact that the state, by statute, gave the garagemen a right that he did not have at common law—the right upon default to sell without notice. At common law the lien was possessory only.
>
> Here the form of the transaction was equivalent to a chattel mortgage. At common law, a chattel mortgagee had the right, upon default, to take possession of the chattel and thenceforth treat it as his own and to sell it if he chose . . .. The statute involved here, unlike that in *Sharrock*, does nothing more than merely acknowl-

a. E.g., Adams v. Southern California First National Bank, 492 F.2d 324 (9th Cir. 1973), certiorari denied 419 U.S. 1006, 95 S.Ct. 325, 42 L.Ed.2d 282 (1974).

edge previous lawful conduct . . . and hence its enactment did not constitute significant state action or involvement.

3. *Sale or Retention of Collateral.* When the secured party repossesses collateral a series of options are available. Under § 9–504 a secured party after default may sell, lease or otherwise dispose of the collateral. Under § 9–505(2) a secured party may propose to retain the collateral in satisfaction of the debtor's obligation. In the case of consumer goods, § 9–505(1) sometimes mandates that the secured party dispose of goods for which the debtor has paid sixty percent of the cash price.

4. *Disposition of Collateral.* Section 9–504 authorizes disposition by public or private proceedings. What factors should influence the secured party in choosing between the two methods of sale? How do the methods differ? Should the secured party be offered such a choice? Why not simply say that any sale must be in a commercially reasonable manner? Does the structure of § 9–504(3) suggest that the secured party's decision to proceed with a public or private sale is not subject to the requirement of commercial reasonableness?

In *Greiner* the secured party could have sold at a private sale without running afoul of § 9–504(3)'s notice requirement. Should his effort to conduct a public sale hurt his position vis-à-vis the debtor? If Article 9 recognized only a single unified method of sale, would mistakes like those in *Greiner* occur?

5. *Notice.* Who is entitled to notice under § 9–504(3)? In Norton v. National Bank of Commerce of Pine Bluff, 240 Ark. 143, 398 S.W.2d 538 (1966), an automobile dealer sold a car to Goldsmith, who executed a promissory note and a conditional sales contract for the unpaid purchase price. The dealer sold the note and contract to bank, endorsed the note and executed a written assignment of the contract. The assignment provided that if Goldsmith should default on the note the dealer would repurchase the contract for the amount due on it. Goldsmith defaulted and bank repossessed and sold the car without notice to the dealer. Was notice to anyone required? Was notice to the dealer required? The court resolved these issues against the bank.

6. *Debtor's Remedies.* In cases like *Norton* and *Greiner,* where the secured party has not complied with Article 9's sales procedures, may the debtor recover damages from the secured party? See § 9–507. Does § 9–507 undermine the court's holding in *Greiner* that a proper sale is a prerequisite to recovery of a deficiency judgment? Compare a rule that presumes the value of collateral sold without proper notice to equal the secured indebtedness, and allows the secured party to overcome the presumption by establishing a different value. Emmons v. Burkett, 256 Ga. 855, 353 S.E.2d 908 (1987).

7. *Secured Party Options. Greiner* illustrates one of the options open to a secured party whose debtor is in default—sale of the collateral, followed by an action against the debtor for the amount of any deficiency. Article 9 offers the secured party other options as well.

Under § 9–501(1), the secured party "may reduce his claim to judgment, foreclose or otherwise enforce the security interest by any available judicial procedure." Why might a secured party prefer suing on the debt to pursuing collateral?

Notes on Special Protections for Consumers

1. Article 9 contains some extra protection for consumers who default on secured obligations. See §§ 9–505, 507. In general, however, Article 9 defers to other state and federal laws on the subject of consumer protection. See § 9–203(4). The Uniform Consumer Credit Code, adopted in approximately ten states, severely limits a secured party's right to a deficiency judgment. UCCC § 5.103. Wisconsin limits the secured party's right to declare a default and to repossess collateral. See generally Grau & Whitford, The Impact of Judicializing Repossession: The Wisconsin Consumer Act Revisited, 1978 Wis.L.Rev. 983. California bans deficiency judgments in connection with automobile (and other) foreclosures. Cal. Civil Code § 1812.5. For an interesting discussion of whether limits on the enforceability of security interests in consumer goods are justifiable, see Schwartz, The Enforceability of Security Interests in Consumer Goods, 26 J.L. & Econ. 117 (1983).

2. Regulation Z, promulgated under the Federal Truth in Lending Act, has been held to require lenders to disclose that a security interest in after-acquired property may cover only property acquired by the debtor within ten days of the loan. See § 9–204(2); Brown v. Termplan, Inc., of East Atlanta, 693 F.2d 1047 (11th Cir. 1982). But see Trust Co. of Columbus v. Cowart, 248 Ga. 691, 286 S.E.2d 23 (1982).

Chapter 3

PRIORITIES

It is in one sense misleading to single out one chapter to cover the subject of priorities—resolution of conflicting claims to the same collateral. Most Article 9 cases raise priority questions. A particular case may turn on whether one of the parties has a perfected security interest, which in turn may depend on when the debtor acquired rights in the disputed collateral. Although such a case might be studied to explore the nature of the "rights-in-the-collateral" requirement, it is, at bottom, a priority case. Two parties are asserting conflicting claims in the same collateral. Priority contests can take many different forms; this Chapter explores some of the basic forms.

A. Buyer vs. Secured Party

Some of the basic rules of §§ 9–301 and 9–307 should by now be familiar. A secured party with an unperfected security interest is on very shaky ground. Under § 9–301(1)(b) an unperfected security interest is subordinate to the rights of a "lien creditor." Section 9–301(3) defines "lien creditor" to include execution creditors as well as the trustee in bankruptcy. Thus an unperfected security interest is usually of no value in bankruptcy. We will defer until Chapters 6 and 7 a more detailed study of the relationship between Article 9 claimants and lien creditors. Under § 9–301(1)(c), an unperfected security interest is subordinate to the rights of a buyer *not* in the ordinary course of business who gives value and receives delivery of the collateral without knowledge of the security interest. Under § 9–307(1), even a perfected security interest is subordinate to rights of a buyer in the ordinary course of business.

LINDSLEY v. FINANCIAL COLLECTION AGENCIES, INC.

Supreme Court of New York, Cattaraugus County, 1978.
97 Misc.2d 263, 410 N.Y.S.2d 1002.

JOSEPH P. KUSZYNSKI, JUSTICE.

A trial before a Jury was held in Cattaraugus County on September 27 and 28, 1978. At the end of plaintiff's case for conversion and trespass, it became clear that no question of fact was in issue—but one of law, specifically whether plaintiff as purchaser of an automobile from a dealer is entitled the protections afforded to consumers under the Uniform Commercial Code (UCC) Section 9–307(1).

The Jury was then discharged and the parties stipulated on the amount of damages if the Court found for the plaintiff. Submitted afterwards were memoranda on the law.

Plaintiff Robert A. Lindsley, had purchased a used 1972 Ford Mustang automobile from H. R. Hunt Corporation, a dealer in new and used cars located in East Aurora, New York on *October 23, 1976* and paid Hunt $2,031.65 for the vehicle.

On or about *March 28, 1972* an earlier owner of the same vehicle, Virgil A. Aughtry, executed in favor of the defendant, Twenty-Nine Thirty-Nine Niagara Street Credit Union, a promissory note, a security agreement, and a standard form financing statement. This financing statement was filed in the Erie County Clerk's Office on April 11, 1972 as provided in UCC. Aughtry then transferred the automobile to one Mary Cooper, who thereafter traded the automobile to plaintiff's seller H. R. Hunt Corporation. This dealer and the Credit Union are located in Erie County.

Aughtry defaulted on his obligation with the defendant Credit Union some time prior to November 1, 1974 and the Credit Union referred the file to its attorney for collection purposes.

Plaintiff testified he had use of the automobile for five months when he received a phone call on *March 30, 1977* from a Shirley DuMont. She informed him in substance, that she represented the defendant Financial Collection Agencies, Inc., which was acting on behalf of the Credit Union. She explained that there was an outstanding security instrument lien on the Ford Mustang, and that the automobile would be repossessed, but she would allow plaintiff several days to investigate his alternatives. Plaintiff stated he called DuMont the following day, and was again informed that the automobile would soon be repossessed. He then advised his attorney as well as H. R. Hunt Corporation concerning the matter. On the night of April 5–6, 1977 the automobile was repossessed by defendants from plaintiff's driveway.

Immediately afterwards plaintiff was informed by letter dated *April 6, 1977* from defendant collection agency of the fact that his automobile had been repossessed by them and that his personal property which was in the vehicle could be reclaimed by him at an address on Chicago Street in Buffalo.

Plaintiff initiated this action by service of a summons and complaint dated *April 7, 1977*, but for unexplained reasons never joined the H. R. Hunt dealership or the prior owners of the automobile as co-defendants.

Article 9 of the UCC controls secured transactions such as the one present in this litigation which was made in favor of the defendant Credit Union. UCC Sections 9–101, 9–102. Attention is particularly called to UCC Section 9–307, entitled "Protection of Buyers of Goods". Subsection (1) reads in relevant part:

"A buyer in ordinary course of business . . . takes free of a security interest *created by his seller* even though the security interest is perfected and even though the buyer knows of its existence." (Emphasis supplied).

It is clear that plaintiff is not protected by UCC Section 9–307(1). Although plaintiff was a buyer in the ordinary course of business, the security interest in question was not "created by his seller", i.e., H. R. Hunt Corporation, but previously by Virgil Aughtry in favor of the Credit Union.

Nor is the plaintiff under the fact pattern herein, afforded any protection under UCC Section 9–307(2) which deals with buyers' protection from existing security interests, since the finance statement covering the automobile was actually filed on April 11, 1972. See UCC 9–307, Comment; National Shawmut Bank v. Jones, 108 N.H. 386, 236 A.2d 484 (1967).

Any attempt to apply UCC Section 2–403 to the facts here is also inappropriate.

This Court concludes that plaintiff's purchase from H. R. Hunt Motor Corporation is subject to the security interest perfected for the benefit of the defendant Credit Union. . . .

The motion of defendants Financial Collection Agencies, Inc. and Twenty-Nine Thirty-Nine Niagara Street Credit Union to dismiss the complaint is granted.

Notes & Questions

1. *Self-Protection.* Could plaintiff in *Lindsley* have protected himself by conducting a U.C.C. search for security interests?

2. *Consumer Buys From Initial Purchaser.* Contrast the *Lindsley* situation with one in which the car does not pass through a dealer's hands before the second purchaser acquires it. In other words, assume that Lindsley acquired the car directly from the initial purchaser. Would § 9–307(1) then provide protection? What about § 9–307(2)? What is the *Lindsley* court's view of § 9–307(2)'s function?

3. *Consensual Transfer?* Does § 9–306(2) provide Lindsley with an argument against the original secured party? Suppose Aughtry had surrendered the car to the Hunt dealership for resale and that the Credit Union knew of the surrender and proposed resale. See In re Woods, 25 B.R. 924 (Bkrtcy.E.D.Tenn.1982) (where secured party knew of the entrusting, entrusting goods to dealer within the meaning of § 2–403(2) was held to authorize sale under § 9–306(2)).

4. Is there any consolation for Mr. Lindsley? Who should he sue?

5. *Farm Products and The Food Security Act of 1985.* Section 9–307(1) excepts from its protection buyers of "farm products from a person engaged in farming operations." Why? Is the buyer of farm products different than other buyers? Are such buyers in less need of protection than other buyers? Are lenders to farmers in greater need of protection? Consider how the typical farmer might be expected to bring goods to market and how the structure of farm goods sales differs from normal retail sales.

Buyers of farm products resisted the farm products exception. Why? Can buyers of farm products quickly search public records to determine if there is a security interest to worry about? Several states enacted nonuniform exceptions to § 9–307 and offered greater protection to farm products buyers. In 1985, Congress entered the field. The Food Security Act of 1985, 7 U.S.C.A. § 1631 (reproduced in the recommended statutory supplement), allows buyers in the ordinary course of farm products to take free of a security interest created by the seller. There are exceptions when the buyer receives pre-sale notification of the security interest or when the state enacts a special central filing system that calls for central filing of security interests in farm goods and registration of likely groups of buyers of farm products and their asserted interests. The registered buyers must receive periodic lists of those farm products in which they claim an interest.

For a Department of Agriculture announcement approving a state's central filing system, see, e.g., 51 Fed.Reg. 45493 (Dec. 19, 1986) (Nebraska).

TANBRO FABRICS CORP. v. DEERING MILLIKEN, INC.

Court of Appeals of New York, 1976.
39 N.Y.2d 632, 385 N.Y.S.2d 260, 350 N.E.2d 590.

BREITEL, CHIEF JUDGE.

In an action for the tortious conversion of unfinished textile fabrics (greige goods), plaintiff Tanbro sought damages from Deering Milliken, a textile manufacturer. Tanbro, known in the trade as a "converter", finishes textile into dyed and patterned fabrics. The goods in question had been manufactured by Deering, and sold on a "bill and hold" basis to Mill Fabrics, also a converter, now insolvent. Mill Fabrics resold the goods, while still in Deering's warehouse, also on a bill and hold basis, to Tanbro.

Deering refused to deliver the goods to Tanbro on Tanbro's instruction because, although these goods had been paid for, there was an open account balance due Deering from Mill Fabrics. Deering under its sales agreements with Mill Fabrics claimed a perfected security interest in the goods.

At Supreme Court, Tanbro recovered a verdict and judgment of $87,451.68 for compensatory and $25,000 for punitive damages. The Appellate Division, by a divided court, modified to strike the recovery for punitive damages, and otherwise affirmed. Both parties appeal.

The issue is whether Tanbro's purchase of the goods was in the ordinary course of Mill Fabrics' business, and hence free of Deering's perfected security interest.

There should be an affirmance. Mill Fabrics' sale to Tanbro was in the ordinary course of business, even though its predominant business purpose was, like Tanbro's, the converting of greige goods into finished fabrics. All the Uniform Commercial Code requires is that the sale be in ordinary course associated with the seller's business (§ 9–307, subd. [1]). The record established that converters buy greige goods in propitious markets and often in excess of their requirements as they eventuate. On the occasion of excess purchases, converters at times enter the market to sell the excess through brokers to other converters, and converters buy such goods if the price is satisfactory or the particular goods are not available from manufacturers. Both conditions obtained here.

Tanbro and Mill Fabrics were customers of Deering for many years. Goods would be purchased in scale on a "bill and hold" basis, that is, the goods would be paid for and delivered as the buyers instructed. When the goods were needed, they were delivered directly where they were to be converted, at the buyers' plants or the plants of others if that would be appropriate. Pending instructions, the sold and paid for goods were stored in the warehouses of the manufacturer, both because the buyers lacked warehousing space and retransportation of the goods to be processed would be minimized.

Mill Fabrics, like many converters, purchased greige goods from Deering on credit as well as on short-term payment. Under the sales notes or agreements, all the goods on hand in the seller's warehouse stood as security for the balance owed on the account. Tanbro was familiar with this practice. It was immaterial whether or not particular goods had been paid for. If the goods were resold by Deering's customers, Deering obtained for a period a perfected security interest in the proceeds of resale for the indebtedness on the open account (Uniform Commercial Code, § 9–306, subds. [2], [3]).

Deering's sales executives advised Tanbro that it had discontinued production of a certain blended fabric. Upon Tanbro's inquiry, the Deering sales executives recommended to Tanbro that it try purchasing the blended fabric from Mill Fabrics, which Deering knew had an excess supply. Ultimately, Tanbro purchased from Mill Fabrics through a broker 267,000 yards at 26 cents per yard. Tanbro paid Mill Fabrics in full.

During October and November of 1969, approximately 57,000 yards of the blended fabric was released by Deering on Mill Fabrics' instructions and delivered to a Tanbro affiliate. There remained some 203,376 yards at the Deering warehouse.

In early January of 1970, Tanbro ordered the remaining fabric delivered to meet its own contractual obligation to deliver the blended fabric in finished state at 60 cents per yard. Deering refused.

By this time Mill Fabrics was in financial trouble and its account debit balance with Deering at an unprecedented high. In mid-January of 1970, a meeting of its creditors was called and its insolvency confirmed.

As noted earlier, under the terms of the Deering sales agreements with Mill Fabrics, Deering retained a security interest in Mill Fabrics' "property" on a bill and hold basis, whether paid for or not. This security interest was perfected by Deering's continued possession of the goods (Uniform Commercial Code, § 1–201, subd. [37]; § 9–305). Tanbro argued that if it had title by purchase its goods were excluded from the security arrangement which was literally restricted to the "property of the buyer", that is, Mill Fabrics. In any event, unless prevented by other provisions of the code, or the sale was not unauthorized, Tanbro took title subject to Deering's security interest.

Under the code (§ 9–307, subd. [1]) a buyer in the ordinary course of the seller's business takes goods free of even a known security interest so long as the buyer does not know that the purchase violates the terms of the security agreement. As defined in the code (§ 1–201, subd. [9]) "a buyer in ordinary course" is "a person who in good faith and without knowledge that the sale to him is in violation of the ownership rights or security interest of a third party in the goods buys in ordinary course from a person in the business of selling goods of that kind but does not include a pawnbroker. 'Buying' may be for cash or by exchange of other property or on secured or unsecured credit and includes receiving goods or documents of title under a preexisting contract for sale but does not include a transfer in bulk or as security for or in total or partial satisfaction of a money debt." Critical to Tanbro's claim is that it purchased the goods in the ordinary course of Mill Fabrics' business and that it did not purchase the goods in knowing violation of Deering's security interest.

Under the code whether a purchase was made from a person in the business of selling goods of that kind turns primarily on whether that person holds the goods for sale. Such goods are a person's selling inventory. (Uniform Commercial Code, § 1–201, subd. [9]; § 9–307, subd. [1]; Official Comment, at par. 2.) Note, however, that not all purchases of goods held as inventory qualify as purchases from a person in the business of selling goods of that kind. The purpose of section 9–307 is more limited. As indicated in the Practice Commentary to that section, the purpose is to permit buyers "to buy goods from a dealer in such goods without having to protect himself against a possible security interest on the inventory" (Kripke, Practice Commentary, McKinney's Cons.Laws of N.Y., Book 62½, Uniform Commercial Code, § 9–307, p. 491, par. 1). Hence, a qualifying purchase is one made from a seller who is a dealer in such goods.

A former Mill Fabrics' employee testified that there were times when Mill Fabrics, like all converters, found itself with excess goods. When it was to their business advantage, they sold the excess fabrics to other converters. Although these sales were relatively infrequent they were nevertheless part of and in the ordinary course of Mill Fabrics' business, even if only incidental to the predominant business purpose. Examples of a nonqualifying sale might be a bulk sale, a sale in distress at an obvious loss price, a sale in liquidation, a sale of a commodity never dealt with before by the seller and wholly unlike its usual inventory, or the like.

The combination of stored, paid for goods, on a hold basis, and the retention of a security interest by Deering makes commercial sense. Mill Fabrics' capacity to discharge its obligation to Deering was in part made possible because it sold off or converted the goods held at the Deering warehouse. Mill Fabrics, as an honest customer, was supposed to remit the proceeds from resale or conversion to Deering and thus reduce, and eventually discharge its responsibility to Deering. Thus, so long as it was customary for Mill Fabrics, and in the trade for converters, to sell off excess goods, the sale was in the ordinary course of business. Moreover, on an alternative analysis, such a sale by Mill Fabrics was therefore impliedly authorized under the code if its indebtedness to Deering was to be liquidated (see Official Comment to § 9–307, par. 2; Draper v. Minneapolis-Moline, 100 Ill.App.2d 324, 329, 241 N.E.2d 342).

All subdivision (1) of section 9–307 requires is that the sale be of the variety reasonably to be expected in the regular course of an on-going business. This was such a case.

Hempstead Bank v. Andy's Car Rental System, 35 A.D.2d 35, 312 N.Y.S.2d 317, stands for no contrary principle. Rightly or wrongly, it was there held as a matter of law, unlike the situation here, that the selling of used rental cars was not in the ordinary course of business for an auto rental company (compare Bank of Utica v. Castle Ford, 36 A.D.2d 6, 9, 317 N.Y.S.2d 542, 544). It may be significant that the used cars were in no sense an "inventory" of a sales business, but the capital inventory of a leasing company, usually subject to extended term financing. . . .

Notes & Questions

1. Secured Party is willing to make a loan to Debtor but has some reservations about Debtor's willingness or ability to transfer the collateral, which consists of equipment. To assure itself maximum protection, Secured Party insists on possession of the collateral. If Debtor sells the equipment to an innocent purchaser, is the sale effective against Secured Party? How does this case differ from *Tanbro Products?*

2. Did the buyer in *Tanbro Products* behave unreasonably? Should it have insisted on seeing the goods before agreeing to purchase them? Was there anything in the storage arrangements that should have raised suspicion?

3. Does *Tanbro Products* cast doubt upon the wisdom of allowing perfection of security interests by possession? Consider Mr. Coogan's comments:

> [*Tanbro Products*] not only reemphasizes that the pledge is a dubious means of giving public notice but also underscores the need . . .

to question the wisdom of another aspect of the current rules of pledge—the exception from the statute of frauds requirement of a security agreement that is signed by the debtor and that describes the collateral. A debtor who surrenders possession may have delivered the property for repair or for safekeeping or on lease. Delivery in and of itself is not proof of purpose; certainly it is not proof of the amount of debt secured or of the terms of the agreement. When the collateral is in the possession of a *bailee,* both the public notice assumption and the exception from the statute of frauds become even more questionable, and the need for a fresh approach becomes correspondingly clearer. It can happen all too easily that the bailee is either unconscious of or unconcerned about his duties as the secured party's "agent" and will allow the debtor to exercise control over the collateral.

Coogan, Article 9—An Agenda for the Next Decade, 87 Yale L.J. 1012, 1035 (1978).

See generally Kripke, Should Section 9–307(1) of the Uniform Commercial Code Apply Against a Secured Party in Possession?, 33 Bus. Law. 153 (1977).

SPECTOR UNITED EMPLOYEES CREDIT UNION v. SMITH

Court of Appeals of North Carolina, 1980.
45 N.C.App. 432, 263 S.E.2d 319.

This is an action to determine whether the plaintiff lender is entitled to possession of personal property used to secure a loan which was subsequently sold to a third party. On 29 April 1976 defendant William Michael Smith purchased an eighteen-foot 1976 Larson motorboat and a 1976 Cox trailer with funds he had obtained from the plaintiff credit union. On the date of purchase, Smith executed a note in the principal amount of $6,500 and a security agreement granting plaintiff a security interest in the boat and trailer. The security agreement stated that its purpose was to secure the note "and all extensions or renewals thereof," and the "payment of all other obligations and liabilities of Debtor to Credit Union whether now held or hereafter acquired . . . including all future advances Credit Union may make to Debtor . . . ." Plaintiff perfected its security interest in the collateral by the timely filing of a financing statement.

Defendant Smith sold the boat and trailer to defendant Herbert Ray on 19 August 1976. Both defendants executed a "Bill of Sale" reciting that defendant Ray was "aware of a lien" on the boat and trailer. On 20 June 1977 plaintiff loaned defendant Smith the principal sum of $6,239.26. Smith executed a note in this amount and another security agreement listing the boat and trailer he had previously sold to Ray as collateral. Of the proceeds loaned to Smith, $5,620.41 were used to pay the balance owed on the 29 April 1976 note and the remaining amount was applied to previous loans made by plaintiff to defendant Smith. In his application for this latter loan, Smith stated that the purpose of the loan was to "catch up on loans and bills." Defendant Smith defaulted on the note of 20 June 1977.

Plaintiff sued the defendants alleging that it was entitled to possession of the boat and trailer under the two security agreements. Both plaintiff and defendant Ray moved for summary judgment under G.S. 1A–1, Rule 56. In ruling on these motions, the trial court considered the pleadings, responses to interrogatories, documents produced, stipulations of the parties and the affidavit of R. W. Hunter, Jr., plaintiff's general manager. From the trial court's judgment denying defendant Ray's motion for summary judgment and granting plaintiff's motion for summary judgment, defendant Ray appeals. . . .

WELLS, JUDGE.

This case presents the problem of interpreting the term "future advance" as it is used in Section 9–307(3) of the North Carolina Uniform Commercial Code. The term is nowhere defined in the Code. G.S. 25–9–307(3) provides:

> A buyer other than a buyer in ordinary course of business (subsection (1) of this section) takes free of a security interest to the extent that it secures future advances made after the secured party acquires knowledge of the purchase, or more than 45 days after the purchase, whichever first occurs, unless made pursuant to a commitment entered into without knowledge of the purchase and before the expiration of the 45-day period.

The parties have stipulated that defendant Ray was not a buyer in the ordinary course of business and that plaintiff's second loan to defendant Smith occurred more than forty-five days after Ray had purchased the collateral from Smith.

We have not found any cases from this State or other jurisdictions interpreting Section 9–307(3) of the Uniform Commercial Code. Subsection (3) was added to the Official Text as part of the 1972 amendments and was effective in North Carolina on 1 July 1976. 1975 N.C. Sess.Laws, ch. 862, § 7. The obvious purpose of the subsection is to define the priorities between a secured party and a purchaser other than a buyer in the ordinary course of business and to encourage the lenders and purchasers affected to shape their business practices on this basis.

> The provision proceeds on the assumption that, after an appropriate grace period, a creditor should know whether the collateral has been sold before making another advance or committing himself to one. Unless he has knowledge to the contrary, the secured party is allowed for 45 days to assume that the debtor still owns the collateral. Advances made with knowledge, or after the 45-day period, may not be secured by the sold collateral . . . .

1 Bender's Uniform Commercial Code Service § 3A.03[c], p. 202 (1979). Thus, under this subsection of the Code, in situations such as the one here a prudent lender would be well-advised to make sure that the

debtor has not transferred or otherwise disposed of the collateral securing the original loan before attempting to expand the obligation covered by the security under the original security agreement's future advances clause. . . .

So the question in the instant case is the nature of the loan transaction of 20 June 1977. The parties agree that if it constituted merely an extension or renewal of plaintiff's obligation of 29 April 1976, it was not a future advance. It is also apparent from the above analysis that, to the extent the second loan may have placed an additional burden on the collateral, it must be considered a future advance. If the second loan was intended by the parties to extinguish the first obligation, the entire amount of the second obligation would be considered a future advance.

Plaintiff relies in large part on Mid-Eastern Electronics, Inc. v. First Nat. Bank of So. Md., 455 F.2d 141 (4th Cir. 1970) in support of its position that the second loan transaction constituted an extension or renewal of the original debt as a matter of law. In that case the issue was whether the creditor's failure to include a future advances clause in its original security agreement caused it to lose its security interest in the collateral following a subsequent exchange of new notes for the old notes. The district court had concluded that new notes were future advances as a matter of law. The Fourth Circuit reversed the district court on this point, holding that the intent of the parties governed and that there was no indication that the parties had intended that the new notes serve any purpose other than to renew or extend the earlier obligation. Likewise, the pre-Code law in North Carolina held that an exchange of notes was presumed not to extinguish the underlying obligation unless the parties intended that such an extinguishment occur. The Code continues the same rule. G.S. 25–3–802(1)(b).

In *Mid-Eastern,* however, no new advances were made to the debtor—there was a mere exchange of notes. The debtor admitted in his deposition that the subsequent transaction constituted a "renewal" of the prior debt. The Court stated that the fact the old notes were returned to the debtor as new notes were issued did not, *in and of itself,* rebut the inference that the original indebtedness had not been extinguished. The *Mid-Eastern* Court distinguished the circumstances present in that case from the situation involved in Safe Deposit Bank & Trust Co. v. Berman, 393 F.2d 401 (1st Cir. 1968), where new notes were issued which increased the debtor's obligation owed to the bank. The *Berman* Court had treated the subsequent loan as a future advance.

It therefore becomes evident that in the case *sub judice,* different factual inferences may be drawn as to the intent of the parties from the circumstances surrounding the 20 June 1977 loan. Supporting the inference that although a part of the loan was intended to pay off the 29 April 1976 obligation, the latter transaction was not intended to simply renew the April 1976 debt is the fact that it involved an actual advance of funds by the credit union which defendant Smith could have used for any purpose. Smith was not obligated to apply any of the proceeds toward the earlier obligation. The June 1977 transaction involved a note for a greater amount than the balance owing on the earlier note and contained somewhat different terms than the previous note. A new security agreement was in fact entered into by the parties. This was not a mere exchange of notes for notes, as was the situation in *Mid-Eastern*. That defendant here used the proceeds of the 20 June 1977 note to satisfy the April 1976 obligation, which was subsequently marked "paid and satisfied," may not itself be conclusive. Lancaster v. Stanfield, supra. When viewed together with the other circumstance mentioned above it does, however, provide some additional evidence that the June 1977 transaction was intended to extinguish the earlier obligation.

On the other hand, there are facts present which support an inference that the 20 June 1977 transaction constituted a renewal of the earlier obligation. Defendant Smith stated that the purpose of the June 1977 loan was to *"catch up* on loans and bills" (emphasis added). One of plaintiff's agents stated during discovery that the purpose of the loan was to "renew and refinance" the earlier obligation. Plaintiff also argues that the execution of a second security agreement with somewhat different terms was mandated by Federal law and that the amount of the second loan differed from the balance owing on the April 1976 note because the second note consolidated three loans which plaintiff had made to defendant. These arguments and explanations should be considered and weighed by the trier of fact at trial. However, on motion for summary judgment they cannot be deemed to conclusively determine the factual issue of the intent of the parties. We agree with defendant Ray, that in light of the other circumstances present in this case, the fact that the parties in their stipulations agreed that the 1977 loan "refinanced" the 1976 note involved an unfortunate and unintended use of this term by counsel for defendant Ray, which should not be deemed determinative.

Summary judgment is appropriate only where the movant has shown that no material issue of fact exists and that he is entitled to judgment as a matter of law. If different material conclusions can be drawn from the evidence, summary judgment should be denied. In the present case, the circumstances surrounding the June 1977 loan transaction do not lead, as a matter of law, to a single conclusion as to the intent of the parties to either renew, enlarge or extinguish the April 1976 note. We therefore affirm the trial court's denial of defendant Ray's motion for summary judgment and reverse the granting of plaintiff's motion for summary judgment.

Affirmed in part and reversed in part.

Notes & Questions

1. *Characterizing Loans.* Consider the issue that the court in *Spector United* finds to be determinative. Is it helpful to think about

loans being either "renewal" loans or being "new" loans? Do the parties to loan transactions necessarily care how the later advances are characterized? If they do not care, how should courts go about determining the "true character" of the later advances?

2. *Protecting Oneself.* Under § 9–307(3) how is a secured party to protect itself from making advances after a debtor has sold collateral to a buyer not in the ordinary course of business? If the secured party makes a physical inspection of the debtor's assets, will this assure priority against a buyer who has bought the collateral but not yet taken delivery?

3. *Intervening Interests.* Sections 9–307(3), 9–301(4), and 9–312(7) were added to the Code in 1972 to clarify the status of advances made after intervening interests in collateral arose. See Chapter 7B infra.

B. Secured Party vs. Secured Party

1. Disputes Over Goods

Section 9–312 is the principal section used to resolve disputes between competing secured parties. To introduce it, please work through the following problems.

1. On January 1, A lends money to debtor and receives a security interest in debtor's property. A does not file or otherwise perfect her security interest. On February 1, B lends money to debtor, receives a security interest and properly files to perfect her security interest. Debtor defaults on his obligations to A and B. Which security interest attached first? Which party is entitled to priority in debtor's property? See §§ 9–312(5)(a), 9–301(1)(a).

2. Same facts except that B knows of A's security interest at the time that B extends credit to debtor.

3. Same facts except that B also never files or otherwise perfects his security interest.

4. On January 1 Debtor, seeking a $10,000 loan, commences negotiations with Secured Party 1. On January 2, in the course of the negotiations, Secured Party 1 files a financing statement covering Debtor's equipment. The parties, however, are unable to reach agreement and no loan is made at this time.

On February 1, Secured Party 2 lends Debtor $20,000 and obtains and perfects a security interest in Debtor's equipment.

On March 1, Secured Party 1 lends Debtor $30,000 and obtains a security interest in Debtor's equipment. Secured Party 1 does not file a new financing statement.

When were the secured parties' security interests perfected? Which Secured Party has priority in Debtor's equipment? See Example 1 to comment 5 to § 9–312.

ALLIS–CHALMERS CREDIT CORP. v.
CHENEY INVESTMENT, INC.

Supreme Court of Kansas, 1980.
227 Kan. 4, 605 P.2d 525.

PRAGER, JUSTICE:

This is a dispute between two secured creditors over the priority of their security interests in an Allis-Chalmers combine. The facts in the case are undisputed and are covered generally by a stipulation of facts filed by the parties in district court. The factual circumstances giving rise to the controversy are set out in chronological order as follows: On November 16, 1970, Lloyd Catlin executed a retail installment contract to Ochs, Inc., a dealer for Allis-Chalmers Corporation, to cover the purchase price of an Allis-Chalmers combine identified as G–7754. This contract was in a total amount of $10,149.44 including the financing charge. There was no provision in the contract for future advances. In the course of the opinion, this will be referred to as contract # 1. This contract was assigned to plaintiff-appellant, Allis-Chalmers Credit Corporation, who financed the transaction. On November 27, 1970, a financing statement covering combine G–7754 was filed by Allis-Chalmers with the register of deeds of Barber County, Kansas.

On December 19, 1970, Cheney Investment Company, Inc., the defendant-appellee, made a cash advance to Lloyd Catlin, taking a security interest (chattel mortgage) in combine G–7754. On December 24, 1970, Cheney Investment filed a financing statement covering combine G–7754 with the Barber County register of deeds. In the course of the opinion, we will refer to the security interest of Cheney Investment as the chattel mortgage. On September 17, 1971, Catlin purchased a new Allis-Chalmers combine G–17992 from Highway Garage and Implement Company, another dealer of Allis-Chalmers. The retail installment contract which created the security interest included both the new combine, G–17992, and the used combine, G–7754. This contract will be referred to in the opinion as contract # 2. Contract # 2 provided that contract # 1 was cancelled and the notation "Payoff ACCC–Wichita $4,542.00" was written on its first page. The balance owing under contract # 1 was included in the purchase price stated in contract # 2. There was no other reference to the prior security agreement or financing statement. On September 29, 1971, Allis-Chalmers Credit Corporation, as assignee of contract # 2 from Highway Garage and Implement Company, filed a financing statement covering both the new combine G–17992 and the used combine G–7754. On February 16, 1972, Allis-Chalmers notifed Cheney Investment of its claim to a senior security interest on combine G–7754, as Cheney had taken possession of that combine when Catlin defaulted on his loan payments to Cheney Investment.

On May 30, 1972, Allis-Chalmers and Cheney Investment executed a letter agreement to allow combine G–7754 to be returned to Catlin, the debtor, with each party to notify the other if Catlin defaulted on either financing agreement. On September 11, 1973, after several revisions and amendments to contract # 2, Catlin sold combine G–17992 and paid Allis-Chalmers $11,641.12, leaving an unpaid blance of $8,300. A new payment schedule was prepared for the balance owing plus a new finance charge. Thereafter, Catlin defaulted on his payments, both to Allis-Chalmers and to Cheney Investment. On March 1, 1974, Cheney Investment sold combine G–7754 at a chattel mortgage sale, having taken possession shortly after Catlin defaulted on the Allis-Chalmers obligation. Allis-Chalmers participated in the sale but was not the purchaser. The sale proceeds totaled $8,560. Subtracting the amount then owing to Cheney Investment and costs, there remained $2,111.80 to satisfy the security interest of Allis-Chalmers.

Following the above events, the plaintiff, Allis-Chalmers, brought this action against Cheney Investment for conversion of combine G–7754, claiming a senior and prior security interest. At that time, Catlin's indebtedness to Allis-Chamers was in the amount of $8,650 plus interest. In its answer, Cheney Investment claimed a first and prior lien against the combine in the amount of $6,093.79 plus interest. All of the above facts were stipulated by the parties. In addition to the stipulation, the case was submitted on the deposition of Richard F. Ellis, vice-president of Allis-Chalmers. In his deposition, Ellis testified that contract # 1 between Ochs, Inc., and Lloyd Catlin was paid off and canceled at the time contract # 2 was executed and the balance owing on contract # 1 was carried forward and became a part of the consideration for contract # 2. He agreed that contract # 2 was a new and separate contract.

 . . . The trial court entered judgment in favor of defendant Cheney Investment, and Allis-Chalmers has appealed to this court.
 . . .

In this case, both of the parties have perfected their respective security interests. Simply stated, the issue to be determined is which of their security interests is entitled to priority over the other. Section 84–9–312(5)(a) governs the priority as between conflicting security interests. Prior to 1975, K.S.A. 84–9–312 provided in part as follows:

"Priorities among conflicting security interests in the same collateral. (1) The rules of priority stated in the following sections shall govern where applicable: . . .

"(5) In all cases not governed by other rules stated in this section . . . priority between conflicting security interests in the same collateral shall be determined as follows:

"*(a) In the order of filing if both are perfected by filing, regardless of which security interest attached first under section 84–9–204(1) and whether it attached before or after filing;*" (Emphasis supplied.)

 . . . As pointed out in the official UCC comment to 84–9–402, this section adopts a system of "notice filing." The notice itself indicates merely that the secured party may have a security interest in the collateral described. The burden is placed upon other persons to make further inquiry from the parties concerned in order to obtain a disclosure of the complete state of affairs. The code philosophy is that a simple, filed notice that the secured party and debtor *may* be financing with respect to collateral described in the financing statement should be a "red flag" warning to third parties not to proceed with any financing on the same collateral of the debtor until investigation is made to see that the road ahead has been cleared. See In re Rivet, 299 F.Supp. 374, 379 (E.D.Mich.1969), citing Professor Roy L. Steinheimer, Jr., of the University of Michigan Law School, in a commentary on 9–402 in 23 M.C.L.A. 467. In his article, Professor Steinheimer suggests that if there is a prior filing, the second lender should do one of the following things:

(1) Insist that the record be cleared by the filing of a termination statement under 9–404, or

(2) Enter into a subordination agreement with the first lender which appropriately apportions priorities in the collateral under 9–316.

The controversy arose in this case, as it has in other cases, because K.S.A. 84–9–312(5)(*a*), as originally adopted, did not have clear and specific language governing the right of a lender to include later advances made in subsequent transactions under the financing statement filed at the time of the original transaction. It should be noted that K.S.A. 84–9–204(5) provided that "[o] bligations covered by a security agreement may include future advances or other value whether or not the advances or value are given pursuant to commitment."

The issue as to the priority of the security interest of a lender, who made advances after the filing of the original financing statement, over the security interest of an intervening creditor came before a Rhode Island superior court in Coin-O-Matic Service Co. v. Rhode Island Hospital Trust Co., 3 U.C.C.Rptr.Serv. 1112 (R.I.Super.Ct.1966). The district court in the present case relied upon *Coin-O-Matic* in holding that the security interest of Cheney Investment was prior to the security interest of Allis-Chalmers. In *Coin-O-Matic*, the debtor gave a security interest in an automobile to the seller, who assigned the debt to Rhode Island Hospital Trust Company which filed a financing statement. One year later, the debtor gave Coin-O-Matic a security interest. It filed a financing statement. The following month, Rhode Island Hospital Trust Company loaned the debtor an additional sum of money, one-third of which was used to pay off the first note to Rhode Island Hospital Trust Company. The first note was cancelled, a new security agreement executed, and a new financing statement filed. When the debtor went into bankruptcy, both Coin-O-Matic Service Company and Rhode Island Hospital Trust Company claimed a prior security interest in the automobile. Rhode Island Hospital Trust Company argued that the first financing statement was sufficient to protect the second contract, as it effectively put the whole world on notice that the collateral was subject to present and future security interests in favor of the filing party. This argument was rejected by the Rhode Island superior court. The *Coin-O-Matic* court first recognized that giving the first-to-file priority in all subsequent transactions placed the lender in an unusually strong position. The court reasoned that, under such a holding, the debtor would be precluded from obtaining a second loan, even to pay off the first, because subsequent lenders would be reluctant to lend money based on the collateral already mortgaged, as their security interest would always be subject to preemption by a subsequent security agreement in favor of the first creditor. The court stated that to construe the UCC to give the first lender an interest in collateral for future advances, absent future advance provisions in the security agreement, would render information obtained under 9–204 irrelevant. The court noted that the first creditor could easily protect future advances by including a future advance provision as authorized by 9–204(5) [now 9–204(3)].

The ultimate conclusion in *Coin-O-Matic* was that a reasonable interpretation of 9–312(5)(*a*) should be that a "single financing statement in connection with a security agreement, when no provision is made for future advances, is not an umbrella for future advances based upon new security agreements, notwithstanding the fact that involved is the same collateral." (3 U.C.C.Rptr.Serv. at 1120.) This portion of the decision in *Coin-O-Matic* caused controversy and widespread criticism of the rule announced therein.

The holding in *Coin-O-Matic*, requiring a future advance clause in the original security instrument in order for future advances to have 9–312 priority, has been rejected by the vast majority of the jurisdictions in subsequent cases. In rejecting *Coin-O-Matic*, those courts generally stress the "notice" or "red flag" function of the code and hold that a financing statement on file is notice to the entire world of present or *future* security interests in the collateral. . . .

The rationale found in James Talcott, Inc. v. Franklin National Bank, 292 Minn. at 290–292, 194 N.W.2d at 784, well illustrates the approach taken by those courts which have rejected the rule adopted in *Coin-O-Matic:*

"Even where the parties originally contemplate a single debt, secured by a single item of property or a single group of items, the secured party and the debtor may enter into further transactions whereby the debtor obtains additional credit and the secured party is granted more security. The validity of such arrangements as against creditors, trustees in bankruptcy, and other secured parties has been widely recognized by many courts.

"Using future-advance clauses and using after-acquired property clauses in the original security agreement are not the only means by which perfected security interests can be obtained in subsequently contracted obligations or in goods the debtor may later come to own. There is nothing exclusive about § 336.9–204(3, 5). Parties may use future-advance and after-acquired clauses, and they are a great convenience. But, if they are not used, there is nothing in the code which prevents the parties from accomplishing the same result by entering into one or more additional security agreements.

". . . The better view holds that, where originally a security agreement is executed, an indebtedness created, and a financing statement describing the collateral filed, followed at a later date by another advance made pursuant to a subsequent security agreement covering the same collateral, the lender has a perfected security interest in the collateral not only for the original debt but also for the later advance." . . .

. . . We have concluded that the district court in this case was not justified in relying upon the decision in *Coin-O-Matic*. The rule of *Coin-O-Matic* was immediately rejected by the UCC permanent editorial board. It conceded that under the 1962 code, as originally adopted, the position of an intervening creditor in reference to a subsequent advance by an earlier secured party was debatable. In order to clarify the matter, the editorial board suggested an amendment to 84–9–312 by the addition of a new subsection (7) which was subsequently adopted in various states. Subsection (7) was adopted by the Kansas legislature by amendment of K.S.A. 84–9–312 in 1975, effective January 1, 1976. The new subsection (7) may be found at K.S.A.1979 Supp. 84–9–312(7) and is as follows:

"(7) If future advances are made while a security interest is perfected by filing or the taking of possession, the security interest has the same priority for the purposes of subsection (5) with respect to the future advances as it does with respect to the first advance. If a commitment is made before or while the security interest is so perfected, the security interest has the same priority with respect to advances made pursuant thereto. In other cases a perfected security interest has priority from the date the advance is made."

The issue has clearly been laid to rest in Kansas by the adoption of the new subsection (7) of K.S.A.1979 Supp. 84–9–312 by the Kansas legislature in 1975. We note the official UCC comment to that section which is printed in the 1979 Supp. at p. 64, and which states as follows:

"7. The application of the priority rules to future advances is complicated. In general, since any secured party must operate in reference to the Code's system of notice, he takes subject to future advances under a priority security interest while it is perfected through filing or possession, whether the advances are committed or non-committed, and to any advances subsequently made 'pursuant to commitment' (Section 9–105) during that period."

Comment (7) is followed by example 5, which sets forth a hypothetical factual situation involving a question of priority which essentially presents the same issue to be decided in this case. It states:

"Example 5. On February 1 A makes an advance against machinery in the debtor's possession and files his financing statement.

On March 1 B makes an advance against the same machinery and files his financing statement. On April 1 A makes a further advance, under the original security agreement, against the same machinery (which is covered by the original financing statement and thus perfected when made). A has priority over B both as to the February 1 and as to the April 1 advance and it makes no difference whether or not A knows of B's intervening advance when he makes his second advance.

"A wins, as to the April 1 advance, because he first filed even though B's interest attached, and indeed was perfected, before the April 1 advance. The same rule would apply if either A or B had perfected through possession. Section 9–204(3) and the Comment thereto should be consulted for the validation of future advances.

"The same result would be reached even though A's April 1 advance was not under the original security agreement, but was under a new security agreement under A's same financing statement or during the continuation of A's possession."

Also note should be taken of the official UCC comment to K.S.A. 1979 Supp. 84–9–402, which states on p. 75 of the 1979 Supp. as follows:

"However, even in the case of filings that do not necessarily involve a series of transactions the financing statement is effective to encompass transactions under a security agreement not in existence and not contemplated at the time the notice was filed, if the description of collateral in the financing statement is broad enough to encompass them. Similarly, the financing statement is valid to cover after-acquired property and future advances under security agreements whether or not mentioned in the financing statement."

It is clear that subsection (7) was adopted by the Kansas legislature to make it clear that K.S.A. 84–9–312(5)(a) should be applied to future advances made by the first creditor, whether such advances are "committed" or "noncommitted" thus making it immaterial whether or not there was a future advance provision in the original security agreement. We regard this amendment as a clarification of the original intent of the legislature when it adopted the Uniform Commercial Code in 1965.

On the basis of the reasoning set forth above, we hold that the security interest of Allis-Chalmers in combine G–7754 is prior and superior to the security interest of the defendant, Cheney Investment, Inc. Under the undisputed facts, the proceeds from the sale of the Allis-Chalmers combine G–7754 totaled $8,650. At the time the suit was filed, Catlin's indebtedness to Allis-Chalmers was in the total amount of $8,650 plus interest. Since the security interest of Allis-Chalmers equals or exceeds the amount of the net proceeds received from the sale of the combine, after expenses of sale, Allis-Chalmers is entitled to apply the net proceeds to its debt. . . .

HOLMES, JUSTICE, dissenting.

I must respectfully dissent. In my opinion the trial court reached the right conclusion in this case and I would adopt the rule and reasoning set forth by the Rhode Island Superior Court in Coin-O-Matic Service Co. v. Rhode Island Hospital Trust Co., 3 U.C.C.Rptr.Serv. 1112 (R.I.Super.Ct.1966), cited and discussed in the majority opinion. . . .

As noted by the majority, a basic theory behind the UCC is one of notice filing and that a notice when filed becomes a red flag to be heeded by all. However, the same applies to the filing made by defendant Cheney Investment, Inc. Their filing is also a red flag to all who might thereafter undertake dealings with the original debtor, Catlin. In the instant case it appears clear that the initial contract and obligation underlying the first filing by Allis-Chalmers was paid and satisfied at the time the second contract was entered into and a second financing statement filed. To say that, lacking a future advance clause as contemplated by the code, life could be breathed back into the first filing when the underlying obligation upon which it was based has been satisfied is difficult to accept.

The majority chooses to follow the majority rule that no future advance clause was necessary in the initial security instrument but concedes that the meaning of the statute (84-9-312[5]), upon which this conclusion rests, was debatable. The UCC permanent editorial board recognized the deficiency and recommended the addition of 9-312(7) to the code. Kansas adopted this new provision, to cover situations like the one before this court, in 1975. However, this case must be determined under the "debatable" meaning of the code prior to that amendment.

Plaintiff could have protected its future advances and its second contract by the notice filed under the first contract, if it had desired to do so, by complying with former 84-9-204(5) and including an after-acquired property and future advance clause in the original security agreement. The official UCC comment to 84-9-204(5) states in part:

"8. Under subsection (5) collateral may secure future as well as present advances when the security agreement so provides. . . .
In line with the policy of this Article toward after-acquired property interests this subsection validates the future advance interest, provided only that the obligation be covered by the security agreement." K.S.A. vol. 7, page 352. . . .

In the instant case the parties appear to have considered the original transaction as a single transaction. No provision was made in the security agreement for future advances or after-acquired collateral. At the time of the second transaction a new combine was purchased, a new contract prepared, the old contract was paid off and cancelled. The case falls squarely within the rationale and holding of *Coin-O-Matic* and the opinion in that case is, in my opinion, a correct application of the UCC provisions as they existed prior to the 1975 amendment to the statute. . . .

SCHROEDER, C. J., and HERD, J., join the foregoing dissenting opinion.

Notes & Questions

1.   Does § 9–312(7) resolve the dispute in *Allis-Chalmers?* Suppose Secured Party 1's initial loan is fully paid off, Secured Party 2 perfects her security interest, and Secured Party 1 then makes additional advances.   Are the future advances in such a case made "while a security interest is perfected by filing?"   Can § 9–312(7) be said to address the issue in *Allis-Chalmers* but not to address the issue in the above hypothetical case?   Is it possible that § 9–312(7) addresses neither dispute?   See comment 7 to § 9–312.

2.   Contrast § 9–312(7)'s treatment of an intervening secured party with § 9–301(4)'s treatment of an intervening lien creditor and § 9–307(3)'s treatment of an intervening buyer.   Do the variations in treatment make sense?

Section 9–307(3), as well as § 9–301(4), were seen to suggest in *Spector United,* supra, that a secured party who contemplates making future advances ought to check to see if the debtor still has physical possession of the collateral.   Do the majority of jurisdictions, in rejecting *Coin-O-Matic,* implicitly adopt a different view of whether a secured party making future advances ought to have to check for intervening U.C.C. filings?   Does it make sense to require a secured party to have to check for sales not in the ordinary course of business but not to have to check for assertions of security interests?

3.   As the court notes, the *Coin-O-Matic* approach has been rejected by most courts.   Indeed, the Bankruptcy Court for the District of Rhode Island has concluded that *Coin-O-Matic* is not good law in its own state.   In re Nason, 13 B.R. 984 (Bkrtcy.D.R.I.1981).   It nevertheless still has some followers.   See ITT Industrial Credit Co. v. Union Bank and Trust Co., 615 S.W.2d 2 (Ky.1981).

In jurisdictions in which *Coin-O-Matic* is not followed, consider a lender who conducts a U.C.C. search and finds Secured Party's financing statement.   Upon inquiry, Secured Party informs the lender that Debtor has no outstanding obligations to Secured Party.   The lender then makes a loan to Debtor.   If Secured Party subsequently makes a loan to Debtor, should Secured Party come ahead of the lender?   If not, does the lender have any choice but to insist that that financing statement be cleared from the files before making a loan?   If the *Coin-O-Matic* rule is rejected, does the addition of future advances clauses to security agreements become superfluous?   If an initial financing statement perfects a security interest in later loans, why bother to insert language in the security agreement that covers future advances?

2. Disputes Involving Less Tangible Forms of Collateral

CHRYSLER CREDIT CORP. v. SHARP

Supreme Court of New York, Erie County, 1968.
56 Misc.2d 261, 288 N.Y.S.2d 525.

This is an action brought against Dorothy Mae Sharp, as buyer, upon a retail installment contract to recover the amount due upon an automobile sales contract and also to recover against the Marine Midland Trust Company of Western New York, the bank which provided floor plan financing to the automobile dealer on the theory of conversion for the reasonable market value of an automobile seized and sold by the said defendant bank. The action against Alfred M. Heintzman, individually, sounding in fraud, has been withdrawn from the consideration of the Court by stipulation. The defendant, Dorothy Mae Sharp, has never been served and her whereabouts are unknown. The determinations are based on a non-jury trial of the issues.

Upon the evidence, in February, 1966, Mrs. Sharp contacted a car dealer in the City of Buffalo, Heintzman-McRae Motors, Inc., through its sales manager, William Peterson, and sought the purchase of a 1963 Chevrolet automobile. On February 16, 1966, she signed a printed form captioned "car order" which was received by the dealer subject to acceptance after a credit investigation by the plaintiff as proposed retail financer. The proposed purchase was, according to records of the plaintiff, phoned into for approval at 9:40 o'clock and approved at 10:30 o'clock by the plaintiff. Thereafter, a formal printed instrument entitled "Retail Installment Contract" was signed by Mrs. Sharp and by the dealer's office manager. The contract follows the form requirements of Article 9, Personal Property Law. It was dated February 16, 1966. On the following day, it was endorsed by the president of the dealer corporation to the plaintiff. Payment of the cash balance received by the dealer from the sale of the retail finance contract to the plaintiff was deposited by the dealer in its deposit account with the defendant bank on February 17, 1966. On February 24, 1966, a financing statement, form UCC–1, was filed in the office of the Clerk of the County of Erie to perfect the security interest of the plaintiff as required by UCC 9–302, subdivision (1)(d), and UCC 9–401, subdivision (1)(b). The retail installment contract contained, in a printed portion, an acknowledgment of delivery and acceptance of the car by the buyer. In fine print on the reverse side under the assignment portion of the contract, the dealer warrants, among other things, that the buyer paid the down payment as stated in the contract. The contract, by its terms, provides for a trade-in which was actually delivered to the dealer at or about the time of signing the contract. It further provided for a cash down payment of $443.00, a payment of $100.00 to be due March 16, 1966, and a thirty payment deferred balance of $1710.70. The $443.00 in cash was in fact not paid on the signing of the contract despite the form recitations. The arrangement between the sales manager and of Mrs. Sharp was that she, as retail purchaser, was to make the cash payment when she received an income tax refund which she expected to receive in the immediate future and that the car was to be left on the lot until the cash payment was made. On or about March 18, 1966, and before the delivery of the car, the defendant, Marine Midland Trust Company of Western New York seized all of the dealer's automobiles then remaining on its lot including the 1963 Chevrolet automobile described in the Sharp contract. The automobile was sold by the bank and the right to the proceeds is the issue to be determined herein. . . .

[W]e find that Mrs. Sharp entered into a contract with the dealer to purchase the car by (1) delivery of her trade-in or exchange of property, (2) by cash, not actually paid but secured by a deferred delivery of the vehicle under a collateral oral agreement, (3) by cash, unsecured, to be paid at a later date, and, (4) by a secured credit agreement sold by the dealer to the plaintiff. The dispute, arising out of the attempt to enforce the secured credit agreement or retail installment contract comes from the contention of the defendant bank that the entire transaction with Mrs. Sharp was executory only, that it was never consummated, title did not pass and it was null and void. The plaintiff, as a retail financer, on the other hand, contends that Mrs. Sharp was a buyer out of inventory in the ordinary course of business on her partly performed contract.

Applying the definitions to the evidence, it may be said that Mrs. Sharp entered into a specific written contract to purchase the car owned by the dealer. She gave valuable consideration in goods, she traded in her old vehicle, and she signed a binding installment contract. She agreed to pay in cash a down payment and a deferred payment. By agreement, orally, she specified the course of her down payment, an anticipated income tax refund, and she certainly, in good faith expected to receive the car and to make her payments upon the evidence, UCC 1–102(3). According to the testimony, she attempted to pay her cash deficiency a few days after the repossession by the bank, but, finding the car gone, abandoned her rights. The sales manager testified without contradiction, that they frequently took and negotiated contracts with the car to be held for a time for the cash down payment, that it was common practice in his twenty years experience in the car business to take contracts without actual receipt of the recited cash down payment. He said he would fire a salesman who failed to do so and that in his experience and opinion a number of dealers would go out of business if they failed to follow this practice.

It is agreed by the parties that both the plaintiff and the defendant have formally perfected security interests and that the value of the collateral is $1,200.00. The question, therefore, becomes one of the priority of rights in the proceeds of the sale of the 1963 Chevrolet automobile. . . . Under the agreement between the defendant bank and the dealer entitled "Floor-Plan Agreement and Signatory Authorization (Inventory)," it is provided in the opening paragraph that the purpose is to finance the dealer's acquisition and/or holding goods, i.e., motor vehicles for use and resale in the course of the dealer's business. It further provides, paragraph 8, as follows "(8) The Dealer agrees that when any item of Goods is sold or otherwise disposed of, the Dealer will account to the Bank for the Proceeds and will deliver to the Bank such Proceeds and such assignments or indorsements as may be requisite or requested by the Bank. The Bank shall be entitled to the Proceeds and shall have a security interest in them. Pending such accounting and delivery, the Dealer will hold the Proceeds in trust for the Bank as the Bank's property, but at the Dealer's risk, in the identical form received and separate and apart from the Dealer's property. Proceeds as used herein means cash and non-cash proceeds, immediate and remote, and includes any debts owing to the Dealer by reason of the sale or other disposition of any Collateral and any cash, checks, trade-ins, accounts, chattel paper, notes, drafts, or other instruments whenever received and any items of Collateral disposed of by the Dealer which are returned to or repossessed by the Dealer." . . .

Under its floor plan agreement, paragraph 12, the bank is completely subrogated to all rights of the dealer in the business transactions and assets of the dealer on insolvency in implementation of the "floating lien" type transaction and for the protection of its rights thereunder. This includes its rights in and to the trade-in and its proceeds, if any, in the rights, if any, and in the contract rights of the dealer against Mrs. Sharp, had they been pursued on the contract, or for damages, (Howarth, supra.).

By the same token, the plaintiff finance company, having furnished new value which has been paid to the dealer on the assignment, and having purchased the chattel paper in due course, is entitled to the returned or repossessed goods under UCC 9–306(5)(b), (c) and (d) and UCC 9–308, provided, as in this case, its interest has been perfected, UCC 9–306(5)(d), UCC 9–302(1)(d), UCC 9–401(1)(b) and UCC 9–312(1). . . .

In making this determination, the Court has, of course, by inference, determined that the buyer of goods was a buyer in the ordinary course of business out of inventory. A discussion of this has been left to the close of this memorandum by reason of the fact that the entire relation of the parties as indicated above relates to whether the irregularities of the transaction would make Mrs. Sharp other than such a buyer. As indicated at the beginning, UCC 1–102 requires a construction of all terms to carry out the underlying purposes and policies set forth in the statute, which is discussed at length in the practice commentaries of McKinney's Consolidated Laws of New York and in the Official Comments. Any interpretation of the entire transaction, where both the retail financer and bank entruster acted in good faith which became so technical as to abort the intention of the Act and where a dealer has acted in relation to all the other parties, buyer, entruster and financer, in such manner as to leave each with damage would undermine the ultimate success of the Act. If there is a usage of trade which exposes an entruster on floor plan to certain risks, these are risks against which he can guard by audits and accounting procedures or he can refuse to knowingly expose himself to the risk with the particular dealer. To fail to place the exposure of such risk with the entruster in such situation would make it impossible for retail finance companies to do business with any dealer unless the entruster were directly a participant. To hold otherwise, would expose the retail financer to a double loss as against at most a partial loss for both. The proliferation of paper work would be a giant step backwards in modern commercial practice. The Court feels a buyer who makes a purchase on a printed form contract in good faith with a full understanding it is a binding contract, who knowingly signs a retail installment payment obligation and trades in an old car in addition must, certainly as to a retail financer furnishing new value on the strength of such contract and as to an entruster giving the dealer wide latitude of sale goods, be deemed a buyer in the ordinary course of business, without regard to the technicalities of when title is to pass pursuant to collateral oral agreements or as to time of delivery and without the necessity of determining whether such delay brings about technically, a bailment, a non-delivery, a repossession or whatever. . . .

The plaintiff shall have judgment against the defendant, Marine Midland Trust Company of Western New York in the amount of $1,200.00 and interest from the 18th day of March, 1966.

Notes & Questions

1. To help isolate the issues in *Sharp,* focus on Chrysler Credit, who purchased the security agreement from the dealer, and on Marine Midland, who financed the dealer's inventory. How does a conflict arise between them over the car and over the amount due on the car-buyer's retail installment contract? If that were the only issue in the case how would § 9–308 resolve it? Is § 9–309 relevant?

Could Marine Midland have improved its position by rephrasing its Floor-Plan Agreement with the dealer? Suppose the agreement recited that Marine was extending credit to the dealer in exchange for a security interest in the dealer's inventory, accounts, and chattel paper. How does this differ from the actual agreement?

2. Why does the court invoke § 9–306(5)? Does analysis of the case under it lead to the same result as analysis under § 9–308?

3. It is common practice for a lender to indicate on leases and security agreements upon which it lends that they are subject to the lender's security interest. Why?

4. (a) Suppose the car dealer in *Sharp* had obtained only a promissory note from Mrs. Sharp, which it then sold to Chrysler Credit. How would your analysis of the case change?

(b) Suppose the car dealer in *Sharp* had sold the car on open account to Mrs. Sharp (the dealer receiving neither chattel paper nor a note) and had then sold the account to Chrysler Credit. How would your analysis of the case change?

CITIZENS BANK & TRUST CO. v. SLT WAREHOUSE CO.

United States District Court, Middle District of Georgia, 1974.
368 F.Supp. 1042, affirmed 515 F.2d 1382.

ELLIOTT, CHIEF JUDGE.

In this action the Plaintiff seeks to recover for losses sustained resulting from shortages in the amount of grain represented by warehouse receipts which it had taken as collateral for loans made by it to the person to whom the receipts had been issued by the Defendant. In its answer the Defendant denies liability to the Plaintiff and by third party action seeks contribution or indemnity from the person to whom its receipts were issued, it being alleged that he is responsible for the shortages.

The case was tried by the Court sitting without a jury on November 29 and November 30, 1973, and this opinion is intended as compliance with the requirements of Rule 52 of the Federal Rules of Civil Procedure.

FINDINGS OF FACT

On or about September 9, 1969 Howell Mathis, d/b/a Iron City Grain and Elevator Company (hereafter Mathis), entered into a field warehousing agreement with SLT Warehouse Company (hereafter SLT), under the terms of which Mathis furnished SLT a warehouse building into which he was to deposit grains and from which SLT was to perform field warehouse services. Mathis deposited grain in the warehouse and received in return warehouse receipts from SLT.

The receipts received by Mathis from SLT were non-negotiable and were understood to be non-negotiable receipts by the Plaintiff, The Citizens Bank and Trust Company (hereafter the Bank), which made numerous loans over a period of several months in 1971 to Mathis based solely upon the receipts which Mathis transferred to them, Mathis being the transferor and the Bank being the transferee of the non-negotiable receipts. The loans totaled over $50,000.00 and the outstanding balance due on the account at the time of trial was $34,938.40 principal and approximately $7,751.08 interest.

The Bank did not file a financing statement as to the receipted grain and made no investigation of Mathis or of the receipted grain.

Although the fact was not known to SLT or to the Bank, it eventually developed that the grain which was covered by the receipts did not belong to Mathis, but instead belonged to certain farmers who had entrusted it to Mathis, and the shortages which were eventually discovered were brought about by Mathis regaining possession of the grains from the warehouse by various surreptitious means (which will be hereafter more fully described) and returning the grain to the farmers, who were the true owners.

Because of some difficulties with Mathis, on November 17, 1971 SLT notified Mathis of SLT's desire to terminate the field warehouse agreement within thirty days. This notice was also sent to the Bank, SLT being aware that the Bank was holding some warehouse receipts issued to Mathis. At this time there was no shortage of grain. During this time SLT had exercised reasonable diligence and care in locking and controlling the warehouse facility, in checking Mathis' withdrawals against the withdrawal slips and in making regular audits to check the balance of grain in the warehouse.

After SLT's letters of November 17, 1971 to Mathis and the Bank various representatives of SLT on a repeated basis attempted to persuade the Bank to require Mathis, the Bank's debtor, to immediately liquidate the grain in the facility in order to pay off the Bank's loan. The evidence shows that the Bank refused to require such a liquidation and went along with a piecemeal liquidation which had been suggested by Mathis. The evidence also shows that had the Bank required such a liquidation at a bulk sale as urged by SLT, the Bank would not have sustained any losses. Further, in January, 1972 representatives of SLT informed the Bank of additional difficulties which SLT had had with Mathis, including certain checks issued by Mathis which were returned for reason of insufficient funds. The checking account on which these bad checks were drawn was carried by Mathis with the plaintiff Bank and the Bank was, therefore, aware of the fact that Mathis was "bouncing" checks. In a further final effort to bring the matter to a head SLT directed a letter to the Bank on January 27, 1972 in which SLT stated that "we hereby advise you that we will not assume any responsibility hereafter for any shortages that may occur in the inventory as a result of the conduct of this customer . . . We have advised you of the severe nature of our prior problems with this customer and neither we nor our bonding company desire to accept further responsibility for the conduct or cooperation of this customer in connection with any further inventory shortage." Even after receipt of this letter the Bank took no action to either investigate Mathis or to investigate the status of the grain in question or to require a bulk liquidation.

In January, 1972 SLT employed a new local agent to look after the warehouse and this agent maintained security over the warehouse on behalf of SLT through a series of locks which were placed on the bins in which the receipted grains were stored and by a lock placed on the power switch which controlled the grain elevator, which was the means by which grain would normally be removed.

As the result of a regular audit made by Mr. Harvey Jay, a field representative of SLT, an initial shortage of grain was discovered in late May, 1972. The shortage of receipted grain discovered by Jay at that time was approximately $35,683.00. When this first shortage was discovered Jay had all of the locks changed on the bins and on the elevator switch and Jay himself retained the only set of keys to these locks. Through his regular audits Jay discovered in August, 1972 that there was an additional shortage of some $8,000.00 in grain, although the new locks still remained on the bins and on the elevator switch.

The evidence makes it clear that the shortages in grain occurred as a result of the fact that Mathis, through a variety of means, took the grain from the warehouse controlled by SLT totally without SLT's knowledge or authority and in a way which was wrongful as to SLT. He did this by bypassing the SLT locks which had been placed on the bin doors by removing the hinges from the doors and loading grain onto trucks by means of a portable auger inserted into the bins and by bypassing the SLT lock which had been placed on the electrical switch which controlled the grain elevator by "hot-wiring" the electrical wires near the switch so that another switch which was supposed to control the operation of another piece of machinery actually controlled the operation of the elevator. These means all circumvented SLT's control and security over the grain. The Court finds as a matter of fact that the shortages were not due to any negligence on the part of SLT, its representatives having taken all precautions which a reasonably prudent warehouseman would have taken in the circumstances.

As has been heretofore noted, the receipted grain which was wrongfully taken by Mathis belonged to the farmers who had entrusted it to him, and after he had wrongfully removed the grain from SLT custody he returned the grain to the rightful owners of it.

CONCLUSIONS OF LAW

A. *Under the circumstances of this case SLT is relieved of liability because the true owners of the grain, the farmers, received back the receipted grain.*

The Uniform Commercial Code, as adopted in Georgia, defines the term "bailee" as meaning:

"the person who by a warehouse receipt, bill of lading or other document of title acknowledges possession of goods and contracts to deliver them." [1]

So, under the facts here presented SLT was a bailee of the grain.

The Georgia Code further provides that:

"The bailee must deliver the goods to a person entitled under the document . . . unless and to the extent that the bailee establishes any of the following:

(a) Delivery of the goods to a person whose receipt was rightful as against the claimant;

. . .

(g) Any other lawful excuse." [2]

1. Georgia Code Annotated § 109A–7–102.

2. Georgia Code Annotated § 1109A–7–403(1).

It is clear here that the farmers whose grain was on receipt and who received back their grain were persons "whose receipt was rightful as against the claimant". This becomes evident from the distinction made between negotiable and non-negotiable warehouse receipts, as set out in the Uniform Commercial Code as adopted in Georgia. This distinction is made clear in the description of the rights accorded to the holder of a warehouse receipt under Title 7 of the Code.

A bona fide purchaser of a *negotiable* warehouse receipt obtains the full protection of the Uniform Commercial Code only if the purchaser obtains the negotiable receipt by *"due negotiation"* and the mechanics of due negotiation are spelled out in the following manner:

"Form of negotiation and requirements of 'due negotiation.'—(1) A negotiable document of title running to the order of a named person is negotiated by his indorsement and delivery. After his indorsement in blank or to bearer any person can negotiate it by delivery alone.

(2)(a) A negotiable document of title is also negotiated by delivery alone when by its original terms it runs to bearer. (b) When a document running to the order of a named person is delivered to him the effect is the same as if the document has been negotiated.

(3) Negotiation of a negotiable document of title after it has been indorsed to a specified person requires indorsement by the special indorsee as well as delivery.

(4) A negotiable document of title is 'duly negotiated' when it is negotiated in the manner stated in this section to a holder who purchases it in good faith without notice of any defense against or claim to it on the part of any person and for value, unless it is established that the negotiation is not in the regular course of business or financing or involves receiving the document in settlement or payment of a money obligation.

(5) Indorsement of a nonnegotiable document neither makes it negotiable nor adds to the transferee's rights.

(6) The naming in a negotiable bill of a person to be notified of the arrival of the goods does not limit the negotiability of the bill nor constitute notice to a purchaser thereof of any interest of such person in the goods." [3]

Any person who obtains a negotiable warehouse receipt by "due negotiation" obtains substantial rights which are described as follows:

"Rights acquired by due negotiation.—

(1) Subject to the following section and to the provisions of 109A–7–205 on fungible goods, a holder to whom a negotiable document of title has been duly negotiated acquires thereby:

(a) title to the document;

(b) title to the goods;

3. Georgia Code Annotated § 109A–7–501.

(c) all rights accruing under the law of agency or estoppel, including rights to goods delivered to the bailee after the document was issued; and

(d) the direct obligation of the issuer to hold or deliver the goods according to the terms of the document free of any defense or claim by him except those arising under the terms of the document or under this Article. In the case of a delivery order the bailee's obligation accrues only upon acceptance and the obligation acquired by the holder is that the issuer and any indorser will procure the acceptance of the bailee.

(2) Subject to the following section, title and rights so acquired are not defeated by any stoppage of the goods represented by the document or by surrender of such goods by the bailee, and are not impaired even though the negotiation or any prior negotiation constituted a breach of duty or even though any person has been deprived of possession of the document by misrepresentation, fraud, accident, mistake, duress, loss, theft or conversion, or even though a previous sale or other transfer of the goods or document has been made to a third person." [4]

However, a *non-negotiable* warehouse receipt such as the warehouse receipts involved in this case cannot be "duly negotiated", as is clearly indicated by the express terms of § 109A–7–502 immediately above quoted.

Robert Braucher in his treatise on warehouse receipts, Documents of Title, § 5.3, at p. 70 (ALI, 1958), states that:

"A non-negotiable document cannot be negotiated; it can only be transferred under this section."

Therefore, there could be no due negotiation of the non-negotiable warehouse receipts involved in this case. More limited rights were acquired by the transferee Bank in this situation, and this is also made clear by the provisions of the Uniform Commercial Code, which provides as follows:

"A transferee of a document, whether negotiable, or nonnegotiable, to whom the document has been delivered but not duly negotiated, acquires the title and rights which his transferor had or had actual authority to convey." [5]

As the Comment of the draftsmen to this section of the Uniform Commercial Code notes:

"It is clear that in the absence of due negotiation a transferor cannot convey greater rights than he himself has, even when the negotiation is formally perfect."

Hence, the plaintiff Bank could obtain no greater rights than Mathis, the Bank's transferor, had authority to convey, and of course,

4. Georgia Code Annotated § 109A–7–502.

5. Georgia Code Annotated § 109A–7–504(1).

the undisputed evidence in this case shows that Mathis had no authority to convey any rights in the farmers' grain.   . . .

There are clear risks involved in the acceptance of non-negotiable receipts as collateral security. Professors White and Summers in their treatise Handbook of the Law under the Uniform Commercial Code, point out that:

> "The field warehouse lender [here the plaintiff Bank] who acquires non-negotiable receipts incurs all the risks that a lender against negotiable documents incurs and in addition incurs the additional title risks that a party acquiring non-negotiable documents incurs. Generally, so far as the debtor's title is defective, so too is the lender's title defective."   Pages 706–707.

Since Mathis had no title to the farmers' grain, he could convey no title under the non-negotiable receipts, and when the farmers, the true owners of the receipted grain, received back the grain the rights of the bank against the warehouse company were defeated. The Bank is left with such remedies as it may have against Mathis, its borrower.

The Bank should have realized that it was incurring a substantial risk of a paramount title in other persons when it accepted the non-negotiable receipts as the sole collateral upon which its loans were based.   . . .

Non-negotiable receipts provided the Bank with an ease and flexibility of procedure which would not have been provided with negotiable receipts, but the Bank should have realized that in accepting non-negotiable receipts it had to rely on the integrity of its borrower. In fact and in law the Bank assumed the risk that Mathis' title was good. It is for this reason that it was incumbent upon the Bank to check Mathis' credit and his grain or to otherwise attempt to perfect a security interest in the grain, none of which was done by the Bank. Indeed, the American Bankers Association has itself indicated the need for such action by a Bank holding non-negotiable receipts by stating:

> "Before a field warehouse arrangement is set up, the typical prospective lender investigates the prospective debtor and the prospective collateral." (White and Summers, supra, p. 706, citing American Bankers Association Credit Policy Committee, A Banker's Guide to Warehouse Receipt Financing (1966)[ ].

The plaintiff Bank must now bear the consequences of its decision to lend funds to a risky borrower based only on the transfer from him of non-negotiable warehouse receipts. SLT should not bear the burden of the Bank's misplaced business judgment, for the Bank should have known that "a warehouseman does not guarantee title to particular goods received by and receipted for by him." *Petzoldt*, supra, 262 F.2d at p. 546.[7]

7. There is an additional factor here which should be noted. Not only did the plaintiff Bank fail to look into Mathis' credit rating and fail to examine the grain when initially making the loans to him, but it continued in its failure after being notified by SLT of the poor risk they considered Mathis to be. Moreover, they con-

B. *SLT is not liable for the wrongful taking by Mathis.*

Although what has already been said in this opinion is dispositive of the issue here presented, there is yet another reason for this decision which the Court feels is worthy of comment.

The degree of care required of a warehouseman under the Uniform Commercial Code is as follows:

"A warehouseman is liable for damages for loss of or injury to the goods caused by his failure to exercise such care in regard to them as a reasonably careful man would exercise under like circumstances but unless otherwise agreed he is not liable for damages which could not have been avoided by the exercise of such care."

Stated otherwise, this simply means that the warehouseman owes the duty of ordinary care in protecting the goods from theft or other wrongful taking.

We have already described the means used by Mathis to take the grain from the warehouse totally without SLT's knowledge or authority, and since we have already determined that SLT was not negligent in its operation or maintenance of the warehouse, it is clear that SLT can have no liability to the plaintiff Bank for a shortage caused in the way the shortage was caused here.   . . .

Notes & Questions

1. There are several possible aspects to the relationships among warehousemen, those who store goods in warehouses, buyers of such goods, and those who lend on the basis that the goods (or related documents) constitute collateral in a secured transaction. These materials cover only those aspects of the warehouse that directly pertain to an Article 9 secured party.

SLT Warehouse Co. involved a field warehouse and non-negotiable warehouse receipts. The secured party lost its contest with the warehouse company because it had no greater interest in the grain than did Mathis, who was storing other farmers' grain. Unlike a field warehouse, a terminal warehouse (for example, a grain elevator) stores goods for many bailors and usually issues negotiable warehouse receipts to the bailor. A negotiable receipt provides that the warehouseman will deliver goods to the bearer of the receipt or to the order of a person named in the receipt (perhaps a purchaser of grain from a farmer who does not require immediate delivery). Negotiable warehouse receipts, which are "documents" within the meaning of § 9–105(f), have a legal status as collateral independent of the goods they represent. Why do such documents exist?

tinually refused to abide by SLT's judgment that they should require an immediate liquidation, which recommendation was made by SLT at times when there was no shortage. The Bank sat on its rights and negligently failed to pursue remedies which were available and which could have made the Bank whole. Under such circumstances the Bank is not entitled to recover.

2. Debtor borrows money from Bank and grants Bank a security interest in equipment. Bank properly perfects its security interest by filing. Debtor then delivers the equipment to a terminal warehouse and receives a negotiable warehouse receipt for the equipment. Debtor takes the receipt to Financer and borrows funds from Financer using the receipt as collateral. Financer takes possession of the receipt. In a dispute between Financer and Bank, who has priority in the equipment? See §§ 9–304(2), 9–309, 7–503(1). Would your analysis of the problem change if the collateral in question were inventory?

3. Goods shipped under bills of lading may generate disputes over collateral similar to those that arise in cases involving warehouse receipts. See §§ 2–505, 7–503. A "bill of lading" is "a document evidencing the receipt of goods for shipment by a person engaged in the business of transporting or forwarding goods . . . ." § 1–201(6). See generally In re Ault, 6 B.R. 58 (Bkrtcy.E.D.Tenn.1980) (§ 2–505(1)(b) provides a security interest to seller shipping under straight bill of lading if goods are conditionally delivered within the meaning of § 2–507(2)).

CITIZENS VALLEY BANK v. PACIFIC MATERIALS CO.

Supreme Court of Oregon, 1972.
263 Or. 557, 503 P.2d 491.

DENECKE, JUSTICE.

The controversy is a bank with a perfected security interest in a negotiable instrument versus an alleged holder in due course of the instrument.

The plaintiff bank financed D & P Construction Co. which assigned the bank its accounts receivable as security. The bank perfected its security interest in the accounts and their proceeds. After the bank's perfection of its security interest, D & P approached Rogers, who owed an account receivable, and induced him to pay D & P his account by giving D & P a promissory note for the amount owed. D & P negotiated this note to defendant Pacific Materials Co. Rogers subsequently paid the note. The money paid is identified and held by a stakeholder. All the dealings with Rogers by D & P were without the knowledge of the bank and the defendant had no actual knowledge of the bank's possible claim to the note.

The trial court held against the bank and it appeals.

The bank contends that the defendant is not a holder in due course because defendant had constructive notice of the bank's security interest in the note by reason of the bank's filing of its security documents. ORS 73.3040(5), part of the chapter on Commercial Paper, provides: "The filing or recording of a document does not of itself constitute notice within the provisions of ORS 73.1010 to 73.8050 to a person who would otherwise be a holder in due course." ORS 79.3090, part of the chapter on Secured Transactions, provides: "Filing under ORS 79.1010 to 79.5070 does not constitute notice of the security interest to such holders [including a holder in due course] or purchasers." We find the defendant did not have notice of the bank's security interest and is a holder in due course.

The bank is correct, however, that the note and the cash payment are proceeds of the bank's collateral in which the bank has a security interest. ORS 79.3060.

The bank stands on ORS 79.3060(2), which provides:

"*Except where ORS 79.1010 to 79.5070 otherwise provide*, a security interest continues in collateral notwithstanding sale, exchange or other disposition thereof by the debtor unless his action was authorized by the secured party in the security agreement or otherwise, and also continues in any identifiable proceeds including collections received by the debtor." (Emphasis added.)

The defendant counters that ORS 79.3090 does "otherwise provide" and we agree.

ORS 79.3090 states:

"Nothing in ORS 79.1010 to 79.5070 limits the rights of a holder in due course of a negotiable instrument or a holder to whom a negotiable document of title has been duly negotiated as provided in ORS 77.5010, or a bona fide purchaser of a security as provided in ORS 78.3010 and such holders or purchasers take priority over an earlier security interest even though perfected. . . . ."

We have found no precedents from other jurisdictions or any statements by the writers precisely on this issue. The wording of the statute, however, seems clear: "[S]uch holders or purchasers take priority over an earlier security interest even though perfected."

Affirmed.

Notes & Questions

1. Does § 9–309, relied on by the court, resolve the dispute? Precisely what security interests does it subordinate to the rights of a holder in due course?

2. Could the court have addressed the issue in *Citizens Valley Bank* under § 9–308? Does Pacific Materials Co., the holder of the note, qualify for the protection afforded by § 9–308? Does § 9–308 purport to resolve a priority contest between the purchaser of a note and a secured party claiming an interest in the account that gave rise to the note? Can both the account and the note exist? See § 9–106.

What is the relationship between § 9–308 and § 9–309?

3. In cases like *Citizens Valley Bank*, a secured party who is first to file and first to perfect finds itself subordinated to a subsequent buyer. Is this result justifiable? Who should win as between bank (the accounts financer) and a later notetaker? What can bank do to protect itself? What can a notetaker do?

4. Does the notetaker prevail because it is important to maintain the negotiability of notes? Does the holder of a negotiable document of title (the warehouse receipt) enjoy the same status as the holder of the negotiable note? Is the notetaker as able to protect itself as is the person who lends and takes a negotiable warehouse receipt as collateral?

5. In *Citizens Valley Bank,* D & P misbehaved by inducing its debtor to execute a note and borrowing on the basis of that note. What role should that misbehavior play in analyzing the case? Consider this situation again in Chapter 6 after studying the law of fraudulent conveyances.

CLARK, ABSTRACT RIGHTS VERSUS PAPER RIGHTS UNDER ARTICLE 9 OF THE UNIFORM COMMERCIAL CODE, 84 Yale L.J. 445–47, 473–79 (1975)

The documentary embodiment of a secured party's rights has intriguing and varying consequences in a number of situations governed by Article 9 of the Uniform Commercial Code. . . . For brevity, and to avoid confusion over the word "documentary," such embodiments of rights are referred to here by a phrase not found in the UCC, "paper rights."

The article will examine problems concerning four specific kinds of paper rights: promissory notes and stock certificates (defined by Article 9 as members of a larger class of paper rights called "instruments"), warehouse receipts (a part of the larger Article 9 class of "documents"), and "chattel paper" (a broad Article 9 classification). Each of these pieces of paper puts its holder in a legal position somewhat different from that of the mere possessor of the underlying or corresponding unembodied form of the right; the holder has a right which has been "concretized" in the paper, rather than remaining an abstract right to the property.

In the case of instruments like promissory notes or stock certificates, the corresponding unembodied right is usually an intangible, a right which does not represent an interest in particular, concrete personal property but which represents instead an interest, defined by a formula or a set of rules, in a legally recognizable locus of value. Consider the situation which gives rise to a promissory note. A consumer's obligation to pay money to a retailer may be called an account receivable or, in UCC terminology, an account. The obligation may of course be satisfied by any of the money, or indirectly by any of the property, owned by the consumer. Furthermore, the retailer may treat the account as intangible property and may sell or hypothecate it. On the other hand, the consumer's obligation may be embodied in more or less definite paper form, as when he gives the retailer a promissory note. The retailer then has a paper right rather than an abstract right.

The shareholder in a corporation finds himself in a similar situation. Traditionally, a shareholder's interest has been represented by a piece of paper, the stock certificate. However, certificates are not required by the laws of all states, and it is quite normal for a shareholder in some types of public corporations to possess a shareholder interest without there being any corresponding certificate. . . .

In the case of the paper rights classed as documents (including warehouse receipts) and chattel paper, the corresponding abstract (i.e., not paperized) right or entitlement is usually in specific *tangible* property, or at least in a defined quantity of tangible property that is "fungible" with similar property. Thus, a secured party may possess a nondocumented interest in specific, tangible goods of a debtor. (It is rare that such a secured party's interest would not be referred to in a writing of some sort, but often enough the writing will not rise to the dignity of a document in the legal sense.) When the debtor of such a secured party bails the particular goods with a warehouseman, the interests of both the debtor and the secured party may become embodied in a warehouse receipt and may thus become a paper right. Similarly, a secured party's security interest in goods may be abstract or it may be represented by what the UCC refers to as "chattel paper." . . .

III. General Considerations: The Evolution of the Tendency to Suppress Abstraction

[T]he Code does not always provide that the secured party who files, even if he files before anyone else perfects, should prevail. Instead, the law often displays a strong preference . . . for paper rights as against earlier established, correlative, abstract rights.

In order to understand why this is so, let us imagine first a society in which all rights are abstract. Though individual human beings have definite and legally recognizable rights to the use and disposition of various pieces of property, none of the rights is evidenced by a piece of paper or in any public or private recording or filing system.[80] In such a society, consider the class of rights that concern property (or complexly and indirectly defined pools of property) not in the physical possession of the individuals having the rights. A potential transferee may not trust the transferor as a source of evidence: The transferor may be lying; he may have the right but be confused as to the various subtle details of its nature; he may have a faulty memory; he may have told a different story to someone else; and so forth. Perhaps most importantly, even if he tries earnestly to describe his right accurately and in detail, his mode of description may vary from one occasion to the next. This shifting and variable characterization of the right is important, for in many unforeseen conflict situations a fixed verbal formula inter-

---

80. There could be various degrees of departure from this extreme. For present purposes, a society's rights could be said to become "less" abstract by virtue of any one or more of the following: an increase in the relative frequency of rights evidenced by pieces of paper (or in some other permanent medium); an increase in the extent to which certain rights are regarded as identified with particular pieces of paper, for which copies are no substitute; and an increase in the number or kind of cases in which access to or the location of such single paper rights is legally controlled.

preted principally in accordance with the customary legal or ordinary meanings given to its component words may be the only, or at least the best, way to resolve the conflict in a neutral and equitable manner.

The fear that the potential transferor may be lying can be mitigated to some extent by getting other individuals to vouch for his ownership of the right. But this procedure is inconvenient. The voucher must both be in a position to know of the transferor's right and be known to or accepted by the transferee as a credible informant. Given a certain common level of need for such vouching, the possible participants in many commercial transactions would be restricted to those persons who have a nexus of personal connections to a satisfactory voucher. Such a system would be economically inefficient, since it needlessly curtails the range of feasible exchange transactions. Moreover, even the statements of an earnest and credible voucher have the same defects as the transferor's statements: His descriptions of the right will tend not to have a fixed formulation.

For the sake of simplicity, one might categorize the various irritations and inefficiencies of a system of totally abstract rights under the two major headings that were previously introduced: "fraud costs" created by the occurrence of the fraudulent transactions which are permitted by this system, and "unfixity costs" created by the lack of a fixed and uniquely embodied or located verbal formulation of the rights.

Because of the inadequacies and costs of the abstract holding of rights, there will naturally be pressures in a legal system to reduce or eliminate this kind of abstraction. A variety of doctrines and devices for facilitating and encouraging the reduction of abstraction, or at least the costs of abstraction, will tend to evolve.

For example, in a system of totally abstract rights a principle might develop to the effect that transferees who are first in time have priority over later, purported transferees of the same rights. Perhaps the chief advantage of this "first in time, first in right" principle is that it provides a decisional rule which promotes conflict resolution and judicial economy. It also reflects, and perhaps is better understood in terms of, the quasi-metaphysical notion that after a right is transferred to one person, there is nothing left to be transferred to a second party. (This notion would apply both to total rights and to partial rights like the interest of a secured party.) At any rate, the contribution which the "first in time, first in right" principle makes by itself to the reduction of both fraud and unfixity costs would appear to be marginal: given the limitations of oral information, even the most thorough investigation by a potential second party may fail to discover prior transfers. . . .

When rights to intangible property, or to tangible property not in possession of the owner, are at issue, what might be called the "paperizing principle" eventually comes into play. The problem of lack of verbal fixity is solved by embodying the abstract right in a fixed verbal formula written down on paper—a formula which, within the restraints imposed by the shifting nature of linguistic meaning itself, provides the same basic stimulus to all readers versed in the language. The basic stimulus may be interpreted and reacted to in different ways by different readers, of course, but the fixity of stimulus reduces the number and range of these variations.

An embryonic form of the paperizing principle at work is the Statute of Frauds. By requiring a writing between the parties to a transaction, unfixity costs are significantly reduced. Fraud costs ought also to be reduced, in that fraud by one of the parties on the other is made somewhat more difficult. . . .

A more developed version of the paperizing principle is found in paper rights which uniquely embody abstract rights, for example, a note, a stock certificate, or a document of title. Only one piece of paper (or one set of papers, if the written material is lengthy) "really" embodies the abstract right; copies may be made, but they are just that—"mere" copies of a note, certificate, etc., not "the" note or certificate. This practice of uniquely embodying rights, together with a standardization of forms of embodiment and the development of rules of transfer and negotiation, further reduces unfixity costs and facilitates the economical transfer of rights through a chain of transferees. Unfortunately, though, despite elaborate rules as to how fraud should be dealt with and who should suffer its consequences, embodiment does relatively little to reduce fraud costs. There are technical and legal impediments to the successful forging of checks and stock certificates, but they can be (and often are) overcome.

Be that as it may, in this stage of evolution of the tendency to suppress abstraction it becomes natural to accord some kind of preferred legal status to transferees who take possession of the paperized right. If, in a given sort of situation, the paperizing of rights becomes common and the elements of the paperization become fairly standard, possession of the paper is a sensible precaution to take. If *A*'s right in some property is evidenced by a single piece of paper, a prudent buyer of the right will want to obtain the piece of paper so as to know exactly what his right consists of and to be able to demonstrate to future transferees what he can sell or hypothecate to them. If the buyer should pay for the right and not bother to obtain the paper, and if *A* later sells the paper to a second innocent buyer, then the second buyer would be given priority in the right over the first, on the grounds that (1) he was more prudent and (2) the paperizing of such rights, since it performs useful economic and legal functions, is to be encouraged.

The same reasons could extend to the situation where the second transferee takes a paper right which was only created after the transfer of the right to the first transferee in abstract form. . . .

Though these remarks about the paperizing principle may suggest a general solution in favor of the holder of the paper rights, there is one additional step in the evolution of the tendency to suppress abstraction which casts doubt on such a result.

That step is the establishment of central recording or filing systems. Not only is the right paperized, but the paper right, a copy of it, or notice of it, is kept in a central system to which potential transferees can make reference. The most obvious examples are the real estate recording systems. Recording is then given preferred legal status: a mortgagee can have an enforceable interest, vis-à-vis the owner who is his debtor, whether or not he records his interest, but he must record to protect himself against third parties. The recording system, in conjunction with such rules, probably reduces the overall amount of fraud that would otherwise result, forcing the fraudulently minded transferor who wants to conceal a prior adverse transfer to resort to attempts at bribing the recording officer or colluding with him.

The evolution of this "recording principle" clearly brings a number of advantages over the stage (not necessarily a temporally prior one) in which the paperizing principle and rules governing possession of tangible property were the only means of forwarding the policies behind the goal of eliminating abstraction. . . . [O]nly the recording principle seems likely to achieve a substantial and decisive reduction of fraud costs. In addition, there is little a priori reason to believe that the costs of achieving the reduction will be exorbitant in relation to the costs of implementing the paperizing principle. Moreover, the recording principle ought to reduce unfixity costs just as well as the paperizing principle. A recording or filing system will reduce mistakes and confusion: the records will either contain, or provide a basis for obtaining, a written description of outstanding rights in the property in question, and a diligent putative transferee may discover that his transferor inadvertently failed to know about, or realize the significance and extent of, a prior adverse interest in the property. Finally, a recording system provides a basis for easily administrable judicial rules, since the recording system will definitively show which of a series of defrauded transferees of the same right was first in time to record. Thus, as a general theoretical matter, the recording principle seems to be the most advanced point in the evolution of the tendency to suppress abstraction, and it suggests a general solution to our priority paradigm (in favor of the first to file) opposite to that (in favor of the paper holder) suggested by the paperizing principle.

Returning from theory to statute, one readily perceives that the UCC provides a mixed system which utilizes—and to some extent synthesizes—all of the chief principles that have developed to reduce the costs of abstraction. The Code expresses, in § 9–312(5), a particular version of the virtually aboriginal first-in-time principle, though a reading of the exceptions to the rule and of the many other rules of and relating to priority in Part 3 of Article 9 convinces one that the principle, in its general and unparticularized form, is virtually useless for the resolution of particular problems. The Code also employs the possession principle, both in making possession of collateral by the secured party an alternative to satisfying the Statute of Frauds [88] in certain cases and by making possession a form of perfection of security interests in tangible collateral and in paper rights.[89] The paperizing principle is reflected in Article 9's particular Statute of Frauds [90] and in the recognition and great importance, exemplified by §§ 9–308(a) and 9–309, that is given to paper rights. Finally, Article 9 is pervaded by references to and reliance upon its notice filing system—an inexpensive streamlined, unified, widely used and highly successful expression of the recording principle—the mechanics of which are elaborately articulated in Part 4 of Article 9.

I have suggested throughout this inquiry that the paperizing principle is rooted in deep psychological needs as well as in more conventionally conceived commercial exigencies. The principle as manifested in practice seems to have acquired a strong and almost unshakeable grip on the thinking and the intuitive reactions of lawyers. But, given the existence of a thoroughly mixed system governing security interests, it is not at all obvious that the paperizing principle, which is a principle less advanced and less perfect than the recording principle, ought to be taken as an infallible rule for the solution of all priority problems involving paper rights. One must look instead for the priority rule which, within a mixed system and in a particular context of commercial practices and expectations, will most efficiently reduce fraud costs and unfixity costs.

Notes & Questions

1. Consider the advantages offered by what Professor Clark describes as "a more developed version of the paperizing principle," one in which "paper rights . . . uniquely embody abstract rights." The unique embodiment of rights, he argues, "reduces unfixity costs and facilitates the economical transfer of rights through a chain of transferees," but does little to reduce fraud costs. Great reductions in fraud costs instead are achieved by the establishment of central recording or filing systems. Given the development of central recording or filing systems for real and personal property, including intangible personal property, should the "unique embodiment" aspect of the paperizing principle be discarded as an evolutionary development that served as a transition to recording systems but is no longer needed in light of the existence of recording systems? Should all interests in property be subject to central filing requirements? all interests in property used as collateral? What additional advantage is gained by the "unique embodiment" aspect of the paperizing principle?

2. In a mixed system such as Article 9, should paper rights be preferred over abstract rights? Does the victory by the holder in due course in *Citizens Valley Bank,* which encourages the paperizing of

88. See § 9–203(1)(a).   90. See § 9–203(1)(a).
89. See § 9–305.

rights, lead to a better economic or legal system than would a victory by the secured party in that case? Are there any costs to favoring the paper right?

3. In one perspective the paperizing principle reflects an advanced stage in the development of rights to intangible property. The use of certificateless shares of stock, see § 8–102(b) (defining "uncertificated security"), and electronic funds transfers (for example, those transfers done through automated teller machines) in lieu of checks or other instruments both suggest greater abstraction of previously tangible property. Are these developments consistent with the view that the paperizing principle arises in a more advanced stage of economic society than purely abstract rights? Or are these developments merely evidence of the triumph of central recording systems as the embodiment of intangible or readily transferable rights? In the case of uncertificated securities, transfer must be registered on the issuer's books. § 8–102(b)(i). Do bank records serve a similar function for electronic funds transfers?[a]

3. Purchase Money Security Interests
GILMORE, THE PURCHASE MONEY PRIORITY, 76 Harv.L.Rev. 1333, 1337–38 (1963)

A recurrent problem in the life history of an enterprise is how to provide for the financing of new equipment free of prior liens. The new equipment may be needed because the business is expanding or shifting to a new line of production or because new inventions have made the old equipment obsolete or because the old equipment has simply worn out. A prior mortgage contains an after–acquired property clause to which the new equipment will be subject. Where bonds have been issued under a corporate mortgage, it will be impossible to procure the assent of the scattered bondholders to a subordination of their lien, so as to make the new financing feasible. It might be argued that as a matter of justice and morals the prior mortgagee or the bondholders ought not to be subordinated without their consent. However that may be, the law's answer has been to provide some more or less complicated method of effecting the subordination. Under pre-Code law, this was most often done by a manipulation of title theory under the system of separate security devices. Most of the specialized devices were recognized as giving the security holder title and not "merely" a lien: this was true of the conditional sale, the security lease (which was the basis of the railroad equipment trust in the version known as the Philadelphia Plan), and the trust receipt. The way of defeating the prior mortgagee, recognized as effective under pre-Code law, was to have the security holder's title to the new equipment come directly from the manufacturer or seller. Thus, conceptually, the title

a. For introductory materials on electronic funds transfers, see R. Speidel, R. Summers, & J. White, Commercial and Consumer Law 1457–71 (3d ed. 1981).

to the equipment never vested in the mortgagor and the lien of the prior mortgage had nothing to bite on.

A solution of this sort was impossible under Article 9, because the Article not only destroyed the system of independent security devices but also refused to recognize any distinction between "title" security interests and "lien" security interests. Nevertheless, the result achieved under the pre-Code law was recognized as sound. The problem was handled as one of priorities and solved by the introduction of the concept of the "purchase money security interest."

Introductory Problems

1. Debtor and Bank agree to enter into a secured transaction under which Debtor grants Bank a security interest in an item of equipment. Before making the loan, Bank checks the U.C.C. records and finds no filings against Debtor. Can you assure Bank that its interest in the equipment will be prior to the interest of all other secured lenders? See § 9–312(4).

2. Debtor wishes to buy equipment from Supplier. He visits Supplier and states, "If you will deliver that equipment to me today, I will pay you tomorrow." Supplier delivers the equipment. On the same day, Debtor goes to Bank, borrows the purchase price of the equipment, and executes a proper financing statement and security agreement. The next day Debtor pays Supplier with the money borrowed from Bank. Does Bank have a purchase money security interest? Does the "enabling" requirement of § 9–107 serve any useful function? See generally Jackson & Kronman, Secured Financing and Priorities Among Creditors, 88 Yale L.J. 1143 (1979).

Suppose in addition that Debtor failed to use the money to pay for the equipment. Would Bank have a security interest? a purchase money security interest?

3. Financer lends Debtor money to purchase goods from Seller. The goods cost $10,000, which Financer pays directly to Seller. Debtor promises to repay financer a total of $11,000. How much of the debt is a purchase money debt? See In re Mid-Atlantic Flange Co., Inc., 26 U.C.C.Rep. 203 (Bkrtcy.E.D.Pa.1979) (only the price).

See generally McLaughlin, Qualifying as a Third-Party Purchase-Money Financier: The Hurdles to Be Cleared, the Advantages to Be Gained, 13 U.C.C.L.J. 225 (1981).

BRODIE HOTEL SUPPLY, INC. v. UNITED STATES

United States Court of Appeals, Ninth Circuit, 1970.
431 F.2d 1316.

HAMLEY, CIRCUIT JUDGE:

Brodie Hotel Supply, Inc. (Brodie), brought this action against the United States to determine which of the parties had priority, under their respective chattel mortgages, to the proceeds of the sale of certain restaurant equipment. The facts were stipulated and the property was sold and proceeds impounded by agreement. The district court granted summary judgment for Brodie and the United States appeals.

In 1959, Brodie sold the restaurant equipment to Standard Management Company, Inc., for use in a restaurant at Anchorage, Alaska. Standard Management went bankrupt. Brodie repossessed the equipment but left it in the restaurant. With the consent of Brodie, James Lyon took possession of the restaurant and began operating it on June 1, 1964. Throughout the summer of 1964, Brodie and Lyon negotiated over the price and terms under which Lyon was to purchase the equipment.

On November 2, 1964, Lyon borrowed seventeen thousand dollars from the National Bank of Alaska and, as security for the loan, which was evidenced by a promissory note, executed a chattel mortgage covering the restaurant equipment. This equipment consisted of 159 separate types of items, including a refrigerator, a dishwasher, an ice cream cabinet, spoons, forks, cups, ladles, pots, pans and assorted glassware and chinaware. The bank assigned its mortgage to the Small Business Administration (SBA), represented in this action by the United States. On November 4, 1964, the bank filed a financing statement, showing the SBA as assignee.

On November 12, Brodie delivered to Lyon a bill of sale covering the equipment. On the same day Lyon executed a chattel mortgage on the equipment, naming Brodie as mortgagee. This mortgage was given to secure the unpaid purchase price of the equipment. Brodie filed a financing statement on November 23, 1964.

Alaska has adopted the Uniform Commercial Code (Code). Under section 9–312(5)(a) of the Code, the general rule of priority, if both interests are perfected by filing, is that the secured party who first files a financing statement (in this case SBA as assignee of the bank) prevails, regardless of when his security interest attached. However, there is a special exception for purchase-money security interests in collateral other than inventory. Brodie had such an interest. Under this exception, the purchase-money security interest prevails over conflicting interests in non-inventory collateral if "the purchase money security interest is perfected [i.e., here it was perfected by filing a financing statement] at the time the debtor receives possession of the collateral or within 10 days after the debtor receives possession." (Code, § 9–312(4)).

On the basis of these stipulated facts, Brodie moved for summary judgment. Brodie contended that although Lyon received possession of the restaurant equipment on June 1, 1964, over five months before Brodie's financing statement was filed, Lyon did not become a "debtor," and the equipment did not become "collateral" until November 12, 1964, when Lyon received the bill of sale and executed Brodie's chattel mortgage. Accordingly, Brodie contended, it was not until November 12, that "the debtor [Lyon] receive[d] possession of the collateral" within the meaning of the statute referred to above. As already indicated, Brodie's financing statement was filed within ten days of that date. The district court agreed with this analysis in granting summary judgment for Brodie.

If, in [Code, § 9–312(4)] the term "debtor" is given the meaning ascribed to it in [Code, § 9–105(1)(d)], Brodie was entitled to priority.[1] It was not until November 12, 1964, that Lyon purchased the equipment and became obligated to pay the purchase price. Until that obligation came into being, Lyon was not Brodie's debtor with power to mortgage the restaurant equipment as collateral for the unpaid purchase price.

But the United States argues that in the context of this case the priority statute [§ 9–312(4)], is ambiguous as to whether "debtor" is used in the sense defined in [§ 9–105(1)(d)], or whether it is used merely to identify an individual in possession, who ultimately becomes indebted to the purchase-money mortgagee. In contending that this "ambiguity" should be resolved in favor of the latter construction, the United States refers to the history and underlying purposes and policies of the Code, the assertedly different language of the prior Uniform Conditional Sales Act, and the fact that, under (Code, § 9–402(1)) a financing statement may be filed before a security agreement is made or a security interest otherwise attaches, notwithstanding the fact that this section refers to "debtor," "secured party," and "security interest."

We are not persuaded that either recourse to the history or consideration of the underlying purposes of the Code supports the Government's position. In our view, the term "debtor" as it is used in this particular priority statute (Code, § 9–312(4)), means "the person who owes payment or other performance of the obligation secured." (Code, § 9–105(d)).[2] Although Lyon might have been liable for the reasonable rental of the equipment or for its return to Brodie, he did not owe performance of an "obligation secured" by the collateral in question until November 12, 1964, and therefore was not a "debtor" for purposes of (Code, § 9–312(4)). Brodie's filing was therefore within the ten-day period and Brodie has priority over the conflicting security interest held by SBA.

The Government has urged us to look at the policy and the purposes of the Code to resolve what it considers to be the ambiguous meaning of "debtor." The Code has granted a specially favored position to the holder of a purchase-money security interest in non-inventory collateral. The holder of such an interest need not follow the notice proce-

1. " '[D]ebtor' means the person who owes payment or other performance of the obligation secured, whether or not he owns or has rights in the collateral, and includes the seller of accounts, contract rights, or chattel paper; where the debtor and the owner of the collateral are not the same person, the term 'debtor' means the owner of the collateral in any provision of the article dealing with the collateral, the obligor in any provision dealing with the obligation, and may include both where the context so requires;" (Code, § 9–105(d)).

2. The Code directs the use of its statutory definitions "unless the context otherwise requires." (Code, § 9–105(1)).

dures which are prescribed for the holders of purchase-money interests in inventory. (Code, § 9–312(3)). Such a holder is also given a special priority position. His interest, perfected second, but within the ten-day grace period, will prevail over any previously perfected security interest. This priority exists even though the framers of the Code knew that the holder of the conflicting security interest would be relying on the possession of the collateral and upon the absence of a prior filing. Similarly, the holder of a purchase-money security interest in non-inventory collateral will have priority over a previously perfected security interest which includes the collateral by virtue of an after-acquired property clause. Code, § 9–312(4), Official Comment 3. Such a holder therefore is not required to search the files to determine the existence of such a conflicting interest in order to be sure of his priority.

The protection which the Code confers upon a purchase-money interest in non-inventory collateral is not unduly extended by a decision giving priority to Brodie's interest. Although it is true that Brodie could have filed a financing statement as soon as Lyon went into possession and thus protected itself, it is also true that the bank, SBA's assignor, could have protected itself by inquiring into Lyon's interest in the equipment before accepting his chattel mortgage. Due to the favored status given by the Code to the holder of a purchase-money interest in non-inventory collateral, we are not convinced that the trial court erred in refusing to impose this burden on Brodie.

Affirmed.

Notes & Questions

1. *The Stakes in* Brodie. A view seemingly contrary to that in *Brodie* has attracted a substantial judicial following. See, e.g., North Platte State Bank v. Production Credit Association, 189 Neb. 44, 200 N.W.2d 1 (1972). Is there anything to be said against the *Brodie* view? Who is put at risk by the view that the purported purchase money lender has ten days from the creation of his debt in which to perfect and that mere possession by the debtor does not trigger the commencement of the ten-day period? Does this view add to the risks of the prior lender with whom the purported purchase money secured party is competing?

2. *Effect of Opposite Result.* Suppose *Brodie* had come out the other way and that the restaurant supply company had been denied purchase money status. What impact would such a holding have on the lending practices of those seeking purchase money status?

3. *The Enabling Requirement.* Does the lender in *Brodie* have a problem under § 9–107, and its definition of purchase money security interest?

KING'S APPLIANCE & ELECTRONICS, INC. v. CITIZENS & SOUTHERN BANK OF DUBLIN

Court of Appeals of Georgia, 1981.
157 Ga.App. 857, 278 S.E.2d 733.

CARLEY, JUDGE.

The instant appeal involves priority between conflicting security interests in the same collateral and interpretation of Code Ann. § 109A–9–312. The relevant facts are as follows: On August 3, 1978, The Citizens and Southern Bank (C&S) filed a financing statement listing itself as the secured party and Randall B. Helton, d/b/a United TV (Helton) as the debtor. The financing statement covered the following types of property: "All equipment of the Debtor of every description used or useful in the conduct of the Debtor's business, now or hereafter existing or acquired, and all accessories, parts and equipment now or hereafter affixed thereto or used in connection therewith. All inventory, accounts receivable and contract rights of borrower whether now or hereafter existing or acquired; all chattel paper and instruments, whether now or hereafter existing or acquired, evidencing any obligation to borrower for payment for goods sold or leased or services rendered; and all products and proceeds of any of the foregoing."

On November 27, 1978, Helton entered into an "Inventory Financing Agreement" with Appliance Buyers Credit Corporation (ABCC) "to finance the acquisition by [Helton] of certain merchandise of inventory from time to time from" King's Appliance & Electronics, Inc. (King's Appliance). On November 29, 1978, ABCC filed a financing statement listing itself as the secured party and Helton as the debtor. The financing statement covered the following property: "Television sets, phonographs, stereos, radios and combinations, tape recorders, organs, pianos and other musical instruments, refrigerators, freezers, ice makers, dish and clothes washers and dryers, ranges, food waste disposers, trash compactors, dehumidifiers, humidifiers, room air conditioners, heating and air conditioning equipment, vacuum cleaners, and other types of mechanical or electrical, commercial, household or industrial equipment and accessories or replacement parts for any of such merchandise." On December 1, 1978, pursuant to Code Ann. § 109A–9–312(3)(d), ABCC sent notification to C&S that it "has or expects to acquire a purchase money security interest in the inventory of [Helton]" and described the inventory by item or type.

Thereafter, King's Appliance apparently began to ship to Helton merchandise which had been financed by ABCC as well as certain merchandise on consignment. The security interest held by ABCC in that part of Helton's inventory financed under the agreement with ABCC was eventually assigned to King's Appliance. When Helton subsequently defaulted on his obligations to both C&S and King's Appliance, C&S took possession of all of Helton's inventory and gave notice of its intent to sell the inventory and apply the amount realized to Helton's indebtedness to it. King's Appliance, contending that as ABCC's assignee it held a perfected security interest in part of the inventory under Code Ann. § 109A–9–302(2), filed a complaint seeking, in effect, a determination that its security interest in the inventory had priority over that of C&S under Code Ann. § 109A–9–312(3). C&S answered and, after discovery, both parties moved for summary judgment. The trial court entered its order granting summary judgment to C&S and denying summary judgment to King's Appliance. The order was based upon the trial court's following interpretation of Code Ann. § 109A–9–312: "Subpart (3)(b)(i) absolutely requires the purchase money secured party to give notification in writing to the holder of the conflicting security interest *before* the date of the filing [of the financing statement] by the purchase money secured party . . . The notice given C&S [dated December 1, 1978] was *after* the filing of the security interest of [ABCC on November 29, 1978] . . . Failure to give a timely notice prevents priority from being accorded the purchase money security interest . . ." King's Appliance appeals, urging that the trial court misconstrued Code Ann. § 109A–9–312(3)(b) and that summary judgment was erroneously granted to C&S and denied to it.

1. Code Ann. § 109A–9–312(3)(b) provides: "A perfected purchase money security interest in inventory has priority over a conflicting security interest in the same inventory and also has priority in identifiable cash proceeds received on or before the delivery of the inventory to a buyer if . . . the purchase money secured party gives notification in writing to the holder of the conflicting security interest if the holder had filed a financing statement covering the same types of inventory, (i) *before the date of the filing made by the purchase money secured party,* or (ii) before the beginning of the 21-day period where the purchase money security interest is temporarily perfected without filing or possession . . ." (Emphasis supplied). The trial court interpreted the emphasized language of this statute as requiring that in order for the purchase money security interest to be afforded priority the notification must be given to the holder of the conflicting security interest *before* the purchase money secured party files (perfects) his interest. While the 1978 amendments to Code Ann. § 109A–9–312(3) are less than a model of clarity, we conclude that the trial court erred in construing Ga.L.1978, pp. 1081, 1111.

Under Ga.L.1962, pp. 156, 406, the former Code Ann. § 109A–9–312(3)(b), in order for a purchase money security interest in inventory to gain priority over a conflicting prior security interest in the same collateral it was necessary that the purchase money secured party notify any other secured party whose security interest was either *known* to him *or* had been *perfected* by a previously filed financing statement covering the debtor's inventory. With reference to timing, under the former law, this notification had to be received by the secured party holding the prior security interest in the inventory *before the debtor received possession of the collateral covered by the purchase money security interest.* The purpose behind this notification system was clear. "The reason for the additional requirement of notification is that typically the arrangement between an inventory secured party and his debtor will require the secured party to make periodic advances against incoming inventory or periodic releases of old inventory as new inventory is received. A fraudulent debtor may apply to the secured party for advances even though he has already given a security interest in the inventory to another secured party. The notification requirement protects the inventory financer in such a situation: if he has received notification, he will presumably not make an advance; if he has not received notification (or if the other interest does not qualify as a purchase money interest), any advance he may make will have priority." Anderson, U.C.C. vol. 4, § 9–312:1, p. 355 (2d Ed. 1977). Thus, because the timing of the notification of a purchase money security interest was tied to *the date the debtor received the possession* of the purchase money financed inventory the previously secured party was afforded adequate protection and the debtor was allowed to secure additional inventory from other sources. See White & Summers, U.C.C., § 25–5, p. 913 (1972).

Current Code Ann. § 109A–9–312(3)(b), which the trial court interpreted as requiring the purchase money secured party to give notification *before* he files his financing statement, is not subject to that interpretation. While the 1978 "amendments" to Code Ann. § 109A–9–312(3) made changes in the notification procedure they did *not* effectuate a change in the timing of the notification. That the notification need not *precede* the filing is clear, if for no other reason than that Code Ann. § 109A–9–312(3)(d) contemplates that the notification may state that a purchase money security interest "has" been acquired in the debtor's inventory. Surely then filing may precede the notification envisioned under the statute. In our opinion the 1978 amendment to Code Ann. § 109A–9–312(3)(b) merely redefines *which holders* of conflicting security interests are entitled to receive notification: those who had filed a financing statement covering the inventory of the debtor prior to the date the purchase money secured party filed his statement and those who had filed statements prior to the beginning of the 21-day period contemplated by Code Ann. § 109A–9–304(5). Thus Ga.L.1978, pp. 1081, 1111, amended the former law only so as *to redefine and limit the class* of secured parties entitled to receive notification of the purchase money security interest to those who had previously *filed* a financing statement covering the same types of inventory. Subsections (i) and (ii) of existing Code Ann. § 109A–9–312(3)(b) are descriptive of the secured parties who must be notified of the subsequent purchase money secured interest; those subsections do not establish that the purchase money secured party must give notification of his interest before he files his financing statement. No other change in the previous law was contemplated or effectuated by the 1978 amendment to Code Ann. § 109A–9–312(3)(b) other than this change in the class of those previously secured parties entitled to receive notification. The timeliness of the notification continues to be determined by the date the debtor *receives possession* of the inventory secured by a purchase money security interest. Under current Code Ann. § 109A–9–312(3)(c) notification is timely if the holder of the conflicting prior security interest receives it no more than five years before the date "the debtor receives possession of the inventory."

In summary, Code Ann. § 109A–9–312(3) provides that a perfected purchase money security interest in inventory has priority over a conflicting prior security interest in the same property if:

(a) The purchase money security is perfected at the time the debtor receives possession of the inventory; and

(b) The purchase money secured party gives written notice to those holders of conflicting prior security interests who have perfected their interest in the same types of inventory before the purchase money secured party perfects his: and

(c) The holder of the previously perfected security interest receives the notification no more than five years before the date the debtor receives possession of the inventory secured by the purchase money interest; and

(d) The notification states that a purchase money security interest in the debtor's inventory, described by item or type, has been or is expected to be acquired.

Insofar as the trial court in the instant case misconstrued Code Ann. § 109A–9–312(3) and granted summary judgment to C&S on the basis of this misconstruction, the judgment must be reversed. . . .

Notes & Questions

1. In *King's Appliance,* the priority contest concerned the rights to the debtor's inventory. Suppose instead that the two secured parties had been feuding over the proceeds of some of the collateral that had been sold. For example, the sale of some appliances might have generated accounts and one of the secured parties might have had a security interest in accounts. Did each secured party have a perfected security interest in the proceeds of the inventory? Which secured party is entitled to priority?

Suppose the dispute in *King's Appliance* had been over equipment instead of inventory. Which secured party would be entitled to priority? Which secured party would be entitled to priority in the proceeds of the equipment?

2. Debtor wishes to buy a $10,000 piece of equipment for which a down payment of $2,000 is required. Secured Party loans Debtor the $2,000, takes back a security interest and immediately files a proper financing statement. Debtor uses the $2,000 to pay Seller, who takes back a security interest to secure the balance of the $8,000 purchase price. Seller files a proper financing statement the next day. Who is entitled to priority in the equipment?

See generally Baker, The Ambiguous Notification Requirement of Revised UCC Section 9–312(3): Inventory Financers Beware!, 98 Banking L.J. 4 (1981).

C. Contests With Prepaying Buyers and Unpaid Sellers

1. Prepaying Buyers

Introductory Problem

Buyer makes a down payment on a refrigerator. Before Seller delivers the refrigerator, Seller becomes insolvent. May Buyer force delivery of the refrigerator? May Buyer get his down payment back? See §§ 2–502, 2–711, 2–716, 2–501. As stated, this is a problem governed solely by Article 2 and a problem not expressly involving the rights of third parties. It becomes somewhat more complex when Seller's creditors, some of whom may be secured, assert their rights.

CHRYSLER CORP. v. ADAMATIC, INC.

Wisconsin Supreme Court, 1973.
59 Wis.2d 219, 208 N.W.2d 97.

This action was commenced on October 21, 1970, by Appellant Chrysler Corporation, seeking to replevin certain goods which it had contracted to purchase from Defendant Adamatic, Inc. Respondent Lakeshore Commercial Finance Corporation was subsequently permitted to intervene on the basis that it claimed a perfected security interest in the goods in question. During the pendency of this action, Adamatic went into receivership and, consequently, Adamatic's receiver, Russell A. Eisenberg, was also permitted to intervene. On February 9, 1972, judgment was entered giving Chrysler possession of the goods but requiring it to pay certain sums to Lakeshore. Chrysler, Lakeshore, and the receiver have all appealed.

The facts of this lawsuit are largely undisputed.

Chrysler owns and operates a plant in Indianapolis, Indiana, where it manufactures alternators and other electrical components for the motor vehicles it assembles elsewhere. Construction of the alternators requires a "stator winder," a highly specialized machine which can wind copper wire around a component part known as the "stator." For several years Chrysler had been purchasing this equipment from an Ohio manufacturer but had been seeking to find a more efficient winding machine. Chrysler engineers discovered that Adamatic was producing an advanced machine at its Milwaukee plant which, while designed for a different purpose, potentially could be converted for use as a stator winder in the Chrysler plant. Chrysler's interest in utilizing the Adamatic machine led to the transactions forming the basis of this lawsuit.

In 1967, Adamatic had entered into various security agreements with Lakeshore, whereby the latter agreed to finance Adamatic's operations and in return took a security interest in Adamatic's inventory and various other assets. The security agreements were duly filed, and it is undisputed that Lakeshore had a valid security interest in Adamatic's inventory at all relevant times.

Chrysler's first transaction with Adamatic, in March 1969, involved a contract calling for Adamatic to produce a prototype six-coil stator winder. Although the proposed machine was based on designs already formulated by Adamatic, it was to be custom built to Chrysler's specifications. The contract also required Adamatic to manufacture a "cell inserter," a separate machine, which was to be used in conjunction with the winder. The original purchase order quoted a price of $77,150 for the two units, but the price was later increased by $4,000 to cover an additional accessory for the cell inserter.

The agreement required Chrysler to make progress payments as the work neared completion. By the time the machines had been completed for shipment, Chrysler had paid 90 percent of the original purchase price. The remaining 10 percent was to be withheld until the goods were delivered and made to perform satisfactorily. Adamatic has never requested payment of this retainage, and it has not been paid.

On February 9, 1970, the completed winder and cell inserter were delivered to the Chrysler plant in Indianapolis. Although the cell inserter evidently performed to contract specifications, the six-coil winder failed to function well enough for production-line use. Over the next few months, Adamatic employees were in almost constant attendance at Chrysler's plant assisting Chrysler engineers in trying to get the winder working. Their attempts were unsuccessful, and on June 9, 1970, Chrysler sent a telegram to Adamatic threatening to cancel the second contract, executed in April 1970, between the parties if the winder could not be made to perform.

Finally, upon Adamatic's suggestion, it was decided to ship the units back to Milwaukee for additional work by Adamatic. By this time, Chrysler had decided that the six-coil winder should be converted for twelve-coil operation. On August 12, 1970, the cell inserter and six-coil winder were shipped back to Adamatic under a non-negotiable bill of lading. On August 20, 1970, Adamatic sent a quotation giving an additional price of $22,410 for the conversion. The quotation was accepted by Chrysler on a change order dated September 11, 1970. Subsequently, the parties executed a "Consigned Material Receipt Agreement," drafted by Chrysler, in which Chrysler purported to retain title to the goods.

Previously, in February, Chrysler had decided to enter into a second transaction with Adamatic involving additional machines of the same type. During that month, personnel from Lakeshore and Adamatic met with Chrysler in Detroit to discuss the financing of the second transaction. At that time, Chrysler was informed of Adamatic's shaky financial condition and the fact that Lakeshore held a security interest in Adamatic's inventory. Lakeshore told Chrysler that it was prepared to lend up to $300,000 to Adamatic if Chrysler would make progress payments on the proposed, second contract.

Chrysler's second contract with Adamatic was entered into in April 1970. A Chrysler purchase order requested Adamatic to produce three twelve-coil stator winders at a price of $83,646.43 per unit. The order, which was accepted by Adamatic, specified that the first machine was to be delivered on September 7, 1970, with the second and third twelve-coil winders to follow at thirty-day intervals. Chrysler agreed to make progress payments after the work was 25 percent complete, in an amount up to 80 percent of the value of the labor and materials put into the machines at that time.

In August 1970, Adamatic requested the first progress payment on the second contract. Chrysler sent an engineer to Milwaukee, who checked the work done and approved a progress payment of $105,761.55, representing 80 percent of the value which had been put into the machines. A payment in that amount was subsequently given to Adamatic, which immediately turned the money over to Lakeshore.

The six-coil winder had been returned in August, and by mid-September, 1970, the three twelve-coil winders were in various stages of construction. Adamatic's financial condition had long been shaky; by September, it had reached a perilous point. Its current balance sheet indicated a net deficit of $135,624.95. In addition, Adamatic had been delinquent for several months in making federal withholding tax payments to the Internal Revenue Service, and the I.R.S. was threatening Adamatic with a tax lien. Moreover, Adamatic was no longer able to pay its suppliers for parts going into the Chrysler machines, and construction was being slowed by suppliers who were withholding delivery. It appears that Adamatic was still operating only because Lakeshore was continuing to make cash advances sufficient to meet Adamatic's payroll.

On September 15, 1970, Lakeshore and Adamatic personnel met to discuss Adamatic's progress on the Chrysler contracts and the company's general financial prospects. At this time, Lakeshore advised Adamatic that it was in default and that unless it found some other source of financing, Lakeshore would be forced to liquidate its loan. Nevertheless, Lakeshore advanced an additional $30,000 to $50,000 to Adamatic, and by October 15, 1970, the loan balance was approximately $340,000. By the time of trial, however, Lakeshore had foreclosed on other secured assets still in Adamatic's possession, and Adamatic presently owes Lakeshore more than $200,000. It was stipulated that Adamatic was in default under its security agreements when this action commenced.

On October 12, 1970, Chrysler sent one of its engineers to Milwaukee in an attempt to expedite delivery of the twelve-coil winders, since the delivery dates for the first two machines had passed. He was told to return at the end of the week, when he could expect to receive the first machine. He returned on Friday, October 16, and the following day the first twelve-coil winder was given a test run at the Adamatic plant. The machine was intended to handle two stators at once, but the tooling for one phase of the operation did not function. Moreover, the machine lacked a paint job and safety guards. Nevertheless, the engineer indicated that he would accept delivery and directed Adamatic to prepare the machine for shipment. Chrysler had arranged for a common carrier truck to be present that day, and the cell inserter was loaded on. Adamatic employees continued to work on the first twelve-coil winder during Saturday, October 17, and on Sunday, the 18th, it operated properly. On Monday, October 19, the truck returned, and the winder was skidded to the Adamatic dock for loading.

At this point, Lakeshore learned that Chrysler was trying to take delivery of the first twelve-coil winder. By telephone, Lakeshore's president directed Adamatic not to ship the machines. Accordingly, Adamatic personnel removed the cell inserter from the truck and moved the winder back into the plant.

Chrysler sought legal advice, and a meeting was held between the attorneys and representatives of Lakeshore and Chrysler on October 20, 1970. The participants in this meeting differ as to what transpired. According to Chrysler's witnesses, Lakeshore demanded that Chrysler renegotiate the price if it wanted delivery of the machines. Lakeshore's president testified, however, that he told Chrysler that Lakeshore had a perfected, security interest in the machines and was asserting its rights to possession.

Chrysler then commenced this replevin action to obtain possession of the machines. On October 21, the sheriff seized the three twelve-coil winders and the cell inserter. At the time of the seizure, the first of the twelve-coil winders was substantially completed. The second was only about half finished, and the third was little more than a naked frame. The sheriff also seized the original six-coil winder, which had been completely stripped of usable parts after its return to Adamatic. In its original complaint, Chrysler declared the value of the goods to be $190,000 and put up a surety bond in twice that amount. Lakeshore immediately sought, and was granted, leave to intervene. Nevertheless, Lakeshore failed to file a sufficient redelivery bond, and the goods were turned over to Chrysler and removed to Indianapolis on or about October 27, [1970].

Adamatic, which had been insolvent for some time before the replevin, shortly thereafter went into receivership.

The trial of this action was held before a jury from November 16 to 23, 1971, and questions were submitted on a special verdict. The jury found that, as to the second contract for the twelve-coil winders, Chrysler had been a buyer in ordinary course of business. The jury further found that Lakeshore wrongfully caused Adamatic to detain the property involved in both transactions and that Chrysler's damages as a result of the detention were $40,000. It also found that Adamatic had been insolvent on the date this action commenced. . . .

HEFFERNAN, JUSTICE.

It should be emphasized that the cause of action is for replevin. The action was brought by Chrysler to gain possession of the machines and for damages against Lakeshore for their wrongful detention. Although there is evidence in the record indicating a breach of contract by the manufacturer, Adamatic, no relief is sought for that. Lakeshore, on the other hand, asserts ownership of the machines because of its prior perfected security agreement with Adamatic. The receiver, representing the general creditors, bases its claim upon Lakeshore's rights as a secured creditor, but in addition asks for an accounting by Lakeshore for any excess which Lakeshore may receive from Chrysler. As an alternative only, the receiver argues that Chrysler's taking of the goods was [a voidable] preference as against the unsecured creditors. No claim is asserted by either creditor against Chrysler for amounts unpaid on the contract price.

The legal issues fall into the natural division between the first contract involving the six-coil winder and the subsequent contract concerned with the three machines that are designated as twelve-coil winders.

The first contract—six-coil winder

. . .

The second contract—twelve-coil winders

. . . In respect to the twelve-coil winders, although there had been a contract entered into at an earlier time, the delivery of the goods was occasioned only by the replevin seizure itself. In the absence of Chrysler's claim, Lakeshore's right to the possession of the twelve-coil winders would be unquestioned.

It was conceded that Lakeshore had loaned substantial sums to Adamatic and, under ch. 409, Stats., had perfected a valid security interest in Adamatic's inventory. It was stipulated by the parties that, prior to the replevin, the twelve-coil winders were a part of that inventory. Had Chrysler not seized the machines under its claim of right, upon Adamatic's default Lakeshore could have taken possession of the machines under sec. 409.503 and sold them under the provisions of sec. 409.504 to satisfy, in part at least, Adamatic's obligations.

The mere physical transfer of the machines from Adamatic to Chrysler does not defeat Lakeshore's right to foreclose on the collateral. A perfected security interest gives the secured creditor rights in the goods themselves, and under the rule of sec. 409.201, Stats., those rights follow the collateral into the hands of subsequent owners.

Applying the principles of the Uniform Commercial Code, it is apparent that Chrysler took physical possession of the machines at a time when Lakeshore would ordinarily be entitled to their possession. Chrysler's possession of the goods is, therefore, subject to Lakeshore's security interest unless some other provision of the Code is sufficient to supersede the rights of Lakeshore.

Chrysler relies upon sec. 409.307(1), Stats., as an exception to the general rule that a purchaser is subject to an outstanding security interest. That section provides:

"A buyer in ordinary course of business . . . takes free of a security interest created by his seller even though the security interest is perfected and even though the buyer knows of its existence."

Chrysler claims to be "a buyer in ordinary course of business." That term is defined by sec. 401.201(9), Stats.:

" 'Buyer in ordinary course of business' means a person who in good faith and without knowledge that the sale to him is in violation of the ownership rights or security interest of a third party in the goods buys in ordinary course from a person in the business of selling goods of that kind but does not include a pawnbroker. 'Buying' may be for cash or by exchange of other property or on secured or unsecured credit and includes receiving goods or documents of title under a pre-existing contract for sale but does not include a transfer in bulk or as security for or in total or partial satisfaction of a money debt."

Chrysler claims that it became a buyer in ordinary course of business at the time it originally contracted to purchase the twelve-coil winders. It further argues that Lakeshore's security interest was cut off at the time of entering into the contract and, at the time it took possession of the machines by replevin, its possession was free and clear of any claims of the secured creditor. Lakeshore and the receiver for the general creditors are united in disputing this claim. They argue that nothing less than a bona fide transfer of the goods could cut off the security interest, and that a replevin cannot constitute a transaction in ordinary course.

The initial question posed is whether one can become a buyer in ordinary course before a sale has occurred. While it is apparent that the contract was a contract to sell, only the position of the creditors can be reconciled with the language of the Uniform Commercial Code.

Under sec. 401.201(9), Stats., "buying" includes receiving goods under a pre-existing contract for sale. The statute is silent on the question of whether "buying" encompasses a situation where there has been a nonreceipt of the goods; but the enumeration in the statute, when reasonably construed, limits buying in ordinary course of business to those situations where a "sale," defined by sec. 402.106(1) as "the passing of title from the seller to the buyer for a price," has occurred. There is no contention that title passed to Chrysler prior to the physical transfer occasioned by the replevin, but, under sec. 401.201(9), the buyer in ordinary course must buy without knowledge that the sale is in violation of the rights of a third party. In the instant case Chrysler, at the time of the replevin, had full knowledge of the perfected security interest of Lakeshore.

The commentators who have written on sec. 401.201(9), Stats., shed but confused elucidation on whether one can become a buyer in ordinary course merely by entering into a contract to buy. Professor Gilmore notes that the Uniform Commercial Code, unlike prior uniform acts, does not require that a buyer actually take delivery to attain the status of buyer in ordinary course of business. 2 Gilmore, Security Interests in Personal Property, p. 696, sec. 26.6. See, also, Warren, Cutting Off Claims of Ownership under the Uniform Commercial Code, 30 Univ. of Chicago L.Rev. 469, 473 (1963). Smith, in his article, Title and the Right to Possession under the Uniform Commercial Code, 10 Boston College Industrial and Commercial L.Rev. 39, 61 (1968), concludes, however, that one cannot be a buyer in ordinary course prior to taking delivery of the goods.

It seems clear that, if there is a sale and the buyer has obtained title to the goods, his status as a buyer in ordinary course will not be defeated merely because he has not taken possession. Such is not our situation here, where Chrysler buttresses its claim as a buyer in ordinary course by asserting the replevin action was a part of the process by which title passed. Moreover, in the contract between the parties, delivery was envisaged as an integral part of the title-passing process.

Although both parties have treated all three twelve-coil winders as being "identified to the contract," the state of the record reveals grave doubt that this is really the fact. Only one machine was in a deliverable state. The other two, at the most, were but incompletely assembled component parts. While the Commercial Code, as pointed out above, does not require that in all cases the buyer actually take delivery in order to have a buyer in ordinary course of business status, sound policy considerations in the instant situation would seem to dictate that the rights of a secured creditor ought not be impaired in the absence of a physical transfer or assignment of the goods. We agree generally with the position submitted by the National Commercial Finance Conference as amicus curiae. It points out that the Code generally gives preference to property interests which are evidenced either by recording or possession and that, to adopt the view of Chrysler, the financier of an inventory would no longer be able to rely on recorded interests and the status of his debtor's inventory. We recognize that this policy argument has been criticized by writers who contend that the commercial reality is that lenders rely not upon inventories or recorded instruments but rather upon the credit ratings of prospective debtors. See, Gordon, The Prepaying Buyer: Second Class Citizenship under Uniform Commercial Code Article 2, 63 Northwestern Univ.L.Rev. 565, 576 (1968); Note, The Uniform Commercial Code and an Insolvent Seller's Possession of Goods Sold, 104 Univ. of Pa.L.Rev. 91, 93.

This court, in Columbia International Corp. v. Kempler, supra, p. 559 of 46 Wis.2d, p. 469 of 175 N.W.2d, took a different position, stressing the policy of this jurisdiction—to place major reliance upon "apparent or ostensible ownership: People should be able to deal with a debtor upon the assumption that all property in his possession is unencumbered, unless the contrary is indicated by their own knowledge or by public records."

Thus, if Chrysler is to be afforded a status as a buyer in ordinary course of business, we conclude that such status must be determined as of the time [it] actually took possession of the goods.

The remedy of replevin is an unusual and drastic mode of recourse to secure the rights of a purchaser; and, from the viewpoint of common knowledge, it is almost absurd to argue that the acquisition of possession by replevin is in the ordinary course of business. It is certainly so in the instant case when we consider sec. 402.402, Stats. (the buyer's right of replevin) and sec. 402.716. Sec. 402.402(3)(a) provides:

"Nothing in this chapter shall be deemed to impair the rights of creditors of the seller:

"(a) Under the provisions of [Article 9] . . .."

The Commercial Code itself specifically negatives Chrysler's contention that the replevin alone can in any way affect the rights of a prior secured creditor. Even if it be argued that these three machines were identified to the contract, sec. 401.201(37), Stats., states:

". . . the special property interest of a buyer of goods on identification of such goods to a contract for sale under s. 402.401 is not a 'security interest' . . .."

Chrysler thus makes the anomalous and unacceptable claim that its buyer's interest gives it a right superior to the holder of an antecedent perfected security interest.

Chrysler is not a buyer in ordinary course of business and holds the machines subject to the security interest of Lakeshore. From the viewpoint of equity, this is an unsatisfactory result, for the record shows that, prior to the replevin, Chrysler had substantially paid the contract price for all the goods involved. Our conclusion, however, is supported by the writings of distinguished commentators, who have pointed out that the Code itself affords but little protection for the prepaying buyer. The Code, however, gives broad latitude whereby a prepaying buyer, acting timely, can enter into suitable arrangements for his own protection.

In the instant case Chrysler was fully aware of the fact that it was not only a buyer but was financing the manufacturing process. It was for that reason it made progress payments on the basis of the work and materials as the manufacturing progressed. By proper negotiations with the other creditors, it might well have protected itself by obtaining a security interest in the goods it had contracted to buy. Lakeshore as a substantial creditor, interested in the well being of Adamatic, might

well have been amenable to a Chrysler proposal that Lakeshore in part
subordinate its security interest. In view of the size of this contract in
proportion to the limited assets of the manufacturer, it was almost
foolhardy for Chrysler to proceed in the face of the perfected security
interest of Lakeshore. . . .

As a result of the replevin action, the machines are presently in the
possession of Chrysler. The taking of the machines by Chrysler under
the circumstances was unlawful. Lakeshore, not Chrysler, was entitled
to possession of the twelve-coil winders. . . .

Notes & Questions

1. Suppose that Chrysler and Adamatic had agreed upon a method
of identifying the equipment being manufactured. Would § 2–502
confer upon Chrysler any rights against Lakeshore? Does it give a
buyer rights against any party other than a seller?

2. Suppose Chrysler were competing with an unsecured creditor of
Adamatic. Would § 2–402 assist Chrysler?

3. The court seems dissatisfied with its finding against Chrysler.
Could Chrysler have protected itself by inserting in its contract with
Adamatic a provision that provided for early passage of title? Would
Chrysler then have been a "buyer in the ordinary course of business"
entitled to the protection of § 9–307(1)? See §§ 2–401, 9–202. Would
insertion of an early passage of title provision deprive Chrysler's
purchase of its "ordinary course" status?

4. The court's own solution to Chrysler's problem points to
Chrysler's taking back a security interest in the machines manufactured by Adamatic. Does Article 9 encompass the creation of a security
interest by a prepaying buyer? Could Chrysler have protected itself by
taking and perfecting an Article 9 security interest in the machines?

5. Suppose Chrysler determined that it wanted to have a *purchase
money* security interest in the machines. Could Chrysler have achieved
purchase money status? Do you see any obstacles in § 9–107? Suppose Chrysler managed to assure that its funds were used to purchase
raw materials for the machines. Would that satisfy the requirements
of § 9–107?

Assume that Chrysler can achieve purchase money status in the raw
materials used to manufacture the machines. Under § 9–314 or § 9–
315, would the security interest continue in the finished machines?
Would the security interest be a purchase money security interest?
Does § 9–312(3) or (4) address this problem?

See generally Jackson & Kronman, A Plea for the Financing Buyer,
85 Yale L.J. 1 (1975); Dolan, The Uniform Commercial Code and the
Concept of Possession in the Marketing and Financing of Goods, 56 Tex.
L.Rev. 1147, 1154–59 (1978).

2. Unpaid Sellers

Introductory Problems

1. Seller sells goods on credit to Buyer. The goods are delivered on February 1. On February 11 Seller discovers that Buyer is insolvent. On February 13 Seller demands that Buyer return the goods. Does § 2–702 help Seller?

2. Same facts as in #1 except that, on the day the goods are delivered, Buyer pays Seller by check. Fifteen days later the check is returned by bank for insufficient funds. May Seller reclaim the goods under § 2–702?

3. How does § 2–507 influence the answer to the above questions? Under § 2–507, how long does one have to reclaim goods?

HOUSE OF STAINLESS, INC. v. MARSHALL & ILSLEY BANK

Supreme Court of Wisconsin, 1977.
75 Wis.2d 264, 249 N.W.2d 561.

FACTS.

Plaintiff-respondent The House of Stainless Steel, Inc. (Stainless) commenced this action against defendant-appellant Marshall & Ilsley Bank (M & I) in regard to certain goods delivered by Stainless to Alkar Engineering Corporation, Lodi, Wisconsin. Stainless alleged priority of claim over these goods against M & I pursuant to sec. 402.702(2), Stats.

On November 1, 1971, Alkar Engineering entered into a general revolving loan and security agreement with M & I, the latter lending money to Alkar and taking back a security interest in ". . . all Debtor's Inventory, documents evidencing Inventory, . . . whether now owned or hereafter acquired, and all proceeds or products of any of them." (This security agreement was properly perfected by the timely filing of financing statements.)

In January, 1973, Stainless shipped certain stainless steel goods to Alkar on open account with an invoice value of $36,130.66. Subsequently Stainless discovered that Alkar had received such goods on credit while insolvent, and demanded in writing the return of said goods from Alkar. (This demand was within ten days of receipt of the goods pursuant to sec. 402.702(2), Stats. On January 17, 1973, notice of this demand was given to M & I.) On January 31, 1973, M & I sold the goods claimed by Stainless to DEC International, Inc.

On July 3, 1973, Stainless commenced this action for conversion against M & I. M & I interposed the following affirmative defenses: (1) That M & I had a perfected security interest in the goods superior to that of Stainless . . ..

Both parties moved for summary judgment, each filing supporting affidavits. The motion of plaintiff Stainless was granted and judgment was entered in its favor in the amount of $36,130.66, plus interest and costs (total $39,954.71). Defendant Marshall & Ilsley Bank appeals from this judgment and the denial by the trial court of the M & I motion for summary judgment.   . . .

ROBERT W. HANSEN, JUSTICE.   . . .

M & I claims priority over Stainless via a perfected security interest in the after-acquired property of Alkar. Under its loan and security agreement dated November 1, 1971, and the financing statements properly filed and recorded in connection therewith, M & I did have a security interest in all of Alkar's inventory, then owned or thereafter acquired. There is no dispute as to the validity of this perfected security interest.

M & I claims priority for its claim under sec. 409.312, Stats., which determines priority among conflicting interests in the same collateral. Our court has held that if, as here, the subject matter of the security interest or collateral constitutes "inventory" of the debtor, ". . . the priority of the security interest is determined by sec. 409.312(3)." Under this section in order for Stainless to have priority, it would have to have a purchase money security interest which requires perfecting its interest at the time the debtor (Alkar) received possession.[10] Additionally, it is contended that such section requires that a prior perfected lender, here M & I, must be given actual notification by a subsequent purchase money lender before the debtor receives possession of the collateral covered by the purchase money security interest.[11]

In the case before us no such notice was given, and the Stainless interest was not perfected by filing of the agreement or of any financing statements covering the property involved. Absent such perfection, M & I sees sec. 409.312, Stats., as giving priority to a secured creditor claiming under an after-acquired property clause in a pre-existing security agreement over a creditor who neglects to perfect his purchase money interest. We will resolve this priority question, infra.

Stainless, as a supplier of goods on credit, claims priority for its claim under sec. 402.702(2), Stats., providing for seller's remedies on discovery of buyer's insolvency. This statute provides a right to reclaim upon demand made within ten days after receipt of the goods.[12]

---

10. Sec. 409.312(3)(a), Stats.1971, providing:

"(3) A purchase money security interest in inventory collateral has priority over a conflicting security interest in the same collateral if:

"(a) The purchase money security interest is perfected at the time the debtor receives possession of the collateral;"

11. Id. with sub. (b) adding: "(b) Any secured party whose security interest is known to the holder of the purchase money security interest or who, prior to the date of the filing made by the holder of the purchase money security interest, had filed a financing statement covering the same items or type of inventory, has received notification of the purchase money security interest [before] the debtor receives possession of the collateral covered by the purchase money security interest;"

12. Sec. 402.702(2), Stats., providing in pertinent part: "Where the seller discovers that the buyer has received goods on credit while insolvent he may reclaim the goods upon demand made within 10 days after the receipt . . .."

It is undisputed that Stainless delivered goods to Alkar and within ten days sought reclamation of said goods.

However, Stainless did not secure possession or repossession of the goods sold and shipped to Alkar. The right to reclaim on discovery of insolvency is subject to an exception where the rights of "a buyer in ordinary course or other good faith purchaser" are involved.[13] Thus, while possessing only voidable title to the goods transferred, Alkar here could transfer title to a good faith purchaser.[14] The trial court here held M & I not to be a "good faith purchaser" drawing a distinction between "goods" and "future goods" and treating differently the M & I interest under its security agreement as to then-held and after-acquired property of Alkar. The issue as to applicability of the exemption to M & I as a "good faith purchaser" is one of law, to be resolved by this court.

We see two issues of law, not one, presented. The first is whether Stainless comes within the provisions of sec. 409.312, Stats., providing a priority for purchase money security interest holders only if such interest is "perfected." Where such creditor fails or neglects to timely perfect his interest as the statute requires, the cases in point clearly agree that the rights of a secured creditor claiming under an after-acquired property clause in a pre-existing security agreement are paramount.

We hold that a seller of goods on credit must perfect his claim to priority, under sec. 409.312, Stats., by filing the agreement and financing statements as there required. We see this result as entirely consistent with the overall purpose of the Uniform Commercial Code of allowing all parties to rely on filed security interests dealing with a debtor's property.[17] Since Stainless does not have a perfected purchase money security interest, sec. 409.312, Stats., provides no basis for a priority claim in the property sold by it to Alkar.

Thus, Stainless' only basis of priority is sec. 402.702, Stats. The second question of law raised on this appeal is whether M & I is a "good faith purchaser" and thus within the exception to the right of reclamation granted by sec. 402.702, Stats. What cases there are dealing with

---

13. Sec. 402.702(3), Stats., providing in pertinent part: "The seller's right to reclaim under sub. (2) is subject to the rights of a buyer in ordinary course or other good faith purchaser under s. 402.403. Successful reclamation of goods excludes all other remedies with respect to them."

14. See: Sec. 402.403(1), Stats., relating to transfer of title to good faith purchaser, and providing: "A purchaser of goods acquires all title which his transferor had or had power to transfer . . . . A person with voidable title has power to transfer a good title to a good faith purchaser for value. . . ."

17. Chrysler Corp. v. Adamatic, 59 Wis. 2d 219, 240, 208 N.W.2d 97, 107 (1973), this court stating: "We agree generally with the position submitted by the National Commercial Finance Conference as amicus curiae. It points out that the Code generally gives preference to property interests which are evidenced either by recording or possession and that, to adopt the view of Chrysler, the financier of an inventory would no longer be able to rely on recorded interests and the status of his debtor's inventory.

this narrow question appear to agree with the affirmative answer sought by M & I on this appeal.

In re Hayward Woolen Co.[18] dealt with the opposing claims of a reclaiming seller on credit and a secured party under provisions identical with those in our Wisconsin law. There, wool goods were delivered to a bankrupt buyer and rights to reclaim these goods were asserted by the sellers, otherwise unsecured, and their assignees. The opposing claimant held a perfected security interest in the after-acquired wool inventory of the bankrupt buyer.

The court in *Hayward* reasoned as follows: Seller's right to reclaim on the ground of buyer's insolvency is subject to the rights of a good faith purchaser under U.C.C. 2–702(3). U.C.C. sec. 2–403(1) provides "a person with voidable title has power to transfer a good title to a good faith purchaser for value." Hayward, the insolvent buyer, is a party having a voidable title. Textile, the party with a security interest in after-acquired collateral, qualifies as a purchaser under U.C.C. sec. 1–201(32, 33).[19] Textile's pre-existing claim constitutes value under U.C.C. sec. 1–201(44)(b).[20] . . .

The court held, therefore, "that Textile, as the holder of a security interest in the debtor's after-acquired inventory, acquired title to the goods remaining in Hayward's possession, as a good faith purchaser for value, and that Textile's rights to such goods are superior to those of the reclamation petitioners. It follows that the reclamation petitions must be denied."[22] . . .

It follows that the trial court order granting the Stainless motion for summary judgment must be reversed and set aside. It likewise follows that the trial court order denying the M & I motion for summary judgment must be set aside. . . .

IN RE SAMUELS & CO., INC.

United States Court of Appeals, Fifth Circuit, En Banc, 1976.
526 F.2d 1238, certiorari denied sub nom. Stowers v. Mahon, 429 U.S.
834, 97 S.Ct. 98, 50 L.Ed.2d 99.

[Samuels, a Texas meat processor, financed its cattle purchases and other operations through weekly loans from C.I.T. and granted C.I.T. a security interest in its inventory, including livestock and carcasses. Cattle farmers, including Stowers, delivered their cattle to Samuels. After slaughter and a 24 hour period during which the carcasses were

---

18. 3 U.C.C.Rep.Serv. 1107 (D.Mass.Ref. 1967).

19. Sec. 401.201(32)(33), Stats., provides:

"(32) 'Purchase' includes taking by sale, discount, negotiation, mortgage, pledge, lien, issue or re-issue, gift or any other voluntary transaction creating an interest in property.

"(33) 'Purchaser' means a person who takes by purchase."

20. Sec. 401.201(44), Stats., provides:

" 'Value' . . . a person gives 'value' for rights if he acquires them:

". . .

"(b) As security for or in total or partial satisfaction of a pre-existing claim;"

22. In re Hayward Woolen Co., supra, at 1111, 1112.

chilled, the meat was graded and a price determined. Checks were then issued to the farmers. On May 23, 1969, before the appellant-farmers' checks had been paid, C.I.T. refused to advance any more funds to Samuels. On the same day Samuels filed a bankruptcy petition. The checks issued in payment for the cattle were dishonored by the drawee bank. After an earlier round of litigation, a panel of the court of appeals held that the farmers' rights to the cattle were prior to C.I.T.'s rights. 510 F.2d 139. Judge Godbold dissented. The court of appeals, sitting en banc, reversed the panel decision and held that C.I.T. had priority in the cattle. In a per curiam opinion, the court adopted Judge Godbold's dissenting opinion, which is reprinted below.]

This case raises one primary question: under the Uniform Commercial Code as adopted in Texas, is the interest of an unpaid cash seller in goods already delivered to a buyer superior or subordinate to the interest of a holder of a perfected security interest in those same goods? In my opinion, under Article Nine, the perfected security interest is unquestionably superior to the interest of the seller. Moreover, the perfected lender is protected from the seller's claims by two independent and theoretically distinct Article Two provisions. My result is not the product of revealed truth, but rather of a meticulous and dispassionate reading of Articles Two and Nine and an understanding that the Code is an integrated statute whose Articles and Sections overlap and flow into one another in an effort to encourage specific types of commercial behavior. The Code's overall plan, which typically favors good faith purchasers, and which encourages notice filing of nonpossessory security interests in personalty through the imposition of stringent penalties for nonfiling, compels a finding that the perfected secured party here should prevail.

My brothers have not concealed that their orientation in the case before us is to somehow reach a result in favor of the sellers of cattle, assumed by them to be "little fellows," and against a large corporate lender, because it seems the "fair" thing to do. We do not sit as federal chancellors confecting ways to escape the state law of commercial transactions when that law produces a result not to our tastes. Doing what seems fair is heady stuff. But the next seller may be a tremendous corporate conglomerate engaged in the cattle feeding business, and the next lender a small town Texas bank. Today's heady draught may give the majority a euphoric feeling, but it can produce tomorrow's hangover.

I. Rights under § 2.403

My analysis begins with an examination of the relative rights of seller and secured party under § 2.403(a).

Section 2.403 gives certain transferors power to pass greater title than they can themselves claim. Section 2.403(a) gives good faith purchasers of even fraudulent buyers-transferors greater rights than the defrauded seller can assert. This harsh rule is designed to promote the greatest range of freedom possible to commercial vendors and purchasers.

The provision anticipates a situation where (1) a cash seller has delivered goods to a buyer who has paid by a check which is subsequently dishonored, § 2.403(a)(2), (3), and where (2) the defaulting buyer transfers title to a Code-defined "good faith purchaser." The interest of the good faith purchaser is protected *pro tanto* against the claims of the aggrieved seller. §§ 2.403(a); 2.403, Comment 1. The Code expressly recognizes the power of the defaulting buyer to transfer good title to such a purchaser even though the transfer is wrongful as against the seller. The buyer is granted the *power* to transfer good title despite the fact that under § 2.507 he lacks the *right* to do so.

The Code definition of "purchaser" is broad, and includes not only one taking by sale but also covers persons taking by gift or by voluntary mortgage, pledge or lien. § 1.201(32), (33). It is therefore broad enough to include an Article Nine secured party. §§ 1.201(37); 9.101, Comment; 9.102(a), (b). Thus, if C.I.T. holds a valid Article Nine security interest, it is by virtue of that status *also* a purchaser under § 2.403(a).

While I shall discuss in detail infra, the implications of C.I.T.'s security interest under Article Nine and under other Article Two provisions, I here note that C.I.T. is the holder of a perfected Article Nine interest which extends to the goods claimed by the seller Stowers.

Attachment of an Article Nine interest takes place when (1) there is agreement that the interest attach to the collateral; (2) the secured party has given value; and (3) the debtor has rights in the collateral sufficient to permit attachment. § 9.204(a).

(1) *The agreement*: In 1963, Samuels initially authorized C.I.T.'s lien in its after-acquired inventory. The agreement between these parties remained in effect throughout the period of delivery of Stowers' cattle to Samuels.

(2) *Value*: At the time of Stowers' delivery, Samuels' indebtedness to C.I.T. exceeded $1.8 million. This preexisting indebtedness to the lender constituted "value" under the Code. § 1.201(44).

(3) *Rights in the collateral*: Finally, upon delivery, Samuels acquired rights in the cattle sufficient to allow attachment of C.I.T.'s lien. The fact that the holder of a voluntary lien—including an Article Nine interest—is a "purchaser" under the Code is of great significance to a proper understanding and resolution of this case under Article Two and Article Nine. The Code establishes that purchasers can take from a defaulting cash buyer, § 2.403(a). Lien creditors are included in the definition of purchasers, § 1.201(32), (33). A lien *is* an Article Nine interest, §§ 9.101, Comment; 9.102(b); 9.102, Comment. The existence of an Article Nine interest presupposes the debtor's having rights in the collateral sufficient to permit attachment, § 9.204(a). Therefore, since a defaulting cash buyer has the power to transfer a security interest to

a lien creditor, including an Article Nine secured party, the buyer's rights in the property, however marginal, must be sufficient to allow attachment of a lien. And this is true even if, *arguendo*, I were to agree that the cash seller is granted reclamation rights under Article Two.

If the Article Nine secured party acted in good faith, it is prior under § 2.403(a) to an aggrieved seller. Under the facts before us, I think that C.I.T. acted in good faith. The Code good faith provision requires "honesty in fact", § 1.201(19), which, for Article Two purposes, is "expressly defined as . . . reasonable commercial standards of fair dealing." §§ 1.201, Comment 19; 2.103(a)(2). There is no evidence that C.I.T. acted in bad faith in its dealings with Samuels, or that Stowers' loss resulted from any breach of obligation by C.I.T. There is no claim that the 1963 security agreement was the product of bad faith. The lender's interest had been perfected and was of record for six years when Stowers' delivery to Samuels occurred. There is no suggestion that the $1.8 million debt owing from Samuels to C.I.T. was the result of bad faith or of a desire to defeat Stowers' $50,000 claim. There is no claim that C.I.T. exercised or was able to exercise control over Samuels' business operations. There is no evidence that C.I.T. authorized or ordered or suggested that Samuels dishonor Stowers' check. There is no contention that C.I.T.'s refusal to extend credit on May 23, the date Samuels filed a voluntary petition on bankruptcy at a time when it owed C.I.T. more than $1.8 million, was violative of an obligatory future advance clause. The Code's good faith provision requires "honesty in fact", § 1.201(19); it hardly requires a secured party to continue financing a doomed business enterprise.

The majority deny that C.I.T. acted in good faith because, they claim, the lender had "intimate" knowledge of Samuels' business operations. The majority's source of information on the scope of C.I.T.'s knowledge is a little puzzling. The Referee in Bankruptcy found only that "C.I.T. knew or should have known of the manner by which the bankrupt bought livestock . . . on a grade and yield basis." In the Matter of Samuels & Co., Inc., No. BK 3–1314 (N.D.Tex., order of Jan. 19, 1972). This factual finding was affirmed by the District Court which reversed the Referee and upheld C.I.T.'s propriety over Stowers. Id., orders of Nov. 24, 1972, and Jan. 16, 1973. Neither the Referee nor the District Court found, nor have the parties alleged, that C.I.T.'s knowledge of Samuels' business extended to knowledge of the debtor's obligations to third party creditors.

However, even if evidence had established that C.I.T. knew of Samuels' nonpayment and of Stowers' claim, C.I.T.'s status as an Article Two good faith purchaser would be unaffected. Lack of knowledge of outstanding claims is necessary to the common law BFP, and is similarly expressly required in many Code BFP and priority provisions. See e.g., §§ 3.302; 6.110; 8.301, 8.302; 9.301(a)(2). But the Code's definition of an Article Two good faith purchaser does not expressly or impliedly include lack of knowledge of third-party claims as an element. The detailed definition of the Article's counterpart of the common law BFP requires only honesty in fact, reasonable commercial behavior, fair dealing. And this describes precisely C.I.T.'s dealings with Samuels: during the period May 13–22—the time when the bulk of Stowers' cattle were delivered and the time of the issuance of the NSF checks—C.I.T.'s advances to Samuels totalled $1 million. The advances were curtailed on May 23 because of Samuels' taking voluntary bankruptcy at a time when its indebtedness to C.I.T. was enormous. The decision to terminate further funding was clearly reasonable. It was also fair, and honest, and, as the majority have failed to grasp, was not the cause of Stowers' suffering. As I note infra in my analysis of rights under Article Nine, the sellers' loss was avoidable through perfection of their security interests in the cattle. If they had perfected, they would not only have been prior to C.I.T. as an Article Nine lender, § 9.312, but also protected against C.I.T. as an Article Two purchaser, § 9.201. As it happens, Stowers did not perfect. I believe the sellers cannot now be permitted to force an innocent, if prosperous, secured creditor to shoulder their loss for them.

II. Rights under § 2.507

The majority opinion devotes much of its concentration and energy to an analysis of the sellers' "reclamation right" under § 2.507 and § 2.702. Relying on an expansive reading of these Sections, the opinion concludes that a cash seller whose right to payment is frustrated through a check ultimately dishonored can "reclaim" proceeds of goods delivered to the buyer despite an interim third-party interest, and despite a year-long delay in seeking reclamation. I am unable to accept this reading of Code policy and requirements.

Although the Code expressly grants a credit seller the right and power to reclaim goods from a breaching buyer, the right is triggered only by specific and limited circumstances; it can be asserted only if an exacting procedure is followed; and the right can never be asserted to defeat the interests of certain third parties who have dealt with the defaulting buyer. § 2.702(b), (c). There is no Code Section expressly granting a similar reclamation right to a cash seller.

The seller's remedies upon breach are enumerated in § 2.703. These provisions do not include or suggest a right or power in a cash seller to recover goods already delivered to a breaching buyer. Nevertheless the courts have read a reclamation right into the Code. It is this judicially-confected right to reclaim goods in which the majority's reclamation analysis is grounded. However, the majority take the reclamation right beyond anything intimated by the Code or heretofore permitted by courts recognizing a cash seller's reclamation right.

The cash seller's right to reclaim has been drawn from the language of § 2.507(b) and § 2.507, Comment 3. I note, first, that the remedy granted by § 2.507(b) is one of seller against buyer, see In re Helms

Veneer Corp., 287 F.Supp. 840 (W.D.Va., 1968). It does not concern rights of seller against third parties. Section 2.507, Comment 3 explains that the seller's rights under § 2.507 must "conform with," the policy set forth in the bona fide purchase section of this Article," i.e., with § 2.403. As I have noted above, under this provision the rights of an aggrieved cash seller are subordinated to those of the buyer's good-faith purchasers, including Article Nine lenders such as C.I.T. Thus, the Code provisions supporting a cash seller's reclamation right expressly preclude recovery by Stowers as against C.I.T.

Moreover, those courts which have permitted reclamation under § 2.507 have invariably adhered to § 2.507, Comment 3's express requirement that demand for return be made within ten days after receipt by the buyer or else be lost.

In the instant case, demand was not made within ten days or ten weeks; it came a full year after delivery to Samuels. The majority excuse this gross noncompliance by finding that the sellers' failure was the product of innocent error, and, in any event, was not required since the "purpose" of the demand rule—protection of purchasers of the delivered goods—was served through C.I.T.'s alleged intimate knowledge of Samuels' business operations.

The Code's ten-day provision is an absolute requirement. There is no exception in the Code Sections or Comments, express or implied, to the statutory period. I would be hesitant to read any extension into a statute of limitations clear and unambiguous on its face, and particularly unwilling to allow an extension some 36 times greater than the statutory maximum. My reluctance is all the greater where the right at issue is not granted by the Code but is rather the product of judicial interpretation of a Comment which, whatever grant of power it may suggest, expressly limits that right to a ten-day life.

The spirit in which the rule was broken seems to me irrelevant. Even conceding that Stowers' noncompliance occurred in absolute good faith, it was nonetheless noncompliance. Mistake of law does not constitute excuse of mistake.

C.I.T.'s apocryphal intimate knowledge of Samuels' business operations is, I believe, also irrelevant to a determination of the validity of Stowers' claim. The majority find the purpose of the ten-day rule to be one of notice to third parties that a claim exists. I have somewhat greater difficulty than my brothers in pinpointing the purpose of the ten-day rule. But I am convinced that the goal is not one of protection or notice to third-party purchasers, for their rights are secure under the Code as against the aggrieved seller even if demand is timely made. §§ 2.507, Comment 3; 2.702(c). The Code does not condition the purchasers' rights on a lack of knowledge of the seller's interest. With or without knowledge, the purchaser rests secure. I am therefore forced to conclude that the ten-day rule serves some function other than notifying third-party takers, and consequently, that even if C.I.T. knew of Stowers' claim, the sellers' obligation under the ten-day rule would not have been excused. And even if knowledge by the purchaser suspended the sellers' duty to make a timely demand, the record in this case is devoid of any hint that C.I.T. knew of Samuels' breach and Stowers' reclamation right.

Moreover, § 2.507 and § 2.702 speak of a right to reclaim goods. Neither provision grants a right to go after proceeds of those goods. Where a right or interest in proceeds is recognized by the Code it is recognized expressly. See e.g., § 9.306. The right granted by § 2.507 is narrowly defined. I am unwilling to imply an extension to such a short-lived and precisely drawn remedy.

Finally, even if there were a right to reclaim proceeds, even if the right had been timely exercised, and even if it could have been exercised despite the transfer of interest to C.I.T., Stowers would have taken subject to C.I.T.'s perfected Article Nine interest. See §§ 9.201, 9.301, 9.306, 9.312. See also my discussion of C.I.T.'s rights and interest under Article Nine, infra.

III. Rights under § 2.511

The majority opinion states that C.I.T.'s interest cannot be found superior to Stowers' because such a finding would violate § 2.511's prohibition on penalizing a seller for accepting as payment a check which is ultimately dishonored. I believe the majority have misconstrued the scope and significance of § 2.511.

Like § 2.507, § 2.511 concerns claims of the seller as against the buyer. See § 2.511(c), § 2.511, Comment 4. On its face it does not affect the rights of third parties taking from the defaulting buyer. Moreover, and more important, the seller is not here "penalized" for taking an N.S.F. check. Such loss as Stowers suffered is the direct result of his failure to comply with Code provisions which, once followed—and regardless of Stowers' acceptance of Samuels' check—would have made his interest invulnerable to claims by C.I.T. See, e.g., §§ 9.107; 9.201; 9.301; 9.312(c), (d).

IV. Rights under Article Nine

I am also unable to agree with the majority's conclusion that, under the Code, Stowers' interest is different from and greater than a security interest. Similarly, I disagree with the theory that by virtue of Stowers' power under Article Two, C.I.T.'s security interest is subject to defeat since it (1) could not attach because the debtor's rights in the collateral were too slight to permit attachment and (2) was subject to defeat even if it attached because a security interest collapses if the debtor's right to the property is extinguished. The majority's result is achieved only by ignoring or circumventing the plain meaning of Article Nine and Article Two.

Prior to the enactment of the Uniform Commercial Code, seller and buyer could agree that, despite buyer's possession, title to goods sold was to remain in the seller until he was paid. Such a reservation of title under the "cash sale" doctrine would defeat not only a claim to the goods by the defaulting buyer, but also the claims of lien creditors of the buyer, for the buyer's naked possession could give rise to no interest to which a lien could attach.

However, the U.C.C. specifically limits the seller's ability to reserve title once he has voluntarily surrendered possession to the buyer: "Any retention or reservation by the seller of the title (property) in goods shipped or delivered to the buyer is limited in effect to a reservation of a security interest." § 2.401(a). See also § 1.201(37). The drafters noted the theory behind this provision: "Article [Two] deals with the issues between seller and buyer in terms of step by step performance or non-performance under the contract for sale and not in terms of whether or not 'title' to the goods has passed." § 2.401, Comment 1.

The majority opinion interprets § 2.401(a) as applying only to "credit" sales, and of no effect where the parties have contracted a "cash" sale. However, the Code provision speaks of "any reservation of title." It does not on its face apply solely to credit sales. There is no authority under the Code for the majority's restrictive interpretation. Numerous courts have, in fact, applied § 2.401 to cash sales. I have been unable to find even one case suggesting that § 2.401 applies only to credit sales.

If the majority were correct, the Section would be merely definitional, for a credit sale is but a sales transaction in which the seller reserves a security interest. However, § 2.401 is not definitional. It is operational and concerns the effect of transfer of possession under a sales contract upon any reservation of title. Neither law nor logic leads me to believe that § 2.401 is correctly interpreted to exclude cash sales.

The majority also suggest that Stowers' interest cannot be characterized as a security interest subject to Article Nine requirements and priorities since, the majority conclude, such interests must be "consensual". While it is true that many interests governed by Article Nine are consensual, §§ 9.102; 9.102, Comment, the Code clearly subjects Article Two security interests arising not by consent but by operation of law to Article Nine. See §§ 2.401(a); 9.113; 9.113, Comment 2. See also §§ 2.326; 9.114; 9.102, Comment 1.

Since Stowers' interest upon delivery of the cattle to Samuels was limited to a security interest subject to Article Nine, §§ 2.401(a); 9.113, the validity of C.I.T.'s Article Nine interest becomes crucial. If C.I.T. is the holder of a perfected Article Nine interest in the collateral claimed by Stowers through its unperfected § 2.401 interest, C.I.T.'s interest will prevail over Stowers', § 9.312(e).

The majority assert that C.I.T. cannot claim an interest in the cattle because Samuels' interest was too slight to permit attachment. See § 9.204(a). As I noted in my discussion of rights under § 2.403, this argument ignores the significance of § 2.403(a) and § 1.201(32), (33).

The Code anticipates a situation where the interest of an unpaid cash seller who has delivered goods to a breaching buyer is subordinated to the interest of "purchasers" of the buyer. Lien creditors are included in the definition of "purchasers"; in order that there *be* lien creditors, the buyer's interest must be great enough to allow attachment. Therefore, however, Samuels' interest upon delivery of the cattle is defined, and however slight or tenuous or marginal it was, it was necessarily great enough to permit attachment of a lien, including C.I.T.'s Article Nine interest.

The majority find that even if attachment occurred, C.I.T.'s interest would be defeated by Stowers' reclamation. The theory behind this argument is that the rights of the Article Nine secured party are at best coextensive with the rights of the debtor; if the debtor loses his rights, the security interest too is lost.

Upon nonpayment Samuels lost the right to retain or dispose of the property, but the Code recognizes that the breaching buyer had the power to encumber, despite nonpayment, so long as he retained possession. §§ 2.403(a); 1.201(32), (33). In the instant case, this power arose as a result of Stowers' delivery, and it did not terminate while the goods remained in Samuels' hands. The whole point of Article Nine is the continuity of perfected security interests *once they have properly attached*, despite subsequent loss of control or possession of the collateral by the debtor. § 9.201. Article Nine does not except an unpaid cash seller from this overall plan. In fact it specifically provides a means for him to perfect and become prior to previous perfected security interests. § 9.312(c), (d).

To hold that a reclaiming seller is given the power to sweep away a security interest which was able to attach only as a direct and Code-approved result of his voluntary act of delivery to the buyer would require ignoring the meaning and interplay of Article Two and Article Nine. Article Two recognizes the continuous vitality and priority of an Article Nine interest over the rights of an aggrieved seller. See §§ 2.403(a); 2.507, Comment 3; 2.702(c). It would be error to believe that a proper analysis of Article Nine could require the extinction of an identical Article Nine interest in the very circumstances specified by Article Two as triggering the priority of lienor over seller. See §§ 2.403(a); 2.507(b); 2.507, Comment 3; 2.702(b), (c); 9.102; 9.107(1); 9.312(c), (d).

Any seeming unfairness to Stowers resulting from the Code's operation is illusory, for the sellers could have protected their interests, even as against C.I.T.'s prior perfected interest, if they had merely complied with the U.C.C's purchase-money provisions. §§ 9.107, 9.312(c), (d). The Code favors purchase-money financing, and encourages it by granting to a seller of goods the power to defeat prior liens. The seller at most need only (1) file a financing statement and (2) notify the prior secured party of its interest before delivery of the new inventory. The procedure is not unduly complex or cumbersome. But whether cumbersome or not, a lender who chooses to ignore its provisions takes a calculated risk that a loss will result.

In the instant case Stowers did not utilize § 9.312's purchase-money provision. The sellers never perfected. Thus, in a competition with a perfected secured party they are subordinated, and, in this case, lose the whole of their interests. See §§ 9.201, 9.301, 9.312(e). . . .

AINSWORTH, CIRCUIT JUDGE, with whom BELL, INGRAHAM, COLEMAN and GEWIN, CIRCUIT JUDGES, join (dissenting): . . .

Is C.I.T. a Good Faith Purchaser Under the Code?

The majority having conceded that the transactions here were sales for cash and payment not having been made to the sellers because the checks were dishonored by the bank after the intervening bankruptcy petition of Samuels, the only point left upon which the majority can possibly rely is that C.I.T. and the trustee were good faith purchasers for value. . . .

. . . The opinion of Judge Ingraham completely refutes C.I.T.'s claim of good faith purchaser for value as follows:

The third question is whether C.I.T. qualifies as a good faith purchaser. Under § 2.403 of the Code, the buyer of goods from a seller is vested with a limited interest that it can convey to a good faith purchaser and thus create in the purchaser a greater right to the goods than the buyer itself had. This is possible even when the buyer obtains the goods as a result of giving a check that is later dishonored or when the purchase was made for cash. But in order to attain this status, the proponent must be a *purchaser* that gives *value* and acts in *good faith*. While C.I.T. gave value for the goods within the meaning of the Code, it failed to meet the test of a purchaser or one acting in good faith.

With regard to C.I.T.'s status as a purchaser, the Code broadly defines this term as one who takes "by sale, discount, negotiation, mortgage, pledge, lien, issue or reissue, gift or any other voluntary transaction creating an interest in property." Texas Business and Commerce Code, § 1.201(32) (1968); *see id.* § 1.201(33). *As noted earlier, C.I.T. does not have an interest in the cattle because its rights in the collateral are derivative of its debtor's rights in it. When Samuels failed to pay for the cattle, its rights in the cattle terminated and thus so did C.I.T.'s.* C.I.T.'s status as a good faith purchaser is also defeated with regard to its acting in good faith. The Code defines good faith as "honesty in fact in the conduct or transaction concerned." Texas Business and Commerce Code, § 1.201(19) (1968). Implicit in the term "good faith" is the requirement that C.I.T. take its interest in the cattle without notice of the outstanding claims of others.

It is true that the evidence does not reveal any breach of an express obligation on C.I.T.'s behalf to continue financing the packing house after Samuels filed a petition in bankruptcy. Nor does the good faith element require the creditor to continue to finance the operation of a business when it is apparent that the business is unprofitable and is going bankrupt. But because of the integral relationship between C.I.T. and Samuels, we do not see how C.I.T. could have kept from knowing of the outstanding claims of others. C.I.T. maintained close scrutiny over the financial affairs of Samuels' operations. C.I.T. had been financing Samuels' packing house operations for at least six years, and the financing involved the flow of millions of dollars. The amount of cash advances made to Samuels was not predetermined or determined arbitrarily, but was calculated only after C.I.T. examined weekly the outstanding accounts and the current inventory of the business. From such a continuous and prolonged study of the business to determine the amount of each weekly advance, C.I.T. must have been intricately aware of the operations and financial status of the business.

Since C.I.T. was so intimately involved in Samuels' financial affairs, it must have known that when it refused to advance additional funds, unpaid checks issued to cattle sellers by Samuels would be dishonored. Samuels' operations were totally dependent on the financing of C.I.T. and both parties knew it. From its enduring involvement in the weekly financing, C.I.T. apparently knew that Samuels was purchasing and processing cattle up until the very time of filing the petition. Knowing that cattle had been purchased and processed immediately preceding its refusal to advance more money, C.I.T. must have known as a result of this refusal that some cattle sellers who had recently delivered their cattle to Samuels would not be paid. Because C.I.T. and Samuels were so intertwined in the management of the financial affairs of the business, we do not think that C.I.T. can plausibly claim, in complete honesty, that it was unaware of the claims of the unpaid cattle sellers. Since C.I.T. was aware of these outstanding claims, it does not qualify as a good faith purchaser.

(Emphasis added.)   510 F.2d at 151–152.

It is important to remember, too, that the Referee in his findings of fact, which were accepted by the district court, held that "C.I.T. knew or should have known of the manner by which the bankrupt bought livestock from the plaintiffs on a grade and yield basis as hereinabove described."

The record does not disclose that any funds were advanced by C.I.T. on the faith of plaintiff's cattle, delivered to Samuels on the eve of its default and bankruptcy petition, being in Samuels' inventory. In fact, it is quite clear that C.I.T.'s decision not to advance funds to Samuels in the week involved directly resulted in Samuels' filing its petition in bankruptcy and the bank thereafter refusing to honor plaintiff's checks in payment of the cattle.

C.I.T.'s intimate knowledge over a long period of years of Samuels' financial affairs, having financed the packer on a weekly basis, shows beyond doubt that C.I.T. knew its decision not to advance further funds to Samuels would result in the cattle farmers involved here not being paid for their cattle. To allow C.I.T. under the guise of a good faith purchaser now to pick up all the proceeds of the cattle farmers' livestock does not comport with section 2.403 of the Code or with any other provision of the U.C.C. Its lien rights to the proceeds of the cattle here, as we have pointed out, were derivative of Samuels' rights. Samuels had no right to the proceeds since it had not paid for the cattle. Therefore, C.I.T. had no right thereto. Thus the majority opinion cannot stand logical scrutiny or the provisions of the Uniform Commercial Code adopted by the Texas Business and Commerce Code.

. . .

Notes & Questions

1. Suppose that Buyer and Seller have contracted for the sale of equipment, the goods have been identified to the contract, and the parties agree that title has passed to Buyer. Buyer has granted Bank a security interest (which Bank perfected) in after-acquired equipment, and Buyer is in default on its loan from Bank. May Bank foreclose on the equipment still held by Seller? Does either § 2–507(2) or § 2–702(2) assist in answering this question? Does § 9–113? Why isn't § 9–113 invoked in *House of Stainless* or *Samuels*?

Does either § 2–507(2) or § 2–702(2) assist in resolving either *House of Stainless* or *Samuels*? How do the two cases differ?

2. According to Judge Godbold, what should the seller in *Samuels* have done to protect itself? Assuming that the seller retained a security interest in the cattle, would the seller have prevailed on the facts of *Samuels*? Suppose that the fight in *Samuels* had been over the cattle themselves. Would that change the benefits obtained by seller if it had a security interest?

3. The immediate holding of *Samuels* was overturned by Congress. Section 196 of the Packers and Stockyards Act, 7 U.S.C.A. § 196, requires large meat packers to hold inventory and its proceeds in trust for the benefit of unpaid cash sellers. A "cash sale" is defined to be a "sale in which the seller does not expressly extend credit to the buyer."

4. In *House of Stainless*, *Samuels*, and *Smoker* (see Chapter 2) are the secured parties or the sellers in a better position to protect themselves? Why should the secured parties be given any interest in goods not yet paid for? Should they equate physical possession of goods by the debtor with those goods' availability as collateral? Could the secured party in either of the above cases reasonably have done so?

5. Should secured parties such as C.I.T. be entitled to "purchaser" status with its attendant benefits? Is C.I.T.'s position analogous to that of other purchasers that the U.C.C. seeks to protect? Did C.I.T. reasonably rely on the Stowers cattle in advancing funds to the debtor?

Should secured parties in C.I.T.'s position only prevail if they can show that they relied on the debtor's possession of assets? In light of other U.C.C. provisions would such reliance be reasonable?

See generally McDonnell, The Floating Lienor As Good Faith Purchaser, 50 S.Cal.L.Rev. 429 (1977); Jackson & Peters, Quest for Uncertainty: A Proposal for Flexible Resolution of Inherent Conflicts Between Article 2 and Article 9 of the Uniform Commercial Code, 87 Yale L.J. 907 (1978).

D. The Rights and Duties of Assignees

Modern financing transactions make frequent use of assignments of contract rights as security interests. The *Michelin Tires* case, which follows, involves the assignment of contract rights to a lender who is financing a construction company's project. The lender wants to be sure that if the construction company defaults on its loan the lender will have as complete an interest as possible in the unfinished property and will be well placed to decide whether to finish, sell, or abandon the project. Similarly, in commercial leasing transactions, the lender often furnishes the lessor with the purchase price of equipment. The lessor leases the equipment to the lessee, whose lease payments are used to retire the debt owed by the lessor to the lender. The lessor assigns to the lender all of its rights under the lease. In such transactions (as in *Michelin Tires*), the lender wishes to minimize the expenses of ownership while retaining the right to retake the leased property if the loan repayment schedule is not met. One common feature of financing leases is a "hell or high water" clause which requires the lessee to pay rent regardless of the performance of the lessor or the leased property. Are such clauses enforceable by the assignee-lender in the event of the equipment's failure? See § 9–206; In re O.P.M. Leasing Services, Inc., 21 B.R. 993, 1005 (Bkrtcy.S.D.N.Y.1982) (yes).

MICHELIN TIRES (CANADA) LIMITED v. FIRST NATIONAL BANK OF BOSTON

United States Court of Appeals, First Circuit, 1981.
666 F.2d 673.

MAZZONE, DISTRICT JUDGE.

This appeal is from a district court's denial of restitution to the plaintiff, a contractual obligor, of monies mistakenly paid to the defendant, an assignee of contract rights. We begin with a summary of the record.

Michelin Tires (Canada) Ltd. ("Michelin"), a Canadian corporation based in New Glasgow, Nova Scotia, and J. C. Corrigan, Inc. ("JCC"), a building contractor, entered into an agreement on June 19, 1970 for the design and installation of a carbon black handling and storage system, which was to form part of a Michelin tire factory under construction in Pictou County, Nova Scotia. Michelin entered into the agreement through its agent, Surveyor, Nenniger & Chenevert ("SNC"), an engineering firm retained by Michelin to procure and supervise the building of the factory.

The construction contract provided that Michelin would make periodic progress payments to JCC in the amount of 90% of each invoice submitted by JCC for work completed. The amounts due were based on a schedule of values of the various parts of the entire project. JCC's invoices were to be submitted first to SNC for its review and certification that the work had been performed and the amount was correct. That certification was contained in an Engineers Progress Certificate ("EPC") and was completed by the SNC project manager. With each invoice, Michelin had the right to require JCC to submit a "Statutory Declaration," or sworn statement, stating the amount JCC owed to subcontractors, suppliers, and others in connection with the work and listing any claims that could result in liens on Michelin's property. If JCC failed to make prompt payments to subcontractors and suppliers, SNC could withhold or nullify its certification and Michelin could deduct from its progress payments to JCC the amount necessary to protect its property from liens.

Prior to signing the construction contract with JCC, neither SNC nor Michelin made inquiries concerning JCC's financial situation. Initially, SNC had requested that JCC provide a performance bond to cover its work, and JCC had requested that Michelin provide a letter of credit to cover the payments due for work performed. Michelin, or SNC, dropped its proposal that JCC be required to provide a performance bond in return for JCC's withdrawal of its request for a letter of credit for Michelin.

The First National Bank of Boston ("FNB"), a commercial bank in Boston, Massachusetts, provided financing to JCC under a longstanding agreement dating from 1960. Under that agreement, FNB agreed to loan JCC an amount not greater than 80% of JCC's outstanding invoices. In return, FNB took a security interest in all JCC's accounts receivable and contract rights—including, of course, JCC's right to receive payments under its contract with Michelin.

On August 14, 1970, two months after the construction contract was executed, JCC assigned its rights under the contract to FNB. The bank notified SNC of the assignment and requested that future JCC invoices be paid directly to FNB. This assignment was acknowledged by SNC on September 3, 1970.

Shortly after JCC's assignment of its contract rights to FNB, Michelin sent FNB the payments it seeks to recover in the instant suit. The first payment was in response to JCC's invoice of August 24, 1970 in the amount of $118,000. JCC presented no EPC and no Statutory Declaration in support of this invoice. SNC prepared an EPC for the invoice and asked JCC to submit a Statutory Declaration with future invoices. Michelin paid 90% of the invoice, to FNB, as provided by the construction contract.

JCC submitted its next invoice on September 23, 1970 in the amount of $187,000. As with the previous invoice, no Statutory Declaration was presented. Michelin withheld payment and asked JCC to submit the Statutory Declaration. JCC did so on October 16, 1970.

JCC then sent Michelin an invoice dated October 22, 1970 in the amount of $313,000, accompanied by a Statutory Declaration and an EPC. Michelin paid 90% of the amounts of the latter two invoices on December 15, 1970, deducting amounts for uncompleted work and for a change order.

Michelin's last payment to FNB was in response to JCC's invoice for $200,000, dated December 21, 1970. JCC sent the corresponding Statutory Declaration to Michelin on January 18, 1971, and Michelin sent its progress payment to FNB on January 20, 1971, including the amount previously withheld for uncompleted work.

It was not until March of 1971 that Michelin learned that JCC had not been paying its subcontractors. Accordingly, the above progress payments were not due under the construction contract, and JCC's Statutory Declarations of October 12, 1970 and January 18, 1971 were fraudulent, JCC made an assignment for the benefit of creditors on April 6, 1971 and was subsequently adjudicated a bankrupt.

The carbon black system was substantially completed by May 1, 1971, and the district court found that JCC performed all the work it could have done prior to May 1, 1971. JCC left, however, a total indebtedness of over $500,000 (Canadian) after its adjudication in bankruptcy.

Throughout this time, FNB maintained its lending relationship with JCC. FNB knew of JCC's financial difficulties. By early 1970, before JCC contracted with Michelin, FNB regarded its loan to JCC as a problem and was concerned about repayment. The bank knew from examining JCC's books that the company's earnings were declining, its trade debt was rising, and its customers were slow to pay. It was further evident from JCC's books that JCC was overstating its income in its reports to the bank. By late August of 1970, the bank was aware that JCC's outstanding indebtedness was greater than the agreed-upon loan ceiling of 80% of JCC's accounts receivable, and a bank officer reminded JCC that loan funds received while JCC was "over-advanced" were to be used only to meet payroll and pay taxes. FNB used the payments it received from Michelin after the assignment to reduce the outstanding amount on its loan to JCC. In October of 1970, FNB sent an inquiry to SNC to verify the accuracy of copies of invoices the bank had received from JCC, used by the bank to calculate the 80% loan ceiling. SNC replied that the invoices were "OK."

The district court specifically found that FNB knew of JCC's contractual obligations to Michelin. Those obligations included prompt payment of subcontractors. FNB, however, did not know that JCC was sending false Statutory Declarations to Michelin, stating under oath that the subcontractors had been paid.

On December 22, 1970, FNB notified JCC that it would extend no further loans to JCC after March 31, 1971 and that JCC should seek financing elsewhere. It was after JCC failed to find a new lender that the company made its assignment for the benefit of creditors on April 6, 1971 and filed a petition in bankruptcy.

After discovering JCC's fraud, Michelin brought this suit to recover the payments it made to FNB, a total of $724,197.60. Michelin asserted it was entitled to restitution under two theories. First, it claimed that since its right to restitution arose from its contract with JCC, the claim could be successfully asserted against FNB, the assignee of contract rights to payment, pursuant to § 9–318(1)(a) of the Uniform Commercial Code (UCC), Mass.Gen.Laws Ann. ch. 106, § 9–318(1)(a).[1] Second, Michelin asserted that FNB was liable because it has been unjustly enriched under traditional restitutionary principles.

The district court tried the case without a jury and upon a stipulated record. In a detailed memorandum, the court found that JCC had breached its contract with Michelin by submitting fictitious invoices and fraudulent Statutory Declarations and by failing to pay its subcontractors when payment was due. It further found that Michelin's payments to FNB had been made in reliance on the fraudulent Statutory Declarations. The district court then ruled, first, that § 9–318(1)(a) does not create a new affirmative cause of action by an account debtor as against an assignee and, second, that since FNB did not know of the fraudulent Statutory Declarations or of JCC's indebtedness to subcontractors, FNB had not been unjustly enriched at the expense of Michelin. This appeal followed.

We affirm because we believe that (1) § 9–318(1)(a) of the UCC was not intended to create a new cause of action by an account debtor against an assignee and (2) the facts the district court found were available to FNB did not put it on notice of JCC's fraud and Michelin's mistake.

I.

Michelin's first argument is that it has an independent cause of action against FNB under § 9–318 of the UCC, Mass.Gen.Laws Ann. ch. 106, § 9–318 (West Supp.1981). That section reads in pertinent part:

1. Michelin's complaint framed this claim as one in breach of contract. On appeal, however, Michelin characterizes the claim as purely restitutionary, although "arising from" its contract with JCC. Apparently, then, Michelin is not attempting to assert that it is entitled to restitution as an alternative remedy for breach of contract. If it were, Michelin would have to show the breach was total, warranting rescission of the contract. See 5 A. Corbin, Corbin on Contracts § 1104 (1964). On the other hand, restitution of property transferred in the course of performance of a contract can be had under equitable principles without regard to the totality of the breach. See Restatement of Restitution § 28, Comment a (1937).

Given our interpretation of § 9–318(1)(a) of the UCC, we need not reach the next question—whether this claim, essentially one in equity, can nevertheless be said to "arise from" the contract.

Defenses Against Assignee; Modification of Contract After Notification of Assignment; Term Prohibiting Assignment Ineffective; Identification and Proof of Assignment.

(1) Unless an account debtor has made an enforceable agreement not to assert defenses or claims arising out of a sale as provided in section 9–206 the rights of an assignee are subject to

(a) all the terms of the contract between the account debtor and assignor and any defense or claim arising therefrom.

In essence, Michelin contends that its restitution claim arises from its contract with JCC, and that § 9–318(1)(a) accordingly permits Michelin to recover from FNB as JCC's assignee. Although Michelin emphasizes the narrow application of this theory to the instant case, the theory rests upon a construction of § 9–318 that would impose full contract liability on assignees of contract rights. Under this view, a bank taking an assignment of contract rights as security for a loan would also receive as "security" a delegation of duties under the contract and the risk of being held liable on the contract in place of its borrower. We do not believe it was the intent of § 9–318(1)(a) to create such a result.

The key statutory language is ambiguous. That "the rights of an assignee are *subject to* . . . (a) all the terms of the contract" connotes only that the assignee's rights to recover are limited by the obligor's rights to assert contractual defenses as a set-off, implying that affirmative recovery against the assignee is not intended. See Englestein v. Mintz, 345 Ill. 48, 61, 177 N.E. 746, 752 (1931), quoted in Anderson v. Southwest Savings & Loan Association, 117 Ariz. 246, 248, 571 P.2d 1042, 1044 (1977):

The words "subject to," used in their ordinary sense, mean "subordinate to," "subservient to," or "limited by." There is nothing in the use of the words "subject to," in their ordinary use, which would even hint at the creation of affirmative rights.

On the other hand, the use of the word "claim" raises the possibility that affirmative recovery was indeed contemplated. However, the section's title and the official Comment support the view that the section does not create affirmative rights. The title reads, "Defenses Against Assignee." Official Comment 1 states in pertinent part:

Subsection (1) makes no substantial change in prior law. An assignee has traditionally been subject to defenses or set-offs existing before an account debtor is notified of the assignment.

Under prior law, an assignee of contract rights was not liable on the contract in the place of his assignor. Wright v. Graustein, 248 Mass. 205, 142 N.E. 797 (1924). Common sense requires that we not twist the "precarious security" [2] of an assignee into potential liability for his assignor's breach.

---

2. This phrase was coined by Professor Gilmore in his article, The Assignee of Contract Rights and His Precarious Security, 74 Yale L.J. 217 (1964). This article

It is evident that § 9–318 has become a red herring in suits against an assignee. We note two cases that have denied account debtors the right to sue. James Talcott, Inc. v. Brewster Sales Corp., 16 UCC Rep.Serv. 1165 (N.Y.Sup.Ct.1975); Meyers v. Postal Finance Co., 287 N.W.2d 614 (Minn.1979). There are also cases that have allowed affirmative claims, at least in limited circumstances. Benton State Bank v. Warren, 263 Ark. 1, 562 S.W.2d 74 (1978); Farmers Acceptance Corp. v. DeLozier, 178 Colo. 291, 496 P.2d 1016 (1972); K Mart Corp. v. First Penn. Bank, 29 UCC Rep.Serv. 70 (Pa.1980).

The decisions permitting an affirmative suit all rely on the pre-UCC case of Firestone Tire and Rubber Co. v. Central Nat. Bank, 159 Ohio St. 423, 112 N.E.2d 636 (1953). There the court required the bank to return payments to an account debtor because, although the bank was innocent of the assignor's fraud, the bank had unwittingly assisted that fraud by independently requesting periodic payment from the account debtor. The bank attached invoices from the assignor to each request thereby impliedly representing that the underlying obligation was valid. The court found that the account debtor relied on the genuineness of the invoices forwarded by the bank. Id. 112 N.E.2d at 639. In the case at hand there was no such reliance. Rather, Michelin established its own system of assuring compliance, including approval of an intermediary, SNC. In addition, they required a Statutory Declaration under oath from JCC. The stipulated record indicates that FNB had no involvement in verifying JCC's performance and was completely unaware of the Statutory Declaration.

Benton State Bank, supra, represented a situation similar to *Firestone*. In *Benton State Bank* the bank advanced progress payments to the assignor. Each request for a progress payment was then forwarded by the bank to the general contractor accompanied by the assignor's certification, a representation similar to the Statutory Declaration submitted by JCC in this case. The court permitted the contractor to recover against the bank because the bank "had solid reasons for suspecting the truth of Harp's [the assignors] assertions, which the bank forwarded to the Warrens [the account debtors], that all past-due bills for labor and materials had been paid." Id., 562 S.W.2d at 76. FNB did not assume an active role in sending JCC's statements to Michelin, nor were they even aware of JCC's misrepresentation to Michelin in any way.

The bank in *K Mart Corp.*, supra, was also actively involved in the relationship between the account debtor and the assignor. In *K Mart*

has been the source of some of the confusion regarding section 9–318. In it, Professor Gilmore analyzes the early case of Firestone Tire and Rubber Co. v. Central National Bank, 159 Ohio St. 423, 112 N.E.2d 636 (1953), and concludes that account debtors should be entitled to sue for repayment of funds mistakenly transferred to assignees even if the transfer was negligent, so long as the assignee has not changed its position. With all due respect to Professor Gilmore, we disagree with this conclusion for the reasons stated in this opinion. We further note, however, that even under Gilmore's analysis, Michelin's suit would fail here since Massachusetts law suggests that a bank's crediting of a debtor's account involves a change of position. Merchants' Insurance Co. v. Abbott, 131 Mass. 397 (1881).

Corp., the court permitted the account debtor, K Mart, to recover from the assignee certain payments made for goods that were later found to be defective. Id. at 707. However, the recovery permitted in *K Mart Corp.* is best viewed as merely anticipated repayment. For nearly 8 years the bank accepted payment from K Mart equal to the value of the assignor's, PSM, invoices *minus* an allowance for defective goods received and paid for in the prior month. The assignor's bankruptcy prevented such an adjustment on the final payment so the court allowed recovery. The court noted "that merely because PSM is bankrupt and can no longer be expected to repay K Mart, the bank may not now *unilaterally ignore its prior understanding, which was clearly in the contemplation of the parties*, and retain funds which should not have been paid to it initially." Id. at 706 (emphasis added). There is no indication that Michelin and FNB agreed to make periodic adjustments depending upon the quality of JCC's performance.

Finally, the Colorado Supreme Court permitted recovery by the account debtor against the assignee in *DeLozier*, supra. The extent of the involvement by the assignee, Farmers Acceptance Corp. ("FAC"), in the underlying contract is ambiguous in that case. The brief opinion indicates that FAC, first used the payment it received from the account debtor to satisfy the personal indebtedness of the assignor and then applied the remainder to the assignor's unpaid account with a materialman. Id., 496 P.2d at 1017. This latter payment to the subcontractor's creditor suggests knowledge and involvement by the assignee that exceeds that of FNB. In the case before us, the stipulated facts indicate that FNB had no involvement in the payments by JCC to its subcontractors. In any event, to the extent that *DeLozier* can be read to permit an affirmative suit against a lender who is completely unrelated to the underlying contract, we decline to follow this departure from traditional common law principles of restitution.

In each of the cases permitting an affirmative suit, with the possible exception of *DeLozier*, the assignee actively participated in the transactions to a degree not approached here. We are aware of no case that has gone beyond those we have cited and actually permitted an affirmative suit against a nonparticipating assignee like FNB. We do not anticipate that the Supreme Judicial Court would extend the law in this way and we are unwilling to do so ourselves. Given the factual distinctions between the cases discussed above and the transactions at issue here, we do not need to reach the issue of whether Massachusetts law would permit suit against an assignee who became more involved in the course of dealings.

While it is our judgment that analysis of the statutory language, taken in context, indicates that no affirmative right was contemplated and further that those cases that have permitted such a right are factually inapposite, we also believe it would be unwise to permit such suits as a matter of policy. As the dissenting justice in *Benton State Bank*, 562 S.W.2d 74, noted, allowing affirmative suits would "make every Banker, who has taken an assignment of accounts for security purposes, a deep pocket surety for every bankrupt contractor in the state to whom it had loaned money." Id. at 77 (Byrd, J., dissenting).

We are unwilling to impose such an obligation on the banks of the Commonwealth without some indication that this represents a considered policy choice. By making the bank a surety, not only will accounts receivable financing be discouraged, but transaction costs will undoubtedly increase for everyone. The case at hand provides a good example. In order to protect themselves, FNB would essentially be forced to undertake the precautionary measures that Michelin attempted to use, independent observation by an intermediary and sworn certifications by the assignor. FNB would have to supervise every construction site where its funds were involved to ensure performance and payment. We simply do not believe that the banks are best suited to monitor contract compliance. The party most interested in adequate performance would be the other contracting party, not the financier. Given this natural interest, it seems likely to us that while the banks will be given additional burdens of supervision, there would be no corresponding reduction in vigilance by the contracting parties, thus creating two inspections where there was formerly one. Costs for everyone thus increase, without any discernible benefit. It is also difficult to predict the full impact a contrary decision would have on the availability of accounts receivable financing in general.

Our holding, of course, is not that § 9–318 *prohibits* claims against the assignee. We hold merely that § 9–318 concerns only the preservation of defenses to the assignee's claims and, as such, is wholly inapposite in an affirmative suit against an assignee. . . .

BOWNES, CIRCUIT JUDGE (dissenting).

I dissent from the majority's holding that Michelin does not have an independent cause of action against First National Bank of Boston (FNB). . . .

I believe that the sounder view is that an account debtor may sue the assignee directly under section 9–318(1)(a) for payments received under the assigned contract. This section provides that an assignee's rights are subject to claims and defenses that the account debtor had against the assignor. The Uniform Commercial Code, as enacted in Massachusetts does not define "claim," but the word "claim" is commonly understood to include original cause [of] action. . . .

It is, in my opinion, incorrect to conclude that the words of limitation, "subject to," foreclose original claims. A party's rights can be subject to whatever affirmative claims or defenses another party might assert. Under section 9–318(1)(a), an assignee's rights to retain payments made to it under an assignment are subject to, or are exposed to, affirmative actions brought by the account debtor to recover payments mistakenly made. The definition of "subject to" taken by the court from Englestein v. Mintz, 345 Ill. 48, 61, 177 N.E. 746, 752 (1931), and Anderson v. Southwest Savings & Loan Association, 117 Ariz. 246, 248,

571 P.2d 1042, 1044 (1977), is too broad. The "affirmative rights" denied to the plaintiffs in those cases were open-ended rights, that is, the plaintiffs were seeking amounts in excess of and unrelated to amounts provided for under the original contracts. In *Englestein*, plaintiff asserted that because his partnership agreement with defendant to purchase part of a parcel of real estate was "subject to" the terms of an earlier contract defendant had with the vendor of the real estate, he was entitled to share as a partner in other purchase transactions defendant had with respect to the parcel. The court rejected the claim, in part on the basis of its definition of "subject to." In *Anderson*, plaintiff sued for breach of implied warranties in the sale of a mobile home, naming as defendants the vendor, the manufacturer, and the vendor's secured creditor. The Arizona court affirmed dismissal of the suit against the secured creditor, reasoning that "subject to" in section 9–318(1)(a) did not expose a secured creditor to such claims against the creditor's assignor. These cases do not reject the result I support, that payments received by an assignee of accounts (FNB) are subject to a claim by an account debtor (Michelin) that payments were mistakenly made because of fraud by the assignor (JCC).

This interpretation of section 9–318(1)(a), that the account debtor has rights of action against the assignee, is the fairest way to reconcile the rights of account debtors and secured creditors, particularly where, as here, credit is advanced through a line of credit. This case boils down to the question of whether the secured creditor or the account debtor should bear the cost of not finding out that JCC falsely claimed that it had paid its subcontractors. The secured creditor is in a better position than the account debtor to determine whether the assignor/ borrower is complying with the terms of the contract in which the creditor has an interest. The reason is that the secured creditor can employ an effective sanction without having to initiate litigation and without risking any loss itself to ensure compliance; it can threaten to cut off credit unless it is satisfied with the borrower's performance. The other party, the account debtor, has no similar sanction. If he is not satisfied, he must litigate and bear the expense of litigation and the sure delay in completion of the contract. The creditor/assignee is not deterred from enforcing compliance by such costs. Obviously, either the secured creditor or the account debtor can make inquiries regarding compliance with the contract, but at some point both will have to rely on the representations of others, which creates opportunities for fraud, as occurred here. The secured creditor is accustomed to looking over the borrower's shoulder on an ongoing basis and can check compliance. By virtue of his control over credit, the creditor can ensure compliance with the contract. The account debtor can only investigate and if it holds up payments, it puts the contract in jeopardy.

The majority contends that holding for appellants will disrupt the free flow of credit because creditors will have additional duties. This argument goes too far because it counsels against any imposition on creditors. Besides, whatever increased credit costs arise will fall on the class truly at fault in these cases—the borrower/assignors.

The majority also stresses the concern that actions under section 9–318(1)(a) will make creditors fully liable for the contracts of their borrowers, which would contravene section 9–317.[1] This case does not present this problem, and this result need not occur. I do not argue that the creditor should be the surety for the assignor. The creditor should be exposed only to the extent that he benefits from the assigned contract rights. Tracking the language of section 9–318(1)(a), whatever rights of payment a secured creditor has are subject to the terms of the contract between the account debtor and the borrower/assignor. The account debtor cannot go beyond the benefits the creditor/assignee obtains under the assignment in an action against the creditor. Whether the account debtor asserts the claim as a counterclaim or as an original claim should be irrelevant.

In reaching a contrary conclusion, the court has relied on the Official Comment to section 9–318 to clarify the supposed conflict between "claim" and "subject to." This reliance is misplaced because the Comment is at least as ambiguous as the language of section 9–318(1)(a) itself. The relevant portion of the Comment reads, "[s]ubsection (1) makes no substantial change in prior law." The argument that the provision for an original right of action in section 9–318(1)(a) would not change prior law substantially is at least as plausible as the majority's argument that it would make a substantial change. . . .

For the foregoing reasons, I would hold that Michelin has a direct cause of action against FNB for the monies it received from Michelin under its assignment from JCC.

Notes & Questions

1. Notice that JCC assigned to FNB its contract rights as security for loans. You will not find the term "contract rights" in the 1972 version of the U.C.C. In the 1962 version of Article 9 there were three types of collateral in which security interests could be perfected only by filing: accounts, contract rights, and general intangibles. A contract right was "any right to payment under a contract not yet earned by performance and not evidenced by an instrument or chattel paper." The definition of general intangibles excluded collateral that qualified as contract rights. For an explanation of the elimination of contract rights as a class of collateral in § 9–106, see "Reasons for 1972 Change" following § 9–106 in the official 1972 U.C.C. text.

1. Mass.Gen.Laws Ann. ch. 106, § 9–317 provides as follows:

Secured Party Not Obligated on Contract of Debtor. The mere existence of a security interest or authority given to the debtor to dispose of or use collateral does not impose contract or tort liability upon the secured party for the debtor's acts or omissions.

2. Could Michelin have protected itself by inserting a clause in its contract with JCC that prohibited JCC from assigning its rights to payment under the contract to anyone? See § 9–318(4). Could FNB have protected itself by insisting that JCC include in its Michelin contract a term by which Michelin agreed not to assert defenses or claims against JCC's assignee? See §§ 9–206, 9–318(1).

3. Suppose that during the term of the Michelin Tire-JCC construction contract, portions of the construction process called for by the contract became extremely expensive. JCC seeks a modification of the contract to call for a less expensive process that would have a slight negative effect on the plant. May JCC and Michelin Tire agree to such a change in a manner that binds FNB? Does this depend on whether the increase in cost of the original process would give JCC a defense in an action by Michelin Tire for damages or to enforce the original contract terms? See § 9–318(2).

Suppose that payments under the Michelin Tire-JCC contract were to be made directly to JCC, who would make loan payments to FNB. JCC, short of cash, proposes to give Michelin Tire a 10% discount on its next few payments if Michelin makes those payments one week ahead of schedule. Can such an agreement be binding on FNB?

The New York version of § 9–318(2) requires that modifications or substitutions be made "in good faith, in accordance with reasonable commercial standards and without material adverse effect upon the assignee's rights under or the assignor's ability to perform the contract. . . ." Does this change the analysis of the above questions?

4. Suppose the payments in *Michelin Tire* went to JCC who was to turn them over to FNB. What risks does FNB run if JCC fails to make the required turnover? What if one of JCC's creditors asserts an interest in the funds before JCC has turned them over to FNB?

5. Suppose the contract between JCC and Michelin contained a clause granting JCC a security interest in all property covered by Article 9 that it furnished or constructed under the contract to secure Michelin's obligations to make payments under the contract. If JCC assigned this contractual right to FNB, must FNB do anything to perfect the security interest? See §§ 9–302(2), 9–405.

6. In Nath v. National Equipment Leasing Corp., 497 Pa. 126, 439 A.2d 633 (1981), an employee who was injured while working on a machine leased to his employer under a financing lease brought suit to recover damages from the lessor. The court stated the issue to be whether § 402A of the Restatement (Second) of Torts applies to financing leases. Section 402A provides for liability of sellers of defective products despite the exercise of all possible care and regardless of the relationship between the injured party and the seller. A previous Pennsylvania case had applied § 402A to "true" leases. Over three dissents the Pennsylvania Supreme Court held § 402A inapplicable to financing leases.

See generally Gilmore, The Assignee of Contract Rights and His Precarious Security, 74 Yale L.J. 217 (1964).

Chapter 4

THE SCOPE OF ARTICLE 9

INTRODUCTION

Although Article 9 reaches an enormous range of secured transactions, there are many important limits on its scope. Each state adopts Article 9 and each state has its own Secretary of State's office for central filings and its own local offices for local filings. The nonfederal nature of Article 9 raises one important question about its limits. To what transactions does each state's version of Article 9 apply? At what point does filing in one state lose legal significance because the secured transaction in question lacks sufficient connection to that state?

This territorial limit on the reach of each state's Article 9 is accompanied by more substantive limits. Some transactions, such as "true leases," are excluded from Article 9 because they are deemed not to be secured transactions. In this area, the critical question is whether a transaction is a true lease or whether it is merely a lease intended as security. Article 9 excludes some transactions that clearly are secured transactions because they are dealt with in other bodies of law. Thus Article 9 does not cover most security interests in real estate. Finally, some secured transactions excluded from Article 9 are not covered by any clearly defined body of rules. As one case below suggests, perfection of security interests in deposit accounts may require conforming to uncodified standards.

Any reasonably large scale or complex secured financing venture is likely to encounter one or more of the limits on Article 9. Although we will not study in detail perfection of security interests in these borderland areas, it is important to be able to recognize when one is dealing with a secured transaction not covered by Article 9. Only then can one begin to search for the rules that do regulate the transaction.

A. The Scope of Each State's Article 9: Multistate Transactions

Consider the "Law Governing" clause of the Security Agreement reproduced in Chapter 2. It states that "This Agreement . . . shall be construed and interpreted in accordance with the law of the State of Illinois. . . ." To what extent does the U.C.C. honor the parties' choice of governing law?

A Pennsylvania bank makes a secured loan to a corporation whose executive offices, chief place of business, and collateral are in California. The parties' lawyers are in New York, and the transaction is negotiated and closed in New York. The security agreement states that it is to be governed by the laws of New York. What law will govern in a dispute over whether a default has occurred under the security agreement? Will a financing statement filed in New York perfect bank's security interest? See §§ 1–105, 9–103. These sections establish, for what should be obvious reasons, that the parties to a secured transaction are not free to choose any appropriate state's law of perfection. Section 9–103 is designed to specify a single state in which to perfect a security interest.

Section 9–103 also deals with a distinct but equally troublesome problem. Suppose a secured party accurately interprets § 9–103 and initially perfects a security interest in the proper state. After initial perfection, however, the circumstances change. The debtor might move the collateral to another state or the debtor might move its executive office or chief place of business to another state. Section 9–103 also encompasses perfection problems that attend such changed circumstances. See § 9–103(1)(c), (d), (2), (3)(e).

1. Initial Perfection of the Security Interest

Introductory Problems

1. Bank makes a secured loan to New Corp. and receives a security interest in New Corp.'s accounts. New Corp.'s largest manufacturing plant is in Connecticut, its chief executive offices are in New York, and its accounting department, which keeps records of New Corp.'s accounts, is located in Pennsylvania. Where must Bank file to perfect its security interest in the accounts? See § 9–103(3). From the viewpoint of prospective lenders interested in information about New Corp.'s secured transactions, which state is the most appropriate place of filing?

2. Secured Party's loan is secured by Debtor's manufacturing equipment. Secured Party is located in New York and Debtor's chief place of business is in New York. The equipment is located in New Jersey and will be used in Debtor's Pennsylvania plant. In what state should Secured Party file its financing statement? See § 9–103(1). That section states, in part, "perfection and the effect of perfection or non-perfection of a security interest in collateral are governed by the law of the jurisdiction where the collateral is when the last event occurs on which is based the assertion that the security interest is perfected or unperfected." To ascertain the correct state of initial filing, one must know which events are eligible to count as "last events." To what events do you think § 9–103(1)(b) is referring? Cf. §§ 9–203, 9–303. On the facts of this problem where should parties interested in Debtor's credit status be expected to look?

Essentially, the "last event" test chooses the location of the collateral as the place of filing for all nonmobile goods. Was a more attractive alternative available? What are the strengths and weaknesses of using the collateral's location as the place of filing? See generally Coogan, The New UCC Article 9, 86 Harv.L.Rev. 477, 555–58 (1973).

JOINT HOLDINGS & TRADING CO., LIMITED v. FIRST UNION NATIONAL BANK OF NORTH CAROLINA

California Court of Appeal, Second District, Division 2, 1975.
50 Cal.App.3d 159, 123 Cal.Rptr. 519.

OPINION

FLEMING, ACTING P. J.—Joint Holdings & Trading Company, Ltd. (plaintiff) and First Union National Bank of North Carolina (Bank) dispute the priority of their competing creditor liens against 42,888 pairs of trousers. Plaintiff asserts priority by virtue of writs of attachment issued in its pending lawsuit against Peter J. Brennan, Inc., and Peter J. Brennan, Inc. of American Samoa; Bank asserts priority for its security interest based on its financing agreements with the Brennan corporations. Bank appeals the judgment which declared its claim to the trousers invalid and its lien subordinate to that of plaintiff.

BACKGROUND

According to the testimony of its managing director Thomas Hood, plaintiff, a Hong Kong corporation, produced partially finished trousers in Taiwan from fabric selected by the Brennan corporations and there sold the trousers to Brennan, who then shipped them to American Samoa for further [finishing]. Thereafter, Brennan shipped the trousers to the United States. The trousers in controversy apparently reached American Samoa in mid-August 1973 and arrived by ship in Los Angeles in mid-October 1973.

In March 1972 and September 1973 Bank and the Brennan corporations entered security agreements encompassing the latter's inventory of trousers as collateral for future loans. On both occasions Bank filed these agreements in North Carolina under legal procedures required to perfect its security interest in that state. Bank later loaned Peter J. Brennan, Inc., more than $1.2 million.

On 12 October 1973 plaintiff sued the Brennan corporations in Los Angeles Superior Court for $424,531.06 owed on sales of trousers and obtained writs of attachment which the sheriff levied on 42,888 pairs of trousers in the possession of a carrier in Los Angeles consigned to defendant Peter J. Brennan, Inc., in North Carolina.

Pursuant to Code of Civil Procedure sections 689 and 689b Bank on 26 October 1973 filed a third-party claim with the sheriff, asserting a paramount security interest in the attached trousers based on its financing agreements with Peter J. Brennan, Inc. Plaintiff petitioned the superior court for a hearing on the validity of Bank's asserted interest, and issue was joined on questions of priority of lien and choice of law.

TRIAL COURT'S FINDINGS

The trial court found the trousers had been shipped by Peter J. Brennan, Inc., from American Samoa via Los Angeles consigned to Peter J. Brennan, Inc., Charlotte, North Carolina. When the trousers arrived in the United States on 12 October 1973, Peter J. Brennan, Inc., already had rights in and owned the trousers. Plaintiff levied its writs of attachment on 12 October and 17 October 1973. On 26 October 1973 Bank asserted a paramount interest in the trousers based on a security interest and on financing statements filed in North Carolina in March 1972 and in California on 25 October 1973 and 1 November 1973.

The court found that Bank's security interest in the trousers did not attach to the trousers in California or in North Carolina, that neither Bank, Peter J. Brennan, Inc., nor Peter J. Brennan, Inc. of American Samoa understood that the trousers were to be kept in any particular state or jurisdiction. Any security interest asserted by Bank was not perfected in any jurisdiction in which the trousers had been located prior to the time they were first attached by plaintiff. The court concluded that any right Bank had in the trousers on 26 October 1973 was subordinate to prior attachment liens secured by plaintiff.

DISCUSSION

(1) Bank contends that under North Carolina law it had a perfected security interest entitled to priority over plaintiff's writs of attachment, that the trial court erred in using the law of California rather than of North Carolina to determine priority of creditor interests. Bank bases its contention on the general conflict-of-laws doctrine that a court should apply the law of the jurisdiction where all material contacts are centered. Bank argues that all material contacts centered in North Carolina in that the parties created the security agreement in North Carolina; they provided that North Carolina law should govern the agreement; the trousers were destined for North Carolina when plaintiff attached them in California; California had no other interest in or contact with the transaction.

However, the Commercial Code does not adopt the general conflict-of-laws doctrine urged [by] Bank. Section 9102 states that the code applies to any secured transaction in personal property "so far as concerns any personal property and fixtures within the jurisdiction of this State." Thus the code adopts the "situs" rule for choice of law. (3 Cal. Commercial Law (Cont.Ed.Bar 1966) p. 23.) The trousers were sited in California when the disputed claims arose.

The general rule of section 9102 is subject to exceptions for multi-state transactions enumerated in section 9103. Bank urges that the second sentence of section 9103, subdivision (3), adopts the general conflict-of-laws doctrine as an exception to the situs rule and should be applied here. That second sentence states: "However, if the parties to the transaction understood at the time that the security interest attached that the property would be kept in this State and it was brought into this State within 30 days after the security interest attached for purposes other than transportation through this State, then the validity of the security interest in this State is to be determined by the law of this State." Bank argues that by negative implication this exception means that when goods are in California for purposes of transit only, then the law of the state to which the goods are destined should apply.

But the language of the Code, read in context, fails to support Bank's position. The second sentence of section 9103, subdivision (3), begins with the word "However," which logically indicates that it is to be read only as an exception to the first sentence: "If personal property . . . is already subject to a security interest when it is brought into this State, the validity of the security interest in this State is to be determined by the law (including the conflict of laws rules) of the jurisdiction where the property was when the security interest attached."

Exception to the situs rule for law applicable to property in California in multi-state transactions is thus based on the law of the jurisdiction where the property was when the security interest attached. And the second sentence is limited to this meaning: Even if the security interest attached while the property was in another jurisdiction, the law of this state determines the validity of the security interest where the property was brought into this state within 30 days after the security interest attached for purposes other than transportation through this state. The second sentence therefore was intended to refer back to California law and the situs rule of section 9102, not to refer to the law of yet another jurisdiction to be determined by the undisclosed intent of the parties to the secured transaction.

Bank finds support for its position in a discussion of section 9103, subdivision (3), by a text commentator, Gilmore, Security Interests in Personal Property (1965) section 22.9, pages 628–631. Gilmore's analysis, however, is premised on a conflict of laws between two Uniform Commercial Code jurisdictions. Gilmore concedes that if the jurisdiction in which the security interest attaches is a non-code jurisdiction, the security interest must be perfected in that jurisdiction (at p. 631). In this case, when the security interest supposedly attached, the trousers were either in Taiwan or American Samoa, non-code jurisdictions. Bank failed to prove perfection of a security interest in either of these two non-code jurisdictions. It would make little sense to give worldwide priority of lien as a result of a filing in one jurisdiction with respect to goods outside that jurisdiction which had never been in the jurisdiction and were wholly unconnected with it. At bench, the North Carolina lien is entitled to little more weight than would be given to one filed in Liberia, Luxemburg, or Lichtenstein.

Bank's burden to protect its security interest in the trousers under the Commercial Code is not difficult. If the trousers are intended for a final destination other than the one where the security interest attaches to the trousers, Bank need only perfect its interest in the jurisdiction where the interest attaches (Taiwan or American Samoa) and in the jurisdiction of intended destination (North Carolina). If the trousers meet unexpected delays, section 9103, subdivision (3), allows Bank four months to perfect the interest in the jurisdiction where the goods are delayed.

Alternatively, Bank could have maintained legal title to or physical control over the trousers.

Furthermore, even assuming that Bank correctly interprets the law, its cause still fails on the facts. The trial court found that Bank and the Brennan corporations did not understand at the time any security interest attached that the trousers would be kept in any particular state or jurisdiction. Bank bore the burden of proof, yet it offered no evidence to establish that the trousers were destined for or would ever reach North Carolina. Addresses on shipping labels do not in themselves establish the intended final destination of the trousers. . . .

Notes & Questions

1. *Post-Entry Dispute.* Suppose the dispute had occurred after the trousers arrived in North Carolina. Would the secured party's filings in North Carolina have served to perfect its security interest in the trousers under Article 9?

2. *Delivery Under F.O.B. Contract.* Debtor and Secured Party are both located in New York. Debtor grants Secured Party a security interest in after-acquired equipment. Secured Party advances funds to Debtor and files a financing statement in New York. Debtor then orders some equipment from a California manufacturer under an f.o.b. place-of-origin contract. (Under such a contract, the California manufacturer bears only the expense and risk of putting the goods into the possession of the carrier. See § 2–319(1)(a). The risk of loss passes to Debtor upon delivery to the carrier. § 2–509(1)(a).) Does Secured Party's New York filing protect her before the goods arrive in New York? Where should Secured Party file to protect herself while the goods are in transit? Does Secured Party's New York filing protect her after the goods arrive in New York? Should Secured Party refile in New York after the goods arrive?

How would your analysis of Secured Party's status change if Secured Party were a purchase money lender? See § 9–103(1)(c). Why is its rule limited to purchase money lenders?

3. *Nonfiling as an Event.* Suppose a lien creditor wishes to challenge the validity of a secured party's security interest. The principal basis of attack is that the secured party never filed a required financing statement to perfect its security interest. If the lien creditor wishes to assert that the security interest is unperfected, how should he determine which state's law governs? Where was the collateral when the "event" "occurred" upon which he bases his assertion of nonperfection?

Can you construct an example in which there will be an event upon which to focus to support an assertion of nonperfection? See § 9–403(2).

4. *Assertions Based on Last Events in Different States.* Debtor has gone bankrupt and the trustee is claiming collateral in which Secured Party claims a perfected security interest. Secured Party bases its assertion of perfection upon a financing statement filed while the goods were in State X. The filing was the last event upon which an assertion of perfection could be based. Secured Party therefore argues that State X's law governs. The trustee counters by asserting that Secured Party's security interest was unperfected because (1) the financing statement filed in State X was defective, and (2) Secured Party failed to file a financing statement thereafter. Before Debtor's bankruptcy, the goods moved from State X to State Y. Which state's law governs the perfection dispute?

See generally Coogan, The New UCC Article 9, 86 Harv.L.Rev. 477 (1973); Murray, Choice of Law and Article 9: Situs or Sense?, 9 Hof.L. Rev. 39 (1980).

2. Post-Perfection Movement of Collateral

IN RE MILLER

United States Bankruptcy Court, District of Oregon, 1974.
14 U.C.C. Rep. Serv. 1042.

HENRY L. HESS, JR., BANKRUPTCY JUDGE. This matter involves a determination of the priorities of the security interests of two creditors and of the rights of the trustee in a 1972 Ford tractor, loader and backhoe. The court has heretofore entered findings of fact. Only the legal issues raised by these findings remain in dispute.

The facts which are material to the issues are briefly as follows.

The defendant, Kenneth C. Miller, was adjudged a bankrupt upon a petition filed by him on October 25, 1973. Prior to April 1, 1973, at a time when the bankrupt was a resident of California, he granted a security interest in the equipment to the defendant, Ford Motor Credit Company (Ford). Ford perfected its security interest in the equipment by filing a financing statement with the Secretary of State of California. On April 1, 1973, the bankrupt removed his residence to Hillsboro, Oregon. On April 15, 1973, he transported the equipment to Hillsboro, Washington County, Oregon. On April 24, 1973, the [bankrupt] granted a security interest in the Ford tractor, loader and backhoe to the defendant, Peerless Pacific Company (Peerless). On April 30, 1973, Peerless filed financing statements with the Secretary of State of Oregon and the proper recording officer of Washington County, Oregon.

At the time of the granting of the security interest to Peerless, it had knowledge that Ford claimed a security interest in the equipment.

Between April 15, 1973, and October 17, 1973, the equipment was continuously located in the State of Oregon. On or about October 17, 1973, the bankrupt removed the equipment to the State of California and notified Ford on or about October 18, 1973, that he had done so. On or about November 15, 1973, Miller removed his residence to the State of California.

On December 10, 1973, Peerless filed a financing statement with the Secretary of State of California evidencing its security interest in the 1972 Ford tractor, loader and backhoe.

At no time material herein did Ford file a financing statement in the State of Oregon nor did it file any continuation statement or financing statement, other than the original financing statement, with the Secretary of State of California.

From the above, it is apparent that the equipment had not been in the State of Oregon for a period of four months at the time that Peerless, with knowledge of the security interest of Ford, took its security interest and filed its financing statements in Oregon. Also, it is apparent that the equipment had remained in Oregon for a period of more than four months before it was returned to California and that Ford had at no time filed a financing statement in the State of Oregon.

It is clear that had the property not been returned to the State of California prior to the petition in bankruptcy, the trustee would have taken title to the 1972 Ford tractor, loader and backhoe, subject only to the security interest of Peerless. Section 70c Bankruptcy Act, 11 USC § 110, ORS 79–1030(3). The fact that Peerless had knowledge of the existence of the claim of a security interest by Ford would not change the result because the Uniform Commercial Code renders knowledge immaterial. ORS 79.3120(5) makes no mention of the matter of knowledge in the determination of priorities. The official comment to the last referred to section makes it clear that priority is a "race of diligence" in which knowledge is irrelevant.

The question then remains whether return of the equipment to California after it had been in Oregon for a period of over four months changed the priorities between the parties. The trustee and Peerless argue that after the four months had expired from the time the equipment was brought to Oregon, the security interest of Ford lapsed and that return of the equipment to California did not have the effect of reviving the security interest of Ford as of the date of the original filing by Ford. Ford contends that its security interest was perfected in California, that the law of California is controlling and that its security interest in California remained unaffected by the fact that the property was for a period of over four months located in Oregon.

Counsel have not furnished to the court any cases directly in point. The California statutes adopting the UCC are identical to the Oregon statutes so far as they are relevant to the question here involved.

ORS 79.1030(3) provides:

"If personal property other than that governed by subsections (1) and (2) of this section is already subject to a security interest when it is brought into this state, the validity of the security interest in this state is to be determined by the law (including the conflict of laws rules) of the jurisdiction where the property was when the security interest attached . . . If the security interest was already perfected under the law of the jurisdiction where the property was when the security interest attached and before being brought into this state, the security interest continues perfected in this state for four months and also thereafter if within the four-month period it is perfected in this state. The security interest may also be perfected in this state after the expiration of the four-month period; in such case perfection dates from the time of perfection in this state. If the security interest was not perfected under the law of the jurisdiction where the property was when the security interest attached and before being brought into this state, it may be perfected in this state; in such case perfection dates from the time of perfection in this state."

When the equipment was brought to Oregon it was subject to the perfected security interest of Ford. It remained subject to Ford's perfected interest for four months. At the end of that period of time, Ford's perfection lapsed, leaving Peerless with the only perfected security interest encumbering the equipment.

"The four month period is long enough for a secured party to discover in most cases that the collateral has been removed and to file in this state; thereafter, if he has not done so, his interest, although originally perfected in the state where it attached, is subject to defeat here by those persons who take priority over an unperfected security interest (see Section 9–301). Under Section 9–312(5) the holder of a perfected conflicting security interest is such a person even though during the four month period the conflicting interest was junior. Compare the situation arising under Section 9–403(2) when a filing lapses." Official Comment to Subsection 3 of ORS 79.1030.

When the equipment was returned to California, California became "this state" and Oregon "the jurisdiction where the property was". Thus, paraphrasing the California UCC, if personal property is already subject to a security interest when it is brought into California, the validity of the security interest in California is to be determined by the law of Oregon. If the security interest was already perfected in Oregon and before being brought into California, the security interest continues perfected in California for four months and also thereafter if within the four-month period it is perfected in California.

In Oregon, the equipment was subject only to the security interest of Peerless. When it was returned to California, it was returned subject to the security interest of Peerless. Ford did not have a perfected security interest in "the jurisdiction where the property was" (Oregon); Peerless did. Consequently, the equipment reached California (this state) subject to "the security interest . . . already perfected under the law of the jurisdiction where the property was when the security interest attached . . ." and just as obviously the equipment arrived in California *not* subject to a security interest unperfected in Oregon.

The Code contemplates that a gap in perfection must be remedied exactly as required by the Code. If it is, the perfection is termed "continuous", and "relates back" to the original perfection date; if it is not remedied as required by the Code, there is a "gap" or a "lapse" and a subsequent perfection does not "relate back" but dates from the later date of perfection and is subject to intervening perfected security interests.

The Official Comment to ORS 79.1030(3) points out "In case of delay beyond the four month period, there is no 'relation back'." The same comment also suggests that the reader "compare the situation arising under Section 9–403(2) when a *filing lapses*" (Emphasis added).

Official Comment Number 3 to ORS 79.4030 is:

"Under the fourth sentence of Subsection (2) the security interest becomes *unperfected* when filing *lapses*. Thereafter, the interest of the secured party is subject to defeat by those persons who take priority over an unperfected security interest (see Section 9–301), and under Section 9–312(5) the holder of a perfected conflicting security interest is such a person even though before lapse the conflicting interest was junior. *Compare the situation arising under Section 9–103(3) when a perfected security interest under the law of another jurisdiction is not perfected in this state within four months after the property is brought into this state."* (Emphasis added.)

ORS 79.3030(2) states:

"If a security interest is originally perfected in any way permitted under ORS 79.1010 to 79.5070 and is subsequently perfected in some other way under ORS 79.1010 to 79.5070, without an intermediate period when it was unperfected, the security interest shall be deemed to be perfected continuously for the purposes of ORS 79.1010 to 79.5070."

The Official Comment to ORS 79.3030 is:

"2. The following example will illustrate the operation of subsection (2) of ORS 79.3030: A bank which has issued a letter of credit honors drafts drawn under the credit and receives possession of the negotiable bill of lading covering the goods shipped. Under subsection (2) of ORS 79.3040 and ORS 79.3050 the bank now has a perfected security interest in the document and the goods. The bank releases the bill of lading to the debtor for the purpose of procuring the goods from the carrier and selling them. Under subsection (5) of ORS 79.3040 the bank continues to have a perfected security interest in the document and goods for 21 days. The bank files before the expiration of the 21-day period. Its security interest now continues perfected for as long as the filing is good. The goods are sold by the debtor. The bank continues to have a security interest in the proceeds of sale to the extent stated in subsection (3) of ORS 79.3060.

"If the successive stages of the bank's security interests succeed each other without an intervening gap, the security interest is 'continuously perfected' and the date of perfection is when the interest first became perfected (i.e., in the example given, when the bank received possession of the bill of lading against honor of the drafts). If, however, there is a gap between stages—for example, if the bank does not file until after the expiration of the 21-day period specified in subsection (5) of ORS 79.3040, the collateral still being in the debtor's possession—then, the chain being broken, the perfection is no longer continuous. *The date of perfection would now be the date of filing (after expiration of the 21-day period); the bank's interest might now become subject to attack under section 60 of the Federal Bankruptcy Act and would be subject to any interests arising during the gap period which under ORS 79.3010 take priority over an unperfected security interest.*

"The rule of subsection (2) of ORS 79.3030 would also apply to the case of collateral brought into this state subject to a security interest which became perfected in another state or jurisdiction. See subsection (3) of ORS 79.1030." (Emphasis added.)

The comment cited above points out that once the gap occurs, subsequent perfection dates from the date of the subsequent perfection, and that the original perfection *is not revived*. The comment specifically applies the rule to ORS 79.1030(3). Consequently, when Ford permitted a gap in perfection to exist in Oregon, Ford's first filing lapsed, and there is no revival.

A major purpose of the UCC was to create uniformity in the creation and perfection of security interests and the priorities to be given to creditors holding security interests in the various states. Under the above view of the UCC, a prospective lender may check the filing records of the state in which the property is located and if he knows that the property has been located in that state for a period of over four months, he can be assured that if he perfects a security interest there it will take priority over any security interest perfected in any other state whether or not prior in time. He is not required to search the filing records of any other state to which the property might later be removed. If the property is later removed, he can maintain his priority by perfecting in the second state within four months. Were the view argued by Ford adopted, a prospective lender could not be assured of priority over security interests earlier perfected in other states to which the property might later be removed without a search of the filing records of all such states. Ford could have maintained its priority status after the property was removed to Oregon by merely filing financing statements in Oregon within four months. This imposes less of a burden than that which would be imposed upon a later lender in another state under Ford's theory.

The court therefore concludes that the title of the trustee to the 1972 Ford tractor, loader and backhoe is subject to the security interest of Peerless but is unencumbered by the security interest of Ford.

Counsel for the trustee may submit an appropriate order.

———

Subsequent to the entry in the above matter of the opinion of the court dated March 7, 1974, the defendant, Ford Motor Credit Company, filed a motion for reconsideration in which it requested the court to reconsider its opinion. The motion was accompanied by a Memorandum of Points and Authorities in response to which the defendant, Peerless Pacific Company, has also filed a Memorandum. The Trustee has informed the court that he concurs with the position taken by Peerless. . . .

Ford's second contention is that the proposed 1972 amendments to UCC § 9–103 indicate that the law prior to the adoption of such amendments made no provision for a lapse of perfection when there has been a removal of the property or the chief place of business of the debtor to another state for a period of more than four months without perfection during this period in the second state. To the contrary, the proposed amendments do not appear to be a change in the law but rather a clarification of the law. There is nothing in the comments to the 1972 amendments indicating any change was intended. . . .

Ford argues that uncertainty will exist for a lender if a dishonest debtor fails to notify him of a change in location of the collateral or the debtor's place of business. Ford, however, recognizes that if the rule contended by it were followed, a lender would have uncertainty as to his priority if the collateral were later removed to another state in which there had been an earlier perfected security interest. Honesty of a debtor is not a relevant factor when recording statutes are involved. Recording statutes are adopted in order that a purchaser or lender need not rely upon the honesty of the seller or borrower. The UCC has determined that there is less of a burden imposed on one who takes a security interest in property to impose upon him the burden of keeping track of the collateral and the debtor than would be the burden upon a later prospective purchaser or lender to check the filing records in fifty states.

Ford contends that under UCC § 9–103(3) removal of the collateral from California to Oregon for a period of more than four months without perfection by it in Oregon may cause a lapse of Ford's security interest in Oregon but not in California. Ford contends that the lapse of a security interest in the state in which the security interest was first perfected is the five year period provided for the filing of a continuation statement under UCC § 9–403(2). If this were true, then

Ford could permit the property to be removed from California to any number of other states, fail to perfect in such other states, and so long as the debtor returned the collateral to California or Ford itself took possession and returned it to California within five years of perfection of its security interest in California, it could then defeat any security interest of any other creditor in any other state which was perfected within the five year period. A rule requiring reperfection in another state within four months from the time collateral or the place of business of the debtor is moved to another state requires some diligence on the part of the holder of a security interest to preserve his priority status. On the other hand, if as urged by Ford, there were no lapse for a period of five years in the state where the property or principal place of business was located at the time the security interest was perfected, all later lenders or purchasers would have to be concerned with searching the records of all states in which the property may have been located within the preceding five years.

While, in connection with the four month rule, it is true that UCC § 9–103(3) speaks only of property "brought into this state" and does not speak of property taken out of "this state", it would seem implicit that each state adopting the UCC sought the uniformity provided in UCC § 1–102(2)(c). It is presumed that by providing when property subject to a perfected security interest comes into "this state" the security interest will be recognized in "this state" for only four months unless the prior security interest is perfected in "this state", it was also intended by those adopting the UCC that property leaving "this state" would be subject to the same rule requiring perfection in the second state within four months.   . . .

For the above reasons, the Motion for Reconsideration filed by Ford is denied.

Notes & Questions

1. *Post-Perfection Movement of Equipment.* Secured Party 1 has a perfected security interest in ordinary equipment located in California. Debtor moves the equipment to Arizona. After two weeks in Arizona, Debtor grants Secured Party 2 a security interest in the same equipment, which Secured Party 2 properly perfects in Arizona. Who has priority in the equipment? Suppose instead of granting a security interest in the equipment Debtor sells the equipment to an Arizona purchaser. Does this case differ in outcome from the first situation? Suppose the dispute occurs five months after removal of the equipment from California and Secured Party never files in Arizona.

2. *Consumer Goods.* Assume again that the collateral moves to Arizona but now assume that the collateral consists of consumer goods and Secured Party has a purchase money security interest. Secured Party never files in Arizona. If there is a dispute over the collateral five months after its removal from California will Secured Party prevail?

3. Miller *Revisited.* How does *In re Miller* differ from the simple case of a debtor moving collateral to a new jurisdiction? Do these differences indicate that Ford should be viewed as losing its security interest or merely losing its priority to Peerless?

4. *First to File.* Can you make an argument that Ford should have prevailed? Which secured party was the first to file?

See generally Kripke, The "Last Event" Test For Perfection of Security Interests Under Article 9 of the Uniform Commercial Code, 50 N.Y.U.L.Rev. 47 (1975).

3. Certificates of Title

COOGAN, THE NEW UCC ARTICLE 9,
86 Harv.L.Rev. 477, 544–50 (1973)

In a connoisseur's list of the most confusing and frustrating problems arising under Article 9, there would surely be a case or two involving a multistate situation and one or more certificate of title statutes. Such statutes are built on the hope that a certificate of title may be able to control property interests in highly mobile goods like automobiles, wherever they may be. Unfortunately, however, not all states have certificate of title laws, much less the same laws, and persons have been known to obtain by fraudulent means two or more certificates of title for a vehicle, on only one of which a security interest was properly noted. When the goods are moved from a certificate state to a noncertificate state or vice versa, and when a number of secured parties or a succession of purchasers enters the picture, perplexities are bound to arise. Revised subsection (2) of 9–103 attempts valiantly to cover the principal situations that may arise. By posing a series of hypotheticals about automobiles, one can test whether the new version succeeds in being reasonably clear and comprehensive.

1. *Protection of Nonprofessional Buyers.*—One major policy decision should be kept in mind with regard to the rules of revised subsection (2): *all* of its provisions are subject to the protection afforded nonprofessional buyers by paragraph (d). If such a buyer relies upon a certificate of title issued by "this state" which does not give him warning to look further, then he is protected regardless of whether a security interest in the car not shown on the certificate was previously perfected in a foreign state through filing or through notation. For the buyer to gain the protection, the certificate upon which he relies must totally fail to indicate that the automobile is subject to any security interest other than those shown; even if the certificate indicates that the automobile *may* be subject to security interests *not shown* on the certificate, the buyer will not be insulated. Furthermore, the buyer must not be in the business of selling automobiles, and he is protected only to the extent that he gives value and receives delivery of the goods after issuance of the certificate in "this state" and without knowledge of the security interest.

The purpose of this overriding protection for the nonprofessional buyer is obvious. This is the class of buyer least able to protect itself. Officers issuing a certificate of title will not always be able to know all the parties who have security interests in other states and will not always be meticulous about either contacting them or listing them on the certificate. Moreover, sellers may transfer fraudulent certificates. Nevertheless, the issuing state has a strong interest in insuring that its certificates will be trusted by those most likely to rely upon them. The professional buyer, on the other hand, is presumed to know the practices of his trade and to be on the alert for the possible existence of security interests whose actual existence is not disclosed.

2. *Priority Where the Security Interest Is Not Perfected in the Removal State.*—Subsection (2) of revised section 9–103 makes clear which rules govern when an automobile in which an unperfected security interest exists in one state is removed to another state where a perfected security interest is created. Suppose that S–1 has an attached and enforceable but unperfected security interest in an automobile situated in X. The vehicle is then brought into Y, and a certificate is there issued noting a security interest in favor of S–2. By virtue of Y's version of existing and revised paragraph 9–302(3)(b), which makes filing unnecessary to perfect a security interest in goods covered by a certificate of title statute, S–2's security interest is thereby perfected without more.

It might be thought obvious that S–2's perfected interest prevails over S–1's temporally prior but unperfected interest. Yet it is not absolutely clear that the priority rules of Part 3 of revised Article 9, as enacted by Y, are intended to cover competing interests when multistate elements are present; one might read them as governing purely domestic transactions only. In any event, revised paragraphs 9–103(2)(a) and (b) make it fairly clear that S–2 does win. Paragraph (a) states that subsection (2) of 9–103 "applies to goods covered by a certificate of title issued under a statute of this state or of another jurisdiction . . .." Paragraph (b) provides that "perfection and the effect of perfection . . . are governed by the law (including the conflict of laws rules) of the jurisdiction issuing the certificate . . .." Since on the facts given, Y was the only state to issue a certificate, paragraph (b) seems to make it plain that the priority rules under Part 3 of Y's revised Article 9 do in fact apply to this multistate situation; therefore, S–2's perfected security interest has priority over the unperfected interest of S–1.

3. *Priority Where Both Security Interests Are Perfected but Only One Is Perfected by Notation on a Certificate of Title.*—The choice of law problem becomes more complicated where one of the competing parties has perfected through notation on a certificate, but the other has perfected through filing. The cases obviously divide into those in which the perfection by filing occurred in the removal state and those in which it occurred in the foreign state. If the perfection was through

filing in the removal state, paragraph (c) of subsection (2) provides that the rights of the holder in the foreign state are controlled by 9–103(1)(d) under which, as we have previously seen, perfection of the security interest continues in the state to which the goods have been removed for a 4-month grace period and then stops unless perfected within the new state during that period. If the perfection in the removal state was through notation on a certificate, on the other hand, then paragraph (b) of subsection (2) provides that perfection of the security interest automatically continues in the foreign state for 4 months *and thereafter* until the vehicle is reregistered in a state other than that from which it originally came. This way of putting the distinction leaves out some refinements. In the case of perfection through filing in the removal state, the 4-month grace period will be cut short under 9–103(1)(d) if the filing ceases to be effective in the original state before the 4 months have expired. In the case of notation on a certificate in the removal state, the prior perfection can at any time be cut short by surrender of the certificate. If the certificate is surrendered, or if more than 4 months after removal the vehicle is reregistered in a state other than that from which it originally came, then paragraph (b) tells us that the automobile is no longer regarded as being covered by the certificate of title. The following two hypotheticals will illustrate these differences between perfection through filing and through notation in the state of removal.

Suppose, first, that S–1's security interest has been perfected through filing in state X. The automobile is then brought into state Y, and, as in the previous case, a certificate is issued in Y to S–2. If the secured parties fight it out within 4 months of removal or before the filing in X becomes ineffective, whichever period is shorter, then S–1 will win. Afterwards S–1 will prevail against S–2 only if S–1 has perfected in Y before expiration of the grace period, or if he perfected in Y before S–2 obtained his certificate (assuming that the latter event occurred after expiration of the grace period). These conclusions are reached by the circuitous route of carefully reading paragraphs (a), (b), and (c) of subsection 9–103(2) and being remitted by paragraph (c) to the familiar grace-period rule of 9–103(1)(d).

The plot thickens, however, if the situation is reversed. Suppose this time that S–1's interest was perfected by notation on a certificate of title issued in X; the automobile comes into Y and S–2 perfects there by filing. Priority will again depend on questions of timing.

Let us first consider the issue where S–2 asserts his claim within 4 months after removal, *or* after 4 months but before the automobile is "registered" in a state other than X, and in either event before the certificate issued in X "is surrendered." Under these circumstances, paragraph 9–103(2)(b) provides that "the law (including the conflict of laws rules)" of state X will govern the existence and effect of perfection. One has a right to be puzzled: what does this pronouncement mean, if X has enacted the revised Code? Should we resort first to X's general conflict of laws rules? If so, the outcome will vary with the actual states which the symbol "X" is taken to represent. Should we, on the other hand, resort first to the conflicts rules of X embodied in X's revised 9–103? If so, we are again told by paragraph (2)(b) to look to "the law (including the conflict of laws rules)" of X. Perhaps the most sensible way to cut through this Gordian knot is to read the mandate as allowing us to treat the transactions as if they had occurred wholly within X, unless X's certificate of title statute has a specific conflicts rule. Assuming no such rule, S–1 would then win under 9–103(2)(b), because only he complied with X's certificate of title statute.

On the other hand, the outcome will be different when S–2 asserts his claim after the 4-month period has expired and after the automobile has been registered in state Y, or in any event after the certificate which S–1 holds has been surrendered. In this situation, even though one's reasoning must be somewhat indirect to arrive at the conclusion that S–2 will win, that conclusion is the proper one.

First of all, 9–103(2)(b) announces that in this case the automobile is "not covered by the certificate of title within the meaning of this section." Read with 9–103(2)(a), which makes any part of subsection (2) applicable only when goods *are* "covered" by a certificate, this surely means that we must leave subsection (2) altogether and look to another relevant subsection of 9–103. If this motor vehicle were an item of equipment or leased inventory, then the announcement of paragraph (2)(b) probably would mean that subsection (3) on mobile equipment or leased inventory would be one's guide. The latter subsection refers us to "the law (including the conflict of laws rules)" of the jurisdiction in which the debtor is located. Assuming that the automobile is a consumer good, however, subsection (3) is inapplicable; and one should probably look to subsection (1), which, as we have seen, refers us to "the law of the jurisdiction where the collateral is when the last event occurs on which is based the assertion that the security interest is perfected or unperfected." The commentary accompanying the revised 9–103 informs one that where collateral is removed from one jurisdiction to another, "maintenance of perfection in the latter jurisdiction or failure to do so is the 'last event' to which the basic rule refers." [160] Since S–1 has failed to maintain his perfection in state Y, the relevant "last event[s]" are S–1's failure to reperfect in Y and S–2's filing there. In sum, if the debtor has followed the automobile—and ignoring the complexities that arise if S–1 and S–2 were dealing with different debtors—then the law of Y will fix priority regardless of whether the automobile is a consumer good covered by the location-of-collateral-at-the-time-of-perfection rule of subsection (1) or a mobile good covered by the location-of-debtor rule of subsection (3). The debtor would be located in Y, and the collateral would be located in Y at the time that S–1's perfection expired and at the time that S–2's perfection became effective. Again, reading the reference to a state's law as meaning its

---

160. See UCC rev. § 9–103, Comment 1.

domestic law in most cases, *S–2* will win, since only he has perfected in *Y.*

4. *Priority Where Both Security Interests Are Perfected by Notation on a Certificate of Title.*—Where the holder of a security interest in the original state and the holder of a security interest in the state to which the goods have been removed have both perfected by notation on a certificate of title, the analysis required by paragraph (b) of subsection (2) is a variation of that given above. Suppose that *S–1's* security interest was perfected by notation on a certificate issued in *X.* The automobile comes into *Y* and *S–2* perfects by notation on a certificate issued in *Y* which neither shows *S–1's* interest nor warns that the automobile may be subject to security interests not shown on the certificate.[161]. A preliminary difficulty in resolving the question of which secured party has priority is determining whether subsection (2) of 9–103 applies at all: paragraph (a) of subsection (2) provides that that subsection applies only to goods covered by *a* certificate of title— but here the automobile is ostensibly covered by *two* certificates. The best solution is probably to read "a" to mean "at least one," as logicians do, so that subsection (2) will apply. For if it does not apply, one consequence will be that a nonprofessional buyer will not be protected against *S–1* if the buyer purchases the automobile in state *Y* in reliance on the *Y* certificate; such a result seems unintended.

Once having decided this much, the potential difficulty in applying paragraph (b) to the *dual* certificate situation, with regard to rights other than those of a nonprofessional buyer, is that it states that "perfection and the effect of perfection or nonperfection of the security interest are governed by the law (including the conflict of laws rules) of the jurisdiction issuing *the* certificate . . . ." (Emphasis added.) Therefore, in order to make sense out of the provision, we must carefully read paragraph (b) twice, once as if the phrase "the certificate" meant the certificate issued in *X*, and once as if it meant the certificate issued in *Y*. For convenience, reading the provision first to apply to the certificate issued in *X*, our analysis is similar to that undertaken above where *S–1* perfected through notation in state *X* and *S–2* perfected through filing in state *Y*. That is, the effect of *S–1's* perfection in state *X* through notation on the certificate issued there, unless *S–1* surrenders that certificate, is to leave him perfected for at least 4 months after the goods have been removed, and thereafter "until the goods are registered in another jurisdiction." Even if registration in the other jurisdiction takes place within the 4-month grace period during which *S–1* is absolutely protected unless he surrenders his certificate, *S–1* will have priority as the first to perfect.

Where the analysis, though not the result, differs from that where *S–2* perfects by filing is either when *S–1* has surrendered his certificate or when the 4-month period has expired and the automobile has been

---

161. Note that the special protection afforded nonprofessional *buyers* by revised 9–103(2)(d) does not apply to other "pur-chasers" (even if also nonprofessional) as that term is defined by the Code. . . .

registered in a jurisdiction other than X. In that event, paragraph (b) tells us that the automobile is no longer "covered by the certificate of title" *issued in X*. However, rather than being remitted to the provisions of subsection (1) on localizable goods or subsection (3) on mobile equipment and inventory as we were before in this situation, we must now make our second reading of paragraph (b) to see if its provisions apply to "the" certificate issued to $S–2$ in state Y. Since that certificate is still effective, the result of our second reading is that the law of Y governs the existence and effect of perfection—so long as the reference to a state's law is taken to mean its domestic law—and thus $S–2$ wins because $S–1$ has not obtained a proper certificate in Y.

B. Leases

Equipment leasing is a multibillion dollar industry in the United States. Everything from airplanes to typewriters is likely to be the subject of a lease agreement between the user and the equipment's titular owner. Why has equipment leasing flourished? In some cases the traditional economic reasons for leasing anything apply. Some students who would prefer to buy housing do not do so simply because they cannot afford the larger capital investment usually required for such a purchase. Similarly, many equipment users cannot afford or do not want to pay for the full useful life of a piece of equipment.

But even those who can afford to choose between leasing and outright purchase may prefer leasing. In recent years tax considerations often favor lease transactions. To illustrate, suppose Corporation X is profitable and is taxed at a 50% rate and Corporation Y is breaking even and has no taxable income. Y has a choice of buying a $10,000 piece of equipment or leasing it from X. If Y buys it from the manufacturer, the investment tax credit and depreciation deduction are wasted, at least temporarily, because Y has no taxable income against which to use the tax benefits. If ownership of the equipment can be placed with X, the tax benefits can be fully utilized and the savings in after-tax purchase price can be passed on to Y in the form of a lower rental rate. By arranging the transaction so that X can use the tax benefits instead of them being wasted on Y, the parties in effect use the federal treasury to finance part of the transaction.

Other reasons may exist for leasing. Companies sometimes have felt that their financial statements appear more profitable if there are fewer borrowings shown even though the borrowings are replaced by lease obligations. Some companies have issued financial covenants limiting their borrowings and feel that leasing may be the only allowable method of acquiring new equipment. A lessor may be able to purchase an item of equipment in bulk at a discount and be able to pass on savings to a lessee who would have had to pay full price for a single item. A lessor may be in a better position than a lessee to realize upon a piece of equipment's residual value or a lessor may have special skill in servicing technical equipment. Each of these factors may induce a company in need of equipment to lease it.

As the case that follows suggests, the line between leasing equipment and buying it is not always clear. And this blurred line leads to problems under Article 9. Simply stated, a true lease (for example, one month's rental of a Hertz car) is not even subject to Article 9. But a so-called financing lease, which is usually for a substantial portion of the useful life of equipment, is treated by Article 9 as a secured transaction. To maximize a financing lessor's rights against third parties, the lessor must file a U.C.C. financing statement. Those who are in doubt as to whether they have true leases or financing leases may file "informational" financing statements. See § 9–408. Despite the availability of the informational filing, many lessors still find themselves litigating over whether they erroneously failed to comply with Article 9.

IN RE MARHOEFER PACKING CO., INC.

United States Court of Appeals, Seventh Circuit, 1982.
674 F.2d 1139.

PELL, CIRCUIT JUDGE.

This appeal involves a dispute between the trustee of the bankrupt Marhoefer Packing Company, Inc., ("Marhoefer") and Robert Reiser & Company, Inc., ("Reiser") over certain equipment held by Marhoefer at the time of bankruptcy. The issue presented is whether the written agreement between Marhoefer and Reiser covering the equipment is a true lease under which Reiser is entitled to reclaim its property from the bankrupt estate, or whether it is actually a lease intended as security in which case Reiser's failure to file a financing statement to perfect its interest renders it subordinate to the trustee.

I

In December of 1976, Marhoefer Packing Co., Inc., of Muncie, Indiana, entered into negotiations with Reiser, a Massachusetts based corporation engaged in the business of selling and leasing food processing equipment, for the acquisition of one or possibly two Vemag Model 3007–1 Continuous Sausage Stuffers. Reiser informed Marhoefer that the units could be acquired by outright purchase, conditional sale contract or lease. Marhoefer ultimately acquired two sausage stuffers from Reiser. It purchased one under a conditional sale contract. Pursuant to the contract, Reiser retained a security interest in the machine, which it subsequently perfected by filing a financing statement with the Indiana Secretary of State. Title to that stuffer is not here in dispute. The other stuffer was delivered to Marhoefer under a written "Lease Agreement."

The Lease Agreement provided for monthly payments of $665.00 over a term of 48 months. The last nine months payments, totaling $5,985.00, were payable upon execution of the lease. If at the end of the lease term the machine was to be returned, it was to be shipped prepaid to Boston or similar destination "in the same condition as when received, reasonable wear and tear resulting from proper use alone excepted, and fully crated." The remaining terms and conditions of the agreement were as follows:

1. Any State or local taxes and/or excises are for the account of the Buyer.

2. The equipment shall at all times be located at

Marhoefer Packing Co., Inc.

1500 North Elm & 13th Street

Muncie, Indiana

and shall not be removed from said location without the written consent of Robert Reiser & Co. The equipment can only be used in conjunction with the manufacture of meat or similar products unless written consent is given by Robert Reiser & Co.

3. The equipment will carry a ninety-day guarantee for workmanship and materials and shall be maintained and operated safely and carefully in conformity with the instructions issued by our operators and the maintenance manual. Service and repairs of the equipment after the ninety-day period will be subject to a reasonable and fair charge.

4. If, after due warning, our maintenance instructions should be violated repeatedly, Robert Reiser & Co. will have the right to cancel the lease contract on seven days notice and remove the said equipment. In that case, lease fees would be refunded pro rata.

5. It is mutually agreed that in case of lessee, Marhoefer Packing Co., Inc., violating any of the above conditions, or shall default in the payment of any lease charge hereunder, or shall become bankrupt, make or execute any assignment or become party to any instrument or proceedings for the benefit of its creditors, Robert Reiser & Co. shall have the right at any time without trespass, to enter upon the premises and remove the aforesaid equipment, and if removed, lessee agrees to pay Robert Reiser & Co. the total lease fees, including all installments due or to become due for the full unexpired term of this lease agreement and including the cost for removal of the equipment and counsel fees incurred in collecting sums due hereunder.

6. It is agreed that the equipment shall remain personal property of Robert Reiser & Co. and retain its character as such no matter in what manner affixed or attached to the premises.

In a letter accompanying the lease, Reiser added two option provisions to the agreement. The first provided that at the end of the four-year term, Marhoefer could purchase the stuffer for $9,968.00. In the alternative, it could elect to renew the lease for an additional four years at an annual rate of $2,990.00, payable in advance. At the conclusion of the second four-year term, Marhoefer would be allowed to purchase the stuffer for one dollar.

Marhoefer never exercised either option. Approximately one year after the Vemag stuffer was delivered to its plant, it ceased all payments under the lease and shortly thereafter filed a voluntary petition in bankruptcy. On July 12, 1978, the trustee of the bankrupt corporation applied to the bankruptcy court for leave to sell the stuffer free and clear of all liens on the ground that the "Lease Agreement" was in fact a lease intended as security within the meaning of the Uniform Commercial Code ("Code") and that Reiser's failure to perfect its interest as required by Article 9 of the Code rendered it subordinate to that of the trustee. Reiser responded with an answer and counterclaim in which it alleged that the agreement was in fact a true lease, Marhoefer was in default under the lease, and its equipment should therefore be returned. . . .

The primary issue to be decided in determining whether a lease is "intended as security" is whether it is in effect a conditional sale in which the "lessor" retains an interest in the "leased" goods as security for the purchase price. 1C Secured Transactions Under U.C.C. § 29A.05[1][C], p. 2939. By defining the term "security interest" to include a lease intended as security, the drafters of the Code intended such disguised security interests to be governed by the same rules that apply to other security interests. See U.C.C. Art. 9. In this respect, section 1–201(37) represents the drafter's refusal to recognize form over substance.

Clearly, where a lease is structured so that the lessee is contractually bound to pay rent over a set period of time at the conclusion of which he automatically or for only nominal consideration becomes the owner of the leased goods, the transaction is in substance a conditional sale and should be treated as such. It is to this type of lease that clause (b) properly applies. Here, however, Marhoefer was under no contractual obligation to pay rent until such time as the option to purchase the Vemag stuffer for one dollar was to arise. In fact, in order to acquire that option, Marhoefer would have had to exercise its earlier option to renew the lease for a second four-year term and pay Reiser an additional $11,960 in "rent." In effect, Marhoefer was given a right to terminate the agreement after the first four years and cease making payments without that option ever becoming operative.

Despite this fact, the district court concluded as a matter of law that the lease was intended as security. It held that, under clause (b) of section 1–201(37), a lease containing an option for the lessee to purchase the leased goods for nominal consideration is conclusively presumed to be one intended as security. This presumption applies, the court concluded, regardless of any other options the lease may contain.

We think the district court's reading of clause (b) is in error. In our view, the conclusive presumption provided under clause (b) applies only where the option to purchase for nominal consideration necessarily arises upon compliance with the lease. See 1C Secured Transactions Under U.C.C. § 29.05[2][b] pp. 2947–49. It does not apply where the lessee has the right to terminate the lease before that option arises with no further obligation to continue paying rent. But see In re Vaillancourt, supra, 7 U.C.C.Rep. 748; In re Royers Bakery, Inc., 1 U.C.C.Rep. 342 (Bankr.E.D.Pa.1963). For where the lessee has the right to terminate the transaction, it is not a conditional sale.

Moreover, to hold that a lease containing such an option is intended as security, even though the lessee has no contractual obligation to pay the full amount contemplated by the agreement, would lead to clearly erroneous results under other provisions of the Code. Under section 9–506 of the Code, for example, a debtor in default on his obligation to a secured party has a right to redeem the collateral by tendering full payment of that obligation.[4] The same right is also enjoyed by a lessee under a lease intended as security. A lessee who defaults on a lease intended as security is entitled to purchase the leased goods by paying the full amount of his obligation under the lease. But if the lessee has the right to terminate the lease at any time during the lease term, his obligation under the lease may be only a small part of the total purchase price of the goods leased. To afford the lessee a right of redemption under such circumstances would clearly be wrong. There is no evidence that the drafters of the Code intended such a result.

We therefore hold that while section 1–201(37)(b) does provide a conclusive test of when a lease is intended as security, that test does not apply in every case in which the disputed lease contains an option to purchase for nominal or no consideration. An option of this type makes a lease one intended as security only when it necessarily arises upon compliance with the terms of the lease.[5]

Applying section 1–201(37), so construed, to the facts of this case, it is clear that the district court erred in concluding that the possibility of Marhoefer's purchasing the stuffer for one dollar at the conclusion of a second four-year term was determinative. Because Marhoefer could have fully complied with the lease without that option ever arising, the district court was mistaken in thinking that the existence of that option alone made the lease a conditional sale. Certainly, if Marhoefer had elected to renew the lease for another term, in which case the nominal purchase option would necessarily have arisen, then the clause (b) test would apply.[6] But that is not the case we are faced with here.

4. Section 9–506 of the Code states:

Debtor's Right to Redeem Collateral

At any time before the secured party has disposed of collateral or entered into a contract for its disposition under Section 9–504 or before the obligation has been discharged under Section 9–505(2) the debtor or any other secured party may unless otherwise agreed in writing after default redeem the collateral by tendering fulfillment of all obligations secured by the collateral as well as the expenses reasonably incurred by the secured party in retaking, holding and pre-paring the collateral for disposition, in arranging for the sale, and to the extent provided in the agreement and not prohibited by law, his reasonable attorneys' fees and legal expenses.

5. This reading of clause (b) is in no way inconsistent with the plain language of that provision since, by its terms, it does not refer to the situation where there are alternate ways of complying with a lease, only one of which results in the nominal purchase option arising.

6. Reiser concedes that had Marhoefer elected to renew the lease after the first

Marhoefer was not required to make any payments beyond the first four years. The fact that, at the conclusion of that term, it could have elected to renew the lease and obtain an option to purchase the stuffer for one dollar at the end of the second term does not transform the original transaction into a conditional sale.

This fact does not end our inquiry under clause (b), however, for the trustee also argues that, even if the district court erred in considering the one dollar purchase option as determinative, the lease should nevertheless be considered a conditional sale because the initial option price of $9,968 is also nominal when all of the operative facts are properly considered. We agree that if the clause (b) test is to apply at all in this case, this is the option that must be considered. For this is the option that was to arise automatically upon Marhoefer's compliance with the lease. We do not agree, however, that under the circumstances presented here the $9,968 option price can properly be considered nominal.

It is true that an option price may be more than a few dollars and still be considered nominal within the meaning of section 1–201(37). Because clause (b) speaks of nominal "consideration" and not a nominal "sum" or "amount," it has been held to apply not only where the option price is very small in absolute terms, but also where the price is insubstantial in relation to the fair market value of the leased goods at the time the option arises.[7] See e.g. Percival Const. Co. v. Miller & Miller Auctioneers, 532 F.2d 166 (10th Cir. 1977) ($8,040 option price found to be nominal); Citicorp Leasing, Inc. v. Allied Institutional, Etc., 454 F.Supp. 511 (W.D.Okla.1977) (option price of $1,253.71 nominal); Chandler Leasing Corp. v. Samoset Associates, 24 U.C.C.Rep. 510 (Bankr.D.Me.1978) ($47,000 option price held nominal). See generally 1C Secured Transactions Under U.C.C. § 29A.05[2][b] ; Annot., 76 ALR 3d 11, 46 (1977).

Here, however, the evidence revealed that the initial option price of $9,968 was not nominal even under this standard. George Vetie, Reiser's treasurer and the person chiefly responsible for the terms of the lease, testified at trial that the purchase price for the Vemag stuffer at the time the parties entered into the transaction was $33,225. He testified that the initial option price of $9,968 was arrived at by taking thirty percent of the purchase price, which was what he felt a four-

term, the transaction would have been transformed into a sale. George Vetie, Reiser's treasurer, testified that the renewal option was actually intended as a financing mechanism to allow Marhoefer to purchase the stuffer at the end of the lease if it desired to do so but was either unable or unwilling to pay the initial purchase price of $9,968.

7. The trustee argues that the determination of whether the option price is nominal is to be made by comparing it to the fair market value of the equipment at the

time the parties enter into the lease, instead of the date the option arises. Although some courts have applied such a test, In re Wheatland Electric Products Co., 237 F.Supp. 820 (W.D.Pa.1964); In re Oak Mfg., Inc., 6 U.C.C.Rep. 1273 (Bankr. S.D.N.Y.1969), the better approach is to compare the option price with the fair market value of the goods at the time the option was to be exercised. In re Universal Medical Services, Inc., 8 U.C.C.Rep. 614 (Bankr.E.D.Pa.1970). See 1C Secured Transactions Under U.C.C. § 29A.05[2][b].

year-old Vemag stuffer would be worth based on Reiser's past experience.

The trustee, relying on the testimony of its expert appraiser, argues that in fact the stuffer would have been worth between eighteen and twenty thousand dollars at the end of the first four-year term. Because the initial option price is substantially less than this amount, he claims that it is nominal within the meaning of clause (b) and the lease is therefore one intended as security.

Even assuming this appraisal to be accurate, an issue on which the bankruptcy court made no finding, we would not find the initial option price of $9,968 so small by comparison that the clause (b) presumption would apply. While it is difficult to state any bright line percentage test for determining when an option price could properly be considered nominal as compared to the fair market value of the leased goods, an option price of almost ten thousand dollars, which amounts to fifty percent of the fair market value, is not nominal by any standard.

Furthermore, in determining whether an option price is nominal, the proper figure to compare it with is not the actual fair market value of the leased goods at the time the option arises, but their fair market value at that time as anticipated by the parties when the lease is signed. 1C Secured Transactions Under U.C.C. § 29A.05[2] [b], p. 2953. Here, for example, Vetie testified that his estimate of the fair market value of a four-year-old Vemag stuffer was based on records from a period of time in which the economy was relatively stable. Since that time, a high rate of inflation has caused the machines to lose their value more slowly. As a result, the actual fair market value of a machine may turn out to be significantly more than the parties anticipated it would be several years earlier. When this occurs, the lessee's option to purchase the leased goods may be much more favorable than either party intended, but it does not change the true character of the transaction.

We conclude, therefore, that neither option to purchase contained in the lease between Marhoefer and Reiser gives rise to a conclusive presumption under section 1–201(37)(b) that the lease is one intended as security. This being so, we now turn to the other facts surrounding the transaction.

III

Although section 1–201(37) states that "[w]hether a lease is intended as security is to be determined by the facts of each case," it is completely silent as to what facts, other than the option to purchase, are to be considered in making that determination. Facts that the courts have found relevant include the total amount of rent the lessee is required to pay under the lease, Chandler Leasing Corp. v. Samoset Associates, supra, 24 U.C.C.Rep. at 516; whether the lessee acquires any equity in the leased property, Matter of Tillery, 571 F.2d 1361, 1365 (5th Cir. 1978); the useful life of the leased goods, In re Lakeshore

Transit-Kenosha, Inc., 7 U.C.C.Rep. 607 (Bankr.E.D.Wis.1969); the nature of the lessor's business, In re Industro Transistor Corp., 14 U.C.C. Rep. 522, 523 (Bankr.E.D.N.Y.1973); and the payment of taxes, insurance and other charges normally imposed on ownership, Rainier National Bank v. Inland Machinery Co., 29 Wash.App. 725, 631 P.2d 389 (1981). See generally 1C Secured Transactions Under U.C.C. § 29A.05[2][e; and Annot., 76 ALR 3d 11 (1977). Consideration of the facts of this case in light of these factors leads us to conclude that the lease in question was not intended as security.

First, Marhoefer was under no obligation to pay the full purchase price for the stuffer. Over the first four-year term, its payments under the lease were to have amounted to $31,920. Although this amount may not be substantially less than the original purchase price of $33,225 in absolute terms, it becomes so when one factors in the interest rate over four years that would have been charged had Marhoefer elected to purchase the machine under a conditional sale contract.[8] The fact that the total amount of rent Marhoefer was to pay under the lease was substantially less than that amount shows that a sale was not intended. 1 Secured Transactions Under U.C.C. § 4A.01.

It is also significant that the useful life of the Vemag stuffer exceeded the term of the lease. An essential characteristic of a true lease is that there be something of value of return to the lessor after the term. 1C Secured Transactions Under U.C.C. § 29A.05[2][c], p. 2959. Where the term of the lease is substantially equal to the life of the leased property such that there will be nothing of value to return at the end of the lease, the transaction is in essence a sale. In re Lakeshore Transit-Kenosha, Inc., supra. Here, the evidence revealed that the useful life of a Vemag stuffer was eight to ten years.

Finally, the bankruptcy court specifically found that "there was no express or implied provision in the lease agreement dated February 28, 1977, which gave Marhoefer any equity interest in the leased Vemag stuffer." This fact clearly reveals the agreement between Marhoefer and Reiser to be a true lease. See Hawkland, The Impact of the Uniform Commercial Code on Equipment Leasing, 1972 Ill.L. Forum 446, 453 ("The difference between a true lease and a security transaction lies in whether the lessee acquires an equity of ownership through his rent payments."). Had Marhoefer remained solvent and elected not to exercise its option to renew its lease with Reiser, it would have received nothing for its previous lease payments. And in order to exercise that option, Marhoefer would have had to pay what Reiser anticipated would then be the machine's fair market value. An option of this kind is not the mark of a lease intended as security. See In re

8. The bankruptcy court found that Reiser was originally willing to sell Marhoefer the stuffer under a conditional sale contract the terms of which would have been $7,225 down and monthly installments of $1,224 over a twenty-four month period. The total payments under such an agreement would have amounted to $36,601, substantially more than the amount Marhoefer was required to pay over four years under the lease.

Alpha Creamery Company, 4 U.C.C.Rep. 794, 798 (Bankr.W.D.Mich. 1967).

Although Marhoefer was required to pay state and local taxes and the cost of repairs, this fact does not require a contrary result. Costs such as taxes, insurance and repairs are necessarily borne by one party or the other. They reflect less the true character of the transaction than the strength of the parties' respective bargaining positions. See also Rainier National Bank, supra, 631 P.2d at 395 ("The lessor is either going to include those costs within the rental charge or agree to a lower rent if the lessee takes responsibility for them.").

IV

We conclude from the foregoing that the district court erred in its application of section 1–201(37) of the Uniform Commercial Code to the facts of this case. Neither the option to purchase the Vemag stuffer for one dollar at the conclusion of a second four-year term, nor the initial option to purchase it for $9,968 after the first four years, gives rise to a conclusive presumption under clause (b) of section 1–201(37) that the lease is intended as security. From all of the facts surrounding the transaction, we conclude that the agreement between Marhoefer and Reiser is a true lease. The judgment of the district court is therefore reversed.

Notes & Questions

1. *Should There Be a Line?* Does it make sense to have a line that differentiates between financing leases and "true leases" that is as fine as the line Article 9 and *Marhoefer Packing* seem to draw? Would some definite, even if imperfect, rule better serve the commercial community?

Is there a useful distinction between a financing lease (i.e., a sale) and a true lease? Are they not just different degrees of a transfer of interest in property?

2. *Distinguishing Characteristics; New U.C.C. Article 2A.* As long as Article 9 distinguishes between kinds of leases, what are the characteristics that separate true leases from financing leases? Consider the following: The lessor's right to retake the equipment at the end of the lease term (the reversionary interest). The lessee's obligation to service the equipment and pay all insurance and tax costs. The lessee's contractual right to purchase the equipment for less than fair market value at the end of the initial lease term. The relationship between the useful life of the equipment and the lease term.

In 1987, a new Article 2A, covering leases, was proposed for the U.C.C. It would amend § 1–201(37) by changing the part of the definition of "security interest" that elaborates upon when a lease is a security interest. The proposed new § 1–201(37) contains the following language:

Amended Section 1–201(37)

(37) "Security interest" means an interest in personal property or fixtures which secures payment or performance of an obligation. The retention or reservation of title by a seller of goods notwithstanding shipment or delivery to the buyer (Section 2–401) is limited in effect to a reservation of a "security interest". The term also includes any interest of a buyer of accounts or chattel paper which is subject to Article 9. The special property interest of a buyer of goods on identification of those goods to a contract for sale under Section 2–401 is not a "security interest", but a buyer may also acquire a "security interest" by complying with Article 9. Unless a consignment is intended as security, reservation of title thereunder is not a "security interest", but a consignment in any event is subject to the provisions on consignment sales (Section 2–326).

Whether a transaction creates a lease or security interest is determined by the facts of each case; however, a transaction creates a security interest if the consideration the lessee is to pay the lessor for the right to possession and use of the goods is an obligation for the term of the lease not subject to termination by the lessee, and

(a) the original term of the lease is equal to or greater than the remaining economic life of the goods,

(b) the lessee is bound to renew the lease for the remaining economic life of the goods or is bound to become the owner of the goods,

(c) the lessee has an option to renew the lease for the remaining economic life of the goods for no additional consideration or nominal additional consideration upon compliance with the lease agreement, or

(d) the lessee has an option to become the owner of the goods for no additional consideration or nominal additional consideration upon compliance with the lease agreement.

A transaction does not create a security interest merely because it provides that

(a) the present value of the consideration the lessee is obligated to pay the lessor for the right to possession and use of the goods is substantially equal to or is greater than the fair market value of the goods at the time the lease is entered into,

(b) the lessee assumes risk of loss of the goods, or agrees to pay taxes, insurance, filing, recording, or registration fees, or service or maintenance costs with respect to the goods,

(c) the lessee has an option to renew the lease or to become the owner of the goods,

(d) the lessee has an option to renew the lease for a fixed rent that is equal to or greater than the reasonably predictable fair market rent for the use of the goods for the term of the renewal at the time the option is to be performed, or

(e) the lessee has an option to become the owner of the goods for a fixed price that is equal to or greater than the reasonably predictable fair market value of the goods at the time the option is to be performed.

For purposes of this subsection (37):

(x) Additional consideration is not nominal if (i) when the option to renew the lease is granted to the lessee the rent is stated to be the fair market rent for the use of the goods for the term of the renewal determined at the time the option is to be performed, or (ii) when the option to become the owner of the goods is granted to the lessee the price is stated to be the fair market value of the goods determined at the time the option is to be performed. Additional consideration is nominal if it is less than the lessee's reasonably predictable cost of performing under the lease agreement if the option is not exercised;

(y) "Reasonably predictable" and "remaining economic life of the goods" are to be determined with reference to the facts and circumstances at the time the transaction is entered into; and

(z) "Present value" means the amount as of a date certain of one or more sums payable in the future, discounted to the date certain. The discount is determined by the interest rate specified by the parties if the rate is not manifestly unreasonable at the time the transaction is entered into; otherwise, the discount is determined by a commercially reasonable rate that takes into account the facts and circumstances of each case at the time the transaction was entered into.

How would the new definition change the analysis or result in *Marhoefer?*

3. *Renewal Options.* Much in *Marhoefer* and in other leasing cases seems to focus on end-of-lease-term purchase options. If lessee has an option to purchase at less than fair market value, but more than a nominal amount, does this suggest that the transaction was a financing lease? Or does it suggest that the transaction had mixed aspects and was in part a sale and in part a true lease? How should courts handle such cases?

Suppose the *Marhoefer* litigation had arisen during the second four year term of the lease, after Marhoefer had renewed the lease in accordance with the letter option. Would the lease then be viewed as a security lease? May a single lease be a true lease during its initial term and a security lease during renewal? What is the effect of the four year renewal option?

4. Should true lease transactions be excluded from Article 9? Do they present the same likelihood of misleading a debtor's subsequent creditors as is presented by an unperfected security interest?

COOGAN, IS THERE A DIFFERENCE BETWEEN A LONG–TERM LEASE AND AN INSTALLMENT SALE OF PERSONAL PROPERTY?, 56 N.Y.U.L.Rev. 1036, 1045–49, 1055 (1981)

In chapter 4A of *Secured Transactions Under the UCC*, I explored at length the various techniques Article 9 uses in dealing with transactions that sometimes are and sometimes are not secured transactions in the usual sense. In short, with respect to consignments, section 2–326 of the UCC requires some form of publicity; the only form that now really makes sense from the consignor's standpoint is a filing under Article 9. Although priorities might be affected by section 9–114, other provisions of Article 9 do not apply unless the consignment is, in fact, one designed for security. The UCC treatment of leases is comparable to that of consignments, except that there is no requirement of publicity for a true lease and section 9–114 priority provisions do not apply to leases. Thus, except where the lease as chattel paper is assigned, only leases for security are subject to Article 9 in any way.

The UCC treats assignments of chattel paper or accounts differently from leases and consignments. The assignor may sell accounts or chattel paper in the same way as inventory is sold—for a cash payment with no strings attached. Alternatively, an assignor may borrow against his accounts or chattel paper. However, distinguishing between an outright sale and a loan can be very difficult in some instances, as when such things as buybacks, guaranties, and warranties are involved. Taking a practical stance, the UCC simplifies this problem in a very acceptable manner; it provides in section 9–102(1)(a) that all assignments for security are true Article 9 security interests, and deems in section 9–102(1)(b) that any sale of accounts or chattel paper creates a security interest even though no true security interest is intended to be created by such a sale, i.e., after the sale the seller-debtor no longer has rights in the collateral and he owes no obligation to be secured—requirements for a security interest under section 1–201(37).

But how does this work out when the assignee is unable to collect on the accounts or chattel paper? Part 5 of Article 9 provides that the holder of a security interest must, on default, "account to the debtor for any surplus [realized from collections], and unless otherwise agreed, the debtor is liable for any deficiency." However, if the owner of accounts or chattel paper has sold them without recourse, such sale usually constitutes a completed transaction, and the seller-assignor no longer has any rights in what would have been the collateral—there is no collateral to be sold on default. Moreover, the seller-assignor ordinarily has no obligation to the assignee to be secured (although there could be an obligation growing out of a breach of warranty, but then what is the collateral?). A partial solution to this problem, which seems to have worked in practice, is incorporated into sections 9–502(2) and 9–504(2). These sections provide that where there is a sale of accounts or chattel paper, i.e., where there is no obligation to be secured, the two principal remedies of part 5 of Article 9 noted above do not apply unless the parties have so provided in the security agreement. Thus, the "debtor" would not be entitled to any surplus on the sale of the "collateral" (it is not his property), nor would he be liable for any deficiency.

Now we may ask, can the UCC, with similar ease, eliminate the distinction it draws between true leases and leases for security? Although it may not be too difficult to fit the filing, statute of frauds, and priority provisions of the UCC to most true leases, I have long taken the position that the remedy provisions of the UCC do not fit a default on a true lease. What might be thought of as the collateral—the equipment—belongs to the lessor, not the lessee. It makes no sense to tell the lessor to sell his own property in order to collect the lessee's obligation to him. Homer [Kripke] says my analysis is wrong; that the lessor is not required to sell the equipment itself, but only the balance of the lease term, which is owned by the lessee (although most lessors, he says would not be adverse also to selling the residual in the equipment, which they do own). Once the remaining lease term is sold, the proceeds could be credited against the lessee's deficiency.

Assuming Homer is right, is it not true that the lease probably will have been terminated, or at least does not the lessor have the right to terminate? Under the UCC and the common law of leasing, once the lease is terminated the lessee has no right, absent a bankruptcy proceeding, to reinstate the lease even by paying accrued rent. Although statutes such as the Saskatchewan Act and our Bankruptcy Code, in section 365, may provide the lessee with a right to cure by paying the amount overdue, the lessee often is unable to do so.

Even if the lease is not terminated or is reinstated, how saleable is a right to use equipment for a limited time? If the lessor sells the equipment, how can we determine what portion of the sale proceeds is attributable to the remaining lease term and what portion was paid for the residual? Perhaps, as Homer suggests, we could work out a statutory formula that would determine such questions. Such a formula, however, does not eliminate the need to distinguish between the very different rights possessed by a lessee under a true lease and by a debtor under a security agreement. . . .

If we should think that collateral (or leased equipment) typically decreases in value to the point where the residual can be disregarded, let us ask an airline that leased one of the early jets or a lessee of an expensive foreign automobile. These lessees found that upon termination of the lease, the equipment was often worth a substantial portion of its original value. Yet, it had to be returned to the lessor, who could bargain hard for renewal of the lease or for a high purchase price. If, on default, it is decided that a true lease exists, then the lessee of equipment with substantial market value is entitled only to the surplus from the sale of the remaining lease term (since that is the only property in which he has rights) and the lessor is awarded all the other proceeds—representing the residual which is now greatly increased in value. If, on the other hand, the transaction had created a security interest, no distinction would be made between the lease term and the residual, and the debtor would receive *all* the surplus in excess of the deficiency. Clearly, then, on default it matters a great deal to the lessor-seller and the lessee-purchaser whether there is a true lease or a secured transaction.

Notes & Questions

1. Could one respond to the difficulty discussed by Mr. Coogan by (a) making Article 9 applicable to all leases and (b) deeming Part 5 of Article 9 (the default provisions) to be inapplicable to true leases? Would an exception from Article 9's coverage be necessary for at least some true leases? Would one expect as much litigation over the lease characterization issue?

2. May one reconcile Article 9's inclusion of various forms of accounts transactions with its exclusion of transactions as closely related as are the various forms of lease transactions?

Note on Consignments As Secured Transactions

A local artisan leaves work with a local art gallery. They agree that the gallery will hold the work for sale under a consignment agreement. The gallery will try to sell the work to the public but may return the work to the artisan without payment if reasonable sales efforts are unsuccessful. Does artisan risk a contest over the work with gallery's secured creditors? How does the consignment agreement differ from other agreements under which suppliers finance the gallery's acquisition of inventory for sale? A major manufacturer of appliances delivers goods to a dealer under a consignment agreement. The manufacturer assumes the risk of resale. The dealer need not pay for the goods until they are sold. Need manufacturer be concerned about a priority contest with dealer's creditors?

W. DAVENPORT & D. MURRAY, SECURED TRANSACTIONS 28–30 (1978)

The hallmark of a true consignment is the absence of any obligation to pay for the goods—or, stated otherwise, the absolute right to return unsold goods. Generally the question of intent is determined from the words used in the consignment agreement. Ascertainment of intent is often difficult. There was, for example, just prior to the turn of the century the famous *Arbuckle Brothers* series of cases. A manufacturer of roasted coffee appointed a firm as its "special selling factor" to handle its goods. Despite frequent use of the word "factor" in the agreement, the courts of last resort of Georgia, Tennessee, and Virginia held the arrangement one of sale, not of agency.[86]

Most consignments, however, will be of the Article 2, not the Article 9, variety. When the delivered goods may be returned by the buyer, even though they conform to the contract, the transaction is a "sale or return" under Section 2–326(1)(b) if the goods are delivered primarily for resale. Section 2–326(2) provides that goods held in a "sale or return" transaction are subject to the claims of the buyer's creditors while in the buyer's possession unless one of three conditions described in Section 2–326(3) obtains: (1) the seller complies with an applicable law permitting a consignor's interest to be evidenced by the posting of a sign, (2) the seller is known to be substantially engaged in selling the goods of others, or (3) the seller complies with the filing provisions of Article 9.

The only sure protection for a consignor under Section 2–326(3) is to file pursuant to the filing provisions of Article 9. The two alternative methods provided are either unavailable or unreliable. Under Section 9–408 of the 1972 Text, a consignor may, in filing, use the terms "consignor" and "consignee" on his financing statement instead of "secured party" and "debtor." The provisions of Part 4 apply as appropriate to the financing statement, but the filing is not of itself a factor in determining whether the consignment is intended as security. If it is determined for other reasons that the consignment is intended as security, however, the security interest of the consignor is perfected by the filing.

A further consideration for a consignor is compliance with the notification requirements concerning prior inventory financers of record. Where the 1962 Text applies, the prudent consignor will comply with the requirements of Section 9–312(3), even if the consignment is not intended as security. Under the 1972 Text, he must comply with the parallel requirements of new Section 9–114.

IN RE LEASING CONSULTANTS, INC.

United States Court of Appeals, Second Circuit, 1973.
486 F.2d 367.

JAMESON, DISTRICT JUDGE:

Respondent-Appellant, First National City Bank (Bank), appeals from an order of the district court affirming, on a petition for review, the order of a referee in bankruptcy directing the Bank to turn over to the Petitioner-Appellee, George Feldman, Trustee in Bankruptcy (Trustee) of Leasing Consultants, Incorporated, (Leasing) the proceeds from the sale of equipment which had been leased by Leasing, located in

---

86. Snelling v. Arbuckle, 104 Ga. 362, 30 S.E. 863 (1898); Arbuckle v. Kirkpatrick, 98 Tenn. 221, 39 S.W. 3 (1897); Arbuckle v. Gates, 95 Va. 802, 30 S.E. 496 (1898). The Supreme Court of Georgia observed that the agreement appeared "to have been drawn for the purpose of enabling Arbuckle Bros. to 'run with the hare, or hold with the hounds,' according as, in the exigencies of a given case, their interests might dictate. . . ." 30 S.E. at 863.

New York, to Plastimetrix Corporation, located in New Jersey. The leases covering the equipment had been assigned to the Bank as security for a loan to Leasing.

The district court held, 351 F.Supp. 1390, on the basis of stipulated facts, that the perfection by the Bank by filing and possession in New York of its security interest in the lease/chattel paper was not a perfection of the Bank's security interest in Leasing's reversionary interest in the leased property, located in New Jersey. Consequently, the Trustee's lien was held superior to the Bank's unperfected security interest in the leased equipment.

Summary of Facts

In March and June of 1969 Leasing entered into eight leases with Plastimetrix covering heavy equipment. The leased equipment was at all relevant times located in New Jersey. Leasing filed financing statements with the Secretary of State of the State of New Jersey covering each transaction, each statement bearing the legend: "THIS FILING IS FOR INFORMATIONAL PURPOSES ONLY AS THIS IS A LEASE TRANSACTION."

On December 15, 1969 Leasing entered into a "Loan and Security Agreement" with the Bank for the financing of its business of purchasing and leasing equipment. The agreement provided in part for the assignment of "a continuing security interest in the lease(s) and the property leased" as collateral security for advances and loans not to exceed 80% of aggregate unpaid rentals.

Pursuant to the security agreement Leasing borrowed money from the Bank in December, 1969 and February, 1970 and assigned as collateral security the eight Plastimetrix leases, each assignment covering all moneys due or to become due under the lease and the "relative equipment" described in the lease. The lease documents were delivered to the Bank.

On December 30 and 31, 1969 the Bank filed financing statements against Leasing with the Secretary of State of the State of New York and the Registrar of the City of New York, Queens County, where Leasing had its principal place of business.[1] No financing statements were filed by the Bank in New Jersey; nor did the Bank take possession of the leased equipment.

On October 14, 1970 Leasing was adjudicated bankrupt by the United States District Court for the Eastern District of New York. On October 30, 1970 Plastimetrix filed a petition under Chapter XI of the Bankruptcy Act in the United States District Court for the District of New Jersey.

---

1. The financing statement covered "continuing security interest in leases and any and all rents due and to become due thereunder, including all related equip-ment described therein, chattel paper represented thereby, accounts receivable therewith and proceeds arising therefrom."

The leases were in default and an offer was made to purchase the Bank's interest in the property for $60,000. On May 21, 1971 the Trustee, the Bank, and the purchaser entered into a stipulation providing for acceptance of the offer and execution of bills of sale by the Trustee and Bank covering all "right, title and interest" in the property, and that the sum of $60,000 "be substituted for the Property" and the "respective rights of the Trustee and of the Bank . . . be impressed upon and relegated to said fund of $60,000 with the same priority and to the same extent as they now have against the Property."

The Trustee petitioned the Referee in Bankruptcy for an order directing the Bank to turn over to the Trustee the sum of $60,000. Under stipulated facts the Trustee and Bank agreed that the question presented was solely one of law—involving the construction of Article 9 of the Uniform Commercial Code—and that the precise issue was:

"Was the Bank required to file a financing statement against the Bankrupt with the Secretary of State of New Jersey in order to perfect a security interest in the leases assigned to it and the equipment leased thereunder by the Bankrupt to Plastimetrix?"

The Referee answered in the affirmative and ordered the Bank to turn over the $60,000, with interest, to the Trustee. On review the district court affirmed.

Decision of District Court

. . .

Based on the stipulation of counsel, the court assumed that the agreements between Leasing and Plastimetrix were "true leases" and not "conditional sales agreements" or devices intended to create only a security interest. Accordingly the court found that the Bank acquired "a security interest in both the right to receive rental payments under the lease and in the reversionary interest in the underlying equipment."

The court held, and the parties agree, that the leases themselves were "chattel papers" (U.C.C. § 9–105(1)(b)) and that the Bank's security interest in the chattel paper was perfected by filing financing statements in New York and taking possession of the leases. U.C.C. § 9–304(1), 9–305, and 9–102(1).

The court held further: "By contrast, the machines themselves constituted 'equipment' located in New Jersey and hence, for perfection purposes, came within the scope of the New Jersey requirements." The Bank having failed to perfect its interest in the reversion in New Jersey, the court concluded that the Trustee "—a lien creditor within the meaning of Uniform Commercial Code § 9–301(3)—has priority over an unperfected security interest under § 9–301(1)(b)."

Emphasizing the distinction between rights under the chattel paper and the reversionary interest in the equipment, the court quoted from Professor Levie as follows:

"In one situation the purchaser of a security agreement may have an advantage over the purchaser of a lease. Where [he] purchases equipment leases, he takes only an assignor's interest in the equipment lease itself. If [he] wishes to be secured by an interest in the goods as well, he must obtain a security interest . . . [in the goods] and perfect it." Levie, Security Interests in Chattel Paper, 78 Yale L.J. 935, 940 (1969).[4]

The district court concluded:

"The distinction between the rights represented by the lease and those represented by the reversionary interest in the equipment is a real one, supported by logic and precedent. To ignore the distinction contributes neither to clarity nor uniformity under the Uniform Commercial Code. Moreover, it may mislead third party creditors. The simple solution for a bank in the situation of petitioner is to file notices as to its interest in the reversion in accordance with the law of the state where the equipment is located."

Contentions of Appellant

Appellant Bank contends that (1) whether the leases be considered "true leases" or security devices, the filing of the security interest in New York (where lessor and the chattel paper were located) covered all of the lessor's rights in the rentals and related equipment wherever located, without a separate filing against the equipment; or (2) alternatively, if a distinction is recognized between a "true lease" and a security device, appellant is entitled to an evidentiary hearing to determine whether the instruments were "true leases" or security interests in the equipment through the device of a lease; and (3) in any event, Leasing in fact had no "reversionary" interests in the property leased to Plastimetrix.

Failure to File Financing Statement in New Jersey

In contending that the filing and physical possession of the lease instruments in New York were sufficient to cover the leased equipment

---

4. The court continued:

"Practical considerations support this conclusion. The property leased was heavy manufacturing equipment. A potential creditor observing these complicated and non-portable machines should be entitled to believe that he could discover all non-possessory interests by consulting the files in the state where the equipment is located. The equipment was obviously of great value; the New Jersey files revealed only that the lessee held it under a lease. Since the lease agreement required each piece of equipment to have a plate affixed indicating that it was the 'property' of the lessor, judgment creditors of the lessor might assume that its reversionary interest in the equipment was of substantial value. Not being alerted to the diminution of value which would be effected by the creditor's security interest, they might then, for example, attach the lessor's interest, relying on an apparently unencumbered and valuable reversionary interest."

located in New Jersey, appellant argues that the "reversionary interest" of Leasing is "an intangible interest, sited at Leasing's domicile in New York, and not in New Jersey." If the reversionary interest in the equipment were characterized as a "general intangible", the Bank's security interest in the equipment would have been perfected when it filed with the New York Department of State and in the county in which Leasing had a place of business. N.Y.U.C.C. §§ 9–103(2), 9–401(1)(c) (McKinney 1964).

The policies of the Code, however, militate against such an interpretation. We agree with the district court that the reversionary interest is an interest in "goods" rather than an interest in intangibles, and that to perfect the security interest in the reversionary interest in the equipment it was necessary to file a financing statement in New Jersey where the equipment was located. N.J.Stat.Anno. 12A:9–102(1) (1962) 9–302, 9–401(1)(c) (Supp.1972).

Obviously the leased property itself is "goods". We conclude, as did the district court, that the future reversionary interest is likewise an interest in goods, whether it represents "equipment" or "inventory" collateral. The drafters of the Code classified collateral mainly according to the nature or use of the underlying entity, rather than the character of its ownership at any given time. Significantly, the examples of "general intangibles" given in the Official Comment to § 9–106 are all types of property that are inherently intangible. And several Code sections and comments suggest that a collateral interest in "goods" remains such even when the goods are leased. See §§ 9–103(2); 9–109(4) and Official Comment 3; 9–304(3); N.Y.U.C.C. 9–109, Practice Commentary 2 (McKinney 1964) (Kripke).

We conclude accordingly that if the instruments were "true leases", the security interest in the leased equipment was not perfected because of the failure of the Bank to file financing statements in New Jersey.

Were Lease Instruments "True Leases"?

In view of our holding that under a true lease the filing of a financing statement in New Jersey would be required, the determination of whether the lease instruments were "true leases" or security agreements is critical. If the agreements were true leases, Leasing was the owner of the equipment. If they were disguised security agreements, Plastimetrix was the owner, and the filing and possession of the agreements in New York would protect the security interest of the Bank.

In assuming that the agreements between the lessor and lessee were in fact "true leases" the district court relied upon a provision in a stipulation of the parties that, "At all times relevant hereto the Bankrupt [Leasing] owned the leased equipment, subject to the claims and interests of the Bank thereto and therein as appears from the exhibits attached to the stipulation."

This stipulation was made prior to submission of the petition to the Referee in Bankruptcy and apparently before the parties were aware that the distinction between a true lease and a security device would be crucial to a determination of this case. It may well be, as appellant argues, that the Bank and Trustee had simply agreed that Leasing was the owner of the equipment, "*vis-a-vis* the Bank [and not *vis-a-vis* Plastimetrix], subject to the rights of the Bank", and that, "Neither the Bank nor the Trustee knew all of the real, complete, underlying agreements between Leasing and Plastimetrix", necessarily involved in determining the nature of the agreements.

In contending that the record supports the conclusion that the agreements were "true leases", appellee relies upon the lease agreements, stipulation of the parties, and the "assumption" of the district court based upon the stipulation. Appellee then argues that the question of whether the agreements were true leases was first raised on appeal and that the case must be decided on the record now before the court. In its reply brief, however, appellant quotes from the brief it submitted to the district court, reading in part: "If this Court concludes the distinction is determinative, it cannot be determined from the Statement and Supplemental Statement, whether the Plastimetrix leases are leases intended as security devices (hence security agreements) or are true leases."

"Whether a lease is intended as security is to be determined by the facts of each case . . .." U.C.C. § 1–201(37). In making this determination the court may properly consider "factors outside of the lease as well as the contents of the lease itself . . .". In Re Walter Willis, Inc., 313 F.Supp. 1274, 1278 (N.D.Ohio 1970), aff'd, 440 F.2d 995 (6 Cir. 1971).

We conclude that the case should be remanded for a determination by the district court, following an evidentiary hearing, whether the lease instruments were in fact "true leases" or lease devices intended as security.

Allocation of $60,000

It appears from the opinion of the district court that at the hearing on the Trustee's petition "the parties stipulated that the $60,000 sum, representing all of creditor's [Bank's] 'right, title and interest' in the equipment be awarded intact either to the trustee as lien creditor or to creditor as secured creditor." The court decided to "honor the agreement to keep the sum intact, even though the $60,000 could be construed to represent two property interests distinguishable under Article 9—an interest in the leasehold, perfected by the creditor, and an unperfected interest in the reversion."

Appellant argues in its reply brief that "Leasing had no 'reversionary' interest in the property leased to Plastimetrix" since the present value of the unpaid lease rentals at the time of the sale exceeded $60,000, and the reversionary interest accordingly had no pecuniary

value. At oral argument appellee contended that the $60,000 repre-
sented the sale price of the equipment itself, and not the leasehold, and
since the Bank had not perfected its security interest in the equipment
it was not entitled to any part of the fund.

We agree with the district court that the $60,000 could properly be
construed to represent the two property interests—the perfected interest in the leasehold and the unperfected interest in the reversion. The
stipulation for the sale covered all the "right, title and interest" of both
the Bank and the Trustee. The lease agreements provide that upon
default the lessor may sell the equipment and that the proceeds, less
expenses, will be credited upon unpaid rentals. The security agreement provides for the assignment to the Bank of a continuing security
interest in both the leasehold and property leased for loans not to
exceed 80% of the aggregate unpaid rentals.

In the event the district court determines upon remand that the
agreements were "true leases", it will then be necessary to consider
further the effect of the stipulations of the parties and determine
whether the $60,000 represents the sale of the leasehold as well as the
sale of the reversionary interest in the equipment. If the court decides
that the $60,000 represents two separate interests, it must determine
the applicability of any stipulation to keep the fund intact and, in the
light of that determination, the proper allocation of the fund. . . .

HAYS, CIRCUIT JUDGE (dissenting):

I would affirm the determination of the trial court for substantially
the reasons given by Judge Weinstein.

Notes & Questions

1. *Focusing the Dispute.* *Leasing Consultants* involves a dispute
over what rights a bank with a perfected security interest in chattel
paper has against the trustee in bankruptcy. In analyzing the court's
decision, it is helpful to recall that all chattel paper includes a right to
payment in addition to a security interest or lease. See § 9–105(1)(b).
Leasing Consultants does *not* involve a dispute over what the bank
should have done to maximize its interest in the right to the stream of
payments represented by Leasing Consultants' chattel paper. To perfect a security interest in that income stream *Leasing Consultants* does
not require Citibank to do anything unusual. It must file a financing
statement covering the chattel paper where Leasing Consultants has its
principal place of business or it must take possession of the chattel
paper.

2. *Different Kinds of Chattel Paper.* The dispute in *Leasing Consultants* is not over the income payments represented by chattel paper
but over the rights to the equipment (or the right to retake the
equipment) inherent in all chattel paper. Although all chattel paper
contains some right to the underlying collateral (equipment in this
case), the two different kinds of chattel paper (security interest chattel
paper and lease chattel paper) give rise to different interests in the

equipment. Can you articulate what those differences are and how they influence the result in *Leasing Consultants*? In particular, please try to understand why the outcome of the case turns on whether the chattel paper includes a true lease or whether it includes a lease intended as security.

3. *Adjusting Lending Practices.* Consider *Leasing Consultants* from the perspective of potential lenders to Leasing Consultants. Suppose a New Jersey bank is interested in lending money to Leasing Consultants and wants to take a security interest in equipment that Leasing Consultants leases to others. Assume that the equipment is in New Jersey and that Leasing Consultants is located in New York. Where should the bank conduct a U.C.C. search if it believes the leases between Leasing Consultants and Leasing Consultants' clients to be true leases? If the bank searches in New Jersey, finds no financing statements and makes the loan, will it rank ahead of a New York lender with a perfected security interest in Leasing Consultants' chattel paper? (Note that such an interest would not show up in a New Jersey search.)

How should the bank's approach to the problem of U.C.C. searches change if it believes that Leasing Consultants' clients are using the equipment under security leases? Is the following statement true? "If the leases are security leases, then any prior lender's perfected security interest in chattel paper will enable it to defeat the New Jersey bank's interest in equipment located in New Jersey."

4. *Distinguishing Between Kinds of Leases.* If a lender's approach to U.C.C. searches turns on whether true leases exist, does this place undue pressure on lender's counsel to determine whether the Leasing Consultants leases are true leases? How should counsel protect its clients who lend in reliance on security interests in a lessor's leased equipment?

5. *The New Jersey Filing.* Why didn't Leasing Consultants' filing against Plastimetrix in New Jersey serve to perfect a security interest in the equipment for Citibank as assignee of Leasing Consultants' rights under its leases?

6. *Who Should Win?* Does *Leasing Consultants* reach a backwards result? Consider the following analysis: A security lease gives the lessor less rights in leased property than does a true lease. Yet under the *Leasing Consultants* case a security lessor's assignee is better off than is the assignee of a true lessor.

See generally Note, In re Leasing Consultants, Inc.: The Double Perfection Rule for Security Assignments of True Leases, 84 Yale L.J. 1722 (1975).

C. Article 9 and Interests in Real Property

1. Fixtures

HOLT v. HENLEY

Supreme Court of the United States, 1914.
232 U.S. 637, 34 S.Ct. 459, 58 L.Ed. 767.

Mr. Justice Holmes delivered the opinion of the court:

This is a petition to the district court, sitting in bankruptcy for leave to remove an automatic sprinkler system and equipment from the premises of the bankrupt, the Williamsburg Knitting Mill Company. It is opposed by the trustee of a mortgage of the plant of the company and the holder of the mortgage notes, and by the trustee in bankruptcy, both of which parties claim the property. The referee, the district court, and the circuit court of appeals, decided in favor of the latter claims. 190 Fed. 871, 113 C.C.A. 87, 193 Fed. 1020. The petitioner, Holt, appeals. The facts are as follows: An agreement to install the sprinkler was signed by Holt on August 28, 1909, and by the bankrupt on October 14, 1909. The installation was begun about December 6, 1909, and finished in the latter part of March, 1910, the equipment consisting of a 50,000-gallon tank on a steel tower, bolted to a concrete foundation, pipes connecting the tank with the mill. By the agreement the system was to remain Holt's property until paid for, and Holt was to have a right to enter and remove it upon a failure to pay as agreed. It also was to be personal property during the same time. A large part of the price has not been paid. But by the Code of Virginia, § 2462, unless registered as therein provided, which this was not, such sales are void as to creditors (construed by the Virginia courts to mean lien creditors only), and as to purchasers for value without notice from the vendee. On November 23, 1909, the mortgage deed was executed, covering the plant on the premises, and that "which may be acquired and placed upon the said premises during the continuance of this trust." The mortgagees claim the system by virtue of this clause and the fact that it had been attached to the soil. As bearing on this last it should be added that there now is a smaller tank on the same steel tower, that supplies the mill for domestic purposes, but this was not put there by Holt. . . .

We turn now to the claim of the mortgagees. This is based upon the clause extending the mortgage to plant that may be acquired and placed upon the premises while the mortgage is in force, coupled with the subsequent attachment of the system to the freehold. But the foundation upon which all their rights depend is the Virginia statute giving priority to purchasers for value without notice over Holt's unrecorded reservation of title; and as the mortgage deed was executed before the sprinkler system was put in, and the mortgagees made no advance on the faith of it, they were not purchasers for value as against Holt. There are no special facts to give them a better position in that regard. But that being so, what reason can be given for not respecting

Holt's title as against them? The system was attached to the freehold, but it could be removed without any serious harm for which complaint could be made against Holt, other than the loss of the system itself. Removal would not affect the integrity of the structure on which the mortgagees advanced. To hold that the mere fact of annexing the system to the freehold overrode the agreement that it should remain personalty and still belong to Holt would be to give a mystic importance to attachment by bolts and screws. For, as we have said, the mortgagees have no equity and do not bring themselves within the statutory provision. We believe the better rule in a case like this, and the one consistent with the Virginia decisions so far as they have gone, is that "the mortgagees take just such an interest in the property as the mortgagor acquired; no more, no less." . . . The case is not like those in which the addition was in its nature an essential indispensable part of the completed structure contemplated by the mortgage. The system, although useful and valuable, can be removed and the works still go on.

Decree reversed.

Notes & Questions

1. *When Would Real Estate Mortgagee Win?* *Holt* involves a dispute between the seller of a sprinkler system under a conditional sales contract and the holder of a real estate mortgage on the entire plant. The mortgage purports to include after-acquired property. Under what circumstances would Justice Holmes have allowed the real estate mortgagee to have priority in later-affixed personal property?

2. *Section 9–313.* The fact pattern in *Holt* is a common one and a system regulating security interests in personal property needs to take account of conflicts between those with security interests in personal property and mortgage holders with blanket liens on real estate and property that becomes attached to the real estate. Article 9's resolution of this problem is contained in § 9–313. How would *Holt* come out under that provision?

3. *Background of § 9–313.* Section 9–313 has an interesting past of its own. The genesis of the 1972 version of § 9–313 is traced in "Reasons for 1972 Change" accompanying the new provision.

As the Code came to be widely enacted, the real estate bar came to realize the impact of the fixture provisions on real estate financing and real estate titles. They apparently had not fully appreciated the impact of these provisions of Article 9 on real estate matters during the enactment of the Code, because of the commonly-held assumption that Article 9 was concerned only with chattel security matters.

The treatment of fixtures in pre-Code law had varied widely from state to state. The treatment in Article 9 was based generally on prior treatment in the Uniform Conditional Sales Act, which, however, had been enacted in only a dozen states. In other states the word "fixture" had come to mean that a former chattel had become real estate for all purposes and that any chattel rights therein were lost. For lawyers trained in such states the Code provisions seemed to be extreme. Some sections of the real estate bar began attempting with some success to have Section 9–313 amended to bring it closer to the pre-Code law in their states. In some states, such as California and Iowa, Section 9–313 simply was not enacted.

Even supporters of Article 9 and of its fixture provisions came to recognize that there were some ambiguities in Section 9–313, particularly in its application to construction mortgages, and also in its failure to make it clear that filing of fixture security interests was to be in real estate records where they could be found by a standard real estate search.

Section 9–313 and related provisions of Part 4 have been redrafted to meet the legitimate criticisms and to make a substantial shift in the law in favor of construction mortgages. The specific changes are described in the 1972 Comments to Section 9–313, and the Comments to the several sections of Part 4.

4. *Tests for Fixture Status.* *Holt* contains its own implicit definition of when personal property becomes so affixed to realty that the interests of a real estate mortgagee attach to the property. Not all states endorsed the test as stated by Justice Holmes. New Jersey employed the "institutional doctrine," under which removal of equipment from a structure would be viewed as causing material injury if it impaired the operation of the institution from which the equipment was removed, even if removal did not physically damage the structure. Lumpkin v. Holland Furnace Co., 118 N.J.Eq. 313, 178 A. 788 (Ct.Err. & App.1935). Under the Pennsylvania "industrial plant mortgage doctrine," all machinery necessary to a manufacturing operation became part of the freehold and there would be material injury whenever any part of the freehold was removed. Central Lithograph Co. v. Eatmor Chocolate Co., 316 Pa. 300, 175 A. 697 (1934). How does Article 9 resolve the question whether an item of personal property has become part of the realty upon which it is located? See § 9–313(1)(a). What consequences turn on this determination?

5. *Problem.* Owner Company contracts with Construction Company for the construction of a new building. The contract calls for progress payments at defined stages of construction. Mortgage Co. agrees to lend the sums needed for the progress payments and obtains a valid mortgage on the land, the building and any fixtures. Mortgage Co. promptly records the mortgage. The mortgage prohibits the removal of any fixtures. Construction Co. then buys the lighting fixtures (which are fixtures under state law) from Lamp Co., grants Lamp Co. a security interest to secure payment, and Lamp Co. immediately files a proper financing statement covering the fixtures in the local real estate office. See § 9–313(1)(b). The fixtures are installed in the building and

the building is soon completed. The fixtures are not readily removable. Is Lamp Co. protected against Mortgage Co.'s mortgage?

Suppose instead that the mortgage was not a construction mortgage. What would Lamp Co.'s rights be?

Suppose the mortgage was not a construction mortgage but that Mortgage Co. was involved in a dispute with Brick Co., a company that furnished bricks for construction of the building, retained a purchase money security interest in the bricks, and made a fixture filing. Who would have priority in the bricks?

2. Security Interests in Real Estate Documents

IN RE BRISTOL ASSOCIATES, INC.

United States Court of Appeals, Third Circuit, 1974.
505 F.2d 1056.

OPINION OF THE COURT

ADAMS, CIRCUIT JUDGE:

The Court is here asked to determine whether a Pennsylvania lender, who takes as collateral for a loan a security interest in a lessor-borrower's lease and in the rents thereunder, must comply with the filing provisions of Article 9 of the Uniform Commercial Code to perfect its interest against attack by a Receiver in bankruptcy.

In 1969, Bristol Associates, Inc. as lessor, entered into an Agreement of Lease, letting certain store premises for a period of 10 years to the Commonwealth of Pennsylvania, agent for the Pennsylvania Liquor Control Board. Two years later, in 1971, in consideration for a loan, Bristol gave Girard Trust Bank a promissory note and, as security, assigned to Girard its interest in the lease. Girard did not record its security interest in the real estate lease by filing a financing statement under Article 9 or make any other public record of the assignment of the lease.

The following year, in 1972, Bristol filed a petition under Chapter XI of the Bankruptcy Act, 11 U.S.C. § 701 et seq. (1966), and a Receiver was appointed. Apart from the first month's rent from the Commonwealth inadvertently paid to Girard, the Receiver retained all rentals and applied them to Bristol's business operations. Girard thereupon filed a reclamation petition with the Bankruptcy Court to recover the rentals paid to the Receiver under the lease that had been assigned. The Bankruptcy Court denied the petition, and the denial was affirmed by the district court. 369 F.Supp. 1 (E.D.Pa.1973).

Under section 70(c) of the Bankruptcy Act, 11 U.S.C. § 110, and section 9–301(3) of the Code, the Receiver assumes the rights of a lien creditor. In this status, the Receiver takes priority over those other creditors of the insolvent debtor who hold unperfected security interests. Unperfected secured parties are relegated to the pool of general creditors.

If the assignment of the lease to Girard is a transaction within the scope of Article 9 and if Girard's interest has not been perfected, then Girard cannot successfully assert its security interest against the Receiver. If, however, the assignment of a lease is excluded from Article 9, the filing and perfection provisions of that Article are not applicable, and Girard's security interest in the lease and in the rents from the lease would not be subordinated to the Receiver.

The apposite statutory provisions and official Comment provide:

§ 9–102 Policy and Scope of Article.

(1) Except as otherwise provided . . . in Section 9–104 on excluded transactions, this Article applies so far as concerns any personal property and fixtures within the jurisdiction of this State

(a) to any transaction (regardless of its form) which is intended to create a security interest in personal property . . ..

(3) The application of this Article to a security interest in a secured obligation is not affected by the fact that the obligation is itself secured by a transaction or interest to which this Article does not apply.

Comment 4. An illustration of subsection (3) is as follows:

The owner of Blackacre borrows $10,000 from his neighbor, and secures his note by a mortgage on Blackacre. This Article is not applicable to the creation of the real estate mortgage. Nor is it applicable to a sale of the note by the mortgagee, even though the mortgage continues to secure the note. However, when the mortgagee pledges the note to secure his own obligation to X, this Article applies to the security interest thus created, which is a security interest in an instrument even though the instrument is secured by a real estate mortgage. This Article leaves to other law the question of the effect on rights under the mortgage of delivery or non-delivery of the mortgage or of recording or non-recording of an assignment of the mortgagee's interest. See Section 9–104(j).

§ 9–104. Transactions Excluded from Article. This Article does not apply . . .

(j) . . . to the creation or transfer of an interest in or lien on real estate, including a lease or rents thereunder.

Comment 2. The exclusion . . . of leases and other interests in or liens on real estate by paragraph (j) merely reiterates the limitations on coverage already made explicit in Section 9–102(3). See Comment 4 to that section.

We are required to apply the law of Pennsylvania to issues such as the one before us. In Re Royal Electrotype Corp., 485 F.2d 394 (3d Cir. 1973). However, the Pennsylvania courts have made no ruling on the interplay of sections 9–102 and 9–104 to resolve the question whether a real estate lease used as collateral falls within the ambit of Article 9.

Therefore, it is incumbent on the federal court not only to apply the relevant state law, but to ascertain what that law, in fact, is.

Our analysis proceeds from the statute. We must give effect insofar as possible to the language and intent of the legislators, giving each section a meaningful interpretation while not eclipsing any other portion of the statute.[3]

The question confronting us here thus becomes whether "an interest in real estate" subsequently employed in a "transaction which is intended to create a security interest" is covered by section 9–102, placing the transaction under the Code, or by section 9–104(j), placing the transaction outside the Code.

The Receiver contends that, when the borrower assigned the lease to the lender, the transaction came within the ambit of Article 9 and its provisions for perfecting security interests. In support of this position, the Receiver advances as a syllogism that Article 9 expressly covers security interests in all personal property; that a lease in Pennsylvania is personal property; and that the transaction in question here therefore falls within Article 9 coverage. Section 9–104(j) would, under this analysis, be read narrowly, exempting from Article 9 only those transactions touching on the real estate itself, such as the creation of a lease or mortgage; subsequent uses of the lease or mortgage, "intended to create a security interest," would not be excluded. Under the Receiver's approach the "transfers" excluded from Article 9 by section 9–104(j) would be only those where no intent to create a security interest was present, for example, transfers of blocks of mortgages and the sale of real estate on which outstanding leases were transferred as part of the sale.

The Receiver would place the lease within the scope of section 9–102, Comment 4, supra, asserting that, analogous to the promissory note, the lease evidences an obligation to pay. Although the Receiver concedes that the underlying lessor-lessee contract is excluded from the Code by section 9–104(j), he nevertheless maintains that its use as security could, under a reasonable interpretation of the language, fall within section 9–102(3). If section 9–104(j) is construed narrowly, claims the Receiver, so that the "transfers" it excludes do not cover

3. Two situations relating to the present case are specifically addressed by Article 9: In one case the provisions of Article 9 control, in the other case the transaction is excluded from coverage. First, had a borrower, such as Bristol, mortgaged its real property to a bank as collateral for a loan, rather than assigning a lease it held as landlord, the Code, under section 9–104(j), explicitly excludes such transaction from its provisions.

On the other hand, where a borrower holds a promissory note in conjunction with a mortgage of real property and then assigns the note as collateral for a loan by a bank, the provisions of Article 9 govern the transaction. The latter situation is the case which the Code includes in section 9–102, Comment 4. Appellant Girard appears to question even this latter application of the Code. But see P. Coogan, W. Hogan & D. Vagts, 1A Secured Transactions Under the Uniform Commercial Code § 23.11 (1973); Warren, Coverage of the Secured Transactions Division of the California Commercial Code, 13 U.C.L.A.L.Rev. 250 (1966).

transfers as security pledges, a consistent reading of the two sections emerges.

Girard argues in opposition that section 9–104(j) explicitly exempts from compliance with the provisions of Article 9 any transfer of an interest in realty, no matter what the purpose. Under this reading of the statute, it becomes irrelevant whether a lease is considered realty or personalty under the state law for other purposes. Even if the lease is deemed personalty, its transfer is claimed by Girard to be the subject of express exclusion from the provisions of Article 9.

Responding to the Receiver's reading of section 9–104(j), Girard suggests that the Receiver would nullify the effect of that section by interpreting it to exclude from Article 9 only transactions which that Article does nor purport to cover, namely, real property transactions and transfers where there is no intent to create a security interest. Girard contends that a proper reconciliation of the two sections results only from interpreting section 9–104(j) to exclude from Article 9 transactions that would otherwise fall within it, such as the transactions involved in the present litigation.

The evolution of the Code since its original enactment, the views of authorities and the realities of the pertinent business practices have persuaded us that the intent of the Legislature was to exclude from the filing and perfection provisions of Article 9 the use of a lease as collateral for a loan.

Sections 9–102 and 9–104 have both been amended since their original enactment. Together, the amendments limit the application of section 9–102 where transactions touch realty and, simultaneously, provide greater explicitness in section 9–104(j), exempting both the creation and transfer of interests in realty. The amendments were proposed in order to clarify the Code as ambiguities in language became evident, rather than to alter the direction or scope of the Code.

As originally enacted in Pennsylvania, section 9–102 did not contain subsection (3). In 1959 subsection (3) was added, accompanied by the explanatory Comment 4. Since the effect produced by Comment 4 was not clear, the Conference of Commissioners on Uniform State Laws and the American Law Institute recommended, in 1962, that the Comment be modified. Before and after the amendment, the relevant portion of Comment 4 read:

> However, when the mortgagee in turn pledges this note *and mortgage* to secure his own obligation to X, this Article is applicable to the security interest thus created in the note *and the mortgage* [which is a security interest in an instrument even though the instrument is secured by a real estate mortgage]. (Emphasis indicates the relevant 1962 deletions; brackets indicate the relevant 1962 addition.)

The changes in wording produced two effects. First, deletion of the references to mortgages distinguishes between the pledge of a note, a separate and distinct contract, and the underlying real estate mortgage. Where a promissory note and mortgage together become the subject of a security interest, only that portion of the package unrelated to the real property is now covered by section 9–102. Second, the added language makes explicit that the promissory note itself falls within the scope of Article 9 by virtue of its status as an instrument.[8] Since a lease of real property is clearly not an instrument, inclusion of its assignment in Article 9 by reason of analogy to the promissory note would be strained. The amendments clarify the rationale of applying Article 9 to the promissory note. They refute the possibility that Article 9 reaches out to encompass every transaction colorably included under section 9–102.

The amendments made to section 9–104 lend further support to the position that the legislators did not intend to include in Article 9 the assignment of a real estate lease. As originally enacted, the Code did not contain section 9–104(j); rather, section 9–104(b) excluded from Article 9 coverage "a landlord's lien or a lien on real estate." Act of April 6, 1953, P.L. 3, § 9–104. Following the recommendation of the Permanent Editorial Board of the Uniform Commercial Code, the Legislature in 1959 adopted the language presently set forth in section 9–104(j). Act of October 2, 1959, P.L. 1023 § 9. The change was promoted by the Board in the interest of "greater clarification and precision as to the types of transactions entirely excluded from the operation of Article 9." 1956 Recommendations of the Editorial Board for the Uniform Commercial Code, 257–58. The language of section 9–104(j) substantially broadens the earlier exclusion by providing that Article 9 does not apply to "the creation or transfer of an interest in or lien on real estate, including a lease or rents thereunder."

Our conclusion, that lenders need not conform to the requirements of Article 9 in order to retain their security interest in a real estate lease assigned to them as collateral, is supported, apparently unanimously, by authorities who have considered this problem. . . .

One final consideration buttresses the conclusion that the lease when used as collateral should be exempted from Article 9. The universal practice of Pennsylvania lenders in these circumstances is to ignore any application of the Code to leases received as collateral. A bank often takes an assignment of a lease or the rents due under a lease as security for a loan. C. Funk, Banks and the Uniform Commercial Code 61 (2d ed. 1964). Collateral of very substantial value is involved in such loans, which are granted regularly and repeatedly in the world of finance. Parties to these loans "are apt to think for good reasons that they are outside the scope of Article 9." Hawkland, 77 Com.L.J. 79, 84 (1972).[12]

---

8. "Instrument" is defined for purposes of Article 9 as "a negotiable instrument, or a security or any other writing which evidences a right to the payment of money and is not itself a security agreement or lease. . . ." 12A Pa.Stat.Ann. § 9–105(g) (1970) (cross references deleted).

12. It was suggested at oral argument without contradiction that lenders believe they are excluded because "literally hun-

While a uniform trade practice does not constitute proof that the legal consequences of the practice are what those in the field take them to be, neither can it be assumed that a legislature which passed the Code and which has considered and passed amendments to it on several occasions would let stand practices or beliefs which it disapproved. In fact, the amendments passed by the Legislature have tended in the other direction, restricting the application of Article 9 when transactions touch real property. (See discussion supra.)

Where language is susceptible of two reasonable meanings, a court, in the commercial field, should choose that interpretation which comports with current universal practice in the business world.

It is argued that by dovetailing the two sections to achieve a wider reach for section 9–104(j) and a resultant narrower scope to section 9–102, sufficient heed is not given to the admonition that the Code be "liberally construed and applied to promote its underlying purposes and policies." 12A Pa.Stat.Ann. § 1–102 (1970). Although the conclusion reached today eliminates from Article 9 a class of secured transactions, it nevertheless would not appear to conflict with the self-proclaimed purposes of the Code, which are generally to "simplify [and] clarify" commercial law, to "permit the continued expansion" of commercial life and to "make uniform" commercial law throughout the United States. Section 1–102(2).

Admittedly, a principal function of Article 9 is to achieve maximum benefit for creditors from the notice-filing provisions. The goal of the filing system is to make known to the public whatever outstanding security interests exist in the property of debtors. Once a transaction falls within the Code, this legislative intent must be given full force in any determination of how the Code applies in a situation. The notice requirements are at the core of Article 9.

In ascertaining whether including or excluding a transaction [from] Article 9 conforms to the legislative intent, however, we must weigh the interest in public notice against the other purposes of the Code, such as uniformity and the promotion of commercial law, and interpret the statute in the light of current commercial and banking practice. On balance, this Court concludes that the drafters who wrote Article 9 and the legislators who enacted it into law intended section 9–104(j) to be interpreted sufficiently broadly to exclude the assignment of a lease and rents thereunder from the operation of Article 9. The burden of those who would propound a different view is to persuade the State Legislature. We should not usurp the legislative function.

The decision of the district court will be reversed, and the case will be remanded for entry of an order consistent with this opinion.

dreds of opinion letters" from attorneys have so informed the banking community.

Notes & Questions

1. *Mortgages as Security.* *Bristol Associates* involved a security interest in a lease. The legal question it poses, however, is of broad commercial importance because it also pertains to the use of home mortgages as security for borrowings by financial institutions. As one commentator describes the problem:

> [T]hrift institutions, including savings and loan associations, savings banks, and credit unions, pledge mortgages and notes of their homeowner borrowers to a commercial bank or mortgage banker as security for their own borrowings. The bank takes delivery of the paper and "warehouses" it until the institution has accumulated a block of mortgages large enough to sell. "Ginnie Maes," the mortgage-backed bonds guaranteed by the Government National Mortgage Association, are also predicated upon the creation of security interests in mortgages. Their integrity and the integrity of the mortgage warehousing practice both depend upon a satisfactory resolution of the problem of governing law.

Note, Security Interests in Notes and Mortgages: Determining the Applicable Law, 79 Colum.L.Rev. 1414, 1415 (1979).

2. *Case Requiring Article 9 Compliance.* The *Bristol Associates* approach to the problem has not received widespread endorsement. For example, in In re Staff Mortgage and Investment Corp., 550 F.2d 1228 (9th Cir. 1977), a retired couple had invested their savings with the bankrupt, a corporation in the business of buying and selling promissory notes secured by trust deeds (mortgages) on real property. The bankrupt had borrowed funds from the couple and, as security, had assigned to them its rights to a note and deed of trust. The assignment was recorded in the real estate records. The court (1) found that the couple's failure to take possession of the note deprived them of a perfected Article 9 security interest and (2) implicitly held that Article 9 applied to the security interest in the note and deed of trust. The trustee in bankruptcy therefore prevailed.

3. *Separating the Note and the Mortgage.* Under *Bristol Associates*, does Article 9 apply to the perfection of a security interest in a note while real property law applies to the perfection of a security interest in the related mortgage? Does it make sense to treat the note as a legal document distinct from the mortgage? Of what importance is the note without the mortgage? Of what importance is the mortgage without the note?

4. *Presumptive Article 9 Coverage?* If *Bristol Associates* presents a close question, should courts incline towards resolving that question in favor of coverage by Article 9 or against such coverage? What lenders are likely to be misled by the failure to perfect in *Staff Mortgage*, supra? If the dispute over perfection arose with any party other than a bankruptcy trustee, could such a party reasonably claim to have been misled by the secured party's failure to perfect?

D. Secured Transactions Beyond the Scope of Article 9

In cases like *Bristol Associates*, courts face a problem of interpretation. Depending upon the interpretation adopted, the secured transaction in question may be included or excluded from Article 9's coverage. In another large class of cases, however, there is no such problem. On its face, Article 9 excludes from its coverage large classes of personal property secured transactions. See § 9–104.

MILLER v. WELLS FARGO BANK INTERNATIONAL CORP.
United States Court of Appeals, Second Circuit, 1976.
540 F.2d 548.

OAKES, CIRCUIT JUDGE:

Arbitrage in foreign exchange—the simultaneous purchase and sale of foreign currency in order to profit from discrepancies between the sales price and the purchase price in separate markets—is a relatively sophisticated form of investment, and properly conducted may be entirely risk-free to the investor. Such a transaction may be equally risk-free, though even more exotic, when it includes the following steps:

(A) the arbitrager borrows dollars from a New York bank;

(B) these dollars are used to purchase Swiss Francs, which are deposited in the arbitrager's time deposit account at a European bank;

(C) simultaneously with step (B), the arbitrager contracts with a Swiss bank to sell the Swiss Francs it has deposited in the European bank (plus the interest, payable in Swiss Francs, accruing in that account) at a date six months in the future—the contractual terms are such that the arbitrager will receive more dollars for his Francs when he sells to the Swiss bank after six months than he paid to obtain the Francs at the date the contract was made;[1]

(D) after six months the Swiss Francs in the time deposit at the European bank (plus interest) are sold to the Swiss bank for dollars in accordance with the contract, and the proceeds are remitted by the Swiss bank to the arbitrager's account at the New York bank;

(E) the New York bank then deducts the principal amount of the sum lent, plus accrued interest, from the arbitrager's account;

(F) the difference between the amount deposited in the arbitrager's New York account in step (D) and the amount deducted from that account in step (E) represents the arbitrager's profit on the transaction.

Involved in this appeal are two such transactions initiated when appellant, Wells Fargo Bank International Corp. ("the New York Bank"),

---

1. The Swiss Bank was obviously speculating that Swiss Francs would rise in value, relative to the dollar, at a rate higher than was contracted for, during the six-month period. The "risk free" nature of this transaction for the arbitrager stems from the fact that it is the Swiss Bank, rather than the arbitrager, that is engaging in the speculation.

loaned $1,000,000 in each case to an international currency dealer, American IBC Corp. (AIBC), which used the proceeds to conduct the two arbitrage transactions in the more exotic form just suggested. The money earned from the foreign currency on the European time deposit, coupled with the price discrepancy on the simultaneous purchase and future sale of Swiss Francs, was to offset the total interest to be paid on the loan and leave the arbitrager, AIBC, with a profit of approximately $2/10$ of one per cent on the overall transaction.[2] This was a profit that was, financially speaking, risk-free, note 1 *supra*. Similarly, the lending bank, the New York Bank, was to obtain a relatively good rate of interest in these transactions which it thought would "automatically unwind" so that in the end it would be repaid its principal and the interest out of the proceeds of the future sale back of the Swiss Francs, purchased and placed on time deposit by AIBC.

Unfortunately, the arbitrager or currency dealer went bankrupt less than four months after the loans were repaid to the lending bank out of the proceeds of the future sales of the Swiss Francs. The United States District Court for the Southern District of New York, Milton Pollack, *Judge*, held that the payments should be set aside as preferential transfers under Section 60(a)(1) of the Bankruptcy Act, 11 U.S.C. § 96(a)(1).[3] . . .

The first transaction. AIBC had a business relationship with the New York Bank, which is an international bank wholly owned by but operated independently from Wells Fargo Bank, N.A., of San Francisco. In April, 1973, AIBC approached the New York Bank with a proposal for a currency arbitrage transaction with the Swiss Credit Bank in Zurich (the Swiss Bank). The New York Bank approved the proposal and on May 3, 1973, loaned AIBC $1,000,000 at 8 per cent interest, to be repaid on November 2, 1973. On May 3, AIBC used the $1,000,000 to purchase 3,240,0000 Swiss Francs from the Swiss Bank and simultane-

---

2. The transactions were designed in such a way that on the two six-month loans of $1,000,000 the arbitrager was to gain a profit of $2,147.70 and $2,977.38, respectively. Miller v. Wells Fargo Bank International Corp., 406 F.Supp. 452, 462 n. 1 (S.D.N.Y.1975).

3. Section 60(a)(1) and (2), 11 U.S.C. § 96(a)(1), (2), provides:

(1) A preference is a transfer, as defined in this title, of any of the property of a debtor to or for the benefit of a creditor for or on account of an antecedent debt, made or suffered by such debtor while insolvent and within four months before the filing by or against him of the petition initiating a proceeding under this title, the effect of which transfer will be to enable such creditor to obtain a greater percentage of his debt than some other creditor of the same class.

(2) For the purposes of subdivisions (a) and (b) of this section, a transfer of property other than real property shall be deemed to have been made or suffered at the time when it became so far perfected that no subsequent lien upon such property obtainable by legal or equitable proceedings on a simple contract could become superior to the rights of the transferee. . . . If any transfer of real property is not so perfected against a bona fide purchase, or if any transfer of other property is not so perfected against such liens by legal or equitable proceedings prior to the filing of a petition initiating a proceeding under this title, it shall be deemed to have been made immediately before the filing of the petition.

ously agreed to resell 3,308,850 Swiss Francs to the Swiss Bank on November 2, 1973, for $1,042,814.37. The difference of 68,850 Swiss Francs in the amount purchased and sold by AIBC was exactly equal to 4.25 per cent per annum interest earned on the six-month time deposit of the 3,240,000 Swiss Francs, a deposit made in Wells Fargo Luxembourg (the Luxembourg Bank), which is a European branch of Wells Fargo Bank, N.A. The time deposit contract was entered into simultaneously with the loan and with the separate purchase and resale agreement with the Swiss Bank.

Everything went smoothly. On November 2, 1973, the Swiss Bank forwarded the resulting $1,042,814.37 to the New York Bank, which credited the AIBC account in the New York Bank with the transfer and debited it with the sum of $1,040,666.67, representing the $1,000,000 principal and 8 per cent interest due on the six-month loan. AIBC's profit on the entire transaction was thus a mere $2,147.70.

On appeal, the New York Bank has employed what might be called a shotgun approach. It claims that it had a valid assignment of a security interest in the Luxembourg time deposit either by virtue of the exchange of correspondence between AIBC and it on April 30 and May 2, respectively,[6] or by virtue of a prior so-called 1970 General Pledge Agreement [7] entered into between AIBC and the New York Bank.

---

6. The April 30, 1973, letter of AIBC to the New York Bank provided:

We confirm to you our borrowing from you and lodging with you as collateral for such borrowing, a Swiss Franc time deposit, as detailed below.

. . .

On May 3, 1973 kindly deliver the sum of $1,000,000 to the Chase Manhattan Bank for credit to the account of Swiss Credit Bank, Zurich, reference American IBC Corp.

Swiss Credit Bank Zurich, is delivering for value May 3, 1973 the sum of 3,240,000 Swiss Francs to Swiss Bank Corp. Zurich in favor of Wells Fargo Luxembourg, ref. American IBC Corp. The Swiss Franc sum is placed on time deposit value May 3, 1973 until November 2, 1973 at an interest rate of 4.25% per annum. This deposit is lodged with you as collateral for the One Million Dollar loan and is subordinated to such loan.

On May 2, 1973, the New York Bank replied in pertinent part to AIBC:

Confirming our telephone conversation of April 30, 1973, we agree to lend you $1,000,000 on May 3rd, 1973, at 8% p. a. on a 360-day basis.

The proceeds of our advance will be transferred to Chase Manhattan Bank, for credit of Swiss Credit Bank, Zurich,

for account of American I.B.C. Corp.

. . .

You have agreed to lodge with us as collateral the Swiss Franc time deposit as outlined in your letter dated April 30, 1973. We are enclosing our usual "Advance Agreement" along with our time note for your execution.

. . .

We wish to quote to your [sic] our telex sent to Wells Fargo Bank, Luxembourg, on May 1, 1973.

. . .

SWISS FRANCS WILL BE CREDITED YOUR ACCOUNT AT SWISS BANK CORP. ZURICH BY ORDER SWISS CREDIT BANK ZURICH BY ORDER AMERICAN I.B.C. 770 LEXINGTON AVE., N.Y. AT MATURITY PAY PRINCIPAL PLUS INTEREST TO SWISS CREDIT BANK ZURICH, ATTENTION MR. RIBI SWISS FRANCS 3,308,850 CREDIT DOLLAR EQUIVALENT 1,042,814.37 TO WFBI FOR ACCOUNT AMERICAN I.B.C. ATTENTION BOLAND.

7. The "General Pledge Agreement" provided in pertinent part:

In consideration of any financial accommodation . . . to be given . . . to the undersigned by WELLS FARGO BANK INTERNATIONAL CORPORATION (hereinafer called Bank), and as

Appellant also claims that the loan in the first transaction was secured by a pledge of the Luxembourg time deposit. Alternatively, appellant claims that AIBC's time deposit at the Luxembourg Bank should be treated as a "special deposit," similar to a trust, running in appellant's favor.

The second transaction. . . . .

A. *First Transaction—Assignment of the Time Deposit.* . . . .

B. *First Transaction—Pledge of the Time Deposit.*

Appellant's last claim with regard to this first transaction is that it had perfected a valid pledge of the AIBC time deposit in the Luxembourg Bank under the 1970 General Pledge Agreement and the New York common law. It is clear, of course, that a loan may be secured through a possessory security interest such as a pledge. The elements of a pledge include an intention to pledge collateral security and possession of the collateral by the pledgee or by a third person acting on the pledgee's behalf for the purposes of securing a debt. Restatement of Security, §§ 5, 8 (1941). It is sufficient that there be notification of the pledge to the third person in possession of the chattel intended to be pledged. Id. § 8, comment *b.* See 53 N.Y. Jurisprudence, supra, Secured Transactions § 39, at 274. To effect a valid pledge of an intangible asset, such as a time deposit, the pledgee, or his agent, must possess formal written evidence of an interest in the intangible which so represents the intangible that the enjoyment, transfer or enforcement of the intangible depends upon possession of the instrument. Restatement of Security, supra, § 1, comment *e.* A valid pledge of such an "indispensable instrument" creates an interest not only in the instrument but in the intangible represented by it. Id. § 2(3). However, where the instrument delivered to the putative pledgee is not indispensable to the transfer or enforcement of the intangible, the interest obtained cannot be a pledge. Id. § 1, comment *e.*

collateral security for the payment of all debts, obligations or liabilities . . . the undersigned hereby assign, transfer to and pledge with Bank . . . all money and property . . . which shall hereafter be delivered or to come into the possession, custody or control of Bank in any manner or for any purpose whatever during the existence of this agreement, and whether held in a general or special account or deposit or for safe-keeping or otherwise, together with any . . . other property which the undersigned are or may hereafter become entitled to receive on account of such . . . other property . . . .

. . .

At any time, without notice, and at the expense of the undersigned, Bank in its name or in the name of its nominee or of the undersigned may, but shall not be obligated to: . . . (3) enter into . . . any agreement in anywise relating to or affecting the collateral, and in connection therewith may deposit or surrender control of such collateral thereunder, accept other property in exchange for such collateral and do and perform such acts and things as it may deem proper, and any money or property received in exchange for such collateral shall be applied to the indebtedness or thereafter held by it pursuant to the provisions hereof; (4) make any compromise or settlement it deems desirable or proper with reference to the collateral; (5) insure, process and preserve the collateral; (6) cause the collateral to be transferred to its name or to the name of its nominee; (7) exercise as to such collateral all the rights, powers and remedies of an owner . . . .

While the district court held that the April 30 and May 2, 1973, correspondence between AIBC and appellant indicate a clear intention to pledge the Swiss Franc time deposit to the New York Bank, see note 6 supra, it concluded that the "issuance by the Luxembourg bank to AIBC of a clean receipt for the time deposit, and the failure of the New York bank to have the receipt recalled or modified to reflect its pledge, are . . . fatal to the [appellant] Bank's pledge claim." 406 F.Supp. at 468–69.[17] Since a valid pledge could be created only by way of delivery of an indispensable instrument pertaining to the bank account itself, Restatement of Security, supra, § 1, comment *e;* G. Gilmore, Security Interests in Personal Property § 7.1 (1965); 21 Harv.L.Rev. 61, 61–62 (1907), and because there was no such delivery of any indispensable instrument to the New York Bank, the district court held that the claim of pledge must fail.

It is, of course, far from certain whether AIBC's time deposit in the Wells Fargo Luxembourg was like the ordinary savings deposit account where a passbook is issued, its delivery constituting a valid pledge. The New York Bank argues that its Telex key and key code constituted the "indispensable instrument" equivalent to a passbook or certificate of deposit in reference to the Luxembourg time deposit.[18] Appellant's argument is that it would be impractical in international banking transactions if methods of depositing and obtaining funds depended on the presentation of an instrument such as a passbook or a certificate of deposit because depositors do not have the time to travel thousands of miles to deposit or withdraw funds located at various banks scattered

---

17. What actually was issued by Wells Fargo Luxembourg was Exhibit 3, which is reproduced as Appendix A hereto.

18. This is a novel contention. Appellant argues that there has never been a "test case" involving "the test key code" because it has worked so well and is so safe and reliable. Appellant also argues that the Telex key code was an "indispensable instrument" under comment *e* to the Restatement of Security § 1 (1941) which reads:

    e. Indispensable instrument. An indispensable instrument as used in the Restatement of this Subject means the formal written evidence of an interest in intangibles, so representing the intangible that the enjoyment, transfer or enforcement of the intangible depends upon possession of the instrument. If the instrument cannot be produced, the interest which it represents can be effectively asserted only by accounting for the absence of the instrument and obtaining as a substitute for it, either a duplicate or some form of court decree. Indispensable instruments include not only negotiable instruments such as promissory notes and bills of exchange,

but also share certificates, bonds, interim certificates, savings bank books and insurance policies. Where the instrument is not an indispensable one, for example, a written assignment of a list of book accounts as security, the interest obtained by the assignee in the accounts is not a pledge.

See also Comment on Section 2(3):

    Where the instrument is an indispensable one but not negotiable, the delivery of the instrument, if made for the purpose of creating a pledge, transfers to the pledgee the pledgor's interest in the intangible represented by the instrument, subject to the pledgor's power to redeem. Where the instrument is not an indispensable one, the delivery may be evidence of an intent to make an assignment of the intangible, but the bailment alone creates an interest in the thing delivered rather than in the intangible represented by it. In the Restatement of this Subject, if an interest is created in an intangible, not represented by an indispensable instrument, it is considered a security assignment rather than a pledge.

across the globe. For this reason, appellant argues, banks in international transactions have adopted more convenient systems for the deposit and withdrawal of funds. In this case the depositor, instead of receiving a passbook from the depository bank, is given an ever-changing "test key" verifying code number which allows the user to deposit and withdraw funds from his account via Telex even though he is thousands of miles away. The New York Bank contends that its test key number, of which it has exclusive knowledge, serves the same purpose and function in international transactions as the traditional "indispensable instrument" does in everyday banking transactions. Because AIBC deposited funds with the Luxembourg affiliate through the use of the New York Bank Telex, and no test key code number was given to AIBC by the New York Bank, appellant claims it retained exclusive control over the deposit or withdrawal of funds from the time deposit account. A witness for the bank testified that AIBC could have sent Telexes or letters to the Luxembourg affiliate, but without the test key code such Telexes would not have affected the disposition of the funds. Therefore, appellant claims, the indispensable instrument in connection with the Luxembourg time deposit was solely the Telex key and Telex key code, not the receipt or contract that was issued to AIBC by Wells Fargo Luxembourg, see note 17 supra. Appellant differentiates time deposit receipts from certificates of deposit, and claims that under the controlling New York law creditors are not entitled to rely on a bank deposit receipt as evidence of ownership of a deposit. See First National Bank v. Clark, 134 N.Y. 368, 372, 32 N.E. 38, 39–40 (1892).

The district court rejected this argument on the basis that the appellant's purported control over disposition of the time deposit account was belied by the documentary evidence. The record includes two examples of mail communication from the Luxembourg Bank to AIBC, including a request for confirmation of receipt of the time deposit contract. But as appellant points out, the mail communication in question did not involve the disposition of the funds. It was simply a request for confirmation of the time deposit receipt. The question is not whether AIBC could *communicate* with the Luxembourg affiliate by other means, but whether by such communication it could have effected the enjoyment, transfer or enforcement of the deposit without use of the Telex key code. While the trial court's findings are not as clear as we would perhaps wish in this respect, the burden was on the appellant to establish that it was secured by pledge and, specifically, to establish that the Telex test key code gave it irrevocable authority over AIBC's account in Luxembourg.

This it did not do. The time deposit account was in the name of AIBC. No instrument indicating the pledge interest of the New York Bank was issued. There is nothing in the record to show that AIBC's contract of deposit was itself insufficient to withdraw the funds or that AIBC could not have obtained access to its time deposit through other documentation, such as duly authenticated signature cards, so as to obviate any need for the bank's Telex test key number. As the district court held, the appellant conducted this transaction in a manner that permitted the bankrupt to make it appear to potential creditors that the Swiss Franc time deposit at Luxembourg was an unencumbered asset. 406 F.Supp. at 471. The primary purpose of the requirement of delivery of the pledged property is to provide notice to creditors that the property in question is no longer free from prior interests of third parties. The Telex key code did not serve this function; nor did it, on the proof presented below, constitute the requisite "indispensable instrument." It is unnecessary for us to determine whether the time deposit contract, or any other documentation received by AIBC, was an indispensable instrument, transfer of which would have constituted the pledge; AIBC did not deliver any such document to the New York Bank. In sum, we agree with Judge Pollack that appellant has failed to show that its interest in the Luxembourg deposits was secured by a pledge. The further conclusion of the district court, that "the assumed pledge was lost as [a] matter of law when the Swiss Francs were forwarded to the Swiss Bank without any notice of a pledge to the New York Bank," 406 F.Supp. at 471, is therefore not necessary to the disposition of this case on appeal. . . .

The judgment of the district court is affirmed.

APPENDIX A

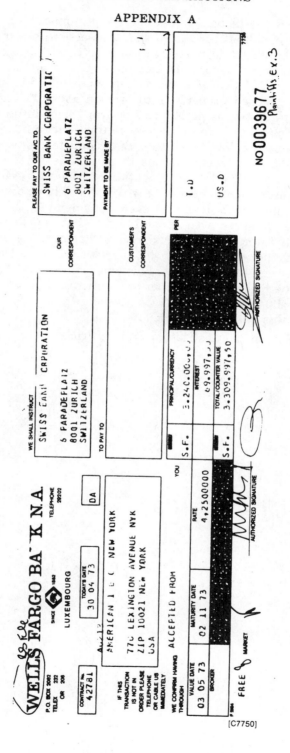

[C7750]

Notes & Questions

1. *Should Deposit Accounts Be Covered?* Should deposit accounts be covered by Article 9? Comment 7 to § 9–104 states: "[D]eposit accounts . . . are often put up as collateral. Such transactions are often quite special, do not fit easily under a general commercial statute and are adequately covered by existing law. . . ." Professor Phillips argues:

> None of these assertions . . . stands up to scrutiny. The transactions are far from "special." On the contrary, a deposit account would in most instances be deemed even more valuable collateral to a potential lender than inventory and accounts whose value as collateral directly results from their easy convertibility into cash. To the extent that a deposit account cannot be utilized as collateral, the debtor is deprived of a major asset on which to borrow; the secured party is constrained to lend less than he otherwise might; and the economic effect is restrictive because potential collateral cannot be used to secure credit.

Phillips, Flawed Perfection: From Possession to Filing Under Article 9—Part I, 59 B.U.L.Rev. 1, 47 (1979). Does *Miller* suggest that secured transactions in deposit accounts are adequately covered by existing law?

2. *Perfecting a Security Interest.* How may a debtor grant a perfected security interest in a deposit account? Does *Miller* suggest surrender of possession of a passbook would constitute perfection? What if the passbook does not note the interest of the secured party? Why is possession of a passbook acceptable as a method of perfection when the various factors relied upon in *Miller* to perfect were not acceptable?

3. *Possession as Perfection.* Does *Miller* reflect the weakness of possession as a method of perfection? Would cases like *Miller* be better handled by requiring a central filing to perfect a security interest?

4. *Relationship to Setoff.* May one view the exclusion of deposit accounts as a way to protect a bank's right of setoff, another transaction excluded from Article 9? Who benefits from the exclusion of deposit accounts? What effect does the exclusion have, when taken in conjunction with the preservation of a bank's right of setoff?

5. *Other Exclusions.* Consider the other § 9–104 exclusions from Article 9. Do any of them raise problems similar to the problems raised by exclusion of deposit accounts?

See generally Coogan, Kripke & Weiss, The Outer Fringes of Article 9: Subordination Agreements, Security Interests in Money and Deposits, Negative Pledge Clauses, and Participation Agreements, 79 Harv.L. Rev. 229 (1965).

Part II

DEBT COLLECTION

Chapter 5

LIMITATIONS ON CREDITOR BEHAVIOR

Most of this book deals with secured credit transactions and topics relating to enforcement of secured and unsecured credit obligations—provisional remedies, fraudulent conveyances, enforcement of judgments, and bankruptcy. But regulation of other aspects of one class of credit transactions, those involving consumers, is of growing importance. This Chapter covers two sets of such regulations, the Fair Credit Reporting Act's restrictions on gathering and disseminating credit information, and the Fair Debt Collection Practices Act's restrictions on nonjudicial collection methods. Other limits on creditor behavior in consumer credit transactions are noted at the end of Chapter 2.

These materials do not include many regulations pertaining to the extension of consumer credit. Consumer credit extensions are subject to substantial regulation, including the disclosures required by the Truth in Lending Act, the antidiscrimination rules imposed by the Equal Credit Opportunity Act, and the interest limitations imposed by some state usury laws. The Truth in Lending Act's disclosure requirements are sufficiently detailed to preclude coverage in a survey debtor-creditor course. The study of regulation of consumer credit obligations is left to contracts courses or to other courses that emphasize consumer protection laws.

A. The Fair Credit Reporting Act

UNITED STATES PRIVACY PROTECTION STUDY COMMISSION, PERSONAL PRIVACY IN AN INFORMATIONAL SOCIETY 55–63, 66–67, 70–71 (1977)

CREDIT BUREAUS: THE GATEKEEPERS

A credit bureau is essentially a clearinghouse for information supplied by credit grantors and collection agencies, and culled by the bureau itself from public records. Although there have been credit bureaus since the late 19th century, the advent of open-end credit coupled with new applications of computers and telecommunications has increased their importance both to the credit grantor and to the consumer.

A credit bureau satisfies one of the credit grantor's basic needs: a centralized source of information about an applicant's ability and willingness to pay. In recent years, automation has enabled some credit bureaus to monitor an individual's performance in a variety of credit relationships, thereby fulfilling another of the credit grantor's needs: to be on the alert for changes in an individual's financial stituation which might affect his ability to meet obligations already incurred.

There are approximately 2,000 credit bureaus in operation today. Although most are small local monopolies serving communities of 20,000 or fewer households, computerization has allowed a few to operate virtually nationwide. The five largest—TRW Credit Data, TransUnion, Credit Bureau, Inc., Chilton Corporation, and Credit Bureau of Greater Houston—together maintain more than 150 million individual credit records. Moreover, because the large nationwide (and regional) bureaus often compete within the same geographic area, a current record on a great many Americans is maintained by more than one bureau.

Except for TRW Credit Data's limitations on the types of public-record information it reports, there is consensus within the industry as to the categories of information on an individual a bureau should maintain and report. These include: *identifying information*, usually the individual's full name, Social Security number, address, telephone number, and spouse's name; *financial status and employment information*, including income, spouse's income, place, position, and tenure of employment, other sources of income, duration, and income in former employment; *credit history*, including types of credit previously obtained, names of previous credit grantors, extent of previous credit, and complete payment history; *existing lines of credit*, including payment habits and all outstanding obligations; *public-record information*, including pertinent newspaper clippings, arrest and conviction records, bankruptcies, tax liens and law suits; and finally *a listing of bureau subscribers that have previously asked for a credit report on the individual.*

Although credit grantors are a credit bureau's principal subscribers, and regulation of the industry is mainly predicated on credit grantors' need to exchange information, other important bureau clients include other credit bureaus, collection agencies, inspection bureaus, insurance companies, employers, landlords, and law enforcement agencies. In other words, a credit bureau report will be available to subscribers with whom the individual has no credit relationship, although it cannot be assumed that the individual himself knows that.

Credit reports are the principal revenue producer for most credit bureaus, but the modern bureau also provides a number of other services. Most have at least a debt collection division. Some automated bureaus "pre-screen" mailing lists to be used in targeted marketing campaigns. Some of the larger automated bureaus offer an account-monitoring service which automatically warns a subscriber if activity in an individual's file indicates that his credit worthiness ought to be reexamined. An unusual payment pattern, charging the limit on several credit cards, and divorce are the kinds of activity that trigger a warning. Finally, some credit bureaus have developed check authorization and medical billing services.

Several factors account for these changes in the credit-reporting industry. Central to the explosive growth of the automated bureaus has been the growth of consumer credit itself, most notably in automobile financing and in the variety of open-end credit plans developed by retailers, by credit-card companies, and, most recently, by commercial banks.

Changes in credit-granting methods bring new forms of credit reporting. The spread of open-end credit redefines the credit risk, which must now be measured by the total amount of credit available to an individual rather than by the amount of debt he has already incurred. As a result, credit grantors are beginning to rely on credit bureaus not only for information to use in making the initial decision to grant or deny credit, but also as monitors of the successful applicant's performance across a variety of credit relationships.

Once credit grantors began to computerize their records, credit bureaus had to follow suit, and a bureau with the capacity to receive and report credit information in computerized form also acquired the capacity to serve multiple markets. This change introduced competition to an industry previously composed of local monopolies. Many local bureaus with manual record keeping and limited geographic coverage have been forced out of business or into cooperative arrangements with other bureaus.

Much of this change has occurred since passage of the Fair Credit Reporting Act which has had its own, independent impact on the industry. Most importantly, the Act encourages specialization. The cost of complying with the Act's requirements regarding investigative reports has forced most of the bureaus that previously performed both credit-reporting and investigative functions to choose one area or the other. As a consequence, the proportion of investigative reports that credit bureaus prepare for employers, for example, has markedly decreased. Finally, the growing percentage of people who abuse credit or try to defraud the credit system influences the kind of services credit bureaus provide. . . .

THE OPERATIONS OF A CREDIT BUREAU

The reach of the credit-reporting industry is illustrated by its trade association's classification of contributors to credit bureau files. It includes: automobile dealers; banks; clothing, department, and variety stores; finance agencies; grocery and home furnishings dealers; insurers; jewelry and camera stores; contractors; lumber, building materials, and hardware suppliers; medical-care providers; national credit-card companies and airlines; oil companies (credit-card divisions); personal services other than medical; mail-order houses; real estate agents; hotel keepers; sporting goods and farm and garden supply dealers; utilities; fuel distributors; government agencies (e.g., the Federal Housing Administration and the Veterans Administration); wholesalers; advertisers; and collection agencies.

CREATING AND MAINTAINING CREDIT BUREAU FILES

When a person applies for credit for the first time, it is unlikely that any credit bureau has a file on him. The credit bureau, however, promptly uses the information given the credit grantor on the individual's application to establish one, or if one already exists, to update it.

For a credit bureau to create its files and keep them current, it must maintain continuing contact with its sources of information. It needs the information credit grantors provide about each of their active accounts, both in routine reports and in the specialized reports described earlier. Its contacts also include other credit grantors; other credit bureaus; employers, landlords, and references listed on the individual's credit application; and often public records and collection agencies.

Legal records, particularly ones pertaining to suits and judgments, bankruptcies, arrests and convictions, divorces, and property transactions, are the most significant public-record sources for a credit bureau's files. Interested parties, such as a credit grantor engaged in a suit, may supply public-record information, and some credit bureaus use public-record reporting services. Newspapers are also sources of public-record information for credit bureaus.

The Fair Credit Reporting Act gives an individual the right to find out the nature and substance of what a credit bureau's file on him contains. Some bureaus interview those who inquire about the contents of their records as a way of developing new information and as a check on information already on file.

Reports from collection agencies pertaining to debts that have been placed for collection are another means of updating a credit file. Because most collection agencies are owned by credit bureaus, and because the fact of having an account placed for collection has great significance for an individual's credit record, this updating procedure is the way credit bureaus often learn about accounts placed for collection by doctors and other collection agency clients who do not routinely disclose information to credit bureaus. . . .

QUALITY CONTROLS

No description can do justice to the dynamic interchange of information that credit reporting represents. Nor can it convey the magnitude of operational problems the bureaus have had to face in recent years. Correctly identifying an individual is chief among the problems that the automated bureaus have had to address. With information from hundreds of sources on literally millions of individuals being compiled and collated in one place, identification methods, some of which partially rely on the Social Security number, must be improved over methods that are adequate in smaller scale operations. Proper matching of information in existing files with information coming from outside sources is especially important, and special efforts have been made to assure it.

Matching reports with inquiries has also been a problem for the large automated bureaus. In the early days of automation, one automated bureau tried to solve it by reporting information on more than one individual when more than one of its files could meet the inquiry's specifications. Recently, some automated credit bureaus have developed sophisticated systems for making sure that inquiries and files are correctly matched. The Commission was not able to determine whether all large credit bureaus have been equally successful in coping with this common problem. One thing that does seem clear is that credit bureaus find the Social Security number a helpful tool for verifying identity.

The Fair Credit Reporting Act requires credit bureaus to have "reasonable procedures" to assure the accuracy of the information they report to their subscribers. The updating procedures described in the preceding section, together with special precautions to assure the accuracy of public-record information, are considered by credit bureaus to constitute "reasonable procedures." The timeliness of information in bureau reports is defined by the Act's statutory standards for obsolete information.

Due to FCRA requirements, space limitations, and rapid decay in the value of certain credit information, credit bureaus must also regularly purge their files. Except for bankruptcies, all "adverse" information more than seven years old is usually purged. While the FCRA only limits the *reporting* of such information, prudent business practice dictates purging it to avoid the cost of storing and segregating it, and to prevent inadvertent reporting of it for which the credit bureau would be liable. One advantage of computerizing credit records is that information can be purged automatically, efficiently, and continuously according to programmed criteria.

The FCRA has promoted completeness of records by giving an individual the right to file an explanatory notice of dispute with a credit bureau when he questions the accuracy of information in its files. Nonetheless, not all credit bureaus include the individual's statement in a credit report. Some simply indicate that a statement of dispute has been filed and that the credit grantor may inquire further if it so desires. The relevance of information in credit reports is determined by the subscribing organizations. Thus, primarily for economic reasons, credit bureaus try to report only information that is both necessary and relevant to the decisions in which their reports are used.

. . .

Uses and Disclosures of the Credit-Reporting File

A credit grantor may ask a credit bureau for a full credit report, for a report of only the information currently held by the bureau, or for a report covering only some specific aspect such as a single credit reference, employment and credit experiences, credit experiences only, or nothing more than previous residential address. In addition, insurance companies and their inspection bureaus may want credit reports for a variety of purposes. They may use a report to confirm the information on an insurance application, or for clues as to an individual's place of employment or previous address. An insurer may also want the substantial information about an individual's current financial situation a credit report provides in order to avoid "overinsuring" him. For inspection bureaus, credit reports are an important source of public-record information which inspection bureaus need but do not regularly compile.

Employers are a third major category of credit report users. In addition to reporting employment history information, an employer may ask a credit bureau to find out such information as the individual's reason for leaving a previous employer and whether the previous employer would rehire him. Employers often ask credit bureaus for information pertaining to an individual's education, including grades and class rank.

Collection agencies are still another major category of credit report users. The FCRA permits them to use a credit report in reviewing or collecting an amount owed on an account. [15 U.S.C. 1681b(3)(A)] A credit report can give a collection agency a great deal of helpful information, such as the debtor's address, place and type of employment, income level, and total outstanding debt. Because notifying employers is a common practice in the collection business, knowing where an individual currently works is especially helpful.

Government agencies are a special subset of credit-bureau subscribers. The FCRA permits government access to credit bureau files for any purpose, including law enforcement, where there is a court order or the information requested is identifying information limited to an individual's name, current and former addresses, and current and former places of employment. Government agencies, however, can still purchase reports like anyone else if they want them for credit or employment-related purposes, or to determine eligibility for certain licenses and benefits. Such access is specifically provided for in the "permissible purposes" section of the FCRA. Federal agencies falling within this last category include the Federal Housing Administration, the Veterans Administration, the Federal Bureau of Investigation, the Civil Service Commission, and the Defense Investigative Service. . . .

Control Over the Collection of Information

. . .

From the Commission's point of view, there are a number of arguments for further government regulation of the collection of personal information by credit grantors. First, an applicant for credit is not well informed about the scope of the inquiry to which he will be subjected. Although most credit application forms state that the credit grantor will verify the information provided in the application, they do not identify which institutions and people will be asked for verification or what additional information will be sought.

Second, and perhaps more important, the more an individual needs credit, the harder it is to withhold any information the creditor may ask for, no matter how irrelevant. With the growing need for credit, the applicant usually worries only about getting it. Later, when he can turn his attention to the import of certain questions, the application process has already been completed.

CONTROL OVER THE CONTENT OF RECORDS

. . .

A serious deficiency of the FCRA is its failure to assure the correction of adverse information erroneously disclosed by a credit grantor to a credit bureau. The situation is even worse with respect to credit cards, where the negative consequences of reporting erroneous adverse information to an independent authorization service can be even more certain than when such information is reported to credit bureaus. Representatives of independent authorization services told the Commission that they and their clients comply with the Fair Credit Reporting Act as far as possible. What this means in practice is that if an individual's credit card is declined at an airport, for example, he will be given the name of the authorization service and left to deal with it directly as best he can. If the authorization service was indeed acting on the basis of erroneous information, the individual will have to suffer until he can get the error corrected.

This example highlights an important point. *As information in systems is used more and more to take preemptive action against individuals, institutional record-keeping policies and practices must become preventive rather than curative.* Emerging information system capabilities and uses are making irrelevant the FCRA approach of rectifying errors made on the basis of inaccurate information *after* the "adverse decision" has been made. . . .

1. Scope of the FCRA

RASOR v. RETAIL CREDIT CO.

Supreme Court of Washington, 1976.
87 Wn.2d 516, 554 P.2d 1041.

UTTER, ASSOCIATE JUSTICE.

This court accepted certification by the Court of Appeals to review a jury verdict and judgment in favor of plaintiff Rasor in her suit alleging violations of the Fair Credit Reporting Act, 15 U.S.C. § 1681 *et seq.* (1970), by defendant Retail Credit Company. Defendant's assignments of error raise questions involving the scope of the act and the elements of damages recoverable under the act.   In support of other assignments of error, defendant argues that the trial court erred in certain of its rulings on the admissibility of evidence and in certain of its instructions to the jury.   Defendant also asserts that alleged misconduct by the jury and by plaintiff's counsel require reversal.   We find no error and affirm the judgment entered below.

At the time of trial, respondent Rasor was a 53-year-old resident of Sandpoint, Idaho, a community of approximately 5,000 persons.   There she operated two businesses, including a motel.   In the fall of 1972, respondent applied for health insurance with Bankers Life & Casualty Company, with which she had other health insurance policies.   The prospective insurer requested appellant Retail Credit Company to prepare a consumer credit report on respondent.   On November 7, 1972, a field representative employed in appellant's Spokane, Washington office, traveled to Sandpoint to conduct an investigation of respondent and ten other persons.   Appellant's employee made the 11 investigations in 4 hours or less one afternoon and spoke with a total of three persons, two partners in a service station and the manager of another service station, in the preparation of his report on respondent.   Based on information from these sources, appellant's report, prepared on November 8, stated in part, "[respondent] has had a reputation of living with more than one man out of wedlock in the past" and "[h]er reputation has suffered because of out of wedlock living arrangements in the recent past."   The document also commented on respondent's drinking habits and concluded this "[i]nformation was carefully confirmed by several long-time residents, in this area, who are businessmen and neighbors."   Although identified on its face as a "HEALTH REPORT", the report contained only two items dealing directly with respondent's health.   The questions "Do you learn of any illness, operation, or injury, past or present?" and "Did you learn of any member of applicant's family (blood relation) having had heart trouble, cancer, diabetes, tuberculosis or mental trouble?" were both answered "No."

On November 14, respondent applied for a Small Business Administration loan to complete the addition of units to her motel.   Approval of the loan was conditioned upon the acquisition of life insurance by respondent to serve as security for the loan.   Accordingly, respondent applied through a local agent for a policy from Guardian Life Insurance Company.   The local insurance agent gave written notice to respondent that "a routine report may be obtained which will provide applicable information concerning character, general reputation, personal characteristics and mode of living", see § 1681d, and the prospective insurer requested from appellant an investigative report on respondent.   Appellant made no new investigation of respondent and mailed a copy of the November 8 report obtained for health insurance purposes to the insurance company.   Following receipt of the report, Guardian Life declined to issue a policy to respondent "due to extensive criticism from inspection which must remain confidential."

After notification from Guardian Life that she could inquire about the report which influenced its decision at appellant's Spokane office, see § 1681m(a), respondent traveled to Spokane on December 20, 1972. She was not allowed to read the report but was informed of its contents, see § 1681g(a), which she found "shocking." With permission from respondent, appellant's employee informed respondent's insurance agent of the substance of the report. The agent then applied for the insurance required to obtain the Small Business Administration loan from two other insurers who offered to issue a policy, but only at a higher premium rate.

On January 9, 1973, respondent made a second trip to appellant's Spokane office and there stated several specific objections to information contained in the November 8 report. As a result, on January 11, an employee of appellant performed a reinvestigation of respondent, see § 1681i(a), contacting ten residents of Sandpoint during the course of an almost day-long inquiry. A second report, based on the reinvestigation stated in part:

> Your applicant has been married and divorced three times and is presently divorced. She has a boyfriend and stated that they each have their own homes and businesses and do not live together, although she admitted he stays overnight occasionally if he is too tired to go home. Sources state that both maintain their own living quarters but are known to stay with each other overnight on an occasional basis. There is no current criticism of this living arrangement.

The new report was sent to the three insurers which had received the November 8 report, with notice that the second report "supplant[s] any previous information we have reported," see § 1681i(d). On February 26, Guardian Life notified the local agent that respondent's case was being reopened in light of the new report. In April 1973, respondent received the policy requested but at an additional premium, calculated by the local agent to be $16.66 per $1,000 of coverage.

Respondent commenced this suit in March 1973 in Superior Court. *See* 15 U.S.C. § 1681p; Ruth v. Westinghouse Credit Co., 373 F.Supp. 468, 469 (W.D.Okl.1974). After 5 days of trial, the court granted appellant's motion to strike respondent's claims for invasion of privacy and libel. The court instructed the jury that if it found the first credit report prepared on November 8 substantially true, the verdict should be for appellant. Alternately, if the jury found the report substantially false, the verdict should be for appellant if it had followed "reasonable procedures" to assure compliance with the Fair Credit Reporting Act. A verdict in favor of respondent for $5,000 was returned.

I

. . .

The threshold question presented is the scope of the Fair Credit Reporting Act. There is no dispute that appellant is a "consumer reporting agency" to which the act applies. See 15 U.S.C. § 1681a(f) (1970); Hoke v. Retail Credit Corporation, 521 F.2d 1079, 1081 (4th Cir. 1975). However, appellant contends that the November 8 report was not a "consumer report" within the meaning of § 1681a(d) because respondent learned of the inaccurate report only when her application for business-related insurance was denied. In view of the clear language of the statute, decisions applying this provision, and administrative interpretation under the act, we conclude that the protections of the act are fully applicable to the November 8 investigatory report.

A "consumer report" is defined as follows:

> any written, oral, or other communication of any information by a consumer reporting agency . . . which is *used or expected to be used or collected in whole or in part* for the purpose of serving as a factor in establishing the consumer's eligibility for (1) credit or insurance to be used primarily for personal, family, or household purposes . . .

(Italics ours.) 15 U.S.C. § 1681a(d) (1970). . . .   The November 8 report prepared by appellant contained information "used . . . expected to be used [and] collected" for the purpose of establishing respondent's eligibility for "insurance to be used primarily for personal . . . purposes." That report was prepared in connection with respondent's application for health insurance. It was not then associated with any business purpose of respondent. Appellant conducted no new investigation in connection with respondent's application for life insurance needed to obtain the Small Business Administration loan, but simply submitted the November 8 report.

This conclusion finds support in several federal cases giving a broad interpretation to the statutory term. In Belshaw v. Credit Bureau of Prescott, 392 F.Supp. 1356, 1359–60 (D.Ariz.1975), the court held that " 'consumer report' must be interpreted to mean any report made by a credit reporting agency of information *that could be used* for one of the purposes enumerated in § 1681a."

> The Act cannot be interpreted as applicable to the activities of credit reporting agencies only when the consumer applies for credit, insurance, or employment, leaving them otherwise free to continue the very practices the Act was designed to prohibit. The Act would afford little protection for the privacy of a consumer if it only regulated credit reporting agencies in the area of their legitimate business activities but left them free to continue their clandestine activities in other areas.

Belshaw v. Credit Bureau of Prescott, supra at 1359. . . .

In addition, administrative interpretation of the term "consumer report" makes it clear that the character of such a report may not be changed by its subsequent use for business purposes. The Federal Trade Commission, charged with enforcement of the Fair Credit Reporting Act, § 1681s, has given the following guidance with respect to this matter:

> *Question*: Is a report on an individual obtained in connection with the extension of BUSINESS CREDIT or writing of business insurance a "consumer report"?

> *Answer*: No. . . . if a report is obtained on an individual for the purpose of determining his eligibility for business credit or insurance, it is not a "consumer report". However, when the information contained in the report was *originally collected in whole or in part for consumer purposes, it is a consumer report* and it may not be subsequently furnished in a business credit or business insurance report.

(Italics ours.) F.T.C., Compliance with the Fair Credit Reporting Act (2d ed. May 7, 1973), 5 CCH Consumer Credit Guide ¶ 11,314, at 59,815.

> A business credit or business insurance report on an individual would be exempt from the Act provided that the information contained in the report was specifically collected for that purpose. *However, if the information was originally collected for consumer purposes and then was subsequently used in a business credit or business insurance report, then such a report would become a consumer report as defined in the Act.*

> We make this distinction because certain large consumer reporting agencies have a substantial quantity of information on individuals which was originally collected for consumer purposes. Congress in passing the legislation did not intend for this information to be used in business reports without being subject to the protective provisions of the Act.

(Italics ours.) [1969–1973 Transfer Binder] CCH Consumer Credit Guide ¶ 99,424, at 89,384–85. (Excerpt from FTC Informal Staff Opinion Letter of May 19, 1971, by Joseph Martin, Jr., General Counsel and Congressional Liaison Officer.) . . .

II

Appellant argues the trial court erred in instructing the jury with respect to damages allowable under the Fair Credit Reporting Act. The pertinent instruction stated in part:

> These damages are such as afford fair and reasonable compensation to the plaintiff for the actual injury which the plaintiff has sustained to her general reputation and good name in the community where known, and for any injury which she has sustained by way of injuries to her feelings or to her credit standing, or any loss of income naturally resulting from such statements published by the defendant.

> . . .

> In determining to what extent a wom[a]n's reputation may have been injured by alleged violation of the act, you must first determine

from the evidence what the reputation of the plaintiff was, as to the trait of character affected by such statement complained of, before the statement was made, and then determine to what extent such reputation was injured.

. . . In assessing the plaintiff's damages, you will take into consideration the mental suffering, if any, produced by such violation of the act.

You may further make such allowance for loss of credit standing or financial loss, if any, as the evidence establishes to a reasonable certainty was sustained by the plaintiff as a natural consequence of the alleged violation of the act.

In essence, appellant contends that damages recoverable under the act are limited to out-of-pocket losses and do not include harm to reputation, injury to feelings, or mental suffering.

Upon a showing of negligent noncompliance with its requirements, alleged by respondent here, see §§ 1681o, 1681e(b), the act provides for the recovery of "an amount equal to . . . any actual damages sustained by the consumer as a result of the failure" of the reporting agency to comply.[2] 15 U.S.C. § 1681o (1970); see 15 U.S.C. § 1681n (1970). The legislative history of the act contains no indication of the scope of the term "actual damages." . . .

Appellant argues that the term "actual damages" was chosen by Congress as part of a formula to limit the liability of credit reporting agencies to damages less than those available under common law libel rules. It is true that the Fair Credit Reporting Act embodies some limitation on liability, but it does not restrict a consumer's recovery as severely as appellant contends. The act precludes consumer actions "in the nature of defamation" based on information disclosed under the act "except as to false information furnished with malice or willful intent to injure such consumer." 15 U.S.C. § 1681h(e) (1970). This provision suggests no more than that Congress intended to restrict the availability of defamation actions and the recovery of defamation damages. However, the trial court's instruction in this case did not contravene the letter or spirit of § 1681h(e) since it was *not* an instruction on libel damages. The striking characteristic of common law libel damages is not that recovery is allowed for injury to reputation but that such injury is often *presumed*. As stated by the United States Supreme Court in Gertz v. Robert Welch, Inc., 418 U.S. 323, 349, 94 S.Ct. 2997, 41 L.Ed.2d 789 (1974):

The common law of defamation is an oddity of tort law, for it allows recovery of purportedly compensatory damages without evidence of actual loss. Under the traditional rules pertaining to

2. We note the court in Ackerley v. Credit Bureau of Sheridan, Inc., 385 F.Supp. 658, 661 (D.Wyo.1974), stated "actual damage is not required in an action to enforce any liability under the [Fair Credit Reporting] Act. [Section 1681n] does not speak in terms of requiring actual damages; rather, it refers to actual damages as only one portion of any award or relief that might be granted."

actions for libel, the existence of injury is presumed from the fact of publication. Juries may award substantial sums as compensation for supposed damage to reputation without any proof that such harm actually occurred.

The trial court's instruction in the present case specifically referred to compensation only for "actual injury," did not suggest that harm was presumed to flow from appellant's acts, and thus did not misapply the "actual damages" language of § 1681*o* in this respect.

The trial court's instruction on damages did state, "[t]he reputation of the plaintiff is presumed to have been good at the time any alleged violation of the act occurred, until the contrary has been established by the evidence." However, this statement does not refer to presumed *injury*, that element of recovery which § 1681h(e) was designed to eliminate in actions under the statute. It has reference only to a condition against which injury to reputation may be measured. This portion of the instruction, then, is also consistent with the act.

Moreover, the limitation of libel recovery embodied in § 1681h(e) does not suggest that "actual damages" under the Fair Credit Reporting Act are limited to out-of-pocket losses. We agree with the reasoning of Justice Tobriner in Weaver v. Bank of America Nat'l Trust & Savings Ass'n, 59 Cal.2d 428, 30 Cal.Rptr. 4, 380 P.2d 644 (1963), where the court construed a statute restricting a drawer's recovery following wrongful dishonor by a bank to "actual damages." After reviewing the history of the statute, the court stated, at page 437, 30 Cal.Rptr. at page 10, 380 P.2d at page 650, "[a]ssuming the purpose of the statute to be the repeal of the common-law presumption of damages, such purpose would not be thwarted by recognition of compensatory damages for actual loss of reputation and impairment of health." See also Levy v. Fleischner, Mayer & Co., 12 Wash. 15, 17–18, 40 P. 384 (1895). Similarly, the intent of Congress in framing the Fair Credit Reporting Act was simply to limit recovery for presumed injury to instances of "malice and willful intent" *and* to allow a fully compensatory award for actual injury in other cases of noncompliance with the act. The two objectives are compatible. The structure of the statute in no way suggests an intent to limit recovery to pecuniary or out-of-pocket losses. A contrary conclusion would diminish much of the effectiveness of this remedial legislation.

In reference to the type of harm suffered, the term "actual damages" has a generally accepted legal meaning. Although it declined to define "actual injury," the United States Supreme Court recently noted the variety of harm which may result when damage is actually sustained.

Suffice it to say that actual injury is not limited to out-of-pocket loss. Indeed, the *more customary types of actual harm* inflicted by defamatory falsehood *include impairment of reputation and standing in the community, personal humiliation, and mental anguish and suffering.* Of course, juries must be limited by appropriate instructions, and all awards must be supported by competent evidence concerning the injury, although there need be no evidence which assigns an actual dollar value to the injury.

Gertz v. Robert Welch, Inc., supra, 418 U.S. at 350, 94 S.Ct. at 3012. It is important to note that although *Gertz* was a defamation action, it is clear that the court's language is not limited to such cases. There is, therefore, no conflict with the restriction on libel actions in § 1681e(h). The statement quoted above describes a limitation on state remedies, *in the form of the elimination of presumed damages*, where knowledge of falsity or reckless disregard for truth was absent. The broad applicability of the language was suggested by the Supreme Court itself when, referring to "actual injury," it noted that "trial courts have wide experience in framing appropriate jury instructions in tort actions." Gertz v. Robert Welch, Inc., supra 418 U.S. at 350, 94 S.Ct. at 3012. Violations of the Fair Credit Reporting Act have been characterized as having a "tortious nature." Ackerley v. Credit Bureau of Sheridan, Inc., 385 F.Supp. 658, 661 (D.Wyo.1974). The court's language is merely descriptive of the type of actual damage likely to flow from the dissemination of false information about a person, as was alleged in the present case. . . . For these reasons, we hold that "actual damages" under the Fair Credit Reporting Act are not limited to out-of-pocket losses, but encompass all the elements of compensatory awards generally, including those stated in the trial court's instruction in the present case. . . .

Notes & Questions

1. *Credit Reports at Common Law.* As *Rasor* suggests, federal law now plays a substantial role in regulating credit reports about consumers. Consider the legal status of credit reports in the absence of legislation. For example, assume that a credit report states that a person is of questionable moral character. If the person believes the statement to be untrue, would the person have a cause of action against the credit reporting agency? Suppose the person concedes that he is of questionable moral character. Would a tort action nevertheless be possible? Does the FCRA eliminate remedies that might be available to persons aggrieved by credit reports in the absence of legislation?

2. *Business vs. Consumer Reports.* Consider the FTC's statement that, "Congress in passing the legislation did not intend for this information to be used in business reports without being subject to the protective provisions of the Act." Why might Congress not have protected business credit reports to the same extent that it protected consumer credit reports? Would some plausible bases for the distinction support a different result in *Rasor?*

3. *Legal Duty Breached.* There is much discussion in *Rasor* of the damages available in a FCRA case. But what legal duty imposed by the Act was breached? Does the Act impose liability for dissemination of false consumer credit information?

4. *Wrongful Purpose.* Suppose Retail Credit Company gathered credit information on unmarried cohabiting individuals not out of a desire to maintain credit files for later use but instead out of a desire to gather and disseminate information to embarrass such individuals. Would dissemination of the information to the local police violate the FCRA? Should such practices violate the Act?

5. *FTC Role.* Section 621 of the FCRA, 15 U.S.C.A. § 1681s, vests the Federal Trade Commission with authority to enforce the act with respect to consumer reporting agencies, and makes a violation of the FCRA a violation of § 5(a) of the Federal Trade Commission Act. The FTC has issued rules entitled Administration of Fair Credit Reporting Act [a] and Statements of General Policy or Interpretations Under the Fair Credit Reporting Act.[b] It also issues Informal Staff Opinion Letters and has produced a booklet, revised in 1977, entitled Compliance with the Fair Credit Reporting Act.[c]

Problems on the Scope of the FCRA

1. Consumer had car insurance from Insurance Company. Before renewing consumer's insurance, Company calls the state's Department of Motor Vehicles (DMV) and receives a report on Consumer which reveals a drunk driving arrest. (It is common for DMVs to sell information to insurance companies.) On the basis of the DMV report, Company doubles Consumer's premiums for the year. Does the FCRA impose any obligations upon the DMV or Insurance Company?

2. Merchant A wishes to check on Customer's credit and knows that Customer has bought on credit from Merchant B. May A call B to ask about his experience with Customer without being subject to the FCRA? See § 603(d)(A), 15 U.S.C.A. § 1681a(d)(A).

3. Smith operates the corner supermarket as a sole proprietorship. Smith needs money for the market and seeks a loan from Bank. Bank asks Dun & Bradstreet for a report on the business, and the report includes Smith's credit history. Does the FCRA cover the transaction?

4. Plaintiff is injured in an automobile accident and brings an action against the tortfeasor. To investigate the validity of plaintiff's claims of liability and damages, the tortfeasor's insurance company requests information from an investigative agency, including information normally found in a credit report. Is the request subject to the FCRA's disclosure requirements? See Houghton v. New Jersey Mfrs. Ins. Co., 795 F.2d 1144 (3d Cir.1986) (not an investigative consumer report since the request only concerned the genuineness of the injured party's personal claim).

a. 36 Fed.Reg. 9293 (May 22, 1971).

b. 38 Fed.Reg. 4945 (Feb. 23, 1973).

c. Issued by the Division of Credit Practices, Bureau of Consumer Protection.

2. Responsibilities of Users of Credit Reports

WOOD v. HOLIDAY INNS, INC.

United States Court of Appeals, Fifth Circuit, 1975.
508 F.2d 167.

LEWIS R. MORGAN, CIRCUIT JUDGE: . . .

I.

Glen Wood, an executive vice president of SAR Manufacturing Company, checked into the Holiday Inn facility at Phenix City, Alabama, during the late afternoon of Feburary 1, 1972. When Wood checked in, he tendered payment for his room by using his Gulf Oil Company credit card. An imprint was made of his card and it was returned to him as was the normal practice.

After Gulf issues a card it continues to evaluate a customer account and, if it concludes from available information that a customer cannot afford to pay, it cancels credit to that customer. In order to facilitate this process, Gulf furnishes to National Data Corporation a list of all credit cancellations. Under the system established by Gulf, Holiday Inns are authorized to contact National Data, which disperses undetailed credit information concerning Gulf credit cards upon inquiry by telephone from properly identified parties authorized to extend credit to Gulf card holders. The information is generally brief and consists of either an authorization or denial of credit.

Gulf maintained a file on Wood. In compiling its information Gulf had received a credit report on the plaintiff from a credit bureau in Tupelo, Mississippi. The report was incomplete in that it did not contain the plaintiff's annual income; in all other respects the credit report was favorable to the plaintiff.

The credit manager of Gulf testified that on January 17, 1972, sixteen days preceding the incident in question, he reviewed the credit file of Wood. Although the file was current at the time he reviewed it, he expressed concern about the increasing amounts which were being charged on the card in relation to Wood's monthly income and made the determination that Wood's card should be placed in the "derog" file. Apparently Wood had not informed Gulf that the credit card was used for business as well as personal expenses. Wood was not notified, but Gulf directed National Data to give the following reply to anyone seeking credit approval on Wood:

Pick up travel card. Do not extend further credit. Send card to billing office for reward.

Sometime during the early morning of February 2, 1972, Jessie Goynes, the "night auditor" of the Phenix City Holiday Inn, called National Data in Atlanta on a toll-free number provided by Gulf in order to confirm the plaintiff's credit card number and receive an authorization to extend credit on the basis of the card. He received a communication from National Data advising him: "Do not honor this sale. Pick up the credit card and send it in for reward."

Wood testified that he was awakened about 5:00 a.m. by Goynes who told Wood that he, Goynes, needed the credit card for the purpose of making another imprint, since the imprint at the time of the registration was indistinct. Goynes came to appellant's room and took his card for the avowed purpose of securing the imprint and with the promise to return it in a few minutes. After 30 minutes Wood became concerned because his card had not been returned and was fearful that someone had taken it under a scheme to fraudulently secure it. Wood then dressed and went to the front desk of the motel where he was told by Goynes that the card was "seized upon the authority of National Data" and that cash payment was required. Goynes refused to call Gulf Oil at appellant's request. Wood then paid in cash and left the motel. Upon returning home Wood called Gulf and explained that he used the card for business purposes. He complained that his account was current and his credit was immediately reinstated.

Goynes, however, stated that after getting the directive from National Data, he telephoned the plaintiff's room at 7:00 a.m., and advised him that he was unable to obtain credit authorization and requested plaintiff to surrender the card. Goynes said that Wood voluntarily complied.

At any rate, Wood's anger and frustration continued to build. Three days later, while he was relating the incident to a friend, he had a heart attack, precipitated apparently by the stress of the incidents surrounding the revocation of credit.

Wood sued the Gulf Oil Corporation, Holiday Inns, Inc., Interstate Inns, Inc. (the owner of the Phenix City Holiday Inn) and Jessie Goynes. Interstate and Goynes denied any negligence or wrongful conduct and asserted by way of cross-claim that they were acting under the direction of Gulf and were therefore entitled to indemnification by Gulf.

After trial, the jury returned a verdict in favor of Wood but apportioned damages in the amounts of $25,000 compensatory damages against Gulf, $25,000 punitive damages against Interstate and Goynes, and $10,000 punitive damages against Holiday Inns. The court then granted the motions of Gulf and Holiday Inns, Inc., for judgments notwithstanding the verdict and granted the motion of Interstate and Goynes for a new trial.

Wood appeals. Interstate and Goynes also appeal the district court's action in overturning the jury's verdict on the cross-claim in their favor through the granting of Gulf's motion for judgment notwithstanding the verdict. . . .

II.

. . .

Wood alleged that Gulf negligently failed to comply with the provisions of the Fair Credit Reporting Act as both a consumer reporting agency and a user of a consumer report. Gulf argues that it was not a consumer reporting agency as defined in 15 U.S.C. § 1681a(f), and the district court so held, apparently as a matter of law.

The Act defines a consumer reporting agency as:

[A]ny person which, for monetary fees, dues, or on a coopertaive nonprofit basis, regularly engages in whole or in part in the practice of assembling or evaluating consumer credit information or other information on consumers for the purpose of furnishing consumer reports to third parties . . . . 15 U.S.C. § 1681a(f).

Gulf vigorously asserts that it falls outside the purview of this statute because no third party was furnished a report. In essence, Gulf contends, and the district court held, that the credit in this case was to be extended only by Gulf, not by Interstate. Hence, while Gulf did terminate Wood's credit vis-a-vis Gulf, it did not make a report advising Interstate as to whether to extend its own credit.

Much of the confusion in this case stems from the multifaceted position of the Phenix City facility, the recipient of Gulf's communication. The Phenix City Holiday Inn accepted the Gulf credit card and was therefore Gulf's representative in facilitating the extension of Gulf's credit. But the Phenix City facility also honored a number of major credit cards, and, in fact, nothing prevented the Phenix City Inn from extending credit on its own account.

The communication by Gulf to the Phenix City Inn was made to a separate business entity. However, the credit to be extended was Gulf's, and the Phenix City facility was merely acting as Gulf's representative in extending the credit. Hence, the communication was not "for the purpose of furnishing consumer reports to third parties." It was merely directed from Gulf to its local representative, made for the purpose of protecting Gulf rather than for the purpose of influencing the Phenix City Inn's own credit decision.

Wood next maintained that Gulf is liable under 15 U.S.C. § 1681m(a) as a user of a credit report. This section provides:

Whenever credit or insurance for personal, family, or household purposes, or employment involving a consumer is denied or the charge for such credit or insurance is increased either wholly or partly because of information contained in a consumer report from a consumer reporting agency, the user of the consumer report shall so advise the consumer against whom such adverse action has been taken and supply the name and address of the consumer reporting agency making the report.

The district court held that there was no evidence that Wood was damaged by Gulf's failure to report the name and address of the reporting agency. Wood renews his argument on appeal, contending that if Gulf had informed him promptly of its decision to terminate his credit, the incident at the Holiday Inn would have been avoided.

Apparently, the only requirement placed upon a "user" of a credit report is the duty to disclose the name and address of the reporting agency when credit is denied. 15 U.S.C. § 1681m. There is no evidence that the actions of Goynes or the reaction of Wood would have been any different if Wood had been told at the time his credit card was withdrawn that Gulf held a favorable credit report from the Tupelo reporting agency.

We need not base our decision upon the timing of the notification, however, for there is no indication that Gulf relied upon this report in making its decision to revoke Wood's credit. Gulf certainly had a credit report in its possession, but there is uncontradicted testimony that this report played no part in Gulf's decision. Of course, the jury would normally be free to disregard the denials of a company holding a credit report that it used the report in evaluating a consumer.

Here, however, there was simply nothing in the consumer report which could have caused Gulf to terminate Wood's credit. Not only was all of the information contained in the report already in Gulf's possession, but the only inference that one could draw from the report was favorable to Wood. Indeed the condition which caused the termination of credit—Wood's monthly income in relation to the charges on his account—was in no way conveyed by the report. Hence, we feel that the district judge properly dismissed the cause of action based upon the "user" provision of the Fair Credit Reporting Act. . . .

[The court then discussed the defendants' liability for breach of the common law duty of the innkeeper to his guests and whether Goynes acted as the agent of the other defendants.]

Notes & Questions

1. *Gaps in the FCRA?* Does *Wood* suggest that there are important gaps in the protections afforded by the FCRA? Should the act cover authorizing entities such as National Data? Should the act (or some other law) require credit grantors to take greater precautions against unwarranted credit denials and card revocations?

2. *Denial for Lack of Information.* Plaintiff applied for an Exxon credit card. Exxon contacted a credit bureau which was unable to furnish sufficient information regarding plaintiff's credit standing. Exxon denied plaintiff's application without stating a reason for the denial. Exxon maintains a procedure whereby it furnishes specific reasons for denial of credit upon receipt of a request for such information. Has Exxon violated the FCRA? See Carroll v. Exxon Co., U.S.A., 434 F.Supp. 557 (E.D.La. 1977) (yes).

3. *Home Sellers and the FCRA.* Smith owns a house in California and has listed the house for sale with Sure Sale Realtors. Buyer makes an offer on the house which includes a proposal that Smith finance $30,000 of the purchase price. Sure Sale tells Smith that such mortgages are common and that Sure Sale will secure a credit report from TRW on Buyer to enable Smith to decide whether Buyer is creditworthy. Sure Sale obtains the report from TRW and forwards it to Smith. The report reveals several outstanding judgments against Buy-

er and, without telling Buyer why, Smith informs Buyer that he will reject Buyer's offer unless Buyer pays all cash or finds his own financing. Buyer refuses and the deal collapses. Have there been any violations of the FCRA?

4. *"Undercover" Information-Gathering.* Smith is a detective seeking to find out financial information about Jones in connection with a divorce case. Smith knows that Snoop Corp. has credit information files on millions of people. He calls his local Snoop office and manages to convince them that he is a merchant in need of information about Jones. Snoop reports that Jones is delinquent on his car payments. Should Smith be worried about FCRA? should Snoop?

3. Standard of Care Imposed Upon Credit Reporting Agencies

BRYANT v. TRW, INC.

United States Court of Appeals, Sixth Circuit, 1982.
689 F.2d 72.

GEORGE CLIFTON EDWARDS, JR., CHIEF JUDGE.

Defendant, a credit reporting agency, appeals from an adverse judgment based on a jury verdict of $8,000 in actual damages and an attorney's fee award of $13,705, which resulted from a suit prosecuted by plaintiff, an individual who was seeking credit for the purpose of a house. The verdict represented a finding that defendant had supplied inaccurate information to a mortgage company and had thereby caused the denial of plaintiff's home loan application. The home loan was eventually approved.

The credit reporting agency was TRW Inc., an Ohio corporation; the prospective mortgagor was an individual named Bennie E. Bryant; and the mortgage company was the Hammond Mortgage Corporation of Southfield, Michigan.

The central issue in this case—which has stirred considerable interest in the credit industry—is whether or not defendant violated section 607(b) of the Fair Credit Reporting Act (FCRA), 15 U.S.C. § 1681e(b), which reads:

> Whenever a consumer reporting agency prepares a consumer report it shall follow reasonable procedures to assure maximum possible accuracy of the information concerning the individual about whom the report relates.

Negligent noncompliance with any requirement of the FCRA gives rise to liability for "any actual damages" and "reasonable attorney's fees," FCRA § 617, 15 U.S.C. § 1681o; willful noncompliance, in addition, gives rise to liability for punitive damages, FCRA § 616, 15 U.S.C. § 1681n.

I

The dispute that resulted in this appeal began to form in August 1976, when plaintiff applied to the Hammond Mortgage Corporation for a federally-insured home loan under a program administered by the Veterans' Administration. At the request of Hammond, defendant prepared a "consumer report" on plaintiff. For the background and outline of the instant litigation, we rely on the opinion of the District Judge:

Beginning sometime in the early 1970's defendant, one of the largest consumer reporting agencies in Michigan, issued consumer reports on plaintiff. On a number of occasions these consumer reports were inaccurate and on a number of occasions plaintiff discussed in person with representatives of defendant his concerns and also went to his creditors, principally retail merchants, in an endeavor to straighten out information sent to defendant on his accounts.

In May of 1976 defendant issued a consumer report in the form of a mortgage report on plaintiff in connection with a mortgage application on a house purchase. This consumer report contained inaccurate information on plaintiff's account with a retail merchant. Plaintiff went to defendant and called its attention to the inaccuracy. The mortgage loan did not close for unrelated reasons.

In August, 1976, plaintiff again signed a mortgage loan application for a home purchase. On September 7, the mortgage company ordered a consumer report in the form of a mortgage report. On September 28, an employee of defendant called the mortgage company to advise that the mortgage report would contain four items of derogatory information on plaintiff. The mortgage company immediately advised plaintiff. Plaintiff the same day went to defendant's office and discussed in detail the four items. Three of these items did not appear in the May report even though at least one of these items related to events prior to May, 1976 and logically should have been part of the May report. Subsequent to September 28 the creditors involved advised defendant the information they previously furnished was erroneous.

At the September 28 personal meeting between plaintiff and a representative of defendant, a memorandum was placed in plaintiff's file which reads:

"9–28–76 Cus' wanted us to re-check Ford Mtr Credit.—showed 6 late charges on most recent clearing (read to mortg. company—file not typed yet). Recleared through adjuster ± FMC.—wanted it shown as pd. acc't.—Gone to Mabel. Told cus. I would review file before it was sent. Also gave him copy of Mgr. attention which is read to creditors. JJW."

The mortgage report was sent to the mortgage company on September 30 in its original form without any further attempt on defendant's part to verify the derogatory items.[3]

The mortgage loan was initially denied on the basis of the mortgage report. Subsequently, with a revision in the mortgage report and through plaintiff's personal efforts the mortgage loan closed.

Plaintiff testified as to the embarrassment, anxiety, humiliation and emotional stress he suffered as a consequence of his difficulties over the two reports. No out-of-pocket expenses or actual dollar losses were proven.

Bryant v. TRW, Inc., 487 F.Supp. 1234, 1346–37 (E.D.Mich.1980).

At the close of evidence, the District Judge read the following, and we think correct, instructions to the jury:

The Fair Credit Reporting Act required that TRW, Inc., when it prepared a consumer report on Bennie Bryant, follow reasonable procedures to assure maximum possible accuracy of the information concerning Mr. Bryant.

If you find that TRW, Inc. was negligent in following the requirements of the law, you should award Mr. Bryant the actual damages sustained by him because of such negligence.

If you find TRW, Inc. willfully failed to follow the requirements of the law, Mr. Bryant is entitled to his actual damages and you may also award punitive damages.

If you find TRW, Inc. followed reasonable procedures you should find for it.

App. 355–56.

The jury returned a verdict of $8,000 in actual damages; it awarded no punitive damages. The trial judge granted plaintiff's motion for attorney's fees in the amount of $13,705, which was calculated on the basis of an hourly rate.

Defendant filed a motion for judgment n.o.v. and an alternative motion for a new trial, arguing principally that section 607(b) of the FCRA does not give rise to liability when a consumer reporting agency, like defendant, accurately reports the information it receives from a

---

3. We do not entirely agree with the District Judge's conclusion in this paragraph and elsewhere in his opinion that, aside from whatever effort it made to check the Ford Motor Co. entry, defendant made no attempt between September 28 and September 30 to verify or recheck the derogatory information contained in the mortgage report. Bryant v. TRW, Inc., 487 F.Supp. 1234, 1237, 1239 (E.D.Mich.1980). The record reflects that the manager of defendant's consumer relations depart-

ment telephonically contacted at least two of the four creditors involved after the meeting of September 28 and before the report was issued. App. 328–29. The two creditors repeated the same information they had conveyed earlier, see id., and defendant, therefore, did not amend the report. But, in addition, the record shows that defendant's employee made no effort to confirm the accuracy of their representations, see id., which were later found by the jury to be inaccurate.

consumer's creditors. The motions were denied. Bryant v. TRW, Inc., 487 F.Supp. 1234 (E.D.Mich.1980).

II

The September 30 mortgage report, as noted by the District Judge in his factual summary, contained "four items of derogatory information on plaintiff." They were:

Ford Motor Credit	4–72 high $3700 auto reported 3–75 paid account, was 17 times 30 days late.
Hughes & Hatchers	open for over 10 years limit $700 high $174 balance $159 was 30 days delinquent is now current.
J.L. Hudsons-time pay	opened 3–75 limit & high $500 balance $285 $22.00 past due 30 days delinquent.
Grinnells	opened 3–76 high $231.16 24 @ $11.96 last paid 8–15–76 due for 7–22–76, as of 9–2–76.

App. 390.

A review of the testimony in this record indicates to us that in the instance of at least two of the four entries set out immediately above, Hudson's and Grinnell's, plaintiff presented evidence from which the jury could have found inaccuracies that contributed meaningfully to the October 26, 1976, denial of plaintiff's home loan application. . . .

III

The critical issue in this appeal, however, is whether or not the case should have been submitted to the jury at all. Defendant does not contest many of the inaccuracies. Its basic defense is that the inaccuracies were those of plaintiff's creditors and that, under section 607(b), all it had to do was report accurately whatever information the creditors furnished.

Thus, it appears to this court that the critical legal issue in this case is whether or not section 607(b) requires a consumer reporting agency to do more than correctly report the information supplied to it by creditors. Reviewing the language and legislative history of the statute, we answer this question affirmatively.

In this regard, section 607(b) provides:

Whenever a consumer reporting agency prepares a consumer report it shall follow reasonable procedures to assure maximum possible accuracy of the information concerning the individual about whom the report relates.

15 U.S.C. § 1681e(b).

Acceptance in full of the position urged on this court by defendant and amicus curiae Associated Credit Bureaus, Inc. would, we believe, serve essentially to repeal by judicial decree a statute that Congress adopted after much consideration in lengthy hearings. Congress chose to require consumer reporting agencies to "follow reasonable procedures to assure *maximum possible accuracy of the information* about whom the report relates."

Although the legislative history of section 607(b) is sketchy and compels neither acceptance nor rejection of defendant's position, two aspects of that history dealing with amendments to the original Senate bill insisted on by the House conferees support a broad reading of the duties imposed by the statute:

    (1)

Procedures to Insure Accuracy

The Senate bill required reporting agencies who prepared investigative reports to follow reasonable procedures to assure the maximum possible accuracy of such report. The House conferees felt that this requirement should be extended to all reporting agencies, whether they prepared investigative reports or conventional credit reports. The Senate conferees felt that this was a reasonable requirement and accepted the House amendment.

116 Cong.Rec. 35940 (1970) (remarks of Sen. Proxmire introducing the conference report).

Investigative consumer reports contain "information on a consumer's character, general reputation, personal characteristics, or mode of living," which is gathered through personal interviews. 15 U.S.C. § 1681a(e). These reports are generally used by employers in their hiring practices and by insurance companies and are put together with greater care than conventional credit reports because of the sensitive and subjective nature of the information involved and the manner in which the information is obtained. See generally Millstone v. O'Hanlon Reports, Inc., 383 F.Supp. 269, 275 (E.D.Mo.1974), aff'd, 528 F.2d 829 (8th Cir. 1976). We are persuaded that by extending to conventional credit reports the requirement of "reasonable procedures to assure maximum possible accuracy," Congress evinced its desire that agencies that assemble conventional credit reports be more than conduits of information and its belief that accurate credit information is as important as accurate personal information.

    (2)

Civil Liability For Negligent Noncompliance

The House amendment to section 617 [15 U.S.C. § 1681o], which was agreed to by the conferees, would establish liability for actual damages sustained as a result of ordinary negligence, instead of only as a result of gross negligence as provided in the Senate bill.

Conf.Rep. No. 1587, 91st Cong., 2d Sess., reprinted in 1970 U.S.Code Cong. & Ad.News 4411, 4416.

This tends to show, we believe, that Congress rejected the imposition of only a nominal standard of care on the credit reporting industry.

In sum, we hold that a consumer reporting agency does not *necessarily* comply with section 607(b) by simply reporting in an accurate manner the information it receives from creditors.

IV

Each case under this statute will vary on the facts, and each must be judged on its own merits. It is clear, as defendant contends, that liability does not flow automatically from the fact that a credit reporting agency, such as defendant, reports inaccurate information. Instead, liability flows from failure to follow "[(1)] *reasonable procedures* [(2)] to assure *maximum possible accuracy of the information* [(3)] *concerning the individual about whom the information relates.*" We agree with the Fifth Circuit and the District Judge that "[t]he standard of conduct by which the trier of fact must judge the adequacy of [consumer reporting] agency procedures is what a reasonably prudent person would do under the circumstances."

The salient facts with respect to the question whether defendant followed reasonable procedures before it issued the mortgage report on September 30 include (1) defendant's prior contact with plaintiff and, in particular, its familiarity with plaintiff's troubled credit history with Husdon's, which centered on two disputes arising from errors made by Hudson's, *see* App. 359–61, 375, and (2) the September 28 meeting between plaintiff and defendant's consumer relations manager, at which plaintiff fervently complained about three and perhaps all four of the four pieces of derogatory information on the tentative report furnished to the Hammond Mortgage Corporation. Absent these facts, we would have a quite different case. However, they exist and are relevant to this case, and the District Judge was correct in admitting them into evidence.

Defendant's effort to "assure maximum possible accuracy of the information" in the mortgage report comprised two phone calls, the record indicates. The calls, one to Hudson's, the other to Grinnell's, simply reconfirmed the information—inaccurate information it turns out—furnished earlier to defendant by the creditors concerned.

On the record of this case, we believe that defendant was required to do more under section 607(b). It would have taken little added effort immediately to advise the creditors of plaintiff's complaints and to request investigation and re-evaluation based on the most recent data. And it would have taken little added effort to ask Hudson's how they calculated that defendant was 30 days delinquent or to ask Grinnell's if any payments had been made after September 2. Although the inaccuracies were eventually corrected, the corrections were made after the rejection of plaintiff's home loan application, his consequent frustration, and the denigration of his name and creditworthiness.

In this record, we call attention to the language of one of the House sponsors of the FCRA.   On October 13, 1970, Representative Sullivan said concerning the Act:

It would be difficult to predict which of the many provisions of H.R. 15073 will turn out to be the most significant from a long-range standpoint;   all of the sections of H.R. 15073 have importance to some aspect of our economy and to the public interest.   But in an era of expanding consumer credit and proliferating techniques for managing or handling such extension of credit, and in view of the increasing importance to the individual of having access to insurance as well as the vital necessity of being able to find employment, I believe that the sections of this bill dealing with credit and personal data reporting will have the greatest overall impact.   *The reason I say that is that with the trend toward computerization of billings and the establishment of all sorts of computerized data banks, the individual is in great danger of having his life and character reduced to impersonal "blips" and key-punch holes in a stolid and unthinking machine which can literally ruin his reputation without cause, and make him unemployable or uninsurable, as well as deny him the opportunity to obtain a mortgage to buy a home.* We are not nearly as much concerned over the possible mistaken turn-down of a consumer for a luxury item as we are over the possible destruction of his good name without his knowledge and without reason.

The loss of a credit card can, of course, be expensive, but, as Shakespeare said, the loss of one's good name is beyond price and makes one poor indeed.   This bill's title VI deals with that problem.

116 Cong.Rec. 36570 (1970) (emphasis added).

We have no doubt from this record that plaintiff offered proofs from which the jury could properly have found that defendant's failure in timely fashion to use "reasonable procedures to assure maximum possible accuracy" occasioned damage to plaintiff's name and consequent anguish and humiliation.   . . .

Notes & Questions

1. *Passing on Tainted Information.*   In *Bryant,* much of the problem resulted from inaccurate information conveyed to a consumer reporting agency by credit grantors.   Should the credit granting merchants in *Bryant* be required to report to the credit bureau that they have reported inaccurate information?   Would a "reasonable procedure" be for TRW contractually to require credit grantors to report developments which lead them to believe that they have previously reported inaccurate information?   See Privacy Commission Report at 82.

2. *Anticipatory Gathering of Information.*   Assume that TRW does not wait for users to request information on a consumer but gathers credit information on consumers for future use.   When a user requests

a consumer report, TRW then furnishes its previously gathered information. Should TRW's obligations under the FCRA differ from those of a consumer reporting agency that awaits a specific request before gathering credit information on a consumer? Does the advance information gathering technique pose added risks of disseminating misleading or irrelevant information?

3. *Accurate But Incomplete Information.* Does *Bryant*'s result depend on a finding that inaccurate information was disseminated? In Pinner v. Schmidt, 805 F.2d 1258 (5th Cir.1986), Pinner was involved in a dispute with Sherwin–Williams. Pinner eventually sued Sherwin–Williams. The credit reporting agency added to its credit report on Pinner a notation of "litigation pending." There was no indication that Pinner was the plaintiff in the pending litigation. The court held that the FCRA's "maximum possible accuracy" standard could be violated by such incomplete information. Compare Austin v. Bankamerica Service Corp., 419 F.Supp. 730 (N.D.Ga.1974) (omitting information that deputy sheriff was sued in his official capacity in report of litigation did not violate the FCRA).

4. *State Laws.* For examples of state laws regulating consumer reporting agencies, see New York's Fair Credit Reporting Act, Gen. Bus.Law §§ 380 to 380–s, California's Consumer Credit Reporting Agencies Act, Cal.Civil Code §§ 1785.1 to 1785.35, and California's Investigative Consumer Reporting Agencies Act, Cal.Civil Code §§ 1786 to 1786.56.

See generally National Consumer Law Center, Fair Credit Reporting Act (1982, 1986 Supp.); 1 Debtor-Creditor Law Ch. 7 (T. Eisenberg ed.).

B. The Fair Debt Collection Practices Act

PUBLIC FINANCE CORP. v. DAVIS

Supreme Court of Illinois, 1977.
66 Ill.2d 85, 4 Ill.Dec. 652, 360 N.E.2d 765.

RYAN, JUSTICE.

In this case Luella Davis (Davis), the defendant and counterclaimant, seeks to recover from Public Finance Corporation (Public Finance), plaintiff and counterdefendant, under the allegations in her amended counterclaim for mental anguish and emotional distress allegedly caused by the agents of Public Finance in attempting to collect money which Davis owed. The circuit court of St. Clair County held that the amended counterclaim failed to state a cause of action. The appellate court affirmed. We granted leave to appeal.

From the pleadings it appears that Davis was indebted to Public Finance on a promissory note executed by her and secured by a security interest in her household goods. She made regular payments on the obligation until August 1, 1974. On February 24, 1975, Davis then being in default, Public Finance filed a complaint seeking judgment against her for the balance due on the note. Davis counterclaimed and, following the allowance of a motion to dismiss the counterclaim, filed an amended counterclaim which is in two counts, both counts seeking recovery on the theory of intentional infliction of severe emotional distress. The sole question to be decided is whether the amended counterclaim stated a cause of action. We find that it did not.

In Knierim v. Izzo (1961), 22 Ill.2d 73, 174 N.E.2d 157, this court recognized the intentional causing of severe emotional distress as a separate and additional tort which one author has been prompted to call a "new tort." (Prosser, Intentional Infliction of Mental Suffering: A New Tort, 37 Mich.L.Rev. 874 (1939).) Although this tort was not recognized in the 1934 Restatement of Torts, the 1948 supplement contained an amended section 46 recognizing the existence of a cause of action based on this theory. (Restatement of Torts sec. 46 (Supp.1948).) The reason for the change as partially stated in the supplement is: "The change in Section 46 is necessary in order to give an accurate Restatement of the present American law. There is a definite trend today in the United States to give an increasing amount of protection to the interest in freedom from emotional distress." Although the 1948 supplement contained the caveat that "[t]he [American Law] Institute expresses no opinion as to whether one who recklessly causes severe emotional distress to another is or is not liable for it," the Institute, in Restatement (Second) of Torts, section 46 (1965), recognizes the existence of a cause of action for severe emotional distress caused by intentional or reckless conduct. *Knierim,* which predated the second Restatement, by innuendo adopted the viewpoint of the 1948 supplement recognizing only a cause of action based on *intentional* conduct. Although recklessness has been rejected in one jurisdiction as a basis for recovery for severe emotional distress (see Alsteen v. Gehl (1963), 21 Wis.2d 349, 124 N.W.2d 312), we do not find the reason for that decision applicable in Illinois. We therefore will test the two counts of the amended counterclaim by the requirements of the cause of action as stated in section 46 of the second Restatement, the decisions of other jurisdictions recognizing the cause of action and by the authors on the subject.

The extensive comments and illustrations to section 46 are helpful in delineating the conduct which gives rise to this cause of action. First, the conduct must be extreme and outrageous. The liability clearly does not extend to mere insults, indignities, threats, annoyances, petty oppressions or trivialities. "It has not been enough that the defendant has acted with an intent which is tortious or even criminal, or that he has intended to inflict emotional distress, or even that his conduct has been characterized by 'malice,' or a degree of aggravation which would entitle the plaintiff to punitive damages for another tort. Liability has been found only where the conduct has been so outrageous in character, and so extreme in degree, as to go beyond all possible bounds of decency . . .." Restatement (Second) of Torts sec. 46, comment *d* (1965).

Second, infliction of emotional distress alone is not sufficient to give rise to a cause of action. The emotional distress must be *severe*. Although fright, horror, grief, shame, humiliation, worry, etc. may fall within the ambit of the term "emotional distress," these mental conditions alone are not actionable. "The law intervenes only where the distress inflicted is so severe that no reasonable man could be expected to endure it. The intensity and the duration of the distress are factors to be considered in determining its severity." Comment *j*. See, also Prosser, Law of Torts sec. 12, at 54 (4th ed. 1971).

Third, reckless conduct which will support a cause of action under the rules stated is conduct from which the actor knows severe emotional distress is certain or substantially certain to result. (Comment *i*.) Liability extends to situations in which there is a high degree of probability that severe emotional distress will follow and the actor goes ahead in conscious disregard of it. Prosser, Law of Torts 60 (4th ed. 1971).

Fourth, as it stated in comment *e*, the extreme and outrageous character of the conduct may arise from an abuse of a position or a relation with another which gives the actor actual or apparent authority over the other or power to affect his interests. This interpretation of the rule is applicable to collecting creditors and would apply to a creditor in its attempt to collect a lawful obligation.

Count I of the amended counterclaim alleges the conduct of Public Finance which Davis claims entitles her to recover. Stripped of the conclusions, it is charged that on or about September 1, 1974, Davis informed Public Finance she was no longer employed, was on public aid and did not have enough money to make regular payments on her obligations; that in order to collect the account Public Finance from September 1, 1974, to April 4, 1975, called Davis several times weekly, frequently more than once a day; that in order to collect the account agents of Public Finance went to Davis' home one or more times a week; that on October 15, 1974, when Davis' daughter was in the hospital, an agent of Public Finance, in order to collect the account, called the defendant at the hospital; that on that day Davis informed the agent of the severity of her daughter's condition, that she, herself, was sick and nervous and asked that Public Finance refrain from calling her at the hospital; that on the same day an agent of Public Finance again called Davis at the hospital; that after an employee of Public Finance induced Davis to write a check and promised that the check would not be processed, Public Finance phoned an acquaintance of Davis and informed her that Davis was writing bad checks; that in November 1974 an employee of Public Finance called at Davis' home and after being told that Davis had no money with which to make a payment, with Davis' permission, used her phone to call Public Finance and to describe and report the items of Davis' household goods; that on that day the employee "failed or refused" to leave Davis' home until her son entered the room.

Count II realleges the conduct of Public Finance alleged in count I and further alleges that Davis suffered from hypertension and a nervous condition; that she was particularly susceptible to emotional distress; that she had frequently informed agents of Public Finance of her condition and that Public Finance had notice that Davis was particularly susceptible to emotional distress.

The conduct alleged is not of such an extreme and outrageous nature as to constitute a basis for recovery under the theory alleged. Davis was legally obligated to Public Finance and was in default in making the payments. As stated in Restatement (Second) of Torts, section 46, comment *g*, in such a case the actor is not liable "where he has done no more than to insist upon his legal rights in a permissible way, even though he is well aware that such insistence is certain to cause emotional distress." A creditor must be given some latitude to pursue reasonable methods of collecting debts even though such methods may result in some inconvenience, embarrassment or annoyance to the debtor. The debtor is protected only from oppressive or outrageous conduct.

In cases wherein courts have permitted the action to be brought or have sustained recovery for severe emotional distress, the collecting tactics of the creditor have involved the use of abusive and vituperative language, shouting and railing at the debtor, repeated threats of arrest and ruination of credit, threats to appeal to the debtor's employer to endanger his employment and accusations of dishonesty. "[L]iability usually has rested on a prolonged course of hounding by a variety of extreme methods." Prosser, Law of Torts 57 (4th ed. 1971).

Returning to the allegations in count I we note that Davis alleges that the course of conduct pursued was in order to collect the account. This Public Finance had a right to do, as long as the methods employed were not outrageous. As to the numerous telephone calls, there is no allegation as to what was said by the person making the calls. The same is true of the allegations of the several visits to Davis' home and of the calls to Davis at the hospital. Davis has not alleged that the agents of Public Finance used abusive, threatening or profane language or that they conducted themselves other than in a permissible manner. There is no allegation concerning these calls or the visits to the house that can serve to characterize Public Finance's conduct as extreme or outrageous. The mere fact that a second call was made to Davis at the hospital after she had requested that they not call her there cannot be so considered, since there is no allegation as to what was said or even that the second call was for the purpose of collecting the past due obligation.

As to the visit of an employee of Public Finance to Davis' home and using her phone to call Public Finance and to inventory and describe her household goods, again we must consider that her obligation was past due and that it was secured by the household goods. Also the allegation that the employee of Public Finance "failed or refused" to leave until Davis' son entered the room contains only an innuendo and not an allegation of any threatening or coercive conduct which could be called outrageous.

We consider the most serious allegation to be the charge that Public Finance induced Davis to write a check for the amount owed with the assurance that the check would not be presented for payment and then subsequently phoned Davis' acquaintance and informed her that Davis was writing bad checks. This conduct was wrong and no doubt caused Davis considerable embarrassment and distress. However, this appears to be a single isolated act. In Lewis v. Physicians and Dentists Credit Bureau, Inc. (1947), 27 Wash.2d 267, 273, 177 P.2d 896, 899, the court stated that persons "who do not pay their bills cannot object to some publicity in connection with attempts to collect them; their tender sensibilities are protected only from 'undue or oppressive publicity.'" Also, in comment j to section 46 it is stated that the intensity and duration of the distress are factors to be considered in determining the severity of the emotional distress. We do not consider that the specific allegation of this single impermissible act consitutes extreme and outrageous conduct calculated to cause severe emotional distress.

There can be no doubt that the conduct of the employees of Public Finance disturbed Davis and possibly caused her emotional distress. The allegations demonstrate that the employees were persistent in their efforts to collect the past due obligation and possibly were persistent to the point of being annoying; however, with the possible exception noted, count I contains no allegation of extreme or excessive conduct. We must therefore hold that count I does not state a cause of action for severe emotional distress.

Even assuming, as we must under the allegations of count II, that Public Finance knew that Davis suffered from hypertension and was nervous the conduct alleged is not actionable. Knowledge that another is peculiarly susceptible to emotional distress may make a person's conduct actionable when it otherwise would not be. "The conduct may become heartless, flagrant, and outrageous when the actor proceeds in the face of such knowledge, where it would not be so if he did not know." (Restatement (Second) of Torts sec. 46, comment f.) However, comment f emphasizes that major outrage, even under such circumstances, is still essential to the tort. As stated above, the complaint contains no allegations of abusive or threatening language or conduct coercive in nature. Public Finance was attempting to collect a legal obligation from Davis in a permissible though persistent and possibly annoying manner.

For the reasons stated we hold that counts I and II of the amended counterclaim do not state a cause of action for either intentional or reckless infliction of severe emotional distress. The judgment of the appellate court is affirmed.

[A dissenting opinion is omitted.]

Notes & Questions

1. *Other Causes of Action?* Were there other causes of action in tort that might have been brought in *Davis?*

2. *Parties Covered by the FDCPA.* (a) Consumer purchases merchandise at a department store, fails to pay when the purchase price is due, and the store dispatches an employee to collect the debt. The employee engages in harassing behavior. Need the store or the employee worry about the FDCPA? See § 803(6), 15 U.S.C.A. § 1692a(6). Assume instead that the department store called its law firm. The law firm dispatches an associate who engages in similar behavior. Need the law firm worry about the FDCPA?

(b) Manufacturer sells goods to a department store for resale to the public. Department store fails to pay and manufacturer employs a debt collection agency to try to collect the debt. Need manufacturer or debt collection agency worry about the FDCPA?

3. *Inadvertent Disclosures.* On January 1, 1978, Joe Smith purchased a refrigerator from Sears and signed a promissory note in which he agreed to pay $50 on the first of each month for 12 months starting with February 1, 1978. Smith, an accountant, used the refrigerator in his office at home where he often discussed business with clients. On February 1, 1978, Sears sold the note to Credit Corporation at a 5% discount.

Smith encountered financial difficulty and failed to pay the $50 due on March 1. Credit Corp. asks the Offer-You-Cannot-Refuse Collection Corp. ("Collection"), a subsidiary of Credit Corp., to collect Smith's overdue debt. On April 1, Tom Jones, an employee of Collection, is given the Smith file. To locate Smith, Jones calls the Sears credit department, tells the person who answers the phone that he, Jones, works for Collection, and asks for Smith's address and telephone number. Jones then calls Smith on the telephone and asks when Smith thinks he will be able to pay. Smith says he is not sure but that Jones should call back in a week. The next day, Jones, eager for quick collection, decides to call Smith again. Jones consults with Collection's counsel about whether such a call is proper. Counsel advises that it is.

Jones places the call, thinks he hears Smith say, "hello," and states, "Smith, we want the money quickly." In fact, Jones had dialed incorrectly and was speaking to a stranger at a meeting of local businessmen and the stranger had a speaker phone turned on. After discovering his error, Jones called Smith and again requested payment.

Has Jones violated the Fair Debt Collection Practices Act and may he be held liable?

BAKER v. G.C. SERVICES CORP.

United States Court of Appeals, Ninth Circuit, 1982.
677 F.2d 775.

SKOPIL, CIRCUIT JUDGE:

Appellant G.C. Services Corp., a debt collection company, appeals from a district court judgment holding that appellant violated the Fair Debt Collection Practices Act, 15 U.S.C. § 1692, by falsely threatened legal action and by failing to inform the debtor that he could dispute a portion of the debt. We affirm.

I.

Appellee Ken Baker was indebted on credit card accounts to Shell Oil Co. and to Chevron U.S.A., Inc. Both accounts were assigned to appellant G.C. Services Corporation for collection. Appellant attempted to collect the amounts owned by Baker by sending three letters and by making several phone calls. One letter stated that:

"It is our policy to attempt to settle these matters out of court before making any decision whether to refer them to an attorney for collection . . . .. Unless we receive your check or money order, we will proceed with collection procedures."

The letter also stated that:

"Verification of this debt, a copy of judgment or the name and address of the original creditor, if different from the current creditor, will be provided if requested in writing within 30 days. Otherwise the debt will be assumed to be valid."

These letters were preprinted form letters regularly used by appellant to solicit payments. Appellant stipulated that its normal procedure for collection of debts of this type is only additional telephone or mail solicitations, and that any legal action would be taken only by the original creditor and not by appellant. The parties stipulated that:

"Defendant obtained the advice and assistance of counsel on the meaning of and compliance with the Fair Debt Collection Practices Act and the correctness of the contents of the [disputed letter]. Defendant's attorneys have, from time to time, met with the staff of the Federal Trade Commission to discuss compliance with the Act."

Baker filed suit for money damages, claiming violations of the Fair Debt Collection Practices Act, 15 U.S.C. § 1692 ("the Act"). Both parties filed cross-motions for summary judgment. The district court rejected most of Baker's claims, but held that appellant had violated the Act by (1) failing to inform Baker that he could dispute any portion of the debt, as well as the entire debt, in violation of 15 U.S.C. § 1692g(a)(3); and (2) by falsely threatening legal action which appellant did not in fact intend to take, in violation of 15 U.S.C. § 1692e(5). The court did not find that Baker had suffered any actual damage. The district court held that a successful plaintiff is entitled to recover statutory damages under the Act even absent proof of actual damages, and awarded Baker $100 in statutory damages as well as $800 in attorney fees.

II.

The issues on appeal are:

(1) Whether Baker, who admitted that he owed the full amount of the debt, had standing to sue under section 1692g of the Act;

(2) Whether the district court erred in holding that appellant had violated section 1692g of the Act, based upon the fact that appellant's notice did not advise the debtor that he could dispute any portion of the debt, as well as the entire debt;

(3) Whether the district court erred in holding that appellant had violated section 1692e of the Act, by threatening to take legal action that it did not intend to take;

(4) Whether the district court erred in rejecting appellant's "bona fide error defense"; and

(5) Whether a debtor is entitled to recover statutory damages and attorney fees absent proof of actual damages.

III.

Appellant argues that the purpose of section 1692g's disclosure requirements is to protect debtors who believe that a debt assigned for collection is improper, and that a debtor who owes all the amounts billed has no standing to assert a violation of section 1692g.

The Act is designed to protect consumers who have been victimized by unscrupulous debt collectors, regardless of whether a valid debt actually exists. 1977 U.S.Code Cong. & Adm.News, 1695, 1696. Section 1692k, which governs a debt collector's civil liability under the Act, provides in pertinent part that "any debt collector who fails to comply with any provision of this subchapter with respect to any person is liable to such person." 15 U.S.C. § 1692k(a). The statute does not make an exception for liability under section 1692g when the debtor does in fact owe the entire debt.

Further, the legislative history supports the contention that a debtor has standing to complain of violations of the Act, regardless of whether a valid debt exists. Representative Frank Annunzio, chairman of the subcommittee that reported out the bill, stated during debate "[t]hat every individual, *whether or not he owes the debt,* has a right to be treated in a reasonable and civil manner." 123 Cong.Rec. 10241 (1977) (emphasis added).

Therefore Baker, even though he stated that he did owe the entire debt, has standing to assert any violations of the Act, including a violation of section 1692g.

IV.

Section 1692g(a) of the Act provides that a debt collector must send the debtor a written notice containing, among other things,

"a statement that unless the consumer, within 30 days after receipt of the notice, disputes the validity of the debt, or any portion thereof, the debt will be assumed to be valid by the debt collector."

15 U.S.C. § 1692g(a)(3). The written notice must also contain

"a statement that if the consumer notifies the debt collector in writing . . . that the debt, or any portion thereof, is disputed, the debt collector will obtain verification of the debt . . . and a copy of such verification . . . will be mailed to the consumer."

15 U.S.C. § 1692g(a)(4).

The clear language of the statute explicitly requires that a debtor shall be given notice that he may "dispute the validity of the debt, or any portion thereof . . . ." 15 U.S.C. § 1692g(a)(3). . . . Congress clearly required the notice to inform the debtor that he could dispute any portion of the debt.

The letters sent by appellant to Baker contained the following statement:

"Verification of this debt, a copy of judgment or the name and address of the original creditor, if different from the current creditor, will be provided if requested in writing within 30 days. Otherwise, the debt will be assumed to be valid."

The district court found that the notice "does not inform [the debtor] that he may dispute only a portion of the debt," and thus violated § 1692g(a)(3). This determination is factual, and it must be upheld on appeal unless it is clearly erroneous. Fed.R.Civ.P. 52(a).

The notice sent by appellant barely informs the debtor that he may even dispute the entire debt. Appellant's notice does contain a statement that verification of the debt will be provided if requested in writing, as required by 15 U.S.C. § 1692g(a)(4). However, the only statement referring to a dispute regarding the validity of the debt, as required by 15 U.S.C. § 1692g(a)(3), is the sentence "[o]therwise the debt will be assumed to be valid." "In evaluating the tendency of language to deceive, the Commission should look not to the most sophisticated readers but to the least." Exposition Press, Inc. v. F.T.C., 295 F.2d 869, 873 (2d Cir. 1961), cert. denied, 370 U.S. 917, 82 S.Ct. 1554, 8 L.Ed.2d 497 (1962). Here, the court should follow the same directive. The language of the notice is simply not sufficient to put a debtor on notice that he could dispute a portion of the debt. A debtor who does owe a valid obligation to the creditor but could dispute finance charges, interest, or have some valid defense, might not be put on notice that he could dispute these additional charges. The district court's finding is not clearly erroneous. Therefore, we affirm the district court's holding that appellant violated section 1692g(a)(3) of the Act.

V.

The Act prohibits a debt collector from using "any false, deceptive, or misleading representation or means" to collect a debt. 15 U.S.C. § 1692e. Among the specific types of conduct prohibited by section 1692e is

"(5) The threat to take any action that cannot legally be taken or that is not intended to be taken."

15 U.S.C. § 1692e(5).

Appellant's second letter stated, in pertinent part:

"It is our policy to attempt to settle these matters out of court before making any decision whether to refer them to an attorney for collection . . . Unless we receive your check or money order, we will proceed with collection procedures."

Appellant's policy, as stipulated in the pretrial order, was not to take legal action in these types of cases, but only to proceed with further telephone and mail solicitation.

The district court found that the language of the notice "create[d] the impression that legal action by defendant is a real possibility . . . [and a consumer could legitimately believe that 'further collection procedures' meant court action when defendant had no intention of pursuing such a course of action." This determination, that appellant threatened to take action that it did not intend to take, is factual and can be overturned on appeal only if clearly erroneous. Fed.R.Civ.P. 52(a). We cannot say this finding is clearly erroneous, and therefore we affirm the court's conclusion that appellant's letter violated section 1692e(5).

VI.

The Act provides a debt collector with a "bona fide error" defense:

"A debt collector may not be held liable in any action brought under this subchapter if the debt collector shows by a preponderance of evidence that the violation was not intentional and resulted from a bond fide error notwithstanding the maintenance of procedures reasonably adapted to avoid any such error."

15 U.S.C. § 1692k(c).

The district court rejected this defense on the merits, stating that appellant had presented no evidence to support the defense. Appellant now states that, with respect to the bona fide error defense, it did not accede to decision on the merits, and that it submitted sufficient evidence to raise a genuine issue of material fact such that summary judgment would be improper. The only evidence presented by appellant in support of the bona fide error defense is the following stipulation:

> "Defendant obtained the advice and assistance of counsel on the meaning of and compliance with the Fair Debt Collection Practices Act and the correctness of the contents of the letter [containing the disputed language]. Defendant's attorneys have, from time to time, met with the staff of the Federal Trade Commission to discuss compliance with the Act."

Reliance on advice of counsel or a mistake about the law is insufficient by itself to raise the bona fide error defense. "§ 1692k(c) does not immunize mistakes of law, even if properly proven." Rutyna v. Collection Accounts Terminal, Inc., 478 F.Supp. 980, 982 (N.D.Ill.1979).

Section 1692k(c) of the Act is nearly identical to the bona fide error defense section under the Truth in Lending Act (TILA), 15 U.S.C. § 1640(c). Carrigan v. Central Adjustment Bureau, Inc., 494 F.Supp. 824, 827 (N.D.Ga.1980). It has been uniformly held that unintentional "clerical errors . . . are the only violations this section [of the TILA] was designed to excuse." Palmer v. Wilson, 502 F.2d 860, 861 (9th Cir. 1974); Haynes v. Logan Furniture Mart, Inc., 503 F.2d 1161, 1167 (7th Cir. 1974) (reliance on advice of counsel insufficient to support defense of bona fide error); Turner v. Firestone Tire & Rubber Co., 537 F.2d 1296, 1298 (5th Cir. 1976) (§ 1640(c) called "the clerical error defense"); Ratner v. Chemical Bank New York Trust Co., 329 F.Supp. 270, 281 (S.D.N.Y.1971); Buford v. American Finance Co., 333 F.Supp. 1243, 1248 (N.D.Ga.1971). In Ratner v. Chemical Bank New York Trust Co., supra, a case in which the defendant similarly contended that an error of law was not intentional within the meaning of § 1640(c), the court stated:

> "It is undisputed that defendant carefully, deliberately—intentionally—omitted the disclosure in question. That defendant . . . mistook the law does not make its action any less intentional."

Id. at 281.

Appellant only presented evidence that, at best, might show it had been mistaken about the law. This is insufficient by itself to support the bona fide error defense pursuant to 15 U.S.C. § 1692k(c). Therefore, we affirm the district court's conclusion that the defense was unavailing.

VII.

The civil liability section of the Act provides:

"(a) Except as otherwise provided by this section, any debt collector who fails to comply with any provision of this subchapter with respect to any person is liable to such person in an amount equal to the sum of—

(1) any actual damage sustained by such person as a result of such failure;

(2)(A) in the case of any action by an individual, such additional damages as the court may allow, but not exceeding $1,000;"

. . .

(3) . . . the costs of the action, together with a reasonable attorney's fee. . . .

15 U.S.C. § 1692k(a). The district court found that Baker had not proved any actual damages, and awarded statutory damages of $100 pursuant to section 1692k(a)(2)(A) and attorney's fees of $800 pursuant to section 1692k(a)(3).

Appellant contends that Baker is not entitled to an award of statutory damages absent proof of actual damages. However, the plain language of the statute does not support appellant's contention. The statute clearly specifies the total damage award as the sum of the separate amounts of actual damages, statutory damages and attorney fees. There is no indication in the statute that award of statutory damages must be based on proof of actual damages.

Further, the Act's damage provisions are very similar to those under the Truth in Lending Act (TILA), 15 U.S.C. § 1640(a). Under TILA, statutory damages are available merely on proof of a violation; no proof of actual damages is required.

The legislative history indicates that the Act is similar to the Truth in Lending Act, but contains no statement that in the Act Congress intended to change the damage provisions. The Senate Report states:

"A debt collector who violates the Act is liable for any actual damages he caused as well as any additional damages the court deems appropriate, not exceeding $1,000."

1977 U.S.Code Cong. & Adm.News, supra at 1700. The section-by-section analysis of the Act's provisions explains the civil liability provisions as follows:

"A debt collector who violates the Act is liable for actual damages plus costs and reasonable attorney's fees. The court may award additional damages of up to $1,000 in individual actions."

Id. at 1702. Neither the Senate Report nor the section-by-section analysis indicate the award of "additional" damages is conditional upon proof of actual damages.

Appellant misstates the legislative history when it states that Congress, in enacting the Act, altered this aspect of the damage provision because of experience with the Truth in Lending Act. TILA provided, in addition to statutory damages, that a minimum statutory recovery of $100 would be available to any debtor who proved a violation. It was only the minimum recovery provision that concerned Congress in the filing of harassment suits under TILA. 1977 U.S.Code Cong. & Adm. News, supra, at 1703.

Policy also supports the award of statutory damages without proof of actual damages. The only actual damages that a plaintiff would be likely to incur would be for emotional distress caused by abusive debt collection practices and, unless the violations are extreme and outrageous, traditional stringent evidentiary hurdles would be difficult to overcome. Further, the legislative history shows that Congress clearly intended that private enforcement actions would be the primary enforcement tool of the Act. See 123 Cong.Rec. 28112–13 (1977) (remarks of Rep. Annunzio); 1977 U.S.Code Cong. & Adm.News, supra at 1700.

Because of the similarity with the Truth in Lending Act and the fact that neither the plain language of the statute nor the legislative history indicates any contrary intent, we affirm the district court's conclusion that statutory damages are available without proof of actual damages.

Affirmed.

Notes & Questions

Does Rasor v. Retail Credit Co., supra, provide appropriate guidance on the question of what constitutes "actual damage" within the meaning of § 1692k(a)(1) [§ 813(a)(1)]?

What factors should guide courts in assessing "additional damages" under § 1692k(a)(2)(A) [§ 813(a)(2)(A)]? May a court refuse to award any additional damages? May punitive damages exceed the $1,000 limit on additional damages?

WHITFORD, STRUCTURING CONSUMER PROTECTION LEGISLATION TO MAXIMIZE EFFECTIVENESS, 1981 Wis.L.Rev. 1018–19, 1022–24

Consumer protection legislation has burgeoned over the past fifteen years. Much of the literature that has considered the effectiveness of this legislation has emphasized its limited impact. Two principal reasons tend to be given for the limited effect. Some commentators have emphasized the limited ability of law to affect consumer transactions because of the influence on those transactions of other economic and social forces. Other commentators, drawing on theories of political economy, argue that most consumer protection legislation was not intended by its drafters and promoters to have much impact on transactions. According to this view the purpose of enacting the legislation is largely symbolic. Symbolic legislation is designed to appear to help consumers, in order to legitimize the current political and economic system, while simultaneously failing to alter significantly the power and economic relations between merchants and consumers.

There is, beyond doubt, a good deal of validity to the views described above. In this article, however, I make the assumption, no doubt also valid, that consumer protection legislation has some effects. The purpose of the article is to propose hypotheses about the relationships between these effects and both the structure of consumer protection legislation and the sanctions for its violation. By structure of legislation I mean a number of details about the legislation which can be varied without significantly altering the manifest or stated purpose of the legislation. Sanctions for violation can also often be varied without altering the stated purpose of the legislation. . . .

I. THE STRUCTURE OF LEGISLATION

. . .

B. *The Importance of Being Specific*

My first proposition respecting the structure of consumer protection legislation is that as the conduct prescribed or proscribed is defined with greater specificity, there will tend to be a greater effect on the voluntary behavior of those regulated. By voluntary behavior I mean action which is not compelled by injunction or similar legal process, even though the action might be motivated in part by fear of legal sanction if it were not taken.

Stated more intuitively, this proposition asserts that if legislation directs merchants to do something particular, many will do it, almost regardless of the provisions for sanctioning violations. Compliance will result from such motives as a general belief in law abidingness and a fear of bad publicity. On the other hand, standardless legislation is unlikely to have much effect on voluntary behavior, because merchants are likely to give themselves the benefit of the doubt in deciding whether their existing practices violate a vague standard, such as unconscionability.

Debt collection is regulated in Wisconsin by a set of rules that can be used to illustrate this proposition. The Wisconsin Consumer Act, which became effective in 1973, contains the following provision pertaining to the harassment of debtors by frequent telephone calls:

> [A] debt collector shall not . . . [c]ommunicate with the customer or a person related to him with such frequency or at such unusual hours or in such a manner as can reasonably be expected to threaten or harass the customer.

The federal Fair Debt Collection Practices Act, which became effective in 1978, contains a similar provision:

> [A] debt collector may not communicate with a consumer in connection with the collection of any debt . . . at any unusual time or place or a time or place known or which should be known to be inconvenient to the consumer.

The federal Act goes on, however, to provide:

> In the absence of knowledge of circumstances to the contrary, a debt collector shall assume that the convenient time for communicating

with a consumer is after 8 o'clock antimeridian and before 9 o'clock postmeridian, local time at the consumer's location.

The proposition asserted above predicts that the more specific federal legislation has more substantial immediate effect on the voluntary behavior of debt collectors than the state legislation, even though the sanctions for violation of the state legislation are more severe than the sanctions for violation of the federal legislation. This difference in impact would be obtained even though the manifest or stated purpose of the two enactments is essentially the same. The difference in the enactments lies in what I have called their structure.

One implication of this proposition is that a statute should contain many specific propositions. At the same time, however, a statute ought to attempt to state its ostensible purpose in generalized terms—as both statutes discussed above have done—since it is highly likely that circumstances will arise that are unforeseen or so idiosyncratic as to be unworthy of specific legislative provision. As a general rule, therefore, statutes should state their principal purposes in general terms, followed by a number of specific applications.

A second implication of the proposition is that a generalized statement of purpose is likely to have more impact in the long run if the legislation provides a relatively easy way to specify its application in particular circumstances. Although a legislature can always amend legislation to specify its application, consumer protection legislation rarely receives such attentiveness from legislatures. Provision for rulemaking is normally desirable, therefore. It is worth noting that the Fair Debt Collection Practices Act, discussed above, specifically prohibits rulemaking by the administrative agencies charged with enforcement responsibility. The proposition asserted here implies that this provision, if it has any effect at all, can only inhibit the overall impact of the Act. . . .

Notes & Questions

Does *Baker* suggest that specific standards will have greater impact than general standards. In *Baker*, what was the collection agency's response to the specific statutory standards? In enforcing the act, did the court draw persuasive support from the details of the act or from more general principles as to what it thought should be prohibited by the act?

For examples of state laws regulating debt collectors, see N.Y.Gen. Bus.Law §§ 600–603; Cal.Bus. & Prof.Code §§ 6850–6956; Cal.Civil Code §§ 1788–1788.32. Efforts to collect debts through normal billing channels are regulated by the Fair Credit Billing Act. 15 U.S.C.A. §§ 1666–1666j.

See generally National Consumer Law Center, Fair Debt Collection (1987); 1 Debtor-Creditor Law Chs. 4, 4A (T. Eisenberg ed.).

Chapter 6

LIMITATIONS ON DEBTORS' AVOIDANCE EFFORTS

Most debtor misbehavior is by those in financial difficulty who take actions that threaten creditors' ability to enforce obligations. Debtors' efforts to avoid repayment occur at different times in the credit transaction process and take different forms. Some debtors will not do anything to frustrate collection efforts until they are sued. They then hide or transfer assets. The law of provisional remedies and the law of fraudulent conveyances both address the issue of the recalcitrant debtor-defendant. Many debtors take action to frustrate collection before litigation commences. Again, they may transfer or hide assets, conduct bargain sales and hide the proceeds, or engage in a variety of other behavior designed to frustrate collection. In these cases, provisional remedies, those that attend the commencement of a lawsuit, are unavailable. The branches of fraudulent conveyance law, including bulk transfer law, offer creditors weapons to deal with such misbehaving debtors and their transferees.

A. Provisional Remedies

1 G. GLENN, FRAUDULENT CONVEYANCES AND PREFERENCES §§ 37, 39 (Rev.Ed.1940)

[The attachment process was connected with . . . "imprisonment for debt" . . .. The original object of an action was to get the defendant into court, to abide the judgment if adverse to him. . . . [At the outset of an action the creditor could obtain a writ of *capias ad respondendum,* issuable as of course in every action of debt, covenant, trespass or case. This authorized the taking of the debtor's body into custody, from which he could be relieved only if he entered an appearance and gave bail to be available for arrest under the *capias ad satisfaciendum* which would issue after any final judgment that might be secured against him. Until this was done, the defendant could not appear or plead; the only thing he could do was to default; and then, being in custody meanwhile, he could be detained under the final *capias ad satisfaciendum.* But there was, in old practice, another method of compelling an appearance. If the defendant could not be found in person within the realm, then his diligent creditor might exert coercive process upon such goods as the fugitive may have left behind him. And so, as agreed by a learned bench, "Our system of attachment on mesne process was derived from the ancient rule of the common law, by which, as part of the service of civil process, goods which were properly subject to distress were allowed also to be taken by a species of distress, and held as *vadii* or pledges to compel the appearance of the defendant." . . .

Originally, as we have seen, the object of the attachment was to secure the debtor's appearance in the action. By the Custom of London, attachment issued only in the case of a non-resident debtor, and served as a substitute for the initial *capias* which has already been mentioned. . . . [So far as England is concerned, this remains as the object of her modern attachment laws . . ..

That is not, however, the law of this country, because here the attachment has undergone a significant change. . . . [In an American commonwealth like New York, the modern purpose of attachment is, "not to compel appearance by the debtor, but to secure the debt or claim of the creditor." And that, it may be said, expresses the general rule with us. Our attachment, first and last, secures the claim of the creditor.

For many years prejudgment attachment was also used as a method of obtaining quasi in rem jurisdiction over a defendant not subject to in personam jurisdiction. In Shaffer v. Heitner, 433 U.S. 186, 97 S.Ct. 2569, 53 L.Ed.2d 683 (1977) and Rush v. Savchuk, 444 U.S. 320, 100 S.Ct. 571, 62 L.Ed.2d 516 (1980), the Supreme Court held that, where the defendant lacked minimal contacts with the forum state, attachment to obtain quasi in rem jurisdiction violated the fourteenth amendment's due process clause.

NORTH GEORGIA FINISHING, INC. v. DI–CHEM, INC.

Supreme Court of the United States, 1975.
419 U.S. 601, 95 S.Ct. 719, 42 L.Ed.2d 751.

MR. JUSTICE WHITE delivered the opinion of the Court.

Under the statutes of the State of Georgia, plaintiffs in pending suits are "entitled to the process of garnishment." Ga.Code Ann. § 46–101.[1] To employ the process, plaintiff or his attorney must make an

---

1. The relevant provisions of the Georgia Code Annotated are as follows:

§ 46–101

"Right to writ; wages exempt until after final judgment

"In cases where suit shall be pending, or where judgment shall have been obtained, the plaintiff shall be entitled to the process of garnishment under the following regulations: Provided, however, no garnishment shall issue against the daily, weekly or monthly wages of any person residing in this State until after final judgment shall have been had against said defendant: Provided, further, that the wages of a share cropper shall also be exempt from garnishment until after final judgment shall have been had against said share cropper: Provided, further, that nothing in this section

shall be construed as abridging the right of garnishment in attachment before judgment is obtained."

§ 46–102

"Affidavit; necessity and contents. Bond

"The plaintiff, his agent, or attorney at law shall make affidavit before some officer authorized to issue an attachment, or the clerk of any court of record in which the said garnishment is being filed or in which the main case is filed, stating the amount claimed to be due in such action, or on such judgment, and that he has reason to apprehend the loss of the same or some part thereof unless process of garnishment shall issue, and shall give bond, with good security, in a sum at least equal to double the amount sworn to be due, affidavit before "some officer authorized to issue an attachment, or the clerk of any court of record in which the said garnishment is filed or in which the main case is being filed, stating the amount claimed to be due in such action . . . and that he has reason to apprehend the loss of the same or some part thereof unless process of garnishment shall issue." § 46–102. To protect defendant against loss or damage in the event plaintiff fails to recover, that section also requires plaintiff to file a bond in a sum double the amount sworn to be due. Section 46–401 permits the defendant to dissolve the garnishment by filing a bond "conditioned for the payment of any judgment that shall be rendered on said garnishment." Whether these provisions satisfy the Due Process Clause of the Fourteenth Amendment is the issue before us in this case.

On August 20, 1971, respondent filed suit against petitioner in the Superior Court of Whitfield County, Ga., alleging an indebtedness due and owing from petitioner for goods sold and delivered in the amount of $51,279.17. Simultaneously with the filing of the complaint and prior to its service on petitioner, respondent filed affidavit and bond for process of garnishment, naming the First National Bank of Dalton as garnishee. The affidavit asserted the debt and "reason to apprehend the loss of said sum or some part thereof unless process of Garnishment issues." [2] The clerk of the Superior Court forthwith issued summons of

payable to the defendant in the suit or judgment, as the case may be, conditioned to pay said defendant all costs and damages that he may sustain in consequence of suing out said garnishment, in the event that the plaintiff shall fail to recover in the suit, or it shall appear that the amount sworn to be due on such judgment was not due, or that the property or money sought to be garnished was not subject to process of garnishment. No person shall be taken as security on the bond who is an attorney for the plaintiff or a nonresident unless the nonresident is possessed of real estate in the county where the garnishment issues of the value of the amount of such bond."

§ 46–103

"Affidavit by agent or attorney

"When the affidavit shall be made by the agent or attorney at law of the plaintiff, he may swear according to the best of his knowledge and belief, and may sign the name of the plaintiff to the bond, who shall be bound thereby in the same manner as though he had signed it himself."

§ 46–104

"Affidavit and bond by one of firm, etc.

"When the debt for recovery of which the garnishment is sought shall be due to partners or several persons jointly, any one of said partners or joint creditors may make the affidavit and give bond in the

name of the plaintiff, as prescribed in cases of attachment."

§ 46–401

"Dissolution of garnishments; bond; judgment on bond

"When garnishment shall have been issued, the defendant may dissolve such garnishment upon filing in the clerk's office of the court, or with the justice of the peace, where suit is pending or judgment was obtained, a bond with good security, payable to the plaintiff, conditioned for the payment of any judgment that shall be rendered on said garnishment. The plaintiff may enter up judgment upon such bond against the principal and securities, as judgment may be entered against securities upon appeal, whenever said plaintiff shall obtain the judgment of the court against the property or funds against which garnishment shall have been issued."

2. The affidavit in its entirety was as follows:

"SUPERIOR COURT OF Whitfield COUNTY GEORGIA, *Whitfield* COUNTY.

"Personally appeared *R.L. Foster*, *President of Di-Chem, Inc.,* who on oath says that he is *President of Di Chem, Inc.,* plaintiff herein and that *North Georgia Finishing, Inc.,* defendant, is indebted to said plaintiff in the sum of $51,279.17 DOL-

garnishment to the bank, which was served that day. On August 23, petitioner filed a bond in the Superior Court conditioned to pay any final judgment in the main action up to the amount claimed, and the judge of that court thereupon discharged the bank as garnishee. On September 15, petitioner filed a motion to dismiss the writ of garnishment and to discharge its bond, asserting, among other things, that the statutory garnishment procedure was unconstitutional in that it violated "defendant's due process and equal protection rights guaranteed him by the Constitution of the United States and the Constitution of the State of Georgia." App. 11. The motion was heard and overruled on November 29. The Georgia Supreme Court,[3] finding that the issue of the constitutionality of the statutory garnishment procedure was properly before it, sustained the statute and rejected petitioner's claims that the statute was invalid for failure to provide notice and hearing in connection with the issuance of the writ of garnishment. 231 Ga. 260, 201 S.E.2d 321 (1973).[4] We granted certiorari, 417 U.S. 907, 94 S.Ct. 2601, 41 L.Ed.2d 210 (1974). We reverse.

The Georgia court recognized that Sniadach v. Family Finance Corp., 395 U.S. 337, 89 S.Ct. 1820, 23 L.Ed.2d 349 (1969), had invalidated a statute permitting the garnishment of wages without notice and opportunity for hearing, but considered that case to have done nothing more than to carve out an exception, in favor of wage earners, "to the general rule of legality of garnishment statutes." 231 Ga., at 264; 201 S.E.2d, at 323. The garnishment of other assets or properties pending the outcome of the main action, although the effect was to " 'impound [them in the hands of the garnishee,' " id., at 263, 201 S.E.2d, at 323, was apparently thought not to implicate the Due Process Clause.

This approach failed to take account of Fuentes v. Shevin, 407 U.S. 67, 92 S.Ct. 1983, 32 L.Ed.2d 556 (1972), a case decided by this Court more than a year prior to the Georgia court's decision. There the Court held invalid the Florida and Pennsylvania replevin statutes which permitted a secured installment seller to repossess the goods sold, without notice or hearing and without judicial order or supervision, but with the help of the sheriff operating under a writ issued by the clerk of the court at the behest of the seller. That the debtor was deprived of only the use and possession of the property, and perhaps

---

LARS, principal, $_____, interest, $_____ attorney's fees, and $_____ cost and that said plaintiff has—a suit pending—*returnable to the* Superior Court of *Whitfield* County, and that affiant has reason to apprehend the loss of said sum or some part thereof unless process of Garnishment issues.

"Sworn to and subscribed before me, this *August* 20, 1971.

　　　　　"*/s/ R.L. Foster,* Affiant.
"*/s/Dual Broadrick,* Clerk

"Superior Court of *Whitfield* County." App 3–4.

3. Appeal was taken in the first instance to the Georgia Supreme Court. That court, without opinion, transferred the case to the Georgia Court of Appeals. The latter court issued an opinion, 127 Ga. App. 593, 194 S.E.2d 508 (1972). The Georgia Supreme Court then issued certiorari, 230 Ga. 623, 198 S.E.2d 284 (1973).

4. Subsequent to the Georgia Supreme Court's decision in this case, a three-judge federal court, sitting in the Northern District of Georgia declared these same statutory provisions unconstitutional. Morrow Electric Co. v. Cruse, 370 F.Supp. 639 (N.D. Ga.1974).

only temporarily, did not put the seizure beyond scrutiny under the Due Process Clause. "The Fourteenth Amendment draws no bright lines around three-day, 10-day, or 50-day deprivations of property. Any significant taking of property by the State is within the purview of the Due Process Clause." Id., at 86, 92 S.Ct., at 1997. Although the length of severity of a deprivation of use or possession would be another factor to weigh in determining the appropriate form of hearing, it was not deemed to be determinative of the right to a hearing of some sort. Because the official seizures had been carried out without notice and without opportunity for a hearing or other safeguard against mistaken repossession, they were held to be in violation of the Fourteenth Amendment.

The Georgia statute is vulnerable for the same reasons. Here, a bank account, surely a form of property, was impounded and, absent a bond, put totally beyond use during the pendency of the litigation on the alleged debt, all by a writ of garnishment issued by a court clerk without notice or opportunity for an early hearing and without participation by a judicial officer.

Nor is the statute saved by the more recent decision in Mitchell v. W.T. Grant Co., 416 U.S. 600, 94 S.Ct. 1895, 40 L.Ed.2d 406 (1974). That case upheld the Louisiana sequestration statute which permitted the seller-creditor holding a vendor's lien to secure a writ of sequestration and, having filed a bond, to cause the sheriff to take possession of the property at issue. The writ, however, was issuable only by a judge upon the filing of an affidavit going beyond mere conclusory allegations and clearly setting out the facts entitling the creditor to sequestration. The Louisiana law also expressly entitled the debtor to an immediate hearing after seizure and to dissolution of the writ absent proof by the creditor of the grounds on which the writ was issued.

The Georgia garnishment statute has none of the saving characteristics of the Louisiana statute. The writ of garnishment is issuable on the affidavit of the creditor or his attorney, and the latter need not have personal knowledge of the facts. § 46–103. The affidavit, like the one filed in this case, need contain only conclusory allegations. The writ is issuable, as this one was, by the court clerk, without participation by a judge. Upon service of the writ, the debtor is deprived of the use of the property in the hands of the garnishee. Here a sizable bank account was frozen, and the only method discernible on the face of the statute to dissolve the garnishment was to file a bond to protect the plaintiff creditor. There is no provision for an early hearing at which the creditor would be required to demonstrate at least probable cause for the garnishment. Indeed, it would appear that without the filing of a bond the defendant debtor's challenge to the garnishment will not be entertained, whatever the grounds may be.[5]

5. Petitioner so asserts, relying on Jackson v. Barksdale, 17 Ga.App. 461, 87 S.E. 691 (1916); Powell v. Powell, 95 Ga. App. 122, 97 S.E.2d 193 (1957). Respondent, without citation of authority states that "Counsel could have attacked the garnishment in other ways either in the State

Respondent also argues that neither *Fuentes* nor *Mitchell* is apposite here because each of those cases dealt with the application of due process protections to consumers who are victims of contracts of adhesion and who might be irreparably damaged by temporary deprivation of household necessities, whereas this case deals with its application in the commercial setting to a case involving parties of equal bargaining power. See also Sniadach v. Family Finance Corp., 395 U.S. 337, 89 S.Ct. 1820, 23 L.Ed.2d 349 (1969). It is asserted in addition that the double bond posted here gives assurance to petitioner that it will be made whole in the event the garnishment turns out to be unjustified. It may be that consumers deprived of household appliances will more likely suffer irreparably than corporations deprived of bank acounts, but the probability of irreparable injury in the latter case is sufficiently great so that some procedures are necessary to guard against the risk of initial error. We are no more inclined now than we have been in the past to distinguish among different kinds of property in applying the Due Process Clause. Fuentes v. Shevin, 407 U.S., at 89–90, 92 S.Ct., at 1998–1999.

Enough has been said, we think, to require the reversal of the judgment of the Georgia Supreme Court. The case is remanded to that court for further proceedings not inconsistent with this opinion.

So ordered. . . .

MR. JUSTICE BLACKMUN, with whom MR. JUSTICE REHNQUIST joins, dissenting. . . .

5. Neither do I conclude that, because this is a garnishment case, rather than a lien or vendor-vendee case, it is automatically controlled by *Sniadach*. *Sniadach*, as has been noted, concerned and reeks of wages. North Georgia Finishing is no wage earner. It is a corporation engaged in business. It was protected (a) by the fact that the garnishment procedure may be instituted in Georgia only after the primary suit has been filed or judgment obtained by the creditor, thus placing on the creditor the obligation to initiate the proceedings and the burden of proof, and assuring a full hearing to the debtor; (b) by the respondent's statutorily required and deposited double bond; and (c) by the requirement of the respondent's affidavit of apprehension of loss. It was in a position to dissolve the garnishment by the filing of a single bond. These are transactions of a day-to-day type in the commercial world. They are not situations involving contracts of adhesion or basic unfairness, imbalance, or inequality. See D.H. Overmyer Co. v. Frick Co., 405 U.S. 174, 92 S.Ct. 775, 31 L.Ed.2d 124 (1972); Swarb v. Lennox, 405 U.S. 191, 92 S.Ct. 767, 31 L.Ed.2d 138 (1972). The clerk-judge distinction, relied on by the Court, surely is of little significance so long as the court officer is not an agent of the creditor. The Georgia system, for me, affords commercial entities all the protection that is required by the Due Process Clause of the Fourteenth Amendment.

or Federal Courts. . . ." Brief for Respondent 5.

6. Despite its apparent disclaimer, the Court now has embarked on a case-by-case analysis (weighted heavily in favor of *Fuentes* and with little hope under *Mitchell*) of the respective state statutes in this area. That road is a long and unrewarding one, and provides no satisfactory answers to issues of constitutional magnitude. . . .

[Concurring opinions by Justices Stewart and Powell, and a dissenting statement by Chief Justice Burger, are omitted.

Notes & Questions

1. *Garnishment.* Garnishment usually refers to the process by which a creditor attaches property that is in the possession of third parties, or debts owed to the defendant. As in *North Georgia*, garnishment involves serving a writ upon a third party possessing property of the defendant or owing a debt to the defendant. Garnishment also may refer to post-judgment efforts to collect funds owed to judgment debtors by serving writs upon third parties. See Chapter 7.

2. *Due Process Limits in Other Contexts.* Due process attacks on other aspects of the debt-collection process include unsuccessful efforts to challenge the self-help provisions of the U.C.C., see Chapter 2, and some successful efforts to challenge post-judgment collection procedures. See Finberg v. Sullivan, 634 F.2d 50 (3d Cir. 1980) (en banc) and Chapter 7. When state action is present a federal civil rights statute, 42 U.S.C.A. § 1983, authorizes damages awards for constitutional violations. Lugar v. Edmondson Oil Co., Inc., 457 U.S. 922, 102 S.Ct. 2744, 73 L.Ed.2d 482 (1982).

3. *Lis Pendens.* Notice of pendency or "lis pendens" is a provisional remedy somewhat different from those scrutinized in the *Sniadach-North Georgia* line of cases. As described by one court:

> Under the common law doctrine of lis pendens, the mere filing of a law suit affecting property imparted constructive notice of the pendency of the suit; one who acquired the property from a party litigant while the suit was pending took the property subject to the outcome of the action, despite having received no actual notice. . . . The genesis of the doctrine has been described as follows:

> > At early common law the principle that a judgment was binding only upon parties to an action was considered to be axiomatic. When this rule was applied to actions which concerned the title or right to possession of specific property, however, the courts often found themselves in the position of rendering hollow judgments, the subject matter of the litigation having been conveyed to a non-participating party prior to the judgment. It was in response to this somewhat embarrassing situation that the doctrine of *lis pendens* developed. . . .

The hardship wrought by application of the common law doctrine of lis pendens is evident. As Professor Casner noted, "Great hardship often arose due to the inability of the purchaser to discover after reasonable search the existence of a suit affecting the title. Deeds in relation to the land were easily found in the title records provided by the recording acts, but the same was not true with respect to suits and actions." 3 A.J. Casner, American Law of Property § 13.12, at 521 (1952) (footnote omitted). In time, the state legislatures enacted statutes designed to ameliorate the harshness of the common law doctrine. In 1902, New Jersey adopted the predecessor of its current lis pendens statute. Its key feature is the provision that any person claiming an interest in the real estate described in the notice of lis pendens through any defendant in the action as to which the notice of lis pendens is filed "shall be deemed to have acquired the same with knowledge of the pendency of the action, and shall be bound by any judgment entered therein as though he had been made a party thereto and duly served with process therein." N.J.Stat.Ann. § 2A:15–7. Further, until a notice of lis pendens is filed "no action, as to which such notice is required, shall . . . be taken to be constructive notice to a bona fide purchaser or mortgagee of . . . the affected real estate." N.J. Stat.Ann. § 2A:15–8.

The statute thus significantly alters the common law doctrine by providing a means for purchasers to obtain actual notice of the pendency of the suit. No longer can the mere filing of the lawsuit itself serve as constructive notice to potential purchasers who would take subject to the outcome of the action. . . . As at common law, however, once the notice of lis pendens is filed, a purchaser of the property takes the property subject to the outcome of the litigation. The filing of a notice of lis pendens "acts as constructive notice to all the world of the pendency of an action involving real property and that a purchaser of that property takes subject to the outcome of the litigation." Wendy's of South Jersey, 170 N.J.Super. at 496, 406 A.2d at 1339.

Chrysler Corp. v. Fedders Corp., 670 F.2d 1316, 1319–20 (3d Cir. 1982). See also N.Y. CPLR §§ 6501, 6511–6515; Cal.Code Civ.Proc. §§ 409–409.8. In *Chrysler Corp.*, the court found that New Jersey's lis pendens provision does not violate due process. Compare Kukanskis v. Griffith, 180 Conn. 501, 430 A.2d 21 (1980) (invalidating a lis pendens statute).

If attachments or garnishments were accomplished through filings (similar to lis pendens filings and to filings made under Article 9), would due process problems be eliminated?

4. *Relief from, and Liability for, Provisional Remedies.* Successful attachment greatly enhances the attaching creditor's bargaining position in settlement negotiations. To balance this effect, and in response to constitutional requirements, attachment statutes frequently contain provisions for prompt relief from attachment. E.g., Cal.Code Civ.Proc. §§ 485.240, 489.310; N.Y. CPLR §§ 6211(b), 6222. Wrongful attachment may lead to an action against the wrongfully attaching creditor. E.g., Cal.Code Civ.Proc. §§ 490.010–490.060.

In California, perceived abuses of the lis pendens statute led to enactment of provisions for the expungement of a lis pendens recorded in bad faith. Cal.Code Civ.Proc. §§ 409.1–409.6. Under the expungement provisions, a party recording a lis pendens must show that the action affects title to real property and that the action was commenced for a proper purpose and in good faith. Id. § 409.1.

Plaintiff files an action alleging an oral promise by defendant to sell real property. Plaintiff records a notice of lis pendens covering the property. The defendant moves for expungement of the lis pendens. The trial court believes plaintiff's case is "pretty thin" but that plaintiff does not lack good faith. May the court order expungement of the notice? See Malcolm v. Superior Court, 29 Cal.3d 518, 174 Cal.Rptr. 694, 629 P.2d 495 (1981) (no); Note, After Malcolm v. Superior Court and Peery v. Superior Court: A Due Process Analysis of California Lis Pendens, 70 Cal.L.Rev. 909 (1982).

READING & BATES CORP. v. NATIONAL IRANIAN OIL CO.

United States District Court, Southern District of New York, 1979.
478 F.Supp. 724.

KEVIN THOMAS DUFFY, DISTRICT JUDGE:

Plaintiffs, Reading & Bates Corporation [hereinafter referred to as "R & B"] and Reading & Bates Exploration Company [hereinafter referred to as "R & B Exploration"], both Delaware corporations, brought this motion to confirm an order of attachment issued *ex parte* by me on August 22, 1979. Defendant, National Iranian Oil Company [hereinafter referred to as "NIOC", a foreign corporation not licensed in New York, cross-moved to vacate the order of attachment and levy.

The complaint in the instant case alleges the unlawful taking and conversion by the defendant of the plaintiffs' oil drilling rig, the "Milton G. Hulme", located in Iranian territorial waters. Jurisdiction of the federal District Court is based on diversity of citizenship. The undisputed facts are as follows:

On November 1, 1977, the plaintiff corporations entered into two contracts with the Oil Services Company of Iran [hereinafter referred to as "OSCO". The first contract, the "Bareboat Charter", chartered the drilling rig to OSCO for three years and the second, the "Drilling Contract" was for operation of the rig. OSCO, at that time, was under a service contract with NIOC dated July 19, 1973. Pursuant to this contract, OSCO was to conduct oil and gas exploration and drilling for NIOC. In turn, NIOC was to supply the oil and gas to members of the International Oil Consortium, also formed in 1973. NIOC provided OSCO's funding for the performance of the service contract. Until approximately November, 1978, invoices sent to OSCO by R & B and R & B Exploration were paid in full.

Thereafter, the parties' interpretation of the facts diverges. The plaintiffs claim that no invoices were paid after November, 1978, save two partial payments in March and May, 1979. They further claim that despite urgent need for an inspection of the rig on February 16, 1979, they were physically prevented from doing so. R & B and R & B Exploration also assert that the failure to make required payments terminated the contract pursuant to its "Termination Clause" and that repeated demands have been made for payment and return of the rig. Finally, they assert that NIOC had complete dominion and control over OSCO and is properly before this Court as its "alter ego."

Defendant, on the other hand, argues, *inter alia*, that substantial payments have been made; that R & B had no right to an inspection; that R & B, in fact, violated the "Bareboat Charter" by attempting to tow the rig from Iranian waters; and that plaintiffs have submitted no evidence of a demand for return of the rig. According to defendant, the contract has not been terminated and, therefore, this cause of action at best sounds in contract; not in conversion. Finally, NIOC persistently argues that it is a separate juridical entity and is not a proper party to this lawsuit.

Both sides concede that there is an arbitration clause in the "Bareboat Charter" between R & B and OSCO. This clause provides that:

> All disputes arising in connection with the present Contract shall be finally settled under the Rules of Conciliation and Arbitration of the International Chamber of Commerce by one or more arbitrators appointed.

Plaintiffs' Exhibit 1 at 14. However, no demand for arbitration has been made by either party.

Upon commencement of the suit the plaintiffs filed a summons and complaint and an *ex parte* application for an order of attachment on August 22, 1979. The attachment application contemplated a levy of approximately $26 million at each of twenty-nine banks holding funds of the defendant. Only one of the banks indicated that it had no funds of defendant. At least four banks indicated that they each possessed funds of the defendant in excess of the amount to be attached. After the order of attachment was granted, pursuant to N.Y.Civ.Prac.Law § 6201, the parties and garnishee banks agreed by stipulation, dated August 31, 1979, to set aside a special fund of approximately $26 million at the Chase Manhattan Bank in lieu of a levy at each of the twenty-nine banks.

As required by N.Y.Civ.Prac.Law § 6211(b), the plaintiffs made the instant motion to confirm the order of attachment within five days by an order to show cause dated August 27, 1979. I heard oral argument on this motion and the defendant's cross-motion to vacate the attachment on September 7th and reserved decision.

This case involves several distinct issues. First, has the plaintiff met its burden of establishing the grounds for attachment, the need for a continuing levy, and the probability of success on the merits as required by N.Y.Civ.Prac.Law § 6223(b)? Second, is NIOC a proper party to this suit as the "alter ego" of OSCO? Third, if NIOC is a proper party, has its immunity to pre-judgment attachment under the Foreign Sovereign Immunity Act, 28 U.S.C. §§ 1602–11, [hereinafter referred to as the "FSIA", been waived by the United States Treaty of Amity with Iran?

At the outset, it should be noted that the provisional remedy of attachment is discretionary with the trial court. Weinstein-Korn-Miller, N.Y.Civil Practice ¶ 6201.03 (1963). It is a harsh remedy which should be construed strictly against those seeking to use it. Siegel v. Northern Boulevard & 80th St. Corp., 31 A.D.2d 182, 183, 295 N.Y.S.2d 804, 806 (1st Dep't 1968). C.P.L.R. § 6223(b) provides that the plaintiff shall have the burden of establishing the grounds for attachment, the need for continuing the levy, and the probability of success on the merits. This provision is specifically made applicable to the motion to confirm the order of attachment via C.P.L.R. § 6211(b). I find that the plaintiff has failed to meet its burden pursuant to Section 6223(b).

Pre-judgment attachments in New York are generally used either to obtain quasi-in-rem jurisdiction over a foreign defendant or to establish security for satisfaction of a potential judgment, or both. In the instant case, plaintiffs contend that there is personal jurisdiction over defendant by virtue of its "doing-business" in New York, N.Y.Civ.Prac.Law § 301 (McKinney), and that

> the purpose of an attachment here is not to obtain jurisdiction in the quasi rem [sic sense, it was done in order to secure any judgment which would be rendered.

Transcript at 50.

When the only purpose for a pre-judgment attachment is security, a different analysis should apply than that used for jurisdictional attachments. In Incontrade, Inc. v. Oilborn International, S.A., 407 F.Supp. 1359 (S.D.N.Y.1976) the Court indicated:

> When jurisdiction already exists, attachment should issue only upon a showing that drastic action is required for security purposes.

Id. at 1361.

Plaintiff has established the grounds for attachment pursuant to C.P.L.R. § 6201. A money judgment has been demanded and would be available against the defendants for conversion and the defendant is a foreign corporation not qualified to do business in New York.

I find, however, that the plaintiff has failed to establish a need to continue the levy under the circumstances of this case. Plaintiffs argue, based on Banco Mercantil y Agricolo, C.A. v. Michel, No. 78–4852 (S.D.N.Y. April 23, 1979), that defendant's unauthorized dominion over the rig to plaintiffs' exclusion, in itself, establishes a continuing need for the levy. I disagree. The defendant in *Banco Mercantil* was an Assistant United States Representative for a Venezuelan bank. She was charged with fraudulently converting bank funds for personal use.

The defendant's unlawful dominion was over funds which she never had a right to possess. In that situation, the Court found a continuing need for the levy.

In contrast, defendant in the instant case did have a right to possess the drilling rig pursuant to the "Bareboat Charter." The dispute here is as to whether or not the contract and, consequently, possession rights were terminated pursuant to specific terms of the Termination Clause. Although continuing to assert that it is not a proper party, NIOC argues that OSCO is still under the terms of its three-year lease and has given no indication that it will fail to return the rig at the end of this period. Under these circumstances, I cannot say that possession of the rig alone is a sufficient need to continue the levy.

Neither can I say that plaintiff has established sufficient insecurity of enforcement of a potential judgment to justify the harsh remedy of pre-judgment attachment. Plaintiffs ask me to accept the possibility that Iran might cut off oil sales to the United States or alter its financial arrangements to require that customers' payments be made outside the United States.[1] The effect of these policy changes would be to reduce NIOC assets in New York. In their brief, plaintiffs indicate that "[there is no way of saying with any reasonable degree of certainty that the events described above will not happen." Plaintiffs' Memorandum in Support of Confirmation of Order of Attachment at 20.

NIOC is presently doing substantial business and is party to many long-term contracts with United States customers. The proceedings in this case indicate that it has at least upwards of $700 million on deposit with New York banking institutions. The possibility that NIOC will remove all of its funds from New York and revise all of its contracts to provide for payments outside of the United States is simply too remote to justify continuing the pre-judgment attachment in this case. Certainly, the plaintiffs' contention that there is no way of saying these events will not happen does not satisfy their burden pursuant to Section 6223(b).

Since I find that plaintiffs have failed to meet the burden of establishing need to continue the levy, I need not determine whether or not they have established probability of success on the merits. Moreover, I need not determine at this time whether or not NIOC is, in fact, the "alter ego" of OSCO. . . .

1. Plaintiffs cite Stromberg-Carlson Corp. v. Bank Melli Iran, 467 F.Supp. 530 (S.D.N.Y.1979) for the proposition that the Court may take judicial notice of the political turmoil in Iran. This may be so. However, I do not feel it appropriate or helpful to do so in the instant case.

NORTHEAST INVESTMENT CO., INC. v. LEISURE LIVING COMMUNITIES, INC.

Supreme Judicial Court of Maine, 1976.
351 A.2d 845.

DUFRESNE, CHIEF JUSTICE.

The plaintiff-appellee, Northeast Investment Co., Inc. (Northeast), by complaint dated August 31, 1973, is seeking from the defendant-appellant, Leisure Living Communities, Inc. (Leisure Living), damages for breach of contract in the amount of $91,666.70 and specific performance of that aspect of the contract under which Northeast claims an option to purchase twenty thousand (20,000) shares of Leisure Living stock. Northeast filed a motion under Rule 4A, M.R.Civ.P. to attach the real estate of Leisure Living in the amount of $100,000.00.[1] On October 30, 1973 a Justice of the Superior Court, after hearing on the motion upon affidavits submitted by both parties, found "that there is a reasonable likelihood that the Plaintiff will recover judgment, including interest and costs, in an amount equal to or greater than $100,000.00," and ordered that "an attachment of the real property may be made against the Defendant's property in the amount of $100,000.00." Following an unsuccessful attempt to have the interlocutory ruling reported to the Law Court, Leisure Living seasonably appealed. We deny the appeal. . . .

Standard—Reasonable likelihood of plaintiff's recovery of judgment

Having determined that the approval of an attachment is an interlocutory order which, nevertheless, is immediately appealable to the Law Court, we must now address the issue, whether Rule 4A was properly applied in the instant case. Such, in turn, must preliminarily

1. Rule 4A. Attachment

"(a) Availability of Attachment. In connection with the commencement of any action under these rules, real estate, goods and chattels and other property may, in the manner and to the extent provided by law, but subject to the requirements of this rule, be attached and held to satisfy the judgment for damages and costs which the plaintiff may recover.

"(c) . . .

No property may be attached unless such attachment for a specified amount is approved by order of the court. Except as provided in subdivision (f) of this rule [ex parte order approving attachment, the order of approval may be entered only after notice to the defendant and hearing and upon a finding by the court that there is a reasonable likelihood that the plaintiff will recover judgment, including interest and costs, in an

amount equal to or greater than the amount of the attachment over and above any liability insurance shown by the defendant to be available to satisfy the judgment.

An action in which attachment of property is sought may be commenced only by filing the complaint with the court, together with a motion for approval of the attachment. The motion shall be supported by affidavit or affidavits meeting the requirements set forth in subdivision (h) of this rule.

. . .

"(h) Requirements for Affidavits. Affidavits required by this rule shall set forth specific facts sufficient to warrant the required findings and shall be upon the affiant's own knowledge, information or belief; and, so far as upon information and belief, shall state that he believes this information to be true."

depend on the quality of showing the Rule compels the plaintiff to make in order to support its entitlement to the requested attachment.

Hence, the immediate issue is, what standard of proof the trial court should apply, when hearing a motion for approval of attachment of real estate, before finding "that there is a reasonable likelihood that the plaintiff will recover judgment, including interest and costs, in an amount equal to or greater than the amount of the attachment over and above any liability insurance shown by the defendant to be available to satisfy the judgment."

The defendant, Leisure Living, contends that the purpose underlying Rule 4A is to prevent a plaintiff from obtaining potentially onerous prejudgment security by way of attachment "when there is a good faith dispute as to the merits [of a claim and when the chances are equal or nearly equal that the plaintiff will not ultimately prevail." It opts for a standard pursuant to which the court could not make the prerequisite finding of "reasonable likelihood" of recovery of judgment "if the court's mind is evenly balanced as to which party will ultimately prevail."

Rule 4A was expanded to cover prejudgment real estate attachments for the purpose of fitting into a State policy of long standing due process safeguards of notice and hearing as an accommodation between the State interest in affording security to creditors and minimal protection to debtors against invalid claims and/or the abuse of excessive attachments. The "likelihood of success" standard will keep the process more in syntony with previous State policy than a "preponderance of the evidence" test.

The term "likelihood of success" connotes mere probability of success or a favorable chance of success.

Clearly, the inquiry into the plaintiff's likelihood of success in the main action requisite to support approval of a prejudgment real estate attachment need not take the form of a full adjudication of the rights of the parties. Such adjudication better be left for determination at the time of trial rather than in the preliminary hearing contemplated by Rule 4A.

The federal cases speak similarly of "likelihood of success" in terms of favorable chance of success. If a claim for which security by means of real estate attachment is requested is not of such insubstantial character that its invalidity so clearly appears as to foreclose a reasonable possibility of recovery, then, such a claim would be within the "likelihood of success" standard required by the Rule. See *Mitchell v. W.T. Grant Company,* 1974, 416 U.S. 600, 94 S.Ct. 1895, 40 L.Ed.2d 406, where it is stated:

"On the contrary, it seems apparent that the seller with his own interest in the disputed merchandise *would need to establish in any event only the probability that his case will succeed . . . .."* (Emphasis ours)

· · ·

*Reasonable likelihood of plaintiff's recovery of judgment in the instant
case*

In order to assess the correctness of the Justice's ruling approving
the attachment, we must first consider the pleadings upon which his
determination was made. The record reveals that Northeast's motion
for allowance of attachment of Leisure Living's real estate in the
amount of $100,000.00 was supported in the Court below by the affidavits of George T. Kattar, president of the plaintiff corporation, while
the defendant's opposition was formulated through affidavits of Bernard J. Mayer, Jr., the then president of the defendant corporation and
John C. Wyman, the defendant's legal representative in a related case
pending in the United States District Court for the District of Massachusetts.

The Kattar affidavits expressly purport to be made on personal
knowledge pursuant to Rule 4A(h) (footnote 1, supra) and contain the
following factual assertions:

On or about February 25, 1970 Mr. Kattar, as president of Northeast, and Mr. J. Allan Bowron, as president of Leisure Living, entered
into an oral agreement the breach of which is the subject of the main
action. It provided in part for Leisure Living to pay Northeast, or
certain other named corporations as might be designated by Mr. Kattar, the sum of fifty thousand ($50,000.00) dollars per year as long as
certain loans and notes payable to James Talcott, Inc. remained unpaid.
In the deal, Northeast was granted the option to purchase twenty
thousand (20,000) shares of Leisure Living stock. The verbal arrangement between the two companies was intended as security in the
purchase by Leisure Living of certain lands owned by Sebago Estates,
Inc. and Gunstock Acres, Inc. in connection with which the loans and
notes payable to James Talcott, Inc. were executed.

Indeed, Northeast undertook to guarantee these Talcott loans and
notes for such time as they remained unpaid, and so did Mr. Kattar,
individually and for Community Investment Corporation, of which
corporation he was president and majority shareholder. In addition
thereto, Mr. Kattar promised new guarantees of said loans and notes
from Tri-State Development Corporation, American Heritage Properties, Inc., The Second Presidential Corporation and Castle Shores, Inc.
Mr. Kattar had a controlling voice in said corporations by reason of his
position of president or his ownership of the majority of the stock. The
loans and guarantees involved in the agreement were in fact made.

In further consideration of Leisure Living's undertaking, Mr. Kattar
individually and for the named corporations, promised to "provide
during the life of said guarantees, such consulting services as Leisure
Living Communities, Inc. would request from time to time."

Pursuant to their contractual obligations, Mr. Kattar and the named corporations "performed numerous consulting services to Leisure Living Communities, Inc. at their request, including but not limited to, assisting with a zoning problem, the purchase of sixty (60) acres of land desired by Leisure Living Communities, Inc., the preparation of a paper giving many suggestions on how to develop property, and the conducting of several sales conferences with salesman."

Leisure Living, so Mr. Kattar's affidavit states, failed to make the payments of fifty thousand ($50,000.00) dollars per year to Northeast since October 25, 1971 and on July 30, 1971 refused Northeast's request to execute the purchase option of twenty thousand (20,000) shares of Leisure Living stock.

Contrary to the Kattar affidavits which are based solely on personal knowledge of alleged positive facts, the Mayer affidavit is founded "upon personal knowledge and upon information and belief based upon careful inquiry" and accentuates the negative.

It alleges that the affiant has no knowledge of any reference oral agreement, because a careful search of the records and other papers of Leisure Living reveals no such agreement nor any act or undertaking pursuant thereto. Mr. Mayer further discloses that he bases part of his affidavit on the information received from an unnamed representative of James Talcott, Inc. to the effect that Talcott's records do not show any such act or undertaking of guaranty as claimed by Northeast and that in the opinion of said Talcott representative

"on February 25, 1970 Northeast Investment Co., Inc. was released from any pre-existing guaranty of indebtedness which might have existed and that no new guaranty was entered into by Northeast Investment Co., Inc. on or after that date."

Mr. Mayer's affidavit further concludes that on the basis of his examination of Leisure Living's records and papers,

"it is my understanding and I therefore believe that the indebtedness to James Talcott, Inc. was assumed by a subsidiary of the company, New England Properties, Inc., and was to be repaid over a considerable period of time well in excess of one year."

Mr. Mayer further states he has no knowledge of any consulting services performed by Northeast or Mr. Kattar subsequent to February 25, 1970.

We need not concern ourselves with the Wyman affidavit as it merely confirms, through Mr. Kattar's deposition, that, whatever agreement there was, it contemplated a period of performance well in excess of one year, a fact which the parties do not seriously dispute.

An analysis of the Mayer affidavit discloses that the facts therein alleged which would tend to dispute affirmatively the plaintiff's cause of action, to wit, "that on February 25, 1970 Northeast Investment Co., Inc. was released from any pre-existing guaranty of indebtedness which might have existed and that no new guaranty was entered into by

Northeast Investment Co., Inc. on or after that date" were not based on the personal knowledge of the affiant, but are stated to be *the opinion of an undisclosed representative of James Talcott, Inc.* Mr. Mayer "made oath that the foregoing statements by him made are true to the best of his knowledge and belief."

Under Rule 4A(h), specific facts sufficient to warrant the findings necessary to the approval of the real estate attachment must be set forth "and [they shall be upon the affiant's own knowledge, information or belief; *and, so far as upon information and belief, shall state that he believes this information to be true.*" (Emphasis supplied). Nowhere, does Mr. Mayer state that he believed the information which he received from the unnamed representative of James Talcott, Inc. to be true. Thus, the Mayer affidavit was deficient in the most important aspect of the facts it purported to present in opposition to the plaintiff's motion for an order permitting the attachment of the defendant's real property, a fact which the Justice below most probably took into consideration in his evaluation of the affidavits upon which he had to make his decision. . . .

We have examined the affidavits submitted to the Court below and, taking into account the positive nature of the plaintiff's affidavits as opposed to the negative aspect of the defendant's counteraffidavits, we are convinced that Northeast has demonstrated a reasonable likelihood of recovery of judgment in its main action, provided it has made a similar showing respecting Leisure Living's affirmative defense of the statute of frauds,[4] which Northeast asserts ineffective by reason of its own part performance of the contract.

IV. *The Statute of Frauds*

That the reference oral agreement was within the class of contracts on which action was prohibited under 33 M.R.S.A. § 51(5) appears clearly. . . .

The agreement called for a $50,000 *annual* payment, thus inferentially implying that payments were to be made for more than one year. Indeed, the payments were to continue "as long as said loans were unpaid and said liabilities in existence." Mr. Kattar in his deposition stated the agreement was to be in effect for five years. Moreover, we take note of the fact the guaranty related to a rather large real estate development project which, in the normal course of events, would not allow its discharge within one year. . . .

But, under certain circumstances, part performance of an unwritten contract may authorize a court of equity to compel specific performance by the other party in contradiction to the positive terms of the statute of frauds on the ground of equitable estoppel based on an equitable

---

4. 33 M.R.S.A. § 51. *Writing required;* "No action shall be maintained in any of the following cases:

. . .

(5) *Agreement not to be performed within one year.* Upon any agreement that is not to be performed within one year from the making thereof; . . . ."

fraud. This Court said in Woodbury v. Gardner, 1885, 77 Me. 68, at 70 and 71:

> "After having induced or knowingly permitted another to perform in part an agreement, on the faith of its full performance by both parties and for which he could not well be compensated except by specific performance, the other shall not insist that the agreement is void. . . . In other words, partial performance [to exclude the operation of the statute of frauds is such a carrying out of the agreement by one party thereto, that fraud would result to him unless the other party be compelled to perform his part of it."

The affidavits in positive terms disclose full performance by Northeast, Mr. Kattar and his interrelated companies, of the oral contract by the execution and continued maintenance of the guaranty agreements, causing a drop in their borrowing power and the loss in the sales force; they further support the rendering of numerous consulting services to Leisure Living. In partial consideration for the guaranty, Leisure Living orally promised the grant of an option to purchase twenty thousand (20,000) shares of Leisure Living stock, the execution of which was never acted upon by Leisure Living although requested on July 30, 1971.

An oral contract relating to the purchase of corporate stock may be enforced specifically under special circumstances as seem present in the instant case, such as that Leisure Living stock has no readily ascertainable market value, cannot be easily obtained from other sources, and is of special interest to Northeast as one of the interrelated corporations engaged in the development of sizable real estate projects. If Northeast is hampered by the bar of the statute of frauds, such loss certainly could not be compensated for adequately by money damages. See Tewksbury v. Noyes, 1941, 138 Me. 127, 23 A.2d 204.

We conclude that Northeast has demonstrated the reasonable likelihood of recovering judgment in its main action within the requirements of Rule 4A(c) to support the approval of a real estate attachment, even though the contract on which its claim is based was an oral one. . . .

Notes & Questions

1. *Cases in Which Attachment May Issue.* Which of the two preceding cases presents the stronger case for attachment? How would *Northeast Investment* come out under the New York law applied in *Reading & Bates*? How would it come out under California law? See Cal.Code Civ.Proc. §§ 483.010, 484.090, 485.010, 492.010. How would *Reading & Bates* come out under California law? under Maine law?

D subjects P to malicious tortious conduct which causes P serious bodily harm. D is likely to hide or dispose of his assets before a judgment can be obtained against him. May P attach any or all of D's assets (a) under New York law? (b) under California law?

Seller and Buyer make a contract for the sale of goods to Buyer. Buyer refuses to accept delivery. Seller sues Buyer for breach of contract. May Seller attach Buyer's assets (a) under New York law? (b) under California law?

In many states, attachment is available in actions based upon contracts but not upon actions sounding in tort. Can you suggest why?

2. *Fraudulent Contracting as Grounds for Attachment.* Former provisions of N.Y. CPLR § 6201 authorized attachment when the plaintiff's complaint alleged fraud in "contracting or incurring" liability, wrongful receipt, retention, or conversion of governmental property, or a cause of action "to recover damages for the conversion of personal property, or for fraud or deceit." Should these grounds for attachment have been repealed?

See generally Kheel, New York's Amended Attachment Statute: A Prejudgment Remedy in Need of Further Revision, 44 Brook.L.Rev. 199 (1978).

Should existing attachment statutes be repealed in favor of a more general standard such as the following:

Attachment is available whenever there is a reasonable likelihood that the plaintiff's ability to enforce any judgment obtained will be compromised by post-filing occurrences and the hardship to the defendant of the attachment is outweighed by the plaintiff's risk of nonenforcement if attachment does not issue.

Is this the standard that existing attachment statutes seek to implement?

3. *The Attaching Creditor's Priority.* (a) On Day 1 creditor obtains an attachment against debtor's equipment. On Day 2 debtor sells the equipment to buyer. On Day 3 creditor obtains a judgment against debtor. Who has priority as to the attached equipment? See N.Y. CPLR § 6203; Cal.Code Civ.Proc. § 488.500; Cal.Civil Code § 2897. What does Article 9 tell you about this problem? Would it make a difference if the attached property were inventory instead of equipment?

(b) On January 1 A files U.C.C. financing statements covering D's inventory in New York and California. On February 1 B attaches D's inventory in New York by having the sheriff deliver a copy of the order of attachment to D (see N.Y. CPLR §§ 6214(a), (c), 6215), and attaches D's inventory in California by filing a notice with the Secretary of State. See Cal.Code Civ.Proc. § 488.405. On February 15 A lends D $15,000 and a proper security agreement is executed. Who has priority in D's inventory?

Suppose the dispute is limited to New York inventory acquired by D after February 15. Who would now have priority? Compare Cal.Code Civ.Proc. §§ 697.530(b), 697.590(b). Cf. N.Y. CPLR § 6214(b).

(c) On January 1 A attaches D's inventory in California by filing a notice with the Secretary of State and attaches D's inventory in New

York by having the sheriff deliver a writ of attachment to D. On March 1, B sells D a new line of inventory on credit (half of the inventory is for California and half is for New York), and retains a purchase money security interest, which B properly perfects. Who has priority in the new line of inventory? Would it make a difference if B delayed perfecting for five days? Compare U.C.C. § 9–301(2).

4. *Methods of Attachment.* New York and California both allow attachment of important classes of property without requiring the sheriff to seize it. E.g., N.Y. CPLR § 6214; Cal.Code Civ.Proc. §§ 488.375, 488.405. To what extent should attachment without seizure be available? What problems accompany allowing nonpossessory attachment?

Should attachment statutes be drafted to mirror the Article 9 system of perfecting security interests? That is, one could allow attachment only by filing in the case of some property (for example, accounts), only by possession in the case of other property (for example, instruments), and by either possession or filing in the case of still other property (for example, inventory and equipment). To what extent would it be appropriate for an attachment statute to mirror Article 9's perfection structure?

See generally Zaretsky, Attachment Without Seizure: A Proposal for A New Creditors' Remedy, 1978 U.Ill.L.Forum 819.

5. *Ex Parte Attachment.* In extreme situations, attachment after notice and hearing may come too late. Consider the California and New York provisions for attachment or other relief without a hearing. N.Y. CPLR §§ 6211, 6301; Cal.Code Civ.Proc. §§ 485.010–485.240, 486.020. Are these provisions constitutional?

6. *Reclamation of Property.* Many states have special procedures for reclaiming specific property in which plaintiff asserts an interest. See N.Y. CPLR §§ 7101–7112; Cal.Code Civ.Proc. §§ 512.010–513.020. When an Article 9 secured party cannot resort to self-help repossession, he is likely to invoke the state's abbreviated statutory reclamation procedure.

7. *Attachment in Federal Court.* Rule 64 of the Federal Rules of Civil Procedure states:

Seizure of Person or Property

At the commencement of and during the course of an action, all remedies providing for seizure of person or property for the purpose of securing satisfaction of the judgment ultimately to be entered in the action are available under the circumstances and in the manner provided by the law of the state in which the district court is held, existing at the time the remedy is sought, subject to the following qualifications: (1) any existing statute of the United States governs to the extent to which it is applicable; (2) the action in which any of the foregoing remedies is used shall be commenced and prosecuted or, if removed from a state court, shall be prosecuted after removal, pursuant to these rules. The remedies thus available include arrest, attachment, garnishment, replevin, sequestration, and other corresponding or equivalent remedies, however designated and regardless of whether by state procedure the remedy is ancillary to an action or must be obtained by an independent action.

B. Fraudulent Conveyances

1. Basic Fraudulent Conveyance Doctrine

CLARK, THE DUTIES OF THE CORPORATE DEBTOR TO ITS CREDITORS, 90 Harv.L.Rev. 505, 506–13 (1977)

The law of fraudulent conveyances, of which the Uniform Fraudulent Conveyance Act (UFCA) is the principal but not exclusive embodiment, allows creditors to set aside certain transfers by debtors. Fraudulent conveyance law has a broad applicability, restricted neither to conveyances—since virtually all transfers of property, and, under the UFCA and under the Bankruptcy Act, the incurrence of obligations, are covered—nor to fraud—since unfair transfers made without deceptive intent are included. Court opinions involving allegedly fraudulent transfers have not infrequently sounded muddled and uncertain notes because of a failure to discriminate among the various distinct ideals that this body of law seeks to implement. Although more than one of these distinct ideals are usually involved in actual cases, what these ideals are, and how closely they are related to the ideal underlying the law of preferential transfers, can be seen through an examination of four simple situations.

1. Debtor grants Friend a mortgage on his small factory in return for a loan of $160,000, which Friend actually makes to Debtor. Debtor, wishing to discourage unpaid trade creditors having $30,000 of claims from litigating them to judgment and seeking execution against the factory, prevails upon Friend to have the recorded mortgage recite that it secures a debt for $200,000, which equals the well-known market value of the factory. The trade creditors' attorneys search the real estate records, discover and give credence to the false mortgage, and, knowing that Debtor has few assets other than the factory, become discouraged and cease pursuing Debtor.

Here, then, is a case of Ur-Fraud, that primeval fraud on creditors than which no greater can be thought. The transfer of the mortgage interest to Friend was known to be false, was intended to thwart legitimate creditors, and actually did so. The keynote of the evil is the *actual deception* or falsehood practiced on the trade creditors to their detriment. By hypothesis, Friend gave full and fair consideration for the extent of the mortgage interest that he could enforce against Debtor. Further, the mortgage interest that he obtained did not actually render Debtor incapable of satisfying the remaining creditors. The ideal offended is simply that of Truth: in connection with transfers of property rights to others, a debtor is forbidden to tell lies to his creditors that will lead to the nonsatisfaction of their claims.

2. Debtor has reached the point where $100,000 of her debts are due and payable, and her entire assets have a fair market value of the same dollar amount. Thinking that she would prefer that her husband and sister rather than her creditors get the benefits of her assets, she makes a deed of gift of all her possessions to those two fortunate relatives, and immediately delivers full and exclusive actual possession of the property to them, relinquishing any use or benefit from the transferred property. She makes no secret of the transaction or of her intentions: she reports the deed of gift in every conceivable recording office, and mails a copy by certified mail to each and every creditor, together with a detailed and psychologically accurate account of her motivations, purposes, and feelings toward her creditors. In this case, Debtor has made a transfer which would clearly be voidable since it was made without fair and full consideration and she was insolvent immediately after the transfer.

The ideal offended by Debtor in the above example is not that of truthful conduct toward creditors. Debtor has been completely open with her creditors and has never tried to deceive them, unless one wants to overstretch the notion of fraud by saying that, when she originally borrowed from her creditors, she "implicitly" promised to satisfy her legal obligations before her moral obligations and personal allegiances, that she has now failed to fulfill this promise, and that the failure is conclusive evidence that the promise was falsely and deceptively given. Instead, it is much simpler, and intellectually more honest, to recognize that another ideal is served by fraudulent conveyance law. The ideal can be captured by a cliche: be just before you are generous. The debtor has a moral duty in transferring his property to give *primacy* to so-called legal obligations, which are usually the legitimate, conventional claims of standard contract and tort creditors, as opposed to the interests of self, family, friends, shareholders, and shrewder or more powerful bargaining parties. I will somewhat hesitantly refer to this as the normative ideal of Respect.

3. Pierce is indebted to Twyne for $400 and to C for $200. Pierce's nonexempt assets are worth only $300. Suppose that Pierce, simply because Twyne is the first to ask that he do so and because he dislikes C, and for no other reason, transfers all of his property to Twyne. Suppose, contrary to the apparent facts in a similar, well-known case, that Pierce makes the transfer openly and with much publicity and fanfare, so that no deception of any sort is practiced on C, and that Pierce does not intend to and never does get a kickback of part of the transferred property or its use or any other kind of benefit from Twyne. Assume also that Twyne's claim is a completely valid, unobjectionable, due and payable, legal obligation of the most conventional sort.

Pierce's transfer to Twyne does not run afoul of the normative ideals of Truth and Respect toward creditors because Pierce has fully and truthfully described the transaction and has given primacy to his legal obligations. It is, however, objectionable for a debtor to satisfy the claims of just one creditor at a time when he lacks sufficient assets to meet his other legitimate and conventional legal obligations. A preferential payment of this sort hinders pro tanto the interest of all the other creditors. In such a situation, a debtor should deal equally with all his creditors. I will dub this principle the ideal of Evenhandedness toward creditors, with the understanding that in using this term the connotation is of equality of treatment of legal obligations in connection with liquidation proceedings. Evenhandedness, in its fullest expression, has two aspects. Whenever a debtor is or is about to become insolvent and thus unable to satisfy all his creditors in full, the debtor should refrain from preferring one creditor over another. Similarly, in such cases creditors should refrain from seeking such a preference. In either instance, transfers resulting in better than equal treatment on the eve of liquidation proceedings should be undone—and may actually be undone in bankruptcy proceedings as voidable preferential transfers.

4. Debtor, who owns 250 shares of stock, sold those shares to her husband for full value in illiquid assets. She was not insolvent at the time of the sale but the stock had been her only liquid asset and as a result of the transaction she had no assets which creditors could easily reach. She made the transfer for the purpose of hindering her creditors but did not deceive them. This transaction would be avoided under the open-ended language of the UFCA, which covers transactions made with actual intent to hinder or delay creditors.

Although the debtor intends and accomplishes a transfer leading to a hindering of her creditors, this case does not strictly offend the ideals of Truth, Respect or Evenhandedness as developed above. The scheme involves no actual deception, for she has truthfully informed all her creditors of the transaction. Moreover, the transfer of the shares is not for less than their fair value, nor does the transfer leave the debtor insolvent, so the transfer does not violate the ideal of Respect. Finally, the scheme results in no preference of any preexisting creditor over the others. Hence, one could say that there may be transactions which are not offensive of the above ideals in their normal applications, but which are yet fraudulent conveyances because they violate the more general expression of the ideal of which all three of the subsumed ideals are specifications. The general ideal might be described as that of Nonhindrance of the enforcement of valid legal obligations against oneself, in connection with transfers of one's property.

In summary, then, fraudulent conveyance law embodies a general ideal, in connection with a debtor's transfers of property rights and incurrences of new obligations, of Nonhindrance of creditors. This vague ideal is made operational through the effectuation of the more specific ideals of Truth, Respect, and Evenhandedness as well as a general, residual prohibition of conduct which hinders creditors in attempting to satisfy their claims.

Notes & Questions

1. *Sources of Fraudulent Conveyance Law.* Commentators often date fraudulent conveyance law from 13 Eliz., ch. 5 (1570), which was an act

> for the avoiding and abolishing of feigned, covinous and fraudulent feoffments, gifts, grants, alienations, conveyances, bonds, suits, judgments and executions . . . which . . . have been and are devised and contrived of malice, fraud, covin, collusion or guile, to the end, purpose and intent, to delay, hinder or defraud creditors and others of their just and lawful actions, suits, debts, accounts, damages, penalties, forfeitures, heriots, mortuaries and reliefs, not only to the let or hinderance of the due course and execution of law and justice, but also to the overthrow of all true and plain dealing, bargaining and chevisance between man and man, without which no commonwealth or civil society can be maintained or continued . . . .

The dominant source of modern fraudulent conveyance law, the Uniform Fraudulent Conveyance Act (UFCA), was proposed in 1918 and is in effect in 23 states, including Michigan, New Jersey, New York, Ohio and Pennsylvania. In 1984 the Commissioners on Uniform State Laws adopted the Uniform Fraudulent Transfer Act (UFTA) as a replacement for the UFCA. In 1985 and 1986 eight states adopted the UFTA. Three of those states, including California, enacted the UFTA to replace the UFCA. States that have not adopted the uniform acts often operate under statutes or common law principles derived from the Statute of Elizabeth.

2. *Applying the UFCA.* Apply the UFCA to the four situations described by Professor Clark. Can you confirm that the first, second, and fourth situations are fraudulent under the UFCA and that the third situation is not? Are the differences in result justifiable?

3. *Sale Plus Hiding Proceeds.* Debtor sells a valuable asset to Purchaser and hides the proceeds from his creditors. May Debtor's creditors pursue the asset under the UFCA? Which act offends the UFCA's principles? Which act is vulnerable to attack?

4. *Bankruptcy.* The Bankruptcy Act contains its own version of the UFCA. 11 U.S.C.A. § 548. In addition, the trustee in bankruptcy may invoke state fraudulent conveyance law to invalidate prebankruptcy transfers. 11 U.S.C.A. § 544(b). These matters are explored in Chapter 14.

5. *Reasons for Fraudulent Conveyance Law.* Why have a law of fraudulent conveyances? Evaluate the following arguments:

(a) It does not matter whether we have a law of fraudulent conveyances. Those debtors who engage in fraudulent conveyances will soon find themselves cut off from access to credit markets. Lenders will not lend funds, suppliers will not ship on credit, and buyers will refuse to make down payments. Those willing to extend credit to misbehaving debtors will do so only at relatively high interest rates which reflect the greater risk of doing business with such debtors. Given that fraudulent conveyance doctrine is a confusing, sometimes archaic area of law we would be better off simply to abolish it. In the long run, there would be no net adverse effect on commercial or consumer credit transactions.

(b) Fraudulent conveyance law is desirable because it contains terms that the parties would agree to in the absence of legal compulsion to do so. If there were no law of fraudulent conveyances, informed creditors and debtors would negotiate credit terms that contain many of the essential provisions of existing fraudulent conveyance doctrine. The preexistence of such a body of doctrine saves the parties the time and effort of negotiating and drafting such terms on a case-by-case basis.

READE v. LIVINGSTON
The Court of Chancery of New York, 1818.
3 Johns. Ch. 481.

THE CHANCELLOR. This case turns upon the validity of the conveyance by Henry G. Livingston to Gilbert Aspinwall.

The bill charges, that Livingston was indebted to John Reade, the plaintiff's intestate, as early as the year 1800, in 6,000 dollars, and that, in August term, 1807, Reade obtained a judgment against H.G.L., for upwards of that sum, and that 3,072 dollars of it remains unpaid. That by deed, dated the 7th of December, 1805, H.G.L. conveyed his lands, to the amount in value of 45,000 dollars, to Aspinwall, in trust for his wife, and that he had no other property to satisfy the balance of the judgment.

The answer of H.G.L., and of his wife, admitted that, in 1800, there were sundry unsettled accounts between the parties, and that they were finally, by rule of Court, referred to referees, and that the judgment upon such reference was rendered, as charged in the bill; they admit further, that the lands included in the deed to Aspinwall, composed the greater part of the real estate of H.G.L., though they deny the lands to be of the value charged. H.G.L. states that, prior to his marriage, and with a view to it, he agreed with his wife's father to settle on her, and her children, 30,000 dollars, and that the deed was executed in pursuance of that agreement. He admits the sum of 1,392 dollars and 92 cents to be still due upon the judgment, and that Reade might have obtained satisfaction out of his personal estate; and he declares, that he was then worth little or no property, though, at the time of his marriage, he was worth 80,000 dollars.

It appears, by the proof taken in the cause, that the judgment was founded upon two bonds dated in the year 1794; that the consideration of them was a farm sold by Reade to H.G.L., and that with the proceeds, or by the exchange of that farm, H.G.L. procured the greater part of the lands included in the deed of settlement. That he was married as early as the year 1791, and that at the date of the judgment he owned personal property to 1,000 dollars; but it does not appear that he possessed any real property free from encumbrance. Valentine Nutter, the wife's father, says, that his wife, Mrs. Nutter, informed him, just previous to the marriage, that H.G.L. had promised to settle 30,000 dollars on his daughter, and that H.G.L. frequently, after the marriage, had admitted the promise, and at last, at the repeated request of the witness, executed the deed.

The deed to Aspinwall contains no reference to, or recital of, any previous agreement; but it is simply a deed in fee, for the consideration of 5,000 dollars, and in trust to convey the lands, and the rents and profits thereof, as the wife of H.G.L., by deed or will, should direct; and, in default of such direction, in trust for her heirs.

I have stated, perhaps, as much of the pleadings and proofs as may be requisite to a full understanding and discussion of the important legal questions involved in the case.

H.G.L. owed the very debt now in question, at the time of the settlement of his real estate upon his wife; and a great part of the lands so settled were purchased with property procured by that same debt. The deed of settlement was not made until 14 years after the marriage, when it is admitted, that, in the mean time, his estate had diminished one half. It had no reference or allusion to any ante-nuptial contract, nor is there any evidence in writing of such an agreement.

Upon such a state of facts, my earliest impressions were against the soundness of the defence; and I apprehend, there is not a case to be met with that gives any colorable support to such a settlement against such a creditor. But after the elaborate argument which has been made in favor of the deed, I have considered it due to the counsel, as well as to the importance of every question of this nature, to look into the cases, and to give to every topic of argument a careful investigation.

The settlement was a voluntary one. There was no portion advanced by, or on behalf of the wife, nor was it founded on any ante-nuptial contract duly ascertained, or on any other valuable consideration. The only attempt at any support of that kind, is the parol promise stated in the answer of H.G.L. to have been made by him previous to his marriage, and which is mentioned also by some of the witnesses. There are several reasons why I think the settlement cannot derive any aid from that parol agreement.

The proof of the agreement consists only of parol declarations and confessions of H.G.L., made after his marriage. . . .

If the present case had, therefore, arisen prior to the statute of frauds, I apprehend it would have been deemed a fraudulent settlement in regard to the existing creditors, from the want of a sufficient connection in point of time, and of correspondence in point of proof, between the settlement and the alleged agreement. And, if it did correspond, the proof of the agreement is defective. To support such a settlement upon no other proof of the prior agreement than the declarations of the husband during coverture, would be to overturn the statute of frauds, and to produce the most lax and dangerous doctrines. Every fraudulent debtor might easily render such doctrines subservient to his views, for he has only to declare that he makes such a settlement in consequence of a prior agreement, and he can then transfer all his estate to his family, and defraud his creditors. But this cannot be the sound rule, and we ought, at least, to require, from the person setting up the settlement, direct and certain proof of the agreement, independent of these interested and suspicious declarations of the party himself.

A settlement after marriage, in pursuance of a valid agreement before marriage, may be good and binding. . . . But these were cases prior to the statute of frauds, (29 Charles II.) which renders void all parol promises, in consideration of marriage; and, therefore, since the statute, it has been determined, that the agreement, to be valid, must be in writing. . . .

If the settlement be considered, as I think it ought to be, unconnected with any ante-nuptial agreement, the simple question then is, whether such a voluntary settlement after marriage, by a party indebted at the time, be not, as against such creditors, absolutely fraudulent and void.

I think this question can be most satisfactorily answered in the affirmative; but the manner in which it has been argued, imposes on me the necessity of reviewing the cases.

As early as the case of Shaw v. Standysh, (2 Vern. 326.) the distinction on the subject of voluntary conveyances seems to have been taken and understood, between creditors existing at the time of the conveyance, and subsequent creditors, and that it was clearly void as to the former, though not as of course against the latter. This was so advanced upon argument in that case; and, perhaps, it was a distinction of common law growth; for it was agreed in *Twyne's case,* (3 Co. 83. a.) that an estate made by fraud shall be avoided only by him who has prior right; but he who hath subsequent right shall not avoid it. But in the Exchequer case of St. Amand v. Barbara, (Comyn's Rep. 255.) a settlement was made upon a child by a party indebted by bond, and who afterwards became also indebted by bond. It was admitted as a doubtful point, whether, if the party had not been indebted at the time, the settlement would have been fraudulent as against the subsequent creditors; but as the party was indebted at the time, the settlement was void against debts contracted afterwards, and all the bond creditors were allowed to come in as against the settlement. If the rule was otherwise, it was said in this case, that the same result would follow in another way; for the subsequent bond creditors would be permitted to stand in the place of the prior bond creditors, and the assets be so marshalled as to satisfy all. . . .

In Stileman v. Ashdown, (2 Atk. 477.) Brown v. Jones, (1 Atk. 190.) Wheeler v. Caryl, (Amb. 121.) and Hylton v. Biscoe, (Ves. 304.) Lord Hardwicke defined what were good settlements after marriage, as against creditors; and he held those good which were made in consideration of a portion paid at the time by, or on behalf of the wife, or in consideration of an agreement by articles before marriage. Such settlements are of equal validity with those made before marriage, in consideration of marriage, and which, it is agreed, are good, even though the party be then indebted. But he said, if the settlement after marriage was in consideration of marriage only, it was voluntary and fraudulent against creditors; and though he was not even indebted at the time, yet if he made the settlement with a view to a future indebtedness, it was equally fraudulent. So, in Ward v. Shallet, (2 Vesey, 18.) he admits a settlement after marriage, in consideration of a portion advanced, or in consideration of the wife parting with a contingent interest secured by her husband's bond, before marriage, to be good; but still he qualifies the admission by saying, there must be no "fraud or great inadequacy."

All the cases assume the position to be undeniable, that the husband must not be indebted at the time of the settlement. They leave no possible doubt on the point. In Middlecome v. Marlow, (2 Atk. 519.) Lord Hardwicke held a post-nuptial settlement good, "there being no proof of the husband being indebted at the time; there was not so much as a single creditor." The settlement in this case was also very reasonable, it being only of the personal estate received from the wife. So, again, in Taylor v. Jones, (2 Atk. 600.) a settlement after marriage on the wife and children was held fraudulent, as to creditors, under the 13th Eliz.; and this case is worthy of notice for the doctrines which it contains. The settlement was held to be fraudulent, as well in respect to creditors after, as before the settlement, for the debtor continued in possession of the property settled; and the statute of Eliz. was held to extend equally to the subsequent creditors who were delayed or defrauded. It was further observed by the master of the rolls, "that it was not material, in that case, what the circumstances of the father were at the time of the settlement, any farther than as evidence to show, if he was in indigent circumstances, that it was made with an intent to commit a fraud."

This case contains also a just observation on the sympathy which is usually excited, or attempted to be excited, in these cases, in favor of the objects of the settlement. "I have always," observes the master of the rolls, "a great compassion for wife and children; yet, on the other side, it is possible, if creditors should not have their debts, their wives and children may be reduced to want.". . .

Lord Hardwicke's decisions are all consistent on this interesting subject. . . .

. . . . He spoke strongly in favor of the superiority of the claims of creditors over family provisions, and observed, that "though an unfortunate case may arise in respect to children, for whom parents are bound by nature to provide, it is impossible to say, the consideration in respect of them is of so high a nature as that of paying just debts, and, therefore, the Court never preferred them to just creditors." In Fitzer v. Fitzer, (2 Atk. 511.) Lord Hardwicke asked the attorney-general if there was an instance in that Court where a conveyance from husband to wife, without any pecuniary consideration moving from the wife, had been held to be good against creditors.

The same rules and distinctions are declared and enforced throughout the subsequent decisions. . . .

It cannot escape observation, that the only question in these cases was respecting the subsequent creditors. There is no doubt, in any case, as to the safety and security of the then existing creditor. No voluntary post-nuptial settlement was ever permitted to affect him; and the cases seem to agree, that the subsequent creditors are let in only in particular cases; as where the settlement was made in contemplation of future debts, or where it is requisite to interfere and set aside the settlement, in favor of the prior creditor, or where the subsequent creditor can impeach the settlement, as fraudulent, by reason of the prior indebtedness. . . .

The conclusion to be drawn from the cases is, that if the party be indebted at the time of the voluntary settlement, it is presumed to be fraudulent in respect to such debts, and no circumstance will permit those debts to be affected by the settlement, or repel the legal presumption of fraud. The presumption of law, in this case, does not depend upon the amount of the debts, or the extent of the property in settlement, or the circumstances of the party. There is no such line of distinction set up, or traced in any of the cases. The attempt would be embarrassing, if not dangerous to the rights of the creditor, and prove an inlet to fraud. The law has, therefore, wisely disabled the debtor from making any voluntary settlement of his estate, to stand in the way of his existing debts. This is the clear and uniform doctrine of the cases, and it is sufficient for the decision of the present cause.

With respect to the claims of subsequent creditors, there is more difficulty in arriving at the conclusion; and I am not called upon in this case to give any definitive opinion, for there are no such creditors before the Court. But since the subject has been examined, I would suggest what appears to me at present, but with my mind still open for further discussion and consideration, to be the better opinion from the cases; it is, that the presumption of fraud as to these creditors, arising from the circumstance, that the party was indebted at the time, is repelled by the fact of these debts being secured by mortgage, or by a provision in the settlement; that if no such circumstance exists, they are entitled to impeach the settlement by a bill properly adapted to their purpose, and charging and proving indebtedness at the time so that their rights will not depend on the mere pleasure of the prior creditors, whether they will or will not impeach the settlement; that the question then arises, To what extent must the subsequent creditors show a prior indebtedness? Must they follow the dictum of Lord Alvanley, and show insolvency, or will it be sufficient to show any prior debt, however small, as is contended for by Mr. Atherley, with his usual ability, in his Treatise on Marriage Settlements? (Ath. Mar. Set. p. 212 to 219.) I should apprehend, that the subsequent creditors would be required to go so far, and only so far, in showing debts, as would be sufficient to raise reasonable evidence of a fraudulent intent. To show any existing debt, however trifling and inevitable, (to which every person is, more or less, subject,) would not surely support a presumption of fraud in fact; no voluntary settlement in any possible case could stand upon that construction. I should rather conclude, that the fraud in the voluntary settlement was an inference of law, and ought to be so, as far as it concerned existing debts; but that, as to subsequent debts, there is no such necessary legal presumption, and there must be proof of fraud in fact; and the indebtedness at the time, though not amounting to insolvency, must be such as to warrant that conclusion. It appears, in all the cases, (and particularly in the decision of Sir Thomas Plumer since the publication of M. Atherley's treatise) that a marked distinction does exist, under the statute of 13 Eliz., between prior and subsequent creditors, in respect to these voluntary settlements; and it is now settled, that the settlement is not void, as of course, against the latter, when there were no prior debts at the time. . . .

If the question rests not upon an actual fraudulent intent, (as is admitted in all the cases,) it must be a case of fraud in law, arising from the fact of a voluntary disposition of property, while indebted; and the inference founded on that fact cannot depend on the particular circumstances, or greater or less degree of pecuniary embarrassment of the party. These are matters for consideration, when we are seeking, as in the case of subsequent creditors, for actual fraud. I apprehend it is, upon the whole, better and safer not to allow a party to yield to temptation, or natural impulse, by giving him the power of placing property in his family beyond the reach of existing creditors. He must be taught by the doctrines of the Court, that the claims of justice are prior to those of affection. The inclination of my mind is strongly in favor of the policy and wisdom of the rule, which absolutely disables a man from preferring, by any arrangement whatever, and with whatever intention, by gifts of his property, his children to his creditors. Though hard cases may arise in which we should wish the rule to be otherwise, yet, as a permanent regulation, more good will ensue to families, and to the public at large, by a strict adherence to the rule, than by rendering it subservient to circumstances, or by making it to depend upon a fraudulent intent, which is so difficult to ascertain, and frequently so painful to infer. . . .

The question does not arise, in this case, as to what extent those voluntary dispositions of property can be reached. Here the land itself exists in the hands of the trustee for the wife; and we have no concern, at present, with the question, how far gifts of chattels, of money, of choses in action, of corporate, of public stock, or of property alienated to a bona fide purchaser, can be affected. The debt in the present case was large, and the disposition extravagant, being of the greater part of the real estate; and we have no evidence of sufficient property left unencumbered. Even if we were to enter into the particular circumstances of the case, I should have no doubt of the justice of the creditor's claim.

I shall, accordingly, decree, that a reference be had to ascertain the balance of principal and interest due to the plaintiff, and that so much of the lands, included in the conveyance to Gilbert Aspinwall, as the master shall judge sufficient to satisfy that amount, with costs, be sold; and that the said G.A. be directed to join in the conveyance, &c. . . . .

Notes & Questions

1. *The Importance of Insolvency.* Chancellor Kent's dictum in *Reade,* that "gifts" by a *solvent* debtor are fraudulent, has been rejected by the UFCA, see § 4, and by most states, including New York. The rule is, however, followed in a few states. See, e.g., Franklin v. Nunnelley, 242 Ala. 87, 5 So.2d 99 (1941); 1 G. Glenn, Fraudulent Conveyances and Preferences § 269 (rev. ed. 1940).

Why does fraudulent conveyance doctrine in most states make so much turn on the debtor's insolvency? Would a better rule be one that proscribes transfers that unduly hinder creditors, whether or not the transfer happens to occur at a time when the debtor is technically insolvent? Is this close to the rule Chancellor Kent was articulating in Reade v. Livingston?

2. *Transfers by Defendants.* Not all of Kent's views on the matter of solvency have been abandoned in New York. Section 273–a of New York's Debtor and Creditor Law states:

> Every conveyance made without fair consideration when the person making it is a defendant in an action for money damages or a judgment in such an action had been docketed against him, is fraudulent as to the plaintiff in that action without regard to the actual intent of the defendant if, after final judgment for the plaintiff, the defendant fails to satisfy the judgment.

What is the effect of this provision? May a defendant give Christmas presents to employees? See McLaughlin, Application of the Uniform Fraudulent Conveyances Act, 46 Harv.L.Rev. 404 (1933). Is § 273–a more restrictive of transfers than was Reade v. Livingston?

3. *Transfers to Related Parties.* A law student's father promises to buy him a color television set if he gets all "A's" in law school. The student does so and the father buys the student a color television. If the father is insolvent at the time of the purchase, may the father's creditors recover from the student? Suppose that under state contract

law the student could enforce his father's promise to reward him. Would that make a difference in analysis under the UFCA? Was there fair consideration at the time of the father's promise? Does that matter? How does this case differ from Professor Clark's second situation? from *Reade?*

4. *Present and Future Creditors.* *Reade* devotes substantial attention to differences in treatment between present and future creditors of a debtor who has made a fraudulent conveyance. How does the UFCA deal with this issue? Does it make sense to distinguish between the two classes of creditors?

5. *The Debtor-in-Possession Problem.* Note the court's mention of retention of transferred property as evidence of fraudulent intent. Cases involving failure to surrender possession of property transferred have played a prominent role in the history of fraudulent conveyance and secured transactions law. The leading fraudulent conveyance case, Twyne's Case, 3 Coke 80b, 76 Eng.Rep. 809 (1601), was decided under the Statute of Elizabeth and involved a secret transfer of all of a debtor's property. The debtor retained possession of the property and later sold some of it. Coke reports that the badges of fraud in the case included (1) the generality of the transfer, "without exception of his apparel, or anything of necessity," (2) the continued possession of the property by the debtor, (3) the secrecy of the transfer, and (4) the transfer occurring while the debtor was defending against an action by creditors.

Aside from Twyne's obvious intent to defraud creditors, his case raises problems that transcend fraudulent conveyance doctrine. Much of Article 9 of the U.C.C. strives to provide creditors with notice of interests in a debtor's property. Perfection by possession and by filing both serve to put creditors on notice of a debtor's transfer of an interest in his property. To some extent Article 9's approval of nonpossessory security interests collides with fraudulent conveyance law's traditional hostility towards transfers not accompanied by a change of possession. See generally Calif.Civil Code §§ 3440 to 3440.9; U.C.C. § 2–402(2).

BULLARD v. ALUMINUM CO. OF AMERICA

United States Court of Appeals, Seventh Circuit, 1972.
468 F.2d 11.

WILLIAM J. CAMPBELL, SENIOR DISTRICT JUDGE.

The defendant Aluminum Company of America (Alcoa) appeals from an order of the district court which granted the motion of the plaintiff, trustee in bankruptcy of the estate of Kritzer Radiant Coils, Inc. (Kritzer Radiant), for summary judgment. The district court held that a transfer of $23,370.60 from the bankrupt to Alcoa was a "fraudulent transfer" under § 67d(2)(a) of the Bankruptcy Act. 11 U.S.C. § 107d(2) (a). Alcoa raises three contentions on appeal: (1) that the transfer was not fraudulent inasmuch as there was no evidence that Alcoa participated in a scheme to defeat the other creditors of Kritzer Radiant or that the transaction involving the transfer of monies was lacking in good faith; (2) that summary judgment was improperly entered since the pleadings and affidavits raised genuine issues of material fact concerning the intentions and motives of Alcoa; and (3) that the district court erred in failing to hold Alcoa had a right under § 67d(6) of the Bankruptcy Act to retain the $23,370.60 as security for repayment of the actual consideration given by Alcoa.

The facts as gleaned from the pleadings, affidavits and from defendant's answers to plaintiff's interrogatories show that on December 1st, 1965, the date of the transfer in question, the bankrupt, Kritzer Radiant, was indebted to Alcoa in the amount of $46,741.20. As of that time 85% of the outstanding capital stock of Kritzer Radiant was owned by Bastian Morely Company, Inc. (Bastian Morely) and the remaining 15% of the stock was held by Henry Kritzer, Sr. Henry Kritzer at that time also owned 15% of the outstanding common stock of Bastian Morely and was a director of that Company. The $46,741.20 debt of Kritzer Radiant, which had been personally guaranteed by Henry Kritzer, had been reduced to a judgment against Kritzer individually and in favor of Alcoa in the Circuit Court of Lake County, Illinois. For a period of time prior to December 1st, 1965, both Kritzer Radiant and Bastian Morely had dealt with Alcoa as a supplier of materials used in manufacturing their products. Bastian Morely was also indebted to Alcoa as of that date in the amount of $11,319.78.

On the critical date of December 1, 1965 an agreement was entered into by and between Kritzer Radiant, Henry Kritzer, Bastian Morely and Alcoa. Pursuant to this agreement, Kritzer Radiant paid to Alcoa $23,370.60 in full satisfaction of the antecedent debt owed Alcoa in the amount of $46,741.20. Additionally, Alcoa released Henry Kritzer from the judgment it had recovered against him in the state court. Finally, Bastian satisfied its debt to Alcoa in the amount of $11,319.78, and ordered from Alcoa additional materials for payment upon receipt. On the date the settlement agreement was executed, Kritzer Radiant was insolvent and there existed creditors of Kritzer Radiant with outstanding claims against it.

The pertinent portion of § 67d(2)(a) of the Bankruptcy Act provides as follows:

> "(2) Every transfer made and every obligation incurred by a debtor within one year prior to the filing of a petition initiating a proceeding under this Act by or against him is fraudulent (a) as to creditors existing at the time of such transfer or obligation, if made or incurred without fair consideration by a debtor who is or will be thereby rendered insolvent, *without regard to his actual intent;* . . . ." (11 U.S.C. § 107d(2)(a) (Emphasis supplied)).

The definition of fair consideration is furnished in § 67d(1)(e) which provides:

> "Consideration given for the property or obligation of a debtor is 'fair' (1) when, in *good faith,* in exchange and as a fair equivalent

therefor property is transferred or an antecedent debt is satisfied, ..." (11 U.S.C. § 107d(1)(e). (Emphasis supplied)).

As the district court indicated in its memorandum opinion, essentially four elements must be present for a transfer to be fraudulent under § 67d(2)(a) of the Act:

    1. The transfer must occur within one year of the initiation of the bankruptcy proceedings;

    2. Creditors of the debtor must exist at the time of the transfer;

    3. The debtor must be insolvent at the time of the transfer; and

    4. There must be a failure of consideration for the transfer.

The bankruptcy petition here was filed on November 22nd, 1966, clearly within one year of the date of the transfer in question. Creditors of Kritzer Radiant were in existence when the transfer was made. Also there is no serious dispute regarding the insolvency of Kritzer Radiant on the date of the transfer. Alcoa then possessed a financial statement of Kritzer Radiant which reflected a negative net worth. Also, some three weeks prior to the execution of the settlement agreement the defendant wrote its attorneys suggesting that certain precautions be undertaken ". . . should either Bastian Morely or Kritzer Radiant Coils go into bankruptcy within four months of the transaction." While it is true that the defendant denied the allegation of insolvency in its answer, we agree with the district court that since Alcoa did not challenge plaintiff's assertion by counter-affidavit nor make any attempt to demonstrate the inaccessibility of information on this question, the issue of insolvency did not present a fact issue precluding the entry of summary judgment.

Thus, the question becomes, under the undisputed facts as set forth above, whether the transfer from Kritzer Radiant to Alcoa was for "fair consideration." Where the transfer is made to extinguish an antecedent debt, the Bankruptcy Act provides that the consideration given must represent a "fair equivalent" for the antecedent debt and must be given in "good faith." 11 U.S.C. §§ 107d(1)(e), 107d(2)(a); see also 4 Collier On Bankruptcy § 67.33. As the defendant itself recognizes, a transfer lacking in good faith is fraudulent within the meaning of the Bankruptcy Act even though fair equivalent may have been present. And the question of good faith depends under the circumstances on whether the "transaction carries the earmarks of an arms-length bargain." Holahan v. Henderson, D.C., 277 F.Supp. 890, aff'd 394 F.2d 177 (5th Cir. 1969).

Considering all the facts that attended this transaction we agree with the district court that the transfer was fraudulent within the meaning of § 67d(2)(a) of the Bankruptcy Act. We find most significant the relationship of the parties to the settlement agreement and the respective allocation of its benefits. Henry Kritzer, the President of the bankrupt as well as a director and stockholder of Bastian Morely, was released entirely and without any consideration on his part from a legally enforceable state court judgment against him. Moreover, Bastian Morely, the principal stockholder of the bankrupt, was permitted to retain its supplier and, for a consideration, extinguished its own antecedent debt to Alcoa. Finally, Alcoa acquired an advantage over the other creditors of the bankrupt at a time when Alcoa was certainly aware of the precarious financial position of Kritzer Radiant. Thus the primary and important benefits of this transaction ran to parties other than the bankrupt. Since transfers made to benefit third parties are not considered as made for "fair" consideration, we agree that on these facts, which are not disputed by the defendant, the transfer here was a fraudulent one within the meaning of § 67d(2)(a) of the Bankruptcy Act.

Alcoa next contends that summary judgment was improper here since there was a fact question raised by the pleadings and affidavits as to the motives and intentions of Alcoa with respect to this transaction. In this regard Alcoa maintains that the transfer here could not have been fraudulent unless Alcoa participated in a scheme to defeat the other creditors of Kritzer Radiant or unless Alcoa acted on bad faith in valuing the properties exchanged. We have been unable to find any support, either statutory or in case law, for this argument. Indeed, the Act itself is to the contrary. A transfer made without "fair consideration", such as the one involved here, represents but one of the several types of fraudulent transfers defined in § 67 of the Act. See 11 U.S.C. § 107d. A transfer is rendered fraudulent under § 67d(2)(a), the section here involved, when made or incurred without fair consideration by a debtor who is or will be thereby rendered insolvent, irrespective of the intent of the parties to the transaction. See 11 U.S.C. § 107d(2)(a); 4 Collier On Bankruptcy § 67.34. The situation that Alcoa refers to, where there is an actual intent to defraud, is specifically covered by § 67d(2)(d) of the Act. Thus, under the section of the Act on which the Trustee proceeded in this case, the motives and intentions of Alcoa are simply immaterial.

Lastly, Alcoa contends that under § 67d(6) of the Bankruptcy Act, it may retain the transferred funds as security for payment of its antecedent debt. See 11 U.S.C. § 107d(6). Under our long-standing rule that issues not presented to the district court cannot be raised for the first time on appeal, we need not consider this question.

For the reasons given the judgment of the district court is hereby affirmed.

Notes & Questions

1. *Adequacy of Consideration Received by the Debtor.* Did the debtor in *Bullard* really receive inadequate consideration from the transactions with Alcoa? Suppose Alcoa had simply agreed to accept half payment on the money owed to it by Kritzer Radiant? Would there have been anything illegal, immoral or fraudulent about such an

arrangement? Is *Bullard* a stronger or weaker case for finding a fraudulent conveyance?

Must every creditor accepting a compromise payment from a financially troubled debtor worry about having to disgorge that payment as a fraudulent conveyance? Is it clear that Alcoa obtained an advantage over other creditors? Can you state precisely what that advantage is? Did Alcoa give anything up to obtain that advantage?

How would *Bullard* come out under § 5 of the UFTA?

2. *Relevance of Consideration Flowing to Third Parties.* Is the real problem in *Bullard* that some of the consideration benefitted parties other than the debtor? Does the discharge of Henry Kritzer's debt to Alcoa benefit the debtor?

3. *Duty of Inquiry.* Suppose one purchases an asset from a financially troubled debtor. Must the purchaser be sensitive to debtor behavior that indicates that the debtor may be trying to hinder his creditors? What duty of inquiry is imposed upon such purchasers? See Alan Drey Co., Inc. v. Generation, Inc., 22 Ill.App.3d 611, 317 N.E.2d 673 (1974) ("to be regarded as a participator in the fraud, it is not necessary that the purchaser have actual knowledge of the debtor's fraudulent intent, but merely a knowledge of facts and circumstances sufficient to excite the suspicions of a prudent man and be put on inquiry, or to lead a person of ordinary perception to infer fraud").

3. In Steph v. Branch, 255 F.Supp. 526 (E.D.Okl.1966), affirmed 389 F.2d 233 (10th Cir. 1968), Branch controlled the debtor when the debtor was sold to the Chandlers for $28,000. At the time of the sale Branch paid all obligations but one then owed by the debtor. The Chandlers paid $5,000 down and signed a promissory note in the amount of $23,000, secured by the debtor's property. The Chandlers then used corporate assets to pay off the note held by Branch. The debtor was insolvent when transfers of assets were made to Branch. The court found that the transfers, totaling $19,594.54, were without fair consideration to the debtor. "The only persons receiving any consideration from these transfers were the Chandlers who obtained a personal consideration in the form of their purchase price note to Branch for the corporate stock . . . being accordingly reduced. But this consideration to the Chandlers for their personal obligation cannot be said to be a consideration to the [corporation whose inventory was being depleted without any consideration to it which activity eventually led to its bankruptcy." Id. at 531.

Did the behavior in *Steph* violate any of Professor Clark's principles of fraudulent conveyance law? Did the behavior in *Bullard* violate any of these principles?

2. Fraudulent Conveyances and Modern Corporate Transactions

TELEFEST, INC. v. VU–TV, INC.

United States District Court, District of New Jersey, 1984.
591 F.Supp. 1368.

BARRY, DISTRICT JUDGE.

The question before the court is whether a security agreement executed on May 6, 1983 for the benefit of intervenor Manufacturers Hanover Trust ("MHT") by defendant VU–TV, Inc. ("VU–TV") and by the company of which VU–TV is a wholly-owned subsidiary, CATV Products, Inc. ("CATV"), constituted a fraudulent conveyance within the meaning of the Uniform Fraudulent Conveyance Act ("UFCA"), as adopted by New Jersey, 25 N.J.S.A. 2–7 through 2–19 ("NJFCA"). If that conveyance was fraudulent, MHT will be impaired to the extent of the fraud in asserting what is otherwise a priority security interest in funds being held by Graphic Scanning, Inc. ("Graphics") for the benefit of VU–TV.

Plaintiff TeleFest, Inc. ("TeleFest") seeks to recover a portion of those funds to recompense the violations of a licensing agreement that it had with defendant VU–TV. Barton Press, Inc. ("Barton"), is a judgment lien creditor, seeking to recover on a contract breached by VU–TV. For the reasons set forth below, I conclude that TeleFest and Barton have failed to prove that the security agreement between MHT and VU–TV amounted to a fraudulent conveyance.

TeleFest entered into a licensing agreement with VU–TV on March 22, 1982. TeleFest licensed to VU–TV the world-wide distribution rights of videotapes of musical performances given at the ChicagoFest Blues Series in 1981. VU–TV agreed to pay TeleFest seventy percent of the gross proceeds of world-wide sales, with a minimum payment of fifty thousand dollars. Simultaneously, the two parties agreed that, in consideration of $7500, VU–TV would distribute another videotape, "Cheap Trick Live at ChicagoFest".

Alleging that VU–TV failed to pay the specified guaranteed amounts and to perform other contractual obligations, TeleFest brought this action on March 4, 1983. VU–TV failed to answer or otherwise appear and, on April 8, 1983, TeleFest was granted an Order of Final Judgment against VU–TV for $57,500, plus costs.

Barton obtained a default judgment against VU–TV on April 19, 1984 in the Superior Court of New Jersey in the amount of $85,323.86. It attempted to levy on that judgment on June 11, 1984, but found that the VU–TV account receivable held by Graphics was affected by restraints imposed by this court on November 22, 1983. Barton sought permission to intervene under Fed.R.Civ.P. 24(b). Notwithstanding the fact that Barton is not indispensable, the motion to intervene was granted because Barton's claim and the main action involve common questions of law and fact.

MHT claims that its security agreement has priority over the judgments of both TeleFest and Barton. The basis for its claim is set forth in the affidavit of MHT Senior Vice–President Joseph Adamko, dated June 4, 1984. According to that affidavit, CATV's predecessor, Gamco Industries, Inc., opened an account and obtained a secured loan from MHT on May 15, 1980. In November, 1980, Gamco sold its assets and changed its name to CATV. The Gamco loan was repaid by January, 1981. In July, 1981, MHT, a New York banking association, agreed to extend a $100,000 unsecured line of credit to VU–TV at two percent over the prime rate of interest in exchange for the personal guarantees of VU–TV's Treasurer, Martin Horak, and its Secretary, Leon Poitrais, and the cross-corporate guarantee of CATV.

An MHT "Credit Facility Review" was conducted in March and April, 1982 in connection with a plan of Horak and Poitrais and a VU–TV and CATV stockholder, Ted Leder, to obtain a $300,000 loan to purchase San Antonio Home Entertainment, Inc. ("San Antonio"). A statement entitled "Credit Department Review", dated March 12, 1982, was issued as part of that effort. The statement described VU–TV's business, its financial condition, and the results obtained through the end of September, 1981 by the company. It concluded that VU–TV was a "company which has recorded strong sales growth and sizeable profit margins, and earnings have been reinvested to increase its equity base." The reviewer also noted that the corporate officers were highly expert and experienced and that the company was positioning itself for expansion to European markets.

MHT agreed to provide the requested loan, but cross-corporate guarantees were to be executed by VU–TV, CATV and San Antonio with each company cross-collateralizing with all assets, including receivables, the loans of the other companies. The collateralization was to cover all outstanding loans, including those that had previously been unsecured. A general security agreement was to be executed and filings on the companies' assets made. In May, 1982, the cross-guarantees of the companies and related documents, prepared by MHT's legal department, were supposedly sent to Horak. Loans were also extended in April and May, 1982 to CATV, which received $300,000, and to San Antonio, which received $20,000.

VU–TV and CATV's cross-guarantees and the UCC filing statements were not executed with the other documents in May and June, 1982. MHT is unable to account for this lapse, but believes that it either failed to prepare those documents, did not receive them back from Horak, or received the documents executed, but "misplaced" them. MHT discovered "sometime in early 1983" that it did not have the desired guarantees. An MHT "Interoffice Letter", dated January 20, 1983, requested the MHT Legal Department to prepare guarantees and UCC filings for VU–TV, CATV and San Antonio.

The loans that had been made to the related companies were renewed by MHT at each maturity date and further loans extended.

As of January, 1983, CATV owed MHT $450,000, VU–TV owed $50,000 and San Antonio owed $17,000. By June, 1983, the loan balances had been reduced, and CATV owed $385,000, VU–TV owed $50,000, and San Antonio owed $15,000. Although MHT filed financing statements for VU–TV accounts receivable on April 15, 1983 with the Clerk of Middlesex County, New Jersey, and on April 18, 1983 with the Secretary of State of New Jersey, it was not until May 6, 1983 that CATV executed a "Guarantee of all Liability and Security Agreement" ("Guarantee"). VU–TV executed a similar agreement, thereby cross-collateralizing the loans extended to the related entities.

A second affidavit of Mr. Adamko, dated October 19, 1983, avers that all of the notes executed by VU–TV and the related entities in favor of MHT are in default. Adamko asserts that because MHT filed its financing statements before TeleFest had the United States Marshal serve a writ of execution upon Graphics—a corporation holding certain monies for the benefit of VU–TV—on June 22, 1983, MHT has a priority of security interest and is entitled to collect any monies held by Graphics for the benefit of VU–TV, up to a total of $450,000.

TeleFest contests the priority of security interest on a number of grounds, one of which is TeleFest's assertion that because MHT obtained the security agreement from VU–TV after the entry of TeleFest's default judgment against VU–TV without fair consideration and at a time when the latter was already insolvent, MHT was the grantee of a fraudulent conveyance within the meaning of the UFCA, as adopted in New Jersey.

TeleFest argues and MHT does not dispute that the security agreement of May 6, 1983 constituted a "conveyance" under § 2–7 of the NJFCA. There is no doubt that, at the very least, the security agreement involved the pledge of "intangible property" pursuant to that section.

The NJFCA contains a provision covering conveyances made where an actual intent to hinder creditors exists, N.J.S.A. 25:2–13, and provisions covering conveyances that are deemed fraudulent without reference to intent. N.J.S.A. 25:2–10 through 12. TeleFest abjures any attempt to prove that there was an intent to defraud creditors when the security agreement was executed, but relies on the three provisions of the NJFCA which read as follows:

25:2–10. What constitutes insolvency fraudulent

Every conveyance made and every obligation incurred by a person who is or will be thereby rendered insolvent is fraudulent as to creditors without regard to his actual intent if the conveyance is made or the obligation is incurred without a fair consideration.

25:2–11. Conveyances by persons in business without fair consideration

Every conveyance made without fair consideration when the person making it is engaged or is about to engage in a business or transaction for which the property remaining in his hands after the conveyance is an unreasonably small capital is fraudulent as to creditors and as to other persons who become creditors during the continuance of such business or transaction without regard to his actual intent.

25:2–12. Incurring debts beyond ability to pay

Every conveyance made and every obligation incurred without fair consideration when the person making the conveyance or entering into the obligation intends to or believes that he will incur debts beyond his ability to pay as they mature, is fraudulent as to both present and future creditors.

TeleFest argues that to the extent that VU–TV's security agreement guaranteed debts incurred by CATV and San Antonio, the agreement was a conveyance or obligation incurred without fair consideration.[2] However, separate and apart from the issue of fair consideration, TeleFest is obliged to show that VU–TV was insolvent at the time of the conveyance to MHT because, in actions to set aside a conveyance as fraudulent to the creditors of the grantor, the burden of proving fraud rests upon the plaintiff. . . .

It is readily apparent then that TeleFest has a heavy burden to show insolvency as the first step in proving a fraudulent conveyance. It has gone some distance in meeting that burden, but hardly far enough to warrant the conclusion that no reasonable jury could find other than that VU–TV was insolvent on May 6, 1983. MHT's characterization of many of the statements in the affidavits presented by TeleFest as hearsay is an accurate one, and it is far from obvious that the material obtained "is more probative on the point for which it is offered than any other evidence which the proponent can procure through reasonable efforts." Fed.R.Evid. 803(24)(B).

There is simply not the abundant clarity, provided through a balancing of available assets and expected liabilities, that on the date of the transfer the grantor of the conveyance was unable to pay its debts as they became due. The most that can be said is that there is evidence that VU–TV may have been paying some debts, e.g. those to the bank, but not others, e.g. rent and wages, as they became due. I cannot say that, as a matter of law, that the state of VU–TV's finances amounted to insolvency for the purpose of determining that there was a fraudulent conveyance.

2. N.J.S.A. 25:2–9 states that fair consideration is given for property or an obligation:

a. When in exchange for such property or obligation, as a fair equivalent therefor, and in good faith, property is conveyed or an antecedent debt is satisfied; or

b. When such property or obligation is received in good faith to secure a present advance or antecedent debt in an amount not disproportionately small as compared with the value of the property or obligation obtained.

Not only is the question of insolvency one of fact, but whether "fair consideration" inhered in a conveyance is also generally a question of fact. . . .

Since insolvency has not been established, the court need not reach the question of fair consideration, but because the parties have forcefully argued their respective views in regard thereto, it will be discussed.

Where a conveyance is supported by an antecedent debt, a grantee of that conveyance may support it when it is attacked as fraudulent by merely pointing to the antecedent debt as the consideration, provided the grantee acted in good faith in accepting it. It is a different case, however, where there is an antecedent debt owed by someone other than the grantor. *See* Annotation, *Transaction in consideration of discharge of antecedent debt owed by one other than grantor as based on "fair consideration" under Uniform Fraudulent Conveyance Act,* 30 A.L.R.2d 1209. It is there stated, at 1210, that

> No case within the scope of this annotation has been discovered wherein the court has upheld a transaction, the consideration for which was the discharge of an antecedent debt owed by one other than the grantor, as based on 'fair consideration' under the Uniform Fraudulent Conveyance Act.

This principle applies not only with regard to a spouse's "conveyance" in consideration of the release of another spouse's debt, *see,* for example, *Hollander v. Gautier,* 114 N.J. 485, 489, 168 A. 860 (Ch. 1933), and the mortgage of partnership property to pay a partner's debts; 30 A.L.R.2d at 1212, but also with regard to a corporation paying the debt of another corporation. Although the case law in this area is sparse, it is more plentiful than the one case cited in the Annotation, *supra,* i.e. *Bennett v. Rodman & English,* 2 F.Supp. 355 (S.D.N.Y.) *aff'd* without opinion, 62 F.2d 1064 (2d Cir.1932). There have been at least three more recent cases that stand for the proposition that a transaction, the consideration for which was an antecedent debt of a corporation owed by one other than the corporate grantor, was not supported by "fair consideration" under the Uniform Fraudulent Conveyance Act.

In *In Re B–F Building Corporation,* 312 F.2d 691 (6th Cir.1963), an insolvent company named B–F owned certain real property, which it leased to Baird–Foerst, also bankrupt and a distributor of General Electric appliances. An individual named Baird was president of and held a controlling interest in both corporations. B–F owned premises occupied by Baird Foerst, but purchased a new site. Its checks in payment for the land were returned for insufficient funds. Baird–Foerst borrowed money from the Central National Bank and B–F defaulted on the land contract. Both companies became financially strapped and B–F decided to assist Baird Foerst by giving the bank from which the latter had borrowed a demand cognovit note for the sum borrowed. The note was endorsed by Baird and indicated that it was secured by the sale of B–F property. The District Court found, after both companies petitioned for bankruptcy, that the execution of the demand cognovit note was fraudulent because unsupported by consideration. B–F was found to owe a considerable sum to General Electric, which argued that payment of another's debt is a transfer without fair consideration. The Sixth Circuit agreed, citing, among other cases, Davis v. Hudson Trust Co., 28 F.2d 740 (3d Cir.1928), a case involving a husband-wife fraudulent conveyance.

In Re B–F Building Corporation, Bennett, Davis, and *Edward Hines W. Pine Co. v. First National Bank,* 61 F.2d 503 (7th Cir.1932), represent a line of cases that support the proposition that, while the agreement of a creditor to extend a debtor's time for payment or forbear suing on a claim constitutes a "valuable" consideration for the promise of a third party to pay a debt, such valuable consideration is not synonymous with "fair" consideration under the statute. Rosenberg, supra at 256. It might well be argued that the case at bar is similar to *In Re B–F Building Corporation,* supra, in that here VU–TV has attempted to affect a conveyance, consideration for which is not primarily a debt that it already owed MHT but, rather, debts owed by two related companies. The rule in *In Re B–F Building Corporation* and the other cases cited is a useful one in that it prevents insolvent corporations from preferring one creditor over another to an extent greater than their actual debt to the creditor preferred. This results in a more equitable distribution of the insolvent corporation's assets when creditors knock at the door of the troubled entity and militates against the insolvent corporation using its remaining assets for the benefit of related entities.

MHT distinguishes *In Re B–F Building Corporation* on two grounds: (1) that the debtor company was demonstrably insolvent at the time of the conveyance and (2) that the court's conclusion that fair consideration had not passed was premised on its finding that "the only thing the bank gave for [the debtor's] demand note . . . was an unsecured and probably worthless note of [debtor's related company]," while here a guarantee was given that cross-collateralized the loan with the corporation's assets. MHT relies upon what it calls the "identity of interest" rule found in *In Re Royal Crown Bottlers of North Alabama,* 23 B.R. 28 (N.D.Ala.1982). There, the court held that an insolvent debtor receives "less than a reasonably equivalent value" when it transfers property for a consideration to a third party, but that

> A clear distinction from this rule exists, however, if the debtor and the third party are so related or situated that they share an 'identity of interests', because what benefits one, will in such case, benefit the other to some degree.

Id. at 30 (footnote omitted).

MHT asserts that the June 4, 1984 Adamko affidavit shows the "close and intertwined relationship" between the parent company and its subsidiaries and that the loans to CATV were based on that close relationship and benefited VU–TV. TeleFest retorts that MHT has the burden of specifically showing how such a benefit accrued to VU–TV from the loans to its parent. It quotes a passage from *Royal Crown Bottlers,* supra which sets out the "identity of interest" rule:

> The ultimate question then becomes one of determining the value of this vicarious benefit and testing it by the measure of 'reasonably equivalent' for the property transferred by the insolvent debtor.

> When the consideration for a transfer passes to the parent corporation of a debtor/subsidiary making the transfer . . . the benefit to the debtor may be presumed to be nominal, in the absence of proof of a specific benefit to it.

I am satisfied that it was intended that a benefit would flow to VU–TV through the loans to CATV and San Antonio ultimately guaranteed by VU–TV. In April, 1982, when MHT was considering whether or not to extend a $300,000 loan to CATV for the purchase of San Antonio, MHT certainly regarded CATV and VU–TV as having an identity of interest. An internal memo from MHT Assistant Vice–President Fasano, dated April 12, 1982, in which that loan is discussed is, in fact, entitled "VU–TV, Inc. CATV Products, Inc." This memo evidences what MHT has consistently argued, i.e. that it always regarded VU–TV and its parent in tandem in its dealing with these companies. Such an outlook is relevant in considering whether the transferee of a conveyance acted in good faith. See generally Good Faith and Fraudulent Conveyances, 97 Harvard Law Review 495 (December 1983). It should also be noted that here the loan transactions were obviously at arm's length, another indicia of the transferee's good faith. Rosenberg, supra at 249.

Even more important than good faith in considering whether fair consideration passed is the nature of the transferor's business and its relationship with its parent. It is clear from the "Credit Department Review" and the Harris memo discussed above that VU–TV was devoted to providing programming for cable television companies, e.g. the ChicagoFest Blues Series. Monies loaned to VU–TV's parent to purchase a cable television system or for other moves directed toward expansion would most probably provide an additional and obviously secure market for VU–TV. The consideration for VU–TV's guarantee of the loans of its parent and sister companies may not have been a direct benefit, but it was a specific enough benefit for a reasonable trier of fact to conclude that fair consideration inhered in the conveyance.

In any event, the notion that a benefit accrues to a subsidiary only when there is a direct flow of capital to that entity the result of its guarantee of a loan to its parent is inhibitory of contemporary financing practices, which recognize that cross-guarantees are often needed because of the unequal abilities of interrelated corporate entities to collateralize loans. As one commentator has noted

> . . . (C)ourts often require a benefit to the guarantor corporation so that the transaction ostensibly fulfills a corporate purpose of the guarantor and is therefore not ultra vires. The concept of 'benefit' cannot, however, be defined precisely. For example, securing a

future sale might constitute a benefit. Consummating a transaction which will improve a corporation's public image might also be said to benefit that company. Since the concept of benefit involves the potential for such a wide range of results, courts have often required that the benefit be 'direct'. It is questionable whether this requirement has helped, however, since courts also vary considerably in their interpretation of the term 'direct.'

Note, Upstream Financing and the Use of the Corporate Guarantee, 53 Notre Dame Lawyer 840, 842 (1978).

Where there are indicia of a bona fide financing arrangement, not designed as a shield against other creditors, the lack of perceptible "direct" benefit to a subsidiary guaranteeing the loan of its parent should not be viewed as tantamount to a lack of "fair consideration" under the UFCA. Indirect benefit provides the necessary "fair consideration".

[Some courts have] rationalized upholding various transfers against fraudulent conveyance challenges by finding that sufficient consideration passed to the transferor because an opportunity had been given to it to escape bankruptcy through the strengthening of an affiliated corporation that received the benefit of the transfer. Such an approach seems indisputably proper when a weak but still solvent entity is rendered insolvent only because of the inclusion of the guaranty on the liability side of the balance sheet. This permits the analysis to focus upon economic reality in the appropriate factual context without rewarding legal laxity or inflexibly ignoring real benefits merely because they have no place on the company's balance sheet.

Such an approach would lead to a finding of fair consideration for a guaranty in a variety of other appropriate contexts. If an alter ego situation presents sufficient consideration, then so should the guaranty of a loan to a third party that is not the alter ego of the guarantor but whose continued health and existence is vitally important to the guarantor—a vital supplier or customer, for example. Under this approach, fair consideration to the guarantor could be found without much difficulty when the loan to the affiliated corporation strengthens its operation sufficiently so that the health of the guarantor is maintained or improved, even though bankruptcy was not imminent.

Rosenberg, supra at 245–246 (footnotes omitted).

The author cites, among other cases, Williams v. Twin City Company, 251 F.2d 678, 681 (9th Cir.1958), in which it is stated that direct consideration running from the creditor to the debtor need not be present for there to be fair consideration. Instead, consideration can run to a third party, so long as it is given in exchange for the promise sought to be enforced. Contemporary corporate practices of vertically and horizontally dividing the integrated operations of what is essentially one enterprise among a number of legally distinct entities, making it necessary for financial institutions to frequently obtain "upstream" and "cross-stream" collateralizations, demand that a broad view of "fair consideration" be taken.

One commentator on the law affecting "upstream" guarantees, in which a subsidiary guarantees the repayment of a loan to a parent corporation, and "cross-stream" guarantees, in which a subsidiary guarantees the repayment by another subsidiary of a common parent corporation, see Coquillette, Guaranty of and Security for the Debt of a Parent Corporation by a Subsidiary Corporation, 30 Case Western L.Rev. 433, 434 & n. 4 (1980), has opined that

> Because Parent and Subsidiary are part of a single economic unit, it is both logical and desirable that Parent be able to borrow based on the value of its subsidiaries' property and assets and that lenders be able to enjoy the full amount of protection which the borrower can make available. Clear legal treatment of these transactions would enable borrowers and lenders to enjoy commercially required confidence in the effectiveness of their arrangements, but the law relating to upstream guaranties and associated grants of security interests is at present difficult to determine and apply.

Id. at 436–437 (footnote omitted). Coquillette also has concluded that it is desirable for indirect benefits to a subsidiary to suffice as "fair consideration":

> The existence of fair consideration is therefore more safely determined by what Subsidiary has obtained in the transaction. Some of the funds obtained by Parent may flow through to Subsidiary. In addition, Subsidiary will receive a right to subrogation to the lender's claim against Parent. If Parent has other subsidiaries, Subsidiary may receive cross-guaranties from other subsidiaries and a right of contribution in the event that it must perform on the guaranty. Subsidiary also receives the intangible benefits of maintaining Parent's financial strength . . .

Id. at 452.

The following hypothetical with "facts" very like those in the instant matter has been posited by yet another commentator in support of the proposition that fair consideration may inhere in a conveyance even though that consideration results only in indirect benefit to the guarantor. A parent corporation, P, which owns two subsidiaries, A and B, asks a bank for a $2 million loan to be used to acquire C, a company that will be integrated into P's manufacturing and marketing system. A and B are required to guarantee the loan to P with equipment, inventory and accounts receivable. Eventually, P, A and B file for reorganization under Chapter XI and then for liquidation.

> The 'fair equivalent' received by A and B may also be sought in benefits which they expected to receive from P's acquisition of C, or other benefits resulting from the over-all corporate relationship. For instance, in our hypothetical case it was believed that the

acquisition of C was desirable because its product line complemented that of A. Bank could argue that A at least expected to benefit by the affiliation with C. In other fact situations the indirect benefits may be even clearer and more substantial. The transaction of which the guaranty is a part may safeguard an important source of supply, or an important customer for the guarantor. Or substantial indirect benefits may result from the general relationship between the parent corporation and its subsidiaries, rather than the particular transaction giving rise to the guaranty.

Consider another hypothetical situation in which a holding company owns 50 subsidiaries, each of which operates a single retail store. Another subsidiary handles buying for the entire chain through a central purchasing system. All advertising and financial functions are also handled centrally, and employees all work under union contracts covering the entire chain. The entire operation is an integrated one from an economic point of view even if the separate corporate identities of the various subsidiaries are carefully preserved, and separate accounting records are carefully maintained for each store. Because of economies of scale, the chain will be able to obtain goods, services and credit on more favorable terms than would be offered to any of the individual corporations. In such a situation, if the holding company borrows in order to open new stores owned by new subsidiaries, existing subsidiaries which guarantee the parent's obligations may well have received substantial indirect benefits which will constitute a fair equivalent consideration, even though the proceeds of the particular loan is used to open new stores, and the existing subsidiaries derive no direct benefit from these particular transactions.

Normandin, "Intercorporate Guaranties and Fraudulent Conveyances" in Personal Property Security Interests Under the Revised UCC 361, 370–371 (1977).

Here, I find that there was "fair consideration" and reject the claim that the guarantee constituted a fraudulent conveyance.[8]

. . .

Notes & Questions

1. *Downstream Guarantees.* Subsidiary S wishes to borrow money from Bank. Bank requires that the loan be guaranteed by S's parent corporation, P. Does such a guarantee raise any problems under the UFCA? How does this situation differ from that at issue in *TeleFest?* What guidance do Professor Clark's principles provide in assessing an "upstream guarantee" under the UFCA?

8. Interestingly, a 1979 Note, The Corporate Guaranty Revisited: Upstream, Downstream, and Beyond—A Statutory Approach, 32 Rutgers L.Rev. 312, 338, stated that ". . . (N)o recent case has been found in which a guaranty was invalidated on the ground of its adverse impact on a creditor."

2. *Valuing Contingent Rights.* In *TeleFest,* the subsidiary granted a security interest to secure a loan to its parent. What rights would the subsidiary have if the secured party relies on its security in the event of the parent company's default? Suppose the lender looked to the subsidiary as a guarantor of the parent's debt. Would the subsidiary have any rights if it paid the parent's obligation? How should contingent rights that guarantors may have, and reciprocal guarantees and reciprocal grants of security, be valued for purposes of determining a debtor's solvency? See Matter of Ollag Construction Equipment Corp., 578 F.2d 904 (2d Cir.1978).

3. *Excess Security.* Note the "not disproportionately small" requirement of UFCA § 3(b). Given that fraudulent conveyance law is designed to protect non-transferee creditors, what is the harm to such creditors if a debtor grants a security interest in property that substantially exceeds the value of the debt secured? If the value of the collateral exceeds that amount of the debt, who enjoys the surplus? See Article 9, Part 5. Should § 3(b) apply when the parties agree that the collateral will also serve to secure any future advances made by the secured creditor?

Should one view § 3(b) as reflecting skepticism about the likelihood of foreclosure actions ever realizing the "true value" of collateral? Need lenders, like MHT in *TeleFest,* who insist on multiple cross-corporate guarantees and grants of security worry, about receiving excess security?

4. *Self–Protection for Creditors.* Need fraudulent conveyance law protect the creditor in *TeleFest?* Is such a creditor in a position to protect itself? Compare the status of a tort creditor or a creditor such as that in the case that follows.

5. *Solvency Again.* If fair consideration is not received for a transfer, construct the arguments for and against treating the transfer as a fraudulent conveyance regardless of the debtor's solvency at the time of the transfer. See UFCA § 5.

UNITED STATES v. TABOR COURT REALTY CORP.

United States Court of Appeals, Third Circuit, 1986.
803 F.2d 1288

Before ALDISERT, CHIEF JUDGE, and HIGGINBOTHAM and HUNTER, CIRCUIT JUDGE.

OPINION OF THE COURT

ALDISERT, CHIEF JUDGE.

We have consolidated appeals from litigation involving one of America's largest anthracite coal producers that emanate from a district court bench trial that extended over 120 days and recorded close to 20,000 pages of transcript. Ultimately, we have to decide whether the court erred in entering judgment in favor of the United States in reducing to judgment certain federal corporate tax assessments made against the coal producers, in determining the priority of the government liens, and in permitting foreclosure on the liens. To reach these questions, however, we must examine a very intricate leveraged buy-out and decide whether mortgages given in the transaction were fraudulent conveyances within the meaning of the constructive and intentional fraud sections of the Pennsylvania Uniform Fraudulent Conveyances Act (UFCA), 39 Pa.Stat. §§ 354–357, and if so, whether a later assignment of the mortgages was void as against creditors.

The district court made 481 findings of facts and issued three separate published opinions: United States v. Gleneagles Investment Co., 565 F.Supp. 556 (M.D.Pa.1983) (Gleneagles I); 571 F.Supp. 935 (1983) (Gleneagles II); and 584 F.Supp. 671 (1984) (Gleneagles III). We are told that this case represents the first significant application of the UFCA to leveraged buy-out financing.

We will address seven issues presented by the appellants and an amicus curiae, the National Commercial Finance Association, and by the United States and a trustee in bankruptcy as cross appellants:

- whether the court erred in applying the UFCA to a leveraged buy-out;

- whether the court erred in denying the mortgage assignee, McClellan Realty, a "lien superior to all other creditors";

- whether the court erred in "collapsing" two separate loans for the leveraged buy-out into one transaction;

- whether the court erred in holding that the mortgages placed by the borrowers on November 26, 1973 were invalid under the UFCA;

- whether the court erred in holding that the mortgages placed by the guarantors were invalid for lack of fair consideration;

- in the government's cross-appeal, whether the court erred in determining that the mortgage assignee, McClellan Realty, was entitled to an equitable lien for municipal taxes paid; and

in the government's and trustee in bankruptcy's cross-appeal, whether the court erred in placing the mortgage assignee, McClellan Realty, on the creditor list rather than removing it entirely.

We will summarize a very complex factual situation and then discuss these issues seriatim.

I.

These appeals arise from an action by the United States to reduce to judgment delinquent federal income taxes, interest, and penalties assessed and accrued against Raymond Colliery Co., Inc. and its subsidiaries (the Raymond Group) for the fiscal years of June 30, 1966 through June 30, 1973 and to reduce to judgment similarly assessed taxes owed by Great American Coal Co., Inc. and its subsidiaries for the fiscal year ending June 30, 1975.

The government sought to collect these tax claims from surface and coal lands owned by the Raymond Group as well as from lands formerly owned by it but which, as a result of allegedly illegal and fraudulent county tax sales, were later owned by Gleneagles Investment Co., Inc. In addition, the government sought to assert the priority of its liens over liens held by others. The district court held in favor of the government on most of its claims and concluded the litigation by promulgating an order of priority of liens on Raymond Group lands.

Raymond Colliery, incorporated in 1962, was owned by two families, the Gillens and the Clevelands. It owned over 30,000 acres of land in Lackawanna and Luzerne counties in Pennsylvania and was one of the largest anthracite coal producers in the country. In 1966, Glen Alden Corporation sold its subsidiary, Blue Coal Corporation, to Raymond for $6 million. Raymond paid $500,000 in cash and the remainder of the purchase price with a note secured by a mortgage on Blue Coal's land. Lurking in the background of the financial problems present here are two important components of the current industrial scene: first, the depressed economy attending anthracite mining in Lackawanna and Luzerne Counties, the heartland of this industry; and second, the Pennsylvania Department of Environmental Resources' 1967 order directing Blue Coal to reduce the amount of pollutants it discharged into public waterways in the course of its deep mining operations, necessitating a fundamental change from deep mining to strip or surface mining.

Very serious problems surfaced in 1971 when Raymond's chief stockholders—the Gillens and Clevelands—started to have disagreements over the poor performance of the coal producing companies. The stockholders decided to solve the problem by seeking a buyer for the group. On February 2, 1972, the shareholders granted James Durkin, Raymond's president, an option to purchase Raymond for $8.5 million. The stockholders later renewed Durkin's option at a reduced price of $7.2 million.

Durkin had trouble in raising the necessary financing to exercise his option. He sought help from the Central States Pension Fund of the International Brotherhood of Teamsters and also from the Mellon Bank of Pittsburgh. Mellon concluded that Blue Coal was a bad financial risk. Moreover, both Mellon and Central States held extensive discussions with Durkin's counsel concerning the legality of encumbering Raymond's assets for the purpose of obtaining the loan, a loan which was not to be used to repay creditors but rather to buy out Raymond's stockholders.

After other unsuccessful attempts to obtain financing for the purchase, Durkin incorporated a holding company, Great American, and assigned to it his option to purchase Raymond's stock. Although the litigation in the district court was far-reaching, most of the central issues have their genesis in 1973 when the Raymond Group was sold to Durkin in a leveraged buy-out through the vehicle of Great American.

A leveraged buy-out is not a legal term of art. It is a shorthand expression describing a business practice wherein a company is sold to a small number of investors, typically including members of the company's management, under financial arrangements in which there is a minimum amount of equity and a maximum amount of debt. The financing typically provides for a substantial return of investment capital by means of mortgages or high risk bonds, popularly known as "junk bonds." The predicate transaction here fits the popular notion of a leveraged buy-out. Shareholders of the Raymond Group sold the corporation to a small group of investors headed by Raymond's president; these investors borrowed substantially all of the purchase price at an extremely high rate of interest secured by mortgages on the assets of the selling company and its subsidiaries and those of additional entities that guaranteed repayment.

To effectuate the buy-out, Great American obtained a loan commitment from Institutional Investors Trust on July 24, 1973, in the amount of $8,530,000. The 1973 interrelationship among the many creditors of the Raymond Group, and the sale to Great American—a seemingly empty corporation which was able to perform the buy-out only on the strength of the massive loan from IIT—forms the backdrop for the relevancy of the Pennsylvania Uniform Fraudulent Conveyance Act, one of the critical legal questions presented for our decision.

Durkin obtained the financing through one of his two partners in Great American.[1] The loan from IIT was structured so as to divide the Raymond Group into borrowing companies and guarantor companies. The loan was secured by mortgages on the assets of the borrowing companies, but was also guaranteed by mortgages on the assets of the guarantor companies. We must decide whether the borrowers' mortgages were invalid under the UFCA and whether there was consideration for the guarantors' mortgages.

The IIT loan was closed on November 26, 1973. The borrowing companies in the Raymond Group received $7 million in direct proceeds from IIT. The remaining $1.53 million was placed in escrow as a reserve account for the payment of accruing interest. The loans were to be repaid by December 31, 1976, at an interest rate of five points over the prime rate but in no event less than 12.5 percent. In exchange, each of the borrowing companies—Raymond Colliery, Blue Coal, Glen Nan, and Olyphant Associates—created a first lien in favor of IIT on all of their tangible and intangible assets; each of the guarantor companies—all other companies in the Raymond Group—created a second lien in favor of IIT on all of their tangible and

---

1. Durkin owned 40% of Great American. Hyman Green owned 10%, and James R. Hoffa, Jr. owned the remaining 50%. Durkin and Green concealed Hoffa's ownership interest in Great American from IIT. Hoffa apparently came into the picture when Durkin attempted to borrow money from the Central States Pension Fund of the International Brotherhood of Teamsters to finance the purchase.

intangible assets. The loan agreement also contained a clause which provided IIT with a priority lien on the proceeds from Raymond's sales of its surplus lands. Finally, the agreement provided that violations of any of the loan covenants would permit IIT to accelerate the loan and to collect immediately the full balance due from any or all of the borrowers or guarantors.

The exchange of money and notes did not stop with IIT's advances to the borrowing companies. Upon receipt of the IIT loan proceeds, the borrowing companies immediately transferred a total of $4,085,000 to Great American. In return, Great American issued to each borrowing company an unsecured promissory note with the same interest terms as those of the IIT loan agreement. In addition to the proceeds of the IIT loan, Great American borrowed other funds to acquire the purchase price for Raymond's stock.

When the financial dust settled after the closing on November 26, 1973, this was the situation at Raymond: Great American paid $6.7 million to purchase Raymond's stock, the shareholders receiving $6.2 million in cash and a $500,000 note; at least $4.8 million of this amount was obtained by mortgaging Raymond's assets.

Notwithstanding the cozy accommodations for the selling stockholders, the financial environment of the Raymond Group at the time of the sale was somewhat precarious. At the time of the closing, Raymond had multi-million dollar liabilities for federal income taxes, trade accounts, pension fund contributions, strip mining and back-filling obligations, and municipal real estate taxes. The district court calculated that the Raymond Group's existing debts amounted to at least $20 million on November 26, 1983. 565 F.Supp. at 578.

Under Durkin's control after the buy-out, Raymond's condition further deteriorated. Following the closing the Raymond Group lacked the funds to pay its routine operating expenses, including those for materials, supplies, telephone, and other utilities. It was also unable to pay its delinquent and current real estate taxes. Within two months of the closing, the deep mining operations of Blue Coal were shut down; within six months of the closing, the Raymond Group ceased all strip mining operations. Consequently, the Raymond Group could not fulfill its existing coal contracts and became liable for damages for breach of contract. The plaintiffs in the breach of contract actions exercised their right of set-off against accounts they owed the Raymond Group. Within seven months of the closing, the Commonwealth of Pennsylvania and the Anthracite Health & Welfare Fund sued the Raymond Group for its failures to fulfill back-filling requirements in the strip mining operations and to pay contributions to the Health & Welfare Fund. This litigation resulted in injunctions against the Raymond Group companies which prevented them from moving or selling their equipment until their obligations were satisfied. Moreover, Lackawanna and Luzerne counties announced their intent to sell the Raymond Group properties for unpaid real estate taxes. Finally, on September

15, 1976, IIT notified the borrowing and guarantor Raymond companies that their mortgage notes were in default. On September 29, 1976, IIT confessed judgments against the borrowing companies for the balance due on the loan and began to solicit a buyer for the Raymond Group mortgages.

New *dramatis personae* came on stage and orchestrated additional financial dealings which led to the purchase of the IIT mortgages. These dealings form the backdrop for additional legal issues to be decided here. Pagnotti Enterprises, another large anthracite producer, was the prime candidate to purchase the mortgages from IIT. In December 1976, James J. Tedesco, on behalf of Pagnotti, commenced negotiations for the purchase. Tedesco signed an agreement on December 15, 1976. Pursuant to the mortgage sale contract—and prior to the closing of the sale and assignment of the mortgages—IIT and Pagnotti each placed $600,000 in an escrow account to be applied to the payment of delinquent real estate taxes on properties listed for the county tax sales or to be used as funds for bidding on the properties at the tax sales.

IIT and Pagnotti agreed that bidding on the properties at the Lackawanna and Luzerne county tax sales would be undertaken by nominee corporations. Pursuant to their agreement, more new business entities then entered the picture. Tabor Court Realty was formed to bid on Raymond's properties at the Lackawanna County tax sale; similarly, McClellan Realty was formed to bid on Blue Coal's lands in Luzerne County. Pagnotti prepaid the delinquent taxes that predated IIT's mortgages to Lackawanna County. On December 17, 1976, Tabor Court Realty obtained Raymond's Lackawanna lands for a bid of $385,000; yet by this date an involuntary petition in bankruptcy had been filed against Blue Coal, a chief Raymond subsidiary, by its creditors. A similar proceeding was instituted against another subsidiary, Glen Nan. Based on the failure of Tabor Court to pay other delinquent taxes, on December 16, 1980, Lackawanna County held a second tax sale of Raymond's lands. At that sale, Joseph Solfanelli, acting on behalf of Gleneagles Investment, bid and acquired Raymond's lands for $535,290.39. These transactions did not stand up. At trial, the parties stipulated that both county tax sales were invalid and that Raymond's lands purportedly sold to Tabor Court and Gleneagles remained assets owned by Raymond.

On January 26, 1977, the sale and assignment of the IIT mortgages took place. Pagnotti paid approximately $4.5 million for the IIT mortgages; at that time, the mortgage balance was $5,817,475.69. Pagnotti thereafter assigned the mortgage to McClellan, thus making McClellan a key figure in this litigation. On December 12, 1977, Hyman Green, one of Durkin's co-shareholders in Raymond, was told that McClellan intended to sell, at a private sale, many of Raymond's assets encumbered as collateral on the IIT mortgages. McClellan did just that—it foreclosed. On February 28, 1978, in a private sale, Loree

Associates purchased the assets from McClellan for $50,000. This sale was not advertised nor were the assets offered to any other parties. Additionally, the sale was not recorded on the books of either Loree Associates or McClellan until May 1983, six months after the start of the litigation below. Nor was this the only private sale. On October 6, 1978, McClellan foreclosed on the stock of Raymond and sold it at a private sale for $1 to Joseph Solfanelli, as trustee for Pagnotti. Again, the sale was not advertised nor was anyone other than Green informed of the sale. No appraisals were obtained for either the stock or the collateral purportedly sold by McClellan at these sales. . . .

II.

The instant action was commenced by the United States on December 12, 1980 to reduce to judgment certain corporate federal tax assessments made against the Raymond Group and Great American. The government sought to assert the priority of its tax liens and to foreclose against the property that Raymond had owned at the time of the assessments as well as against properties currently owned by Raymond. The United States argued that the IIT mortgages executed in November 1973 should be set aside under the Uniform Fraudulent Conveyance Act and further that the purported assignment of these mortgages to Pagnotti should be voided because at the inception Pagnotti had purchased the mortgages with knowledge that they had been fraudulently conveyed.

As heretofore stated, after a bench trial, the district court issued three separate published opinions. In Gleneagles I, 565 F.Supp. 556 (1983), the court concluded, *inter alia,* that the mortgages given by the Raymond Group to IIT on November 26, 1973 were fraudulent conveyances within the meaning of the constructive and intentional fraud sections of the Pennsylvania Uniform Fraudulent Conveyances Act, 39 Pa.Stat. §§ 354–357. In Gleneagles II, 571 F.Supp. 935 (1983), the court further held that the mortgages to McClellan Realty were void as against the other Raymond Group creditors. In its third opinion, 584 F.Supp. 671 (1984), the court set out the priority of the creditors. The court granted McClellan and Tabor Court an equitable lien ahead of the creditors for the Pennsylvania municipal taxes they paid in Raymond's behalf prior to the 1976 Lackawanna county tax sale of Raymond's properties. However, the court placed McClellan, as assignee of the IIT mortgages, near the bottom of the list of creditors. The trustee in bankruptcy of Blue Coal and Glen Nan argues that McClellan's rights are totally invalidated and that McClellan has no standing whatsoever as a creditor.

The Raymond Group—four coal mining companies that executed the mortgages (Raymond Colliery, Blue Coal, Glen Nan, and Olyphant Associates) as well as interrelated associated companies that had placed guarantee mortgages and subsidiaries of such associated companies—has appealed. As heretofore stated, all these mortgages, subsequently invalidated by the district court, had been granted to IIT on November 26, 1973 and assigned by IIT to appellant McClellan. For the purpose of this appeal, we shall refer to the Raymond Group as "appellants", or "McClellan". . . .

Jurisdiction was proper in the trial court, 28 U.S.C. §§ 1340, 1345. We are satisfied that jurisdiction on appeal is proper based on 28 U.S.C. § 1291. Although one or two parties have questioned the timeliness of McClellan's appeal based on a contention that partially defective service of McClellan's motion for a new district court trial failed to toll the running of the 60–day period for filing appeals under Rule 4(a)(1) of the Federal Rules of Appellate Procedure, we are satisfied that this was not fatal. See Thompson v. INS, 375 U.S. 384, 84 S.Ct. 397, 11 L.Ed.2d 404 (1964).

III.

McClellan initially challenges the district court's application of the Pennsylvania Uniform Fraudulent Conveyances Act (UFCA), 39 Pa. Stat. §§ 351–363, to the leveraged buy-out loan made by IIT to the mortgagors, and to the acquisition of the mortgages from IIT by McClellan. The district court determined that IIT lacked good faith in the transaction because it knew, or should have known, that the money it lent the mortgagors was used, in part, to finance the purchase of stock from the mortgagors' shareholders, and that as a consequence of the loan, IIT and its assignees obtained a secured position in the mortgagors' property to the detriment of creditors. Because this issue involves the interpretation and application of legal precepts, review is plenary.

In applying section 353(a) of the UFCA, the district court stated:

> The initial question . . . is whether the transferee, IIT, transferred its loan proceeds in good faith. . . . IIT knew or strongly suspected that the imposition of the loan obligations secured by the mortgages and guarantee mortgages would probably render insolvent both the Raymond Group and each individual member thereof. In addition, IIT was fully aware that no individual member of the Raymond Group would receive fair consideration within the meaning of the Act in exchange for the loan obligations to IIT. Thus, we conclude that IIT does not meet the standard of good faith under Section 353(a) of the Act. See e.g., Cohen v. Sutherland, 257 F.2d [737] at 742 [(2d Cir.1958)] (transferee's knowledge that the transferor is insolvent defeats assertion of good faith); Epstein v. Goldstein, 107 F.2d 755, 757 (2d Cir.1939) (transferee's knowledge that no consideration was received by transferor relevant to the issue of good faith).

565 F.Supp. at 574.

McClellan argues that "the only reasonable and proper application of the good faith criteria as it applies to the lender in structuring a loan is one which looks to the lender's *motives* as opposed to his *knowledge*."

Br. for appellants at 17. McClellan argues that good faith is satisfied when "the lender acted in an arms-length transaction without ulterior motive or collusion with the debtor to the detriment of creditors." Id.

Section 354 of the UFCA is a "constructive fraud" provision. It establishes that a conveyance made by a person "who is or will be thereby rendered insolvent, is fraudulent as to creditors, without regard to his actual intent, if the conveyance is made . . . without a fair consideration." 39 Pa.Stat. § 354. Section 353 defines fair consideration as an exchange of a "fair equivalent . . . in good faith." 39 Pa. Stat. § 353. Because section 354 excludes an examination of intent, it follows that "good faith" must be something other than intent; because section 354 also focuses on insolvency, knowledge of insolvency is a rational interpretation of the statutory language of lack of "good faith." McClellan would have us adopt "without ulterior motive or collusion with the debtor to the detriment of creditors" as the good faith standard. We are uneasy with such a standard because these words come very close to describing intent.

Surprisingly, few courts have considered this issue. In Epstein v. Goldstein, 107 F.2d 755, 757 (2d Cir.1939), the court held that because a transferee had no knowledge of the transferor's insolvency, it could not justify a finding of bad faith, implying that a showing of such knowledge would support a finding of bad faith. In Sparkman and McClean Co. v. Derber, 4 Wash.App. 341, 481 P.2d 585 (1971), the court considered a mortgage given to an attorney by a corporation on the verge of bankruptcy to secure payment for his services. The trial court found that the transaction had violated section 3 of the UFCA (here, section 353) because it had been made in bad faith. On appeal the Washington Court of Appeals stated that "prior cases . . . have not precisely differentiated the good faith requirement . . . of fair consideration [in UFCA section 3] from the actual intent to defraud requirement of [UFCA section 7]." Id. at 346, 481 P.2d at 589. The court then set forth a number of factors to be considered in determining good faith: 1) honest belief in the propriety of the activities in question; 2) no intent to take unconscionable advantage of others; and 3) no intent to, or knowledge of the fact that the activities in question will, hinder, delay, or defraud others. Id. at 348, 481 P.2d at 591. Where "any one of these factors is absent, lack of good faith is established and the conveyance fails." Id. See also Wells Fargo Bank v. Desert View Bldg. Supplies, Inc., 475 F.Supp. 693, 696–97 (D.Nev.1978) (lender lacked good faith when exchanging its securities for preexisting loans in context of an impending bankruptcy), aff'd mem., 633 F.2d 225 (9th Cir.1980).

We have decided that the district court reached the right conclusion here for the right reasons. It determined that IIT did not act in good faith because it was aware, first, that the exchange would render Raymond insolvent, and second, that no member of the Raymond Group would receive fair consideration. We believe that this determination is consistent with the statute and case law.

McClellan and amicus curiae also argue that as a general rule the UFCA should not be applied to leveraged buy-outs. They contend that the UFCA, which was passed in 1924, was never meant to apply to a complicated transaction such as a leveraged buy-out. The Act's broad language, however, extends to any "conveyance" which is defined as "every payment of money . . . and also the creation of any lien or incumbrance." 39 Pa.Stat. § 351. This broad sweep does not justify exclusion of a particular transaction such as a leveraged buy-out simply because it is innovative or complicated. If the UFCA is not to be applied to leveraged buy-outs, it should be for the state legislatures, not the courts, to decide.

In addition, although appellants' and amicus curiae's arguments against general application of the Act to leveraged buy-outs are not without some force, the application of fraudulent conveyance law to certain leveraged buy-outs is not clearly bad public policy.[2] In any event, the circumstances of this case justify application. Even the policy arguments offered against the application of fraudulent conveyance law to leveraged buy-outs assume facts that are not present in this case. For example, in their analysis of fraudulent conveyance law, Professors Baird and Jackson assert that their analysis should be applied to leveraged buy-outs only where aspects of the transaction are not hidden from creditors and the transaction does not possess other suspicious attributes. See Baird and Jackson, Fraudulent Conveyance Law and Its Proper Domain, 38 Vand.L.Rev. 829, 843 (1985). In fact, Baird and Jackson conclude their article by noting that their analysis is limited to transactions in which "the transferee parted with value when he entered into the transaction and that transaction was entered in the ordinary course." Id. at 855 (footnote omitted). In the instant case, however, the severe economic circumstances in which the Raymond Group found itself, the obligation, without benefit, incurred by the Raymond Group, and the small number of shareholders benefited by the transaction suggest that the transaction was not entered in the ordinary course, that fair consideration was not exchanged, and that the transaction was anything but unsuspicious. The policy arguments set forth in opposition to the application of fraudulent conveyance law

2. A major premise of the policy arguments opposing application of fraudulent conveyance law to leveraged buy-outs is that such transactions often benefit creditors and that the application of fraudulent conveyance law to buy-outs will deter them in the future. See Baird and Jackson, Fraudulent Conveyance Law and Its Proper Domain, 38 Vand.L.Rev. 829, 855 (1985). An equally important premise is that creditors can protect themselves from undesirable leveraged buy-outs by altering the terms of their credit contracts. Id. at 835. This second premise ignores, however, cases such as this one in which the major creditors (in this instance the United States and certain Pennsylvania municipalities) are involuntary and do not become creditors by virtue of a contract. The second premise also ignores the possibility that the creditors attacking the leveraged buy-out (such as many of the creditors in this case) became creditors before leveraged buy-outs became a common financing technique and thus may not have anticipated such leveraged transactions so as to have been able to adequately protect themselves by contract. These possibilities suggest that Baird and Jackson's broad proscription against application of fraudulent conveyance law to leveraged buy-outs may not be unambiguously correct.

to leveraged buy-outs do not justify the exemption of transactions such as this.[3]

IV.

McClellan next argues that under section 359(2) of the UFCA, it is entitled to a lien superior to all other creditors on Raymond's property. Br. for appellants at 27. Once again, review of this issue is plenary. *Universal Minerals,* 669 F.2d at 102.

A.

Section 359 establishes a two-tier system to protect certain purchasers from the effects of the UFCA. Section 359(1) permits a purchaser who has paid "fair consideration without knowledge of the fraud at the time of the purchase" to maintain the conveyance as valid against a creditor. 39 Pa.Stat. § 359(1). Section 359(2) of the Act specifies that a "purchaser who, without actual fraudulent intent, has given less than a fair consideration for the conveyance or obligation may retain the property or obligation as security for repayment." 39 Pa.Stat. § 359(2).

In *Gleneagles II,* the district court found that Pagnotti, who purchased the IIT mortgages for $4,047,786 and transferred them to McClellan Realty, was not entitled to protection under section 359(1). The court determined that although Pagnotti had given a "fair equivalent" for the IIT mortgages, it did not do so without knowledge of the fraud at the time of the purchase. 571 F.Supp. at 952.

In *Gleneagles III,* the district court concluded that McClellan, Pagnotti's assignee, was not entitled to the partial protection of section 359(2). The court stated that although it had found in *Gleneagles II* that Pagnotti had not acted in good faith in acquiring the IIT mortgages, this was not equivalent to a finding that Pagnotti had given "less than fair consideration." 584 F.Supp. at 682. The court, however, also implied that notwithstanding its finding that Pagnotti had not acted with "actual fraudulent intent," it had not "purchased the IIT mortgages in good faith." Id. The court ruled that good faith is at least required to merit protection under section 359(2). The court therefore found that Pagnotti was not entitled to such protection. Id.

McClellan faults this reasoning with an argument that, at least facially, seems persuasive. It argues that the district court's finding that Pagnotti acted with knowledge of the fraud means that Pagnotti acted without good faith and therefore paid "less than fair considera-

---

3. It should also be noted that another basic premise of the Baird and Jackson analysis is that as a general matter fraudulent conveyance law should be applied only to those transactions to which a rational creditor would surely object. Baird and Jackson, at 834. Although a rational creditor might under certain circumstances consent to a risky but potentially beneficial leveraged buy-out of a nearly insolvent debtor, no reasonable creditor would consent to the intentionally fraudulent conveyance the district court correctly found this transaction to be. Thus, the application of fraudulent conveyance law to the instant transaction appears consistent even with Baird and Jackson's analysis.

tion" as defined by section 353 of the Act. Therefore, McClellan reasons, absent a finding of "actual fraudulent intent," it is entitled to protection under section 359(2).

Admittedly, section 359(2) is inartfully drafted and a literal reading of the section could conceivably command this result. We believe, however, that the public policy behind the UFCA compels a different interpretation. The Act protects both *purchasers* and *third parties*. We see a distinction here. The Act protects those *purchasers*, who, without actual fraudulent intent and without a lack of good faith, have paid less than a fair equivalent for the property received. Conversely, the Act does not protect purchases having a fraudulent intent or a lack of good faith. We are not satisfied that the UFCA affords third parties greater protection than purchasers. The purposes of the Act would be nullified if third parties who in bad faith paid less than a fair equivalent could take the property in a better position than an original purchaser who at the outset had engaged in a fraudulent transfer.

We are most uneasy with an interpretation that would deny rights to the purchaser, Pagnotti, but confer them on its assignee, McClellan. Such a literal reading of the statute's language would require us to ignore the statute's purpose. We are reminded of Judge Roger J. Traynor's advice, "We need literate, not literal judges."

B.

Moreover, we find support in analogizing to the federal bankruptcy laws. Section 548(c) of the Bankruptcy Code—the successor to section 67(d)(6) of the Bankruptcy Act—provides that a transferee or obligee of a fraudulent transfer or obligation who takes for value and in good faith may retain the interest transferred or the obligation incurred. 11 U.S.C. § 548(c).[4] This section of the Bankruptcy Code thus closely tracks section 359(2) of the UFCA. Indeed, bankruptcy's leading commentator explains that: "The major similarity between the Bankruptcy Code and the UFCA is reflected in the portion of subsection [548(c)] that permits the good faith transferee or obligee to retain his lien." 4 Collier on Bankruptcy ¶ 548.07, at 548–65 (15th ed. 1986). McClellan acknowledges that "[t]he fraudulent conveyance provisions of the Code are modeled on the UFCA, and uniform interpretation of the two statutes [is] essential to promote commerce nationally. Cohen v. Sutherland, 257 F.2d 737, 741 (2d Cir.1958). . . ." Br. for appellants at 29.

In two cases similar to the one at bar, courts have denied protection to lenders under section 67(d) of the Bankruptcy Act because, although their conduct was not intentionally fraudulent, the lenders exhibited a lack of good faith. In re Allied Development Corp., 435 F.2d 372, 376 (7th Cir.1970); In re Venie, 80 F.Supp. 250, 256 (W.D.Mo.1948). The

4. "Fair consideration" is defined under
. . . . the Bankruptcy Code as an exchange
of fair equivalents in good faith.

same principles should apply here to deny protection to Pagnotti where the record supports the district court's findings that Pagnotti lacked good faith. See The Uniform Fraudulent Conveyance Act in Pennsylvania, 5 U.Pitt.L.Rev. 161, 186 (1939) (Section 359(2) language "without actual fraudulent intent" should mean without knowledge).

C.

McClellan next challenges the district court's finding that as Pagnotti's assignee, it too, lacked good faith, and therefore was disqualified from protection under the Act. McClellan states that "[t]he District Court never suggests, much less finds, that McClellan's dealings with IIT concerning its purchase of the mortgages were anything but at arms-length." Br. for appellants at 25. The district court's determination that McClellan lacked good faith is a factual finding reviewed on the clearly erroneous standard.

Although McClellan attempts to distance itself from Pagnotti, the party that purchased the mortgages from IIT and assigned them to McClellan, it cannot do this successfully. A well-recognized rule provides that an assignee gets only those rights held by its assignor and no more. The district court clearly held that Pagnotti did not obtain the mortgages in good faith. Gleneagles II, 571 F.Supp. at 952. The court supported its findings with facts from the record. See id. at 952–56. Because McClellan's rights as an assignee are no greater than Pagnotti's and because McClellan does not show how the district court's finding of Pagnotti's lack of good faith was clearly erroneous, McClellan is charged with the same quality of faith.[5] . . .

E.

McClellan next contends that the district court erred in not crediting McClellan for that portion of the IIT loan that was not passed through to Raymond's shareholders: although "the District Court acknowledged that $2,915,000, or approximately 42 percent, of the IIT loan proceeds originally went for the benefit of . . . creditors, IIT and McClellan received no credit therefor in regard to the partial validity of their liens." Br. for appellants at 28. McClellan argues the district court determined that "[t]he wrong committed upon the creditors . . . [was] the diversion of some 58 percent of the loan proceeds from the IIT loan to [Raymond's] shareholders." Id. at 29. It concludes that to

---

5. McClellan also argues that under section 359(3), no duty was imposed on it, or its assignor, Pagnotti, to make an inquiry into the circumstances of the sale. Section 359(3) provides that:

   (3) Knowledge that a conveyance has been made as a gift or for nominal consideration shall not by itself be deemed to be knowledge that the conveyance was a fraud on any creditor of the grantor, or impose any duty on the person purchas-

ing the property from the grantee to make inquiry as to whether such conveyance was or was not a fraud on any such creditor.

39 Pa.Cons.Stat. § 359(3). However, Pagnotti's knowledge went far beyond mere knowledge "that a conveyance has been made as a gift or for nominal consideration." See Gleneagles II, 571 F.Supp. at 952–58.

invalidate the entire mortgage would be to provide Raymond's creditors with a "double recovery." Id. at 28. We understand the dissent to agree with McClellan's analysis when noting that " 'creditors have causes of action in fraudulent conveyance law only to the extent they have been damaged.' " (citations omitted).

McClellan and, by implication, the dissent mischaracterize the district court's findings and conclusions regarding the fraudulent nature of the IIT loans. The district court did not determine that the loan transaction was only partially—or, to use McClellan's formulation, 58%—fraudulent. Nor did the district court conclude that Raymond's creditors had been wronged by only a portion of the transaction. Instead, the district court stated that:

> McClellan Realty's argument rests on the incorrect assumption that some portions of the IIT mortgages are valid as against the Creditors. In *Gleneagles I,* 565 F.Supp. at 580, 586, this Court found that IIT and Durkin engaged in an intentionally fraudulent transaction on November 26, 1973. The IIT mortgages are therefore invalid in their entirety as to creditors.

Gleneagles III, 584 F.Supp. at 683. In essence, the district court ruled that the *aggregate* transaction was fraudulent, notwithstanding the fact that a portion of the loan proceeds was allegedly used to pay existing creditors.

This determination is bolstered by the fact that most of the $2,915,000 allegedly paid to the benefit of Raymond's creditors went to only one creditor—Chemical Bank. In *Gleneagles I,* the district court found that $2,186,247 of the IIT loan proceeds were paid to Chemical Bank in satisfaction of the mortgage that Raymond had taken to purchase Blue Coal (a Raymond subsidiary). See 565 F.Supp. at 570, 571 (findings 132(k) and 140). The purpose of this payment is of critical significance:

> The Gillens and the Clevelands [Raymond's shareholders] required satisfaction of the Chemical Bank mortgage as a condition of the sale of their Raymond Colliery stock at least in part because Royal Cleveland had personally guaranteed repayment of that loan.

Id. at 571 (finding 141). McClellan does not challenge this finding on appeal. Thus, of the $2.9 million allegedly paid to benefit Raymond's creditors, $2.2 million were actually intended to benefit Raymond's shareholders and to satisfy a condition for the sale. The remaining amounts allegedly paid to benefit Raymond's creditors were applied to the closing costs of the transaction. See id. at 570 (finding 133).

On this record, the district court's characterization of the transaction as a whole as fraudulent cannot reasonably be disputed. The court's consequent determination that the "IIT mortgages are . . .

invalid in their entirety as to creditors" is supported by precedent. See *Newman v. First National Bank*, 76 F.2d 347, 350–51 (3d Cir.1935).[6]

Moreover, as the district court correctly noted, it sits in equity when fashioning relief under the UFCA. *Gleneagles III*, 584 F.Supp. at 682. Consequently, our review of the district court's action is severely limited. *Evans v. Buchanan*, 555 F.2d 373, 378 (3d Cir.1977), cert. denied, 434 U.S. 880, 98 S.Ct. 235, 54 L.Ed.2d 306 (1977).

The district court determined that "[t]he Creditors . . . would not be placed in the same or similar position which they held with respect to the Raymond Group in 1973 merely by replacing the $4,085,500 of IIT loan proceeds that were misused on November 26, 1973." *Gleneagles III*, 584 F.Supp. at 681. We agree with the district court and are persuaded that this court's decision in *Newman* controls. In *Newman* we held that where a creditor was prevented from recovering on its judgment as a result of a fraudulent scheme between the debtor and another creditor, a judgment obtained by the defrauding creditor was totally void. We stated that "[i]f we extract from the fraudulent actors every advantage which they derived from their fraud and restore the creditor to the position which lawfully belonged to it at the time the fraud was perpetrated and give it all rights which, but for the fraud, it had under the law, we feel that equity would adequately be done." *Id.* at 350. Here, the district court found that only by voiding the entire amount could the creditors be placed in the same position they held before the November 26, 1973 misuse of the loans. To the extent that this determination was based on facts, we do not view them as clearly erroneous; to the extent the conclusion was based on law, we find no error. Consequently, we do not believe that the district court's equitable remedy was "arbitrary, fanciful, or unreasonable," or the product of "improper standards, criteria, or procedures." *Evans*, 555 F.2d at 378.

For the above reasons, therefore, we will not disturb the district court's determination that McClellan is not entitled to a "lien superior to all other creditors" as the assignee of all or part of the IIT mortgages. . . .

VI.

McClellan next faults the district court's determination that the Raymond Group was rendered insolvent by "the IIT transaction and the instantaneous payment to the selling stockholders of a substantial portion of the IIT loan in exchange for their stock." *Gleneagles I*, 565 F.Supp. at 580. McClellan disputes the method of computation used by

---

6. On broadly analogous facts, the *Newman* court found that a defendant bank's fraudulent conduct rendered its judgment against a debtor "wholly void":

Therefore, the whole of it should be set aside. Setting aside only the more vicious part (the $3,500 sham loan) is not enough. *It was the act of the Bank in obtaining the judgment by fraud not the amount of the judgment that defeated the [creditor] recovering on its judgment.*

Newman v. First National Bank, 76 F.2d 347, 350–51 (3d Cir.1935) (emphasis added).

the district court. The question of insolvency is a mixed question of law and fact. Our review of the legal portions of the issue is plenary, while review of the factual portion is according to the clearly erroneous standard. *Universal Minerals,* 669 F.2d at 102.

A.

Section 352 of the UFCA defines insolvency as "when the present, fair, salable value of [a person's] assets is less than the amount that will be required to pay his probable liability on his existing debts as they become absolute and matured." 39 Pa.Stat. § 352(1). As heretofore stated, the district court calculated the Raymond Group's existing debts as "at least $20,000,000 on November 26, 1973." Gleneagles I, 565 F.Supp. at 578. The court then compared Raymond's debt to the "present, fair, salable value" of its assets and found the Group insolvent. Id. at 578–80. In doing so, the court relied on *Larrimer v. Feeney,* where the Pennsylvania Supreme Court stated:

> A reasonable construction of the . . . statutory definition of insolvency indicates that it not only encompasses insolvency in the bankruptcy sense i.e. a deficit net worth, but also includes a condition wherein a debtor has insufficient presently salable assets to pay existing debts as they mature. If a debtor has a deficit net worth, then the present salable value of his assets must be less than the amount required to pay the liability on his debts as they mature. A debtor may have substantial paper net worth including assets which have a small salable value, but which if held to a subsequent date could have a much higher salable value. Nevertheless, *if the present salable value of [his] assets [is] less than the amount required to pay existing debts as they mature the debtor is insolvent.*

411 Pa. 604, 608, 192 A.2d 351, 353 (1963) (emphasis supplied, citation omitted). Guided by this teaching, the court found that: (1) the Raymond Group's coal production, which had been unprofitable since 1969, "could not produce a sufficient cash flow to pay the company's obligations in a timely manner"; (2) the sale of the Raymond Group's surplus lands, which had provided a substantial cash flow, was "abruptly cut off" by the terms of the IIT agreement; and (3) sale of its equipment could not generate adequate cash to meet Raymond's existing debts as they matured. Gleneagles I, 565 F.Supp. at 579–80. These determinations are the factual components of the insolvency finding; McClellan contends that at least one of the findings is clearly erroneous.

. . .

VIII.

Finally, McClellan challenges the district court's invalidation of the guarantee mortgages. The district court invalidated these mortgages because the guarantors did not receive fair consideration. 565 F.Supp. at 577.

McClellan, relying on Telefest, Inc. v. VU–TV, Inc., 591 F.Supp. 1368 (D.N.J.1984), argues that the guarantors were so closely associated with the borrower companies that they received sufficient indirect consideration from the benefits to the borrowing companies. In *Telefest,* however, the existence of fair consideration was undisputed. See id. at 1370. The court held that the cross-collateral guarantor company also benefitted from the fair consideration provided to the borrowers. Id. at 1378– 79. The consideration in the underlying transaction here, however, was determined to be deficient. Any indirect benefit to guarantor companies deriving from that consideration would, *a fortiori,* also be deficient. The district court did not err in so holding. . . .

A. LEON HIGGINBOTHAM, JR., CIRCUIT JUDGE, concurring in part and dissenting in part.

I concur in the majority's judgment that Pennsylvania's fraudulent conveyance laws may be applied to a leveraged buyout where, as here, a few shareholders seek to use it as a device to benefit themselves and take advantage of the creditors of a clearly faltering corporation. Since I find that the purposes underlying Pennsylvania's fraudulent conveyance law dictate that only a portion of the disputed transfer of funds be set aside, however, I must dissent from that part of the majority's opinion which declares the IIT mortgage loans wholly void.

The basic objective of fraudulent conveyance law is to preserve estates and to prevent them from being wrongfully drained of assets. See Melamed v. Lake County National Bank, 727 F.2d 1399, 1401 (6th Cir.1984). Fraudulent conveyance law is not intended to add to estates for the unjustified benefit of creditors. In fact, "creditors have causes of action in fraudulent conveyance law only to the extent they have been damaged." A/S Kreditt–Finans v. Cia Venetico De Navegacion, 560 F.Supp. 705, 711 (E.D.Pa.1983), aff'd, 729 F.2d 1446 (3d Cir.1984). IIT made four separate loans totaling $8,530,000. Of this, $4,085,000 was passed through Raymond Group companies to shareholders and $1,530,000 was retained by IIT as an interest reserve as part of the invalid transaction. However, $2,915,000 was used to pay existing debts (including an existing mortgage loan owned by Chemical Bank). To the extent that the IIT funds were used to pay existing creditors, the assets available to creditors generally were not diminished and the Raymond Group's estate was not improperly depleted. I would therefore hold that only the transfer of the $4,085,000 between IIT and the Raymond Group's shareholders and the creation of the $1,530,000 interest reserve for IIT should be set aside.

BAIRD & JACKSON, FRAUDULENT CONVEYANCE LAW AND ITS PROPER DOMAIN, 38 Vand.L.Rev. 829, 832–36, 850–54 (1985)

. . . Identifying the precise reach of fraudulent conveyance law is the crucial inquiry in several important legal disputes, such as whether a foreclosure of a debtor's equity of redemption or a leveraged buyout is a fraudulent conveyance. These cases are strikingly different from gratuitous transfers or transfers intended to defraud. It is not clear that permitting the debtor to engage in a leveraged buyout, for instance, is against the long-term interests of the creditors as a group. Because fraudulent conveyance law's use of "fair consideration" is not limited solely to cases in which fraudulent intent can be presumed, a view has recently gained currency that suggests the core principle of fraudulent conveyance law is that creditors should be able to set aside transfers by insolvent debtors that harm the creditors as a group. Under such view, this principle, which covers both transfers made with fraudulent intent and gifts, should inform construction of a section such as section 4 of the Uniform Fraudulent Conveyance Act. But, just as a view of section 4 that treats it as a surrogate of section 7's intentional fraud standard is too narrow, we believe this competing principle is too broad.

To establish this, we start from a simple, but important, proposition. After a debtor has borrowed money, his interests conflict with those of his creditors. A debtor has an incentive to take risks that he did not have before he borrowed. He enjoys all the benefits if a risky venture proves successful, but he does not incur all the costs if the venture fails. Every transfer he makes that has the effect of making an asset less like cash benefits the debtor at his creditors' expense. Creditors rely upon existing legal rules and contractual terms to limit unwarranted risk-taking by their debtor. Creditors, however, do not want to place too many restraints on their debtor. Creditors lend money in the first instance because the debtor has entrepreneurial skills that they do not have. To take advantage of the debtor's skills, creditors must give their debtor a certain amount of freedom. To give the debtor the power to make correct decisions, creditors must to some extent give him the power to make wrong decisions. Allowing creditors to escape the consequences of their debtor's bad decisions after the fact has costs as well as benefits. To decide whether the benefits justify the rule, one must also be sensitive to the costs that rule brings.

A creditor would not want to impose all possible restraints upon a debtor, even if the absence of a restraint exposes the creditor to the risk that the debtor will injure it. Fraudulent conveyance law is a restraint that the law imposes upon debtors for the benefit of creditors by giving creditors the power to void transactions. The power of creditors to set aside transactions after the fact limits the ability of debtors to engage in the transactions in the first instance. This power is unobjectionable if the transaction—such as a gift by an insolvent debtor—always injures creditors. But often the transaction—such as a leveraged buyout—might or might not injure creditors. If one applies fraudulent conveyance law to leveraged buyouts, one might protect some creditors who were injured after the fact, but one might work counter to the interests of those creditors who, before the fact, would have wanted their debtor to have the power to enter into such transactions.

Treating transfers by a debtor that make creditors as a group worse off as fraudulent conveyances is overbroad because many ordinary transfers that a debtor makes do this. Like any other creditor remedy, fraudulent conveyance law must have some limits. Indeed, in considering a legal rule such as fraudulent conveyance law, overbroad rules may be more pernicious than underbroad rules. It is easier for creditors to contract into prohibitions on conduct by a debtor than it is to contract out. If fraudulent conveyance law does not cover a certain kind of activity, yet creditors want to prohibit it, it can be prohibited contractually. Myriad restrictions in loan agreements, for example, perform this function. If certain activity is prohibited by a few large creditors, other creditors (including nonconsensual creditors) may be able to profit by the monitoring of the debtor undertaken by those whose contracts do prohibit such activity. Yet, contracting *out* of a rule that prohibits conduct, such as fraudulent conveyance law, is much harder. To be effective, the consent of all creditors must be reached. And in the unlikely case that all creditors *did* so agree, the trustee in bankruptcy could still seek to upset the transfer under section 548 of the Bankruptcy Code.

Thus, we believe, one must be careful in deciding where to place the reach of fraudulent conveyance law. In establishing its limits, one must recognize that the debtor-creditor relationship is essentially contractual.[20] A creditor acquires certain rights to control its debtor's actions. The more rights the creditor acquires, the lower its risk and the lower the interest rate it enjoys. Not all the rights that the creditor wants, or that the debtor would agree to give it, however, can be bargained for explicitly. Sometimes these rights (such as priority

---

20. Many claimants are, of course, non-consensual, but we think that fact is unimportant in discussing the bases of fraudulent conveyance law. In the first place, we think that debtor-creditor law should presumptively give all creditors the set of rights they would bargain for if they could, and if they had the time and sophistication to do it. "Nonconsensual" creditors, be they tort or tax, would not necessarily want different limits of restraint than would consensual creditors. Indeed, in many respects, their interests in controlling the debtor are identical. As a result, the limits that consensual creditors would impose on investments by a debtor also largely will protect nonconsensual claimants because of the congruence in their interests. To be sure, their interests are not always congruent. For example, certain actions by a debtor (such as safety measures) may affect only tort claimants directly. In those cases, other legal rules might be desirable to place monitoring burdens on the consensual creditors. See, e.g., Note, Tort Creditor Priority in the Secured Credit System: Asbestos Times, the Worst of Times, 36 Stan.L.Rev. 1045 (1984). These controls, however, are not likely to be imposed via fraudulent conveyance law. Finally, to focus on the protections nonconsensual creditors would want is a species of a larger inquiry, which implicates, inter alia, questions such as whether limited liability for corporations should apply to nonconsensual creditors.

rights with respect to a debtor's assets) affect third parties as well and should be subject to legal constraints. The ambition of the law governing the debtor-creditor relationship, including fraudulent conveyance law, should provide all the parties with the type of contract that they would have agreed to if they had had the time and money to bargain over all aspects of their deal. Fraudulent conveyance law, in other words, should be viewed as a species of contract law, representing one kind of control that creditors generally would want to impose and that debtors generally would agree to accept.

. . .

IV. THE LEVERAGED BUYOUT

Assume that Firm owes its general creditors 4 million dollars and has no secured debt. Firm's managers decide to acquire it, and the old shareholders agree to sell their shares for 1 million dollars. The managers put up 200,000 dollars of their own money and borrow 800,000 dollars from Bank. They agree to give Bank a security interest in all of Firm's assets to support the loan. The managers then proceed to use that money to buy the stock in the hands of all the shareholders. When the transaction is over, the managers own all the stock, the old shareholders are cashed out, and Firm has 4.8 million dollars in debt. The general creditors take a second priority position to Bank. As a result, the pool of assets available to satisfy their loans is 800,000 dollars smaller.

. . .

Even under the narrowest view of fraudulent conveyance law, the leveraged buyout may be a fraudulent conveyance. The managers and the old shareholders are made better off (by virtue of having a highly leveraged investment) and the general creditors are made worse off. The transaction "hinders" the creditors in the sense that it leaves them with fewer assets than before, and this may be the intent behind the transaction. In that case, the transaction could be attacked using section 7 of the Uniform Fraudulent Conveyance Act. But before determining whether a leveraged buyout should be treated as a section 7 fraudulent conveyance, which requires a messy inquiry into intent, the transaction should be examined to see whether it falls within any of the other existing sections. There are two sections containing per se rules that might lead to the characterization of the leveraged buyout as a fraudulent conveyance. One, embodied in section 4 of the Uniform Fraudulent Conveyance Act, provides that any transfer made by a debtor while insolvent without receiving fair consideration is a fraudulent conveyance. In a better world, a leveraged buyout never would run afoul of this provision. If the old shareholders and managers were informed fully (which, of course, they are not), the price paid for the stock would be the difference between the value of all the assets of the firm and all the liabilities. If the assets were worth less than the

liabilities, the managers would not be willing to pay a positive price for
Firm.

. . .

As a matter of sound practice, lawyers must ensure that a firm
acquired in a leveraged buyout is not insolvent or rendered insolvent
and that managers and others put up enough capital so that the firm is
not too thinly capitalized.[51]   An important conceptual question is
whether a leveraged buyout in fact presents fraudulent conveyance
problems or comes under a per se rule that turns out to be overbroad as
applied to this particular case. A firm that incurs obligations in the
course of a buyout does not seem at all like the Elizabethan deadbeat
who sells his sheep to his brother for a pittance.

The question, in other words, is whether a corporate debtor that
incurs additional debt in a leveraged buyout can be presumed either to
be engaging in a manipulation by which it (or its shareholders) will
profit at its creditors' expense or in some other transfer that its
creditors would almost always want to ban. At one level, the answer to
this question is straightforward. This transaction does hinder the
general creditors of Firm. After the transaction, the general creditors
are less likely to be paid. Before the transaction, a 1 million dollar
cushion protected the general creditors. After the buyout, the general
creditors had only a 200,000 dollar cushion. If Firm lost only a few
hundred thousand dollars, the general creditors would discover that
they would not be repaid in full.

Moreover, Firm, or more precisely, its owners (the old and new
shareholders), benefit to the extent that the general creditors are
disadvantaged. Before the transaction, the shareholders as a group
had invested 1 million dollars to enjoy the profits of a firm with assets
worth 5 million dollars. After the transaction, the shareholders as a
group have 200,000 dollars at risk (instead of 1 million dollars), yet they
still enjoy the profits generated by assets of 5 million dollars.[53] Their
investment of course is riskier, but a portion of these risks has been
passed on to the general creditors. To the extent that the general
creditors are made worse off by facing a riskier secured loan, the
beneficiaries must be the shareholders.

It thus might seem a good thing that these transactions appear to
trigger sections of existing fraudulent conveyance statutes. But we
doubt this is the case. These transactions do not seem to be clearly to
the detriment of creditors, nor did we always see creditors treating such
transactions as events of default in their loan agreements, even before

51. Lawyers also face obstacles imposed by other legal principles. For example, various state corporation codes forbid distributions to shareholders while a firm is insolvent. See, e.g., Cal.Corp.Code § 501 (West 1977) (prohibiting distributions to shareholders if the corporation is, or is likely to become, unable to meet its liabilities as they mature). While such rules do not affect the rights of Bank, they might not allow the old shareholders to keep the money they receive from the transaction.

53. Because of higher debt service, the profits of the firm will be somewhat less, but this reduction is almost certain to be offset by the shareholders' investment being so much smaller.

the issue was moved to the domain of fraudulent conveyance law. With the buyout may come more streamlined and more effective management. Among other things, a going-private transaction may save the costs of complying with relevant federal securities statutes.

A leveraged buyout is analogous to the simple case in which the firm issues new preferred debt and then uses the proceeds as a dividend for the existing shareholders. Debt instruments commonly control this conduct. If in a particular case those creditors who were in a position to control this conduct did not, one might conclude that these creditors should not be able to set this transaction aside. If they had the knowledge and the sophistication to control such conduct, but did not, there seems to be little reason for fraudulent conveyance law to control it for them. Indeed, as long as these creditors were not controlling this kind of debtor misbehavior through other kinds of monitoring devices, one might infer that none of the other creditors should be able to set it aside either. Although they may not actually have confronted the issue, their interests and those of other, better positioned creditors ought to coincide. As long as the creditors who could bargain and prevent the buyout do not (or do not ensure that they are cashed out when the buyout takes place), one might infer that the fraudulent conveyance remedy did not advance the interests of all the creditors.

If creditors who bargained did limit the ability of the debtor to incur preferred debt to create dividends for shareholders, one might argue that the fraudulent conveyance remedy is an appropriate off-the-rack term that creditors should presumptively have. A difficulty with this approach, however, is that the fraudulent conveyance remedy is very hard to contract out of. Even if it were in the interests of everyone that the leveraged buyout take place, a debtor would not be able to ensure that the transaction would be immune to a fraudulent conveyance attack. In bankruptcy, the trustee has the power to set aside the entire transaction, even if at the time of the actual transaction every existing creditor waived its right to set the transaction aside. It may make sense for the trustee to have the power to set aside fraudulent conveyances without looking to the rights of any actual creditors. The costs of establishing the rights of actual creditors may not be worth the benefits of having a rule that is more finely tuned. Nevertheless, the inability of creditors to contract around the fraudulent conveyance remedy when it is in their interest may suggest that fraudulent conveyance law should be applied in bankruptcy to a narrow range of cases in which there is little chance that creditors would find the transfer in their interest. In those cases in which it is not clear whether creditors would want to prevent the activity, all the creditors may be protected if a single one prohibits the transaction. The fraudulent conveyance remedy is far easier to contract into than it is to contract out of.

Notes & Questions

1. *The Scope of Fraudulent Conveyance Law.* If transfers for low consideration sometimes harm creditors and sometimes do not, how should we decide which transfers (other than those with fraudulent intent) are within the domain of fraudulent conveyance law? Consider the following factors:

(a) *The Scope of the Transaction.* Should the scope of the transaction affect the applicability of the law? Without wishing to scrutinize every transaction that harms creditors, should courts be amenable to scrutinizing transactions, like leveraged buyouts, that work massive changes in firm ownership and have massive effects on creditor welfare?

(b) *The Parties.* Should courts be especially wary of management-generated leveraged buyouts? Why not simply leave it to creditors to protect themselves? Should the rules change if the bulk of a corporation's debt is owed to involuntary tort creditors rather than to sophisticated banks? Where does the tax collector, the moving creditor in *Tabor Court Realty,* fit in?

(c) *After-the-Fact Developments.* Must courts limit their focus to the facts at the time of transfer? Or should subsequent developments influence the characterization of the transfer? Will they regardless of the stated legal rule?

(d) *Transferee's Knowledge.* Given an arm's length loan transaction, should creditor knowledge of the intended use of the loan proceeds matter? In a large loan transaction, should creditor knowledge of the intended use of the proceeds be presumed?

(e) *Notice and Waiting Period.* Would some of the objections to leveraged buyouts be removed if creditors received notice and a substantial waiting period were required? Compare the approach of U.C.C. Article 6 to the problem of bulk transfers, infra.

2. *Liability of Transferees.* (a) Note that in *Tabor Court Realty,* McClellan, an entity somewhat removed in the transactions from IIT, seeks to defend the Raymond Group's grant of mortgages to IIT that secured IIT's loan to the Raymond Group. IIT's loan was used to finance the purchase of Raymond by Great American and Durkin. Why does McClellan care about the validity of the grant of mortgages from the Raymond Group to IIT?

(b) Consider the court's treatment of the question whether McClellan, Pagnotti's assignee, was entitled to the protection of UFCA § 9(2). Since Pagnotti did not have "actual fraudulent intent," how could the court, consistent with the statute, deny McClellan § 9(2)'s protection? Why does the court feel the need to interpret § 9(2) the way it does?

(c) If the grant of mortgages to IIT was a fraudulent conveyance may the government obtain a money judgment against IIT even though IIT later transferred the mortgages? See UFTA § 8(b), (c), (d).

3. *The Need for a Judgment.* In *TeleFest* and *Tabor Court Realty,* the attacking creditors had judgments. The UFCA has been interpreted to allow creditors without judgments to rely on it. See American Surety Co. v. Conner, 251 N.Y. 1, 166 N.E. 783 (1929); cf. Fed.Rule Civ.Proc. 18(b) (no judgment needed). In light of the remedies available under § 10 of the UFCA, what is the relationship between prejudgment fraudulent conveyance remedies and provisional remedies such as attachment or replevin? Should a fraudulent conveyance be viewed as one of the circumstances that justifies prejudgment attachment? See UFTA § 7(a)(2).

C. Bulk Transfers

Bulk transfer doctrine may be viewed as responding to gaps in traditional fraudulent conveyance doctrine. Fraudulent conveyance rules operate after the fact. They only come into play after a conveyance, however broadly defined, has occurred. One can conceive of invoking fraudulent conveyance principles to enjoin a pending or future transfer, but cases in which creditors have the advance notice needed for such action must be rare. Once a conveyance has occurred, creditors may not be able to pursue a bona fide transferee. Even if the initial transferee is not bona fide, there may be obstacles to recovery. The transferee may himself have transferred the assets upon which creditors are relying. Or an intermediate non-bona fide transferee may not be susceptible to a money judgment. Thus in many cases fraudulent conveyance doctrine will not be available in time to serve creditors' needs. Consider the extent to which bulk transfer laws, now contained in Article 6 of the U.C.C., respond to the limitations inherent in fraudulent conveyance doctrine.

Introductory Problems

1. Eastern Auto Parts (EAP) has retail stores in New York, Pennsylvania, and New Jersey. Jennie's Auto Boutique (JAB) wishes to purchase all of the inventory in EAP's Pennsylvania stores. Need EAP or JAB worry about Article 6? Suppose instead that the proposed transaction involved a chain of restaurants selling all of the equipment in its Pennsylvania stores. See § 6–102.

2. If one is about to engage in a transaction covered by Article 6, what must one do? See §§ 6–104, 6–105. Suppose a transferee asks for the list required under § 6–104 and is told by the seller that there are no creditors. May the transferee rely on this representation?

3. Who counts as a creditor entitled to notification under Article 6? See §§ 1–201(12), 6–109.

NATIONAL BANK OF ROYAL OAK v. FRYDLEWICZ

Court of Appeals of Michigan, 1976.
67 Mich.App. 417, 241 N.W.2d 471.

Per Curiam.

Defendant National Unclaimed Furniture Showrooms (National) appeals a judgment of $17,356.76 granted in plaintiff's favor after a bench trial in Oakland County Circuit Court.

This litigation arose out of the transfer by Edward Frydlewicz to National of inventory in which plaintiff had a security interest. In December, 1968, Edward Frydlewicz asked plaintiff for a loan in the total amount of $20,027 to pay for inventory for his business, King Furniture & Appliance Mart. This business establishment, located at 126 East 14 Mile Road, Clawson, Michigan, was a retail outlet for King Distributors, Inc., which sold furniture wholesale and was owned and operated by Frydlewicz.

The security agreement gave plaintiff a security interest in all inventory located at King Furniture & Appliance Mart, 126 East 14 Mile Road. The security interest attached on December 31, 1968. Plaintiff filed a financing statement for the inventory with the Oakland County register of deeds. Repayment of the underlying loan was guaranteed by Edward and Elizabeth Frydlewicz, individually, and by King Distributors, Inc., by Edward Frydlewicz its president. The repayment of the loan was to be by 60 monthly installments commencing in February, 1969. Monthly installment payments, totalling $2,670.24, were made as scheduled through September, 1969, after which Frydlewicz was declared bankrupt.

In the interim on March 6, 1969, Frydlewicz contracted with National to lease the King Furniture & Appliance Mart. As a pre-condition to the agreement to lease the premises, National agreed to purchase all of the King Furniture & Appliance Mart inventory. Accordingly, an item-by-item inventory was conducted by the parties of the merchandise which consisted of damaged furniture and odds and ends. Defendant purchased this entire inventory for $13,603.24. When defendant purchased this inventory and leased the premises in Clawson, it changed the name of the business establishment to National Unclaimed Furniture Showrooms and removed all of the old King Furniture signs.

When the sale of inventory at King Furniture & Appliance Mart was being negotiated, Frydlewicz verbally represented to defendant that there were no liens of any kind against the inventory. National neither requested a written statement from Frydlewicz that there were no liens against the inventory nor gave notice to anyone of the inventory purchase.

National became aware of plaintiff's security interest in the inventory on May 14, 1970, when plaintiff served National with a writ of attachment against the inventory located at the furniture showroom on

14 Mile Road in Clawson. Apparently, National had made no attempt to investigate whether a security interest existed in the inventory. The stipulated statement of facts indicates that, on prior occasions, National had purchased wholesale lots of merchandise from King Distributors, Inc.

At trial and on appeal, the dispute requires the interaction of the Uniform Commercial Code (UCC) provisions on secured transactions and bulk transfers. Plaintiff's status under article 9 of the UCC, M.C. L.A. § 440.9101 et seq.; M.S.A. § 19.9101 et seq., is that of an un-perfected secured creditor. Plaintiff failed to perfect its interest when it filed the financing statement with the Oakland County register of deeds rather than with the Secretary of State, as M.C.L.A. § 440.9401; M.S.A. § 19.9401 requires.

National's status is the dispositive issue in the case. Under the instant facts, one of three legal positions could be ascribed to National: (1) a buyer in ordinary course of business, (2) a buyer not in ordinary course of business or (3) a transferee in bulk. If National is a buyer in the ordinary course of business, UCC § 9–307(1), M.C.L.A. § 440.9307(1); M.S.A. § 19.9307(1), would give its interest in the disput-ed merchandise priority over plaintiff's unperfected security interest. As a buyer not in the ordinary course of business, National's interest would be subordinated to plaintiff's interest.

Normally, as a transferee in bulk, National would be entitled to priority over plaintiff's unperfected security interest. Pursuant to UCC § 9–301(1)(c), M.C.L.A. § 440.9301(1)(c); M.S.A. § 19.9301(1)(c), "an un-perfected security interest is subordinate to the rights of in the case of goods, . . ., a person who is not a secured party and who is a transferee in bulk". However, National failed to satisfy the require-ments necessary under the bulk transfer provisions of UCC art. 6 to assert a claim of priority as a transferee in bulk. Specifically, UCC § 6–104(1) requires:

"Except as provided with respect to auction sales (section 6–108), a bulk transfer subject to this article is ineffective against *any creditor* of the *transferor* unless:

"(a) The *transferee requires the transferor to furnish a list of his existing creditors* prepared as stated in this section; and

"(b) The parties prepare a schedule of the property transferred sufficient to identify it; and

"(c) The transferee preserves the list and schedule for 6 months next following the transfer and permits inspection of either or both and copying therefrom at all reasonable hours by any creditor of the transferor, or files the list and schedule in the office of the secretary of state."   M.C.L.A. § 440.6104(1); M.S.A. § 19.6104(1). (Emphasis supplied.)

It was undisputed at trial that National did not request Frydlewicz to furnish a list of his creditors.

The trial court found National to be a transferee in bulk and, therefore, to be subordinate to plaintiff's rights in the disputed merchandise. The court relied in part on an admission in National's trial brief that it was not a "buyer in ordinary course of business".

While we do not rely on this ill-conceived admission, we find from the record that National was, as the trial court held, a transferee in bulk. A bulk transfer is

> "any transfer in bulk and not in the ordinary course of the transferor's business of a major part of the materials, supplies, merchandise or other inventory (section 9–109) of an enterprise subject to this article." M.C.L.A. § 440.6102(1); M.S.A. § 19.6102(1).

The items transferred must be inventory, i.e. held "for sale or lease." M.C.L.A. § 440.9109(4); M.S.A. § 19.9109(4). Here, the furniture transferred clearly represented the entire inventory held for sale by the King Furniture and Appliance Mart.

The transferor enterprise must have as its "principal business . . . the sale of merchandise from stock." M.C.L.A. § 440.6102(3); M.S.A. § 19.6102(3). Here, the transferor was a retail furniture store. The transfer must not be in the ordinary course of the transferor's business, and the items transferred must constitute a "major part" of the transferor's inventory. "Major part" has been defined as "meaning something more than 50%". Coogan, Hogan, Vagts, Secured Transactions Under the UCC, § 22.06(1)(c), p. 2287. Whether "major" is a quantitative or qualitative determination remains an open question; one which courts have approached on an ad hoc basis. Id. Ordinary course means day-to-day operation. The bulk sale must be an extraordinary event, one occurring a few times in the life of a merchant.

> "The plain meaning of the statute is that when a storekeeper disposes of a substantial part of his stock in trade in bulk, and selling in bulk sales is not the usual and ordinary way in which he conducts his business from day to day, the sale falls within the statute." Jubas v. Sampsell, 185 F.2d 333, 334 (C.A. 9, 1950).

The closing of a retail store and bulk sale of its stock, both whole and damaged items, constitutes such an extraordinary transaction. Further, the instant case is prototypical of the situation which the bulk sales law was promulgated to remedy. The law attempts to protect a creditor from a "merchant, owing debts, who sells out his stock in trade to anyone for any price, pockets the proceeds, and disappears leaving the creditors unpaid." UCC § 6–101, Official Comment 2(b). Here Frydlewicz sold his inventory for less than its value and declared bankruptcy. But for the bulk sales law plaintiff might be without a remedy.

Some question exists as to the scope of "enterprise" where, as here, the transferor is a retail outlet owned by a wholesaler. Does "enterprise" represent the entire business or each outlet for purposes of determining whether the sale is of a "major part" of the inventory? In the instant case, "enterprise" must be construed as representing the retail outlet so as to effectuate the purpose enunciated above. Plaintiff's dealings with the transferor, Frydlewicz, concerning only his Appliance & Furniture Mart and its inventory. The Mart was, at all times, considered a separate entity. The interaction of the secured transaction and bulk transfer provisions of the MUCC, therefore, require that plaintiff be protected against loss of collateral by the coverage of the bulk transfer notice provisions.

National's second claim on appeal is that the trial court incorrectly calculated National's liability to plaintiff. The court awarded plaintiff $17,356.76. National argues that it is liable to plaintiff for the transferred property or the extent of value of the property in the hands of the transferee, who is acting as a trustee. This value, National claims, is $13,603.24, the amount which National paid to Frydlewicz.

Where the remedy utilized is money damages, the amount of the award is the fair market value of the transferred items. National Grocer Co. v. Plotler, 167 Mich. 626, 133 N.W. 493 (1911), Watkins v. Angus, 241 Mich. 690, 696, 217 N.W. 894 (1928). National cites the general principle that where no question is raised that the amount paid by the transferee was not the fair value, the amount paid represents the maximum liability. Cornelius v. J & R Motor Supply Corporation, 468 S.W.2d 781, 784 (Ky.1971), Waterman v. Perrotta, 144 Colo. 117, 355 P.2d 313 (1960). Here, however, the fair market value of the collateral was in issue. As plaintiff notes, the agreed statement of facts shows that National did not pay market value for the furniture. Inasmuch as the bulk transfers law is designed to prevent transfers in defraud of creditors, whenever the transfer is made at less than the wholesale cost, value should automatically be put in question. National paid Frydlewicz an agreed "wholesale cost, less ten per cent". In addition, National set aside, in lieu of bond, merchandise valued at "not less than Twenty Thousand Dollars", rather than $13,603.24, the amount claimed to be the maximum liability. The amount awarded by the court was within the parties' estimates, and we will not overturn it.

. . .

IN RE MCBEE

United States Court of Appeals, Fifth Circuit, 1983.
714 F.2d 1316.

Before THORNBERRY, GEE and WILLIAMS, CIRCUIT JUDGES.

JERRE S. WILLIAMS, CIRCUIT JUDGE.

This case concerns the determination of the rights of three secured creditors: National Bank of Texas ("National Bank"), West Texas Wholesale Supply Company ("Wholesale Supply"), and RepublicBank–Austin ("RepublicBank"). It raises novel questions of perfection and priorities in an unusual factual setting, including a bulk sale which did not comply with Article 6 of the Uniform Commercial Code and the subsequent bankruptcy of the transferee of the assets in question.

I. FACTS

From January, 1979, until May 5, 1980, Joe Ben Colley, who is not a party to these proceedings, owned and operated a business known as the Oak Hill Gun Shop. In January 1979, Cynthia K. McBee approached National Bank for a loan and represented to it that she was Colley's partner in the Oak Hill Gun Shop. As found by the bankruptcy court for the Western District of Texas, 20 B.R. 361, no partnership in fact existed; McBee lent her "creditworthiness" in assisting Colley to obtain a loan for his sole proprietorship. A loan was extended to "Oak Hill Gun Shop" as debtor, but signed by McBee as "partner". National Bank filed a U.C.C.–1 financing statement with the Secretary of State of the State of Texas solely under the name Oak Hill Gun Shop. The financing statement purported to collateralize all present and after acquired inventory of the gun shop.

Subsequently, Wholesale Supply, an inventory supplier, extended goods on credit and filed the financing statement on April 22, 1980, specifying "Joe B. Colley d/b/a Oak Hill Gun Shop" as debtor. The U.C.C.–1, signed by Colley, covered all inventory, proceeds and accounts receivable and also all equipment, furniture and fixtures used in the debtor's place of business.

On May 5, 1980, Colley assigned his interest in the Oak Hill Gun Shop to Cynthia K. McBee. The assignment included any "partnership interest" Colley had in the gun shop. The assignment agreement provided that McBee in the transfer of the business would comply with the provisions of Article 6 of the Texas Uniform Commercial Code dealing with bulk transfers. McBee never in fact complied with these provisions, including Section 6.105 which requires notification of the bulk transfer to the transferor's creditors. Tex.Bus. & Comm.Code Ann. § 6.105 (Vernon 1968).

Thereafter, McBee sought and obtained a loan from RepublicBank. RepublicBank filed a U.C.C.–1 financing statement on July 16, 1980, naming "C.K. McBee dba Oak Hill Gun Shop" as debtor. The statement filed by RepublicBank covered "All accounts, contract rights . . . inventory . . . whether now owned or hereafter acquired."

II. PROCEEDINGS BELOW

McBee filed a petition in bankruptcy on October 22, 1980. On January 31, 1981, the trustee in bankruptcy conducted an auction sale of all the remaining inventory of the Oak Hill Gun Shop. Subsequently, on February 19, National Bank filed its Motion for Distribution of Cash Collateral, by which it asked the bankruptcy court to distribute some $40,000 in proceeds from the auction sale, with payment being made first to National Bank in full discharge of its claim, and the balance, if any, being paid to Wholesale Supply and RepublicBank in the order of their priority.

On April 8, 1981, National Bank filed its Motion to Establish Bar Date by which it asked the bankruptcy court to establish a deadline for the filing of objections to National Bank's Motion for Distribution of Cash Collateral. Thereafter, the bankruptcy court established April 30 as the bar date. RepublicBank did not file a timely objection to National Bank's motion for distribution of cash collateral before the bar date deadline; it did, however, timely object to Wholesale Supplies' similar Motion for Payment of Sum on April 20.

At the beginning of the May 7 hearing on National Bank's motion, RepublicBank sought leave to file an objection. In support of its effort to file an objection after the bar date, RepublicBank claimed that newly discovered evidence provided it grounds for the first time to object to National Bank's claimed priority. After argument by all counsel, the bankruptcy court granted RepublicBank's motion for leave to file objection. The bankruptcy court then proceeded to trial and, after the presentation of evidence and the submission of briefs by all parties, entered its opinion and order here on appeal.

The bankruptcy court held that under the Uniform Commercial Code, as adopted by Texas, Wholesale Supply had first priority in the fund created by the trustee in bankruptcy's sale of the gun shop inventory followed by RepublicBank's right to satisfy its claim with the remainder. In so concluding, the court held that National Bank's claim to first priority was without merit inasmuch as it had failed to perfect its security interest. Both National Bank and RepublicBank appeal the bankruptcy court's determination, asserting their respective claims to priority in the proceeds of the sale of the bankrupt's assets.[5]

We disagree with the court's conclusion that National Bank failed to perfect its security interest, under Section 9.402(g) of the Texas Uniform Commercial Code. Tex.Bus. & Comm.Code Ann. § 9.402(g) (Vernon 1968 & Supp.1982–1983). Thus, priority among all three perfected creditors must be determined. After considering the specific provisions of Article 6, we find that by virtue of the non-complying bulk transfer of the gun shop, transferor Colley's creditors—National Bank and Wholesale Supply—retained their security interest in the inventory of the gun shop to the extent of the value of the inventory existing at the time of the bulk sale. We find nothing in the Code which would limit this interest to the specific inventory transferred at the earlier time but still traceable as remaining at the time of bankruptcy, as argued by RepublicBank. Thus, in accordance with the following discussion, we find that National Bank is to be granted first priority to the extent of the value of the collateral transferred, with priority in the remainder to Wholesale Supply. RepublicBank's priority is limited to the excess value, if any, of the sale proceeds over the value of the inventory which

5. Wholesale Supply did not appeal from the bankruptcy court's order. It did, however, participate in the appeal. At oral argument, Wholesale Supply took the position that the bankruptcy court erred in giving it first priority in the bankrupt's assets; it argued that National Bank should properly be afforded first priority and that it should properly have been relegated to a position of second priority.

existed when the business was transferred and which was transferred
in bulk.

. . .

2. *Priorities*

The general rule, of course, is that priorities of perfected security
claims are determined in the order of filing. Having found National
Bank's interest perfected, the order of priority in accordance with the
"first to file" rule is clear: first, National Bank, followed by Wholesale
Supply, and then RepublicBank.[9] This determination of general priorities, however, does not end our inquiry.

The collateral at issue here is the gun shop inventory held by *McBee*
at the time of bankruptcy. RepublicBank, the last creditor in time to
file, clearly held a security interest in *McBee*'s inventory. On the other
hand, National Bank and Wholesale Supply, the initial creditors to file,
held a security interest in the inventory, including "after-acquired
property,"[10] of the gun shop when owned by *Colley*. This intervening
bulk sale of the gun shop and its inventory from Colley to McBee raises
the question of whether, and to what extent, the transferor's creditors,
National Bank and Wholesale Supply, retain priority over the transferee's subsequent creditor, here RepublicBank. This question must be
analyzed in light of the fact that the bulk sale from Colley to McBee
was not made in accordance with the requirements of Article 6 of the
U.C.C., dealing with bulk sales.

Article 6 of the U.C.C. defines, in general terms, the rights, liabilities and responsibilities of the parties to a bulk sale. As adopted in
Texas, Section 6.105[11] requires that the transferee give notice to the
transferor's creditors, in accordance with Section 6.107,[12] *before* the

---

9. Wholesale Supply might possibly
have asserted the "purchase money security interest" exception to this rule, to gain
first priority over National Bank despite
the latter's earlier filing.   Tex.Bus. &
Comm.Code § 9.312(c) (Vernon 1968 &
Supp.1982–1983). Wholesale Supply, however, does not assert such priority. It concedes that it took its security interest subject to National's prior interest and should
have second priority.

10. All three secured creditors executed
security instruments covering after-acquired property. See Borg–Warner Acceptance Corp. v. Wolfe City National
Bank, 544 S.W.2d 947, 950 (Tex.Civ.App.—
Dallas 1976) ("all inventory" automatically
includes after-acquired inventory).

11. Section 6.105 provides:

§ 6.105. Notice to Creditors

   In addition to the requirements of the
preceding section, any bulk transfer subject to this chapter except one made by
auction sale (Section 6.108) is ineffective

against any creditor of the transferor
unless at least ten days before he takes
possession of the goods or pays for them,
whichever happens first, the transferee
gives notice of the transfer in the manner and to the persons hereafter provided (Section 6.107).

12. Section 6.107 states:

§ 6.107. The Notice

(a) The notice to creditors (Section 6.105)
shall state:

   (1) that a bulk transfer is about to be
made; and

   (2) the names and business addresses
of the transferor and transferee, and all
other business names and addresses used
by the transferor within three years last
past so far as known to the transferee;
and

   (3) whether or not all the debts of the
transferor are to be paid in full as they
fall due as a result of the transaction,

bulk transfer is made. This before-the-fact notice provision affords the transferor's creditors an opportunity to act before the sale to protect their security interests. Another protection, afforded by Section 6.106,[13] is a requirement upon the transferee to see that the relevant part of the proceeds of the sale finds its way into the hands of the transferor's creditors. Texas is among the minority of jurisdictions which has adopted this optional provision, providing further remedial concern for a transferor's creditors in a bulk sale.

The provisions of Article 6, if complied with, also protect the transferee and his future creditors. Secured creditors of the transferor cannot assert any claims against the transferee or his property after a complying bulk transfer; the transferee will not "pay twice" for property thus freed from prior security interests. Similarly, the transferee obtains clear title to the transferred assets and may obtain credit on the unencumbered property. The transferee's creditors also need not be concerned with the possibility that prior creditors, in the chain of title, will assert previously perfected interests in the transferee's property.

If the provisions of Article 6 are not complied with, Sections 6.104 and 6.105 state that the transfer is "ineffective" against the transferor's creditors. Tex.Bus. & Comm.Code Ann. §§ 6.104, 6.105 (Vernon 1968). The term "ineffective" is nowhere explicitly defined in the Code, nor by Texas case law. In the immediate case, it is conceded that the transfer from Colley to McBee did not comply with Article 6, despite the fact

---

and if so, the address to which creditors should send their bills.

(b) If the debts of the transferor are not to be paid in full as they fall due or if the transferee is in doubt on that point then the notice shall state further:

(1) the location and general description of the property to be transferred and the estimated total of the transferor's debts;

(2) the address where the schedule of property and list of creditors (Section 6.104) may be inspected;

(3) whether the transfer is to pay existing debts and if so the amount of such debts and to whom owing;

(4) whether the transfer is for new consideration and if so the amount of such consideration and the time and place of payment; and

(5) if for new consideration the time and place where creditors of the transferor are to file their claims.

(c) The notice in any case shall be delivered personally or sent by registered mail or certified mail to all the persons shown on the list of creditors furnished by the transferor (Section 6.104) and to all other persons who are known to the transferee to hold or assert claims against the transferor.

13. This section provides:

§ 6.106. Application of the Proceeds

In addition to the requirements of the two preceding sections:

(1) Upon every bulk transfer subject to this chapter for which new consideration becomes payable except those made by sale at auction it is the duty of the transferee to assure that such consideration is applied so far as necessary to pay those debts of the transferor which are either shown on the list furnished by the transferor (Section 6.104) or filed in writing in the place stated in the notice (Section 6.107) within thirty days after the mailing of such notice. This duty of the transferee runs to all the holders of such debts, and may be enforced by any of them for the benefit of all.

(2) If any of said debts are in dispute the necessary sum may be withheld from distribution until the dispute is settled or adjudicated.

(3) If the consideration payable is not enough to pay all of the said debts in full distribution shall be made pro rata.

that McBee had covenanted to comply with the bulk transfer provisions. The bankruptcy court examined the policies underlying Articles 6 and 9, as well as other specific provisions in both articles, and concluded that the term "ineffective" meant that the creditor's original interest and rights are unaffected by the transfer, and continue in the collateral as they would have if the collateral were still owned by the transferor. The court thus concluded that Colley's perfected creditors [15] retained their interest in the collateral, despite the transfer, and retained priority over transferee McBee's non-purchase money [16] creditors. We agree that these pre-transfer interests retain priority to the extent of the value of the inventory-collateral transferred in the noncomplying bulk sale.

In the absence of a bulk sales law, creditors generally would lose all security interest in collateral once transferred to a new owner; [17] the secured creditor's recourse would lie against the debtor-transferor, including an interest in any proceeds received by the transferor from the bulk sale.[18] In many cases, this would leave the secured creditor without any effective remedy. The value received upon transfer might be far less than that of the transferred collateral, or by the time the creditor learned of the transfer little, if any, of the sales proceeds might be recoverable from the debtor-transferor.

Article 6 of the U.C.C., as adopted by Texas, changes the relative position of the parties affected by a bulk sale. "The Bulk Transfers Act and related predecessors were enacted for the protection of creditors who sell goods and merchandise to others on credit for inventory and resale." Anderson & Clayton Co. v. Earnest, 610 S.W.2d 846, 848 (Tex. Civ.App.—Amarillo 1980). As summarized above, Article 6 places certain requirements upon the parties to the bulk sale. These require-

---

15. The court had, erroneously, found only Wholesale Supply to have a perfected security interest. As we concluded, supra, National Bank's interest was perfected as well.

16. RepublicBank does not maintain that it possessed a "purchase money security interest." Under Article 9, these security interests hold a special position as an exception to the "first-to-file" rule. That is, if properly created, purchase money security interests may have priority over previously filed and perfected security interests. See Tex.Bus. & Comm.Code Ann. §§ 9.302(a), 9.312(c)(d), (Vernon 1968 & Supp.1981–1983).

17. See generally, J. White & R. Summers, Uniform Commercial Code 768 (2d ed. 1980).

18. Article 6 does not contain any general rules of priority among creditors. Article 9, on secured transactions, sets out these rules. Among these are provisions which attempt to define the extent to which a security interest follows the proceeds of a sale of collateral and/or the collateral itself. See, e.g., Tex.Bus. & Comm.Code Ann. §§ 9.306, 9.312.

RepublicBank argues that the provisions of Article 9 alone are relevant, and that the bankruptcy court's reliance on Article 6 is misplaced. We strongly disagree. Clearly, Article 9, covering secured transactions, sets forth the general principles for determining security conflicts. Article 6, by contrast, sets forth specific rules to govern the limited context of bulk sales. If the immediate case did not involve a bulk sale, Article 6 would be of no relevance. Yet this is not the case at hand. The bulk sale between Colley and McBee directly gives rise to RepublicBank's claim that National Bank and Wholesale Supply's prior perfected interests did not attach to McBee's interest in the gun shop. Accordingly, the specific provisions of Article 6 must be scrutinized in determining the validity of RepublicBank's claim.

ments serve to notify the transferor's creditors of the intended sale, thus permitting the creditors to protect their security interests *before* the transfer.   They also protect the transferee and his subsequent creditors by bringing to light and terminating all prior security claims to the transferred property.

Had Article 6 been complied with, transferor-Colley's secured creditors—National Bank and Wholesale Supply—would have retained no interest in the gun shop in McBee's hands.   There is no evidence, however, of any attempt at compliance, although McBee had contracted to do so in her sale agreement with Colley.   As a result, Colley's secured creditors were left without the benefit of Article 6's remedial provisions, most notably those requiring notice to the transferor's creditors.   Furthermore, these creditors, National Bank and Wholesale Supply, were unable to avail themselves of the additional remedial provision, Section 6–106, adopted in a minority of jurisdictions including Texas, which requires a transferee to see that the relevant part of the proceeds of the sale finds its way into the hand of the transferor's creditors.

The Code provides that this total noncompliance makes the transfer "ineffective" as to the transferor's creditors.   Given the remedial purpose behind Article 6, particularly as adopted in Texas, it is clear that by "ineffective" the Code drafters intended that the pre-transfer security interests survive the transfer, despite the fact that the collateral is no longer owned by the debtor.   RepublicBank argues that this result is untenable, particularly with regard to new property purchased by the transferee and never owned by the transferor.   At first glance, this argument is appealing: how can a debtor-transferor give his secured creditors an interest in property he no longer owns and, more significantly, in post-transfer property acquired by the transferee which the transferor never owned?

Upon analysis, however, the facial logical persuasiveness and the equitable underpinning of this argument disappears.   The transferor gives his creditors a security interest in *his* property which may, as in the immediate case, cover "after-acquired property."   It is Article 6, which provides as a "sanction for non-compliance" that the transfer is ineffective against creditors of the transferor.   Tex.Bus. & Comm.Code Ann. § 6.106 official comment 2 (Vernon 1968).   If this result were not reached, the remedial purposes behind Article 6 would be severely, if not wholly, undercut.   The entire Article could be ignored with impunity; the remedial notice provisions, which serve to awaken unknowing creditors to press their claims before transfer, would be avoided.   Clearly, a transferee cannot complain if, by his non-compliance, the transferor's creditors' claims attach to his property as they had prior to sale.

The immediate case proves the importance of the statutory requirement.   Transferee McBee cannot complain.   She was aware of National Bank's interest in the inventory and after-acquired property of the gun shop, yet she breached her specific covenant to comply with Article 6 in her sale agreement with Colley. Nor can the transferee's creditors be heard to complain of the protections afforded the transferor's creditors. The transferee's creditors should inquire as to a debtor's source of title where circumstances warrant. See Tex.Bus. & Comm.Code Ann. § 9.402(g) official comment 8 (Vernon Supp.1982–1983). Where, as in the immediate case, a bulk transfer has recently taken place, a subsequent creditor can and should inquire as to whether the transfer complied with Article 6. We find that the underlying policies of the Code are best supported by an interpretation which favors the unknowing prior creditor over the subsequent potential creditor. It is more equitable to place the burden on the potential subsequent creditor to check Article 6 compliance upon application for credit than to require constant vigilance of a prior creditor who, in the absence of notification, may rightfully assume that no bulk transfer cutting off his security interest has occurred.

We find further support for our conclusion in the statutory pattern. The transferor's creditor is not saved harmless forever in a noncomplying bulk transfer. Article 6 limits the period in which a transferor's creditor may assert a security interest to six months after the non-complying bulk transfer, unless there has been concealment of the transfer. Tex.Bus. & Comm.Code Ann. § 6.111 (Vernon 1968). This limitations period evidences a policy that at some point a diligent creditor should realize that a transfer has occurred absent concealment of that fact and despite his lack of notice. If the prior creditor does not exercise such diligence, his security interest in the transferred property is lost. This time limitation was met in this case by National and Wholesale Supply.[19] The time limitation supports our conclusion that Article 6 is a reasonable and balanced provision in preserving the security interests of the transferor's creditors effective against the transferee.

RepublicBank relies upon two cases interpreting the Alabama version of the U.C.C. as compelling an opposite result: Bill Voorhees Co. v. R & S Camper Sales, 605 F.2d 888 (5th Cir.1979); Get It Kwik of America v. First Alabama Bank, 361 So.2d 568 (Ala.App.1978). We find these cases significantly distinguishable. Both cases held that the transferee was not *personally liable* for the transferor's *original debt* because of the transferee's noncompliance with Article 6. *Bill Voorhees,* supra, 605 F.2d at 890 (citing *Get It Kwik* for this proposition). Our conclusion today is not in conflict with these holdings. The question of personal liability is not before us. We found, *supra,* that

---

19. In the immediate case, the transfer occurred on May 5, 1980. The transferor's creditors asserted their interest in the gun shop's inventory here at issue in October 1980, before the six-month period expired. We agree with the bankruptcy court that the four-month period for refiling upon a name change of the debtor under Article 9, Tex.Bus. & Comm.Code Ann. § 9.402(g) (Vernon 1982–1983), does not apply here.

If this general Article 9 provision applied, it would in effect reduce the specific provision in Article 6 from six to four months. Where, as here, a specific section of the Code applies to a particular situation, the specific provision should govern. Thus, the six-month period in Article 6, relating to non-complying bulk sales, was correctly applied by the bankruptcy court.

noncompliance with Article 6 results in the retention of the transferor's creditors' *security interest in the collateral* despite its transfer to a new owner. Colley's creditors, National Bank and Wholesale Supply, have not sought relief on the ground that McBee was personally liable for Colley's business debt, as had the creditors in *Bill Voorhees* and *Get It Kwik.* As recognized in the cited cases, these theories of recovery are narrowed to specific liabilities. A transferor's creditor may be entitled to recover the value of the *collateral* even though the transferee is not personally liable for the debt. Cf. Anderson & Clayton Co. v. Earnest, 610 S.W.2d 846, 848 (Tex.Civ.App.—Amarillo 1980) (transferor's creditors' relief is obtained primarily from and against the asset transferred in bulk; personal liability of the transferee arises only under limited circumstances); *Get It Kwik,* supra (transferee not personally liable under Alabama U.C.C., but transferor's creditor entitled to recover value of transferred collateral under a conversion theory).

The sagacity behind this distinction is self evident. Noncompliance with Article 6 without the saving provisions would deprive transferor's creditors of the opportunity to secure their interests existing at the time of the transfer. They would be deprived, in the absence of compliance, of the *value of the collateral* which is transferred. As we interpret Article 6, its policies and specific provisions rendering the transfer "ineffective" are furthered by permitting the secured creditor to recover this value. But, it is questionable whether Article 6 goes further to contemplate the clearly greater "sanction" of personal liability, which might result in the transferor creditor's receipt of more value than that which was transferred.

Further, the Alabama U.C.C. construed in *Bill Voorhees Co.* and *Get It Kwik* does not adopt the optional remedial provision, Section 6.106, adopted in Texas. Both this Court in *Bill Voorhees Co.,* supra, 605 F.2d at 891, and the Alabama court in *Get It Kwik,* supra, 361 So.2d at 571, found this absence significant in reaching the conclusion that personal liability does not arise under the U.C.C. as adopted in Alabama. As analyzed in *Bill Voorhees Co.,* supra, 605 F.2d at 891, the optional remedy provision as contained in the Texas law "evidence[s] a legislative intention to treat the transferee like a trustee" who "must account for the bulk property or be held accountable for the proceeds of its sale." While the Texas courts might only extend personal liability in narrow circumstances, despite the adoption of Section 6.107 in their U.C.C., they clearly have adopted this "trustee" analysis of a transferee in a non-complying bulk transfer. As stated by one court:

> "Failure of the purchaser to comply with the Bulk Sales Law fixes his liability as that of a receiver, and he becomes bound to see that the property, or its value, is applied to the satisfaction of claims of the creditors of the seller. In other words, he becomes a trustee, charged with the duties and liabilities of a trustee. Under the law he is charged with liability only to the extent of the value of the

property received by him and his liability is to all the creditors pro rata."

Anderson & Clayton Co. v. Earnest, 610 S.W.2d 846, 848 (Tex.Civ. App.—Amarillo 1980) (quoting Southwestern Drug Corp. v. McKesson and Robbins, 172 S.W.2d 485, 487 (Tex.1943).

RepublicBank argues that Section 6.110 protects its interest from those of the transferor's creditors. Section 6.110 provides that:

> When the title of a transferee to property is subject to a defect by reason of his noncompliance with the requirements of this chapter, then:
>
> (1) a purchaser of any of such property from such transferee who pays no value or who takes with notice of such noncompliance takes subject to such defect, but
>
> (2) a purchaser for value in good faith and without such notice takes free of such defect.

Tex.Bus. & Comm.Code Ann. § 6.110 (Vernon 1968). RepublicBank reasons that: (1) there is no finding or evidence that it had notice of McBee's failure to comply with Article 6; (2) the term "purchaser" includes a secured party such as RepublicBank under U.C.C. §§ 1.201(32), (33); and therefore (3) its interest is held free of any prior security interests by operation of Section 6.110(2).

This argument is not persuasive. While it is true under the Code that the general term "purchaser" may include a secured party, we find it clear that the term as used in Section 6.110 was not intended to include secured creditors.

As we find, supra, Article 6 clearly contemplates that transferors' creditors retain their security interest in the transferred collateral in the event of total noncompliance. This contemplated result would be frustrated were an extensive reading given to the term "purchaser" in Section 6.110 to cover subsequent creditors. Further we doubt whether a subsequent creditor could assert a claim that it took its interest "without notice." If a prior security interest is perfected, the burden is on the subsequent creditor to search for that claim. His failure to receive actual notice cannot be held as a defense to the priority of the prior perfected lien. Since Article 6 clearly provides that after a non-complying bulk transfer the transferor creditors' security interests remain effective, such interests may not be cut off by a broad reading of Section 6.110 at odds with the specific purpose behind Article 6.

RepublicBank further argues that Article 9 of the Code limits Colley's creditors' security interests to the particular collateral in the stock in trade at the time of the bulk transfer and remaining with McBee at the time of bankruptcy. The argument is that the security interest does not extend to any new inventory even if of lesser value than that transferred. The contention is not persuasive. Nothing in Article 9 limits this interest to the *particular* inventory which was transferred between Colley and McBee. Rather, as recognized in the very case relied upon by RepublicBank, Article 9 compels a contrary conclusion. *Get It Kwik,* supra, said:

> The vast majority of jurisdictions hold that when a security interest is taken in the inventory of a business, after acquired inventory is automatically covered unless it is clearly set out that only certain items of inventory are to be covered. See In re Nickerson & Nickerson, Inc., 9 U.C.C.Rep. 886, 329 F.Supp. 93 (DCD Neb.1971).

> As the court in *In Re Page,* 16 U.C.C.Rep. 501, 504 (DCMD Fla. 1974), stated:

>> "Needless to say, any reasonable secured party would be fully aware that this type of business presupposes a constant change in the inventory. Therefore, it is obviously unreasonable to assume that anyone would have received or acquired or intended to acquire a security interest in an inventory with the rigid limitation that it should be limited to the same items which made up the inventory on the date the document was executed."

> This approach is consistent with the general liberal philosophy of the U.C.C. and is certainly the prevailing and accepted commercial practice in financing retail merchandising businesses.

361 So.2d at 573–74. Texas adheres to the majority rule that an interest in inventory is generally assumed to cover after-acquired inventory, and that a secured party's interest in the new inventory remains perfected. See Borg–Warner Acceptance Co. v. Wolfe City National Bank, 544 S.W.2d 947, 950 (Tex.Civ.App.—Dallas 1976) (citing §§ 9.108, 9.203, 9.204 of the Texas U.C.C.).

In the immediate case, all of the secured parties had a security interest in the after-acquired property. By virtue of transferee McBee's failure to comply with Article 6, this security interest in the ever-changing inventory-collateral remained effective. RepublicBank's contention that Colley's creditors' interest, if any, was limited to the actual inventory transferred and which remained with the gun shop at the time of bankruptcy is therefore without merit. While National Bank and Wholesale Supply's priority is limited to the overall *value* of the inventory transferred in bulk to McBee,[20] it is not limited to the actual inventory remaining and traceable to the bulk sale.[21]

---

20. The trustee in bankruptcy is not a party to this proceeding. We note, however, that under the Bankruptcy Act an after-acquired property interest in collateral to the extent of the value of the collateral at a set pre-bankruptcy date may only be valid against the trustee. 11 U.S.C. § 547. Thus, under the Act, a secured creditor—even without an intervening bulk sale—might not be able to enforce his "floating" lien for the greater value of inventory at the time of bankruptcy. See J. White & R. Summers, Uniform Commercial Code 1007–11 (2d ed. 1980). Without deciding whether the result we reach is required by this section of the Bankruptcy Act, we note its consistency with the result we reach under the U.C.C.

21. RepublicBank argues that § 9.306 limits Colley's creditors' perfected security interests to the precise inventory which remained from the transfer because there was insufficient evidence that the new inventory was purchased directly and exclusively from the *proceeds* of the sale of the guns as is required to maintain continued perfection under that section. We reject

We thus conclude that National Bank, as first, and Wholesale Supply, as second, are entitled to priority in the inventory of transferee McBee given the latter's noncompliance with Article 6. Their security interest in the inventory of Oak Hill Gun Shop remained perfected and attached to the inventory after the transfer to McBee.

IV. CONCLUSION

The bankruptcy court erred in concluding that under § 9.402(g) of the Texas U.C.C. National Bank's security interest in the gun shop collateral was unperfected. Accordingly, all three creditors held perfected security interests. We also conclude that the security interests of National Bank and Wholesale Supply remained perfected and attached to the gun shop inventory despite its bulk transfer to McBee, in light of McBee's failure to comply with Article 6 of the U.C.C., as adopted in Texas. These prior, perfected interests retained their priority over the later security interest filed by RepublicBank in the same inventory, to the extent of the value of the inventory-collateral transferred from Colley to McBee. Accordingly we remand to the bankruptcy court with instructions to enter an order granting priority first to National Bank, to the extent of the value of the inventory-collateral transferred to McBee, and then to Wholesale Supply; RepublicBank's priority is limited to the excess value, if any, of the inventory-fund over that of the inventory transferred to McBee.

Reversed and Remanded.

Notes & Questions

1. *Effect of a Defective Transfer.* What do §§ 6–104 and 6–105 mean when they deem defective bulk transfers to be "ineffective against any creditor?" Should Article 6 contain a more detailed list of remedies? Was the remedy in *National Bank* the most appropriate? Were the creditors made better off as the result of the defective bulk transfer than they would have been if the parties had complied with Article 6?

2. *Treatment of Transferees.* Compare the treatment of the transferees in *National Bank* with the UFCA's treatment of transferees. Are transferees treated more harshly under Article 6 than under the UFCA? If Article 6 is a branch of fraudulent conveyance law, is there any reason not to borrow the UFCA's treatment of transferees?

RepublicBank's proffered application of § 9.306(b) to the issue at hand. Here, the "original collateral" included not only presently-owned inventory but after-acquired inventory as well. This sort of floating lien, as discussed *supra*, reflects the commercial reality that inventory is fluid. Constant refiling, to achieve perfection, could not have been contemplated by the Code's drafters. The Code provides a special mechanism for subsequent purchase money security creditors to obtain priority over prior, floating liens in inventory. See Tex.Bus. & Comm.Code Ann. § 9.312(c) (Vernon Supp.1982–1983). RepublicBank's subsequent security interest, however, does not fit into this special priority category.

3. *Utility of Notice.* Given that Article 6 requires notice to the creditors of a debtor about to engage in a bulk transfer, what good does such notice do the notified creditors? Does Article 6 merely provide the mechanics for a game in which a debtor taunts existing creditors by telling them that the assets they were relying on are now being sold? Put another way, what should a creditor receiving notice of a bulk transfer do?

4. *Avoiding Article 6.* Suppose debtor wants to engage in a bulk transfer but wishes to avoid Article 6's notice requirements. Instead of selling assets to transferee, debtor grants transferee a security interest in the assets to secure a loan from transferee. Debtor then defaults on the loan and transferee forecloses on the assets. Does Article 6 cover such a transaction?

5. *Transferor's Creditors vs. Transferee's Creditors.*

(a) *McBee* raises a priority question in which two innocent parties, the transferor's creditor and the transferee's creditor, are competing over the same assets. Should the approach to this contest differ from the approach to contests between the transferee and the transferor's creditors?

(b) Would or should anything in *McBee* be analyzed differently if the transferee's creditor had been unsecured? Could it simply act as if the fraudulent transfer had never occurred?

(c) Would analysis in *McBee* be furthered by resort to the commingling rules of § 9–315?

6. *The Wisdom of Article 6.* Should Article 6 be repealed? By its terms, it seems to protect only those unsecured creditors who are looking to a debtor's assets to assure repayment. Given Article 9, would any sane unsecured creditor derive comfort from the existence of assets, even assets unencumbered at the time credit is extended? What costs does Article 6 impose? Who is likely to incur liability under it?

Is there a relationship worth exploring between bulk transfer problems and problems raised by leveraged buyouts?

Chapter 7

POST–JUDGMENT COLLECTION CONCERNS

Useful analogies exist between the creation, perfection, and enforcement of an Article 9 security interest and the issues that arise in enforcing a judgment. Questions about the scope of Article 9 (which secured transactions does it govern?) are analogous to questions about the property any particular form of judgment enforcement mechanism may reach. In most jurisdictions, the judgment lien that arises upon docketing a judgment creates a specific interest only in real property. Other methods must be used to establish enforceable interests in personal property. Some property, even though not exempt, is beyond the reach of existing enforcement mechanisms.

Enforcement procedures also have mechanical differences. The method by which a judgment creditor obtains an interest in specific real property usually differs from the method by which the creditor obtains an interest in chattels or less tangible assets such as chattel paper. The methods by which judgment creditors obtain interests in specific property that are valid against third parties bear a close relationship to the methods by which an Article 9 secured party perfects a security interest. Indeed, one might ask whether there should be any difference between methods of perfection for purposes of Article 9 and methods of levy for purposes of enforcing a judgment. The first part of this Chapter deals with methods of enforcing judgments.

Like any Article 9 secured party, a judgment creditor must worry about competitors asserting interests in the property to which he is looking for satisfaction of a judgment. Competition among judgment creditors and between judgment creditors and other creditors can be no less keen than competitions involving Article 9 secured parties. The second part of this Chapter deals with priorities in property sought to be reached by judgment creditors.

RIESENFELD, COLLECTION OF MONEY JUDGMENTS IN AMERICAN LAW—A HISTORICAL INVENTORY AND A PROSPECTUS, 42 Iowa L.Rev. 155, 156–63 (1957)

GENERAL CLASSIFICATION OF COLLECTION TECHNIQUES AND THE IMPACT OF THE COMMON LAW TRADITION

In classifying the legal effects of a final personal judgment for the recovery of money it might be helpful to distinguish between its intrinsic effects as authoritative and conclusive disposition of the cause of action and the litigated issues between the parties pertaining thereto and the extrinsic attributes which are bestowed thereon by the common

345

law (and the classical statutes that are deemed to have become part of it) for the purpose of enabling the judgment creditor to proceed to a forced but orderly collection. The latter effects may be divided into three great categories, *viz.*:

> (1) *Executability* (by means of assorted writs or process).

> (2) *Actionability* (by constituting a cause of action for an action of debt or civil action in general).

> (3) *Creation of lien* (by "encumbering" specifically defined interests in land of the debtor).

Actually this classification is the result of the development of certain common law concepts and doctrines which require some further discussion. Moreover, as will be seen, equity also added to the arsenal of collection remedies by entertaining creditors' suits to compel or facilitate the satisfaction of judgments in cases calling for such intervention.

The *common law,* in its mature or classical stage, provided for the execution of money judgments by means of two principal writs known by the names of *fieri facias* and *elegit.* The former writ, which was of uncertain but ancient origin, commanded the sheriff to cause the judgment to be satisfied out of the judgment debtor's goods and chattels and was executed by seizure and sale. *Elegit,* on the other hand, was an innovation introduced by the Statute of Westminster II in the course of the great reform legislation of Edward I and authorized the judgment creditor to obtain satisfaction not only out of his debtor's goods and chattels, but also out of the use of a moiety of his lands. The goods and chattels were transferred to the judgment creditor at a reasonable price, while the use of half of the lands was assigned to him in the form of a tenancy for a term determined by an appraisal of its annual value (so-called tenancy by *elegit*).

The availability of *fieri facias* and *elegit* resulted in the obsolescence of another writ or, perhaps more accurately, agglomerate of writs traditionally designated as *levari facias* after the command to the sheriff contained therein to "levy" on the debtor's chattels and lands. This remedy was actually perhaps the most ancient enforcement method in English law and seemingly dated back to the days when compulsory process was given only as a means of constraint and not as a means of true satisfaction. Gradually, however, *levari facias* was transformed in some instances into a true collection proceeding. This occurred with respect to the enforcement of recognizances and with respect to at least certain judgments recovered in the royal courts. Unfortunately the latter aspect of the evolution is quite obscure, and at any rate the significance of *levari facias* as a method of execution of money judgments ceased, owing to the competition by *fieri facias* and *elegit.*

The *executability* of a money judgment at common law by means of a suitable writ—whether *levari facias, fieri facias* or *elegit*—was limited in time. According to English practice in the eighteenth century the judgment creditor was entitled to sue out a writ of execution upon "signing final judgment" without awaiting its formal entry in the judgment roll or its docketing and lost such right upon the expiration of a year and a day, counted from such signing date. The reason for this limitation was the presumption that after such time the judgment was satisfied. This presumption could be overcome in real actions by resort to the writ of *scire facias,* while in personal actions originally an action in debt on the judgment was required, to obtain a new execution. The Statute of Westminster II, however, extended *scire facias* to personal actions and henceforth money judgments could either be renewed by an action of debt or revived by writ of *scire facias.* The two methods differed in many respects, especially as to venue. *Scire facias* had to be brought in the county where the original action was laid, while the action on the judgment had to be brought in Middlesex county because it was to be pursued in the county where the record was located.

The *actionability* of the judgment, consequently, was originally extremely important in view of the limited executability. The subsequent availability of *scire facias* reduced the importance of the actionability of domestic judgments. Still there were certain procedural considerations why the actionability of domestic judgments remained of practical utility.

The *executability* of the judgment by means of *fieri facias* was not deemed at common law to create a charge of such judgment on the debtor's chattels. Rather such binding effect was held to arise only upon the suing out of the writ as of the date specified in its teste. This rule was modified in this latter respect by the Statute of Frauds which postponed the binding effect of the writ of *fieri facias* to the time of its delivery to the sheriff.

Contrariwise, the executability of a judgment by means of the writ of *elegit* was deemed to constitute the judgment itself a charge upon the moiety of the debtor's lands which, at least in the eighteenth century, was designated as a legal lien. This lien was independent of the possession by the judgment creditor and matured into a tenancy by *elegit* upon execution of the writ by the sheriff. While originally the sheriff had to place the creditor into actual possession, in later days delivery of legal possession was held to be sufficient, leaving the tenant to his remedy by ejectment. At common law the judgment lien related back to the first day of the term in which the judgment was rendered. But subsequently the rule was altered by statute in order to prevent frauds and to protect bona fide purchasers. The Statute of Frauds specified that "as against purchasers bona fide for valuable consideration of lands . . ." judgments should be considered as such and constitute a charge only from the time as they shall be signed in compliance with the statute and a later statute added the further qualification that the judgments should affect purchasers and mortgagees only upon proper entering and docketing thereof. As these rules applied only for the benefit of purchasers, it was concluded that as between judgment creditors the relation back theory was still in force and that therefore creditors obtaining judgments in the same term acquired liens of equal rank, permitting the creditor who resorted first to *elegit* to gain priority. Although the common law did not allow satisfaction out of lands by means of a sale of the moiety, the chancery during the eighteenth century started decreeing such sale when the creditor had to resort to equity to overcome fraudulent conveyances.

In the course of time *equity* came to intervene in aid of execution in situations where the legal process available to the creditor was either frustrated through fraud or concealment on the side of the debtor or was inadequate for other reasons. In order to fully appreciate the growth of this branch of the law, however, it must be realized that those remedies which since Pomeroy are commonly classified as creditors' suits constituted by no means the only occasions where the Chancery accorded assistance to creditors in the collection of their claims; rather the classical and by far most important and comprehensive instances of "creditors' bills" were those by which creditors sought payment of their claims from executors or administrators or out of assets in the hands of an heir, devisee or successor of such heir or devisee when in equity or by statute they were entitled to such collection. In the latter cases the grant of relief generally was not conditioned upon a previous judgment at law and execution sued out and returned *nulla bona,* since with respect to most of these claims an action at law would have been unavailable to the creditors. . . .

Many uncertainties and doubts existed also in regard to the extent to which equity would intervene on behalf of judgment creditors for the purpose of enabling them to satisfy their claims out of assets not reachable by the writs of *fieri facias* and *elegit.* Reference has already been made to the fact that the Chancery went all out in this respect in connection with the administration of decedents' estates and its creation of a doctrine of "equitable assets", i.e., assets which could be reached solely by the aid of the court of equity and only on a basis of equality for all creditors. Outside of this branch of equity, however, intervention was much more hesitating and limited. To be sure, the Statute of Frauds itself had extended the writ of *elegit* to the beneficial interest in land of a *cestui* under a trust and insofar obviated the need for equitable assistance. But that statute did not apply to other equitable interests in land. Equity therefore was willing to aid judgment creditors of a mortgagor at least to the extent of permitting them to redeem. Yet overzealous reliance on the maxim that equity follows the law proved to be somewhat of an obstacle to the development of equitable proceedings permitting resort to other types of assets, especially choses in action such as corporate stock and debts. Although during the first part of the eighteenth century the chancellors tended to take a liberal attitude toward the creditors, even in *inter vivos* cases of this type, subsequent cases showed reluctance to follow these precedents.

Generally speaking, however, the foregoing discussion can be summed up in the conclusion that equity gradually developed various remedies to facilitate and supplement the execution process. It can therefore be stated that a fourth great class of the legal effects of a money judgment under English law is its capacity to serve as a basis for equitable proceedings in aid of execution. . . .

There is no question that the law of enforcement of money judgments in any jurisdiction in the United States still bears to some extent the earmarks of the common law pattern. Yet everywhere profound transformations have taken place and the existing law of creditors' remedies shows such a perplexing and ever-increasing variety of sports that attempts of functional classification must of necessity end in bitter frustration. The only common denominator or standard of comparison possible is the common law system and all descriptions of the American systems must be in terms of deviation from that model. . . .

A. Methods of Creating Post–Judgment Interests in Specific Property

McCAHEY v. L.P. INVESTORS

United States Court of Appeals, Second Circuit, 1985.
774 F.2d 543

WINTER, CIRCUIT JUDGE:

The plaintiff, Cynthia McCahey, appeals from Judge Platt's dismissal of her complaint for failure to state a claim, Fed.R.Civ.P. 12(b)(6). McCahey seeks injunctive, declaratory, and monetary relief on the grounds that New York's post-judgment remedies deprived her of property without due process. We affirm.

BACKGROUND

1. *The Underlying Dispute*

Because the complaint was dismissed for failure to state a claim, we accept its allegations as true.

According to the complaint, McCahey is a single mother of three children. She and her family are dependent for support on the Aid to Families with Dependent Children program ("AFDC"). On October 13, 1982, L.P. Investors obtained a default judgment against McCahey for unpaid rent in the amount of $1,979.61. McCahey had notice of the proceeding but did not appear. She does not contest the validity of the judgment.

To collect the judgment, L.P. Investors hired a collection agency, Affiliated Credit Adjusters, which in turn hired an attorney, Allen Rosenthal. On June 14, 1983, Rosenthal telephoned McCahey and asked her to pay the judgment. McCahey refused, explaining that she did not have sufficient funds and was wholly dependent on AFDC. As evidence of her dependent status, she told Rosenthal her public assistance case number.

Rosenthal ascertained that McCahey had a checking account at the Island State Bank. The sole source of funds for the account was AFDC. On July 6, the bank received a restraining notice from Rosenthal directing it to stop all payments on the account. Shortly after July 12, McCahey received a letter from the bank informing her that her account had been restrained. The bank charged her $10 for this notice. Soon thereafter, McCahey called the bank and informed a bank employee that her account consisted entirely of welfare money. The bank employee told McCahey that welfare money was exempt from seizure and promised to contact Rosenthal. About July 18, the bank employee informed McCahey that Rosenthal did not believe the account contained only welfare money. The employee also informed McCahey that the bank would nevertheless no longer honor the restraining notice.

Also on July 18, McCahey received a formal Notice to Judgment Debtor from Rosenthal. New York law requires that such a notice be sent to judgment debtors whenever their property is restrained. The Notice disclosed the name of the judgment creditor and information about the underlying judgment. It also informed the judgment debtor that property of the debtor has been taken, that some forms of property are exempt from seizure (one example given is welfare such as AFDC), that the debtor may contact "the person sending this notice" or a lawyer or Legal Aid, and that there is a procedure to get property back if the property is exempt.

As suggested by the form, McCahey contacted "the person sending this notice," i.e. Rosenthal, and informed him that the money in the account was welfare money and thus exempt from seizure. Rosenthal asked her to send him a copy of her welfare check. McCahey's next check arrived on August 15, and she then sent Rosenthal a copy.[1]

On August 26, at the direction of Rosenthal, the Sheriff of Suffolk County served an execution on the bank. Three days later, the Sheriff sent another Notice to Judgment Debtor to McCahey, but McCahey did not receive it. On August 30, the bank turned over $35.13 to the Sheriff. On September 19, the Sheriff turned over the money to Rosenthal. Rosenthal received only $11 because of sheriff's fees. When he called the bank to determine why he had received only $11, the bank again informed him that the money in the account was exempt. Nonetheless, on October 4, 1983, the bank paid the Sheriff the entire balance in the account, $406.82.

At some later date, the plaintiff contacted the Legal Aid Society, as the Notice to Judgment Debtor had recommended. Rather than invoke the procedures provided by New York statute to recover levied property, however, the Legal Aid lawyer attempted to intervene in litigation pending before Judge Lasker, Deary v. Guardian Loan Co., 534 F.Supp. 1178 (S.D.N.Y.1982). In that case, Judge Lasker had declared unconstitutional the predecessor statutes of the ones at issue in the instant case

---

1. Rosenthal claims that he never received the copy of the check.

and had retained jurisdiction over the issue of whether the instant statutes were constitutional.[2] Leave to intervene in *Deary* was denied to McCahey. Nevertheless, Rosenthal returned McCahey's money as a consequence of the attempted intervention.[3]

McCahey then instituted the present action to recover for the loss of the use of her money for four and one-half months.[4] She claims that during this period she fell behind in her rent and utility payments, skimped on food and clothing, and was afraid to use her bank account.

2. *New York's Current Post–Judgment Remedies*

In *Deary,* Judge Lasker found that New York's earlier post-judgment remedies violated due process because they did not provide notice to the debtor that: (i) property had been seized, (ii) such property might be exempt from seizure, or (iii) there were procedures available to contest the seizure. 534 F.Supp. at 1187–88. After Judge Lasker's decision, the New York legislature enacted the revisions at issue in this case. The revised statutory scheme is set out in the appendices to this opinion.

The current process of enforcing money judgments begins when the attorney for the judgment creditor issues a restraining notice to the holder of the judgment debtor's property. The restraining notice includes information about the underlying action and informs the recipient that transfer of property by the debtor is punishable as contempt of court. If the restraining notice is sent to someone other than the judgment debtor, a copy of it must also be mailed to the judgment debtor within four days of service of the notice.

In addition to the information supplied by the restraining notice, the notice sent to the judgment debtor must state:

NOTICE TO JUDGMENT DEBTOR

Money or property belonging to you may have been taken or held in order to satisfy a judgment which has been entered against you. Read this carefully. YOU MAY BE ABLE TO GET YOUR MONEY BACK

State and federal laws prevent certain money or property from being taken to satisfy judgments. Such money or property is said to

---

2. The case was eventually settled, without a ruling by Judge Lasker on the constitutionality of the statutes at issue in the instant case.

3. Rosenthal claims that he returned the money when McCahey attempted to intervene in *Deary* because that was the first time that he had received a sworn document claiming an exemption.

4. The issue of mootness arises in cases similar to the present one, because the judgment creditor frequently returns the debtor's property before judgment is rendered upon the constitutionality of the legislation in question. That has occurred in this case as well. However, McCahey's claim is not moot because she continues to demand compensatory and punitive damages for her temporary loss of funds. Memphis Light, Gas & Water Div. v. Craft, 436 U.S. 1, 8, 98 S.Ct. 1554, 1559, 56 L.Ed. 2d 30 (1978).

be "exempt". The following is a partial list of money which may be exempt:

1. Supplemental security income (SSI);

2. Social security;

3. Public assistance (welfare);

4. Alimony or child support;

5. Unemployment benefits;

6. Disability benefits;

7. Workers' compensation benefits;

8. Public or private pensions; and

9. Veterans benefits.

If you think that any of your money that has been taken or held is exempt, you must act promptly because the money may be applied to the judgment. If you claim any of your money that has been taken or held is exempt, you may contact the person sending this notice.

Also, YOU MAY CONSULT AN ATTORNEY, INCLUDING LEGAL AID IF YOU QUALIFY. The law (New York civil practice law and rules, article four and sections fifty-two hundred thirty-nine and fifty-two hundred forty) provides a procedure for determination of a claim to an exemption.

In order to obtain possession of the restrained property, the attorney issues an execution to the sheriff. The execution states essentially the same information as the restraining notice. The sheriff then levies on the property by serving the execution on the person in possession. That person must turn over the property to the sheriff "forthwith." If the execution does not state that a Notice to Judgment Debtor has been sent within the prior year by the attorney, then the sheriff must send yet another Notice within four days of levy. The sheriff must hold the property for at least fifteen days before turning it over to the judgment creditor.

The judgment debtor has two procedures for disputing seizures. First, by serving notice on the judgment creditor and the sheriff prior to the application of the property to the debt, the judgment debtor can start a "special proceeding" to adjudicate rights in the property. Second, at any time, on its own motion or on that of any interested party, the court can issue protective orders.

If the debtor makes a motion to adjudicate his rights in the property, the creditor has eight days to file a response. However, the court may shorten that time for cause shown.

DISCUSSION

1. *The Analytic Framework*

We first discuss the analytic framework in which McCahey's challenge to the New York post-judgment remedies must be addressed. We of course assume that McCahey's bank account was exempt from seizure, N.Y.Soc.Serv.L. § 137 (McKinney 1983), and constituted a property interest of which she could not be deprived, even temporarily, without due process. Fuentes v. Shevin, 407 U.S. 67, 84–85, 92 S.Ct. 1983, 1996, 32 L.Ed.2d 556 (1972).

Supreme Court decisions addressing due process limits on post-judgment remedies are so scant that Endicott–Johnson Corp. v. Encyclopedia Press, Inc., 266 U.S. 285, 45 S.Ct. 61, 69 L.Ed. 288 (1924), is still frequently cited. The Court held there that a judgment debtor is not constitutionally entitled to notice and a hearing prior to a wage garnishment. The Court viewed the existence of the underlying judgment as sufficient "notice of what will follow." Id. at 288, 45 S.Ct. at 62, quoting Ayres v. Campbell, 9 Iowa 213, 216 (1859).

Notwithstanding *Endicott,* post-judgment remedies have been repeatedly challenged under the due process clause in the last decade,[5] largely on the grounds that *Endicott* never considered the existence of property exempt under state law from execution that might neverthe-

5. See, e.g., Dionne v. Bouley, 757 F.2d 1344 (1st Cir.1985) (Rhode Island remedies held unconstitutional); Duranceau v. Wallace, 743 F.2d 709 (9th Cir.1984) (Washington child support collection remedy constitutional); Nelson v. Regan, 731 F.2d 105 (2d Cir.), cert. denied, — U.S. —, 105 S.Ct. 175, 83 L.Ed.2d 110 (1984) (IRS refund intercept program unconstitutional); Finberg v. Sullivan, 634 F.2d 50 (3d Cir. 1980) (en banc) (Pennsylvania remedies unconstitutional); Brown v. Liberty Loan Corp., 539 F.2d 1355 (5th Cir.1976), cert. denied, 430 U.S. 949, 97 S.Ct. 1588, 51 L.Ed.2d 797 (Florida wage garnishment remedies constitutional); Neeley v. Century Finance Co., 606 F.Supp. 1453 (D.Ariz. 1985) (Arizona remedies unconstitutional); Haines v. General Motors Corp., 603 F.Supp. 471 (S.D.Ohio 1984) (Kentucky remedies constitutional); Reigh v. Schleigh, 595 F.Supp. 1535 (D.Md.1984) (Maryland remedies held unconstitutional); Clay v. Fisher, 584 F.Supp. 730 (S.D.Ohio 1984) (Ohio remedies held unconstitutional); Jahn v. Regan, 584 F.Supp. 399 (E.D. Mich.1984) (IRS refund intercept program partially unconstitutional); Harris v. Bailey, 574 F.Supp. 966 (W.D.Va.1983) (Virginia remedies unconstitutional); Deary v. Guardian Loan Company, 534 F.Supp. 1178 (S.D.N.Y.1982) (New York remedies held unconstitutional); Community Thrift Club, Inc. v. Dearborn Acceptance Corp., 487 F.Supp. 877 (N.D.Ill.1980) (Illinois wage garnishment unconstitutional); Betts v. Tom, 431 F.Supp. 1369 (D.Hawaii 1977) (Hawaii remedies held unconstitutional); Huggins v. Deinhard, 134 Ariz. 98, 654 P.2d 32 (1982) (Arizona remedies constitutional); In Re Marriage of Wyshak, 70 Cal. App.3d 384, 138 Cal.Rptr. 811 (1977) (California remedies constitutional); Taylor v. Madigan, 53 Cal.App.3d 943, 126 Cal.Rptr. 376 (1976) (California remedies constitutional); Gedeon v. Gedeon, 630 P.2d 579 (Colo.1981) (Colorado remedies constitutional); Coursin v. Harper, 236 Ga. 729, 225 S.E.2d 428 (1976) (Georgia remedies unconstitutional); City Finance Co. v. Winston, 238 Ga. 10, 231 S.E.2d 45 (1976) (Georgia remedies unconstitutional); Antico v. Antico, 241 Ga. 294, 244 S.E.2d 820 (1978) (Georgia revised remedies constitutional); Wanex v. Provident State Bank, 53 Md.App. 409, 454 A.2d 381 (1983) (Maryland remedies constitutional); Warren v. Delaney, 98 A.D.2d 799, 469 N.Y.S.2d 975 (1983) (New York remedies unconstitutional); Cole v. Goldberger, Pedersen & Hochron, 95 Misc.2d 720, 410 N.Y.S.2d 950 (1978) (New York remedies unconstitutional); Mullins v. Main Bank & Trust, 592 S.W.2d 24 (Tex.Civ.App.1979) (Texas remedies constitutional).

less be seized by a creditor if notice and an opportunity to be heard are not accorded the debtor. *Endicott's* rationale assumed that the judgment resolved all outstanding issues between the debtor and the creditor, collection being a ministerial act. However, the judgment does not resolve whether certain property is exempt, Finberg v. Sullivan, 634 F.2d 50, 56–57 (3d Cir.1980) *(en banc),* and subsequent Supreme Court decisions have implied that *Endicott* is not the last word on the subject.

Griffin v. Griffin, 327 U.S. 220, 66 S.Ct. 556, 90 L.Ed. 635 (1946), involved the collection of past-due alimony payments arising out of a divorce decree. The Court held that a judgment directing issuance of execution for collection of the unpaid alimony violated due process because it had been obtained *ex parte* and had cut off defenses available to the husband. Although the majority opinion did not refer to *Endicott,* debate has arisen over the effect of *Griffin* on *Endicott's* vitality as a precedent.

The expansion of the due process limitations on prejudgment remedies has also led to a closer scrutiny of post-judgment remedies because of the partial analogy between the two. While some ambiguity exists, it is generally believed that pre-judgment *ex parte* attachments are constitutional if issued by a neutral judicial officer on the basis of factual representations regarding the merits of the plaintiff's claim and immediately followed by notice to the defendant and by an opportunity to contest the seizure. See Jonnet v. Dollar Savings Bank, 530 F.2d 1123, 1129–30 (3d Cir.1976); Scott, Constitutional Regulation of Provisional Creditor Remedies: The Cost of Procedural Due Process, 61 Va.L. Rev. 806, 832–33 (1975).[7] Of course, the law of pre-judgment remedies, while suggestive, does not automatically govern post-judgment remedies, which are available only after all doubt as to liability has been erased.

The majority of courts that have recently considered the due process aspects of post-judgment remedies have adopted a balancing analysis derived from Mathews v. Eldridge, 424 U.S. 319, 334, 96 S.Ct. 893, 902, 47 L.Ed.2d 18 (1976). As Justice Powell explained:

> [R]esolution of . . . whether . . . procedures provided . . . are constitutionally sufficient requires analysis of the governmental and private interests that are affected. More precisely, our prior decisions indicate that identification of the specific dictates of due process generally requires consideration of three distinct factors: First, the private interest that will be affected by the official action; second, the risk of an erroneous deprivation of such interest through the procedures used, and the probable value, if any, of additional or substitute procedural safeguards; and finally, the Government's interest, including the function involved and the fiscal and adminis-

---

7. Some courts have interpreted the pre-judgment cases as requiring prior notice and hearing when wages are gar- nished. See, e.g., Brown, 539 F.2d at 1366; Neeley, 606 F.Supp. at 1461.

trative burdens that the additional or substitute procedural requirement would entail.

Id. at 334–35, 96 S.Ct. at 902–03 (citations omitted). We agree that the
balancing analysis is applicable.

The creditor's interests are straightforward: a swift, sure and inexpensive mechanism for collecting judgments. This interest is most
directly served by allowing creditors to reach bank accounts and other
liquid assets, because seizure of those assets is the lowest-cost method of
satisfying judgments.

The debtor's interest in preserving non-exempt property for his or
her own use is of course subservient to the creditor's judgment. However, the debtor has a clearly legitimate interest in protecting exempt
property from seizure.

The state has several interests in the matters at hand. First, it has
an interest in providing inexpensive and rapid methods of collecting
judgments, as part of its more general interest in ensuring compliance
with its laws. Second, it has an interest in the efficient use of judicial
resources, so they are not wasted in proceedings of little value. Finally,
the state has an interest in seeing that laws exempting property from
seizure are not evaded.

McCahey challenges the New York procedures on five grounds, all
rooted in due process. She claims: (i) judgment debtors are entitled to
notice and a hearing before seizure of their property; (ii) if pre-seizure
remedies are not required, seizure may occur only on the order of a
neutral judicial officer after disclaimer by the judgment debtor of
knowledge of any exemptions; (iii) the New York Notice to Judgment
Debtor does not adequately explain the procedure for pressing an
exemption claim; (iv) by recommending that the debtor contact "the
person sending this notice," the New York Notice to Judgment Debtor
misleads the debtor into thinking that "the person," who will usually
be the attorney for the creditor, will protect the debtor's rights; and (v)
the New York procedure for adjudicating exemption claims does not
provide a sufficiently prompt opportunity to contest the levy.

2.   *The Requirements of Due Process for Post–Judgment Seizure of a
     Debtor's Property*

The district court concluded that post-judgment remedies satisfy due
process requirements if they provide: (i) notice to judgment debtors
that their property had been seized, (ii) notice to judgment debtors of
exemptions to which they may be entitled; and (iii) a prompt opportunity for judgment debtors to challenge the seizure and assert their
exemptions. *Deary,* 534 F.Supp. at 1187–88. The majority of courts
have reached similar conclusions, see, e.g., Finberg, 634 F.2d at 59–62;
Dionne v. Bouley, 757 F.2d 1344, 1354 (1st Cir.1985), and we also believe
these requirements strike a fair balance between the competing interests.

It is certainly clear that judgment debtors are entitled to at least this much protection. Providing post-seizure notice of the fact of the seizure is an elemental requirement of due process, see Mullane v. Central Hanover Bank & Trust Co., 339 U.S. 306, 70 S.Ct. 652, 94 L.Ed. 865 (1950), and, because the assets cannot thereafter be transferred or hidden by the debtor without court authority, post-seizure notice adds little to the cost of collection. Providing notice of possible exemptions and a prompt opportunity to be heard on claims of exemption add costs to the collection of judgments but also enhance the likelihood that the exemptions provided under state law will be recognized.

McCahey argues that additional procedural protections must be accorded debtors before seizure: specifically notice and a hearing. We disagree. That level of procedural protection for debtors is not constitutionally required even in the case of pre-judgment attachments, when liability has not been determined. A fortiori, it can hardly be required where the creditor's claim has been finally confirmed by a court, and where the risk that the debtor will conceal assets is stronger than in the pre-judgment context. For those reasons, we agree with the great majority of courts that have considered and rejected this suggestion.

McCahey also suggests that if *ex parte* orders are permitted, they must be issued only by neutral judicial officers on the basis of affidavits submitted by judgment creditors disclaiming knowledge of the existence of any exemptions the debtor may assert. We believe neither step is required by due process, because their cost is outweighed by any benefits they might produce. The need for involving a neutral judicial officer is minimal because of the existence of the underlying judgment, which, even if rendered by default, involved a court at some point in the process. *Finberg,* 634 F.2d at 62; *Brown,* 539 F.2d at 1369; see *Scott,* 61 Va.L.Rev. at 853–56. A requirement that the creditor swear to ignorance of any possible exemptions likewise adds little but cost. Even if the debtor asserts an exemption to the creditor before seizure, the creditor still has a right to have that assertion adjudicated. See, e.g., *Finberg,* 634 F.2d at 62; *Cole,* 410 N.Y.S.2d at 956. Moreover, the debtor is in the best position to provide evidence of the exemption and may legitimately be required to carry the burden of proving its existence. See, e.g., McCormick on Evidence 950 (3d ed. 1984) ("where the facts with regard to an issue lie peculiarly in the knowledge of the party, that party has the burden of proving the issue"); Fed.R.Civ.P. 8(c) (burden on defendant to prove payment, discharge in bankruptcy, and license). We thus conclude that New York's statutory scheme provides sufficient notice and otherwise meets due process standards as far as the initial seizure is concerned.

3. *The Adequacy of New York's Required Notice to Judgment Debtor*

We turn now to McCahey's more specific objections to the New York procedures. She argues that the statutorily required Notice to Judgment Debtors is constitutionally inadequate because it does not apprise the judgment debtor of the specific steps to be taken in order to adjudicate exemption claims.

The Notice states: "The law (New York sections fifty-two hundred thirty-nine and fifty-two hundred forty) provides a procedure for determination of a claim to an exemption." McCahey argues that instead of referring the debtor to the relevant statutes, the notice should provide specific information about the time, place, or method for making a motion to perfect the exemption claim and obtain a protective order. Brief of Appellant at 23.

We are not persuaded even that this additional information would be helpful, much less that it is constitutionally required. Elaborate explanation of the procedures for asserting an exemption may so confuse a layman that he or she may be put off by the complexities and simply allow the seizure. Indeed, McCahey states in her brief that the very notice she challenges as being too sparse was "too difficult for her to understand." Brief of Appellant at 20. A fuller recitation of New York motions practice would hardly clarify matters. The recommendation in capital letters that the debtor contact an attorney or Legal Aid, in combination with notice of the existence of procedures to test claims of exemption, is a sufficient and efficient notice to judgment debtors of their rights.

It is true that New York might rewrite this legislation in the hope of simplifying it so laymen might act as their own counsel. This has been attempted in a number of states,[8] and New York itself provides relatively simple procedures for contesting pre-judgment attachments.[9]

New York of course *could* provide simplified procedures for hearing these claims. However, we find no support for the assertion that New York *must* provide such procedures as a requirement of due process. No matter how laudatory the goal, judicial experience with *pro se* litigants offers no guarantee that a simplified procedure for use by laymen is better than a more complex procedure used by lawyers.

8. Connecticut provides a simple procedure for judgment debtors who are natural persons to claim exemptions when their bank accounts are seized. When a bank receives an execution on an account, the bank is required to forward the execution and a simple exemption claim form to the account owner. The debtor has 15 days to return the form to the bank. If the form is returned, the bank forwards the claim to the clerk of the court, who schedules a hearing on the short motion calendar, usually for the following Monday. Conn.Gen. Stat. § 52–367b (1983).

Under California law, the creditor sends the execution and the exemption claim form to the debtor. The debtor has 10 days to claim an exemption, by sending the form to the court clerk. If the debtor does so, the creditor has 10 days to file a motion for a hearing. If the creditor fails to re-

quest a hearing within 10 days, the account is returned to the debtor. A hearing must be held not more than 20 days after the creditor files his motion for a hearing. Cal.Civ.Proc.Code §§ 703.020, 703.520, 703.550, 703.570 (1985).

A number of other states have provided simplified procedures for claiming exemptions. See, e.g., Minn.Stat. § 571–41 (1984); Ohio Rev.Code.Ann. § 2716.06 (Page 1984); Okla.Stat. tit. 12 § 1174 (West 1985).

9. After obtaining an *ex parte* pre-judgment attachment, the plaintiff must move within five days after levy to have the order confirmed. Failure to do so results in the lapse of the attachment. The plaintiff not only has to make the motion for confirmation, but also bears the burden of proof at the hearing. CPLR §§ 6211, 6223.

Absent such a guarantee, the requirements of due process do not dictate use of one method rather than another.

In support of her claim for a more elaborate notice, McCahey relies heavily upon Memphis Light, Gas & Water Division v. Craft, 436 U.S. 1, 98 S.Ct. 1554, 56 L.Ed.2d 30 (1978). In that case, the Court ruled that the notice a power company provided customers before it turned off their service was insufficient for purposes of due process. The notice made no mention "of a procedure for the disposition of a disputed claim." Id. at 13, 98 S.Ct. at 1562. The Court went on to state that "notice is given to thousands of customers of various levels of education, experience, and resources. Lay consumers of electric service, the uninterrupted continuity of which is essential to health and safety, should be informed clearly of the availability of an opportunity to present their complaint. In essence, recipients of a cutoff notice should be told where, during which hours of the day, and before whom disputed bills appropriately may be considered." Id. at 15 n. 15, 98 S.Ct. at 1563 n. 15.

We do not believe that *Memphis Gas* alters our analysis in the present case. First, the Court also stated that a new notice developed by Memphis Gas "may be entirely adequate." Id. at 15 n. 16, 98 S.Ct. at 1563 n. 16. That notice "lists 'methods of contact' and states in part that trained 'Credit Counselors are available to clear up any questions, discuss disputed bills or to make any needed adjustments. There are supervisors and other management personnel available if you are not satisfied with the answers or solutions given by the Credit Counselors.'" Id. at 15 n. 16, 98 S.Ct. at 1563 n. 16. We believe the notice McCahey received is functionally equivalent to the second notice in *Memphis Gas.*

In addition, there is a difference between the complexity of proving an exemption claim and the complexity of disputing a utility bill. A single company providing a dispute resolution procedure for a single type of dispute is more able to develop simple methods of resolving those disputes than is a state providing procedures to enforce its judgments against various sorts of property.

McCahey also relies on Nelson v. Regan, 560 F.Supp. 1101 (D.Conn. 1983), aff'd 731 F.2d 105 (2d Cir.), cert. denied, ___ U.S. ___, 105 S.Ct. 175, 83 L.Ed.2d 110 (1984). That case involved joint taxpayers who were entitled to tax refunds where one of them was also delinquent in child support payments. They successfully claimed that the notice they received from the Internal Revenue Service informing them that their refunds were being seized for the support payments was insufficient because, *inter alia,* it did not explain how to dispute the seizure. In *Nelson,* however, there were no regularized procedures for asserting defenses of which notice could be given. Id. at 1106. In the present case, procedures for claiming an exemption exist. Moreover, the child support intercept program affected the second taxpayer, who was not subject to the judgment and who became involved only because of the joint return. Notice that procedures exist to assert exemptions and a recommendation to seek legal counsel thus meet the constitutional standards for post-judgment remedies.

McCahey next argues the Notice to Judgment Debtors violates due process because its recommendation that the judgment debtor "contact the person sending this notice" is misleading. She argues that this recommendation leads the debtor into believing that "the person sending this notice," usually the attorney for the judgment creditor, will protect the debtor's rights. She also claims that the notice must state that mere contact with the sender does not necessarily protect exempt property from seizure.

Although we view McCahey's assertions as to the behavioral responses of judgment debtors with a degree of skepticism, we also believe that the Notice is misleading only if the initial recommendation is viewed in isolation. That recommendation does not stand alone but is immediately followed by bold type recommending that the debtor contact a lawyer or Legal Aid. We believe this second recommendation eliminates any harmful implications of the prior statement by clearly indicating an alternative course of action if satisfaction is not achieved.

McCahey stresses that she called Rosenthal, as the form recommended, and was led by him to believe that he would resolve the dispute. This, she claims, is proof of the constitutional defectiveness of the notice. However, she also followed the recommendation that the judgment debtor contact an attorney or Legal Aid. Her own case, therefore, hardly demonstrates that the form is so poorly drafted as to lead debtors into complete reliance on the creditor's attorney.

We further note that recommending contact with the creditor's attorney is not bad practical advice for many judgment debtors, who may be able to avoid the most painful consequences by working out an agreeable method of satisfaction. We add this observation, not out of any belief in the generosity of collection agencies, but out of recognition that legal processes have costs for them also which may be reduced through negotiation with debtors.

4. *The Requirement of a Prompt Hearing*

McCahey argues finally that New York's post-judgment procedures are defective because they do not guarantee a prompt post-seizure hearing. We agree that due process requires that a judgment debtor be afforded an opportunity for a hearing on an exemption claim within a matter of days. *Finberg,* 634 F.2d at 59; *Dionne,* 757 F.2d at 1353. McCahey has failed to demonstrate that New York does not provide her with that opportunity.

It is true that the statutory scheme in question does not provide a mandatory outside time limit on according a hearing on an exemption claim. It is also true that the majority of courts that have squarely addressed the issue has stated that only a mandatory period can withstand constitutional scrutiny.[10]

In each of these cases, however, with the exceptions of *Dionne* and *Neeley*,[11] the judgment debtors had resorted to the state procedures to regain their property before they brought a constitutional challenge in federal court. In each case, moreover, the time that elapsed exceeded what the court decided was the constitutionally permissible maximum. McCahey, on the other hand, made no effort to recover her property by using New York's procedures. We are therefore not faced with a concrete example of the New York statute in action, and we are unwilling to invalidate a statute because it might, but need not, be applied in an unconstitutional manner.

The New York statute on its face provides an opportunity for a prompt hearing. The only specific time limit on special proceedings, CPLR § 5239, and motions, CPLR § 5240, requires the respondent to be served with the petition or motion papers at least eight days before the hearing. CPLR §§ 403(b), 2214(b). Both periods, however, may be shortened for cause. CPLR §§ 403(b), 2214(d).

It would hardly strain the bounds of statutory construction for New York courts to hold that exemption claims must be heard expeditiously under the New York statutes. Such claims might be treated as presenting "cause" because of due process requirements, and judgment debtors would then have their claims heard within a matter of days. Indeed, in Banks v. Leef, 120 Misc.2d 1083, 467 N.Y.S.2d 156 (1983), the judgment debtor was able to obtain an order to show cause with a return date only 10 days after the levy was served on the garnishee, a period of time consistent with most of the caselaw.

McCahey relies heavily on Barry v. Barchi, 443 U.S. 55, 99 S.Ct. 2642, 61 L.Ed.2d 365 (1979), which involved a horse trainer whose horse was discovered to have been drugged during a race and whose license was suspended for 15 days pursuant to New York law. The Court invalidated the statute because it specified no time limit within which a

10. See, e.g., *Dionne*, 757 F.2d at 1353 ("one might expect that it would be fortuitous whether the state judge before whom a hearing is sought treated the matter as requiring immediate attention, absent any provision of law specifying the debtor's procedural rights"); *Finberg*, 634 F.2d at 59 (15 days too long); *Neeley*, 606 F.Supp. at 1467 ("the hearing must be commenced between 5 days after the request . . . and the 14th day after the request"); *Reigh*, 595 F.Supp. at 1556 ("all the courts examining this question have concluded, a prompt judicial hearing on this question in these circumstances is one which will take place within two weeks or less from the time the claim of exemption is filed"); *Clay*, 584 F.Supp. at 733 ("an ad hoc method of providing hearings does not sat- isfy due process because . . . [t]here is no statutory time limit on setting the hearing"; 38 days too long); *Harris*, 574 F.Supp. at 971 ("a mandated period of time, will help ensure that the exemption issue will be decided before any hardship results"; a few days may be too long).

11. In *Dionne*, the court observed that "Rhode Island law is silent as to any right of a judgment debtor to be heard after an attachment is made." 757 F.2d at 1352. In *Neeley*, the court noted that the statutes in question, would, by their own terms, not afford the judgment debtor a hearing for more than a month after the debtor requested it. 606 F.Supp. at 1467. New York's statutes are clearly distinguishable.

hearing must be held and allowed the board to wait until thirty days after the hearing to issue a final order. Given that loss of the license destroyed the trainer's livelihood, the Court held that hearings had to be held and concluded "without appreciable delay." Id. at 66, 99 S.Ct. at 2650.

Unlike *Barchi,* there is no basis in this case to hold that New York post-judgment remedies prevent judgment debtors from having their claims heard "without appreciable delay." CPLR § 5239 or CPLR § 5240 do not specify a time period for ruling on exemption claims, but neither do they explicitly give the courts thirty days to delay a ruling. *Barchi* is therefore not controlling.

The present case is controlled, or at least informed, by Carey v. Sugar, 425 U.S. 73, 96 S.Ct. 1208, 47 L.Ed.2d 587 (1976) *(per curiam).* That case involved an attack on the constitutionality of New York's prejudgment attachment statute. The plaintiffs contended that the hearing provided on a motion to vacate the attachment was inadequate because the hearing would be concerned only with the question whether the " 'attachment is unnecessary to the security of the plaintiff,' § 6223, and would not require the plaintiff to litigate the question of the likelihood that it would ultimately prevail on the merits." Id. at 77, 96 S.Ct. at 1210. The statutory language superficially supported the plaintiffs' argument in stating: "If, after the defendant has appeared in the action, the court determines that the attachment is unnecessary to the security of the plaintiff, it shall vacate the order of attachment." CPLR § 6223 (McKinney 1980). Nevertheless, the case was remanded because two New York trial courts had held that the statute should not be so narrowly construed. The Court stated: "[i]t would be unwise for this Court to address the constitutionality of the New York attachment statutes, for decision on that issue may be rendered unnecessary by a decision of the New York courts as a matter of state law." 425 U.S. at 78, 96 S.Ct. at 1210. We think that it would be just as unwise to hold CPLR §§ 403, 2214 facially unconstitutional because of a lack of a mandatory time limit. We therefore choose to await a concrete example of its application by New York courts to a judgment debtor.

We have examined McCahey's other claims and have determined them to be without merit.

Affirmed.

. . .

KEARSE, CIRCUIT JUDGE, dissenting:

I respectfully dissent from the majority's holding that the statutorily required "Notice to Judgment Debtor" ("Notice") sent to plaintiff Cynthia McCahey satisfies due process. While the current form of the notice used in New York for notifying judgment debtors that their property has been seized and that they may contest the seizure of exempt property is an improvement over the postjudgment remedies held constitutionally deficient in Deary v. Guardian Loan Co., 534

F.Supp. 1178 (S.D.N.Y.1982), I do not believe the New York legislature has cured all of the constitutional infirmities of the prior notice.

As the Supreme Court has stated, " 'An elementary and fundamental requirement of due process in any proceeding which is to be accorded finality is notice reasonably calculated, under all the circumstances, to apprise interested parties of the pendency of the action and afford them an opportunity to present their objections.' " Memphis Light, Gas & Water Division v. Craft, 436 U.S. 1, 13, 98 S.Ct. 1554, 1562, 56 L.Ed.2d 30 (1978) (quoting Mullane v. Central Hanover Trust Co., 339 U.S. 306, 314, 70 S.Ct. 652, 657, 94 L.Ed. 865 (1950)). In *Memphis Light,* the Court held that a utility's notification of the termination of utility service did not meet this standard because it failed to advise the customer of the availability of a procedure for protesting the proposed termination. The Court held that utility customers, who were "of various levels of education, experience, and resources," were constitutionally entitled to "be informed clearly of the availability of an opportunity to present their complaint." Id., 436 U.S. at 15 n. 15, 98 S.Ct. at 1563 n. 15. The Court specified the minimum notice required by due process as follows: "In essence, recipients of a cutoff notice should be told where, during which hours of the day, and before whom disputed bills appropriately may be considered." Id.

I agree with the *Deary* court that the principles stated in *Memphis Light* are equally applicable in determining the notice to which a New York judgment debtor is constitutionally entitled. Here, as in *Memphis Light,* the affected individuals are of various levels of education, experience and resources, and should be given notice of both the exemptions to which they may be entitled and the procedures for asserting those exemptions.

The New York legislature, in amending the prior statutory scheme in light of *Deary,* has included in the form of notice only the section numbers of the statutory provisions that govern objections to the seizure of exempt property and has included no disclosure of what those procedures are. In my view, the information thereby given the judgment debtor does not meet the minimum constitutional requirements. I do not find, as does the majority, that the present Notice is substantially the equivalent of a revised form of notice developed by the *Memphis Light* utility which the Supreme Court thought "may be entirely adequate." *Memphis Light,* 436 U.S. at 15 n. 16, 98 S.Ct. at 1563 n. 16. The new notice in *Memphis Light* actually described "methods of contact" and stated that trained credit counselors were available "to clear up any questions, discuss disputed bills or to make any needed adjustments." *Id.* Thus, the new notice apparently satisfied the Court's requirement that customers be told before whom disputed bills appropriately might be resolved. By contrast, the New York Notice does not clearly tell judgment debtors the agency from which they are most likely to get relief—*i.e.,* the state courts. I think it an unreasonable assumption that all judgment debtors, of whatever level of education and experience, will understand the mere reference to two sections of the New York Civil Practice Law and Rules as an instruction that they may go to court and obtain a prompt hearing on their claim.

Nor do I view it as sufficient that the Notice indicates that judgment debtors may talk to the person sending the notice or to an attorney of their own. While in some cases contacting the attorney who sent the notice may well be the easiest practical solution, and while we have no desire to multiply proceedings unnecessarily, I believe that a debtor who sees that as the first course of action recommended by the Notice may well be materially misled. The facts of this very case show that the judgment creditor's attorney simply may disregard advice even from disinterested third parties such as bank officials, and may refuse to wait for promised evidence from the debtor that the property in question is in fact exempt. And although the majority states that McCahey did not rely on this part of the Notice but contacted Legal Aid as well, the record indicates that she apparently did not contact Legal Aid until some 2½ months after she received the Notice to Judgment Debtor, and then only after her bank had paid the Suffolk County Sheriff the entire balance in her account. Thus, McCahey may well have been misled by the Notice into believing that the first course of action listed—contacting the person who sent it—identified the person before whom the disputed claim of exemption might appropriately be resolved.

In sum, I would hold that the requirements of due process, as set out in *Memphis Light,* require that, at a minimum, the Notice to Judgment Debtor should tell judgment debtors to what court they should go to seek relief from the seizure, and that the present statement that the debtor may contact the person who sent the notice should be modified to make clear that this is a practical route, not a sure one.

Notes & Questions

1. *Garnishment and After-Acquired Property. McCahey* illustrates one important method of reaching a debtor's property, service of notice or a writ on a third party in control of the property. See also N.Y. CPLR §§ 5201, 5222, 5231, 5232; Cal.Code Civ.Proc. §§ 700.040, 700.140, 700.170. If a third party is served with a writ of garnishment (or levy of an execution in a state using terminology similar to New York's), does the writ cover debts that become owing to the debtor at some future date? See N.Y. CPLR § 5232(a); Cal.Code Civ.Proc. § 701.010(b)(1)(B).

2. *The Value of Receiving Notice and Objecting to Execution.* In *McCahey,* the debtor received the notice required by CPLR § 5222(e) (quoted in the opinion) and duly objected to the creditor's lawyer. What good did it do her? Is there anything in the CPLR sections regulating execution of judgments that prevented the bank from turning over the entire contents of the account to the creditor? Once a

claim of exemption is asserted by the debtor, is the judgment creditor required to come into court and disprove the claim of exemption? Or must the judgment debtor initiate the relevant proceedings? Which procedure is preferable?

Assume that the judgment debtor instead receives a copy of the execution and notice as required by CPLR § 5232(c). The debtor believes that some exempt money is at risk. Should the debtor notify the sheriff? If the debtor objects to the sheriff what should the sheriff do?

3. *Enforcement Against Property Owned by the Debtor.* Often, of course, a judgment creditor will try to reach tangible personal property that the debtor possesses or will possess. Consider the case of Creditor, who has a $50,000 judgment against Debtor. Debtor has the following nonexempt property:

(a) a stereo system worth $5,000,

(b) business equipment worth $10,000,

(c) a $10,000 debt owed to Debtor by Smith, who borrowed the money and orally promised to repay it.

How should Creditor go about enforcing the judgment so as to maximize its rights against any third parties to whom Debtor might sell or otherwise transfer property while Creditor's enforcement effort is pending? See N.Y. CPLR §§ 5202(a), 5232; Cal.Code Civ.Proc. §§ 697.510, 697.520, 697.530, 697.710, 697.730, 697.740, 699.510, 700.070.

4. *Lessor's Rights.* Leasing Corp. is in the business of purchasing computer equipment and leasing it to businesses. Manufacturer has a substantial money judgment against Leasing and finds that Leasing's only significant unencumbered assets are the lease obligations owed to Leasing by Leasing's customers, Leasing's interests in the leased computers, and several checks in Leasing's possession made payable to Leasing by Leasing's customers. How should Manufacturer request the sheriff to levy against Leasing's assets? Does it matter whether the leases between Leasing and its customers are "true" leases or "financing" leases? Does New York's execution law address these issues? See Cal.Code Civ.Proc. § 700.100(c). Recall In re Leasing Consultants, Chapter 4.

5. *Pre- and Post-Judgment Comparison.* Compare state law's method of creating post-judgment liens in classes of property with its method of creating perfected security interests in classes of collateral. Should there be any differences beween the two methods for establishing interests that are valid against third parties?

6. *Judgment Liens.* In New York, docketing of a judgment in the office of the county clerk creates a lien on the debtor's real property in the county. In almost all states docketing in some public office creates what is called a "judgment lien" on real property, with potential effects on purchasers, mortgagees, heirs, and donees. E.g., Cal.Code Civ.Proc. § 697.310. Judgment liens are enforced either by foreclosure proceed-

ings (as when a mortgage is foreclosed) or through levy and sale under a writ of execution. See N.Y. CPLR § 5236; Cal.Code Civ.Proc. §§ 701.510, 701.540. For provisions regulating execution sales of personal property, see N.Y. CPLR § 5233; Cal.Code Civ.Proc. §§ 701.510 to 701.680.

With respect to securities and goods covered by negotiable documents, U.C.C. §§ 8–317 and 7–602 provide rules governing the enforcement of judgments.

B. Priorities

ROBINSON v. WRIGHT

Supreme Court of Colorado, 1932.
90 Colo. 417, 9 P.2d 618.

BUTLER, J.

W. Ed. Wright, Jr., as executor of the estate of W. Ed. Wright, deceased, obtained judgment against B.E. Robinson for possession of personal property. Robinson says that the judgment was erroneous.

On February 9, 1928, an execution was issued out of the district court of Weld county on a judgment against Lacey H. Mathews, and on the same day the execution was placed in the hands of Robinson, as sheriff of that county. On March 22 of the same year, Wright sold and delivered to Mathews an automobile and a team of mules, taking from him, at the same time and as part of the same transaction, two chattel mortgages to secure the payment of part of the purchase price. The mortgages were recorded on April 10. Four days thereafter Robinson, by virtue of the execution, levied upon the automobile and the mules, taking them from the possession of Mathews. Thereupon Wright brought suit for possession of the property.

1. At common law an execution bound the debtor's personal property from the time the execution was awarded. 23 C.J. p. 490. To prevent the embarrassment to trade resulting from this rule, an English statute provided that no writ of execution should bind the debtor's property, except from the time of the delivery of the writ to the sheriff. Similar statutes have been passed quite generally in the United States. Id. We have such a statute in Colorado. C.L. § 5913. The lien thus created is not a secret lien, for the statute requires the sheriff, upon receipt of the writ, to indorse thereon, and to enter in a book kept for that purpose in his office, the exact time when the writ was received; and the statute declares that such book "shall be a public record and open to the inspection of the public."

It has been held repeatedly that under the statute an execution lien upon the personal property of the debtor attaches upon receipt of the execution by the sheriff. The same effect is given to an execution issued by a justice of the peace and in the hands of a constable.

2. Ordinarily an execution lien has priority over chattel mortgage liens and other liens thereafter acquired. See cases cited above. How-

ever, counsel for Wright says that there are two reasons why the judgment should be affirmed, notwithstanding the rule just stated. Of these in their order:

(1) It is contended that the lien of the execution became subordinate to the lien of the chattel mortgage by reason of the fact that the execution was permitted to lie in the hands of the sheriff for more than sixty days, without any attempt or effort to make a levy.

The proper office of an execution is to enforce the collection of a judgment, not to create a security. If, because of any direction by, or of any understanding with, the execution creditor, the sheriff delays making a levy upon the debtor's property, the lien is held to be waived during the period of such delay. There was no such express direction or understanding in the present case. True, where the sheriff delays an unreasonable time to make a levy, it is presumed, in the absence of an explanation for such delay, that the delay was caused by direction of the execution creditor. But in the present case the circumstances reasonably explain the delay in making the levy. Mathews did not acquire the property until March 22. He lived on a farm some distance from the county seat. The chattel mortgage was not recorded until April 10; and, so far as the record discloses, that was the first notice the execution creditor had that Mathews owned the property. Four days thereafter the execution was levied. The trial court held that the lien of the execution was not waived. The ruling was right. In the circumstances, the delay was not unreasonable; it therefore raised no presumption that the failure to levy sooner was due to any direction by the execution creditor.

(2) The two chattel mortgages are purchase-money mortgages; and it is said that purchase-money mortgages have priority over prior liens.

We have held that a mortgage of land executed by a purchaser thereof contemporaneously with the acquisition of the title, or afterwards as part of the same transaction, is entitled to preference over all other claims or liens through the mortgagor, even though prior in time. Emery v. Ward, 68 Colo. 373, 191 P. 99. The reason for the rule is that the execution of the deed and mortgage being practically simultaneous acts, the title does not for a single moment rest in the purchaser unincumbered by the mortgage.

But counsel for Robinson contend that the rule applicable to real estate mortgages does not apply in the case of chattel mortgages, because real estate mortgages, though not recorded, are valid, not only between the parties, but as to third persons with notice; whereas unrecorded chattel mortgages, they say, are not valid as to third persons, even though they have actual notice thereof, and therefore between the giving and the recording of a chattel mortgage there is an interval of time when the purchaser has an unincumbered title to which a prior lien attaches. Blatchford v. Boyden, 122 Ill. 657, 13 N.E. 801, cited by counsel, seems to recognize such distinction between real estate mortgages and chattel mortgages. We do not take the view that there is a valid distinction between them. It is a mistake to suppose that in this state unrecorded chattel mortgages are void as to third persons with actual notice thereof. The statute is to the contrary. C.L. § 5086. The reason for the rule that we are considering applies equally to real estate mortgages and chattel mortgages, and, by the weight of authority, the same rule applies to both. See cases collected in 11 C.J. p. 648. A chattel mortgage, whether recorded or unrecorded, is valid as between the mortgagor and the mortgagee, and in cases such as the one at bar the passage of title to the purchaser and the creation of the lien of the purchase-money mortgage are simultaneous.

In the present case the automobile and mules were acquired after the execution was received by the sheriff. An execution lien attaches not only to property owned at the time the execution was so received, but to property acquired thereafter while the writ is in force. 23 C.J. p. 494. In this respect, the execution lien in the present case is similar to the lien of a chattel mortgage covering after-acquired property. In Indian Creek Coal Mining Co. v. Home Savings & Merchants' Bank, 80 Colo. 96, 249 P. 499, 502, the Routt-Pinnacle Company gave to the bank, as trustee, a mortgage covering after-acquired property. Thereafter the Indian Creek Company sold and delivered to the Routt-Pinnacle Company certain chattels, and as part of the same transaction leased to that company certain land. The lease reserved a lien upon the personal property to secure the payment of all moneys due to the Indian Creek Company under the lease. We held such provisions in the lease to be, in effect, a "mortgage or form of security," and that the Indian Creek Company's lien was superior to the lien of the mortgage as to the property thus sold. We said: "The Routt-Pinnacle Company acquired its interests after it had given the mortgage to the bank, and they are subject thereto only because of the provision therein that it shall attach to after-acquired property. In such case the mortgage grasps only what the mortgagor gets, and takes subject to all the reservations in the grant to him and all liens and other incumbrances granted by him as a part of his transaction of purchase. The mortgagee gets a windfall and has no equity in it. The cases are very numerous. United States v. N.O.R.R., 12 Wall. 362, 20 L.Ed. 434, is enough. Even if the property comes into the hands of the mortgagor subject to a lien which is good against him, though for want of formalities it is not good against his subsequently attaching creditors and third persons, it is nevertheless prior to the lien of a mortgage under an after-acquired property clause. Harris v. Youngstown Bridge Co., 90 F. 322, 33 C.C.A. 69, where many other cases are cited. The United States court in Colorado has so held, in spite of the Chattel Mortgage Acts. Frank v. D. & R.G.R. Co. (C.C.) 23 F. 123. The lease from the Indian Creek Company to the Routt-Pinnacle Company was one transaction with the bill of sale of the personalty, and contained the above provision that the lessee should not remove any of the improvements, buildings, machinery, or equipment until it had paid all moneys due under the provisions of the lease. The mortgage attached to the property subject to all this. . . . The objection that the property on which the Indian Creek Company claims the lien is not sufficiently described in the lease is not tenable. The lease, bill of sale, and inventory must be read together—the bill of sale and lease describe the property in general terms and the inventory specifically; the description is there full and complete. That the bill of sale and inventory are not recorded is not available to a mortgagee who claims under the after-acquired clause. *United States v. N.O.R.R.,* supra." . . .

We conclude that in the present case the two purchase-money chattel mortgages have priority over the execution lien.

The judgment is affirmed.

Notes & Questions

1. *Establishing a Lien.* In most states delivery of a writ of execution to the sheriff does not establish a lien upon personal property. No lien arises until the sheriff levies upon property. Under California's enforcement-of-judgments law a judgment lien on many important classes of personal property (including accounts receivable, equipment, and inventory) is created by filing a notice of judgment lien in the office of the Secretary of State. Cal.Code Civ.Proc. § 697.510. The Secretary of State maintains an Article 9-like file of judgment liens and, upon request, issues certificates showing the existence of any judgment liens against a debtor. Id. § 697.580. A judgment creditor also may follow a more traditional path by obtaining a lien created by a levy under a writ of execution. Id. § 697.520.

Which system of post-judgment lien creation is preferable?

2. *Creation of Lien under Current Law.* How would *Robinson* come out under N.Y. CPLR § 5202? See also N.Y. CPLR § 5230(d). Under Cal.Code Civ.Proc. § 697.590(a)? Suppose the chattel mortgagee was aware that the debtor was in financial difficulty. Would she be able to satisfy the "fair consideration" requirement of CPLR § 5202? Recall UFCA § 3.

What body of law would today resolve the priority contest between the chattel mortgagee in *Robinson* and the judgment creditor? Compare Cal.Code Civ.Proc. §§ 697.530(b), 697.590(b), 697.740. Should the court's reliance on the purchase money status of the mortgages survive enactment of Article 9?

3. *Priorities Between Competing Judgment Creditors.* On January 1, Creditor A delivers a writ of execution to the sheriff. On January 10, Creditor B delivers a writ of execution to the sheriff. On January 15, the sheriff levies on debtor's property to enforce Creditor B's judgment and sells the property. Who is entitled to priority in the proceeds? Does the execution sale purchaser have to worry about Creditor A's interest? See N.Y. CPLR § 5234; Weinstein, Korn, Miller, New York Civil Practice § 5234.03. Compare Cal.Code Civ.Proc. §§ 697.600, 697.610, 697.730, 697.740, 701.630, 701.640.

Should judgment creditors, like holders of security interests, always be ranked? Consider the following provision:

> Liens of all judgments obtained in actions for damages growing out of a common disaster or occurrence shall be equal in rank or priority regardless of the date of the rendition of the verdict or the entering of the judgment. However, this Code section shall apply only to judgments obtained in actions which are filed within 12 months from the date of the happening of the disaster or occurrence giving rise to the cause of action.

Ga.Code Ann. § 110–507.1(a) (1982 Supp.).   Is this preferable to a general rule that ranks judgment creditors' interests in order of execution, levy, or judgment?

Should judgment creditors rank ahead of other creditors? Or, once a judgment has been obtained, should all creditors of a debtor share equally in the assets available for distribution? What is the status under the Georgia provision of a security interest obtained prior to one judgment but after another?

DICK WARNER CARGO HANDLING CORPORATION v. AETNA BUSINESS CREDIT, INC.

United States Court of Appeals, Second Circuit, 1984.
746 F.2d 126.

Before FRIENDLY, PIERCE and WINTER, CIRCUIT JUDGES.

FRIENDLY, CIRCUIT JUDGE.

This troubling case, a diversity action removed from a Connecticut state court, is here for the second time. See 700 F.2d 858 (2d Cir.1983). Although the facts are stated in Judge Blumenfeld's first opinion, 538 F.Supp. 1049 (D.Conn.1982), and in this court's opinion on the appeal therefrom, they must be recapitulated in summary fashion.

On April 10, 1979, Aetna and Best Banana entered into a financing arrangement evidenced by a General Loan and Security Agreement, an Accounts Receivable Rider, a further Rider, and a Continuing Letter of Credit Agreement (collectively, the "Agreements"). Aetna agreed to lend money to Best Banana in its discretion and to obtain letters of credit to enable Best Banana to make purchases from overseas suppliers. In paragraph (2) of the General Loan and Security Agreement, Best Banana, as debtor, granted Aetna a security interest in certain property, including its inventory, accounts and other receivables, as well as "[a]ll contract rights and general intangibles including . . . deposit accounts whether now owned or hereafter created or acquired." As regards the obligations secured, paragraph (2) broadly provided that the grant of security was

> [f]or the purpose of collateralizing any and all sums loaned or advanced by Aetna to Debtor and any and all other Obligations or liabilities of any and every kind, including all liabilities arising under agreements and contracts of guaranty, now or hereafter

owing and to become due from Debtor to Aetna, including all interest thereon, howsoever created, evidenced, acquired or arising whether under this Agreement or any other instruments, obligations, contracts or agreements of any and every kind, now or hereafter existing or entered into between the Debtor and Aetna or otherwise and whether direct, indirect, primary, secondary, fixed or contingent (herein collectively referred to as "Obligations")[.]

Among the obligations of Best Banana thus secured were its undertakings in the Agreements (1) to repay to Aetna the principal amount of any advances, together with interest thereon; (2) to indemnify Aetna for any liability, loss or expense incurred as a result of or in connection with any letter of credit or Aetna's application therefor; (3) to pay Aetna $7,500 a month as a "minimum charge," although this obligation was to be reduced to the extent of interest on the advances and commissions on the letters of credit actually due; and (4) to reimburse Aetna for its expenses in enforcing or protecting its security interest or its rights under any of the Agreements "or in respect of any of the transactions to be had thereunder."

In order to perfect its security interest in the collateral, Aetna filed financing statements on April 13 and 17, 1979. It then advanced certain funds to Best Banana and on April 23 applied to Nordic American Bank ("Nordic") for the issuance of an irrevocable letter of credit ("L/C") in the amount of $1,104,000 for the benefit of an Ecuadoran banana shipper, Exportadora Constructora Regional, Ltda. ("Exportadora").

The L/C having been issued, Exportadora made two shipments of bananas to Best Banana in June 1979, with delivery in Virginia, where plaintiff Dick Warner Cargo Handling Corporation ("Warner") unloaded them pursuant to an agreement with Best Banana. The latter claimed the bananas were defective and Aetna requested Nordic not to honor the L/C. Nordic complied. On October 31, 1980, Exportadora began an action in New York against Nordic, Aetna and Best Banana, in which it alleged that the letter of credit had been wrongfully dishonored.

Meanwhile, Warner, which had not been paid for its services in unloading the shipments, sued Best Banana in a Virginia court and was awarded a judgment of $80,651.86 in November 1979. Warner then brought an action in the Hartford, Connecticut, Superior Court to collect the judgment through garnishment of Best Banana's credit balance with Aetna, described below. Garnishment process was served on January 11, 1980, and judgment was rendered on June 25, 1980, against Best Banana as defendant and Aetna as garnishee. When Aetna refused satisfaction, Warner instituted a *scire facias* action against it in the Superior Court, which Aetna removed to the District Court for Connecticut pursuant to 28 U.S.C. § 1441(a).

Pursuant to the Agreements, Best Banana's collections on its encumbered accounts had been deposited in a "lockbox" bank account and forwarded to Aetna for credit against its various obligations. Prior to the garnishment, $399,366.02 had been remitted to Aetna, some $353,576.91 of which was used to discharge Best Banana's current indebtedness for advances, interest, and other charges. This left $45,789.11 as a net credit balance, which, under the Agreements, Aetna held as additional security for obligations of Best Banana that might later accrue. Warner's garnishment was aimed at this credit balance, thereby raising the question whether the priority to which Aetna's perfected security interest would normally be entitled *vis-a-vis* a later judicial lien extended to obligations which had been undertaken before, but matured after, the creation of the lien (to wit, Best Banana's obligations to reimburse Aetna for its attorneys' fees and other expenses incurred in defending Exportadora's and Warner's suits and to pay "minimum monthly charges"), or to obligations which had been undertaken before the creation of the lien but which might or might not become due at some future date (the obligation to indemnify Aetna for any liability on the dishonored L/C).

. . .

Judge Blumenfeld construed this court's opinion as requiring him to determine whether the various obligations that Aetna claimed to be secured by the collateral related to "advances" of the sort specified in § 9–301(4) of the New York U.C.C. so as to take priority over a lien creditor like Warner. Section 9–301(4), which was added to the U.C.C. in 1972 and adopted by New York in 1977, provides that:

> [a] person who becomes a lien creditor while a security interest is perfected takes subject to the security interest only to the extent that it secures advances made before he becomes a lien creditor or within 45 days thereafter or made without knowledge of the lien or pursuant to a commitment entered into without knowledge of the lien.

In an unpublished ruling, the judge concluded that Aetna's post-garnishment expenses for attorneys in the Exportadora action and in this one constituted advances within that section. He also ruled, although this turned out to have no practical importance, that Aetna's potential liability on the L/C would be or result from an advance qualifying for priority over Warner under § 9–301(4) and that the "minimum charges" of $7,500 a month for interest and commissions that had accrued after the garnishment would not. Finding that Aetna, subsequent to January 11, 1980, had paid $48,785.12 for attorneys' fees and expenses, as against the $45,789.11 it owed Best Banana, the court determined that the fund sought to be garnished had been exhausted and dismissed Warner's action with prejudice. Warner has appealed from this dismissal. Aetna has cross-appealed from the judge's ruling in respect of the "minimum charges" accruing after the garnishment.

DISCUSSION

The district court felt constrained, on remand, with much justification, to apply U.C.C. § 9–301(4) in deciding the priority it should accord the obligations Aetna claimed to be secured by the collateral relative to Warner's lien. Warner enthusiastically accepts this approach, but insists that, with respect to the attorneys' fees and Aetna's exposure on the L/C, the judge reached the wrong result since these were not "advances" or, if they were, were not among the four categories protected by § 9–301(4), and that, under the plain words of the statute, a lien creditor is entitled to priority over any security interest other than advances so protected, leaving unprotected even non-advances. . . . Our own examination of the question has led us to conclude that section 9–301(4) is essentially irrelevant to the determination of Aetna's rights. In our opinion, section 9–301(4) was not meant broadly to affect the general rule establishing the priority of obligations undertaken by the debtor to a lender and embodied in a perfected security interest before another person became a lien creditor, see U.C.C. § 9–301(1)(b), but was designed only to except from that rule a narrow class of transactions not at all of the nature of those here at issue. Hence, we agree with the district court that Warner's action should be dismissed, although we reach that result by different reasoning.

When a prospective borrower and a lender meet to set up a financing structure, they agree on many things. The lender often makes immediate advances and sets up a program, mandatory or discretionary, for future ones. In return, the borrower undertakes various obligations—not only to repay the advances, but to pay interest and to indemnify the lender against various expenses that he may be obliged to make. Most such expenditures do not constitute "advances" as that term is commonly used; in the ordinary meaning of language, "advances" are sums put at the disposal of the borrower—not expenditures made by the lender for his own benefit. See, e.g., Black's Law Dictionary 48 (5th ed. 1979). We will call the debtor's obligations to pay interest and to indemnify the lender for various expenses incurred by him obligations for "non-advances." It cannot be that if the lender perfects his security interest with respect to such obligations, he is not entitled to protection against a subsequent lien creditor when, as here, the obligations relate to transactions that had occurred long before the lien attached.

The necessity for this conclusion is most readily illustrated by the common arrangement whereby a debtor makes a secured promise to pay interest on his secured debt. No one could plausibly argue that a debtor's periodic incurring of an obligation to pay interest was the receipt of an "advance" by him. Yet, on Warner's literal reading, § 9–301(4) would give priority to a lien creditor over a lender's perfected security interest not only as to interest on protected advances accruing *after* the creation of a lien,[2] a result which we regard as inconsistent with the basic purposes of the U.C.C., but also as to the debtor's obligation to pay interest that accrued *before* the levy, a result that could not possibly have been deliberate. A review of the circumstances and commentary accompanying the 1972 amendments to the U.C.C., which added § 9–301(4), convinces us that no such result was intended, the letter of that section notwithstanding.

In keeping with Article 9's general policy of validating the "floating lien," § 9–204(5) of the 1962 Code[3] provided that the obligations secured by a security interest could relate not only to present loans and "future advances" but also to "other value." Obligations of the latter sort correspond to what we have called "non-advance obligations." Cf. 2 R. Alderman, A Transactional Guide to the Uniform Commercial Code § 7.22 at 957 (2d ed. 1983) (distinguishing "future value" from "future advances"). Nothing in the U.C.C. limited the protection offered by filing and perfection to obligations securing "advances," and the instruments here must be typical of millions in which creditors have properly sought such protection. There does not appear to have been any doubt that a perfected interest securing a non-advance obligation undertaken by the debtor before the creation of a judicial lien would take priority thereover, under §§ 9–201 and –301(1)(b),[4] even though the obligation had not become due until after the creation of the lien. Had this case arisen under the 1962 Code, we should thus have thought it clear beyond peradventure that Aetna would prevail. The question is whether this conclusion survives enactment of § 9–301(4).

The most authoritative statement of the background of that section, paragraph (5) of the "Reasons for 1972 Change" appended to the Official Comment on § 9–312, begins by noting that "[t]he priority of *future advances* against an intervening party has been the subject of much discussion and disagreement" (emphasis added). A review of this controversy confirms the limited scope of the intended change. The protagonist in the debate was Peter F. Coogan, a prominent Boston

2. This view appears to be taken by Carlson & Shupack, Judicial Lien Priorities Under Article 9 of the Uniform Commercial Code (pt. 1), 5 Cardozo L.Rev. 287, 356 & n. 294 (1984). They accurately predict that their position as to the status of post-lien interest "may strike some as surprising and, perhaps, alarming."

3. Section 9–204(3) is the corresponding provision in the 1972 version.

4. Section 9–201 ("General Validity of Security Agreement") stated that,

[e]xcept as otherwise provided by this Act a security agreement is effective according to its terms between the parties, against purchasers of the collateral and against creditors.

Notwithstanding the broad reference to effectiveness against creditors, § 9–301(1)(b) "otherwise provided" that

an unperfected security interest is subordinate to the rights of . . . a person who becomes a lien creditor . . . before [the security interest] is perfected[.]

Taken together, these sections—which are so far as here relevant the same as their 1972 counterparts—imply that a security interest perfected *before* the creation of a lien is not subordinate thereto. See R. Henson, Secured Transactions Under the Uniform Commercial Code § 5–2 at 74 (1973); Note, Priority of Future Advances Lending under the Uniform Commercial Code, 35 U.Chi.L.Rev. 128, 136 (1967). For brevity's sake, we shall refer to this implication as the rule stated in § 9–301(1)(b).

lawyer particularly versed in commercial law and a member of the National Sponsors' Subcommittee on Article 9. Mr. Coogan advanced an ingenious argument that would have permitted a lien creditor to prevail, even under the unamended Code, over a prior-perfected security interest to the extent that it secured advances made subsequent to the creation of the lien. As conceived by Mr. Coogan, a secured party who made multiple advances pursuant to a security agreement acquired a corresponding multiplicity of security interests, one per advance, the priority of each of which relative to the lien must be determined separately. See Coogan & Gordon, The Effect of the Uniform Commercial Code upon Receivables Financing, 76 Harv.L.Rev. 1529, 1549–51 (1963).

Coogan put a case, see id. at 1549, in which (1) a secured party advanced $100 on January 1 under a filed agreement giving him security in the debtor's accounts; (2) a creditor levied on the collateral on February 1; and (3) the secured party advanced an additional $500,000 on February 10. Under his "separate security interests" theory, the secured party would have *two* interests in the collateral, securing, respectively, the debtor's obligations to repay $100 and $500,000. Under § 9–301(1)(b) of the 1962 Code, the security interest securing the January 1 advance would have defeated the lien. Coogan argued, however, that, in the absence of a binding commitment to lend, the February 10 interest, securing the $500,000 advance would not. Under the rule that a security interest cannot be perfected until it attaches, *see* § 9–303(1), the second interest would not have been perfected until the secured party made the second advance, thereby supplying the "value," see § 1–201(44)(a), without which an interest could not attach under former § 9–204(1).[6] Hence, the judicial lien created on February 1 would have priority over the interest securing the February 10 advance, although it would remain subordinate to the January 1 security interest, which attached and was perfected on that date as a result of the contemporaneous advance.

Responding to Coogan's analysis, Professor Gilmore, in his deservedly influential treatise, Security Interests in Personal Property (1965), argued "for the idea of 'one security interest' over that of 'separate security interests.' " § 35.6 at 937 n. 5. On this view, a security agreement providing for multiple advances would create a single interest, which, having attached and become perfected upon the *initial* advance,

> may thereafter fluctuate as to the amount of the obligation secured, whenever [the debtor] pays down part of the loan or whenever [the secured party] makes further advances; it does not become a new or separate security interest simply because the outstanding unpaid balance of the loan varies from time to time.

6. This requirement persists in § 9–203(1)(b) of the 1972 Code.

Id. at 938. Combined with the priority rule stated in § 9–301(1)(b), this would mean that the secured party in Coogan's hypothetical would date the perfection of his (single) interest from January 1 and therefore prevail against the lien creditor even as to the February 10 advance. . . .

The elegance of Professor Gilmore's conception gives it considerable theoretical appeal. But whatever the ultimate merits of the Coogan–Gilmore debate, it is clear that both sides to the controversy were concerned only with the problems of future advances in the ordinary sense of those words and that it occurred to neither to question the established priority of non-advance obligations under § 9–301(1)(b).

The focus on future advances continued in 1972, when sections 9–301(4), –307(3), and –312(5), dealing, respectively, with lien creditors, certain purchasers of collateral, and rival secured parties, were added to the Code. Sections 9–301(4) and –307(3), generally accepted Coogan's conclusion that security interests relating to advances created subsequent to the intervention of a third party as a lien creditor or purchaser should be subordinated to the interest of the third party. As regards the intervening lien creditor, the "Reasons for 1972 Change," supra, observed that

> [i]t seems unfair to make it possible for a debtor and secured party with knowledge of the judgment lien to squeeze out a judgment creditor who has successfully levied on a valuable equity subject to a security interest, by permitting later enlargement of the security interest by an additional advance, unless the advance was committed in advance without such knowledge. Proposed Section 9–301(4) provides that a lien creditor does not take subject to a subsequent advance unless it is given or committed without knowledge, but there is an exception protecting future advances within 45 days after the levy regardless of knowledge.

On this formulation it is tolerably clear that § 9–301(4) was intended to protect lien creditors by giving them a special priority *only* against security interests securing certain sorts of future advances; nothing suggests an intention to upset the general rule as to non-advance obligations in § 9–301(1)(b).

It is particularly instructive to compare § 9–307(3), which, according to the "Reasons for 1972 Change," was to deal with the "similar" problem that arose where the intervening party was a buyer (other than a buyer in the ordinary course of business) of collateral subject to a security interest. There the perceived unfairness to the buyer was dealt with by providing that he

> takes free of a security interest to the extent that it secures future advances made after the secured party acquires knowledge of the purchase, or more than 45 days after the purchase, whichever first occurs, unless made pursuant to a commitment entered into without knowledge of the purchase and before the expiration of the 45 day period.

Unlike § 9–301(4), § 9–307(3) leaves no room to argue that the intervening buyer takes free of a security interest securing obligations such as those here at issue, whether or not they are within the four categories of protected future advances. We cannot think of any reason why a levying creditor should stand better in that respect.

In light of the foregoing, we think the conclusion is irresistible that a drafting failure occurred with respect to § 9–301(4). The draftsmen of the 1972 amendments had no thought that they were addressing the problem of the relative priority of interests securing obligations not involving advances and judicial liens. They made this plain in § 9–307(3); there is not the slightest reason to think they intended anything different with respect to § 9–301(4). Upholding Aetna's position here in no way countenances action by "a debtor and secured party with knowledge of the judgment lien to squeeze out a judgment creditor who has successfully levied on a valuable equity subject to a security interest, by permitting later enlargement of the security interest by an additional advance," the evil at which the 1972 changes were aimed. We have been instructed that when the "plain meaning" of statutory language leads to "absurd or futile results," we should look "beyond the words to the purpose" and, indeed, that we should do this "even when the plain meaning did not produce absurd results but merely an unreasonable one 'plainly at variance with the policy of the legislation as a whole.'" United States v. American Trucking Ass'ns, 310 U.S. 534, 543, 60 S.Ct. 1059, 1063 (1940) (quoting Ozawa v. United States, 260 U.S. 178, 194, 43 S.Ct. 65, 67, 67 L.Ed. 199 (1922)). A literal application of § 9–301(4), which would subordinate a prior-perfected security interest to a judicial lien insofar as the former secures a non-advance obligation relating to a transaction prior to the levy, like that of the debtor to pay interest or even to reimburse the creditor for attorneys' fees incurred reasonably and in good faith with respect to loans made prior to the imposition of the lien or otherwise protected from it, would yield results so plainly unreasonable and inconsistent with commercial practice that such an interpretation must be avoided. We thus deem it appropriate to read that section in the slightly changed manner set forth in the margin,[9] thereby bringing it in line with § 9–307(3), in order to carry out the purpose announced in the "Reasons for 1972 Change" and to avoid an unintended consequence of the words chosen. On such a construction the relative priority of Aetna's interest, insofar as it secured Best Banana's non-advance obligations relating to protected advances, and of Warner's garnishment lien must be determined under the general rule of § 9–301(1)(b), not the special provision regarding future advances in § 9–301(4). As under the 1962 Code, Aetna's prior-perfected security interest should prevail against the lien, notwithstanding that the obligations, relating to transactions before the

---

9. A person who becomes a lien creditor while a security interest is perfected takes free of the security interest to the extent that it secures advances made more than 45 days after he became a lien creditor, unless made without knowledge of the lien or pursuant to a commitment entered into without knowledge of the lien.

date of garnishment, became due only subsequent thereto. Thus, while we accept Warner's argument that Aetna's payments for attorneys' fees and other litigation expenses are not protected advances within the letter of § 9–301(4) since they were neither "advances" in the ordinary meaning of language nor made pursuant to a prior commitment to Best Banana, they nevertheless take priority over Warner's lien.[10] It is unnecessary to decide whether Aetna's placing itself at risk in connection with the L/C transaction for which Best Banana would indemnify it constituted an advance. If it did, as seemingly would be the case, Aetna would be protected even under the letter of section 9–301(4) since Aetna's action long antedated January 11, 1980, the date on which Warner served garnishment process; alternatively, if it were considered not to constitute an advance, its priority is also protected under what we deem the proper construction of § 9–301(4). We prefer not to decide whether Aetna's right to enforce Best Banana's obligation to pay "minimum monthly charges" for interest and commissions, which is clearly not a protected advance under § 9–301(4), should nevertheless receive priority because of Aetna's perfection of its security interest.

. . .

On the appeal, the judgment is affirmed. The cross-appeal is dismissed. No costs.

Notes & Questions

1. *Judgment Creditors v. Secured Parties.* On January 1 Debtor grants Secured Party a security interest in all of his present and after-acquired personal property to secure a loan and Secured Party properly files a financing statement. On January 10 the sheriff receives a writ of execution against Debtor. On January 20 Debtor buys collateral from a third party. On January 30 the sheriff levies upon the collateral pursuant to the writ of execution. Does Secured Party's security interest have priority over Judgment Creditor's execution lien? When was the security interest perfected? When did Judgment Creditor obtain a lien on the collateral? See Cal.Code Civ.Proc. § 697.530(a).

Recall from Chapter 2 that there is some difficulty in deciding when a debtor has "rights in the collateral" for purposes of Article 9. Is there an analogous problem under statutes regulating the enforcement of judgments? Suppose Debtor orders goods from Seller under an f.o.b. destination contract. At the time Seller places the ordered goods in the hands of the shipper, does Debtor have "rights in the collateral" for purposes of Article 9? Does Debtor have a sufficient interest in the goods so that the sheriff may enforce a judgment against Debtor's interest in those goods? Is there anything to be said for a system under which "rights in the collateral" for purposes of Article 9 do not arise simultaneously with the existence of rights reachable by judgment creditors?

10. The result would be different if the attorneys' fees related to advances not within any of the four categories protected by § 9–301(4).

2. Recall that U.C.C. § 9–301(1) subordinates the rights of an unperfected security interest to those of "a creditor who has acquired a lien . . . by attachment, levy or the like." Suppose that Debtor, Secured Party, and Judgment Creditor in Note 1 are in California and that, instead of obtaining a writ of execution followed by levy, Judgment Creditor acquired a judgment lien on the relevant collateral by filing on January 10 a notice with the Secretary of State. Who has priority? See Cal.Code Civ.Proc. § 697.590. Suppose instead that Secured Party delayed filing until January 15. Now who would have priority? How does § 697.590 differ from § 9–301(2)?

3. *The Analysis in* Dick Warner Cargo. Consider the following:

> Judge Friendly's opinion could have been motivated by a serious misconception. He seems to have thought that if *postlien* interest and collection expense produce a security interest junior to the judicial lien, then *prelien* interest must be junior as well. Therefore, he supposes that his decision is necessary to save the priority of interest obligations that have accrued before the judicial lien attaches.

> This is not a real concern. . . . [W]e may use [the negative implication of § 9–301(1)(b)] to establish that a perfected security interest for accrued interest has priority over a subsequent lien.

Schroeder & Carlson, Future Nonadvance Obligations under Article 9 of the UCC: Legitimate Priority or Unauthorized Squeeze–Out?, 102 Banking L.J. 412, 428–29 (1985).

4. *The Timing and Structure of Collection Expenses.* Suppose that secured party in *Dick Warner Cargo* had not incurred collection expenses at the time of the conflict but intended to do so. How would analysis of the relative priority change? Should the secured party be able to run up an unlimited amount in collection expenses after the judicial lien arises and retain priority as to the full amount? Should Aetna continue to enjoy priority with respect to the monthly minimum $7,500 charges?

MARYLAND NATIONAL BANK v. PORTER–WAY HARVESTER MANUFACTURING CO.

Supreme Court of Delaware, 1972.
300 A.2d 8.

BIFFERATO, JUDGE:

This is an appeal from denial by the Superior Court of the petition of Maryland National Bank (Bank) to set aside an execution sale of certain farm equipment sold by Porter-Way Harvester Manufacturing Company (Porter-Way) to Warren Callaway.

The issues raised in this appeal concern the Superior Court's interpretation of Article 9, Secured Transactions, Uniform Commercial Code. The specific issues are: (1) Does the financing statement filed by the Bank meet the requirements of 5A Del.C. § 9–402(1); and (2) Is a prior creditor's security interest affected by an execution sale?

In 1971, Callaway purchased from Porter-Way cultivators, mobile viners, motor vehicles, and other farm equipment. As a condition of the contract of sale, Callaway arranged financing through the Bank. The Bank thereafter perfected a purchase money security interest by complying with the Delaware recording statutes. 21 Del.C. § 2335; 5A Del.C. § 9–402. The financing statements included the following phrase as the description of the types (*or* items) of property that were to be considered collateral:

> "Equipment of all kinds, including equipment now owned by Debtor and equipment hereafter acquired by Debtor."

Subsequently, Porter-Way perfected a security interest on the same equipment covered under the Maryland National Bank's recorded lien.

On February 24, 1970, after obtaining a judgment against Callaway, Porter-Way caused the farm equipment secured by its lien to be sold by the Sheriff at execution sale. On March 4, 1970, the Bank petitioned the Superior Court to set aside the sale, contending that the attachment of the perfected security interest which they held continued in the goods, notwithstanding the disposition thereof by the sheriff's sale. Porter-Way denied this and claimed that the Bank was not a senior lien holder because the description of the goods in the recorded financing statement was too general.

The Superior Court held that the financing statement was adequate and that its description of the goods therein met the requisites of 5A Del.C. § 9–402(1). The Court also found that the involuntary sale of Callaway's collateral resulted in the extinguishment of the previously perfected liens, leaving the Bank as senior lien holder, however, with the recourse of first priority in the distribution of the proceeds. Both parties have appealed. . . .

II

The second issue raised on this appeal is whether a prior creditor's security interest remains in effect after an execution sale.

The alienability of the debtor's rights is dealt with in Section 5A Del.C. § 9–311 which provides:

> "The debtor's rights in collateral may be voluntarily or involuntarily transferred (by way of sale, creation of a security interest, attachment, levy, garnishment or other judicial process) notwithstanding a provision in the security agreement prohibiting any transfer or making the transfer constitute a default."

It is the position of the Bank that only the debtor's rights may be alienated in an involuntary disposition of goods; and that the security interest of a lienholder continues in the property even after a sheriff's sale. . . .

We find unpersuasive the contention that an execution sale does not extinguish a previous security interest in collateral.

The official Uniform Commercial [Code] Comment upon § 9–311 [Comment 2 to § 9–311, A.L.I.], which deals with alienability of debtor's rights explains that:

> "in all security interests the debtor's interest in the collateral remains subject to claims of creditors who take appropriate action. *It is left to the law of each state to determine the form of 'appropriate process'*." (Emphasis added)

There is no statutory provision in Delaware for the "appropriate process" to be followed by a creditor intending to limit the interest in secured property acquired by a purchaser at a sale.

It has long been settled by case law in this State that a creditor may levy against a secured property in the hands of a debtor with the resultant proceeds being distributed on the basis of priority of liens. In turn, under the established case law of this State, the title acquired by the purchaser at the sale is free and clear of all liens theretofore existing. In 2 Woolley on Delaware Practice § 1072(d), p. 736, the author states:

> "When goods and chattels levied upon and sold under either fi fa or vend. exp. are covered by a chattel mortgage placed upon them either before or after levy, they are sold free and discharged from the lien of the mortgage, and the proceeds are applied first, to the costs of the sale, and the balance distributed according to the priority of the respective liens."

It appears, therefore, that it was the intent of the Legislature to forbear concerning the enactment of any statutory provision for the "appropriate process" contemplated by § 9–311, in order that our case law remain determinative of the issue of alienability of debtor's rights. The silence of the commentators as to any change made by § 9–311 to existing Delaware law contributes to the conclusion that § 9–311 made no change in Delaware's long-standing policy in the matter. Certainly, if a reversal of law was sought the Act itself or the commentators would have made mention of such an important change.

We agree with the policy of the law thus established. Chattels sold at an execution sale should be sold free and clear of all encumbrances in order to ensure the highest price and to stimulate bidding. The creditor with the highest priority is not prejudiced in his reliance on the value of the chattel to secure the debt since he is satisfied first from the proceeds.

We find that Altec Lansing v. Friedman Sound, Inc., supra, and First National Bank of Glendale v. Sheriff of Milwaukee County, supra, are clearly distinguishable. In Florida and Wisconsin, at the time these cases were decided, the legislatures of both states had enacted statutes to supplement § 9–311 of the Uniform Commercial Code. Their legislatures sanctioned the continuance of the security interest for the lienholder in collateral purchased at an execution sale. As we have seen, such legislation has not been enacted in Delaware.

Moreover, the Florida and Wisconsin rules interfere with the general policy of the Code to eliminate stumbling blocks in commercial transactions. Certainly, prospective bidders at a sheriff sale would be discouraged from bidding on property with an encumbered title.

We conclude, therefore, that the Superior Court correctly held that the sale extinguished the Bank's lien under § 9–311, according it, however, a priority position as to the proceeds. The contrary rule would discourage prospective bidders by requiring them, in effect, to make lien searches before bidding.

For the forgoing reasons, the judgment below is affirmed.

Notes & Questions

1. *Execution Sales and § 9–311.* Professor Riesenfeld reports that, "Prior to the adoption of U.C.C. § 9–311 there existed great disparity among the jurisdictions on the question whether and under what conditions the interests of a chattel mortgagor or conditional buyer of a chattel were subject to levy and sale on execution." S. Riesenfeld, Creditors' Remedies and Debtors' Protection 196 (4th ed. 1987). Most jurisdictions now permit an execution sale of the debtor's interest in collateral subject to the perfected security interest. See id. at 197. Suppose a purchaser at an execution sale in such a jurisdiction has no notice of an Article 9 security interest. (When would a diligent search fail to reveal a security interest?) Is the purchaser's interest subordinate to the security interest? See National Shawmut Bank of Boston v. Vera, 352 Mass. 11, 223 N.E.2d 515 (1967) (yes). See generally N.Y. CPLR §§ 5233, 5234, 5239; Cal.Code Civ.Proc. §§ 701.630, 701.640, 701.810.

Is the rule articulated in *Maryland National Bank* preferable to a rule allowing the security interest to survive an execution sale?

2. *Effect of Levy on a Secured Party's Right to Possession.* Debtor is in default on payments owing to Secured Party. The sheriff has levied on the collateral to enforce Creditor's money judgment against Debtor. Does the levy take precedence over Secured Party's right to possession of the collateral upon default? See William Iselin & Co. v. Burgess & Leigh, Limited, 52 Misc.2d 821, 276 N.Y.S.2d 659 (Sup.Ct. 1967) (no).

3. *Levy as an Event of Default.* Debtor is not in default on payments owing to Secured Party. The security agreement provides, however, that it shall be an event of default for Debtor to allow an execution or levy to attach to Secured Party's collateral. If the sheriff levies, is Secured Party entitled to repossess the collateral? Is the answer to this question affected by whether the jurisdiction permits execution sales subject to security interests?

See generally Justice, Secured Parties and Judgment Creditors—
The Courts and Section 9–311 of the Uniform Commercial Code, 30 Bus.
Law. 433 (1975).

C. Property Beyond the Reach of Creditors

1. Nonexempt Property Interests Beyond the Reach of Creditors

ADAMS v. DUGAN

Supreme Court of Oklahoma, 1945.
196 Okl. 156, 163 P.2d 227.

WELCH, JUSTICE.

This action was brought to enjoin the sale of land under execution.
The trial court sustained demurrer to plaintiff's petition. The petition
alleged that plaintiff is the qualified and acting executor of the estate of
Walter Barr Steedman, deceased, and is also the testamentary trustee
of the real property under a trust thereof established by the will of such
decedent. A copy of the will to which reference was made was attached
to the petition. The same contained the following provisions:

"All the real property which I am possessed of at the time of my
death, I bequeath and devise unto Mack B. Adams, to have and to hold
the same in trust upon the terms and conditions for the uses and
purposes, and with the powers and duties following, that is to say:

"First: To hold, possessed, manage and control the said estate and
every part thereof, in the same manner as if I were living, and the
trustee shall have power to sell, mortgage, convey, lease, and dispose of
the same upon such terms and in such manner and for such length of
time and for such prices as to my said trustee shall seem meet and
proper, and I give and grant unto my said trustee full power and
authority to invest and reinvest all moneys, which may come into his
hands in such manner, in such securities, or other property as to my
said trustee shall seem meet and proper, and all such property which
shall be so acquired shall be imbued with the same trust as the original.

"Second: And the trustee shall pay the income of the said trust to
my wife, Kathryn Bell Steedman, until her death, in the event that I
die first.

"Third: At the death of my wife, in the event that I die first, or
upon my death, in the event that she dies first, the income of said trust
shall be paid to my children, George Ward Steedman, (Mrs) Reba
Adams, and Aubrey Earl Steedman. If at the time of my death, in the
event that my wife dies first or upon her death in the event that I die
first, one or more of my children shall be dead or whenever one of my
children shall die during the time that the children are receiving the
income of the said trust, then in that event the issue or issues of said
child shall receive that child's proportionate share by right of representation or per stirpes but if there be no living blood descendants of my

child then that child's portion shall be divided between the other beneficiaries. This, is in the event that my children shall not have sold their beneficial interest in the estate in the manner that I have hereinafter set out, if they have so sold then that grantee shall take the child's share.

"Fourth: In the event that one or more of my children should desire to sell their beneficial interest in the trust estate it is my wish and desire that they be so allowed. To sell their interest it shall be necessary for them to cause to be made a written instrument signed and acknowledged before some officer authorized to take acknowledgments, said instrument to be executed by the parties and then served upon the trustee, who shall acknowledge receipt upon the instrument and it shall then be recorded in the Recording Office under both real property conveyances and also personal property conveyances in every county

(Signed Walter Bar Steedman)

wherein any of the trust property may be located.

"Fifth: Eleven (11) years after the death of my wife in the event that I die first or eleven (11) years after my death in the event that she dies first the trust herein created shall at once cease and the trustee shall pay over and deliver the property constituting the trust estate both principal and accumulated interest free from the trust, to my then living children or to their grantees if they have sold their share, or if they have not sold their share but have died to the persons whom they have designated in their last will and testament, or if they do not make a will or do not provide for disposition of this property, then it shall go to their living issue, if they have any, per stirpes or by right of representation, if they do not leave any issue then that deceased child's portion shall be distributed between the other persons entitled thereto. In the event that none of my children shall be alive at that time nor designate anyone to take the property, nor have sold their share, nor leave any living issue then the property shall be paid over and distributed by the trustees to the persons who would then be my heirs at law as the same may be determined by the laws of the State of Oklahoma in force at that time in like manner as if I had then died intestate.

"In the event that I should die before my wife and she should elect to take one-third ($\frac{1}{3}$) of my property as provided by the laws of descent and distribution of the State of Oklahoma, as she has a right to do, rather than take under this will it is expressly provided that this shall in no manner render the balance of this will void but it is my intention that in such event the remaining two-thirds ($\frac{2}{3}$) shall be kept in the trust and the income therefrom shall be paid to my children as I have above set out."

It is further alleged that the administration of the estate of Walter Steedman is pending in the county court of Kiowa County, Oklahoma, and has not been closed and the assets have not been distributed; that there are debts and allowed and unpaid claims against the estate which, together with widow's allowance and expense of administration, will necessitate a sale of all or a part of the real estate involved for the purpose of payment thereof.

It is further alleged that the defendant sheriff of Kiowa County, Oklahoma, has levied upon said real estate under execution issued out of the District Court of Oklahoma County, Oklahoma, in a cause wherein Florence Steedman had obtained a personal judgment against George Steedman. The levy so made was upon "the following described interest in said real estate of said debtor situated in Kiowa County, State of Oklahoma, to-wit: "The undivided beneficial interest of said George Steedman, being the same person as George Ward Steedman, as remainderman, in and to the estate, and in the trust created under the last will of Ward Barr Steedman, deceased, including an undivided one-third interest as remainderman in and to the following described real estate, to-wit, . . . " (land description omitted).

It is further alleged that said George Steedman has no interest in the real estate subject to levy and sale upon execution, and that such levy and effort to sell thereunder would operate to cloud plaintiff's title.

The trial court sustained defendant's demurrer to such petition and dismissed the cause, resulting in this appeal by plaintiff.

The question presented here is whether George Steedman had an interest in the land which is subject to levy and sale under execution.

It is obvious from the terms of the will that the legal title to the land is vested in plaintiff, Mack B. Adams, and that there is thereby created an active trust. 60 O.S.A. § 144, and Hill v. Hill, 49 Okl. 424, 152 P. 1122. The trustee is given full power of sale. That holds true as to any portion of the real estate remaining even though the widow might elect to take under the statutes of descent and distribution.

The will does not provide that George Steedman shall receive any part or portion of the specific real estate described in the return of levy. The levy is sought to be made upon the real estate. The will vests title thereto in plaintiff Adams as trustee. George Steedman can never own an interest in that specific property except, first, the same is not sold by the trustee, and, second, that said George Steedman be living at the end of the trust period. In view of those contingencies it is little more than mere speculation to assume or anticipate that he will ever receive any part or interest in the specific realty. As to George Steedman's present interest in this land it is but little more if any than a mere contingent expectancy. At best then, George Steedman can be classed only as a contingent remainderman.

The great weight of authority is to the effect that such contingent interest is not subject to levy and sale under execution.

In discussing the rule in 23 C.J., pages 335 and 336, the notes to the text state one of the sound reasons for the rule as follows: "The reason given is that such a policy would encourage gambling and speculation and that the purchasers at such sales would not put a high estimate on the possibility of the defendant in execution afterward acquiring any interest in the land and that the danger of sacrifice is a strong reason for not subjecting contingent interests to sale under execution.

In 33 C.J.S., Executions, page 169, subsec. d of § 36, under executory devises, it is stated: ". . . However, such a devise subject to a condition which makes the estate wholly contingent and a mere possibility cannot be reached on execution." . . .

A statement helpful in many respects herein is found in 33 C.J.S., Executions, page 175, a part of subsec. c of § 41, as follows: ". . . Under many of the statutes, the rule is laid down that where the legal title is vested in the trustee under a passive, simple, or dry trust, with no duty except to convey to the person ultimately entitled, the interest of the cestui que trust is subject to seizure and sale under execution; but where the land is held by the trustee under an active trust, requiring the continuance of the legal title in him to enable him to perform his duties, the equitable estate is not subject to execution. It is also the generally accepted doctrine in the United States, in construing statutes based on 29 Car. II, that in order to subject the equitable estate of a cestui que trust to execution at law, the trust must be clear and simple, and for the benefit of the debtor alone, and that equitable interests held jointly with another person are not subject to sale under execution." . . .

We are in accord with the statement in 33 C.J.S., Executions, page 167, § 36, to the effect that the general rule is that all possible interests in land, contingent or otherwise, which are real and substantial are subject to seizure and sale on execution and that generally if the interest is assignable it is subject to execution. Where the contingencies are such, however, as to render the interest in the specific property a mere remote possibility the difficulty in determining the value of the interest for sale upon execution gives strong practical and legal reasons for denial of the right to so levy. Especially so where sacrifice of the judgment debtor's expectancy is probably without substantial benefit to the judgment creditor.

Under the facts here the value to be placed upon the contingent interest of George Steedman in this real estate can be nothing more than speculation and the benefits to be gained by the judgment creditor are equally so. We conclude that the legal title of the trustee who must retain the same in the full performance of his active trust should not be subjected to the cloud of such an effort to sell under execution.

The judgment is reversed, and the cause remanded, with directions to overrule defendant's demurrer to plaintiff's petition, and to proceed consistent with the views herein expressed.

GIBSON, C.J., and OSBORN, BAYLESS, DAVISON, and ARNOLD, JJ., concur.

HURST, V.C.J., dissents.

HURST, VICE CHIEF JUSTICE (dissenting).

The majority opinion is based upon the assumption that the interest of George Steedman in the lands levied upon is at most a contingent remainder. I think it is a vested remainder.

1. Our statutes do not define vested and contingent remainder, though they refer to them. 60 O.S.1941, ch. 2. We must look, then, to the general law for the distinctions.

In Black's Law Dictionary, 3d Ed., a vested remainder is defined as one "limited to a certain person at a certain time or upon the happening of a necessary event", and a contingent remainder is defined as one "limited to take effect to a dubious and uncertain person, or upon a dubious and uncertain event." Similar definitions may be found in many cases and text books. See 23 R.C.L. 497, 499; 33 Am.Jur. 525, 529; 21 C.J. 980, 981; 31 C.J.S. Estates, § 69, pp. 88, 90. A vested remainder is an estate, while a contingent remainder is not an estate but is a mere possibility or prospect of an estate.

There are three classes of vested remainders, (a) those absolutely vested, (b) those subject to being partly divested by opening and letting in other remaindermen, and (c) those subject to being completely divested. Simes, § 57; Restatement, Property, § 157; Tiffany, § 319.

The remainder here is either a contingent remainder or a vested remainder of the third class—one subject to complete defeasance. The difference between the two, broadly speaking, is stated in an annotation on the subject in 131 A.L.R. 712, as follows: "If the condition on which the estate depends is precedent, the estate is contingent; if subsequent, it is vested, subject to defeasance." To the same effect, see 23 R.C.L. 509, § 43; 33 Am.Jur. 544, § 88; Page on Wills, 2d Ed., § 1116. . . .

The interest of George Steedman in the lands fits the definition of a vested remainder and not that of a contingent remainder as stated by Black, above. The three remaindermen, children of testator, are "certain persons." The event which entitles them to come into possession of the estate is a "necessary event." Their mother is certain to die, and eleven years are certain to elapse after her death. It would seem, then, that the remainder interest should be considered vested unless the other provisions of the will clearly indicate that the testator intended it to be contingent. The fact that the remaindermen are expressly given the right to dispose of their interest, either by grant or will, so that the grantee or beneficiary under the remainderman's will would have an absolutely vested interest, thus rendering the other conditions inapplicable, is indicative of an intention on the part of the testator that the interests of the three children shall be vested rather than contingent. I do not believe that any of the provisions establish an intention on the part of testator that the remainder interests be contingent. . . .

While authorities may be found to support any position that may be taken on some of the questions above mentioned, I think the view supported by the better and more recent authorities is that the interest of the three named children of testator is a vested remainder subject to complete defeasance by the happening of conditions subsequent, such as sale of the property by the executor to pay the debts of testator, or sale by the trustee under the power given in the will, or death of a remainderman intestate and without issue and without having conveyed his interest. A careful study of the cases cited in the majority opinion convinces me that they do not support the conclusion reached.

. . .

3. The final question is whether the interest of George Steedman as cestui que trust in the trust estate—a chose in action as distinguished from his interest in the land—has been levied upon, and, if so, whether it can be sold under the execution. Appellant states that such interest has not been levied upon, while the appellees contend to the contrary. It will be observed that the return refers to the one third beneficial interest of George Steedman in the "trust therein created." I believe this is in addition to his interest as remainderman in the land. The appellees contend that such an interest or chose in action is subject to levy under a general execution, and cite 60 O.S.1941 §§ 146, 298, and 23 C.J. 343; 33 C.J.S., Executions, § 41.

Section 146 has reference to the title of the beneficiary of a trust in land. The Corpus Juris citation, relied upon, has reference to a passive trust in land. These authorities are, therefore, not in point. Section 298 provides: "The execution, in whole or in part, of any trust power, may be adjudged for the benefit of the creditors or assignees of any person, entitled as one of the beneficiaries of the trust, to compel its execution, when his interest is transferable." This section does not have reference to a general execution. Rather, it has reference to a special proceeding in the court having jurisdiction of the trust estate that has for its purpose the execution or enforcement of the trust power in favor of creditors or assignees of a beneficiary when the interest of the beneficiary is transferable. Such a chose in action does not constitute "lands, tenements, goods and chattels" that may be levied upon under 12 O.S.1941 §§ 733, 751, but the remedy of the creditors of the beneficiary is by a special proceeding in the court that has jurisdiction over the trust estate under authority of section 298, above, and under authority of 12 O.S.1941 § 841.

For the foregoing reasons, I dissent in so far as the majority holds that the interest of the three children in the land is not subject to sale on execution, and I agree that the interest in the trust estate as such (a chose in action) is not subject to sale on execution.

Notes & Questions

1. *The Problem of Executing Against Future Interests.* In Meyer v. Reif, 217 Wis. 11, 258 N.W. 391 (1935) a judgment creditor sought to reach Reif's interest in a trust created by Reif's grandmother's will. The income of the trust was to be dedicated to the education and support of Reif until he reached twenty-five years of age, if he lived so

long, and then the fund with any accumulations was to be turned over to him. If Reif did not reach twenty-five years of age, the fund was to go to his mother and, if she were not living, to the grandmother's heirs then living. After deciding that under Wisconsin law Reif had an interest in the trust fund that was subject to transfer and assignment, the court stated:

> It would seem that the relief that should be granted to a plaintiff in equity in a situation such as is here involved is to adjudge a lien on the defendant's interest in the fund in the trustee's hands, enjoin the cestui que trust from assigning, pledging, or incumbering his interest therein, adjudge that in case the cestui que trust arrives at the age of twenty-five years the trustee satisfy the plaintiff's judgment out of the fund before paying the fund or any part thereof over to the cestui que trust or any other person, and enjoin the trustee from paying over a portion of the fund sufficient to satisfy plaintiff's judgment in any other manner. . . . To grant the relief above suggested would protect the plaintiff and be fairer to the cestui que trust than to sell his interest in the fund. A sale as ordinarily made on execution or pursuant to judgment would carry the interest in the fund and thus carry the whole fund when the cestui que trust arrived at the age of twenty-five, if he reached that age. The uncertainty of his arriving at that age would prevent the bidding of an amount at all commensurate with the amount of the fund, and such a sale would be likely to work injustice to the cestui que trust through carrying the amount of the fund in excess of the amount due on the plaintiff's judgment.

Should the court in *Adams v. Dugan* have ordered relief similar to that ordered in *Meyer*?

To the extent that *Adams* and *Meyer* represent efforts by judgment creditors to reach after-acquired property, are any extraordinary remedies necessary? Could a judgment creditor simply wait until the debtor acquires an interest in a trust or estate? See Cal. Code Civ.Proc. §§ 683.020, 683.120(b); N.Y. CPLR § 211(b) (20 year statute of limitations on enforcement of judgment). At common law a judgment became dormant a year and a day after its signing. To revive the judgment a creditor had to obtain a writ of *scire facias*. As the above statutes suggest, the period of time during which a judgment remains enforceable is regulated by statutes that vary substantially from state to state.

2. How would *Adams* and *Meyer* come out under New York's CPLR? under Cal.Code Civ.Proc.? See §§ 695.010, 695.030, 699.720(a)(9), (b), 709.020.

3. *Other Contingent Interests.* Do the reasons one can offer for keeping certain future interests beyond the reach of creditors justify limiting creditor access to other classes of property? Should creditors be able to reach a debtor's contingent tort claim? See Cal.Code Civ. Proc. §§ 695.030(b)(2), 699.720(a)(3), 704.140, 708.410, 708.480.

See generally Halbach, Creditors' Rights in Future Interests, 43 Minn.L.Rev. 217 (1958).

Notes on Spendthrift Trusts

1. Putting aside the future interest question in *Adams*, suppose the document creating the trust had contained a clause prohibiting the transfer or alienation of Steedman's interest in the trust. Would a court enforce the settlor's wish to prevent Steedman's creditors from reaching the trust?

In Nichols v. Eaton, 91 U.S. 716, 23 L.Ed. 254 (1875), a testamentary trust devised real and personal property to trustees, directed them to pay the income from the trust to Eaton, and provided that if Eaton should alienate or dispose of his interest in the trust, or should become bankrupt or insolvent, the trust should cease and the trustees should apply the trust to the support of Eaton's wife and children. The trustees also were authorized, in their discretion, to transfer to Eaton up to one-half of the trust fund and, even after forfeiture, to pay funds to Eaton. Eaton, who had no wife or children, made a general assignment for the benefit of creditors and was declared a bankrupt. Eaton's creditor argued that this effort to secure for Eaton the enjoyment of property "free from liability for his debts" was void on grounds of public policy, as being in fraud of the rights of creditors. The Supreme Court, in an opinion by Justice Miller, found that Eaton's creditor could not reach his interest in the trust:

> It is believed that every State in the Union has passed statutes by which a part of the property of the debtor is exempt from seizure on execution or other process of the courts; in short, is not by law liable to the payment of his debts. This exemption varies in its extent and nature in the different States. In some it extends only to the merest implements of household necessity; in others it includes the library of the professional man, however extensive, and the tools of the mechanic; and in many it embraces the homestead in which the family resides. This has come to be considered in this country as a wise, as it certainly may be called a settled, policy in all the States. To property so exempted the creditor has no right to look, and does not look, as a means of payment when his debt is created; and while this court has steadily held, under the constitutional provision against impairing the obligations of contracts by State laws, that such exemption laws, when first enacted, were invalid as to debts then in existence, it has always held, that, as to contracts made thereafter, the exemptions were valid.

> This distinction is well founded in the sound and unanswerable reason, that the creditor is neither defrauded nor injured by the application of the law to his case, as he knows, when he parts with the consideration of his debt, that the property so exempt can never be made liable to its payment. Nothing is withdrawn from this liability which was ever subject to it, or to which he had a right to

look for its discharge in payment. The analogy of this principle to the devise of the income from real and personal property for life seems perfect. In this country, all wills or other instruments creating such trust-estates are recorded in public offices, where they may be inspected by every one; and the law in such cases imputes notice to all persons concerned of all the facts which they might know by the inspection. When, therefore, it appears by the record of a will that the devisee holds this life-estate or income, dividends, or rents of real or personal property, payable to him alone, to the exclusion of the alienee or creditor, the latter knows, that, in creating a debt with such person, he has no right to look to that income as a means of discharging it. He is neither misled nor defrauded when the object of the testator is carried out by excluding him from any benefit of such a devise.

Nor do we see any reason, in the recognized nature and tenure of property and its transfer by will, why a testator who *gives*, who gives without any pecuniary return, who gets nothing of property value from the donee, may not attach to that gift the incident of continued use, of uninterrupted benefit of the gift during the life of the donee. Why a parent, or one who loves another, and wishes to use his own property in securing the object of his affection, as far as property can do it, from the ills of life, the vicissitudes of fortune, and even his own improvidence, or incapacity for self-protection, should not be permitted to do so, is not readily perceived.

Erwin Griswold attributed the growth of the so-called "spendthrift trust" to Nichols v. Eaton and the Supreme Court's influence. See E. Griswold, Spendthrift Trusts § 29 (2d ed. 1947). See also Broadway National Bank v. Adams, 133 Mass. 170, 43 Am.Rep. 504 (1882).

2.   Most states honor spendthrift trust provisions, but they vary in the extent to which they limit creditor access to a debtor's interest in a trust. New York contains one interesting set of limits. New York's CPLR § 5205(c), (d) and Estates, Powers, and Trusts Law § 7–1.5 [a] in effect make every trust a spendthrift trust with respect to judgment creditors. Note the provision in § 5205(d) excluding from the income exemptions parts of personal property that the court "determines to be unnecessary for the reasonable requirements of the judgment debtor and his dependents." Professor Powell comments:

By this route, as applied by New York courts, a creditor can reach the income of a beneficiary-debtor to the extent that it can be proved that such income exceeds that which the beneficiary needs to continue living in the manner to which he is accustomed! This

---

a. EPTL § 7–1.5 states in part:

(a) The interest of the beneficiary of any trust may be assigned or otherwise transferred, except that:

(1) The right of a beneficiary of an express trust to receive the income from property and apply it to the use of or pay

it to any person may not be transferred by assignment or otherwise unless a power to transfer such right, or any part thereof, is conferred upon such beneficiary by the instrument creating or declaring the trust. . . .

"station-in-life" rule has seldom given a creditor any payment on his claim, either in New York or in other states having a similar provision. . . . Trusts of this type are usually created by persons of substantial wealth for the benefit of a wife or children, all of whom have been accustomed to relatively luxurious living. No provable surplus above that needed to continue the accustomed mode of life is to be expected.

Powell, The Rule Against Perpetuities and Spendthrift Trusts in New York: Comments and Suggestions, 71 Colum.L.Rev. 688, 699 (1971).

California's Probate Code states:

§ 15300.   Restraint on transfer of income

Except as provided in Sections 15304 to 15307, inclusive, if the trust instrument provides that a beneficiary's interest in income is not subject to voluntary or involuntary transfer, the beneficiary's interest in income under the trust may not be transferred and is not subject to enforcement of a money judgment until paid to the beneficiary.

§ 15301.   Restraint on transfer of principal

(a) Except as provided in subdivision (b) and in Sections 15304 to 15307, inclusive, if the trust instrument provides that a beneficiary's interest in principal is not subject to voluntary or involuntary transfer, the beneficiary's interest in principal may not be transferred and is not subject to enforcement of a money judgment until paid to the beneficiary.

(b) After an amount of principal has become due and payable to the beneficiary under the trust instrument, upon petition to the court under Section 709.010 of the Code of Civil Procedure by a judgment creditor, the court may make an order directing the trustee to satisfy the money judgment out of that principal amount. The court in its discretion may issue an order directing the trustee to satisfy all or part of the judgment out of that principal amount.

§ 15303.   Transferee or creditor of beneficiary; power to compel trustee to pay any amount; liability of trustee to creditor

(a) If the trust instrument provides that the trustee shall pay to or for the benefit of a beneficiary so much of the income or principal or both as the trustee in the trustee's discretion sees fit to pay, a transferee or creditor of the beneficiary may not compel the trustee to pay any amount that may be paid only in the exercise of the trustee's discretion.

(b) If the trustee has knowledge of the transfer of the beneficiary's interest or has been served with process in a proceeding under Section 709.010 of the Code of Civil Procedure by a judgment creditor seeking to reach the beneficiary's interest, and the trustee pays to or for the benefit of the beneficiary any part of the income or principal that may be paid only in the exercise of the trustee's discretion, the trustee is liable to the transferee or creditor to the extent that the payment to or for the benefit of the beneficiary impairs the right of the transferee or creditor. This subdivision does not apply if the beneficiary's interest in the trust is subject to a restraint on transfer that is valid under Section 15300 or 15301.

(c) This section applies regardless of whether the trust instrument provides a standard for the exercise of the trustee's discretion.

(d) Nothing in this section limits any right the beneficiary may have to compel the trustee to pay to or for the benefit of the beneficiary all or part of the income or principal.

§ 15306.5. Court order directing trustee to satisfy judgments; payment to which beneficiary entitled; limitations

(a) Notwithstanding a restraint on transfer of the beneficiary's interest in the trust under Section 15300 or 15301, and subject to the limitations of this section, upon a judgment creditor's petition under Section 709.010 of the Code of Civil Procedure, the court may make an order directing the trustee to satisfy all or part of the judgment out of the payments to which the beneficiary is entitled under the trust instrument or that the trustee, in the exercise of the trustee's discretion, has determined or determines in the future to pay to the beneficiary.

(b) An order under this section may not require that the trusteee pay in satisfaction of the judgment an amount exceeding 25 percent of the payment that otherwise would be made to, or for the benefit of, the beneficiary.

(c) An order under this section may not require that the trustee pay in satisfaction of the judgment any amount that the court determines is necessary for the support of the benefciary and all the persons the beneficiary is required to support.

(d) An order for satisfaction of a support judgment, as defined in Section 15305, has priority over an order to satisfy a judgment under this section. Any amount ordered to be applied to the satisfaction of a judgment under this section shall be reduced by the amount of an order for satisfaction of a support judgment under Section 15305, regardless of whether the order for satisfaction of the support judgment was made before or after the order under this section.

(e) If the trust gives the trustee discretion over the payment of either principal or income of a trust, or both, nothing in this section affects or limits that discretion in any manner. The trustee has no duty to oppose a petition to satisfy a judgment under this section or to make any claim for exemption on behalf of the beneficiary. The trustee is not liable for any action taken, or omitted to be taken, in compliance with any court order made under this section.

(f) Subject to subdivision (d), the aggregate of all orders for satisfaction of money judgments against the beneficiary's interest in the trust may not exceed 25 percent of the payment that otherwise would be made to, or for the benefit of, the beneficiary.

§ 15307. Income in excess of amount for education and support; application to creditor's claim

Notwithstanding a restraint on transfer of a beneficiary's interest in the trust under Section 15300 or 15301, any amount to which the beneficiary is entitled under the trust instrument or that the trustee, in the exercise of the trustee's discretion, has determined to pay to the beneficiary in excess of the amount that is or will be necessary for the education and support of the beneficiary may be applied to the satisfaction of a money judgment against the beneficiary. Upon the judgment creditor's petition under Section 709.010 of the Code of Civil Procedure, the court may make an order directing the trustee to satisfy all or part of the judgment out of the beneficiary's interest in the trust.

See also Cal.Code Civ.Proc. §§ 695.030(b)(1), 699.720(a)(8), (b), 709.010.

HELMSLEY–SPEAR, INC. v. WINTER

Supreme Court of New York, Appellate Division, First Dept., 1980.
74 A.D.2d 195, 426 N.Y.S.2d 778, affirmed 52 N.Y.2d 984, 438 N.Y.S.2d 79, 419
N.E.2d 1078 (1981).

SILVERMAN, JUSTICE:

This is an appeal by defendant Winter and his wife from an order of the Supreme Court denying their motion to vacate an attachment with respect to defendant Winter's interest in the Helmsley-Spear, Inc. Employees' Profit Sharing Plan and Trust.

Defendant Winter had been an employee of plaintiff Helmsley-Spear, Inc. The complaint alleged that while so employed he had engaged in a course of fraud, involving false invoices from alleged suppliers, misappropriations of checks, and kickbacks from suppliers, resulting in damages to plaintiff of $665,549. Winter was indicted with respect to some of these transactions, acquitted as to some, and convicted of grand larceny with respect to the theft of two checks totalling $8,584. That conviction has recently been affirmed by this Court. . . . In the present action, partial summary judgment has been granted in plaintiff's favor with respect to the amounts involved in the transactions for which defendant Winter has been convicted, and the remainder of the case has not yet been determined.

On September 25, 1975, an order of attachment issued out of the Supreme Court in the amount sued for. That attachment was levied by the sheriff on the proceeds of the Trust (as well as other property). Thereupon, the Trust paid over to the sheriff pursuant to the attachment the sum of $20,924.59 "which represent the sole and complete interest of Frank Winter in the Helmsley-Spear, Inc. Employees' Profit Sharing Plan and Trust." Defendant Winter does not attack the validity of the original attachment order, but he and his wife have moved to vacate the attachment so far as applicable to the moneys paid to the sheriff by the Trust on the ground that that money is exempt from the claims of creditors. In our view, this money is exempt, and, therefore, the motion to vacate the levy of the attachment with respect to these funds should have been granted. . . .

Nor can the case be considered as if the levy were on money actually in possession of defendant Winter. The garnishees were the trustees of the Trust with respect to funds "held or controlled" by the trustees. CPLR § 5201(c)[2]. The fact that, if once the funds were in Winter's hands they would theoretically be subject 100% to the claims of creditors, does not alter the exemption, if any, so long as the funds are held by the Trust. Otherwise there would be no meaning to the provisions of CPLR § 5205(d)[1] exempting from application to the satisfaction of a money judgment 90% of the payments from a trust, or CPLR § 5205(c) exempting property "while held in trust."

Coming then to the main question, whether defendant Winter's interest in the Trust, to the extent that it was valid, is subject to the claims of creditors, we find exemptions from such claims in the Employees Retirement Income Security Act of 1974 ("ERISA," 29 U.S.C. § 1001 et seq.), and in the terms of the Trust itself, and to the extent of 90% in our state statute, CPLR § 5205(d)[1].

The Appellate Division in the Second Department has recently held that vested benefits from a pension trust are not exempt from execution under ERISA but are exempt to the extent of 90% under the state statute. National Bank of North America v. International Brotherhood of Electrical Workers, 69 A.D.2d 679, 419 N.Y.S.2d 127. Justice Rabin dissented on the ground that in his view, the entire trust was exempt under ERISA. With due respect we agree with Justice Rabin.

ERISA provides in § 206(d) [29 U.S.C. § 1056(d)]:

(d)(1) Each pension plan shall provide that benefits provided under the plan may not be assigned or alienated.

In general, it is only property which can be assigned or alienated that is subject to the claims of creditors. See e.g., CPLR § 5201(a).

The Internal Revenue Service has promulgated regulations pursuant to ERISA to the effect "that benefits provided under the plan may not be . . . assigned . . . alienated or subject to attachment, garnishment, levy, execution or other legal or equitable process." (1 FTR § 1.401(a)(13)(b)(1) (1980)). "It is well settled that the construction given statutes and regulations by the agency responsible for their administration, if not irrational or unreasonable, should be upheld." Matter of Howard v. Wyman, 28 N.Y.2d 434, 438, 322 N.Y.S.2d 683, 686, 271 N.E.2d 528, 531.

The Trust instrument itself provides:

SECTION 3.6. *Inalienability of benefits.* The right of any person to receive any payment from the trust fund becoming payable to him under the provisions of this Plan shall not be subject to alienation or assignment and . . . should such right be subjected to attachment, execution, garnishment, acquestration [*sic*] or other legal, equitable or other process, it shall *ipso facto* pass and be transferred to such one or more as may be appointed by the Committee from among the beneficiaries, if any, of the participant with respect to whom such right arises, and the spouse, blood relatives or dependents of such participant and in such shares and proportions as the Committee may appoint . . . .

Even if ERISA did not exempt these funds from the claims of creditors, our state statute would still exempt 90% of them. CPLR § 5205(c) exempts from application to the satisfaction of a money judgment "[a]ny property while held in trust for a judgment debtor, where the trust has been created by, or the fund so held in trust has proceeded from a person other than the judgment debtor . . . ." This apparently applies to the principal of the Trust. See CPLR

§ 5205(d)[1]. CPLR § 5205(d)[1] then declares to be exempt "ninety per cent of the income or other payments from a trust the principal of which is exempt under subdivision (c)," except as determined to be unnecessary for the reasonable requirements of the judgment debtor and his dependents. The Appellate Division, Second Department, in the *National Bank of North America* case, supra, 69 A.D.2d 679, 419 N.Y.S.2d 127, was unanimous in its view that at least this 90% was exempt.

It is argued that the statutory exemptions should not apply to the claims of tort creditors, and particularly to the claims of tort creditors who are settlors of the allegedly exempt trust. We see nothing in the statutes carving out such an exception. And we note "strong public policy against forfeiture of employee benefits manifested by the Employee Retirement Income Security Act of 1974 (ERISA) (U.S. Code, tit. 29, § 1001 et seq.)" Post v. Merrill Lynch, Pierce, Fenner & Smith, Inc., 48 N.Y.2d 84, 88, 421 N.Y.S.2d 847, 849, 397 N.E.2d 358, 360.

We therefore think that defendant Winter's interest in the Trust was not subject to attachment on the claims here sued on. . . .

FEIN, JUSTICE PRESIDING, and CARRO, JUSTICE, dissent in an opinion by FEIN, JUSTICE PRESIDING. . . .

We agree with the majority that the language of the pertinent CPLR provisions, "ERISA" and the trust instrument itself, is to the effect that the corpus of such trust and the income therefrom are exempt from attachment, with the possible exception of 10% thereof (CPLR Section 5205[d1]; National Bank of North America v. International Brotherhood of Electrical Workers, 69 A.D.2d 679, 419 N.Y.S.2d 127). However, unlike the majority, we do not find that this is dispositive. The issue in this case is not, as the majority suggests, whether an exception should be carved out from such exemptions in favor of tort creditors. The narrower issue with which we are presented is whether a faithless employee, who has stolen from his employer during the period of time that the employer has contributed to the pension funds, may rely upon the statutory exemption to preclude the employer from enforcing a judgment for the money stolen against the corpus and/or the interest from such fund after it has vested. We have concluded that as a matter of public policy the exemption statutes and the provisions of the trust indenture were not designed for this purpose. . . .

The purpose of the provisions in the CPLR and other statutes exempting spendthrift trusts from attachment or other enforcement is to insure that the beneficiary will not fritter away the moneys provided for his or her needs. The exemption was not designed to permit the beneficiary to steal from his employer and to hide behind the exemption statute when the employer seeks recovery of the ill-gotten gains by reaching for funds originally provided by the employer.

The same analysis applies with respect to "ERISA". That statute and the exemptions contained therein were designed to insure that an employee who worked loyally for an employer with a pension plan would not find himself without any pension because of some action or inaction by the employer or the fiduciary by way of mismanagement, wasting, looting or arbitrary vesting rules. The statute was not designed to aid thieves in retaining their loot.

Plainly, the exemption provision contained in the trust indenture here in issue was not intended to provide a shield to one in Winter's position. . . .

The express language of the exemption statute and of trust indentures designed to preclude attachment or other interference by creditors and others has been held not to bar enforcement of the rights of wives and children to support. In Matter of Chusid, 60 Misc.2d 462, 301 N.Y.S.2d 766, affd. 35 A.D.2d 655, 314 N.Y.S.2d 354, the restrictions against alienation in a testamentary trust were held not to preclude enforcement against the proceeds of court orders in favor of the wife and children for support, reaching both principal and interest. Public policy required such a result despite the testamentary language and pertinent statutes prohibiting alienation.

The *Chusid* court gave a future direction as to periodic payments despite the restrictions in the Will. The exemption provisions of "ERISA" and of private and public pension trust agreements cannot, as a matter of public policy, bar enforcement of the right of the wife and children to support. (Cogollos v. Cogollos, 93 Misc.2d 406, 402 N.Y.S.2d 929; Matter of Wanamaker v. Wanamaker, 93 Misc.2d 784, 401 N.Y.S.2d 702; Matter of M.H. v. J.H., 93 Misc.2d 1016, 403 N.Y.S.2d 411). There are obviously strong public policy considerations in favor of insuring the support of wives and children. Public policy also requires the conclusion that the exemption statutes and the trust agreement may not be interpreted to shield an employee, proven to be a thief, from the reach of remedies designed for the enforcement of judgments. . . .

Notes & Questions

1. *The State Law Result.* Suppose that *Helmsley-Spear* arose solely as a matter of state law, without the complications added by ERISA. What result?

2. *The Effect of ERISA.* As *Helmsley-Spear* suggests, courts disagree over whether pension benefits covered by ERISA are reachable by creditors. In In re Daniel, 771 F.2d 1352 (9th Cir. 1985), cert. denied 475 U.S. 1016, 106 S.Ct. 1199, 89 L.Ed.2d 313 (1986), a debtor claimed an exemption in a pension and profit-sharing plan and relied, in part, on an ERISA-mandated antialienation provision in the plan. The court held that such provisions are effective in bankruptcy only if they are enforceable under state law as spendthrift trusts. Does this more accurately interpret the plain language of the antialienation provisions than does *Helmsley-Spear*? Does this mean the preservation of one's federally guaranteed pension rights depends on the intricacies of state spendthrift trust law?

In the case of court ordered alimony and child support, there is less disagreement. Courts long have been willing to allow spouses and children to reach interests in debtors' interests in trusts, even in spendthrift trusts, 2 A. Scott, The Law of Trusts § 157.1 (3d ed. 1967), and ERISA does not seem to have changed this attitude. See, e.g., American Telephone and Telegraph Co. v. Merry, 592 F.2d 118 (2d Cir. 1979). Other creditors who may be able to penetrate spendthrift trusts include those who furnish necessities to the beneficiary, those who perform services that increase or preserve the beneficiary's interest, and governments. See A. Scott, supra, §§ 157.2–157.4.

3. *The New Trusts.* Do the "trusts" in which ERISA pension funds are kept bear a substantial relationship to the "trusts" that are the subject of traditional state trust law? Should the rules governing trusts generally be made applicable to modern pension plan trusts?

If one decides that retirement trust funds should be exempt, should Individual Retirement Accounts (IRAs) and interests in Keogh plans also be exempt? IRAs and Keogh plans are usually established by an employee or sole proprietor. Since the person establishing the fund also is the beneficiary, traditional spendthrift trust principles would not be applicable to keep interests in these retirement accounts beyond the reach of creditors.[b]

4. *The Scope of ERISA's Protection.* In Franchise Tax Board v. Construction Laborers Vacation Trust, 679 F.2d 1307 (9th Cir. 1982), vacated on other grounds 463 U.S. 1, 103 S.Ct. 2841, 77 L.Ed.2d 420 (1983), the California Franchise Tax Board levied against money held in trust for union members by a vacation trust fund, seeking to collect unpaid personal income taxes. The trust agreement contained an anti-alienation clause and specified that the accumulated money shall be exempt from the claims of creditors. After acknowledging that ERISA does not expressly protect vacation trusts from creditors' claims (ERISA's prohibition on alienation applies only to pension funds and not to all employee welfare benefit plans), the court stated:

> Extending similar protection to vacation funds is consistent with the statute, however, if not demanded by it. Both types of ERISA plans have the same goal: to provide accumulated money to a worker for future beneficial use. The worker's money deserves trust protection from dissipation regardless of the purpose for which the money has been set aside under ERISA.

Cf. Cal.Code Civ.Proc. § 704.113 (vacation credit exemption).

5. *Pensions Currently Being Paid.* In the case of pensions in "current pay" status, the real issue in cases like *Helmsley-Spear* may be mostly logistical. A judgment creditor would like to be able to serve a garnishment order on the caretaker of the pension fund. The order

b. See In re Howerton, 21 B.R. 621 (Bkrtcy.N.D.Tex.1982); In re Clark, 18 B.R. 824 (Bkrtcy.E.D.Tenn.1982); Loh water, Who Can Attach Your IRA?, Nat'l Law J., Apr. 19, 1982, at 22. But see Cal. Code Civ.Proc. § 704.115 (limited exemption for Keogh and IRA plans).

would direct the caretaker to pay a portion of each period's pension payments directly to the creditor. On one level, a court that denies such an order is merely creating an administrative headache. Once the pension payment is received by the judgment debtor, is there anything in ERISA that precludes creditor access to the entire amount of the pension payment? But the administrative headache is likely to be expensive one, raising the costs of credit. Each pay period will generate a race in which the debtor attempts to spend or hide funds before the judgment creditor can reach them. What policy interest is served by the refusal to allow a garnishment order to operate directly against the pension fund caretaker? Would such policies be better served through an exemption of funds once received by the debtor?

May judgment creditors reach a debtor's interest in a pension fund *before* the fund reaches pay status? What if the pension plan gives the debtor the option to withdraw funds at age 62? What if the plan authorizes withdrawal upon termination of employment?

2. Exemptions

As *Helmsley-Spear* illustrates, states expressly place some property beyond the reach of creditors. See, e.g., N.Y. CPLR §§ 5205, 5206; Cal.Code Civ.Proc. §§ 704.010–704.210. Homesteads and life insurance are prominent features of most exemption systems but these and other exempt categories vary widely from state to state. The Bankruptcy Act contains its own list of exemptions which are available in circumstances discussed in Chapter 10C.

Where statutes, like New York's, list exemptions by specific types of property, it is tempting for debtors to crowd as much of their assets as possible into exempt categories. Courts have not been eager to scrutinize the circumstances under which wealth comes to be contained in exempt categories of property, see Chapter 10C, or the amount of wealth in such categories. For example, in In re Westhem, 642 F.2d 1139 (9th Cir. 1981), the court interpreted a California provision which then exempted "[n]ecessary household furnishings and appliances and wearing apparel, ordinarily and reasonably necessary to, and personally used by, the debtor and his resident family." The court held that this language protected a diamond engagement ring valued at $3,000.

Consider the following items of property and decide which are exempt under (1) New York (or your state's) law, and (2) § 522(d) of the Bankruptcy Act:

  (a) $250 per month used to pay rent on an apartment
  (b) a $1,500 car subject to a $500 security interest
  (c) $2,000 in furniture subject to a $1,000 security interest
  (d) a $500 stereo
  (e) a $1,000 radio
  (f) a $250 television set
  (g) $2,000 worth of kitchen utensils

Do the lists of exemptions need revision?

STATE v. AVCO FINANCIAL SERVICE OF NEW YORK, INC.

Court of Appeals of New York, 1980.
50 N.Y.2d 383, 429 N.Y.S.2d 181, 406 N.E.2d 1075.

FUCHSBERG, JUDGE.

The Attorney-General, acting on a consumer complaint, instituted this special proceeding under subdivision 12 of section 63 of the Executive Law to enjoin respondent Avco's use of a security clause in a loan agreement form. The petition alleged that the clause was illegal and void as against public policy on the theory that it constituted an impermissible waiver of the personal property exemption afforded a judgment debtor under CPLR 5205 (subd. [a]). Special Term summarily declared the clause invalid for this reason. Although the Appellate Division, over a single dissent, affirmed the order and judgment, it did so on the ground that the provision was unconscionable (70 A.D.2d 859, 418 N.Y.S.2d 52). We now reverse, holding that it is not illegal and that the determination of unconscionability was improperly made without any opportunity for an evidentiary presentation as to the commercial and bargaining context in which the clause appears.

The clause at issue is one regularly inserted by Avco, a finance company, in its loan agreements. Its terms unmistakably provide: "This loan is secured by . . . all household goods, furniture, appliances, and consumer goods of every kind and description owned at the time of the loan secured hereby, or at the time of any refinance or renewal thereof, or cash advanced under the loan agreement secured hereby, and located about the premises at the Debtor's residence (unless otherwise stated) or at any other location to which the goods may be moved."

It is not denied that this language must be understood to create a security interest in items of personal property which include the ones made exempt from the reach of a judgment creditor by CPLR 5205 (subd. [a]). From its inception, this statute—along with its venerable antecedents—has embodied the humanitarian policy that the law should not permit the enforcement of judgments to such a point that debtors and their families are left in a state of abject deprivation (see Stewart v. Brown, 37 N.Y. 350, 351; Griffin v. Sutherland, 14 Barb 456, 459).

It is well recognized, however, that simply because the law exempts such property from levy and sale upon execution by a judgment creditor does not mean that the exemption statute was intended to serve the far more paternalistic function of restricting the freedom of debtors to dispose of these possessions as they wish (see Montford v. Grohman, 36 N.C.App. 733, 245 S.E.2d 219; Mutual Loan & Thrift Corp. v. Corn, 182 Tenn. 554, 188 S.W.2d 345; Swan v. Bournes, 47 Iowa 501, 503; 1 Jones, Chattel Mortgages and Conditional Sales [6th ed],

§ 114). No statute precludes exempt property from being sold; nor is there any which expressly interdicts the less drastic step of encumbering such property. So, for example, while contractual waivers of a debtor's statutory exemptions are usually held to be void (see Caravaggio v. Retirement Bd. of Teachers' Retirement System, 36 N.Y.2d 348, 357–358, 368 N.Y.S.2d 475, 329 N.E.2d 165; Kneettle v. Newcomb, 22 N.Y. 249), the law has not forbidden a debtor to execute a mortgage upon the property so protected and thus create a lien which may be foreclosed despite the property's exempt status (see Banking Law, § 356 [governing security interests in household furniture]; Uniform Commercial Code, § 9–102, subd. [1]; Matter of Brooklyn Loan Corp. v. Gross, 259 App.Div. 165, 166, 18 N.Y.S.2d 179; Emerson v. Knapp, 129 App.Div. 827, 114 N.Y.S. 794; 6 Weinstein-Korn-Miller, N.Y.Civ.Prac., par. 5205.7).[3] The clause here permits no more and, hence, cannot be said to contravene the exemption statute.

The Attorney-General nevertheless argues that the clause should be invalidated under the doctrine of unconscionability. The contention, as accepted by the majority of the Appellate Division, is that "the inequality of bargaining position and the granting to the creditor of enforcement rights greater than those which the law confers upon a judgment creditor armed with execution, lead inevitably to the conclusion that the absence of choice on the part of the debtor left him with no recourse but to grant to his creditor rights which, in good conscience, the law should not enforce" (70 A.D.2d 859, 860, 418 N.Y.S.2d 52). The clause is also alleged to be unconscionable in that its broad terms create security interests even in items not sold or financed by Avco and function mainly as an *in terrorem* device to spur repayment.

In this connection, we note initially that the statute under which this proceeding was brought (Executive Law, § 63, subd. 12) lists "unconscionable contractual provisions" as a type of "fraudulent" conduct against which the Attorney-General is authorized to move. Furthermore, an application for injunctive or other relief under this provision is one which may properly look to the exercise of a sound judicial discretion (State of New York v. Princess Prestige Co., 42 N.Y. 2d 104, 108, 397 N.Y.S.2d 360, 366 N.E.2d 61). But the petition here provided no opportunity for the operation of such discretion on the issue of unconscionability since it alleged only that the clause per se was "illegal" and "void as against public policy and contrary to law", theories which, as we have seen, are not consonant with established law. Indeed, the only ground presented to nisi prius was that the clause violated CPLR 5205 (subd. [a]); the petitioner never raised an unconscionability argument until it arrived at the Appellate Division.

As a general proposition, unconscionability, a flexible doctrine with roots in equity (see Chesterfield v. Janssen, 2 Ves.Sen. 125, 155–156; 28

3. Notably, too, the Legislature has thrice declined to adopt an amendment to section 356 of the Banking Law which would have made security interests in household furniture invalid and unenforceable (see N.Y. State Assembly, 1979 Banking Comm. Bill Mem. on A 5538).

Eng.Rep. 82, 100 [Ch. 1750]; Hume v. United States, 132 U.S. 406, 411, 10 S.Ct. 134, 136, 33 L.Ed. 393), requires some showing of "an absence of meaningful choice on the part of one of the parties together with contract terms which are unreasonably favorable to the other party" (Williams v. Walker-Thomas Furniture Co., D.C.Cir., 350 F.2d 445, 449). The concept, at least as defined in the Uniform Commercial Code— which both parties seem to agree governs the transactions at issue here—is not aimed at "disturbance of allocation of risks because of superior bargaining power" but, instead, at "the prevention of oppression and unfair surprise" (McKinney's Cons. Laws of N.Y., Book 62½, Uniform Commercial Code, § 2–302, Official Comment 1).   To that extent at least it hailed a further retreat of *caveat emptor*.

By its nature, a test so broadly stated is not a simple one, nor can it be mechanically applied (see White and Summers, Handbook on the Uniform Commercial Code [2d ed], p. 151).   So, no doubt precisely because the legal concept of unconscionability is intended to be sensitive to the realities and nuances of the bargaining process, the Uniform Commercial Code goes on to provide: "When it is claimed or appears to the court that the contract or any clause thereof may be unconscionable the parties shall be afforded a reasonable opportunity to present evidence as to its commercial setting, purpose and effect to aid the court in making the determination" (Uniform Commercial Code, § 2–302, subd. 2).

That such evidence may be crucial is made plain too by the drafters' own explication of unconscionability as "whether   . . .   the clauses involved are so one-sided as to be unconscionable under the circumstances existing at the time of the making of the contract" (McKinney's Cons. Laws of N.Y., Book 62½, Uniform Commercial Code, § 2–302, Official Comment 1; see Wilson Trading Corp. v. David Ferguson, Ltd., 23 N.Y.2d 398, 403–404, 297 N.Y.S.2d 108, 244 N.E.2d 685).   And, in the light of this dependency upon the particular circumstances surrounding a transaction, courts and commentators have consistently construed subdivision 2 of section 2–302 to mandate at least the opportunity for an evidentiary hearing.   . . .

Accordingly, the order of the Appellate Division should be reversed and the petition should be dismissed, without costs, with leave to the petitioner to commence a new proceeding, if it be so advised.   . . .

Notes & Questions

1. *Waiver of Exemptions.* If a debtor's interest in exempt property may be alienated through the grant of a security interest, followed by foreclosure, why should not the debtor's interest also be waivable by contract? Does it make sense to allow grants of security to accomplish indirectly what direct transactions could not accomplish? Compare UFCA § 1 (conveyance includes grant of security). Does the New York approach to exemptions favor sophisticated creditors like Avco at the

expense of unsophisticated trade creditors and other small creditors? See also Cal.Code Civ.Proc. §§ 703.010, 703.040.

2. *The FTC Rule.* The Federal Trade Commission has adopted a rule making it an unfair trade practice to obtain from a consumer an obligation that waives or limits exemptions from attachment or execution "unless the waiver applies solely to property subject to a security interest executed in connection with the obligation." 16 C.F.R. § 444.2.

Should secured transactions like that in *Avco* be distinguished from grants of security made in return for purchase money loans? Should those secured creditors who satisfy U.C.C. § 9–107's definition of purchase money security interest be able to foreclose upon otherwise exempt property?

3. *Notice to Debtors.* Should Avco have to inform debtors that they are surrendering what would otherwise be exempt property? Compare N.Y. CPLR §§ 5222, 5232, 5234 (requiring notice of possible exemptions to judgment debtors whose assets are being garnished).

4. Is the security interest taken by Avco vulnerable to attack as a fraudulent conveyance?

5. The Bankruptcy Act contains an interesting and heavily litigated provision, § 522(f), that enables bankruptcy debtors to avoid certain security interests in exempt property. See Chapter 10.

EDWARDS v. HENRY
Court of Appeals of Michigan, 1980.
97 Mich.App. 173, 293 N.W.2d 756.

Before DANHOF, C.J., and R.B. BURNS and MACKENZIE, JJ.

Per Curiam.

The defendant was evicted from the apartment she rented from the plaintiff, leaving the rent in arrears in the amount of $177.10. The plaintiff brought an action in small claims court for the rent and other damages and received a default judgment of $193.30, including costs. The plaintiff immediately sought garnishment of the defendant's checking account in the Michigan National Bank. Pursuant to the writ of garnishment, the bank removed the $103.96 in the defendant's checking account to an escrow account, and eventually delivered that amount to the district court.

The defendant's income at the time was derived from ADC benefits and wages of $72 per week from her part time job. Acting upon the defendant's motion for post-judgment relief, the district court determined that the defendant's ADC benefits were exempt from garnishment despite their being comingled with wages in the checking account, citing Pease v. North American Finance Corp., 69 Mich.App. 165, 244 N.W.2d 400 (1976). Applying a formula based on the relative amounts of the defendant's benefits and wages, the court ordered $43.96 of the garnished account returned to the defendant and the remaining $60 paid to the plaintiff in partial satisfaction of the judgment. The remainder of the judgment was settled by a large voluntary payment from the defendant and a court ordered plan for discharging the balance in installments.

The district court rejected the defendant's claim that subchapter II of the Consumer Credit Protection Act (CCPA), 15 U.S.C. §§ 1671–1677, exempted from garnishment that portion of her account monies attributable to her wages. On direct appeal to the circuit court, the orders of the district court were affirmed. She appeals by leave granted. The plaintiff has filed no responsive brief.

The CCPA provides, in pertinent part:

"(a) The Congress finds:

"(1) The unrestricted garnishment of compensation due for personal services encourages the making of predatory extensions of credit. Such extensions of credit divert money into excessive credit payments and thereby hinder the production and flow of goods in interstate commerce.

"(2) The application of garnishment as a creditors' remedy frequently results in loss of employment by the debtor, and the resulting disruption of employment, production, and consumption constitutes a substantial burden on interstate commerce.

"(3) The great disparities among the laws of the several States relating to garnishment have, in effect, destroyed the uniformity of the bankruptcy laws and frustrated the purposes thereof in many areas of the country.

"(b) On the basis of the findings stated in subsection (a) of this section, the Congress determines that the provisions of this subchapter are necessary and proper for the purpose of carrying into execution the powers of the Congress to regulate commerce and to establish uniform bankruptcy laws."   15 U.S.C. § 1671.

"For the purposes of the subchapter:

"(a) The term 'earnings' means compensation paid or payable for personal services, whether denominated as wages, salary, commission, bonus, or otherwise, and includes periodic payments pursuant to a pension or retirement program.

"(b) the term 'disposable earnings' means that part of the earnings of any individual remaining after the deduction from those earnings of any amounts required by law to be withheld.

"(c) The term 'garnishment' means any legal or equitable procedure through which the earnings of any individual are required to be withheld for payment of any debt."   15 U.S.C. § 1672.

"(a) Except as provided in subsection (b) of this section and in section 1675 of this title, the maximum part of the aggregate disposable earnings of an individual for any workweek which is subjected to garnishment may not exceed

"(1) 25 per centum of his disposable earnings for that week, or

"(2) The amount by which his disposable earnings for that week exceed thirty times the Federal minimum hourly wage prescribed by section 206(a)(1) of Title 29 in effect at the time earnings are payable,

whichever is less. In the case of earnings for any pay period other than a week, the Secretary of Labor shall by regulation prescribe a multiple of the Federal minimum hourly wage equivalent in effect to that set forth in paragraph (2)." 15 U.S.C. § 1673.

The question on appeal is whether subchapter II of the CCPA shelters from garnishment that portion of a worker's checking account funds attributable to her wages and falling within the statute's maximum.

The defendant urges us to follow the lead of a Utah county court and answer the question in the affirmative. We find, however, that the reported cases available to us are much more persuasive and do not favor the defendant's position. Three of these cases are particularly notable, each making a slightly different point against extension of the statute's reach to the "wages" filling an earner's account.

John O. Melby & Company Bank v. Anderson, 88 Wis.2d 252, 254, 276 N.W.2d 274 (1979), examined the findings and statements of purpose set forth in 15 U.S.C. § 1671 and concluded that the Congress had focused in subchapter II on abuse of the wage garnishment remedy by the consumer credit industry and the injuries that befall debtors whose employers are compelled to withhold wages. The *Anderson* Court also commented that the statute's reference to the "workweek" and "pay period" as bases for computing the maximum allowable garnishment served to illustrate the Congressional intent to affect only the passing of wages from employer to employee.

Our question was also answered in the negative by Dunlop v. First National Bank of Arizona, 399 F.Supp. 855 (D.Ariz.1975). The District Court in that case pointed out that the provisions considered here were only part of a larger single enactment, which in subchapters I and III, 15 U.S.C. §§ 1601–1665 and 15 U.S.C. §§ 1681–1681t, "specifically address[es] . . . problem areas within which financial institutions have a role to play". That Court continued, "Where Congress has specifically used a term . . . in certain places within the statute . . . and excluded it in another . . . the court should not read that term into the excluded section". 399 F.Supp. at 856.

The *Dunlop* Court pointed out that the "administrative red tape" involved in following portions of weekly paychecks into bank accounts would be "staggering". 399 F.Supp. at 856, fn. 7. This concern was more directly before the Court in Usery v. First National Bank of Arizona, 586 F.2d 107 (CA 9, 1978), in which the Secretary of Labor, seeking to enforce subchapter II under the authority granted him by 15 U.S.C. § 1676, sought to compel a bank to calculate the portion of wage earners' accounts attributable to protected wages before honoring garnishment orders. The Court made virtually the same analysis of the

CCPA that was set out in *Anderson* and *Dunlop*. In considering the only textual support claimed by the defendant here, the Court said:

> "The definition of earnings as compensation 'paid or payable' in section 302(a) is not inconsistent with this view, and is quite consistent with an interpretation that confines the duty to apply the exemption exclusively to the employer or those in the position of the employer. The term 'paid' as applied to the employer will cover those amounts which have been accrued on the employer's books, and thus are 'paid' in the accounting sense, even though such funds have not yet been transmitted to the employee. This construction is an adequate explanation for the use of the terms 'paid or payable.' Moreover, we find it unreasonable to use the single word 'paid' as the basis for the sweeping extension of the Act advocated by the Department." 586 F.2d at 110.

To the Secretary's claim that his interpretation of the statute that he was charged to enforce was entitled to deference, the *Usery* Court responded, "[T]he agency's interpretation departs so widely from the statutory mandate that it is explicable more easily as an organic reflex to extend its own jurisdiction than as a reasoned interpretation of the statute". 586 F.2d at 111.

The defendant points out that statutory restrictions on garnishment of money paid or payable as veterans' or Social Security benefits have been held to protect those funds on deposit citing Philpott v. Essex County Welfare Board, 409 U.S. 413, 93 S.Ct. 590, 34 L.Ed.2d 608 (1973), and Porter v. Aetna Casualty & Surety Co., 370 U.S. 159, 82 S.Ct. 1231, 8 L.Ed.2d 407 (1962). It is her claim that the CCPA should be interpreted so as to afford an equal degree of protection to funds earned in private employment.

This argument was rejected in each of the three cases we have considered in this opinion. The *Usery* Court pointed out that the statute protecting veterans' benefits expressly provides shelter "either before or after receipt by the beneficiary". 38 U.S.C. § 3101a. It went on to comment that 42 U.S.C. § 407, at issue in *Philpott*, protects Social Security payments from "execution, levy, attachment, garnishment, or other legal process", while the CCPA refers only to garnishment of wages. 586 F.2d at 111.

We believe that there exists a significant difference between the purposes underlying the protection of government benefits and that upon which the CCPA is based. Recipients of government benefits are by definition deemed to be entitled to them by need or merit. In a sense, the government has an interest in the money it distributes even after it has passed into the hands of the recipient. Veterans' benefits are also exempt from state and Federal taxation. In that connection, the Supreme Court of the United States has said:

> "These payments are intended primarily for the maintenance and support of the veteran. To that end neither he nor his guardian is obliged to keep the moneys on his person or under his roof. As

the immunity from taxation is continued after the payments are received, the usual methods of receipt must be deemed available so that the amounts paid by the Government may be properly safe-guarded and used as the needs of the veteran may require." Lawrence v. Shaw, 300 U.S. 245, 250, 57 S.Ct. 443, 81 L.Ed. 623 (1937).

In conclusion, we note that where there exists no split of authority in the Federal courts concerning the interpretation of a Federal statute, state courts should be very cautious in differing with the prevailing view in that system, if they do not feel themselves precluded altogether from doing so. The CCPA has never, to our knowledge, been afforded by a Federal court the reach the defendant would ask to give it. For this reason and for the reasons set forth above, we affirm the lower court.   . . .

Notes & Questions

1. *The Interests Protected.* Under one vision of the federal provision limiting garnishment, its purpose is to prevent deterioration of the employer-employee relationship due to wage garnishments. After wages have been paid to the employee, cases like *Edwards* argue, the federal provision no longer serves any function. If this accurately portrays Title II of the CCPA, does it make sense to allow garnishment of any wages owed by employers? Are employers likely to care about the *amount* garnished or the *fact* of garnishment? If employers are inconvenienced by the fact of garnishment (independent of amount), what role does the monetary limitation in § 1673 play? Could one argue that it evidences an intent to see that employees keep enough of their wages to live on?

2. *Administrative Considerations.* Consider the administrative problems in tracing current wages once they are commingled with an employee's other funds. Do these problems differ in kind from those involved in tracing proceeds of collateral into deposit accounts?

3. *State Laws.* For state provisions limiting wage garnishment, see N.Y. CPLR §§ 5205(d)(1), 5231(b); Cal.Code Civ.Proc. §§ 704.070, 706.010 to 706.154.

Chapter 8

THE FEDERAL GOVERNMENT AS CREDITOR

The federal government acts in several capacities that lead to its becoming a creditor. In its capacity as tax collector the government must be the largest unpaid creditor in the United States. In a fiscal year, the Internal Revenue Service establishes and closes millions of delinquent accounts. In its capacity as loan guarantor and creditor under business, mortgage assistance, and other programs, the government becomes involved with thousands of other delinquent debtors.

To what extent should the government be treated differently than other creditors? To what extent should the federal government's rights against debtors and competing creditors be shaped by state law? These are the principal questions addressed in this Chapter.

A. The Federal Income Tax Lien

Note on When the Tax Lien Arises

Internal Revenue Code (IRC) § 6321 makes "demand" a prerequisite to the amount of tax due becoming a lien on the taxpayer's property. IRC § 6303 requires that the Secretary or his delegate, "as soon as practicable, and within 60 days, after the making of an assessment of a tax pursuant to section 6203, give notice to each person liable for the unpaid tax, stating the amount and demanding payment thereof." IRC § 6322 states that the lien imposed by § 6321 shall arise at the time assessment is made. The notice and demand employed by the IRS gives the taxpayer ten days to make payment. Cf. IRC § 6331(a) (IRS may levy ten days after notice and demand).

These provisions make demand a prerequisite to the creation of the lien, assessment a prerequisite to the creation of the lien, and assessment a prerequisite to demand. A lien that arises as the result of a proper demand will relate back to the date of assessment.[a] "Consequently, a tax lien arises when three events have happened: (1) a tax assessment has been made; (2) the taxpayer has been given notice of the assessment stating the amount and demanding its payment; and (3)

---

a. IRC § 6203 states:

The assessment shall be made by recording the liability of the taxpayer in the office of the Secretary in accordance with rules or regulations prescribed by the Secretary. . . .

The timing and method of assessment depend on whether the taxpayer acknowledges or challenges his tax liability. Filing a tax return acknowledging a tax liability in excess of payments results in almost immediate assessment. In this case assessment consists of recording the liability on a list kept in an IRS Regional Service Center. When the tax due emerges after the government alleges an understatement of liability, assessment may come much later, see generally W. Plumb, Federal Tax Liens 14–18 (3d ed. 1972), but the government may accelerate assessment to protect its interests. IRC §§ 6861, 6862.

the taxpayer has failed to pay the amount assessed within ten days after the notice and demand." M. Saltzman, IRS Practice and Procedure ¶ 14.06, at 14–26, 14–27 (1981).

UNITED STATES v. GLOBE CORP.

Supreme Court of Arizona, 1976.
113 Ariz. 44, 546 P.2d 11.

STRUCKMEYER, VICE CHIEF JUSTICE.

The Valley Gin Company, as plaintiff in the Superior Court, commenced this action to determine the proper party to receive $15,694.10, the balance of the proceeds from crops grown on land leased by the Globe Corporation to Lee Wong Farms, Inc. The Superior Court, after authorizing the deposit of the fund with the court, awarded the Valley Gin Company $635.40 as costs and attorneys' fees from the fund and ordered that the Valley Gin Company be dismissed from the action. Both the United States and the Globe Corporation were named defendants. Both filed motions for summary judgment. The court below denied the motion of the United States and granted the motion of the Globe Corporation. The United States has appealed. The judgment is set aside and this cause is remanded with directions.

The facts are not in dispute. Lee Wong Farms, Inc. leased certain lands from the Globe Corporation. The lease, dated December 29, 1966, was for four years and provided for an annual rental of $45,000 payable in equal installments on January 1 and August 1 of each year. Pursuant to the lease, Lee Wong Farms, Inc. was in possession of the demised property in April of 1970, at which time it planted a cotton crop scheduled for harvest in late 1970. The cost of planting and growing the crop was advanced by the Valley Gin Company. In the summer of 1970, Lee Wong Farms, Inc. encountered financial difficulty and was unable to meet its obligations. Consequently, the Valley Gin Company took over the harvesting and processing of the crop and satisfied its claim from the proceeds. The balance was interpleaded with the result as stated.

The United States claimed the fund by reason of certain tax liens filed during June and July of 1970. Globe claimed the fund because Lee Wong Farms, Inc. failed to make the rental payment due August 1, 1970. Globe has asserted both a statutory and a contractual landlord's lien on the fund, either of which it claims is entitled to priority over the federal tax liens. The United States on appeal contends that the statutory landlord's lien was inchoate (was not a perfected security interest) at the time the federal tax liens were filed, that the contractual landlord's lien did not constitute a properly protected security interest under the Uniform Commercial Code, and that neither the statutory landlord's lien nor the contractual landlord's lien is entitled to priority over the federal tax liens. . . .

By the United States Internal Revenue Code, § 6321, there is created a lien in favor of the United States upon all property and rights to property belonging to any person who neglects or refuses to pay his tax liability after demand. The lien arises at the time the assessment is made and continues until the liability for the assessed amount is satisfied or becomes unenforceable by reason of lapse of time. Internal Revenue Code, § 6322. The liens asserted by the United States are based on taxes assessed during May and June of 1970 and recorded pursuant to the authority of § 6323 during June and July of 1970.

Globe asserts a statutory lien by reason of A.R.S. § 33–362(C), reading:

"C. The landlord shall have a lien for rent upon crops grown or growing upon the leased premises, . . . and the lien shall continue for a period of six months after expiration of the term of the lease."

As stated, the United States' position is that Globe's lien was not a perfected security interest and therefore it was not entitled to priority over the federal liens.

Under Arizona law, a landlord has a lien for rent upon crops grown or growing on the leased premises until the rent is paid, A.R.S. § 33–362(C), supra, and the lien attaches at the beginning of the tenancy. The lien is for rent due or to become due, Murphey v. Brown, 12 Ariz. 268, 100 P. 801 (1909). The landlord acquires a fixed, specific lien in the amount of the rent due on his tenant's goods and property rather than a mere claim for priority of payment. The lien exists independent of any proceedings.

While agreeing that the Arizona law is as stated, the United States urges that merely because the landlord's lien attaches at the beginning of the tenancy does not mean that it is so perfected as to have priority over the federal tax lien. As to this, a lien may be classified by the state as choate (specific and perfected) so as to defeat other state liens, but whether it is sufficient to defeat a federal tax lien is a question of federal law.

To have priority over a federal tax lien, a state lien must be choate under federal law. United States v. State of Vermont, 377 U.S. 351, 84 S.Ct. 1267, 12 L.Ed.2d 370 (1964); United States v. Security Trust & Savings Bank, 340 U.S. 47, 71 S.Ct. 111, 95 L.Ed. 53 (1950); T.H. Rogers Lumber Company v. Apel, 468 F.2d 14 (10th Cir. 1972). To be choate under federal law, the identity of the lienor, the identity of the property subject to the lien and the amount of the lien must be certain.

Globe's position is that the choate doctrine is no longer applicable because the Federal Tax Lien Act of 1966 was adopted subsequent to the cited cases and that it set new standards for determining when a state lien prevails over a federal tax lien. It is argued that Globe's statutory lien qualifies for priority under the Federal Tax Lien Act of 1966 for either of two reasons. First, because Globe qualifies as a holder of a "security interest" under the Internal Revenue Code §§ 6323(a) and 6323(h)(1).

Section 6323(a) provides that:

"[t]he lien imposed by section 6321 shall not be valid as against any . . . holder of a security interest . . . until notice thereof which meets the requirements of subsection (f) has been filed by the Secretary or his delegate."

Section 6323(h)(1) defines a "security interest" as:

"any interest in property acquired by contract for the purpose of securing payment or performance of an obligation or indemnifying against loss or liability. A security interest exists at any time (A) if, at such time, the property is in existence and the interest has become protected under local law against a subsequent judgment lien arising out of an unsecured obligation, and (B) to the extent that, at such time, the holder has parted with money or money's worth."

However, while Globe's statutory landlord's lien arises out of the landlord-tenant relationship, the lien is not within the meaning of § 6323(a).

The purpose of the Federal Tax Lien Act was to conform the internal revenue laws with the developments in the Uniform Commercial Code, Senate Report No. 1708, House Report No. 1884, 89th Congress, 2d Session (1966). The security interest referred to in the tax act must therefore be read in conjunction with the Uniform Commercial Code.

Article nine of the Uniform Commercial Code does not apply to this statutory lien. A.R.S. § 44–3102(B). A lien which is not protected as a security interest by the Uniform Commercial Code is not a security interest within the meaning of § 6323(a) of the Federal Tax Lien Act. Because Globe's statutory lien was not protected as a security interest under the Uniform Commercial Code, it is not entitled to priority under § 6323(a) of the Federal Act.

Globe also contends that its statutory lien qualifies for a priority status under the provisions of § 6323(c).

Section 6323(c)(1) reads:

"To the extent provided in this subsection, even though notice of a lien imposed by section 6321 has been filed, such lien shall not be valid with respect to a security interest which came into existence after tax lien filing but which—

(A) is in qualified property covered by the terms of a written agreement entered into before tax lien filing and constituting—

(i) a commercial transactions financing agreement,

(ii) a real property construction or improvement financing agreement, or

(iii) an obligatory disbursement agreement, and

(B) is protected under local law against a judgment lien arising, as of the time of tax lien filing, out of an unsecured obligation."

Section 6323(c)(3)(A) defines a "real property construction or improvement financing agreement" as:

"an agreement to make cash disbursements to finance—

(i) the construction or improvement of real property,

(ii) a contract to construct or improve real property,

or

(iii) *the raising or harvesting of a farm crop* or the raising of livestock or other animals.

For purposes of clause (iii), the furnishing of goods and services shall be treated as the disbursement of cash." (Emphasis supplied)

Globe contends that it meets the requirements of § 6323(c)(1) since it had entered into a written agreement of lease before the government's lien was filed, which agreement required it to furnish to Lee Wong Farms the lands upon which it raised and harvested a farm crop. Globe construes the word "goods" as including farm lands and so concludes it is entitled to priority status. But we think such a construction is contrary to the meaning of the word "goods" as personal property. Words must be accorded their obvious and natural meaning.

There are, however, other reasons for denying Globe priority status. The disbursements covered in § 6323(c)(3) were discussed in Senate Report No. 1708, supra. The types of financing agreements covered:

"are generally those involving disbursements to an owner of a property for the construction or improvement of real property, or to a builder for a contract to construct or improve real property, as well as disbursements for the raising or harvesting of farm crops or the raising of livestock or other animals. Protection is limited to interests arising from cash disbursements by the lender except in the case of the financing of a farm crop, livestock, or other animals, where the disbursement may also be in the form of the supplying of goods or services." Senate Report No. 1708, supra page 8, U.S. Code Cong. & Admin. News 1966, pp. 3722, 3729.

The House also refers to the types of disbursements covered:

"a person financing a farm crop is protected to the extent of the value of the seed he furnishes to the farmer to plant a wheat crop and the value of the use of a combine to harvest that crop, as well as cash disbursements he makes to provide funds to pay farm laborers needed to plant and harvest the crop." House Report No. 1884, supra, page 43.

There is no indication whatsoever that the rent for farm lands is included within the coverage.

Furthermore, the term "qualified property" includes only:

"in the case of subparagraph (A)(iii), property subject to the lien imposed by section 6321 at the time of tax lien filing and the crop or the livestock or other animals referred to in subparagraph (A)(iii)." Internal Revenue Code § 6323(c)(3)(B)(iii).

Globe's farm lands are not subject to the lien created by § 6321 and are not entitled to priority over the federal tax liens under Internal Revenue Code § 6323(c).

Since the Federal Tax Lien Act does not give Globe's lien a priority, this case must be determined by the principle first in time, first in right. The priority of the liens depends on the time they became specific and perfected. In House Report No. 1884, cited supra, at page 35, the choate doctrine as expressed in United States v. City of New Britain, Conn., supra, is specifically retained in the new § 6323(a); that is, the state lienor is protected if at the time notice of the tax lien is filed the identity of the lienor, the property subject to the lien, and the amount of the lien are all established. Several federal cases have applied the choate doctrine since 1966. See, e.g., Texas Oil & Gas Corporation v. United States, 466 F.2d 1040 (5th Cir. 1972); T.H. Rogers Lumber Company v. Apel, supra. The choate doctrine is still viable and must be met by a lienor in order to prevail over a federal tax lien.

Globe's statutory lien does not meet the choate principle. The amount of Globe's lien was not certain and specific within the meaning of the applicable federal law. True, Globe's lien related back to the date of the making of the lease, the beginning of the tenancy, and was good for all State purposes. Still, under federal law, its lien was inchoate in June and July when the federal tax lien was filed.

"It is clear that Lawler's lien for rent cannot be paid out of the fund interpleaded before the Government's tax lien. Section 6321 does not confer a priority on the lien it creates, but the lien created by its language did attach to all of Walker's property, pursuant to § 6322, when the assessment was made on August 31, 1956. While under Virginia law Lawler has a specific and not merely inchoate lien, which relates back to July 1, 1949, the beginning of the tenancy, and good for all state purposes, under federal law his lien was inchoate at the time the federal tax lien arose and was duly recorded on October 26, 1956, in the proper offices. At the time the federal tax lien attached to Walker's property, he was not in default in the payment of rent, and the distress warrant and writ of attachment were not issued until several months thereafter. Lawler's lien had not been perfected in a federal sense when the federal tax lien came into existence. His lien was only 'a *caveat* of a more perfect lien to come.'" United States v. Lawler, 201 Va. 686, 112 S.E.2d 921 at 926 (1960).

Globe also argues that it has a contractual landlord's lien which constitutes a protected security interest and, therefore, it has priority over the federal tax liens. The United States agrees that if Globe had properly recorded its interest in the leased premises it would have had priority over the federal liens, but because Globe only recorded its lease under the index for leases in the Maricopa County Recorder's Office, and not under the index for secured transactions, the lease was not properly recorded as a security interest. Globe replies that it was not required to record its security agreement in order to obtain a priority because A.R.S. § 44–3104(2) excludes landlord's liens from the filing requirements of the Uniform Commercial Code. We, however, are of the opinion that *contractual* landlord's liens are not excluded from the filing requirements of the Uniform Commercial Code.

The principal test as to whether a transaction falls within Article 9 of the Uniform Commercial Code is whether the transaction was intended to have effect as security. Official Comment 1 to U.C.C. § 9–102 (A.R.S. § 44–3102). Excluded are security interests that arise by statute or common law and not by the consent of the parties. Those cases which have considered the landlord's lien exclusion have concluded that landlord's liens arising out of contract are not excluded from the filing requirements. The reasoning of these cases is persuasive. While statutory liens and liens arising from operation of law are excluded from filing by A.R.S. § 44–3104(2), a lien granted a lessor by contract is not excluded by the Uniform Commercial Code. Since the Code's filing requirements apply, Globe's contractual landlord's lien must have been properly filed to have priority.

Arizona enacted the Uniform Commercial Code, A.R.S. § 44–2201 et seq., effective January 1, 1968. Pursuant to the Code, A.R.S. § 44–3123, a financing statement must be filed to perfect all security interests with certain exceptions not here applicable. A.R.S. § 44–3140(A)(1) provided at the time Globe filed its lease that:

> "The proper place to file in order to perfect a security interest is as follows:
>
> 1. When the collateral is . . . farm products . . . then in the office of the county recorder in the county of the debtor's residence or if the debtor is not a resident of this state then in the office of the county recorder in the county where the goods are kept, and in addition when the collateral is crops in the office of the county recorder in the county where the land on which the crops are growing or to be grown is located." Laws 1967, Ch. 3, § 5.

Since both the debtor's residence and the county in which the land is located was Maricopa County, the financing statement had to be filed in the Maricopa County Recorder's Office. Globe filed its lease with the Maricopa County Recorder on February 6, 1970.

A.R.S. § 44–3141(A) provided at the time Globe filed its lease that:

> "A financing statement is sufficient if it is signed by the debtor and the secured party, designates by typing or printing the names and mailing addresses of both the debtor and the secured party and contains a statement indicating the types, or describing the items, of collateral. A financing statement may be filed before a security agreement is made or a security interest otherwise attaches. When the financing statement covers crops growing or to be grown, or timber to be cut, or goods which are or are to become fixtures, the statement must also contain a description of the real estate con-

cerned. *A copy of the security agreement is sufficient as a financing statement if it contains the above information and is signed by both parties."* Laws 1967, Ch. 3, § 5. (Emphasis supplied)

Unfortunately, the lease is not a part of the record before this Court and, therefore, we are unable to determine whether the lease was sufficient as a financing statement within the meaning of § 44–3141(A).

A.R.S. § 11–462, as it read at the time Globe filed its lease, provided for an index of leases, but not for an index of secured transactions. We also find nothing in the record before us to establish that the Maricopa County Recorder's Office kept an index of secured transactions in February of 1970, when Globe filed its lease. Accordingly, we cannot say whether, as the United States argues, Globe's lease was improperly filed under leases. This case must, therefore, be set aside and remanded to the Superior Court.

If it is determined that Globe's lease was sufficient as a financing statement, the Superior Court must then determine whether the Maricopa County Recorder's Office had established an index for the filing of financing statements under the Uniform Commercial Code at the time Globe filed its lease. If there was an index for financing statements and Globe did not direct that its lease be filed as a financing statement, the court below shall enter judgment in favor of the United States, for we consider the law is correctly set forth in In re Leckie Freeburn Coal Company, supra at 1046.

"When dealing with a multi-purpose document, it is incumbent upon the filing party to disclose to the Clerk the purpose for recording. In the present case the record does not show that Appellants had directed the Clerk to record the lease as a financing statement when they paid the filing fee. . . .

. . . To allow constructve [sic] notice in this case would defeat the purposes of the recording statutes. One object of filing a financial statement is to insure a bona fide purchaser that his title will not be encumbered. For the Court to hold that the filing of this instrument as a lease provided constructive notice to those searching the records for a financing statement would be wholly illogical."

. . .

It is ordered that the judgment herein is set aside and this cause is remanded with directions.

Notes & Questions

1. *The Effect of A Tax Lien Filing.* (a) Secured Party has a perfected security interest in an existing piece of Debtor's equipment. The IRS then assesses a deficiency and files a notice of tax lien. Who prevails in a priority contest between Secured Party and the IRS?

Now assume that the IRS assessed a deficiency before perfection of the security interest but filed a notice of tax lien after perfection. Who would prevail?

Assume that the IRS both assessed and filed before perfection of the security interest. Who would prevail?

(b) Secured Party has done everything it can do to perfect a security interest in Debtor's equipment but Debtor has not yet acquired rights in the equipment. After Secured Party has taken all the other steps necessary to perfect, the IRS files a notice of tax lien. Debtor then acquires the equipment. Who prevails as between Secured Party and the IRS? See Glass City Bank v. United States, 326 U.S. 265, 66 S.Ct. 108, 90 L.Ed. 56 (1945) (IRS wins).

2. *Effect of Filing on Purchasers and Judgment Creditors.* C is a judgment creditor of D, and has had a writ of execution delivered to the sheriff. P is a purchaser who pays fair consideration for goods purchased from D. How will C and P fare in contests with the IRS if (a) the IRS files a notice of tax lien after C delivers the writ of execution to the sheriff and P purchases the goods, and (b) the IRS files a notice of tax lien before C delivers a writ of execution to the sheriff and P purchases the goods? See IRC § 6323; Treas.Reg. §§ 301.6323(b)–1, 301.6323(h)–1.

Treasury Regulation § 301.6323(h)–1(g) defines "judgment lien creditor" (see IRC § 6323(a)) to be:

> a person who has obtained a valid judgment, in a court of record and of competent jurisdiction, for the recovery of specifically designated property or for a certain sum of money. In the case of a judgment for the recovery of a certain sum of money, a judgment lien creditor is a person who has perfected a lien under the judgment on the property involved. A judgment lien is not perfected until the identity of the lienor, the property subject to the lien, and the amount of the lien are established. Accordingly, a judgment lien does not include an attachment or garnishment lien until the lien has ripened into judgment, even though under local law the lien of the judgment relates back to an earlier date. If recording or docketing is necessary under local law before a judgment becomes effective against third parties acquiring liens on real property, a judgment lien under such local law is not perfected with respect to real property until the time of such recordation or docketing. If under local law levy or seizure is necessary before a judgment lien becomes effective against third parties acquiring liens on personal property, then a judgment lien under such local law is not perfected until levy or seizure of the personal property involved. . . .

3. *Perfected Lien.* Suppose the landlord in *Globe* had perfected the contractual lien that he claimed the tenant granted him in the crops. Would the landlord then necessarily have prevailed over the government's tax lien? See IRC § 6323(a), (h).

4. *Unperfected Security Interests.* May an unperfected security interest prevail over a tax lien, notice of which is filed after the security interest attached? See IRC § 6323(h)(1). In such cases, does it matter whether the government obtains actual knowledge of the un-

perfected security interest? See Dragstrem v. Obermeyer, 549 F.2d 20 (7th Cir. 1977) (no).

May an unperfected *purchase money* security interest prevail over a tax lien, notice of which is filed after the security interest attached? May an unperfected purchase money security interest prevail over a tax lien, notice of which is filed *before* the security interest attached? In General Motors Acceptance Corp. v. Wall, 239 F.Supp. 433 (W.D.N.C. 1965), the holder of a conditional sale contract (GMAC) on an automobile claimed priority over a federal tax lien filed before the conditional sale. The conditional sale contract was not recorded in the debtor's county as required by state law. Relying on a state supreme court case, the court held that "reservation of title in favor of the seller under a conditional sale contract is effective to give priority to the seller against federal tax liens filed against the purchaser both before and after the conditional sale contract is entered into, even though the conditional sale contract was never recorded. . . . [T]he taxpayer-purchaser had no property right in the vehicle to which the tax lien of the Government could attach." Should this theory survive enactment of Article 9? See also Robinson v. Wright, Chapter 7.

DONALD v. MADISON INDUSTRIES, INC.

United States Court of Appeals, Tenth Circuit, 1973.
483 F.2d 837.

LARAMORE, SENIOR JUDGE.

The question presented by this appeal involves the relative priority of a Federal tax lien and a private security interest to the proceeds from the sale of certain property of a taxpayer-debtor, Madison Industries. Resolution of this question devolves to an interpretation and application of section 6323(c) of the Internal Revenue Code of 1954, as amended.

To the extent relevant herein, the facts disclose that in 1966, Madison Industries (taxpayer) borrowed $40,000 from First National Bank of Madison, Kansas (First National). As collateral for the loan, taxpayer executed a "security interest" in

all inventory, accounts, machinery, equipment, finished products and products being manufactured. Also everything connected with said business in any way.

In November 1968, the 1966 First National note was transferred to Alliance Capital Corporation of Fort Worth, Texas (Alliance Capital). Because Alliance Capital extended additional credit to the taxpayer, a replacement promissory note and security agreement were executed granting Alliance Capital a security interest in the following items:

All items of personal property, wherever situated, including, but not limited to: cars, trucks, inventory, accounts receivable, equipment used in connection with manufacturing, tools, finished products, work in process, now owned or purchased as a replacement, or purchased as new equipment in the future. This is intended to cover everything owned by this business in any fashion.

Thereafter, these security agreements were assigned to Paul Donald, plaintiff-appellant. On December 12, 1969, the Internal Revenue Service filed its first notice of tax liens against the taxpayer in the appropriate state and local offices. In July, August and September of 1970, First National made additional loans to the taxpayer based on new security agreements, which were ultimately assigned to Donald in September, 1971. The government seized all of the taxpayer's property on September 9, 1970, but three days later released all of it back to the taxpayer, except for six trailers (five manufactured by taxpayer and one trade-in) and one pick-up truck.

In November 1970, Donald initiated the present action in the District Court of Lyons County, Kansas, seeking to enjoin the United States from disposing of the taxpayer's assets then in possession of the Internal Revenue Service. The United States removed the action to the United States District Court and filed a cross-complaint asking for an adjudication of the relative priorities of the various liens on taxpayer's property. By agreement between the parties, the assets in issue were sold at a private sale and the $11,000 proceeds deposited in the Court Registry. From a decision in favor of the United States, Donald has prosecuted the present appeal.

The lower court found the basic issue herein to be whether the appellant's security interest was "choate" at the time the Federal tax liens were filed. Pursuant to a thesis tendered by the government, resolution of this "choateness" issue was seen as being dependent on whether the property subject to the security agreements was described with sufficient "specificity," i.e., was it "identifiable." Based in part on an interpretation of Illinois v. Campbell, 329 U.S. 362, 67 S.Ct. 340, 91 L.Ed. 348 (1946), the District Court concluded that the security agreement's coverage of "finished goods" was not sufficiently specific, since that description encompassed a class of goods which was constantly changing and only identifiable at some particular point in time. As a result, the security interest was found to be "inchoate," and thus inferior to the Federal tax lien in priority.

A review of the pertinent Federal law in this area convinces us that we must reject as inappropriate and out-of-date the legal criteria advanced by the government and adopted by the lower court for resolution of the lien priority issue presented herein. While we do not find the "choateness doctrine" totally obsolete, it appears that the government would have us revitalize the doctrine to its pristine form by completely ignoring the Federal Lien Act of 1966, and emasculating significant elements of section 6323 which were specifically designed to alter the effects of said doctrine. We cannot concur in such a scheme.

Moreover, even if this case had arisen prior to the Federal Lien Act, we would harbor grave doubts as to whether the choateness doctrine would have dictated the degree of specificity which the government

would have us find. Our dubiousness stems from the government's
reliance on the "specificity" criteria in Illinois v. Campbell, supra, a
case arising under the Federal insolvency priority statute, R.S. § 3466,
which was later construed as giving virtually absolute priority to
Federal liens in insolvency situations, unless the secured party had
already gained either possession or title to the property. United States
v. Gilbert Associates, 345 U.S. 361, 73 S.Ct. 701, 97 L.Ed. 1071 (1953).
Appellee correctly points out that United States v. Security Trust and
Savings Bank, 340 U.S. 47, 71 S.Ct. 111, 95 L.Ed. 53 (1950), also applied
the general choateness doctrine to a case involving the predecessor tax
lien priority statute, and in United States v. R.F. Ball Construction Co.,
355 U.S. 587, 78 S.Ct. 442, 2 L.Ed.2d 510 (1958), it was established that
the doctrine is also applicable to a consensual lien created by contract
between the parties.

However, the government fails to note that in United States v.
Vermont, 377 U.S. 351, 84 S.Ct. 1267, 12 L.Ed.2d 370 (1964), the
Supreme Court explicitly held that the degree of "specificity" required
under the Federal tax lien provisions is not as great as that which is
necessary in cases involving insolvent debtors under R.S. § 3466—such
as Illinois v. Campbell, supra. In fact, it was held in *Vermont* that to
be choate a state lien need not attach to specifically identified portions
of a taxpayer's property, as it must in the case of a lien on an insolvent
debtor, but instead may cover "all property and rights to property,
whether real or personal, belonging to such [taxpayer]." 377 U.S., at
352, 84 S.Ct., at 1267. Since this all-encompassing description was
found sufficient to establish the identity of the property subject to the
lien for purposes of the choateness doctrine in *Vermont*, we fail to see
how the descriptions herein, "finished goods" (among others), could be
faulted as being too broad or unspecific.

In any event, we no longer need rely solely on *Vermont* and its
predecessors to light the way, for Congress provided us with new guide
posts in the Federal Lien Act of 1966. Section 6323 deals generally
with the "validity and priority [of Federal tax liens] against certain
persons," while subsection (c) specifically addresses itself to "protection
for certain commercial transactions financing agreements." Section
6323(c)(1) provides, in pertinent part, that:

. . . even though notice of a lien imposed by section 6321 has been
filed, such lien shall not be valid with respect to a security interest
which came into existence after tax lien filing but which—(A) is in
qualified property [defined in (c)(2)(B)] covered by the terms of a
written agreement entered into before tax lien filing and constituting—(i) a commercial transactions financing agreement [defined in
(c)(2)(A)] . . . and . . . (B) is protected under local law
against a judgment lien arising, as of the time of tax lien filing, out
of an unsecured obligation.

For purposes of sections 6323 and 6324, section 6323(h)(1) defines a "security interest" as meaning:

> . . . any interest in property acquired by contract for the purpose of securing payment or performance of an obligation or indemnifying against loss or liability. A security interest exists at any time (A) if, at such time, the property is in existence and the interest has become protected under local law against a subsequent judgment lien arising out of an unsecured obligation, and (B) to the extent that, at such time, the holder has parted with money or money's worth.

Subsection 6323(c)(2)(B) states, that the "term 'qualified property,' when used with respect to a commercial transactions financing agreement, includes only commercial financing security [collateral] *acquired by the taxpayer before the 46th day after the date of tax lien filing*," (emphasis added). "Commercial financing security" (collateral) is defined by subsection 6323(c)(2)(C) as including "inventory," which the committee reports state "include raw materials and goods in process as well as property held by the taxpayer primarily for sale to customers in the ordinary course of his trade or business." H.R.Rep.No.1884, 89th Cong., 2d Sess. 41 (1966), reprinted at 1966-2 Cum.Bull. 844.

Subsection 6323(c)(2)(A) defines a "commercial transaction financing agreement," as relevant herein, as "an agreement (entered into by a person in the course of his trade or business)—(i) to make loans to the taxpayer to be secured by commercial financing security [here, inventory] acquired by the taxpayer in the ordinary course of his trade or business, . . . but such an agreement shall be treated as coming within the term only to the extent that such a loan or purchase [made pursuant to the agreement which was entered into before tax lien filing] is made before the 46th day after the date of tax lien filing or (if earlier) before the lender or purchaser had actual notice or knowledge of such tax lien filing."

In addition, subsection 6323(i)(2) provides, as interpreted by the committee reports, that "[i]f local law permits one person to acquire by substitution the rights of another with respect to any lien or interest dealt with here, then the person substituted is to stand in the shoes of the person he replaces with regard to Federal tax liens." H.R.Rep.No. 1884, supra; (1966-2 Cum.Bull. 823). Thus, the rules set out above are applicable to appellant even though the original security agreements were between the taxpayer and First National and Alliance Capital, as long as his substitution was valid under local law. The government has not suggested that it was not.

Summarizing the foregoing definitions and rules as applicable herein, it is apparent that the appellant's security interest will take priority over the filed Federal tax lien if the following requisites are met:

1. The "security interest" stems from a written agreement which

(a) was entered into before the Federal tax lien was filed, and

(b) qualifies as a "commercial transactions financing agreement" under section 6323(c)(2)(A)(i);

2. The loans were made pursuant to the written agreement within 45 days of the tax lien filing or prior to receiving actual notice or knowledge that the tax lien had been filed, i.e., disbursements or loans after receipt of actual notice or 45 days, whichever is sooner, are unprotected;

3. The written agreement covered "qualified property"—here inventory—which was "acquired" by the taxpayer within 45 days of the tax lien filing; and

4. State law gives the security interest holder priority over a judgment lien by an unsecured creditor, as of the time the Federal tax lien is filed.

Before measuring the facts of this case against these requisites, it appears appropriate at this juncture to further answer the government's initial allegation of insufficient specificity in view of the above criteria, and make several other pertinent observations.

First, it should be noted that the definition of "qualified property" specifically includes "inventory," and the committee reports indicate that said term encompasses everything from raw materials to finished products. Neither the Code nor the committee reports imply that these elements of inventory need to be specifically described or perpetually up-dated as to exact identity and amount of each, as the government suggests. In fact, exactly the opposite implication can be drawn from the face of the statute. Since subsection 6323(c) provides that collateral acquired by the taxpayer-debtor within 45 days *after* the tax lien filing will be subject to the lienor's priority if, among other conditions, the written agreement was entered into *prior* to the tax lien filing, it is evident that Congress envisioned the security agreements being allowed to describe collateral in broad enough terms that after-acquired property could automatically become subject to the creditor's lien without a constant rewriting of the agreement as to exact quantities and specific identities of items currently covered by the agreement. In other words, if we required the government's suggested degree of specificity, it would be impossible to ever have property acquired during the 45-day grace period become subject to the creditor's prior lien since the security agreement is not allowed to be rewritten after the tax lien filing. Such a result is clearly not consistent with the intent of the statute, and this fact alone would contradict the government's assertion.

We need not rely solely on the logical inferences of the statutory structure, however, since both the definition of a security interest, § 6323(h)(1)(A), and § 6323(c)(1)(B) explicitly provide that the standard of security perfection is dependent on "local law," i.e., if the security interest is sufficiently perfected under state law to be protected against an unsecured creditor's judgment lien, then it shall also be considered "perfected" for Federal tax lien priority purposes. Thus being directed to "local law," we find that the degree of specificity of description required by the Uniform Commercial Code (UCC) as adopted by Kansas, whose law is applicable herein, is set out in Kan.Stat.Ann. § 84–9–110 as follows:

> Except in the case of a description of real estate concerned with goods which are or are to become fixtures, for purposes of this article *any description of personal property or real estate is sufficient whether or not it is specific if it reasonably identifies what is described.* phasis added.

The official comment for this provision explains that "under this rule courts should refuse to follow the holdings, often found in the older chattel mortgage cases, that descriptions are insufficient unless they are of the most exact and detailed nature, the so-called 'serial number' test." As a result, it is readily apparent that the UCC does not require, but instead rejects the degree of specificity which the government suggests is necessary. Based on this fact and the logical inferences of the statutory structure, we must conclude that the collateral herein was described with sufficient specificity to make it reasonably identifiable at the appropriate point in time—45 days after the tax lien filing.

Secondly, it is apparently necessary to clarify the scope of subsection 6323(c) since both parties virtually ignored it and the lower court found it inapplicable because "it speaks of a 'security interest which came into existence after tax lien filing,' and the security interest of plaintiff here came into existence before tax lien filing." While it is true that the plaintiff-appellant's security interest was "in existence" prior to the tax lien filing with respect to that collateral which the taxpayer had acquired prior to said filing, it is also true that a portion of the security interest did not "come into existence" until after the filing with respect to any after-acquired property. This result stems from the fact that the security interest ordinarily attaches automatically to new collateral the moment it is acquired, and hence cannot be "perfected" with respect thereto, until "the debtor has rights in the collateral." Uniform Commercial Code, Kan.Stat.Ann. §§ 84–9–204(1) and 84–9–303(1). This evolving security interest is, however, frozen after the 45th day with respect to loans already made and the value of property "acquired" by that time. Section 6323(c)(2)(A) and (B). Thus, we must also dismiss as wholly untenable appellant's contention that when a security interest comes into existence is solely dependent on when the loans are made and not when the property to which it attaches is acquired, since both the UCC and section 6323 make it clear that the security interest is perfected only as it attaches to the after-acquired property. Moreover, it is apparent that subsection 6323(c) defines the outer-limits of a creditor's protection, and it is obvious that a lien would not forfeit the benefits of its standards or avoid its requisites simply because there had been no changes in the status of the security interest during the 45-day grace period. As a result, section 6323(c) is determinative of the lien priorities herein.

Returning now to an application of the above conditions of priority to the facts of this case, it is apparent that the first and second requisites are met, i.e., the 1966 First National and 1968 Alliance Capital security agreements were entered into prior to the December 12, 1969 tax lien filing and qualify under section 6323(c)(2)(A)(i), and the relevant loans were made pursuant to these agreements within 45 days of the tax lien filing. Appellant also endeavors to base his priority on security agreements which First National entered into with the taxpayer in July, August and September of 1970 and were subsequently assigned to appellant in September 1971. Since these security agreements were entered into *after* the tax lien filing by some eight months or more (one day after would be just as fatal), appellant clearly can draw no support from these documents with respect to the December 1969 tax lien. Section 6323(c)(1). However, they would be relevant to any tax liens filed after their execution.

Similarly, there does not appear to be any problem with meeting the fourth requirement that the security interest have priority under local law over a judgment lien arising out of an unsecured obligation, as of the time of tax lien filing. The required steps for perfection under U.C.C., Kan.Stat.Ann. §§ 84–9–302 to 84–9–306 appear to have been met herein, and the government has not suggested otherwise. Although this "state priority" issue is measured as of the time of tax lien filing, it is pertinent to note that because a judgment lienor, like a secured creditor, could not attach his lien to after-acquired property until said property is, in fact, "acquired," the judgment lien could not possibly be perfected *prior* to the security holder's interest being perfected. Thus, if a security holder has priority at the time of the tax lien filing, he will retain that priority during the 45-day grace period as to after-acquired property.

The third requisite, however, presents questions of less certainty. Five of the trailers in issue were not completed until some eight months after the Federal tax lien was filed. The sixth was a trade-in. The government contends that the phrase "came into being or existence" should be used interchangeably with the word "acquired" in subsection 6323(c)(2)(B)'s limitation on "qualified property," i.e., only collateral which "came into existence" before the 46th day after the tax lien filing would be subject to the security holder's priority. As a result, the government maintains that the trailers in issue are not "qualified property" since they did not "come into existence" within 45 days of the tax lien filing.

The effect of the government's construction, as we understand it, would be a finding that any items which constituted "goods-in-process" on the 45th day (subject to the security holder's lien priority) would no longer be counted as "qualified property" (priority collateral) if on the

46th day the taxpayer added a coat of paint or some other finishing touches which would now place the items in the category of "finished products." That is to say, since the items were not "in existence" as "finished products" on the 45th day after tax lien filing, none of their value would be subject to the lien holder's priority when they are subsequently completed, although said finished products admittedly: (1) would have been subject to his priority if they had been "in existence" on the 45th day, rather than the 46th, and (2) contain substantial materials which were owned by the taxpayer on the 45th day. We cannot concur with such an interpretation of the statute.

While we find it evident from the face of the statute that property not yet owned or "acquired" by the debtor-taxpayer by the 45th day after the tax lien filing, such as purchases of new raw materials or new equipment, would not be subject to the creditor's priority, we find it equally clear that where property owned by the debtor within the 45-day period subsequently undergoes transformations in character and form, such as the evolution of raw materials into final products and eventually cash proceeds, as occurred herein, the creditor does not lose his security interest in the value of that property which was owned on the 45th day. Implicit in this conclusion, however, is the fact that the creditor would have no rights to the "value-added" to the product after the 45th day by the addition of either labor or *parts subsequently acquired.*

It is with some surprise—although the inappropriateness and invalidity of the bulk of the government's contentions should have put us on notice—that we find our foregoing conclusions strongly supported by the government's own Proposed Treasury Regulation § 301.6323(c)–1(d), which provides, in relevant part, that:

> . . . qualified property consists solely of commercial financing security acquired by the taxpayer-debtor before the 46th day after the date of tax lien filing . . . . Inventory is acquired by the taxpayer when title passes to him. *Identifiable proceeds, which arise from the collection or disposition of qualified property by the taxpayer, are considered to be acquired at the time such qualified property is acquired if the secured party has a continuously perfected security interest in the proceeds under local law.* The term "proceeds" includes whatever is received when collateral is sold, exchanged, or collected. For purposes of this paragraph, the term "identifiable proceeds" does not include money, checks and the like which have been commingled with other cash proceeds. *Property acquired by the taxpayer after the 45th day following tax lien filing, by the expenditure of proceeds, is not qualified property.* phasis added.

It is evident from the preceding proposed regulation that not only cash proceeds from the disposition of the pre-46th day collateral are qualified property, but also that which may be received in exchange for said property. Consequently, the trade-in trailer involved herein would constitute qualified property to the extent that its value reflects an exchange for property owned by the taxpayer before the 46th day after the tax lien filing. However, it should be noted that the proposed regulation suggests that once protected collateral is reduced to cash proceeds, it may not be reinvested in similar products and still be considered qualified property. We concur in this conclusion, for while we accept the commercial necessity of allowing continued production of that which is in process, we also recognize the necessity of ending the perpetuity of the taxpayer's liens by payment of his debts and tax obligations with the consequent funds.

Thus, the crucial fact which should have been determined in this case was an analysis of what portion of the finished products' value was attributable to the inclusion of property which was owned by the taxpayer before the 46th day after the tax lien filing. . . .

Accordingly, in the interest of justice we remand this case with directions to the District Court for further proceedings in accordance with this opinion.

Notes & Questions

1. *Importance of Pre-Filing Commitment and Future Advances Clause.* In *Donald*, does it matter whether the bank's advances made after the government filed notice of its tax lien were made pursuant to a pre-filing commitment to lend? Does it matter whether the original security agreement contained a future advances clauses?

2. *Equipment vs. Inventory.* If the collateral in *Donald* had consisted of equipment instead of inventory, would the bank have had any protection under IRC § 6323(c)? under § 6323(d)?

3. *Choate Liens.* Compare *Donald*'s attitude towards the choate lien doctrine with that of *Globe*, supra. Are the differences in attitude supportable?

4. Consider the following problem: [b]

Lender (a commercial bank) and Borrower (a contractor) on June 1 sign a security agreement, and file a financing statment, covering the contract rights which Borrower has against the owner of the underlying project and providing for non-mandatory working capital advances from time to time as payments are earned. No money is advanced on that date and no part of the contract right has yet become an account. On June 2 a tax lien is filed. . . . On June 30 Borrower has "earned" an unpaid progress payment, and Lender makes an advance. On June 48 (just to be clear that we are beyond the 45 day period) a second progress payment is earned but unpaid, and Lender makes a second advance. If everything (including Borrower's business life) stopped right there, and if the project's

b. From Dauer & Stern, UCC § 9–301(4) [1972] vs. IRC § 6323(c)(1)(A)(ii) [1966], 8 Toledo L.Rev. 51, 62–63 (1976).

owner began a "stakeholder" action against both Lender and the IRS to determine which of them had the prior right to each of the two progress payments, what outcome would there be?

In most states a judgment lien applies only to real property. Does § 9–301(4) of the U.C.C. provide the protection required by IRC § 6323(c)(1)(B)?

Is Lender's security for the second advance perfected as of the date the tax lien is filed? Does this matter?

5. *Bankruptcy.* The validity of the federal tax lien in bankruptcy depends upon analysis of 11 U.S.C.A. § 545 which invalidates many statutory liens. See Chapter 14.

B. The Government As Nontax Creditor

UNITED STATES v. KIMBELL FOODS, INC.

Supreme Court of the United States, 1979.
440 U.S. 715, 99 S.Ct. 1448, 59 L.Ed.2d 711.

[A secured party, Kimbell, was competing with the Small Business Administration (SBA), a federal agency, over the proceeds of collateral. Under state law, the secured party's interest was prior to that of the SBA. The government argued that an independent federal rule of priority was necessary to protect the federal interest. The Court, in an opinion by Justice Marshall, held that the source of the priority rule should be federal. The opinion then discussed whether a federally mandated rule should adhere to the state's priority system.]

The Government argues that effective administration of its lending programs requires uniform federal rules of priority. It contends further that resort to any rules other than first in time, first in right and choateness would conflict with protectionist fiscal policies underlying the programs. We are unpersuaded that, in the circumstances presented here, nationwide standards favoring claims of the United States are necessary to ease program administration or to safeguard the Federal Treasury from defaulting debtors. Because the state commercial codes "furnish convenient solutions in no way inconsistent with adequate protection of the federal interest[s]," United States v. Standard Oil Co., supra, 332 U.S., at 309, 67 S.Ct., at 1609, we decline to override intricate state laws of general applicability on which private creditors base their daily commercial transactions.

A

Incorporating state law to determine the rights of the United States as against private creditors would in no way hinder administration of the SBA and FHA loan programs. In United States v. Yazell, supra, this Court rejected the argument, similar to the Government's here, that a need for uniformity precluded application of state coverture rules to an SBA loan contract. Because SBA operations were "specifically and in great detail adapted to state law," 382 U.S., at 357, 86

S.Ct., at 509, the federal interest in supplanting "important and carefully evolved state arrangements designed to serve multiple purposes" was minimal. Id., at 353, 86 S.Ct., at 507. Our conclusion that compliance with state law would produce no hardship on the agency was also based on the SBA's practice of "individually negotiat[ing] in painfully particularized detail" each loan transaction. Id., at 345–346, 86 S.Ct., at 503. These observations apply with equal force here and compel us again to reject generalized pleas for uniformity as substitutes for concrete evidence that adopting state law would adversely affect administration of the federal programs.

Although the SBA Financial Assistance Manual on which this Court relied in *Yazell* is no longer "replete with admonitions to follow state law carefully," id., at 357 n. 35, 86 S.Ct., at 509; SBA employees are still instructed to, and indeed do, follow state law. In fact, a fair reading of the SBA Financial Assistance Manual, SOP 50–10 (SBA Manual), indicates that the agency assumes its security interests are controlled to a large extent by the commercial law of each State. Similarly, FHA regulations expressly incorporate state law. They mandate compliance with state procedures for perfecting and maintaining valid security interests, and highlight those rules that differ from State to State. E.g., 7 CFR §§ 1921.104(c)(1), 1921.105, 1921.106, 1921.107, 1921.108, 1921.111, 1930.5, 1930.8, 1930.9, 1930.14, 1930.17, 1930.27 (1978). To ensure that employees are aware of new developments, the FHA also issues "State supplements" to "reflect any State statutory changes in its version of the UCC." § 1921.111(c); see, e.g., §§ 1802.80, 1904.108(d), 1930.46(d)(3). Contrary to the Government's claim that the FHA complies only with state procedural rules, Reply Brief for United States in No. 77–1644, p. 7, the agency's reliance on state law extends to substantive requirements as well. Indeed, applicable regulations suggest that state rules determine the priority of FHA liens when federal statutes or agency regulations are not controlling. 7 CFR §§ 1872.2(c), 1921.111(b), 1930.43, 1930.44, 1930.46(d)(1), (3) (1978); see also § 1955.15(d).

Thus, the agencies' own operating practices belie their assertion that a federal rule of priority is needed to avoid the administrative burdens created by disparate state commercial rules.[28] The programs already conform to each State's commercial standards. By using local lending offices and employees who are familiar with the law of their respective localities, the agencies function effectively without uniform procedures and legal rules.

28. The differences between the rules, moreover, are insignificant in comparison with the similarities. All States except Louisiana have enacted Art. 9 of the UCC with minor variations. See Model UCC 1–2 (1979 pamphlet). As Judge Friendly observed in United States v. Wegematic Corp., 360 F.2d 674, 676 (CA2 1966):

"When the states have gone so far in achieving the desirable goal of a uniform law governing commercial transactions, it would be a distinct disservice to insist on a different one for the segment of commerce, important but still small in relation to the total, consisting of transactions with the United States."

Nevertheless, the Government maintains that requiring the agencies to assess security arrangements under local law would dictate close scrutiny of each transaction and thereby impede expeditious processing of loans. We disagree. Choosing responsible debtors necessarily requires individualized selection procedures, which the agencies have already implemented in considerable detail. Each applicant's financial condition is evaluated under rigorous standards in a lengthy process. Agency employees negotiate personally with borrowers, investigate property offered as collateral for encumbrances, and obtain local legal advice on the adequacy of proposed security arrangements. In addition, they adapt the terms of every loan to the parties' needs and capabilities. Because each application currently receives individual scrutiny, the agencies can readily adjust loan transactions to reflect state priority rules, just as they consider other factual and legal matters before disbursing Government funds. As we noted in United States v. Yazell, 382 U.S., at 348, these lending programs are distinguishable from "nationwide act[s] of the Federal Government, emanating in a single form from a single source." (Footnote omitted.) Since there is no indication that variant state priority schemes would burden current methods of loan processing, we conclude that considerations of administrative convenience do not warrant adoption of a uniform federal law.

B

The Government argues that applying state law to these lending programs would undermine its ability to recover funds disbursed and therefore would conflict with program objectives. In the Government's view, it is difficult "to identify a material distinction between a dollar received from the collection of taxes and a dollar returned to the Treasury on repayment of a federal loan." Brief for United States in No. 77–1359, p. 22. Therefore, the agencies conclude, just as "the purpose of the federal tax lien statute to insure prompt and certain collection of taxes" justified our imposition of the first-in-time and choateness doctrines in the tax lien context, the federal interest in recovering on loans compels similar legal protection of the agencies' consensual liens. However, we believe significant differences between federal tax liens and consensual liens counsel against unreflective extension of rules that immunize the United States from the commercial law governing all other voluntary secured creditors. These differences persuade us that deference to customary commercial practices would not frustrate the objectives of the lending programs.

That collection of taxes is vital to the functioning, indeed existence, of government cannot be denied. McCulloch v. Maryland, 4 Wheat. 316, 425, 428, 431, 4 L.Ed. 579 (1819); Springer v. United States, 102 U.S. 586, 594, 26 L.Ed. 253 (1881). Congress recognized as much over 100 years ago when it authorized creation of federal tax liens. Act of July 13, 1866, ch. 184, § 9, 14 Stat. 107, recodified as amended in 26 U.S.C. §§ 6321–6323. The importance of securing adequate revenues to discharge national obligations justifies the extraordinary priority accorded federal tax liens through the choateness and first-in-time doctrines. By contrast, when the United States operates as a moneylending institution under carefully circumscribed programs, its interest in recouping the limited sums advanced is of a different order. Thus, there is less need here than in the tax lien area to invoke protective measures against defaulting debtors in a manner disruptive of existing credit markets.

To equate tax liens with these consensual liens also misperceives the principal congressional concerns underlying the respective statutes. The overriding purpose of the tax lien statute obviously is to ensure prompt revenue collection. The same cannot be said of the SBA and FHA lending programs.[34] They are a form of social welfare legislation, primarily designed to assist farmers and businesses that cannot obtain funds from private lenders on reasonable terms. We believe that had Congress intended the private commercial sector, rather than taxpayers in general, to bear the risks of default entailed by these public welfare programs, it would have established a priority scheme displacing state law. Far from doing so, both Congress and the agencies have expressly recognized the priority of certain private liens over the agencies' security interests, thereby indicating that the extraordinary safeguards applied in the tax lien area are unnecessary to maintain the lending programs.

The Government's ability to safeguard its interests in commercial dealings further reveals that the rules developed in the tax lien area are unnecessary here, and that state priority rules would not conflict with federal lending objectives.[37] The United States is an involuntary creditor of delinquent taxpayers, unable to control the factors that make tax collection likely. In contrast, when the United States acts as a lender or guarantor, it does so voluntarily, with detailed knowledge of the borrower's financial status. The agencies evaluate the risks associated with each loan, examine the interests of other creditors, choose the security believed necessary to assure repayment, and set the terms of every agreement. By carefully selecting loan recipients and tailoring

34. Congress did not delineate specific priority rules in either the tax lien statute prior to 1966, the insolvency statute, or the statutes authorizing these lending programs. Accordingly, the Government urges that we establish identical priority rules for all three situations. This argument overlooks the evident distinction between lending programs for needy farmers and businesses and statutes created to guarantee receipt of debts due the United States. We, of course, express no view on the proper priority rules to govern federal consensual liens in the context of statutes other than those at issue here.

37. We reject the Government's suggestion that the choateness and first-in-time doctrines are needed to prevent States from "undercutting" the agencies' liens by creating "arbitrary" rules. Brief for United States in No. 77–1359, pp. 24–25. Adopting state law as an appropriate federal rule does not preclude federal courts from excepting local laws that prejudice federal interests. See, e.g., RFC v. Beaver County, 328 U.S., at 210, 66 S.Ct., at 995; De Sylva v. Ballentine, 351 U.S., at 581, 76 S.Ct., at 980; United States v. Little Lake Misere Land Co., 412 U.S., at 596, 93 S.Ct., at 2398. The issue here, however, involves commercial rules of general applicability, based on codes that are remarkably uniform throughout the Nation. See n. 28, supra.

each transaction with state law in mind, the agencies are fully capable of establishing terms that will secure repayment.

The Government nonetheless argues that its opportunity to evaluate the credit worthiness of loan applicants provides minimal safety. Because the SBA and FHA make loans only when private lenders will not, the United States believes that its security interests demand greater protection than ordinary commercial arrangements. We find this argument unconvincing. The lending agencies do not indiscriminately distribute public funds and hope that reimbursement will follow. SBA loans must be "of such sound value or so secured as reasonably to assure repayment." 15 U.S.C. § 636(a)(7); see 13 CFR § 120.2(c)(1) (1978). The FHA operates under a similar restriction. 7 CFR § 1833.35 (1978). Both agencies have promulgated exhaustive instructions to ensure that loan recipients are financially reliable and to prevent improvident loans. The Government therefore is in substantially the same position as private lenders, and the special status it seeks is unnecessary to safeguard the public fisc. Moreover, Congress' admonitions to extend loans judiciously supports the view that it did not intend to confer special privileges on agencies that enter the commercial field. Accordingly, we agree with the Court of Appeals in No. 77–1359 that "[a]s a quasi-commercial lender, [the Government] does not require . . . the special priority which it compels as sovereign" in its tax-collecting capacity. 557 F.2d, at 500. . . .

C

In structuring financial transactions, businessmen depend on state commercial law to provide the stability essential for reliable evaluation of the risks involved. Cf. National Bank v. Whitney, 103 U.S. 99, 102, 26 L.Ed. 443 (1881). However, subjecting federal contractual liens to the doctrines developed in the tax lien area could undermine that stability. Creditors who justifiably rely on state law to obtain superior liens would have their expectations thwarted whenever a federal contractual security interest suddenly appeared and took precedence. . . .

IV

Accordingly, we hold that, absent a congressional directive, the relative priority of private liens and consensual liens arising from these Government lending programs is to be determined under nondiscriminatory state laws. In No. 77–1359, the Court of Appeals found that Texas law gave preference to Kimbell's lien. We therefore affirm the judgment in that case. . . .

Notes & Questions

1. *Choateness Doctrine.* Does *Kimbell Foods* provide guidance as to the extent to which the choateness doctrine survives enactment of the Federal Tax Lien Act?

2. *Other Federal Entities.* Rust v. Johnson, 597 F.2d 174 (9th Cir. 1979), certiorari denied 444 U.S. 964, 100 S.Ct. 450, 62 L.Ed.2d 376, involved the question whether a city's lien on property may be enforced without first protecting the interest of the Federal National Mortgage Association (FNMA), which held a mortgage on the same property. FNMA is a privately owned, federally chartered corporation that operates as "a reserve market for mortgage investors . . . to facilitate the distribution of investment capital available for home mortgage financing." Id. at 177. FNMA enjoys certain federally granted privileges, including an exemption from having to qualify to do business in any state and an immunity from state taxes.

The city argued that state law should govern the dispute. In rejecting the city's argument, the court distinguished *Kimbell Foods* as follows:

> In a recent case involving the lending functions of the Small Business Administration (SBA) and the Farmers Home Administration (FmHA), the Supreme Court followed the same approach and held that "the prudent course is to adopt the ready-made body of state law as the federal rule of decision until Congress strikes a different accommodation." United States v. Kimbell Foods, Inc., 440 U.S. 715, 717, 99 S.Ct. 1448, 1452, 59 L.Ed.2d 711 (1979). We note, however, that Congress has indicated an intent to have state law govern interests held by the SBA and FmHA. See 15 U.S.C. § 646 and 7 U.S.C. § 1981(d), as amended (Supp.). Moreover, the SBA and FmHA operate under a set of rules and regulations which allow them to individually tailor their loans.
>
> FNMA, on the other hand, has little or no contact with its mortgagors and it does not individually negotiate the mortgage contracts it receives. As a secondary market facility, FNMA buys mortgages which are of such quality, type and class as those which meet the general purchase standards of private institutional investors. See 12 U.S.C. § 1719(a)(1), as amended (Supp.). Thus, it appears that FNMA operates on an entirely different plane and under a more elastic set of regulations than either the SBA or FmHA. To subject it to the same rules which govern the lending programs of the SBA and FmHA would either limit the types of mortgages which FNMA can purchase or require the corporation to participate in the negotiations between its assignor and the mortgagor. This would impair the liquidity in the home mortgage market which Congress hoped to achieve by creating FNMA and, by restricting the mortgages available to FNMA, it would be contrary to the express intent of Congress which has been to expand rather than to limit the corporation's market.
>
> This is not a case where Congress has allowed the federal interest to be subject to state law. Compare 15 U.S.C. § 646 and 7 U.S.C. § 1981(d), as amended (Supp.). Nor is it a case where the federal instrumentality can easily protect itself by including a

clause in the mortgage contract stating that it is exempt from state law because FNMA is not a party to the original contract. Consequently, we believe that state law should not be applied as the federal rule of decision in cases involving the lending functions of FNMA and that existing federal law should control.

Under federal law, as it is set forth in this opinion, the action of the City to collect payment on the bond without protecting the federal interest was an unconstitutional exercise of state power over property of the United States.

Should it matter in *Rust* that the mortgages FNMA purchases are usually purchased from holders that have assured that the mortgages are perfected and recorded in accordance with state law?

Notes on the Federal Priority—11 U.S.C.A. § 3713

Federal law has given the United States some priority in collecting all debts (not just taxes) since 1789. The federal priority statute was amended in 1982 and codified as 11 U.S.C.A. § 3713. It now reads:

§ 3713. Priority of Government claims

(a)(1) A claim of the United States Government shall be paid first when—

(A) a person indebted to the Government is insolvent and—

(i) the debtor without enough property to pay all debts makes a voluntary assignment of property;

(ii) property of the debtor, if absent, is attached; or

(iii) an act of bankruptcy is committed; or

(B) the estate of a deceased debtor, in the custody of the executor or administrator, is not enough to pay all debts of the debtor.

(a)(2) This subsection does not apply to a case under title 11.

(b) A representative of a person or an estate (except a trustee acting under title 11) paying any part of a debt of the person or estate before paying a claim of the Government is liable to the extent of the payment for unpaid claims of the Government.

1. *Relationship Between the Federal Tax Lien and the Federal Priority.* Assume that a lien is perfected under state law in a manner that assures priority over the federal tax lien. May the United States obtain priority for the tax debt by invoking § 3713? See Nesbitt v. United States, 445 F.Supp. 824 (N.D.Cal.1978), affirmed 622 F.2d 433 (9th Cir.1980), cert. denied 451 U.S. 984, 101 S.Ct. 2315, 68 L.Ed.2d 840 (1981) (yes, where lien not yet reduced to possession).

2. *When Does § 3713 Apply?* (a) Consider the events that trigger application of § 3713. Bankruptcy law no longer contains "acts of bankruptcy" (see Chapter 10). How should courts decide what events mandate application of § 3713? Should they rely on events that would have been "acts of bankruptcy" under the superseded bankruptcy law? Or should they rely on events that may allow creditors to force debtors

into involuntary bankruptcy under the new bankruptcy act? See 11 U.S.C.A. § 303(h); Chapter 10.

Other questions also attend the circumstances under which § 3713 applies:

> Although the first clause of Section 3466 [now § 3713] appears to give the Government priority "[w]henever any person indebted to the United States is insolvent," the Supreme Court, viewing the provision as a whole, has determined that, except in the case of a decedent's estate, something more than insolvency is required. The insolvency of a living debtor must have been manifested by (1) a "voluntary assignment" made by one not having sufficient property to pay his debts, (2) the attachment of the estate and effects of an absconding, concealed, or absent debtor, or (3) the commission of an act of bankruptcy (even though not followed by a bankruptcy proceeding). These acts, in general, involve a divestment of the debtor's property for the benefit of his creditors; the Supreme Court has therefore generalized in repeated dicta that the "priority does not attach while the debtor continues the owner and in possession of the property," but applies only "when the possession and control of the estate of the insolvent is given to any person charged with the duty of applying it to the payment of the debts of the insolvent, as the rights and priorities of creditors may be made to appear." Hence, outside of bankruptcy, the federal insolvency priority has been applied almost exclusively to insolvent decedents' estates, general assignments for creditors, general receiverships, liquidations of insolvent corporations, and comparable collective proceedings for the administration of the assets of an insolvent.
>
> Nevertheless, some lower courts have applied the insolvency priority to situations in which acts of bankruptcy have been committed that did not involve or lead to collective proceedings of any kind—e.g., a debtor making a fraudulent conveyance or a preferential transfer, or the Government or another creditor obtaining a lien through legal proceedings or distraint that has not been duly vacated or discharged.

Plumb, The Federal Priority in Insolvency: Proposals for Reform, 70 Mich.L.Rev. 3, 12–14 (1971).

(b) What is a "case under title 11" within the meaning of § 3713(a)(2)? Does it include proceedings related to title 11 proceedings? See Chapter 17. Does it make sense to limit the federal government's priority to nonbankruptcy proceedings? Does not this provide all other creditors with an incentive to force debtors into bankruptcy?

3. *Treatment of Representatives and Transferees.* A hopelessly insolvent debtor who has committed an act that triggers operation of § 3713 sells property to Buyer. Need Buyer worry about the government asserting an interest in the property? What is the effect of § 3713 in such a case? See also In re Wabash Power Association, Inc.,

77 B.R. 991 (Bankr.S.D.Ind.1987) (government threatening directors of corporation indebted to U.S. with personal liability under § 3713(b)).

4. *Conforming to Commercial Practice.* Does *Kimbell Foods*, supra, suggest that courts should be willing to deny the United States the priority contained in § 3713? In United States v. S.K.A. Associates, Inc., 600 F.2d 513 (5th Cir. 1979), the SBA relied on § 3713 to assert priority over a landlord's lien. The court stated:

> Justice Marshall in his very detailed opinion for a unanimous court in *Kimbell* sought to carefully instruct Government agencies that in their commercial lending activities they are subject to "customary commercial practices," and should fare no better, and no worse, than a private lender. . . .
>
> . . . The Supreme Court's meticulous rationale in *Kimbell* rejecting every Government argument for favored treatment makes so much good sense that it should be applied effectively. To hold that federal law adopts state commercial law in a dispute between lienholders when the debtor is solvent, but not when he is insolvent, would deprive private lenders of equanimity when it is most needed. We, therefore, reject the argument that § [3713] gives the Government as a secured lienholder a priority over other lienholders that it would not enjoy under state commercial law.

5. "The extent to which the sovereign will yield, and in whose favor, is not a question which is capable of a simple solution. Above all, it is not capable of a solution, on whatever level of complexity, which will endure for all time or even for a generation. As the role and function of the central government change from generation to generation, so will the answers which are, for a time, proposed to these questions. Anyone who reviews the present state of the controversy will be tempted to conclude that the fault lies with the slothfulness of Congress or with the incompetence of the Supreme Court. If Congress would pass a statute, all would be well. Or if the Supreme Court would for once explain what it means in a reasoned opinion, all would be, if not well, at least much better, but Congress refuses to legislate and the Supreme Court has, in recent years, mostly restricted itself to cryptic per curiam opinions. It is just possible that wisdom has been on the side of Congress and the Supreme Court."

2 Gilmore § 40.1, at 1047–48.

Part III

BANKRUPTCY

Chapter 9

INTRODUCTION TO INSOLVENCY PROCEEDINGS

A. An Overview of State Law Alternatives to Bankruptcy

SHIMM, THE IMPACT OF STATE LAW ON BANKRUPTCY, 1971 Duke L.J. 879, 881–94

STATE LAW AS AN ALTERNATIVE TO BANKRUPTCY

What nonbankruptcy options are open to the distressed debtor and his creditors for the resolution of his financial difficulties?

Composition and Extension. The oldest, simplest, and perhaps the most satisfactory state-sanctioned technique for comprehensively resolving the insolvent debtor's difficulties with his creditors is the informal, out-of-court settlement, which may take the form of either of two common law contractual devices: the composition or the extension. Requiring the concurrence of the debtor and no more than two of his creditors—although ideally it should embrace them all, and this may be exacted as a condition of participation by the assenting creditors—the composition is an agreement that binds the parties to make and accept, respectively, a specified partial payment in full satisfaction of claims owed by the debtor to these creditors. Alternatively, under the extension, the parties may agree only to a variation or extension of the time scheduled for payment of the assenting creditors' claims. In either event, these creditors are barred from the pursuit of other remedies against the debtor until the stipulated or a reasonable time for his modified performance has elapsed, and once the debtor has complied with the newly agreed-upon terms, the underlying claims are discharged.

This procedure is relatively quick and inexpensive, and its attraction is strongest in those cases where the debtor's financial distress is of a temporary and nonrecurrent nature and his creditors expect that a partial remission or a temporary postponement of their claims against him will insure his survival and the continuation of their favorable business relations with him. But the composition and the extension are, it should be emphasized, entirely consensual devices—which means that they affect only those parties who subscribe to them—and hence

434

they lose their effectiveness and their appeal as insolvency-administration techniques to the extent that creditors do not or will not participate in them.

Since the principles of contract law that govern the composition and the extension obtain uniformly throughout the Anglo-American jurisprudential world, no distinctive variations in the form or incidents of these devices were discovered among the eight states that comprised the sample for the Brookings study.[a] Interviews with persons intimately involved in and concerned with the phenomenon of insolvency, furthermore, have tended to confirm their expected popularity. Indeed, the composition and the extension have found wide favor among not only debtors and those with debtor-oriented perspectives, but also among creditors and their coterie. Thus, major creditors ascribed to the composition an almost unparalleled efficacy as a debt-collection technique, placing it virtually in a class by itself in terms of cost and speed, as well as size of return—particularly when used against delinquent business debtors. In the judgment of their attorneys, too, this device was clearly regarded as the most promising tack to take against such debtors; in fact, in one state—New York—it was so characterized by 100 percent of these respondents. Against delinquent individual debtors, however, creditors' attorneys generally rated the composition as somewhat inferior a device to proceedings under chapter XIII of the Bankruptcy Act for the collection of their client's claims, especially in those states—like Alabama, Illinois, and Maine—where these latter proceedings are more commonly used and presumably more familiar to the bar.

Debt-pooling. Distantly related to the extension, in that it relies on creditor acquiescence for its effectiveness, is an insolvency administration technique that has recently enjoyed some vogue—or notoriety— among consumer-debtors and that is variously known as debt-pooling, debt-adjustment, debt-prorating, debt-management, debt-counseling, debt-liquidating, debt-consolidation, debt-lumping, financial management, or budget-planning—to mention some of the more usual designations. Under this arrangement the financially distressed debtor undertakes regularly to pay a specified part of his salary or wages to an agent who, generally for a fee, promises to try to persuade his creditors to accept ratable shares of this payment until their claims against the debtor are fully satisfied. Not uncommonly this agent purports to counsel the debtor in matters of money management as well, with an eye to preventing the recurrence of similar episodes of financial stringency.

Like the more conventional and familiar extension, debt-pooling suffers from the fact that creditor cooperation cannot be compelled. The gravity of this weakness has been compounded by the fact that the debtor is frequently neither aware nor sufficiently apprised of it and

a. See D. Stanley & M. Girth, Bankruptcy: Problem, Process, Reform (1971).

may, accordingly, in reliance upon deceptive advertising, be detrimentally misled in dealings with his creditors. Nor does this exhaust the debtor's possible debt-pooling woes. Since only rarely are professional or ethical standards prescribed for those who proffer debt-pooling services, the debtor-client commonly has found himself between Scylla and Charybdis—either legal advice tendered by a not-completely-disinterested layman, or lack of counsel concerning the validity of his creditors' claims and the availability and desirability of alternative modes of debt settlement. Moreover, since the fees charged usually have been uncontrolled as to amount or application and the safeguards against misuse of the collected funds have been few, the debtor's financial burden not infrequently has been increased by debt-pooling rather than diminished. And creditors, too, have had no assurance that they will be treated fairly.

Disturbed by these and other reported and potential shortcomings and abuses, many states have begun to look askance at debt-pooling and take appropriate remedial measures. Thus, some twenty-eight jurisdictions have by statute absolutely prohibited or drastically curtailed debt-pooling, except as an adjunct of legal counseling or banking practice or as a nonprofit community service. At least sixteen other states have circumscribed and regulated its practice with statutory provisions regarding licensing, inspection, posting of surety bonds, accounting, record-keeping, and service fees, the violation of which has been made punishable by fine or imprisonment or both. And without the benefit of direct legislative sanction, some states have, additionally or alternatively, judicially imposed restraints that render debt-pooling operations difficult, if not impossible.   . . .

Assignment for the Benefit of Creditors. The resemblance of state-sanctioned techniques of insolvency administration to bankruptcy is most pronounced where creditor acquiescence is not left to the vagaries of free choice, but rather is coerced. The most significant of these techniques in terms of extent of use is the assignment for the benefit of creditors. Stemming doctrinally from the law of trusts, the assignment effects a transfer of all of the debtor's nonexempt assets to an assignee in order that they may be promptly liquidated and their proceeds distributed among his creditors. Despite its tendency incidentally to hinder and delay particular creditors in the collection of their claims, the assignment, because it redounds to the benefit of creditors in general, historically has enjoyed universal judicial approbation, absent demonstrable fraud.

The common law recognized in the debtor an unqualified right not only to designate the assignee, but also to dictate virtually all the terms of the assignment. Thus, if he wished, the debtor could, among other things, execute but a partial transfer of his assets,[b] prefer certain of his creditors and exclude others, condition participation upon release by

---

b. See, however, the suggestion in V. Countryman, Debtor and Creditor 206 (2d ed. 1974), that at common law an effective assignment required the debtor to transfer all of his nonexempt property.

creditors of the unpaid balance of their claims against him, and endow a friendly assignee with broad latitude in the administration of the assignment. Although such free-wheeling principles have continued in some states exclusively to determine the validity and incidents of the assignment, they have, owing to their susceptibility to abuse, been supplemented or superseded in forty-one jurisdictions by statutory regulations that may not only prescribe prophylactic formal standards and affect dispositive provisions, but introduce a measure of judicial control as well. Thus, detailed rules rather than the debtor's predilections may now govern such matters as the execution and recordation of the assignment; the appointment of the assignee and his duties; permissible fees; the posting of surety bonds; the filing of schedules of assets and liabilities; the notification of interested parties; the proof and allowance of claims; the collection, liquidation, and distribution of the estate; the dischargeability of unpaid obligations; fees; and the keeping of records and rendering of reports—all of which may be scrupulously enforced by a watchful court.

The salient advantage of the assignment, common law and statutory alike, vis-à-vis consensual insolvency administration techniques lies in its capacity to immunize the debtor's assets against individual creditor process and thus diminish the likelihood of their inequitable disposition or dissipation. Its principal shortcoming, on the other hand, lies in its incapacity—as a rule—to release the debtor of the unpaid balance of his creditors' claims against him. This failing is not universal, however, and where a discharge provision can effectively be incorporated, the assignment begins closely to approach functional equivalency with bankruptcy and seems to be the insolvency-liquidation technique of choice where recourse to the Bankruptcy Act's avoiding provisions are not strongly indicated. . . .

Interviews with interested and knowledgeable persons in [the eight states covered by the Brookings study] have disclosed a comparatively high degree of satisfaction with the assignment. Thus, among creditors' attorneys, it was regarded less favorably than only the composition, and about on a par with proceedings under chapter XI of the Bankruptcy Act, as a device for the collection of their clients' claims against business debtors—although not against individual debtors. And among major creditors themselves, although the assignment did not recommend itself significantly in terms of cost, speed, or size of return, such mention as it did receive in these respects was generally positive—particularly in Texas and California. It may be worthy of note that the assignment was cited as a source of difficulty in insolvency administration that should be legislatively corrected by the federal district judges of but two of the states—Illinois and California—in which statutory controls are either nonexistent or ineffectual.

Receivership. An ancillary equitable remedy that has long been employed in aid of both the dissolution and the rehabilitation of insolvent corporations is the general receivership. Envisaged initially as a means of forestalling an uneconomic creditors' "race of diligence" and substituting in its stead methodical procedures for liquidating and distributing the insolvent debtor's estate, this technique came eventually to be the principal vehicle for corporate reorganization. Now largely superseded in this latter function by section 77 and chapter X of the Bankruptcy Act, the equity receivership, commonly codified in or regulated by statute, is almost completely confined to its original role, in which its utility as an insolvency-administration device seems directly to be related to both the quality and the quantity of the judicial supervision that it is accorded.

All eight of the states embraced by the Brookings study statutorily authorize the judicial appointment and supervision of a receiver for an expiring corporation. Nevertheless, the receivership does not appear to be a widely popular or well regarded liquidation device. Thus, it was mentioned with notable infrequency by creditors' attorneys who were asked in interviews to list the devices used by their clients in collecting claims against business debtors. Indeed, in only one state—Maine—did the receivership seem clearly to enjoy more than nominal vogue and be viewed with anything approaching general favor. It may be significant to recall, in this connection, that Maine is one of those states in which the assignment has not been subjected to statutory control and in which the assignment appears to play a relatively inconsequential role in debtor-creditor relationships.

Wage-Earner Trusteeship. To answer the peculiar needs of the insolvent wage earner for rehabilitative relief, a few states have innovated a distinctive species of voluntary statutory personal receivership—the so-called wage-earner trusteeship. Typically the enabling statutes require the debtor regularly to remit the nonexempt portion of his earnings to a court-designated and supervised trustee for ratable distribution among his creditors until their claims are fully satisfied. Although somewhat reminiscent of chapter XIII proceedings under the Bankruptcy Act, in that their most dramatic effect is the immunization of the debtor's property—primarily his wages—from creditor process, these proceedings are by no means identical. On the positive side, the wage-earner trusteeship is locally administered and, therefore, probably more convenient for the debtor; furthermore, it is less costly than chapter XIII proceedings; and, finally, it does not depend on creditor consent for its effectiveness. Contraposed to these advantages for the debtor, however, the trusteeship is less flexible—in that it cannot in theory embrace less than all of the debtor's nonexempt earnings; moreover, it confers a narrower measure of relief—in that it neither permits the debtor to reject onerous contracts, nor spares him the burden of further defending debt-collection actions, nor stops the running of interest on claims against him, nor permits the discharge of his unpaid obligations under any circumstances. . . .

B. Assignments for the Benefit of Creditors

FIRST FEDERAL SAVINGS & LOAN ASSOCIATION OF COEUR D'ALENE v. MARSH

Supreme Court of Washington, 1943.
19 Wn.2d 438, 143 P.2d 297.

JEFFERS, JUSTICE.

This action involves the right of Ola T. Marsh and Ward Marsh, her husband, to redeem certain property located in Spokane, from a foreclosure sale had in the case of First Federal Savings & Loan Association of Coeur d'Alene, a corporation, plaintiff, v. Gael G. Marsh et al., defendants. The only evidence introduced was record evidence. . . .

In April, 1937, Gael G. Marsh and wife made, executed and delivered to J.L. Cooper & Company, their promissory note and real estate mortgage to secure the note. The mortgage covered lot 10, block 27, Jerome Park Addition to Spokane. The mortgage was duly recorded April 2, 1937, in the office of the auditor of Spokane county. On October 20, 1938, the mortgage was duly assigned to First National Savings & Loan Association of Coeur d'Alene. The assignee foreclosed the mortgage in 1941, and became the purchaser of the property at a sale held December 13, 1941. A certificate of sale was issued to the purchaser, which subsequently was assigned to G.E. Lovell, respondent herein.

On November 2, 1937, Gael Marsh and wife executed a common-law assignment for the benefit of creditors to Chas. F. Cowan. This assignment included in the property conveyed to the trustee the property covered by the Cooper mortgage, together with other property with which we are not concerned. The assignment was filed for record in the office of the auditor of Spokane county on November 4, 1937.

On October 26, 1937, Gael Marsh and wife executed a quit-claim deed to Chas. F. Cowan, as trustee for the benefit of creditors. This deed covered the property here in question, and was filed for record on November 5, 1937. On October 24, 1939, Chas. F. Cowan, as trustee, executed a quitclaim deed to Charles F. Hafer, his successor as trustee. This deed was filed November 10, 1939.

On November 5, 1937, Bonded Adjustment Company, a corporation, which had taken no part in the common-law assignment, secured a judgment against Gael Marsh and wife for some three hundred dollars, in the superior court for Spokane county. This judgment, as appears from the stamp on the original, was not filed until November 12, 1937. Thereafter, pursuant to an execution duly issued, the sheriff levied upon and sold lot 10, block 27, Jerome Park Addition to Spokane, this being the same property covered by the mortgage and included in the common-law assignment. At this sale, the judgment creditor, Bonded Adjustment Company, became the purchaser for the sum of ten dollars. The certificate of sale issued to the purchaser was, on November 24,

1942, assigned to Ola T. Marsh, mother of Gael Marsh, and on December 3, 1942, a sheriff's deed was issued to Ola T. Marsh.

On December 7, 1942, Ola T. Marsh gave notice in writing to the sheriff of Spokane county of her intention to redeem from the mortgage sale on December 14, 1942. While we have not checked the exact time, it seems to be conceded that December 14, 1942, was the last day on which a redemption might be had from the foreclosure sale had on December 13, 1941.

While in view of the conclusions we have reached it does not become material, it may be stated that Ola T. Marsh did not, at the time of serving her notice of intention to redeem, or at any other time, tender to the sheriff a sufficient sum of money to redeem the property, or any sum. The sheriff, upon receipt of the notice, notified Mr. Lovell, who, on December 11, 1942, filed a petition in the foreclosure proceedings, wherein he asked that the sheriff be restrained from accepting a redemption or issuing a certificate of redemption to Ola T. Marsh, for the reason that Mrs. Marsh was not a redemptioner, in that she had no lien on the property by virtue of any judgment, decree, or mortgage.

A temporary restraining order was issued, restraining the sheriff from delivering to Ola T. Marsh a certificate of redemption until Tuesday, December 15th, at which time the sheriff was directed to appear and show cause why the temporary restraining order should not remain in full force, pending final hearing. On December 15th, Mr. Lovell moved to dismiss his petition and quash the temporary restraining order, on the ground that the controversy had ended. On December 16th the court quashed the restraining order, but did not dismiss the petition.

On December 16, 1942, Ola T. Marsh and husband and Gael G. Marsh and wife filed an answer and cross-complaint to Mr. Lovell's petition. The answer, in addition to certain denials, set up in substance the record as hereinbefore set out, and then in paragraph 5 alleged: "That the lien of the judgment of November 12, 1938, [judgment of Bonded Adjustment Company against Gael Marsh and wife] was superior in every respect to the common law assignment aforesaid, and was a lien on said real estate, and the said Ola T. Marsh was, and is, legally entitled to redeem from said mortgage sale of December 13, 1941."

By their cross-complaint, Ola T. Marsh and husband asked that they be decreed to be legally entitled to redeem from the foreclosure sale.

At the time of filing her answer and cross-complaint, Ola T. Marsh filed a motion asking that the sheriff be restrained from issuing a sheriff's deed to the property, and on the same day a restraining order was issued, ordering the sheriff and Mr. Lovell to appear in court on December 23rd and show cause why the restraining order should not be made permanent.

It was apparently after this restraining order was issued that the one procured by Mr. Lovell was quashed, and it was apparently because of the objection made by counsel for Ola T. Marsh that the court refused to dismiss the Lovell petition, although subsequently, on December 19th, it was dismissed.

Lovell and wife filed an answer to the Marsh cross-complaint, wherein it was alleged that Ola T. Marsh had never redeemed from the foreclosure sale, and that the time for redemption had expired; that Ola T. Marsh and husband were not redemptioners, and at no time had a right to redeem.

When the case came on for hearing, because the petition of Mr. Lovell had been dismissed, the case was treated as an original action on the issues raised by the cross-complaint of Ola T. Marsh and husband and the answer of Mr. Lovell. The court, after hearing the cause and considering the argument of counsel, entered a judgment dismissing the cross-complaint of Ola T. Marsh and quashing the restraining order whereby the sheriff was restrained from issuing a sheriff's deed. Motions for judgment notwithstanding the memorandum decision and for new trial were made and denied, and this appeal by Ola T. Marsh and husband followed.

Appellants' assignments of error are: The court erred (1) in its decree that Ola T. Marsh and husband were not redemptioners; (2) in rendering a judgment in favor of G.E. Lovell and wife; (3) in rendering judgment against appellants for costs; (4) in denying appellants' motion for new trial; (5) in denying appellants' motion for judgment notwithstanding the court's memorandum decision; (6) in not holding that the common-law assignment of Gael G. Marsh and wife was void and in holding that it was valid.

The trial court made and filed a very comprehensive memorandum decision, from which it appears that the court concluded that the common-law assignment was valid and passed to the trustee title to the property here involved; that such assignment becoming effective prior to November 12th, when the Bonded Adjustment Company judgment was filed, that judgment never became a lien on the property; and that as Ola T. Marsh had no lien on the property, she was not a redemptioner and not entitled to redeem.

We are of the opinion that the principal question to be decided in this case is whether or not Ola T. Marsh and husband were in fact redemptioners, and as such entitled to redeem from the foreclosure sale.

Rem.Rev.Stat. § 445–1, provides in part as follows:

"The lien of judgments upon the real estate of the judgment debtor shall commence as follows: -

"(a) . . . judgments of the superior court for the county in which the real estate of the judgment debtor is situated, from the time of the entry thereof."

The judgment of Bonded Adjustment Company, upon which Ola T. Marsh relies to establish her right to redeem, could not have become a lien upon the property of Gael Marsh, the judgment debtor, until November 12, 1937, the date the judgment was filed.

We are of the opinion the common-law assignment, if valid, became effective on November 5, 1937, that being the date of the filing of the deed from Gael Marsh and wife to Chas. F. Cowan. We make the last statement, not with the idea that it is the announcement of any general rule, but because of the lack of evidence in this case as to just when it may have been the intention of the parties to make the assignment effective.

Any debtor owning property has, as an incident of ownership, an inherent common-law right to make a voluntary assignment of such property for the equal benefit of his creditors. 6 C.J.S. Assignments for Benefit of Creditors, p. 1227, § 6.

We have long recognized the right of an insolvent debtor to make a common-law assignment for the benefit of creditors.

We stated in Endicott-Johnson Corporation v. Bloom, 175 Wash. 606, 27 P.2d 1069, 1072:

> "From the beginning it has been the rule in this state that a debtor, though insolvent, may in good faith prefer one or more of his creditors over all other creditors, even to the extent of the exhausting of his assets. This court adopted that rule in Turner v. Iowa National Bank, 2 Wash. 192, 26 P. 256, and has never departed from it. . . .

> "Since a debtor may so prefer a creditor or creditors by a direct conveyance, there appears to be no valid reason why the conveyance may not be to a trustee for the benefit of those to be preferred. Indeed, such conveyances to trustees were upheld in both the Vietor [Vietor v. Glover, 17 Wash. 37, 48 P. 788, 40 L.R.A. 297] and the McAvoy [McAvoy v. Jennings, 44 Wash. 79, 87 P. 53] cases."

Let us now examine some of the authorities relative to the rights or title acquired by the trustee under such an assignment.

In 2 R.C.L. 655, § 13, under the general heading "Assignments for the Benefit of Creditors," we find the following statement: "The broad rule is that a general assignment for the benefit of creditors passes to the assignee all property and every right of the assignor."

In the same volume, at p. 659, the following rule is announced: "Broadly stated the rule is that title passes to the assignee at the moment when the assignment is complete, subject to all liens which have attached before that time, and to no others. Thus a judgment obtained prior to an assignment for the benefit of creditors may be a lien on the real estate of the assignor, but one obtained subsequent thereto is no lien, for the title has passed to the assignee, and the judgment can have no retroactive effect."

We have followed the rule last above announced, as indicated by the case of Gilbert v. Morgan Lumber Co., 87 Wash. 293, 151 P. 785, 787, wherein we stated: "The bill of sale with the conditions annexed was in the nature of a general assignment for the benefit of the creditors of the assignor, and the rule is general in such cases that the assignment passes to the assignee all title to the property then vested in the assignor, and vests in the assignee title to the property *superior to that of any person save those who have prior thereto acquired some specific lien upon it.* Contrary, therefore, to the appellant's contentions, we think it acquired no lien upon or right to the property in virtue of the purported sheriff's sale. *Since the title to the property was not then vested in the execution debtor, but was vested in another for the benefit of third persons, it was not subject to levy and sale as the property of the execution debtor."* (Italics ours.)

Appellants contend that the common-law assignment is void on its face as to Bonded Adjustment Company, a non-consenting creditor, and to support this contention they point out some twelve provisions of the assignment which they claim are invalid and which make the assignment as a whole invalid.

What are the rights of appellants as non-consenting creditors, in so far as this assignment is concerned?

In McAvoy v. Jennings, 44 Wash. 79, 87 P. 53, 55, we quoted from Vietor v. Glover, 17 Wash. 37, 48 P. 788, 40 L.R.A. 297, as follows: " 'It is the established law of this state that an individual, although insolvent or in failing circumstances, may pay or secure one or more creditors to the exclusion of others equally meritorious, even if by doing so he exhausts the whole of his property.' "

The opinion continues, referring to the Vietor case:

"It was also said that the manner of giving the preference was immaterial, that it might be given by deed or in any mode which effects a legal transfer of the property . . . citing Bump on Fraudulent Conveyances (3d Ed.), page 186. It was further said: 'The right to prefer manifestly involves the right to designate the creditors, or class of creditors, to be preferred; and it therefore follows that the only ground on which the unpreferred creditors can justly complain is that the claims of the preferred creditors are not bona fide and real.' Then, if an insolvent debtor has a right to prefer one class of creditors to the extent of the absolute exclusion of another class, by a diversion of the funds of the estate by payments made to the preferred class which exhausts such funds, it must follow that he has a right to make such payments upon such terms as he sees fit to impose. If the terms are not agreed to by the creditor, the only result is that he will not become a preferred creditor. In this instance, if the respondent's assignor, the bank, had not been incorporated in the agreement by being placed upon the list of creditors to whom the payments should be made, he could not have complained under the law which has been announced by this court. He certainly is not in any better position by reason of his having been placed among the creditors. The right, in the absence of a fraud upon the creditors by payment of claims which are not bona fide, to make such payments as the debtor sees fit to make, it seems to us must logically carry with it the right to make the agreement which is the basis of this action."

In the case of Endicott-Johnson Corporation v. Bloom, 175 Wash. 606, 27 P.2d 1069, 1071, we stated the question to be answered, as follows: "May an individual debtor, though insolvent, in *good faith* execute a trust mortgage to secure all of his creditors ratably which will be good as against one or more creditors, who, refusing to accept under the mortgage, seek to subject the mortgaged property to the payment of their claims, thereby securing to themselves priority over all other creditors?" (Italics ours.)

. . .

We then quoted from 12 R.C.L. 574: " 'It is immaterial that other creditors may by the preference be delayed or wholly prevented from obtaining payment; for such is the natural result of the transaction; but a distinction is drawn between the inevitable result of a legal act, *and a bad intent.*' " (Italics ours.)

The opinion continues:

"The question of what is a bad intent which will invalidate such a conveyance, seems to be of vital importance here. . . .

"To indicate a bad intent, there must be a hindering of creditors by the debtor for his own advantage in some way, such as a conveyance in trust for his own use and benefit, or a hindering which leaves the debtor free to make disposition of the property according to his own will or for his own purposes. Perhaps, in addition to that, any device which has for its primary purpose the preventing and averting of legal action by creditors, thus rendering the courts helpless to enforce just demands, would, in most cases, indicate the bad intent which the law condemns."

It seems to us, then, that in the instant case before appellants can successfully attack the assignment in question, it must appear upon the face of the instrument itself that it was made by the assignors with a bad or fraudulent intent to unreasonably delay and hinder their creditors. The presumption is that it was made with an honest intent.

The assignment contains some twenty-one numbered paragraphs or provisions. It is apparent from a study of the instrument that it is a form designed to cover many situations, among which is one where the trustee is to operate and carry on the business of the assignors. The assignment therefore contains provisions relative to the manner in which the trustee may operate and carry on such business. Inasmuch as there was no business to be carried on in the instant case, the only property conveyed to the trustee being certain real estate, there are some provisions in the assignment which do not strictly apply to this case. However, the fact that there may be provisions in the assignment which are not applicable to the trust created, or even provisions which are invalid, would not necessarily require that the entire assignment be declared invalid, if those provisions which are valid can be separated from those which are not, without defeating the general intent and purpose of the assignment. See Endicott-Johnson Corporation v. Lurie, 152 Wash. 653, 278 P. 693.

It is apparent to us that the general purpose of the assignment was to transfer to the trustee all the property of the assignors, to the end that the trustee reduce the property to money as soon as possible, taking into consideration the character of the property and the best interests of the creditors, and distribute the proceeds, less certain expenses and costs of administration, ratably among all the creditors. . . .

We now come to some of the provisions claimed by appellants to be invalid. Paragraph 6a provides:

"To Have And To Hold all of said property above mentioned, whether real, personal or mixed, and wheresoever situated, unto the said assignee, its successors and assigns, for the uses hereinafter mentioned, that is to say:

"The assignee shall take immediate possession of the trust estate, as full owner thereof and shall have and possess the same power to use, control, manage, mortgage, hypothecate and dispose of the same as the assignee shall in its legal judgment deem to be for the best interest of the creditors of the assignors."

Paragraph 7: "It Is Further Agreed that the assignee shall reduce the property herein conveyed to money as soon as the same can wisely, prudently and properly be done, taking into consideration the character of the property and using the assignee's best legal judgment. The assignee has the right to continue the business of the assignors and to use and sell the same either on cash or credit, as the assignee, in its best legal judgment, shall deem best."

Paragraph 8a: "It Is Further Agreed that the assignee may employ such agents, attorneys, labor and incur such expenses and purchase such materials as shall in its opinion, be necessary and proper for the economical and faithful administration of the trust herein created."

Paragraph 8: "It Is Further Agreed that the assignee may, if it shall deem it best, continue the business of the assignor, with the right to buy and sell new merchandise and incur all reasonable costs and expenses in connection therewith, and to give credit in the conduct of said business, to the end and in so far as may be reasonably necessary to reduce the properties of the assignor to money as soon as the same can wisely, prudently and properly be done."

Appellants contend that the above provisions relative to the right of the assignee to continue the business of the assignors are void, as are also the provisions giving to the assignee the right to sell the property for cash or credit, to buy and sell new merchandise and give credit. It is plain to us that the provisions were meant to apply to a situation where the assignee was to carry on the business of the assignors, and can be considered as surplusage in the instant case.

However, we do not believe it can be said, as a legal proposition, that the provisions for carrying on a business are invalid, as we are of the opinion such provisions are entirely consistent with an honest intent to make the property bring as much as possible for the benefit of the creditors, and only authorizes the trustee to continue the business for such length of time as may be reasonably necessary to reduce the property to money, in a wise and prudent manner. See 6 C.J.S., Assignments for Benefit of Creditors, p. 1277, § 92. . . .

After a careful examination of the assignment, we are satisfied that it cannot be said as a legal proposition that it shows other than a good intent on the part of the assignors to vest title to their property in the assignee, to the end that the assignee sell the property as soon as the same can be done, taking into consideration the nature of the property and the best interests of the creditors, and thereafter distribute the proceeds ratably to all the creditors who have notified the assignee in writing of the amount and character of their claims, and whose claims have not been rejected by the assignee, as in the assignment provided. . . .

We are entirely in accord with the conclusions reached by the trial court, that the instrument is a valid assignment, and as such passed to the trustee all the right, title and interest in and to the property here involved which the assignors had; that the assignment was complete at least not later than November 5, 1941, when the quitclaim deed to Mr. Cowan, as trustee, was filed for record, and consequently the judgment of Bonded Adjustment Company never became a lien on the property, as Gael Marsh and wife, on November 12, 1941, the date the judgment was filed, had no title or interest in the property to which a lien could attach.

It follows, then, that appellants, having no lien on the property by virtue of any judgment, decree or mortgage, were not redemptioners, and therefore not entitled to redeem from the mortgage foreclosure sale. . . .

The judgment of the trial court is affirmed.

Notes & Questions

1. *Statutory and Common Law Assignments.* New York, like many other states, has detailed provisions regulating assignments for the benefit of creditors. N.Y. Debtor and Creditor Law §§ 2–24. But, at least in New York, a *partial* assignment may be a valid common law assignment despite noncompliance with statutory requirements. 5 Debtor-Creditor Law ¶ 24.02[C] [2][b][vi]. (T. Eisenberg ed.) For many years California had a statutory scheme regulating assignments, but in Bumb v. Bennett, 51 Cal.2d 294, 333 P.2d 23 (1959), the court held that a common law assignment for the benefit of creditors may be valid despite noncompliance with the statutory requirements. The statutory

assignment provisions were repealed in 1980. 1980 Cal.Stats., ch. 135. Other statutory provisions continue to influence the terms and effects of common law assignments. E.g., Cal.Code Civ.Proc. §§ 493.010 et seq.; 1800; 1954.1.

2. *Conditions Upon Participation.* What conditions may a debtor-assignor impose upon a particular creditor's participation in an assignment? May an assignor require that secured creditors surrender their security or forfeit their right to participate in the estate? May an assignor condition a creditor's participation in the estate upon the creditor's agreement to release the debtor from liability for any deficiency that remains after distribution of the assigned estate? May a state statute provide for release of claims against the debtor following a valid assignment of the debtor's property?

3. *Assignee's Powers.* What powers does an assignee for the benefit of creditors possess? See U.C.C. § 9–301(3); N.Y. Debtor and Creditor Law § 15(6). At common law, the assignee lacked power to challenge preferences or fraudulent conveyances or to assert the rights of lien creditors. See S. Riesenfeld, Creditors' Remedies and Debtors' Protection 440 (4th ed. 1987).

4. *Pre-Assignment Preferences.* Debtor has five creditors, including C, whom Debtor dislikes. Hopelessly insolvent, Debtor liquidates all of his assets and distributes them pro rata to all creditors other than C. Outside of bankruptcy, does C have any remedy? Should C have a remedy under a provision like New York Debtor and Creditor Law § 15(6–a), which follows:

The court shall have power:

. . .

6–a. To authorize an assignee to bring an action, which he is hereby empowered to maintain, against any person, who with reasonable cause to believe the assignor was insolvent as defined in section thirteen of this act, has within four months of the assignment received a voluntary transfer from the assignor of money or property for or on account of an antecedent debt, the effect of which transfer is to enable the creditor to obtain a greater percentage of his debt than some other creditor of the same class, and the assignee may recover the property so transferred or its value. For the purpose of this section a transfer shall be deemed to have been made when it is so far perfected that no creditor having a judgment on a simple contract without special priority (whether or not such a creditor exists) could have obtained an interest superior to that of the transferee therein. A transfer not so perfected prior to the assignment shall be deemed to have been made immediately before the assignment.

Consider later whether C may force Debtor into bankruptcy and seek to recover the payments to the other creditors? See Bankruptcy Act §§ 303(h)(2), 543.

California has a provision allowing for recovery of preferences paid prior to an assignment for the benefit of creditors, but it applies only to *general* assignments. Cal.Code Civ.Proc. § 1800. If a debtor may make an assignment for the benefit of selected creditors, does it make sense to have a provision allowing for the recovery of preferences that precede a general assignment?

5. *Continuing the Business.* On the question whether an assignee may be authorized to continue the assignor's business, see also F.H. Roberts Co. v. Hopkins, Inc., 296 Mass. 519, 6 N.E.2d 837 (1937) (limiting debtor's authority to instruct assignee to continue the business). Why do debtors want to have their assignees continue the business after the date of the assignment?

POBRESLO v. JOSEPH M. BOYD CO.

Supreme Court of the United States, 1933.
287 U.S. 518, 53 S.Ct. 262, 77 L.Ed. 469.

MR. JUSTICE BUTLER delivered the opinion of the Court.

Chapter 128 of the Wisconsin Statutes, 1929, regulates and controls voluntary assignments for the benefit of creditors and also contains provisions relating to the discharge of insolvent debtors. By this appeal we are called on to decide whether as construed below the provisions of that chapter which relate to voluntary assignments for the benefit of creditors and especially a clause contained in § 128.06 conflict with the National Bankruptcy Act. The clause declares: "No creditor shall, in any case where a debtor has made or attempted to make an assignment for the benefit of creditors, or in case of the insolvency of any debtor, by attachment, garnishment or otherwise, obtain priority over other creditors upon such assignment being for any reason adjudged void, or in consequence of any sale, lien or security being adjudged void." [1]

1. Section 128.06 follows.

"All voluntary assignments or transfers whatever . . . for the benefit of or in trust for creditors shall be void as against the creditors of the person making the same unless the assignee shall be a resident of this state and shall, before taking possession of the property assigned and before taking upon himself any trust conferred upon him by the instrument of assignment, deliver to the county judge or court commissioner of the county in which such assignor or some one of the assignors at the time of the execution of such assignment shall reside . . . a bond . . . in a sum not less than the present value of the assets of such assignor, . . . with two or more sufficient sureties . . . ; and the bond shall be conditioned that such assignee shall faithfully discharge the several trusts reposed in him by such assignment and diligently and faithfully collect and reduce to money the property assigned to him and account for and pay over to the several parties, then being creditors of the assignor, all moneys that shall come into his hands from the effects of such assignor after deducting the necessary expenses of performing the several trusts mentioned in the assignment, as settled and allowed by the circuit court, and abide the order of said court. But no assignment shall be void because of any defect, informality or mistake therein or in the bond, inventory or list of creditors accompanying the same; and the court or judge may direct the amendment of the assignment or of any other such paper to effect the intention of the assignor or assignee, and any such amendment shall relate back to the time of the execution of the paper to which it is made. No mistake in filing a copy instead of an original or any like mistake or inadvertent failure to comply with the

The Boyd Company, a Wisconsin corporation, March 23, 1931, made a voluntary assignment of all its property to assignees for the benefit of its creditors. They immediately took possession, and the circuit court of Dane county on the same day assumed jurisdiction declaring in its order that it did so pursuant to chap. 128. Appellant, a non-assenting creditor, brought suit against the assignor and prayed judgment for more than $2,500. September 1, 1931, she instituted garnishment proceedings against the assignees, asserting that the assignment was void because of failure to comply with chap. 128 in several particulars and because that chapter was repugnant to the Bankruptcy Act. Thereafter the assignor amended the assignment to authorize the judge of the circuit court, in case of resignation of the assignees, to appoint a trustee. The assignees resigned, and the court appointed appellee Samp as sole trustee. He answered the garnishment and admitted that he had the property conveyed by the assignment but denied that he had possession or control of any property in which the assignor had an interest. Appellant, having recovered judgment against the assignor for $2,645, moved for judgment against the garnishees. The court found that the assignees had received property belonging to the assignor in excess of appellant's judgment and had transferred the same to the trustee, and ordered that it be applied to satisfy the judgment. The supreme court reversed and directed that the garnishee action be dismissed. 242 N.W. 725.

In view of the construction, theretofore put upon chap. 128 by the state supreme court, it is evident that the assignment did not have the effect of instituting proceedings contemplating discharge of assignor from its debts.

In Re Tarnowski (1926) 191 Wis. 279, 210 N.W. 836, 49 A.L.R. 686, 9 Am.Bankr.Rep. (N.S.) 284, the supreme court declared that, as to all matters comprehended within the Bankruptcy Act, the state insolvency laws had been by it completely superseded and said (p. 283): "The statutes of this state relating to the subject of bankruptcy are suspended during the existence of the federal Bankruptcy Act, and . . . such statutes afford the courts of this state no power or authority to discharge debtors from their debts." In Hazelwood v. Olinger Bldg. Dept. Stores (1931) 205 Wis. 85, 236 N.W. 591, the court pointed out that the Wisconsin statute under consideration is essentially different from the Arkansas statute before us in International Shoe Co. v. Pinkus, 278 U.S. 261, 49 S.Ct. 108, 73 L.Ed. 318, and, speaking through Chief Justice Rosenberry, said (p. 88): "In Re Tarnowski . . . it was

provisions of this chapter shall avoid the assignment. No creditor shall, in any case where a debtor has made or attempted to make an assignment for the benefit of creditors, or in case of the insolvency of any debtor, by attachment, garnishment or otherwise, obtain priority over other creditors upon such assignment being for any reason adjudged void, or in consequence of any sale, lien or security being adjudged void; but in all such cases the property of such insolvent debtor shall be administered for the ratable benefit of all his creditors under the direction of the court by the assignee or by any receiver of said property and estate appointed as hereinafter provided."

held that the right to make a voluntary assignment for the benefit of
creditors is a personal right inherent in the ownership of property, and
existed at common law independent of the statute; that, while the
discharge of a bankrupt from his debts constitutes the very essence of
the Bankruptcy Law, the discharge of a debtor is no part of an
assignment law; that part of the chapter relating to discharge is
entirely superseded by the federal act, and has, under present conditions, no efficacy; and, further, that a creditor filing his claim and
accepting his pro rata share of the proceeds under a voluntary assignment does not waive his right to object to the debtor's discharge. As a
condition of filing a claim under the Arkansas statute, the creditor was
required to agree that payment of a pro rata share of the assets of the
insolvent's estate should discharge his claim. It is hardly necessary to
point out the wide difference between the statute of Arkansas and that
of Wisconsin as construed by this court." In the case at bar the court
again declared that the provisions in chap. 128 that apply to such
voluntary assignments are severable from those that relate to the
discharge of insolvent debtors. It reiterated that the federal Act
superseded the latter. And it held that, as there was an attempt to
make an assignment for the benefit of creditors, the quoted clause of
§ 128.06 prevented garnishment, even though the assignees had failed
to follow some of the procedural details prescribed by chap. 128.

There is slight need to refer more specifically to the differences
between this case and International Shoe Co. v. Pinkus, supra. There
the proceedings in the chancery court were under the state insolvency
law (Crawford & M. Dig., §§ 5885–5893) and not under the law governing voluntary assignments for the benefit of creditors. Id., §§ 486–
493. Upon the entry of the shoe company's judgment against him,
Pinkus sought discharge from his debts under the insolvency law and to
that end procured the entry of a decree under which his creditors were
prohibited from having any payment out of his property except upon
stipulation for his full release. As shown by our decision in that case,
the Arkansas insolvency law not only related to the subject of bankruptcies but actually dealt with essential features of that subject which
are covered by the Act now in force. It not only governed discharge of
the bankrupt debtor but imposed conditions which trammeled and
made against equal distribution of his property.

In the case now before us the Wisconsin statutory provisions relating to discharge of insolvent debtors were not invoked. There is
nothing in the assignment, the application to the circuit court to take
jurisdiction or its order thereon to suggest that the discharge of the
assignor was contemplated. The provisions regulating the administration of trusts created by voluntary assignments for the benefit of
creditors apply whether the assignor is solvent or insolvent. They do
not prevent creditors from bringing action against the debtor or require
those seeking to participate in the distribution of the estate to stipulate
for his discharge. And, quite in harmony with the purposes of the
federal Act, the provisions of chap. 128 that are regulatory of such

voluntary assignments serve to protect creditors against each other and go to assure equality of distribution unaffected by any requirement or condition in respect of discharge.

A proceeding under the Arkansas law derives its force solely from legislation that involves a judicial winding up of an insolvent estate and the discharge of the debtor. Such a law is within the field of the federal Act. Indeed, the declaration: "Proceedings commenced under State insolvency laws before the passage of this Act shall not be affected by it" ([July 1, 1898] chap. 541, 30 Stat. at L. 566) suggests that Congress intended to supersede these local enactments. See Re Sievers (D.C.) 91 Fed. 366; Star v. Johnson (Tex.Civ.App.) 44 S.W. (2d) 429. On the other hand the Wisconsin law merely governs the administration of trusts created by deeds like that in question which do not differ substantially from those arising under common law assignments for the benefit of creditors. The substantive rights under such assignments depend upon contract; the legislation merely governs the execution of the trusts on which the property is conveyed. And as proceedings under any such assignment may be terminated upon petition of creditors filed within the time and in the manner prescribed by the federal Act (George M. West Co. v. Lea Bros., 174 U.S. 590, 43 L.Ed. 1098, 19 S.Ct. 836, 2 Am.Bankr.Rep. 463), it is apparent that Congress intended that such voluntary assignments, unless so put aside, should be regarded as not inconsistent with the purposes of the federal Act. It follows that the above quoted provision of § 128.06 is valid and effective to prevent garnishment of funds in the hands of the trustee.

Judgment affirmed.

Notes & Questions

1. *Power to Discharge.* Part of New York's statute regulating assignments for the benefit of creditors, Debtor and Creditor Law § 15(14), states that the court shall have power:

> On proof of a composition between the assignor and his creditors, to discharge the assignee and his sureties from all further liability to the compounding creditors appearing or duly cited, and to authorize the assignee to release the assets to the assignor; provided, however, that if there be any creditors not assenting to the composition, the court shall determine what proportion of the fund shall be paid to or reserved for creditors not assenting, which shall not be less than the sum or share to which they would be entitled if no composition had been made, and may decree distribution accordingly . . . .

Is this provision constitutional? Would it be constitutional without the clause mandating a minimum distribution to nonassenting creditors?

2. *Effect of Discharge.* An assignment for the benefit of creditors states that a creditor may receive a payment from the assignee only if the creditor agrees to a discharge of the full amount of any claim the creditor has against the debtor. May state courts enforce such a

provision against an assenting creditor who participates in the distribution by the assignee and who later sues the debtor in an effort to obtain a judgment for the deficiency? May a dissenting creditor challenge the provision in court and force his own participation in the distribution without complying with the condition contained in the instrument of assignment?

C. Introduction to Bankruptcy

1. Constitutional Limits on Bankruptcy Legislation

Article I, § 8, cl. 4 of the Constitution empowers Congress to "establish uniform laws on the subject of bankruptcies throughout the United States."[c] As interpreted in Hanover National Bank v. Moyses, 186 U.S. 181, 22 S.Ct. 857, 46 L.Ed. 1113 (1902), the uniformity limitation does not prevent incorporation of state law into federal bankruptcy provisions despite the fact that such incorporation means that similar bankruptcy proceedings may lead to different results in different states. Bankruptcy law is uniform "when the trustee takes in each state whatever would have been available to the creditors if the bankrupt law had not been passed. The general operation of the law is uniform although it may result in certain particulars differently in different states." Id. at 190, 22 S.Ct., at 861. Thus a bankruptcy law that incorporates state exemption provisions does not violate the uniformity requirement. Under the Regional Rail Reorganization Act Cases, 419 U.S. 102, 95 S.Ct. 335, 42 L.Ed.2d 320 (1974), a bankruptcy statute may confine its operations to a single region where all covered bankrupt entities happen to be located. Railway Labor Executives' Association v. Gibbons, 455 U.S. 457, 102 S.Ct. 1169, 71 L.Ed.2d 966 (1982), the only Supreme Court case to invalidate a bankruptcy law for lack of uniformity, struck down the Rock Island Railroad Transition and Employee Assistance Act because it covered only one of several railroads then in reorganization.

Can you suggest why the Court has been so reluctant to invalidate bankruptcy laws for lack of uniformity when laws lead to different results in different states?

However many other theoretical limitations restrict Congress's bankruptcy power, only a few have led to invalidation of bankruptcy legislation. As interpreted in reorganization cases, the fifth amendment's takings clause limits Congress's bankruptcy power to alter or interfere with the rights of secured creditors. See Chapter 11. For a brief period there was doubt about Congress's authority to regulate municipal bankruptcies. In Ashton v. Cameron County Water Improvement District, 298 U.S. 513, 56 S.Ct. 892, 80 L.Ed. 1309 (1936), the Supreme Court invalidated, as an interference with state sovereignty, a 1934 municipal bankruptcy law. But in United States v. Bekins, 304

c. See generally Nadelmann, On the Origin of the Bankruptcy Clause, 1 Am.J. Leg.Hist. 215 (1957).

U.S. 27, 58 S.Ct. 811, 82 L.Ed. 1137 (1938), in a shift that may be attributable to changes in Court personnel, the Court sustained a similar law. The Bankruptcy Reform Act of 1978 contains an updated municipal bankruptcy law. 11 U.S.C.A. §§ 901–946.

Under Sturges v. Crowninshield, 17 U.S. (4 Wheat.) 122, 4 L.Ed. 529 (1819), when no national bankruptcy law is in effect, states may regulate insolvency. Their effectiveness in doing so is limited by the requirement that states not impair the obligation of contracts. This limits the ability of state insolvency laws to deal with obligations entered into prior to enactment of such laws. At the Constitutional Convention, an effort failed to place upon Congress the same prohibition concerning impairing contracts as was placed upon the states. When national bankruptcy legislation is in effect, Stellwagen v. Clum, 245 U.S. 605, 38 S.Ct. 215, 62 L.Ed. 507 (1918) and other cases, including *Pobreslo*, supra, indicate that state laws are abrogated only to the extent that they undermine federal law.

2. Prior Bankruptcy Legislation

Commencing in 1800, Congress often considered or enacted bankruptcy legislation during periods of depression or financial unrest, and repealed the legislation shortly after enactment. The Bankruptcy Act of 1800 was repealed in 1803, the Bankruptcy Act of 1841 was repealed in 1843, and the Bankruptcy Act of 1867 was repealed in 1878. Since 1898, however, the United States continuously has had a comprehensive bankruptcy law, one completely revised by the Bankruptcy Reform Act of 1978.

Bankruptcy laws have served different interests at different times. The 1800 Act "followed closely the existing English Bankruptcy Act and applied only to traders, [and other intermediaries], it was purely a creditors' measure . . . ." C. Warren, Bankruptcy in United States History 13–14 (1935). The act provided only for involuntary bankruptcy petitions. Debtors, without the collusion of some creditors, could not voluntarily avail themselves of its benefits. Only wearing apparel and beds and bedding were exempt. Bankruptcy Act 1800, ch. 19, § 5, 2 Stat. 23. Creditors holding security for their debts received no greater proportion of their debts than unsecured creditors. Id. § 31, 2 Stat. 30. Discharge from debts required the consent of two-thirds in number and value of the creditors. Id. § 36, 2 Stat. 31.

A depression commencing in 1819 generated pressure for another bankruptcy act but the proposed act differed from past bankruptcy legislation.

In 1820–1821, a bankruptcy bill of 64 sections (53 pages) was introduced in the Senate of the 16th Congress; and there then arose a contest which lasted for twenty years. Heretofore, the only bankruptcy system known in England or in this country was one applicable to traders alone, and one in which action must originate with the creditor. Now, for the first time in the history of the world, legislation was proposed to benefit debtors at large, instead of

merely to enable creditors to reach the property of merchants and
traders.

C. Warren, supra, at 27. The proposal was not enacted but the shift in
attitude it represented survived.

The 1841 Act, enacted during another period of financial distress,
provided for voluntary bankruptcies and extended bankruptcy relief to
the nontrader classes. Bankruptcy Act 1841, ch. 9, § 1, 5 Stat. 440–41.
Merchants, retailers, bankers, factors, brokers, underwriters and
marine insurers were vulnerable to involuntary bankruptcy proceedings. Id. § 1, 5 Stat. 441–42. The act contained a list of federal
exemptions which included necessary household and kitchen furniture,
other articles and necessaries "having reference in the amount to the
family, condition, and circumstances of the bankrupt," all not to exceed
$300 in value, plus wearing apparel. Id. § 3, 5 Stat. 443. Discharge
was available to the debtor unless a majority in number and value of
his creditors objected. Id. § 4, 5 Stat. 443.

The Panic of 1857 and the financial dislocations that accompanied
the Civil War combined to generate pressure for a third bankruptcy act,
one finally enacted in 1867. The 1867 Act provided for both voluntary
and involuntary bankruptcy by and against a broad class of debtors and
extended bankruptcy coverage to corporations. Bankruptcy Act 1867,
ch. 176, §§ 11, 37, 39, 14 Stat. 521, 535–36. The 1867 Act was the first
to incorporate state exemptions into bankruptcy and made such exemptions available in addition to property that had been exempt under the
1841 Act (with an increase in total value to $500). Id. § 14, 14 Stat.
522–23. On the effective date of the act, discharge from debts did not
require the assent of creditors. Id. § 29, 14 Stat. 531–32. In bankruptcy proceedings commenced more than one year from the effective date
of the act, however, a majority in value and number of creditors had to
approve a discharge for those debtors whose assets did not pay off fifty
per cent of the claims against the estate. Id. § 33, 14 Stat. 533.

The 1898 Act maintained the broad availability of voluntary and
involuntary bankruptcy proceedings. It was the first bankruptcy law
to incorporate state exemptions without also granting federal exemptions to all debtors. Bankruptcy Act 1898, ch. 541 § 6, 30 Stat. 548.
Discharge became available without the need for creditor consent and
without any requirement that a minimum amount be repaid to creditors. Id. § 14, 30 Stat. 550. The 1898 Act tried to minimize the
expenses of bankruptcy administration, a major cause of discontent
with the 1867 Act. See H.R. Rep. No. 65, 55th Cong., 2d Sess. 44–47
(1897).

With several amendments, the 1898 Act survived until 1978. The
most important amendments, added during the 1930's Depression,
covered corporate reorganizations and wage earners' plans. In 1938,
the Chandler Act replaced these new provisions with Chapters X, XI,
XII, and XIII and added a new chapter to cover municipal bankruptcies.
Act of June 22, 1938, ch. 575, 52 Stat. 840.

3. The Bankruptcy Reform Act of 1978 and Amendments

In 1970 Congress established a Commission on the Bankruptcy Laws of the United States to "study, analyze, evaluate, and recommend changes" to the Bankruptcy Act of 1898. Act of July 24, 1970, Pub.L. No. 91–354, 84 Stat. 468. The Commission's Report, issued in 1973, laid the groundwork for several proposed bankruptcy bills, including the bill that was enacted in 1978 as the Bankruptcy Reform Act, with an effective date of October 1, 1979. The act has had two major amendments. Congress enacted the Bankruptcy Amendments and Federal Judgeship Act of 1984, Pub.L.No. 98–353, 98 Stat. 380, to rework bankruptcy court jurisdiction and make many other minor amendments. It enacted the Bankruptcy Judges, United States Trustees, and Family Farmers Bankruptcy Act of 1986, Pub.L.No. 99–554, 100 Stat. 3088, in part to provide family farmers with a nonliquidating bankruptcy proceeding more tailored to their needs.

The new act and amendments divide bankruptcy law into Chapters 1, 3, 5, 7, 9, 11, 12, and 13. Chapter 9 covers municipal bankruptcy and is not covered by these materials. Chapters 7, 11, 12, and 13 are in a sense the operative bankruptcy chapters. All private bankruptcy proceedings must be initiated under one of these chapters and may not be conducted under more than one of these chapters at any particular time. It is common to speak of a debtor as "being in Chapter 7" (or Chapter 11, 12, or Chapter 13). Cases brought under one chapter may be converted to another chapter. See §§ 706, 1112, 1208, 1307. Section 348 sets forth some of the effects of conversion. Some proceedings may be brought under more than one chapter. For example, many individual business debtors may choose to file under Chapter 7, Chapter 11, or Chapter 13.

Chapter 7 provides for a "straight" or liquidating bankruptcy—all nonexempt assets are gathered by the trustee, converted to cash, and the proceeds are distributed to creditors. Chapter 11 provides for the reorganization of businesses but individuals also are eligible to file under Chapter 11. In Chapter 11, a rehabilitation plan is proposed and, upon acceptance, it becomes the guiding document for the debtor's relations with its creditors. Assets are not necessarily marshalled and sold and the business may continue to operate, often with the debtor or its management in control. Chapter 13 provides for the restructuring of the debts of individuals. Again, assets are not necessarily collected and liquidated. The debtor proposes a plan to rearrange the structure of his debts by extending payment schedules or by reducing the principal amount of the debt. Chapter 12 is similar to Chapter 13 but changes provisions that were thought inappropriate for bankruptcies filed by family farmers.

Chapters 1, 3 and 5 provide the infrastructure of bankruptcy law and apply generally to all proceedings. Section 103 sets forth rules regulating the applicability of chapters. For example, § 103(a) states that Chapters 1, 3 and 5 are applicable to proceedings brought under

Chapter 7, 11, 12, or 13. Chapter 1 contains a list of definitions and other general provisions. Chapter 3 regulates case administration. It contains rules covering commencement of a case, the procedures for selecting and compensating trustees and other officers, and some of the powers arising upon commencement of a case. Chapter 5 regulates creditors' claims, debtors' duties and benefits, and determines what property becomes part of the bankruptcy estate for distribution to creditors.

Bankruptcy proceedings are conducted in special bankruptcy courts located in each federal judicial district. Their jurisdiction and procedures are discussed in Chapter 17.

4. The Operation of Bankruptcy Law

As the following Table [d] suggests, there has been a dramatic rise in the number of bankruptcy filings. Some attribute the rise to recessionary trends in the economy, others point to bankruptcy provisions that have become more favorable to debtors.

Bankruptcy Filings During the Twelve Month Periods Ended June 30, 1975 through 1986

Year	Total Filings	Chapter			
		7	11	13	Other
1975	254,484	209,330	3,975	41,178	1
1976	246,549	209,067	3,901	33,579	2
1977	214,399	181,194	3,782	29,422	1
1978	202,951	168,771	3,991	30,185	4
1979	226,476	183,259	3,774	39,442	1
1980	360,957	275,090	5,866	79,996	5
1981	360,329	265,718	7,827	86,778	6
1982	367,866	255,095	14,058	98,705	8
1983	374,734	251,319	21,206	102,201	8
1984	344,275	232,778	20,023	91,460	13
1985	364,536	244,647	21,420	98,452	17
1986	477,856	332,675	24,442	120,726	13

Fewer than one per cent of bankruptcy filings are involuntary petitions.[e]

All studies reveal that a liquidating bankruptcy is, in Professor Gilmore's words, "a disaster for everyone concerned except the law-

---

d. Adapted from Admin. Off. U.S. Cts., Annual Report of the Director 1982, at 14; id. 1986, at 35. The figures for 1981 and 1982 differ between the two reports because the Administrative Office changed its way of counting bankruptcies filed by husbands and wives. Id. 1983, at 12 (Table 9 n.*).

e. 1982 Report at 396 (Table F2B).

yers." [f] In fiscal 1977, unsecured creditors received only about five per cent of their allowed claims. Twenty-three per cent of the estate went to pay administrative and related expenses. Secured creditors fared substantially better.[g]

Introductory Questions

1. What features of a bankruptcy law prompt debtors to file bankruptcy petitions? See §§ 362, 522, 524, 727.

2. Are there any reasons not to file for bankrupcty? See §§ 523, 541, 727(a)(8), (9).

3. How does one commence a bankruptcy case? See §§ 301–303. May any debtor file a case under any chapter? See § 109.

4. What happens upon the filing of a bankruptcy petition? See §§ 362, 541, 701, 341, 343.

---

f. 2 Gilmore, § 45.3, at 1288.

g. Admin. Off. U.S. Cts., Tables of Bankruptcy Statistics During Fiscal Year Ending June 30, 1977 (Tables F. 5 & F. 6).

Chapter 10

COMMENCEMENT OF THE CASE
AND THE ESTATE

A. Involuntary Proceedings

Introductory Note

Like most issues that arise in bankruptcy, the Act's treatment of involuntary bankruptcy may be analyzed from two overlapping but distinct perspectives. First, one may view the bankruptcy process in isolation from the rest of the legal world. Actors within and without the bankruptcy process often behave in a manner that reflects such a perspective. The existence of separate bankruptcy courts reinforces this attitude. This perspective may be viewed as encompassing intrabankruptcy issues, including those in the *Reid* case, infra, such as whether a sufficient number of creditors have filed an involuntary petition, and which creditors count as claimholders for purposes of § 303.

But bankruptcy also may be viewed as a process within a larger body of debtor-creditor (and other) law. In analyzing a bankruptcy issue in this perspective, one may wish to ask how the issue would be dealt with in a nonbankruptcy proceeding. Study of the nonbankruptcy model then may be contrasted with treatment of the issue in bankruptcy to assess whether there is any net benefit from the bankruptcy rule and the necessity of maintaining what amounts to two separate systems of debtor-creditor relations. It often is tempting to resolve intrabankruptcy issues by resorting to the nonbankruptcy standard. Absent some important reason, should the result in bankruptcy match the result that would be obtained in a nonbankruptcy setting?

Which of the issues discussed below should be viewed as intrabankruptcy system issues? Which require analysis of nonbankruptcy alternatives?

When Are Involuntary Bankruptcy Proceedings Necessary or Appropriate?

1. *Bankruptcy's Advantages.* Given that bankruptcy involves real costs, see, e.g., §§ 326, 330, 331, that reduce the amounts available for distribution to creditors, what circumstances would lead creditors to force an unwilling debtor into involuntary bankruptcy rather than to pursue their state law remedies? Consider the following factors:

(a) The bankruptcy court's collection and enforcement mechanisms. §§ 363, 542, 543, 704(1). These should be contrasted with the collection mechanisms available under state law, as noted in

Chapters 6 and 7. Does the Bankruptcy Act offer significant advantages?

(b) Creditors may prefer a bankruptcy setting for reasons other than the rights such a proceeding provides against the debtor. Creditors may fear each other as much or more than they fear the debtor and may look to bankruptcy proceedings as a way to nullify other creditors' leads in the collection process. One creditor with a head-start in filing suit against the debtor may be on the verge of obtaining a substantial portion of the debtor's assets. Or the debtor simply may prefer paying one creditor to paying the others.

(c) Bankruptcy law may contain a substantive rule that favors (or disfavors) particular creditors. For example, § 545(3), (4) invalidates in bankruptcy landlords' liens on a lessee's property. This suggests that many landlords should favor a nonbankruptcy setting for resolving disputes. For creditors competing with landlords, however, § 545 may provide sufficient reason to resort to bankruptcy.

If state law limits collection mechanisms, favors creditors who win races to courthouses, and allows debtors to prefer one creditor over others, should bankruptcy law impose a different set of rules?

2. *The Old Acts of Bankruptcy.* Section 3 of the Bankruptcy Act of 1898 read in part as follows:

Acts of Bankruptcy

a. Acts of bankruptcy by a person shall consist of his having (1) concealed, removed, or permitted to be concealed or removed any part of his property, with intent to hinder, delay, or defraud his creditors or any of them, or made or suffered a transfer of any of his property, fraudulent under the provisions of section 67 or 70 of this Act; or (2) made or suffered a preferential transfer, as defined in subdivision a of section 60 of this Act; or (3) suffered or permitted, while insolvent, any creditor to obtain a lien upon any of his property through legal proceedings or distraint and not having vacated or discharged such lien within thirty days from the date thereof or at least five days before the date set for any sale or other disposition of such property; or (4) made a general assignment for the benefit of his creditors; or (5) while insolvent or unable to pay his debts as they mature, procured, permitted, or suffered voluntarily or involuntarily the appointment of a receiver or trustee to take charge of his property; or (6) admitted in writing his inability to pay his debts and his willingness to be adjudged a bankrupt.

b. A petition may be filed against a person within four months after the commission of an act of bankruptcy. . . .

c. It shall be a complete defense to any proceedings under the first act of bankruptcy to allege and prove that the party proceeded against was not insolvent as defined in this Act at the time of the filing of the petition against him. If solvency at such date is proved by the alleged bankrupt, the proceedings shall be dismissed. In such proceedings the burden of proving solvency shall be on the alleged bankrupt.

The following statement from the Commission Report, pt. I, at 14, summarizes some of the problems with old § 3.

The Commission has encountered a generally prevalent opinion in the business community that a major factor explaining the smallness of distributions in business bankruptcies is the delay in the institution of proceedings for liquidation until assets are largely depleted. Debtors are reluctant to file voluntary petitions until after the situation has become hopeless, and creditors are obliged to allege and prove the commission of one of six acts of bankruptcy. For most of these acts the petitioner must be able to establish that the debtor was insolvent at the time the act was committed. Insolvency is defined in the Act as insufficiency of the debtor's property at a fair valuation to pay his debts. It is frequently difficult for a debtor's creditors to establish this fact, and the debtor is entitled to jury trial of the issue of whether he committed an act of bankruptcy.

The demand for a jury trial delays the disposition of the involuntary petition, and not infrequently the estate suffers a further diminution in value during the interim between the filing of the petition and the ultimate resolution of the issues raised by the petition and answer thereto. While a receiver may be appointed during the interim, the creditor must post a bond to protect the debtor in the event that the petition and the receivership have resulted in damage to the debtor. The receivership itself adds to the cost of administration when an adjudication does ensue.

Compare the standards for granting petitioning creditors relief under old § 3 with the standards contained in § 303(h) of the new bankruptcy act. Which set of standards best defines the circumstances when a federal bankruptcy proceeding becomes a useful or necessary adjunct to state debt collection laws? Is it necessary or appropriate to allow creditors access to federal bankruptcy proceedings whenever the debtor is generally not paying his debts as they become due? Why is not state law sufficient to deal with this form of debtor behavior?

Consider the following:

New § 303(h) removes much of the unnecessary bulk of old § 3. But it does so at substantial cost. For it is arguable that § 3 better reflects the spirit in which the bankruptcy law should operate than does § 303. There is no obvious reason to offer creditors the opportunity to displace state collection mechanisms merely because the debtor is not paying his debts. Under § 3, involuntary bankruptcy proceedings required one of the listed acts of bankruptcy. The debtor had to be doing something more than not paying his bills on time. The acts-of-bankruptcy requirement implemented this idea by requiring some instance of debtor misbehavior that suggested a genuine need for resort to a federal bankruptcy proceeding. Undoubtedly, the acts enumerated in § 3 needed some refinement. But it is far from clear that the entire concept should have been scrapped. Its elimination portends a major shift in attitude towards involuntary bankruptcy. Any creditor or group of creditors who feels the debtor is not paying quickly enough may bypass state collection law and trigger a federal bankruptcy.

3. *Failure to Pay One Debt.* May failure to timely pay a single debt satisfy the requirements of § 303(h)(1)? See In re Blaine Richards & Co., Inc., 16 B.R. 362 (Bkrtcy.E.D.N.Y.1982) (yes, under appropriate circumstances). Should the weighty mechanism of a federal bankruptcy proceeding be available without some stronger showing that state law is inadequate to handle the task of collecting a single debt?

4. *Economic Analysis of Involuntary Bankruptcy.* Scholars sometimes seek to justify or explain the existence of a set of legal rules on the ground that the rules reflect the bargain the parties would have reached through private negotiation. R. Posner, Economic Analysis of Law (3d ed. 1986). In the bankruptcy area, Professor Jackson has attempted to explain the existence of a government enforced set of bankruptcy rules on this ground. He argues that a collective system like bankruptcy, in which all unsecured claims are treated alike, offers creditors three advantages. It reduces the individual collection risks of each creditor; they need not worry about who wins the race to the courthouse. It may increase the pool of assets to which creditors may look for repayment by preventing "a piecemeal dismantling of a debtor's business by the untimely removal of necessary operating assets." Third, a collective proceeding may be administratively more efficient. Professor Jackson concludes:

> The three considerations I have described above make it likely that a general unsecured creditor will agree to a collective system in lieu of a scheme of individualistic remedies. No single creditor, however, would agree to be bound to this collective system unless it were a compulsory system binding all other creditors: to allow the debtor to contract with other creditors on an opt-out basis would destroy the advantages of a collective proceeding.

Jackson, Bankruptcy, Non-Bankruptcy Entitlements, and the Creditors' Bargain, 91 Yale L.J. 857, 864, 866 (1982).

May one apply this method of analysis to the Bankruptcy Act's treatment of involuntary bankruptcy? If creditors would approve a collective system akin to the bankruptcy system, what sort of rules would they opt for to regulate access to that system? Would nonpayment of a single debt trigger access? Would creditors require some showing beyond generally not paying one's debts as they become due?

How would the creditors' bargain model work to deal with invocation of bankruptcy by involuntary creditors, such as tort claimants?

See generally Honsberger, Failure to Pay One's Debts Generally As They Become Due: The Experience of France and Canada, 54 Am. Bankr.L.J. 153 (1980).

IN RE ZADOCK REID

United States Court of Appeals, Seventh Circuit, 1985.
773 F.2d 945.

Before WOOD, CUDAHY and FLAUM, CIRCUIT JUDGES.

FLAUM, CIRCUIT JUDGE.

This case involves an appeal by a debtor from the district court's grant of an emergency application for the appointment of an interim trustee to take possession of the debtor's personal assets for the benefit of creditors. The main issue presented is whether the district court properly granted the creditor's application for the appointment of an interim trustee pursuant to 11 U.S.C. § 303(g) (1982). We reverse and remand.

I.

On June 29, 1984, the petitioning creditors-appellees, Dale R. Schmid, D.D.S., Ralph F. Schmid, Katherine G. Dengler, and Michael Overfield (the "creditors") filed an involuntary petition against Zaddock & Co., Inc. ("Zaddock"). On July 2, 1984, the district court appointed an interim trustee, Nathan Yorke ("Yorke"), to manage the company's business. One week later, the interim trustee held a hearing at which the president and principal shareholder of Zaddock, J.B.W. Reid ("Reid"), was examined. Except for questions as to his name and legal residence, Reid declined to answer all of the questions posed by counsel for the interim trustee, claiming his constitutional right against self-incrimination.

On July 13, 1984, the same creditors filed another involuntary petition against Reid individually, alleging that the creditors had claims in excess of $5,000 that were not contingent as to liability and that arose out of several demand notes. The creditors further alleged upon information and belief that Reid had commingled his assets with those of Zaddock.

On July 17, 1984, the creditors filed an emergency application for the appointment of an interim trustee against Reid. The creditors claimed that the court had to appoint an interim trustee in order to preserve the property of Reid's estate or to prevent loss to the estate pursuant to 11 U.S.C. § 303(g) (1982). Specifically, the creditors alleged that Reid may have been transferring certain of Zaddock's assets to foreign jurisdictions, that the interim trustee appointed to manage Zaddock believed that Reid had commingled his assets with those of Zaddock, and that Reid had implied that substantial assets of Zaddock were in Jamaican banks. After a review of the evidence presented at a hearing on the creditors' application, the district court concluded that

Reid totally controlled and directed Zaddock and that he had commingled his individual funds with those of the corporation. The court appointed Yorke as an interim trustee and set bond at $10,000.

On appeal, Reid challenges the appointment of the interim trustee, claiming that: (1) the creditors did not have standing to file the involuntary petition, (2) the creditors did not sustain their burden of proving that an interim trustee was imperative for the preservation of Reid's estate, (3) the creditors did not establish that Reid had commingled his assets with those of Zaddock, and (4) the $10,000 bond set by the district court was insufficient to indemnify Reid against possible loss to his property.

II.

Reid's first argument to this court is that the petitioning creditors did not have standing to file the involuntary petition in bankruptcy against the debtor because they did not meet the Bankruptcy Code's requirements for a creditor entitled to commence such a petition. We will proceed to scrutinize carefully the creditors' filing of the involuntary petition in this case because the courts have held that the filing of an involuntary petition is an extreme remedy with serious consequences to the alleged debtor, such as loss of credit standing, inability to transfer assets and carry on business affairs, and public embarrassment. See, e.g., In re First Energy Leasing Corp., 38 B.R. 577, 585 (Bankr.E.D.N.Y.1984); In re McMeekin, 18 B.R. 177, 177–78 (Bankr.D. Mass.1982). Since we agree with Reid that the creditors did not have standing to bring the involuntary petition, we must reverse the district court's appointment of the interim trustee.

Section 303(b)(1) of the Bankruptcy Act of 1978, as amended by the Bankruptcy Amendments and Federal Judgeship Act of 1984, provides that an involuntary case may be commenced against a debtor by three or more creditors, "each of which is . . . a holder of a claim against such person that is not contingent as to liability or the subject of a bona fide dispute . . . ." 11 U.S.C.A. § 303(b)(1) (West Supp.1985).[1] Prior to this amendment, a creditor only had to meet the requirement that his claim not be contingent as to liability in order to file an involuntary petition. 11 U.S.C. § 303(b)(1) (1982). The 1984 amendment to section 303(b)(1), which added the requirement that the creditors' claims not be the subject of a bona fide dispute became effective on July 10, 1984. Bankruptcy Amendments and Federal Judgeship Act of 1984, Pub.L. No. 98–353, § 553(b), 98 Stat. 392 (1984). Since the involuntary petition in the present case was filed on July 13, 1984, three days after the amendment to section 303(b)(1) had taken effect, the creditors were required to show that their claims were not contingent as to liability or the subject of a bona fide dispute.

---

1. Section 101(4)(A) of the Bankruptcy Act of 1978 defines a "claim" as a right to payment, whether or not such right is reduced to judgment, liquidated, unliquidated, fixed, contingent, matured, unmatured, disputed, undisputed, legal, equitable, secured, or unsecured. 11 U.S.C. § 101(4)(A) (1982).

In the present case, we find that the creditors' claims are "the subject of a bona fide dispute."[2] Before the 1984 amendment to section 303(b)(1) added the requirement that a creditor's claim not be the subject of a bona fide dispute, there were numerous cases holding that a creditor did have standing to bring an involuntary petition even if his claim was disputed. See, e.g., In the Matter of Covey, 650 F.2d 877, 881–82 (7th Cir.1981); In re Dill, 30 B.R. 546, 549 (Bankr. 9th Cir.1983), aff'd, 731 F.2d 629, 631 (9th Cir.1984); In re Marshall, 37 B.R. 108, 110 (Bankr.S.D.Fla.1984); In re Longhorn 1979–II Drilling Program, 32 B.R. 923, 926 (Bankr.W.D.Okla.1983). Several courts however, expressed doubt that Congress really intended for a creditor to be able to bring a claim under section 303(b)(1) when that claim was subject to serious dispute. See, e.g., In re B.D. International Discount Corp., 701 F.2d 1071, 1076 (2d Cir.), cert. denied, 464 U.S. 830, 104 S.Ct. 108, 78 L.Ed.2d 110 (1983); *In re First Energy Leasing*, 38 B.R. at 582. In *In re First Energy Leasing*, the bankruptcy court explained that it felt constrained by the expansive grant of eligibility in section 303(b)(1) to allow a creditor to file an involuntary petition even if the claim was disputed. 38 B.R. at 582. However, the court noted that the dilemma in which it found itself could be resolved if Congress would define the term "contingent" in such a way so as to subsume "disputed" claims. Id. The court concluded that it was reticent to take such a step in the absence of some basis in either the statute or its legislative history. Id. See also 2 King, Collier on Bankruptcy ¶ 303.08[11][b], at 303–33, 303–36 (15th ed. 1984) (the 1984 amendment to section 303(b)(1) holding that creditors with claims in "bona fide dispute" cannot file an involuntary petition changes reasoning and result of a significant number of cases dealing with disputed claims).

Since Congress amended section 303(b)(1) in 1984, a creditor cannot bring a claim that is subject to a bona fide dispute. In the present case, we hold that the creditors' claims that Reid was commingling his assets with those of Zaddock were the subject of a bona fide dispute. Throughout all of the proceedings, Reid has not admitted his liability as to any of the creditors' claims nor has he ever executed any guaranty or document rendering him personally liable for the company's debts. Although the creditors, at the hearing held before the district court to

2. Reid argues that the creditors' claims, which are based on Reid's personal liability as an alter ego of the corporate debtor, Zaddock, are contingent as to liability since Reid's liability for the company's debts could only arise upon the occurrence of an extrinsic event—a finding of personal liability by a competent judicial tribunal. See In re Turner, 32 B.R. 244, 247–48 (Bankr.D.Mass.1983). We note that the cases appear to be in conflict as to whether a creditor, whose right to payment depends on the obtaining of a judgment, is qualified to file an involuntary petition. Compare In re Turner, 32 B.R. at 247–48 (holding such claims to be contingent); In re All Media Properties, Inc., 5 B.R. 126, 133 (Bankr.S.D.Tex.1980) (same), aff'd, 646 F.2d 193 (5th Cir.1981) with In re Longhorn 1979–II Drilling Program, 32 B.R. 923, 927–29 (Bankr.W.D.Okla.1983) (holding such claims to be noncontingent); In re Dill, 30 B.R. 546, 549 (Bankr. 9th Cir.1983) (same), aff'd, 731 F.2d 629 (9th Cir.1984). However, we need not decide whether the creditors' claims in the present case are contingent as to liability because we find that they are the subject of a bona fide dispute.

determine whether the court should appoint an interim trustee, produced evidence that checks from Zaddock's corporate account were issued to Reid, this evidence does not support the conclusion that Reid commingled his assets with those of Zaddock, especially when these checks could have been compensation for Reid's services to the corporation or merely loans to Reid. We conclude that the creditors' allegations that Reid commingled his assets with those of Zaddock and that Reid is personally liable for the company's debts are claims subject to a bona fide dispute,[3] and thus that the creditors did not have standing to bring their involuntary petition.

In conclusion, we reverse the district court's grant of the creditors' involuntary petition for the appointment of an interim trustee and remand the case to the district court for further proceedings consistent with this opinion.

CUDAHY, CIRCUIT JUDGE, concurring:

I agree that the petitioning creditors have not established the absence of a bona fide dispute with respect to their claims against Zadock Reid. I would therefore expressly authorize the district court on remand to conduct further evidentiary proceedings to determine whether the dispute as to Reid's liability is bona fide.

HARLINGTON WOOD, JR., CIRCUIT JUDGE, dissenting.

Not being prepared to depart from Chief Judge McGarr's legal and practical view of this case, I must respectfully dissent.

The petitioning creditors filed an emergency application for the appointment of an interim trustee on the basis that Reid had commingled his personal assets with those of Zaddock Co., Inc., the subject of a related bankruptcy. After an evidentiary hearing Judge McGarr determined that those allegations were correct and that the corporate veil, a very transparent one, should be pierced. Reid, it was found, totally controlled the corporations and had used the corporate assets as his own. Judge McGarr, in coming to this conclusion, received no help from Reid as Reid declined to testify on the grounds that he might incriminate himself.

The interim trustee appointed in the Zaddock bankruptcy did testify. He told of his unavailing search for original corporate books and records. Nevertheless he was able to determine that there was corporate indebtedness of about $5,000,000, much of which was due and owing these petitioning creditors. The interim trustee also determined that during one period of time Reid had used about $45,000 of corporate funds for his and his wife's personal and family expenses. In addition, based on information from two persons formerly associated with the

3. We note that there has not yet been a judicial determination that the corporate veil should be pierced, thereby rendering Reid personally liable for the company's debts. As the creditors acknowledged in their brief before this court, the district court's decision to appoint an interim trustee based on the evidence submitted by the creditors was only a preliminary factual determination and was not an adjudication on the merits of the dispute.

corporation, the interim trustee had reason to believe that there were three banks in Jamaica in which Reid had personal accounts but which contained corporate funds. This confirmed the petitioners' allegation, based on what Reid himself had previously indicated, that there were substantial corporate funds in Jamaica. There is no need, however, for our present purposes to reexamine all the evidence in detail. The evidence is sufficient, in my judgment, to fully support Judge McGarr's findings and actions, the seriousness of which he fully understood. Judge McGarr appointed Nathan York, interim trustee in the corporate bankruptcy, as interim trustee of Reid's personal estate because of his already existing knowledge of the circumstances. If it turns out that an interim trustee is unnecessary the trusteeship can be terminated.

The majority holds that the allegations of commingling which would make Reid personally liable for the unpaid corporate notes, are claims subject to a bona fide dispute and therefore under Section 303(b)(1) cannot constitute a basis for involuntary bankruptcy. The mere fact that Reid does not admit raiding the corporation does not make it a bona fide or legitimate dispute. Judge McGarr resolved any doubt there may have been by finding that the petitioners' allegations were in fact true and fully justified appointing an interim trustee.

Under the bona fide dispute rule as viewed and applied by the majority these hapless creditors will have standing when that standing may likely be worthless. Judge McGarr is being told not to shut the barn door until it is absolutely certain that the horse is already gone. The evidence strongly suggests that in the meantime any personal or corporate assets that Reid may still have may become conveniently out of his creditors' reach in sunny Jamaica, but not out of his.

Notes & Questions

1. *Allocating the Risk of Error.* How should the bankruptcy system approach the question of the possibility of "incorrect" involuntary bankruptcy filings? Should the system be indifferent as between erroneously subjecting a debtor to a bankruptcy proceeding and erroneously denying the debtor's creditors access to the bankruptcy proceeding they wish to commence? Can one view the multiple creditor requirement of § 303 (in some cases) as an effort to be sure that a debtor "belongs" in bankruptcy?

2. *Debtor's Strategy.* Suppose the filing of a successful involuntary bankruptcy petition would stand a good chance of ruining the debtor's business (perhaps the business in question is a law firm). The debtor is in a dispute with the creditor over the amount of the claim. Debtor says she owes $10, creditor claims to be owed $10,000. Should the debtor change her position and assert that she owes $0 instead of $10?

3. *The Governing Factors.* What factors should a court take into account in deciding whether a dispute is bona fide? Should a simple denial of liability by the debtor suffice? Should the court conduct a brief examination of the merits of the creditor's claim? Is it likely that

the district court did that in *Reid?* Should the Court of Appeals have examined the merits of the dispute more closely?

4. *The Creditors' Bargain.* If one were to apply the creditors' bargain model to this problem, see supra, what standard would an unsecured creditor vote for? Where would such a creditor want the risk of error to fall—on the side of erroneously allowing or erroneously disallowing an involuntary bankruptcy? Can a creditor approach this question without being told what kind of claim he has?

5. *The Consequences to the Creditor of an Erroneous Involuntary Petition.* Assume that on remand in *Reid* the district court concludes that the involuntary petition should be dismissed. What problems would such a decision raise for those dealing with Reid during the interim period between the filing of the involuntary petition and the time at which the court found in favor of Reid? See §§ 507(a)(2), 502(f), 549(b). What problems arise for a debtor in Reid's position who has a valid defense to the involuntary filing? Section 303(e), (i) of the Bankruptcy Act may provide some relief for debtors who prevail against efforts to force them into involuntary bankruptcy.

6. *The Infrequency of Involuntary Petitions.* Only about one percent of bankruptcy filings are involuntary petitions. Why? Does the infrequency of involuntary filings render them unimportant?

7. *Triggering Phrases.* Note that some Bankruptcy Act provisions become operative after the "order for relief," (see § 341) whereas many other provisions are triggered by "the filing of the petition," e.g., § 362, or the "commencement of the case." E.g., § 541. In a voluntary case, the commencement of the case, the filing of the petition, and the order for relief appear to be synonymous. In an involuntary case, commencement of the case under § 303 by filing a petition is distinct from the order for relief. See § 303(h).

B. Assets of the Estate

Section 541 contains the standards for determining whether property is "property of the estate." In a Chapter 7 (liquidating) bankruptcy, property of the estate is distributed to the debtor's creditors. § 726. (The debtor may keep his exempt property. § 522.) Thus, inclusion of property in the estate usually means that the debtor must surrender the property for the benefit of creditors. Exclusion from the estate usually leaves property available to the debtor. The debtor's future earnings constitute the most important class of property not included in Chapter 7 estate. Cf. § 541(a)(6). How should one approach the question of the assets to be included in a debtor's estate? Should creditors be able to reach in bankruptcy any assets that they could not reach outside of bankruptcy?

The Background of § 541

Section 70a of the Bankruptcy Act of 1898, states in part:

> a.   The trustee of the estate of a bankrupt . . . shall . . . be vested by operation of law with the title of the bankrupt as of the date of the filing of the petition initiating a proceeding under this Act, except insofar as it is to property which is held to be exempt, to all of the following kinds of property wherever located . . . (5) property, including rights of action, which prior to the filing of the petition he could by any means have transferred or which might have been levied upon and sold under judicial process against him, or otherwise seized, impounded, or sequestered: *Provided,* That rights of action ex delicto for libel, slander, injuries to the person of the bankrupt or a relative, whether or not resulting in death, seduction, and criminal conversation shall not vest in the trustee unless by the law of the State such rights of action are subject to attachment, execution, garnishment, sequestration, or other judicial process . . . (6) rights of action arising upon contracts, or usury, or the unlawful taking or detention of or injury to his property . . . ..

Perceived difficulties with § 70a, noted below, led to enactment of § 541.

The Commission Report, pt. 1, at 193–94, endorsed the following analysis by Professor Countryman:

> On balance, there is little to justify the distinctions made in sections 70a(5) and (6) among: (1) types of property which vest in the trustee regardless of transferability or vulnerability to creditors' process; (2) those which vest only if subject to creditors' process; and (3) those which vest if either transferable or subject to creditors' process. The results are far from uniform and very often are the products of archaic state rules harking back to the days when causes of action and other nonpossessory interests were generally regarded as nontransferable or to equally archaic state statutes governing attachment, garnishment and execution. Even where the state law may be said to reflect some special concern for debtors, such concern is so haphazard that it should not be embodied in what is supposed to be a uniform bankruptcy law.

> It would be preferable to replace sections 70a(5) and (6) with a single provision giving the trustee title, as of the date of bankruptcy . . . .. If the trustee then finds that there is no effective way he can sell and assign a particular type of property without delaying the closing of the estate he can abandon it. (Or, alternatively, the Bankruptcy Act could authorize the trustees to make an effective transfer of property nontransferable under nonbankruptcy law.) To the extent that it is thought, as a matter of federal bankruptcy policy, that certain amounts of types of property should be saved to aid in the bankrupt's rehabilitation, that is a matter for a separate,

federal bankruptcy exemption policy. It should not be a reason for cluttering up section 70a with references to nonuniform state law on transferability and reach of judicial process.

The House Report on the Bankruptcy Act states:

> The bill makes significant changes in what constitutes property of the estate. Current law is a complicated melange of references to State law, and does little to further the bankruptcy policy of distribution of the debtor's property to his creditor in satisfaction of his debts. The Bankruptcy Commission explored the subject and the need for change in depth, and it is not necessary to repeat that discussion here.

> The bill determines what is property of the estate by a simple reference to what interests in property the debtor has at the commencement of the case. This includes all interests, such as interests in real or personal property, tangible and intangible property, choses in action, causes of action, rights such as copyrights, trade-marks, patents, and processes, contingent interests and future interests, whether or not transferable by the debtor. . . .

> These changes will bring anything of value that the debtors have into the estate. The exemption section will permit an individual debtor to take out of the estate that property that is necessary for a fresh start and for the support of himself and his dependents. . . .

> Paragraph (1) also has the effect of overruling Lines v. Frederick. . . .

House Report at 175–76, 368. How does § 541(a) differ from § 70a? Which provision provides the sounder approach? Were there other ways to deal with the confusing guidance in § 70a? Why is it important to have nationwide uniformity in defining what assets are included in the bankruptcy estate? Does bankruptcy law tolerate nonuniformity in other important areas? Does § 541(a)'s broad reach introduce new problems?

LINES v. FREDERICK

Supreme Court of the United States, 1970.
400 U.S. 18, 91 S.Ct. 113, 27 L.Ed.2d 124.

Per Curiam. This case presents the question of whether a bankrupt wage earner's vacation pay, accrued but unpaid at the time of the filing of his petition, passes to the trustee in bankruptcy as "property" under § 70a(5) of the Bankruptcy Act, 30 Stat. 565, as amended, 11 U.S.C.A. § 110(a)(5). The facts are not in dispute. Respondent Frederick, employed by a large manufacturing company, had accrued vacation pay of $137.28 at the time he filed his petition. He could collect this sum either during the annual period when his employer shut down the plant in which he worked, or on final termination of his employment. Respondent Harris had accrued vacation pay of $144.14, which he could draw either on termination or under a conventional voluntary vacation plan of his employer. In each case, the referee in bankruptcy made a "turnover order" requiring the bankrupt to pay to the trustee on receipt all of his accrued vacation pay, less one-half of that part accrued during the 30 days prior to the filing of the petition (the deducted sum being exempt under Cal.Code Civ.Proc. § 690.11 (Supp.1970)).

The District Court affirmed the referee in both cases, but the Court of Appeals for the Ninth Circuit reversed, holding that accrued but unpaid vacation pay is not "property" under the statute, and therefore finding it unnecessary to decide whether such accrued pay meets the further statutory requirement of being "transferable." As the Court of Appeals noted, its decision was squarely in conflict with that of the Court of Appeals for the Fifth Circuit in Kolb v. Berlin, 356 F.2d 269.

In Segal v. Rochelle, 382 U.S. 375, 379, 86 S.Ct. 511, 515, 15 L.Ed.2d 428, we said that "[t]he main thrust of § 70a(5) is to secure for creditors everything of value the bankrupt may possess in alienable or leviable form when he files his petition. To this end the term 'property' has been construed most generously and an interest is not outside its reach because it is novel or contingent or because enjoyment must be postponed." But we pointed out that " '[i]t is impossible to give any categorical definition to the word "property," nor can we attach to it in certain relations the limitations which would be attached to it in others.' "

The most important consideration limiting the breadth of the definition of "property" lies in the basic purpose of the Bankruptcy Act to give the debtor a "new opportunity in life and a clear field for future effort, unhampered by the pressure and discouragement of pre-existing debt. The various provisions of the Bankruptcy Act were adopted in the light of that view and are to be construed when reasonably possible in harmony with it so as to effectuate the general purpose and policy of the act." Local Loan Co. v. Hunt, 292 U.S. 234, 244–245, 54 S.Ct. 695, 699, 78 L.Ed. 1230 (citations omitted).

In Segal v. Rochelle, supra, the question was whether loss-carry-back tax refunds arising out of business losses immediately prior to bankruptcy but not collected until the end of the calendar year were property subject to a turnover order in favor of the trustee. In that case, as in this one, the problem of classification for purposes of the Bankruptcy Act could not be resolved simply by reference to the time when the right to the payment "vested," or to definitions of property drawn from other areas of the law. The Court looked to the purposes of the Act and concluded that the tax refund claim was "sufficiently rooted in the pre-bankruptcy past and so little entangled with the bankrupt's ability to make an unencumbered fresh start that it should be regarded as 'property' under § 70a(5)." 382 U.S., at 380, 86 S.Ct., at 515.

Applied to the set of facts before us here, the principles reflected in the earlier cases compel a decision for the bankrupt. In *Segal,* a business had ceased to operate and the task of the trustees in bankruptcy was to marshal whatever assets were left for distribution to the creditors. The tax refund claim, arising out of the operations of the business and specifically out of the losses that had precipitated its failure, was such an asset. By contrast, the respondents here are wage earners whose sole source of income before and after bankruptcy, is their weekly earnings. The function of their accrued vacation pay is to support the basic requirements of life for them and their families during brief vacation periods or in the event of layoff. Since it is a part of their wages, the vacation pay is "a specialized type of property presenting distinct problems in our economic system." Sniadach v. Family Finance Corp., 395 U.S. 337, 340, 89 S.Ct. 1820, 1822, 23 L.Ed.2d 349. Where the minimal requirements for the economic survival of the debtor are at stake, legislatures have recognized that protection that might be unnecessary or unwise for other kinds of property may be required. See, e.g., the Consumer Credit Protection Act, § 301, 82 Stat. 163, 15 U.S.C.A. § 1671.

The wage-earning bankrupt who must take a vacation without pay or forgo a vacation altogether cannot be said to have achieved the "new opportunity in life and [the] clear field for future effort, unhampered by the pressure and discouragement of preexisting debt," Local Loan Co. v. Hunt, supra, which it was the purpose of the statute to provide.

The motion of respondent Harris to proceed *in forma pauperis* is granted. The motion of respondent Frederick to dispense with printing his brief in opposition is granted. The petition for certiorari is granted and the judgment is affirmed.

THE CHIEF JUSTICE is of the opinion that the petition for writ of certiorari should be denied.

MR. JUSTICE HARLAN, dissenting. In my view this case is another instance in which the pressure of an overcrowded docket has led the Court to deal summarily with an issue which, if deserving of our attention at all, is deserving of full-dress treatment. Moreover, the Court disposes of the case despite the opaqueness of the record and the uncertainty with regard to relevant California law.

Under the terms of respondent Frederick's employment, his employer credited him with one day's vacation pay for each month's work. From September 15, the date of bankruptcy, to December 23, the beginning of the shutdown and the enforced "vacation," Mr. Frederick presumably became entitled to a little over three days' pay. The same amount would have accrued to a person starting work on the date of bankruptcy with no debts or assets, the paradigm of "an unencumbered fresh start." Indeed, the order not only permitted Mr. Frederick a *fresh* start; it gave him a *head* start, to the extent of half a day's pay. Segal v. Rochelle, 382 U.S. 375, 86 S.Ct. 511, 15 L.Ed.2d 428 (1966), and Local Loan Co. v. Hunt, 292 U.S. 234, 54 S.Ct. 695, 78 L.Ed. 1230 (1934), therefore tend to support the position of the trustee rather than "compel a decision for the bankrupt."

However, respondents can muster forceful arguments in their support, even on the assumption that the accrued vacation pay was subject to the claims of creditors—a point of California law which the court below found it unnecessary to decide.

Since the question tendered for review is close and has split the courts of appeals, I would set the case for argument.

Notes & Questions

1. *Interpreting "Property."* How does § 541 overrule *Lines v. Frederick?* After enactment of § 541, does it remain open to a court to interpret a debtor's interest in an asset as not being "property" within the meaning of the Bankruptcy Act? A state divorce court found the debtor's medical degree and license to have a "current value" of $300,000 and awarded the debtor's spouse $60,000 of that value. If the debtor files a petition, are the degree and license property of the estate? See In re Lynn, 18 B.R. 501 (Bkrtcy.D.Conn.1982) (no).

In Chicago Board of Trade v. Johnson, 264 U.S. 1, 44 S.Ct. 232, 68 L.Ed. 533 (1924), the bankrupt was a member of the Chicago Board of Trade. A member who has paid all assessments, has no outstanding claims held against him by members, and has not impaired or forfeited his membership may, upon payment of a fee and subject to Board approval, transfer his membership. The bankrupt's membership was worth $10,500. The Supreme Court of Illinois had held "that the membership is not property or subject to judicial sale," basing its conclusion on the restrictions upon obtaining and transferring memberships. The Court held that the membership became part of the bankrupt's estate, but that the trustee's interest in the membership was subject to the rights of creditors who had properly objected to the transfer. Under § 541, may assets that are not "property" under state law become part of the estate?

2. *Post-Petition Assets.* On January 1, 1982 Debtor files a voluntary petition in bankruptcy. On January 2, 1982 Debtor wins $75,000 in a golf tournament. Does the $75,000 become an asset of the bankruptcy estate? Suppose that instead of winning the $75,000 Debtor inherited it on January 2. See § 541(a)(5)(A). Why the different treatment?

3. *Keeping Assets Out of the Estate.* Evaluate the following strategies for keeping assets beyond the reach of the trustee in bankruptcy in light of § 541(c):

(a) Secured Party inserts in the security agreement a clause that reads: "Debtor's interest in any property covered by this agreement automatically terminates upon the filing of a petition in bankruptcy."

(b) Secured Party inserts in the security agreement a clause that reads: "Debtor's interest in any property covered by this agreement automatically terminates if Debtor's assets fail to exceed Debtor's liabilities by at least $1,000."

(c) Debtor has a liquor license, transfer of which requires approval by a state authority. May the state revoke the liquor license upon the filing of a bankruptcy petition?

(d) The settlor of a trust fears that Debtor, if given outright control over money, will squander it. The settlor therefore provides that Debtor, the beneficiary, cannot sell, encumber, or transfer Debtor's interest in the trust.

EANES v. SHEPHERD

United States District Court, Western District of Virginia, 1983.
33 B.R. 984, reversed without opinion 735 F.2d 1354 (4th Cir.1984).

JAMES H. MICHAEL, JR., BANKRUPTCY JUDGE.

Appellants, Robert Clay and Janice Tew Eanes, bring this appeal challenging the final decision of the United States Bankruptcy Court for the Western District of Virginia handed down in a Memorandum Opinion and Order dated August 13, 1982. The question presented on appeal is whether the Bankruptcy Court erred in holding that the appellant-debtor may not exempt from the property of the bankrupt estate a personal injury cause of action. Appellants also contend that the Bankruptcy Court erred in failing to dismiss the joint objections filed by Jesse W. and Elizabeth F. Shepherd to appellants' claim of exempt property for failure to file within the time prescribed by Local Bankruptcy Rule 4005. Having been fully briefed, this appeal is now ripe for disposition.

On February 25, 1982, Robert C. Eanes, the appellant-debtor (hereinafter debtor) filed a petition constituting an order for relief under Chapter 7 of the United States Bankruptcy Code, 11 U.S.C. § 101 et seq. Debtor listed a cause of action for personal injury arising from an automobile accident as a contingent and unliquidated claim for damages for personal injury on Schedule B–2 filed with the petition. He also listed this claim among exempt property shown on Schedule B–4 filed with the petition. The debtor contends that his personal injury cause of action is exempt property under applicable state law pursuant to 11 U.S.C. § 522(b)(2)(A) of the Bankruptcy Code with up to the amount of $4,375.00 specifically claimed as exempt by virtue of § 34–4 of the Code of Virginia pursuant to the homestead deed filed in the Clerk's Office of the Circuit Court of Fluvanna County prior to the date of filing of the petition.

The trustee appointed in this case declined to object to the debtor's claim of exemption for his personal injury cause of action. However, several creditors of the debtor did file objections to the debtor's claim that the value of the personal injury cause of action was exempt property in so far as the value exceeds the amount of $4,375.00 claimed under the homestead exemption and deed. The joint objections filed by Jesse W. and Elizabeth F. Shepherd were filed with the court sixteen days following the date of the meeting of creditors, allegedly in violation of Local Bankruptcy Rule 4005.

On November 14, 1980, the debtor sustained personal injuries as a result of an automobile accident. The debtor maintains that these injuries gave rise to a legal cause of action against the negligent parties for damages he sustained including, but not limited to, lost earnings, pain and suffering, medical costs, diminished future earning capacity, and the cost of future medical treatments and operations necessitated by the injury. The statute of limitations for such a cause of action would not expire until after the date of filing of appellant's petition in Bankruptcy.

Debtor argued in the court below that his unliquidated, contingent claim for personal injury constituted property "exempt" under the law of Virginia, because such a property was not assignable by the debtor nor subject to any form of creditor process under Virginia law. Debtor contended that the provisions of § 522(b)(2), which state in pertinent part that "notwithstanding § 541 of this title, an individual debtor any exempt from property of the estate . . . any property that is exempt under state or local law that is applicable on the date of filing of the petition . . .", permit him to look to judicial, as well as statutory law for the determination of what property may be exempted.

The creditors argued that Virginia Code § 34–3.1 (1981 Cum.Supp.), which states that, "no individual may exempt from the property of the estate the property specified in subsection (d) of § 522 of the Bankruptcy Reform Act, except as may otherwise be expressly permitted under this title" is the exclusive source of permitted exemptions, and since no express exemption for personal injury claims is stated in Title 34, the claim must be included in the bankrupt estate. Creditors further argued that, even if resort to common law is permitted, such personal injury claims are subject to creditor process and are therefore not property subject to exemption.

The Bankruptcy Court rejected debtor's arguments, holding that Virginia Code § 34.3–1 controls what property may be held exempt from a bankrupt estate, and since there is no provision in Title 34 expressly permitting an individual to exempt a personal injury claim, debtor's claim for personal injury did not constitute an exemption within the meaning of 11 U.S.C. § 522. Both in the court below, and on appeal, the debtor submits that under 11 U.S.C. § 522, all applicable law of the state or locality, judicial and statutory, is an appropriate source for the determination of what property of the bankrupt may be taken as an exemption, and secondly, that under Virginia common law, claims for personal injury have long been recognized as non-transferable and immune from creditor process, thereby rendering such claims exempt from inclusion in the debtor's estate.

Under the Bankruptcy Reform Act of 1978, 11 U.S.C. § 101 et seq., the definition of the bankrupt's estate was changed. 11 U.S.C. § 541 defines the bankrupt's estate to include all legal and equitable interest in property, including property of the debtor needed for a fresh start. Whether the property of the estate may be given exempt status is determined by provisions of § 522 of the Code which begins, "[N]otwithstanding § 541 of this title, an individual debtor may exempt from property of the estate . . .". Thus, under the Code, even property held to be exempt will initially become property of the estate and will remain in the estate until such time as the exemption is taken. Consequently, 11 U.S.C. § 541(a)(1) makes the debtor's unliquidated and contingent right of action for damages for personal injury property of the bankrupt estate. The question becomes whether the claim may be exempted from the estate under 11 U.S.C. § 522(b)(2)(A).

Section 522 states in pertinent part:

(b) Notwithstanding section 541 of this Title, an individual debtor may exempt from property of the estate—

(1) property that is specified under subsection (d) of this section, unless the State law that is applicable to the debtor under paragraph (2)(A) of this subsection specifically does not so authorize; or, in the alternative,

(2)(A) any property that is exempt under Federal law, other than subsection (d) of this section, or State or local law that is applicable on the date of the filing of the petition at the place in which the debtor's domicile has been located for the 180 days immediately preceding the date of the filing of the petition, . . .

11 U.S.C. § 522(b).

Thus, Congress, after creating a "federal" exemption in the Code, deemed it appropriate to allow each state the opportunity to "opt out" of the exemptions listed in § 522(d) or mandate its own exemption laws. As a result, the Virginia General Assembly enacted Virginia Code § 34–3.1 (1982 Cum.Supp.) which opted Virginia out of the "federal" exemptions and denied Virginia debtors the right to choose the federal exemptions stated in § 522(d).

Section 522 provides in pertinent part that, "notwithstanding § 541 of this title, an individual debtor may exempt from property of the estate . . . any property that is exempt under federal law other than subsection (d) of this section or state or local law that is applicable on the date of the filing of the petition . . .". Thus, although the Virginia General Assembly has denied Virginia debtors the exemptions set forth in § 522(d), Virginia debtors may, in accordance with § 522(b) (2)(A) exempt from property of the estate property that is exempt under federal law, other than the exemptions listed in § 522(d), or property exempt under state or local law. Consequently, in order for this court to determine that appellants are entitled to the exemption, this court must find that Mr. Eanes' personal injury cause of action is exempt under federal non-bankruptcy law or applicable state and local law.

In deciding the question presented, the Bankruptcy Court reasoned that since nowhere in Title 34 of the Virginia Code is a contingent and unliquidated personal injury claim an expressly permitted exemption, such a claim is therefore not exempt under Bankruptcy Code § 522(b).

In so holding, the Bankruptcy Court apparently relied on Virginia Code § 34–3.1 (1982 Cum.Supp.), and the holding in In re Dummitt, 2 B.R. 136 (Bkrtcy.W.D.Va.1980), which held that no exemption exists unless the express language of Title 34 so provides.

Section 34–3.1 reads as follows:

Property specified in Bankruptcy Reform Act not exempt. No individual may exempt from the property of the estate in any bankruptcy proceeding the property specified in subsection (d) of § 522 of the Bankruptcy Reform Act, except as may otherwise be expressly permitted under this Title.

Virginia Code § 34–3.1 (1982 Cum.Supp.). Reliance on this statute is misplaced. 11 U.S.C. § 522(b)(1), the authority for this "opting out" statute, does not give the states the power to "opt out" of § 522 in its entirety, but the power is clearly limited by its language to excluding only the federal exemption specified in § 522(d). Bass v. Thacker, 5 B.R. 592 (Bkrtcy.W.D.Va.1980). See also Farmer's & Merchants Bank v. Boyd, 11 B.R. 690 (Bkrtcy.W.D.Va.1981). This court also finds the Bankruptcy Court's reasoning in *In re Dummitt*, supra, which held that no exemption exists unless permitted by the express language of Title 34 of the Virginia Code, to be erroneous and not supported by Virginia law. First, no Virginia case or statute stands for the proposition that exemptions only exist where expressly provided for in Title 34. In addition, numerous exemptions are provided for in other titles of the Virginia Code. 11 U.S.C. § 522(d) grants a property exemption to the debtor's right to receive public assistance benefits. A review of the statutes under Title 34 reveals no exemption for welfare benefits. However, Virginia Code § 63.1–88 (1980 Repl.Vol.) specifically exempts public assistance from the operation of bankruptcy laws. Similarly, compensation to crime victims (§ 19.2–368.–12(A)), Workmen's Compensation (§ 65.1–82), Life Insurance (§ 38.1–482), and Industrial Sick Benefits (§ 38.1–488), have each been given legislative protection as an exemption from the bankrupt estate, although Title 34 fails expressly to accord such properties exempt status. Consequently, this court finds no basis for the Bankruptcy Court's holding that exemptions are limited to those expressly provided for in Title 34 of the Virginia Code. Property is exempt under 11 U.S.C. § 522(b) if exempt under federal non-bankruptcy law or statutory or judicial Virginia law. In Re Ford, 3 B.R. 559 (Bkrtcy.Md.1980) aff'd, 638 F.2d 14 (4th Cir.1981).

Appellants contend that Mr. Eanes' unliquidated contingent claim for personal injury constitutes property that is exempt under the law of Virginia because such property is not assignable or subject to being reached by any form of creditor process under Virginia law. Appellees do not argue that Mr. Eanes' cause of action would not be exempt if neither assignable or subject to any form of creditor process under Virginia law, but rather assert that Mr. Eanes' claim is subject to several types of creditor process.

Appellees agree that a personal injury claim cannot be assigned. Virginia Code § 8.01–26 (1977 Repl.Vol.); City of Richmond v. Hanes, 203 Va. 102, 122 S.E.2d 895 (1961). They also agree that a contingent personal injury claim is not tangible personal property subject to levy or execution. Virginia Code § 8.01–478 (1977 Repl.Vol.). Finally, appellees concede that garnishment procedures would not apply to a personal injury claim. Lynch v. Johnson, 196 Va. 516, 84 S.E.2d 419 (1954).

Appellees submit, however, that a creditor can reach a contingent personal injury cause of action by way of writ of *fieri facias,* pursuant to Virginia Code § 8.01–501 (1977 Repl.Vol.). Appellees' theory, however, is necessarily premised upon the ground that Virginia Code § 8.01–501 is broad enough to include a "chose in action". See Evans v. Greenhow, 56 Va. (15 Gratt.) 153 (1859). However, in Dillard v. Collins, 66 Va. (25 Gratt.) 343 (1874), the Virginia Supreme Court of Appeals defined a "chose in action" to include only those "rights of action founded on contracts, or for injuries to property, and not rights of action for torts . . .". Moreover, the Virginia Supreme Court, in Boisseau v. Bass, 100 Va. 207, 209, 40 S.E. 647 (1902), specifically excluded contingent claims as property subject to the lien under Va. Code § 8.01–501 (1977 Repl.Vol.): "a debt which has a present existence, although payable in the future, may be subjected to a lien of *fieri facias,* but not a debt which rests upon a contingency which may or may not happen, and over which the court has no control." In *Boisseau,* the Virginia Supreme Court held that the interest of an assured in a life insurance policy, which was dependent for its continued existence on voluntary payments to be made in the future, was not an interest or estate that could be reached by the lien of *fieri facias.* Accordingly, such "properties" are exempt from creditor process. Appellees' contention that *Dillard v. Collins,* supra, predates passage of and contravenes the present wording of Virginia Code §§ 8.01–546, 547, 548, and 550 is not applicable. A review of these Code sections reveals that they pertain to tangible things, not contingent and unliquidated causes of action.

Finally, appellees submit that the statutory scheme of Virginia Code § 8.01–66.2 et seq. (1977 Repl.Vol.), illustrates how a contingent and unliquidated personal injury claim may be subjected to creditor process. Section 8.01–66.2 imposes a lien on the claim of a person who sustains personal injuries caused by the alleged negligence of another in favor of a hospital or physician who treats the injured person. Code § 8.01–66.9 creates a similar lien for the benefit of the Commonwealth in certain instances. However, Virginia Code § 8.01–66.11 (1977 Repl.Vol.), provides that no liability to pay these liens may exist against one alleged to have caused these injuries until the claim is reduced to settlement or judgment.

Despite appellees' contention, this court finds that Virginia Code § 8.01–66.1 et seq. represents specially created exemptions to the general rule that contingent personal injury claims are not subject to creditor process. Code § 8.01–66.2 establishes a limited lien ($500.00 in the case of a hospital, and $100.00 for each physician, nurse, or physical therapist) for professional services rendered by a hospital or physician, similar to an attorney's lien created when professional services are rendered. It is apparent that the Virginia General Assembly, realizing the immunity of contingent personal injury claims to general forms of creditor process, created a remedy for certain creditors by establishing a limited statutory lien on the proceeds of a personal injury claim. Absent such a statute, these designated creditors would be forced to collect their debts from other of the debtor's non-exempt assets.

This court's decision, to reverse the lower court, comports with the policy of the new Bankruptcy Act, to give liberal construction to exemption claims, particularly where the state has "opted out" of the federal exemption scheme. Cheeseman v. Nachman, 656 F.2d 60 (4th Cir.1981). In *Cheeseman* the court construed 11 U.S.C. § 522(m) to require that Virginia's statutory definition of "householder" (Virginia Code § 34.1) be interpreted to permit both spouses, rather than one spouse, to claim a homestead exemption despite the intent of the state legislature. The court stated that the "fresh start" policy of the Bankruptcy Act mandated a broad and liberal construction of debtor's exemptions. This court's ruling also comports with two recent, and factually analogous, decisions of the Bankruptcy Court holding that an unliquidated and contingent personal injury cause of action is exempt under § 522(b)(2)(A) because it is neither assignable nor subject to the reach of creditor process under Virginia law. In re Musgrove, 7 B.R. 892 (Bkrtcy.W.D.Va.1981); In re Tignor, 21 B.R. 219 (Bkrtcy.E.D.Va. 1982). In *Musgrove,* the Bankruptcy Court applied in its reasoning, "the line of authority that best comports with the underlying policies of the Bankruptcy Code and the current law on the subject in Virginia . . . ." in allowing the debtor to exempt a personal injury claim against his employer, brought under the Federal Employer's Liability Act. . . .

Accordingly, an appropriate Order will this day enter, reversing the August 13, 1982, Memorandum Opinion and Order of the Bankruptcy Court and remanding this action to the Bankruptcy Court for further proceedings not inconsistent with this Memorandum Opinion.

Notes & Questions

1. *Property Reachable under State Law.* Recall from Chapter 7 New York's CPLR § 5201(b), which states in part:

(b) *Property against which a money judgment may be enforced.* A money judgment may be enforced against any property which could be assigned or transferred, whether it consists of a present or future right or interest and whether or not it is vested, unless it is exempt from application to the satisfaction of the judgment.

CPLR §§ 5205 and 5206 contain express exemptions for specific classes of real and personal property. In disputes arising in New York outside of bankruptcy, does § 5201(b) effectively add to the debtor's package of exempt assets?

2. *The Old Act's Approach.* Under § 70a(5) of the old bankruptcy act, the trustee probably could not reach Eanes' personal injury claim in bankruptcy because the interest is neither transferable nor leviable. Given old § 70a(5), it probably did not matter whether state law expressly deemed an asset exempt or deemed assets beyond the reach of creditors by some provision like N.Y. CPLR § 5201(b). Does inclusion in the estate depend on whether state law expressly exempts assets or instead relies on some provision similar to CPLR § 5201(b) to protect them? Should anything turn on that?

Does the existence of a provision like CPLR § 5201(b) raise doubts about the Bankruptcy Act's focus on exemptions as the exclusive method for allowing the debtor to retain property? Does the new Act attach importance to a single concept—exemption—when state law uses differently phrased concepts—nontransferability and inalienability—to effectively treat assets as exempt? But see In re Musgrove, 7 B.R. 892 (Bkrtcy.W.D.Va.1981) (equating nonassignability under state law with exempt status under state law). See also § 522(b)(2)(B) (referring to property "exempt from process" under state law); Cal.Code Civ.Proc. § 704.210.

3. *Other Contingent Interests.* Recall Adams v. Dugan, Chapter 7, and creditors' inability in many states to reach a debtor's contingent interest in property. May creditors reach such interests in a bankruptcy proceeding? See In re Hicks, 22 B.R. 243 (Bkrtcy.N.D.Ga.1982) (seemingly not).

4. *Pension Interests.* Recall from Chapter 7 that the Internal Revenue Code provides favorable tax treatment for qualified pension plans which include qualified trusts. Internal Revenue Code § 401(a)(13) states in part: "A trust shall not constitute a qualified trust under this section unless the plan of which such trust is a part provides that benefits provided under the plan may not be assigned or alienated." Given § 401(a)(13) and § 541(c)(2) of the Bankruptcy Act (which honors spendthrift trust clauses), participants in many qualified pension plans may not have to worry about § 541's broad definition of property of the estate.

But many individuals are covered by pension plans that are not qualified and that need not necessarily contain a spendthrift trust type provision.[a] Even for those with qualified plans, is there some danger of

a. Many pension plans that are not qualified under IRC § 401(a) may be required to have provisions limiting assignment or alienation of benefits under the plan. The labor law title of the Employee Retirement Income Security Act of 1974 (ERISA) applies to many pension plans that are not qualified. Section 206(1) of ERISA's labor title, 29 U.S.C.A. § 1056(d)(1), provides that "Each pension plan shall provide that benefits provided under the plan may not be assigned or alienated." But § 206(d)(1) only applies to "pension plans," which § 3(2) of the labor title, 29 U.S.C.A. § 1002(2),

creditors reaching pension rights if state law does not honor spendthrift trust clauses? Cf. Regan v. Ross, 691 F.2d 81 (2d Cir. 1982) (when debtor wishes to use pension benefits to fund a Chapter 13 plan, benefits become part of estate even where state honors spendthrift trusts). Note that in many states a trust created by a settlor for her own benefit does not qualify as a spendthrift trust. Thus, a pension fund set up by a worker for herself may become part of the bankruptcy estate if state law would not treat it as a spendthrift trust. In re Graham, 726 F.2d 1268 (8th Cir. 1984); In re Goff, 706 F.2d 574 (5th Cir. 1983).

C. Exemptions

Dissatisfaction with state exemption systems, see Chapter 7, led to proposals for a set of federal exemptions to be available in bankruptcy. The House version of the Bankruptcy Reform Act of 1978 contained a system of federal exemptions that would have been available to all debtors regardless of state law. The Senate balked at this provision, leading to a compromise contained in § 522(b) and (d). The Bankruptcy Act contains a set of federal exemptions in § 522(d), but § 522(b) authorizes states to deprive debtors of the opportunity to avail themselves of the federal exemptions. Most states have enacted statutes prohibiting debtors from using the federal bankruptcy exemptions.

LOCKWOOD v. EXCHANGE BANK
Supreme Court of the United States, 1903.
190 U.S. 294, 23 S.Ct. 751, 47 L.Ed. 1061.

MR. JUSTICE WHITE, . . . delivered the opinion of the court:

The general exemption of property from levy or sale, authorized by article 9, § 1, ¶ 1, of the present Constitution of the state of Georgia (that of 1877), is "realty or personalty, or both, to the value in the aggregate of $1,600." By article 9, § 3, ¶ 1, of the same Constitution, a debtor is vested with power to waive or renounce in writing this right of exemption, "except as to wearing apparel, and not exceeding $300 worth of household and kitchen furniture and provisions." The mode

limits to plans maintained by an "employer or by an employee organization." The term "employer" does not appear to include governmental entities. Id. § 3(5), (9), 29 U.S.C.A. § 1002(5), (9). In addition, § 206(d)(1)'s requirements do not apply to unfunded plans "maintained by an employer primarily for the purpose of providing deferred compensation for a select group of management or highly compensated employees" or to certain tax exempt organizations. Id. § 201, 29 U.S.C.A. § 1051.

One other complication exists in sorting out the vulnerability of pension rights to creditor attacks. The language employed in § 206(d)(1) and in IRC § 401(a)(13) does not expressly state that pension benefits must be kept beyond the reach of creditors. The Internal Revenue Service, however, has interpreted § 401(a)(13) to mean that a trust will not be qualified unless the plan of which the trust is a part provides that benefits provided under the plan may not be anticipated, assigned (either at law or equity), alienated or subject to attachment, garnishment, levy, execution or other legal or equitable process. Treas.Reg. § 1.401(a)–13(b). See Chapter 7C.

of enforcement of a waiver of exemption is provided for in § 2850 of the Code of 1895, reading as follows:

"In all cases when any defendant in execution has applied for and had set apart a homestead of realty and personalty, or either, or where the same has been applied for and set apart out of his property, as provided for by the Constitution and laws of this state, and the plaintiff in execution is seeking to proceed with the same, and there is no property except the homestead on which to levy upon the ground that his debt falls within some one of the classes for which the homestead is bound under the Constitution, it shall and may be lawful for such plaintiff, his agent, or attorney, to make affidavit before any officer authorized to administer oaths that, to the best of his knowledge and belief, the debt upon which such execution is founded is one from which the homestead is not exempt, and it shall be the duty of the officer in whose hands the execution and affidavit are placed to proceed at once to levy and sell, as though the property had never been set apart. The defendant in such execution may, if he desires to do so, deny the truth of the plaintiff's affidavit by filing with the levying officer a counter affidavit."

The question presented on the record before us may be stated in similar language to that which was used by the district judge—the correctness of whose decision in the case at bar is now for review—in the course of his opinion in Re Woodruff, 96 Fed. 317, as follows (p. 318):

"Has the bankruptcy court jurisdiction to protect or enforce against the bankrupt's exemption the rights of creditors not having a judgment or other lien, whose promissory notes or other like obligations to pay contain a written waiver of the homestead and exemption authorized and prescribed by the Constitution of the state, or are such creditors to be remitted to the state courts for such relief as may be there obtained?"

The provisions of the bankruptcy act of 1898 which control the consideration of the question just propounded are as follows: By clause 11 of § 2 courts of bankruptcy are vested with jurisdiction to "determine all claims of bankrupts to their exemptions." Section 6 provides as follows:

"Sec. 6. This act shall not affect the allowance to bankrupts of the exemptions which are prescribed by the state laws in force at the time of the filing of the petition in the state wherein they have had their domicil for the six months or the greater portion thereof immediately preceding the filing of the petition."

By clause 8 of § 7 the bankrupt is required to schedule all his property, and to make "a claim for such exemptions as he may be entitled to." By clause 11 of § 47 it is made the duty of the trustees to "set apart the bankrupt's exemptions and report the items and estimated value thereof to the court as soon as practicable after their appoint-

ment." By § 67 it is provided, among other things, that the property of
the debtor fraudulently conveyed, etc., "shall, if he be adjudged a
bankrupt, and the same is not exempt from execution and liability for
debts by the law of his domicil, be and remain a part of the assets and
estate of the bankrupt," etc. In § 70 is enumerated the property of the
bankrupt which is to vest in the trustee as of the date of the adjudication in bankruptcy, "except in so far as it is to property which is
exempt."

Under the bankruptcy act of 1867 it was held that property generally exempted by the state law from the claims of creditors was not part
of the assets of the bankrupt, and did not pass to the assignee, but that
such property must be pursued by those having special claims against
it, in the proper state tribunals. Thus, speaking of the act of 1867, Mr.
Justice Bradley (Re Bass, 3 Woods, 382, 384, Fed.Cas. No. 1,091) said:

> "Not only is all property exempted by state laws, as those laws
> stood in 1871, expressly excepted from the operation of the convey-
> ance to the assignee, but is added in the section referred to, as if *ex
> industria* that 'these exceptions shall operate as a limitation upon
> the conveyance of the property of the bankrupt to his assignee, and
> in no case shall the property hereby excepted pass to the assignee,
> or the title of the bankrupt thereto be impaired or affected by any of
> the provisions of this title.'

> "In other words, it is made clear as anything can be that such
> exempted property constitutes no part of the assets in bankruptcy.
> The agreement of the bankrupt in any particular case to waive the
> right to the exemption makes no difference. He may owe other
> debts in regard to which no such agreement has been made. But
> whether so or not, it is not for the bankrupt court to inquire. The
> exemption is created by the state law, and the assignee acquires no
> title to the exempt property. If the creditor has a claim against it,
> he must prosecute that claim in a court which has jurisdiction over
> the property, which the bankrupt court has not."

We think that the terms of the bankruptcy act of 1898, above set
out, as clearly evidence the intention of Congress that the title to the
property of a bankrupt, generally exempted by state laws, should
remain in the bankrupt, and not pass to his representative in bankruptcy, as did the provisions of the act of 1867, considered in Re Bass. The
fact that the act of 1898 confers upon the court of bankruptcy authority
to control exempt property in order to set it aside, and thus exclude it
from the assets of the bankrupt estate to be administered, affords no
just ground for holding that the court of bankruptcy must administer
and distribute, as included in the assets of the estate, the very property
which the act, in unambiguous language, declares shall not pass from
the bankrupt, or become part of the bankruptcy assets. The two
provisions of the statute must be construed together, and both be given
effect. Moreover, the want of power in the court of bankruptcy to
administer exempt property is, besides, shown by the context of the act;

since, throughout its text, exempt property is contrasted with property not exempt, the latter alone constituting assets of the bankrupt estate subject to administration.   The act of 1898, instead of manifesting the purpose of Congress to adopt a different rule from that which was applied, as we have seen, with reference to the act of 1867, on the contrary, exhibits the intention to perpetuate the rule, since the provision of the statute to which we have referred in reason is consonant only with that hypothesis.

Though it be conceded that some inconvenience may arise from the construction which the text of the statute requires, the fact of such inconvenience would not justify us in disregarding both its letter and spirit.   Besides, if mere arguments of inconvenience were to have weight, the fact cannot be overlooked that the contrary construction would produce a greater inconvenience.   The difference, however, between the two is this: That in the latter case—that is, causing the exempt property to form a part of the bankruptcy assets—the inconvenience would be irremediable, since it would compel the administration of the exempt property as part of the estate in bankruptcy; whilst in the other, the rights of creditors having no lien, as in the case at bar, but having a remedy under the state law against the exempt property, may be protected by the court of bankruptcy, since, certainly, there would exist in favor of a creditor holding a waiver note, like that possessed by the petitioning creditor in the case at bar, an equity entitling him to a reasonable postponement of the discharge of the bankrupt, in order to allow the institution in the state court of such proceedings as might be necessary to make effective the rights possessed by the creditor.

As, in the case at bar, the entire property which the bankrupt owned is within the exemption of the state law, it becomes unnecessary to consider what, if any, remedy might be available in the court of bankruptcy for the benefit of general creditors, in order to prevent the creditor holding the waiver as to exempt property from taking a dividend on his whole claim from the general assets, and thereafter availing himself of the right resulting from the waiver to proceed against exempt property.

The judgment of the District Court is reversed, and the proceeding is remanded to that court with directions to overrule the exceptions to the trustee's assignment of homestead and exemption, and to withhold the discharge of the bankrupt, if he be otherwise entitled thereto, until a reasonable time has elapsed for the excepting creditor to assert, in a state tribunal, his alleged right to subject the exempt property to the satisfaction of his claim.   And it is so ordered.

Notes & Questions

1.   Lockwood *and the New Bankruptcy Act.*   The legislative history of § 541(a) states that "Paragraph (1) has the effect of overruling Lockwood v. Exchange Bank   .   .   .   because it includes as property of

the estate all property of the debtor, even that needed for a fresh start. After the property comes into the estate, then the debtor is permitted to exempt it under proposed 11 U.S.C.A. 522, and the court will have jurisdiction to determine what property may be exempted and what remains as property of the estate." House Report at 368.

What is the effect of the new Act on *Lockwood*'s holding that otherwise exempt assets may be available to creditors if state law so allows? See § 522(e). Does it make sense to allow states to opt out of the federal system of exemptions and then to prohibit states from limiting the exemptions provided as they please? Does § 522(e) make sense only in the context of a universally available system of federal exemptions?

2. *Pension Exemption.* When the legislative history of § 541(a) was written, § 522(d)(10), which protects pensions, was part of the Bankruptcy Act and the opt out provision in § 522(b) was not. Does this suggest an interpretation of § 541 that might save some pensions (and other assets) from becoming part of the estate? Consider the following:

EISENBERG, BANKRUPTCY LAW IN PERSPECTIVE, 28 UCLA L.Rev. 953, 972–73 n. 60 (1981)

In states where state law now precludes resort to federal exemptions, on the surface debtors appear to be no worse off than they were under the old bankruptcy act. Under the old act, state law determined a debtor's bankruptcy exemptions. Bankruptcy Act of 1898 § 6. Upon further analysis, however, debtors are likely to be worse off under the new act than under the old. Under the old law, exemptions did not provide the only legitimate route through which debtors could keep assets despite bankruptcy. Courts allowed debtors to keep additional nonexempt assets out of the estate by construing such assets not to be "property" within the meaning of § 70a of the old act, see Lines v. Frederick; Chicago Board of Trade v. Johnson, 264 U.S. 1, 44 S.Ct. 232, 68 L.Ed. 533 (1923); Page v. Edmunds, 187 U.S. 596, 23 S.Ct. 200, 47 L.Ed. 318 (1903), or by straining to read state law in a manner that would avoid satisfying one of § 70's requirements for inclusion of an asset in the bankruptcy estate. See In re Schmelzer, 480 F.2d 1074 (6th Cir. 1973). Under the new act, § 541, which determines the assets to be included in the bankruptcy estate, was intended to be all inclusive. All of the debtor's assets are to be in the estate and the exemption provisions alone determine what the debtor is permitted to keep. See S.Rep. No. 95–989, 95th Cong., 2d Sess. 82 (1978); H.R.Rep. No. 95–595, 95th Cong., 1st Sess. 175–76, 367–68 (1977) . . .. The Senate and House Reports expressly state that § 541 is intended to overrule Lines v. Frederick. Thus, Congress meant to foreclose the method of keeping assets out of the bankruptcy estate through interpretation of the term "property." Debtors who may only avail themselves of state exemptions are at least in this respect in a worse theoretical position than under the old act.

Notwithstanding the Senate and House Reports, the Lines v. Frederick method—keeping assets out of the estate through construction of the term "property"—may, and perhaps should, survive enactment of the new law. The act includes in the estate a comprehensive list of items, all of which are characterized as "property" or an "interest in property." 11 U.S.C. § 541(a). Courts that construed the term "property" in the old act to keep assets out of the bankruptcy estate will not find congressional disapproval of those results in § 541's text. Only the legislative history reveals the plan in this area. And the legislative history can be viewed as more equivocal than it first seems. The statements in the House and Senate Reports about the all inclusive scope intended for § 541 were made at a time when the House version of the bankruptcy reform bill contained a system of federal exemptions that was available in bankruptcy regardless of state law. A system of federal exemptions that could not be stripped away by the states may have been viewed as fair compensation to debtors for the all inclusive nature of § 541. Once § 522 was recast on the eve of passage, and after preparation of the House and Senate Reports, the trade-off between federal exemptions and a broad view of § 541 arguably should no longer govern. . . . Courts would then have no definite statements about the scope of § 541 in the context of the final act with its provision allowing states to opt out of the federal exemption system.

3. *Excepted Creditors.* New York's CPLR § 5205(a) prefaces its list of exempt personal property with the following language:

> The following personal property . . . is exempt from application to the satisfaction of a money judgment except where the judgment is for the purchase price of the exempt property or was recovered by a domestic, laboring person or mechanic for work performed by that person in such capacity . . ..

What is the effect of Bankruptcy Act § 522(c) on this provision and similar provisions providing for "excepted creditors" in other states? Does it make sense to allow states to opt out of the federal exemption system in bankruptcy and to impose such a limitation on the state exemption systems that Congress implicitly endorsed by enacting the opt out language in § 522(b)?

See generally Woodward, Exemptions, Opting Out, and Bankruptcy Reform, 43 Ohio St.L.J. 335 (1982).

4. *Federal Nonbankruptcy Exemptions.* Section 522(b)(2)(A) allows a debtor who relies on state exemptions to also exempt property exempt under nonbankruptcy federal laws. Such federal exemptions include social security benefits and certain other retirement or disability programs. The federal limitation on wage garnishment, 15 U.S.C.A. § 1673(a), does not apply to Chapter 13 cases. Id. § 1673(b). May a debtor exempt assets in an Individual Retirement Account? See, e.g., In re Talbert, 15 B.R. 536 (Bkrtcy.W.D.La.1981) (depends on state law).

5. *Exemptions in Joint Cases.* The existence of state and federal exemption systems, and the Bankruptcy Act's authorization of joint bankruptcy cases, see § 522(m), generated questions about some debtors' efforts to invoke both exemption systems. As amended in 1984, § 522(b) now expressly prohibits one debtor in a joint case from selecting state exemptions while the other debtor selects federal exemptions.

Notes on Constitutional Issues Under § 522

In providing a federal list of exemptions in § 522(d), but allowing states to opt out of the federal exemption system, Congress created novel tensions and opportunities. The new system already has generated several constitutional questions.

1. In In re Sullivan, 680 F.2d 1131 (7th Cir. 1982), certiorari denied 459 U.S. 992, 103 S.Ct. 349, 74 L.Ed.2d 388, an Illinois debtor requested that the court declare unconstitutional the portion of § 522(b) that permits states to prohibit their residents from using the federal exemptions provided in § 522(d). In denying relief, the court relied on Hanover National Bank v. Moyses, 186 U.S. 181, 22 S.Ct. 857, 46 L.Ed. 1113 (1902), which had sustained the provision of the Bankruptcy Act of 1898 that incorporated state exemption laws into federal bankruptcy law.[b]

2. May a state condition the availability of § 522(d)'s exemptions upon the debtor waiving some rights that would otherwise be available in bankruptcy? For example, may a state limit a debtor to state exemptions unless the debtor agrees to waive the automatic stay of § 362? Cf. In re Davis, 16 B.R. 62 (Bkrtcy.D.Md.1981) (seemingly not).

3. May a state provide debtors greater exemptions in bankruptcy than it provides debtors in nonbankruptcy proceedings? For example, New York's Debtor and Creditor Law §§ 282–284 provides *bankrupt* debtors with a motor vehicle exemption of $2,400. Nonbankrupt debtors are entitled no similar allowance under CPLR § 5205 and the federal exemption system limits the motor vehicle exemption to $1,200. Several other states have enacted similar measures. See Woodward, supra, at 369–71.

See generally Stern, State Exemption Law in Bankruptcy: The Excepted Creditor As a Medium for Appraising Aspects of Bankruptcy Reform, 33 Rutgers L.Rev. 70 (1980); Vukowich, Debtors' Exemption Rights Under the Bankruptcy Reform Act, 58 N.C.L.Rev. 769 (1980).

---

b. *Sullivan* casts doubt upon the authority of a bankruptcy court decision finding constitutional flaws in the Illinois exemption system. See In re Balgemann, 16 B.R. 780 (Bkrtcy.N.D.Ill. 1982). But see In re Locarno, 23 B.R. 622 (Bkrtcy.D.Md.1982) (finding state opt-out statute unconstitutional because it unfairly discriminated against nonhomeowner debtors by denying exemption comparable to homestead exemption).

1. Lien Avoidance

IN RE HALL
United States Court of Appeals, 11th Circuit, 1985.
752 F.2d 582.

Before KRAVITCH and ANDERSON, CIRCUIT JUDGES, and ATKINS, DISTRICT JUDGE.

KRAVITCH, CIRCUIT JUDGE:

These four cases were consolidated for appeal because they involve common issues of bankruptcy law. The two questions presented are: (1) whether debtors in bankruptcy whose property exemptions are defined by Georgia law may use 11 U.S.C. § 522(f) to avoid liens that encumber the property they seek to exempt; and (2) whether debtors who opt to file for Chapter 13 rehabilitation are entitled to use that same provision. The courts below ruled in favor of the debtors on both questions. We affirm.

I.

On June 4, 1982, plaintiffs in Register v. Kennesaw Finance Co., No. 84–8067, voluntarily filed a petition for relief under Chapter 13 of the Bankruptcy Code. One of plaintiffs' creditors, defendant Kennesaw Finance Company, held a nonpossessory, nonpurchase-money security interest in the Registers' household goods and furniture as collateral for a loan extended to plaintiffs. The indebtedness on the loan greatly exceeded the value of the collateral. After they filed for bankruptcy, plaintiffs brought this action in bankruptcy court to avoid defendant's security interest under 11 U.S.C. § 522(f) (1982), because the lien prevented plaintiffs from exempting from the estate the property it encumbered. The bankruptcy court granted plaintiffs' motion for summary judgment, and the district court affirmed this ruling. Defendant brought this appeal, seeking reinstatement of the lien.

The other three cases arose in a similar fashion. Each case involved the same defendant; they were thus consolidated for determination in both the bankruptcy court and the district court. Plaintiffs in Ronald Hall v. Finance One, No. 84–8132, filed their Chapter 13 petition on April 4, 1982. Stubblefield v. Finance One, No. 84–8066, began when plaintiffs sought relief under Chapter 13 on April 1, 1982. February 2, 1982, was the date on which plaintiffs filed their Chapter 13 petition in Donald Hall v. Finance One, No. 84–8065. Shortly after their petitions were filed, plaintiffs in each case sought to avoid defendant's nonpossessory, nonpurchase-money security interests in their household goods and furniture pursuant to section 522(f), claiming the liens impaired exemptions to which plaintiffs were entitled. In none of the cases did the value of property covered by the liens equal or exceed the amount of the loan outstanding. The bankruptcy court ordered the liens avoided and the district court affirmed. This appeal ensued.

II.

Appellants contend that the Georgia Legislature has defined the exemptions to which plaintiffs claim they are entitled in a way that prevents them from using the federal lien-avoidance statute, section 522(f). Specifically, they point out that Georgia law permits a debtor in bankruptcy to exempt property only if it is not encumbered by a lien. To evaluate their argument properly, we first explore the statutory scheme of property exemptions to which debtors in bankruptcy can avail themselves.

Upon the filing of a petition in bankruptcy, all of the debtor's legal and equitable interests in property, with few exceptions not relevant here, become property of the estate. 11 U.S.C. § 541(a) (1982). After the property comes into the estate, the debtor is allowed to exempt certain items under 11 U.S.C. § 522(b) (1982). Congress specified the kinds and amount of property that may be exempted in section 522(d). In addition, debtors may retain property defined as exempt by other federal laws. 11 U.S.C. § 522(b)(2)(A). Once the property is removed from the estate, the debtor may use it as his own. Liens valid in bankruptcy that cover exempt property, however, are preserved, and creditors holding such liens may enforce them against exempt property. 11 U.S.C. § 522(c)(2) (1982). Section 522(f), however, permits a debtor to avoid certain kinds of liens encumbering particular kinds of property to the extent that the lien impairs an exemption. Section 522(f) provides:

> Notwithstanding any waiver of exemptions, the debtor may avoid the fixing of a lien on an interest of the debtor in property to the extent that such lien impairs an exemption to which the debtor would have been entitled under subsection (b) of this section, if such lien is—
>
> (1) a judicial lien; or
>
> (2) a nonpossessory, nonpurchase-money security interest in any—
>
> > (A) household furnishings, household goods, wearing apparel, appliances, books, animals, crops, musical instruments, or jewelry that are held primarily for the personal, family, or household use of the debtor or a dependent of the debtor;
> >
> > (B) implements, professional books, or tools, of the trade of the debtor or the trade of a dependent of the debtor; or
> >
> > (C) professionally prescribed health aids for the debtor or a dependent of the debtor.

Thus, section 522(f) permits the debtor to enjoy an exemption even if property has been fully encumbered by a lien.

The new Bankruptcy Code permits states to "opt out" of the federal list of exemptions described in section 522(d), making them inapplicable to their residents who file petitions for relief under the bankruptcy laws. 11 U.S.C. § 522(b)(1).[1] The Georgia Legislature has taken advantage of this opportunity and enacted a statute precluding a debtor from using the federal list of exemptions. O.C.G.A. § 44–13–100(b). Thus, debtors who file for bankruptcy in Georgia may claim only those exemptions allowed by state law. The Georgia exemption relied upon by the debtors in this case provides as follows:

> (a) In lieu of the exemption provided in Code Section 44–13, any debtor who is a natural person may exempt, pursuant to this article, for purposes of bankruptcy, the following property:
>
> . . .
>
> (4) The debtor's interest, not to exceed $200.00 in value in any particular item, in household furnishings, household goods, wearing apparel, appliances, books, animals, crops, or musical instruments that are held primarily for the personal, family, or household use of the debtor or a dependent of the debtor. The exemption of the debtor's interest in the items contained in this paragraph shall not exceed $3,500.00 in total value;

O.C.G.A. § 44–13–100(a)(4).

Appellants' claim is that the Georgia Legislature has defined the exemptions to preclude debtors from avoiding liens under section 522(f). They assert that the phrase "debtor's interest" as used in the exemption statute indicates that a debtor may exempt property only to the extent of his or her equity. Thus, because Georgia law forbids the debtor to exempt property to the extent it is encumbered by a lien, the liens do not impair exemptions to which the debtors are entitled under section 522(b), as required by the language of section 522(f). In support, creditors rely on McManus v. Avco Financial Services (Matter of McManus), 681 F.2d 353 (5th Cir.1982), and Giles v. Credithrift of America (In Re Pine), 717 F.2d 281 (6th Cir.1983), cert. denied, ___ U.S. ___, 104 S.Ct. 1711, 80 L.Ed.2d 183 (1984). In *McManus,* the Fifth Circuit reviewed efforts by Louisiana debtors to avoid liens covering their household goods and furnishings. Louisiana had enacted an exemption statute and opted out of the federal exemption scheme. As part of the statute, the Louisiana Legislature included a provision forbidding debtors to exempt household goods and furnishings held subject to a chattel mortgage. Observing that Congress's authorization in section 522(b) for the states to enact their own exemption statutes

1. Section 522(b) provides in part:

(b) Notwithstanding section 541 of this title, an individual debtor may exempt from property of the estate either—

(1) property that is specified under subsection (d) of this section, unless the State law that is applicable to the debtor under paragraph (2)(A) of this subsection specifically does not so authorize; or, in the alternative,

(2)(A) any property that is exempt under Federal law, other than subsection (d) of this section, or State or local law that is applicable on the date of the filing of the petition at the place in which the debtor's domicile has been located for the 180 days immediately preceding the date of the filing of the petition, or for a longer portion of such 180–day period than in any other place;

. . .

was indeed a broad one, 681 F.2d at 355, the Fifth Circuit determined that Louisiana's decision to exclude encumbered property from its exemption scheme was permissible. Id. at 357. Section 522(f) allows the debtor to avoid only those liens encumbering property that is exempt under section 522(b), and property subject to a chattel mortgage was defined as not exempt. Therefore, the court reasoned, the lien avoidance provision could not be used in that case because the lien did not impair an exemption to which the debtor was entitled under section 522(b). Id.[2] The Sixth Circuit employed similar reasoning to reach the same conclusion in *Giles,* when construing Georgia and Tennessee statutes that, according to the court, allowed exemptions only to the extent of the debtor's equity. The court observed that by enacting the opt-out scheme without limitation, Congress expressed its preference for state control of exemptions. 717 F.2d at 284.

We agree that the lien-avoidance power is tied directly to the exemption provision, section 522(b). We do not believe, however, that this compels the result urged by the creditors in this case. In our opinion, the appellants' reasoning conflicts with the purpose of section 522(f). This section operates to permit a debtor to avoid the fixing of a lien on property if that avoidance would allow the debtor to enjoy an exemption. Brown v. Dellinger (In re Brown), 734 F.2d 119, 125 (2d Cir. 1984). Thus, the very purpose of the statute is to permit debtors to claim, as exempt, property completely or partially secured by an otherwise valid lien. To permit states to inhibit the operation of the lien-avoidance provision simply by defining all lien-encumbered property as "not exempt" would render the statute useless, a result inconsistent with the well-established principle of statutory construction requiring that all parts of an act be given effect, if at all possible.

It is true that the statute prescribes that debtors may not invoke their powers under section 522(f) except to affect property that is exempt under section 522(b). There may, however, be several reasons why a debtor cannot exempt property. A state may decide in enacting its list of exemptions that a particular kind of property, furniture for example, will not be exempt. We assume for purposes of this case that there is nothing in the Bankruptcy Code that prohibits such a classification.[3] Likewise, the state legislature may determine that lien-encumbered property cannot be exempted, even if the particular kind of property that is encumbered by the lien is defined as exempt. We do not suggest that states are prohibited from defining lien-encumbered property as not exempt. Any such decision would, however, be subject

2. Judge Dyer, sitting by designation, dissented from the majority's conclusion. He concluded that Congressional authorization to opt out of the federal list of exemptions did not empower the states to enact legislation that conflicts with section 522(f). 681 F.2d at 357–59.

3. The extent to which a state's list of property exemptions may provide less for the debtor than does the federal list contained in section 522(d), see infra note 6, is not before this court today, and we do not intimate any view on this issue.

to the provisions of section 522(f).[4] Thus, property encumbered by judicial liens and nonpossessory, nonpurchase-money security interests could still be exempted, notwithstanding the state's classification of lien-encumbered property as not exempt.[5]

The language of the "opt-out" provision contained in section 522(b)(1) does not suggest a contrary result. But see Giles, 717 F.2d at 284 (Congress expressed preference for state control of exemptions by enacting the "opt-out" provision without limitation; therefore, it is doubtful that Congress intended section 522(f) to limit the kind of property states could define as exempt). In granting the states the power to opt out of the federal list of exemptions, Congress did not appear to place any limits on the states' ability to do so.[6] This broad grant of power, however, does not mean that Congress authorized the states to enact legislation that conflicts with any other provision of the Bankruptcy Code. Rather, the import of the provision is merely that a state may decide to require that its debtors rely upon state-defined exemptions, instead of the list of federal exemptions contained in section 522(d). Cf. In re Storer, 13 B.R. 1, 3 (Bankr.S.D.Ohio 1980) (drawing a distinction between an exemption and the operation of a lien upon an exemption; with respect to the latter, no state may deprive a debtor of the right to avoid a lien authorized by the Bankruptcy Code).

The legislative history of the new Bankruptcy Code supports our view that the lien-avoidance provision was intended to apply to state exemptions, notwithstanding state limitations on the ability of debtors to exempt lien-encumbered property. The Senate version of the bill would have entitled debtors to property exemptions defined by state law. The bill also contained a lien-avoidance section identical to the one codified at 11 U.S.C. § 522(f), and, in the report accompanying the bill, the Senate described the provision as allowing debtors to exempt property "to the extent that the property could have been exempted in the absence of the lien." S.Rep. No. 989, 95th Cong., 2d Sess., 76 (1978), reprinted in 1978 U.S.Code Cong. & Ad.News 5787, 5861. The bill that originally passed the House would have enabled a debtor to choose between the federal list that was ultimately codified at 11 U.S.C. § 522(d) and state exemptions, and also contained a lien-avoidance provision. The House's description of section 522(f) is identical to that contained in the Senate report. H.R.Rep. No. 595, 95th Cong., 2d Sess., 362 (1978), reprinted in 1978 U.S.Code Cong. & Ad.News, 5963, 6318.

---

4. Conflicts between state and federal law must be resolved in favor of the federal provision. U.S. Const., Art. VI, cl. 2; see Perez v. Campbell, 402 U.S. 637, 91 S.Ct. 1704, 29 L.Ed.2d 233 (1971). . . .

5. There are, of course, other liens that encumber property, such as purchase-money security interests and statutory liens, and section 522(f) would not operate to allow exemptions for property covered by these liens if the state has decided that lien-encumbered property is not exempt.

6. Indeed, at least two circuit courts have made this observation in upholding the constitutionality of state laws that provided for less exemptions than did the federal law. Rhodes v. Stewart, 705 F.2d 159 (6th Cir.1983), cert. denied, ── U.S. ──, 104 S.Ct. 427, 78 L.Ed.2d 361 (1984); Matter of Sullivan, 680 F.2d 1131 (7th Cir. 1982), cert. denied, 459 U.S. 992, 103 S.Ct. 349, 74 L.Ed.2d 388 (1983).

In our opinion, it is important that both the Senate and the House considered the debtor's lien-avoidance power in conjunction with exemptions defined by state law. This evidences that debtors' lien-avoidance powers would not be eviscerated by state-defined exemptions. See Haines, Section 522's Opt–Out Clause: Debtors' Bankruptcy Exemptions in a Sorry State, 1984 Ariz.St.L.J. 1, 30–31. Hence we doubt that Congress intended that states could limit the debtor's power as appellants suggest. Of course, the compromise exemption scheme that ultimately passed and is now codified contains a federal list of exemptions, but allows states to deny their residents these exemptions, a result not contemplated by either the House or Senate bill. As discussed previously, however, we do not believe that this compromise changes our analysis.

The legislative history further reveals that Congress enacted section 522(f) as a response to what it viewed as unconscionable creditor practices in the consumer loan industry. H.R.Rep. No. 595, supra, at 126–27; 1978 U.S.Code Cong. & Ad.News, 6087–88. Congress evidenced its concern about overreaching creditors who obtained nonpossessory, nonpurchase-money security interests covering a substantial part of debtors' otherwise exempt property. Congress found that debtors usually granted blanket security interests, and agreed to waive their right to exempt property, without understanding the consequences of their actions. The property subject to these liens often was of little value to the creditors, because of its low resale value, but its replacement cost to debtors was usually high. Accordingly, creditors, although they did not view the property as a source of funds to which they could turn in the event of default, often used the threat of foreclosure to coerce debtors into making payments. Under section 522(f), debtors can now protect themselves from this practice by avoiding these liens in bankruptcy. In addition, Congress hoped that the lien-avoidance provision would leave enough property in the hands of the debtor to insure a "fresh start" after discharge. These concerns are equally applicable to debtors who must rely on state exemptions. *McManus,* 681 F.2d at 359 (Dyer, J., dissenting). Although Congress may have undercut the purpose of the exemption scheme by permitting states to opt-out, we disagree that Congress meant to allow unlimited state action on this matter. We hold, therefore, that the Georgia exemptions do not preclude the operation of section 522(f).[8]

. . .

8. Indeed, at least two bankruptcy courts, apparently troubled by the result achieved by the Sixth Circuit in *Pine,* have undertaken to write lengthy opinions on the operation of section 522(f) on exemptions defined by state law. Matter of Lewis, 38 B.R. 113 (Bankr.S.D.Ohio 1984) (distinguishing *Pine*); In re Law, 37 B.R. 501 (Bankr.S.D.Ohio 1984) (outcome controlled by *Pine* but court undertook extensive explanation of why the *Pine* court's conclusion was incorrect).

Notes & Questions

1. *State Control Over Exemptions.* Suppose Georgia decided that the class of property at issue in *Hall* should not be exempt at all. Is there anything preventing Georgia from eliminating the exemptions entirely, thereby precluding any argument that § 522(f) can be used to avoid a lien? If Georgia may eliminate the exemptions entirely, does it make sense to prevent Georgia from granting them in part? Is § 522(f) another provision that, interpreted as in *Hall*, makes sense only in the context of a single uniform system of exemptions? Does this mean that the *McManus* interpretation (discussed in *Hall*) is preferable?

2. *Property Covered.* Note the similarity in phrasing between the items protected by § 522(f)(2) and the items listed in § 522(d)(3), (4), (6), and (9). Does § 522(f) apply to any class of property that is not included in the corresponding provisions of § 522(d)? See generally Augustine v. United States, 675 F.2d 582 (3d Cir.1982). Does it apply to automobiles, which are listed in § 522(d) but not in one of the § 522(d) sections that is incorporated into § 522(f)(2)?

3. *Debtor's Additional Powers.* Note also the debtor's powers to recover or exempt property under § 522(g), (h).

4. *Constitutional Overtones.* In United States v. Security Industrial Bank, 459 U.S. 70, 103 S.Ct. 407, 74 L.Ed.2d 235 (1982), the Supreme Court held that § 522(f)(2) does not apply to security interests acquired before the Bankruptcy Reform Act's effective date and suggested that serious fifth amendment problems would arise if Congress gave § 522(f) retroactive effect. See Chapter 11.

2. Converting Property to Exempt Categories

IN RE ADLMAN

United States Court of Appeals, Second Circuit, 1976.
541 F.2d 999.

GURFEIN, CIRCUIT JUDGE:

This is an appeal from an order of the United States District Court for the Eastern District of New York, Thomas C. Platt, Judge, which affirmed a judgment of the Bankruptcy Court, Boris Radoyevich, Bankruptcy Judge, denying appellant, Lois Adlman, a discharge in bankruptcy pursuant to section 14c(4) of the Bankruptcy Act, 11 U.S.C. § 32(c)(4). The discharge was denied on the ground that appellant, within twelve months preceding the filing of her petition in bankruptcy, transferred property with the intent to hinder, delay or defraud her creditors.

The evidence presented at the hearing before the Bankruptcy Judge showed that appellant's husband, Edward C. Adlman, was engaged in 1972 and 1973 in the purchase and development of real property in Pennsylvania and was a general partner in the limited partnership known as Leesport Gardens Company ("Leesport").

The Bankruptcy Judge found that Lois Adlman "is a housewife and that she was not engaged in any business. Her husband had put her in as a limited partner in Leesport but she did nothing other than sign the partnership certificate and go on a guaranty of the Bank's loan."

On October 23, 1972, Leesport obtained a loan from the Bank of Pennsylvania. In connection with this loan, appellant and her husband executed and delivered to the Bank of Pennsylvania a continuing guarantee of any loans which the bank might make to Leesport. Appellant testified that she executed this instrument at the request of her husband because her husband explained that it was something needed in business and that it was important to have both their signatures under the law of Pennsylvania.

During the year 1973, the financial position of Mr. Adlman deteriorated. On October 12, 1973, appellant sold the family home in Sands Point, New York, to which she had always held the title in her own name, to an aunt and uncle of her husband for the sum of $125,000, subject to a first mortgage. She realized approximately $60,000 from the sale. A lease was entered into between the Adlmans and the new owners, and the Adlmans continued to live in the house.

Appellant owned insurance policies on the lives of her husband and her father and was beneficiary of these policies. Under Section 166 of the New York Insurance Law, these policies constituted assets exempt from creditors.[1]

Shortly before and simultaneously with the closing of title, appellant drew checks on her checking account to pay $52,653.40 of loans outstanding on these insurance policies and to pay $7,663.22 in premiums on these policies. Appellant testified that she made these payments because her husband was in poor health and because she was concerned that the policies might lapse and that she would be unable to obtain other insurance. She testified, without contradiction, that her husband felt that eventually things would get better. She was not examined by the objecting creditor on whether she knew enough about her husband's affairs to know that he was insolvent or even on whether

---

1. Section 166(1) of the New York Insurance Law provides in relevant part as follows:

"If any policy of insurance has been or shall be effected by any person on his own life in favor of a third person beneficiary, or made payable, by assignment, change of beneficiary or otherwise, to a third person, such third person beneficiary, assignee or payee shall be entitled to the proceeds and avails of such policy as against the creditors, personal representatives, trustees in bankruptcy and receivers in state and federal courts of the person effecting the insurance. If any policy of insurance has been or shall be effected by any person upon the life of another person in favor of the person effecting the same or made payable, by assignment, change of beneficiary or otherwise, to such person, the latter shall be entitled to the proceeds and avails of such policy as against the creditors, personal representatives, trustees in bankruptcy and receivers in state and federal courts of the person insured; if the person effecting such insurance shall be the wife of the insured, she shall be entitled to the proceeds and avails of such policy as against her own creditors, trustees in bankruptcy and receivers in state and federal courts."

But see also note 9 and accompanying text for an exception.

she knew the extent of his obligations, but only on whether she knew she was in "financial difficulty."

On March 22, 1974, approximately five and one-half months after the payment of these loans and premiums, appellant and her husband filed voluntary petitions in bankruptcy and were adjudicated bankrupts. Appellant's schedules showed liabilities of $4,091,725.20 and no assets other than life insurance policies having a face value of $275,000, which she claimed as exempt property under the New York Insurance Law.

On November 27, 1974, the Bank of Pennsylvania, one of appellant's creditors on a loan of $25,000, filed a complaint with the Bankruptcy Court objecting to appellant's discharge. See Bankruptcy Rule 404. The complaint alleged that appellant's husband had submitted to the bank, with the knowledge and consent of appellant, false financial statements misrepresenting the assets and liabilities of appellant and her husband, and that the bank had relied on these statements in extending credit to the Adlmans. The complaint also alleged that the conveyance of the Sands Point house by appellant was made "without valid consideration" and with the purpose and intent of hindering, delaying and defrauding the creditors of appellant and her husband.[2] The Bankruptcy Judge found that appellant and her husband did not intend to deceive the bank in submitting financial statements, and he therefore dismissed those portions of the complaint which requested that a discharge be denied on the ground that appellant had submitted false financial statements. Appellant's husband was granted a discharge. However, the Bankruptcy Judge denied appellant a discharge on the ground that she had sold the Sands Point house, repaid loans on her life insurance policies and prepaid the insurance premiums with the intent to hinder, delay and defraud her creditors.

The Bankruptcy Judge found that at the time appellant sold the Sands Point house, she was insolvent because of her liabilities of $4,091,725.20, which arose from her guarantees of her husband's obligations. He further found that appellant's husband, in October 1973, had little or no income, that he was under tremendous financial pressure, and that he wanted to sell the Sands Point house "because he felt it would be the wisest thing to do at that particular time." Indeed, he found specifically "[t]hat the defendant sold the Sands Point house, which she continues to occupy with her husband, to David and Dorothy Adlman, on October 12, 1973, repaid loans on various policies of life insurance, and paid premiums, some in advance of their due dates, in order to secure protection for herself and her children."[3] He found that "[t]he husband had had a history of illness." But he also found

2. The complaint also alleged that "the sums purportedly paid to the bankrupt for the transfer of said property were used to pay the debts of the bankrupt and her husband to the prejudice of the creditors herein." But the Bankruptcy Judge failed to find that the transfer of the house was, itself, a fraudulent transaction. The failure to so find was contrary to the gravamen of the complaint.

3. We note that no premium was paid more than 10 weeks before it was due.

that she did these things "for the purpose of removing such assets from the reach of her creditors." He finally recorded both as a finding of fact and as a conclusion of law that the transfer of the house, the repayment of loans, and the payment of premiums were done "with the intent to hinder, delay or defraud her creditors, all as specified in Section 14c(4) of the Bankruptcy Act."

In the Bankruptcy Judge's memorandum opinion accompanying his decision, he seemed to assume that the $125,000 purchase price of the house was a fair consideration. Indeed, there was no evidence which indicated that the house was sold for less than fair consideration. He also recognized that almost $40,000 of the $60,000 paid to the insurance companies was apparently paid before receipt of money from the sale of the house and that only $20,147.12 was paid to the insurance companies on the day of the closing.

Apparently recognizing the validity of the sale of the house, standing by itself, the Bankruptcy Judge noted that appellant was under no personal obligation to repay the loans on the insurance policies, since they "are considered advancements of the sums payable under the policy and if not repaid are merely deducted from the amount payable when the policy, by its provisions, matures", and that the repayment of the loans did not enhance the bankrupt's estate available to her creditors. He made no specific finding that Mrs. Adlman was lying when she testified that she was afraid that the insurance might lapse. He concluded, nevertheless, that repayment of the policy loans was made "with actual intent to hinder, delay or defraud the bankrupt's creditors," supporting his conclusion by stating that "[i]t was plainly her intention to remove such funds from the reach of her creditors by placing the same in an exempt cat[e]gory." He cited as his authority In re Hirsch, 4 F.Supp. 708 (S.D.N.Y.1933). He also noted that the payments of the premiums could be set aside as fraudulent under Section 276 of the New York Debtor and Creditor Law, which makes fraudulent such conveyances as are made with actual intent to hinder, delay or defraud creditors.[4]

The Bankruptcy Judge made no finding of extrinsic facts to support the conclusion that there was an *actual* intent to defraud her creditors. He appears to have found sufficient ground for denying a discharge in the mere fact that her intention was to place the funds in the exempt category.

The District Court affirmed simply on the ground that "[t]he Bankruptcy Judge could well have and apparently did infer the requisite intent from such facts [the house sale, repayment of insurance loans and premium payments] along with all of the other evidence in the case." Though Judge Platt did not specify what the relevant "other

4. Section 276 provides as follows:

"Every conveyance made and every obligation incurred with actual intent, as distinguished from intent presumed in law, to hinder, delay, or defraud either present or future creditors, is fraudulent as to both present and future creditors."

evidence" was, he felt that he "must" accept the Bankruptcy Judge's findings of fact unless clearly erroneous under Bankruptcy Rule 810.[5] He made no independent review of the authorities.

We think the courts below incorrectly assumed that a transfer prior to bankruptcy of non-exempt assets *ipso facto* compels the conclusion that there was an *actual* intent to "hinder, delay or defraud creditors" and that such transfer compels denial of a discharge in bankruptcy under § 14c(4) of the Act. Hence we reverse.

We begin with the well-accepted principle that the Bankruptcy Act was intended to permit the honest debtor to get a new start in life free from debt, and that section 14 of the Act must be construed strictly against the objectors and liberally in favor of the bankrupt.

More specifically, in order to deny a discharge under section 14c(4) of the Act, 11 U.S.C. § 32(c)(4), the court must find that property was transferred or removed with *actual* intent to hinder, delay or defraud creditors. Halpern v. Schwartz, 426 F.2d 102, 104 (2d Cir. 1970). Constructive fraudulent intent, such as would suffice to set aside a transfer under section 67 of the Act, 11 U.S.C. § 107, or under section 70e, 11 U.S.C. § 110e, cannot be the basis for the denial of discharge.

The distinction between constructive intent involved in a transfer without consideration while insolvent and "actual intent" to hinder, delay or defraud creditors is well recognized, though not always easy of definition. The difficulty of proving "actual intent" to defraud was made manifest in Feist v. Druckerman, 70 F.2d 333 (2d Cir. 1934), a decision concurred in by Judges Learned Hand, Swan and Augustus N. Hand.[6]

5. One Court of Appeals, in reversing an affirmance of the District Court of findings of a Referee in Bankruptcy, indicated that whether property was conveyed under Section 14c(4) might be "an ultimate question of fact" to which the "clearly erroneous" rule would not apply. Minnick v. Lafayette Loan & Trust Co., 392 F.2d 973, 977 (7th Cir. 1968). See Stewart v. Ganey, 116 F.2d 1010, 1013 (5th Cir. 1940); In re Pioch, 235 F.2d 903 (3d Cir. 1956); Costello v. Fazio, 256 F.2d 903, 908 (9th Cir. 1958). Both *Pioch* and *Costello* were noted by us in In re Tabibian, 289 F.2d 793, 795 (2d Cir. 1961).

6. In *Feist*, the bankrupt, several months before bankruptcy, obtained the full surrender value of an insurance policy he owned jointly with his brother and deposited his share of the proceeds in his personal account. Two months before the filing of the petition, he paid to his son $3500, which was virtually all the money he had in the bank at this time. Furthermore, several months prior to the filing of the petition, the bankrupt conveyed to his wife his entire interest in a lot worth $50,000, which he had owned jointly with his wife. This conveyance was made without consideration, and at the time it was made the bankrupt was apparently insolvent. The bankrupt stated that his wife had agreed to assume the $7,000 balance of the mortgage which was on the property and to pay the arrears in taxes, amounting to $8,000. But the trial court "entirely disbelieve[d]" this testimony and found that there was no such understanding between the bankrupt and his wife. The trial court found that the bankrupt had actual intent to defraud his creditors by making the above-mentioned transfers, and set aside the transfer of the bankrupt's interest in the lot pursuant to Section 276 of the Debtor and Creditor Law. 6 F.Supp. 751 (E.D.N.Y.1933).

On appeal, however, this court, in an opinion by Judge Augustus N. Hand, found that the evidence was insufficient to warrant a finding of actual fraud. The court stated that

"[i]n view of the false statement of [the bankrupt] as to such a vital matter as an

The reluctance of the courts to find actual intent by a bankrupt to defraud his creditors is illustrated by decisions holding that the exchange by the bankrupt, on the eve of bankruptcy, of non-exempt property for exempt property, is not itself a fraud on his creditors and cannot be the basis for a denial of a discharge absent extrinsic evidence of fraud. Forsberg v. Security State Bank, 15 F.2d 499, 502 (8th Cir. 1926). See Wudrick v. Clements, 451 F.2d 988, 989–90 (9th Cir. 1971); Grover v. Jackson, 472 F.2d 589, 590 (9th Cir. 1973). As the court stated in Forsberg v. Security State Bank, supra, 15 F.2d at 502, "before the existence of [any] fraudulent purpose can be properly found, there must appear in evidence some facts or circumstances which are extrinsic to the mere facts of conversion of non-exempt assets into exempt and which are indicative of such fraudulent purpose." [7]

In Doethlaff v. Penn Mutual Life Insurance Co., 117 F.2d 582 (6th Cir.), cert. denied, 313 U.S. 579, 61 S.Ct. 1100, 85 L.Ed. 1536 (1941), it was held that the payment of life insurance premiums by a debtor who was insolvent did not constitute a fraud on creditors. We cited *Doethlaff* with approval in Schwartz v. Seldon, 153 F.2d 334, 336 (2d Cir. 1945), where this court upheld the exemption of a life insurance policy on the assumption that the bankrupt himself had paid off loans on the policy while insolvent. We stated that even if the bankrupt had repaid the loans, "the policy would not lose its exempt character unless the payment constituted a transfer made with 'actual intent' to defraud creditors, as required by § 166 [of the N.Y. Insurance Law] if exemption is to be defeated." Id.[8] We concluded that "the record contains no

assumption by [his wife] of the mortgage and in view also of the transfer of property to his wife and son and of his conversion of his life insurance policy, all within six months of the filing of the petition in bankruptcy, there is some reason to hold that an inference of 'actual intent' to defraud creditors 'as distinguished from intent presumed in law,' should be drawn and that accordingly the conveyance should be set aside under the provisions of section 276 of the New York Debtor and Creditor Law."

But Judge Hand went on to state that

"[w]e are, however, inclined to think that the testimony when taken alone was not sufficient to prove actual fraud, and that a cause of action under section 276 of the New York Debtor and Creditor Law must fail."

70 F.2d at 334.

7. For an example of the type of extrinsic evidence needed to show actual fraud, see Kangas v. Robie, 264 F. 92 (8th Cir. 1920). In that case the bankrupt's claim to a homestead exemption was denied where the evidence established that he obtained the purchase price of the homestead by buying merchandise on credit immediately

prior to bankruptcy and using the proceeds of the merchandise to buy the homestead, rather than pay his suppliers. As the Ninth Circuit noted in Wudrick v. Clements, supra, 451 F.2d at 990: "A different case would be presented if on the eve of bankruptcy a debt were created with no intention of repaying the creditor, either by purchasing goods on credit or borrowing money without security." In the instant case, by contrast, Mrs. Adlman paid the premiums and repaid the loans with money that was derived from an asset which she had owned for many years.

8. In Schwartz v. Seldon, repayments of loans on the bankrupt's life insurance policies were made while he was insolvent. The referee found that the *bankrupt* had repaid the loans "with actual intent to hinder, delay or defraud creditors" and entered an order that the bankrupt pay the trustee the amount of the loans or turn over the policies so that the trustee might realize the amount out of their cash surrender values. There was a question whether the *wife* of the bankrupt rather than the bankrupt himself had repaid the loans. The quoted passage is based on the alternative assumption by the court that

evidence justifying an inference of 'actual intent' to defraud creditors." Furthermore, we noted that "[e]ven the conversion of nonexempt property into exempt property by an insolvent contemplating bankruptcy has been held a transaction not intended to defraud creditors in the absence of evidence of extrinsic fraud," citing Forsberg v. Security State Bank, supra. Id. at 337.

In the case at hand, there is no evidence of any extrinsic fraud committed by the appellant in the payment of premiums on her life insurance policies and the repayment of loans. Indeed, the Bankruptcy Judge specifically found that appellant made these payments "in order to secure protection for herself and her children." It is true that the Bankruptcy Judge also found that these payments were made "for the purpose of removing such assets from the reach of her creditors" and "with intent to hinder, delay and to defraud her creditors." But it is evident that the Bankruptcy Judge misconceived the law in reaching these conclusions, since nowhere did he find any evidence of fraud other than the mere payments themselves, and his citation of In re Hirsch, supra, was, as we shall see below, reliance on an authority wrongly reasoned. Absent convincing evidence of extrinsic fraud, it was incorrect as a matter of law for the Bankruptcy Judge to conclude that appellant had actual intent to defraud her creditors. See Schwartz v. Seldon, supra. Although the judge may also have concluded as a matter of *fact* that appellant intended to defraud her creditors, we are not bound to accept such a finding, since it was induced by an erroneous view of the law.

Appellee argues, however, that under *New York* law, appellant's payments of loans on her policies and prepayments of premiums would be considered as having been made with actual intent to defraud creditors. Section 166(4) of the New York Insurance Law provides that "[e]very assignment or change of beneficiary, or other transfer, shall be valid, except in cases of transfer with actual intent to hinder, delay or defraud creditors, as such actual intent is defined by article ten of the debtor and creditor law . . . ."[9] Appellee argues that Baxter House, Inc. v. Rosen, 27 A.D.2d 258, 278 N.Y.S.2d 442 (2 Dep't 1967), indicates that New York courts would hold that the mere payment of premiums by an insolvent debtor, without more, constitutes actual intent to defraud creditors within the meaning of Section 166(4). We disagree.

Baxter House involved an appeal from the dismissal of a complaint. Rosen, it was alleged, paid premiums on a life insurance policy while

the bankrupt, himself, had repaid the loans while insolvent.

9. Before the "actual intent" language came into § 166 of the Insurance Law, the former Section 55–a of the Insurance Law (McKinney 1937), enacted by [1927] N.Y. Laws, ch. 468, § 1, excepted only "cases of transfer with the intent to defraud creditors," without the word "actual." This court construed the earlier statute as well as the latter to except only transfers with "actual intent." Schwartz v. Seldon, supra, 153 F.2d at 337. Purvin v. Grey, 294 N.Y. 282, 62 N.E.2d 72 (1945), may, perhaps, be thought *contra* with respect to former section 55–a, but the New York Court of Appeals disclaimed any intention of interpreting section 166(4), the statute now before us. Id., at 286, 62 N.E.2d 72.

insolvent "actually intending to defraud his creditors." The court below held that Section 166 applied only where there was an assignment of the policy or a change of beneficiary. 47 Misc.2d 77, 80, 262 N.Y.S.2d 378 (Sup.Ct.1965). The Appellate Division reversed, holding that even though there was no such assignment or change of beneficiary a cause of action was stated for voiding the payment of the premiums. Since the complaint specifically alleged "actual intent," there was no occasion for the Appellate Division, in merely sustaining the complaint, to discuss the meaning of "actual intent." The case is inapposite. Indeed, we have seen that in Schwartz v. Seldon, supra, this court viewed New York law in a manner contrary to appellee's contention. Nor have we found later New York cases which cast doubt on that view of New York law. . . .

The order of the District Court affirming the Bankruptcy Judge's denial of a discharge is reversed, and the case is remanded to the District Court with instructions to grant appellant a discharge.

MOORE, CIRCUIT JUDGE (dissenting):

The only issue on this appeal is whether Mrs. Adlman ("bankrupt") converted non-exempt property into exempt property *with intent to* "hinder, delay or defraud" her creditors under 11 U.S.C. § 32(c). Whether or not the bankrupt did act with such actual intent is a purely factual question, properly resolved by the trier of facts—here, the bankruptcy judge—and not subject to reversal on appeal unless clearly erroneous.

Once the evidence established some reasonable ground to believe that the bankrupt acted with intent to defraud creditors in violation of § 32(c) (and I believe that the undisputed facts of the sale to and leaseback from relatives of realty with continued occupancy thereof, with proceeds used to *prepay* life insurance premiums constituted such reasonable ground), the burden of proof shifted to the bankrupt to demonstrate to the court's satisfaction that a discharge was warranted. In making its factual finding, the bankruptcy judge was free to consider circumstantial evidence, and was in the best possible position to determine the question of motive since the bankrupt testified in person and at some length before the court.

In light of the record, it can hardly be argued that Bankruptcy Judge Radoyevitch's finding of actual intent was "clearly erroneous". On the contrary, it is amply supported by the testimony presented to the Court, and the undisputed facts alone are indicative of a scheme to defraud creditors. The sale and leaseback was not an arm's length transaction; the immediate conversion of the proceeds into exempt property was not for the purpose of paying premiums due and owing on the policy, but rather for the *prepayment* of future premiums. It is conceded that the bankrupt was counselled in this course of action by a spouse who was an experienced, albeit not necessarily successful businessman. The court could fairly infer from all of the above that there was actual intent to place assets beyond the reach of creditors, and under such circumstances, discharge was properly denied. . . .

Notes & Questions

1. *The Issue.* Consider two questions: (1) Whether the debtor should be denied a discharge because he converted property to an exempt category on the eve of bankruptcy? (2) Whether the converted property should be recoverable by the estate? Which question does *Adlman* address? Does the answer to one necessarily dictate an answer to the other?

2. *The Stakes.* If cases such as *Adlman* seem questionable, is there something more going on than an unabashed desire to assist bankrupts? Consider the stakes in *Adlman.* If Mrs. Adlman lost on the "intent to defraud" issue what were the consequences? See Bankruptcy Act § 727(a)(2). Should the stakes be so high? Compare the New York Insurance Law sanction for a finding of intent to defraud. Section 166(4)(a) of the Insurance Law states, in part: "the amount of premiums or other consideration paid with actual intent to defraud creditors . . . together with interest on such amount, shall enure to the benefit of creditors from the proceeds of the policy or contract . . . ." If this were the only penalty for debtors in Mrs. Adlman's position, would courts be so reluctant to find fraudulent intent? Should federal law pile on devastating additional consequences such as denial of a discharge? [c]

3. *The Law.* The new Bankruptcy Act's legislative history states: "As under current law, the debtor will be permitted to convert nonexempt property into exempt property before filing a bankruptcy petition. The practice is not fraudulent as to creditors, and permits the debtor to make full use of the exemptions to which he is entitled under the law." Senate Report at 76; House Report at 361. For the view that this summary of the law does not accurately reflect Texas exemption law, see In re Reed, 11 B.R. 683 (Bkrtcy.N.D.Tex.1981), affirmed 700 F.2d 986 (5th Cir. 1983). See also In re Schwingle, 15 B.R. 291 (W.D.Wis. 1981) (construing old bankruptcy act). The Fifth Circuit in *Reed,* supra, alluded to this legislative history in finding that an eve-of-bankruptcy conversion to exempt property will lead to denial of a discharge but that it will not cause the exempt property acquired in the conversion to lose its exempt status. Is this a sound approach to the conversion problem?

4. *What Should the Law Allow?* Consider the following:

[A] limit on prebankruptcy exemption planning, even if it worked, would be perceived as unfair to some debtors. It generates unequal treatment between the sophisticated debtor and the unsophisticated debtor. The unsophisticated debtor who waits until the eve-of-

c. See generally Eisenberg, Bankruptcy Law in Perspective: A Rejoinder, 30 UCLA L.Rev. 617, 621 n. 18 (1983).

bankruptcy to take advantage of his exemptions will be frustrated. A determined, well-advised debtor will convert his assets to exempt property prior to whatever vulnerable period a bankruptcy act imposes on such conversions.

Eisenberg, Bankruptcy Law in Perspective, 28 UCLA L.Rev. 953, 996 (1981). Can you respond to this argument?

5. *Source of Law.* Is *Adlman* based on the court's construction of federal bankruptcy law or on the court's interpretation of New York's debtor-creditor law? Under the new Act, is the effectiveness of prebankruptcy conversion of assets to exempt categories governed by state law if state exemptions are chosen and by federal law if federal exemptions are chosen?

D. Turnover of Property

UNITED STATES v. WHITING POOLS, INC.

Supreme Court of the United States, 1983.
462 U.S. 198, 103 S.Ct. 2309, 76 L.Ed.2d 515.

JUSTICE BLACKMUN delivered the opinion of the Court.

Promptly after the Internal Revenue Service (IRS or Service) seized respondent's property to satisfy a tax lien, respondent filed a petition for reorganization under the Bankruptcy Reform Act of 1978, hereinafter referred to as the "Bankruptcy Code." The issue before us is whether § 542(a) of that Code authorized the Bankruptcy Court to subject the IRS to a turnover order with respect to the seized property.

I

A

Respondent Whiting Pools, Inc., a corporation, sells, installs, and services swimming pools and related equipment and supplies. As of January 1981, Whiting owed approximately $92,000 in Federal Insurance Contribution Act taxes and federal taxes withheld from its employees, but had failed to respond to assessments and demands for payment by the IRS. As a consequence, a tax lien in that amount attached to all of Whiting's property.[1]

On January 14, 1981, the Service seized Whiting's tangible personal property—equipment, vehicles, inventory, and office supplies—pursuant to the levy and distraint provision of the Internal Revenue Code of 1954.[2] According to uncontroverted findings, the estimated liquidation

---

1. Section 6321 of the Internal Revenue Code of 1954, 26 U.S.C. § 6321, provides:

"If any person liable to pay any tax neglects or refuses to pay the same after demand, the amount . . . shall be a lien in favor of the United States upon all property and rights to property, whether real or personal, belonging to such person."

2. Section 6331 of that Code, 26 U.S.C. § 6331 provides:

"(a) Authority of Secretary

"If any person liable to pay any tax neglects or refuses to pay the same within 10 days after notice and demand, it shall be lawful for the Secretary to collect such tax (and such further sum as shall be sufficient to cover the expenses

value of the property seized was, at most, $35,000, but its estimated going-concern value in Whiting's hands was $162,876. The very next day, January 15, Whiting filed a petition for reorganization, under the Bankruptcy Code's Chapter 11, 11 U.S.C. §§ 1101 *et seq.* (1976 ed., Supp. V), in the United States Bankruptcy Court for the Western District of New York. Whiting was continued as debtor-in-possession.[3]

The United States, intending to proceed with a tax sale of the property,[4] moved in the Bankruptcy Court for a declaration that the automatic stay provision of the Bankruptcy Code, § 362(a), is inapplicable to the IRS or, in the alternative, for relief from the stay. Whiting counterclaimed for an order requiring the Service to turn the seized property over to the bankruptcy estate pursuant to § 542(a) of the Bankruptcy Code.[5] Whiting intended to use the property in its reorganized business.

B

The Bankruptcy Court determined that the IRS was bound by the automatic stay provision. In re Whiting Pools, Inc., 10 B.R. 755 (Bkrtcy.1981). Because it found that the seized property was essential to Whiting's reorganization effort, it refused to lift the stay. Acting under § 543(b)(1) of the Bankruptcy Code,[6] rather than under § 542(a), the court directed the IRS to turn the property over to Whiting on the condition that Whiting provide the Service with specified protection for its interests. 10 B.R., at 760–761.[7]

of the levy) by levy upon all property and rights to property . . . belonging to such person or on which there is a lien provided in this chapter for the payment of such tax. . . .

"(b) Seizure and sale of property

"The term 'levy' as used in this title includes the power of distraint and seizure by any means. . . . In any case in which the Secretary may levy upon property or rights to property, he may seize and sell such property or rights to property (whether real or personal, tangible or intangible)."

3. With certain exceptions not relevant here, a debtor-in-possession, such as Whiting, performs the same functions as a trustee in a reorganization. 11 U.S.C. § 1107(a) (1976 ed., Supp. V).

4. Section 6335, as amended, of the 1954 Code, 26 U.S.C. § 6335, provides for the sale of seized property after notice. The taxpayer is entitled to any surplus of the proceeds of the sale. § 6342(b).

5. Section 542(a) provides in relevant part:

"[A]n entity, other than a custodian, in possession, custody, or control, during the case, of property that the trustee

may use, sell, or lease under section 363 of this title, or that the debtor may exempt under section 522 of this title, shall deliver to the trustee, and account for, such property or the value of such property, unless such property is of inconsequential value or benefit to the estate." 11 U.S.C. § 542(a) (1976 ed., Supp. V).

6. Section 543(b)(1) requires a *custodian* to "deliver to the trustee any property of the debtor transferred to such custodian, or proceeds of such property, that is in such custodian's possession, custody, or control on the date that such custodian acquires knowledge of the commencement of the case."

The Bankruptcy Court declined to base the turnover order on § 542(a) because it felt bound by In re Avery Health Center, Inc., 8 B.R. 1016 (D.W.D.N.Y.1981) (§ 542(a) does not draw into debtor's estate property seized by IRS prior to filing of petition).

7. Section 363(e) of the Bankruptcy Code provides:

"Notwithstanding any other provision of this section, at any time, on request of an entity that has an interest in property used, sold, or leased, or proposed to be

The United States District Court reversed, holding that a turnover order against the Service was not authorized by either § 542(a) or § 543(b)(1). App. to Pet. for Cert. 46a. The United States Court of Appeals for the Second Circuit, in turn, reversed the District Court. 674 F.2d 144 (1982). It held that a turnover order could issue against the Service under § 542(a), and it remanded the case for reconsideration of the adequacy of the Bankruptcy Court's protection conditions. The Court of Appeals acknowledged that its ruling was contrary to that reached by the United States Court of Appeals for the Fourth Circuit in Cross Electric Co. v. United States, 664 F.2d 1218 (1981), and noted confusion on the issue among bankruptcy and district courts. 674 F.2d, at 145 and n. 1. We granted certiorari to resolve this conflict in an important area of the law under the new Bankruptcy Code.

II

By virtue of its tax lien, the Service holds a secured interest in Whiting's property. We first examine whether § 542(a) of the Bankruptcy Code generally authorizes the turnover of a debtor's property seized by a secured creditor prior to the commencement of reorganization proceedings. Section 542(a) requires an entity in possession of "property that the trustee may use, sell, or lease under § 363" to deliver that property to the trustee. Subsections (b) and (c) of § 363 authorize the trustee to use, sell, or lease any "property of the estate," subject to certain conditions for the protection of creditors with an interest in the property. Section 541(a)(1) defines the "estate" as "comprised of all the following property, wherever located: (1) . . . all legal or equitable interests of the debtor in property as of the commencement of the case." Although these statutes could be read to limit the estate to those "interests of the debtor in property" at the time of the filing of the petition, we view them as a definition of what is included in the estate, rather than as a limitation.

A

In proceedings under the reorganization provisions of the Bankruptcy Code, a troubled enterprise may be restructured to enable it to operate successfully in the future. Until the business can be reorganized pursuant to a plan under 11 U.S.C. §§ 1121–1129 (1976 ed., Supp. V), the trustee or debtor-in-possession is authorized to manage the property of the estate and to continue the operation of the business.

used, sold, or leased by the trustee, the court shall prohibit or condition such use, sale, or lease as is necessary to provide adequate protection of such interest. In any hearing under this section, the trustee has the burden of proof on the issue of adequate protection." 11 U.S.C. § 363(e) (1976 ed., Supp. V).

Pursuant to this section, the Bankruptcy Court set the following conditions to pro-

tect the tax lien: Whiting was to pay the Service $20,000 before the turnover occurred; Whiting also was to pay $1,000 a month until the taxes were satisfied; the IRS was to retain its lien during this period; and if Whiting failed to make the payments, the stay was to be lifted. 10 B.R., at 761.

See § 1108. By permitting reorganization, Congress anticipated that the business would continue to provide jobs, to satisfy creditors' claims, and to produce a return for its owners. H.R.Rep. No. 95–595, p. 220 (1977), U.S.Code Cong. & Admin.News 1978, p. 5787. Congress presumed that the assets of the debtor would be more valuable if used in a rehabilitated business than if "sold for scrap." Ibid. The reorganization effort would have small chance of success, however, if property essential to running the business were excluded from the estate. See 6 J. Moore & L. King, Collier on Bankruptcy ¶ 3.05, p. 431 (14th ed. 1978). Thus, to facilitate the rehabilitation of the debtor's business, all the debtor's property must be included in the reorganization estate.

This authorization extends even to property of the estate in which a creditor has a secured interest. § 363(b) and (c); see H.R.Rep. No. 95–595, p. 182 (1977). Although Congress might have safeguarded the interests of secured creditors outright by excluding from the estate any property subject to a secured interest, it chose instead to include such property in the estate and to provide secured creditors with "adequate protection" for their interests. § 363(e), quoted in n. 7, supra. At the secured creditor's insistence, the bankruptcy court must place such limits or conditions on the trustee's power to sell, use, or lease property as are necessary to protect the creditor. The creditor with a secured interest in property included in the estate must look to this provision for protection, rather than to the nonbankruptcy remedy of possession.

Both the congressional goal of encouraging reorganizations and Congress' choice of methods to protect secured creditors suggest that Congress intended a broad range of property to be included in the estate.

B

The statutory language reflects this view of the scope of the estate. As noted above, § 541(a) provides that the "estate is comprised of all the following property, wherever located: . . . all legal or equitable interests of the debtor in property as of the commencement of the case." 11 U.S.C. § 541(a)(1).[8] The House and Senate Reports on the Bankruptcy Code indicate that § 541(a)(1)'s scope is broad.[9] Most important, in the context of this case, § 541(a)(1) is intended to include in the estate any property made available to the estate by other provisions of the Bankruptcy Code. See H.R.Rep. No. 95–595, p. 367

---

8. Section 541(a)(1) speaks in terms of the debtor's "interests . . . in property," rather than property in which the debtor has an interest, but this choice of language was not meant to limit the expansive scope of the section. The legislative history indicates that Congress intended to exclude from the estate property of others in which the debtor had some minor interest such as a lien or bare legal title.

. . .

9. "The scope of this paragraph [§ 541(a)(1)] is broad. It includes all kinds of property, including tangible or intangible property, causes of action (see Bankruptcy Act § 70a(6)), and all other forms of property currently specified in section 70a of the Bankruptcy Act." H.R.Rep. No. 95–595, p. 367 (1977); S.Rep. No. 95–989, p. 82 (1978).

(1977). Several of these provisions bring into the estate property in which the debtor did not have a possessory interest at the time the bankruptcy proceedings commenced.

Section 542(a) is such a provision. It requires an entity (other than a custodian) holding any property of the debtor that the trustee can use under § 363 to turn that property over to the trustee. Given the broad scope of the reorganization estate, property of the debtor repossessed by a secured creditor falls within this rule, and therefore may be drawn into the estate. While there are explicit limitations on the reach of § 542(a),[12] none requires that the debtor hold a possessory interest in the property at the commencement of the reorganization proceedings.

As does all bankruptcy law, § 542(a) modifies the procedural rights available to creditors to protect and satisfy their liens.[14] In effect, § 542(a) grants to the estate a possessory interest in certain property of the debtor that was not held by the debtor at the commencement of reorganization proceedings.[15] The Bankruptcy Code provides secured creditors various rights, including the right to adequate protection, and these rights replace the protection afforded by possession.

C

This interpretation of § 542(a) is supported by the section's legislative history. Although the legislative reports are silent on the precise issue before us, the House and Senate hearings from which § 542(a) emerged provide guidance. Several witnesses at those hearings noted, without contradiction, the need for a provision authorizing the turnover of property of the debtor in the possession of secured creditors. Section 542(a) first appeared in the proposed legislation shortly after these

---

12. Section 542 provides that the property be usable under § 363, and that turnover is not required in three situations: when the property is of inconsequential value or benefit to the estate, § 542(a), when the holder of the property has transferred it in good faith without knowledge of the petition, § 542(c), or when the transfer of the property is automatic to pay a life insurance premium, § 542(d).

14. One of the procedural rights the law of secured transactions grants a secured creditor to enforce its lien is the right to take possession of the secured property upon the debtor's default. Uniform Commercial Code § 9–503, 3A U.L.A. 211 (1981). A creditor's possessory interest resulting from the exercise of this right is subject to certain restrictions on the creditor's use of the property. See § 9–504, 3A U.L.A. 256–257. Here, we address the abrogation of the Service's possessory interest obtained pursuant to its tax lien, a secured interest. We do not decide whether any property of the debtor in which a third party holds a possessory interest in-

dependent of a creditor's remedies is subject to turnover under § 542(a). For example, if property is pledged to the secured creditor so that the creditor has possession prior to any default, 542(a) may not require turnover. See 4 L. King, Collier on Bankruptcy ¶ 541.08[9], p. 541–53 (15th ed. 1982).

15. Indeed, if this were not the effect, § 542(a) would be largely superfluous in light of § 541(a)(1). Interests in the seized property that could have been exercised by the debtor—in this case, the rights to notice and the surplus from a tax sale, see n. 4, supra—are already part of the estate by virtue of § 541(a)(1). No coercive power is needed for this inclusion. The fact that § 542(a) grants the trustee greater rights than those held by the debtor prior to the filing of the petition is consistent with other provisions of the Bankruptcy Code that address the scope of the estate. See, e.g., § 544 (trustee has rights of lien creditor); § 545 (trustee has power to avoid statutory liens); § 549 (trustee has power to avoid certain post-petition transactions).

hearings. See H.R. 6, § 542(a), 95th Cong., 1st Sess., introduced January 4, 1977. See generally Klee, Legislative History of the New Bankruptcy Code, 54 Am.Bankr.L.J. 275, 279–281 (1980). The section remained unchanged through subsequent versions of the legislation.

Moreover, this interpretation of § 542 in the reorganization context is consistent with judicial precedent predating the Bankruptcy Code. Under Chapter X, the reorganization chapter of the Bankruptcy Act of 1898, as amended, §§ 101–276, 52 Stat. 883 (1938) (formerly codified as 11 U.S.C. §§ 501–676 (1976 ed.)), the bankruptcy court could order the turnover of collateral in the hands of a secured creditor. . . . Nothing in the legislative history evinces a congressional intent to depart from that practice. Any other interpretation of § 542(a) would deprive the bankruptcy estate of the assets and property essential to its rehabilitation effort and thereby would frustrate the congressional purpose behind the reorganization provisions.[17]

We conclude that the reorganization estate includes property of the debtor that has been seized by a creditor prior to the filing of a petition for reorganization.

III

A

We see no reason why a different result should obtain when the IRS is the creditor. . . .

B

Of course, if a tax levy or seizure transfers to the IRS ownership of the property seized, § 542(a) may not apply. The enforcement provisions of the Internal Revenue Code of 1954, 26 U.S.C. §§ 6321–6326 (1976 ed. and Supp. V), do grant to the Service powers to enforce its tax liens that are greater than those possessed by private secured creditors under state law. But those provisions do not transfer ownership of the property to the IRS.

The Service's interest in seized property is its lien on that property. The Internal Revenue Code's levy and seizure provisions, 26 U.S.C. §§ 6331 and 6332, are special procedural devices available to the IRS to protect and satisfy its liens, United States v. Sullivan, 333 F.2d 100, 116 (CA3 1964), and are analogous to the remedies available to private secured creditors. See Uniform Commercial Code, § 9–503, 3A U.L.A. 211–212 (1981); n. 14, supra. They are provisional remedies that do not determine the Service's rights to the seized property, but merely bring the property into the Service's legal custody. At no point does

---

17. Section 542(a) also governs turnovers in liquidation and individual adjustment of debt proceedings under Chapters 7 and 13 of the Bankruptcy Code, 11 U.S.C. §§ 701–766, 1301–1330 (1976 ed., Supp. V). See § 103(a). Our analysis in this case depends in part on the reorganization context in which the turnover order is sought. We express no view on the issue whether § 542(a) has the same broad effect in liquidation or adjustment of debt proceedings.

the Service's interest in the property exceed the value of the lien. United States v. Rogers, 461 U.S. at 690–91, 103 S.Ct. at 2141; id., at 724, 103 S.Ct. at 2158 (concurring in part and dissenting in part); see United States v. Sullivan, 333 F.2d, at 116 ("the Commissioner acts pursuant to the collection process in the capacity of lienor as distinguished from owner"). The IRS is obligated to return to the debtor any surplus from a sale. 26 U.S.C. § 6342(b). Ownership of the property is transferred only when the property is sold to a bona fide purchaser at a tax sale. See Bennett v. Hunter, 9 Wall. 326, 336, 19 L.Ed. 672 (1870); 26 U.S.C. § 6339(a)(2); Plumb, 13 Tax.L.Rev., at 274–275. In fact, the tax sale provision itself refers to the debtor as the owner of the property after the seizure but prior to the sale.[19] Until such a sale takes place, the property remains the debtor's and thus is subject to the turnover requirement of § 542(a).

IV

When property seized prior to the filing of a petition is drawn into the Chapter 11 reorganization estate, the Service's tax lien is not dissolved; nor is its status as a secured creditor destroyed. The IRS, under § 363(e), remains entitled to adequate protection for its interests, to other rights enjoyed by secured creditors, and to the specific privileges accorded tax collectors. Section 542(a) simply requires the Service to seek protection of its interest according to the congressionally established bankruptcy procedures, rather than by withholding the seized property from the debtor's efforts to reorganize.

The judgment of the Court of Appeals is affirmed.

Notes & Questions

1. *Result in Chapter 7 Case.* Would the Court's analysis or result change if *Whiting Pools* were not a reorganization case? Does anything in § 542 support a different turnover standard in Chapter 7 cases than is followed in Chapter 11 cases? Isn't § 542 essentially a mechanical provision designed to get all property under the trustee's control? Compare § 362(d)(2) (taking into account debtor's equity in property and property's necessity to an effective reorganization).

2. *Undersecured Creditors.* Should the result in *Whiting Pools* change if the seized assets were worth less than the $92,000 owed to the IRS? For purposes of the court's analysis, should the assets be valued in Whiting Pools' hands ($163,000) or at their value in the IRS's hands ($35,000)? What approach should a court take when there is disagreement over whether the seized assets exceed the amount owed to the seizing party? Does anything in § 542 turn on whether the debtor has an equity in the seized property?

19. See 26 U.S.C. § 6335(a) ("As soon as practicable after seizure of property, notice in writing shall be given by the Secretary to the owner of the property"), and § 6335(b) ("The Secretary shall as soon as practicable after the seizure of the property give notice to the owner").

3. *Incentives.* Consider the incentives created by the decision in *Whiting Pools.* Under the Court's approach, the critical date for purposes of § 542 is not the date of repossession or levy but rather the date of sale by the IRS or by a secured party. How should this ruling affect creditor behavior? Will creditors now rush to sell property as soon as possible after foreclosure? If so, might this not lead to property fetching lower prices than it would in a sale conducted at a more leisurely pace?

If creditors as a group were designing a bankruptcy system would they want a system where sale was the magic date for purposes of avoiding involvement with the bankruptcy court? Would they want a date where possession were the trigger? Or would they prefer a system with no magic date? Are there reasonable alternatives? How about a provision requiring turnover of all property (or its proceeds) repossessed within ninety days prior to the filing of a bankruptcy petition? Would that be a fairer approach? Would it generate less litigation?

Are there theoretical problems with the use of the sale date to define when § 542 applies? Suppose a creditor, unlike the IRS in *Whiting Pools,* is content to repossess property and has no desire to sell it. Will this creditor always be subject to a turnover order if his debtor subsequently goes bankrupt? How far back in time does § 542 reach?

4. *The Relationship Between § 542 and § 363.* One of the differences between § 543, which deals with custodians, and § 542, which deals with the more general obligation of all other parties to turn over property to the trustee, is that § 542 only requires the turnover "of property that the trustee may use, sell or lease under section 363 . . .." Section 363(e), in turn, provides that "on request of an entity that has an interest in property . . . to be used, sold, or leased, by the trustee, the court shall prohibit or condition such use, sale, or lease as is necessary to provide adequate protection of such interest." In *Whiting Pools,* the Court seems to equate § 542's reference to § 363 with a requirement that, upon request of a party, the turnover order must be conditioned upon furnishing adequate protection. Does § 542's reference to § 363 necessarily incorporate § 363's adequate protection standard? Or may one interpret the reference to define only the classes of property that must be turned over, without addressing the question of the protection to be afforded to the entity surrendering possession?

Why isn't a custodian's turnover obligation in § 543 limited to an obligation to turn over property that the trustee may use, sell, or lease under § 363?

5. *Attached Property.* Is property subject to a valid attachment order property of the estate? What if the creditor has proceeded to the stage of obtaining a judgment in the dispute that gave rise to the attachment? Does the method of attachment matter? Does property's status for bankruptcy purposes turn on whether the attachment is accomplished by physical possession of the property? Would the results

change if the attachment is accomplished by filing a notice of attachment with the Secretary of State?

6. *The Relationship Between § 542 and Interests Arising Under the U.C.C.* C is a secured creditor of Debtor. Prior to bankruptcy, Debtor is in default under the security agreement. The security agreement provides that in the event of default, the secured party is entitled to the collateral. Does the collateral become part of the estate? Would it matter if the secured party perfected by possession? Suppose instead that the event of default was the filing of the bankruptcy petition. See § 541(c).

Is property subject to a "special property and an insurable interest" under U.C.C. § 2–501(1) subject to a turnover order? See In re International Horizons, Inc., 21 B.R. 414 (N.D.Ga.1982) (no).

See generally Nowak, Turnover Following Prepetition Levy of Distraint Under Bankruptcy Code § 542, 55 Am.Bankr.L.J. 313 (1981).

Chapter 11

EFFECT OF COMMENCEMENT UPON TRANSACTIONS

The two principal immediate effects of the commencement of a bankruptcy case are the establishment of the estate, discussed in Chapter 10, and the automatic stay on actions against the debtor and the estate. See § 362. Before examining the automatic stay and some less automatic effects of commencement, such as the trustee's power to assume or reject executory contracts, it is helpful to examine some of the constitutional limitations on the bankruptcy process. Both the turnover requirement of § 542, discussed in Chapter 10D, and the automatic stay limit a secured party's or a lien creditor's rights against specific property. In a series of cases in the 1930's, the Supreme Court articulated some fifth amendment limitations on the degree to which bankruptcy law may interfere with rights in specific property.

A. The Constitutional Contours of Affecting Property Interests in Bankruptcy

LOUISVILLE JOINT STOCK LAND BANK v. RADFORD

Supreme Court of the United States, 1935.
295 U.S. 555, 55 S.Ct. 854, 79 L.Ed. 1593.

MR. JUSTICE BRANDEIS delivered the opinion of the Court:

[This case dealt with the question of Congress's power to modify the rights of a mortgagee. The Frazier-Lemke Act, a 1934 amendment to then § 75 of the bankruptcy law, provided that a farmer who has been unable to obtain the necessary consents to a composition may, upon being adjudged a bankrupt, acquire alternative options in respect to mortgaged property.]

1. By paragraph 3, the bankrupt may, if the mortgagee assents, purchase the property at its then appraised value, acquiring title thereto as well as immediate possession, by agreeing to make deferred payments as follows: 2½ per cent within two years; 2½ per cent within three years; 5 per cent within 4 years; 5 per cent within 5 years; the balance within six years. All deferred payments to bear interest at the rate of 1 per cent per annum.

2. By paragraph 7, the bankrupt may, if the mortgagee refuses his assent to the immediate purchase on the above basis, require the bankruptcy court to "stay all proceedings for a period of five years, during which five years the debtor shall retain possession of all or any part of his property, under the control of the court, provided he pays a reasonable rental annually for that part of the property of which he retains possession; the first payment of such rental to be made within

six months of the date of the order staying proceedings, such rental to be distributed among the secured and unsecured creditors, as their interests may appear, under the provisions of this Act. At the end of five years, or prior thereto, the debtor may pay into court the appraised price of the property of which he retains possession: Provided, That upon request of any lien holder on real estate the court shall cause a reappraisal of such real estate and the debtor may then pay the reappraised price, if acceptable to the lien holder, into court, otherwise the original appraisal price shall be paid into court and thereupon the court shall, by an order, turn over full possession and title of said property to the debtor and he may apply for his discharge as provided for by this Act: Provided, however, That the provisions of this Act shall apply only to debts existing at the time this Act becomes effective."

. . .

It is true that the position of a secured creditor, who has rights in specific property, differs fundamentally from that of an unsecured creditor, who has none; and that the Frazier-Lemke Act is the first instance of an attempt, by a bankruptcy act, to abridge, solely in the interest of the mortgagor, a substantive right of the mortgagee in specific property held as security. But we have no occasion to decide in this case whether the bankruptcy clause confers upon Congress generally the power to abridge the mortgagee's rights in specific property. Paragraph 7 declares that "the provisions of this Act shall apply only to debts existing at the time this Act becomes effective." The power over property pledged as security after the date of the Act may be greater than over property pledged before; and this Act deals only with pre-existing mortgages. Because the Act is retroactive in terms and as here applied purports to take away rights of the mortgagee in specific property, another provision of the Constitution is controlling.

Fourth. The bankruptcy power, like the other great substantive powers of Congress, is subject to the Fifth Amendment. Under the bankruptcy power Congress may discharge the debtor's personal obligation, because, unlike the States, it is not prohibited from impairing the obligation of contracts. But the effect of the Act here complained of is not the discharge of Radford's personal obligation. It is the taking of substantive rights in specific property acquired by the Bank prior to the Act. In order to determine whether rights of that nature have been taken, we must ascertain what the mortgagee's rights were before the passage of the Act. We turn, therefore, first to the law of the State.

. . .

As here applied it has taken from the Bank the following property rights recognized by the law of Kentucky:

1. The right to retain the lien until the indebtedness thereby secured is paid.

2. The right to realize upon the security by a judicial public sale.

3. The right to determine when such sale shall be held, subject only to the discretion of the court.

4. The right to protect its interest in the property by bidding at such sale whenever held, and thus to assure having the mortgaged property devoted primarily to the satisfaction of the debt, either through receipt of the proceeds of a fair competitive sale or by taking the property itself.

5. The right to control meanwhile the property during the period of default, subject only to the discretion of the court, and to have the rents and profits collected by a receiver for the satisfaction of the debt.

Strong evidence that the taking of these rights from the mortgagee effects a substantial impairment of the security is furnished by the occurrences in the Senate which led to the adoption there of the amendment to the bill declaring that the Act "shall apply only to debts existing at the time this Act becomes effective." The bill as passed by the House applied to both pre-existing and future mortgages. It was amended in the Senate so as to limit it to existing mortgages; and as so amended was adopted by both Houses pursuant to the report of the Conference Committee. This was done because, in the Senate, it was pointed out that the bill, if made applicable to future mortgages, would destroy the farmers' future mortgage credit.

Sixth. Radford contends that these changes in the position of the Bank wrought pursuant to the Act, do not impair substantive rights, because the Bank retains every right in the property to which it is entitled. The contention rests upon the unfounded assertion that its only substantive right under the mortgage is to have the value of the security applied to the satisfaction of the debt. It would be more accurate to say that the only right under the mortgage left to the Bank is the right to retain its lien until the mortgagor sometime within the five-year period, chooses to release it by paying the appraised value of the property. A mortgage lien so limited in character and incident is of course legally conceivable. It might be created by contract under existing law. If a part of the mortgaged property were taken by eminent domain a mortgagee would receive payment on a similar basis. But the Frazier-Lemke Act does not purport to exercise the right of eminent domain; and neither the law of Kentucky nor Radford's mortgages contain any provision conferring upon the mortgagor an option to compel, at any time within five years, a release of the farm upon payment of its appraised value and a right to retain meanwhile possession, upon paying a rental to be fixed by the bankruptcy courts.

Equally unfounded is the contention that the mortgagee is not injured by the denial of possession for the five years, since it receives the rental value of the property. It is argued that experience has proved that five years is not unreasonably long, since a longer period is commonly required to complete a voluntary contract for the sale and purchase of a farm; or to close a bankruptcy estate; or to close a railroad receivership. And it is asserted that Radford is, in effect, acting as receiver for the bankruptcy court. Radford's argument ignores the fact that in ordinary bankruptcy proceedings and in equity receiverships, the court may in its discretion, order an immediate sale and closing of the estate; and it ignores, also, the fundamental difference in purpose between the delay permitted in those proceedings and that prescribed by Congress. When a court of equity allows a receivership to continue, it does so to prevent a sacrifice of the creditor's interest. Under the Act, the purpose of the delay in making a sale and of the prolonged possession accorded the mortgagor is to promote his interests at the expense of the mortgagee.

Home Bldg. & L. Asso. v. Blaisdell, 290 U.S. 398, 54 S.Ct. 231, 78 L.Ed. 413, 88 A.L.R. 1481, upon which Radford relies, lends no support to his contention. There the statute left the period of the extension of the right of redemption to be determined by the court within the maximum limit of two years. Even after the period had been decided upon, it could, as was pointed out, "be reduced by order of the court under the statute, in case of a change in circumstances . . ." (p. 447); and at the close of the period, the mortgagee was free to apply the mortgaged property to the satisfaction of the mortgage debt. Here, the option and the possession would continue although the emergency which is relied upon as justifying the Act ended before November 30, 1939.

Seventh. Radford contends further that the changes in the mortgagee's rights in the property, even if substantial, are not arbitrary and unreasonable, because they were made for a permissible public purpose. That claim appears to rest primarily upon the following propositions: (1) The welfare of the Nation demands that our farms be individually owned by those who operate them. (2) To permit widespread foreclosure of farm mortgages would result in transferring ownership, in large measure, to great corporations; would transform farmer-owners into tenants or farm laborers; and would tend to create a peasant class. (3) There was grave danger at the time of the passage of the Act, that foreclosure of farms would become widespread. The persistent decline in the prices of agricultural products, as compared with the prices of articles which farmers are obliged to purchase, had been accentuated by the long continued depression and had made it impossible for farmers to pay the charges accruing under existing mortgages. (4) Thus had arisen an emergency requiring congressional action. To avert the threatened calamity the Act presented an appropriate remedy. Extensive economic data, of which in large part we may take judicial notice, were submitted in support of these propositions. . . .

The province of the Court is limited to deciding whether the Frazier-Lemke Act as applied has taken from the Bank without compensation, and given to Radford, rights in specific property which are of substantial value. As we conclude that the Act as applied has done so, we must hold it void. For the Fifth Amendment commands that, however great the Nation's need, private property shall not be thus taken even for a wholly public use without just compensation. If the public interest requires, and permits, the taking of property of individual mortgagees in order to relieve the necessities of individual mortgagors, resort must be had to proceedings by eminent domain; so that, through taxation, the burden of the relief afforded in the public interest may be borne by the public.

Reversed.

WRIGHT v. VINTON BRANCH OF THE MOUNTAIN TRUST BANK OF ROANOKE

Supreme Court of the United States, 1937.
300 U.S. 440, 57 S.Ct. 556, 81 L.Ed. 736.

JUSTICE BRANDEIS delivered the opinion of the Court.

[In response to *Radford*, Congress enacted a new Frazier-Lemke Act, which was soon challenged by a secured creditor. The Court summarized the facts as follows:] Wright, a Virginia farmer, gave in 1929 a mortgage deed of trust of his farm to secure a debt now held by the Vinton Branch of the Mountain Trust Bank. In March, 1935, he filed a petition under § 75 of the Bankruptcy Act . . .. When the proceedings were begun, the debt secured by the deed of trust had matured and was in default, and the trustee, at the request of the beneficiary, had advertised the property for sale pursuant to the terms of the deed of trust and the provisions of the Virginia Code. The debtor's petition prayed, among other things, "that all proceedings against him by way of pending and advertised foreclosures of his farming lands, or by other methods contrary to the provision" of the Act be stayed. The petition, "appearing to be in proper form and to have been filed in good faith," was referred to the Conciliation Commissioner as required by § 75. On July 27, 1935, the debtor made a proposal for composition; but it was not accepted by the mortgage creditor. On October 8, 1935, Wright filed an amended petition under subsection (s) of § 75 as amended by the new Frazier-Lemke Act; and asked to be adjudged a bankrupt and to have all the benefits of the provisions of said sub-section (s) as so amended and approved August 28, 1935.

[The Court then stated that the opinion in *Radford* enumerated five important substantive rights in specific property which had been taken. After noting that *Radford* did not hold that the deprivation of any one of these rights would have rendered the first Frazier-Lemke Act invalid "but that the effect of the statute in its entirety was to deprive the mortgagee of his property without due process of law," the Court analyzed the new Frazier-Lemke Act's treatment of the five rights.]

It is not denied that the new Act adequately preserves three of the five above enumerated rights of a mortgagee. "The right to retain the lien until the indebtedness thereby secured is paid" is specifically covered by the provisions in paragraph 1, that the debtor's possession, "under the supervision and control of the court," shall be "subject to all existing mortgages, liens, pledges, or encumbrances," and that: "All such existing mortgages, liens, pledges, or encumbrances shall remain in full force and effect, and the property covered by such mortgages, liens, pledges, or encumbrances shall be subject to the payment of the claims of the secured creditors, as their interests may appear."

"The right to realize upon the security by a judicial public sale" is covered by the provision in paragraph 3 that at the termination of the stay:

". . . upon request in writing by any secured creditor or creditors, the court shall order the property upon which such secured creditors have a lien to be sold at public auction."

The new Act does not in terms provide for "The right to protect its [the mortgagee's] interest in the property by bidding at such sale whenever held. . . ." But the committee reports and the explanations given in Congress make it plain that the mortgagee was intended to have this right. We accept this view of the statute.

Fourth. The claim that sub-section (s) is unconstitutional rests mainly upon the contention that the Act denies to a mortgagee the "right to determine when such sale shall be held, subject only to the discretion of the court." The assertion is that the new Act in effect gives to the mortgagor the absolute right to a three-year stay; and that a three-year moratorium cannot be justified. The three-year stay is specified in the following provisions:

"When the conditions set forth in this section [Section 75] have been complied with, the court shall stay all judicial or official proceedings in any court, or under the direction of any official, against the debtor or any of his property, for a period of three years." Par. 2.

"At the end of three years, or prior thereto, the debtor may pay into court the amount of the appraisal of the property of which he retains possession, including the amount of encumbrances on his exemptions, up to the amount of the appraisal, less the amount paid on principal." Par. 3.

Whether, in view of the emergency, an absolute stay of three years would have been justified under the bankruptcy power, we have no occasion to decide. There are other provisions in the statute affecting the mortgagor's right to possession. Their phraseology is lacking in clarity. But we are of opinion that, while the Act affords the debtor, ordinarily, a three-year period of rehabilitation, the stay provided for is not an absolute one; and that the court may terminate the stay and order a sale earlier. . . .

The mortgagor's right to retain possession during the stay is specifically limited by paragraph 3, which provides: "If, however, the debtor at any time fails to comply with the provisions of this section, or with any orders of the court made pursuant to this section, or is unable to refinance himself within three years, the court may order the appointment of a trustee, and order the property sold or otherwise disposed of as provided for in this Act."

Thus, for example, the debtor's tenure under the stay is subject to the requirement that he pay "a reasonable rental semiannually for that part of the property of which he retains possession." Paragraph 2. Under the last-quoted provision of paragraph 3, if the debtor defaults in this obligation "at any time," the court may thereupon order the property sold. Likewise, the property while in the debtor's possession is kept, according to paragraph 2, at all times "in the custody and under the supervision and control of the court;" and, also under paragraph 2: "The court, in its discretion, if it deems it necessary to protect the creditors from loss by the estate, and/or to conserve the security, . . . may, in addition to the rental, require payments on the principal due and owing by the debtor to the secured or unsecured creditors, as their interests may appear, in accordance with the provisions of this Act, and may require such payments to be made quarterly, semiannually, or annually, not inconsistent with the protection of the rights of the creditors and the debtor's ability to pay, with a view to his financial rehabilitation."

Paragraph 3 authorizes the court to have the property sold if "at any time" the debtor should fail to comply with orders of the court issued under its power to require interim payments on principal, or otherwise in the course of its "supervision and control" of his possession. Paragraph 3 also provides that "if . . . the debtor at any time . . . is unable to refinance himself within three years," the court may close the proceedings by selling the property. This clause must be interpreted as meaning that the court may terminate the stay if after a reasonable time it becomes evident that there is no reasonable hope that the debtor can rehabilitate himself within the three-year period.

Finally, the intention of Congress to make the stay terminable by the court within the three years is shown also by paragraph 6, which declares the Act an emergency measure, and provides that:

"if in the judgment of the court such emergency ceases to exist in its locality, then the court, in its discretion, may shorten the stay of proceedings herein provided for and proceed to liquidate the estate."

. . .

Fifth. It is urged that subsection (s) is unconstitutional because there is taken from the mortgagee "the right to control meanwhile the property during the period of default, subject only to the discretion of the court, and to have the rents and profits collected by a receiver for the satisfaction of the debt."

(a) The argument is that possession by the mortgagor during the stay is necessarily less favorable to the mortgagee than possession by a receiver or trustee would be. This is not true. The mortgagor is in default, but it is not therefore to be assumed that he is a wrongdoer, or incompetent to conduct farming operations. The legislation is designed to aid victims of the general ecomomic depression. The mortgagor is familiar with the property, and presumably vitally interested in preserving ownership thereof and ready to exert himself to the uttermost to that end. It is not unreasonable to assume that, under these circumstances, the interests of all concerned will be better served by leaving him in possession than by installing a disinterested receiver or trustee. For the mortgagor holds possession charged with obligations imposed for the benefit of the mortgagee as fully as if the property were in the possession of a receiver or trustee, and there is probably a saving of expense. In order to protect the creditor's interests, the possession is at all times subject to the supervision and control of the court; and, if the debtor, "at any time," fails to comply with orders of the court issued in the exercise of its supervisory power to protect the mortgagee against waste or other abuse of his possession by the mortgagor, the court may order the property sold. The farmer's proceeding in bankruptcy for rehabilitation, resembles that of a corporation for reorganization. As to the latter it is expressly provided that the debtor may, to some extent, be left in possession, 11 U.S.C.A. § 207(c); and it is common practice to appoint as receivers one of the officials of the corporation. . . .

(c) The disposition of the rental required to be made is said to involve denial of the mortgagee's rights. Paragraph 2 provides: "Such rental shall be paid into court, to be used, first, for payment of taxes and upkeep of the property, and the remainder to be distributed among the secured and unsecured creditors, and applied on their claims, as their interests may appear."

It is suggested that payment of taxes and keeping the property in repair take the income from the mortgagee, and that the mortgagor alone may be benefited thereby; that if the mortgagor exercises the option to purchase the property at its appraised value, he will secure the property free of tax liens which otherwise might have accrued against it. But it must be assumed that the mortgagor will not get the property for less than its actual value. The Act provides that upon the creditor's request the property must be reappraised, or sold at public auction; and the mortgagee may by bidding at such sale fully protect his interest. Non-payment of taxes may imperil the title. Payments for upkeep are essential to the preservation of the property. These payments prescribed by the Act are in accordance with the common practice in foreclosure proceedings where the property is in the hands of receivers.

. . . A court of bankruptcy may affect the interests of lien holders in many ways. To carry out the purposes of the Bankruptcy Act, it may direct that all liens upon property forming part of a bankrupt's estate be marshalled; or that the property be sold free of encumbrances and the rights of all lien holders be transferred to the proceeds of the sale. Despite the peremptory terms of a pledge, it may enjoin sale of the collateral, if it finds that the sale would hinder or delay preparation or consummation of a plan of reorganization. Continental Illinois

National Bank & Trust Co. v. Chicago, Rock Island & Pacific Ry. Co., 294 U.S. 648, 680, 681, 55 S.Ct. 595, 608, 79 L.Ed. 1110. It may enjoin like action by a mortgagee which would defeat the purpose of subsection (s) to effect rehabilitation of the farmer mortgagor. For the reasons stated, we are of opinion that the provisions of subsection (s) make no unreasonable modification of the mortgagee's rights; and hence are valid. . . .

Notes & Questions

1. *The Limits Imposed by* Radford. What constitutional limits does *Radford* impose upon the extent to which a bankruptcy law may affect secured creditors' interest in property? Consider the following assertions:

(a) The secured creditor has the right to have the value of its secured position maintained through the proceedings. See 2 Collier on Bankruptcy ¶ 362.01, at 362–15 (L. King ed. 15th ed. 1982).

(b) "In context, Justice Brandeis' comments suggest that the holding of [*Radford*] is only that the modification of secured creditors' rights effected by the Frazier-Lemke Act was too substantial to permit the Act to be applied retroactively. Thus, the famous statement that the bankruptcy power is subject to the fifth amendment must be taken to mean nothing more than that the fifth amendment, through either the due process or the takings clause, is the constitutional foundation for the proposition that statutes that retroactively disrupt settled expectations may be subject to particularly attentive judicial scrutiny." Rogers, The Impairment of Secured Creditors' Rights in Reorganization: A Study of the Relationship Between the Fifth Amendment and the Bankruptcy Clause, 96 Harv.L.Rev. 973, 985 (1983).

2. *Limiting the Sale of Collateral.* In Continental Illinois National Bank & Trust Co. v. Chicago, Rock Island & Pacific Railway Co., 294 U.S. 648, 55 S.Ct. 595, 79 L.Ed. 1110 (1935), a railroad filed a petition seeking reorganization under then § 77 of the Bankruptcy Act. A group of creditors owned notes of the debtor secured by bonds granting liens on portions of the debtor's property. The debtor filed a petition requesting the district court to determine whether it should enjoin the holders of the secured notes, in the event of a default, from selling any of the collateral. The district court granted the requested relief and the secured creditors appealed, challenging the constitutionality of the order.

Having satisfied itself that § 77, "in its general scope and aim," is within Congress's bankruptcy clause power, the Court found the act conferred power to enjoin a sale where the sale would hinder and probably prevent an effective reorganization plan. The Court continued:

> The injunction here in no way impairs the lien, or disturbs the preferred rank of the pledgees. It does no more than suspend the

enforcement of the lien by a sale of the collateral pending further action. It may be, as suggested, that during the period of restraint the collateral will decline in value; but the same may be said in respect of an injunction against the sale of real estate upon foreclosure of a mortgage; and such an injunction may issue in an ordinary proceeding in bankruptcy. . . . A claim that injurious consequences will result to the pledgee or the mortgagee may not, of course, be disregarded by the district court; but it presents a question addressed not to the power of the court but to its discretion—a matter not subject to the interference of an appellate court unless such discretion be improvidently exercised. So far as constitutional power is concerned, there is no difference between an injunction restraining the enforcement of a real-estate mortgage and one restraining the enforcement of a pledge by the sale of collateral security.

On similar grounds the Court found the injunction did not violate the due process clause of the fifth amendment.

Speaking generally, it may be said that Congress, while acting without power to impair the obligation of contracts by laws acting directly and independently to that end, undeniably, has authority to pass legislation pertinent to any of the powers conferred by the Constitution, however it may operate collaterally or incidentally to impair or destroy the obligation of private contracts. . . . And under the express power to pass uniform laws on the subject of bankruptcies, the legislation is valid though drawn with the direct aim and effect of relieving insolvent persons in whole or in part from the payment of their debts. . . .

The injunction here goes no further than to delay the enforcement of the contract. It affects only the remedy.

In *Continental Illinois*, the collateral seemed to be worth substantially more than the debt, 294 U.S. at 658–60, 55 S.Ct. at 598–99, but given the collateral's status as part of a financially troubled railroad, substantial questions as to the collateral's value must have existed.

3. *Abolition of Secured Creditor's Priority in Bankruptcy.* May Congress deem all security ineffective in bankruptcy? *Radford* seems to establish that the fifth amendment limits Congress's power to regulate security interests in a bankruptcy proceeding. It and subsequent cases suggest that there is a faint line separating permissible and impermissible regulation or alteration of security interests. The first Frazier-Lemke Act fell on one side of that line; the second on the other.

It may assist one's thinking about that line to focus on property interests that are somewhat more tangible than mortgages and security interests. Consider a tangible piece of property, a car. If you own a car and Congress passes a law (presumably for the public good) containing pollution limitations that makes your car unusable (or worthless), has the fifth amendment been violated? Suppose the law merely reduces the value of your car by requiring periodic inspections or some

safety-related repair or modification? In the context of the car regulation, would there be a faint line dividing fifth amendment violations
from lawful regulation that is similar to the faint line in the *Radford*
set of cases? Or is the car case an easy one? If it is, what are its
implications for the regulation of security interests in bankruptcy?

Could one argue that a bankruptcy rule regulating security interests
is less burdensome than the car regulation laws? Does a bankruptcy
law ever totally "take" a security interest?

4. *The Retroactivity Factor.* Notice the Court's emphasis in *Radford* on the retroactive nature of the Frazier-Lemke Act. Consider
again the car law but assume that it applies only to cars purchased
after the effective date of the law. (Such a law might provide a model
for thinking about a bankruptcy law affecting only newly created
security interests.) Does the prospective nature of the law change the
constitutional analysis? Would there be any chance of such a law
violating the fifth amendment? Consider the law from the perspective
of a car dealer and its effect on the value of cars in that dealer's
inventory on the date the law becomes effective. Has there been a
taking of the dealer's property? If a bankruptcy law applies only to
future security interests, does it nevertheless unduly interfere with
someone's property interest? Consider such a law's effect on the value
of property which previously could have been used as collateral for
secured loans.

In United States v. Security Industrial Bank, 459 U.S. 70, 103 S.Ct.
407, 74 L.Ed.2d 235 (1982), debtors sought to avoid liens on their
property by invoking § 522(f) of the Bankruptcy Act. The lienholder
claimed that § 522(f) is unconstitutional. In holding that § 522(f)
should not be applied to liens that predate the effective date of § 522(f),
the Court, in an opinion by Justice Rehnquist, alluded to the constitutional problem it sought to avoid by so construing § 522(f).

"It may be readily agreed that § 522(f)(2) is a rational exercise of
Congress' authority under Article I, Section 8, Clause 4, and that this
authority has been regularly construed to authorize the retrospective
impairment of contractual obligations. Hanover National Bank v.
Moyses, 186 U.S. 181, 188, 22 S.Ct. 857, 860, 46 L.Ed. 1113 (1902). Such
agreement does not, however, obviate the additional difficulty that
arises when that power is sought to be used to defeat traditional
property interests. The bankruptcy power is subject to the Fifth
Amendment's prohibition against taking private property without compensation. Louisville Joint Stock Land Bank v. Radford, 295 U.S. 555,
55 S.Ct. 854, 79 L.Ed. 1593 (1935). Thus, however 'rational' the exercise
of the bankruptcy power may be, that inquiry is quite separate from
the question whether the enactment takes property within the prohibition of the Fifth Amendment.

"The government apparently contends (Brief for the United States,
at 30–32) that because cases such as Arnett v. Kennedy, 416 U.S. 134,
94 S.Ct. 1633, 40 L.Ed.2d 15 (1974) and Goldberg v. Kelly, 397 U.S. 254,

90 S.Ct. 1011, 25 L.Ed.2d 287 (1970) defined 'property' for purposes of the Due Process Clause sufficiently broadly to include rights which at common law would have been deemed contractual, traditional property rights are entitled to no greater protection under the takings clause than traditional contract rights. It argues that 'bankruptcy principles do not support a sharp distinction between the rights of secured and unsecured creditors.' Brief for the United States, at 31. However 'bankruptcy principles' may speak to this question, our cases recognize, as did the common law, that the contractual right of a secured creditor to obtain repayment of his debt may be quite different in legal contemplation from the property right of the same creditor in the collateral. Compare Hanover National Bank v. Moyses, supra, with Louisville Joint Stock Land Bank v. Radford, supra, and Kaiser-Aetna v. United States, 444 U.S. 164, 100 S.Ct. 383, 62 L.Ed.2d 332 (1979).

"Since the governmental action here would result in a complete destruction of the property right of the secured party, the case fits but awkwardly into the analytic framework employed in Penn Central Transportation Co. v. New York City, 438 U.S. 104, 98 S.Ct. 2646, 57 L.Ed.2d 631 (1978) and Prune Yard Shopping Center v. Robins, 447 U.S. 74, 100 S.Ct. 2035, 64 L.Ed.2d 741 (1980), where governmental action affected some but not all of the 'bundle of rights' which comprise the 'property' in question. The government argues that the interest of a secured party such as was involved here is 'insubstantial,' apparently in part because it is a nonpurchase-money, non-possessory interest in personal property. The 'bundle of rights' which accrues to a secured party is obviously smaller than that which accrues to an owner in fee simple, but the government cites no cases supporting the proposition that differences such as these relegate the secured party's interest to something less than property. And our decisions in *Radford*, supra, and Armstrong v. United States, 364 U.S. 40, 80 S.Ct. 1563, 4 L.Ed.2d 1554 (1961), militate against such a proposition. . . .

"In *Armstrong*, materialmen delivered materials to a prime contractor for use in constructing navy personnel boats. Under state law, they obtained liens in the vessels. The prime contractor defaulted on his obligations to the United States, and the government took title to and possession of the uncompleted hulls and unused materials, thus making it impossible for the materialmen to enforce their liens. We held that this constituted a taking:

'"The total destruction by the government of all compensable value of these liens, which constitute compensable property, has every possible element of a Fifth Amendment 'taking' and is not a mere 'consequential incidence' of a valid regulatory measure."' 364 U.S., at 48, 80 S.Ct., at 1568–69.

"The government seeks to distinguish *Armstrong* on the ground that it was a classical 'taking' in the sense that the government acquired for itself the property in question, while in the instant case the government has simply imposed a general economic regulation which in effect transfers the property interest from a private creditor to a private debtor. While the classical taking is of the sort that the government describes, our cases show that takings analysis is not necessarily limited to outright acquisitions by the government for itself.

"The government finally contends that because the resale value of household goods is generally low, and because creditors therefore view the principal value of their security as a lever to negotiate for reaffirmation of the debt rather than as a vehicle for foreclosure, the property interests involved here do not merit protection under the takings clause. While this contention cannot be dismissed out of hand, it seems to run counter to the state's characterization of the interest as property, to our reliance in other 'takings' cases on state law characterizations, see, e.g., Kaiser-Aetna v. United States, supra, 444 U.S. 164, 179, 100 S.Ct. 383, 392, 62 L.Ed.2d 332 and also to at least some of the implications of *Radford,* supra, and *Armstrong,* supra.

"The foregoing discussion satisfies us that there is substantial doubt whether the retroactive destruction of the appellees' liens in these cases comports with the Fifth Amendment. . . ."

5. *Distinguishing Between Secured and Unsecured Creditors.* If the fifth amendment does limit Congress's power to affect interests of secured creditors, does it also limit Congress's power to affect interests of unsecured creditors? How are they different? Are unsecured creditors' rights under the UFCA and bulk transfer laws different in kind from secured creditors' rights in collateral? Is an unsecured creditor's right to recover a money judgment against a defaulting debtor unworthy of constitutional protection? If it is worthy of protection, how can the right be reconciled with the debtor's ability to obtain a discharge of most unsecured debts merely by going through a bankruptcy proceeding?

6. *Bankruptcy Clause Limits.* Professor Rogers has argued that the takings clause and the due process clause do not impose substantive limitations on congressional exercise of the bankruptcy power. "Instead, the principal source of substantive limitations on bankruptcy legislation is the bankruptcy clause itself, and hence the constitutionality of a statute adopted under the bankruptcy clause depends only on whether the measure falls within the scope of the powers conferred by the bankruptcy clause." Rogers, supra, at 997–98. If this view is accepted, how should we go about deciding the limits on Congress's power under the bankruptcy clause?

See generally Note, Constitutionality of Retroactive Lien Avoidance Under Bankruptcy Code Section 522(f), 94 Harv.L.Rev. 1616 (1981); Comment, The Secured Creditor's Right to Full Liquidation Value in Corporate Reorganization, 42 U.Chi.L.Rev. 510 (1975).

B. The Automatic Stay

KENNEDY, AUTOMATIC STAYS UNDER THE NEW BANKRUPTCY LAW, 12 U.Mich.J.Law Ref. 3, 10 (1978)

In Mueller v. Nugent,[1] decided shortly after the enactment of the Bankruptcy Act of 1898, the United States Supreme Court declared that a petition in bankruptcy is "a *caveat* to all the world, and in effect an attachment and injunction." This judicial gloss, much quoted and applied since, was an early recognition that a stay of creditors from collecting their claims against the debtor and his property from and after the filing of a petition under the Bankruptcy Act is indispensable to bankruptcy administration. Unless the creditors are stayed, the debtor's estate will be dismembered and the objective of equality of distribution defeated. The fresh start sought by the bankrupt in invoking the bankruptcy laws is likely to be compromised by permitting the continuation of actions against him. All the property of the bankrupt in his possession is brought into the custody of the bankruptcy court by the filing of the petition, and no interference with that custody can be countenanced without the court's permission. The bankruptcy court's control has been buttressed with statutory power and inherent power as a court of equity to enjoin litigation and acts of creditors and others insofar as necessary to effectuate bankruptcy objectives. . . .

A petition filed under Title 11 triggers an automatic stay under section 362, just as the filing of a petition does under the previous Act and the Rules of Bankruptcy Procedure. As under prior law, the stay becomes operative immediately whether the petition is voluntary or involuntary. When a petition is filed by husband and wife in a joint case, the stay takes effect with respect to both debtors and their property and the property of their estates. Unlike prior law, section 362 does not recognize or permit any different effect to be given the stay because of the chapter under which the case was commenced. Any rule that would prescribe a different procedure for enforcing or obtaining relief from a stay by reference to the chapter under which the case was brought would be vulnerable to challenge as in conflict with Title 11. While the new bankruptcy legislation imposes some limitations on the stay not found in the previous law, section 362 is notable for enlarging the scope of the stay as it applies in liquidation cases so that it generally is given the same effect as the stay now has in debtor relief cases.

Introductory Problems

1. Some questions involving the automatic stay involve seemingly straightforward application of § 362. For example, Debtor files a voluntary Chapter 7 petition on February 1. On February 8, Debtor receives a paycheck at work. May creditors take action to collect out of

1. 184 U.S. 1, 14 (1901).

that paycheck without violating the automatic stay? May the Debtor's spouse seek to collect alimony or child support out of the paycheck without violating the automatic stay? Suppose the spouse's actions pose a serious threat to the orderly administration of the estate? See § 105.

2. On January 31, Creditor lends Debtor $1,000 and is granted a security interest in Debtor's equipment. On February 1, Debtor files a voluntary bankruptcy petition. May Creditor take action to perfect his security interest? Suppose Creditor is a purchase money lender? See §§ 362(b)(3), 546(b).

3. On January 1, 1980, Debtor injured Smith in an automobile accident. Smith has been diligently seeking legal advice and gathering data and plans to file suit before the statute of limitations for tort claims expires. Thirty days before the limitations period expires, Debtor files a voluntary petition in bankruptcy. May Smith commence his lawsuit? See § 108(c), cf. IRC § 6503(b) (suspending collection limitations period for period assets are in control of court).

4. How long may the stay remain in effect without court action? See § 362(e). with court action?

5. Debtor, who filed a Chapter 7 petition on February 1, has contracts with A and B. Debtor breached his contract with A on January 1 and on February 2. May A take legal action against Debtor without violating the automatic stay?

B's contract includes the grant to B of a security interest. May B perfect the security interest on February 2? May he repossess the collateral on February 2? Would anything change if default on B's contract occurred on February 2?

MATTER OF M. FRENVILLE CO., INC.

United States Court of Appeals, Third Circuit, 1984.
744 F.2d 332, cert. denied 469 U.S. 1160, 105 S.Ct. 911, 83 L.Ed.2d 925 (1985).

Before SEITZ, CHIEF JUDGE, STEWART, ASSOCIATE JUSTICE (Retired) *, and ADAMS, CIRCUIT JUDGE.

OPINION OF THE COURT

ADAMS, CIRCUIT JUDGE.

This is an appeal by Avellino & Bienes (A & B) from a ruling by the district court, affirming the judgment of the bankruptcy court, that A & B's action against M. Frenville Co., Inc. and Rudolf Frenville, Sr. was barred by the automatic stay provision of the Bankruptcy Reform Act of 1978 (the Code), 11 U.S.C. § 362(a)(1) (1982). The critical issue is whether the automatic stay provision applies to situations in which the acts of the debtor occurred before the filing of the bankruptcy petition

* Justice Potter Stewart, Associate Justice (retired) of the United States Supreme Court sitting by designation.

yet the cause of action stemming from those acts arose post-petition.
For the reasons set forth, we reverse the district court's judgment.

I.

The facts of this case are undisputed. A & B is a certified public
accounting firm located in New York City. From 1977 to 1979 A & B
was engaged by M. Frenville Co., Inc. as an independent auditor and
accountant. As part of its duties, A & B prepared certified financial
statements of the company for fiscal years 1978 and 1979.

In July 1980, creditors of Frenville filed an involuntary petition for
bankruptcy against the company under chapter 7 of the Bankruptcy
Reform Act of 1978, 11 U.S.C. §§ 701 et seq. (1982). In January 1981,
creditors also filed involuntary petitions under chapter 7 of the Code
against two principals of the company: Rudolph Frenville, Sr. and
Rudolph Frenville, Jr.[1]

The Chase Manhattan Bank, N.A., the Fidelity Bank, Fidelity International Bank and Girard International Bank (the banks) filed suit in
the Supreme Court of New York on November 16, 1981, against A & B.
The complaint alleged that A & B negligently and recklessly prepared
the Frenville financial statements, that the statements were false, and
that because of their reliance on the statements, the banks had collectively suffered losses in excess of five million dollars.

As a result of the suit by the banks, A & B filed a complaint on
January 10, 1983, in the Bankruptcy Court for the District of New
Jersey, which was administering the Frenvilles' chapter 7 proceedings.
In the bankruptcy court, A & B sought relief from the automatic stay
provision of § 362(a) in order to include the Frenvilles as third-party
defendants in the New York state proceeding. The purpose of the
third-party complaint was to obtain indemnification or contribution
from the Frenvilles for any loss suffered by A & B as a result of the suit
by the banks.

The bankruptcy judge held the automatic stay provision of § 362(a)
was applicable to A & B's suit because the Frenvilles' liability, if any,
resulted from their pre-petition acts. Moreover, the bankruptcy judge
refused to grant relief from the automatic stay as provided in § 362(d)
of the Code.[2] The district court affirmed the bankruptcy judge's order
that the automatic stay barred A & B's action for indemnification or
contribution.

1. M. Frenville Co., Inc. will be referred
to as "Frenville." M. Frenville Co., Inc.
and Rudolph Frenville, Sr. collectively will
be referred to as the "Frenvilles." Rudolph Frenville, Jr., although involved in
the bankruptcy proceedings, is not a party
to A & B's proposed action.

2. Since we hold that the automatic
stay, by its own terms, is inapplicable in
the present case, we need not reach the
issue of whether relief from the stay was
warranted.

II.

We must decide today whether the automatic stay of § 362(a) of the Code is applicable when the debtor's acts which form the basis of a suit occurred pre-petition but the actual cause of action which is being instituted did not arise until after the filing of a bankruptcy petition. The automatic stay provision provides that

> (a) Except as provided in subsection (b) of this section, a petition filed under section 301, 302, or 303 of this title . . . operates as a stay, applicable to all entities, of—

> > (1) the commencement or continuation, including the issuance or employment of process, of a judicial, administrative, or other proceeding against the debtor that was or *could have been commenced before* the commencement of the case under this title, or to recover a claim against the debtor that *arose before* the commencement of the case under this title;

11 U.S.C. § 362(a)(1) (emphasis added).

The automatic stay provision of § 362(a) is one of the fundamental protections provided to a debtor by the Code. Congress' intent in enacting § 362(a) is clear—it wanted to stop collection efforts for all antecedent debts. Congress intended that the debtor obtain a fresh start, free from the immediate financial pressures that caused the debtor to go into bankruptcy.

Yet despite the broad reach of the automatic stay, it is not all encompassing. Section 362(b), for example, provides exemptions from the automatic stay. As a further restriction, the Code requires that the proceeding stayed "was or could have been commenced" before filing or that the proceeding was based on a claim that arose pre-petition. § 362(a)(1); see In re York, 13 B.R. 757, 758 (Bankr.D.Me.1981). Proceedings or claims arising post-petition are not subject to the automatic stay. See, e.g., Turner Broadcasting System, Inc. v. Sanyo Electric, Inc., 33 B.R. 996, 999–1000 (N.D.Ga.1983); In re Powell, 27 B.R. 146, 147 (Bankr.W.D.Mo.1983); In re Anderson, 23 B.R. 174, 175 (Bankr. N.D.Ill.1982); In re York, 13 B.R. 757, 758–59 (Bankr.D.Me.1981). In *Anderson*, for example, the debtor signed a contract for shipping services with several shipping companies on August 1, 1981. On November 12, 1981, the debtor filed a petition for relief under chapter 13 of the Code. Three months after the petition was filed the shipping companies commenced suit, alleging that the debtor had submitted fraudulent shipping charges. The court held that the automatic stay did not apply. Although the parties had signed the contract pre-petition, the alleged fraud did not begin until December 24, 1981, a month after the petition was filed. Since the shipping companies' claim arose post-petition, the bankruptcy court declared that § 362(a) was inapplicable.

Only proceedings that could have been commenced or claims that arose before the filing of the bankruptcy petitions are automatically stayed. It is undisputed that the Frenvilles' acts which ultimately led to A & B's suit for indemnification or contribution occurred in 1978 or 1979, well before the chapter 7 petitions were filed. Section 362(a)(1), however, refers to "proceedings" and "claims" against, not acts done by, the debtor. Pre-petition acts by a debtor, by themselves, are not sufficient to cause the automatic stay to apply. In most cases, the claim or cause of action will arise simultaneously with the underlying act. But to the extent that the harm is separated from the underlying conduct, at least for purposes of § 362(a), Congress has focused on the harm, rather than the act. Cf. *Anderson,* 23 B.R. at 175 ("The fact that a contract was executed among the parties [pre-petition] is not sufficient basis to hold that the claim arose prior to filing."); In re THC Financial Corp., 686 F.2d 799, 804 (9th Cir.1982) (although express indemnity agreement arose pre-petition, the related unjust enrichment claim arose post-petition). Thus, unless A & B could have proceeded with its suit before the bankruptcy petitions were filed in July 1980,[4] or had a claim against the Frenvilles which arose before that date, the automatic stay is inapplicable.

The proceeding which A & B sought to institute was an action for indemnity or contribution in New York state court. According to New York law, a third-party complaint for contribution or indemnity may be commenced at the time the defendant (in the present case A & B) serves his answer in the suit brought by the plaintiff (here, the banks), but not before. N.Y.Civ.Prac.Law § 1007 (McKinney 1976);[5] see also Blum v. Good Humor Corp., 57 A.D.2d 911, 394 N.Y.S.2d 894 (N.Y.App.Div. 1977); Taca International Airlines, S.A. v. Rolls Royce of England, Ltd., 47 Misc.2d 771, 263 N.Y.S.2d 269, 272 (N.Y.Sup.Ct.1965) (indemnification suit "could not be commenced by defendants until after service of their answer"); Musco v. Conte, 22 A.D.2d 121, 254 N.Y.S.2d 589, 595 (N.Y.App.Div.1964). In the present situation, A & B could not bring a proceeding for indemnification or contribution until it filed its answer in the suit instituted by the banks on November 16, 1981, some fourteen months after the filing of the bankruptcy petitions. Consequently, A & B's suit cannot be stayed by the "proceeding" language of § 362(a)(1).

The applicability of the automatic stay, therefore, depends on whether A & B's claim arose pre-petition. The Code defines a "claim" as a

---

4. For convenience, we will refer to the earlier July 1980 petition against Frenville as the filing date for both petitions; nothing of consequence occurred between July 1980 and January 1981.

5. N.Y.Civ.Prac.Law § 1007 states (in pertinent part):

After the service of his answer, a defendant may proceed against a person not a party who is or may be liable to him for all or part of the plaintiff's claim against him, by serving upon such a person a summons and third-party complaint and all prior pleadings served in the action.

(A) right to payment, whether or not such right is reduced to judgment, liquidated, unliquidated, fixed, contingent, matured, unmatured, dispute[d], undisputed, legal, equitable, secured, or unsecured; or

(B) right to an equitable remedy for breach of performance if such breach gives rise to a right to payment, whether or not such right to an equitable remedy is reduced to judgment, fixed, contingent, matured, unmatured, disputed, undisputed, secured, or unsecured;

11 U.S.C. § 101(4) (1982).

Congress intended the definition of a claim to be very broad; the legislative history states:

> The definition is any right to payment, whether or not reduced to judgment, liquidated, unliquidated, fixed, contingent, matured, unmatured, disputed, undisputed, legal, equitable, secured or unsecured. . . . By this broadest possible definition and by the use of the term throughout the title 11, especially in subchapter I of chapter 5, the bill contemplates that all legal obligations of the debtor, no matter how remote or contingent, will be able to be dealt with in the bankruptcy case. It permits the broadest possible relief in the bankruptcy court.[6]

At first glance, A & B might be thought to have had an unliquidated, contingent, unmatured and disputed claim pre-petition. While all of these adjectives may describe A & B's cause of action against the Frenvilles, the threshold requirement of a claim must first be met—there must be a "right to payment." § 101(4)(A). One court noted that "although the code definition of claim has been drafted in extremely broad terms, such definition may not confer the status of a claimant upon a petitioning creditor who has no right to payment." In re First Energy Leasing Corp., 38 B.R. 577, 581 (Bankr.E.D.N.Y.1984); see also In re McMeekin, 16 B.R. 805, 808 (Bankr.D.Mass.1982).

Thus we must determine at what point A & B had a "right to payment" for its claim for indemnification or contribution. Of course, if A & B is found liable to the banks, it would have a right to payment from the Frenvilles (assuming liability for the moment), albeit a disputed and unliquidated one. The crucial issue, however, is when did A & B's right to payment arise, for the automatic stay provision applies only to claims that arise pre-petition. See In re Thomas, 12 B.R. 432, 433 (Bankr.S.D.Iowa 1981) ("The existence of a 'claim' turns on when it arose.").

The present case is different from one involving an indemnity or surety contract. When parties agree in advance that one party will indemnify the other party in the event of a certain occurrence, there

6. H.R.Rep. No. 595, 95th Cong., 2d Sess. 309, reprinted in 1978 U.S.Code Cong. & Ad.News 5963, 6266; see also S.Rep. No. 989, 95th Cong., 2d Sess. 21–22, reprinted in 1978 U.S.Code Cong. & Ad.News 5785, 5807–08 (virtually identical statement).

exists a right to payment, albeit contingent,[7] upon the signing of the agreement. See In re THC Financial Corp., 686 F.2d 799, 802–04 (9th Cir.1982); In re All Media Properties, Inc., 5 B.R. 126, 133 (Bankr.S.D. Tex.1980), aff'd, 646 F.2d 193 (5th Cir. (Unit A) 1981) (per curiam). Such a surety relationship is the classic case of a contingent right to payment under the Code—the right to payment exists as of the signing of the agreement, but it is dependent on the occurrence of a future event. See *All Media,* 5 B.R. at 133. A & B, however, had no indemnity agreement with the Frenvilles. Accordingly, cases holding that a claim arises upon the signing of an indemnity agreement are inapposite.

We must ascertain when a right to payment for an indemnity or contribution claim arises where there is no specific agreement. Although "claim" is defined by § 101(4), the Code does not define when a right to payment arises. Thus, while federal law controls which claims are cognizable under the Code, the threshold question of when a right to payment arises, absent overriding federal law, "is to be determined by reference to state law." Vanston Bondholders Protective Committee v. Green, 329 U.S. 156, 161, 67 S.Ct. 237, 239, 91 L.Ed. 162 (1946); see also In re McMeekin, 16 B.R. 805, 808 (Bankr.D.Mass.1982); In re Thomas, 12 B.R. 432, 433 (Bankr.S.D.Iowa 1981).[8]

We look to New York law to ascertain at what point A & B's claim arose. For both separate actions and third-party complaints, a claim for contribution or indemnification does not accrue at the time of the commission of the underlying act, but rather at the time of the payment of the judgment flowing from the act. See Blum v. Good Humor Corp., 57 A.D.2d 911, 394 N.Y.S.2d 894, 896 (N.Y.App.Div.1977); Taca International Airlines, S.A. v. Rolls Royce of England, Ltd., 47 Misc.2d 771, 263 N.Y.S.2d 269, 272 (N.Y.Sup.Ct.1965). Although such a claim does not mature until payment is made, the New York Civil Practice Code permits a defendant to institute a third-party claim against a party who may be liable to him for all or part of the plaintiff's claim after service of his answer. N.Y.Civ.Prac.Law § 1007 (McKinney 1976). In circumstances similar to the present case, one court declared:

> Technically a claim for indemnity does not arise until the prime obligation to pay has been established. . . . Nevertheless, for the sake of fairness and judicial economy, [N.Y.Civ.Prac.Law § 1007]

7. Bankruptcy judges have defined a contingent claim as a claim which becomes due only on the occurrence of a future event. See, e.g., In re Dill, 30 B.R. 546, 549 (Bankr. 9th Cir.1983). One frequently cited definition of contingent is that "claims are contingent as to liability if the debt is one which the debtor will be called upon to pay only upon the occurrence or happening of an extrinsic event." In re All Media Properties, Inc., 5 B.R. 126, 133 (Bankr.S.D. Tex.1980), aff'd, 646 F.2d 193 (5th Cir. (Unit A) 1981) (per curiam).

8. If there were some overriding federal policy, we might have the power to develop federal law. See In re Beck Indus., Inc., 725 F.2d 880, 891 (2d Cir.1984); In re Johns–Manville Corp., 36 B.R. 743, 751 n. 4 (Bankr.S.D.N.Y.), appeal denied, 39 B.R. 234 (S.D.N.Y.1984). A bankruptcy proceeding stemming from a mass tort—such as exposure to asbestos—may be a case in which the application of federal law is indicated.

allows third-party actions to be commenced in certain circumstances before they are technically ripe, so that all parties may establish their rights and liabilities in one action. . . . Moreover, there is no justification for permitting a claim of indemnity where the primary action which might be the source of the right to indemnity . . . is not even pending.

Burgundy Basin Inn v. Watkins Glen Grand Prix Corp., 51 A.D.2d 140, 379 N.Y.S.2d 873, 880 (1976 N.Y.App.Div.) (citations omitted).

In the case at bar, A & B had an unmatured, unliquidated, disputed claim when the banks brought suit against it in New York state court. Until the banks instituted suit, however, A & B did not have any claim or cause of action based on indemnity or contribution against the Frenvilles. Since the banks' suit began some fourteen months after the filing of the Frenvilles' involuntary chapter 7 proceedings, A & B's claim, as well as its cause of action, arose post-petition. Although arguably A & B may have had some claim at the time the Frenvilles gave it allegedly false information, it did not have a claim for indemnification or contribution until the banks filed their suit. Thus, by its very terms, the automatic stay provision of § 362(a) is inapplicable to A & B's suit.

III.

Our decision today is in keeping with the policy of the Code. Congress has determined that only those claims which arise pre-petition[9] can be discharged in a chapter 7 proceeding.[10] Since claims arising post-petition are not dischargeable, there is no compelling reason to stay judicial proceedings predicated on such claims.

IV.

We conclude that the automatic stay does not apply to A & B's proposed action against the Frenvilles.[11] Therefore, the district court's

---

9. Technically, the date crucial for discharge (as opposed to the automatic stay) is the date of the bankruptcy court's order for relief. In the present case, the bankruptcy judge entered orders for relief within a month of the filing of the petitions.

10. 11 U.S.C. § 727(b) (1982) provides that:

Except as provided in section 523 of this title, a discharge under subsection (a) of this section discharges the debtor from all debts that arose before the date of the order for relief under this chapter, and any liability on a claim that is determined under section 502 of this title as if such claim had arisen before the commencement of the case, whether or not a proof of claim based on any such debt or liability is filed under section 501 of this title, and whether or not a claim based

on any such debt or liability is allowed under section 502 of this title.

Other discharge provisions in the Code are 11 U.S.C. §§ 944, 1141, 1328, 15727 (1982).

11. Should A & B succeed in obtaining a judgment against the Frenvilles in the New York proceeding, the provisions of § 362(a)(3) and (4) would be applicable. See Turner Broadcasting System, Inc. v. Sanyo Electric, Inc., 33 B.R. 996, 1000 n. 2 (N.D.Ga.1983); In re Powell, 27 B.R. 146, 147 (Bankr.W.D.Mo.1983); In re Anderson, 23 B.R. 174, 175 (Bankr.N.D.Ill.1982); In re York, 13 B.R. 757, 758–59 (Bankr.D.Me. 1981).

11 U.S.C. § 362(a)(3) and (4) (1982) provide:

(a) Except as provided in subsection (b) of this section, a petition filed under

judgment will be reversed and the matter remanded for proceedings consistent with this opinion.

Notes & Questions

1. *Reaction to* Frenville. One court summarizes criticism of *Frenville* as follows:

> (1) *Frenville* mistakenly applied state law rather than federal bankruptcy law, to determine whether creditors' claims arose. . . .

> (2) Congress intended an extremely broad definition of "claim" for bankruptcy administration, which would include a subrogation claim. . . .

> (3) Equality among creditors under bankruptcy law is frustrated if a surety by waiting to file suit for recovery against a debtor, could prejudice the rights of other creditors.

Acevedo v. Van Dorn Plastic Machinery Co., 68 B.R. 495, 497 (Bkrtcy. E.D.N.Y.1986). Evaluate these criticisms.

2. *Nonindemnity Actions.* Suppose the action against Frenville were a routine tort action based on events that occurred before the filing of the bankruptcy petition but giving rise to harm after the filing of the petition. Should analysis of the automatic stay issue change? Would such a case affect the criticisms in Note 1?

Suppose that the action were one of a series of thousands of tort actions based on a common cause (e.g., prepetition exposure to asbestos) but giving rise to claims both before and after the filing of the petition.

IN RE THE MINOCO GROUP OF COMPANIES, LTD.

United States Court of Appeals, Ninth Circuit, 1986.
799 F.2d 517.

Before ANDERSON and NORRIS, CIRCUIT JUDGES, and COPPLE, DISTRICT JUDGE.

NORRIS, CIRCUIT JUDGE:

Appellants First State Underwriters Agency of New England and First State Insurance Company (collectively, "First State") are affiliated insurance companies that issued prepaid excess officers and directors liability policies to The Minoco Group of Companies ("Minoco"). The policies provided coverage only for "claims made" from November 24, 1982, through July 1, 1984, but permitted either party to cancel the policies at any time upon thirty days' notice. In November 1983, two

section 301, 302, or 303 of this title . . . operates as a stay, applicable to all entities, of—

. . .

(3) any act to obtain possession of property of the estate or of property from the estate;

(4) any act to create, perfect, or enforce any lien against property of the estate;

Thus, A & B will have to seek relief from the automatic stay to collect any judgment it might obtain.

months after Minoco filed a voluntary petition for reorganization under Chapter 11 of the Bankruptcy Code (the "Code"), 11 U.S.C. §§ 1101–1174 (1982), First State gave Minoco notice of cancellation of the policies. Minoco then brought this action in bankruptcy court seeking a declaratory judgment that cancellation of the policies was automatically stayed by section 362(a) of the Code, as well as an injunction prohibiting First State from cancelling the policies.

After an evidentiary hearing, the bankruptcy court made a finding of fact that if First State were permitted to cancel the policies, Minoco would be required to indemnify present and former officers and directors for legal expenses and judgments which arise from their activities as officers and directors.[1] The bankruptcy court also found that cancellation of the policies would render reorganization of Minoco more difficult, if not impossible, for two reasons: (a) the difficulty of attracting and retaining competent personnel to serve as officers and directors, and (b) the increase in claims against the debtor's estate resulting from claims for indemnification by present and former officers and directors. On the basis of these findings, the bankruptcy court declared that cancellation of the policies was automatically stayed by section 362(a) and enjoined First State from effecting a cancellation. The district court affirmed. Exercising jurisdiction under 28 U.S.C. § 158(d), we affirm on the ground that the filing of the bankruptcy petition automatically stayed cancellation of the policies under section 362(a)(3) of the Code.

Section 362(a)(3) provides that the filing of a bankruptcy petition operates as a stay of "any act to obtain possession of property of the estate or of property from the estate or to exercise control over property of the estate." "Property of the estate" is defined in section 541(a) of the Code as "all legal or equitable interests of the debtor in property as of the commencement of the case." The legislative history makes it plain that "[t]he scope of this paragraph [section 541(a)] is broad. It includes all kinds of property, including tangible or intangible property. . . ." S.Rep. No. 95–989, 95th Cong., 1st Sess. 82 (1978), reprinted in 1978 U.S.Code Cong. & Admin.News 5787, 5868. In In re Bialac, 712 F.2d 426 (9th Cir.1983) we said that section 541(a)'s definition of property "was intended to be broad and all-inclusive," id. at 430, and

---

1. The insuring clause of the policies provides as follows:

First State Insurance Company, in consideration of the payment of the premium and in reliance upon the statements in the application made a part hereof and subject to all of the terms, conditions, and exclusions of this policy, agrees:

(a) with the Directors and Officers of the Company that, if during the policy period any claim or claims are made against the Directors and Officers for a Wrongful Act, the Insurers shall pay on behalf of such Directors and Officers all loss which such Directors and Officers shall become legally obligated to pay, except for such loss which the Company shall indemnify the Directors or Officers;

(b) with the Company that, if during the policy period any claim or claims are made against the Directors or Officers of the Company for a Wrongful Act, the Insurers shall pay on behalf of the Company, all loss for which the Company may be required or permitted by law to indemnify the Directors or Officers.

"an interest is not outside its reach because it is novel or contingent or enjoyment must be postponed." Id. at 431 (quoting Segal v. Rochelle, 382 U.S. 375, 379, 86 S.Ct. 511, 515, 15 L.Ed.2d 428 (1966)).

First State argues on appeal that the excess officers and directors liability policies are not "property of the estate" within the meaning of section 541(a) because the policies benefit only the officers and directors, not Minoco. We disagree. As the bankruptcy court found,[2] the policies also benefit Minoco because the policies insure Minoco against indemnity claims made by officers and directors. Moreover, First State's position is contrary to the case law. For example, in A.H. Robins Co. v. Piccinin, 788 F.2d 994 (4th Cir.1986), the Fourth Circuit held that a products liability policy issued to the debtor was "property of the estate" within the meaning of section 541(a). The Fourth Circuit stated:

> Under the weight of authority, insurance contracts have been said to be embraced in this statutory definition of "property." In re Davis, 730 F.2d 176, 184 (5th Cir.1984). For example, even the right to cancel an insurance policy issued to the debtor has uniformly been held to be stayed under section 362(a)(3). Lam, Cancellation of Insurance: Bankruptcy Automatic Stay Implications, 59 Am.Bankr. L.J. 267 (1985) (extensively reviewing the cases to this effect). A products liability policy of the debtor is similarly within the principle: it is a valuable property of the debtor, particularly if the debtor is confronted with substantial liability claims within the coverage of the policy in which case the policy may well be, as one court has remarked in a case like the one under review, "the most important asset of [the debtor's] estate," In re Johns Manville Corp., 40 B.R. 219, 229 (S.D.N.Y.1984).

Id. at 1001.

The reasoning of the Fourth Circuit in *A.H. Robins* applies to this case with full force. For the purposes of the automatic stay, we see no significant distinction between a liability policy that insures the debtor against claims by *consumers* and one that insures the debtor against claims by *officers and directors*. In either case, the insurance policies protect against diminution of the value of the estate. As the Fourth Circuit understood, liability policies meet the fundamental test of whether they are "property of the estate" because the debtor's estate is worth more with them than without them. See Jackson, Translating Assets and Liabilities to the Bankruptcy Forum, 14 J.Legal Stud. 73, 99 (1985). Accordingly, cancellation of the insurance policies by First State was automatically stayed by section 362(a)(3).

We reject First State's contention that this case is governed, not by section 541(a), but by section 541(b). Under subsection (b), property held by the debtor solely for the benefit of another does not constitute

---

2. First State does not challenge on appeal the bankruptcy court's findings of fact.

property of the estate. The legislative history to subsection (b) manifests Congressional concern that funds which the debtor holds in constructive trust for another should not be parceled out among the creditors:

> Situations occasionally arise where property ostensibly belonging to the debtor will actually be held in trust for another. For example, if the debtor has incurred medical bills that were covered by insurance, and the insurance company had sent payment of the bills to the debtor before the debtor had paid the bill for which the payment was reimbursement, the payment would actually be held in constructive trust for the person to whom the bill was owed.

H.R.Rep. No. 595, 95th Cong., 2d Sess. 368 (1978), reprinted in 1978 U.S. Code Cong. & Admin.News 5963, 6324. Liability policies, however, are not held in constructive trust by the insured for the benefit of potential claimants; they are held by the insured as protection against claims that may be asserted against the insured. It is conceivable that at some point Minoco would receive money from First State for payment to officers and directors in satisfaction of indemnification claims, in which event section 541(b) might come into play. But that question is not before us in this appeal.

First State contends that Minoco never demonstrated irreparable harm from cancellation. This point is meritless. The automatic stay comes into play upon the filing of a bankruptcy petition whether or not the debtor would suffer irreparable harm in the absence of the stay. First State also makes myriad assertions concerning Minoco's unstable corporate management and alleged misrepresentations by Minoco's officers and directors. While these assertions might have supported a demonstration of "cause" for relief from the stay under section 362(d), First State never submitted a motion in bankruptcy court for relief from the stay and does not argue on appeal that it was entitled to such relief. Although First State's assertions may stand as monuments to a missed opportunity, they are irrelevant to our decision in this case: that cancellation of liability insurance policies is automatically stayed by section 362(a).

Affirmed.

Notes & Questions

1. *The Showing Necessary to Obtain Relief From the Automatic Stay.* Since the automatic stay applies in *Minoco,* First State Underwriters must seek relief from the automatic stay to cancel the insurance policy. In seeking such relief, what argument should First State Underwriters make? Consider the following: "By the terms of the insurance contract we had the right to cancel the policy by giving thirty days' notice. With the court's permission, we hereby do so. Therefore, the contract should terminate within thirty days." Should the court accept this argument as a basis for granting relief from the stay and permitting First State Underwriters to send a cancellation notice?

What showing would a secured or unsecured creditor have to make to obtain relief from the stay?

2. *The Role of Motive.* In evaluating a creditor's request for relief from the stay, does the motive behind the request matter? Suppose the insurance could show that it would have cancelled the policy whether or not the debtor was in bankruptcy. Or suppose it concedes that it is cancelling solely because the debtor is in bankruptcy. Would either of these motives make a difference?

3. *Redrafting Contracts in Light of* Minoco. Can First State Underwriters redraft its contract to avoid the problem in *Minoco?* Suppose it rewrites its contracts to state that insurance protection automatically expires at the end of thirty days (or one year) unless both parties agree to renew. Is there anything in the Bankruptcy Act that prevents the expiration from taking effect? Could a bankruptcy court require First State Underwriters to renew? See § 105.

4. *Supply Contracts.* Purchaser signs an agreement with Supplier agreeing to purchase all of the widgets it needs from Supplier. Either party may cancel the contract by giving thirty days' notice. If Supplier files for bankruptcy may Purchaser terminate the contract? Cf. In re Computer Communications, Inc., 824 F.2d 725 (9th Cir.1987) (no).

5. *Incentives.* Does *Minoco* give some companies an incentive to prefer bankruptcy to a nonbankruptcy setting? Is this desirable?

6. *Picketing.* Corporation and Union are in a labor dispute. Corporation files a petition under Chapter 11 of the Bankruptcy Act and Union pickets Corporation, Union's sole demand being that it wants Corporation to pay higher wages. Does the automatic stay apply to the union's activity? Cf. Petrusch v. Teamsters, Local 317, 667 F.2d 297 (2d Cir.), cert. denied 456 U.S. 974, 102 S.Ct. 2238, 72 L.Ed.2d 848 (1982) (per curiam) (relying on anti-injunction provision of Norris-La Guardia Act to overturn lower court's issuance of an injunction).

C. Adequate Protection (§ 361)

When a party seeks relief from the automatic stay, the requirement of "adequate protection" often will play a key role in determining whether the relief sought will be obtained. See § 362(d). The Bankruptcy Act describes adequate protection in § 361.

IN RE MUREL HOLDING CORP.

United States Circuit Court of Appeals, Second Circuit, 1935.
75 F.2d 941.

L. HAND, CIRCUIT JUDGE.

This appeal is from an order in bankruptcy denying a motion to vacate a stay of the prosecution of a suit in foreclosure in the state court; it arises upon the following facts: The Metropolitan Life Insurance Company held a mortgage upon an apartment house in the borough of Manhattan amounting to $400,500, owned as cotenants by the two corporations which are the petitioners herein. There was a second mortgage upon the same property, but for the purposes of this case it may be disregarded, for it was executed between the present co-owners and a company which holds all their stock. The mortgage being in default, the mortgagee filed a bill of foreclosure in the Supreme Court of New York on December 8th, 1934, and Leighton was appointed receiver of the rents. Immediately thereafter the owners filed petitions under section 77B of the Bankruptcy Act (11 U.S.C.A. § 207), and procured an ex parte stay against the foreclosure. The mortgagee and the receiver moved to vacate this on December 19th, 1934, and the judge denied their motion on January 16th, 1935. They appeal from this order. When the bill was filed the defaults on the mortgage amounted to nearly $100,000; about $20,000 of taxes and assessments, $43,000 of interest and $36,000 of amortization payments. The properties were assessed at $540,000, and the rentals came to $3,600 a month. On December 26, 1934, the debtors filed with the court a "plan of reorganization" under subdivision (a) of section 77B, 11 U.S.C.A. § 207(a), by which the second mortgagee was to provide $11,000, to be used by the debtors to alter the "line C" apartments in the building; this advance to have priority over all liens but the arrears of taxes and such new taxes as fell due during the nine months that the alterations were in progress. The debtors estimated that during this period there would be a slight deficit in interest and taxes, but that thereafter the "line C" apartments would be much more readily leasable. The expected rentals should then come to $59,346 and the expenses would be only $20,400, leaving a yearly surplus of $38,946. Against this there would be taxes of $14,280 and interest of $22,027.50, leaving a surplus of $2638.50; enough to discharge existing arrears of taxes and leave about $3,000 at the end of ten years. In consideration of these expected benefits the mortgagee was to release the amortization payments ($9,000 per annum) and extend the due date; it was to receive its interest, 5½%, and all taxes were to be paid, both those in arrears and those to accrue. The mortgagee refused to consider this plan.

The argument and the briefs have taken a wide range, being for the most part directed to the powers of the court. We do not find it necessary to discuss the points raised, because it seems to us that though for argument we assume that the judge had power to grant the stay, there was not enough before him to justify one. The debtors' assumption is that under section 77B not only may a company effect a reorganization among its creditors, when two-thirds of each class consent, but that it may compel its unwilling creditors to accept a moratorium, though some of the classes refuse in toto. That was perhaps intended in subdivision (b)(5), 11 U.S.C.A. § 207(b)(5), but the power if it exists at all, is much hedged about. Normally it was expected that consents should be obtained. If they were not, the plan must "provide adequate protection for the realization by them," the dissenting class, "of the full value of their interest, claims, or liens". This may be done in four ways: (a) The liens may be merely kept in statu quo, the

reorganization not going so deep down into the title, so to say, but being confined to the equity. That is not this case. (b) The property may be sold free and clear and the liens attach to the proceeds. This was a not uncommon course in bankruptcy when the court was in possession. Regardless of whether it may now apply to a case where it is not, nothing of the sort is here proposed. (c) The value of the liens may be appraised and paid, or, if the objectors prefer, the same course might be taken with any new securities which shall be offered to them in reorganization. This again was not adopted here. (d) The last is not, properly speaking, a "method" at all; it merely gives power generally to the judge "equitably and fairly" to "provide such protection," that is, "adequate protection," when the other methods are not chosen. It is this alone which the debtors here invoke. In construing so vague a grant, we are to remember not only the underlying purposes of the section, but the constitutional limitations to which it must conform. It is plain that "adequate protection" must be completely compensatory; and that payment ten years hence is not generally the equivalent of payment now. Interest is indeed the common measure of the difference, but a creditor who fears the safety of his principal will scarcely be content with that; he wishes to get his money or at least the property. We see no reason to suppose that the statute was intended to deprive him of that in the interest of junior holders, unless by a substitute of the most indubitable equivalence.

If therefore subdivision (c)(10), 11 U.S.C.A. § 207(c)(10), may be applied to a situation like this, the stay so authorized, like any other, lies in the court's discretion; prima facie the creditor may go on to collect; if his hand is to be held up, the debtor must make a clear showing. The liens of the taxes and the first mortgage now are nearly $500,000 and the property is assessed for only $540,000; it has not been able to pay its way for several years. The amount to be advanced is a mere trifle compared with the debts; its effect is wholly speculative, based upon the expectations of those who have everything to gain and nothing to lose. The mortgagee is to be compelled to forego all amortization payments for ten years and take its chances as to the fate of its lien at the end of that period, though it is now secured by a margin of only ten per cent. It does not seem to us that this setting authorized any stay; it should appear that the plan proposed has better hope of success; full details may not be necessary, but there must be some reasonable assurance that a suitable substitute will be offered. No doubt less will be required to hold up the suit for a short time until the debtor shall have a chance to prepare; much depends upon how long he has had already, and upon how much more he demands. But a stay should never be the automatic result of the petition itself, and we cannot see that there was here anything else of substance.

Order reversed.

UNITED SAVINGS ASSOCIATION OF TEXAS v. TIMBERS OF INWOOD FOREST ASSOCIATES, LTD.

Supreme Court of the United States, 1988.
___ U.S. ___, 108 S.Ct. 626, 98 L.Ed.2d 740.

JUSTICE SCALIA delivered the opinion of the Court.

Petitioner United Savings Association of Texas seeks review of an en banc decision of the United States Court of Appeals for the Fifth Circuit, holding that petitioner was not entitled to receive from respondent debtor, which is undergoing reorganization in bankruptcy, monthly payments for the use value of the loan collateral which the bankruptcy stay prevented it from possessing. In re Timbers of Inwood Forest Assocs., 808 F.2d 363 (1987). We granted certiorari, 481 U.S. ___ (1987), to resolve a conflict in the Courts of Appeals regarding application of §§ 361 and 362(d)(1) of the Bankruptcy Code, 11 U.S.C. §§ 361 and 362(d)(1) (1982 ed. and Supp. IV). . . .

I

On June 29, 1982, respondent Timbers of Inwood Forest Associates, Inc. executed a note in the principal amount of $4,100,000. Petitioner is the holder of the note as well as of a security interest created the same day in an apartment project owned by respondent in Houston, Texas. The security interest included an assignment of rents from the project. On March 4, 1985, respondent filed a voluntary petition under Chapter 11 of the Bankruptcy Code, 11 U.S.C. § 101 et seq. (1982 ed. and Supp. IV), in the United States Bankruptcy Court for the Southern District of Texas.

On March 18, 1985, petitioner moved for relief from the automatic stay of enforcement of liens triggered by the petition, see 11 U.S.C. § 362(a), on the ground that there was lack of "adequate protection" of its interest within the meaning of 11 U.S.C. § 362(d)(1). At a hearing before the Bankruptcy Court, it was established that respondent owed petitioner $4,366,348.77, and evidence was presented that the value of the collateral was somewhere between $2,650,000 and $4,250,000. The collateral was appreciating in value, but only very slightly. It was therefore undisputed that petitioner was an undersecured creditor. Respondent had agreed to pay petitioner the postpetition rents from the apartment project (covered by the after-acquired property clause in the security agreement), minus operating expenses. Petitioner contended, however, that it was entitled to additional compensation. The Bankruptcy Court agreed and on April 19, 1985, it conditioned continuance of the stay on monthly payments by respondent, at the market rate of 12% per annum, on the estimated amount realizable on foreclosure, $4,250,000—commencing six months after the filing of the bankruptcy petition, to reflect the normal foreclosure delays. In re Bear Creek Ministorage, Inc., 49 B.R. 454 (1985) (editorial revision of earlier decision). The court held that the postpetition rents could be applied to these payments. See id., at 460. Respondent appealed to the District Court and petitioner cross-appealed on the amount of the adequate protection payments. The District Court affirmed but the Fifth Circuit en banc reversed.

We granted certiorari to determine whether undersecured creditors are entitled to compensation under 11 U.S.C. § 362(d)(1) for the delay caused by the automatic stay in foreclosing on their collateral.

II

When a bankruptcy petition is filed, § 362(a) of the Bankruptcy Code provides an automatic stay of, among other things, actions taken to realize the value of collateral given by the debtor. The provision of the Code central to the decision of this case is § 362(d), which reads as follows:

"On request of a party in interest and after notice and a hearing, the court shall grant relief from the stay provided under subsection (a) of this section, such as by terminating, annulling, modifying, or conditioning such stay—

"(1) for cause, including the lack of adequate protection of an interest in property of such party in interest; or

"(2) with respect to a stay of an act against property under subsection (a) of this section, if—

"(A) the debtor does not have an equity in such property; and

"(B) such property is not necessary to an effective reorganization."

The phrase "adequate protection" in paragraph (1) of the foregoing provision is given further content by § 361 of the Code, which reads in relevant part as follows:

"When adequate protection is required under section 362 . . . of this title of an interest of an entity in property, such adequate protection may be provided by—

"(1) requiring the trustee to make a cash payment or periodic cash payments to such entity, to the extent that the stay under section 362 of this title . . . results in a decrease in the value of such entity's interest in such property;

"(2) providing to such entity an additional or replacement lien to the extent that such stay . . . results in a decrease in the value of such entity's interest in such property; or

"(3) granting such other relief . . . as will result in the realization by such entity of the indubitable equivalent of such entity's interest in such property."

It is common ground that the "interest in property" referred to by § 362(d)(1) includes the right of a secured creditor to have the security applied in payment of the debt upon completion of the reorganization; and that that interest is not adequately protected if the security is depreciating during the term of the stay. Thus, it is agreed that if the apartment project in this case had been declining in value petitioner would have been entitled, under § 362(d)(1), to cash payments or additional security in the amount of the decline, as § 361 describes. The crux of the present dispute is that petitioner asserts, and respondent denies, that the phrase "interest in property" also includes the secured party's right (suspended by the stay) to take immediate possession of the defaulted security, and apply it in payment of the debt. If that right is embraced by the term, it is obviously not adequately protected unless the secured party is reimbursed for the use of the proceeds he is deprived of during the term of the stay.

The term "interest in property" certainly summons up such concepts as "fee ownership," "life estate," "co-ownership," and "security interest" more readily than it does the notion of "right to immediate foreclosure." Nonetheless, viewed in the isolated context of § 362(d)(1), the phrase could reasonably be given the meaning petitioner asserts. Statutory construction, however, is a holistic endeavor. A provision that may seem ambiguous in isolation is often clarified by the remainder of the statutory scheme—because the same terminology is used elsewhere in a context that makes its meaning clear, see, e.g., Sorenson v. Secretary of Treasury, 475 U.S. 851, 850 (1986), or because only one of the permissible meanings produces a substantive effect that is compatible with the rest of the law . . .. That is the case here. Section 362(d)(1) is only one of a series of provisions in the Bankruptcy Code dealing with the rights of secured creditors. The language in those other provisions, and the substantive dispositions that they effect, persuade us that the "interest in property" protected by § 362(d)(1) does not include a secured party's right to immediate foreclosure.

Section 506 of the Code defines the amount of the secured creditor's allowed secured claim and the conditions of his receiving postpetition interest. In relevant part it reads as follows:

> "(a) An allowed claim of a creditor secured by a lien on property in which the estate has an interest . . . is a secured claim to the extent of the value of such creditor's interest in the estate's interest in such property, . . . and is an unsecured claim to the extent that the value of such creditor's interest . . . is less than the amount of such allowed claim. . . .

> "(b) To the extent that an allowed secured claim is secured by property the value of which . . . is greater than the amount of such claim, there shall be allowed to the holder of such claim, interest on such claim, and any reasonable fees, costs, or charges provided for under the agreement under which such claim arose."

In subsection (a) of this provision the creditor's "interest in property" obviously means his security interest without taking account of his right to immediate possession of the collateral on default. If the latter were included, the "value of such creditor's interest" would increase, and the proportions of the claim that are secured and unsecured would alter, as the stay continues—since the value of the entitlement to use the collateral from the date of bankruptcy would rise with the passage of time. No one suggests this was intended. The phrase "value of such creditor's interest" in § 506(a) means "the value of the collateral." H.R.Rep. No. 95–595, pp. 181, 356 (1977); see also S.Rep. No. 95–989, p. 68 (1978). We think the phrase "value of such entity's interest" in § 361(1) and (2), when applied to secured creditors, means the same.

Even more important for our purposes than § 506's use of terminology is its substantive effect of denying undersecured creditors postpetition interest on their claims—just as it denies *over*secured creditors postpetition interest to the extent that such interest, when added to the principal amount of the claim, will exceed the value of the collateral. Section 506(b) provides that "*[t]o the extent that* an allowed secured claim is secured by property the value of which . . . is greater than the amount of such claim, there shall be allowed to the holder of such claim, interest on such claim." (Emphasis added.) Since this provision permits postpetition interest to be paid only out of the "security cushion," the undersecured creditor, who has no such cushion, falls within the general rule disallowing postpetition interest. See 11 U.S.C. § 502(b)(2). If the Code had meant to give the undersecured creditor, who is thus denied interest on his *claim*, interest on the value of his *collateral*, surely this is where that disposition would have been set forth, and not obscured within the "adequate protection" provision of § 362(d)(1). Instead of the intricate phraseology set forth above, § 506(b) would simply have said that the secured creditor is entitled to interest "on his allowed claim, or on the value of the property securing his allowed claim, whichever is lesser." Petitioner's interpretation of § 362(d)(1) must be regarded as contradicting the carefully drawn disposition of § 506(b).

Petitioner seeks to avoid this conclusion by characterizing § 506(b) as merely an alternative method for compensating oversecured creditors, which does not imply that no compensation is available to undersecured creditors. This theory of duplicate protection for oversecured creditors is implausible even in the abstract, but even more so in light of the historical principles of bankruptcy law. Section 506(b)'s denial of postpetition interest to undersecured creditors merely codified pre-Code bankruptcy law, in which that denial was part of the conscious allocation of reorganization benefits and losses between undersecured and unsecured creditors. "To allow a secured creditor interest where his security was worth less than the value of his debt was thought to be inequitable to unsecured creditors." Vanston Bondholders Protective Committee v. Green, 329 U.S. 156, 164 (1946). It was considered unfair to allow an undersecured creditor to recover interest from the estate's unencumbered assets before unsecured creditors had recovered any principal. See id., at 164, 166; Ticonic Nat. Bank v. Sprague, 303 U.S. 406, 412 (1938). We think it unlikely that § 506(b) codified the pre-Code rule with the intent, not of achieving the principal purpose and function of that rule, but of providing oversecured creditors an alternative method of compensation.   Moreover, it is incomprehensible why Congress would want to favor undersecured creditors with interest if they move for it under § 362(d)(1) at the inception of the reorganization process—thereby probably pushing the estate into liquidation—but not if they forbear and seek it only at the completion of the reorganization.

Second, petitioner's interpretation of § 362(d)(1) is structurally inconsistent with 11 U.S.C. § 552. Section 552(a) states the general rule that a prepetition security interest does not reach property acquired by the estate or debtor postpetition. Section 552(b) sets forth an exception, allowing postpetition "proceeds, product, offspring, rents, or profits" of the collateral to be covered only if the security agreement expressly provides for an interest in such property, and the interest has been perfected under "applicable nonbankruptcy law." Section 552(b) therefore makes possession of a perfected security interest in postpetition rents or profits from collateral a condition of having them applied to satisfying the claim of the secured creditor ahead of the claims of unsecured creditors. Under petitioner's interpretation, however, the undersecured creditor who lacks such a perfected security interest in effect achieves the same result by demanding the "use value" of his collateral under § 362. It is true that § 506(b) gives the *over*secured creditor, despite lack of compliance with the conditions of § 552, a similar priority over unsecured creditors; but that does not compromise the principle of § 552, since the interest payments come only out of the "cushion" in which the oversecured creditor *does have* a perfected security interest.

Third, petitioner's interpretation of § 362(d)(1) makes nonsense of § 362(d)(2). On petitioner's theory, the undersecured creditor's inability to take immediate possession of his collateral is always "cause" for conditioning the stay (upon the payment of market rate interest) under § 362(d)(1), since there is, within the meaning of that paragraph, "lack of adequate protection of an interest in property." But § 362(d)(2) expressly provides a different standard for relief from a stay "of an act against property," which of course includes taking possession of collateral. It provides that the court shall grant relief "if . . . (A) the debtor does not have an equity in such property (i.e., the creditor is undersecured); *and* (B) such property is not necessary to an effective reorganization." (Emphasis added.) By applying the "adequate protection of an interest in property" provision of § 362(d)(1) to the alleged "interest" in the earning power of collateral, petitioner creates the strange consequence that § 362 entitles the secured creditor to relief from the stay (1) if he is undersecured (and thus not eligible for interest under § 506(b)), *or* (2) if he is undersecured *and* his collateral "is not necessary to an effective reorganization." This renders § 362(d)(2) a practical nullity and a theoretical absurdity. If § 362(d)(1) is interpreted in this fashion, an undersecured creditor would seek relief under § 362(d)(2) only if its collateral was not depreciating (or it was being compensated for depreciation) and it was receiving market rate interest on its collateral, but nonetheless wanted to foreclose. Petitioner offers no reason why Congress would want to provide relief for such an obstreperous and thoroughly unharmed creditor.

Section 362(d)(2) also belies petitioner's contention that under-secured creditors will face inordinate and extortionate delay if they are denied compensation for interest lost during the stay as part of "adequate protection" under § 362(d)(1). Once the movant under § 362(d)(2) establishes that he is an undersecured creditor, it is the burden of the *debtor* to establish that the collateral at issue is "necessary to an effective reorganization." See § 362(g). What this requires is not merely a showing that if there is conceivably to be an effective reorganization, this property will be needed for it; but that the property is essential for an effective reorganization *that is in prospect*. This means, as many lower courts, including the en banc court in this case, have properly said, that there must be "a reasonable possibility of a successful reorganization within a reasonable time." 808 F.2d, at 370–371, and nn. 12–13, and cases cited therein. The cases are numerous in which § 362(d)(2) relief has been provided within less than a year from the filing of the bankruptcy petition. And while the bankruptcy courts demand less detailed showings during the four months in which the debtor is given the exclusive right to put together a plan, see 11 U.S.C. § 1121(b), (c)(2), even within that period lack of any realistic prospect of effective reorganization will require § 362(d)(2) relief.

III

A

Petitioner contends that denying it compensation under § 362(d)(1) is inconsistent with sections of the Code other than those just discussed. Petitioner principally relies on the phrase "indubitable equivalent" in § 361(3), which also appears in 11 U.S.C. § 1129(b)(2)(A)(iii). Petitioner contends that in the latter context, which sets forth the standards for confirming a reorganization plan, the phrase has developed a well-settled meaning connoting the right of a secured creditor to receive present value of his security—thus requiring interest if the claim is to be paid over time. It is true that under § 1129(b) a secured claimant has a right to receive under a plan the present value of his collateral. This entitlement arises, however, not from the phrase "indubitable equivalent" in § 1129(b)(2)(A)(iii), but from the provision of § 1129(b)(2)(A)(i)(II) that guarantees the secured creditor "deferred cash payments . . . of a value, *as of the effective date of the plan*, of at least the value of such (secured claimant's) interest in the estate's interest in such property." (Emphasis added.) Under this formulation, even though the undersecured creditor's "interest" is regarded (properly) as solely the value of the collateral, he must be rendered payments that assure him that value *as of the effective date of the plan*. In § 361(3), by contrast, the relief pending the stay need only be such "*as will result in the realization* . . . of the indubitable equivalent" of the collateral. (Emphasis added.) It is obvious (since §§ 361 and 362(d)(1) do not entitle the secured creditor to immediate payment of the principal of his collateral) that this "realization" is to "result" not at once, but only upon completion of the reorganization. It is *then* that he must be assured "realization . . . of the indubitable equivalent" of his collateral. To put the point differently: similarity of outcome between § 361(3) and § 1129 would be demanded only if the former read "such other relief . . . as will give such entity, *as of the date of the relief,* the indubitable equivalent of such entity's interest in such property."

Nor is there merit in petitioner's suggestion that "indubitable equivalent" in § 361(3) connotes reimbursement for the use value of collateral because the phrase is derived from In re Murel Holding Corp., 75 F.2d 941 (CA2 1935), where it bore that meaning. *Murel* involved a proposed reorganization plan that gave the secured creditor interest on his collateral for 10 years, with full payment of the secured principal due at the end of that term; the plan made no provision, however, for amortization of principal or maintenance of the collateral's value during the term. In rejecting the plan, *Murel* used the words "indubitable equivalence" with specific reference not to interest (which was assured), but to the jeopardized principal of the loan:

> "Interest is indeed the common measure of the difference (between payment now and payment 10 years hence), but a creditor who fears the safety of his principal will scarcely be content with that; he wishes to get his money or at least the property. We see no reason to suppose that the statute was intended to deprive him of that in the interest of junior holders, unless by a substitute of the most indubitable equivalence." Id., at 942.

Of course *Murel,* like § 1129, proceeds from the premise that in the confirmation context the secured creditor is entitled to present value. But no more from *Murel* than from § 1129 can it be inferred that a similar requirement exists as of the time of the bankruptcy stay. The reorganized debtor is supposed to stand on his own two feet. The debtor in process of reorganization, by contrast, is given many temporary protections against the normal operation of the law.

Petitioner also contends that the Code embodies a principal that secured creditors do not bear the costs of reorganization. It derives this from the rule that general administrative expenses do not have priority over secured claims. See §§ 506(c); 507(a). But the general principle does not follow from the particular rule. That secured creditors do not bear one kind of reorganization cost hardly means that they bear none of them. The Code rule on administrative expenses merely continues pre-Code law. But it was also pre-Code law that undersecured creditors were not entitled to postpetition interest as compensation for the delay of reorganization. Congress could hardly have understood that the readoption of the rule on administrative expenses would work a change in the rule on postpetition interest, which it also readopted.

Finally, petitioner contends that failure to interpret § 362(d)(1) to require compensation of undersecured creditors for delay will create an inconsistency in the Code in the (admittedly rare) case when the debtor proves solvent. When that occurs, 11 U.S.C. § 726(a)(5) provides that postpetition interest is allowed on unsecured claims. Petitioner contends it would be absurd to allow postpetition interest on unsecured claims but not on the secured portion of undersecured creditors' claims. It would be disingenuous to deny that this is an apparent anomaly, but it will occur so rarely that it is more likely the product of inadvertence than are the blatant inconsistencies petitioner's interpretation would produce. Its inequitable effects, moreover, are entirely avoidable, since an undersecured creditor is entitled to "surrender or waive his security and prove his entire claim as an unsecured one." United States Nat. Bank v. Chase Nat. Bank, 331 U.S. 28, 34 (1947). Section 726(a)(5) therefore requires no more than that undersecured creditors receive postpetition interest from a solvent debtor on equal terms with unsecured creditors rather than ahead of them—which, where the debtor is solvent, involves no hardship.

B

Petitioner contends that its interpretation is supported by the legislative history of §§ 361 and 362(d)(1), relying almost entirely on statements that "[s]ecured creditors should not be deprived of the benefit of their bargain." H.R.Rep. No. 95–595, at 339; S.Rep.No. 95–989, at 53. Such generalizations are inadequate to overcome the plain textual indication in §§ 506 and 362(d)(2) of the Code that Congress did not wish the undersecured creditor to receive interest on his collateral during the term of the stay. If it is at all relevant, the legislative history tends to subvert rather than support petitioner's thesis, since it contains not a hint that § 362(d)(1) entitles the undersecured creditor to postpetition interest. Such a major change in the existing rules would not likely have been made without specific provision in the text of the statute, cf. Kelly v. Robinson, 479 U.S. ___, ___ (1987); it is most improbable that it would have been made without even any mention in the legislative history.

Petitioner makes another argument based upon what the legislative history does *not* contain. It contends that the pre-Code law gave the undersecured creditor relief from the automatic stay by permitting him to foreclose; and that Congress would not have withdrawn this entitlement to relief without any indication of intent to do so in the legislative history, unless it was providing an adequate substitute, to wit, interest on the collateral during the stay.

The premise of this argument is flawed. As petitioner itself concedes, Brief for Petitioner 20, the undersecured creditor had no absolute entitlement to foreclosure in a Chapter X or XII case; he could not foreclose if there was a reasonable prospect for a successful rehabilitation within a reasonable time. Thus, even assuming petitioner is correct that the undersecured creditor had an absolute entitlement to relief under Chapter XI, Congress would have been faced with the choice between adopting the rule from Chapters X and XII or the asserted alternative rule from Chapter XI, because Chapter 11 of the current Code "replaces Chapters X, XI and XII of the Bankruptcy Act" with a "single chapter for all business reorganizations." S.Rep.No. 95–989, at 9; see also H.R.Rep. No. 95–595, at 223–224. We think § 362(d)(2) indicates that Congress adopted the approach of Chapters X and XII. In any event, as far as the silence of the legislative history on the point is concerned, that would be no more strange with respect to alteration of the asserted Chapter XI rule than it would be with respect to alteration of the Chapters X and XII rule.

Petitioner's argument is further weakened by the fact that it is far from clear that there was a distinctive Chapter XI rule of absolute entitlement to foreclosure. At least one leading commentator concluded that "a Chapter XI court's power to stay lien enforcement is as broad as that of a Chapter X or XII court and that the automatic stay rules properly make no distinctions between the Chapters." Countryman, Real Estate Liens in Business Rehabilitation Cases, 50 Am.Bankr.L.J. 303, 315 (1976). Petitioner cites dicta in some Chapter XI cases suggesting that the undersecured creditor was automatically entitled to relief from the stay, but the courts in those cases uniformly found in addition that reorganization was not sufficiently likely or was being unduly delayed. Moreover, other Chapter XI cases held undersecured creditors not entitled to foreclosure under reasoning very similar to that used in Chapters X and XII cases. The at best divided authority under Chapter XI removes all cause for wonder that the alleged departure from it should not have been commented upon in the legislative history.

. . .

The Fifth Circuit correctly held that the undersecured petitioner is not entitled to interest on its collateral during the stay to assure adequate protection under 11 U.S.C. § 362(d)(1). Petitioner has never sought relief from the stay under § 362(d)(2) or on any ground other than lack of adequate protection. Accordingly, the judgment of the Fifth Circuit is

Affirmed.

Notes & Questions

1. *Family Farmer Provisions.* Read the forms of adequate protection listed in § 1205(b). Do they provide a sounder drafting approach to the problem in *Timbers?*

2. *The Interest to Be Adequately Protected.* What is it that § 362(d) requires to be adequately protected? Is it the likelihood of timely payments to the creditor? Is it the position the secured party would have been in had the automatic stay not been in effect? Or is it the position the secured party would have been in had the automatic stay not been in effect and had no default occurred? Do these standards

differ? Which standard does § 361(1) and (2) contemplate? Which does *Murel Holding* contemplate?

3. *The Importance of the Value of the Collateral.* Consider the effect of the value of the property at issue in *Murel.* If its value had substantially exceeded the amount of the debt it secured, would Judge Hand have issued his famous dictum about indubitable equivalence? Does "indubitable equivalence" in *Murel Holding* represent a reasonable likelihood that the secured party will recover the collateral or its value on the date of bankruptcy?

If there is a large gap between the value of collateral and the amount owed to the creditor, is it necessary that the debtor offer the creditor additional security or periodic payments? Do §§ 362 and 361 always require that the secured party be given something in addition to the secured party's preexisting lien? Or may the court simply conclude that existing arrangements offer the secured party adequate protection?

4. *The Other Branches of § 361.* What assumptions about the nature of "adequate protection" are inherent in § 361's specific illustrations of adequate protection in subsections (1) and (2)? Do they suggest that secured creditors can be adequately protected if they are given a reasonable likelihood of recovering their collateral or its value? Or do they reflect the view that secured creditors must be compensated for the additional risk of participating in a risky reorganization and for the lost opportunity to reinvest funds?

5. *Incentives Created by Timbers.* How will the decision in *Timbers* affect secured party behavior? Would they be expected to change their nonbankruptcy behavior? How? May parties to a contract influence the adequate protection issue through their agreement? Consider the following provision in a security agreement covering a truck.

> The parties agree that in the event of Debtor's insolvency or bankruptcy it will be difficult to accurately appraise the value of the collateral. They therefore deem it in their mutual interest to agree upon a reasonable figure to reflect the periodic depreciation in the value of the collateral. In the event Secured Party is prevented from repossessing the collateral, the parties agree that the monthly depreciation in the value of the collateral shall be deemed to be three percent of the purchase price of the collateral.

6. *Adequate Protection Gone Wrong.* What happens if the adequate protection furnished turns out to be inadequate? See § 507(b); Chapter 12B.

Note on Use, Sale or Lease of Property (§ 363)

When the trustee or the debtor in possession resists a secured party's request for relief from the automatic stay, it is usually because the estate can make use of the property. The Bankruptcy Act outlines the trustee's power to use, sell or lease property in § 363. Note that under § 363(e) a party may request that its interest in property to be used be adequately protected. When the trustee both resists relief from the automatic stay and seeks to use collateral, do §§ 362(d) and 363(e), taken together, impose any greater protective burdens than would § 362(d) standing alone? What is the specific interest that § 363(e) seeks to adequately protect?

D. Executory Contracts and Unexpired Leases (§ 365)

Many aspects of the trustee's power to assume or reject executory contracts are dealt with in § 365. That section, however, does not define the term "executory contract." The following excerpt is from the leading discussion of the meaning of the term.

COUNTRYMAN, EXECUTORY CONTRACTS IN BANKRUPTCY: PART I, 57 Minn.L.Rev. 439, 450–52, 458–61 (1973)

II.　WHAT IS AN EXECUTORY CONTRACT?

As Professor Williston has said, "All contracts to a greater or less extent are executory. When they cease to be so, they cease to be contracts." But that expansive meaning can hardly be given to the term as used in the Bankruptcy Act or even to the Act's occasional alternative reference to contracts "executory in whole or in part." The concept of the "executory contract" in bankruptcy should be defined in the light of the purpose for which the trustee is given the option to assume or reject. Similar to his general power to abandon or accept other property, this is an option to be exercised when it will benefit the estate. A fortiori, it should not extend to situations where the only effect of its exercise would be to prejudice other creditors of the estate.

A.　Contracts Performed by the Nonbankrupt

Executory contracts, in the sense in which Professor Williston spoke, abound in a bankruptcy proceeding. One example is the contract under which the nonbankrupt party has fully rendered the performance to which the bankrupt is entitled, but which the bankrupt has performed only partially or not at all. Such a contract will give the nonbankrupt party a provable claim in the bankruptcy proceeding, whether it is liquidated or unliquidated and whether it is absolute or contingent as to liability. The trustee's option to assume or reject should not extend to such contracts. The estate has whatever benefit it can obtain from the other party's performance and the trustee's rejection would neither add to nor detract from the creditor's claim or the estate's liability. His assumption, on the other hand, would in no way benefit the estate and would only have the effect of converting the claim into a first priority expense of administration and thus of preferring it over all claims not assumed—a prerogative which the Bankruptcy Act has never been supposed to have vested in either the trustee or the court. . . .

B. Contracts Performed by the Bankrupt

Another example of a contract executory in the Willistonian sense which should not be treated as an executory contract within the meaning of the Bankruptcy Act is a contract which the bankrupt has fully performed, but which the nonbankrupt party has performed only partially or not at all. The bankrupt's claim to further performance under such a contract obviously is an asset which in most instances will pass to the trustee under § 70a(5) or (6). It is fairly obvious from the terms of the Act alone that such claims in favor of the bankrupt were not viewed as executory contracts. Obviously, the trustee's assumption of the underlying contract would add nothing to his title to the claim. And it would make no sense to say, as § 63c does of executory contracts, that the trustee's rejection of a contract fully performed by the bankrupt "shall constitute a breach of such contract." Nor could the other contracting party, who has received full performance from the debtor, have much of a claim under provisions in the chapters providing that upon rejection of an executory contract any person injured by the rejection shall be deemed a creditor.

Since the bankrupt's claim against the other party is an asset which will pass to the trustee, it is one which the trustee can accept or abandon just as he can accept or abandon noncontractual claims. But his acceptance of the asset merely leaves the other party's liability where § 70a of the Act has already transferred it, while his abandonment of it merely leaves the other party liable to the bankrupt as he was before bankruptcy. . . .

C. Contracts Unperformed on Both Sides

Thus, by a process similar to one method of sculpting an elephant, we approach a definition of executory contract within the meaning of the Bankruptcy Act: a contract under which the obligation of both the bankrupt and the other party to the contract are so far unperformed that the failure of either to complete performance would constitute a material breach excusing the performance of the other.

Such a contract, similar to the contract under which the other party has fully performed but the bankrupt has not, represents a claim against the estate. But here that claim may be reduced or totally eliminated if the trustee rejects the contract, because the other party is required to mitigate damages by an amount approximating the value of the performance he is spared by the trustee's rejection. In addition, such a contract, like the one under which the bankrupt has fully performed but the other party has not, represents an asset of the estate to the extent that it carries the unperformed obligation of the other party. But if the trustee elects to assume the contract, as when he accepts other assets to which he takes the title of the bankrupt under § 70a, he takes it *cum onere* and must render that performance which the bankrupt had contracted to perform as a condition to receiving the benefits of the contract. Whether in a given case the trustee will assume or reject depends, presumably, on his comparative appraisal of the value of the remaining performance by the other party and the cost to the estate of the unperformed obligation of the bankrupt, although the Act is silent on that point. . . .

Notes & Questions

1. Consider Professor Countryman's analysis of contracts that have been fully performed by the nonbankrupt. Is it true that because "[s]uch a contract will give the nonbankrupt party a provable claim in the bankruptcy proceeding," that "[t]he trustee's option to assume or reject should not extend to such contracts"? Might there be contracts that the nonbankrupt party has fully performed that the trustee should be given authority to assume despite the fact that performance is due only from bankrupt? What about contracts that will maintain good relationships with an important supplier in a reorganization? Could not the overall benefits to the estate exceed the costs of complying with any particular contract? See also In re Jolly, 574 F.2d 349, 351 (6th Cir. 1978), certiorari denied, 439 U.S. 929, 99 S.Ct. 316, 58 L.Ed.2d 322 (if objectives of rejection have already been, or cannot be, accomplished through rejection, contract is not executory).

2. What is the justification for authorizing the trustee to reject executory contracts? Is it that the debtor, in a nonbankruptcy setting, could have breached the contract, and the trustee should enjoy the same opportunity? Does § 365 give the trustee the same set of rights that the debtor would have enjoyed in a nonbankruptcy setting? Or does it give the trustee the same set of rights the debtor would have enjoyed in a nonbankruptcy setting, plus the additional right to act as if the debtor had not experienced any financial difficulty? If the nonbankrupt party is being made to bear the additional risk of dealing with a debtor in financial difficulty, should this be taken into account in assessing any rights the nonbankrupt party may have under § 365?

RICHMOND LEASING CO. v. CAPITAL BANK, N.A.

United States Court of Appeals, Fifth Circuit, 1985.
762 F.2d 1303.

Before GEE, JOHNSON and DAVIS, Circuit Judges.

PER CURIAM:

In this Chapter 11 bankruptcy reorganization, the appellants, bank creditors of the debtor in possession, Richmond Leasing Company (RLC), challenge the district court's affirmance of the bankruptcy court's approval of RLC's decision to assume an amended lease under § 365 of the Bankruptcy Code. We conclude that the district court did not err in approving the assumption of the lease as a valid business judgment of the debtor, and thus we affirm.

The debtor in possession, RLC, is in the business of leasing railroad cars. It is a wholly-owned subsidiary of Richmond Tank Car (RTC), which manufactures railroad cars. The lease that forms the subject matter of this appeal is part of a larger transaction in which RLC and its parent corporation, RTC, both played a part. RTC manufactured and sold 402 railroad cars to General Electric Credit Corporation (GECC). GECC in turn leased the railroad cars back to RTC's subsidiary, RLC, for a twenty-year term. Under the lease agreement between GECC and RLC, dated June 1, 1982, RLC agreed to pay GECC approximately $1.8 million every six months, beginning on June 30, 1983. RLC also granted GECC a security interest in RLC's subleases of the cars to third parties. There was some suggestion at the hearing that GECC may have paid RTC a premium price for the cars and RLC may in turn have leased them from GECC at a premium. The 402 cars covered by the lease make up less than ten percent of RLC's inventory.

On January 7, 1983, before the first payment was due under this lease, RLC filed its petition in bankruptcy. In April 1983, RLC and GECC offered for court approval a renegotiated lease that RLC proposed to assume. Under the amended lease, GECC agreed to waive existing defaults in the lease [2] and to reduce the rent due under the lease through 1986 to quarterly payments of $500,000 or 85% of the gross quarterly revenues generated by the 402 cars, whichever was less; however, the quarterly payments were not to average less than $400,000 for two consecutive quarters. From 1986 through 2002, the quarterly payments were to increase to $937,500. In exchange, RTC agreed to issue preferred stock to GECC periodically, and GECC placed restrictions upon RTC's ability to encumber its property, buy stock, make loans, guarantee obligations, dilute its stock, dispose of its fixed assets at less than fair market value, lease property, merge with or be purchased by another company, or dispose of its receivables out of the ordinary course of business, without GECC's consent. The amended lease designates RTC's violation of these restrictions as an event of default. RTC's bankruptcy is an event of default under both the original and the amended leases.

After a hearing, the bankruptcy court approved the joint application of RLC and GECC for authority to amend and assume the lease. The court's order provided that the automatic stay imposed by 11 U.S.C. § 362 would be lifted automatically in the event of RLC's default, after GECC notified the court and all parties in interest. On appeal from the bankruptcy court, the district court affirmed the bankruptcy court's approval of the assumption of the lease.

The bank creditors raise several points in their appeal to this Court. We shall consider those points in turn.. . . .

---

2. The district court correctly held that RLC was not in default of its obligations under the lease, since no payment was yet due. RLC's filing for bankruptcy was an event of default under the lease, but under the provisions of 11 U.S.C. § 365(b)(2), that default would have had no effect in bankruptcy. However, RLC's bankruptcy would have triggered RTC's obligations as a guarantor of the June 1982 lease, so the waiver of defaults represented some consideration flowing from GECC to RTC.

RLC's Exercise of Business Judgment and Adequate Assurance of Future Performance

The bank creditors invite us to overturn the district court's holding that the bankruptcy court did not clearly err when it found that RLC's assumption of the amended lease was a proper exercise of its business judgment. The bank creditors urge us to hold that the business judgment question, as a mixed question of law and fact, is subject to *de novo* review. We have noted above that the decision whether assumption of the lease represented a proper exercise of business judgment depended entirely upon resolution of a factual dispute as to whether RLC could generate sufficient revenues in the future to cover its obligations under the lease. The parties did not dispute the legal standard to be applied in § 365 cases, nor could they. It is well established that "the question whether a lease should be rejected . . . is one of business judgment." Group of Institutional Investors v. Chicago, Milwaukee, St. Paul & Pacific Railroad Co., 318 U.S. 523, 550, 63 S.Ct. 727, 742, 87 L.Ed. 959 (1943). See also Matter of Minges, 602 F.2d 38, 42–43 (2d Cir.1979). "As long as assumption of a lease appears to enhance a debtor's estate, court approval of a debtor-in-possession's decision to assume the lease should only be withheld if the debtor's judgment is clearly erroneous, too speculative, or contrary to the provisions of the Bankruptcy Code. . . ." Allied Technology, Inc. v. R.B. Brunemann & Sons, 25 B.R. 484, 495 (Bankr.S.D.Ohio 1982).

The parties did not dispute whether doubts about RLC's financial stability had achieved a critical mass sufficient to render RLC's assuming the lease an improper exercise of business judgment; instead they disputed whether the doubts about RLC's financial status were justified. Thus this issue is properly considered under the "clearly erroneous" standard of review. The bankruptcy court heard extensive testimony on direct examination and cross-examination of financial experts and company officers. It was called upon to determine whether a projection of future income based on RLC's revenues was more accurate than one based on cash flows, whether certain types of income were sufficiently assured to be considered as available to pay RLC's lease obligations, whether an incipient upward turn in the railroad car leasing business was likely to continue in the long term, and whether the administrative claim that might result from RLC's default on the amended lease would be so large that possible prejudice to RLC's unsecured creditors mandated a more cautious business approach than that taken in assuming the lease. The bankruptcy court's findings reflect its decisions on these disputed factual matters. It did not clearly err.

Similarly, the parties do not dispute that 11 U.S.C. § 365(b)(1)(C) requires a debtor in possession [7] to provide adequate assurance of future performance when it assumes a lease. Nor do they dispute the legal

---

7. A debtor in possession enjoys the powers of a trustee under 11 U.S.C. § 1107, except those withheld by 11 U.S.C. § 1106.

standard for determining adequate assurance. In In Re Sapolin Paints, Inc., 5 B.R. 412, 420–21 (Bankr.E.D.N.Y.1980), the court traced the phrase "adequate assurance" as it is used in § 365 to the "adequate assurance" defined in § 2–609(1) of the Uniform Commercial Code:

> The terms "adequate assurance of future performance" are not words of art; the legislative history of the Code shows that they were intended to be given a practical, pragmatic construction.

> The phrase first appears in the legislation proposed by the Commission on Bankruptcy Laws. . . .

> The Commission Report explains the language "adequate assurance of future performance" as follows:

> "The language 'is adopted from Uniform Commercial Code § 2–609(1).' What constitutes 'reasonable time thereafter' for curing defaults or an 'adequate assurance of future performance' must be determined by consideration of the facts of the proposed assumption. Cf. Official Comment 4 to Uniform Commercial Code § 2–609 (1972 Edition). It is not intended, however, that any non-debtor party should acquire greater rights in a case under the act than he has outside the act." Report of the Commission on Bankruptcy Laws of the United States, H.R.Doc. No. 93–137, 93d Cong., 1st Sess. Pt. II 156–57 (1973).

> Section 2–609 of the Uniform Commercial Code, from which the bankruptcy statute borrows its critical language, provides that "when reasonable grounds for insecurity arise with respect to the performance of either party, the other may in writing demand adequate assurance of future performance. . . ." The Commentaries to the Code note that " 'adequate' assurance is to be 'defined by commercial rather than legal standards.' " Official Comment 3 To Uniform Commercial Code § 2–609 (1972 Ed.). What constitutes "adequate assurance" is to be determined by factual conditions; the seller must exercise good faith and observe commercial standards; his satisfaction must be based upon reason and must not be arbitrary or capricious.

Courts have consistently determined whether a debtor offered adequate assurance of future performance by considering whether the debtor's financial data indicated its ability to generate an income stream sufficient to meet its obligations, the general economic outlook in the debtor's industry, and the presence of a guarantee. See, e.g., Seacoast Products, Inc. v. Spring Valley Farms, 34 B.R. 379, 381 (Bankr.M.D.N.C.1983); In re Berkshire Chemical Haulers, Inc., 20 B.R. 454, 458–59 (Bankr.Mass.1982); In re Lafayette Radio Electronics Corp., 9 B.R. 993, 1000 (Bankr.E.D.N.Y.1981). The bankruptcy court considered just such factual matters in this case.

The bank creditors contend that the bankruptcy court erred when it credited the testimony of RLC's witnesses projecting RLC's future profitability rather than the testimony of the bank creditors' witnesses.

That dispute is essentially factual and is subject to review under the "clearly erroneous" standard. We affirm the district court's holding that the bankruptcy court did not clearly err when it made this determination.

RLC's Granting GECC Greater Rights Under the Amended Lease

The bank group contends that the bankruptcy court erred when it approved RLC's assumption of the amended lease on the ground that § 365 of the Bankruptcy Code requires that the debtor grant the creditor no greater rights under the amended lease than under the original lease. This argument misconstrues the requirements of § 365.

We first observe that the amended lease significantly reduces RLC's short-term obligations to GECC. In exchange for this concession, GECC receives additional benefits under the amended lease largely from RLC's parent corporation, RTC, in the form of stock and increased control over the way RTC conducts its business. The consideration flowing from RTC to GECC cannot affect any interest of the bank creditors that RLC's bankruptcy proceeding protects.[8] Under the amended agreement, RLC provides GECC additional consideration only in the sense that it agrees that RTC's default on its new obligations to GECC will permit GECC to terminate the agreement and repossess its cars from RLC.

Section 365 is intended to provide a means whereby a debtor can force another party to an executory contract to continue to perform under the contract if (1) the debtor can provide adequate assurance that it, too, will continue to perform, and if (2) the debtor can cure any defaults in its past performance. The provision provides a means whereby a debtor can force others to continue to do business with it when the bankruptcy filing might otherwise make them reluctant to do so. The section thus serves the purpose of making the debtor's rehabilitation more likely.

In this context, it becomes clear that in the typical case under § 365, if anyone objects to the debtor's assumption of the contract it will be the other party to the executory contract, not the debtor's creditors who are strangers to the transaction. Thus, the often-repeated statement that the debtor must accept the contract as a whole means only that the debtor cannot choose to accept the benefits of the contract and reject its burdens to the detriment of the other party to the agreement. See In re Holland Enterprises, Inc., 25 B.R. 301 (Bankr.E.D.N.C.1982); In re LHD Realty Corp., 20 B.R. 717 (Bankr.S.D.Ind.1982). Similarly, the other party cannot hold out for concessions from the debtor beyond those required to provide adequate assurance. See In re Lafayette Radio Electronics Corp., 9 B.R. 993, 998 (E.D.N.Y.1981). We conclude

---

8. The bank creditors contend that RTC, to which they have also lent money, is itself in default of its obligations to them and may file for bankruptcy in the future. If the bank creditors want court supervi- sion of RTC's activities, they can commence an involuntary bankruptcy case against RTC if the requirements of 11 U.S.C. § 303 are met.

that RLC's recognizing an event of default in RTC's failure to perform the new covenants, which were included in the amended lease in order to assure GECC that RTC would perform its guarantee, is part of RLC's offer of adequate assurance of future performance to GECC. See In re Kennesaw Dairy Queen Brazier, 28 B.R. 535, 536 (N.D.Ga.1983) (stating, "The fact that debtors may cure defaults and reinstate contracts or leases also is perhaps the clearest example of the modification of an executory contract or unexpired lease.").

Moreover, to the extent that the amended lease represents a true renegotiation of the obligations of RLC, RTC and GECC, it falls entirely outside of § 365's concern. 11 U.S.C. §§ 1107 and 1108, taken together, authorize a debtor in possession to operate the business of the debtor. Nothing in the Code suggests that the debtor may not modify its contracts when all parties to the contract consent. Although § 1107 provides that a court may limit the debtor's exercise of the rights of the trustee, including the § 1108 right to operate the business, in the absence of special circumstances or a specific Code provision, we see no reason to require the debtor to do more than justify its actions under the "business judgment" standard if creditors object.[9] More exacting scrutiny would slow the administration of the debtor's estate and increase its cost, interfere with the Bankruptcy Code's provision for private control of administration of the estate, and threaten the court's ability to control a case impartially. See In re Airlift International, Inc., 18 B.R. 787, 789 (Bankr.S.D.Fla.1982); In re Curlew Valley Assocs., 14 B.R. 506, 509–514 (Bankr.D.Utah 1981). This business judgment standard thus does not differ from the business judgment inquiry already undertaken and resolved in favor of the amended lease under § 365. Accordingly, the bankruptcy court did not err in approving the lease as amended, and we affirm the district court's order on this point.

Lease as a Sub Rosa Plan of Reorganization

The bank creditors contend that the amended lease goes beyond what is permissible in the assumption of a lease and establishes, *sub rosa*, a plan of reorganization, allowing GECC and RLC to circumvent the plan confirmation requirements of Chapter 11. The bank creditors complain that the lease does not expressly restrict payment due under the amended lease to the revenues generated by the GECC rail cars; the order approving the lease provides for the automatic lifting of the § 362 stay if there is a default; in the event of default, the lease permits GECC to assert a large administrative claim that would affect the proportion of assets that could be allocated to other creditors under a plan of reorganization; and the amended lease restricts RTC's actions and names as an event of default RTC's filing for bankruptcy, so that, in the event of RTC's bankruptcy, a consolidation with RLC's case would be more difficult.

9. 11 U.S.C. § 1104 permits the appointment of a trustee, of course, in the event of debtor misconduct.

We do not doubt that a debtor can assume a lease under its original, pre-bankruptcy terms without creating a sub rosa plan of reorganization, so long as such an assumption is a valid exercise of a debtor's business judgment. Thus, we need not greatly concern ourselves with the alleged debilitating effects of GECC's rights, under the amended lease, to look to sources other than revenues from the GECC cars for payment, to assert a large administrative claim in the event of default,[13] or to consider RTC's bankruptcy as an event of default: the original lease afforded GECC all those advantages, and the bankruptcy court determined that they do not render assumption of the amended lease an improper business decision. The lifting of the automatic stay and the restrictions on RTC's actions, even were we to combine them with the advantages under the original lease, do not alter creditors' rights, dispose of assets, and release claims to the extent proposed in the wide-ranging transaction disapproved in In re Braniff Airways, Inc., 700 F.2d 935 (5th Cir.1983). Although the disposition of a "crown jewel" asset might, in combination with other factors, severely restrict a future reorganization plan so as to amount to a *sub rosa* plan of reorganization even though all or substantially all of the debtor's assets were not involved in the transaction, that is not the case here. We will not make a mountain out of the molehill of restrictions included in the amended lease.

Notes & Questions

1. *The Fairness of the Power to Reject.* Should a trustee be able to reject a profitable contract simply because a better, more profitable deal is available elsewhere? Does use of the rejection power create an unfair asymmetry for those who contract with potential bankrupts? If the contract is favorable to the bankrupt, the trustee assumes it and the nonbankrupt party bears the burden of his bad deal. If the contract is favorable to the nonbankrupt party, the trustee rejects it and the nonbankrupt party is left with a claim for breach of contract against a bankrupt debtor. Should this asymmetry be tempered by a rule limiting the trustee's power to reject to cases in which the contract is actually burdensome to the estate?

13. We believe that the bankruptcy court's discretion under 11 U.S.C. § 503 is broad enough to reject administrative claims that result from inequitable conduct, including entering into agreements in bad faith, when the inequitable conduct prevents the estate's receiving the benefit that the court envisioned when it approved an agreement. See generally In re Allied Artists Industries, Inc., 35 B.R. 737 (Bankr. S.D.N.Y.1983). The bankruptcy court's order in this case astutely reserves the right to exercise this discretion when and if GECC presents an administrative claim. If, as the bank creditors fear, GECC en- gages in the sharp practice of urging one interpretation of the amended lease's waiver of existing defaults before bankruptcy court approval and another thereafter, principles of estoppel should come into play.

Moreover, we keep in mind that creditor misconduct has traditionally formed the basis for equitable subordination of a creditor's priority status. See generally Allied Technology, Inc. v. R.B. Brunemann & Sons, 25 B.R. 484, 499 (Bankr.S.D.Ohio 1982); Matter of Multiponics, Inc., 622 F.2d 709 (5th Cir.1980).

2. *Debtor's Opportunity Costs.* Is there a relationship worth exploring between the "business judgment" rule in the area of executory contracts and the issues that arise in determining what is "adequate protection" within the meaning of § 361, discussed supra? The business judgment rule seems to put the bankruptcy estate in the position to pursue more profitable alternatives if its investment in or commitment to a contract proves to be costly when measured from the perspective of other available opportunities. That is, the power to reject even profitable contracts enables the bankruptcy estate to take into account its "opportunity costs" in deciding whether to assume or to reject an executory contract. The expense to the estate of pursuing opportunities that are available only upon breach of an existing contract is drastically reduced in bankruptcy because unsecured creditors, including the nonbankrupt party to a rejected executory contract, receive only a fraction of the face amount of their claims. When compared with the nonbankruptcy setting, the bankruptcy estate is being built up at the expense of the nonbankrupt party to an executory contract.

Contrast this treatment with that of secured creditors seeking adequate protection under § 361. The protection furnished secured creditors does not always include protection for the investment opportunities lost by their inability to retake collateral and reinvest the proceeds of its sale.

Do the executory contract and adequate protection rules, taken together, suggest that the estate is entitled to have its opportunity costs taken into account but those who deal with the estate are not so entitled? Is this justifiable on the ground of trying to maximize the estate for the benefit of all unsecured creditors?

3. *Terminating Contracts With a Bankrupt Debtor: Default and Contractual Provisions.* Often a debtor seeking to assume a contract will have defaulted on one or more duties imposed by the contract. Or the contract itself will make bankruptcy or financial distress an event of default. The notes that follow explore the extent to which a prebankruptcy default or a contractual provision can deprive the debtor of the power to assume an executory contract.

Notes on § 365(b): Default and Adequate Assurance

As *Richmond Leasing* indicates, in the usual case it is the nonbankrupt party to a contract that objects to the debtor's assumption of the contract. Put yourself in the position of a nonbankrupt party who has an executory contract with the debtor. Would you rather have the bankrupt default before bankruptcy or would you prefer what contracting parties usually prefer, that the bankrupt at all times fully honor his commitments under the contract? See § 365(b)(1) and consider it in light of a case like In re General Oil Distributors, Inc., 18 B.R. 654 (Bkrtcy.E.D.N.Y.1982). There the debtor, General, sought bankruptcy court authorization to assume its executory contract for the sale of oil to New York City. The contract called for General to deliver 5.7 million gallons of fuel oil to city facilities, including the Staten Island Ferry, at a fixed price. A drop in oil prices made the contract a valuable asset of the debtor. Prior to the filing of its bankruptcy petition, General had failed to make a scheduled delivery of oil needed to run the ferry. Due to the drop in oil prices, the city suffered no monetary damages. Applying § 365(b)(1), the court refused to approve the debtor's request to assume the contract,

> . . . [I]nasmuch as this default engendered no monetary damages, it follows that there is nothing to cure. Accordingly, General could assume the contract provided it could provide adequate assurance of future performance. . . .

> The concept of adequate assurance of future performance is one borrowed from section 2–609ᶜ of the Uniform Commercial Code. . . . Accordingly, the case law under U.C.C. section 2–609 has been held applicable to section 365(b)(1)(C). . . .

> In general section 365(b)(1) attempts to strike a balance between the interest of the estate in preserving (or disposing of at a profit) a valuable asset and the interest of the nondebtor party to the contract in receiving its bargained for performance. . . .

> Applying the foregoing to the case at bar, the Court cannot ignore the reality of who the nondebtor party to this contract is. It is the City of New York; and the oil is needed that the Staten Island Ferry might run and that several waste treatment plants might be able to process refuse prior to its disposal at sea. Nor can this Court ignore the precarious financial position that General has been shown to be in; nor the fact that General has defaulted on past deliveries; nor the fact that General is presently out of oil and out of money . . . .

Suppose that, prior to bankruptcy, General managed to scrape by and make its scheduled deliveries to New York City. Would the bankruptcy court then have any authority to refuse to approve General's assumption of the contract? Should courts engage in a balancing process under § 365 whether or not the debtor is in prebankruptcy default?

Might U.C.C. § 2–609 be used by parties to contracts with nondefaulting bankrupt debtors to extract some promise of assurance of future performance? May such parties argue that the debtor's bank-

c. Section 2–609 states in part:

(1) A contract for sale imposes an obligation on each party that the other's expectation of receiving due performance will not be impaired. When reasonable grounds for insecurity arise with respect to the performance of either party the other may in writing demand adequate assurance of due performance and until he receives such assurance may if com- mercially reasonable suspend any performance for which he has not already received the agreed return. . . .

(4) After receipt of a justified demand failure to provide within a reasonable time not exceeding thirty days such assurance of due performance as is adequate under the circumstances of the particular case is a repudiation of the contract.

ruptcy gives them "reasonable grounds for insecurity" within the meaning of § 2–609(1), and that this reasonable ground entitles them to adequate assurance from the trustee or the debtor-in-possession under the contract to be assumed—whether or not there has been a prebankruptcy default?

Suppose the trustee or the debtor assumes an executory contract and later breaches it.   See §§ 503(b), 507(a)(1).

Notes on Section 365's Anti-Avoidance Provisions

Many provisions in § 365 directly address efforts by parties to avoid having to deal with bankrupt debtors.   This Note explores § 365's treatment of those who seek to minimize contractual dealings with bankrupts.

1.   To start, apply § 365 to the following problem:

Debtor is party to a contract with Gyro Supply Co. under which Gyro is obligated to deliver five gyroscopes every other month for one year. Debtor is obligated to pay for the delivered gyroscopes thirty days after delivery.   At Gyro's insistence the following terms are part of the supply contract:

I.   Conditions on Gyro's Obligations

(1) In the event of:

> Debtor's dissolution, termination of existence, insolvency or business failure; appointment of a receiver of all or any part of the property of Debtor; an assignment for the benefit of creditors by Debtor; the calling of a meeting of creditors of Debtor; or the commencement of any proceeding under any bankruptcy or insolvency laws by or against Debtor or any guarantor, surety or endorser for Debtor,

all of Gyro's obligations to perform under this contract shall automatically terminate without further notice to Debtor.

II.   Constructive Breach

(1) Debtor shall be deemed in material breach of this contract upon the happening of any of the following events or conditions:

> (a) Debtor's failure to pay when due any indebtedness due under this contract.

> (b) Debtor's dissolution, termination of existence, insolvency or business failure, the appointment of a receiver of all or any part of the property of Debtor; the calling of a meeting of creditors by Debtor; the calling of a meeting of creditors of Debtor; or the commencement of any proceeding under any bankruptcy or insolvency laws by or against Debtor or any guarantor, surety or endorser for Debtor.

III. Assignment

Debtor's rights and obligations under this contract may not be assigned or assumed without the prior written consent of Gyro. Debtor will give Gyro at least thirty days notice of any proposed assignment.

IV. Termination

Either party may terminate this contract on thirty days written notice to the other party.

At the time of Debtor's bankruptcy petition, Debtor was fifteen days late on one of the payments due to Gyro. In addition, Debtor's financial condition on the date of bankruptcy was such that it was in default under other financial covenants of the supply contract. May Debtor's trustee in bankruptcy assume the contract? On the date of the bankruptcy petition, Gyro sends a letter to Debtor exercising its right to terminate the supply contract thirty days thereafter. If Gyro is sending this letter solely because of the Debtor's bankruptcy, will the letter be effective to terminate the contract thirty days later?

Debtor also is the supplier of video game components to Curari, a manufacturer of video games. Debtor and Curari are in the midst of a long-term supply contract that is favorable to Debtor. The contract contains an anti-assignment provision similar to that in the Gyro contract. Debtor now lacks the manufacturing capacity to fulfill the Curari contract. May the trustee assign the contract to another supplier of video game components?

2. *Drafting Around § 365's Anti-Avoidance Provisions.* Sections 365(b)(2), (e)(1), & (f)(3) all limit a party's contractual freedom to terminate relationships with a debtor who files a bankruptcy petition. Are such provisions justifiable? How should an entity concerned about dealing with bankrupts draft its contracts to take account of § 365? Based on § 365(b), should it add the following clause: "Any default in any of the terms of this agreement automatically terminates this agreement."?

Consider the avoidance technique suggested by the following excerpt:

> Even in cases in which the general rules of contract law would not call a duty non-delegable . . . the parties are free to draft their own anti-delegation clause. In this respect, parties are free to contract into their own creation of a property rule. . . . This could be done either directly as a matter of assignment ("A cannot assign his obligation to deliver wheat to me"), or indirectly, as a term of the contract ("A must deliver to me wheat grown on A's farm, located at Blackacre, Kansas"). Games such as this may be played under the Bankruptcy Code, which, while striking down anti-assignment clauses, requires the assignee to give adequate assur-

ances of performing the terms of the contract. Bankruptcy Code
§ 365(f)(2).

Jackson, Bankruptcy, Non-Bankruptcy Entitlements, and the Creditors'
Bargain, 91 Yale L.J. 857, 896–97 n. 178 (1982). Can you redraft the
Gyro contract to reduce Gyro's risks in bankruptcy?

3. *Modifying the Terms of An Assumed Contract.* In In re U.L.
Radio Corp., 19 B.R. 537 (Bkrtcy.S.D.N.Y.1982), a lease provision limited the use of the leased premises to the sale of electrical appliances.
The buyer of the bankrupt tenant's leasehold wanted to operate a
restaurant. The court ordered the lease modified to accommodate the
buyer. Contra, In re Pin Oaks Apartments, 7 B.R. 364 (Brktcy.S.D.Tex.
1980).[d]

What are the limits on a debtor's authority to assume or assign a
contract in bankruptcy? See § 365(c), (e).

4. *Pretextual Terminations.* Suppose an entity's contract with a
bankrupt does not contain a clause automatically terminating the
contract in the event of bankruptcy. May the nonbankrupt party to a
contract use some other event of default under the contract as a pretext
for termination when its real concern is the existence of the bankruptcy
proceeding? Does anything in § 365 prevent a party from taking
actions motivated by a debtor's bankruptcy? Does it not simply focus
on contractual terms? Does anything else in the Bankruptcy Act
prevent such action?

How effective is § 362's automatic stay in preventing such terminations? If it is only the stay that prevents termination, should the
nonbankrupt contracting party be entitled to adequate protection of its
interests? What form should such protection take?

In In re Blackwelder Furniture Co., Inc., 7 B.R. 328 (Bkrtcy.
W.D.N.C. 1980), a major furniture retailer filed a Chapter 11 petition
and had its plan of reorganization approved. Subsequent to confirmation of the plan, some of the retailer's most important suppliers refused
to deal with the retailer. There were no long term contracts between
the retailer and the suppliers. The retailer filed a complaint with the
bankruptcy court claiming that the suppliers should be permanently
enjoined from terminating their relationships with the retailer.

> Blackwelder claims and alleged that the defendants have refused
> to deal with it because of its filing under Chapter 11 of the Bank-
> ruptcy Code, and that said refusals on said grounds are illegal and
> unlawful. It urges this Court to find that the defendants have
> unlawfully discriminated against the debtor (Blackwelder) and that
> they have therefore violated the letter and spirit of the Bankruptcy
> Code and should be enjoined, pursuant to and by authority of section
> 105 of the Code . . . from further violation.

---

d. See generally Simpson, Leases and   ors of Strict Performance, 38 Bus. Law. 61
the Bankruptcy Code: Tempering the Rig-   (1982).

May the court grant Blackwelder any relief? (It found that it may.) See also In re Ike Kempner & Brothers Inc., 4 B.R. 31 (Bkrtcy.E.D.Ark. 1980).

5. *Excepted Contracts.* Why do § 365's anti-avoidance provisions contain exceptions for loans and other financial contracts? See § 365(c) (2), (e)(2)(B). Is this because loans of money are such individualized transactions that lenders willing to lend to a nonbankrupt party should not be forced to lend to that party's legal successor, whether that successor be a trustee or a debtor-in-possession? Why should suppliers be forced to extend credit to bankrupts when money lenders are not?

Note on the General Problem of Avoiding Entanglements With Bankrupts

The anti-avoidance provisions of § 365 share a common goal with numerous other bankruptcy provisions. Section 365's limitations prevent a party, through contract, from avoiding dealings with a bankrupt entity. Sections 362, 542 and 543 require parties who have property in which the debtor has an interest to deal with the estate. Section 541(c) limits contract provisions that seek to keep property out of the estate. Taken together, all of these provisions can be viewed as limiting efforts by those who have engaged in transactions with the debtor to disengage themselves from dealings with the debtor in the event of bankruptcy proceedings. One question these sections raise, explored at various points in these materials, is whether parties should be prohibited from taking measures to avoid involvement with the debtor in the event of bankruptcy.

But they also raise a question as to their own effectiveness. Given the array of bankruptcy anti-avoidance measures, how much room is left for unsecured parties and their lawyers to minimize the risk of becoming involved with or injured by a bankruptcy proceeding? How can prepaying or other buyers protect themselves against a seller's bankruptcy? One possible technique is to make sure any advance payments go into a segregated escrow account, with appropriate conditions put upon release of the funds. Can you think of any other techniques?

How can credit sellers protect themselves from potential bankruptcy by buyers? Is the letter of credit a useful device to assure that, after shipment, a seller need not worry about a debtor's bankruptcy because the bank's obligation to honor the letter of credit is independent of any obligation of the debtor? (Can letters of credit be rejected by the trustee as executory contracts?) What other techniques are available to sellers?

To the extent escrows and letters of credit minimize the risk of suffering a loss because of a seller's or buyer's bankruptcy, they seem to undermine the anti-avoidance measures contained in the Bankruptcy Act. Can the anti-avoidance measures be expected to work so long as these avoidance techniques are honored? Is the net effect of the system that those creditors with sophisticated planning ability, and with the expertise and funds to set up escrows and letters of credit, will avoid entanglement in bankruptcy, and less sophisticated creditors, particularly small trade creditors, will routinely be entangled in bankruptcy proceedings?

See generally Countryman, Executory Contracts in Bankruptcy: Part I, 57 Minn.L.Rev. 439 (1973), Part II, 58 Minn.L.Rev. 479 (1974); Fogel, Executory Contracts and Unexpired Leases in the Bankruptcy Code, 64 Minn.L.Rev. 341 (1980).

WHEELING–PITTSBURGH STEEL CORPORATION v. UNITED STEELWORKERS OF AMERICA, AFL–CIO–CLC

United States Court of Appeals, Third Circuit, 1986.
791 F.2d 1074.

Before: ADAMS, SLOVITER, and MANSMANN, CIRCUIT JUDGES.
SLOVITER, CIRCUIT JUDGE.

I.

ISSUE

In NLRB v. Bildisco & Bildisco, 465 U.S. 513, 104 S.Ct. 1188, 79 L.Ed.2d 482 (1984), the Supreme Court held that the debtor-in-possession may reject its collective bargaining agreements, subject to the approval of the bankruptcy court which must balance the equities of the affected parties. Thereafter, following considerable debate and controversy, Congress enacted section 1113 of the Bankruptcy Code, 11 U.S.C. § 1113 (Supp. II 1984), which establishes the procedures to be followed and the conditions that must be met before the bankruptcy court may authorize such a rejection. On May 31, 1985, Wheeling–Pittsburgh Steel Corp., a debtor-in-possession under Chapter 11 of the Bankruptcy Code, sought authorization in the bankruptcy court to reject its collective bargaining agreements with the United Steelworkers of America, AFL–CIO–CLC ("Union" or "Steelworkers"). After a four-day hearing, the bankruptcy court authorized Wheeling–Pittsburgh to do so, finding that it had satisfied the requirements of the statute. The district court affirmed that order, and the Union appeals. Before us are important matters of first impression for an appellate court regarding the interpretation of the statute. Amici Curiae briefs have been filed by the American Federation of Labor and Congress of Industrial Organizations, and the Glass, Pottery, Plastics and Allied Workers International Union, AFL–CIO–CLC.

II.

FACTUAL BACKGROUND

Wheeling–Pittsburgh is the seventh largest steel manufacturing corporation in the United States. In the late 1970's, Wheeling–Pittsburgh began a major capital investment program to become one of the most modern and efficient major United States producers. The price of such efficiency was heavy borrowing. Wheeling–Pittsburgh's long-term debt increased from $170 million at the end of 1979 to $527 million at the end of 1984. A 1982 recession adversely affected the steel industry. The Company's losses in 1982, 1983 and 1984 and the need to pay principal and interest due on the modernization loans substantially weakened its financial position.

For some years, Wheeling–Pittsburgh and other major steel corporations, organized as the "Steel Company Coordinating Committee", have engaged in coordinated collective bargaining with the Steelworkers, and, as a result, their workers' wages and benefits were generally the same. Wheeling–Pittsburgh's average gross labor costs (including wages, benefits, current pension costs and other benefits for retirees, and payroll taxes) under the 1980 collective bargaining agreement were about $25 per hour. Because of its financial problem, Wheeling–Pittsburgh asked the Union for concessions twice in 1982. The April concession consisted of a $1.65 an hour reduction in labor costs in return for entitlement to preferred stock which each employee could redeem when s/he quit, died or retired.

The December 1982 concession was made as part of a new three and a half year collective bargaining agreement scheduled to expire on July 31, 1986. It is that contract that is the subject of the dispute at issue before us. The Union agreed to concessions that reduced the average labor cost to $18.60 an hour at its lowest point. In return, Wheeling–Pittsburgh agreed to a profit sharing plan. The new agreement provided for gradual restoration of the Union concessions so that the average labor cost per hour would return to $25. By the end of 1984, the average labor cost had been restored to $21.40, and further restorations were due in 1985.

At the end of 1984, Wheeling–Pittsburgh again asked for concessions, this time the cancellation of all scheduled restorations. The Union agreed to defer restorations while its accounting firm, Arthur Young & Co., analyzed Wheeling–Pittsburgh's financial reports to determine the extent of its financial distress. When Arthur Young confirmed Wheeling–Pittsburgh's condition, the Union agreed to defer restorations indefinitely. In mid-January 1985, Wheeling–Pittsburgh asked the Union for a fourth reduction in labor cost. The Union, however, refused to make further concessions until Wheeling–Pittsburgh gained concessions from its lenders, who had made none to that date.

After mediation efforts, Wheeling–Pittsburgh issued a restructuring proposal on March 8, 1985, which sought concessions from the Union, the lenders, and shareholders. It asked the Union for a labor cost of approximately $19 for three years and cancellation of the restorations, with the employees to receive preferred or common stock in Wheeling–Pittsburgh in return. Wheeling–Pittsburgh asked all of its lenders for a 100% moratorium on principal payments for 1985–1986, and some of its lenders for an additional 50% moratorium for 1987–1989, and/or reductions in interest, with the lenders to be given common stock in return. Significantly, the Company did not propose pledging its current assets for past debts. Wheeling–Pittsburgh also proposed a continued suspension of dividends to its preferred stockholders, elimination of preemptive rights for its common stockholders, and dilution of their present holdings to the extent necessary to compensate labor and lenders for their sacrifices.

The Union's counter-offer to Wheeling–Pittsburgh called for a two-year contract with labor costs of $19.50 the first year and $20.00 the second year; cancellation of the scheduled restorations; common stock as compensation; the right to appoint a member of Wheeling–Pittsburgh's Board of Directors; and Wheeling–Pittsburgh's promise not to pledge its current assets to the banks to secure the old debt. The Union believed the current assets were the "life preserver" needed to keep the Company and the employees' jobs afloat in the event of economic difficulties.

The lenders' counter-proposal to Wheeling–Pittsburgh called for deferment of about $210 million in outstanding indebtedness; $40 million in additional credit over the next four years; and Wheeling–Pittsburgh's pledging its current accounts receivable and inventory (about $300 million in value) to secure the entire debt. Neither the Union nor the lenders were willing to compromise on their respective positions concerning the pledge of current assets to secure the old loans, and the restructuring proposal collapsed. Wheeling–Pittsburgh filed a Chapter 11 petition for bankruptcy on April 16, 1985.

Thereafter, on May 9, 1985, Wheeling–Pittsburgh presented its proposal to the Union for modifying the current collective bargaining agreement. Wheeling–Pittsburgh proposed a five-year contract which included the following items: an average labor cost not to exceed $15.20 an hour; a reduction in medical and insurance benefits, as part of the employment cost adjustment; elimination of supplemental unemployment benefit guarantees for employees with 20 or more years' service and cost-of-living adjustments; elimination of various other prior obligations, including payments of the pension plan, redemption fund and cash dividends on preferred stock; and elimination of the profit sharing plan. These proposals were accompanied by five-year forecasts far more pessimistic than those that had accompanied the restructuring proposal the Company had offered two months earlier in March, before the bankruptcy.

The Union hired Lazard Freres & Co. and Arthur Young & Co. to assist it in evaluating the Wheeling–Pittsburgh proposal and formulating a response. The financial advisors sought certain financial information from Wheeling–Pittsburgh, which provided some, but not all, of the requested information. On May 24, Wheeling–Pittsburgh announced it would provide no additional information, demanded the Union's response by May 30, and threatened to seek authorization to reject the agreement. When the Union replied that it could not respond until it had all the requested information, Wheeling–Pittsburgh filed its application with the bankruptcy court for authorization to reject the collective bargaining agreement on May 31, 1985.

The bankruptcy court held a hearing on Wheeling–Pittsburgh's motion from June 17–21, 1985. On July 17, 1985, it issued a decision authorizing Wheeling–Pittsburgh to reject the agreement. Wheeling–Pittsburgh did so, and announced that it would institute a $17.50 labor cost, effective immediately, and make various other changes. In response, the Union commenced a strike on July 21, 1985. It also appealed the decision of the bankruptcy court to the District Court for the Western District of Pennsylvania, which affirmed the bankruptcy court decision on August 28, 1985. The Union filed a timely appeal to this court.

On October 15, 1985, Wheeling–Pittsburgh and the Steelworkers reached a settlement which ended the strike. The settlement, which we need not describe in detail, included, *inter alia,* a new collective bargaining agreement providing for a labor cost of $18.00 per hour, to be effective "up to and including 10 days following the entry of an order confirming a plan of reorganization." Some of the other features of the agreement were a price escalation clause under which a labor cost bonus will be paid in relationship to increases in Wheeling–Pittsburgh's product prices; a pension relief program to aid retirees and beneficiaries in the likely event the current pension plan is terminated; and an employee buy-out protection plan for employees whose jobs have been permanently terminated as a result of reorganization. The Union received the right to "nominate" a member of Wheeling–Pittsburgh's Board of Directors, and several joint management-union committees were created. The settlement agreement also resolved various disagreements between Wheeling–Pittsburgh and the Union arising out of Wheeling–Pittsburgh's petition for bankruptcy and rejection of the 1983 collective bargaining contract and the resulting strike. Most significantly for present purposes, the settlement provided that if the Union were successful in reversing the courts' order authorizing rejection of the collective bargaining agreement, it would assert claims for lost pay of plant guards and others who worked during the strike. . . .

V.

BACKGROUND OF 11 U.S.C. § 1113

The Union argues that both the bankruptcy court and the district court misinterpreted and misapplied 11 U.S.C. § 1113, the statute enacted by Congress in response to the Supreme Court's opinion in NLRB v. Bildisco & Bildisco, 465 U.S. 513, 104 S.Ct. 1188, 79 L.Ed.2d 482 (1984). A review of that opinion and the available legislative history of section 1113 are thus essential to consideration of the parties' contentions.

In *Bildisco,* the Court held that a collective bargaining agreement is an executory contract subject to rejection by a debtor-in-possession under section 365(a) of the Bankruptcy Code. It also held that "because of the special nature of a collective-bargaining contract," a somewhat stricter standard than the traditional "business judgment" standard should govern the decision of the bankruptcy court to allow rejection of a collective bargaining agreement. Id. at 524, 104 S.Ct. at 1195. However, the Court rejected the argument of the Union and the NLRB that the standard for approval of the debtor's rejection should be the "very strict standard" adopted by the Second Circuit in Brotherhood of Railway, Airline & Steamship Clerks v. REA Express, Inc., 523 F.2d 164, 167–69 (2d Cir.), cert. denied, 423 U.S. 1017, 96 S.Ct. 451, 46 L.Ed. 2d 388 (1975), which required a showing that "rejection of the collective-bargaining agreement is necessary to prevent the debtor from going into liquidation." NLRB v. Bildisco & Bildisco, 465 U.S. at 525, 104 S.Ct. at 1196. The Supreme Court viewed this standard as "fundamentally at odds with the policies of flexibility and equity built into Chapter 11 of the Bankruptcy Code." Id. Instead, it approved the standard first used in In re Brada Miller Freight System, Inc., 702 F.2d 890 (11th Cir.1983), that the bankruptcy court should permit rejection if "the debtor can show that the collective-bargaining agreement burdens the estate, and that after careful scrutiny, the equities balance in favor of rejecting the labor contract." NLRB v. Bildisco & Bildisco, 465 U.S. at 526, 104 S.Ct. at 1196. . . .

When the Supreme Court announced its decision in *NLRB v. Bildisco & Bildisco* on February 22, 1984, labor groups mounted an immediate and intense lobbying effort in Congress to change the law. . . .

In the fall of 1983, even before the *Bildisco* decision, several members of Congress had expressed concern that some companies were using the bankruptcy law as a " 'new collective bargaining weapon.' " Rosenberg, supra, at 312 (quoting Daily Labor Report (BNA) No. 194 at A–6 (October 5, 1983)). At hearings of the Labor Management Relations and Labor Standards Subcommittees of House Education and Labor Committee, "six airline unions testified that employers were improperly using federal bankruptcy law." Rosenberg, supra, at 312. The *Bildisco* decision was announced on February 22, 1984 at the same time as a crisis in the federal bankruptcy system loomed. The Bankruptcy Act of 1978 had been declared unconstitutional in Northern Pipeline Construction Co. v. Marathon Pipe Line Co., 458 U.S. 50, 102 S.Ct. 2858, 73 L.Ed.2d 598 (1982), and the "interim rule" under which the bankruptcy courts had been kept in operation was due to expire March 31, 1984. See Pullium, supra, at 396–97; Rosenberg, supra, at 309–13; White, supra, at 1191. Labor advocates thus saw an opportunity to change the outcome of the *Bildisco* decision. . . .

As enacted, the new section on collective bargaining agreements, section 1113, provides that a debtor-in-possession may assume or reject a collective bargaining agreement only by following the provisions of the statute. See 11 U.S.C. § 1113(a). The subsections at issue in this appeal read as follows:

> (b)(1) Subsequent to filing a petition and prior to filing an application seeking rejection of a collective bargaining agreement, the debtor in possession or trustee (hereinafter in this section 'trustee' shall include a debtor in possession), shall—
>
>> (A) make a proposal to the authorized representative of the employees covered by such agreement, based on the most complete and reliable information available at the time of such proposal, which provides for those necessary modifications in the employees benefits and protection that are necessary to permit the reorganization of the debtor and assures that all creditors, the debtor and all of the affected parties are treated fairly and equitably; and
>>
>> (B) provide, subject to subsection (d)(3), the representative of the employees with such relevant information as is necessary to evaluate the proposal.
>
> (2) During the period beginning on the date of the making of a proposal provided for in paragraph (1) and ending on the date of the hearing provided for in subsection (d)(1), the trustee shall meet, at reasonable times, with the authorized representative to confer in good faith in attempting to reach mutually satisfactory modifications of such agreement.
>
> (c) The court shall approve an application for rejection of a collective bargaining agreement only if the court finds that—
>
>> (1) the trustee has, prior to the hearing, made a proposal that fulfills the requirements of subsection (b)(1);
>>
>> (2) the authorized representative of the employees has refused to accept such proposal without good cause; and
>>
>> (3) the balance of the equities clearly favors rejection of such agreement.

11 U.S.C. § 1113(b) & (c) (Supp. II 1984). . . .

VI.

DISCUSSION

A. *Whether Consideration of the Proposal Can be Pretermitted*

At the outset, we must consider the Union's argument that Wheeling–Pittsburgh failed to make the threshold showing needed under section 1113 to entitle it to reject the collective bargaining agreement. The Union asserts that undisputed evidence showed that Wheeling–Pittsburgh could have adhered to that agreement for its remaining 13 months and still have had sufficient cash to operate for both the short and long term. It further asserts that even if assets were reduced by some $80 million as a result of the adherence to the labor contract, creditors could not rationally have preferred liquidation to reorganization. Accordingly, the Union contends that no modification could be "necessary", and that the bankruptcy court erred in even evaluating Wheeling–Pittsburgh's proposal under section 1113.

We need not decide in this part the validity of the Union's characterization of the state of the record, because we do not agree with the Union's statutory analysis in regard to the procedure to be followed. Nowhere in the statute is there a requirement that the bankruptcy court make a preliminary determination regarding the necessity of any changes in the collective bargaining agreement before the debtor's proposal must be made or evaluated. The statutorily mandated sequence of steps to be followed after a Chapter 11 petition has been filed is: the trustee (or debtor-in-possession) who seeks to reject a collective bargaining agreement must make a proposal for modification thereto "prior to filing an application for rejection;" the court must schedule a hearing within a specified time for consideration of the application for rejection; the trustee and the Union must negotiate during the interval between the making of the proposal and the hearing; and the court must rule on the application within 30 days of the [hearing,] subject to agreed upon extensions.

The only provision for any preliminary determination appears in section 1113(e). At the same time that Congress overturned the part of *Bildisco* that held that a debtor could unilaterally reject a labor contract, and provided instead that the agreement remains in force until the bankruptcy court has authorized its rejection, Congress recognized that there might be immediate problems of an emergency nature in individual cases. Thus, section 1113(e) provides that the bankruptcy court may authorize interim changes in the terms, conditions, wages, benefits or work rules provided by a collective bargaining agreement if the court finds, following a hearing, that an interim change is "essential to the continuation of the debtor's business, or in order to avoid irreparable damage to the estate." 11 U.S.C. § 1113(e).

The focus for the ultimate issue of the debtor's application for rejection is different. In section 1113(c), the statute directs the court to determine whether the "proposal" meets the substantive standard of section 1113(b)(1). The bankruptcy court correctly recognized, "[T]he question is *not* simply whether Wheeling–Pittsburgh can continue to pay the $21.40 rate required by the current *collective bargaining agreement* and still emerge with enough cash in hand at the expiration of the contract term to meet current operational expenses," but instead is "whether it is necessary for Wheeling–Pittsburgh to pay the $15.20 rate found in its *proposal* in order to successfully reorganize." In re Wheeling Pittsburgh, 50 B.R. at 978 (emphasis in original).

Of course, when the bankruptcy court considers whether a specific proposal of modifications is "necessary" under the substantive standard set forth in section 1113, it will have to decide if the debtor has shown that any modifications are necessary. However, we reject the Union's suggestion that the legislative history showing an intent to overrule, in part, the *Bildisco* opinion should also be interpreted as requiring the bankruptcy court to make a preliminary determination independent of the statutorily required sequence of steps. The statutory language clearly requires that necessity *vel non* must be evaluated in the context of a specific proposal of modifications, and the statute does not either explicitly or implicitly provide for pretermitting evaluation of the debtor's proposal.

B. *Whether the Proposed Modifications Were "Necessary" and Treated All Parties "Fairly and Equitably"*

Under section 1113(b)(1), the debtor's proposal antecedent to its filing an application for rejection of a collective bargaining agreement must be one that "provides for those necessary modifications in the employees benefits and protections that are necessary to permit the reorganization of the debtor and assures that all creditors, the debtor and all of the affected parties are treated fairly and equitably." 11 U.S.C. § 1113(b)(1)(A). The Union's contention that Wheeling–Pittsburgh's proposal was neither "necessary" nor treated all parties "fairly and equitably" was rejected by both the bankruptcy court and the district court.

The parties offer widely varying interpretations of "necessary". Because the statute contains no definition, we must turn to the legislative history for enlightenment. . . .

In *Bildisco,* the Supreme Court had rejected the Second Circuit's "stringent test" for "necessity" to be used in adjudicating petitions to reject labor contracts. Instead, the Supreme Court opted for a test which permitted rejection if "the equities balance in favor of rejecting the labor contract." *Bildisco,* 465 U.S. at 526, 104 S.Ct. at 1196.

It was this lenient standard that caused the labor forces to mobilize on Congress. The day the *Bildisco* decision was announced, Representative Rodino, Chairman of the House Judiciary Committee with jurisdiction over bankruptcy legislation, introduced a bill to overturn that decision. 130 Cong.Rec. H809 (daily ed. February 22, 1984). He decried "[t]he balancing-of-the-equities standard adopted by the Supreme Court" because it would give "no special weight to collective bargaining interests and the significant concerns underlying the national labor policy." Id. at H780.

The February bill was ultimately incorporated into a comprehensive bankruptcy bill, H.R. 5174, known as the Bankruptcy Amendments of 1984. See generally id. at H1721–23, H1795–1854 (daily ed. March 19, 21, 1984) (House debate). The expanded bill passed the House on March 21. When it reached the Senate, Senator Thurmond offered an amendment which would have "preserve[d] the balancing of the equities standard for rejection of such contracts." Id. at S6082 (May 21, 1984). Senator Packwood offered a substitute amendment which required the trustee's proposal to make the "minimum modifications in [the] employees' benefits and protections that would permit the reorganization," id. at S6181–82 (daily ed. May 22, 1984), and was recognized to represent the position of organized labor on this issue. See id. at S6192, S6194 (daily ed. May 22, 1984) (remarks of Sens. DeConcini and Thurmond); id. at S8898 (daily ed. June 29, 1984) (remarks of Sen. Kennedy). Senator Packwood based his proposal on the approach suggested by Professor Vern Countryman of the Harvard Law School. See id. at S6181 (daily ed. May 22, 1984) (quoting Bordewieck & Countryman, The Rejection of Collective Bargaining Agreements by Chapter 11 Debtors, 57 Am.Bankr.L.J. 293 (1983)). This approach argues for a strong presumption against rejection of labor contracts on the ground that rejection seriously undercuts fundamental aspects of federal labor policy which should be permitted "only in extraordinary cases." See 130 Cong.Rec. S6185 (daily ed. May 22, 1984) (quoting Bordewieck & Countryman, supra, at 299–300).

As noted previously, the Senate bill went to conference without any collective bargaining provision, but the Conference Committee eventually emerged with the provision now embodied in the language of section 1113. To ascertain the meaning of the language ultimately adopted, it is instructive to examine the language of the proposals that were rejected. Senator Thurmond's amendment would have permitted rejection of a labor contract if the court found, *inter alia,* "that the inability to reach an agreement threatens to impede the success of the [debtor's] reorganization." 130 Cong.Rec. S6084 (daily ed. May 21, 1984). The Thurmond proposal stems from the language of *Bildisco,* where the Court said, "Since the policy of Chapter 11 is to permit successful rehabilitation of debtors, rejection should not be permitted without a finding that the policy would be served by such action." *Bildisco,* 465 U.S. at 513, 104 S.Ct. at 1191.

In contrast, the Rodino bill would have conditioned rejection of a collective bargaining agreement on a showing that absent such rejection "the jobs covered by such agreement will be lost and any financial reorganization of the debtor will fail." 130 Cong.Rec. H1942 (daily ed. March 26, 1984) (remarks of Rep. Rodino). This stems from the language of the Second Circuit's *REA Express* opinion that rejection should be authorized only when the debtor shows that "unless the agreement is rejected, the [employer] will collapse and the employees will no longer have their jobs." *REA Express,* 523 F.2d at 172.

The Packwood amendment, supported by labor, provided that the debtor's proposal should contain "the minimum modifications in such employees' benefits and protections that would permit the reorganization." 130 Cong.Rec. S6181–82 (daily ed. May 22, 1984). As a substitute for this clause, the Conference Committee proposed, and section 1113 provides, that the debtor's proposal provide "for those necessary modifications in the employees' benefits and protections that are necessary to permit the reorganization of the debtor." § 1113(b)(1)(A). This was seen as a victory for labor.

The contemporaneous remarks of the conferees made it clear that the provision was based on the substance of Senator Packwood's proposal. Thus, Senator Thurmond, who presented the conference report to the Senate, explained that the Senate conferees had been required to accept a bankruptcy bill, if there was to be one at all, that contained "a labor provision acceptable to organized labor", and that the provision was one whose "procedures *and standard* are essentially the same as those of the Packwood amendment." Id. at S8888 (daily ed. June 29, 1984) (emphasis added). Senator Packwood himself was "pleased that the approach contained in the amendment I offered was, for the most part, adopted by the conferees." Id. at S8898. . . .

The legislative history illuminates two aspects of the court's inquiry into necessity: (1) the standard to be applied, i.e., "*how* 'necessary' " must the proposed modifications be, and (2) the object of the "necessary" inquiry, i.e., " 'necessary' *to what.*"

The "necessary" standard cannot be satisfied by a mere showing that it would be desirable for the trustee to reject a prevailing labor contract so that the debtor can lower its costs. Such an indulgent standard would inadequately differentiate between labor contracts, which Congress sought to protect, and other commercial contracts, which the trustee can disavow at will. The congressional consensus that the "necessary" language was substantially the same as the phrasing in Senator Packwood's amendment, which looked to the "minimum modifications . . . that would permit the reorganization," requires that "necessity" be construed strictly to signify only modifications that the trustee is constrained to accept because they are directly related to the Company's financial condition and its reorganization. We reject the hypertechnical argument that "necessary" and "essential" have different meanings because they are in different subsections. The words are synonymous.

The question of " 'necessary' to what" is not easily answered by reference to the statutory language which merely provides "necessary to permit the reorganization of the debtor." It is significant that the Thurmond amendment, which the conferees did not accept, and *Bildis-*

co, which they clearly sought to modify, seemed directed to the successful rehabilitation of the debtor, which suggests focus on the long-term
economic health of the debtor. While we do not suggest that the
general long-term viability of the Company is not a goal of the debtor's
reorganization, it appears from the legislators' remarks that they
placed the emphasis in determining whether and what modifications
should be made to a negotiated collective bargaining agreement on the
somewhat shorter term goal of preventing the debtor's liquidation, the
mirror image of what is "necessary to permit the reorganization of the
debtor." This construction finds additional support in the conferees'
choice of the words *"permit* the reorganization," which places the
emphasis on the reorganization, rather than the longer term issue of
the debtor's ultimate future.

It is also important to note that the requirement that the proposal
provide only for "necessary" modifications in the labor contract is
conjunctive with the requirement that the proposal treat "all of the
affected parties . . . fairly and equitably." The language as well as
the legislative history makes plain that a bankruptcy court may not
authorize rejection of a labor contract merely because it deems such a
course to be equitable to the other affected parties, particularly creditors. Such a construction would nullify the insistent congressional
effort to replace the *Bildisco* standard with one that was more sensitive
to the national policy favoring collective bargaining agreements, which
was accomplished by inserting the "necessary" clause as one of the two
prongs of the standard that the trustee's proposal for modifications
must meet.

In its challenge to the court's finding that the debtor's proposal
satisfied the "necessary" prong, the Union contends that Wheeling–
Pittsburgh's available and projected cash shows that no modifications
at all were necessary. Although the Company's cash position may be a
relevant factor, it is not the only factor in determining whether any
modifications are necessary. As the bankruptcy court pointed out, the
cash availability to which the Union points was created by the reorganization proceeding. In re Wheeling–Pittsburgh, 50 B.R. at 977. Congress cannot have intended the bankruptcy court to hold all other
parties at bay, while pointing to the resulting cash as the reason why
no modifications to the labor contract are needed.

The Union next argues that Wheeling–Pittsburgh's proposal did not
contain only "those necessary modifications . . . necessary to permit
the reorganization of the debtor", not only because the Company failed
to prove a need for relief from the collective bargaining agreement, but
also because the proposal (1) called for a five-year agreement with
drastically reduced labor costs, (2) was based on conservative projections under which labor cost reductions in the amount proposed would
be needed only if Wheeling–Pittsburgh's actual experience conformed
to the "worst case" scenario, and (3) failed to contain a "snap back"
provision for additional compensation to the employees if Wheeling–

Pittsburgh's performance turned out to be better than predicted. The Union is on firmer ground with this argument.

The Union's uncontradicted evidence was that a five-year contract was neither the practice of Wheeling–Pittsburgh nor that of the steel industry in general. In fact, a Vice–President of Wheeling–Pittsburgh who was its labor negotiator admitted that he had tried to get the Union to agree to a five-year term in bargaining but had been unsuccessful. JA at 140. Nonetheless, the bankruptcy court found "that the five year term is necessary for the debtor's reorganization" because "Wheeling–Pittsburgh's period of reorganization likely will last *at least* five years," labor stability would be necessary during the reorganization period, and "there is no evidence as to how labor stability can be achieved with a contract of less than five years' duration." In re Wheeling–Pittsburgh, 50 B.R. at 979.

The bankruptcy court accepted the Company's pessimistic projection of its performance over the next five years because of its findings that the United States steel industry is in "very critical shape; the price of steel . . . has declined; rising steel imports have cut into the domestic steel market despite federal 'dumping' laws; steel plant shutdowns are growing more numerous . . .; and the most optimistic forecasts predict only relatively small market improvements." Id. at 978. These conditions, and the fact that Wheeling–Pittsburgh has sustained significant losses over the last three years, led the court to reject the optimistic assessment of the Union's experts. Id. at 978–79.

We do not understand the Union to challenge the necessity of drastically lower labor costs if the "worst case" scenario eventuates. In any event, a reviewing court might be hard-pressed to regard such a finding as clearly erroneous.

The Union's principal emphasis is on the failure of the proposal to contain any "snap back" provision which would increase employees' wages or benefits in the event the Company performed more favorably than anticipated. The Union claims that each of the three prior agreements it had made with Wheeling–Pittsburgh in which it granted concessions had contained either profit sharing and/or equity in compensation for concessions made. Moreover, the proposal that Wheeling–Pittsburgh had given the Union in March 1985, immediately preceding the bankruptcy, had contained such a feature.

Wheeling–Pittsburgh has offered no credible explanation why its proposal did not contain a "snap back" provision. Even more troubling is the fact that the bankruptcy court's discussion of "necessity" does not even mention this issue. The court confined its consideration of the absence of a "snap back" provision to its discussion of the second prong of the standard, whether the proposal treated all affected parties "fairly and equitably." In failing to focus on the Union's contention about the "snap back" provision when deciding whether the modifications were "necessary", the bankruptcy court erroneously treated the two prongs of the standard as disjunctive rather than conjunctive. We find it difficult, on the basis of this record, to accept the court's finding that it was "necessary" to modify an existing labor contract by providing an unusually long five-year term at markedly reduced labor costs based on a pessimistic five-year projection without at least also providing for some "snap back" to compensate for workers' concessions. Such a finding cannot be sustained in light of the court's failure to consider the Union's argument regarding a "snap back" in the context of the "necessary" inquiry.

Furthermore, it appears that the bankruptcy court was still applying a substantive standard closer to, if not taken directly from, *Bildisco* rather than a standard informed by the legislative history. The court consistently framed the issue and goal in terms of "*successful* reorganization", see id. at 978, in a manner which implied it was looking to the long-term economic health of the Company rather than the feasibility of reorganization as such.

Nor can we say with certainty that the district court recognized the appropriate standard of "necessity", since at times it referred to the goal of "prevention of the debtor going into liquidation," see In re Wheeling–Pittsburgh, 52 B.R. at 1003, but it also approved the standard of "necessity" used by the bankruptcy court. *Id.* The district court appeared to regard the congressional response to *Bildisco* as limited to prevention of the trustee's unilateral rejection of the contract before formal rejection by the bankruptcy court. Id. at 1004. Apparently, the court failed to appreciate Congress' substantial modification of the standard for rejection.

Moreover, the district court treated the bankruptcy court's findings of "necessity" as factual findings, subject only to "clearly erroneous" review. The finding as to whether the modifications were "necessary" should have been reviewed as a mixed question of law and fact. To the extent that the bankruptcy court applied the wrong statutory standard and failed to consider all of the relevant factors in making its finding of necessity, it committed an error of law. Therefore, we are obliged to return the case to that court.

The Union again points to the absence of a "snap back" provision in arguing that the bankruptcy court erred in finding that the proposal met the second prong of the substantive standard. This requires that the proposal "assure[ ] that all creditors, the debtor and all of the affected parties are treated fairly and equitably." 11 U.S.C. § 1113(b) (1)(A). The Union argues that Wheeling–Pittsburgh's proposed modifications were not "fair and equitable" to the employees because the lack of a "snap back" provision in a five-year agreement predicated on worst-case assumptions meant that any improvement in the Company's position over this long period would not be shared by the employees.

The "fair and equitable" determination will often be based on subsidiary findings of fact, reviewable under the clearly erroneous standard, but also entails the exercise of discretion in making the required balancing. In reviewing the latter aspect of the determination, we must look to whether the bankruptcy court considered the correct factors, and gave them appropriate weight in the circumstances.

Congressional intent with regard to the meaning of "fair and equitable" is reflected in the comments of Congressman Morrison who stated that:

> language that requires assurance that "All creditors, the debtor and other affected parties are treated fairly and equitably." . . . would ensure that, where the trustee seeks to repudiate a collective bargaining agreement, the covered employees do not bear either the entire financial burden of making the reorganization work or a disproportionate share of that burden, but only their fair and equitable share of the necessary sacrifices.

130 Cong.Rec. H7496 (daily ed. June 29, 1984). As Senator Packwood explained:

> The second requirement of the proposal—that it assure fair and equitable treatment for all creditors, the debtor and other affected parties . . . guarantees that the focus for cost cutting must not be directed exclusively at unionized workers. Rather the burden of sacrifices in the reorganization process will be spread among all affected parties. This consideration is desirable since experience shows that when workers know that they alone are not bearing the sole brunt of the sacrifices, they will agree to shoulder their fair share and in some instances without the necessity for a formal contract rejection.

130 Cong.Rec. S8898 (daily ed. June 29, 1984).

The bankruptcy court recognized that the focus of inquiry as to "fair and equitable" treatment should be whether the Company's proposal would impose a disproportionate burden on the employees.[3] In re Wheeling–Pittsburgh, 50 B.R. at 980. The Union does not challenge the articulation of the standard, but instead contends that the court misapplied the standard when it concluded that "[t]he burden on the Union employees is not disproportionate from the burden on other affected parties." Id.

It has been suggested by some commentators that the court should undertake "a comparison of the concessions asked of the Union, on a dollar or percentage basis, with those sought from other affected parties." Ehrenwerth & Lally–Green, supra, at 955. From the debtor's standpoint, it may be possible to compare the amount or percentage of its cost reduction from various sources during reorganization. But when examining the fairness and equity to the parties who are making concessions, as section 1113 also requires us to do, we are uncertain of the basis for comparison in either dollar or percentage terms.

3. Although there is "fair and equitable" language in other sections of the bankruptcy statute, the construction of these words in § 1113 is not aided by reference to the other sections. For example, "fair and equitable" is specifically defined in 11 U.S.C. § 1129(b)(2) in terms of priority of claims, patently inapplicable here.

Of course, wage reductions by one group of employees, such as hourly unionized workers, can be compared with wage reductions by another group, such as non-unionized salaried employees. The bankruptcy court stated that "salaried employees have been without wage increases since about 1981, and took a 10% reduction in 1982, half of which was restored in 1984." In re Wheeling–Pittsburgh, 50 B.R. at 980. The court did not directly compare this concession to that made by the hourly workers, who had been at a $25 rate in 1982 when first asked to make concessions, and who were at a $21.40 rate at the time of the bankruptcy in 1984 when Wheeling–Pittsburgh made its proposal for a $15.20 rate. Nonetheless, the court's findings that the salaried employees are leaving for better paying jobs elsewhere and that the Company has difficulty finding qualified replacements may satisfactorily support its conclusion that no further sacrifices from the salaried employees are warranted, id., even though it failed to make the possible comparison between the concessions of the different groups of employees in dollar amount or percentages.

On the other hand, we do not know whether the percentage of interest foregone by creditors during reorganization may fairly be considered comparable with the percentage of reductions in wages taken by workers. We cannot accept *ipso facto* the commentators' suggestion that such matters are capable of comparison by percentage or in dollars. Neither the bankruptcy court nor the district court discussed this issue, and the bankruptcy court referred to the concessions in absolute, rather than relative, terms. In referring to the projected reorganization plan, it stated that "Creditors . . . are to be subjected to a 50% loss amounting to losses of some $250 million, with the 50% balance payable over 10 years." Id. at 980. The Union's witnesses referred to the employees' sacrifice during the projected five-year term as close to $600 million. JA at 581. Considerably more economic expertise would have to be addressed to the comparability of the concessions of each group before we could fault the court for failing to make a direct comparison between creditors and labor on a dollar or percentage basis.

There are, however, other comparisons that the court did not adequately consider. The Union argues that even if the sacrifices made by the workers and the creditors are viewed as proportionate in the event the Company's worst-case forecast proves to be accurate, the workers would suffer disproportionately to the creditors if the Company in fact fared better than its forecast. Under Wheeling–Pittsburgh's proposal, labor costs would remain frozen. One of the Union's witnesses, a general partner with the investment banking firm of Lazard–Freres & Company, testified that based on his experience with other Chapter 11 reorganizations, excess cash beyond what was needed to operate would go to pay off the creditors. JA at 583. The bankruptcy court did not discredit this testimony. Its only discussion of what seems on its face to be a serious inequity was as follows:

It is relevant to note that the proposal also does *not* provide for any downward adjustment below the $15.20 in the event the Company continues to lose money. The steel industry and this Company are in serious financial trouble. It might not be inequitable to ask hourly employees to share in future shortfalls, but that has not been done. In any event, the proposal provides cost stability for the Company, and also provides wage stability for Union workers.

50 B.R. at 980 (emphasis in original).

This is not persuasive. The workers did not ask for or need "wage stability" at a rate they considered substandard. Therefore, such "stability" cannot be considered to be a benefit to them to compensate for the absence of any share of better-than-anticipated recovery. Similarly, since the entire proposal was predicated on a worst-case economic scenario, there was no record basis from which the bankruptcy court could hypothesize a possible need for "any downward adjustment." Equity demands that concessions and benefits to the various interested parties be examined from a realistic standpoint and on the basis of record evidence.

The district court did not independently discuss the "fair and equitable" issue. It simply quoted the bankruptcy court's opinion and added that:

Our review of the record does not produce a conviction that the proposed plan will place a burden upon the employees disproportionate from that burden on other affected parties or that Judge Bentz's conclusion . . . [that it is fair and equitable] constitutes a mistake which requires correcting by this Court.

In re Wheeling–Pittsburgh, 52 B.R. at 1005. However, as we pointed out above, the proposal's failure to provide workers a share in a possible recovery, is particularly significant in this case since the proposal asked workers to take substantial reductions over a five-year period based on extremely pessimistic forecasts. The bank creditors argue that the proposal contains a "snap back" in that the Union's claim as a pre-petition unsecured creditor for the reduction in wages and benefits during the 13 month period left on the old contract, could be repaid at a higher level. But an unsecured claim is not equivalent in kind to a "snap back", which is based on the principle that all of the concessions sought may not turn out to be necessary. In the circumstances of this case, the bankruptcy court's failure to recognize the need for some parity in this regard flaws the court's conclusion that the proposal was "fair and equitable." Therefore, we cannot affirm the district court's order approving the debtor's rejection of the collective bargaining agreement.

C. *Whether the Procedural Test of Section 1113 Was Satisfied*

Section 1113 imposes on a debtor certain procedures when it presents its proposal for modifications of the collective bargaining agreement. A debtor must provide "the representative of the employees with such relevant information as is necessary to evaluate the proposal," 11 U.S.C. § 1113(b)(1)(B), and "meet . . . to confer in good faith in attempting to reach mutually satisfactory modifications." 11 U.S.C. § 1113(b)(2). The purpose of the requirement that the debtor supply the relevant information was intended to encourage negotiation between the Company and the Union rather than permit a unilateral repudiation. See, e.g., 130 Cong.Rec. S8990 (daily ed. June 29, 1984) (remarks of Sen. Moynihan). We agree with the Union that the debtor must meet its negotiating obligation before the court may approve its rejection of the labor contract.

The Union asserts that the bankruptcy court erred in ruling that Wheeling–Pittsburgh satisfied the procedural requirements of section 1113. It complains that the three-week period that it was given to evaluate Wheeling–Pittsburgh's proposal was inadequate and that Wheeling–Pittsburgh did not provide it with the necessary relevant information. The bankruptcy court rejected the Union's contentions, finding that "a three week negotiation period by itself is not inherently unreasonable." In re Wheeling–Pittsburgh, 50 B.R. at 976.

We agree with that court that the time for negotiation must depend on the circumstances of the particular case. However, the court was unduly concerned about the need for haste, stating "[t]hree weeks was sufficient time in this emergent situation." Id. at 982. Section 1113(e) provides an adequate procedure to cope with an emergency situation, and Wheeling Pittsburgh made no application under this section. Thus, the need for haste in itself cannot support the finding that Wheeling Pittsburgh met its negotiating obligation.

The court also found that Wheeling–Pittsburgh did provide the Union with the information necessary to evaluate the proposal. Id. at 976–77. Although the Union argues, with some persuasion, that the bankruptcy court misinterpreted the evidence, we would not be prepared to hold the court's finding to be clearly erroneous. However, because the court may have given undue weight to the factor of the need for haste, and the district court failed to recognize that possibility, we will direct that on remand the bankruptcy court reconsider its findings in this respect as well.

VII.

SUMMARY

In summary, we hold that the case before us is not moot because there remains the outstanding issue of the status of the claims of the plant guards. We hold that section 1113 does not require the bankruptcy court to examine the necessity of proposed modifications to the collective bargaining contract independently of its consideration of the proposal that has been made. We further hold that the bankruptcy court erred in its interpretation and application of the "necessary" standard, because it failed to give due regard to Congress' intent that "necessity" be strictly construed and failed to address the absence of a "snap back". Moreover, the district court erred in limiting its review of the bankruptcy court's finding in this regard under the clearly erroneous standard. We hold that the reasons given by the bankruptcy court in concluding that the proposal was "fair and equitable" cannot adequately support its conclusion because the court failed to give any persuasive rationale for the disproportionate treatment of the employees who were being asked to take a five-year agreement under a worst-case scenario without any possibility for restoration or share in the event of a better-than-anticipated recovery.

For the foregoing reasons, we will vacate the order of the district court and remand to that court with directions that it remand this case to the bankruptcy court for such further proceedings as may be appropriate under the circumstances. The Union, the principal bank creditors, and Wheeling–Pittsburgh are to share costs on appeal equally.

Notes & Questions

1. *Damages for Breach of a Collective Bargaining Agreement.* Recall that the bankruptcy law's remedy for the nonbankrupt party to a rejected executory contract is to deem the rejection a breach. § 365(g). Section 502(c) seems to require that all traditional contractual remedies be reduced to a monetary amount. What is to be the remedy for loss of collective bargaining provisions covering job descriptions, discipline and grievance procedures, meal time, dress rules and the numerous other provisions that might be found in a collective bargaining agreement? Does the difficulty in quantifying these benefits support the special treatment of collective bargaining agreements?

2. *Balancing the Equities in Other Cases.* Does § 1113 contain a framework that would be useful for contracts other than collective bargaining agreements? Consider the requirement that the court balance the equities.

3. *The Necessary Requirements.* How can one be certain whether any provision is "necessary" for a successful reorganization? Surely the best one can hope for is that a modification will improve the chances for a successful reorganization. How much of an improvement of the chances for a successful reorganization should be sufficient to satisfy the necessary requirement? Would a four-year contract, subject to renegotiation, significantly have reduced the chances for a successful reorganization of Wheeling–Pittsburgh?

4. *The Snap Back Provision.* Is Wheeling–Pittsburgh's failure to include a snap back provision an "unnecessary" modification of the collective bargaining agreement? Suppose none of the prior agreements had contained restoration provisions. Can failure to include any term be a modification of an agreement?

5. *The Union's Power to Reject a Proposed Modification.* Under § 1113(c)(2), one of the requirements for approving rejection of a collective bargaining agreement is that the union refuse to accept the proposal "without good cause." Is it possible for a union to have good

cause for rejecting a proposal that complies with the requirements of § 1113(b)? Or is the good cause standard simply a way of allowing the union to reject a proposal that does not conform with § 1113(b)? Could the court approve such a nonconforming proposal under § 1113(c)? Or could a reasonable difference with an employer about the necessity of a modification or its degree constitute good cause?

6. *The Equities in* Wheeling–Pittsburgh. In comparing the union's sacrifices with those of other interested parties, is the court's focus too narrow? Why should only large bank creditors make concessions? Why not all of a company's suppliers and creditors?

Chapter 12

APPORTIONING THE ESTATE

A. Claims

To participate in a bankruptcy distribution a creditor must have a "claim." See § 726(a). The term "claim" is defined broadly in § 101(4) and includes unliquidated, contingent, unmatured, and disputed rights to payment. Claims that satisfy the broad definition of § 101(4) participate in a bankruptcy to the extent that they are allowed under § 502.

The Bankruptcy Act distinguishes between "secured claims" and "unsecured claims." A creditor with a claim has a secured claim (and is a secured creditor) to the extent that the claim is secured by a "lien" on property. "Lien" is defined in § 101 to mean "charge against or interest in property to secure payment of a debt or performance of an obligation." This definition is broad enough to include all Article 9 security interests, a conclusion confirmed by § 101's definition of "security interest" as a "lien created by an agreement." The two other classes of liens defined by the Bankruptcy Act are "judicial liens" and "statutory liens". Thus any creditor with a lien—an interest in specific property to secure payment or other performance—may have a secured claim. In particular, Article 9 secured parties, lien creditors (as that term is used in Article 9), and statutory lienholders (e.g., mechanics' lienholders) all have secured claims within the meaning of the Act.

Under § 506(a), any secured creditor whose lien is not worth the full amount of the debt owed to the creditor has two separate claims in bankruptcy. Such a creditor has a secured claim to the extent of the value of the property subject to the lien, and an unsecured claim to the extent that the debt owed to the creditor exceeds the value of the property subject to the lien. For example, an Article 9 secured party who is owed $1,000 and whose collateral is worth $700 has a secured claim in bankruptcy of $700, and an unsecured claim in bankruptcy of $300.

1. The Priority of Secured Claims

Although it is widely understood that secured creditors, to the extent of the value of their collateral, come first in the order of bankruptcy distribution, bankruptcy law nowhere specifies this result. The new act, in a somewhat opaque fashion, authorizes disposition of property to secured creditors in § 725. The Act's legislative history states, in part: "The section is in lieu of a section that would direct a certain distribution to secured creditors." House Report at 382. Whether statutorily prescribed or not, secured creditors and other lienholders usually have the top priority in bankruptcy. Is this justifiable?

SCHWARTZ, SECURITY INTERESTS AND BANKRUPTCY PRIORITIES: A REVIEW OF CURRENT THEORIES, 10 J.Leg.St. 1, 2, 7–13, 22–25, 27–28, 30–31 (1981)

If an insolvent debtor's business is liquidated, its secured creditors may take property subject to their liens before any other creditors are paid. Congress has also created six classes of "priority" creditors, the most important of which are expenses of administration (first priority), wage and employee-benefit claims up to limited amounts (third and fourth priority) and taxes (sixth priority). Each priority class is paid in full, to the extent available assets exist, before the next class is paid. Finally, "general" creditors, those without security interests or priority status, receive payment if payment is possible. As this priority list suggests, secured creditors do much better than general creditors in bankruptcy liquidations.

The principal justification for a distribution scheme that seemingly advantages the sophisticated and relatively affluent, who often take security, at the expense of the relatively poor and unsophisticated, who often do not, is that the institution of secured debt is efficient. Lawyers commonly make this claim in a slightly different form, asserting that the ability of firms to give security increases the amount of credit available to the firms, but the implicit premise is that the gains to firms and secured creditors from additional credit exceed the costs that security may occasionally impose on priority and general creditors. This efficiency justification has prevailed; the accepted wisdom holds that the current bankruptcy priority list is normatively desirable. . . .

II. EFFICIENCY EXPLANATIONS OF SHORT-TERM SECURED DEBT

A. *The Problem*

Firms issue and creditors buy secured debt when the private gains from doing so exceed the costs. An efficiency explanation of secured debt must show when this is so and also that the social gains from security exceed the social costs. The conventional efficiency story is that high risk firms prefer issuing security because it enables them to borrow, and creditors prefer buying it because it enables them to make loans they otherwise would refuse. Security has these properties because it reduces the risks of creditors in the event of default, largely by allowing the secured party to take the property subject to its security interest and sell it to reduce or eliminate the debt. As we have seen, the power to seize and sell often survives the debtor's bankruptcy.

This conventional story seems unpersuasive if creditors (*i*) can learn of and react to the existence of security; (*ii*) can calculate risks of default reasonably precisely; (*iii*) are risk-neutral; and (*iv*) have homogeneous expectations respecting default probabilities. . . . If all creditors are informed, the secured creditor will charge a lower interest rate because it is secured, whereas the unsecured creditors will charge higher interest rates because the pool of assets available to satisfy their claims has shrunk. The debtor's total interest bill is thus unaffected by the existence of security. Since the issuance of secured debt is itself costly, however, the debtor would be worse off with security than without it. Firms would never sell secured debt. . . .

B. *Monitoring Costs*

. . . The monitoring-cost explanation for the existence of secured debt attempts to show how security actually can increase the costs of unsecured creditors by *less* than it reduces the costs of secured creditors, even if the assumptions made above of creditor knowledge, ability, risk neutrality, and homogeneous expectations hold. Recall that interest rates are partially a function of the risk of default, and that this risk is itself a function of the riskiness of the debtor's business. Suppose a firm borrows money at an interest rate that accurately reflects the risk of its enterprise. After the loan is made, the firm pursues a higher risk project for which a higher interest rate would have been charged. The firm has thus retroactively reduced the interest rate it faces; it is borrowing at a low risk rate for a high risk project. Firms with limited shareholder liability sometimes would so act because they would capture most of the gains if a high risk project pays off but bear only part of the losses if it does not. Creditors would bear the rest of these losses.

Creditors know that debtors have incentives to reduce interest rates retroactively by taking greater risks. To prevent or limit such debtor misconduct, they can (and do) monitor debtors—that is, watch and police them. Monitoring, however, is expensive. A security interest is then explicable as a device to reduce creditor monitoring costs. If a creditor is fully secured, it need only monitor to ensure that the assets subject to its security interest are not dissipated; it need not monitor the debtor's entire business to prevent the debtor from taking risks not justified by the operative interest rate.

. . . [A]lthough security may reduce the secured party's monitoring costs, it seems likely to increase the monitoring costs of unsecured creditors. The existence of security raises the expected cost of default for unsecured creditors by reducing the available asset pool and thus creates incentives for these parties to monitor more extensively. A monitoring-cost theory therefore must also explain why the secured creditor gains more from security than the unsecured creditors lose from it.

A way to show that security can reduce a firm's net credit costs is to focus on the methods by which a firm can behave in a more risky fashion after a loan is made. Sometimes, taking greater risks requires a firm to exchange assets for other assets. A firm that wants to switch from making lathes to making amphibious cars, for example, will need different machinery. A security interest in the firm's property would impede such a substitution of assets by drying up the market for the firm's equipment. The code provides, in § 9–306(2), that "a security interest continues in collateral notwithstanding sale, exchange or other disposition thereof unless the disposition was authorized by the secured party . . . ." In consequence, people would be deterred from purchasing equipment from misbehaving firms. Since asset substitution is an important method of behaving more riskily after a loan is made, security reduces the risk of a debtor's misbehaving. Most significantly, it reduces this risk not only for secured parties but for anyone who extends credit to the firm. The increase in monitoring costs that unsecured creditors experience as a result of security may thus be less than the decrease in monitoring costs that the secured party incurs; indeed, where asset substitution is the principal method of behaving more riskily, the absolute level of monitoring by unsecured creditors could decline.

This explanation of the existence of secured debt, however, is unpersuasive when applied to short-term financing because the kind of monitoring for which security is supposedly a substitute often seems unnecessary in this case. Suppose that creditors can observe at relatively low cost the significant asset substitutions by a debtor that materially alter the riskiness of the debtor's enterprise. A creditor can react to the possibility of such substitutions in two ways: it can monitor its debtor fairly extensively to reduce the likelihood of the debtor's misbehavior, or it can rely on the sanction of lost good will to induce the debtor not to misbehave. A firm that behaves in a riskier fashion after a loan is made shows itself to be untrustworthy, and its ability to obtain future loans is impaired. Lost good will would seem of particular concern to a debtor that primarily uses short-term financing. Such a firm must enter the credit market frequently and is likely to regard the good-will cost from asset substitutions as high in relation to the retroactive interest-rate reduction that those substitutions produce on existing loans. Thus the creditors of such a firm probably would choose to incur the relatively low cost of invoking the good-will sanction by observing whether significant asset substitutions have occurred, rather than the relatively high cost of policing to prevent this form of misbehavior. Security interests are expensive, however, and seem substitutes only for the high cost version of monitoring—that is, policing for preventive purposes. Creditors have an incentive to enage in this form of policing during long-term financing situations, where the debtor's good-will costs from misbehavior are relatively less. The monitoring-cost explanation therefore predicts that firms may issue secured debt when much of their financing is long-term but will seldom do so when they primarily use short-term credit. The relatively large amount of short-term secured debt issued by retailers thus constitutes a serious counterexample to the monitoring-cost theory.

That short-term debt sometimes has many of the characteristics of long-term debt is an insufficient response to this difficulty. Short-term debt is considered long-term debt for some purposes when a debtor and particular creditor form a relatively permanent association. As an example, a bank may finance a particular retailer for many years, taking security interests in its (everchanging) inventory and accounts receivable. Banks, however, extend funds on a periodic basis in such relationships and will terminate if the firm behaves more riskily. Moreover, such a creditor can conveniently learn of important changes in its debtors' businesses. Thus even in these "long-term" financing situations the good-will costs of debtor misbehavior seem sufficiently high to make questionable the monitoring-cost explanation for the existence of secured debt. . . .

E. Risk Aversion, Uncertainty, and Heterogeneous Expectations

1. *Risk Aversion.* Security interests might increase welfare if they helped shift risks from more to less risk-averse creditors. . . .

The risk-aversion explanation seems plausible, but has two serious difficulties. First, it fails to show why creditors respond to risk aversion by taking security. Taking security is costly, so risk-averse creditors may prefer to buy low risk debt directly rather than buy high risk debt and reduce its risk by mortgages. Since much low risk debt exists, the risk-aversion explanation is incomplete. Second, given what is known about the goals that corporate managers actually pursue, explaining the existence of secured debt as a response to differential levels of risk aversion among creditors seems either mistaken or tautological. To perceive the nature of this difficulty, recall that risk aversion in individuals is explained by the diminishing marginal utility of money theory. This theory provides that each additional dollar a person receives generates less utility for him than the addition of earlier dollars did because later dollars are used to satisfy less urgent needs. Because money has diminishing marginal utility, a person seeking to maximize his or her expected utility would not be indifferent between equal prospects of gain or loss. The person would lose more utility if the loss materialized than he or she would gain if prospects were successful. That is, for an ordinary person the expected utility of being given an equal chance of winning or losing the same amount would be less than the utility of not gambling. The assumptions that individuals maximize expected utility and that money has diminishing marginal utility thus imply individual risk aversion, not risk neutrality.

Many of a firm's business creditors, however, are likely to be corporations that are operated by managers whose scope of operation is to some extent independent of shareholder preferences. What utility function these managers maximize is a controversial and unresolved question. Economists and lawyers commonly assume that the managers try to maximize the market value of the corporation's stock. This goal implies risk neutrality. . . . Suppose next that the assumption of corporate managers maximizing share values is abandoned. There is no other widely accepted or easily defensible assumption of what goals corporate managers pursue to take its place. Given this theoretical and empirical vacuum, an argument that security is a response to differential levels of risk aversion among creditors becomes tautological: it proves the existence of security by presupposing differential levels of risk aversion, and it proves the existence of differential levels of risk aversion by showing that security exists. . . .

. . .

2. *Uncertainty.* Security interests also could increase welfare if they reduced creditor uncertainty. In this connection, the assumption made in Part II–A above that little uncertainty exists seems unrealistic; a creditor calculating the risk of default must predict the ratio of its debt to existing debt at the time of default as well as the size of the then available asset pool, but these predictions are difficult to make precisely. A security interest may reduce this uncertainty because secured creditors have only to know whether assets will exist to satisfy their claims. Thus the lower interest rates that accompany secured debt may partly be a function of the greater certainty that security generates. Since the existence of secured debt seems not to increase uncertainty for a firm's other creditors, that fraction of the secured creditors' lower interest charge attributable to a reduction in uncertainty is a net gain to the firm. Firms, the explanation goes, issue secured debt to capture this gain.

This explanation, however, generates predictions that the facts seem not to confirm and fails to explain why creditors respond to uncertainty by taking security. First, the uncertainty explanation predicts that, other things equal, firms will issue as much secured debt as they can; for if security always generates net interest-rate reductions, firms always have an incentive to capture them. Firms, however, often seem not to issue as much secured debt as their assets would justify. This counterexample cannot be dismissed by arguing that the costs of taking security sometimes exceed the gains of a reduction in uncertainty and sometimes do not. In the absence of further evidence, such a response is tautological. It asserts only that security will exist when security is efficient—its gains in reducing uncertainty exceed its costs—and will not exist when it is inefficient. . . .

3. *Heterogeneous Expectations Respecting Default.* The argument in Part II–A that security fails to generate net gains for a firm presupposed that the firm's creditors assigned equal probabilities to default. If this assumption is relaxed, security may increase welfare. . . . And to generalize, it is always efficient for the firm to secure the creditor that assigns the highest probability to default.

This explanation initially seem plausible because a firm's creditors could assign different probabilities to the likelihood of default. The probability that a firm will default is a function, *inter alia*, of the length and size of loans and not all of a firm's debt is likely to be of the same length and size. The heterogeneous-expectations explanation, however, is difficult to confirm with the sparse data that now exist.

The explanation predicts that long-term or large debt will be secured more frequently than short-term or small debt, but the issue is not length or size simpliciter but whether length or size differs enough to generate different default probabilities on the part of creditors. Thus the explanation is not necessarily disconfirmed by the practice of firms, whose financing is primarily short-term, often to issue some secured debt. For particular debtors, a six-month loan may be long-term if the question is default probability. Nor is the explanation necessarily disconfirmed by the practice of some firms never to sell secured debt although they obtain credit for different periods or in different magnitudes. Such firms may nevertheless pose similar probabilities of default because of their earning capacities or other factors. The heterogeneous-expectations explanation is thus similar to the uncertainty explanation. It is internally coherent but is weakened by apparent counterexamples that themselves could conceivably be dissolved by adequate empirical investigation. . . .

III. DISTRIBUTIONAL EXPLANATIONS

A. *The "Offensive" Distributional Explanation*

Distributional explanations for the existence of secured debt are of two related kinds—the "offensive" and the "defensive." The former relaxes the assumption made in Part II-A that a firm's unsecured creditors are aware of security and react to its issuance by raising their interest rates. Suppose that some of these creditors fail to do this. Firms would then have an incentive to issue secured debt because they would benefit from the lower interest rates secured creditors would charge but not be harmed by higher interest rates charged elsewhere. In this circumstance, secured debt redistributes wealth from uninformed creditors (who fail to react to security) to firms. Firms would then be anxious to make secured loans, so demand for these loans would increase; thus secured creditors—primarily banks and finance companies—would share some of the gains made at the expense of the uninformed creditors.

This distributional explanation predicts that firms will issue secured debt only when a substantial number of their creditors are uninformed. The prediction has some empirical support. Consider retailers in consumer markets. A retailer's creditors include not only its financers and sellers but also its customers and employees. A customer who buys from a retailer has a potential warranty claim. Further, hard goods, such as appliances or cars, often are bought with service contracts or under the standard repair or replacement warranty. Customers who have made partial or full payment would be entitled to restitution if the goods are defective. Retailers are debtors respecting consumer-warranty claims; that is, customers have potential claims against retailers for money or services, and the retailers have a corollary potential liability. If assets are withdrawn from the pool otherwise available to satisfy the warranty claims of customers and devoted to the claims of different creditors, the purchase risks of the customers are increased; their claims against firms will be more difficult to satisfy. Purchases from "secured firms" are, consequently, less attractive than purchases from unsecured firms, so the secured firms should command lower prices. These lower prices are the product-market equivalent of the higher interest rates that unsecured creditors in financial markets charge to a firm that issues secured debt. But if retail customers are unaware of the existence of security, their demand for the goods of secured firms will be unaffected by it. These customers consequently will pay higher prices than they should pay, as measured by their own (informed) preferences. The excess will be shared by retailers and their financers.

Employees are creditors for their wages and should receive higher wages, other things equal, from secured than from unsecured firms because security makes the former firms more risky to deal with. Retail employees, however, are less likely to be organized than manufacturing employees and more likely to be employed on a casual or seasonal basis. Retail employees may therefore have relatively less power and knowledge than manufacturing employees to demand higher wages from secured firms, with the result that these firms (and their financers) may capture some of the wealth of the employees.

The offensive distributional explanation seems correctly to predict that firms will issue secured debt when a substantial number of their creditors are uninformed. It apparently predicts wrongly the absence of security, however, in cases when most of a firm's creditors would be aware of security and could react to its existence. As Part II–B showed, when creditors are informed and capable, security generates no reductions in net interest rates for the firm. Thus the offensive distributional explanation predicts that those industrial firms whose sellers, buyers, and financers all seem sophisticated will rarely secure the debt they sell. In practice, however, these firms often issue some secured debt. This explanation therefore is also unconvincing.

Notes & Questions

1. *The Relative Cost of Secured Credit.* Consider Professor Schwartz's initial arguments that (a) the reduced risks that secured creditors gain are offset by the increased risks to which unsecured creditors are exposed, and (b) given this relationship, the debtor is worse off with security than without it because the issuance of secured debt is costly. In assessing this argument, should one ask not whether secured debt is costly to issue, but whether it is *more* costly to issue than unsecured credit? For example, suppose an unsecured loan takes the form of a complex agreement with many financial covenants, including definitions of long and short term assets and liabilities, restrictions on net worth, and restrictions on dividends and borrowings. Is the negotiation and issuance of such an unsecured loan necessarily less costly than issuance of a secured loan without such financial

covenants?　What implications does this have for the foregoing analysis?

2.　*Monitoring Costs.*　Consider the "monitoring cost" explanation for the existence of secured credit.　It seems to assume that the interest rate at which a firm borrows initially accurately reflects the risk of the enterprise but does not accurately reflect the risk of prospective debtor misbehavior.[a]　In light of all the other contingencies that one is willing to view as being reflected in the initial interest rate, should one assume that the rate does not reflect the likelihood of prospective debtor misbehavior?

3.　*Does the Bankruptcy Setting Make a Difference?*　Consider the following two questions: (1) Why do creditors take, and debtors issue, secured credit?　(2) Why do secured creditors rank first in a bankruptcy proceeding?　One could treat these questions as being indistinguishable, as the above excerpt seems to.　That is, one could search for the reasons (efficiency-based or other) justifying secured credit's existence and then treat the discovered justification as supporting secured creditors' bankruptcy priority.　The above excerpt suggests that it may be difficult to find such a justification for the existence of secured credit but seems willing to allow that justification to carry over into a justification for the bankruptcy priority.

Should one separate the question of why secured credit exists from the question whether secured creditors should have priority status in bankruptcy?　If one settles on a satisfactory explanation for the existence of secured credit, should that explanation necessarily carry over into supporting bankruptcy priority?

4.　*Should Bankruptcy Law Follow State Law?*　Should a bankruptcy draftsman think along either of the following lines?　(1) I'm not sure what the justification is for secured credit but, given that all the states want to allow it, there ought to be a pretty damning case against it before it is not given a top priority in bankruptcy.　(2) I'm not sure what the justification is for secured credit, but if a secured party's interest in property is not honored in bankruptcy there would be serious constitutional problems.　It is not worth taking the chance of invalidation to test whether the economy would be better off with a bankruptcy system that did not honor security interests in property.

5.　*Nonconsensual Liens.*　The discussion in the Schwartz excerpt, and most other discussions of the secured creditor's priority in bankruptcy, focus almost exclusively on the status of consensual security interests.　What are the economic or social welfare explanations of the priority given to other secured claims?　Why are judicial liens and statutory liens (to some extent) honored in bankruptcy?　Would refusal to honor them be unconstitutional?

a.　But see Jackson & Kronman, Secured Financing and Priorities Among Creditors, 88 Yale L.J. 1143, 1150 (1979) (recognizing interest rate increase as means of dealing with threat of debtor misbehavior).

2. Unsecured Claims

VANSTON BONDHOLDERS PROTECTIVE
COMMITTEE v. GREEN

Supreme Court of the United States, 1946.
329 U.S. 156, 67 S.Ct. 237, 91 L.Ed. 162.

MR. JUSTICE BLACK delivered the opinion of the Court.

December 2, 1930, a Kentucky District Court appointed an equity receiver of Inland Gas Corporation to take complete and exclusive control, possession, and custody of all of Inland's properties, and enjoined Inland's officers from paying its debts. At that time there was no interest unpaid on Inland's first mortgage bonds. February 1, 1931, semiannual interest coupons fell due on these bonds. The debtor could not pay; the court did not direct the receiver to pay. The indenture trustee, acting under the terms of the indenture, promptly declared the entire principal due and payable despite the previous assumption of custody of the estate by the federal court. In 1935, the same District Court approved a creditor's petition for reorganization under § 77B of the Bankruptcy Act, and at a subsequent date the reorganization was continued as a Chapter X proceeding. The indenture provides for payment of interest on unpaid interest. Inland is insolvent, but its assets are sufficient to pay the first mortgage bondholders in full, including the interest on interest. Should interest on interest be paid, however, subordinate creditors would receive a greatly reduced share in the reorganized corporation. These latter concede that the first mortgage bondholders should receive simple interest on the principal due them, but challenge their right to be paid interest on interest [2] which fell due after the court took charge of Inland, and which interest the Court, out of consideration for orderly and fair administration of the estate, directed the receiver not to pay on the due date. It is this controversy which we must determine.

The first mortgage indenture document was written and signed in New York, designated a New York bank as trustee, and provided for payment of the bonds and attached interest coupons at the office of the trustee in New York or, at the option of the bearer, at a bank in Chicago, Illinois. . . . Inland was organized under the corporation laws of Delaware. Its principal place of business was in Kentucky, and the property mortgaged was located in that state. . . .

A purpose of bankruptcy is so to administer an estate as to bring about a ratable distribution of assets among the bankrupt's creditors. What claims of creditors are valid and subsisting obligations against the bankrupt at the time a petition in bankruptcy is filed is a question which, in the absence of overruling federal law, is to be determined by reference to state law. But obligations, such as the one here for interest, often have significant contacts in many states, so that the

2. The claims for interest on interest
amount to some $500,000.

question of which particular state's law should measure the obligation seldom lends itself to simple solution. In determining which contact is the most significant in a particular transaction, courts can seldom find a complete solution in the mechanical formulae of the conflicts of law. Determination requires the exercise of an informed judgment in the balancing of all the interests of the states with the most significant contacts in order best to accommodate the equities among the parties to the policies of those states. Certainly the part of this transaction which touched New York, namely, that the indenture contract was written, signed, and payable there, may be a reason why that state's law should govern. But apparently the bonds were sold to people all over the nation. And Kentucky's interest in having its own laws govern the obligation cannot be minimized. For the property mortgaged, was there; the company's business was chiefly there; its products were widely distributed there; and the prices paid by Kentuckians for those products would depend, at least to some extent, on the stability of the company as affected by the carrying charges on its debts. But we need not decide which, if either, of these two states' laws govern the creation and subsistence and validity of the obligation for interest on interest here involved. For assuming, arguendo, that the obligation for interest on interest is valid under the law of New York, Kentucky, and the other states having some interest in the indenture transaction, we would still have to decide whether allowance of the claim would be compatible with the policy of the Bankruptcy Act.

In determining what claims are allowable and how a debtor's assets shall be distributed, a bankruptcy court does not apply the law of the state where it sits. Erie R. Co. v. Tompkins, 304 U.S. 64, 58 S.Ct. 817, 82 L.Ed. 1188, 114 A.L.R. 1487, has no such implication. That case decided that a federal district court acquiring jurisdiction because of diversity of citizenship should adjudicate controversies as if it were only another state court. But bankruptcy courts must administer and enforce the Bankruptcy Act as interpreted by this Court in accordance with authority granted by Congress to determine how and what claims shall be allowed under equitable principles. And we think an allowance of interest on interest under the circumstances shown by this case would not be in accord with the equitable principles governing bankruptcy distributions.

When and under what circumstances federal courts will allow interest on claims against debtors' estates being administered by them has long been decided by federal law. The general rule in bankruptcy and in equity receivership has been that interest on the debtors' obligations ceases to accrue at the beginning of proceedings. Exaction of interest, where the power of a debtor to pay even his contractual obligations is suspended by law, has been prohibited because it was considered in the nature of a penalty imposed because of delay in prompt payment—a delay necessitated by law if the courts are properly to preserve and protect the estate for the benefit of all interests involved. Thus this Court has said: "We cannot agree that a penalty in the name of interest should be inflicted upon the owners of the mortgage lien for resisting claims which we have disallowed. As a general rule, after property of an insolvent passes into the hands of a receiver or of an assignee in insolvency, interest is not allowed on the claims against the funds. The delay in distribution is the act of the law; it is a necessary incident to the settlement of the estate." Thomas v. Western Car Co., 149 U.S. 95, 116, 117, 13 S.Ct. 824, 37 L.Ed. 663. Courts have felt that it would be inequitable for anyone to gain an advantage or suffer a loss because of such delay. Sexton v. Dreyfus, 219 U.S. 339, 346, 31 S.Ct. 256, 258, 55 L.Ed. 244. Accrual of simple interest on unsecured claims in bankruptcy was prohibited in order that the administrative inconvenience of continuous recomputation of interest causing recomputation of claims could be avoided. Moreover, different creditors whose claims bore diverse interest rates or were paid by the bankruptcy court on different dates would suffer neither gain nor loss caused solely by delay.

Simple interest on secured claims accruing after the petition was filed was denied unless the security was worth more than the sum of principal and interest due. Sexton v. Dreyfus, supra. To allow a secured creditor interest where his security was worth less than the value of his debt was thought to be inequitable to unsecured creditors. . . . But where an estate was ample to pay all creditors and to pay interest even after the petition was filed, equitable considerations were invoked to permit payment of this additional interest to the secured creditor rather than to the debtor.

. . .

In this case, where by order of the court interest was left unpaid, we do not think that imposition of interest on that unpaid interest can be justified by "an application of equitable principles." See Dayton v. Stanard, 241 U.S. 588, 590, 36 S.Ct. 695, 696, 60 L.Ed. 1190. Prior to the beginning of the equity receivership, Inland would have never owed interest on interest unless and until it had breached its obligation to pay simple interest promptly—on the date it was due. Before the receivership began, a failure by Inland to pay coupons on the date they were due might have breached an existing obligation. This breach would have imposed upon Inland, under the terms of the covenant, a duty to pay interest on the interest it had failed to pay. But when the equity receivership intervened, these interrelated obligations were drastically changed. The obligation to make prompt payment of simple interest coupons was suspended. In fact, both Inland and the receiver were ordered by the court not to pay the coupons on the dates they were, on their face, supposed to have been paid. The contingency which might have created a present obligation to pay interest on interest—i.e., a free decision by the debtor that it would not or could not pay simple interest promptly—was prohibited from occurring by order of the court. That order issued for a good cause, we may assume: to preserve and protect the debtor's estate pending a ratable distribution among all the creditors according to their interests as of the date the receivership began. The extra interest covenant may be deemed added compensation for the creditor or, what is more likely, something like a penalty to induce prompt payment of simple interest. In either event, first mortgage bondholders would have been enriched and subordinate creditors would have suffered a corresponding loss, because of a failure to pay when payment had been prohibited by a court order entered for the joint benefit of debtor, creditors, and the public. Such a result is not consistent with equitable principles. For legal suspension of an obligation to pay is an adequate reason why no added compensation or penalty should be enforced for failure to pay.

Affirmed.

MR. JUSTICE FRANKFURTER, with whom MR. JUSTICE JACKSON joins, concurring; MR. JUSTICE BURTON having concurred in the opinion of the Court also joins in this opinion. . . . One way of putting our problem is to ask whether the bankruptcy court executing the policy of Congress could recognize a claim for interest on coupons and allow it to share in the distribution of the bankrupt's assets. But thus to frame the question is to avoid the crucial preliminary inquiry whether any obligation exists to be recognized. For nothing comes into a bankruptcy court to which congressional policy can apply unless it is an obligation created by applicable State law. And no obligation finds its way into a bankruptcy court unless, by the law of the State where the acts constituting a transaction occur, the legal consequence of such a transaction is an obligation to pay. Where a transaction in its entirety occurs in one State, it is clearly the law of that State that determines if an obligation is born, whether the question becomes relevant in a bankruptcy court or in any other court. But the mere fact that an agreement is made in one State by citizens of a second State for performance in a third and affecting individuals in all forty-eight States does not change the principle inherent in our federal scheme, that the existence of a debt comes about not by federal law but by force of some State law, even though the right to enforce the debt, if it exists, may raise federal questions if bankruptcy ensues. Bankruptcy legislation is superimposed upon rights and obligations created by the laws of the States. We do not reach considerations of policy in bankruptcy administration until there are rights, created by applicable local law, to be recognized.

This brings us to the immediate situation. This is not a case where damages are claimed, in the form of interest, for the detention of monies due. In such a situation the right to interest and its measure become matters for judicial determination. The claim here asserted is based solely on the terms of the agreement. The covenant for interest on interest was entered into by the parties in New York. The dominant place of performance was also New York. In the circumstances, if the words of the indenture created an obligation, they did so only if the law of New York says they did. Williston, Contracts, § 1792. If New

York outlawed such a covenant, neither Kentucky nor Delaware nor the States in which bonds were sold or where bondholders reside could give effect to an obligation which never came into being. And the ultimate voice of New York law, the New York Court of Appeals, speaking through Judge Cardozo, stated it as settled law that "a promise to pay interest upon interest is void . . . ." Newburger-Morris Co. v. Talcott, 219 N.Y 505, 510, 114 N.E. 846, 847. This view of the New York law is supported by the great weight of Judge Mack's authority. American Brake Shoe & Foundry Co. v. Interborough Rapid Transit Co., (DCNY) 11 F.Supp. 418–420. But see American Brake Shoe & Foundry Co. v. Interborough Rapid Transit Co., D.C., 26 F.Supp. 954, contra. However, it is not for us to ascertain independently whether the law of New York deemed a nullity the agreement that was here sought to be made the basis of a claim. We would not have brought the case here on that issue. The Circuit Court of Appeals made such an investigation and concluded that in New York the undertaking to pay interest was void. We accept this finding and conclude that since no obligation was created there was no claim provable in bankruptcy. And so we are not now called upon to decide whether as a matter of bankruptcy administration an agreement to pay interest on interest, where it is an obligation enforceable by State law, is enforceable in bankruptcy. That is a question that can arise only where such an obligation arose under State law. The opposite is the assumption in the case before us. . . .

Notes & Questions

1. *Allowance-of-Claims Problem.* On the date of the petition, the debtor owes the following:

to creditor A:	$900	overdue principal on a loan
	$100	prepetition overdue interest
to creditor B:	$850	overdue principal
	$100	overdue interest
	$50	overdue interest on interest
to creditor C:	$500	overdue principal
	$500	principal overdue by virtue of a clause accelerating the maturity of the entire debt
to landlord:	$500	overdue rent
	$5,000	rent overdue due to an acceleration clause
	$200	attorney's fees that the lease characterizes as rent

> to taxing
> authority: $500   in delinquent taxes
> $300   in penalties
> $200   in interest (The tax code describes pen-
>   alties and interest as "additional tax-
>   es.")

Which claims are allowed? See §§ 501, 502. How would your answers change if the particular claim arose after the filing of the bankruptcy petition?

2. *State Law and Bankruptcy Claims.* What should be the relationship between state law and claims in bankruptcy? Should validity under state law be a prerequisite to allowing a claim in bankruptcy? Is there any alternative? When should bankruptcy law disallow claims despite their validity under state law? Should bankruptcy law treat differently claims that state law treats as equals?

Consider these issues in light of the treatment of similar issues that arise in deciding what property becomes property of the estate, studied in Chapter 10. In determining the scope of the bankruptcy estate, we saw (a) that some assets that creditors may reach under state law may not necessarily be reachable in a bankruptcy proceeding, and (b) that some assets that creditors could not reach under state law may nevertheless be reachable in a bankruptcy proceeding. Are there some claims that nonbankruptcy law honors that should not be honored in bankruptcy, and some claims that nonbankruptcy law does not honor that should be honored in bankruptcy? Are the criteria for departure from state law the same with respect to the estate and claim issues?

3. *Tort Claims: Manifested and Unmanifested.* Manville Corporation filed a petition under Chapter 11 because of present and future tort claims of former workers exposed to asbestos. Which of the following classes of workers have claims against Manville?

(a) Workers who have money judgments against Manville based on their exposure.

(b) Workers who have filed lawsuits against Manville but whose suits have not yet been adjudicated.

(c) Workers who have been diagnosed as having asbestos-related diseases but who have not yet made any demand of Manville for compensation.

(d) Workers who have been exposed to asbestos but who do not yet show any signs of asbestos-related diseases.

See § 502(c).

4. *What Is a Claim?* (a) *The Role of State Law.*

The . . . bankruptcy petitions of asbestos manufacturers like Manville Corp. and UNR Industries [have] been the source of much academic and public interest since the early 1980s. At the core of the debate is the status of "future" asbestos victims. These are people who have had their contact with asbestos in the past, but who, as of the date of the relevant bankruptcy petition, have not yet manifested any injury. . . .

That there has been a debate, however, is largely due to a confusion of the role of nonbankruptcy law. Although it properly gives content to words in the Bankruptcy Code such as *claim* or *arose* that delimit those entitled to participate in bankruptcy's collective proceeding, there is no particular reason to think that one should resort to nonbankruptcy law to define those words. To be sure, courts must resort to nonbankruptcy law to determine who is entitled to participate in the distribution of assets, but nothing in this process suggests that one also must look at what state law *calls* some asserted claim. Doing so would confuse attributes (where nonbankruptcy rules play a crucial role) with labels (where nonbankruptcy rules should play no role). In the contested issue in the bankruptcies of Manville and UNR, for example, the attributes are (1) whether the right being asserted, based on an asbestos-related tort, is cognizable under state law (it is); (2) whether such a cause of action has some value at the time of the bankruptcy proceeding (it does, if it is not barred by the statute of limitations); and (3) whether such a cause of action arises out of the past of the debtor (it does). If those attributes are present, then the person is—and should be—a creditor holding a claim within the meaning of the Bankruptcy Code. How state law chooses to label those attributes (for any number of a variety of nonbankruptcy reasons) is of no moment.

T. Jackson, The Logic and Limits of Bankruptcy Law 47–49 (1986).

Should the reasons why state law might refuse to treat an unmanifested tort claim as not stating a current cause of action matter? What are those reasons? Consider the following:

(1) "a plaintiff should not be deprived of a remedy [by allowing a statute of limitations to run] before receiving clear warning that an invasion of a legal right has occurred." Bibler, The Status of Unaccrued Tort Claims In Chapter 11 Bankruptcy Proceedings, 61 Am.Bankr.L.J. 145, 164 (1987).

(2) "Given the widespread recognition of the inability of toxic tort victims to realize their rights have wrongfully been invaded until symptoms of their insidious diseases become manifest, it is not surprising that courts and commentators agree that the practical difficulties of identifying and giving constitutionally adequate notice to thousands of contingent future claimants are almost certainly insurmountable." Id. at 168–69.

(b) *The Stakes.* What is at stake when a potential cause of action is or is not treated as a claim for bankruptcy purposes? Assume that one decides that unmanifested tort claims are not claims entitled to participate in a bankruptcy. What is the effect of this decision on a person with such a claim? Should the person be pleased or displeased?

Assume that one decides that unmanifested tort claims are claims that may participate in a bankruptcy and be discharged by it. Should companies with possibly dangerous products file for bankruptcy periodically to limit the tort consequences of harms their products may cause?

In In re Amatex Corp., 755 F.2d 1034, 1041 (3d Cir.1985), the debtor sought appointment of a guardian ad litem to represent the interests of prospective unknown asbestos claimants. The district court denied the request and the court of appeals reversed, stating:

> Bankruptcy Judge King based his recommendation to deny Amatex' motion to appoint a legal representative for future claimants on a determination that such individuals as yet had no cognizable claims under the Code. Therefore, he believed, future claimants are not "creditors" and their claims may not be discharged, or even affected, in a reorganization plan. We need not reach the merits of these conclusions in order to ascertain that future claimants do have a sufficient interest to require some representation during the reorganization proceedings. Whether or not future claimants have claims in the technical bankruptcy sense that can be affected by a reorganization plan, such individuals clearly have a practical stake in the outcome of the proceedings. Indeed, Judge King observed that the interests of the future claimants could be adversely affected if Amatex failed to rehabilitate itself and was liquidated. . . .

The court went on to rely on § 1109(b) of the Code to authorize appointment of a guardian.

5. *Acceleration of Principal.* (a) *The Rule.* Section 502(b)(2)'s legislative history states:

> Section 502(b) . . . contains two principles of present law. First, interest stops accruing at the date of the filing of the petition, because any claim for unmatured interest is disallowed under this paragraph. Second, bankruptcy operates as the acceleration of the principal amount of all claims against the debtor. One unarticulated reason for this is that the discounting factor for claims after the commencement of the case is equivalent to contractual interest rate on the claim. Thus, this paragraph does not cause disallowance of claims that have not been discounted to a present value because of the irrebuttable presumption that the discounting rate and the contractual interest rate (even a zero interest rate) are equivalent.

House Report at 352–53. Why does bankruptcy operate to accelerate the principal amount of all claims against the debtor?

(b) *Justification for the Acceleration Rule.* Professor Jackson states:

> This [acceleration of principal] rule is consistent with the effort to maintain as closely as possible relevant nonbankruptcy attributes in a bankruptcy proceeding. If an insolvent debtor were being dismembered by creditors outside of bankruptcy, any loan agree-

ment worth its salt would have default and acceleration provisions that would afford the lender its opportunity to share in the spoils without having to wait until the maturing date fifteen years hence, at which time, under a system of individualistic grab remedies, the debtor's assets would be long gone. The decision of a debtor (or its creditors) to liquidate in bankruptcy should change nothing: it represents the kind of event that would trigger such default and acceleration.

T. Jackson, supra, at 38. Can one be faithful to preserving nonbankruptcy entitlements and allow for acceleration of all debts?

Consider the following:

If bankruptcy law were to fully mirror state law entitlements, however, it would accelerate only those claims with acceleration clauses. Acceleration clauses do not accompany many credit extensions, particularly informal, short-term extensions. Institutional lenders demand such clauses but they are not the only lenders. And even they will negotiate with some debtors over the details of the acceleration clause. Lawyers often negotiate terms such as how many days an otherwise defaulting debtor has to cure. If state law entitlements should dominate the area, a single bankruptcy rule is unnecessary even if the state rule applies only to a few lenders.

One can even imagine situations in which the parties bargain over the acceleration clause itself. Bankruptcy's automatic inclusion of acceleration would then sharply depart from the state law outcome. A debtor who can avoid an acceleration clause in one loan is a more attractive candidate for a loan from a later lender than is a debtor who has a massive acceleration clause. . . .

Nor is it clear that all lenders attach great importance to having an acceleration clause. A lender worth more than its salt might relax about liquidation of a debtor's assets so long as the debtor has prospects of acquiring future assets that will satisfy the lender's debt. This is, of course, not true of lenders to a dissolving corporation. They must be paid now or never. Lenders to individuals, however, need not worry about an entity liquidating under state law. If an individual debtor sells off all its assets but later has regular income that enables the debtor to pay the lender's debt, the lack of an acceleration clause is not a serious problem for the lender.

Bankruptcy's acceleration principle becomes more explicable when one accounts for a unique feature of bankruptcy: its power to discharge debts. To discharge a debt in bankruptcy, one must measure the debt's worth now and forever. No post-liquidation payments will be made to the creditor who has lent money to an individual and who, through custom, oversight, or negotiation, has not demanded an acceleration clause. Because of the discharge, the creditor's claim must be currently valued for bankruptcy purposes. . . . [T]he existence of the discharge, and not merely the need to preserve state law rights, necessitates the valuation.

Eisenberg, A Bankruptcy Machine That Would Go of Itself, 39 Stan.L. Rev. 1519, 1529–30 (1987). Even accepting the need to accelerate debts, should the terms of the accelerated debts (their interest rate and period) be ignored?

6. *Post-Petition Interest:* (a) *Unsecured Claims.* The general rule in bankruptcy is that unsecured claims for post-petition interest are not allowed. Why? Was *Vanston* decided on that ground? Suppose the debtor's estate is large enough to pay post-petition interest claims. See § 726(a)(5); Sexton v. Dreyfus, 219 U.S. 339, 31 S.Ct. 256, 55 L.Ed. 244 (1911); Littleton v. Kincaid, 179 F.2d 848, 852 (4th Cir. 1950) (post-petition interest allowed). What would be the effect of a rule that allowed post-petition interest to accrue? Consider two separate cases: (a) All creditors' claims accrue post-petition interest at the same rate. (b) Creditors' claims accrue interest at a different rate or some creditors' claims call for interest and others do not.

(b) *Secured Claims.* Secured lenders receive more favorable treatment on the issue of post-petition interest. See § 506(b). This obviously makes it desirable for secured creditors to be substantially oversecured. But see Uniform Fraudulent Conveyance Act § 3(b) (excess security can be a fraudulent conveyance). Which creditors are likely to benefit most from grants of post-petition interest to secured creditors? See, e.g., IRC § 6321 (granting federal government a tax lien on all of a debtor's real and personal property). Sections 724(a) and 726(a)(4) impose some limits on taxing authorities' beneficial position. Note that they do not apply to Chapter 11, Chapter 12, or Chapter 13 cases. See § 103.

There is an unexpected twist on the rule allowing post-petition interest to oversecured creditors. When the oversecured claim is non-consensual (e.g., a tax lien or a judgment lien), there is authority for disallowing post-petition interest. See In re Ron Pair Enterprises, Inc., 828 F.2d 367 (6th Cir. 1987) (relying on pre–1978 Act law). Compare In re Best Repair Co., Inc. v. United States, 789 F.2d 1080 (4th Cir. 1986) (opposite result reached, relying on the plain language of § 506(b)). Is there a justification for treating nonconsensual secured claims worse than consensual secured claims?

7. *Special Limitations on Claims.* Consider § 502(b)'s treatment of lease obligations and employment contracts. Why are these claims singled out for special limitations? Are there other claims that should be considered for similar treatment? Debtor has a ten-year supply contract with supplier. The contract is highly favorable to supplier and the normal measure of contract damages would give supplier a claim of $2 million for its breach by debtor. If debtor rejects the contract, should supplier be limited to damages or a claim that reflects only the first year of the contract? Only the first three years? How does supplier differ from the landlord claims dealt with in § 502(b)(6) and the employee claims dealt with in § 502(b)(7)?

Kuehner v. Irving Trust Co., 299 U.S. 445, 57 S.Ct. 298, 81 L.Ed. 340 (1937), involved a challenge to a prior bankruptcy law provision limiting landlords' claims to three years' rent. The landlord argued that any surplus over the three years' rent limitation, even if subordinate to the claims of other creditors, had to be given priority over the interests of stockholders in the bankrupt firm. The Court found the three years' limitation to be within the bankruptcy power and not to violate the fifth amendment's due process guaranty.

> We cannot pronounce the limit set upon petitioners' claim arbitrary or unreasonable. It is well known that leases of business properties, particularly retail business properties, commonly run for long terms. The longer the term the greater the uncertainty as to the loss entailed by abrogation of the lease. Testimony as to present rental value partakes largely of the character of prophecy, and, although that value is the cardinal factor in the measure of damages for which petitioners contend, it is obvious that, since the landlord is not bound to relet the premises for the unexpired term of the lease, that factor may have little real bearing upon the realities of the case. And, in any event, the possibility of the landlord's using the premises for his own purposes, their sale, their condemnation for public use, or their loss by foreclosure, renders an estimate of present rental value highly uncertain. Add to this the fact that bankruptcies multiply in hard times, and that estimates of rental value are made upon the basis of what a new tenant will pay in an era of economic depression, and the estimate becomes even more unreliable. Whatever courts, in the absence of a statutory formula, might feel compelled to adopt as the measure of damage in such a case, we cannot hold that Congress could not reasonably find that an award of the full difference between rental value and rent reserved for the remainder of the term smacks too much of speculation and that a uniform limit upon landlords' claims will, in the long run, be fair to them, to other creditors, and to the debtor. . . .

> The petitioners say that by limiting their claim they are put upon a different basis from other creditors. A sufficient ground for the distinction is that petitioners get back their property. In other words, they have lost merely a bargain for the use of real estate whereas merchandise creditors, lenders, and others, recover in specie none of the property or money which passed from them to the debtor. . . .

B. Priorities and Distribution

There are many reasons why a bankruptcy law may choose to favor a particular creditor and many ways in which to implement the decision to favor a creditor. Some creditors may be viewed as entitled to protection because they have added value to the debtor's estate. This is often the justification given for honoring mechanics' liens in bankruptcy. Cf. § 545. Other creditors may be favored because not to do so would flirt with disaster or be viewed as unfair. Thus, a debtor's alimony and child support obligations are deemed not dischargeable in bankruptcy. See § 523(a)(5). Still other creditors receive favored treatment because they are needed to successfully complete a bankruptcy proceeding. Those who work for the debtor after the petition is filed are entitled to an administrative priority under §§ 503 and 507.

Note that in each of the above cases a different technique is employed to favor a chosen creditor. Some creditors' debts are deemed not dischargable. Other creditors are allowed to enforce their liens. And other creditors are simply given a priority among those unsecured creditors who participate in a bankruptcy.

Which creditors should bankruptcy law single out for favored treatment? Which technique for favoring a creditor is the most appropriate? Should bankruptcy law do anything to disrupt the system of priorities among creditors that state law has created.

1. Administrative Priority

READING CO. v. BROWN

Supreme Court of the United States, 1968.
391 U.S. 471, 88 S.Ct. 1759, 20 L.Ed.2d 751.

MR. JUSTICE HARLAN delivered the opinion of the Court.

On November 16, 1962, I. J. Knight Realty Corporation filed a petition for an arrangement under Chapter XI of the Bankruptcy Act, 11 U.S.C. §§ 701–799. The same day, the District Court appointed a receiver, Francis Shunk Brown, a respondent here. The receiver was authorized to conduct the debtor's business, which consisted principally of leasing the debtor's only significant asset, an eight-story industrial structure located in Philadelphia.

On January 1, 1963, the building was totally destroyed by a fire which spread to adjoining premises and destroyed real and personal property of petitioner Reading Company and others. On April 3, 1963, petitioner filed a claim for $559,730.83 in the arrangement, based on the asserted negligence of the receiver. It was styled a claim for "administrative expenses" of the arrangement. Other fire loss claimants filed 146 additional claims of a similar nature. The total of all such claims was in excess of $3,500,000, substantially more than the total assets of the debtor.

On May 14, 1963, Knight Realty was voluntarily adjudicated a bankrupt and respondent receiver was subsequently elected trustee in bankruptcy. The claims of petitioner and others thus became claims for administration expenses in bankruptcy which are given first priority under § 64a(1) of the Bankruptcy Act, 11 U.S.C. § 104(a)(1). The trustee moved to expunge the claims on the ground that they were not for expenses of administration. It was agreed that the decision whether petitioner's claim is provable as an expense of administration would establish the status of the other 146 claims. It was further agreed that, for purposes of deciding whether the claim is provable, it would be assumed that the damage to petitioner's property resulted from the negligence of the receiver and a workman he employed. The United States, holding a claim for unpaid prearrangement taxes admittedly superior to the claims of general creditors and inferior to claims for administration expenses, entered the case on the side of the trustee.

The referee disallowed the claim for administration expenses. He also ruled that petitioner's claim was not provable as a general claim against the estate, a ruling challenged by neither side. On petition for review, the referee was upheld by the District Court. On appeal, the Court of Appeals for the Third Circuit, sitting en banc, affirmed the decision of the District Court by a 4–3 vote. We granted certiorari, 389 U.S. 895, because the issue is important in the administration of the bankruptcy laws and is one of first impression in this Court. For reasons to follow, we reverse.

Section 64a of the Bankruptcy Act provides in part as follows:

> "The debts to have priority, in advance of the payment of dividends to creditors, and to be paid in full out of bankrupt estates, and the order of payment, shall be (1) the costs and expenses of administration, including the actual and necessary costs and expenses of preserving the estate subsequent to filing the petition . . . .."

It is agreed that this section, applicable by its terms to straight bankruptcies, governs payment of administration expenses of Chapter XI arrangements. Furthermore, it is agreed that for the purpose of applying this section to arrangements, the words "subsequent to filing the petition" refer to the period subsequent to the *arrangement* petition, and the words "preserving the estate" include the larger objective, common to arrangements, of operating the debtor's business with a view to rehabilitating it.

The question in this case is whether the negligence of a receiver administering an estate under a Chapter XI arrangement gives rise to an "actual and necessary" cost of operating the debtor's business. The Act does not define "actual and necessary," nor has any case directly in point been brought to our attention. We must, therefore, look to the general purposes of § 64a, Chapter XI, and the Bankruptcy Act as a whole.

The trustee contends that the relevant statutory objectives are (1) to facilitate rehabilitation of insolvent businesses and (2) to preserve a maximum of assets for distribution among the general creditors should the arrangement fail. He therefore argues that first priority as "necessary" expenses should be given only to those expenditures without which the insolvent business could not be carried on. For example, the trustee would allow first priority to contracts entered into by the receiver because suppliers, employees, landlords, and the like would not enter into dealings with a debtor in possession or a receiver of an insolvent business unless priority is allowed. The trustee would exclude all negligence claims, cn the theory that first priority for them is not necessary to encourage third parties to deal with an insolvent business, that first priority would reduce the amount available for the general creditors, and that first priority would discourage general creditors from accepting arrangements.

In our view the trustee has overlooked one important, and here decisive, statutory objective: fairness to all persons having claims against an insolvent. Petitioner suffered grave financial injury from what is here agreed to have been the negligence of the receiver and a workman. It is conceded that, in principle, petitioner has a right to recover for that injury from their "employer," the business under arrangement, upon the rule of respondeat superior. Respondents contend, however, that petitioner is in no different position from anyone else injured by a person with scant assets: its right to recover exists in theory but is not enforceable in practice.

That, however, is not an adequate description of petitioner's position. At the moment when an arrangement is sought, the debtor is insolvent. Its existing creditors hope that by partial or complete postponement of their claims they will, through successful rehabilitation, eventually recover from the debtor either in full or in larger proportion than they would in immediate bankruptcy. Hence the present petitioner did not merely suffer injury at the hands of an insolvent business: it had an insolvent business thrust upon it by operation of law. That business will, in any event, be unable to pay its fire debts in full. But the question is whether the fire claimants should be subordinated to, should share equally with, or should collect ahead of those creditors for whose benefit the continued operation of the business (which unfortunately led to a fire instead of the hoped-for rehabilitation) was allowed.

Recognizing that petitioner ought to have some means of asserting its claim against the business whose operation resulted in the fire, respondents have suggested various theories as alternatives to "administration expense" treatment. None of these has case support, and all seem to us unsatisfactory.

Several need not be pursued in detail. The trustee contends that if the present claims are not provable in bankruptcy they would survive as claims against the shell. He also suggests that petitioner may be able to recover from the receiver personally, or out of such bond as he posted. Without deciding whether these possible avenues are indeed open, we merely note that they do not serve the present purpose. The "master," liable for the negligence of the "servant" in this case was the business operating under a Chapter XI arrangement for the benefit of creditors and with the hope of rehabilitation. That benefit and that rehabilitation are worthy objectives. But it would be inconsistent both with the principle of respondeat superior and with the rule of fairness in bankruptcy to seek these objectives at the cost of excluding tort creditors of the arrangement from its assets, or totally subordinating

the claims of those on whom the arrangement is imposed to the claims
of those for whose benefit it is instituted.   . . .

In any event, we see no reason to indulge in a strained construction
of the relevant provisions, for we are persuaded that it is theoretically
sounder, as well as linguistically more comfortable, to treat tort claims
arising during an arrangement as actual and necessary expenses of the
arrangement rather than debts of the bankrupt. In the first place, in
considering whether those injured by the operation of the business
during an arrangement should share equally with, or recover ahead of,
those for whose benefit the business is carried on, the latter seems more
natural and just.   Existing creditors are, to be sure, in a dilemma not of
their own making, but there is no obvious reason why they should be
allowed to attempt to escape that dilemma at the risk of imposing it on
others equally innocent.

More directly in point is the possibility of insurance. An arrangement may provide for suitable coverage, and the court below recognized
that the cost of insurance against tort claims arising during an arrangement is an administrative expense payable in full under § 64a(1) before
dividends to general creditors. It is of course obvious that proper
insurance premiums must be given priority, else insurance could not be
obtained; and if a receiver or debtor in possession is to be encouraged
to obtain insurance in adequate amounts, the claims against which
insurance is obtained should be potentially payable in full.   In the
present case, it is argued, the fire was of such incredible magnitude
that adequate insurance probably could not have been obtained and in
any event would have been foolish; this may be true, as it is also true
that allowance of a first priority to the fire claimants here will still
only mean recovery by them of a fraction of their damages.   In the
usual case where damages are within insurable limits, however, the
rule of full recovery for torts is demonstrably sounder.

Although there appear to be no cases dealing with tort claims
arising during Chapter XI proceedings, decisions in analogous cases
suggest that "actual and necessary costs" should include costs ordinarily incident to operation of a business, and not be limited to costs
without which rehabilitation would be impossible.   It has long been the
rule of equity receiverships that torts of the receivership create claims
against the receivership itself; in those cases the statutory limitation to
"actual and necessary costs" is not involved, but the explicit recognition
extended to tort claims in those cases weighs heavily in favor of
considering them within the general category of costs and expenses.

In some cases arising under Chapter XI it has been recognized that
"actual and necessary costs" are not limited to those claims which the
business must be able to pay in full if it is to be able to deal at all.   For
example, state and federal taxes accruing during a receivership have
been held to be actual and necessary costs of an arrangement.   The
United States, recognizing and supporting these holdings, agrees with
petitioner that costs that form "an integral and essential element of the

continuation of the business" are necessary expenses even though priority is not necessary *to* the continuation of the business. Thus the Government suggests that "an injury to a member of the public—a business invitee—who was injured while on the business premises during an arrangement would present a completely different problem [i.e., could qualify for first priority]" although it is not suggested that priority is needed to encourage invitees to enter the premises.

The United States argues, however, that each tort claim "must be analyzed in its own context." Apart from the fact that it has been assumed throughout this case that all 147 claimants were on an equal footing and it is not very helpful to suggest here for the first time a rule by which lessees, invitees, and neighbors have different rights, we perceive no distinction. No principle of tort law of which we are aware offers guidance for distinguishing, within the class of torts committed by receivers while acting in furtherance of the business, between those "integral" to the business and those that are not.

We hold that damages resulting from the negligence of a receiver acting within the scope of his authority as receiver give rise to "actual and necessary costs" of a Chapter XI arrangement. . . .

Mr. Justice Marshall took no part in the consideration or decision of this case.

Mr. Chief Justice Warren, with whom Mr. Justice Douglas joins, dissenting. . . .

On other occasions, this Court has observed that "[t]he theme of the Bankruptcy Act is 'equality of distribution' . . .; and if one claimant is to be preferred over others, the purpose should be clear from the statute." Nathanson v. NLRB, 344 U.S. 25, 29, 73 S.Ct. 80, 97 L.Ed. 23 (1952); see Sampsell v. Imperial Paper Corp., 313 U.S. 215, 219, 61 S.Ct. 904, 907, 85 L.Ed. 1293 (1941). More particularly, the Act expressly directs that eligible negligence claims are to share *equally* with the unsecured claims in a pro rata distribution of the debtor's nonexempt assets. Bankruptcy Act §§ 63a(7), 65a, 11 U.S.C. §§ 103(a)(7), 105(a). Departing from this statutory scheme, the Court today singles out one class of tort claims for special treatment. After today's decision, the status of a tort claimant depends entirely upon whether he is fortunate enough to have been injured after rather than before a receiver has been appointed. And if the claimant is in the select class, he may be permitted to exhaust the estate to the exclusion of the general creditors as well as of the wage claims and government tax claims for which Congress has shown an unmistakable preference. In my view, this result frustrates rather than serves the underlying purposes of a Chapter XI proceeding, and I would not reach it without a clear indication that Congress so intended.

Congress enacted Chapter XI as an alternative to straight bankruptcy for individuals and small businesses which might be successfully rehabilitated instead of being subjected to economically wasteful liquidation. The success of a Chapter XI proceeding depends largely on two factors: first, whether creditors will take the chance of permitting an arrangement; second, whether other businesses will continue to deal with the distressed business. With respect to the first of these considerations, today's decision will undoubtedly discourage creditors from permitting arrangements, because it subjects them to unpredictable and probably uninsurable tort liability. I do not believe the statutory language requires such an interpretation. I would construe § 64a(1) with reference to the second consideration mentioned above. In my opinion, the Court would reach a result more in line with congressional intent and the Bankruptcy Act generally by regarding as administrative costs only those costs required for a smooth and successful arrangement. Accordingly, the administrative cost priority should be viewed as a guaranty to the receiver and those who deal with or are employed by him that they will be paid for their goods and services. Any broader interpretation will discourage creditors from permitting use of the rehabilitative machinery of Chapter XI and tend to force distressed businesses into straight bankruptcy.

It is equitable, the Court believes, that the general creditors (and wage and tax claimants) bear the loss in this case because they have "thrust" an insolvent business upon petitioner for their own benefit. I respectfully submit that this is a most unfair characterization of arrangements. An economically distressed businessman seeks an arrangement for his own and not for his creditors' benefit. Of course the creditors will benefit if the arrangement is successful, just as they would have benefited if the businessman had been successful without resorting to an arrangement. But a business in arrangement is no more thrust on the public than is any other business enterprise which is conducted for the mutual prosperity of the owners, the wage earners and the creditors. Realistically, the only difference is that a business administered under Chapter XI has not been prosperous. If the arrangement is successful, the owners, wage earners and creditors will all benefit; if it is not, they will all be injured. Thus, I would not distinguish in this case between petitioner and the other general creditors, none of whom was responsible for the catastrophe for which all of them must sustain some loss. Instead, in deciding this case, I would adhere to the Act's basic theme of equality of distribution.

The Court states that its decision will encourage Chapter XI receivers to obtain "adequate" insurance. The Court fairly well concedes, however, that in this case "adequate" insurance "probably could not have been obtained and in any event would have been foolish." In other words, so far as this Court knows, the insurance taken out by the receiver in this case was in fact "adequate," in the sense that no reasonable receiver could or should obtain fire insurance in the amount of $3,500,000 on the assumption that his workman might accidentally cause a fire of the proportions which occurred here. Moreover, quite apart from the case at bar, there is absolutely no indication that today's decision is needed to encourage receivers to obtain insurance. I see no basis in the Act or in sound policy for a ruling that the creditors of an estate under a Chapter XI arrangement become involuntary insurers against a liability which probably would not and should not be insurable by more traditional means. . . .

Notes & Questions

1. *Is* Reading Co. *"Right"*? Professor Jackson analyzes the case as follows:

> It is fruitful to recharacterize the underlying dispute in *Reading Co. v. Brown* as essentially one of whether the transfer of ownership from the corporation to its creditors should be deemed to occur at the moment bankruptcy is filed or at the moment the process is over. Consider, first, the case of a liquidating corporation. Such a corporation, if it were to dissolve outside bankruptcy, would parcel out its assets as the final step in the dissolution process. Tort claims that accrued after the decision to dissolve but before the actual dissolution would presumably share pro rata with the other general creditors in the distribution. No postdissolution torts would be committed by the corporation because by definition the corporation would no longer exist.
>
> This analogy supports the dissenting view of Chief Justice Warren. The bankruptcy process may be part of a *decision* to dissolve, but its commencement is not tantamount to a dissolution. Justice Harlan's view is supported by a slightly different analogy whereby the decision to invoke bankruptcy is itself a triggering event that transfers ownership of the corporation to its creditors. The corporation in bankruptcy is then like a corporation held by shareholders. Any debts that the corporation incurs during the bankruptcy proceeding have priority over prepetition unsecured claims because debts take priority over equity claims. Upon completion of the bankruptcy process and dissolution of the corporation the tort claims that arose during the bankruptcy proceeding would have priority over the prepetition claims of the general creditors, which are viewed, for purposes of bankruptcy law, as equity owners.

T. Jackson, supra, at 154–55. Consider two other possible methods of dealing with a financially failing debtor under state law. As noted in Chapter 9, state law allows debtors to assign all of their assets to a trustee for the benefit of creditors and allows creditors to place failing debtors in receivership. Which of the (now four) possible state law analogies is the most appropriate for *Reading Co.* to follow? See generally Eisenberg, A Bankruptcy Machine That Would Go of Itself, supra, at 1523–24. Should we just invent an independent bankruptcy rule? What considerations should inform that bankruptcy rule?

2. *Obligations to Employees.* (a) *Benefits Accruing Over Time.* A Chapter 11 debtor filed a petition on March 5, 1980. Under the debtor's collective bargaining agreement vacation pay to employees become due and owing on July 15, 1980. The agreement obligates the debtor to pay vacation pay to its employees with at least six months

service who are "on the active payroll of the Company on July 15 of any year" or laid off and later recalled after July 15th, but prior to December 31st of that same year. To what extent, if any, is the vacation pay entitled to priority as an administrative expense under §§ 503 and 507? Do the priorities set forth in § 507 affect one's analysis of this question? See In re Schatz Federal Bearings Co., Inc., 5 B.R. 549 (Bkrtcy.S.D.N.Y.1980) (adminstrative priority limited to portion of vacation pay attributable to days worked after March 5, 1980).

(b) *One-Shot Benefits.* If the dispute in *Schatz,* supra, had been about severance pay obligations triggered by post-bankruptcy lay-offs, should the entire amount of severance pay be deemed an administrative expense? Should that depend upon the terms under which employees accrue severance pay rights?

3. *Implementing Priorities.* If one accepts that bankruptcy law should favor administrative expenses, is the § 507(a)(1) priority the best way to accomplish that goal? Why not make adminstrative expenses nondischargeable? What effect would nondischargeability have on (a) debtors' decisions to file petitions, and (b) creditors' attitudes towards administrative expenses?

4. *The Order of Priorities.* Does the current order of priorities within the Bankruptcy Act make sense? On what grounds should one unsecured creditor's claim be preferred to that of another unsecured creditor? Are there unsecured creditors who are equally deserving of priority but who receive no favored treatment under the Act?

If creditors were designing the Bankruptcy Act's priority system, would they include priorities similar to those contained in § 507?

Consider the case of a financially troubled major automobile company (Chrysler), airline (Braniff or Continental), or other business that deals with the public. In the case of an automobile company would a priority for warranty claims help the company to keep selling cars despite the lack of confidence in the company? Should airline passengers who pay for tickets in advance be given a priority in bankruptcy? Will this encourage passengers to keep dealing with the airline and thereby improve the airline's chances for financial recovery?

5. *Honoring Prepetition Claims.* May a company in bankruptcy honor prepetition warranty claims or tickets to preserve good will as an asset of the estate? May the company honor these claims by treating them as transactions in the ordinary course of business, which a debtor-in-possession is generally entitled to conduct? See generally Note, Consumer Warranty Claims Against Companies in Chapter 11 Reorganizations, 14 U.Mich.J.L.Ref. 347 (1981).

6. *Section 724(b).* As of the date of the petition, debtor owes the following amounts:

   (1) $300 to wage earner for wages overdue by one month

   (2) $500 to First Secured Party (FSP)

(3) $100 to New York State (NYS), for back taxes

(4) $100 to Second Secured Party (SSP)

FSP, NYS, and SSP all have perfected interests in debtor's equipment, which is worth $750. Under state law, FSP is prior to NYS and SSP, and NYS is prior to SSP. If the equipment is the estate's only asset, what amount is each creditor entitled to? What if the equipment were worth $850? See § 724(b). The "simplicity" of § 724(b) makes obsolete some charming circular priority problems that existed under the old bankruptcy law.[b]

IN RE CALLISTER

United States Bankruptcy Court, District of Utah, 1981.
15 B.R. 521, affirmed 13 Bankr.Ct.Dec. 21 (10th Cir. 1984).

RALPH R. MABEY, BANKRUPTCY JUDGE.

FACTUAL AND PROCEDURAL BACKGROUND

This case raises issues concerning the superpriority provision of 11 U.S.C. Section 507(b).

Debtor, the sole proprietor of a trucking business, filed a petition under Chapter 11 on December 12, 1980. Ingersoll-Rand Financial Corporation (Rand), which holds a security interest in three tractors and two trailers, filed a complaint seeking relief from the automatic stay on January 2, 1981. A hearing was held January 23. At that time, the parties stipulated that the collateral was worth $129,000, that the debt owing was $106,248, and that debtor would pay $1,232 per month beginning February 1 to Rand. Debtor also agreed to insure the equipment as required in the security agreements. A procedure was established for lifting the stay in the event of default. The court ruled that Rand was adequately protected under this arrangement. Two payments were made, but debtor defaulted May 1, and the stay was lifted June 5. The case was converted to Chapter 7 on August 5.

Meanwhile, counsel for debtor filed an application for allowance and payment of fees in the amount of $9,052 under 11 U.S.C. Section 331. Counsel for the unsecured creditors committee likewise requested fees in the amount of $2,994. Rand objected, claiming that the fees might be allowed but not paid because it was entitled to a superpriority under 507(b).

Hearings were held August 18 and 19. The evidence showed that two of the three tractors underwent repair from January to June and therefore conferred no benefit on the estate. The third tractor was used for approximately three weeks but it caught fire and was de-

---

b. See In re American Zyloptic Co., 181 F.Supp. 77 (E.D.N.Y. 1960); In re Quaker City Uniform Co., 238 F.2d 155 (3d Cir. 1956), certiorari denied 352 U.S. 1030, 77 S.Ct. 595, 1 L.Ed.2d 599 (1957); 2 Gilmore, ch. 39.

stroyed. Through inadvertence, no insurance was in force to indemnify this casualty.[9] The trailers were used without mishap.

Debtor values the collateral, as of June 5, at $89,600. This is the value "as is" without repairs or payment of repair bills. In his view, with the exception of the burned tractor, minimal depreciation has occurred. The decline in value is attributable to the uninsured loss and depression in prices.

Rand values the collateral, as of the same time, and also "as is," at $63,900. In its view, substantial depreciation, independent of the accident, has taken place.

The court values the collateral as of June 5 at $68,900. Subtracting costs of repair in the amount of $7,097 leaves $61,803. Hence, the collateral has dwindled in worth by $67,197. At least four factors account for this decrease. The uninsured loss equals $19,411. Error in the stipulation is responsible for $33,447. Market forces caused a loss of $7,993. Use caused a loss of $6,346. Because of the error in the stipulation, the allowed secured claim on January 23 was $95,553, not $106,248. The allowed secured claim on June 5 was $61,803, for a reduction of $33,750.

These facts raise several issues which may be classified under the headings of statutory construction, allowance, and rank. Under statutory construction: May a creditor ineligible for an administrative claim under 11 U.S.C. Section 503(b) qualify for superpriority status under 507(b)? Under allowance: Are losses caused by failure to obtain insurance, an error in the stipulation, market forces, and depreciation recompensable under 507(b)? Under rank: Does the superpriority take precedence over interim fees under 331? Under what, if any, circumstances may fees be paid notwithstanding the existence of or potential for a superpriority? These questions are discussed below.

IS THE SUPERPRIORITY AN ADMINISTRATIVE EXPENSE OR SOMETHING MORE?

The superpriority provision is found in 507(b) which states:

If the trustee, under Section 362, 363, or 364 of this title, provides adequate protection of the interest of a holder of a claim secured by a lien on property of the debtor and if, notwithstanding such protection, such creditor has a claim allowable under subsection (a) (1) of this section arising from the stay of action against such property under Section 362 of this title, from the use, sale, or lease

9. Debtor was accustomed to buying fleet not single truck insurance. Bankruptcy, however, altered his course of dealing. His casualty insurance expired on January 26. His usual carrier, for reasons unclear in the record (but see the motion for turnover filed February 12), did not write a renewal. Faced with the stipula- tion and a need to change carriers, he contacted the Herbert Stockman Agency. There was a mis-understanding concerning the scope of coverage; debtor believed he had arranged for casualty insurance; the policy was written for liability insurance. Debtor learned of the mixup when he called to report his claim on the tractor.

of such property under Section 363 of this title, or from the granting of a lien under Section 364(d) of this title, then such creditor's claim under such subsection shall have priority over every other claim under such subsection.

11 U.S.C. Section 507(a)(1) gives priority to "expenses allowed under Section 503(b)" which include, in part, "the actual, necessary costs . . . of preserving the estate."

Debtor maintains that only creditors who have claims under 503(b) *and* who lose adequate protection may enjoy the benefit of 507(b). This view draws support from the face of 507(b) which speaks of "a claim allowable under subsection (a)(1) of this section" which in turn refers to 503(b). But 507(b), on closer analysis, is the proverbial prism in the fog. A review of its language, history, and relation to adequate protection, however, may elucidate its meaning.

The Language of 507(b)

The use of property for the estate creates an administrative claim under 503(b). Curbing repossession of property through the stay, without more, may not lead to the same result. Section 507(b), however, treats property used and property subject to the stay, implying that both, so long as they lose adequate protection, meet the standards of 503(b). Indeed, commentators appear to equate inadequate protection with allowability under 503(b). See, e.g., 3 Collier on Bankruptcy ¶ 507.05 at 507-46 (15th ed. 1980) ("In essence, [507(b)] affords a superpriority to post-petition creditors in whose case the protection given by the trustee is inadequate to protect the creditor's interest *thereby resulting in an administrative expense claim under Section 503(b)(1)(A)* ") (emphasis supplied). The facts, however, may belie this assumption. Here, for example, debtor needed the equipment, but circumstance, for the most part, kept it idle. If the equipment has not been an "actual, necessary cost . . . of preserving the estate," does it nevertheless qualify as a superpriority because its *use is implicit* in 507(b)? . . .

The parties seek a ruling that the superpriority must be allowed either as an administrative expense or as a guarantee of adequate protection. But neither approach is satisfactory. The statute is a confederation of principles; it cannot be "construed" to favor one at the expense of another; it should be interpreted to account for the merits of all. Hence, equitable considerations, arising from the facts of each case, should be examined. The rights and importance of other interests must be weighed. The manner in which adequate protection was provided and the role of the superpriority as a "backstop" should be considered.

PROBLEMS OF ALLOWANCE

The Uninsured Loss

Rand argues that adequate protection in the form of a stipulation to procure insurance was afforded; noncompliance resulted in the uninsured destruction of the tractor; therefore adequate protection failed and 507(b) comes into play.

True, the superpriority is born when adequate protection fails. But whether adequate protection has failed depends upon whether and how it has been provided. In this regard, Rand may misconceive the purpose of adequate protection which shelters creditors "from any impairment in value attributable to the stay. The stay does not cause, but it may forestall a creditor from preventing or mitigating a decline in value. Some harm to collateral however may be unavoidable with or without the stay. Likewise, creditors may acquiesce in some harm to collateral for business or other reasons notwithstanding the stay. In these situations and others which may arise, any impairment in value may not be attributable to the stay. Hence, not every decline in value must be recompensed, only those which, but for the stay, could be and probably would be prevented or mitigated." In re Alyucan Interstate Corp., supra at 1126.

The uninsured loss may not have been attributable to the stay for at least two reasons. First, the risk occasioned by the stay, and for which protection in the form of insurance was afforded, was that the tractor, before repossession, would be damaged. There was, however, another risk at work, *viz.*, the risk of inadvertently failing to obtain insurance. Protection against this risk was not and indeed could not have been afforded.

If this risk were allocated between debtor and Rand outside bankruptcy, naturally, it would be borne by debtor, who, as between the two innocent parties, was in a better position to prevent the inadvertence. But the risk must be allocated not only between debtor and Rand, but also between Rand and other administrative claimants. As between these parties, Rand was in a better position to prevent the mistake and therefore arguably it should suffer the loss.

Second, the loss which flowed not from the accident, but from the oversight, while unprotectible under 361, was preventable by Rand. The security agreements permit Rand, when the debtor does not obtain insurance, to pay the premium and charge the account. Under 11 U.S.C. Section 506(b), when the creditor is oversecured, this supplements the allowed secured claim, increasing the lien entitled to protection. Although the fact of reorganization invites more than ordinary diligence by creditors, Rand did not ascertain whether insurance was bought, nor did it exercise its right to default under the stipulation. Indeed, Rand, from one view, may have "acquiesced" in the harm to its collateral.

Nevertheless, deciding whether loss is attributable to the stay, using the abstraction of "cause," in this case, is speculative. The conflict between debtor, Rand, and administrative claimants may be overdrawn. The debtor is a debtor in possession, the fiduciary representative of the estate. The interest of administrative claimants is his stewardship. Even absent court order, this includes the procurement of insurance. A rule which might relax this duty, where possible, should be avoided. Cf. Reading Co. v. Brown, 391 U.S. 471, 483, 88 S.Ct. 1759, 1765, 20 L.Ed.2d 751 (1968). The assertion that the failure to insure was preventable while compelling under other circumstances, is not convincing on these facts. A degree of reliance upon stipulations is warranted, and Rand, with less than a month to act, did not sleep on its rights. These considerations mandate allowance of the uninsured loss as a superpriority. . . .

Market Forces

Both sides acknowledge the interposition of the market: several carriers have folded and are liquidating their equipment; newer models are more attractive to entrepreneurs. This combination of circumstances has lowered prices.

The property at stake and its susceptibility to market forces are factors to be considered in determining adequate protection. See, e.g., In re Alyucan Interstate Corp., supra 12 B.R. 803, 7 B.C.D., at 1125 ("[P]rotection may vary if the property is real or personal, tangible or intangible, perdurable or perishable, or if its value is constant, depreciating, or subject to sudden or extreme fluctuations"). Arguably, Rand should have accounted for these forces in negotiating the stipulated interim payments. But the collapse of freighters and the inauguration of products are not readily foreseeable. In this regard, Rand, like debtor, is at the mercy of events beyond its control. Rand did not speculate on the market at the expense of the estate; it was reasonably prompt in obtaining relief from the stay and mitigating damage. The loss resulting from market forces therefore "ought not equitably to be saddled on [Rand] but on [the estate] for whose supposed benefit the restraint was imposed." In re New York, New Haven & Hartford R. Co., 147 F.2d 40, 48 (2d Cir. 1945).

Depreciation Through Use

Since the trailers were used and useful to the estate, debtor, in principle, should not object to loss through depreciation as a superpriority. The question is how much loss. The stipulation provided for interim payments, which if paid, from February to May, would have totalled $4,928. Actual depreciation equalled $6,346. Should Rand receive the amount it bargained for in the stipulation or the amount of real loss? Equity recommends the former. Rand was not bereft in bankruptcy. It had the background and tools to insure that payments were commensurate with depreciation. Indeed, if it had calculated depreciation based upon the security agreements, the amount would have been $9,300. This figure, unlike the stipulated payments, approximates the real loss. The court is reluctant to penalize the estate for an error which could have been remedied by Rand. The depreciation allocable to superpriority is therefore $4,928 minus payments received in the amount of $2,464 or $2,464. . . .

PROBLEMS OF RANK

Rand argues that the superpriority has precedence over claims allowed under 503(b). Attorneys fees may be allowed under 503(b)(2). Thus no fees may be paid until the superpriority is satisfied. This argument is flawed, however, for several reasons.

Fees are allowed under 11 U.S.C. Section 330 and classified as administrative expenses under 503(b)(2). But while other administrative expenses must wait until confirmation, 11 U.S.C. Section 1129(a)(9), or liquidation, 11 U.S.C. Section 726, for reimbursement,[38] fees are payable on an interim and therefore a preeminent basis under 331. Not only the statutory scheme but also reasons of policy support this preeminence of fees under 331.

Lenders like Rand may be involuntarily harnessed to the ordeal of reorganization, but fee claimants voluntarily contribute to the ideal of rehabilitation. Section 331 encourages this volunteerism and, as an inducement to work for the estate, is a vital provision of the Reform Act which places the burden of administration upon trustees, creditor committees, and their professional representatives. Absent this incentive, it would be difficult to assure continued efficient management. See, e.g., 2 Collier on Bankruptcy, supra ¶ 331.02 at 331–5. Requests for adequate protection in Chapter 11 are ubiquitous; each raises the spectre of a superpriority. If the superpriority, in turn might preempt interim fees, it would jeopardize the further provision of services. The result would not be attractive. The administrators might mutiny: but the case, whether in Chapter 11 or in a superseding Chapter 7, would not care for itself. They might cut corners: but this would cause delay, which is anathema to creditors, especially those holding a superpriority who are waiting for confirmation or liquidation. They might demand exorbitant retainers at the beginning of each case: but for most debtors this either would be impossible or would decrease their chances for rehabilitation.

These dangers do not dictate that in every instance fees must be paid ahead of the superpriority. Section 331 says that fees "may" be paid on an interim basis. There is a presumption, for the reasons outlined above, that they will be paid notwithstanding the existence of a superpriority. This presumption may be strengthened, for example,

---

38. With the exception of 331, the Code is silent as to when administrative claims are payable. As a practical matter, and under the auspices of prior case law, the court may permit the payment of operating expenses as they are incurred in a reorganization.

where a trustee or his representative who is requesting fees was installed at the behest of a creditor entitled to a superpriority. Cf. In re Hotel Associates, Inc., 6 B.R. 108, 114 (Bkrtcy., E.D.Pa. 1980). But it is rebuttable under appropriate equitable circumstances. Cf. 2 Collier on Bankruptcy, supra ¶ 331.01 at 331–3 ("The genesis of interim compensation is rooted in the equity powers of the bankruptcy court"). These circumstances, however, are not present in this case.

It Is Therefore Ordered:

1.   Rand is allowed a superpriority in the amount of $29,868.

2.   Fees of counsel for debtor and the unsecured creditors committee which have been previously allowed shall be paid forthwith.

Notes & Questions

1. *The Opposite View.* In In re Flagstaff Foodservice Corp., 739 F.2d 73 (2d Cir.1984), debtor owed creditor $22 million on the date of the bankruptcy petition, a claim secured by assets worth $42 million. After the petition, the bankruptcy court authorized the debtor to borrow additional sums from the creditor, the loans to be secured by a superpriority interest in all present and future property of the estate. The bankruptcy court's order stated that all obligations to the creditor shall have priority over all debts or obligations, including all administrative expenses, of the kind specified in §§ 503(b) and 507(b) of the Bankruptcy Code. During the Chapter 11 proceedings the creditor advanced an additional $9 million to the debtor and there was not enough in the estate to pay off the $9 million. During the proceedings, the bankruptcy court awarded interim fees to attorneys and accountants representing the debtor and one of the creditors' committees. The court of appeals, rejecting *Callister,* found the interim fee awards to be in error. Referring to § 506(c), the court held that any fees payable from the secured creditor's collateral must be for services which were for the benefit of the secured creditor rather than the debtor or other creditors. The court did note that attorneys may secure a portion of their fee in advance.

Which approach to interim fees is preferable? Are there foreseeable adverse consequences to either *Callister* or *Flagstaff?*

2. *Adequate Protection.* Does *Callister* implicitly express a view on what it is that § 362 adequately protects? Is *Callister*'s treatment of the secured party at odds with *Radford,* Chapter 11A?

3. *Cause of Loss.* Consider *Callister*'s discussion of "cause." Suppose the loss of the uninsured tractor were attributable to an event that a "normal" insurance policy would not have covered. Would the secured party then lose its superpriority claim to the extent the collateral was reduced in value by the loss event? What would be the implications of such a holding?

4. *Debtor's Discretion.* Suppose a debtor that manufactures automobiles wishes to honor warranty claims. May it treat them as an

administrative expense entitled to priority? Does it matter whether the problems giving rise to the warranty claims arose before or after the filing of the bankruptcy petition?

2. Equitable Subordination

TAYLOR v. STANDARD GAS & ELECTRIC CO.

Supreme Court of the United States, 1939.
306 U.S. 307, 59 S.Ct. 543, 83 L.Ed. 669.

MR. JUSTICE ROBERTS delivered the opinion of the Court.

The question presented is whether the District Court abused its discretion in approving the compromise of a claim by a parent against a subsidiary corporation and a plan of reorganization based upon the compromise, in proceedings under § 77B of the Bankruptcy Act. The Circuit Court of Appeals, by a divided court, approved the District Court's order.

The petitioners are a committee for the protection of preferred stockholders. The respondents are the trustee of the debtor, Deep Rock Oil Corporation (a Delaware corporation whose business was that of producing, refining, and selling gasoline, oil, and other petroleum products from lands located in Oklahoma, Kansas, Texas, and Arkansas), a reorganization committee, representing noteholders and certain holders of preferred stock, and Standard Gas and Electric Company, which owns practically all of the common stock of the debtor, claiming as a creditor.

The debtor was organized in 1919 to take over the properties then being operated by one C. B. Shaffer. Standard Gas & Electric Company, hereinafter called Standard, then had investments in various utility properties but had never been interested in oil. Byllesby & Company, hereinafter called Byllesby, an investment banking corporation which controlled Standard, entered into a contract with Shaffer whereby he was to organize the debtor corporation and to be paid by that corporation for his properties $15,580,000 made up of cash, a note, and preferred and common stock of the company. . . .

. . . From its organization Deep Rock was, most of the time, "two jumps ahead of the wolf," as one of Standard's officers testified. The common stock went into a voting trust which gave Standard and Shaffer equal control. Shaffer undertook the management of the properties and business. After two years Standard became dissatisfied with Shaffer's management and he severed his connection with the company selling his common stock to Standard and surrendering to Deep Rock 50,000 shares of preferred stock which was cancelled.

Thenceforward the debtor was under the complete control and domination of Standard through ownership of the common stock. Standard's officers, directors, and agents always constituted a majority of the Board. . . . All of the fiscal affairs of the debtor were wholly controlled by Standard, which was its banker and its only source of financial aid.

Deep Rock was placed in the hands of a receiver in March 1933 and the present proceeding under § 77B of the Bankruptcy Act was instituted in June 1934. Standard filed a claim as a creditor in the receivership and in the bankruptcy proceedings, which the receivers and the trustee resisted. The claim was referred to a master, before whom trial lasted many months. All the witnesses were officers, directors or agents of Standard, or its affiliates, and officers of the debtor. All the documentary evidence came from the books and records of Standard and Deep Rock. The basis of claim was an open account which embraced transactions between Standard and Deep Rock from the latter's organization in 1919 to the receivership in 1933. The account consists of thousands of items of debit and credit. . . .

The account contains debits to Deep Rock in excess of $52,000,000 and credits of approximately $43,000,000 leaving a balance shown to be due Standard of $9,342,642.37, which was the amount of the claim presented. Cash payments by Standard to Deep Rock, or to others for its account, as shown by the books, total $31,804,145.04. Management and supervision fees paid or credited to Management Corporation amount to $1,219,034.83. Interest charges by Standard to Deep Rock on open account balances total $4,819,222.07. Rental charges upon a lease to Deep Rock of oil properties owned by a Standard subsidiary but claimed by petitioners to belong, in equity, to Deep Rock, amount to $4,525,000. Debits by Standard to Deep Rock of the amounts of dividends declared by Deep Rock to Standard, but not paid, reached the sum of $3,502,653. In addition there are hundreds of debits and credits representing other intercompany items.

Two preferred stockholders were permitted to intervene in the proceedings and they joined in the trustee's objections to the claim. Many transactions entered in the account were attacked as fraudulent and it was asserted that as Standard had made Deep Rock its mere agent or instrumentality it could not transmit itself from the status of the proprietor of Deep Rock's business to that of creditor. The hearings before the master were closed, but before he made any report, and as a result of negotiations initiated by the reorganization committee organized at the instance of Byllesby, representing approximately eighty-two per cent. of the noteholders and sixty per cent. of the preferred stockholders of Deep Rock, Standard proposed a compromise of its claim. . . .

Months later the reorganization committee presented an amended plan which, as modified by the Court, contemplated the compromise of Standard's claim at $5,000,000, as before, and the organization of a new company which should issue $10,000,000 par value of debentures and 520,000 shares of common stock. These securities were to be distributed as follows: The new issue of debentures was to go to the holders of the old notes. In lieu of interest on the old notes accumulated to

January 1, 1937, totaling $2,300,000, the noteholders were to receive $1,200,000 in cash and 40,000 shares of common stock; interest accruing subsequent to January 1, 1937, was to be paid in cash. The old preferred stockholders were to receive 100,000 shares of common stock and Standard was to receive for its claim 380,000 shares of common stock. Thus there was allocated to Standard approximately seventy-three per cent., to the old preferred stockholders nineteen per cent., and to the noteholders eight per cent. of the common stock. . . .

The petitioners insist that the appraisal upon which the plan was based was inordinately low and that, for this reason alone, the plan should not have been approved. The appraisal was supported by substantial evidence and the values shown by it were approved and adopted by the District Court and by the Circuit Court of Appeals. We accept the concurrent findings of the two courts that the value of the debtor's assets does not exceed $17,000,000.

As the debentures to be issued to the noteholders, plus the cash they are to get, total $11,200,000, the equity remaining in the property is not over $5,800,000. Standard's share of this equity will be seventy-three per cent., or $4,234,000, and will give it complete control of the new company. The preferred stockholders will receive nineteen per cent. or $1,020,000,—a minority interest without representation on the board of directors. The question is whether, within the bounds of reason and fairness, such a plan can be justified. We think the history of Standard's dealings with Deep Rock requires a negative answer.

Without going into the minutiae of the transactions between the two companies, enough may be stated to expose the reasons for our decision. As has been stated, Standard came into complete control of Deep Rock in 1921. From the outset Deep Rock was insufficiently capitalized, was topheavy with debt and was in parlous financial condition. Standard so managed its affairs as always to have a stranglehold upon it.

At organization Deep Rock had cash working capital of only about $6,600,000 and a mortgage indebtedness of $12,000,000, the interest and sinking fund requirements of which were nearly $2,000,000 a year. . . . So inadequate was Deep Rock's capitalization that, in the period from organization to 1926, the balance due on open account to Standard grew to more than $14,800,000. Standard determined to place some of this indebtedness of Deep Rock with the public. In order to do so it had to improve Deep Rock's balance sheet. This it did by purchasing 80,000 shares of preferred stock for which it credited Deep Rock $7,223,333.33. It then bought $7,500,000 face value two year six per cent. notes for $7,273,750, which were sold to the public through a syndicate organized by Byllesby. Deep Rock's requirements of additional capital persisted and, by the spring of 1928, the open account and a note which Deep Rock had given Standard for advances totaled over $11,000,000. As the two-year notes held by the public were maturing, Standard found it necessary to make a new offering. There still remained nearly $2,000,000 of first mortgage bonds outstanding which had to be retired to make an unsecured note issue salable. Standard, therefore, determined that Deep Rock's balance sheet must again be put in such shape that notes could be sold. It accordingly purchased common stock from Deep Rock to the amount of the then open balance and commuted 90,000 shares of the preferred stock, which it held, into common. It caused Deep Rock to issue $10,000,000 of six per cent. notes which were sold by a syndicate organized by Byllesby and applied the proceeds to the redemption of the two-year notes and the outstanding mortgage bonds. This financing, however, merely changed the character of Deep Rock's funded indebtedness and gave it no new working capital. This $10,000,000 note issue is the one now outstanding. As before, Deep Rock's resources were wholly insufficient for its business and the open account began again to build up so that between February 1928 and February 1933, the date of receivership, the account had grown to $9,342,642.37.

No dividends were paid on preferred stock until 1926. In that and the following year existing arrearages were paid by Standard, for Deep Rock's account, in the amount of $1,435,813. Between 1928 and 1931 Standard advanced Deep Rock, for payment of preferred dividends, $1,106,706.

During the period between 1926 and 1929 Deep Rock declared dividends on its common stock in a total of $3,064,685.50. Of these dividends $1,946,672 was charged by Standard, as owner of common stock, against Deep Rock in the open account. Standard took new common stock for dividends to the amount of $1,015,437.50 and advanced Deep Rock cash to pay dividends to outside holders of common stock in the sum of $102,576. Against the total of $2,645,095 advanced by Standard to pay Deep Rock's dividends, Standard credited payments received from Deep Rock in the open account in the sum of $927,500.

These dividends were declared in the face of the fact that Deep Rock had not the cash available to pay them and was, at the time, borrowing in large amounts from or through Standard. . . .

During the whole period from 1919 to the receivership, Standard charged Deep Rock interest at the rate of seven per cent. per annum compounded monthly on the balance shown by the open account. During the entire period the Management Corporation charged Deep Rock with round annual sums for management and supervision of Deep Rock's affairs which totaled $1,219,034.83, all of which Standard assumed and charged into the open account.

It is impossible within the compass of this opinion to detail the numerous other transactions evidenced by the books of the two companies many of which were to the benefit of Standard and to the detriment of Deep Rock. All of them were accomplished through the complete control and domination of Standard and without the participation of the preferred stockholders who had no voice or vote in the management of Deep Rock's affairs. . . .

Petitioners invoke the so-called instrumentality rule,—under which, they say, Deep Rock is to be regarded as a department or agent of Standard,—to preclude the allowance of Standard's claim in any amount. The rule was much discussed in the opinion below. It is not, properly speaking, a rule, but a convenient way of designating the application in particular circumstances of the broader equitable principle that the doctrine of corporate entity, recognized generally and for most purposes, will not be regarded when so to do would work fraud or injustice. This principle has been applied in appropriate circumstances to give minority stockholders redress against wrongful injury to their interests by a majority stockholder. It must be apparent that the preferred stockholders of Deep Rock assert such injury by Standard as the basis of their attack on the decree below. We need not stop to discuss the remedy which would be available to them if § 77B of the Bankruptcy Act had not been adopted for we think that, by that section, the court, in approving a plan, was authorized and required, as a court of equity, to recognize the rights and the status of the preferred stockholders arising out of Standard's wrongful and injurious conduct in the mismanagement of Deep Rock's affairs.

. . . In the present case there remains an equity after satisfaction of the creditors in which only the preferred stockholders and Standard can have an interest. Equity requires the award to preferred stockholders of a superior position in the reorganized company. The District Judge, we think, properly exercised his discretion in refusing to approve the first offer of compromise and concomitant plan because it partly subordinated preferred stockholders to Standard. The same considerations which moved him to reject that plan required the rejection of the new offer and the amended plan.

Deep Rock finds itself bankrupt not only because of the enormous sums it owes Standard but because of the abuses in management due to the paramount interest of interlocking officers and directors in the preservation of Standard's position, as at once proprietor and creditor of Deep Rock. It is impossible to recast Deep Rock's history and experience so as even to approximate what would be its financial condition at this day had it been adequately capitalized and independently managed and had its fiscal affairs been conducted with an eye single to its own interests. In order to remain in undisturbed possession and to prevent the preferred stockholders having a vote and a voice in the management, Standard has caused Deep Rock to pay preferred dividends in large amounts. Whatever may be the fact as to the legality of such dividends judged by the balance sheets and earnings statements of Deep Rock, it is evident that they would not have been paid over a long course of years by a company on the precipice of bankruptcy and in dire need of cash working capital. This is only one of the aspects in which Standard's management and control has operated to the detriment of Deep Rock's financial condition and ability to function. Others are apparent from what has been said and from a study of the record.

If a reorganization is effected the amount at which Standard's claim is allowed is not important if it is to be represented by stock in the new company, provided the stock to be awarded it is subordinated to that awarded preferred stockholders. No plan ought to be approved which does not accord the preferred stockholders a right of participation in the equity in the Company's assets prior to that of Standard, and at least equal voice with Standard in the management. Anything less would be to remand them to precisely the status which has inflicted serious detriment on them in the past.

Reversed.

COMSTOCK v. GROUP OF INSTITUTIONAL INVESTORS

Supreme Court of the United States, 1948.
335 U.S. 211, 68 S.Ct. 1454, 92 L.Ed. 1911.

MR. JUSTICE JACKSON delivered the opinion of the Court.

Since 1933 the Missouri Pacific, the New Orleans, Texas and Mexico Railway Co. and a number of affiliated railroad corporations have been in reorganization under the Bankruptcy Act, 11 USCA § 205, 3 FCA title 11, § 205. A second plan of reorganization, approved by the Interstate Commerce Commission, was before the District Court for the Eastern District of Missouri. Comstock then, in 1944, made objection to allowance of a claim of approximately 10 million dollars by the Missouri Pacific, one debtor corporation, against another, the New Orleans, which, during the 10 years of proceedings, had been unchallenged. The issues raised by his objection were severed from other problems of reorganization which do not concern us here. . . .

"The objector prayed that the Missouri Pacific claim for $10,565,227 and interest against the New Orleans be disallowed; that it be determined that the New Orleans was not indebted to the Missouri Pacific, and in the alternative, that all claims of the Missouri Pacific against the New Orleans be subordinated in the reorganization to the New Orleans capital stock interest."

Special emphasis has been placed on the fact that under control of the Missouri Pacific dividends were paid by the subsidiary at a time when it was borrowing money represented by this claim. It is clear from the findings that the dividends were paid out of current earnings or surplus, and not in violation of law or contract. Only in 1929 did New Orleans earn currently sufficient to pay its dividends. Nevertheless in all three years there was sufficient earned surplus legally to permit dividends. Heavy investments in improvements may require borrowings for dividends; but no law or public policy requires a corporation to finance capital additions out of earnings or to pass dividends because of low current earnings when past earnings are available for dividend purposes. These past earnings may be used to compensate the capital that produced them, and capital additions may be made from funds borrowed or raised by issues of capital securities, so long as the authorizations required in the case of railroads are obtained. No question is raised as to the authority to borrow.

While the contemporaneous borrowing to pay for capital additions, and payment of dividends, is not in itself illegal, it would, of course, come under the ban of the *Taylor* decision if it were carried out in breach of good faith for the advantage of the holding company to the detriment of the subsidiary. But the findings of good faith, fair dealing and freedom from fraud or overreaching cover the dividend policy as well as other questioned transactions. Such being the facts, the allowance of the claim is not error of law.

The findings here do not stop with holding that the questioned transactions were intended to and did benefit the system as a whole. An overall benefit to the system might be attained at the injury of one of its units and the security holders of that unit. But here the finding of good faith and of benefit applies to the New Orleans and its security holders as well as to the system generally. The finding is unequivocal that the control of Missouri Pacific not only was "in good faith and with due regard to its obligations, legal and equitable, to the New Orleans and its security holders," but also that its control of the Gulf Coast Lines "was beneficial and advantageous to the New Orleans and the holders and pledgees of its securities." The criticised transactions are thus not only exonerated of evil or illegal intent but are also established as beneficial rather than injurious to the interests which now challenge them. The findings to that effect are entitled to special weight where, as here, they are based on the District Judge's complete familiarity with the case. Affirmed by the Circuit Court of Appeals, they are, under the rule concerning concurrent findings, and on the basis of our grant of certiorari, conclusive in this Court.

Disallowance of petitioner's objections on such findings was not error of law. . . .

MR. JUSTICE MURPHY, with whom MR. JUSTICE BLACK, MR. JUSTICE DOUGLAS and MR. JUSTICE RUTLEDGE agree, dissenting. . . .

Comstock's objection No. 19, which is our sole concern, related to the validity and priority of a $10,565,226.78 claim filed by the Missouri Pacific (hereinafter called MOP) against its subsidiary New Orleans, Texas and Mexico Railway Co. (hereinafter called NOTM) in the joint reorganization proceedings. It appears that MOP had acquired the controlling interest in NOTM's common stock in 1924 and had completely dominated and controlled NOTM until the reorganization proceedings began in 1933. MOP's claim against NOTM was based upon "cash advances for operation, interest payments, etc., at various times from March, 1929, to February, 1933, both inclusive." Most of the NOTM stock which MOP held was pledged as security for the class of MOP 5¼% secured bonds which Comstock owned, the pledge constituting 82% of the outstanding shares of NOTM's sole class of stock. MOP sought to put its claim against NOTM ahead of the claims of the holders of these MOP bonds who looked to the NOTM common stock for security.   The revised plan of reorganization gave effect to MOP's desire in this respect.   . . .

III.

The District Court found that during the period from March, 1929, to February, 1933, MOP advanced to NOTM the net sum, after deducting principal payments, of $10,565,226.78—which constitutes the claim in issue.   Included in these advances was the greater portion of the $2,795,000 loaned to NOTM between November 30, 1928, and November 27, 1931, to make additions and improvements to the railroad properties of NOTM and other related subsidiaries.   But each time one of these advances was made, there was an almost simultaneous payment of a dividend by NOTM on its stock, which was largely owned by MOP.   . . .

It is said, however, that MOP's   . . .   action in making these loans and receiving back the dividends followed a natural pattern of a company devoted to improving the properties of its subsidiaries, there being merely a "near coincidence as to the dates of certain dividends and advances."   Reference is made in this respect to the relationship which MOP bears to the various companies in the Gulf Coast Lines system (hereinafter called GCL).   In 1924, MOP acquired a controlling interest in NOTM and thereby inherited complete control of the GCL system, the rail lines of which are interlaced with others in the MOP system.   NOTM at all times has been primarily a holding company owning all the stocks and bonds of the fourteen subsidiary companies constituting the GCL group, NOTM itself operating only about 11% of the total GCL mileage.   Of the GCL operating companies, the St. Louis, Brownsville and Mexico Railway Co. (hereinafter called Brownsville) is the most important, operating about one-third of the GCL mileage and contributing from 61% to 84% of the group's income during the period in question.   NOTM is the only one of the GCL group which has securities outstanding in the hands of the public.

According to the District Court findings, MOP's policy in advancing the $2,795,000 to NOTM was to reimburse NOTM's treasury for additions and betterments to the properties of the GCL system.   NOTM acted as banker for that system.   The GCL subsidiaries were not in a position from 1925 to 1930 to finance their own improvements except out of earnings and by borrowing from NOTM.   Most of their freight revenues were cleared through NOTM; as these items were received by NOTM, they were credited against the obligations created by the loans from NOTM to the subsidiaries.   But since the total requirements of the subsidiaries for operating expenses, dividends and improvements were in excess of the receipts, the unpaid accounts mounted.   Finally MOP had to begin loaning money to NOTM to cover these accounts.   It is in this way that MOP's advances are said to have been directed toward the improvement program of the GCL system.

It is vigorously denied that these MOP advances were in any way used to pay for the almost simultaneous dividends from NOTM to MOP, such a contention being termed "superficial" and contrary to "basic principles of accounting." In support of that denial, an illustration is used. Assume that NOTM receives $200,000 cash from net earnings on January 31, when it is known that this amount will be needed to pay a bill for a new freight yard for a subsidiary. NOTM also knows that on April 1 a $100,000 cash dividend to MOP will be due. Instead of borrowing to pay for the new freight yard, NOTM uses the $200,000 cash for that purpose. Then, three days prior to the dividend date, NOTM borrows $100,000 from MOP to reimburse the NOTM treasury in part for the investment in the new freight yard. This saves NOTM about two months' interest on $100,000 of the money spent for the freight yard. The fact that a $100,000 cash dividend is paid three days after the $100,000 loan is thought to be a mere coincidence, the dividend and the loan having no connection.

But in this illustration it is obvious that NOTM has insufficient cash to finance both the $200,000 freight yard and the $100,000 dividend. It has to borrow money for one purpose or the other. But to say that it here borrows $100,000 to help pay for the freight yard is unrealistic. NOTM has enough cash to pay for the freight yard and it uses the cash just for that purpose. Two months later it has the choice of (1) borrowing $100,000 and paying the dividend, or (2) not borrowing the money and not paying the dividend. It chooses the former course of action. By such action, NOTM has borrowed money to pay a dividend.

The foregoing illustration indicates what the record in this case amply demonstrates—namely, that the MOP advances found by the District Court to have been for the payment of GCL improvements were in reality advances for the payment of dividends by NOTM, dividends which for the most part went to MOP. Considered as a separate entity, NOTM rarely had enough income from the time MOP acquired control in 1924 to the start of reorganization in 1933 to pay the regular dividends; loans were essential if MOP was to continue to receive its share of these dividends.

Year	Net income	Dividends
1925	$839,679.00	$1,038,198
1926	1,393,806.58	1,038,198
1927	937,098.90	1,038,198
1928	742,058.00	1,038,198
1929	1,153,257.54	1,038,198
1930	854,139.71	1,038,198
1931	*399,487.80	1,038,198
1932	(−951,607.76)	None

* After deduction of $3,155,000 for that portion of the dividends on Brownsville stock held by NOTM which was unpaid in 1931. . . .

The consolidated picture of NOTM and its GCL subsidiaries was equally indicative of the lack of an ability to pay dividends to MOP without borrowing.

Year		Net income	Dividends
1925	....	$2,547,633	$1,038,198
1926	....	1,783,278	1,038,198
1927	....	(−202,438)	1,038,198
1928	....	956,433	1,038,198
1929	....	845,064	1,038,198
1930	....	674,950	1,038,198
1931	....	(−1,122,422)	1,038,198

Care was taken, however, to avoid the appearance of borrowing from MOP to pay dividends to MOP, a practice of doubtful legality. Whenever it was found that NOTM had inadequate income to meet a prospective dividend payment, MOP officers would direct Brownsville, NOTM's principal subsidiary, to take steps to declare a dividend on its stock, all of which was held by NOTM. Usually this dividend was the precise amount by which NOTM lacked money to pay its own dividend. But Brownsville invariably was unable to make a cash payment of its dividends to NOTM and many of its pre-1931 dividend declarations were considered collected by NOTM only at the expense of leaving unpaid Brownsville's debts to NOTM for essential supplies. These paper dividend declarations were capped in 1931 when Brownsville was ordered to declare dividends to NOTM of $4,155,000; in that year Brownsville earned but $398,000. The Bureau of Accounts of the Interstate Commerce Commission in 1936 informed NOTM that these 1931 dividends were declared at a time when NOTM was aware that Brownsville "was without funds to pay it, and even on the basis of past experience the earnings of the company, had business continued good, would not have been adequate to make the payment until some future date." This fact rendered the dividends improper under Commission rules. And while it was too late to correct the income accounts of NOTM which had already been closed, NOTM was directed to write off the unpaid portion of the 1931 dividends (some $1,400,000) through profit and loss.

This 1931 incident grew out of the fact that NOTM was operating that year at a great loss. It began that year with a profit-and-loss balance of only $709,000 and operated at a loss of $606,000. It also had to charge off $875,000 to correct its former inadequate depreciation accruals. By the end of 1931, NOTM would have shown a debit profit-and-loss balance of $772,000 or more. MOP, of course, was demanding payment of the usual $1,038,000 dividend for the year. "The problem was solved as it had been solved in previous years—by milking the Brownsville. But this time the milking would have to be thorough. . . . The solution found was to cause the Brownsville to declare an extraordinary dividend of $3,500,000—a dividend seven times the par value of the stock upon which it was declared. Other Brownsville dividends to the N. O. T. & M. brought the total for the year to $4,155,000, enough to fill up the N. O. T. M.'s profit-and-loss deficit and to enable the latter to declare a $1,038,000 dividend in favor chiefly of the Missouri Pacific." S.Rep.No. 25, Part 9, 76th Cong. 3d Sess. p. 10.

Thus the Brownsville dividend declarations gave NOTM earned surpluses on paper without giving it any cash with which to pay its dividends to MOP. Dividends declared by Brownsville were entered as income to NOTM even though they were not paid. An ostensible legal basis was thereby established for a declaration of dividends to MOP. NOTM would then borrow money from MOP to pay for those dividends. This again was largely a paper transaction. The earned surplus upon which the Court today places great reliance in affirming the District Court's findings was but a figment of the MOP imagination. . . .

By advancing to NOTM $2,795,000, MOP received back $2,654,000 in dividends within a few days after the various loans, making a total net advance of $141,000. MOP's cash position was unaffected by these various transactions, the NOTM dividends merely giving it a paper profit and loss balance out of which to declare its own dividends. Hence MOP, like NOTM, was forced to borrow money; it did so from outside sources. Yet MOP now seeks to claim nearly all of the $2,795,000 plus interest, an aggregate of about $4,795,000, for engaging in these bookkeeping transactions and for extending credit to the extent of $141,000.

NOTM's fiscal affairs in this respect have certainly not "been conducted with an eye single to its own interests" within the meaning of the Deep Rock doctrine. . . . Compelling a subsidiary to pay dividends under these circumstances is the type of mismanagement by a parent which leads to the subordination of the resulting indebtedness. . . .

Notes & Questions

1. *The Statute.* See § 510(c). Does the type of equitable subordination ordered in *Standard Gas & Electric* (subordination of debt to preferred stockholders' interests) survive enactment of the Bankruptcy Act?

2. *Dealings With Affiliated Corporations.* What duty does or should a parent owe to a subsidiary and the creditors of that subsidiary? What expectations should creditors have in dealing with affiliated corporate groups? Should mere unequal benefit taint intercorporate transfers? With respect to these questions, is *Comstock* consistent with *Standard Gas & Electric?*

If state law does not contain a doctrine of equitable subordination, should bankruptcy law?

3. *Relationship to Fraudulent Conveyance Law.* If corporate parents or individual shareholders misuse controlled corporate entities, are the abusive transactions subject to attack under state fraudulent con-

veyance law (and, in bankruptcy, under § 548 as well)? Consider the following:

> A . . . likely explanation of equitable subordination appears when one lifts the assumption about simple transactions. In fact, many of the equitable subordination cases—Pepper v. Litton is the classic example—involved an incredibly complex series of controlling party transfers and other transactions. It would be extremely difficult and costly, if not impossible, to attempt to analyze separately each step in the series, to assess all the evidence relating thereto, to make numerous separate findings as to insolvency and fairness of consideration, and to draw conclusions as to the proper amount of recovery at each step under the apparently exacting tests of the UFCA. Though fraudulent conveyance law conceivably could be broadened to sanction a gestalt approach comparable to the step transactions doctrine in tax law, rather than to require a transaction-by-transaction analysis and legal conclusion in all cases, it has seemed less violent to tradition to invoke a more obviously amorphous doctrine to which the label "equitable" is attached.

Clark, The Duties of the Corporate Debtor to Its Creditors, 90 Harv.L. Rev. 505, 530–31 (1977). Are the special opportunities for abuse by insiders now adequately covered by the special preference rules for insiders contained in § 547 (studied in Chapter 14)? If the complexity of tracing particular transactions justifies equitable subordination, should the doctrine apply in all cases, whether or not abusive behavior can be isolated?

How would a fraudulent conveyance attack have fared in *Standard Gas & Electric* and *Comstock?* Are there gaps in fraudulent conveyance law that one may view the doctrine of equitable subordination as filling?

4. *Remedies.* If equitable subordination is an appropriate adjunct to basic fraudulent conveyance doctrine, is subordinating the creditor's claim the appropriate remedy? What other remedies are possible? Consider the following:

> [T]he three [possible plausible interpretations of equitable subordination doctrine] will be labelled the Full Subordination Rule, the Offset Rule, and the Constructive Distribution Rule. Under the Full Subordination Rule, invocation of the doctrine automatically and invariably implies full subordination of all creditor claims of the controlling party, and nothing else. As a result, the insider may in some cases be penalized in an amount greater than the unjust advantage he reaped from his controlling position. The second and third interpretations are supposed to be corrective but not punitive—the controlling party is subordinated only to the extent of the unfair advantage taken of the corporation. Under the Offset Rule, the nonpunitive objective is construed to mean that the amount of the unjust benefit will be deducted from the insider's legitimate creditor claim and then the estate will be distributed pro rata.

Finally, under the Constructive Distribution Rule the pro rata
shares would be computed as if the tainted transaction had not
occurred and the controlling party is then considered to have already received an anticipatory distribution in the amount of his
unjust benefit.

Clark, supra, at 519–20. Which remedial rule is the most appropriate?

5. *Consolidation.* When the affairs of two corporate entities are
inextricably intertwined, courts may order consolidation of their bankruptcy proceedings, which effectively treats the corporations as a single
entity with common creditors. See generally Note, Substantive Consolidation in Bankruptcy: A Flow of Assets Approach, 65 Calif.L.Rev. 720
(1977). What standards should govern substantive consolidation?
What is the relationship among consolidation, equitable subordination,
and fraudulent conveyance doctrine?

6. *Piercing the Corporate Veil in Bankruptcy.* Given the holding in
favor of equitable subordination in *Standard Gas & Electric,* should
Deep Rock's creditors push one step farther and seek to impose liability
upon Deep Rock's corporate parent for debts incurred by Deep Rock?
When will nonbankruptcy law allow corporate veils to be pierced?
Should a bankruptcy court allow piercing whenever a state court would
as a matter of state corporate law? May a bankruptcy court pierce a
corporate veil selectively, reaching a shareholder or corporate parent
for some creditors but not for all creditors? Does anything in the
Bankruptcy Act authorize imposing liability upon an entity other than
the bankrupt? See generally Long v. McGlon, 263 F.Supp. 96
(D.S.C.1967) (relying on § 70c, now § 544(a), to impose liability on
individual shareholders); Henderson v. Rounds & Porter Lumber Co.,
99 F.Supp. 376 (W.D.Ark.1951) (relying in part on state court decision
finding that bankrupt's corporate parent was liable to bankrupt's
creditors).

Proposals for Automatic Subordination of Affiliate Claims

Section 4–406 of the bankruptcy law recommended by the Commission on the Bankruptcy Laws of the United States read in part as
follows:

(a) *Subordinated Classes of Claims.* The following claims are
subordinated in payment to all other nonsubordinated but allowable
claims:

. . .

(2) any claim, whether secured or unsecured, of any principal
officer, director, or affiliate of a debtor, or of any member of the
immediate family of such officer, director, or affiliate . . ..

In effect, the provision would have subordinated the claims of parents
against subsidiaries to all other claims against subsidiaries. Professor

Landers supported such a proposal and Professor (now Judge) Posner disapproved of it. This led to the following exchange: [c]

Professor Landers: Rarely, if ever, does a court question the major premise of the subordination doctrine that, absent one or more . . . subordinating factors, the claims of parent and affiliated corporations must be allowed to compete with claims of outside creditors for the assets of the bankrupt. The premise is vulnerable to two separate attacks. First, since the owners of the enterprise are concerned with maximizing return on their investment commensurate with the desired risk, any loan to the subsidiary or affiliate must be designed to maximize overall profits and thus is inherently more like risk capital than ordinary debt. Given that it is essentially risk capital, the "debt" owed to the related corporation should not be permitted to share *pari passu* with the true debts owed to other creditors. Second, since the enterprise owner is concerned with maximizing return on his entire investment, decisions regarding the operation of the subsidiary or affiliate will be made with that goal in mind—not with a view to ensuring that the subsidiary will function as a viable corporate entity. . . . [T]he economic reality of the situation gives rise to a presumption that the parent has not used its control in the best interests of the subsidiary. To ensure that creditors are treated fairly, the claim of the parent of affiliate must be subordinated.

Professor Posner: In effect, Landers is proposing that the only kind of investment that a corporation may make in an affiliated corporation is an equity investment. This is . . . objectionable as undermining the overall efficiency of the investment process. Parent corporations are sometimes the most efficient lenders to their affiliates because the enterprise relationship may enable the parent to evaluate the risk of a default at a lower cost than an outsider would have to incur. A rule that placed heavier liabilities on a parent lender than on an outside lender might thus distort the comparative advantages of these two sources of credit.

The proposed rule is a dubious one even from the excessively narrow standpoint of protecting creditors of the affiliate receiving the loan. The parent may extend credit to its subsidiary on terms more advantageous to the latter than an independent creditor would offer because the parent fears that its own creditworthiness would suffer if the subsidiary becomes insolvent. The availability of loans thus reduces the risk that the subsidiary will in fact default. If the parent is not allowed to make a "real" loan to a subsidiary—if in effect the only permitted method of rescue is a contribution of equity capital—the added risks of this method of rescue may deter the

c. Landers, A Unified Approach to Parent, Subsidiary, and Affiliate Questions in Bankruptcy, 42 U.Chi.L.Rev. 589, 598–99 (1976); Posner, The Rights of Creditors of Affiliated Corporations, 43 U.Chi.L.Rev. 499, 518, 523–24 (1976); Landers, Another Word on Parents, Subsidiaries and Affiliates in Bankruptcy, 43 U.Chi.L.Rev. 527, 536–38 (1976).

parent from trying to salvage the subsidiary. If so, the creditors of the subsidiary will be hurt. There is, to be sure, another side to the coin. The parent may make the loan merely to conceal the subsidiary's precarious state and thereby attract new creditors who, but for the loan, would have been warned away by slow payment or other symptoms of financial distress that the loan may mask. But this possibility indicates only that parent-subsidiary lending is susceptible of abuse, and not that creditors in general would be benefited by a rule of automatic subordination of the parent's loan to the rights of independent creditors.

. . . Although a rule of automatic subordination would be inappropriate, a creditor should be permitted to show that the parent's loan misled him regarding the amount of the assets the corporation had available for repayment of his loan. He may have reasonably believed that the corporation had the usual equity capitalization for a corporation of its size and line of business. If these reasonable expectations were defeated because the parent supplied capital to the corporation in the form of a loan rather than equity, the parent should be estopped to deny that the loan is actually part of the subsidiary's equity capital. . . .

In all cases in which estoppel is successfully invoked some competing group of creditors [in this case creditors of the parent who relied on the debt owed by the subsidiary as an asset] will be disadvantaged whose expectations may have been just as reasonable as those of the creditors invoking estoppel. But to the extent that enforcing the estoppel or misrepresentation principle will discourage borrowers from using the corporate form to mislead creditors, creditors in general will benefit—as will society since the costs of credit transactions will be lower, and hence interest rates will be lower for any given level of risk.

Professor Landers: Professor Posner . . . suggests that the parent is sometimes the most efficient lender because of its lower information costs. This argument cannot be taken seriously. In fact, virtually all the cases involve loans or advances that an outside lender would not make at all or, at least, would not make on equally favorable terms. A better explanation is that the parent has an additional incentive to make the loan insofar as it seeks to preserve its investment in the subsidiary. . . . Advances from the parent sometimes benefit existing creditors by infusing new resources and staving off bankruptcy. But such advances obviously harm subsequent creditors, who would otherwise never have become creditors, and often harm existing creditors, for whom a postponed bankruptcy may mean a lower realization. . . .

Professor Posner's test, by requiring voluntary creditors seeking subordination to show either that their information costs were too high or that they were misled, would require individualized proof by each creditor of facts unique to its transactions. While Professor

Posner does suggest treating groups of creditors as a class, misrepresentation is not the kind of claim that lends itself readily to class adjudication. Indeed, the pressures of class adjudication have been largely responsible for the elimination of the need to prove reliance in securities fraud class actions. Insofar as other creditors are concerned, the duty to investigate will presumably vary in part according to the amount of the transaction and the creditor's prior dealings with the bankrupt. Professor Posner proposes no effective mechanism for proving such matters.

    . . . As a practical matter, Professor Posner's proposal would deter all but the largest creditors from seeking subordination because of disproportionate costs. And, ironically, it is these largest creditors who, because they were in the best position to investigate the facts, are least likely to warrant subordination.

Notes & Questions

1. Judge Posner concedes that certain forms of corporate behavior should trigger subordination of parent corporation debt claims but rejects any general rule requiring subordination. Consider the circumstances under which he would allow subordination. Would his criteria allow for subordination in *Standard Gas & Electric* or *Comstock?* Should they?

2. Could one modify the automatic subordination proposal to make it more appealing to those wishing to protect creditors holding claims against the entity whose debt would be subordinated? Consider a rule that would establish a presumption in favor of subordination but that would allow the parent corporation to rebut the presumption by evidence showing that it conducted its relationships with its subsidiary at arm's length.

3. Is the basic difference between Landers and Posner a different perception of the real world? Landers seems to assume that parent corporations routinely manipulate debt relationships with subsidiaries to their own advantage. Posner seems to view such misdealings as exceptional rather than the norm. Which view more accurately reflects reality? If questionable dealings are common, would an absolute rule be preferable to current doctrine? Would a presumption in favor of subordination be preferable? Would the costs imposed by Posner's approach yield a sufficient return in terms of singling out those cases in which subordination should be ordered?

Chapter 13

DISCHARGE

WEISTART, THE COSTS OF BANKRUPTCY, 41 Law & Contemp.Probs. 107, 108–12 (1977)

I would suggest that in structuring the legal system for debtor-creditor relationships in our society, most of us would favor the establishment of a formal system for the collective settlement of the obligations of overburdened debtors. And after we consider the various alternative arrangements that might be devised, we would likely conclude that the state should play a central role in the administration of the system. This would be our conclusion, I believe, whether we were voting as debtors or as creditors, or from a more disinterested perspective. For the moment we should leave aside the question whether our system would allow the debtor to be discharged from his debts with something less than full satisfaction of the obligations. A discharge is not an inseparable part of bankruptcy, as evidenced by the fact that the bankruptcy systems of many European countries operate without it. In the absence of a discharge we would use our system to arrange for the extension of debts and perhaps to facilitate voluntary compromises of creditors' claims. . . .

Our . . . debate is likely to heat up somewhat when we turn our attention to the question whether we should permit a court-ordered discharge of certain debts. It is one thing to authorize the government to intervene to facilitate plans for the extension and voluntary compromise of obligations; it may be quite another matter to force the creditor to accept less than complete satisfaction. We can approach the issue as being whether such a compulsory settlement involving less than the full obligations should ever be required, leaving until later the question which debts should be dischargeable.

The arguments against permitting discharge are likely to have a decided philosophical overtone. Granting discharges may erode the degree of responsibility with which the debtor approaches his affairs and may lessen his incentive to avoid overextension. To the extent that we remove the penalty for insolvency we may actually nudge debtors down the path of imprudence and thus foster the tragedies that attend the disintegration of personal estates. Finally, it would be urged that a contract is a contract, and a creditor who gave fair consideration to his debtor is entitled to the promised return, even if he is required to wait for its receipt.

There are other considerations, however, which are likely to prompt us to accept discharges in some circumstances. For example, we must recognize that some debts are simply uncollectible. The clearest case is one in which the productive capacity of a wage earner is destroyed by a debilitating illness or other tragedy that forces the individual to rely upon state support or private largesse for his continued existence. Obligations may have been accumulated that both the debtor and creditor assumed would be paid out of future earnings. Here the notion of the efficiency of the bankruptcy remedy again comes into play. Rather than require each individual creditor to pursue a costly investigation to discover that his claim is uncollectible, we can use the bankruptcy system to establish that fact by a single inquiry. The granting of discharge will also foreclose vindictive or otherwise unnecessary collection actions. . . .

Other situations will require a much different focus. At some point we will want to examine the theory of the fresh start, which encourages liberal dispensations from prior debts. The notion of giving the overextended but honest debtor a second chance is fundamental to our existing system and has prompted new proposals for further reforms to improve the debtor's post-bankruptcy position.[3] While the fresh-start doctrine in our existing system seems to be buoyed primarily by humanitarian concerns, we might want to inquire whether there is not also some economic justification for liberalized access to bankruptcy discharges. The point to be investigated is whether excessive debt, with its attendant pressure on family and emotional stability and job security, does not so inhibit productivity that there would be a net social gain from terminating costly collection actions, excusing the debts, and giving the poorer-but-wiser debtor a second chance.

As we move from the cases of uncollectible debts, in which bankruptcy serves a cost-saving function, to the cases in which we investigate its effects on productivity, the debate about the wisdom of discharges will intensify appreciably. For the present it is enough to suggest that we have crossed the threshold of the discharge question and established that nondischargeability is not an inviolable concept.

Those who would urge that the discharge in bankruptcy violates the basic sanctity of contract must also be prepared to deal with an extensive body of nonbankruptcy law that weighs against that position. Bankruptcy is not the only context in which the dischargeability of obligations is recognized. Indeed, the general law of contracts accepts that there are circumstances in which a party may be excused from commitments that otherwise have all the attributes of a valid contract. Decisions in this area were first categorized under the doctrine of impossibility, which in its early formulations authorized a court to discharge a contractual obligation if performance had been rendered impossible, provided that the court found that the promisor had not assumed the particular risk and that he was not the cause of the circumstances which prevented performance. A leading case in this

---

3. Among the reforms that appear to be intended to enhance the debtor's fresh start are those which prohibit postbankruptcy reaffirmations, invalidate a debtor's attempt to waive his exemptions, and further restrict the classes of nondischargeable debts.

area is the 1863 English decision in Taylor v. Caldwell.[4] Taylor contracted to rent Caldwell's music hall for a future date. Taylor planned to stage a musical event and, of course, anticipated making a profit by charging admission. Before the agreed-upon date, the hall was destroyed by fire. When Taylor later sued for the damages which resulted from Caldwell's failure to perform, the court concluded that there was no liability. In the court's view Caldwell's duty to deliver the hall was by implication conditional upon its continued existence. As that condition was not satisfied, Caldwell was discharged from his contract.

Since the time of Taylor v. Caldwell the trend has been toward increasing liberalization of the grounds for excuse. One important development in this area was the adoption of section 2–615 of the Uniform Commercial Code, which shifts the emphasis in sale-of-goods contracts from a requirement of objective impossibility to a standard that requires a showing that "performance . . . has been made *impracticable* by the occurrence of a contingency the non-occurrence of which was a basic assumption on which the contract was made . . .."

On the surface it might appear that many debtors who come to the bankruptcy court would otherwise be entitled to a discharge under these principles. Not infrequently the precipitating cause of bankruptcy is major illness or other catastrophe that destroys the debtor's income. Could it not be said that the occurrence of these unexpected events made it impossible for the debtor to perform according to the original terms of his credit contracts? In the same vein, wasn't the debtor's continued earning capacity a basic assumption on which the contract was made? Whatever the appeal of this analysis, it is not generally recognized in the cases applying the impossibility doctrine. We can find authoritative statements to the effect that personal insolvency, whatever the cause, does not discharge performance under a contract, whether the agreement calls for the payment of money or some other type of exchange. Many older cases suggest that the intervening conditions must indicate "objective impossibility," which is to say it must be shown that no person could have rendered the required performance.

Much is troubling about the defense of impossibility. One might wonder whether Taylor v. Caldwell would have been decided the same way if it had arisen in an economic setting in which sophisticated forms of business interruption insurance were available to landlords who rented music halls. But even if we choose not to question the origins of the doctrine, it is not at all clear that we must accept that the distinction between insolvency and other types of impossibility is inevitable. Some suggest that the distinction represents a policy decision that a contrary result would encourage personal irresponsibility. But

4. 3 Best & Sm. 826, 122 Eng.Rep. 309.

that is hardly compelling in cases in which the insolvency is precipitated by such external causes as an illness or economic recession.[8]

T. JACKSON, THE LOGIC AND LIMITS OF BANKRUPTCY LAW (1986) 228–37, 243, 255–57

The Normative Underpinnings of a Fresh–Start Policy

Two Partial Justifications for the Nonwaivable Right of Discharge: Risk Allocation and Social Safety Nets

In considering why society would deem it desirable to allow individuals to discharge virtually all their debts in exchange for surrendering
a portion of their total wealth, recent scholarly treatments of discharge
law have focused on whether the debtor or the creditor is the superior
risk bearer and whether discharge should be presumptively available.
For example, in one of the first serious efforts to consider the extent to
which discharge should be available, Theodore Eisenberg offers an
explanation that, although not presented in these terms, would support
a general presumption of *non* dischargeability.[12] He suggests that risk
bearing is the main issue underlying the right of discharge: "A discharge system provides a technique for allocating the risk of financial
distress between a debtor and his creditors." That suggestion, in turn,
draws on recent theoretical work on risk allocation in cases of contractual impossibility. That work has suggested that when the contract is
silent, risk should be placed on the party best able to bear it. A party's
ability to bear risk, in turn, depends both on its capacity to avoid
deleterious events and on its ability to insure efficiently against those
events. Although he concludes that the superior insurer cannot be
determined a priori, Eisenberg suggests that the debtor should be
presumed to be the superior risk bearer because he is in "greater
control of [his] financial activities than any particular lender" and thus
better able to judge when he is taking on too much credit.

Yet the conclusion that the debtor is likely to be the superior risk
bearer is by no means beyond question. Discharge may be viewed as a
form of limited liability for individuals—a legal construct that stems
from the same desires and serves the same purposes as does limited
liability for corporations. Richard Posner identifies two reasons why
limiting the liability of corporations is sensible.[16] First, creditors of an
enterprise are in a better position to appraise the risks of extending

---

8. I believe that there may be an entirely different explanation for the insolvency
exception. Much of the law on impossibility evolved during the period when governments were establishing a separate institutional framework for dealing with
insolvency problems. Courts considering
private contract litigation in which insolvency was raised as a defense may well
have concluded that they should defer to
those legal mechanisms specifically designated to effectuate the settlement of debts.

12. See Eisenberg, "Bankruptcy Law in
Perspective," 28 *UCLA L.Rev.* 953, 976–91
(1981); see also Weistart, "The Costs of
Bankruptcy," Law & Contemp. Probs., Au-
tumn 1977, at 107 (discussing by analogy to
contract impossibility whether discharge is
desirable).

16. See Posner, "The Rights of Creditors of Affiliated Corporations," 43 *U.Chi.
L.Rev.* 499, 507–09 (1976). See generally
Halpern, Trebilcock, & Turnbull, "An Economic Analysis of Limited Liability in Cor-

credit to an enterprise than are its shareholders and hence are superior risk bearers. Second, limited liability may be advantageous—at least in the case of publicly held corporations with widely dispersed owner- ship—because the shareholders are likely to be more risk averse than the creditors and thus willing to pay to have the creditors bear a greater share of the risk.

Both of these reasons could also support limited liability for individ- uals. As to the first, the creditors of an individual, having gained experience through dealing with many debtors, may be more adept than the individual at monitoring his borrowing. This argument contradicts Eisenberg's analysis. Moreover, Posner's second justifica- tion for limited liability may be especially powerful with respect to individuals. To the extent that individuals can invest their capital in securities and various other income-producing assets, they can further their desire to avoid risk by diversifying their holdings. Yet an individual's capital may consist largely of *human* capital—especially in the case of a young person—and this particular form of property cannot readily be diversified by investing in assets with different risk charac- teristics. Thus, like business associations that find the corporate form and its accompanying limited liability worth the increase in the cost of credit, individuals may also derive a net benefit from the limited liability that discharge affords them.

Even if we could determine whether the debtor or his creditor is more likely to be the superior risk bearer in any particular situation, risk-allocation analysis of this sort yields no more than a presumption. Such an analysis cannot explain why the presumption should be frozen into a nonwaivable right of discharge. Indeed, businesses commonly contract out of the presumption that creditors are better risk bearers than the shareholders. The corporate form is merely an alternative to other forms of conducting business—such as sole proprietorships and partnerships—in which the liability of the equity owners is not limited by statute. Guarantees and similar arrangements, moreover, permit circumvention of limited liability by contract even when the corporate form is used. Risk-allocation analysis by itself suggests no reason why this elective feature should not apply as well to the limited liability of individuals.

If contract law does not provide a pertinent analogy, another area of law might. The nonwaivability of the right of discharge might be justified—although only partially—by the existence of various social insurance programs, such as unemployment insurance, Medicare, and Social Security. By this, I do not mean to imply that discharge is justified simply because it resembles other paternalistic social programs that have gained general acceptance. Instead, I mean only that against the background of general social programs bankruptcy's fresh-start policy may be justified in part because it reduces the "moral hazard"

poration Law," 30 U.Toronto L.J. 117 (1980) (discussing justifications for the lim- ited liability of corporations); R. Clark, Corporate Law ch. 1 (1986) (same).

that those social programs create. The existence of social welfare programs leads individuals to undervalue the costs of engaging in risky activities today because they can depend on society to bear a portion of the costs that may arise tomorrow. A person who breaks his legs while mountain climbing may be entitled to unemployment benefits, food stamps, health care, and the like. The knowledge that such assistance is available invites the individual to discount (although not to anything like zero) the costs of possible future injury when deciding whether to climb. Accordingly, such programs can be viewed as a form of social insurance, paid for in the form of general taxes. Because the "rate" that any individual pays for the insurance is not geared to the probability that he will engage in a risky activity, such insurance creates what is commonly referred to as a *moral hazard:* a situation in which individuals systematically—and rationally—underestimate the real costs of engaging in a risky activity because some of those costs are borne by someone else.

If there were no right of discharge, an individual who lost his assets to creditors might rely instead on social welfare programs. The existence of those programs might induce him to underestimate the true costs of his decisions to borrow. In contrast, discharge imposes much of the risk of ill-advised credit decisions not on social insurance programs but on creditors. The availability of a limited nonwaivable right of discharge in bankruptcy therefore encourages creditors to police extensions of credit and thus minimizes the moral hazard created by safety-net programs. Because creditors can monitor debtors and are free to grant or withhold credit, the discharge system contains a built-in checking mechanism. . . .

Volitional and Cognitive Justifications

Perhaps the most general question raised by bankruptcy discharge is whether the nonwaivability of the right of discharge, although it inhibits a borrower's individual autonomy, does not in fact faithfully protect his interests and those of noncontracting parties. To my mind, the answer is a qualified yes. I will argue in this section that a key to bankruptcy discharge policy has to do with inherent biases—uncorrected by marketplace constraints—in the ways most individuals make decisions that lead them to overconsume and undersave. This view, in turn, is based on available evidence that suggests that many people systematically fail to pursue their own long-term interests when making decisions about whether to spend today or save for tomorrow. It is important to be precise about the problem I am identifying. The problem cannot be simply that people come to regret some of their actions because they or their circumstances have changed over time. Rather, in order to justify nonwaivability, it must be shown that individuals *systematically* misjudge (or ignore) their own interests and that this bias consistently leads them in one direction—to consume too much and save too little. . . .

More specifically, a legal rule discouraging the extension of credit might be the best means to assist individuals in controlling impulsive credit decisions. A nonwaivable right of discharge controls impulsive credit decisions by encouraging creditors to monitor borrowing. Other less intrusive rules would not be nearly as effective in controlling an individual's urge to buy or borrow on credit. Consider, for example, a rule that allowed an individual to decide for himself whether to be subject to a legally enforceable right of discharge. For such a rule to work, the individual's decision would have to be irrevocable—either it would have to be enforceable by some form of specific performance or the individual would have to face some nontrivial penalty for reneging on his initial choice. Otherwise, an individual in the grip of an impulse could revoke his decision to embrace or forego the right of discharge, just as a smoker can revoke his New Year's resolution not to smoke whenever he is seized with the urge to light up. Moreover, even if the decision were made irrevocable, problems would remain in setting limits on *when* the decision would have to be made. We are all relatively constant consumers of credit. As a result, the choice might be deferred beyond the time a nonimpulsive individual would choose. Conversely, the election itself might be made impulsively.

Thus, although the law might respond to the problem of impulsive credit behavior by letting individuals choose whether or not to waive the right of discharge, the problem may better be handled by means of a legal rule that uniformly disallows waiver. This kind of rule is justified by the kind of hypothesized Rawlsian original position touched on in looking at bankruptcy's compulsory collective system of debt-collection rules in Chapter 1: if the members of society had gathered together before the fact and had anticipated the human tendency toward impulsive behavior, they would have devised a rule that denied them the opportunity to behave impulsively in the future.[33]

Incomplete Heuristics: A Cognitive Justification. Whereas impulsive behavior is volitional, there is a closely related cognitive feature of decision making that makes the need for a legal rule perhaps more evident. Individuals appear to make choices by processing information in a way that consistently underestimates future risks. This problem—which I shall call the problem of *incomplete heuristics*—provides a powerful argument that most individuals, *whether or not* they are prone to impulsive behavior or have undergone personality shifts, would favor a legal rule making discharge nonwaivable. Like impulsiveness, incomplete heuristics may lead the individual to favor present consumption in a way that does not give due regard to his long-term desires and goals. Likewise, incomplete heuristics would justify the decision to adopt a universal nonwaivable right of discharge on a Rawlsian ground: if individuals in the "original position" had recognized that they would face informational constraints when making

---

33. See J. Rawls, A Theory of Justice 136–42 (1971) (discussing the concept of the "veil of ignorance").

credit decisions, they would probably have chosen a system that would make some of the consequences of their borrowing avoidable. . . .

Rational Behavior and the Notion of Externalities

The above justifications for societal intervention in individuals' credit decisions rest on the claims that most people suffer distortions in making those decisions caused by defects in their volitional and cognitive processes, that they would agree in advance to protect against them, and that creating a nonwaivable right of discharge is a fairly effective way to achieve that protection. Another justification for a uniform, nonwaivable discharge rule, however, derives from the possibility that waiver of the right of discharge will generate externalities. The cost to the debtor of waiving that right might not reflect the costs to third parties of such a decision. To avoid these externalities, which individuals might systematically ignore if permitted to do so, it might be appropriate to impose a nonwaivable discharge rule. Such a rule helps curtail the costs otherwise imposed on a wide range of people— from family and friends, to business associates, to society in general. . . .

Thus the question really is: why is the special trigger rule applicable to human capital a federal rule? That question is less a bankruptcy law issue than it is an issue of general federal versus state regulation. Perhaps the answer in federalizing fresh-start law as it relates to human capital has to do with a belief that impulsive behavior, incomplete heuristics, and externalities generate a standard problem with respect to human capital that is amenable to a uniform, nationwide rule. Moreover, although no clear conceptual line separates one form of wealth from another, it is not surprising that federal bankruptcy law has traditionally afforded distinctive protection to human capital. Of the various forms of wealth, human capital not only is the least diversifiable but also has the most direct bearing on the future well-being of the individual and the people who depend on him. Yet even though human capital may be especially deserving of protection through bankruptcy law, it does not follow that such special protection is equally justifiable in all cases. If an individual holds large amounts of wealth in the form of human capital but has few other existing assets, he may justly be required to have the proceeds of his human capital subject to at least certain debts—in particular, debts such as student loans, which the individual incurred in order to acquire human capital. In contrast, younger people can make perhaps the most persuasive claim to having their human capital stringently protected, since they are at an age when they are more likely to make decisions that will later induce regret. Whatever the cause of regretted decisions—be it impulsiveness, incomplete heuristics, or something else— someone who is fifty-five years old is less likely to experience such regret than someone who is twenty. Hence, discharge policy, in theory at least, should treat younger debtors more generously than older ones.

How does this observation translate into policy? It seems to call for a scheme that would protect a decreasing portion of one's wealth as one grows older. A focus on protecting human capital arguably reflects that policy. As one advances in age, the portion of one's wealth that consists of human capital is likely to decrease, while the value of one's other assets is likely to increase. Accordingly, limiting discharge to the freeing of human capital may in fact achieve the goal of protecting youth from later regret.

Concern for externalities may supply another reason why the protection of human capital is at the core of bankruptcy's discharge policy. Consider human capital in relation to durable forms of wealth. Like durable goods, human capital is consumed over time. These assets differ, however, in other respects. A durable good can be seized and its consumption halted abruptly: if an individual is deprived of his automobile, its future consumption value for him falls to zero and he will have to spend a certain amount of money to reacquire it or obtain a replacement. By contrast, in a world in which slavery is prohibited, human capital can be seized only by seizing its proceeds—that is, by garnishing wages if and when they are earned. Yet an individual has considerable control over the amount of future earnings derived from his existing human capital. If discharge did not protect human capital, many individuals would counter attempts at garnishment by substituting leisure, which creditors cannot reach, for wages. As suggested in the previous chapter, the debtor may not internalize the full cost of this substitution. By largely exempting human capital from the bankruptcy estate, society avoids this undesirable externality.

More subtle but equally important are the problems of measuring the present value of human capital. These problems probably cannot be solved with any degree of precision.[6] Although human capital is in some sense an existing asset, an individual can augment it by replacing leisure, which is something an individual can enjoy but his creditors

---

6. This may be illustrated by the following example. Assume that an individual was a salesman prior to his bankruptcy. Assume further that his creditors have a claim on all his human capital "existing" prior to bankruptcy, but no claim on his "future" human capital. Following bankruptcy, the individual goes to medical school and becomes a doctor. What portion of his wages as a doctor is a consequence of human capital in existence at the time of his bankruptcy? The question cannot easily be answered, because there is no simple measure of what portion of his human capital was acquired after bankruptcy, other than the *cost* of attending medical school. Yet that cost is unreliable as a determinant of value, in part because the cost itself (including tuition, lost wages, lost leisure, and "pain and suffering") is hard to calculate and in part because the degree of consumer surplus attributable to education is hard to measure. These problems arise in other contexts. For example, in community property (and perhaps other) states, courts must resolve to what extent a spouse can lay claim to his partner's income stream as a doctor because he was married to her while she attended medical school. See In re Marriage of Sullivan, 37 Cal.3d 762, 691 P.2d 1020, 209 Cal.Rptr. 354 (1984); Mahoney v. Mahoney, 91 N.J. 488, 453 A.2d 527 (1982); Krauskopf, "Recompense for Financing Spouse's Education: Legal Protection for the Marital Investor in Human Capital," 28 U.Kan.L.Rev. 379 (1980). Moreover, the problem exists even if the individual does not change fields of work: one's growth in a profession over time cannot sensibly be treated entirely as an asset in existence at the beginning of one's career.

cannot reach, with labor (including further education). Treating an individual's lifetime income stream as an existing form of wealth fails to account for this substitutability. Thus, to say that human capital is in existence at the time of bankruptcy does not mean that creditors are entitled to claim all of the debtor's measureable future income as an existing asset because some of that income will depend on future efforts by the debtor to acquire human capital—efforts over which the creditors have no control and that society does not require. . . .

Notes & Questions

1. *Discharge and Impossibility.* Consider the relationship between the bankruptcy discharge and the doctrine of impossibility in contract law. Footnote 8 of the Weistart excerpt suggests that courts hearing contract cases may have become inhospitable to an insolvency defense because bankruptcy mechanisms exist to handle cases in which insolvency is the issue. Suppose one resolves that, at least on some occasions, insolvency, whether through bankruptcy law or traditional contract doctrine, ought to relieve the debtor of her duty to perform. Which mechanism, bankruptcy or contract doctrine, is the most appropriate one through which to implement that decision? Does it make a difference?

2. *Scope of Relief.* One obvious difference is that contractual impossibility doctrine relieves the debtor of only a single obligation. The bankruptcy discharge leads to more sweeping relief. Is the bankruptcy result supportable on the ground that insolvency with respect to a single obligation can be equated with inability to perform any financial obligation and, therefore, the system might as well relieve the debtor of all debts rather than requiring a series of individual lawsuits by creditors in which the insolvency defense is raised? If insolvency were a recognized contract defense would a series of lawsuits be necessary or likely?

3. *Price to the Debtor.* Is bankruptcy law a superior mechanism because it requires the insolvent to surrender all nonexempt property and contract impossibility doctrine does not? Is the surrender requirement a crude way of testing for whether the debtor really believes himself unable to perform his financial obligations?

4. *Discharge and the Social Safety Net.* Consider Professor Jackson's argument that if there were no right to a discharge, an individual who lost his assets might rely instead on social welfare programs. Does this also suggest the need for a set of nonwaivable exemptions in (or outside of) bankruptcy? One important wrinkle is that exemptions focus on existing assets and the discharge protects future earnings.

5. *Discharge and Creditor's Incentives.* The availability of a discharge encourages creditors to monitor debtors. If personal bankruptcies are caused primarily by unexpected medical bills, deaths, or accidents, how will creditor monitoring be affected. Does this affect the nonwaivability issue? Recall that § 303 of the Consumer Credit Protec-

tion Act, 15 U.S.C.A. § 1673, limits garnishments of earnings to 25% of a debtor's weekly disposable earnings. See Chapter 7C. Could whatever legitimate functions a discharge serves be equally well served by a rule limiting the amount of a debtor's future wages that creditors may reach? See also Chapter 15 (which discusses Chapter 13 plans).

6. *Statutory Provisions.* In a Chapter 7 case, the conditions to a discharge are set forth in § 727(a). Section 727(b), in conjunction with §§ 523 and 524, sets forth the effect of a discharge. Note that corporations are ineligible for Chapter 7 discharges. § 727(a)(1). Why?

Differences between discharge under Chapter 7 and discharge under Chapter 13 are explored in Chapter 15.

A. Effect on Liens

In United States National Bank v. Chase National Bank, 331 U.S. 28, 33–34, 67 S.Ct. 1041, 1044, 91 L.Ed. 1320 (1947), the Court summarized what have traditionally been regarded as the "several avenues of action open to a secured creditor of a bankrupt."

> (1) He may disregard the bankruptcy proceeding, decline to file a claim and rely solely upon his security if that security is properly and solely in his possession. . . . (2) He must file a secured claim, however, if the security is within the jurisdiction of the bankruptcy court and if he wishes to retain his secured status, inasmuch as that court has exclusive jurisdiction over the liquidation of the security. . . . (3) He may surrender or waive his security and prove his entire claim as an unsecured one. . . . (4) He may avail himself of his security and share in the general assets as to the unsecured balance. . . .

The statement of the first two avenues requires some elaboration. If the secured creditor disregards the proceeding, as she is entitled to, the creditor will only have recourse to the security to enforce its claim after bankruptcy. No deficiency judgment will be allowed. Second, it is not necessary to file a secured claim to retain a security interest after bankruptcy. See § 506(d)(2). See generally Matter of Lindsey, 823 F.2d 189 (7th Cir.1987); Chandler Bank of Lyons v. Ray, 804 F.2d 577 (10th Cir.1986).

LONG v. BULLARD

Supreme Court of the United States, 1886.
117 U.S. 617, 6 S.Ct. 917, 29 L.Ed. 1004.

MR. CHIEF JUSTICE WAITE delivered the opinion of the court:

The material facts appearing in this record are as follows:

In the month of December, 1869, parts of lots 5 and 6, in square 90 of the City of Macon, were set off under the laws of Georgia to Betsey A. Long, the wife of Francis M. Long, as a homestead. The property was at the time incumbered by a mortgage made by Francis M. Long to the Ocmulgee Building Association. Proceedings were afterwards had to foreclose this mortgage, and to save the property from sale Francis M. Long applied to Daniel Bullard for a loan of money. This loan was made at usurious interest, and Long and his wife executed to Bullard their joint note, dated November 18, 1872, for $1,220 payable twelve months after date, and conveyed to him the homestead property by a deed absolute on its face as security. On the 29th of May, 1873, Francis M. Long was adjudged a bankrupt, and on the 15th of April, 1874, he received his discharge. In his schedules the debt to Bullard, with its security on the homestead premises, was duly entered. On the 28th of June, 1873, the same premises were set apart to the bankrupt to be retained by him under the bankrupt law as being exempt under the state law from levy and sale upon execution. Bullard did not prove his debt in the bankrupt proceedings.

On the 9th of February, 1878, Bullard brought suit in the Superior Court of Bibb County, Georgia, to subject the property to the payment of his debt. In his bill he alleged that the money he loaned was used to pay off the prior incumbrance on the homestead, and he claimed a valid lien on that account. He also set forth the bankruptcy of Francis M. Long, and the assignment of the property to him under the bankrupt law as a homestead.

Long and his wife in their answer stated that the deed to Bullard was void for usury in the debt for which it was given as security; that only $727.94 of the amount actually lent by Bullard was used to pay off the prior incumbrance; that the money was lent to the husband and not to the wife; and that the husband had been discharged in bankruptcy. Upon these facts, it was insisted that the homestead rights of Mrs. Long and her children were superior to the claim of Bullard under his conveyance, and that the property could not be sold to pay him.

Upon the trial the court charged the jury, in substance, that there could be no personal recovery against the husband upon the note, but that the property could be subjected to the payment of the amount due, as the discharge of Long in bankruptcy did not release the lien of the mortgage. This was excepted to by the Longs. A verdict was returned in favor of Bullard for the amount of money actually lent, excluding the usurious interest. Thereupon the Longs moved for a new trial, on the ground, among others, of error in the instructions to the jury as to the effect of the discharge in bankruptcy. This motion was granted, but only because the property was subjected to the payment of a larger sum than was used to pay off the prior incumbrance. From the order granting a new trial, Bullard took a writ of error to the supreme court, where it was adjudged April 19, 1882, that the judgment of the superior court granting the new trial be affirmed, "unless the plaintiff in error will write off from his verdict in the court below the sum of $300." The only questions decided on this writ of error, as shown by the opinion, were such as related to the right of Bullard to recover the full amount of his loan, instead of the amount used to pay off the incumbrance on the homestead.

When the case got back to the trial court the specified amount was "written off," and a decree entered accordingly for a sale of the property to pay what remained due according to the verdict as reduced. Francis M. Long thereupon excepted to the decree, among other things, because the property ordered to be sold "constitutes and is his home- stead, exempted, set apart, and secured to him by the Bankrupt Court of the United States . . . in a bankruptcy proceeding in that court . . . as against this said debt of complainant's, and all others of said defendant then existing, . . . said homestead being set apart, al- lowed, and secured to the defendant, then bankrupt, under and by virtue of § 5045 of the Revised Statutes . . . and which said exemp- tion was valid against said debt of said complainant under and by virtue of said Act of Congress, and said part of said decree charging said exemption with the payment of said debt of complainant's and directing a sale . . . is in contravention and in violation of that Act of Congress;" and because the decree charging the property with the debt "is in violation of his discharge in bankruptcy as shown in the record and proceedings in this cause, and his rights under the same as declared by and set out in § 5119 of the Revised Statutes . . . and is in conflict with and in derogation of that Act of Congress." Another writ of error from the supreme court was thereupon sued out by Francis M. Long and Betsey A. Long, but the court being of the opinion "that the judgment pronounced in this case when it was here at the last term was conclusive on the questions there presented, and that the decree in the court below now excepted to was in conformity with that judgment, and that a failure on the part of Long and wife to except to the overruling of these motions for a new trial, on other grounds than that on which it was allowed, was conclusive against them, and could not now be reopened," affirmed the decree. To reverse that judgment this writ of error was brought.

It perhaps sufficiently appears that a determination of the question as to the effect of the discharge in bankruptcy upon the right of Bullard to enforce a lien upon the property in existence at the time of the commencement of the proceedings in bankruptcy was necessarily in- volved in the decision of the supreme court which is here under review, and that this decision was adverse to the right set up by Long. This being the case, we have jurisdiction, but there cannot be a doubt of the correctness of the decision. By section 5119 of the Revised Statutes the discharge releases the bankrupt only from debts which were or might have been proved, and by section 5075 debts secured by mortgage or pledge can only be proved for the balance remaining due after deduct- ing the value of the security, unless all claim upon the security is released. Here the creditor neither proved his debt in bankruptcy nor released his lien. Consequently his security was preserved notwith- standing the bankruptcy of his debtor. ˙The dispute in the court below was as to the existence of the lien at the time of the commencement of the proceedings in bankruptcy. That depended entirely on the state laws, as to which the judgment of the state court is final and not subject to review here.

The setting apart of the homestead to the bankrupt, under section 5045 of the Revised Statutes, did not relieve the property from the operation of liens created by contract before the bankruptcy. It is not the decree in this case which constitutes the lien on the property, but the conveyance of Long and wife before the bankruptcy.

The judgment is affirmed.

Notes & Questions

1. *Discharge's Effect on Liens.* The legislative history of § 522 states, in part: "The bankruptcy discharge will not prevent enforcement of valid liens. The rule of Long v. Bullard, 117 U.S. 617, 6 S.Ct. 917, 29 L.Ed. 1004 (1886), is accepted with respect to the enforcement of valid liens on nonexempt property as well as on exempt property." House Report at 361.

Since §§ 501, 502 and 506(a) of the Bankruptcy Act now allow secured claims to participate in bankruptcy, should the post-bankruptcy survival of security interests and other liens be reexamined?

IN RE BELL

United States Court of Appeals, Sixth Circuit, 1983.
700 F.2d 1053.

KRUPANSKY, CIRCUIT JUDGE.

This action joins the legal issue of whether redemption of secured collateral in a Chapter 7 bankruptcy proceeding may be achieved through installment payments.

Debtors, Thomas and Louise Bell (Bells), were parties to a purchase money security agreement with General Motors Acceptance Corporation (GMAC) covering a 1978 Chevrolet Van. The agreement contemplated that the Bells would pay the balance of the purchase price, approximately $6,000 together with financing charges, in equal monthly installments. At the time debtors filed a joint petition in Bankruptcy on March 28, 1980, under Chapter 7 of the Bankruptcy Reform Act of 1978 (Bankruptcy Act), 11 U.S.C. § 701 et seq., the fair market value of the Van exceeded the outstanding balance on the agreement by approximately $1,000, the debtors had tendered all monthly installments on their obligation to GMAC and had otherwise not defaulted upon any term of the contract.[1] The Van became property of the estate subsequent to which the debtors exempted their equity and the trustee abandoned the estate's interest. GMAC filed a complaint to reclaim the Van and debtors counterclaimed seeking authorization from the bankruptcy court to retain possession of the Van upon continued

---

1. "Default" as predicated upon a provision of the security agreement which authorized GMAC to immediately repossess the Van upon the filing of a bankruptcy petition (bankruptcy clause) is discussed hereafter.

payment of monthly installments. The Bankruptcy Court permitted installment redemption, In re Bell, 8 B.R. 549 (Bkrtcy.E.D.Mich.1981), and the District Court reversed, In re Bell, 15 B.R. 859, 7 B.C.D. 219 (E.D.Mich.1981).

The Bankruptcy Reform Act of 1978 authorizes a Chapter 7 debtor to redeem certain secured property:

> An individual debtor may, whether or not the debtor has waived the right to redeem under this section, redeem tangible personal property intended primarily for personal, family, or household use, from a lien securing a dischargeable consumer debt, if such property is exempt under section 522 of this title or has been abandoned under section 554 of this title, by paying the holder of such lien the amount of the allowed secured claim of such holder that is secured by such item.

11 U.S.C. § 722. This provision generally permits a debtor to redeem tangible secured personal property by paying the creditor the approximate fair market value of said property, or the amount of the claim, whichever is less. However, § 722 is facially silent as to the mechanics of redemption and, particularly, on whether the redemption may be accomplished through installment payments. The weight of authority has denied installment redemption.

The bankruptcy redemption provision, § 722, is a legislative derivative of the redemption provision of 9–506, Uniform Commercial Code. The official comment to 9–506 provides:

> "Tendering fulfillment" obviously means more than a new promise to perform the existing promise; it requires payment in full of all monetary obligations then due and performance in full of all other obligations then matured.

The legislative history of § 722 does not reflect a Congressional intent which contemplated anything other than an intent to incorporate the fundamental requirement of "lump sum" redemption as suggested in the underlying UCC provision upon which § 722 was predicated.

More importantly, the redemption remedy of § 722 must be construed *in pari materia* with the reaffirmation provision, 11 U.S.C. § 524(c), which pertinently provides:

> (c) An agreement between a holder of a claim and the debtor, the consideration for which, in whole or in part, is based on a debt that is dischargeable in a case under this title is enforceable only to any extent enforceable under applicable nonbankruptcy law, whether or not discharge of such debt is waived, only if—
>
> . . .
>
> (4) In a case concerning an individual, to the extent such debt is a consumer debt that is not secured by real property of the debtor, the court approves such agreements as—

. . .

(B)(i) entered into in good faith; and (ii) in settlement of litigation under section 524 of this title, or providing for redemption under section 722 of this title.

Section 524(c) authorizes a Chapter 7 debtor to seek renegotiation of the terms of the security agreement with the creditor thereby creating an alternative method pursuant to which a debtor may attempt to retain possession of secured collateral. Such an alternative, obviously attractive to the debtor financially unable to redeem the secured collateral through a lump-sum payment, is the equitable complement to § 722. See: In re Cruseturner, supra, 8 B.R. at 583 et seq. Simply, a debtor incapable or unwilling to tender a lump-sum redemption and redeem the secured collateral for its fair market value may reaffirm with the creditor; contrawise, a debtor confronted with a creditor unwilling to execute a renegotiation may retain the secured collateral by redeeming it for its fair market value, which value may be substantially less than the contractual indebtedness. However, § 524(c) facially contemplates that the creditor, for whatever reason, may reject any and all tendered reaffirmation offers; § 524(c) envisions execution of an "agreement" which, by definition, is a voluntary undertaking. See: In re Whatley, supra, 16 B.R. at 396. Accordingly, if a debtor is authorized by the bankruptcy court to redeem by installments over the objection of the creditor, such practice would render the voluntary framework of § 524(c) an exercise in legislative futility. See: In re Miller, supra, 4 B.R. at 307–08. Phrased differently:

Of course, if Section 722 payments could be made by installment, no debtor would ever have reason to reaffirm under Section 524(c)(4)(B) (ii), since, by right, he could obtain under Section 722 the same end—continuing possession of his property—under the same terms— payment by installment—for what would often be a significantly lower price. Thus, installment payments under Section 722 would render useless Congress' carefully laid scheme for voluntary agreement under Section 524—clearly indicating that Congress had no intention to allow such payments under Section 722.

In re Hart, supra, 8 B.R. at 1022.

Further, authorization of installment redemption would interpose into Chapter 7 a procedure which Chapter 7 is ill-equipped to implement. A Chapter 7 proceeding, whereby the debtor is discharged through liquidation, may conclude prior to the expiration of the installment payment period. A default by the debtor subsequent to discharge—possibly predicated upon a waste of the collateral, inability to meet the monthly installments or lack of motivation to continue payments on a rapidly depreciating collateral such as a vehicle—would burden the creditor with the expense and effort of reapplying to the bankruptcy court for relief. See: In re Hart, supra, 8 B.R. at 1022–23 (rapidly depreciating collateral). A bankruptcy court's inability to effectively monitor the installment program and to expeditiously and meaningfully enforce the installment redemption raises serious issues

of adequate creditor protection. See: In re Cruseturner, supra, 8 B.R.
at 588 ("Chapter 7 bankruptcies are just not equipped with the procedure to enforce redemptions in installments").   . . .

Debtors posit that preclusion of installment redemption will precipi-
tate situations wherein a Chapter 7 debtor will possess no viable
method of retaining possession of secured collateral. However, a debtor
may avoid such an untenuous position by initially filing a petition for
bankruptcy under Chapter 13 or converting an existing Chapter 7
proceeding to a Chapter 13 proceeding. Chapter 13 is designed to
provide a debtor with a fresh start through rehabilitation, unlike
Chapter 7 which provides a fresh start through liquidation. As such,
Chapter 13 authorizes redemption by installment over an objection by
the creditor (a "cram down"), the very result sought in the action at
bar.   11 U.S.C. § 1325(a)(5).   . . .

Lastly, the debtors maintain that no default had occurred under the
terms of the security agreement and that, upon the trustee's abandonment of the Van under 11 U.S.C. § 554, the debtors reacquired the
collateral since they held the primary possessory interest. Debtors
posit that they enjoyed the same rights after abandonment as before
the filing of the bankruptcy petition including the right to continue
monthly installments so long as no default, as defined by the security
agreement, intervened. Under this theory, the right to continued
possession of the secured collateral emanates from the security agreement rather than under a § 722 redemption. However, it has been
recognized that a return of abandoned property to the party with the
primary possessory interest (usually the debtor) merely provides that
debtor with time to enforce his right to redeem the property under
§ 722 or to seek a reaffirmation of the agreement under § 524(c). The
automatic stay of 11 U.S.C. § 362(a)(5) continues in effect, and prevents
repossession by the creditor until the case is closed, dismissed, or
discharge is granted or denied pursuant to 11 U.S.C. § 362(c)(2). Analyzing the relationship between § 362(a)(5) (debtors protection of the
automatic stay) and § 554 (abandonment), the Court in In re
Cruseturner has summarized:

Accordingly, Section 362(a)(5) grants the debtor time to enforce
rights in his property given him under Sections 722 and 524(c).

The effect of Section 362(a)(5) is to provide the debtor with
separate protection of his property. This enables him to exercise his
right to redeem either by acquiring refinancing or by otherwise
gathering the necessary funds, or to negotiate a reaffirmation.
Unless earlier relief is requested by the creditor, the creditor may
not repossess property, despite any abandonment by the trustee,
until one of the three acts specified in Section 362(c)(2) occurs   . . .
The application of Section 362 to exempt property and abandoned
property is co-extensive with the redemption right given in Section
722, for this right extends to exempt property as well as to nonexempt property which may be abandoned by the trustee. Likewise,

the stay will cover property which may be the subject of reaffirmation agreements.

8 B.R. at 592.

Further, a serious issue exists as to whether the debtors held the primary possessory interest in the Van upon abandonment. The security agreement authorized GMAC to immediately repossess the Van upon the filing of a bankruptcy petition (bankruptcy clause). While this bankruptcy clause was initially inoperative under 11 U.S.C. § 541(c)(1), and the Van had become property of the estate under 11 U.S.C. § 544 irrespective of such clause, the § 541(c) prohibition against such a bankruptcy clause has been held inoperable once the asset has been abandoned from the estate. See: In re Schweitzer, supra, 19 B.R. at 865 et seq. Accordingly, the bankruptcy clause became effective upon abandonment, the debtors were in default of the security agreement and therefore no longer entitled to the primary possessory interest in the Van.

Further, a discharge of the debtor's personal liability on the security agreement through bankruptcy constructively vitiated Paragraph 6 of the security agreement which provides that "buyer shall be liable for a deficiency." Negation of the creditor's right to seek personal liability precipitated a default so as to empower GMAC with the primary possessory right to the Van.

In sum, this Court concludes that redemption and reaffirmation constituted the exclusive methods pursuant to which the Bells could retain possession of the secured collateral. The sole method of redemption available to a Chapter 7 debtor under § 722 is a lump-sum redemption. Accordingly, the judgment of the district court is Affirmed.

Notes & Questions

1. Why did GMAC foreclose on the van?

2. *Variations on Bell's Facts.* (a) *No Abandonment.* Suppose the trustee in *Bell* had not abandoned the Van under § 554. (Why did the trustee abandon it?) In Riggs National Bank of Washington, D.C. v. Perry, 729 F.2d 982 (4th Cir.1984), the debtor had been tardy on over half of his car payments. The secured creditor argued that the debtor breached the sales agreement by commencing a bankruptcy proceeding, and that this default constituted cause for relief from the automatic stay. The court rejected this and other arguments, distinguishing *Bell* on the ground that in *Bell* the trustee had abandoned the property.

(b) *Post–Discharge Effort to Foreclose.* Suppose the debtor maintains possession of the collateral during the bankruptcy proceeding and receives a discharge. May the secured party wait until after the discharge to foreclose based on the filing of the bankruptcy petition as an event of default? Is this situation covered by the rule in *Long v. Bullard,* supra, approved in the Bankruptcy Act's legislative history?

Several courts have questioned *Bell* and its applicability to post-discharge reclamation efforts. E.g., In re Winters, 69 B.R. 145 (Bkrtcy.D. Or.1986) (Bankruptcy Code voids provision in security agreement designating filing of bankruptcy as default); In re Carey, 51 B.R. 294 (Bkrtcy.D.D.C.1985) (questioning *Bell*).

3. *Assuming the Contract.* Could the Bells have assumed the contract with GMAC and thereby relied on § 365(b), (e) to avoid the effect of the bankruptcy default clause in the GMAC agreement? If the van were new enough would there be an argument that the transaction with GMAC involved an executory contract? Should debtors be spared the effect of "ipso facto" and bankruptcy default clauses only if there is an assumable executory contract?

4. *Assignment of Wages.* Local Loan Co. v. Hunt, 292 U.S. 234, 54 S.Ct. 695, 78 L.Ed. 1230 (1934), addressed the important question whether a prebankruptcy assignment of wages survived a bankruptcy discharge.

> Whether an assignment of future earned wages constitutes a lien within the meaning of § 67(d) of the bankruptcy act [which provided that liens are not affected by the Act], is a matter upon which the decisions of the state and federal courts are not in complete accord; although by far the larger number of cases and the greater weight of authority are in the negative. We do not stop to review the state decisions. · . . .
>
> The earning power of an individual is the power to create property; but it is not translated into property within the meaning of the bankruptcy act until it has brought earnings into existence. An adjudication of bankruptcy, followed by a discharge, releases a debtor from all previously incurred debts, with certain exceptions not pertinent here; and it logically cannot be supposed that the act nevertheless intended to keep such debts alive for the purpose of permitting the creation of an enforceable lien upon a subject not existent when the bankruptcy became effective or even arising from, or connected with, pre-existing property but brought into being solely as the fruit of the subsequent labor of the bankrupt. . . .
>
> . . . Undoubtedly, . . . cases hold . . . that in Illinois an assignment of future wages creates a lien effective from the date of the assignment, which is not invalidated by the assignor's discharge in bankruptcy. The contention is that even if the general rule be otherwise, this court is bound to follow the Illinois decisions, since the question of the existence of a lien depends upon Illinois law.
>
> We find it unnecessary to consider whether this contention would in a different case find support in § 34 of the Judiciary Act of 1789 . . . since we are of opinion that it is precluded here by the clear and unmistakable policy of the bankruptcy act. . . .
>
> One of the primary purposes of the bankruptcy act is to "relieve the honest debtor from the weight of oppressive indebtedness and

permit him to start afresh free from the obligations and responsibilities consequent upon business misfortunes." . . . Local rules subversive of that result cannot be accepted as controlling the action of a federal court.

. . . Confining our determination to the case in hand, and leaving prospective liens upon other forms of acquisitions to be dealt with as they may arise, we reject the Illinois decisions as to the effect of an assignment of wages earned after bankruptcy as being destructive of the purpose and spirit of the bankruptcy act.

See also § 552; In re Miranda Soto, 667 F.2d 235 (1st Cir. 1981) (applying *Local Loan Co.* under new Bankruptcy Act).

IN RE REAGAN

United States Court of Appeals, Fifth Circuit, 1984.
741 F.2d 95.

Before CLARK, CHIEF JUDGE, JOLLY, and DAVIS, CIRCUIT JUDGES.

PER CURIAM:

This is an appeal from a district court's affirmance of the bankruptcy court's denial of secured status to a claim against a debtor. Because we find the present assignment of a future right to a share in a public employee retirement fund can create a valid secured claim in bankruptcy and that the right in the fund is property of the estate, we reverse the judgment of the district court.

I

Gus H. Reagan and Doris J. Reagan (debtors) filed a voluntary petition for relief under Chapter 13 of the Bankruptcy Code on August 26, 1980. Debtors listed in their schedule of debts one in the amount of $2,658.87 owed to Austin Municipal Federal Credit Union (Credit Union). This debt, incurred by debtors pursuant to an "open ended credit plan" with Credit Union, was primarily secured by funds contained in Doris Reagan's retirement fund account. That account, consisting of amounts withheld from her salary checks earned as a nurse at the municipal hospital, contained a total of $6,591.83.

Doris Reagan's right to possess and receive any benefits from the retirement fund was expressly contingent upon her termination of employment as a municipal employee. The ordinance governing the municipal retirement fund contained the following language relating to assignments of the fund as collateral:

> None of the funds, provided in the Retirement system are assignable, with the exception that assignment of funds may be made to the Austin Municipal Credit Union, . . . *provided any assignments shall not become enforceable until such time as the employee involved is actually entitled to possession of such funds.* City of Austin Retirement and Pensioning Ordinance, No. 72 0331–A. [emphasis added]

The Open End Credit Plan Agreement pursuant to which the debtors assigned Doris Reagan's retirement fund to Credit Union provides:

> Upon notice given or notice received by the maker or any co-maker of his separation from employment by the City of Austin, the entire indebtedness of the undersigned shall become immediately due and payable at the option of the Credit Union without notice, and I/we, the maker and co-makers, hereby sell, assign and transfer to the Austin Municipal Federal Credit Union, its successors and assigns, any and all sums of money which may be due me/us at such time by the City of Austin as wages or salaries, as well as any and all sums in my/our City Retirement Fund . . . such sale, assignment and transfer, however, to be only to the extent of all my/our obligations to the Credit Union, proceeds to be applied at Credit Union's discretion.

On its face, the assignment is valid under the pertinent ordinance. The issues are: (1) whether Doris Reagan's retirement fund is property of the bankruptcy estate, and (2) whether Credit Union's claim against the debtors is secured by the fund even though Doris Reagan's right to possession of the fund is contingent upon termination of her employment.

II

Section 541 of the Bankruptcy Code defines the bankrupt's estate to include "all the following property, wherever located: (1) . . . all legal or equitable interests of the debtor in property as of the commencement of the case." Reagan's retirement fund consisted solely of accumulated monies withheld from her salary checks, plus interest. Federal income and social security taxes on the fund have already been paid. The fund will become Reagan's legal property upon her separation from city employment. She presently is possessed of a legal right of assignment, albeit a limited one, and an equitable interest evidenced by her vested future rights. It therefore qualifies as property of the estate under § 541.

Sections 522 and 541(c)(2), as they read at the time of this proceeding, allow a debtor to retain certain assets which would otherwise be considered property of the estate. Section 522(d) listed property that a debtor may exempt if he chooses the federal law exemptions. Section 522(b) permits the debtor to choose state law exemptions instead of federal law exemptions. Debtors here chose the state exemptions. Texas law does not exempt retirement funds. Matter of Goff, 706 F.2d 574, 579 (5th Cir.1983).

Section 541(c)(2) provides that property subject to restrictions on alienation which are enforceable "under applicable nonbankruptcy law" never enters the property of the estate. In Matter of Goff, this court held that "applicable nonbankruptcy law" did not include an ERISA plan exemption, but that Congress intended to exclude from the property of the estate only "spendthrift trusts" traditionally protected against creditors under applicable state law. 706 F.2d at 580.

The *Goff* court explained that trust funds protected against the reach of creditors in most states are those created to provide monies for the maintenance of a beneficiary, upon which the settlor has placed "spendthrift" restrictions securing the fund from creditors and the beneficiary's own improvidence. Id. at 580. Those not so protected, in Texas and most other states, are trusts created by a settlor for his own benefit, even though they contain a spendthrift clause purporting to restrain alienation or assignment. Id. at 587. The retirement fund in this case which Reagan's contributions created for her own benefit is expressly assignable to a credit union under Texas law. The fund therefore cannot be considered a spendthrift trust of the sort traditionally beyond the reach of a creditor credit union, thus section 541(c)(2) does not prevent it from passing into the estate.

The bankruptcy court held that, despite the broad reach of § 541, equitable considerations counselled against including the retirement fund in the property of the estate. The court stated that such inclusion would frustrate the Bankruptcy Act's stated purpose of affording the debtor an unencumbered fresh start. This analysis reverts to pre-Code assessments of the legal nature of an asset in light of the purposes of the Bankruptcy Act. But as this court explained in Matter of Goff, § 541 of the Bankruptcy Code supplanted this analysis. It includes in the property of the estate all property of the debtor, even property needed for a fresh start. The exemptions and exclusions in the Code are designed to meet the purpose of retaining for the debtor property sufficient for a fresh start. In this case those exceptions and exclusions are inapplicable to the retirement fund. It therefore is included in property of the estate.

III

The district court, affirming the bankruptcy court, denied secured status to Credit Union's claim. The court relied on 11 U.S.C. § 502(b), which states:

> (b) The Court . . . shall allow such claim in such amount except to the extent that—
>
> > (1) such claim is unenforceable against the debtor, and unenforceable against property of the debtor, under any agreement or applicable law for a reason other than because such claim is contingent or unmatured.

The court reasoned that Doris Reagan was not entitled to the retirement fund until termination of her employment with the city, and that the security agreement was unenforceable until "the employee involved is actually entitled to possession of such funds." He therefore found the security interest to be unenforceable, and affirmed the bankruptcy judge's order holding Credit Union's claim unsecured. We disagree with the court's answer to this novel question.

The district court misperceived the significance of the "claim" language of § 506(b)(1). An accepted interpretation of the first part of this section is:

> When the debtor and the creditor might have come to some agreement whereby the creditor would not be permitted to assert his claim against the debtor, that claim will remain unenforceable in the bankruptcy case and, under section 502(b)(1), would not for that reason be allowed to share in a distribution of the debtor's assets.

3 Collier on Bankruptcy, ¶ 502.02[1] at 502–28 (15th ed. 1983). The security agreement here did not forbid Credit Union to assert its claim against the Reagans for the loan it had made them.[1] Rather, it recognized the indebtedness and made an assignment of Reagan's interest in the retirement fund as security for the loan. That the security interest was to vest in Reagan or Credit Union in the future does not affect the present enforceability of the underlying claim or render the claim unsecured. The district court's construction confuses the claim and the security for the claim. Its interpretation of 11 U.S.C. § 502(b)(1) was erroneous.

Reagan could not prevail even if the district court's theory were proper. Reagan got Credit Union's money and gave in exchange a present assignment of her future rights in the retirement fund. That presently operative assignment created the security Credit Union claims. Though Credit Union cannot convert the security to cash until Reagan is separated from her employment, it is entitled above all other claimants to assert in bankruptcy its security interest in the assigned fund. Section 502(b)(1) literally would erect no bar even if it applied to the security. Credit Union's assignment security is presently unenforceable only because Reagan's rights to the funds have not matured by separation. This would be the precise situation covered by the "other than" words of section 502(b)(1).

The claim of Credit Union should be treated as secured by the assigned interest in Reagan's retirement fund to the extent of the Reagan's obligation to the Credit Union.[2] That security interest, along with any other interests in the fund, will become enforceable upon the termination of Doris Reagan's employment by the municipality.

Notes & Questions

1. Is *Reagan* consistent with *Local Loan Co. v. Hunt?*

2. How do *Reagan* and *Bell* square with the justifications for discharge discussed in the Weistart and Jackson, excerpts, supra?

1. We note that if it had, the proper course would have been to disallow the claim entirely, rather than to relegate it to unsecured status.

2. The proof in this case showed that there was more money in the retirement fund than the amount of the Credit Union's claim, and that the City's eventual contributions could only increase the fund. Therefore, it appears that Credit Union's claim was fully secured by Reagan's otherwise unassignable and indefeasible future right to receive her share of the fund.

B. The Scope of the Discharge

1. The Concept of Claim

OHIO v. KOVACS

Supreme Court of the United States, 1985.
469 U.S. 274, 105 S.Ct. 705, 83 L.Ed.2d 649.

JUSTICE WHITE delivered the opinion of the Court.

Petitioner State of Ohio obtained an injunction ordering respondent William Kovacs to clean up a hazardous waste site. A receiver was subsequently appointed. Still later, Kovacs filed a petition for bankruptcy. The question before us is whether, in the circumstances present here, Kovacs' obligation under the injunction is a "debt" or "liability on a claim" subject to discharge under the Bankruptcy Code.

I

Kovacs was the chief executive officer and stockholder of Chem–Dyne Corp., which with other business entities operated an industrial and hazardous waste disposal site in Hamilton, Ohio. In 1976, the State sued Kovacs and the business entities in state court for polluting public waters, maintaining a nuisance, and causing fish kills, all in violation of state environmental laws. In 1979, both in his individual capacity and on behalf of Chem–Dyne, Kovacs signed a stipulation and judgment entry settling the lawsuit. Among other things, the stipulation enjoined the defendants from causing further pollution of the air or public waters, forbade bringing additional industrial wastes onto the site, required the defendants to remove specified wastes from the property, and ordered the payment of $75,000 to compensate the State for injury to wildlife.

Kovacs and the other defendants failed to comply with their obligations under the injunction. The State then obtained the appointment in state court of a receiver, who was directed to take possession of all property and other assets of Kovacs and the corporate defendants and to implement the judgment entry by cleaning up the Chem–Dyne site. The receiver took possession of the site but had not completed his tasks when Kovacs filed a personal bankruptcy petition.[1]

Seeking to develop a basis for requiring part of Kovacs' postbankruptcy income to be applied to the unfinished task of the receivership, the State then filed a motion in state court to discover Kovacs' current income and assets. Kovacs requested that the Bankruptcy Court stay those proceedings, which it did.[2] The State also filed a complaint in the

---

1. Kovacs originally filed a reorganization petition under Chapter 11 of the Bankruptcy Code, 11 U.S.C. § 1101 et seq., but converted the petition to a liquidation bankruptcy under Chapter 7. See 11 U.S.C. § 1112.

2. The Bankruptcy Court held that the requested hearing was an effort to collect money from Kovacs in violation of the automatic stay provision. See 11 U.S.C. § 362. It entered a specific stay as well. The District Court affirmed, ruling that Ohio was trying to enforce a judgment obtained before filing of the bankruptcy petition. The Court of Appeals for the Sixth Circuit also found the hearing

Bankruptcy Court seeking a declaration that Kovacs' obligation under the stipulation and judgment order to clean up the Chem–Dyne site was not dischargeable in bankruptcy because it was not a "debt," a liability on a "claim," within the meaning of the Bankruptcy Code. In addition, the complaint sought an injunction against the bankruptcy trustee to restrain him from pursuing any action to recover assets of Kovacs in the hands of the receiver. The Bankruptcy Court ruled against Ohio, In re Kovacs, 29 B.R. 816 (SD Ohio 1982), as did the District Court. The Court of Appeals for the sixth circuit affirmed, holding that Ohio essentially sought from Kovacs only a monetary payment and that such a required payment was a liability on a claim that was dischargeable und r the bankruptcy statute. In re Kovacs, 717 F.2d 984 (1983). We granted certiorari to determine the dischargeability of Kovacs' obligation under the affirmative injunction entered against him.

. . .

III

Except for the nine kinds of debts saved from discharge by 11 U.S.C. § 523(a), a discharge in bankruptcy discharges the debtor from all debts that arose before bankruptcy. § 727(b). It is not claimed here that Kovacs' obligation under the injunction fell within any of the categories of debts excepted from discharge by § 523. Rather, the State submits that the obligation to clean up the Chem–Dyne site is not a debt at all within the meaning of the bankruptcy law.

For bankruptcy purposes, a debt is a liability on a claim. § 101(11). A claim is defined by § 101(4) as follows:

"(4) 'claim' means—

"(A) right to payment, whether or not such right is reduced to judgment, liquidated, unliquidated, fixed, contingent, matured, unmatured, disputed, undisputed, legal, equitable, secured, or unsecured; or

"(B) right to an equitable remedy for breach of performance if such breach gives rise to a right to payment, whether or not such right to an equitable remedy is reduced to judgment, fixed, contingent, matured, unmatured, disputed, undisputed, secured, or unsecured."

The provision at issue here is § 101(4)(B). For the purposes of that section, there is little doubt that the State had the right to an equitable remedy under state law and that the right has been reduced to judgment in the form of an injunction ordering the cleanup. The State argues, however, that the injunction it has secured is not a claim

barred. In re Kovacs, 681 F.2d 454 (1982). In that court's view, while § 362(b) allowed governmental units to continue to enforce police powers through mandatory injunctions, it denied them the power to collect money in their enforcement efforts. Because of the later filing by Ohio of a complaint to declare that Kovacs' obligations were not claims under bankruptcy, we granted certiorari, vacated the judgment of the Court of Appeals, and remanded to that court to consider whether the dispute over the stay was moot. 459 U.S. 1167, 103 S.Ct. 810, 74 L.Ed.2d 1010 (1983). As far as we are advised, the Court of Appeals has taken no action on the remand.

against Kovacs for bankruptcy purposes because (1) Kovacs' default was a breach of the statute, not a breach of an ordinary commercial contract which concededly would give rise to a claim; and (2) Kovacs' breach of his obligation under the injunction did not give rise to a right to payment within the meaning of § 101(4)(B). We are not persuaded by either submission.

There is no indication in the language of the statute that the right to performance cannot be a claim unless it arises from a contractual arrangement. The State resorted to the courts to enforce its environmental laws against Kovacs and secured a negative order to cease polluting, an affirmative order to clean up the site, and an order to pay a sum of money to recompense the State for damage done to the fish population. Each order was one to remedy an alleged breach of Ohio law; and if Kovacs' obligation to pay $75,000 to the State is a debt dischargeable in bankruptcy, which the State freely concedes, it makes little sense to assert that because the cleanup order was entered to remedy a statutory violation, it cannot likewise constitute a claim for bankruptcy purposes. Furthermore, it is apparent that Congress desired a broad definition of a "claim" and knew how to limit the application of a provision to contracts when it desired to do so.[4] Other provisions cited by Ohio refute, rather than support, its strained interpretation.[5]

The courts below also found little substance in the submission that the cleanup obligation did not give rise to a right to payment that renders the order dischargeable under § 727. The definition of "claim" in H.R. 8200 as originally drafted would have deemed a right to an equitable remedy for breach of performance a claim even if it did not give rise to a right to payment.[6] The initial Senate definition of claim was narrower,[7] and a compromise version, § 101(4), was finally adopted. In that version, the key phrases "equitable remedy," "breach of performance," and "right to payment" are not defined. See 11 U.S.C. § 101. Nor are the differences between the successive versions explained. The legislative history offers only a statement by the sponsors of the Bankruptcy Reform Act with respect to the scope of the provision:

"Section 101(4)(B) . . . is intended to cause the liquidation or estimation of contingent rights of payment for which there may be an alternative equitable remedy with the result that the equitable remedy will be susceptible to being discharged in bankruptcy. For

4. See 11 U.S.C. § 365 (assumption or rejection of executory contracts and leases).

5. Congress created exemptions from discharge for claims involving penalties and forfeitures owed to a governmental unit, 11 U.S.C. § 523(a)(7), and for claims involving embezzlement and larceny. § 523(a)(4). If a bankruptcy debtor has committed larceny or embezzlement, giving rise to a remedy of either damages or equitable restitution under state law, the resulting liability for breach of an obligation created by law is clearly a claim which is nondischargeable in bankruptcy.

6. H.R. 8200, 95th Cong., 1st Sess., 309–310 (House Committee print 1977), as reported September 8, 1977.

7. See S. 2266, 95th Cong., 1st Sess., 299 (1977), as introduced October 31, 1977.

example, in some States, a judgment for specific performance may be satisfied by an alternative right to payment in the event performance is refused; in that event, the creditor entitled to specific performance would have a 'claim' for purposes of a proceeding under title 11." [8]

We think the rulings of the courts below were wholly consistent with the statute and its legislative history, sparse as it is. The Bankruptcy Court ruled as follows, In re Kovacs, 29 B.R., at 816:

"There is no suggestion by plaintiff that defendant can render performance under the affirmative obligation other than by the payment of money. We therefore conclude that plaintiff has a claim against defendant within the meaning of 11 U.S.C. § 101(4), and that defendant owes plaintiff a debt within the meaning of 11 U.S.C. § 101(11). Furthermore, we have concluded that that debt is dischargeable."

. . . As we understand it, the Court of Appeals held that, in the circumstances, the cleanup duty had been reduced to a monetary obligation.

We do not disturb this judgment. The injunction surely obliged Kovacs to clean up the site. But when he failed to do so, rather than prosecute Kovacs under the environmental laws or bring civil or criminal contempt proceedings, the State secured the appointment of a receiver, who was ordered to take possession of all of Kovacs' nonexempt assets as well as the assets of the corporate defendants and to comply with the injunction entered against Kovacs. As wise as this course may have been, it dispossessed Kovacs, removed his authority over the site, and divested him of assets that might have been used by him to clean up the property. Furthermore, when the bankruptcy trustee sought to recover Kovacs' assets from the receiver, the latter sought an injunction against such action. Although Kovacs had been ordered to "cooperate" with the receiver, he was disabled by the receivership from personally taking charge of and carrying out the removal of wastes from the property. What the receiver wanted from Kovacs after bankruptcy was the money to defray cleanup costs. At oral argument in this Court, the State's counsel conceded that after the receiver was appointed, the only performance sought from Kovacs was the payment of money. Tr. of Oral Arg. 19–20. Had Kovacs furnished the necessary funds, either before or after bankruptcy, there seems little doubt that the receiver and the State would have been satisfied. On the facts before it, and with the receiver in control of the site,[10] we cannot fault the Court of Appeals for concluding that the cleanup order

8. 124 Cong.Rec. 32393 (1978) (remarks of Rep. Edwards); see also id., at 33992 (remarks of Sen. DeConcini).

10. We were advised at oral argument that the receiver at that time was still in possession of the site, although he was contemplating terminating the receivership. Tr. of Oral Arg. 4, 56–57. We were also advised that it was difficult to tell exactly who owned the property at 500 Ford Boulevard and that although the trustee did not formally abandon the property, he did not seek to take possession of it. Id., at 55, 58.

had been converted into an obligation to pay money, an obligation that was dischargeable in bankruptcy.[11]

IV

It is well to emphasize what we have not decided. First, we do not suggest that Kovacs' discharge will shield him from prosecution for having violated the environmental laws of Ohio or for criminal contempt for not performing his obligations under the injunction prior to bankruptcy. Second, had a fine or monetary penalty for violation of state law been imposed on Kovacs prior to bankruptcy, § 523(a)(7) forecloses any suggestion that his obligation to pay the fine or penalty would be discharged in bankruptcy. Third, we do not address what the legal consequences would have been had Kovacs taken bankruptcy before a receiver had been appointed and a trustee had been designated with the usual duties of a bankruptcy trustee.[12] Fourth, we do not hold that the injunction against bringing further toxic wastes on the premises or against any conduct that will contribute to the pollution of the site or the State's waters is dischargeable in bankruptcy; we here address, as did the Court of Appeals, only the affirmative duty to clean up the site and the duty to pay money to that end. Finally, we do not question that anyone in possession of the site—whether it is Kovacs or another in the event the receivership is liquidated and the trustee abandons the property, or a vendee from the receiver or the bankruptcy trustee—must comply with the environmental laws of the State of Ohio. Plainly, that person or firm may not maintain a nuisance, pollute the waters of the State, or refuse to remove the source of such conditions. As the case comes to us, however, Kovacs has been dispossessed and the State seeks to enforce his cleanup obligation by a money judgment.

The judgment of the Court of Appeals is

11. The State relies on Penn Terra, Ltd. v. Department of Environmental Resources, 733 F.2d 267 (CA3 1984). There, the Court of Appeals for the Third Circuit held that the automatic stay provision of 11 U.S.C. § 362 did not apply to the State's seeking an injunction against a bankrupt to require compliance with the environmental laws. This was held to be an effort to enforce the police power statutes of the State, not a suit to enforce a money judgment. But in that case, there had been no appointment of a receiver who had the duty to comply with the state law and who was seeking money from the bankrupt. The automatic stay provision does not apply to suits to enforce the regulatory statutes of the State, but the enforcement of such a judgment by seeking money from the bankrupt—what the Court of Appeals for the Sixth Circuit concluded was involved in this case—is another matter.

12. . . . Had no receiver been appointed prior to Kovacs' bankruptcy, the trustee would have been charged with the duty of collecting Kovacs' nonexempt property and administering it. If the site at issue were Kovacs' property, the trustee would shortly determine whether it was of value to the estate. If the property was worth more than the costs of bringing it into compliance with state law, the trustee would undoubtedly sell it for its net value, and the buyer would clean up the property, in which event whatever obligation Kovacs might have had to clean up the property would have been satisfied. If the property were worth less than the cost of cleanup, the trustee would likely abandon it to its prior owner, who would have to comply with the state environmental law to the extent of his or its ability.

Affirmed.

JUSTICE O'CONNOR, concurring.

. . . I write separately to address the petitioner's concern that the Court's action will impede States in enforcing their environmental laws.

To say that Kovacs' obligation in these circumstances is a claim dischargeable in bankruptcy does not wholly excuse the obligation or leave the State without any recourse against Kovacs' assets to enforce the order. Because "Congress has generally left the determination of property rights in the assets of a bankrupt's estate to state law," Butner v. United States, 440 U.S. 48, 54, 99 S.Ct. 914, 918, 59 L.Ed.2d 136 (1979), the classification of Ohio's interest as either a lien on the property itself, a perfected security interest, or merely an unsecured claim depends on Ohio law. That classification—a question not before us—generally determines the priority of the State's claim to the assets of the estate relative to other creditors. Cf. 11 U.S.C. § 545 (trustee may avoid statutory liens only in specified circumstances). Thus, a State may protect its interest in the enforcement of its environmental laws by giving cleanup judgments the status of statutory liens or secured claims.

The Court's holding that the cleanup order was a "claim" within the meaning of § 101(4) also avoids potentially adverse consequences for a State's enforcement of its order when the debtor is a corporation, rather than an individual. In a Chapter 7 proceeding under the Bankruptcy Code, a corporate debtor transfers its property to a trustee for distribution among the creditors who hold cognizable claims, and then generally dissolves under state law. Because the corporation usually ceases to exist, it has no postbankruptcy earnings that could be utilized by the State to fulfill the cleanup order. The State's only recourse in such a situation may well be its "claim" to the prebankruptcy assets.

For both these reasons, the Court's holding today cannot be viewed as hostile to state enforcement of environmental laws.

Notes & Questions

1. *Losing But Winning.* Is the State of Ohio better off having lost this case than if it had won it? Is one better placed in a bankruptcy to have an interest that is nondischargeable and not a claim, or to have one that is both a claim and dischargeable?

What can the state do to enhance its position in bankruptcy after *Kovacs?*

2. *Abandoning Property.* Recall that in *Bell,* supra, the trustee abandoned property of the estate, thereby allowing GMAC to foreclose its lien. In Midlantic National Bank v. New Jersey Department of Environmental Protection, 474 U.S. 494, 106 S.Ct. 755, 88 L.Ed.2d 859 (1986), the trustee sought to abandon property for a different reason.

The property used by the *Midlantic* debtor was a waste oil facility that the debtor had operated in violation of a state operating permit by accepting more than 400,000 gallons of oil contaminated with PCB, a highly toxic carcinogen. The NJDEP ordered the debtor to cease operations at the site. Before the negotiations between the debtor and the NJDEP concluded the debtor filed a Chapter 11 petition. The next day the NJDEP issued an administrative order requiring the debtor to clean up the site. The case was converted to Chapter 7 and the debtor sought to abandon the property, including the costs of cleaning it up.

The Supreme Court, in a 5–4 decision, held that abandonment could not be supported. It relied on pre–1978 Act law limiting the trustee's § 554 abandonment power to protect legitimate state or federal interests. It concluded, "The Bankruptcy Court does not have the power to authorize an abandonment without formulating conditions that will adequately protect the public's health and safety." The effect of denying the abandonment power seems to have been that the debtor's assets would all be consumed in cleaning up the site, leaving nothing for creditors.

3. What is the relationship between the issues in *Kovacs* and *Midlantic?*

See generally Baird & Jackson, Kovacs and Toxic Wastes in Bankruptcy, 36 Stan.L.Rev. 1199 (1984).

2. Exceptions

Section 523 contains a substantial lists of debts that are ineligible for discharge in at least a Chapter 7 bankruptcy. What rationale or rationales underlie the list of nondischargeable debts?

Notes & Questions

1. *Who Benefits from Nondischargeability?* Once one concludes that nondischargeability of some debts is appropriate, two separate questions arise. The first question, which § 523(a) addresses in some detail, is which debts should not be discharged? The second question is which creditors should benefit from the finding of nondischargeability? Section 523(a) offers the obvious answer—the creditor who benefits is the creditor whose debt is nondischargeable. Is the obvious answer the correct answer for all debts? If the goal of nondischargeability is to discourage the incurrence of such debts, could the same deterrent effect be obtained by distributing the benefit of a nondischargeable debt among all the innocent unsecured creditors? Does § 523(a) protect some creditors from their own lack of prudence in extending credit to the debtor?

2. *Consolidation Loans.* In three separate transactions, debtor borrowed $100, $200, and $300 from Finance Co. Rather than repay the loans when due, debtor obtained from Finance Co. a consolidation loan in the amount of $1,000, with $600 of the new loan being applied to repay the old loans. In obtaining the consolidation loan, debtor

furnished a materially false financial statement. In a subsequent bankruptcy proceeding, to what extent is the consolidation loan dischargeable? See § 523(a)(2); In re Danns, 558 F.2d 114 (2d Cir. 1977). Compare In re Carter, 11 B.R. 992 (Bkrtcy.M.D.Tenn.1981) (entire renewal loan not dischargeable where prior loans had matured and were overdue).

See generally Zaretsky, The Fraud Exception to Discharge Under the New Bankruptcy Code, 53 Am.Bankr.L.J. 253 (1979).

3. *Taxes and § 523(a)(1).* Section 6672 of the Internal Revenue Code provides:

> Any person required to collect, truthfully account for, and pay over any tax imposed by this title who willfully fails to collect such tax, or truthfully account for and pay over such tax, or willfully attempts in any manner to evade or defeat any such tax or the payment thereof, shall, in addition to other penalties provided by law, be liable to a penalty equal to the total amount of the tax evaded, or not collected, or not accounted for and paid over.

In United States v. Sotelo, 436 U.S. 268, 98 S.Ct. 1795, 56 L.Ed.2d 275 (1978), a case involving an objection to discharge under § 17a of the old bankruptcy act, the Court analyzed § 6672 as follows:

> [T]he "penalty" language of Internal Revenue Code § 6672 is [not] dispositive of the status of the . . . debt under Bankruptcy Act § 17a(1)–(e). The funds here involved were unquestionably "taxes" at the time they were "collected or withheld from others." . . . That the funds due are referred to as a "penalty" when the Government later seeks to recover them does not alter their essential character as taxes for purposes of the Bankruptcy Act, at least in a case in which, as here, the § 6672 liability is predicated on a failure to pay over, rather than a failure initially to collect, the taxes.

If a debtor fails to pay federal withholding taxes, may the debtor obtain a discharge for amounts owing under § 6672? See § 523(a)(1), (a)(7); In re Dickey, 10 B.R. 9 (Bkrtcy.W.D.Tenn.1980) (no discharge).

4. *Credit Binges and the Background of § 523(a)(2)(B).*

R. SCOTT. It seems to me that Allen Farnsworth reminded us of our basic failure, the failure to consider the merits. The economists ask for an enumeration of the benefits of abolishing the fraud exception. Their argument is that if the fraud exception is abolished, there will be an increase in the amount of fraud. Policing against that fraud will be costly for creditors, and there is some evidence that those costs will fall on those consumer-debtors whom the proposal is designed to protect. Consequently, the proposal, viewed in that light, doesn't make any sense. The argument is probably correct.

Unfortunately, it misses the point. The point is that the abolition of the fraud exception is not premised on the notion that the fraud exception prevents consumer fraud. Rather it reflects the belief that the fraud exception is a vehicle for creditor fraud. Of course, this assumption may well be gratuitous, but there are some rather explicit data to support it. Marjorie Girth was alluding a moment ago to the classic case.

MANNE. For our record, will you repeat the classic case?

R. SCOTT. Yes. A creditor will say to a borrower, "List some of your debts," and the debtor replies, "How many?" The creditor responds, "Well, there are three spaces; put down three creditors." Subsequently that list will be used to prevent discharge when it is discovered that, indeed, the debtor had a dozen additional creditors.

Well, one may respond, as Mike Jensen would, "That's easy; that's creditor fraud. We'll solve that." But that is trying to solve one legal problem in a vacuum. It narrows the inquiry in such a way that it becomes meaningless. From our perspective as lawyers, the cost of policing against that creditor fraud is quite high, because of the existence of other legal rules. They may be archaic, but nonetheless there's the parole evidence rule, among others, which prevents the kind of testimony which could demonstrate that the creditor has been fraudulent. So one can develop an argument (which should be tested) that the costs of policing this kind of creditor fraud exceed the costs that would be imposed by the abolition of the exception to discharge of loans gained through fraudulent financial statements. And that's the argument behind this proposal.

Discussion, 41 Law & Contemp.Probs. 123, 169–70 (1977). How well does § 523(a)(2)(B) deal with the "classic case?"

The 1984 amendments added § 523(a)(2)(C), which presumes that consumer "credit binges" to acquire "luxury goods or services" shortly before bankruptcy are tainted by fraud or falsity within the meaning of § 523(a)(2)(A), and therefore are not dischargeable.

5. *Criminal Penalties and § 523(a)(7).* In Kelly v. Robinson, 479 U.S. ___, 107 S.Ct. 353, 93 L.Ed.2d 216 (1986), the Court interpreted § 523(a)(7) to except from discharge any condition a state criminal court imposes as part of a criminal sentence, including restitution obligations. Section 523(a)(9) denies discharges of debts arising out of drunk driving incidents.

6. *The Exceptions to Discharge and Bankruptcy Policy.* Do the exceptions to discharge square with the theories of discharge discussed in the Weistart and Jackson excerpts, supra?

BOYLE v. ABILENE LUMBER, INC.
United States Court of Appeals, Fifth Circuit, 1987.
819 F.2d 583.

Before CLARK, CHIEF JUDGE, GARWOOD and HILL, CIRCUIT JUDGES.

GARWOOD, CIRCUIT JUDGE:

Appellant Christopher Boyle ("Boyle") appeals a bankruptcy court decision, affirmed by the district court, holding that Boyle was personally liable on debts for supplies incurred by two Texas corporations Boyle controlled and that these debts were not dischargeable in bankruptcy. The courts below ruled that a Texas statute addressing the use by contractors of construction funds created a trust for bankruptcy purposes and that Boyle, who had used funds advanced for specific projects on other projects, but was not found to have done so fraudulently, could not discharge debts owed to unpaid creditors. Because we conclude that the Texas statute does not suffice to constitute Boyle's conduct a fiduciary defalcation for purposes of the nondischargeable debt exception of the Bankruptcy Code, we reverse.

I.

Appellant owned and operated two corporations in the Abilene, Texas area. Christopher Boyle Builder, Inc. ("Boyle Builder"), was engaged in the residential construction business and at times had several construction jobs underway simultaneously. Boyle's other corporation, Abilene Home Energy, Inc. ("Home Energy"), evaluated the insulation and other weatherproofing in existing homes and installed insulating materials to make homes more energy efficient. Both corporations purchased materials on credit from, *inter alia*, Abilene Lumber, Inc. ("Abilene Lumber"). The courts below found that Boyle executed a personal "guaranty agreement" in favor of Abilene Lumber for purchases made by each corporation.

Beginning in late 1981, Boyle Builder began to encounter financial problems. In September 1982, Abilene Lumber filed mechanic's and materialman's liens on four houses built by Boyle Builder, but later released two of these liens. In 1983, Boyle's primary lender, Abilene National Bank ("the Bank") instituted foreclosure proceedings and attempted to collect a deficiency. Boyle and his businesses filed this bankruptcy proceeding on June 7, 1984.

Abilene Lumber had supplied but not been paid for materials it identified through invoice job descriptions as having been purchased (1) by Home Energy, without describing any specific projects for which the supplies were acquired, and (2) by Boyle Builder for four houses it had constructed, with specific invoices traceable to each building project. Abilene Lumber filed a complaint requesting the bankruptcy court to determine the dischargeability of these five debts, and the issue came to trial on March 14, 1985.

The court held that none of the debts were dischargeable. In evaluating the Boyle Builder purchases, the court focused on four houses constructed by that firm and concluded that Boyle Builder had financed building three with loans from the Bank and the fourth with construction payments from the individual for whom the house was being built.[1] The court concluded Boyle was personally liable for $15,528.33 in credit purchases from Abilene Lumber made by Boyle Builder and for $1,851.31 in credit purchases by Home Energy.

The bankruptcy court found, and the district court agreed, that Boyle Builder had deposited all loan proceeds and construction contract payments into a single business checking account, into which it also deposited the proceeds of other work, and that Boyle Builder had not used any system to segregate loan or construction contract payment funds in order to ensure that they were used only on the construction project for which the corporation received them but, instead, had merely drawn checks on its account as bills fell due without regard to the source of the funds.

The courts below held that all five debts were nondischargeable because, first, a Texas statute[2] treats funds loaned or paid under a construction contract to finance an improvement on specific real property as funds the builder holds in trust for the benefit of those unpaid creditors who contributed labor or material to the project, and, second, because provisions of the Bankruptcy Code state that an individual's debts "for fraud or defalcation while acting in a fiduciary capacity" cannot be discharged.[3] There was no finding, and indeed no evidence, that Boyle or either of his corporations acted fraudulently, or that there were any agreements with Abilene Lumber, the Bank, or the homeowner which either required segregation of the funds, or otherwise by force of their own terms, and apart from the Texas statute, made Boyle or his companies fiduciaries of the funds. Indeed, there is no finding or evidence that Boyle or his corporations breached any of their agreements in any way other than by failing to pay the amounts claimed.

Appellant challenges the conclusions of the district court on three grounds, substantially as follows: (1) that the Texas statute does not suffice to constitute Boyle's conduct a fiduciary defalcation for purposes of the Bankruptcy Code debt discharge exception; (2) that the courts below erred in finding the entire claim of Abilene Lumber was nondischargeable rather than only an amount equal to appellant's actual "misapplication" on each particular project; and (3) that the claim

---

1. The four houses are identified here by the addition to the City of Abilene in which each was located. The totals of the funds provided for construction and owed to Abilene Lumber established by the court below were as follows:

Property	Source of funds	Amount provided	Amount owed Abilene Lumber
Coronado Estates	Owner	$ 69,791	$ 8,574.20
Mesquite Forest	Bank	$ 67,920	$ 3,473.75
Hunters Creek	Bank	$ 58,400	$ 1,274.92
Lytle Shores	Bank	$150,000*	$ 2,205.46
TOTAL		$346,111	$15,528.33

* The bankruptcy court described this as an approximate amount.

2. 3 Tex.Prop.Code Ann. ch. 162 (§§ 162.001 to .033) (Vernon 1984) (discussed and quoted below).

3. 11 U.S.C. § 523(a)(4) (discussed and quoted below).

against Home Energy did not in any event fall within the scope of the Texas statute.

We agree with appellant's first contention. Because it is dispositive of this dispute, we need not decide and do not reach his remaining claims.

II.

A. *The Texas construction funds statute*

We examine first the Texas construction funds statute, 3 Tex.Prop. Code Ann. §§ 162.001 to .033 (Vernon 1984), which provides in pertinent part as follows:

"Section 162.001

"(a) Construction payments are trust funds under this chapter if the payments are made to a contractor or subcontractor or to an officer, director, or agent of a contractor or subcontractor, under a construction contract for the improvement of specific real property in this state.

"(b) Loan receipts are trust funds under this chapter if the funds are borrowed by a contractor, subcontractor, or owner or by an officer, director, or agent of a contractor, subcontractor, or owner for the purpose of improving specific real property in this state, and the loan is secured in whole or in part by a lien on the property.

"Section 162.002

"A contractor, subcontractor, or owner, or an officer, director, or agent of a contractor, subcontractor, or owner, who receives trust funds or who has control or direction of trust funds, is a trustee of the trust funds.

"Section 162.003

"An artist, laborer, mechanic, contractor, subcontractor, or materialman who labors or who furnishes labor or material for the construction or repair of an improvement on specific real property in this state is a beneficiary of any trust funds paid or received in connection with the improvement.

"Section 162.004

" . . . .

"(b) The Texas Trust Act . . . does not apply to any trust created under this chapter. . . .

"Section 162.031

"(a) Except as provided by Subsection (b), a trustee who, with intent to defraud, directly or indirectly retains, uses, disburses, or otherwise diverts trust funds without first fully paying all obligations incurred by the trustee to the beneficiaries of the trust funds has misapplied the trust funds.

"(b) A trustee may use trust funds to pay the trustee's reasonable overhead expenses that are directly related to the construction or repair of the improvement.

"Section 162.032

"(a) A trustee who misapplies trust funds amounting to less than $250 commits an offense punishable by confinement in jail for not more than two years and by a fine of not more than $500 or by the confinement without the fine.

"(b) A trustee who misapplies trust funds amounting to $250 or more commits an offense punishable by imprisonment in the Texas Department of Corrections for not more than 10 years."

Applying the statute to the facts of this case, the courts below correctly concluded that section 162.001 reached the funds loaned by the Bank for three projects and paid by the owner under a construction contract on the fourth project and that Abilene Lumber's credit sales to Boyle Builder for these four homes, by which Abilene Lumber furnished building materials for "an improvement on specific real property," placed the creditor within the class of beneficiaries described by section 162.003. While we are inclined to view the sales to Home Energy as not addressed by the Texas statute, we treat this fifth claim *arguendo* as though it also were within its coverage, although our discussion will be only in terms of the Boyle Builder claims.[4]

The actual language of the Texas statute, we emphasize, provides only for a criminal penalty and then only if the holder of construction funds "retains, uses, disburses, or otherwise diverts trust funds without first fully paying all obligations" to the named classes of creditors "*with intent to defraud.*" The statute contains no provision requiring the fund holder to segregate funds by source and project; it does not prohibit the commingling of funds; it does not bar use of funds provided for one project to pay bills incurred on another project if this is done without an "intent to defraud"; and it does not prohibit a fund holder from paying, without any fraudulent intent, creditors on one

---

4. Neither the findings of the bankruptcy court and district court nor the record below make reference to any identifiable pool of funds provided under a construction contract or loaned to Home Energy for improvements on "*specific* real property," a fundamental prerequisite for the application of sections 162.001 and 162.003. Indeed, the only testimony about the Home Energy purchases indicated they were not traceable to a specific property but, instead, included equipment used on more than one project and purchases for projects other than the four homes involved in this case. Consequently, we find no support for

the conclusion of the courts below that Abilene Lumber's claim against Home Energy was analogous to its claims against Boyle Builder, which were based on materials supplied for construction or improvements on specific, identified real property as to which Boyle Builder had received construction loan proceeds secured by the respective properties or construction contract advances. Our decision that the debt discharge exception of section 523(a)(4) is inapplicable on other grounds, however, makes it unnecessary to remand for further findings on this issue respecting Home Energy.

project with surplus funds left over from earlier work and then using
the funds provided for that later project on still other work. In short,
the statute does not create "red," "blue," and "yellow" dollars each of
which can only be used for the "red," "blue," or "yellow" construction
project. Although cases construing the statute have expanded its reach
beyond its express language, the above-referenced limitations in the
statute's actual terms are relevant in determining what *fiduciary*
duties are imposed on the fund holder and the manner in which the
state's statutory construction funds "trust" interacts with the Bankruptcy Code debt discharge exception for those debts arising from
fiduciary activities.

B. The Bankruptcy Code's nondischargeable debt provision

The general policy of bankruptcy law favors allowing the debtor to
discharge debts and to make a fresh start. This policy, however, is
subject to exceptions for certain types of debts, including those arising
from a debtor's malfeasance. The specific exception relied upon by
both courts below is provided in 11 U.S.C. § 523(a)(4), which, like its
predecessor statute, bars discharge of those debts a debtor incurs
through "defalcation while acting in a fiduciary capacity." Although
the language of section 523(a)(4) does not precisely parallel that of its
predecessor statute, for purposes of this appeal we assume that Congress did not intend to narrow the substantive content of this particular
debt discharge exception by enacting section 523(a)(4), and we apply
decisions construing the predecessor section as though they were equally applicable to section 523(a)(4).

The plain language of the statute and limited evidence of congressional intent [10] indicate that the pertinent debt discharge exception was
intended to reach those debts incurred through abuses of fiduciary
positions and through active misconduct whereby a debtor has deprived
others of their property by criminal acts; both classes of conduct
involve debts arising from the debtor's acquisition or use of property
that is not the debtor's.

Cases construing the Bankruptcy Act's exceptions to debt dischargeability are "consistent with the well-established principle that
exceptions to discharge should be limited to those clearly expressed in
the statute." Angelle v. Reed (In re Angelle), 610 F.2d 1335, 1339 (5th
Cir.1980). Those exceptions expressed in the Act are generally to be
"narrowly construed . . . against the creditor and in favor of the
bankrupt." Murphy & Robinson Investment Co. v. Cross (In re Cross),

---

10. The most significant passage in the
legislative history addressing subsection
523(a)(4) is the following:

"Paragraph (4) excepts debts for embezzlement or larceny. The deletion of
willful and malicious conversion from
§ 17a(2) of the Bankruptcy Act is not
intended to effect a substantive change.
The intent is to include in the category

of non-dischargeable debts *a conversion
under which the debtor willfully and ma-
liciously intends to borrow property* for a
short period of time with no intent to
inflict injury but on which injury is in
fact inflicted." 1978 U.S.Code. Cong. &
Ad.News 6320 (reprinting H.Rep. No.
595, 95th Cong., 2d Sess. 364; emphasis
added).

666 F.2d 873, 879–80 (5th Cir.1982). These same principles should apply to the Bankruptcy Code.

This Court has on three occasions examined the relationship between the predecessor statute to section 523(a)(4) and state construction fund "trust" statutes other than the Texas act. We held on two occasions that the state statutes did not create a trust for purposes of the Bankruptcy Code. *Cross,* supra (holding Georgia statute did not create a trust cognizable for purposes of section 35(a)(4)); *Angelle,* supra (reaching this result construing a similar Louisiana statute). In one opinion, we determined that the state statute did operate to create a trust that could be recognized under the standards of the debt discharge exception. Carey Lumber Co. v. Bell, 615 F.2d 370 (5th Cir.1980) (finding that Oklahoma statute did create a trust for purposes of section 35(a)(4)).

In each decision, we were guided by the Supreme Court's holdings that the exception applies only to a "technical trust . . . [which] must exist prior to the act creating the debt and without reference to that act." *Angelle,* supra, at 1338. Like the Texas statute, the Georgia and Louisiana laws involved in *Cross* and *Angelle* provided only for criminal penalties and did not bar a contractor's use of funds for other purposes. Unlike the Texas statute, the Oklahoma lien law found to create a trust for purposes of the debt discharge exception strictly limited the use of construction funds to the project for which the funds were loaned or advanced, *expressly prohibiting* any other use.[14] There is no comparable provision in the Texas statute.

We found that the state statutes in *Cross* and *Angelle* imposed no obligations on the holder of construction funds unless and until creditors were unpaid after fund diversion had occurred. In that event, the statutes only provided for criminal sanctions. Therefore, we held that these statutes did not create trusts fulfilling the debt discharge requirement "that the trust arise prior to the act creating the debt." *Angelle,* supra, at 1340; see also *Cross,* supra, at 881. Unlike those two statutes, however, section 162.001 of the Texas statute does flatly state that construction funds are "trust funds." Consequently, our analysis of the Texas statute for debt discharge purposes is not directly controlled by these three earlier decisions.

We now turn to consider some of the decisions dealing with state law effects of the Texas statute, and then decisions concerning the debt discharge exception as applied to construction fund statutes in other states.

C. *Other decisions*

. . .

14. " 'Such trust funds shall be applied to the payment of said valid lienable claims and *no portion thereof shall be used for any other purpose* until all lienable claims due and owing shall have been paid.' " *Carey,* supra, at 373 n. 2 (quoting the Oklahoma statute; emphasis added).

Our review of these decisions indicates that this Court has not previously resolved whether the Texas statute creates a trust for purposes of the debt discharge exception. Our decisions involving the statutes of other states, however, like those of other courts confronting similar state statutes, have applied strict standards in deciding whether such statutory trusts meet the fiduciary debt discharge exception.

The Ninth Circuit held that California's construction funds statute (resembling the Louisiana statute in *Angelle*) did not establish a trust for bankruptcy purposes. Runnion v. Pedrazzini (In re Pedrazzini), 644 F.2d 756 (9th Cir.1981). The *Pedrazzini* opinion recognizes that a trust imposed by a statute may be effective to make a debt nondischargeable, concluding that the manner of creation of the trust is not controlling but emphasizing that, "[r]ather, the focus should be on whether true fiduciary responsibilities have been imposed." 644 F.2d at 758 n. 2. See also Schlecht v. Thornton (In re Thornton), 544 F.2d 1005 (9th Cir. 1976) (holding Oregon statute did not create a fiduciary relationship). . . .

State lien laws have been held to create trusts for purposes of section 523(a)(4) or its predecessor in a limited number of cases. We so held respecting the Oklahoma statute in *Carey*, but as previously noted that statute, *unlike* the Texas statute, expressly prohibits any non-project use of the funds prior to payment of all project expenses, *whether or not* all such expenses are thereafter paid. The Tenth Circuit also reached this result respecting the New Mexico statute in Allen v. Romero (In re Romero), 535 F.2d 618 (10th Cir.1976). But we distinguished *Romero* and declined to follow it in *Angelle*, supra, at 1340 n. 11, and the Ninth Circuit also rejected *Romero*. *Pedrazzini*, supra, at 759 (agreeing with "the Fifth Circuit's criticism" of *Romero*).

In *Angelle*, we discussed Besroi Construction Corp. v. Kawczynski (In re Kawczynski), 442 F.Supp. 413 (W.D.N.Y.1977), in which the district court found a contractor to be a fiduciary for purposes of the debt discharge exception under the New York statute, which in addition to providing for criminal penalties "requires a contractor to keep detailed records of advances and to segregate funds advanced." *Angelle*, supra, at 1339. . . .

III.

Our resolution of this case arises from our examination of the precise duties imposed on a fund holder by the Texas statute. Although the statute labels these funds as "trust funds," this label does not carry the day, because the "scope of the concept fiduciary under [11 U.S.C. § 523(a)(4)] is a question of federal law." *Angelle*, supra, at 1338.

Our review of the Texas statute and decisions interpreting it reveal that the statute may serve several purposes for state law, but state-law rights created by the statute do not control the issue before us. Further, the Texas statute provides that the Texas Trust Act, governing trusts generally (other than constructive or resulting trusts) is inapplicable to it.   The actual *fiduciary* duties imposed by the construction fund statute amount to only a single restriction: the fund holder may not, "*with intent to defraud*," use such funds for other purposes without first fully paying all obligations to the named classes of claimants. Only the diversion of funds "*with intent to defraud*" triggers the criminal provisions of this statute, and it does so regardless of whether the builder subsequently pays all project claims (unlike the statute in *Angelle*).   Under the Texas statute, such a fraudulent "diversion" is *wrongful when made* by, for example, the corporate officer, notwithstanding that thereafter the corporate builder may pay all project claims.   By contrast, where the builder later pays the claims, the nonfraudulent "diverter" is untouched by the Texas statute.   Although the statute has been construed to put a nonfraudulent diverter in the position of a personal guarantor, that is not equivalent to holding that nonfraudulent "diversion" is itself *wrongful,* as we believe is required by section 523(a)(4).

If no fraudulent intent exists, the Texas statute does not prohibit or make wrongful the contractor's mere use of the funds other than on the project for which the funds were provided or loaned; it does not require any segregation of funds; it does not obligate the fund holder to maintain the separate identity of any trust res; it imposes no bookkeeping obligations on the fund holder.   And it does not allow a personal liability claim if the contractor uses all the "red" dollars loaned to pay bills arising from the "yellow" project so long as he expends on the "red" project an amount equal to the total of funds advanced.   *Cf. Dixie Masonry,* supra.   In these respects, the Texas statute is distinguishable on its face from the Oklahoma statute in *Carey* and the New York statute in *Kawczynski,* both of which were found effective to create a trust for purposes of the debt discharge exception.   Oklahoma's statute specifically forbade any diversion of construction funds, with or without fraudulent intent and whether or not the project expenses were subsequently paid, and New York's statute required fund holders to segregate construction funds.

Following the example of the Ninth Circuit, we have studied the Texas construction funds statute to determine "whether true fiduciary responsibilities have been imposed." *Pedrazzini,* supra, at 758 n. 2.   As *Angelle* teaches, for this purpose we must look to whether the "diversion" was *wrongful* when done, not to what the results are if subsequently some project debts are not paid.   Under the Texas statute, the "diversion" is *wrongful when done only* if it is done with intent to defraud.   Otherwise, the sole consequence—and this resulting from judicial construction rather than express statutory provisions—is that the "diverter" becomes a personal guarantor.   If the claims are paid by the corporate builder, this status may be immaterial; but if they are not, this does not mean that the nonfraudulent diversion was *wrongful when made. Angelle.*

There being no finding or evidence of fraud on Boyle's part, nor any basis for any theory of fiduciary defalcation other than the Texas statute itself, we hold that it was error to sustain Abilene Lumber's objection to the discharge of these debts of Boyle.

Accordingly, we reverse the courts below and order that appellee's objections to the discharge of these debts of Boyle be denied.

Reversed.

Notes & Questions

1. *Different Kinds of Trusts.* Why differentiate for bankruptcy purposes, as *Boyle* and other cases do, between trust relationships that pre-exist the alleged wrongful behavior and trust relationships that arise as a result of the wrongful behavior? Do the policies underlying nondischargeability support such a distinction?

2. *All or Nothing?* Even if the debts in *Boyle* are dischargeable, should bankruptcy law grant the creditors in *Boyle* priority treatment? Under § 523, if a debt is nondischargeable, the creditors are free to pursue the debtor for full repayment. If it is dischargeable, the creditors receive only their pro rata share of the bankruptcy distribution. In cases like *Boyle,* does § 523 operate in too much of an "all or nothing" fashion? Is there a middle ground? Are the creditors in *Boyle* less deserving of priority than the creditors who receive priority treatment under § 507?

3. *The Meaning of Defalcation.* What is a "defalcation" within the meaning of § 523(a)(4)? In Central Hanover Bank & Trust Co. v. Herbst, 93 F.2d 510 (2d Cir. 1937), a receiver of real property presented an account to the court for settlement, which the court approved. Without waiting for the time to appeal from the order approving the accounting to expire, the receiver spent the funds. An appeal resulted in disallowance of the accounting. The receiver later filed a voluntary bankruptcy petition and the question arose whether the debt owing due to the misspent funds was dischargeable. On appeal, Judge Learned Hand stated:

> In the case at bar the bankrupt had not been entirely innocent—not, for instance like the victim of an employee—though possibly one may acquit him of deliberate wrongdoing. A judge had awarded him the money, and prima facie he was entitled to it; but he knew, or if he did not know, he was charged with notice . . . that the order would not protect him if reversed . . . .. We do not hold that no possible deficiency in a fiduciary's account is dischargeable . . . ..
>
> All we decide is that when a fiduciary takes money upon a conditional authority which may be revoked and knows at the time that it may, he is guilty of a "defalcation" though it may not be a "fraud," or an "embezzlement," or perhaps not even a "misappropriation."

4. *Alimony, Child Support, and § 523(a)(5).* In In re Spong, 661 F.2d 6 (2d Cir. 1981), the issue was whether a debt for legal services rendered to a debtor's former spouse in connection with a divorce proceeding is nondischargeable because it is a debt "for alimony to, maintenance for, or support of" a former spouse within the meaning of § 523(a)(5). The alimony exception dates from Audubon v. Shufeldt, 189 U.S. 575, 577–80, 21 S.Ct. 735, 736–37, 45 L.Ed. 1009 (1901), where the Court held that debts arising out of the husband's natural and legal duty to support his wife were not dischargeable. Congress codified this result in 1903 and continued it in § 523(a)(5). Under the old bankruptcy law and under state law, it appears that payments to a spouse's divorce attorney are alimony. The court rejected the debtor's claim that the debt was dischargeable because it was not owed to the spouse or had been assigned within the meaning of § 523(a)(5).

Note on the Relationship Between State Trust Law and Bankruptcy

Recall that § 541(c)(2) enables state trust law to keep a debtor's beneficial interest in a trust out of the debtor's bankruptcy estate. By its operation, § 541(c)(2) relies on state trust law in a way that can be expected to benefit bankrupt debtors. By contrast, the provision at issue in *Boyle*, now § 523(a)(4), relies on trust principles to allow some debts to survive the debtor's discharge in bankruptcy. Should state trust law have such powerful potential in a bankruptcy proceeding?

Is *Boyle* an understandable effort to limit the role of state law in this area? Was the Texas provision at issue in *Boyle* unreasonable? If not, what interest is served by refusing to honor it in bankruptcy? Could Texas enact a statute that would result in the debts not being dischargeable?

C. Reaffirmation

IN RE HIRTE
United States Bankruptcy Court, District of Oregon, 1986.
71 B.R. 249.

ELIZABETH L. PERRIS, BANKRUPTCY JUDGE.

Debtors have requested Court approval of an agreement to reaffirm their $2,890.44 unsecured debt to the Chase Manhattan Bank, N.A. ("Bank"). The Debtors entered into the reaffirmation agreement in order to settle a dischargeability claim by the Bank. The amount reaffirmed equals the sum that the Debtors charged to their Bank credit card within fifty days prior to their bankruptcy. At the time the Court held the Debtors' discharge hearing, Bank's dischargeability claim was time barred under 11 U.S.C. § 523(c) and Bankruptcy Rule 4007(c) because Bank failed to either timely file a complaint or obtain an extension of time within which such complaint could be filed.

The issue which the Court must resolve is whether it should approve a reaffirmation agreement which is a good faith settlement of a claim of nondischargeability if such claim could not be successfully pursued by the creditor at the time of the discharge hearing because of the statute of limitations contained in § 523(c) and Bankruptcy Rule 4007(c). For reasons discussed hereafter, the Court concludes that such a reaffirmation agreement should not be approved.

Section 524(d)(2) precludes the Court from approving a reaffirmation agreement unless the Court finds that the agreement does not impose "an undue hardship on the debtor or a dependent of the debtor; and (ii) [is] in the best interest of the debtor." § 524(c)(6)(A).

Utilizing legislative history, the cases which have interpreted the term "best interest of the debtor" have focused primarily on whether the reaffirmation agreement is financially or economically beneficial to the debtor. In re Avis, 3 B.R. 205, 1 CBC2d 667 (Bankr.S.D.Ohio 1980); In re Jenkins, 4 B.R. 651 (Bankr.E.D.Va.1980). The Court must apply the "best interest" test as of the time of the discharge hearing since no earlier time is specified by the statute and "the statutory reaffirmation scheme is to be strongly construed so as to protect the interests of debtors." In re Roth, 38 B.R. 531, 537 (Bankr.N.D.Ill.) aff'd, 43 B.R. 484 (N.D.Ill.1984). While it is understandable that debtors may enter into the reaffirmation agreement regarding an unsecured debt while dischargeability litigation is still a possibility, once the deadline passes without such a complaint being filed, the Court cannot find that it is in the debtor's best interest to pay the unsecured obligation which had been discharged. In re Leonard, 12 B.R. 91 (Bankr.D.Md.1981).

This conclusion is bolstered by the 1984 amendment to § 524(c). In cases filed prior to the effective date of the 1984 amendments to Bankruptcy Code, the Court could approve a reaffirmation agreement if it either was a good faith settlement of dischargeability litigation, or was in the best interests of the debtor and would not cause undue hardship. See former 11 U.S.C. § 524(c)(4)(B) (1982). Congress chose to delete the provision allowing the Court to approve reaffirmation agreements which fell into the former category. Thus, the Bank's cries that the agreement at issue represents a good faith settlement of dischargeability litigation are insufficient to compel approval of the reaffirmation agreement.

For the foregoing reasons,

IT IS HEREBY ORDERED, that the reaffirmation agreement between the Debtors and the Bank is not approved.

Notes & Questions

1. *Why Reaffirm?* From a debtor's perspective, what is the difference between entering into a reaffirmation agreement and voluntarily paying amounts owed to a creditor? Why would debtors prefer to reaffirm rather than simply pay the debt without obligating themselves to do so?

Should the debtor's joining in a reaffirmation petition be evidence that reaffirmation is in the debtor's "best interest" within the meaning of § 524(c)(6)? What other reasons should courts credit in reaffirmation proceedings? May the court approve a reaffirmation petition where the debtor reaffirms to prevent liability of a codebtor? See In re Berkich, 7 B.R. 483 (Bkrtcy.E.D.Pa.1980) (debt guaranteed by mother and secured by lien on mother's real estate could not be affirmed); In re Avis, 3 B.R. 205 (Bkrtcy.S.D.Ohio 1980) (debtor could not reaffirm to protect cosigners who were friends). Is the court's interpretation of "best interest" in *Hirte* too narrow?

2. *Reaffirmation and Waiver.* A binding reaffirmation, in effect, waives the debtor's right to a discharge of the reaffirmed debt. Should a debtor be able to waive discharge of a debt in advance of bankruptcy? Suppose a creditor is willing to charge a lower interest rate in exchange for the debtor's waiver. Why should the law prevent the parties from entering into such a transaction? If the answer is that creditors would take advantage of debtors, perhaps a protection mechanism similar to that contained in § 524 could be made available for advance waivers of discharge. Is the system of reaffirmation and nonwaiver consistent with the theories of discharge discussed in the Weistart and Jackson excerpts, supra?

3. *The Role of Attorneys.* How does analysis of reaffirmation change if the debtor is represented by an attorney? See § 524(c)(3). Should the system be different? Who will benefit?

4. *Post–Discharge Reaffirmation.* Debtors filed a voluntary petition and were granted a discharge under § 727. They then sought to reaffirm a discharged obligation. May the court allow reaffirmation? See § 524(c). If not, may the debtors seek revocation of their discharge under § 727(d)? See In re McQuality, 5 B.R. 302 (Bkrtcy.S.D.Ohio 1980).

D. Discrimination

DUFFEY V. DOLLISON

United States Court of Appeals, Sixth Circuit, 1984.
734 F.2d 265.

Before ENGEL, KEITH and WELLFORD, CIRCUIT JUDGES.

ENGEL, CIRCUIT JUDGE.

The precise issue presented by this appeal is whether Ohio's Motor Vehicle Financial Responsibility Act, Ohio Revised Code §§ 4509.01–.99 (Baldwin 1975), as it has been applied to the Duffeys, conflicts with section 525 of the Bankruptcy Act of 1978, 11 U.S.C. § 525 (1982), thereby violating the Supremacy Clause of the United States Constitution. U.S. Const. art. VI, cl. 2.

Motor vehicle financial responsibility laws, which require motorists to maintain some type of automobile insurance or otherwise to furnish proof of financial responsibility, have been enacted in nearly all states.

Some states compel all drivers to furnish proof that they are adequately insured as a precondition to the issuance of driver's or automobile licenses. E.g., Mich.Comp.Laws Ann. §§ 500.3101–.3179 (1983). Other states, such as Ohio, have enacted less comprehensive laws which require proof of financial responsibility only when a driver has failed, within a reasonable time, to satisfy a judgment for damages arising from an automobile accident or has been convicted of certain serious traffic offenses.[2] . . .

The validity of the Ohio statute is a matter of great concern to those interested in keeping irresponsible drivers off the highways as well as to those individuals who, voluntarily or involuntarily, go into bankruptcy. While we have been furnished no Ohio statistics, the general pervasiveness of the problem is well illustrated by the stipulated findings in Henry v. Heyison, 4 B.R. 437 (E.D.Pa.1980). There, the court noted that in one year, 12,000 drivers in Pennsylvania had their driver's licenses suspended as the result of unsatisfied motor vehicle tort judgments. Id. at 439 n. 4. Of those 12,000 drivers, 300 had reported that their motor vehicle tort judgments were discharged in bankruptcy proceedings. Id.

This appeal is particularly important because several bankruptcy courts that have considered whether the Ohio Motor Vehicle Financial Responsibility Act unconstitutionally conflicts with federal bankruptcy laws have reached opposite conclusions. Compare In re Cerny, 17 B.R. 221, 224 (Bkrtcy. N.D.Ohio 1982) ("[T]he [Ohio] statute is being applied nondiscriminatorily and is therefore consistent with 11 U.S.C. § 525.") with In re Shamblin, 18 B.R. 800, 803 (Bkrtcy.S.D.Ohio 1982) ("Ohio's [statute] is discriminatory and in violation of § 525 of the Bankruptcy Code.") and In re Duffey, 13 B.R. 785, 788 (Bkrtcy.S.D.Ohio 1981) (Ohio's financial responsibility law and policy discriminates against bankrupts and hence violates section 525 of the Bankruptcy Code).
. . .

Finally, the present controversy is significant because it involves a potential conflict between important state and federal interests: state concern for public safety and federal concern for establishing uniform bankruptcy laws. Clearly if these competing interests are incompatible, the Supremacy Clause dictates that we resolve the conflict in favor of federal law. Good policy and good sense, however, suggest the desirability of accommodating both interests if this can reasonably be achieved.

I.

The facts here are stipulated. On June 18, 1979, a judgment of $912.76, arising from an auto accident, was entered against George

2. As of September, 1982, eleven states had such "future proof" laws: Florida, Mississippi, Nebraska, Nevada, New Hampshire, Ohio, Oregon, South Dakota, Tennessee, Texas, and Washington. Traffic Safety Department, American Automobile Ass'n, Digest of Motor Laws (49th ed. 1983).

Duffey in the Municipal Court of Franklin County, Ohio. This judgment was not satisfied within 30 days and, consequently, Mr. Duffey's operator's license and vehicle registration were suspended on July 28, 1980, by the Registrar of Motor Vehicles, Dean Dollison, pursuant to Ohio Revised Code section 4509.37. On May 23, 1980, a judgment of $1,131.90, arising from an auto accident, was entered against Shari Duffey in the Franklin County Municipal Court. This judgment also was not satisfied within 30 days, resulting in the suspension of Mrs. Duffey's driving privileges on October 28, 1980.

The Duffeys, on January 27, 1981, filed a voluntary joint bankruptcy petition under Chapter 7 of the Bankruptcy Act. A copy of their bankruptcy petition, which listed the unsatisfied accident-related judgments in the schedule of debts, was sent by the Duffeys to Registrar Dollison with the request that he reinstate their driving privileges. Dollison, while recognizing that the judgment debts were subject to discharge and that the Duffeys could not be required to satisfy or reaffirm the debt as a condition to reobtaining their licenses, nevertheless refused to vacate the order of suspension until the Duffeys had filed evidence of financial responsibility as required under Ohio Revised Code section 4509.40.

On February 24, 1981, the Duffeys brought suit in bankruptcy court in the Southern District of Ohio for reinstatement of their driving privileges. In that action the Duffeys argued that Ohio's requirement of proof of financial responsibility, as it applies to individuals whose unsatisfied tort judgments have been stayed or discharged by bankruptcy, unconstitutionally conflicts with the federal bankruptcy provision prohibiting the discriminatory treatment of bankrupts, 11 U.S.C. § 525 (1982). The bankruptcy judge agreed that the challenged provisions of the Ohio Motor Vehicle Financial Responsibility Act conflict with the Bankruptcy Act and ordered the Registrar to reinstate the Duffeys' driving privileges. The Registrar appealed this decision to the United States District Court for the Southern District of Ohio. In a carefully considered opinion, United States District Judge John D. Holschuh reversed the decision of the bankruptcy court and held that Ohio's financial responsibility requirement does not violate section 525 of the Bankruptcy Act because the state statute applies equally to bankrupts and nonbankrupts. We affirm.

II.

The Supreme Court, in Perez v. Campbell, 402 U.S. 637, 91 S.Ct. 1704, 29 L.Ed.2d 233 (1971), stated that "[d]eciding whether a state statute is in conflict with a federal statute and hence invalid under the Supremacy Clause is essentially a two-step process of first ascertaining the construction of the two statutes and then determining the constitutional question whether they are in conflict." Id. at 644, 91 S.Ct. at 1708. In making this decision a reviewing court must "determine whether a challenged state statute 'stands as an obstacle to the accomplishment and execution of the full purposes and objectives of Congress.'" Id. at 649, 91 S.Ct. at 1711 (quoting Hines v. Davidowitz, 312 U.S. 52, 67, 61 S.Ct. 399, 404, 85 L.Ed. 581 (1941)). Applying the *Perez* approach, we therefore first ascertain the construction of the Ohio Motor Vehicle Financial Responsibility Act and section 525 of the Bankruptcy Act, and then determine whether the statutes conflict.

A.

The Ohio Motor Vehicle Financial Responsibility Act provides that "[w]henever any person fails within thirty days to satisfy a judgment rendered within this state, upon written request of the judgment creditor or his attorney," the court must forward a certified copy of the judgment to the registrar of motor vehicles. Ohio Rev.Code Ann. § 4509.35 (Baldwin 1975). Upon receipt of a certified copy of the unsatisfied judgment, the registrar shall "suspend the license and registration and nonresident's operating privilege of any person against whom such judgment was rendered, except as provided in sections 4509.01 to 4509.78 of the Revised Code." Ohio Rev.Code Ann. § 4509.37 (Baldwin 1975). Driving privileges must remain suspended for seven years; however, "[t]he registrar shall vacate the order of suspension *upon proof that such judgment is stayed,* or satisfied in full . . . *and upon such person's filing with the registrar of motor vehicles evidence of financial responsibility* in accordance with section 4509.45 of the Revised Code." Ohio Rev.Code Ann. § 4509.40 (Baldwin 1975) (emphasis added). Proof of financial responsibility must be maintained for three years and may be given by filing a certificate of insurance, a surety bond, a certificate of deposit, or a certificate of self-insurance. Ohio Rev.Code Ann. § 4509.45 (Baldwin 1975).

The Ohio Supreme Court has not authoritatively construed the Motor Vehicle Financial Responsibility Act. Consequently, we look to lower court decisions in Ohio construing the statute, and to the language of the Act itself. It has been observed that the purpose of the Act is to "provide sanctions which would encourage owners and operators of motor vehicles on Ohio highways to obtain liability insurance sufficient in amount to protect others who might be injured through the negligent operation of a motor vehicle." Iszczukiewicz v. Universal Underwriters Insurance Co., 182 F.Supp. 733, 735 (N.D.Ohio 1960). Following the United States Supreme Court's decision in Perez v. Campbell, 402 U.S. 637, 91 S.Ct. 1704, 29 L.Ed.2d 233 (1971), the former version of Ohio's Motor Vehicle Financial Responsibility Act was declared unconstitutional to the extent that it required payment of a tort judgment as a condition to restoration of driving privileges, even though the underlying judgment was stayed, or discharged in bankruptcy. Weaver v. O'Grady, 350 F.Supp. 403, 407 (S.D.Ohio 1972). The Act as it is now written cures that defect. Ohio Rev.Code Ann. § 4509.40 (Baldwin 1975). However, bankruptcy does not relieve the judgment debtor of the requirement of posting proof of future financial responsibility. House v. O'Grady, 35 Ohio Misc. 20, 299 N.E.2d 706 (Ct.C.P. Franklin County 1973).

The Ohio Act has as its object the protection of the public from financially irresponsible motorists who have proved unwilling or unable to satisfy a judgment arising from an automobile accident. The statute embodies a "one-bite" approach to achieving this purpose by permitting motorists the privilege of driving without any proof of financial responsibility until they incur an accident-related judgment and fail to satisfy it within 30 days.

B.

Section 525 of the Bankruptcy Act of 1978 provides that:

a governmental unit may not deny, revoke, suspend, or refuse to renew a license, permit, charter, franchise, or other similar grant to, condition such a grant to, discriminate with respect to such a grant against, deny employment to, terminate the employment of, or discriminate with respect to employment against, a person that is or has been a debtor under this title or a bankrupt or a debtor under the Bankruptcy Act, or another person with whom such bankrupt or debtor has been associated, solely because such bankrupt or debtor is or has been a debtor under this title or a bankrupt or debtor under the Bankruptcy Act, has been insolvent before the commencement of the case under this title, or during the case but before the debtor is granted or denied a discharge, or has not paid a debt that is dischargeable in the case under this title or that was discharged under the Bankruptcy Act.

11 U.S.C. § 525 (1982). This section has yet to be authoritatively construed by the United States Supreme Court. However, the legislative history indicates that section 525, "codifies the result of Perez v. Campbell, 402 U.S. 637, 91 S.Ct. 1704, 29 L.Ed.2d 233 (1971), which held that a State would frustrate the Congressional policy of a fresh start for a debtor if it were permitted to refuse to renew a drivers license because a tort judgment resulting from an automobile accident had been unpaid as a result of a discharge in bankruptcy." S.Rep. No. 989, 95th Cong., 2d Sess. 81, reprinted in 1978 U.S.Code Cong. & Ad.News 5787, 5867. Therefore when construing section 525, it is helpful to examine the *Perez* holding.

In *Perez*, the petitioners filed a voluntary bankruptcy petition two days before judgment was entered against them for personal injuries and property damages which arose from an automobile collision. The judgment was discharged in bankruptcy by order of the district court. Nevertheless, the State of Arizona suspended the Perezes' driving privileges pursuant to a statute which provided for such suspension when an accident-related judgment went unsatisfied for 60 days. In order to regain their privileges, the Perezes were required to satisfy the judgment and give proof of future financial responsibility. Unlike the Ohio Act, the Arizona statute required satisfaction of the judgment even though it was discharged in bankruptcy or its collection stayed. Id. at 638–42, 91 S.Ct. at 1705–1707.

In considering whether the Arizona law unconstitutionally conflicted with the Bankruptcy Act, the Court noted that "the validity of [the] limited requirement that some drivers post evidence of financial responsibility for the future in order to regain driving privileges is not questioned here." Id. at 642, 91 S.Ct. at 1707. The only issue the Court examined was whether a State may enact a statute "providing that a discharge in bankruptcy of [an] automobile accident tort judgment shall have no effect on the judgment debtor's obligation to repay the judgment creditor, at least insofar as such repayment may be enforced by the withholding of driving privileges by the State." Id. at 643, 91 S.Ct. at 1708. The majority determined that the statute jeopardized the "fresh start" objectives of the Bankruptcy Act by providing creditors leverage for collection of judgments which had been discharged in bankruptcy. Id. at 646–48, 91 S.Ct. at 1710–10. In the majority's view, one of the primary purposes of the Bankruptcy Act "is to give debtors 'a new opportunity in life and a clear field for future effort, unhampered by the pressure and discouragement of preexisting debt.'" Id. at 648, 91 S.Ct. at 1710 (quoting Local Loan Co. v. Hunt, 292 U.S. 234, 244, 54 S.Ct. 695, 699, 78 L.Ed. 1230 (1934)). Because the Arizona law obstructed these objectives, it was found to be invalid under the Supremacy Clause. Id., 402 U.S. at 656, 91 S.Ct. at 1714.

Thus the *Perez* decision, which section 525 of the Bankruptcy Act codifies, specifically left open the issue we now consider: whether bankrupts who have discharged an accident-related judgment can be required, as a condition to the restoration of driving privileges suspended prior to the bankruptcy, to post evidence of financial responsibility. The legislative history indicates that section 525 was intended by Congress to incorporate further refinements of the *Perez* doctrine:

> [T]he enumeration of various forms of discrimination against former bankrupts is not intended to permit other forms of discrimination. The courts have been developing the *Perez* rule. This section permits further development to prohibit actions by governmental or quasi-governmental organizations that perform licensing functions, such as a State bar association or a medical society, or by other organizations that can seriously affect the debtors' livelihood or fresh start. . . .

S.Rep. No. 989, supra, at 81, 1978 U.S. Code & Ad.News at 5867. It appears that section 525 is intended to ensure that bankrupts are not deprived of a "fresh start" because of governmental discrimination against them, based "solely" on the bankruptcy. Senate Report 989 specifies that "the effect of . . . section [525], and of further interpretations of the *Perez* rule, is to strengthen the anti-reaffirmation policy found in section 524(b). Discrimination based solely on nonpayment could encourage reaffirmations, contrary to the expressed policy." Id. The House further noted regarding Section 525:

[T]he purpose of the section is to prevent an automatic reaction
against an individual for availing himself of the protection of the
bankruptcy laws. Most bankruptcies are caused by circumstances
beyond the debtor's control. To penalize a debtor by discriminatory
treatment as a result is unfair and undoes the beneficial effects of
the bankruptcy laws. However, in those cases where the causes of a
bankruptcy are intimately connected with the license, grant, or
employment in question, an examination into the circumstances
surrounding the bankruptcy will permit governmental units to
pursue appropriate regulatory policies and take appropriate action
without running afoul of bankruptcy policy.

H.R.Rep. No. 595, 95th Cong., 1st Sess. 165 reprinted in 1978 U.S.Code
Cong. & Ad.News 5963, 6126 (footnote omitted). Therefore, we agree
with the district court's conclusion that "the primary purpose of section
525 of the Bankruptcy Code is to prevent the government either from
denying privileges to individuals solely as a reaction to their filing
bankruptcy or from conditioning the grant of privileges on the bankrupt's reaffirmation of certain debts." Duffey v. Dollison, No. C–2–81–
1154, slip op. at 8 (S.D.Ohio Aug. 13, 1982). It is thus necessary to
determine whether the Ohio Financial Responsibility Act impedes the
accomplishment of, or frustrates, these Congressional objectives.

. . .

The Duffeys contend that Ohio law requires them to post proof of
financial responsibility "solely" because they have not paid a debt that
is dischargeable in bankruptcy. Therefore in the Duffeys' view, the
Ohio Act violates section 525 of the Bankruptcy Act because section 525
specifically prohibits states from using the failure to pay a debt as the
basis for denying a driver's license. . . .

We recognize that the portion of the Ohio Act which suspends
motorists' driving privileges for failure to satisfy a judgment is not
triggered unless a judgment creditor requests in writing that a certified
copy of the unsatisfied judgment be forwarded to the Registrar. Ohio
Rev.Code Ann. § 4509.35 (Baldwin 1975). It is conceivable that under
certain circumstances not present here, a creditor might attempt to use
this ability to initiate license suspension proceedings to coerce a debtor
into reaffirming all or part of a judgment that is stayed by the
Bankruptcy Act.

However under the facts of this case, the Duffeys could not have
been coerced into reaffirming the stayed judgments because the judgments had been certified to the Registrar and the requirement of
furnishing proof of financial responsibility had been fixed *before* the
Duffeys filed in bankruptcy. Once the judgment were certified, the
Duffeys could not have regained their driving privileges without furnishing proof of financial responsibility even by paying the judgments.
Thus, at that juncture, the judgment creditors could do nothing further
to benefit or inconvenience the Duffeys; there was no leverage which
could have induced the Duffeys to reaffirm their debts. As applied

here the Ohio Act, which depends on judgment creditors to initiate license suspension proceedings, employs a reasonable method for relieving the state of the burden of policing every accident-related judgment. Ohio simply has chosen in civil cases to place the responsibility for reporting unsatisfied tort judgments on the party in the best position to know whether a judgment has been satisfied, and with the greatest incentive to notify the Registrar of nonpayment.[5]

The Duffeys would have us hold that the Ohio Motor Vehicle Financial Responsibility Act violates section 525 because the Act fails to treat a bankrupt as though he or she had never incurred a dischargeable, accident-related tort judgment. Under such an interpretation, once a judgment is discharged or stayed, states would be absolutely prohibited from imposing or continuing any burden, whether a reaffirmation of liability or the imposition of financial responsibility requirements. We believe that this reads more into section 525 than Congress intended.

As the district court correctly noted:

[N]either the language of the statute nor its legislative history indicates that section 525 was intended by Congress to erase all traces of a discharged debt and thereby foreclose the imposition of any future responsibility requirements. To the contrary, the legislative history of section 525 contemplates both the consideration of the circumstances surrounding bankruptcy and the valid imposition of future financial responsibility requirements.

Duffey v. Dollison, No. C-2-81-1154, slip op. at 10 (S.D.Ohio Aug. 13, 1982). This conclusion is amply supported by the legislative history. Senate Report 989 specifically observes that section 525 "does not prohibit consideration of other factors, *such as future financial responsibility or ability,* and does not prohibit imposition of requirements such as net capital rules, if applied nondiscriminatorily." S.Rep. No. 989, supra, at 81, 1978 U.S.Code Cong. & Ad.News at 5867 (emphasis added).
. . .

The Ohio Financial Responsibility Act in no way discriminates against bankrupts, or penalizes them for filing in bankruptcy. The Act provides that "any person" who fails to satisfy an accident-related judgment within 30 days shall have his or her driving privileges suspended by the Registrar. Ohio Rev.Code Ann. §§ 4509.35, .37 (Baldwin 1975). The statute applies without exception to *any* person who fails to satisfy a judgment for whatever reason, whether because of unwillingness, inadvertence, or inability to pay. Once a judgment has been certified to the Registrar for nonpayment, the debtor's obligation to furnish proof of financial responsibility becomes fixed. Thereafter, neither payment of the debt, reaffirmation, nor bankruptcy can relieve

5. This statutory scheme thus complements the provisions of the Motor Vehicle Responsibility Act pertaining to criminal traffic cases. Ohio courts are required to initiate license suspension by notifying the Registrar whenever a person has been convicted of, pleads guilty to, or forfeits bail for certain serious traffic offenses. Ohio Rev.Code Ann. §§ 4507.16, 4509.31 (Baldwin 1975).

the debtor of this requirement. Judgment debtors such as the Duffeys who seek relief under the bankruptcy laws are therefore treated no differently from any other judgment debtor. Indeed it is this lack of discrimination to which the Duffeys take exception. By arguing that bankrupts who have proved to be irresponsible drivers should be excused from the requirement of posting proof of financial responsibility, the Duffeys in effect ask this court "to go beyond the fresh start policy of *Perez* and . . . give a debtor a head start over persons who are able to satisfy their unpaid judgment debts without resort to a discharge in bankruptcy." In re Cerny, 17 B.R. 221, 224 (Bkrtcy.N.D. Ohio 1982). We do not believe that section 525 was intended by Congress to afford debtors in bankruptcy such preferential treatment.

We therefore hold that Ohio's "one-bite" approach to the imposition of financial responsibility requirements, as applied to the Duffeys, violates neither the *Perez* holding nor its statutory codification, section 525 of the Bankruptcy Act. . . .

Our ruling here is a relatively narrow one. We uphold the Ohio Act where the requirement to furnish proof of financial responsibility has become fixed, through certification to the Registrar, prior to bankruptcy. Where the obligation has thus become fixed, neither payment of the judgment, nor arrangement with the creditor, nor bankruptcy can relieve the debtor of the requirement of furnishing proof of financial responsibility. In this respect the Ohio Act does not have the effect of discriminating between those who are bankrupt and those who are not. It cannot induce the bankrupt to reaffirm a discharged debt, or to pay thereafter, for neither action can affect the legal requirement to post proof of financial responsibility.

The judgment of the district court is Affirmed.

Notes & Questions

1. *Discriminatory Impact.* Should it matter in *Duffey* what percentage of those to whom the financial responsibility requirement applies in fact went through bankruptcy? Suppose it turns out that 95% of those to whom the provision applies had been bankrupt? How should courts deal with the situation left open in *Duffey*, that in which the financial responsibility law might have been used to coerce a debtor into reaffirming a debt?

2. *Perez & § 525.* The legislative history of § 525 states:

This section . . . codifies the result of *Perez v. Campbell*

. . . ..

. . . It does not prohibit consideration of other factors, such as future financial responsibility or ability, and does not prohibit imposition of requirements such as net capital rules, if applied nondiscriminatorily.

In addition, the section is not exhaustive. The enumeration of various forms of discrimination against former bankrupts is not intended to permit other forms of discrimination. . . . This section permits further development to prohibit actions by governmental or quasi-governmental organizations that perform licensing functions, such as a State bar association or a medical society, or by other organizations that can seriously affect the debtors' livelihood or fresh start, such as exclusion from a union on the basis of discharge of a debt to the union's credit union. . . .

House Report at 366–67; Senate Report at 81. Does § 525 really codify *Perez*? Could one view it as undermining at least part of the *Perez* holding?

3. *Nonbankruptcy Law.* If it is a good idea to prevent governments from discriminating against former bankrupts, why not go one step further and adopt the Bankruptcy Commission's proposal to prohibit discrimination by private parties? Does § 525 establish a questionable incentive for some to file bankruptcy who might not otherwise be inclined to do so?

In In re Alessi, 12 B.R. 96 (Bkrtcy.N.D.Ill.1981), the Illinois Racing Board denied the debtors' application for a license to race horses after the debtors filed a Chapter 7 petition. Prior to the filing of the bankruptcy petition, the Board had held a hearing at which allegations were made concerning the debtors' weak financial condition, including their issuance of checks not covered by sufficient funds. The Board found that:

The accumulation of unpaid obligations by Alessi in the racing industry, especially the debts to persons for whom Alessi has driven and with whom he has owned horses, subjects Alessi to influence and power by those persons and endangers the integrity of the sport of horse racing.

Was the license lawfully denied? The bankruptcy court sustained the denial but stated: "We take no position on what the order of this Court might have been if the creditors to whom money was owed were not themselves directly involved in horse racing or if the debts had not been incurred in the case of horses which are themselves the object of control of the Racing Board." Did the debtors increase their chances of obtaining the license by filing in bankruptcy? Should they be able to? Compare In re Anderson, 15 B.R. 399 (Bkrtcy.S.D.Miss.1981) (prohibiting state tax commission from requiring payment of indebtedness due it as a condition to renewing liquor permit and supplying debtor with alcoholic beverages).

4. *Employment Discrimination.* Section 525(b), added to the Bankruptcy Act in 1984, prohibits private employers from discriminating against bankrupts. To what extent may employers take into account past financial responsibility in hiring and promotion under § 525(b)?

Chapter 14

THE TRUSTEE'S POWERS

2 GILMORE, SECURITY INTERESTS IN PERSONAL PROPERTY § 45.2, at 1286–89 (1965)

The central figure in the pattern of bankruptcy administration under the Act of 1898 was the bankruptcy trustee, who was conceived as being not merely the passive representative of the unsecured creditors but their champion. Common law and statutory assignees for the benefit of creditors had always been thought of as standing in the debtor-assignor's shoes: claims which were good against the assignor were good against the assignee. From the beginning, the federal bankruptcy trustee had greater powers. In carrying out his function of assembling the bankrupt's assets and selling them, he was given a double capacity. In one capacity he acquired whatever property rights the bankrupt had before the institution of the proceeding. In his other capacity he acquired, or inherited, whatever rights the bankrupt's creditors had. Thus a claimed interest in the bankrupt's property was not necessarily good against the trustee simply because, under applicable state law, the claimant could have recovered the property from the bankrupt. To be good against the trustee the claim had to be effective not only against the bankrupt but against his other creditors. In his role as champion of the unsecured creditors, it was not only the trustee's right but his duty to seek to invalidate as many property claims as he could, since each defeated claim brought more assets into the estate and increased the fund for distribution.

It is impossible to understand anything about the climate of bankruptcy law without an appreciation of the trustee's statutory personality. He might have been designed as an official whose primary duty was to hold the scales in even balance between the creditors who claimed property interests and the creditors who had no such claims. It had been, after all, a basic premise of the act that property rights were to be respected; the trustee could have been charged with the duty of seeing that they were respected. Instead, the trustee became a sort of devil's advocate, whose function was to resist, by every available device and stratagem, the assertion of such claims against the estate.

"Equality is equity" is a beguiling slogan. In the context of bankruptcy proceeding, ideal equality might seem to lie in having all creditors share equally, without regard to their pre-bankruptcy status. The Bankruptcy Act did not go—could not, it may be, constitutionally have gone—that far. Nevertheless, bankruptcy law has always inclined in that direction. In the structure of the act there is a sort of built-in tension between the basic prescription that security rights are

687

to be recognized and the administrative procedures which insure that they will be recognized to the smallest degree possible. . . .

It is manifestly to the advantage of all creditors, secured and unsecured, who have claims against an insolvent to keep the foundering enterprise out of bankruptcy. Everybody knows this. It is much better for the creditors to reach a negotiated settlement—which may lead to a salvage operation and which in any case will avoid the crippling expense of bankruptcy administration. No doubt many more cases are settled by informal creditors' committees than ever reach the bankruptcy courts. But the tactical situation of a secured creditor in such negotiations is decisively affected by the status that his security interest will have if the other creditors (or the debtor himself) decide on the last resort of filing a bankruptcy petition. Thus the theoretical question whether a security interest is, or is not, vulnerable to the avoiding powers of the bankruptcy trustee is an intensely practical question in all cases of actual or threatened insolvency and not merely in the insignificant minority of cases which, all hope abandoned, go on to adjudication.

§ 45.3. **The bankruptcy trustee's powers.** Our subject is the trustee's powers to invalidate security interests in bankruptcy. The proposition that he can invalidate security transfers which were, for some reason, unenforceable against, or voidable by, the bankrupt needs no discussion. Of course he can: if the mortgage of Blackacre was extorted by blackmail, if the mortgagor was forced to sign at gun-point, if the loan was usurious, the mortgagor's trustee will stoutly resist the claims of our hypothetical blackmailing, gun-wielding usurer. Let us pass on to the security transfer which is entirely valid and enforceable between the parties but which can nevertheless be invalidated by the trustee, either in his own right or in the right of the bankrupt's creditors. . . .

Introduction to the Trustee's Principal Avoiding Powers

In thinking about the trustee's powers to invalidate transactions, one may subdivide those powers into those that track state law and those that enable the trustee to attack transactions not vulnerable under state law. One of the trustee's powers, contained in § 544(b), authorizes him to avoid transfers that unsecured creditors could have avoided under nonbankruptcy law. Note that § 544(b) does not specify the transfers that can be avoided by enumerating them. The transfers that the trustee may avoid under § 544(b) are simply those that unsecured creditors may avoid under state law. If state law confers no avoidance powers upon unsecured creditors (as, for example, in the form of bulk transfer and fraudulent conveyance laws), then § 544(b) is of little use to the trustee.

Section 544(a) elevates the trustee to the status of lien creditor. Even if a debtor has no lien creditors, the trustee may act as if he were a lien creditor. In this sense, and unlike § 544(b), § 544(a) puts the trustee in a better position than the debtor's creditors are in under nonbankruptcy law. But note that § 544(a) shares an important feature with § 544(b). It only confers a *status* upon the trustee. To decide what rights attach to that status one must look to state law. Thus, even though § 544(a) confers lien creditor status, if state law gives lien creditors no interests in the debtor's property, § 544(a) is of little value to the trustee.

While § 544 confers creditor status upon the trustee and leaves the consequences of those statuses to state law, §§ 545 and 547 go one important step further. Both of these sections in effect undermine various transactions that, under state law, are valid against both unsecured and lien creditors. Indeed, § 545's primary function is to invalidate certain liens that are provided by state statutes. Section 547, the preference section, covers a broad range of transactions. But the feature that most distinguishes it from § 544 is its greater independence from state law. (Even § 547 is not wholly independent of state law. See if you understand why when you examine § 547 infra). Section 547 contains its own set of characteristics that taint transactions and it is the trustee's most important avoiding power.

In summary, § 544(b) confers upon the trustee whatever powers state law confers upon unsecured creditors to invalidate transactions. Section 544(a) gives the trustee whatever status state law gives to lien creditors. Sections 545 and 547 give the trustee sets of powers that transcend state law.

A. The Trustee as Creditor (§ 544(a) and (b))

IN RE VERCO INDUSTRIES

United States Court of Appeals, Ninth Circuit, 1983.
704 F.2d 1134.

BOOCHEVER, CIRCUIT JUDGE.

This appeal from the Bankruptcy Appellate Panel, 10 B.R. 347, presents a novel issue as to whether a debtor-in-possession which invalidated a sale for failure to comply with bulk transfer laws and retained the sale property for the benefit of the estate's creditors, may recover the balance owed on the sale free from the buyer's claim of set-off. Because the buyer is entitled to a set-off we reverse in part.

I.

Facts

The material facts are undisputed. On December 21, 1979, Verco Industries ("Verco") closed a sale to Spartan Plastics ("Spartan") of machinery, tools, and a building lease used in manufacturing practice bombs for the military. Verco tendered a bill of sale for the personal property, an assignment of its leasehold interest in the manufacturing facility, and a covenant not to compete. Spartan's consideration consisted of $125,595 cash, $85,000 worth of castings, a $36,860 prepaid sublease, assumption of approximately $20,000 of Verco's outstanding obligations, and a promissory note back to Verco for $31,545. The promissory note was increased to $37,310 following Verco's assignment of a rental deposit on the leasehold interest sold to Spartan. Spartan immediately provided all the promised consideration except for payment of the promissory note which was not due until July 1, 1980. Spartan's failure to pay the note is the subject of the present appeal.

On July 23, 1980, Verco filed for bankruptcy under Chapter 11 of the Bankruptcy Code and became a debtor-in-possession with basically the same powers as a trustee in bankruptcy. See 11 U.S.C. § 1107 (Supp.1981). Acting pursuant to 11 U.S.C. § 544 (Supp.1981), Verco sued Spartan in bankruptcy court to invalidate the transfer of personal property called for in the sale on the grounds that it violated provisions of California's bulk transfer and fraudulent conveyance laws, Cal.Com. Code §§ 6105 & 6107 (Deering Supp.1982), and Cal.Civ.Code § 3440 (Deering 1972). Verco also sought to enforce payment of the $37,110 promissory note pursuant to 11 U.S.C. § 541 (Supp.1981), which makes a bankruptcy trustee or debtor-in-possession the successor in interest to the debtor's property.

The bankruptcy court invalidated the transfer as against Verco's creditors because Spartan had failed to satisfy the notice provisions of California's bulk transfer laws, Cal.Com.Code §§ 6105 & 6107 and had violated Cal.Civ.Code § 3440, by failing to take possession of the property within a commercially reasonable time. The court ordered that the debtor-in-possession retain the property for the benefit of the estate under 11 U.S.C. §§ 550 & 544(b) (Supp.1981). The court also concluded that because the transfer was invalid and Verco retained possession of the property, Spartan was relieved of its obligation to pay the promissory note.

Verco appealed the promissory note ruling to the three-judge Bankruptcy Appellate Panel ("panel") for the Ninth Circuit pursuant to 28 U.S.C. § 160 (Supp.1981). The panel reversed the bankruptcy court, holding that, as a debtor-in-possession, Verco need not elect between invalidating the property transfer[1] on behalf of the creditors under 11 U.S.C. § 544(b) and recovering the full sale price on behalf of the debtors' estate under 11 U.S.C. § 541(a)(1).

Raising the issue *sua sponte*, two of the panel judges also concluded that Spartan had no right of set-off against Verco for the consideration it paid on the goods retained by Verco. The third panel member concurred in the panel's decision to allow Verco to recover on the note but differed on the last issue, arguing that Spartan was entitled to a set-off under 11 U.S.C. § 553(a) (permitting a set-off of mutual debts that arose before commencement of the case).

---

1. Because Spartan conceded at oral argument before the bankruptcy panel that the transfer could have been invalidated for violating California's bulk transfer provisions, the panel proceeded on that ground alone without reference to Spartan's alleged violation of Cal.Civ.Code § 3440's "possession" requirement. We do the same.

Spartan appeals, arguing that: (1) the promissory note was unenforceable after Verco invalidated the transfer and retained the property; or (2) it has a right of set-off for the consideration it paid on the goods retained by Verco.

II.

Recovery on the Note

The bankruptcy panel found that Verco, as debtor-in-possession, could recover the amount of the promissory note from Spartan despite the fact that it had successfully set aside the transfer of assets. It is undisputed that a debtor-in-possession has the powers of a trustee in bankruptcy, 11 U.S.C. § 1107, and ascends to the rights of creditors to set aside a non-complying bulk transfer under 11 U.S.C. § 544(b) as well as acquiring all the debtor's legal rights and remedies under 11 U.S.C. § 541(a)(1). We agree with the panel below that Verco may assert both of these rights and recover the property and the amount due on the note.

The California bulk transfers law is designed to protect the creditors of the transferor. Failure to give the notice required under section 6107 renders any bulk transfer fraudulent and void against any creditor of the transferor. Cal.Com.Code § 6105; Danning v. Daylin, Inc., 488 F.2d 185, 187 (9th Cir. 1973). The transfer is not void, however, as between the parties to the transaction. Cooley v. Brennan, 102 Cal. App.2d 952, 228 P.2d 104 (1951). The transferor may maintain an action for the purchase price of the assets despite a violation of the bulk transfer laws, Jeffery v. Volberg, 159 Cal.App.2d 815, 324 P.2d 964 (1956); Escalle v. Mark, 43 Nev. 172, 183 P. 387 (1919), and the sale will not be set aside as to the transferor's right to recover the purchase price even if the transferor's creditors make claims on all or part of the transferred assets. Clifton v. Dunn, 208 Ga. 326, 66 S.E.2d 735 (1951). We think it clear that had bankruptcy not intervened, Verco's creditors would have been able to set aside the sale to Spartan as to them without depriving Verco of its right to payment of the promissory note. We see no reason why the intervening bankruptcy of Verco should alter this situation given that Verco assumes both of these rights upon becoming debtor-in-possession. . . .

III.

Set-Off

Although we acknowledge that Verco has a valid claim for the unpaid amount of the note from Spartan, we also believe that Spartan would have a claim against Verco for the loss it suffered when the transfer was set aside. In Misty Management Corp v. Lockwood, 539 F.2d 1205 (9th Cir. 1976), this court stated that even where the transferee is responsible for the transfer being invalidated as fraudulent, that factor does not prevent the transferee from asserting a claim against the transferor:

> Older versions of the Bankruptcy Act did contain provisions penalizing recipients of a fraudulent conveyance. Those provisions have been eliminated, however, and the modern view is that a *transferee guilty of fraudulent behavior* may nevertheless prove a claim against a bankrupt estate, once he returns the fraudulently conveyed property to the estate. . . . A rule to the contrary would allow the estate to recover the voidable conveyance and to retain whatever consideration it had paid therefor. Such a result would clearly be inequitable.

539 F.2d at 1214 (emphasis added) (citations omitted). Similarly, we find that to allow Verco to recover the entire purchase price without allowing Spartan a claim against the estate would result in an "inequitable" double recovery.

The bankruptcy panel's attempt to distinguish *Misty* on the ground that the debtor-transferor was the non-complying party misreads *Misty's* facts. *Misty* clearly involved "a transferee guilty of fraudulent behavior." Id. Verco's contention that *Misty* is an inapplicable "fraudulent conveyance case" is also unpersuasive. Both are bankruptcy cases in which the transferees' conduct led to the transfers being set aside pursuant to the same section of the Bankruptcy Act. (In *Misty*, the transfer was set aside pursuant to § 70(e) of the old Act, the predecessor to § 544(b), the provision employed in this case.) Although the rationale for invalidating the transfers in the two situations is somewhat different, the same inequitable result is involved in both instances. Accordingly, Spartan has a claim against the estate which may be set-off against Verco's recovery on the note.

We note that Spartan was not guilty of any actual fraud in connection with the transfer of assets. At most, Spartan was negligent in failing to take immediate possession of the subject property and in failing properly to circulate notice of the bulk transfer to Verco's creditors. Spartan concedes that Verco is entitled to invalidate the transfer and retain the property for the benefit of its creditors. Spartan's negligence is not relevant, however, to whether Spartan is entitled to a set-off. See *Misty*, 539 F.2d at 1214. . . .

Section 553 of the Bankruptcy Code permits "a creditor to offset a mutual debt owing by such a creditor to the debtor that arose before the commencement of the case . . . against a claim of such a creditor that arose before the commencement of the case. . . ." The timing and mutuality elements must both be satisfied to establish a set-off under the section. 4 Collier On Bankruptcy ¶¶ 553.04, 553.05, 553.08 (15th ed. 1982).

We agree with the concurring member of the bankruptcy panel that both elements are satisfied here:

The estate's claim is based on a note given by Spartan Plastics to Verco Industries before the commencement of the case. Any claim Spartan Plastics can establish that arises from recovery of the fraudulently conveyed property "shall be determined, and shall be allowed . . . the same as if such claim had arisen before the date of the filing of the petition." 11 U.S.C. § 502(h). Thus the timing elements of section 553 are satisfied.

"To be mutual, the debts must be in the same right and between the same parties, standing in the same capacity." 4 Collier on Bankruptcy, 15th ed. p. 553–22. A claim that is deemed to have arisen before bankruptcy is by necessary implication deemed to have been owed to the estate's predecessor, here Verco Industries. Thus, from a pre-bankruptcy perspective, the two debts were between the same parties in their corporate capacities. . . . Spartan's debt under the note is to the estate; Spartan's claim, when fixed, will be against the estate. Mutuality is therefore satisfied.

A set-off claim would not defeat the estate's invalidation of the transfer because the claim is not allowable under 11 U.S.C. § 502(d) until after the property has been surrendered to the estate. We also agree with the concurring panel member that although the "right" to seek set-off is a legal issue, the "amount" of any set-off presents a factual question that must be determined on remand. The amount of the claim will presumably bear the same relationship to the total purchase price of $305,765 as the value of the bulk sales property bore to the total consideration tendered by Verco.

We find no support for Verco's contention that section 502(h) only serves to reinstate an existing claim where property is recovered by the trustee. As noted in Collier:

the import of Section 502(h) is that where a claim is allowable as provided in that section, its status is as a claim in existence on the date of the filing of the petition regardless of when, after the petition, the trustee has taken the necessary action and recovered.

3 Collier, supra, ¶ 502.08, at 502–92 n. 6. We also find no support for Verco's contention that where a transferor is blameless, no claim may be proven against it.

CONCLUSION

The decision of the bankruptcy panel is reversed in part, and the matter is remanded to the bankruptcy trial court to determine the amount of Spartan's set-off.

Notes & Questions

1. *The Basics of § 544(b).* Although *Verco* involves some other issues, please be sure you understand the basic issue of how § 544(b) enables the trustee to attack a defective bulk transfer. To test your understanding, consider the following situation. Debtor borrows $1,000

from Lender and grants Lender a security interest in Debtor's equipment. Debtor has other creditors, all of whom are unsecured. Lender allows thirty days to pass before perfecting its security interest. Six months later, Debtor files a bankruptcy petition. May Debtor's trustee in bankruptcy invalidate Lender's security interest under § 544(b)? Suppose that during the thirty day period when Lender's security interest was unperfected, a tort claimant became a lien creditor with respect to the same equipment. Would the trustee then be able to invalidate Lender's security interest in bankruptcy? Will § 544(b) ever enable the trustee to invalidate a perfected security interest?

2. *Flawed Perfection.* Suppose Lender in Question 1 never perfected its security interest. Would it be vulnerable under § 544(b)? Suppose Lender perfected its security interest one day before the filing of the bankruptcy petition?

3. *Actual Creditor Required.* Note that § 544(b) refers to transfers voidable by a creditor holding an unsecured claim and that § 544(a) specifies that the trustee obtains the rights of creditors or purchasers whether or not they exist. What would be the effect of not requiring an actual creditor in § 544(b)?

4. *Why Have § 544(b)?* Is the basic rule of § 544(b) (and old § 70e) a necessary consequence of having a bankruptcy law? Suppose one had a bankruptcy proceeding in which the trustee could not invoke the rights of actual creditors. Could a bankruptcy law rationally let such creditors invoke their state law rights at their own initiation and in their own behalf? Why should all of the unsecured creditors represented by the trustee benefit in bankruptcy from rights that only particular creditors could have benefited from outside of bankruptcy?

LEWIS v. MANUFACTURERS NATIONAL BANK OF DETROIT

Supreme Court of the United States, 1961.
364 U.S. 603, 81 S.Ct. 347, 5 L.Ed.2d 323.

MR. JUSTICE DOUGLAS delivered the opinion of the Court.

The bankrupt borrowed money from respondent on November 4, 1957, giving as security a chattel mortgage on an automobile. In Michigan, where the transaction took place, mortgages were void as against creditors of the mortgagor unless filed with the Register of Deeds with a special dispensation to purchase-money mortages if filed within 14 days of the execution of the mortgage. This mortgage, however, was not a purchase-money mortgage; and though executed on November 4, 1957, it was not recorded until November 8, 1957.

Over five months later—on April 18, 1958—the borrower filed a voluntary petition in bankruptcy and an adjudication of bankruptcy followed, petitioner being named trustee.

There was no evidence that any creditor had extended credit between November 4, the date of the execution of the mortgage, and

November 8, the date of its recordation. But since the mortgage had not been recorded immediately, the referee held that it was void as against the trustee. The referee relied upon § 70, sub. c of the Bankruptcy Act, 11 U.S.C. § 110, which, so far as material here, reads:

> "The trustee, as to all property whether or not coming into possession or control of the court, upon which a creditor of the bankrupt could have obtained a lien by legal or equitable proceedings at the date of bankruptcy, shall be deemed vested as of such date with all the rights, remedies, and powers of a creditor then holding a lien thereon by such proceedings, whether or not such a creditor actually exists."

He ruled that § 70, sub. c "clothes the Trustee with the rights of a creditor who could have obtained a lien at the date of bankruptcy whether or not such a creditor exists." He concluded that under Michigan law a creditor could have taken prior to the mortgage had he extended credit during the four-day period when the mortgage was "off record" and that therefore the trustee can claim the same rights, even though there was no such creditor. The District Court overruled the referee and the Court of Appeals affirmed the District Court. 275 F.2d 454. The case is here on a petition for a writ of certiorari which we granted because of a conflict between that decision and Constance v. Harvey, 215 F.2d 571, decided by the Court of Appeals for the Second Circuit . . . ..

Petitioner's case turns on the words, "upon which a creditor of the bankrupt could have obtained a lien . . . whether or not such a creditor actually exists," contained in § 70; sub. c. . . .

The predecessor of the present § 70, sub. c was § 47(a)(2) of the Bankruptcy Act, as amended by the 1910 Act which provided in relevant part:

> ". . . such trustees, as to all property in the custody or coming into the custody of the bankruptcy court, shall be deemed vested with all the rights, remedies, and powers of a creditor holding a lien by legal or equitable proceedings thereon; and also, as to all property not in the custody of the bankruptcy court, shall be deemed vested with all the rights, remedies, and powers of a judgment creditor holding an execution duly returned unsatisfied." 36 Stat. 840.

That language was held to give the trustee the status of a creditor "as of the time when the petition in bankruptcy is filed." Bailey v. Baker Ice Machine Co., 239 U.S. 268, 276, 36 S.Ct. 50, 54, 60 L.Ed. 275.

In 1938 the relevant provisions of § 47(a)(2) were transferred to § 70, sub. c with no material change.

In 1950 § 70, sub. c was recast to read as follows:

> ". . . The trustee, as to all property of the bankrupt at the date of bankruptcy whether or not coming into possession or control of the court, shall be deemed vested as of the date of bankruptcy

with all the rights, remedies, and powers of a creditor then holding a lien thereon by legal or equitable proceedings, whether or not such a creditor actually exists." 64 Stat. 26.

Thus the distinction between property in the possession of the bankrupt as of the date of bankruptcy and other property was abolished; and the trustee was given the status of a creditor holding a lien through legal or equitable proceedings as to both types of property. This 1950 Amendment, however, created an anomaly. The House Report accompanying a 1952 amendment that cast § 70, sub. c in its present form states:

". . . it is now recognized that the amendment did not accurately express what was intended. Since the trustee already has title to all of the bankrupt's property, it is not proper to say that he has the rights of a lien creditor upon his own property. What should be said is that he has the rights of a lien creditor upon property in which the bankrupt has an interest or as to which the bankrupt may be the ostensible owner. Accordingly, the language of section 70c has been revised so as to clarify its meaning and state more accurately what is intended."

We think that one consistent theory underlies the several versions of § 70, sub. c which we have set forth, viz., that the rights of creditors—whether they are existing or hypothetical—to which the trustee succeeds are to be ascertained as of "the date of bankruptcy," not at an anterior point of time. That is to say, the trustee acquires the status of a creditor as of the time when the petition in bankruptcy is filed. We read the statutory words "the rights . . . of a creditor [existing or hypothetical] then holding a lien" to refer to that date.

This construction seems to us to fit the scheme of the Act. Section 70, sub. e enables the trustee to set aside fraudulent transfers which creditors having provable claims could void. The construction of § 70, sub. c which petitioner urges would give the trustee power to set aside transactions which no creditor could void and which injured no creditor. That construction would enrich unsecured creditors at the expense of secured creditors, creating a windfall merely by reason of the happenstance of bankruptcy.

It is true that in some instances the trustee has rights which existing creditors may not have. Section 11, 11 U.S.C. § 29, gives him two years to institute legal proceedings regardless of what limitations creditors might have been under. Section 60, 11 U.S.C. § 96, 11 U.S.C.A. § 96, gives him the right to recover preferential transfers made by the bankrupt within four months whether or not creditors had that right by local law. A like power exists under § 67, sub. a, 11 U.S.C. § 107, as respects the invalidation of judicial liens obtained within four months of bankruptcy and when the bankrupt was insolvent. Section 67, sub. d, 11 U.S.C. § 107, sub. d, carefully defines transactions which may be voided if made "within one year prior to the filing" of the petition.

Congress in striking a balance between secured and unsecured creditors has provided for specific periods of repose beyond which transactions of the bankrupt prior to bankruptcy may no longer be upset—except and unless existing creditors can set them aside. Yet if we construe § 70, sub. c as petitioner does, there would be no period of repose. Security transactions entered into in good faith years before the bankruptcy could be upset if the trustee were ingenious enough to conjure up a hypothetical situation in which a hypothetical creditor might have had such a right. The rule pressed upon us would deprive a mortgagee of his rights in States like Michigan, if the mortgage had been executed months or even years previously and there had been a delay of a day or two in recording without any creditor having been injured during the period when the mortgage was unrecorded.

That is too great a wrench for us to give the bankruptcy system, absent a plain indication from Congress which is lacking here.

Affirmed.

MR. JUSTICE HARLAN. As the judge who wrote for the Court of Appeals in Constance v. Harvey, 215 F.2d 571, I think it appropriate to say that I have long since come to the view that the second opinion in Constance, 215 F.2d 575 was ill-considered. I welcome this opportunity to join in setting the matter right.

Notes & Questions

1. *Security Interests and § 544(a).* Apply § 544(a) to the situation of Lender in Question 1, following *Verco*, supra. Would its effect change if Lender had never perfected its security interest? What if Lender perfected one day before the filing of the bankruptcy petition?

2. *The Timing of the Hypothetical Extension of Credit.* Section 544(a), the successor to § 70c, specifies the time at which the trustee is deemed to have extended credit to the debtor. In light of the nationwide adoption of Article 9, does the date on which the trustee is deemed to have extended credit to the debtor matter to the extent that it mattered under the personal property security system at issue in *Lewis*? Are there any situations in which the date of deemed credit extension will matter? (Hint: Consider a prebankruptcy fraudulent conveyance that is fraudulent only as against existing creditors, all of whom have been paid off prior to bankruptcy. Is such a transaction vulnerable under § 544(b)?)

3. *Why Invalidate Unperfected Security Interests?* As the questions illustrate, § 544(a) enables the trustee to invalidate unperfected security interests. Is this justifiable? Outside of bankruptcy would any of the unsecured creditors who benefit from the trustee's use of § 544(a) be able to attack an unperfected security interest?

4. *Why Confer Hypothetical Creditor Status on the Trustee?* What would be the effect of requiring an actual creditor who could invalidate a secured party's interest before the trustee would be entitled to invoke

§ 544(a)? In Pacific Finance Corp. v. Edwards, 304 F.2d 224 (9th Cir. 1962), the court interpreted § 70c to require the trustee to produce an actual creditor who could obtain a lien.

We believe that the word "creditor" in the foregoing quoted language means an *actual* creditor. Such construction is confirmed by the remainder of § 70, sub. c which provides that the trustee "shall be deemed vested as of such date with all the rights, remedies, and powers of a creditor then holding a lien thereon by such proceedings, whether or not such a creditor actually exists." The clause "whether or not such a creditor actually exists" refers only to a "creditor then holding a lien thereon." Under our construction of § 70, sub. c the Trustee is empowered to exercise the powers given him even if no actual creditor has obtained a lien, but he cannot do so if no actual creditor could have obtained a lien.

Does § 544(a) overrule *Pacific Finance?*

5. *The U.C.C. & § 544(a).* What is the relationship between § 544(a) of the Bankruptcy Act and U.C.C. § 9–301(1)(b) & (3)? Are there differences between the rights they confer upon trustees in bankruptcy? Would any cases come out differently if the trustee in bankruptcy were not included in the definition of lien creditor in § 9–301(3)? See generally 2 Gilmore § 45.3.2, at 1296.

6. *Post-Bankruptcy Perfection.* If bankruptcy occurs after the grant of a security interest and before perfection of the security interest, may the secured party perfect after the bankruptcy petition has been filed? See §§ 546(b), 362(a)(5), 362(b)(3).

IN RE SASSARD & KIMBALL, INC. (MOORE v. BAY)

United States Court of Appeals, Ninth Circuit, 1931.
45 F.2d 449.

NORCROSS, DISTRICT JUDGE.

This is an appeal from an order made by the court below reversing a ruling of the referee in bankruptcy holding a certain chattel mortgage void as to all creditors.

The facts are stipulated, and those material are as follows: At all times important to be considered in this case Sassard & Kimball, Inc., was a corporation engaged in the business of a merchant selling automobiles, automobile parts and accessories. On the 31st day of December, 1929, the corporation filed a voluntary petition in bankruptcy, and on the same date appellant was appointed receiver for the estate of the bankrupt, and upon qualifying, took into his possesison all property claimed to be a part of the estate, including that covered by a certain chattel mortgage in question. On November 23, 1928, the bankrupt executed a chattel mortgage as security for the payment of a certain promissory note for $10,000, payable thirty days after date to the assignor of appellee. The mortgage was acknowledged of date November 30, 1928, the affidavit of good faith was executed December

5, 1928, and the instrument filed for record and recorded by the county recorder of Los Angeles county on December 19, 1928.   The chattel mortgage covered a certain Studebaker service car, a Ford roadster, the furniture, showroom, and shop equipment of the bankrupt.   Prior to the execution or filing of the mortgage no notice of intention to mortgage the stock in trade, fixtures, and equipment belonging to the mortgagor was recorded in accordance with the provisions of section 3440 of the Civil Code of California.   In relation to the mortgage, the proceeding presents three classes of creditors of the bankrupt: (1) Those existing at the date of the mortgage; (2) those who became such between the date of the mortgage and its recordation; (3) those so becoming subsequent to the recording of the mortgage.

Section 3440 of the Civil Code of California provides that a chattel mortgage "will be conclusively presumed to be fraudulent and void as against the existing creditors . . .   unless at least seven days before the consummation of such . . .   mortgage, the . . .   mortgagor . . .   shall record in the office of the county recorder . . .   a notice of said intended . . .   mortgage," setting out the particulars of its proposed effect and purpose.

It is clear that the mortgage, by reason of the provisions of the statute, is void as to creditors of the first class, and it is conceded it is also void as to those of the second class.   As held by decisions of the Supreme Court of California, the mortgage would be valid as against creditors of the third class.

It is the contention of appellant that, under section 70e of the Bankruptcy Act of 1898 (11 U.S.C.A. § 110(e)), the mortgage in question, being void as to one creditor or class of creditors, is void in toto at the suit of the trustee.

Section 70e of the Bankruptcy Act reads: "The trustee may avoid any transfer by the bankrupt of his property which any creditor of such bankrupt might have avoided, and may recover the property so transferred, or its value, from the person to whom it was transferred, unless he was a bona fide holder for value prior to the date of the adjudication. Such property may be recovered or its value collected from whoever may have received it, except a bona fide holder for value.   For the purpose of such recovery any court of bankruptcy as defined in this title, and any State court which would have had jurisdiction if bankruptcy had not intervened, shall have concurrent jurisdiction."

There is no express language in this section which specifically gives to any unsecured creditor of a bankrupt any greater rights or any secured creditor any less right than he had before adjudication in bankruptcy.   The rights of a trustee in bankruptcy to "avoid any transfer" are no greater than those of a creditor or particular class of creditors.   It is clear, we think, that a trustee in bankruptcy is limited in his control and disposition of the estate of the bankrupt to the rights of creditors as such rights existed and could be enforced under the state law prior to the time proceedings in bankruptcy were instituted.   This is not a case of an ordinary transfer of property in whole or in part in fraud of creditors, but a case of a transfer made void by statute only as to a specific class of creditors. In National Bank v. Moore, 247 F. 913, 919, this court said: "The trustee in the interest of the general creditors may therefore contest any claim of lien that a judgment creditor might contest if bankruptcy had not intervened."

In the case at bar, only judgment creditors of the first or second class specified could have successfully contested the mortgage had not bankruptcy intervened.

We quote with approval the following from the memorandum opinion of Judge Killits filed in the court below: "In 1910, the Bankruptcy Act was amended to make clear the position of the Trustee. It seems to have been the theory of the Referee that the effect of this amendment, which gave the Trustee the status of an execution creditor, so far affected the status of the creditors of each of the three classes, as against the mortgage, as to place them all on the same level of superiority. In this we are very clear that the Referee was wrong. There is nothing whatever in the cause for, or the language of the amendment of 1910 to produce such a result. The Trustee indeed represents all creditors, but only as their respective interests in the property under administration were fixed by local law when the bankruptcy proceedings intervened, and it is his duty to administer and distribute accordingly as he finds at that time liens or inferiorities of respective creditors were established. If at that time any creditors had no inchoate right under existing state laws to reduce his claim to judgment and thereby establish a lien by execution superior to an existing and recorded mortgage, he is bound in distribution to recognize the latter's superior position. It is said, as a settled law in federal courts, that there is so much of local nature entering into chattel mortgages that federal courts accept as decisive the state law fixing the priority of such encumbrance. . . .

MOORE v. BAY

Supreme Court of the United States, 1931.
284 U.S. 4, 52 S.Ct. 3, 76 L.Ed. 133.

MR. JUSTICE HOLMES delivered the opinion of the court.

The bankrupt executed a mortgage of automobiles, furniture, showroom, and shop equipment that is admitted to be bad as against creditors who were such at the date of the mortgage, and those who became such between the date of the mortgage and that on which it was recorded, there having been a failure to observe the requirements of the Civil Code of California, § 3440. The question raised is whether the mortgage is void also as against those who gave the bankrupt credit at a later date, after the mortgage was on record. The Circuit Court of Appeals affirmed an order of the District Judge giving the mortgage priority over the last creditors. 45 F.2d 449. Whether the court was right must be decided by the Bankruptcy Act, since it is superior to all state laws upon the subject.

The trustee in bankruptcy gets the title to all property which has been transferred by the bankrupt in fraud of creditors or which prior to the petition he could by any means have transferred, or which might have been levied upon and sold under judicial process against him. Act of July 1, 1898, c. 541, § 70 (U.S.Code, title 11, § 110, 11 U.S.C.A. § 110). By section 67a (U.S.Code, title 11, § 107(a), 11 U.S.C.A. § 107(a)) claims which for want of record or for other reasons would not have been valid liens as against the claims of the creditors of the bankrupt shall not be liens against his estate. The rights of the trustee by subrogation are to be enforced for the benefit of the estate. The Circuit Courts of Appeal seem generally to agree, as the language of the Bankruptcy Act appears to us to imply very plainly, that what thus is recovered for the benefit of the estate is to be distributed in "dividends of an equal per centum   .   .   .   on all allowed claims, except such as have priority or are secured."   .   .   .

Decree reversed.

IN RE PLONTA

United States Court of Appeals, Sixth Circuit, 1962.
311 F.2d 44.

CECIL, CHIEF JUDGE.

This is an appeal from the United States District Court for the Western District of Michigan, Southern Division. The controversy grows out of the bankruptcy of Eugene (Dean) W. Plonta. Sears, Roebuck and Co., the appellant, claims to be a secured creditor of the bankrupt Plonta. Wadsworth Bissell, trustee in bankruptcy, is the appellee. The parties will be referred to as the Bankrupt, Sears and Trustee, respectively.

The pertinent facts are not in dispute and may be stated as follows: The Bankrupt purchased a 22-foot cabin cruiser from Sears on a conditional sales contract April 30, 1956. The cruiser was in kit form and by agreement between the purchaser and seller, the boat hull, engine, parts, and equipment were to be shipped for assembly to North Shore Marina, Incorporated, at Grand Haven, Ottawa county, Michigan. The various parts and equipment arrived at the marina about the middle of May, 1956. The boat was completed and given a trial run on July 3rd or 4th.

After the trial run, the boat remained at the marina for the installation of some additional items of equipment purchased by the Bankrupt and for which he paid the marina. On June 13, 1956, the Bankrupt executed and delivered a promissory note to Sears, for the balance of the purchase price and gave a chattel mortgage to Sears covering the boat and equipment as security for the payment of the note. The chattel mortgage was filed in the office of the Register of Deeds of Muskegon county, Michigan, June 21, 1956. The mortgage was not filed with the Register of Deeds of Ottawa county, the county in which North Shore Marina was located. At all times pertinent to this litigation, the Bankrupt was a resident of Muskegon county.

The installation of the additional equipment was completed about the middle of August. At this time, the Bankrupt took the boat to the Muskegon Yacht Club, in Muskegon county, docked it there one night and then returned it to North Shore Marina, in Grand Haven. It was then taken to a marina in Bear Lake channel, in Muskegon county, and left there two or three nights and again returned to Grand Haven. The Bankrupt traveled back and forth between North Shore Marina and Bear Lake channel until the latter part of August. At this time he was able to rent docking facilities in the channel. The boat remained here until October, when it was returned to the marina in Grand Haven and stored for the winter.

During the following year 1957, although the Bankrupt sometimes used the boat, it was continuously kept at the marina in Grand Haven for repairs and storage. On December 16, 1957, Sears repossessed the boat in foreclosure of its chattel mortgage and paid North Shore Marina its accumulated storage, repair and upkeep charges against the Bankrupt. About two hours after the repossession, the Bankrupt filed his petition in bankruptcy. The time relation between these two events was coincidental and not a race for priority. Subsequent to the repossession, Sears sold the boat for $2300, which was considered to be its fair and reasonable value.

The history of the litigation is as follows: On January 13, 1959, the Trustee filed a petition to require Sears to turn the $2300 over to the bankrupt estate. There was a hearing on this petition and the referee found from the facts above stated that the location of the boat for the purpose of filing a chattel mortgage, under Michigan Statutes Annotated 26.929, Comp.Laws 1948, § 566.140, was Ottawa county, Michigan. He further found that the mortgage was invalid as to the Trustee for failure to file with the Register of Deeds, of Ottawa county, and ordered Sears to turn over $2300 to the estate. There was a petition for review of this order and on review the District Judge adopted the referee's findings of fact and conclusions of law and sustained his order.

Later counsel for Sears moved to set aside this order and for reconsideration of its petition for review. In the meantime, the Supreme Court of Michigan had decided the case of Schueler v. Weintrob, 360 Mich. 621, 105 N.W.2d 42, in which it was held that repossession by a mortgagee prior to the time of filing a petition in bankruptcy was in legal effect equivalent to filing in the county of location (M.S.A. 26.929) and deprived the Trustee in Bankruptcy of any rights under section 70, sub. c of the Bankruptcy Act. (Sec. 110, sub. c, Title 11, U.S.C.)

A motion was then filed on behalf of the Trustee for the court to receive additional testimony or remand the matter to the referee to take testimony concerning the extension of credit to the Bankrupt between the date of the execution of the mortgage on June 13, 1956, and the repossession of the property on December 16, 1957. The court sustained the motion and remanded the case to the referee for the purpose of taking further evidence. Upon hearing the referee found that within the interim period involved, Albert B. Doherty extended credit to the Bankrupt in the amount of $10, without knowledge of the mortgage and it was unpaid. The referee concluded that the existence of this interim creditor invalidated the mortgage as a security document pursuant to section 70, sub. e (Sec. 110, sub. e(1), Title 11, U.S.C.) of the Bankruptcy Act and that the benefits of the invalidity inured to all the general creditors of the Bankrupt. The turnover order of $2300 was again entered. On petition for review, the District Judge affirmed the order of the referee. In a subsequent order, the motion of Sears to vacate the original order of the court, dated October 20, 1960, was denied.

The first question presented for our consideration is whether, under the law of Michigan, the chattel mortgage should have been filed in Ottawa county, as well as Muskegon county. The Michigan Statute (M.S.A. 26.929) provides: "Every mortgage or conveyance intended to operate as a mortgage of goods and chattels which shall hereafter be made which shall not be accompanied by an immediate delivery and followed by an actual and continued change of possession of the things mortgaged, shall be absolutely void as against the creditors of the mortgagor, and as against subsequent purchasers or mortgagees in good faith, unless the mortgage or a true copy thereof shall be filed in the office of the register of deeds of the county where the goods or chattels are located, and also where the mortgagor resides . . .."

The referee found and concluded, from the facts as stated herein, that Ottawa county was the county of location and under the Michigan statute the mortgage should have been filed there. . . .

The mortgage then was invalid, under the Michigan statute (M.S.A. 26.929) as to creditors of the Bankrupt. After the opinion of the court on the question of the necessity of filing the mortgage in Ottawa county, it seemed that Sears' security might be salvaged by the decision of the Supreme Court of Michigan, in Schueler v. Weintrob, 360 Mich. 621, 105 N.W.2d 42, to which reference is heretofore made. . . .

Section 70, sub. e(1) of the Bankruptcy Act (110, sub. e(1), Title 11, U.S.C.) provides: "A transfer made or suffered or obligation incurred by a debtor adjudged a bankrupt under this title which, under any Federal or State law applicable thereto, is fraudulent as against or voidable for any other reason by any creditor of the debtor, having a claim provable under this title, shall be null and void as against the trustee of such debtor."

The following facts, as found by the referee, are substantiated by the evidence: The mortgage was not filed in Ottawa county as required by the Michigan statute. Albert B. Doherty became a creditor in the amount of ten dollars July 20, 1957, when the mortgage was off record and his claim was provable against the Bankrupt under the Bankruptcy

Act. The conclusion of the referee, sustained by the District Judge, that the mortgage being invalid under the Michigan statute as to interim creditor Doherty, was null and void as against the Trustee, is a correct application of the law. . . .

So far as we have been able to ascertain the amount of the credit extended is immaterial and the validity or invalidity of the chattel mortgage is not affected by the size of the creditor's claim. Neither is it material that the debt was not scheduled or that the creditor did not know of the existence of the chattel; nor is it necessary to prove that the creditor would not have extended the credit if he had known of the mortgage. Counsel for the appellant have cited no authorities in support of these claims.

Finding no error in the record the judgment of the District Court is affirmed.

Notes & Questions

1. *Reaction to* Moore. "The rule of Moore v. Bay is that a transaction which is voidable by a single creditor, however small his claim, is, under § 70(e) [now § 544(b)], entirely void as to the trustee in bankruptcy. The rule has been often criticized and rarely defended. It has been suggested that the 'rule' is really not set forth in the opinion. It has been suggested that the case, even if it did embody the 'rule,' should not be taken seriously because Justice Holmes was over ninety years when he wrote the opinion. These suggestions fail to take into account that the Court was unanimous and that the mandate was clear even if the opinion was ambiguous and inadequate. At all events, neither Congress nor the Supreme Court has ever sought to change the rule, which may be taken as a permanent feature of our bankruptcy law."
2 Gilmore, § 45.3.1, at 1290.

2. *The Significance of Small Claims.* Would *Plonta* have come out differently if Doherty had not been owed $10? Does it make sense for so much to turn on the existence of a creditor with a de minimis claim? Does the *Moore-Plonta* rule survive in the Bankruptcy Act? The legislative history states:

> Subsection [544(b)] is derived from current section 70e. It gives the trustee the rights of actual unsecured creditors under applicable law to void transfers. It follows Moore v. Bay . . . and overrules those cases that hold section 70e gives the trustee the rights of secured creditors.

Senate Report at 85. Would § 544(b) mandate the same result in *Plonta*? To what other situations will *Moore's* rule apply?

3. *Assumptions About Creditor Behavior.* What assumptions about unsecured creditor behavior underlie the *Moore* rule? As you may have gathered from reading *Moore* and *Plonta,* the systems of personal property security in effect in those cases differ from the now dominant system, Article 9. Under some of these pre-U.C.C. systems, a grant of a security interest in property could be attacked by specified classes of

unsecured creditors. In *Moore,* under what was then California law, these classes included unsecured creditors whose loans preceded recordation of the personal property mortgage. Under such security systems, unsecured creditors could derive substantial comfort from searching the public record for security interests in the property of those to whom they wished to lend. If such interests existed but were not of record at the time of the unsecured loan, their subsequent recordation could not adversely affect the unsecured lender's access to the property used as security. In short, some of the old personal property security systems encouraged unsecured lenders to rely on the absence of recorded interests in the debtor's property.

Do these observations about the nature of personal property security systems suggest a rationale for the *Moore* rule? One way to state the *Moore* rule is that vulnerability to any unsecured creditor renders an interest in the debtor's property vulnerable to all unsecured creditors (through the trustee). Does *Moore* assume that, for every unsecured creditor actually found, there may be many others who are not found or who do not speak up but who may have relied on the lack of public record of security interests to extend unsecured credit to the debtor? *Moore,* it can then be argued, protects the unknown unsecured creditors who have been misled about the debtor's financial status by whatever defects (such as the delayed filing in *Moore)* led to a secured creditor's vulnerability to a single unsecured claim. See generally Eisenberg, A Bankruptcy Machine That Would Go of Itself, 39 Stan.L.Rev. 1519, 1530–32 (1987); T. Jackson, The Logic and Limits of Bankruptcy Law 79–82 (1986).

If the above is a rationale for the *Moore* rule, does it enjoy continued validity today? Article 9 replaced the personal property security systems involved in *Moore* and *Plonta.* Under it, should unsecured creditors derive any comfort from searching the public record for notice of security interests? How can an unsecured creditor rely on any of the debtor's property for repayment when, outside of bankruptcy, a security interest (even an unperfected security interest) will almost always defeat the claims of unsecured creditors?

In short, do *Moore* and Article 9 reflect the same assumptions about the extent to which unsecured creditors may rely on the public record for notice of adverse interests in specific property?

4. *The Effect of* Moore. Is it possible that a creditor whose interest in property is eliminated under the rule of Moore v. Bay may be better off than if the interest had been partly sustained? Suppose under applicable bulk transfer law a transfer is defective as to existing creditors but not as to future creditors. The transfer, which consists of property worth $20,000, occurs on January 1, 1984, at which time the debtor owes unsecured creditors $15,000. Between January 1 and February 1, the debtor incurs an additional $20,000 in unsecured debt. How much of the $20,000 transfer would the transferee of the bulk

transfer be able to keep outside of bankruptcy? In bankruptcy, with *Moore* applicable, how much does he get of the $20,000?

5. Does the answer to the above question turn on whether the trustee "inherits" the fraudulent transfer for the benefit of all creditors? Could the transfer be avoided solely for the benefit of those who could have avoided it outside of bankruptcy? What does *Moore* suggest? See §§ 551, 554.

B. Fraudulent Conveyances

IN RE HULM

United States Court of Appeals, Eighth Circuit, 1984.
738 F.2d 323, cert. denied, 469 U.S. 990, 105 S.Ct. 398, 83 L.Ed.2d 331.

Before BRIGHT, ARNOLD and FAGG, CIRCUIT JUDGES.

FAGG, CIRCUIT JUDGE.

The questions in this case are (1) whether a foreclosure of a mortgage pursuant to the North Dakota statutory scheme, involving a judicial foreclosure sale and issuance of a sheriff's deed following expiration of a redemption period, effects a transfer of an interest of the debtor in property within the meaning of 11 U.S.C. § 548(a), which permits the bankruptcy trustee to avoid a fraudulent transfer of an interest of the debtor in property, and, if so, (2) whether absent improprieties the price received for property at a judicial foreclosure sale provides a reasonably equivalent value for the transfer of the debtor's interest under 11 U.S.C. § 548(a)(2)(A) as a matter of law. We hold that foreclosure of a mortgage pursuant to the North Dakota statutory scheme effects a transfer of an interest of the debtor in property, and that on remand the bankruptcy court must conduct an evidentiary hearing to determine whether the sale price at the judicial foreclosure sale which occurred in this case provided a reasonably equivalent value in exchange for the transfer of the debtor's interest.

George Hulm and Linda Heikes granted a mortgage on residential property to First Federal Savings & Loan Association of Bismarck on November 24, 1978, to secure a note for $61,000. Hulm and Heikes failed to make payments as required, and on November 12, 1981, a notice of intention to foreclose was served. A complaint commencing the foreclosure action was served on December 31, 1981, a default judgment foreclosing the mortgage was entered on February 4, 1982, and the house was sold at a judicial foreclosure sale on March 4, 1982. First Federal purchased the property at the foreclosure sale for $64,443.64, an amount which represented the unpaid balance of the note, accrued interest, and statutory costs awarded in the foreclosure action. On July 9, 1982, following expiration of the statutory period for redemption, a sheriff's deed was issued to First Federal, giving it title to the property. Hulm filed his petition in bankruptcy on July 26, 1982.

First Federal filed this adversary action seeking a determination that the property was not a part of Hulm's bankruptcy estate and a modification of the automatic stay so that First Federal could proceed with eviction proceedings under state law. Heikes had already been evicted. The trustee contended that the mortgage foreclosure should be set aside because it was a preferential transfer under 11 U.S.C. § 547 or a fraudulent transfer under 11 U.S.C. § 548. The bankruptcy court rejected both contentions, but only the fraudulent transfer question is presented to us on appeal.

The principal rules governing fraudulent transfers are found in 11 U.S.C. § 548, which provides in pertinent part:

> (a) The trustee may avoid any transfer of an interest of the debtor in property, or any obligation incurred by the debtor, that was made or incurred on or within one year before the date of the filing of the petition, if the debtor—
>
> . . .
>
> (2)(A) received less than a reasonably equivalent value in exchange for such transfer or obligation; and
>
> (B)(i) was insolvent on the date that such transfer was made or such obligation was incurred, or became insolvent as a result of such transfer or obligation. . . .

There appears to have been no real dispute concerning whether Hulm fell within the insolvency requirement of section 548(a)(2)(B)(i). Similarly, there is no doubt that the judicial foreclosure sale, the expiration of the redemption period, and issuance of the sheriff's deed all occurred within one year before Hulm's bankruptcy petition was filed. As a consequence, we are not asked to decide in this appeal precisely when during the foreclosure process the transfer took place. We are concerned with the remaining elements of a fraudulent transfer, i.e., whether the mortgage foreclosure procedures in this case effected a transfer of an interest of the debtor in property and whether a reasonably equivalent value was received in exchange for the transfer.

The bankruptcy court held that absent a showing of fraud or collusion the sale price at a judicial foreclosure sale is a reasonably equivalent value for the property transferred, and that since there was no such showing in the present case, any transfer resulting from the foreclosure sale could not be set aside under 11 U.S.C. § 548(a). On appeal the district court held that sale of the property at the foreclosure sale was a transfer within the meaning of 11 U.S.C. § 548(a), and then, after discussing the facts involved, concluded that the sale price was a reasonably equivalent value. At that time, however, no evidentiary hearing had been conducted concerning the issue of reasonably equivalent value. Although the bankruptcy court and the district court focused on the total price received for the property at the sale, it is more accurate to consider the value received for Hulm's interest, which comprised less than all rights in the property. This point is not of practical significance, however, since examination of the adequacy of the total sale price necessarily subsumes the issue of the adequacy of the value received for Hulm's interest.

On appeal Hulm and the trustee contend that the district court erred in its determination that the sale price at the foreclosure sale was a reasonably equivalent value under 11 U.S.C. § 548(a)(2)(A). In its cross-appeal First Federal contends that the transfer of Hulm's interest occurred when the mortgage was recorded and perfected under state law on November 29, 1978, more than one year before Hulm's bankruptcy petition was filed. First Federal also contends that actual market value is irrelevant because absent a showing of fraud or collusion the sale price at a judicial foreclosure sale is a reasonably equivalent value for the property transferred as a matter of law.

The question of whether the judicial foreclosure of a mortgage effects a transfer within the meaning of section 548(a) is a question of federal law. See McKenzie v. Irving Trust Co., 323 U.S. 365, 369–70, 65 S.Ct. 405, 407–08, 89 L.Ed. 305 (1945). Thus, to aid in determining whether the foreclosure of the mortgage was a transfer of an interest of the debtor in property, we turn to the definition of transfer found in 11 U.S.C. § 101(41): " '[T]ransfer' means every mode, direct or indirect, absolute or conditional, voluntary or involuntary, of disposing of or parting with property or with an interest in property, including retention of title as a security interest." If at the time of the mortgage foreclosure Hulm held an interest in the property, the language of section 101(41) clearly establishes that the mortgage foreclosure procedure in this case effected a transfer. Section 101(41) expressly includes involuntary transfers, and neither section 101(41) nor section 548(a) indicates that to fall within their terms the transfer had to be made by Hulm himself.

The term "interest of the debtor in property" is not defined in the Bankruptcy Code, however, and thus we look to state law to determine whether the debtor had an interest in property. See Butner v. United States, 440 U.S. 48, 55, 99 S.Ct. 914, 918, 59 L.Ed.2d 136 (1979); Johnson v. First National Bank of Montevideo, 719 F.2d 270, 273 (8th Cir.1983), cert. denied, ___ U.S. ___, 104 S.Ct. 1015, 79 L.Ed.2d 245 (1984). We have no difficulty in concluding that under North Dakota law Hulm had an interest in the property at the time of its sale, and at least until expiration of the redemption period. The mortgage held by First Federal was only a defeasible conveyance giving it the right to satisfy Hulm's unpaid debt from the property. See Pioneer Credit Co. v. Latendresse, 286 N.W.2d 445, 447 (N.D.1979). As a mortgagee, First Federal did not have a title interest in the property. Aure v. Mackoff, 93 N.W.2d 807, 811 (N.D.1958). Hulm remained the legal owner of the property until foreclosure, and his interest was alienable. Knowlton v. Coye, 76 N.D. 478, 37 N.W.2d 343, 347 (1949). Hulm's interest also included the right to possession of the property until the end of the redemption period, see N.D.Cent.Code § 28–24–11, and the right to the excess of the value of the property over First Federal's mortgage, see N.D.Cent.Code § 32–19–10. At the foreclosure sale Hulm's interest was transferred, subject to redemption. Hulm's equity of redemption was likewise an interest in the mortgaged property which could be conveyed. See Robar v. Ellingson, 301 N.W.2d 653, 657 (N.D.1981). Issuance of the sheriff's deed terminated Hulm's interest in the property. See N.D.Cent.Code § 32–19–09.

In support of its contention that the transfer of Hulm's interest in the property occurred when the mortgage was perfected, First Federal cites 11 U.S.C. § 548(d)(1) which provides:

> For the purposes of this section, a transfer is made when such transfer becomes so far perfected that a bona fide purchaser from the debtor against whom such transfer could have been perfected cannot acquire an interest in the property transferred that is superior to the interest in such property of the transferee, but if such transfer is not so perfected before the commencement of the case, such transfer occurs immediately before the date of the filing of the petition.

This section only determines when a transfer is deemed to have occurred, not whether a certain occurrence is a transfer of an interest of the debtor in property. See McKenzie v. Irving Trust Co., supra, 323 U.S. at 369–70, 65 S.Ct. at 407–08. Hence, the transfer of an interest accomplished by Hulm's granting the mortgage to First Federal occurred, by the terms of section 548(d)(1), when the mortgage was perfected. But as we have already noted, Hulm retained an interest in the property after the mortgage was perfected. Section 548(d)(1) is in no way inconsistent with our conclusion that separate and distinct interests in property may be transferred at different times. It is our view that foreclosure of the mortgage under the North Dakota statutory scheme effected a transfer of the interest retained by Hulm after he granted a mortgage to First Federal.

We now turn to the issue of whether a reasonably equivalent value was received for Hulm's interest in property which was transferred as a result of the mortgage foreclosure. The bankruptcy court relied on In re Madrid, 21 B.R. 424, 427 (Bankr. 9th Cir.1982), and concluded that absent a showing of fraud or collusion the sale price at a judicial foreclosure sale is a reasonably equivalent value for the property transferred as a matter of law. The bankruptcy court did not hold an evidentiary hearing in order to develop a record from which a determination could be made whether the price bid at the foreclosure sale provided a reasonably equivalent value for Hulm's interest in the property. In support of the bankruptcy court's holding, First Federal has cited only the bankruptcy appellate panel's decision in In re Madrid, supra, 21 B.R. at 427. While the Ninth Circuit affirmed that decision, In re Madrid, 725 F.2d 1197 (9th Cir.1984), in doing so the court expressly declined to adopt the reasoning of the bankruptcy appellate panel. Id. at 1199.

We disagree with the approach taken by the bankruptcy court. We do not believe that the sale price at a regularly conducted foreclosure sale, although absent fraud or collusion, can automatically be deemed to provide a reasonably equivalent value in exchange for the interest of the debtor transferred within the meaning of section 548(a). In our view, the question of whether the sale price provided a reasonably equivalent value cannot be answered without an evidentiary hearing. Accordingly, we vacate the judgment of the district court and remand to the bankruptcy court for an evidentiary hearing and for a determination of whether the sale price at the foreclosure sale provided a reasonably equivalent value in exchange for the transfer of Hulm's interest in the property.

We are aware of expressed concern that the result we have reached will affect the strategies of purchasers at judicial foreclosure sales. See In re Madrid, 725 F.2d 1197, 1202 (9th Cir.1984); Abramson v. Lakewood Bank & Trust Co., 647 F.2d 547, 550 (5th Cir.1981) (Clark, J., dissenting), cert. denied, 454 U.S. 1164, 102 S.Ct. 1038, 71 L.Ed.2d 320 (1982). The Bankruptcy Code provisions are clear, however, and direct the result we have reached. Hence, policy considerations cannot affect the outcome in this case, but must be addressed, if at all, by Congress.

Notes & Questions

1. *Relationship to State Law.* The issue in *Hulm* began to attract widespread attention after the Fifth Circuit's decision in Durrett v. Washington National Ins. Co., 621 F.2d 201 (5th Cir.1980), where the court held, under prior bankruptcy law, that a foreclosure sale constituted a transfer and that a price that was approximately 57.5% of the property's fair market value was not a "fair equivalent" for the transferred property.

If state fraudulent conveyance law that may be used by the trustee under § 544(b) does not render a transfer fraudulent, should § 548 be viewed as doing so? How might the approach of a state court in a nonbankruptcy setting differ from that of a bankruptcy court?

Should *Hulm* and *Durrett* be viewed as ways of "fixing" weaknesses in state foreclosure law? Is that an appropriate use of Congress's bankruptcy power?

2. *Some Subsequent Developments.* (a) Some of the provisions in the Bankruptcy Amendments and Federal Judgeship Act of 1984 seem to endorse the *Durrett* rule.[b] They were in fact part of a package of amendments intended to overturn *Durrett* through the following (unenacted) amendment to § 548(d)(2):

(D) A secured party or third party purchaser who obtains title to an interest of the debtor in property pursuant to a regularly conducted noncollusive foreclosure, power of sale, or other proceeding or provision of nonbankruptcy law permitting or providing for the realization of security upon default of the borrower under a mortgage, deed of trust, security agreement or other lien, whether before or after the date of the filing of the petition, gives reasonably equivalent

---

b. They include an amendment to what is now § 101(48) adding that transfer includes "foreclosure of the debtor's equity of redemption," and an amendment to § 548(a) adding "voluntarily or involuntarily."

value to the debtor within the meaning of this section if such creditor or third party purchaser bids in the full amount of the debt secured by such mortgage, deed of trust, security agreement or other lien at such foreclosure sale.

130 Cong.Rec. S6081–6082, S6118, S6122, S6127 (Daily ed., March 21, 1984).

In the late scramble to pass the bankruptcy amendments, this provision was deleted and the provisions that sound favorable to *Durrett* survived. In "legislative history" inserted into the Congressional Record three months after passage of the 1984 bankruptcy amendments, Senators Dole and DeConcini disavowed any support that might be gleaned for *Durrett*. 130 Cong.Rec. S13771–13772 (Daily ed., October 5, 1984).

(b) The proposed substitute for the UFCA, the Uniform Fraudulent Transfer Act, which would amend only *state* fraudulent conveyance law, disapproves of the *Durrett* result.

3. *Reasons for § 548.* Why restate in bankruptcy a power that creditors have under state law, and a power that the bankruptcy trustee may invoke through § 544(b)? When will the trustee be able to rely on § 548 but not on § 544(b)? When will the trustee be able to rely on § 544(b) but not on § 548?

4. *Transferees (§§ 548, 550).* In many cases the trustee will be able to proceed either under § 544(b) or under § 548. When will the provision chosen make a difference? Assume that the debtor has made a pre-bankruptcy fraudulent conveyance that is vulnerable under both §§ 544(b) and 548. Under which provision should the trustee proceed? Recall UFCA § 9 and compare Bankruptcy Act §§ 548(c) and 550.

C. Preferences (§ 547)

The simple primitive or classical preference was the ordinary course payment of his debt by an insolvent. Let us assume that X has assets of $1000 and liabilities of $10,000; he has ten creditors, each of whom has a $1000 claim. If X now pays creditor A in full, we say that A has received a preference. He has been paid, his fellow creditors have not been paid and X has no remaining assets. It should be emphasized that there is not the slightest hint of dishonesty in the A–X transaction. X has paid a debt, which is what a debtor should do, and A has received payment in satisfaction of his claim, which is what a creditor should do. Nor is there any depletion of A's estate from a balance sheet point of view: his assets and his liabilities have both been reduced by the same amount. This is a quite different transaction from the dishonest debtor's attempt to conceal his assets by putting them in the name of his wife or his brother-in-law. It is of course true that creditors B through J will get nothing if the A–X transaction is allowed to stand. If it can be avoided and X's assets divided ratably among all his creditors, each of them will get $100.

The idea that unlucky participants in an unanticipated catastrophe should bear an equal burden of the losses may be as old as the idea of law itself. In pre-insurance days, maritime law developed the institution of general average under which the owners of ship and cargo share ratably, according to the value of their investments, in whatever assets may be salvaged from the wreck. Anglo-American common law, however, did not seize on the maritime law analogy to provide a comparable protection to the creditor of an insolvent enterprise. There was no common law doctrine which made preferences unlawful or voidable. To make them so was one of the principal objects of the nineteenth century bankruptcy acts.

2 Gilmore, § 45.3.5, at 1298. If the common law (and, today, state law generally) did not undermine preferences why should it be a goal of bankruptcy law to do so?

1. The Basic Preference Rules

IN RE DUFFY

United States Bankruptcy Court, Southern District of New York, 1980.
3 B.R. 263.

HOWARD SCHWARTZBERG, BANKRUPTCY JUDGE.

The trustee in bankruptcy has invoked the voidable preference provisions under the Bankruptcy Reform Act of 1978, 11 U.S.C. § 547(b) to set aside and recover from Avis Rent A Car System, Inc. ("Avis") a $400 payment made by the bankrupt, as a lessee of an Avis vehicle, pursuant to a postdated check delivered by the debtor more than 90 days before the filing of the petition for relief, but which was cashed within the 90-day period.

In its answer to the trustee's complaint in this adversary proceeding Avis denies the preferential payment and affirmatively alleges that the payment was made more than 90 days before the filing of the petition. Avis also contends that the payment was made by the debtor for new value and was a substantially contemporaneous exchange within the meaning of this exception under Code § 547(c)(1). . . .

The undisputed facts established at the trial are as follows:

FINDINGS OF FACT

1. The debtor filed his voluntary petition for relief under Chapter 7 of the Bankruptcy Reform Act of 1978 on November 2, 1979. The commencement of this case for relief constituted an order for relief under Chapter 7, as prescribed under 11 U.S.C. § 301.

2. Prior to such petition the debtor had been a lessee of an automobile from Avis on a long term basis at a monthly rental charge of $209.27 per month, including tax, pursuant to a written lease dated January 24, 1979. There is no proof that the debtor ever made any payments under this lease other than the $400 payment in question.

3. Apparently some time in July, 1979, the debtor had a conversation with one Howard Krebs, an Avis representative, with regard to the debtor's arrears in rental payments, which resulted in the debtor's forwarding to Avis a $400 check postdated to August 3, 1979, enclosed in a letter dated July 30, 1979 (Exhibit "A").

4. This letter reads as follows:

"Dear Mr. Krebs:

As per our phone conversation on Monday morning (30 July 79), I have enclosed my check for $400.00.

Please note that this check is post dated 3 Aug. 1979 as agreed to in our conversation.

I will call you on 15th of August 1979 to let you know the status of another 400 dollar payment within a month's time. Thank you so much for your help in this matter.

Peter L. Duffy"

5. The check cleared and was honored by the drawee bank on August 6, 1979, which was 88 days before the debtor filed his petition for relief (Exhibit "1").

6. There is no evidence that Avis ever declared that the debtor was in default under its rental agreement with the debtor or that it ever requested the debtor to surrender possession of the leased vehicle.

7. The $400 payment by the debtor to Avis was on account of an antecedent debt owed by the debtor before such payment was made.

8. Avis presented no evidence to rebut the presumption of the debtor's insolvency for the 90 days preceding the filing of the petition for relief, as prescribed under 11 U.S.C. § 547(b)(4).

9. The $400 payment to Avis enabled Avis to receive more than it would receive if the payment had not been made and Avis received payment of its debt by way of distribution in this case, as specified in 11 U.S.C. § 547(b)(5).

DISCUSSION

From the foregoing facts, this court must first determine whether or not the $400 payment by the debtor to Avis accrued within the proscribed 90-day period so as to trigger the voidable preference provisions under 11 U.S.C. § 547(b). If the 90-day requirement has been met, reference must then be made to the exception to the trustee's avoiding power referred to by Avis in its answer, namely, a substantially contemporaneous exchange for a new value given to the debtor, as delineated under 11 U.S.C. § 547(c)(1).

WHEN THE TRANSFER OCCURS

That a payment of a debt by check is a transfer of property is manifestly expressed in the broad definition of "transfer" under the Bankruptcy Code, 11 U.S.C. § [101(50)]. It is clear that payment of the debt did not occur when the debtor delivered the postdated check to Avis. A check itself does not vest in the payee any title to or interest in the funds held by the drawee bank. See U.C.C. § 3–409. The check is simply an order to the drawee bank to pay the sum stated and does not constitute a transfer and delivery of the fund until it is paid. The date of payment, and not the date of delivery is crucial in determining when the preferential transfer occurred. Klein v. Tabatchnick, 610 F.2d 1043 [2d Cir. 1979]; In re Lyon, 121 F. 723 [2d Cir. 1903]. The Second Circuit Court of Appeals, in In re Lyon, stated at page 726:

> ". . . the mere giving of the post dated checks was not payment, certainly not such as would constitute a transfer of property, within the language of section 60a, 30 Stat. 562."

Avis argues that once the check is paid, payment should revert to the date the check was delivered, citing Flint v. United States, 237 F.Supp. 551 [D.C.Idaho 1964] and Clark v. Commissioner of Internal Revenue, 253 F.2d 745 [3rd Cir. 1958]. These tax cases are inapposite since they address the issue of when a cash basis taxpayer is entitled to deduct a business expense. For income tax purposes, the delivery of a check is treated in the same manner as a cash payment. The concept of the timing of a transfer of property within the framework of the preference provisions requires a different focus.

"CONTEMPORANEOUS EXCHANGE" EXCEPTION

Having found that the $400 payment was the only rental payment shown to have been made with respect to the debtor's obligation to Avis, and that it amounted to a preferential payment of an antecedent indebtedness, there next remains for consideration the affirmative defense that the transfer was a contemporaneous exchange for new value within the meaning of Code § 547(c)(1), which provides as follows:

> "(c) The trustee may not avoid under this section a transfer—
>
> (1) to the extent that such transfer was—(A) intended by the debtor and the creditor to or for whose benefit such transfer was made to be a contemporaneous exchange for new value given to the debtor; and
>
> (B) in fact a substantially contemporaneous exchange;"

Avis argues that it gave new value to the debtor when it accepted the $400 payment because of its forbearance from repossessing the leased vehicle.

The term "new value" is defined in Code § 547(a)(2) as follows:

> "(2) 'new value' means money or money's worth in goods, services, or new credit, or release by a transferee of property previously transferred to such transferee in a transaction that is neither void nor voidable by the debtor or the trustee under any applicable law, *but does not include an obligation substituted for an existing obligation;*" (Emphasis added)

The basic concept underlying bankruptcy legislation, and of particular significance in dealing with preferences is the fundamental goal of equality of distribution. See House Report No. 595, 95th Cong., 1st Sess. 177, 178 (1977), U.S.Code Cong. & Admin.News 1978, p. 5787. A creditor who gives new value in exchange for the receipt of a payment from the debtor has not depleted the debtor's estate to the detriment of other creditors. In the instant case, a forebearance by Avis from repossessing the rented vehicle does not enhance the value of the debtor's estate. The debtor's continued right to drive the rented vehicle is not an asset of benefit to his creditors that could reasonably offset the diminution of his estate upon the payment of the $400.

Indeed, the net effect was that upon the debtor's payment of $400 for an antecedent obligation, Avis extended credit by forebearance from its right to reclaim possession immediately and substituted instead its right to reclaim possession for nonpayment of the debt at some future undetermined date. An obligation substituted for an existing obligation is expressly excluded from the definition of "new value". See 11 U.S.C. § 547(a)(2). While Avis' forebearance from reclaiming possession of the rented vehicle might constitute consideration to support a contract, it is nevertheless not "new value" within the meaning of Code § 547(c)(1) as defined in Code § 547(a)(2). Such forebearance was of no economic solace to the creditors of this estate.

CONCLUSIONS OF LAW

1. The $400 payment made by the debtor to Avis pursuant to the check postdated to August 3, 1979 constituted a voidable preference within the meaning of 11 U.S.C. § 547(b).

2. Avis has not established that the preferential transfer in question was a contemporaneous exchange for new value to the debtor so as to amount to an exception within the meaning of 11 U.S.C. § 547(c)(1).

3. The trustee in bankruptcy is entitled to an order directing Avis to return the $400 payment made to it by the debtor as a voidable preference.

Notes & Questions

1. *Other Preferential Transactions.* *Duffy* illustrates the payment of an overdue debt to a creditor within the 90 day preference period. What transactions other than a straightforward voluntary transfer of assets might be vulnerable as preferential? Consider the following:

(a) In *Duffy,* suppose that instead of paying Avis $400, the debtor had, within 90 days of bankruptcy, granted Avis a security interest in $400 worth of the debtor's property.

(b) Suppose that within 90 days of bankruptcy an unsecured creditor of Duffy attached property owned by Duffy.

(c) Suppose that within 90 days of bankruptcy Duffy gave his daughter $400.

2. *Delayed Grant of Security.* One year before bankruptcy, Debtor borrows money from Lender and grants Lender a security interest in Debtor's equipment. Eleven months later, when he hears that debtor is in financial difficulty, Lender files a financing statement to perfect his security interest. Should this transaction be preferential? What is the effect of § 547(e)(2)? Suppose instead that the borrowing and grant of security occurred thirty-five days before bankruptcy, with the financing statement being filed five days later. What is the effect of § 547(e)? What if no financing statement is filed? Does § 547 overlap with § 544(a)?

3. *New Value.* For appellate court agreement that forebearance does not constitute "new value" within the meaning of § 547(c)(1), see Drabkin v. A.I. Credit Corp., 800 F.2d 1153 (D.C.Cir.1986).

BARASH v. PUBLIC FINANCE CORP.

United States Court of Appeals, Seventh Circuit, 1981.
658 F.2d 504.

JAMESON, DISTRICT JUDGE.

This consolidated appeal involves eight bankruptcy cases in which Barry M. Barash, Chapter 7 Trustee for the debtors, sought recovery of alleged preferential transfers. In each case the bankruptcy court found in favor of the defendant creditor. The cases were consolidated on appeal to the district court, which affirmed the decision of the bankruptcy court in all cases.

The sole issue on appeal is whether installment payments voluntarily made by a debtor to an undersecured creditor in the ordinary course of the debtor's financial affairs within the 90 days preceding bankruptcy, but not more than 45 days after their due date, are preferences which may be avoided by the Trustee under Section 547 of the Bankruptcy Code. This is a case of first impression in this circuit; nor do we find that any other circuit court has passed on the question.

I. *Factual Background*

In each of the eight cases regular installment payments were made to a creditor within 90 days of an order for relief, 11 U.S.C. § 301. In each case the value of the creditor's collateral was less than the debt it secured. In all but one case, however, the value of the collateral exceeded the amount of payments made during the 90-day period preceding bankruptcy. All of the payments in question were voluntary, some made through automatic payroll deductions, others by direct payment from the debtor. The bankruptcy court found that none of the payments were made to cure defaults or eliminate arrearages. All of the accounts in question were considered current.[1] . . . The district court affirmed the decisions without an opinion.

1. The following chart summarizes the transactions:

In resolving the issue presented on this appeal, it is necessary to determine (1) whether the installment payments were preferences under the Bankruptcy Code; and (2) if so, whether the statutory exception removes the transactions from the operation of the preference rules.

II. *Elements of a Preference*

The Bankruptcy Code prescribes five requirements for a preference, all of which must be met for the Trustee to avoid a transfer. A transfer is preferential if it is (1) to a creditor, (2) on account of a pre-existing debt, (3) made while the debtor is insolvent, (4) made on or within 90 days before the date of filing the petition, or made between 90

Footnote 1—Continued

Trustee for Dennis v. Public Finance

Description of security: household goods and furniture, 1974 Ford pickup truck and 1974 Suzuki motorcycle.
Date of loan: March 28, 1979.
Date of bankruptcy: April 10, 1980.
Amount paid in last 90 days: $166.
Value of Collateral: The parties stipulated that Public was undersecured.
Balance due creditor at bankruptcy: $4,652.43.

Trustee for Millington v. First Galesburg National Bank & Trust Company

Description of security: 1979 Pontiac Firebird.
Date of loan: March 23, 1979.
Date of bankruptcy: March 31, 1980.
Amount paid in last 90 days: $553.06.
Value of collateral: retail—$5,950; wholesale—$4,925.
Balance due creditor at bankruptcy: gross—$7,122.18, net payoff balance—$6,005.08.

Trustee for Millington v. Associates Finance, Inc.

Description of security: household goods and furniture.
Date of loan: August or September, 1979.
Date of bankruptcy: March 31, 1980.
Amount paid in last 90 days: $342.
Value of collateral: $1,200.
Balance due creditor at bankruptcy: $3,306.

Trustee for Millington v. Midwest Employees Credit Union

Description of security: $25.34 on deposit at credit union.
Date of loan: December 16, 1978.
Date of bankruptcy: March 31, 1980.
Amount paid in last 90 days: $103.04.

Value of collateral: $25.34.
Balance due creditor at bankruptcy: $847.27.

Trustee for Nelson v. Farmers and Mechanics Bank

Description of security: 1976 Ford pick-up truck and 1979 Dodge Colt.
Date of loan: 1979 (2 loans).
Date of bankruptcy: April 2, 1980.
Amount paid in last 90 days: $381.84.
Value of collateral: $6,400.
Balance due creditor at bankruptcy: $9,200.

Trustee for Nelson v. Household Finance Corporation

Description of security: household goods and furniture.
Date of loan: May 23, 1979.
Date of bankruptcy: April 2, 1980.
Amount paid in last 90 days: $75.
Value of collateral: $2,000.
Balance due creditor at bankruptcy: $2,467.93.

Trustee for Carter v. Leath & Company

Description of security: furniture.
Date of loan: 1978–1979.
Date of bankruptcy: April 2, 1980.
Amount paid in last 90 days: $75.
Value of collateral: $300.
Balance due creditor at bankruptcy: $479.

Trustee for Harding v. Gates Credit Union

Description of security: 1978 Dodge.
Date of loan: June 15, 1978.
Date of bankruptcy: April 8, 1980.
Amount paid in last 90 days: $984.90.
Value of collateral: retail—$5,225; wholesale—$4,425 (stipulated).
Balance due creditor at bankruptcy: $5,353.07.

days and one year before the date of filing the petition if the creditor was an insider who had reasonable cause to believe the debtor was insolvent, and which (5) enables the creditor to receive more than he would receive if the estate were liquidated under Chapter 7. 11 U.S.C. § 547(b).

There is no dispute that the first four elements of a preference are established in each case. The installment payments were all made by a debtor to a creditor, on a pre-existing debt, within 90 days of the bankruptcy filing. The debtors are presumed insolvent during the 90-day period, 11 U.S.C. § 547(f), and no evidence was presented to rebut the presumption. Appellees argue, however, that they have not improved their position vis-a-vis other creditors, as required by § 547(b)(5). The Trustee, on the other hand, contends that the payments received within the 90-day period enabled the creditors to receive a greater proportion of their respective debts than they would if the estate were liquidated under Chapter 7.

As noted above, the debts in all of these cases are undersecured. 11 U.S.C. § 506(a) separates undersecured creditors' claims into two parts: a secured component and an unsecured component. A creditor has a secured claim only to the extent of the value of his collateral. Any remaining balance is an unsecured claim. The effect of § 506(a) is to classify claims, not creditors, as secured and unsecured. In other words, a single undersecured creditor has both a secured claim and an unsecured claim, each of which is considered in its respective class.
. . .

Except for two cases involving valuation of automobiles, it is agreed that the unsecured components of the debts exceed the amounts of the asserted preferences. The Trustee argues that the payments must be charged against the unsecured claims, and therefore the payments enabled the creditors to receive a greater proportion of their unsecured claims than other unsecured claimants.

Appellees, on the other hand, assert that in all but one case, where the debt is partially secured by a minimal balance in a credit union share account, because the value of the collateral exceeds the payments during the 90-day period, they did not receive more than they would have upon liquidation. The answer to these opposing contentions will depend on which component of the debts, secured or unsecured, the payments should be charged against. . . .

. . . A principal goal of the preference provisions is the assurance of equal distribution among creditors. H.R.Rep. 95–595, 95th Cong., 1st Sess. 178 (1977), reprinted in 5 U.S.Code Cong. & Admin. News 6138–39 (1978); 4 Collier on Bankruptcy [Collier] ¶ 547.03[1 (15th ed.1980). Section 547(b)(5) is aimed at achieving that goal. The "greater distribution requirement" of § 547(b)(5) is discussed in 4 Collier ¶ 547.35. The discussion emphasizes the comparison between what a creditor actually received in an alleged preference and what other creditors of the same class would have received upon liquidation had the questioned transfer not been made. This explanation alone, however, does not adequately clarify the statutory scheme.

For example, if upon liquidation unsecured creditors would be paid 20% of their claims (based on remaining assets and scheduled claims after secured creditors are paid), to defeat a trustee's avoidance rights a creditor would have to show only that the payments received during the 90-day period do not exceed 20% of the creditor's unsecured claim. This sole comparison, however, does not account for what happens thereafter. If the payments made were less than 20%, there would be no preference and the creditor would keep the payments and later also receive a pro-rata share of the balance of his claim. In the final analysis, this would violate the fundamental principle of equal distribution among a class of claims.

Section 547(b)(5) is directed at transfers which *enable* creditors to receive more than they would have received had the estate been liquidated and the disputed transfer not been made. As long as the transfers diminish the bankrupt's estate available for distribution, creditors who are allowed to keep transfers would be enabled to receive more than their share. The creditors in the instant case must account for the payments they received during the 90 days preceding the bankruptcy filing, or they will ultimately receive a larger share of their *unsecured* claims than other unsecured creditors. Of course, they will still receive the full benefit of their collateral as to their secured claims.

III. *Normal Course of Business Exceptions: § 547(c)(2)*

[The court found that the payments were not made within 45 days after the debts were incurred. In 1984 Congress eliminated the 45–day requirement from § 547(c)(2).]

IV. *Valuation of Collateral*

The payments here in dispute are preferential to the extent they are credited to the unsecured components of the debts. Payments on secured claims do not diminish the estate, i.e., they do not enable a creditor to receive more than he would under the liquidation provisions of the Code. Section 506(a) provides that a debt is secured only to the extent of the value of the collateral. Any remaining amount is an unsecured claim. Valuation of collateral is thus crucial to determining the amount of the preferences. See In re Conn., supra, 9 B.R. 435.

In all but two of the cases it is undisputed that the unsecured component of the debt exceeds the payments made during the preference period. In Trustee for Millington v. First Galesburg National Bank and Trust Co. and Trustee for Harding v. Gates Credit Union, however, all of the payments during the 90 days preceding the bankruptcy filings may not be preferential, depending on what values are used for the automobiles securing the debts. In the *Millington* case, the bank contends that the NADA retail value of the car, $5,950, is proper. The net payoff is $6,005, so the amount of the preference would be only $55 and the bank would not have to account to the Trustee for the remaining $498 received during the preference period. The Trustee argues that the wholesale value, $4,925, should be used. In that case, the entire $553 received by the bank during the 90-days would be recovered by the Trustee. A similar problem exists in the *Harding* case. If retail value is used, only $128 of the total $984 paid would be preferential, but if wholesale value applies, $928 would be avoidable by the Trustee.

The legislative history of § 506(a) indicated that no fixed formula exists for establishing the value of collateral. Congress did not necessarily contemplate the use of forced sale or liquidation value; nor is fair market value always appropriate. "Courts will have to determine value on a case-by-case basis, taking into account the facts of each case and the competing interests in the case." H.R.Rep. No. 95–595, supra, at 356, 5 U.S.Code Cong. & Admin.News at 6312. Value should be determined by the purpose of the valuation and the proposed disposition or use of the property. S.Rep. No. 95–989, supra, at 68, 5 U.S.Code Cong. & Admin.News at 5854.

The present record does not enable us to determine the appropriate value of the cars in these cases. On remand the bankruptcy court should determine the value of the automobiles in light of the competing interests of the parties and the proposed use or disposition of the cars by the secured creditors. The choice of values is not restricted to NADA wholesale or retail, but depends on the facts and circumstances of each case.

V. *Conclusion*

We hold that regular installment payments on consumer debts, made within 90 days preceding the filing of a bankruptcy petition, may be avoided as preferential transfers to the extent the payments are credited to unsecured claims. The bankruptcy court must determine the value of collateral on a case-by-case basis to ascertain the extent of the preferences, in keeping with the bifurcation of debts into secured and unsecured claims under 11 U.S.C. § 506(a). The exception for normal transactions in 11 U.S.C. § 547(c)(2) extends only to situations where payment is made within 45 days after the debtor first becomes legally bound to pay.

Reversed and remanded.

Notes & Questions

1. *Seemingly Pro–Rata Payment Before Bankruptcy. Barash* illustrates § 547(b)(5) as applied to payments to undersecured creditors. Consider prebankruptcy payments to unsecured creditors. Debtor owes three unsecured creditors $100 each and has $150 available. Just prior to bankruptcy, Debtor pays one of the creditors $50. Is this payment preferential? See In re K. Pritchard Co., 17 B.R. 508 (Bkrtcy.S.D.Ala. 1981) (no preference where creditor did not file a claim for the balance

of his debt).   In applying § 547(b)(5), should one take into account the administrative expenses of a bankruptcy proceeding?

2.   *Contractual Performance as a Preference.*   Debtor agrees to sell goods to Buyer.   Buyer pays for the goods in advance.   Shortly before bankruptcy, debtor delivers the goods in accordance with the contract. Is this a preference?   See In re Lewis W. Shurtleff, Inc., 778 F.2d 1416 (9th Cir.1985) (whether transfer of property in accordance with contract was preferential depends on whether damages claim for failure to comply with contract for transfer of property exceeded value of property transferred).

3.   *The Amendment to § 547(c)(2).*   The 1984 elimination of the 45-day requirement from § 547(c)(2)'s exception means that all ordinary course payments, including those at issue in *Barash,* are no longer subject to preference attack.   What kind of payments remain vulnerable to preference attacks?

4.   *Insiders.*   In a preference attack brought by the trustee, the defendants were the parents of the debtor's fiancee, who had lived with the debtor for five years.   Are the defendants covered by § 547's insider provisions?   See In re Montanino, 15 B.R. 307 (Bkrtcy.D.N.J.1981) (yes).

2.   The Other Basic Exceptions

To recover a preferential transfer under the old bankruptcy act, the trustee had to do something more than satisfy the requirements of what is now § 547(b).   Old § 60a defined the preference in much the same way as does § 547(b), but old § 60b limited the trustee's avoidance powers.   It stated:

> Any such preference may be avoided by the trustee if the creditor receiving it or to be benefited thereby or his agent acting with reference thereto has, at the time when the transfer is made, reasonable cause to believe that the debtor is insolvent.

The requirement that the trustee show that the recipient of a preference have reasonable cause to believe that the debtor was insolvent generated much criticism.   The Commission on Bankruptcy Laws stated that this requirement "more than any other, has rendered ineffective the preference section of the present Act."   Commission Report, pt. I, at 204.

Partial elimination of the "reasonable cause to believe" requirement makes the new preference power very broad.   In part to temper its reach, it became necessary to add a new set of explicit exceptions to the preference section.   (Only § 547(c)(4) has statutory antecedents in the old act.)   In the preceding and following cases, consider whether the old § 60b requirement would save much unnecessary litigation that can be expected to occur under the new act.   Does the new set of exceptions do a better job of sorting out those prebankruptcy transfers that should be undone?   Would the trustee in *Arnett,* which follows, have bothered to sue under old § 60?   Should he have sued?

IN RE ARNETT
United States Court of Appeals, 6th Circuit, 1984.
731 F.2d 358.

Before JONES and WELLFORD, CIRCUIT JUDGES, and MILES, DISTRICT
JUDGE.

MILES, DISTRICT JUDGE.

This is an appeal in bankruptcy. Plaintiff, the trustee in bankruptcy, appeals the order of the district court, 17 B.R. 912, affirming the
decision of the bankruptcy court declining to set aside as a preferential
transfer the security interest held by defendant-appellee Security Mutual Finance Corporation ("Security Mutual") in property of the debtors
in bankruptcy and co-defendants-appellees in this proceeding, Burton
and Charlotte Arnett.

On December 10, 1980, the Arnetts obtained a consolidation loan
from Security Mutual, granting to Security Mutual a lien on their 1978
Volkswagen, which was at that time subject to a prior perfected lien
held by defendant-appellee American National Bank ("ANB"). The
loan obtained from Security Mutual thus included an amount sufficient
to pay off the prior security interest. On December 10 or 11, 1980,
Security Mutual mailed a check for the outstanding balance of the lien
to ANB, requesting ANB to release its lien and forward the certificate
of title to the vehicle to Security Mutual. ANB deposited the check on
December 19, 1980. Because of the delayed holiday mails and employee absences, however, ANB did not release its lien and forward the
certificate of title until January 9, 1981. Upon receiving the release,
Security Mutual applied to the State of Tennessee Department of Motor
Vehicles to note its lien on the certificate, as required by T.C.A. 55–3–
119. The lien was perfected on January 12, 1981, 33 days after the
granting of the security interest to Security Mutual.

On February 25, 1981, the Arnetts filed a voluntary petition for
relief under Chapter 7 of the Bankruptcy Code, 11 U.S.C. § 701 et seq.
The trustee filed suit to set aside Security Mutual's lien on the
Volkswagen as a voidable preference under 11 U.S.C. § 547(b). The
parties agreed to allow the vehicle to be sold to the debtors for $3,601.47
pending the outcome of this proceeding.

The bankruptcy judge ruled that Security Mutual's perfection of its
security interest was "substantially contemporaneous" with the loan
transaction, notwithstanding the 33–day hiatus and thus, that the
transaction fell within the exception to the trustee's avoidance powers
found at 11 U.S.C. § 547(c)(1). See, In re Arnett, 13 B.R. 267 (Bkrtcy.
E.D.Tenn.1981). The trustee unsuccessfully appealed to the district
court, which upheld the bankruptcy court's decision. This appeal
followed.

The sole issue before this Court is whether a delay of 33 days in
perfection of a security interest is a "substantially contemporaneous

exchange" under 11 U.S.C. § 547(c)(1), thus excepted from the trustee's avoidance powers. Although the lower courts have been wrestling with this problem for some time, the issue has not yet been addressed by any of the circuit courts of appeals. . . .

All five elements [of § 547(b)] are prerequisites to the finding of a voidable preference. Barash v. Public Finance Corp., 658 F.2d 504 (7th Cir.1981). The parties concede that these elements are present. However, Security Mutual and ANB point to the exceptions to the trustee's avoidance powers contained in subsection (c)(1). That subsection provides:

(c) The Trustee may not avoid under this section a transfer—

(A) intended by the debtor and the creditor to or for whose benefit such transfer was made to be a contemporaneous exchange for new value given to the debtor; and

(B) in fact a substantially contemporaneous exchange;

Relying on 11 U.S.C. §§ 547(c)(3) and 547(e)(2)(A) and (B), the trustee contends that the contemporaneous exchange exception is inapplicable beyond 10 days of creation of Security Mutual's security interest, and thus, that the lien may be avoided. Section 547(c)(3), the so-called "enabling loan" provision, excepts from the trustee's avoidance powers security interests in property acquired by the debtor which are perfected within 10 days of creation. Section 547(e)(2) establishes when the "transfer" of a security interest is deemed to occur:

(2) For the purposes of this section, except as provided in paragraph (3) of this subsection, a transfer is made—

(A) [at the time such transfer takes effect between] the transferor and the transferee, if such transfer is perfected at, or within 10 days after, such time;

(B) at the time such transfer is perfected, if such transfer is perfected after such 10 days;

Not persuaded that the 10-day limit established by the above two sections was incorporated *sub silentio* into the contemporaneous exchange exception, both the bankruptcy judge and the district judge ruled that "contemporaneity" is a question of fact to be evaluated in light of the parties' intent, the reasons for delay, and the risks of fraud and misrepresentation. The construction given to section 547(c)(1) by the lower courts in this case requires examination of all circumstances surrounding the transaction giving rise to the transfer. Thus, where delayed perfection of a security interest may be satisfactorily explained, and in the absence of dilatoriness or negligence on the part of a transferee, the transfer may still be found "substantially contemporaneous" with the exchange of new value to the debtor, regardless of the lapse of time.

. . .

The legislative history of section 547(c)(1) is sparse. The Comment to the section provides in its entirety as follows:

The first exception [§ 547(c)(1)] is for a transfer that was intended by all parties to be a contemporaneous exchange for new value, and was in fact substantially contemporaneous. Normally, a check is a credit transaction. However, for the purposes of this paragraph, a transfer involving a check is considered to be "intended to be contemporaneous," and if the check is presented for payment in the normal course of affairs, which the Uniform Commercial Code specifies as 30 days, U.C.C. § 3–503(2)(a), that will amount to a transfer that is "in fact substantially contemporaneous."

H.R.Rep. No. 595, 95th Cong., 1st Sess. 373 (1977) [hereinafter cited as H.R. 595], U.S.Code Cong. & Admin.News 1978, pp. 5787, 6329.

In enacting the "contemporaneous exchange" exception, Congress intended to codify decisions under the old bankruptcy act which had held that, when a cash sale was intended, acceptance of a check instead of cash did not change the character of the transaction, so long as the check was cashed within a reasonable period of time. See, e.g., Engstrom v. Wiley, 191 F.2d 684 (9th Cir.1951); Engelkes v. Farmers Cooperative Co., 194 F.Supp. 319 (N.D.Iowa 1961). Some have stated that the provision also codified Dean v. Davis, 242 U.S. 438, 37 S.Ct. 130, 61 L.Ed. 419 (1917), which held that there was no preference where a loan was intended by both parties to be a secured loan even though the mortgage was not actually executed until seven days after the loan was made. See, e.g., In re Advance Glove Mfg. Co., 25 B.R. 521 (Bkrtcy. E.D.Mich.1982); In re Martella, 22 B.R. 649 (Bkrtcy.D.Colo.1982). Whether *Dean v. Davis* survived passage of the Bankruptcy Reform Act of 1978, and was codified into section 547(c)(1) has been questioned, however. In re Murray, 27 B.R. 445 (Bkrtcy.M.D.Tenn.1983).

Nonetheless, it is clear that the classic exception to avoidance intended by Congress to be reflected in section 547(c)(1) is the exchange of goods or other "value" for a check. Such transactions are generally intended to be cash transactions, although some extension of credit is necessarily involved until the check is negotiated. . . .

Although the legislative history reveals that even a 30–day delay between receipt and negotiation of a check does not preclude a substantially contemporaneous exchange, standard commercial practices appropriate to the transfer of negotiable instruments are not necessarily commensurate with those involving security interests. Congress has given security interests specialized treatment both in sections 547(c)(3) and 547(e)(2). That Congress explicitly enacted a 10–day limitation for the perfection of security interests in order to preserve "relation back", and yet accepted a 30–day period as appropriate to the negotiation of checks indicates an intent to differentiate the two types of "transfers" under the Bankruptcy Reform Act.

However, since neither the literal language of section 547(c)(1) nor the legislative history explicitly reveals whether expansion of the classic check transaction reflected in section 541(c)(1) was intended to include transfers of security interests more than 10 days after their creation, consideration of the statutory context is necessary.

Two elements are crucial to the establishment of the contemporaneous exchange exception: 1. The parties must intend that the exchange be substantially contemporaneous; 2. the exchange must *in fact* be substantially contemporaneous. 11 U.S.C. § 547(c)(1); Butz v. Pingel, 17 B.R. 236 (Bkrtcy.S.D.Ohio 1982). There is no dispute here that the parties intended a contemporaneous exchange when the loan was obtained through the granting of a security interest to Security Mutual. Further, the parties do not dispute that the "transfer" here pertinent occurred when Security Mutual perfected its security interest 33 days later. In any case, section 547(e)(2) resolves any doubt by providing that the "transfer" of a security interest not perfected until after 10 days is deemed to occur at the date of perfection. Moreover, under Tennessee law, Security Mutual's lien was invalid until recorded on a certificate of title. T.C.A. 55–3–114, 123, 125, 126. Thus, the key inquiry is whether the exchange was "in fact" substantially contemporaneous.

The issue has frequently arisen in the context of the relationship between section 547(c)(1) and (c)(3). As previously noted, section 547(c)(3) excepts from avoidance so-called "enabling loans", or "purchase money loans", and prescribes a 10–day limit for perfection of security interests taken in such transactions. Some purchase-money lenders, having failed to meet the prescribed 10–day deadline, have argued that perfection of the purchase-money security interest was nonetheless substantially contemporaneous with the giving of "new value" to the debtor. See, e.g. In re Davis, 22 B.R. 644 (Bkrtcy.M.D.Ga.1982); In re Enlow, 20 B.R. 480 (Bkrtcy.Ind.1982); In re Burnette, 14 B.R. 795 (Bkrtcy.E.D.Tenn.1981); In re Christian, 8 B.R. 816 (Bkrtcy.M.D.Fla. 1981); In re Merritt, 7 B.R. 876 (Bkrtcy.W.D.Mo.1980).

As *Davis* notes, one line of cases holds that section 547(c)(1) is merely cumulative with section 547(c)(3), so that a transfer which occurs more than 10 days after the cash advance, thus not qualifying under section 547(c)(3), may nonetheless be deemed substantially contemporaneous under section 547(c)(1). In re Burnette, supra; In re Hall, 14 B.R. 186 (Bkrtcy.S.D.Fla.1981). Judge Kelley, the presiding bankruptcy judge in both this case and in *Burnette*, has concluded that section 547(c)(3) is simply one type of contemporaneous exchange, and that section 547(c)(1), although not intended to reach the transfer of security interests, may be read broadly to cover such situations as the present. In re Burnette, supra, at 802–803. The practical effect of an expansive reading in the "enabling loan" context is to give creditors "two bites at the apple." In re Davis, supra at 647.

Most courts, however, have concluded that an expansive reading of section 547(c)(1) renders section 547(c)(3) redundant and superfluous in the enabling loan context, and thus, is an unwarranted and erroneous construction. In re Murray, 27 B.R. 445 (Bkrtcy.Tenn.1983); In re

Davis, supra; In re Vance, 22 B.R. 26 (Bkrtcy.D.Idaho 1982); In re Enlow, supra; In re Merritt, supra. These courts have been persuaded that Congress intended section 547(c)(3) to be the exclusive provision applicable in the enabling loan context. "Expressio unius est exclusius alterius."

Although this case does not involve an "enabling loan", we are also persuaded that expansion of section 547(c)(1)'s reference to contemporaneity beyond 10 days in the context of transfers of security interests is erroneous. The particular problems posed by the delay between creation and perfection of security interests were well recognized by Congress. One of the principal purposes of the Bankruptcy Reform Act is to discourage the creation of "secret liens" by invalidating all transfers occurring within 90 days prior to the filing of the petitions. Thus, creditors are discouraged from waiting until the debtor's financial troubles become all-too-manifest before recording security interests. Section 547(e)(2)(A) and (B) reflect this concern by providing that a transfer of a security interest relates back to the date of the underlying transaction if perfection occurs no more than 10 days afterwards; if perfection occurs more than 10 days later, the transfer is deemed to occur at the date of perfection.

The lower courts' broad reading of section 547(c)(1) effectively negates section 547(e)(2). Assuming the interval between creation and perfection to straddle the 90–day cutoff, although a security interest is perfected more than 10 days after the underlying transaction, and is thus voidable as a preference, the transfer might still be preserved if it is found to be part of a "substantially contemporaneous" exchange. Such hopeless conflict cannot have been intended by Congress.

Further, the evidentiary problems inherent in an expansive reading of section 547(c)(1) embody a Pandora's box of evils, even if no risk of fraud or misrepresentation was present in this case.

> [S]uch a stance invites litigation over the question when in fact a transfer is "substantially contemporaneous". There are no objective standards for determining this fact and the courts are having great difficulty in determining the issue, creating much uncertainty in the law. In re Vance, supra at 28.

The lower courts noted that the facts of this case cry out for application of the contemporaneous exchange exception. However, the lower courts' conviction that delayed perfection of the security interest resulted from fortuitous circumstances entirely beyond Security Mutual's control and unattributable to negligence is not entirely well-founded. Under Tennessee's expedited title procedure, T.C.A. 55–3–114, discharge of a lien may be noted upon the certificate of title within 72 hours from demand.* Thus, Security Mutual is to some extent responsible for its own predicament. Although there can be no doubt

---

* Several states have adopted expedited title procedures similar to Tennessee's. Florida also permits recordation of the lien on the certificate within 72 hours after demand. . . .

that the parties' clear intent to effectuate a contemporaneous exchange was frustrated, the statute nonetheless requires that the exchange *in fact* be contemporaneous. Section 547(c)(1)(B). . . .

In light of the explicit grace periods provided for perfection of security interests in sections 547(e)(2) and 547(c)(3), Congress has clearly struck the balance in favor of repose in this area of the law. Case-by-case development of the contemporaneous exchange exception would quickly result in uncertainty and protracted litigation, delaying, not expediting, the satisfaction of creditors' claims and the debtor's return to financial health. The policies of discouraging creditors "from racing to the Courthouse to dismember the debtor during his slide into bankruptcy" and facilitating equality of distribution would be severely eroded under the lower courts' construction of the statute. H.R. 595.

In conclusion, we believe the District Court and the Bankruptcy Court erred in ruling that Security Mutual's perfection of its security interest 33 days after granting a loan to the Arnetts was part of a substantially contemporaneous exchange of new value. Section 547(e) (2)(B) explicitly provides that a security interest perfected more than 10 days after its creation does not relate back and is deemed to have occurred on the date of perfection. The applicability of section 547(c)(1) to delayed perfection of security interests is thus limited to 10 days. The transfer of Security Mutual's security interest is not excepted from the trustee's avoidance powers, and may be set aside as a voidable preference.

Because the bankruptcy judge found no preference, he did not reach the cross-claim of Security Mutual against ANB in related proceedings. Thus, remand is necessary for additional findings to comply with Bankr.Rule 7052 . . . ..

Reversed and remanded for further proceedings.

WELLFORD, CIRCUIT JUDGE, dissenting:

I would affirm District Judge Frank Wilson and the Bankruptcy Judge in this case. I agree with them that the credit transaction involved comes within the meaning of a "contemporaneous exchange" under 11 U.S.C. § 547(c)(1), and that Security Mutual Finance Corporation's perfecting of its lien and security interest, although delayed, was excepted from the preference provisions of § 547(b). Not only is it clear that the transaction in dispute was intended to be contemporaneous, but appellee Security Mutual acted diligently under the circumstances to protect its security position under the law.

Judge Wilson deemed it to be essentially, a question of fact as to whether a transaction extending beyond ten days is "substantially contemporaneous" under the law. The Bankruptcy Court decided the question in accordance with the *clear intent of the parties.* . . .

Notes & Questions

1. *Brief Delays as Not Contemporaneous.* In National City Bank of New York v. Hotchkiss, 231 U.S. 50, 34 S.Ct. 20, 58 L.Ed. 115 (1913), a bank made an unsecured loan to a brokerage firm in the morning and later found out that the firm was in financial trouble. That afternoon, the bank sought and received security for the morning loan. The Court found the grant to be preferential. In Dean v. Davis, 242 U.S. 438, 37 S.Ct. 130, 61 L.Ed. 419 (1917), the parties negotiated a secured loan but the mortgage securing the loan was not recorded until one week later. The Supreme Court found no preference since the "mortgage was provided to secure a substantially contemporaneous advance." How does § 547(c)(1) affect these cases?

2. *§ 547(c)(3).* Bank lends Debtor $10,000 to buy a car. The next day Bank and Debtor execute a security agreement designating any car purchased by Debtor as collateral for the loan. Bank immediately takes proper steps to perfect its security interest. The next day Debtor buys a new car, using the loan from Bank. Is there a preference under § 547(b)? Does the exception in § 547(c)(3) apply?

3. *Small Consumer Debts.* The 1984 Amendments added a new preference exception in § 547(c)(7) for consumer debts involving transfers of less than $600.

Note on § 547(c)(4)

The legislative history of § 547(c)(4) states:

> The fourth exception codifies the net result rule in section 60c of current law. If the creditor and the debtor have more than one exchange during the 90-day period, the exchanges are netted out according to the formula in paragraph (4). Any new value that the creditor advances must be unsecured in order for it to qualify under this exception.

Senate Report at 88. Does § 547(c)(4) codify a rule that focuses merely on the "net result" of exchanges during the 90-day preference period? Consider the following transactions that occur within the 90-day period, at a time when debtor already owes creditor $100. (a) Creditor lends debtor an additional $100. (b) Debtor repays creditor $50. Does the order in which steps (a) and (b) occur matter for purposes of § 547? Should the order matter? See In re Fulghum Construction Corp., 706 F.2d 171 (6th Cir. 1983) (only subsequent advances are protected by § 547(c)(4); broader net result rule applied by courts under old act does not survive).

3. Section 547(e)(3) and Inventory and Receivables Financing

IN RE EBBLER FURNITURE AND APPLIANCES, INC.

United States Court of Appeals, Seventh Circuit, 1986.
804 F.2d 87.

Before FLAUM and EASTERBROOK, CIRCUIT JUDGES, and SWYGERT, SENIOR CIRCUIT JUDGE.

FLAUM, CIRCUIT JUDGE.

This suit involves an issue of first impression in this circuit. We are asked to define the word "value" as used in 11 U.S.C. § 547(c)(5). We affirm the bankruptcy court and district court in their use of "cost" as the proper measurement in this case. However, we remand this case for further proceedings to determine the precise amount of the preference payment that the defendant received.

I.

The present action is by the trustee in bankruptcy under 11 U.S.C. §§ 547(b) and (c)(5) (1986), to recover preference payments received by the defendant. Ebbler Furniture and Appliance, Inc. ("Ebbler"), filed a voluntary petition for relief pursuant to the Chapter 7 liquidation provisions of the Bankruptcy Code.

The appellant, Alton Bank & Trust Co. ("the Bank"), was the inventory financier for Ebbler. Although the security agreement is not in the record, it appears that the security agreement granted the Bank a security interest in Ebbler's inventory, and accounts receivable. The record is unclear as to whether the security interest covered proceeds and whether it was properly perfected.

The bankruptcy court made the following factual findings. Purchases made by the debtor within ninety days prior to bankruptcy totaled $170,911.33. The cost of goods sold during the ninety day period equaled $214,065.19. The ending inventory, as of the date of filing bankruptcy, was $67,000.00. The cost of the beginning inventory ninety days prior to the filing of the bankruptcy was calculated by the bankruptcy court in the following manner.

cost of goods sold	($214,065.19)
+ ending inventory	($ 67,000.00)
− purchases	($170,911.33)
beginning inventory	$ 110,000.00

The bankruptcy court also found that there were $19,000 worth of accounts receivable, subject to the Bank's security interest. These receivables were added to beginning inventory. The bankruptcy court then concluded:

> 12. On the basis on [sic] the foregoing figures, the creditor Bank received a preference as described in 11 U.S.C. § 547(c)(5) of approximately $75,000.00, i.e., the difference between what the

Bank received on account of the debt it was owed ($204,571.61), less the debtor's beginning inventory ($110,000.00) and its accounts receivable ($19,000).

In re Ebbler Furniture & Appliances, Inc., No. 84–0150 (Bankr.S.D.Ill. 1985) (unpublished order).

The bankruptcy court noted that a discrepancy existed in the amount of $15,000 as to the value of the ending inventory. Consequently, the bankruptcy court reduced the preference by $15,000.00, and found a preference of $60,000.00.

Beginning approximately three to four months before filing its petition, Ebbler conducted a going out of business sale. Ebbler ceased doing business on November 30, 1983. At that time Ebbler was indebted to the Bank in the amount of $50,000 and had $67,000 in inventory (valued on a cost basis). The Bank repossessed $50,000 worth of inventory and sold it at cost applying the $50,000 proceeds to the debt.

Finally, and perhaps most important for purposes of this appeal, the bankruptcy court determined that the parties "were relying on the cost basis of the inventory in evaluating the security for the indebtedness." Id.

II.

. . .

B.

The issue presented is the interpretation of "value" as used in § 547(c)(5) of the Bankruptcy Code.[1] Section 547(c)(5) applies to situations where a secured creditor does not have sufficient collateral to cover his outstanding debt. Subparagraph five (5) codifies the "improvement in position test" and overrules an earlier line of cases such as Grain Merchants of Indiana, Inc. v. Union Bank & Savings Co., 408 F.2d 209 (7th Cir.), cert. denied, 396 U.S. 827, 90 S.Ct. 75, 24 L.Ed.2d 78 (1969). Section 547(c)(5) prevents a secured creditor from improving its position at the expense of an unsecured creditor during the 90 days

---

1. This section states that:

(c) The trustee may not avoid under this section a transfer—

5) that creates a perfected security interest in inventory or a receivable or the proceeds of either, except to the extent that the aggregate of all such transfers to the transferee caused a reduction, as of the date of the filing of the petition and to the prejudice of other creditors holding unsecured claims, of any amount by *which the debt secured by such security interest exceeded the value of all security interests for such debt on the later of*—

(A)(i) with respect to a transfer to which subsection (b)(4)(A) of this section applies, 90 days before the date of the filing of the petition; or

(ii) with respect to a transfer to which subsection (b)(4)(B) of this section applies, one year before the date of the filing of the petition; or

(B) the date on which new value was first given under the security agreement creating such security interest. . . .

11 U.S.C. § 547(c)(5) (emphasis added).

prior to filing the bankruptcy petition. See generally 4A Collier on Bankruptcy ¶ 547.41, p. 547–133 (15th ed.).

The first step in applying section 547(c)(5) is to determine the amount of the loan outstanding 90 days prior to filing and the "value" of the collateral on that day. The difference between these figures is then computed. Next, the same determinations are made as of the date of filing the petition. A comparison is made, and, if there is a reduction during the 90 day period of the amount by which the initially existing debt exceeded the security, then a preference for section 547(c)(5) purposes exists. See generally 4A Collier on Bankruptcy ¶ 547.41. The effect of 547(c)(5) is to make the security interest voidable to the extent of the preference. Id. at p. 547–134. Of course, if the creditor is fully secured 90 days before the filing of the petition, then that creditor will never be subject to a preference attack.

C.

The language of section 547(c)(5), the "value of all security interest for such debt," was purposely left without a precise definition. See generally H.R. No. 595, S.Rep. No. 989, 95th Cong., 2d Sess., reprinted in 1978 U.S.Code Cong. & Ad.News, 5787, 6176; N. Cohen, "Value" Judgments: Account Receivable Financing and Voidable Preferences Under the New Bankruptcy Code, 66 Minn.L.Rev. 639, 653 (1982) (hereinafter "Cohen"); *In re Beattie*, 31 B.R. 703, 714 (W.D.N.C.1983). Furthermore, it has been persuasively argued that the other Bankruptcy Code sections' definitions of "value" would not be useful for section 547(c)(5) purposes. Cohen, supra, at 651–654. Thus, the only legislative guidance is "that we are to determine value on case-by-case basis, taking into account the facts of each case and the competing interests in the case." Matter of Lackow Bros., Inc., 752 F.2d 1529, 1532 (11th Cir.1985), *citing* H.R.Rep. No. 545, 95th Cong., 1st Sess. 356 (1977) reprinted in 1978 U.S.Code Cong. & Ad.News 5787, 6312.

The method used to value the collateral is crucial in determining whether or not the bank received a preference. The Bank urges that we adopt an "ongoing concern" [2] value standard, which, in this case, would be cost plus a 60% mark-up. The Bank relies on *Lackow Bros.*, supra, as authority for the use of this definition of value. We find *Lackow Bros.* readily distinguishable. There, the only evidence of value before the court was ongoing concern value. As the Eleventh Circuit stated: "The only evidence in the record of value for the

---

2. The authors of Collier on Bankruptcy suggest that in a liquidation case under chapter 7, "it would seem that liquidation value should be used, although other standards of value may be appropriate under certain circumstances. In a case under chapter 9, 11, or 13, it would seem that a going concern value should be used although liquidation value may be appropriate in certain cases." 4A Collier on Bankruptcy ¶ 547.41, at 547–135; *Lackow Bros.*, 752 F.2d at 1532. We deem it inappropriate to bind this circuit to these distinctions at the present time. We note, however, that the Eleventh Circuit has cited this distinction, although commenting that it "is not set in cement." Id. We believe that the definition of "value" should be individualized and variable enough so as to be tailored to each situation.

ninetieth day prior to the filing of the bankruptcy is the ongoing concern value; therefore, this is the *only* standard of valuation that can be applied to determine if Creditor's position improved. . . . ." *Lackow Bros.* at 1532.

Another view as to how value should be defined is proposed by Professor Cohen. He proposes an after-the-fact determination of value. In his article discussing accounts receivable, Cohen argues that the courts should look at the actual manner in which the collateral was liquidated, i.e. cost or ongoing concern. Whatever method is used to dispose of the collateral, Cohen argues, should be used to value the collateral 90 days before the filing of the bankruptcy petition. *Cohen,* supra, at 664. At least one circuit has found Cohen's reasoning useful, though not necessarily adopting it as a rigid rule. Matter of Missionary Baptist Foundation, 796 F.2d 752, 761–62 (5th Cir.1986).

In *Missionary Baptist Foundation,* supra, the appellate court remanded to the district court for factual determinations as to whether or not the bank improved its position during the preference period. Id. at 761. The court noted, however, that merely remanding for factual findings may not be sufficient in light of the ambiguous meaning of "value" in section 547(c)(5). Id. at 761–62. The Fifth Circuit quoted with approval Cohen's admonition of an individualized approach in defining value and his hindsight solution of the problem. We follow the Fifth Circuit's lead and hold that under Section 547(c)(5) value should be defined on a case by case basis, with the factual determinations of the bankruptcy court controlling.

D.

In the present case we affirm the bankruptcy court's use of cost as the method for valuing the collateral for 547(c)(5) purposes. The bankruptcy court found that the parties were using a cost basis for valuing the security. Furthermore, when the Bank removed inventory with a *cost* of approximately $50,000, about a week before the petition was filed, Ebbler was given credit for that amount—$50,000. We do not find the bankruptcy court's factual findings so clearly erroneous as to warrant reversal. In re Kimzey, 761 F.2d 421, 423 (7th Cir.1985).

Using these factual findings the bankruptcy court applied cost as the legal definition of "value." We affirm the use of this definition as applied to these facts.

III.

We remand to the bankruptcy court, however, for a determination as to the amount of the preference. The bankruptcy court found, weighing the conflicting evidence, that a preference of $60,000 existed. It is not clear why the bankruptcy court did not consider the $43,000 in cash which the debtor had in hand at the time of filing the bankruptcy petition.

The bankruptcy court held that the Bank had a security interest in the inventory and accounts receivable. The bankruptcy court's opinion is silent as to whether or not this security agreement covered cash proceeds, and whether or not the $43,000 in actuality was cash proceeds of the inventory. It must also be determined if these interests were properly perfected. The only evidence in the record is Mr. Ebbler's testimony that all the proceeds from sales of inventory were deposited into an account at the Bank. The bank statement shows that on the 90th day prior to the bankruptcy the account contained $43,000. Depending on the court's findings on these issues an adjustment downward in the amount of the preference might be appropriate.

IV.

For the reasons set forth we affirm the use of cost as a basis for defining value in section 547(c)(5) of the Bankruptcy Code. We remand, however, for a determination as to how the debtor's cash on hand affected the preference amount.

EASTERBROOK, CIRCUIT JUDGE, concurring. . . .

"Value" is defined for a purpose, which sets limits on the admissible standards of appraisal even though it does not govern all cases. Section 547(c)(5) requires the court to find whether the secured creditor improved its position at the expense of other investors during the 90 days before the filing of the petition in bankruptcy. This calls for two appraisals, one on the day of filing and one 90 days earlier, using the same method each time, to see whether there was an improvement in position. The only standard that might plausibly be used in this case is wholesale cost of goods, because that is the only standard that could have been applied on both dates.

Wholesale cost is also the appropriate standard as a rule because wholesale and retail goods are different things. A furniture store, a supermarket, or the manufacturer of a product (the three situations are identical) uses raw materials purchased at wholesale to produce a new item. In the retailing business the difference between the wholesale price and the retail price is the "value added" of the business. It is the amount contributed by storing, inspecting, displaying, hawking, collecting for, delivering, and handling warranty claims on the goods. This difference covers the employees' wages, rent and utilities of the premises, interest on the cost of goods, bad debts, repairs, the value of entrepreneurial talent, and so on. The increment of price is attributable to this investment of time and other resources. The Bank does not have a security interest in these labors. It has an interest only in its merchandise and cash on hand.* The value of its interest depends on what the Bank could do, outside of bankruptcy, to realize on its

---

* The Bank's interest in the proceeds of sales is not the same as an interest in the whole retail price for unsold inventory. An ongoing financing arrangement provides for operating expenses, too, to come out of proceeds. The security interest on any given day covers only identified proceeds, an asset that is identifiable and significantly smaller than the wholesale or retail value of the entire inventory.

security. See Thomas H. Jackson, Avoiding Powers in Bankruptcy, 36
Stan.L.Rev. 725, 756–77 (1984). What it could do is seize and sell the
inventory. It would get at most the wholesale price—maybe less
because the Bank would sell the goods "as is" and would not offer the
wholesaler's usual services to its customer. The Bank does not operate
its own furniture store, and if it did it would still incur all the costs of
retailing the goods, costs that would have to be subtracted from the
retail price to determine the "value" of the inventory on the day the
Bank seized it. Cf. Contrail Leasing Partners, Ltd. v. Consolidated
Airways, Inc., 742 F.2d 1095, 1101 (7th Cir.1984); Uniform Commercial
Code § 9–504(1)(a).

To give the Bank more than the wholesale value is to induce a spate
of asset-grabbing among creditors, which could make all worse off. If
the Bank gets the whole increment of value (from wholesale to retail)
during the last 90 days, other creditors may respond by watching the
debtor closely and propelling it into bankruptcy when it has a lower
inventory (and therefore less "markup" for the Bank to seize). The
premature filing may reduce the value of the enterprise. There are
other defensive measures available to creditors. The principal function
of § 547(c)(5) is to reduce the need of unsecured creditors to protect
themselves against the last-minute moves of secured creditors. It
would serve this function less well if goods subject to a security interest
were appraised at their retail price.

Too, the Bank's security interest does not reach the "going concern"
value of the debtor; it had security in the *goods,* not in the *firm.* To
value the inventory in a way that reflects "going concern" value is to
give the Bank something for which it did not contract. At all events,
this wrinkle does not make a difference. If Ebbler had been sold as a
going venture 90 days before the filing of the bankruptcy petition, the
buyer of the business would have paid only wholesale price for Ebbler's
inventory. If Ebbler had been at the peak of health, the buyer would
have paid no more for inventory. A buyer would not have paid retail,
because it would have had to invest the additional time and money
necessary to obtain the retail price. So whether Ebbler is valued as a
defunct business or as a going business sold to a hypothetical buyer on
the critical date, wholesale is the right valuation, because it reflects the
price that a willing buyer would pay after arms'-length negotiation.
(The "going concern" value of Ebbler is reflected in its name, reputation, customer list, staff, and so on—things in which the Bank did not
have a security interest.)

To put this differently, a willing buyer of a flourishing retail or
manufacturing business will not pay more than the wholesale price for
inventory of goods or parts on hand, because this buyer could purchase
the same items on the market from the original sellers. Why pay
Ebbler $500 for a sofa when you can get the same item for $200 from its
manufacturer? Nothing would depend on whether Ebbler planned to
stay in business. The court therefore properly does not allow the
outcome of this case to turn on the fact that Ebbler chose a Chapter 7

liquidation rather than a Chapter 11 reorganization. Chapter titles are of little use in valuing assets under § 547(c)(5). A "liquidation" may be a sale of the business en bloc as an ongoing concern, and a "reorganization" may be a transition from one line of business to another. . . .

Notes & Questions

1. *Why Was an Exception Needed?* Why is it that an exception under § 547(c) was needed in *Ebbler?* Under what line of analysis was there a preference within the meaning of § 547(b)? See § 547(e)(3). Suppose the debtor's inventory and receivables had stopped changing (no further assets were sold) prior to the preference period but had fluctuated in value (through market fluctuation) during the preference period. Would there be a preference problem? The legislative history of § 547 states:

> Subsection (e) determines when a transfer is made, for the purposes of the preference section. . . . Paragraph (3) specifies that a transfer is not made until the debtor has acquired rights in the property transferred. This provision, more than any other in the section, overrules *DuBay* and *Grain Merchants*. . . .

House Report at 374.

2. *The Overruling of* Grain Merchants. As *Ebbler* and the legislative history suggest, § 547 was intended to overrule a line of cases, headed by *Grain Merchants*, holding that security interests in shifting inventory and receivables did not constitute preferences under prior bankruptcy law. One line of analysis in the old cases was that the transfer occurred at the time the secured party filed its financing statement. Since the filing preceded the preference period, no transfer of an interest in inventory or receivables occurred during the preference period. Another line of analysis relied on the "substitution of collateral" doctrine. "[A] transfer of accounts receivable to the secured creditor made during the four months prior to bankruptcy is not considered preferential where the accounts transferred are substituted for prior released accounts." *Grain Merchants*, 408 F.2d at 217. Another line of reasoning regarded accounts receivables and inventory as a single asset (with possibly changing components) so that perfection of an interest in inventory or receivables protected the secured party even as the original inventory or receivables were replaced by after-acquired inventory or receivables.

Should *Grain Merchants* be overruled? Consider the following:

> If one is going to have a bankruptcy proceeding to which anyone will wish to come, one had better be prepared to examine and to threaten to undo at least some pre-bankruptcy transactions. Otherwise nothing will be left for unsecured creditors. As a general principle this seems to justify a preference provision.
>
> Although this theory supplies an appropriate rationale for upsetting eve-of-bankruptcy payments and grants of security, the classic bankruptcy preferences, it offers no justification for the new preference rule unfavorable to accounts receivable and inventory lenders.

The article 9 secured party enters the preference period having done all one can to secure an interest in collateral. Secured lenders' treatment in bankruptcy causes displeasure not because of their eve-of-bankruptcy activity but because their interests in the bankrupt's assets can be perfected far in advance with preemptive rights as against subsequent creditors. Section 547's treatment of inventory and receivables financing must be justified on some other ground.

The most popular ground seems to be that, absent some such limitation, secured lenders would fare "too well" in bankruptcy compared with unsecured creditors. "Equality is equity." For example, the National Bankruptcy Conference, a private group involved in bankruptcy reform, noted disapprovingly that under the old bankruptcy law, "it appears that no perfected Article 9 after-acquired property interest in inventory, receivables or any other type of property can ever be set aside in bankruptcy." Yet this straightforward suggestion that too much is too much is also an incomplete justification for the new act's subordination of inventory and receivables secured lending.

Lawmakers face a difficult decision in choosing the ideal ranking of secured and unsecured creditors in a bankruptcy proceeding. Rightly or wrongly, bankruptcy law generally accepts secured lending as a credit vehicle and honors it in bankruptcy. Given this decision, and unsecured lenders' freedom to choose borrowers, a bankruptcy system that fully honors the article 9 security interests of inventory and receivables secured lenders does not seem less equitable than section 547's treatment of inventory and receivables lenders. If it is "equitable" to honor secured credit transactions in all other contexts, notions of fairness cannot require any particular treatment of inventory and receivables. Indeed, since an inventory or receivables lender must follow the article 9 notice system to achieve secured status in bankruptcy, all lenders may discover the likelihood of not being able to seek satisfaction out of the secured lender's inventory or receivables collateral. Even without notice, absent a security interest of their own, other lenders would be foolish to rely on particular assets of the debtor. Finally, both groups know the rules of the game when they extend credit. If the rules favor secured lenders, unsecured lenders should not be able to cry "foul" after the fact. One cannot justify the new act's treatment of inventory and receivables financing on the ground of equity between secured and unsecured lenders.

A final effort to justify the new rules rests on the larger econom-ic view that, regardless of the equities, the economy as a whole benefits more from dividing the debtor's assets between the secured and unsecured lenders than from allowing secured lenders to obtain them all. From an economic perspective that encompasses both secured and unsecured lenders, however, the bankruptcy rule proba-bly does not matter. If inventory and receivables lenders fare well under article 9 and bankruptcy law, unsecured lenders will have to charge higher interest rates (explicitly or in higher prices of goods sold on open credit) or lend more carefully (at greater cost) to obtain the same return on their investments given the greater bankruptcy losses they would incur if they continued to follow their prior lending practices. Debtors' reliance on unsecured borrowing may decrease because of the higher cost of money, thereby slowing the presumably desirable flow of unsecured credit. But this damping effect on the flow of credit is matched by an increase in reliance on the inventory and receivables lenders whose cost of doing business is decreased by their favorable treatment in bankruptcy. If differences in the costs of engaging in secured and unsecured credit transactions are ignored, the decrease and corresponding increase will result in no net change in the cost of funds. If one really wishes to justify a particular preference rule on the basis of its widespread economic effects, one would need to know the relative elasticity of demand for the relevant types of secured and unsecured credit and the increased costs associated with more careful lending by the relevant lenders. Indeed, one might also need to know who in the economy really bears the cost of credit increases. Absent such information, and neither Congress, the Commission on Bankruptcy Laws, nor the National Bankruptcy Conference, suggest its existence, one cannot justify the new preference rule on the ground that it has anything other than short term beneficial effects for a chosen group of lenders.

Eisenberg, Bankruptcy Law in Perspective, 28 UCLA L.Rev. 963–66 (1981). Should it matter in *Ebbler* that a going-out-of-business-sale had been conducted?

3. *Post-Petition Collateral.* Consider the relationship between § 552 and § 547. Under § 547, a secured party's interest in inventory and receivables acquired by the debtor during the 90-day period is vulnerable to attack. Does § 552(b) suggest that the secured party has a less vulnerable interest in inventory and receivables acquired after the commencement of the case? Is a security interest in such collateral vulnerable to attack under § 547 by virtue of § 547(e)(3)? If so, when will § 552(b) serve to save an otherwise vulnerable interest in post-petition property? Cf. In re DiToro, 17 B.R. 836 (Bkrtcy.E.D.Pa.1982) (deeming mortgagee to be entitled to certain post-petition rents by virtue of mortgage foreclosure).

KRONMAN, THE TREATMENT OF SECURITY INTERESTS IN AFTER–ACQUIRED PROPERTY UNDER THE PROPOSED BANKRUPTCY ACT,
124 U.Pa.L.Rev. 110, 144–47 (1975)

The floating lien . . . should not receive unlimited protection. In particular, there are two situations in which a secured party should not be permitted to claim as collateral for his loan the full value, measured on the date of bankruptcy, of the inventory or receivables securing it.

First, a secured party obviously should be denied rights in his collateral to the extent that the value of such collateral increased, during the period immediately preceding bankruptcy, because of his own fraudulent or manipulative conduct. A creditor whose loan is secured by receivables sometimes uses his power or influence to persuade his debtor to conduct a "fire sale" of all available inventory at prices well below cost, in order to "pump" the receivables and thereby swell the value of the collateral securing his loan. Such a creditor gains an unfair advantage over the debtor's other creditors, secured as well as unsecured, and diminishes the total value of the bankrupt's estate. Conduct of this sort should be discouraged.

Secondly, and not as obviously, a secured party should be denied the benefit of any "windfall" increase in the value of his collateral during the immediate pre-bankruptcy period. Such a windfall could result from an unexpected and extraordinary flurry of sales which dramatically increased the total value of the outstanding receivables. Since the secured party did not bargain for a windfall of this type, he has not given anything to the debtor's estate, by way of consideration, that might entitle him to appropriate to himself the entire benefit of the windfall. A windfall increase in the value of the bankrupt's estate should benefit all creditors equally so that the consequences of the vicissitudes of commercial life will be moderated rather than exaggerated in bankruptcy.

The policy of protecting the floating lien on after-acquired inventory and receivables in all but the two situations just described is best served by focusing not on the state of mind of the secured party, or on the technical chronology of each transfer, but rather on fluctuation in the overall value of the collateral securing the floating lien. In almost all cases, the total value of the debtor's inventory and receivables will decline in the period preceding bankruptcy. When it increases instead, the increase will almost always be due to manipulative conduct by the secured party or a windfall outside "the normal course of a business declining into bankruptcy."

This presumption, like all others, does not hold true in every case. Weaving the preference net more finely to catch the distinction between "good" and "bad" increases in the value of collateral would, however, require refinement of the two-point net improvement test that would undoubtedly make proving the existence of a voidable preference more difficult. This difficulty would increase the likelihood of "tedious, asset-exhausting litigation" that would only deplete the estate. In sum, there must be "a straight policy choice between the rough and ready provisions of [section 4–607(d)] a (which, it is thought, will work reasona-

---

a. Section 4–607(d) was an early version of the improvement-in-position test now codified in § 547.

bly well in all but the unusual case) and the desire to do justice case by case."

This argument is well put. As the draftsmen themselves recognized, however, the two-point test embodied in section 4–607(d) would condemn many "improvements of position" whose increase was due neither to manipulative conduct on the part of the secured party nor to a windfall gain outside the normal course of business. Such "improvements" would occur, for example, in most seasonal industries, in which the volume of inventory and receivables fluctuates dramatically but regularly during the course of the business year.

Imagine the situation, under section 4–607(d), of a secured party who makes a loan to a toy manufacturer in November and takes as collateral the manufacturer's receivables, including those to arise in the future. When he makes the loan, the secured party may not be disturbed that his loan is presently under-collateralized; he anticipates that a rapid but normal expansion in the volume of his debtor's receivables during the holiday season will bring the value of the collateral up to the amount of the loan. The near certainty of such an expansion is part of the consideration inducing the secured party to make his loan in the first place. The expansion is not an unanticipated and unbargained-for windfall. Nevertheless, when the manufacturer files a bankruptcy petition in January, the lender will learn, much to his dismay, that he has received a voidable preference which the manufacturer's trustee is empowered to recover for the benefit of the bankrupt's unsecured creditors.

This result seems unfair and is certainly inconsistent with the policy underlying section 4–607(d). The two-point net improvement test should be modified to avoid the result in this case without significantly increasing the likelihood of expensive and time-consuming litigation in cases in which a true preference has been given and should be set aside.

One new approach would be to state the basic premise of section 4–607(d) in the form of an explicit but rebuttable presumption. The premise is, of course, that "[i]n the *normal* course of a business declining into bankruptcy the position of an inventory or receivables lender, far from improving, will almost certainly deteriorate." The trustee would be entitled to rely on the presumption, but a secured party could rebut it in the unusual case in which his improvement in position was entirely attributable to events occurring in the normal and anticipated course of his debtor's business.

Notes & Questions

1. *Windfalls.* Why should a secured lender be denied the benefit of "windfall" increases in the value of collateral? Should the lender be spared the loss generated by windfall decreases in the value of collateral? Doesn't the interest rate agreed upon by the lender and the debtor try to take account of unexpected risks and benefits?

2. *Manipulative Conduct.* If the central problem addressed by the new act's treatment of inventory and receivables financing is manipulative conduct by secured lenders, why not draft a rule that addresses only such conduct? Does § 547 leave inventory and receivables lenders free to engage in at least some manipulative conduct?

4. Section 547(e)(3) and Other After-Acquired Property

The improvement in position test of § 547(c)(5) *could* have been limited to capturing increases in the value of inventory and receivables. But § 547's structure, which relies on § 547(e)(3) to weaken the interests of secured parties and other lienholders, seems to reach many other transactions as well. Suppose that six months before bankruptcy debtor borrows money from secured party and grants secured party a security interest in a blue truck and any replacements of the blue truck. Secured party properly perfects. During the preference period, debtor replaces the blue truck with a red truck. In bankruptcy, may the trustee invoke § 547(e)(3) to avoid secured party's interest in the red truck? Does it matter whether the red truck is of equal value to the blue truck? Suppose the blue truck was replaced simply because it was wearing out.

Suppose that instead of trading in the blue truck the debtor sells it for cash. Assuming that secured party can trace the cash, does his interest in it survive bankruptcy? Are all proceeds and after-acquired property received during the 90-day period subject to preference attack by virtue of § 547(e)(3)? If so, does § 547(e)(3) constitute an unconstitutional interference with the rights of secured parties? See Chapter 11A.

Does § 552(b) suggest that Congress thought certain interests in after-acquired property and proceeds would survive enactment of § 547?

IN RE RIDDERVOLD

United States Court of Appeals, Second Circuit, 1981.
647 F.2d 342.

FRIENDLY, CIRCUIT JUDGE:

David B. and Susan R. Riddervold filed voluntary petitions in the Bankruptcy Court for the Northern District of New York for relief under Chapter 7 of the Bankruptcy Reform Act of 1978 (the Code) on December 3, 1979. A month later they filed a complaint against four judgment creditors. . . . A . . . cause of action asserted on behalf of David B. Riddervold (hereafter Riddervold) that between September 3 and December 3, 1979, one of the defendants, the Saratoga Hospital, had caused monies to be deducted from his wages by virtue of an income execution served on his employer in the amount of $260; that such monies constituted preferences which Riddervold's trustee could have avoided; that if the trustee had avoided these payments, Riddervold could have exempted them under the blanket exemption of

§ 522(d)(5), to wit, $400 plus any unused amount of the exemption provided in § 522(d)(1); but that the trustee had not attempted and would not attempt to recover the alleged preferences. In its answer Saratoga Hospital prayed for judgment dismissing the second cause of action. Bankruptcy Judge Mahoney granted this prayer, and an appeal was taken directly to this court by agreement purportedly pursuant to the authority of 28 U.S.C. § 1293(b). . . .

The Hospital's claim here at issue arose from medical treatment rendered to Susan R. Riddervold in 1976 and 1977. When the Hospital's bill was not paid, at least in full, it obtained a New York state court judgment, in the amount of $1,410.50 against Mr. Riddervold on March 17, 1977, which it recorded in the office of the Saratoga County Clerk. On January 17, 1978, it served an "income execution" pursuant to this judgment upon Riddervold's employer, the State of New York, under N.Y.C.P.L.R. § 5231. Under this execution the State made two payments aggregating $227 to the Hospital from wages otherwise payable to Riddervold within 90 days of the petition in bankruptcy. Riddervold contends that these payments constituted preferences which his trustee could have avoided under § 547 and that since the trustee has not taken and will not take proceedings to that end, Riddervold is entitled to do so under § 522(h).[2] The validity of this contention depends on applying the section of the 1978 Code relating to preferences, § 547, to the result of the action taken by the Hospital under N.Y.C.P.L.R. § 5231.

Section 547 of the 1978 Code completely rewrote § 60, the preference section of the Act of 1898 as amended, and removed or altered related material that had previously been dealt with in the lien provision, § 67. The key provision for this case is § 547(b). This allows the trustee to "avoid any transfer of property of the debtor", to or for the benefit of a creditor, for or on account of an antecedent debt, made while the debtor was insolvent[3] and within specified periods, here 90 days, before the filing of the petition and that enables the creditor to receive "more than such creditor would receive if—

(A) the case were a case under chapter 7 of this title;

(B) the transfer had not been made; and

(C) such creditor received payment of such debt to the extent provided by the provisions of this title."

Apparently the Riddervolds' exemptions exceeded their debts so that the Hospital would have received nothing under this test. Section

---

2. This provides:

(h) The debtor may avoid a transfer of property of the debtor or recover a set off to the extent that the debtor could have exempted such property under subsection (g)(1) of this section if the trustee had avoided such transfer, if—

(1) such transfer is avoidable by the trustee under section 544, 545, 547, 548,

549, or 724(a) of this title or recoverable by the trustee under section 553 of this title; and

(2) the trustee does not attempt to avoid such transfer.

3. Section 547(f) creates a presumption of insolvency during the 90 days preceding the filing of the petition.

101(40) broadly defines "transfer" to include "every mode, direct or indirect, absolute or conditional, voluntary or involuntary, or [sic] disposing of or parting with property or with an interest in property, including retention of title as a security interest." We quote in the margin the pertinent provisions of N.Y.C.P.L.R. § 5231 entitled "Income Execution." [4] Since the income execution was issued on January 17, 1978, it is safe to assume that the steps to and including the levy on the employer occurred long before the 90 days prior to the bankruptcy petition of December 3, 1979. Riddervold has not claimed the contrary.

There is a dearth of authority on the question whether payments by an employer during the crucial period—then four months—to a judgment creditor who had levied on the employer before the beginning of that period under N.Y.C.P.L.R. § 5231 and its predecessors, N.Y.C.P.A. § 684 and § 1391 of the N.Y. Code of Civil Procedure, constituted preferences under § 60 of the Bankruptcy Act of 1898 if the other requirements of that section were met. Indeed we have been cited to

---

4. § 5231. Income execution.

(a) Form. An income execution shall specify, in addition to the requirements of subdivision (a) of section 5230, the name and address of the person from whom the judgment debtor is receiving or will receive money; the amount of money, the frequency of its payment and the amount of the installments to be collected therefrom; and shall contain a notice to the judgment debtor that he shall commence payment of the installments specified to the sheriff forthwith and that, upon his default, the execution will be served upon the person from whom he is receiving or will receive money.

(b) Issuance. Where a judgment debtor is receiving or will receive more than eighty-five dollars per week from any person, an income execution for installments therefrom of not more than ten percent thereof may be issued and delivered to the sheriff of the county in which the judgment debtor resides or, where the judgment debtor is a non-resident, the county in which he is employed.

(c) Service upon debtor. Within twenty days after an income execution is delivered to the sheriff, the sheriff shall serve a copy of it upon the judgment debtor, in the same manner as a summons or, in lieu thereof, by certified mail return receipt requested provided additional copies are sent by regular mail as follows: (i) to the debtor; and (ii) to the debtor in care of his last known employer. If service is by mail as herein provided, the person effecting service shall retain the receipt together with a post office certificate of mailing as proof of such service.

(d) Levy upon default or failure to serve a debtor. If a judgment debtor fails to pay installments pursuant to an income execution served upon him for a period of twenty days, or if the sheriff is unable to serve an income execution upon the judgment debtor within twenty days after the execution is delivered to the sheriff, the sheriff shall levy upon the money that the judgment debtor is receiving or will receive by serving a copy of the income execution, indorsed to indicate the extent to which paid installments have satisfied the judgment, upon the person from whom the judgment debtor is receiving or will receive money personally within the county in the same manner as a summons or by certified mail return receipt requested, except that such service shall not be made by delivery to a person authorized to receive service of summons solely by a designation pursuant to a provision of law other than rule 318.

(e) Withholding of installments. A person served with an income execution shall withhold from money then or thereafter due to the judgment debtor installments of ten percent thereof and pay them over to the sheriff. If such person shall fail to so pay the sheriff, the judgment creditor may commence a proceeding against him for accrued installments. If the money due to the judgment debtor consists of salary or wages and his employment is terminated by resignation or dismissal at any time after service of the execution, the levy shall thereafter be ineffective, and the execution shall be returned, unless the debtor is reinstated or re-employed within ninety days after such termination.

none.[5] Such cases as have been called to our attention or been found by our own research dealt with the provision of § 67 invalidating liens obtained within the four-months period rather than the recovery of preferences; they arose when the creditor sought modification of a stay of state court proceedings so as to enable him to collect moneys in the hands of the employer or the sheriff and the bankrupt opposed.

Early in his judicial career Judge L. Hand held in In re Sims, 176 F. 645 (S.D.N.Y.1910), that moneys withheld from the bankrupt's salary under a levy under § 1391 of the New York Code of Civil Procedure more than four months old at the date of the bankruptcy and still in the hands of the sheriff at the date of adjudication belonged to the creditors, whereas post-adjudication earnings of the bankrupt did not. On the former point he reasoned that the execution operated as a "continuing levy". In re Beck, 238 F. 653 (S.D.N.Y.1915), involved a portion of Beck's salary retained by the city paymaster pursuant to an execution under the same statute also long antedating the bankruptcy. Without referring to In re Sims, supra, and in misplaced reliance on Clarke v. Larremore, 188 U.S. 486, 23 S.Ct. 363, 47 L.Ed. 555 (1903), not a garnishment case, where the judgment, levy and execution all occurred within the four-months period, Judge Hough held that the trustee was entitled to such moneys still in the paymaster's hands as represented retentions during the four-month period. He argued that "there could be no levy upon Beck's salary until there was a salary to levy upon. Therefore the date of levy is coincident with the date of accruing wage." However, he also held that if the debtor did not receive a discharge, amounts retained after the beginning of the four-months period and indeed after the adjudication should be payable to the judgment creditor. . . .

In principle it does not appear to us that the State's paying $227 to the hospital during the 90-day period now provided by § 547(b)(4)(A) constituted a "transfer of property of the debtor." This is not because Riddervold took no action to cause the payments to be made, since "transfer" is defined to include an involuntary transfer. It is rather because after the sheriff has taken the step described in N.Y.C.P.L.R. § 5231(d), the debtor has no property or interest in property subject to the levy which can be transferred. Service of the income execution on the employer in effect works a novation whereby the employer owes 10% of the employee's salary not to the employee but to the sheriff for the benefit of the judgment creditor. This view is substantiated by the provision in N.Y.C.P.L.R. § 5231(e) that if the employer fails to pay the

5. Under § 60(b) of the 1898 Act only the trustee could avoid a preference. In view of the accepted learning that "[a] preference is not an act evil in itself but one prohibited by the Bankruptcy Act in the interest of equality of division," Canright v. General Finance Corp., 35 F.Supp. 841, 844 (E.D.Ill.1940), aff'd, 123 F.2d 98 (7 Cir. 1941), see 4 Collier, Bankruptcy ¶ 547.01 (15th ed.1980), it is not clear why the 1978 Code extended the power to avoid preferences to bankrupts. However, it unquestionably did, subject to certain restrictions set forth in § 522(g), none of which is applicable here.

sheriff, the judgment creditor may sue the employer to recover accrued installments.

It is true that the employer comes under no liability to pay the sheriff until the wages are earned. Indeed the last sentence of N.Y.C.P. L.R. § 5231(e) expressly provides for this eventuality of stating that if "employment is terminated by resignation or dismissal . . ., the levy shall thereafter be ineffective." But this does not require us to hold that the portion of the salary subject to the income execution vests in the employee for a fleeting second after it has been earned, when in fact the employer becomes bound at that very time to pay it to the sheriff.

We emphasize that we are here concerned with payments which were not made simply in discharge of a lien [6] but were pursuant to an execution levied many months before the beginning of the 90-day period. Our decision follows the "continuing levy" principle announced by Judge L. Hand and adopted by Judge Mayer under the Act of 1898 scores of years ago. It seems also to conform to the intimations of Clarke v. Larremore, supra, 188 U.S. at 488–90, 23 S.Ct. at 364–365, that when a writ of execution under a valid lien has been fully executed by payment to the execution creditor, a subsequent bankruptcy does not affect the creditor's rights. To be sure, these cases were decided under the Act of 1898 but we find nothing in the language or the policy of the 1978 Code that forbids their continued application.

Affirmed.

Notes & Questions

1. *Relationship to* Grain Merchants. Based on Judge Friendly's reasoning in *Riddervold,* is it clear that § 547 overrules *Grain Merchants*? See also In re Kendrick & King Lumber, Inc., 14 B.R. 764 (Bkrtcy.W.D.Okl.1981) (security interest in tax refund received after petition was filed not subject to preference attack). Based on *Riddervold,* could one argue that after perfection of a security interest "the debtor had no property or interest in property" subject to the security interest which can be transferred? Is the debtor's interest in his wages in *Riddervold* less substantial than a debtor's interest in property subject to a security interest? Why aren't the wages merely a form of encumbered after-acquired property? Several cases have rejected *Riddervold.* E.g., In re Perry, 48 B.R. 591 (Bkrtcy.M.D.Tenn.1985).

2. *Wages Earned and Garnished Before Preference Period.* Suppose that wages are garnished and earned before the preference period and paid to the creditor during the preference period. See In re Conner, 733 F.2d 1560 (11th Cir.1984) (no preference).

6. We note that if an income execution under N.Y.C.P.L.R. § 5231 was a statutory lien, § 547(c)(6) would bar avoidance since the conditions of § 545 for avoiding the fixing of such liens were not met. However, § 5231 procedures do not create a statutory lien, as defined by § 101(38), since an income execution does not arise "solely by force of a statute."

See generally Weisberg, Commercial Morality, the Merchant Character, and the History of the Voidable Preference, 39 Stan.L.Rev. 3 (1986).

5. Section 9–306(4): Article 9 Proceeds in Bankruptcy

IN RE GIBSON PRODUCTS OF ARIZONA

United States Court of Appeals, Ninth Circuit, 1976.
543 F.2d 652, certiorari denied 430 U.S. 946, 97 S.Ct. 1583,
51 L.Ed.2d 794 (1977).

HUFSTEDLER, CIRCUIT JUDGE:

On this appeal we must referee a collision between the "proceeds" provision of the Uniform Commercial Code (U.C.C. § 9–306(4), A.R.S. § 44–3127(D)[1]) and the bankruptcy trustee's power to avoid preferences under Section 60 of the Bankruptcy Act. The provisions collide under circumstances that place the creditor, asserting a perfected security interest in the debtor's bank account, in the dimmest equitable light: If the creditor prevails, it receives \$19,505.27 from the debtor's

---

1. For convenience, we refer hereafter solely to U.C.C. § 9–306, rather than to the Arizona statute adopting the U.C.C. We also use the text of U.C.C. § 9–306 prior to the 1972 amendments because Arizona did not adopt the 1972 amendments until 1975, effective January 1, 1976, a date long after this litigation began. (Arizona Laws of 1975, Ch. 65.) The 1972 amendments, even if applicable, do not affect the issues in this case.

In pertinent part, U.C.C. § 9–306 provided:

"(1) 'Proceeds' includes whatever is received when collateral or proceeds is sold, exchanged, collected or otherwise disposed of. The term also includes the account arising when the right to payment is earned under a contract right. Money, checks and the like are 'cash proceeds'. All other proceeds are 'non-cash proceeds'.

(2) Except where this Article otherwise provides, a security interest continues in collateral notwithstanding sale, exchange or other disposition thereof by the debtor unless his action was authorized by the secured party in the security agreement or otherwise, and also continues in any identifiable proceeds including collections received by the debtor.

(3) The security interest in proceeds is a continuously perfected security interest if the interest in the original collateral was perfected but it ceases to be a perfected security interest and becomes unperfected ten days after receipt of the proceeds by the debtor unless

(a) a filed financing statement covering the original collateral also covers proceeds; or

(b) the security interest in the proceeds is perfected before the expiration of the ten day period.

(4) In the event of insolvency proceedings instituted by or against a debtor, a secured party with a perfected security interest in proceeds has a perfected security interest

(a) in identifiable non-cash proceeds;

(b) in identifiable cash proceeds in the form of money which is not commingled with other money or deposited in a bank account prior to the insolvency proceedings;

(c) in identifiable cash proceeds in the form of checks and the like which are not deposited in a bank account prior to the insolvency proceedings; and

(d) in all cash and bank accounts of the debtor, if other cash proceeds have been commingled or deposited in a bank account, but the perfected security interest under this paragraph (d) is

(i) subject to any right of set-off; and

(ii) limited to an amount not greater than the amount of any cash proceeds received by the debtor within ten days before the institution of the insolvency proceedings and commingled or deposited in a bank account prior to the insolvency proceedings less the amount of cash proceeds received by the debtor and paid over to the secured party during the ten day period."

account on proof that the debtor, within ten days of the insolvency, deposited $10 in the account from the sale of a hair drier in which the creditor had a perfected security interest. The district court affirmed the bankruptcy judge's order awarding $19,505.27 to the secured creditor. We reverse because we conclude that the operation of U.C.C. § 9–306(4)(d) created a voidable preference by the transfer to the creditor of a perfected security interest in the cash deposited in the debtor's account that exceeded the amount of the creditor's proceeds.

The creditor, Arizona Wholesale Supply Co. ("Wholesale") sold General Electric and Proctor-Silex appliances to the debtor, Gibson Products of Arizona ("Gibson"). Wholesale has a perfected security interest in the appliances. On January 13, 1972, Gibson initiated Chapter XI proceedings. During the ten-day period immediately preceding the institution of these proceedings, Gibson deposited $19,505.27 in its bank account. During the same period, Gibson deposited in the account $10 from the sale of a Proctor-Silex dryer.[3] At the time insolvency proceedings were instituted, Gibson was indebted to Wholesale in the amount of $28,800 for the appliances it had sold to Gibson and for which it has perfected security interests. . . .

The proceeds section of the Code generally follows the pre-Code law that a security interest continues in any identifiable proceeds received by the debtor from the sale or other disposition of the collateral. The Code's new twist is extending the creditor's security interest to commingled funds without specifically tracing the creditor's proceeds into the fund, when the debtor has become insolvent. (U.C.C. § 9–306(4)(d).) No collision between the proceeds provision of the Code and the preference sections of the Bankruptcy Act occurs when the creditor's perfected security interest in his collateral is attached to the proceeds from the sale or other disposition of the collateral if (1) his interest was initially perfected in the collateral more than four months before bankruptcy, and (2) he can identify the proceeds to which his security interest has attached. Under these circumstances, the creditor has priority over later creditors when he first perfected his security interest, and his priority relates back to his initial perfection. (Cf. DuBay v. Williams (9th Cir. 1969) 417 F.2d 1277, 1286–87.) The problem arises in the U.C.C. § 9–306(4)(d) situation because that subsection gives the secured creditor a perfected security interest in the entire amount deposited by the debtor within ten days before bankruptcy without limiting the interest to the amount that can be identified as the proceeds from the sale of the creditor's collateral. With respect to the funds that are not the creditor's proceeds, the creditor has no security interest except that conferred by U.C.C. § 9–306(4)(d). His interest in these nonproceeds arises upon the occurrence of two events: (1) insol-

---

3. No other sales during the 10-day period were proved, regardless of the disposition of the proceeds. Under these circumstances, some alternative interpretations of U.C.C. § 9–306(4)(d) were not advanced and are not before us. Wholesale tried, but failed to prove that the proceeds from the sale of some television sets were also deposited in the account during the ten-day period.

vency proceedings instituted by or against a debtor, and (2) commingling of some of the proceeds from his collateral with the debtor's cash on hand or with other deposits in his debtor's bank account.   His security interest is limited to an "amount not greater than the amount of any cash proceeds received by the debtor within ten days before institution of the insolvency proceedings" and is subject to the additional set-offs in Section 9–306(4)(d).

The draftsmen's intent was not to deliver a security bonanza to any secured creditor.   As Professor Gilmore observes: "It goes without saying that a provision of state law which purported to give a secured creditor greater rights in the event his debtor's estate was administered in bankruptcy than he would have apart from bankruptcy would be invalid.   However, . . .   § 9–306(4) does not in the least aim at such a result.   Indeed, § 9–306(4) is the reverse of such a statute, since it sharply cuts back the secured party's rights when insolvency proceedings are initiated."   (2 G. Gilmore, Security Interests in Personal Property ¶ 45.9, at 1337–38 (1965).)   The intent was to eliminate the expense and nuisance of tracing when funds are commingled and to limit the grasp of secured creditors to the amount received during the last ten days before insolvency proceedings, which, the draftsmen assumed, would usually be less than the same creditor could trace if he had a grip on the entire balance deposited over an unlimited time.   (Id. at 1340.)   On that assumption, awarding a perfected security interest to the secured creditor, good for a short time on the entire balance, gives the secured creditor no windfall to the detriment of general creditors. On our facts, the contrary is true.

When confronted with an analogous situation, the Seventh Circuit limited the secured creditor's interest to those proceeds in the bank account traceable to the sale of the creditor's collateral.   The Seventh Circuit's theory was that the term "any cash proceeds" used in Section 9–306(4)(d) does not refer to all receipts from any source deposited in the bank account, but, instead, refers to "proceeds" as defined in Section 9–306(1), and thus the phrase means "cash proceeds from the sale of collateral in which the creditor had a security interest."   (Fitzpatrick v. Philco Finance Corp. (7th Cir. 1974) 491 F.2d 1288, 1291–92.)

Although we reach a similar result, we reject the Seventh Circuit's reasoning because, in our view, that construction impermissibly bends the language and structure of Section 9–306.   The general definition of "proceeds" in Section 9–306(1) cannot be transplanted into Section 9–306(4) shorn of its statutory freight.   The statute divides "proceeds" into two categories, "identifiable" and "commingled," i.e., nonidentifiable proceeds, and alters the reach of a perfected security interest, depending upon whether the proceeds are identifiable or nonidentifiable.   (Compare § 9–306(4)(a), (b), (c) with § 9–306(4)(d).)   Section 9–306(4)(d) deals only with nonidentifiable cash proceeds.   If the cash proceeds could be "identified," i.e., had not been commingled, the secured party would have a perfected security interest in the whole fund under Section 9–306(4)(b), just as he did in pre-Code days, without any of the limitations imposed by Section 9–306(4)(d). Under the Code scheme, the secured creditor also has a perfected security interest under subsection (d) when he cannot identify his proceeds in the commingled fund, as long as he can show that some of his proceeds were among those in the commingled fund.

We leave the language of Section 9–306(4) as it was drafted and apply Section 60 of the Bankruptcy Act to resolve the problem. As defined by Section 60a(1), a preference is "[1] a transfer . . . of the property of a debtor [2] to or for the benefit of a creditor [3] for or on account of an antecedent debt, [4] made or suffered by such debtor while insolvent and [5] within four months before the filing . . . [of bankruptcy], [6] the effect of which transfer will be to enable such creditor to obtain a greater percentage of his debt than some other creditor of the same class." Section 60a(2) of the Bankruptcy Act provides that "a transfer of property . . . shall be deemed to have been made or suffered at the time when it became so far perfected that no subsequent lien upon such property obtainable by legal or equitable proceedings on a simple contract could become superior to the rights of the transferee." As we held in DuBay v. Williams, supra, 417 F.2d at 1287:

> " 'Transfer' for the purpose of section 60a(2) is thus equated with the act by which priority over later creditors is achieved and not with the event which attaches the security interest to a specific account."

With respect to Wholesale's security interest in the proceeds from the sale of the collateral, no later creditor could obtain priority over Wholesale from the time its financing statement was filed and further perfected pursuant to Section 9–306(3), at least until Wholesale's proceeds were commingled with that of other secured creditors or with cash from other sources deposited in Gibson's bank account. Wholesale's security interest in those proceeds relates back to its initial financing statement. (Cf. DuBay v. Williams, supra, 417 F.2d at 1287–88.) However, Wholesale had no interest in cash other than its own proceeds, and hence no priority over later creditors in such cash, until (1) some part of Wholesale's proceeds were deposited with other cash in Gibson's bank account, (2) within ten days of Gibson's filing its Chapter XI petition. The effect of Section 9–306(4) is thus to transfer to Wholesale a security interest in the cash in Gibson's bank account which does not derive from the sale of its collateral. In this situation, the act that gives Wholesale priority and the events that attach the security interest to the questioned asset occur at the same time. The transfer cannot occur earlier than ten days before the institution of bankruptcy. The transfer of the excess, above the wholesaler's proceeds, is a preference unless we can say that the transfer was neither for nor on account of an antecedent debt. We cannot avoid the conclusion that the transfer was on account of an antecedent debt.

Wholesale could not qualify for Section 9–306(4) treatment absent the antecedent debt; moreover, the transfer does not happen unless the debt owed exceeds the payments made to the creditor during the ten-day period before the bankruptcy petition has been filed.

The result is that Wholesale cannot successfully assert its claim under U.C.C. § 9–306(4)(d) to thwart the trustee's power to set that interest aside as a preference. However, the conclusion does not necessarily also follow that the creditor loses his security interest both in the proceeds from the sale of his collateral and in the nonproceeds in the debtor's bank account. In his contest with the trustee, he only loses his claim to the amounts in excess of his proceeds because only that amount is a preference. His security interest in the whole account, subject to the limitations of U.C.C. § 9–306(4), is valid except that the trustee can avoid it. To the extent that a creditor is able to identify his proceeds to trace their path into the commingled funds, he will be able to defeat *pro tanto* the trustee's assertion of a preference.

By this construction of Section 60 of the Bankruptcy Act and Section 9–306(4) of the U.C.C., we do violence neither to statute nor to substantial justice among the parties. The creditor's security interest in the whole account under Section 9–306(4) is *prima facie* valid, except as to the trustee, and, as to him, the creditor's security interest is presumptively preferential. The creditor can rebut the presumption by appropriately tracing his proceeds. We think that it is fair to place the burden on the creditor to identify his own proceeds and thus to defeat, in whole or in part, the trustee's claim of preference. The creditor is in a better position than the trustee to trace his proceeds; moreover, if the creditor wants to avoid both the limitations of U.C.C. § 9–306(4)(d) and the burden of proof in a potential contest with the trustee, all he needs to do is to prevent commingling of his proceeds and thus to follow U.C.C. § 9–306(4)(a)–(c).

Reversed and remanded for further proceedings consistent with the views herein expressed.

Notes & Questions

1. *The Nonbankruptcy Result.* Assume that, in a nonbankruptcy setting, Debtor sells collateral worth $90,000 and deposits the $90,000 in receipts in an account that already has $10,000 in it. Does the depositing of the $90,000 mean that these proceeds have become unidentifiable? Does it mean that they have become commingled? What does *Gibson Products* suggest about the meanings of these terms? May proceeds be both identifiable and commingled? See *C.O. Funk & Sons, Inc.*, Chapter 2B.

2. *Bankruptcy.* Assume the same facts but also that 30 days after the deposit the Debtor goes bankrupt. What are the secured party's rights in Debtor's bank account?

3. *The Meaning of "Proceeds."* How does *Gibson Products* interpret the term "proceeds" in § 9–306(4)? Is the court's view consistent with the way the term is used elsewhere in Article 9?

4. *The Effect of § 547.* Does *Gibson Products'* finding of a preference continue to be valid after enactment of § 547? Under § 547, may the trustee claim both the $19,505 in proceeds that was deposited in the debtor's account within ten days of bankruptcy *and* the $10 in proceeds from the Proctor-Silex dryer? Are all proceeds received within 90 days before bankruptcy recoverable by the trustee as a preference?

D. Statutory Liens (§ 545)

In sorting through bankruptcy law's dealings with statutory liens, there are a few questions worth isolating. One question, addressed in the excerpt that follows, is whether bankruptcy law should invalidate liens that are effective only in times of financial distress. See § 545(1). A separate, preliminary question is what liens should count as "statutory liens" for purposes of bankruptcy. This question seems fairly raised in each of the cases that follow. As to those liens that are found to be statutory liens and that are effective in nonbankruptcy settings, a third question arises. How "strong" must the lien be before it will pass the test of § 545(2) and be honored in bankruptcy?

JACKSON, BANKRUPTCY, NON–BANKRUPTCY ENTITLEMENTS, AND THE CREDITORS' BARGAIN, 91 Yale L.J. 857, 902–06 (1982)

What, if anything, is wrong with state-created priorities and bankruptcy statutory liens? Surprisingly little critical attention has been directed to this inquiry. Two questions, however, seem to be raised. First, is there any justification at all for a state's attempt to prefer a given type of creditor in bankruptcy? Second, if there is a justification for such an attempt, is there any reason to believe that the use of state-created priorities and bankruptcy statutory liens is not a proper way to implement those desired preferences?

Several reasons, other than simply political expedience or special interest group pressure, may explain a state's desire to provide a level of protection to certain types of claimants, instead of leaving the issue to the area of consensual security interests. First, non-consensual claimants, such as tort creditors, pose special problems to which application of a consensual model seems largely inapplicable. Should a state believe that a certain level of deterrence is desirable to protect against certain behavior, a system of priority entitlements to "victims" of that behavior may help the state achieve that goal, at least with respect to some types of torts. By giving non-consensual tort claimants priority over general unsecured creditors, those general creditors (whose chance of repayment has been made more risky than under a proportional payment scheme) will have an increased incentive to monitor the debtor to reduce the likelihood of such torts occurring in the first place.

Second, a state may have reason to believe that, with respect to a particular class of claimants, there is systematic advantage-taking of them by other creditors, because of an informational disparity or other reasons. Intervention by a state, in giving this class of claimants priority entitlements, may be a way of addressing a form of market inefficiency. Finally, the state is itself likely to be a claimant (often-times, as in its taxing capacity, a non-consensual one), in which case the level of priority it provides is a part of the cost calculus it has decided on in setting its rates (whether tax rates or otherwise).

There may be inefficient interferences by a state as well, due to politically-motivated causes. But the relevant point is that state inter-ventions may sometimes be efficient or otherwise justified and, in any event, are generally recognized in bankruptcy. The bankruptcy law upholds state-created entitlements unless the entitlement is directed specifically at the bankruptcy process. Unless there is some reason to believe that inefficiently motivated instances of state interference are more common with respect to state-created priorities or bankruptcy statutory liens than with respect to other forms of state-created entitle-ments, inquiry into the validity of an entitlement should first be directed at the *form* of the intervention. The relevant inquiry is whether there is anything particularly undesirable about state-created priorities or bankruptcy statutory liens that justifies the blanket prohi-bition against them in the bankruptcy process and that distinguishes them from other forms of non-bankruptcy entitlements.

State-created priorities and bankruptcy statutory liens attempt to direct allocative entitlements in bankruptcy, but in this respect they are indistinguishable from other types of non-bankruptcy entitlements routinely recognized in bankruptcy. The difficulty with state-created priorities and bankruptcy statutory liens is that they suffer from the same "bankruptcy incentive" problems previously discussed in connec-tion with ipso facto clauses. Since the rules of the bankruptcy process set the minimum level of entitlements against which non-bankruptcy "workouts" must be evaluated, a creditor enjoying a state-created priority effective only in bankruptcy will demand to be treated similar-ly outside of bankruptcy as well. A creditor with such a priority might push for initiation of the bankruptcy process when it is not in the aggregate interests of the creditors to do so. But because a creditor with a state-created priority does not necessarily have that priority right outside of the bankruptcy process, he must negotiate with the other creditors in order to receive that preferential treatment. These negotiations, because they are likely to involve a number of unsecured creditors, may involve free-rider problems that will not only make negotiations costly but also may lead ultimately to an inefficient use of the bankruptcy process. Moreover, unlike the case of consensually negotiated agreements, there is no persuasive reason to believe that this state of affairs involves policing or other sorts of efficiencies that may justify retention of the system. Therefore, at our creditors' bar-gain meeting, if it were clear that a particular creditor was going to receive a state-created priority or bankruptcy statutory lien, we would expect the creditors as a group to view it as in their interest to give that creditor a lien that is valid both in and out of bankruptcy. Refusing to recognize state-created priorities and bankruptcy statutory liens simply requires a state that wishes to give someone a "priority" to do so by means of an entitlement that is good in and out of bankruptcy.

The puzzle with respect to state-created priorities and bankruptcy statutory liens is why a state would ever enact an entitlement that is good only in bankruptcy. Part of the answer is that, at least based on reported cases from the last twenty-five years or so, few such statutes have been passed. Ironically, bankruptcy law's failure to recognize entitlements only good in bankruptcy may be viewed as justified, not on the ground that it is protective of something fundamental to the bankruptcy process itself, or even of general unsecured creditors, but rather on the ground that it protects claimants in the aggregate (and ultimately the debtor) against presumptively illogical actions by state governments, which accrue to no one's advantage.

From another perspective, however, the greater irony may be that bankruptcy law's obsession with formulating a rule on the subject may have done more harm than good. For while the prohibition on state-created entitlements good only in bankruptcy may occasionally strike down an aberrant state statute designed to create an irrational form of entitlement, the presence of the federal rule has, meanwhile, led to substantial confusion in its application. For if an entitlement is enforceable both in and out of bankruptcy, there is no reason, stemming from the justifications underlying condemnation of state-created priorities or bankruptcy statutory liens, to refuse recognition of the entitlement. The failure to recognize this simple point has led to a variety of confusing and ill-considered decisions by appellate courts. The rule against state-created priorities and bankruptcy statutory liens, if correctly understood, may be harmless and even occasionally beneficial. But since the reasons for the rule are misperceived, the resulting misapplications may engender more uncertainty than continuation of the rule is worth.

ELLIOTT v. BUMB

United States Court of Appeals, Ninth Circuit, 1966.
356 F.2d 749, certiorari denied 385 U.S. 829, 87 S.Ct. 67, 17 L.Ed.2d 66.

ELY, CIRCUIT JUDGE:

On or about November 15, 1962, a written "Agency Franchise and Trust Agreement" was executed by and between Van's Market and Security Currency Services, Ltd. In the agreement, Security appointed Van's as its "Agent for the purpose of issuing Money Orders" and Van's agreed to hold all proceeds for the face value of money orders issued, plus fifty percent of the fees therefrom, in trust for Security and entirely separate and apart from other funds in Van's possession.[1]

1. The agreement provided:

Neither of the two companies fared well financially. On October 15, 1963, Van's executed a general assignment for the benefit of creditors to the Credit Managers Association of Southern California and ceased to do business. Subsequently, on November 19, 1963, an Involuntary Petition in Bankruptcy was filed against Van's and it was adjudged a bankrupt on March 5, 1964. Peter M. Elliott is the duly appointed, qualified, and acting trustee of Van's estate. Security filed a petition under the provisions of Chapter XI of the Bankruptcy Act on January 16, 1964, and its bankruptcy was adjudicated. A.J. Bumb is the trustee in bankruptcy for Security.

There is due to Security from Van's the sum of $3,109.16, proceeds from the sale of money orders and checks sold by Van's as agent for Security in the amount of $3,092.99 and an additional sum of $16.17 in fees for the sale of certain checks. The obligation flows from transactions occurring before October 15, 1963, the date of Van's assignment for the benefit of creditors. All the money orders and checks sold by Van's were honored and paid by Security. The Credit Managers Association presently holds $2,014.99 which was on deposit in Van's bank account prior to October 15, 1963 and which was received by Van's from its sale of money orders for Security. The balance due, $1,094.17, was commingled by Van's with its other assets.

Elliott, trustee of Van's, applied for an order that Bumb (Security's trustee), the Credit Managers Association, and the Corporations Commissioner for the State of California show cause why orders should not be entered declaring "any statutory lien" in favor of Bumb, Security, or the Corporations Commissioner, with respect to any funds of the estate of Van's, to be null and void pursuant to section 67c(2) of the Bankruptcy Act, 11 U.S.C. § 107(c)(2) (1964),[4] and ordering the Credit Managers Association to remit to Elliott, for Security, the funds which it held. The order to show cause was issued on September 18, 1964, and in answer, Bumb asserted that his claim to the money properly rested upon Security's status as the beneficiary of a trust fund under the

"[1. Agent shall accept responsibility and liability for properly issuing all Money Orders and shall account for and remit all proceeds for face value issued plus 50% of fees therefrom to Security; Agent shall hold all said moneys in trust for Security entirely separate and apart from other funds in possession of Agent until remitted. Agent shall twice weekly render to Security, a true and correct written statement of all funds received to date of report by Agent, accompanied by all said funds. Agent shall be solely and wholly liable and accountable for all moneys received by Agent pursuant to this Agreement up to and until Agent delivers physical possession thereof to Security or its designated depositary. Agent shall maintain accounts and records of all transactions and same shall be maintained by Agent not less than two years from date of said transactions.]"

4. "(c) Where not enforced by sale before the filing of a petition initiating a proceeding under this title, and except where the estate of the bankrupt is solvent: . . . .

"(2) the provisions of subdivision (b) of this section to the contrary notwithstanding, statutory liens created or recognized by the laws of any State for debts owing to any person, including any State or any subdivision thereof, on personal property not accompanied by possession of, or by levy upon or by sequestration or distraint of, such property, shall not be valid against the trustee: . . .."

express provisions of section 12300.3 of the California Financial Code.[5] He alleged that the California statute created a true trust and not a statutory lien which would be unenforceable under section 67c(2) of the Bankruptcy Act. The Referee in Bankruptcy, rejecting Bumb's contentions, held that any trust claimed to have been created in favor of Security pursuant to sections 12300.3 and 12300.4 [6] of the California Financial Code was, as against Van's, wholly invalid and that the funds

5. "§ 12300.3

All funds received by a licensee or its agents from the sale of checks, drafts, money orders, or other commercial paper serving the same purpose and for the purpose of paying bills, invoices, or accounts of an obligor, equal in amount to the face value of such instruments or equal to the amount to be paid, shall constitute trust funds owned by and belonging to the person from whom they were received or a licensee who has paid the checks, drafts, money orders or other commercial paper serving the same purpose, for which the funds of such persons have been received by the agent but not transmitted to such licensee or deposited in the trust account of such licensee. If a licensee or an agent of a licensee shall commingle such funds with those of his own, all assets of such agent shall be impressed with a trust in favor of said purchaser or the licensee in an amount equal to the aggregate funds received or which should have been received by the agent from such sale. Such trust shall continue until an amount equal to said funds is separated from those of the agent and transmitted to the licensee or deposited in the trust account of licensee. An amount equal to all such trust funds shall be deposited in a bank or banks in an account or accounts in the name of the licensee designated 'trust account,' or by some other appropriate name indicating that the funds are not the funds of the licensee or of its officers, employees, or agents. Such funds, or, in the event of the commingling of such funds by licensee or its agent with those of the licensee or its agent, an amount of funds of such licensee or of its agent equal thereto, shall constitute trust funds as herein provided and shall not be subject to attachment, levy of execution or sequestration by order of court except by a payee, or bona fide assignee, or bona fide holder in due course of a check, draft, or money order sold by a licensee, or except by an obligor for whom a licensee is acting as an agent in paying bills. Funds in said account, together with funds and checks on hand and in the hands of agents held for the account of the licensee, at all times shall be at least equal to the aggregate liability of the licensee on

account of checks sold and bills, invoices, and accounts accepted for payment.

"Nothing in this law shall be construed to prevent a purchaser, a holder in due course, the payee of a check, draft or money order sold by the licensee in the usual course of his business, or an obligor for whom the licensee is acting as an agent in paying bills of the obligor, from taking any legal action necessary to enforce any claims which said purchaser, holder in due course, payee, or obligor may desire to take including the right to levy attachment or execution.

"In the event a license under this law shall be suspended or terminated the licensee shall immediately deposit in said trust account an amount which with funds therein contained shall be equal to the outstanding checks sold and bills unpaid."

6. "§ 12300.4

Prior to such separation and transmittal to the licensee or deposit by its agent such funds received by said agent may be used by said agent for the sole purpose only of the making of change or cashing of checks in the normal course of its business. All such funds received by said agent to the date of deposit or transmittal as required below or an amount equal to such funds must be separated from those of the agent and transmitted to, or deposited in the trust account of, the licensee not less than every third business day. If an agent owns or operates, either directly or indirectly, more than two locations for the sale of checks, drafts, money orders, or other commercial paper serving the same purpose and/or for the receipt of money for the purpose of paying bills, invoices or accounts of an obligor, and handles trust funds in any three-day period equal to or in excess of securities to be deposited as provided in Section 12223, said agent shall transmit to, or deposit in the trust account of, the licensee directly from each such location of such agent such funds not later than the end of the next business day following receipt; such funds to be in form of cash or checks cashed in the normal course of business only.

"Where the total amount of such funds held by an agent does not exceed one thouin question should remain assets of Van's estate, free and clear of any right, title, lien, or other interest whatsoever in favor of the estate of Security. He directed that the $2,014.99 held by the Credit Managers Association be released to Elliott for the estate of Van's. On review, the District Court reversed the Referee's decision, holding that proceeds from the sale of money orders and checks by Van's as agent for Security, whether deposited to a trust account or commingled with assets of Van's, constituted trust funds not subject to the provisions of section 67c of the Bankruptcy Act. Elliott made a timely appeal, properly invoking our jurisdiction under 11 U.S.C. § 47 (1964). . . .

There are actually two amounts to which we must direct our consideration, (1) the $2,014.99 on deposit in Van's bank account prior to the assignment for the benefit of creditors and which represents segregated funds received for money orders sold by Van's as agent for Security; and (2) the balance of the $3,109.16 due to Security, $1,094.17, which was commingled by Van's with its other assets.

As to the identifiable sum of $2,014.99, the District Court made the correct determination in favor of Security's trustee. Although one may become bankrupt, property which is held by him in trust belongs to the beneficiary of the trust. 4 Collier, Bankruptcy ¶ 70.25[2] (14th ed.1964) [hereinafter called Collier]; 3 Remington, Bankruptcy § 1212 (Henderson ed.1957). Apart from the provisions of the California Financial Code, the segregated amount is corpus of a trust. The bankrupts' written agreement was a valid trust agreement under California law. See Cal.Civ.Code §§ 2221, 2222. While no trust corpus existed as of the time of the agreement, it has been held, in equity, that if parties intend to create a trust at a future time when the corpus comes into being, the trust should take effect at such future time and the equitable interest pass to the beneficiary. I Bogert, Trusts and Trustees § 113, pp. 575–76 (2d ed.1965). Generally, the question of whether a trust is established is one to be resolved by the application of state law. See Jaffke v. Dunham, 352 U.S. 280, 281, 77 S.Ct. 307, 1 L.Ed.2d 314, (1957). Although no California court has ruled directly upon the question in a cause involving such an explicit trust agreement as that made by the bankrupts here, the California Supreme Court has written, "A mere promise to obtain money and thereupon hold it in trust does not create a trust *until it is at least so far executed that the money has been obtained in accordance with the promise.*" Molera v. Cooper, 173 Cal. 259, 262, 160 P. 231 (1916). (Emphasis added.) From the quoted

sand dollars ($1,000) in a calendar week, the commissioner may, in his discretion, by written order permit the agent to transmit or deposit such funds in periods in excess of 3 days but not more than 10 days.

"If, after reasonable notice from licensee, an agent shall fail to transmit or deposit the funds, or an amount equal thereto, or to report to the licensee, as herein provided without just cause, or if an agent shall use any of such funds, directly or indirectly,

for any purpose other than is permitted herein, licensee shall immediately terminate such agency and within five (5) days thereafter notify the commissioner in writing of the reason for such termination, setting forth the name and address of the agency location. No agent so terminated shall be permitted to become an agent of the licensee or any other licensee except as provided in Section 12301.4 of the Financial Code."

language, it must be inferred that California courts would hold, under the terms of the explicit agreement here, that a trust actually came to be established upon the receipt of those corpus funds which were so clearly anticipated in the agreement precisely defining their trust quality and manner of handling.   . . .

As to the remaining $1,094.17, commingled with other money, our determination is fraught with more difficulty.   Under the provisions of the California statute all assets of Van's would be impressed with a trust in favor of Security in an amount equal to the aggregate funds received from the sale of the checks and money orders and the trust would remain until payment of the amount due to Security.   Cal.Fin. Code § 12300.3.   By impressing a trust on all assets of the agent, the statute would relieve check and money order principals from the burden of tracing commingled funds.   Generally such burden falls upon the beneficiary of a trust.   In re J.M. Acheson Co., 170 F. 427 (9th Cir. 1909).   As Collier has written:

> "The basic idea of the trust doctrine as applied in bankruptcy is a fair and reasonable identification of the property or fund so as not to harm other creditors.   It is not enough, therefore, to show merely that the funds or property came into the bankrupt's hands or went into the bankrupt's business or, by the better view, even that the funds or property are contained somewhere within the bankrupt's estate.   If the trust fund or property cannot be identified in its original or substituted form, the *cestui* becomes merely a general creditor of the estate, for the prevailing rule in trusts is that 'a beneficiary who cannot find the trust property has no lien or charge spread over the entire estate of the faithless trustee.'"

4 Collier ¶ 70.25[2], pp. 1216–18.   (Citations omitted.)

In this case, however, the state statute undertakes to dispense with the beneficiary's need to trace.   Generally, state law governs the determination of whether a beneficiary has sufficiently identified trust property, but,

> "There is the further question, and this a federal one: what is the distribution contemplated by the Bankruptcy Act in the situation at bar?   State trust law must not be allowed to pervert or override the distributive provisions of the Bankruptcy Act.   A state rule which purports to fasten a general lien on a person's estate in the event of insolvency or a general liquidation must be regarded as a priority in disguise and incompatible with the order of distribution prescribed for bankruptcy.   The adoption of § 64a(5) and § 67c of the Bankruptcy Act was intended to make clear that state rules of priority of distribution must yield in bankruptcy cases to that prescribed by the Act."

4 Collier ¶ 70.25[2], pp. 1224–1225.   In an early case, after recognizing that under applicable state law the owner of a trust fund was entitled to a preference as to the entire body of the estate of an insolvent trustee when the trustee had mingled the trust fund with his own

property, the court held that federal bankruptcy law could not allow such a preference and that the beneficiary, unable to trace the trust property, must share in the estate on the same basis as general creditors. John Deere Plow Co. v. McDavid, 137 F. 802, 812 (8th Cir. 1905). Since the time of that decision, Congress has made even clearer its intent that state law shall not be permitted to confer preference on one class of the creditors of one adjudged a bankrupt under federal law, even though the state may have the highest public purpose in attempting to do so. See, e.g., 2 U.S.Code Cong. & Ad.News p. 1973 (1952). So it is that section 64 of the Bankruptcy Act eliminates all state-created priorities save one (rent). 11 U.S.C. § 104 (1964). And statutory liens not accompanied by "possession of" or by "levy upon" the property subject to lien before the filing of the petition in bankruptcy are invalidated by section 67c(2) of the Bankruptcy Act. 11 U.S.C. § 107(c)(2) (1964).

If state law is contrary to federal bankruptcy law, the state law must yield. Giving effect to the provisions of section 12300.3, which would impress a trust upon commingled funds, would open the door to state creation of priorities in favor of various classes of creditors by labeling such priorities as "trusts". This would tend to thwart or obstruct the scheme of federal bankruptcy. It may be true that Congress was aware of statutory trusts when it made its most recent amendments to the bankruptcy law, for courts were previously confronted with state statutory trusts in bankruptcy cases. E.g., In re Treister & Son, Inc., 145 F.Supp. 144 (S.D.N.Y.1956); Albert Pick Co. v. Travis, 6 F.Supp. 486 (E.D.N.Y.1933). We cannot believe, however, that Congress contemplated that if trust funds are commingled with other assets of one subsequently declared bankrupt under federal law, a state statute may impress a trust on all assets of the bankrupt's estate to the extent of the amount due the beneficiary. We find no prior case authority which would have adequately warned Congress of the possibility of such a result, and we have pointed to direct authority for the opposite conclusion. John Deere Plow Co. v. McDavid, supra. We hold that the provisions of section 12300.3 of the California Financial Code, insofar as they would establish a trust on the commingled funds, are in such conflict with the federal bankruptcy scheme that they cannot be given effect in the case at bar. The cause is remanded so as to afford to appellee the opportunity to attempt to trace the sources of the commingled funds.

Affirmed in part, reversed in part.

Notes & Questions

1. *The Meaning of "Statutory Lien."* Is the California statute at issue in *Elliott* a statutory lien? Are all state laws creating trusts to be treated as statutory liens in bankruptcy and subjected to analysis under § 545? If they are to be subjected to such scrutiny, will they fare any better than did the trust in *Elliott?* Are there material differences

between the statutory liens invalidated by § 67c(2), as in effect in *Elliott,* and the liens invalidated by new § 545? How will § 545(2)'s bona fide purchaser test apply in cases like *Elliott?* Is any lien valid against a bona fide purchaser of money?

2. *The State's Goals.* What is wrong with what the state was trying to accomplish in *Elliott?* Was it creating a lien, such as that condemned by § 545(1), that is only effective in bankruptcy? Is there a case to be made for statutes like Cal.Financial Code § 12300.3? If so, will such statutes be of any value if they are invalid in bankruptcy?

3. *Tracing.* Elliott undermines only the part of § 12300.3 that "undertakes to dispense with the beneficiary's need to trace." Does *Elliott* therefore merely amount to a holding that bankruptcy law, somehow, somewhere, specifies principles of trust tracing? What if California trust law does not require a beneficiary to be able to trace to specific property but instead allows beneficiaries to recover whatever property they happen to find in the hands of their trustees? Would such a rule, allowing automatic tracing into commingled funds, violate any bankruptcy principles? Compare U.C.C. § 9–306(4).

4. *Commentary.* Professor Jackson comments on *Elliott:*

The holding misperceives the nature of the inquiry. All state-created entitlements act in favor of some group of creditors, but bankruptcy law generally recognizes them nonetheless. The inquiry, which *Elliott v. Bumb* ignored, is whether the statute applied only in bankruptcy. Without further inquiry into the efficiencies of a *particular* application of statutory trust doctrine there is nothing to suggest that these impressed trusts should be considered contrary to bankruptcy policy.

Jackson, supra, at 906 n. 228.

IN RE SABERMAN

United States Bankruptcy Court, Northern District of Illinois, 1980.
3 B.R. 316.

ROBERT L. EISEN, BANKRUPTCY JUDGE.

AAA Building Maintenance Co., (AAA) is a building contractor and a creditor. AAA has filed an objection to the Chapter 13 wage earner plan of Henry Dean Saberman, the debtor herein. The plan as proposed contemplates a sale of the debtor's real estate and provides for payment in full to secured creditors and a composition payment to unsecured creditors. AAA objects to this plan because the terms of the plan do not provide for payment in full for the work on debtor's residence. It is undisputed that the real estate was improved as a result of the labor and materials provided by the claimant.

AAA was engaged to provide certain improvements to the debtor's premises. The date last worked on this job was May 5, 1978. AAA filed its mechanics' lien for $1400 in January or February of 1980, subsequent to debtor's filing of its Chapter 13 petition.

The issues presented here are whether the mechanics' lien is avoidable as the debtor asserts and if so, whether and to what extent a Chapter 13 debtor may exercise the avoiding powers of a trustee. AAA asserts that an Illinois mechanics' lien may be perfected subsequent to the filing of a bankruptcy petition and its interest must therefore be recognized as a secured obligation. If the creditor prevails on the perfection issue, the issue of the debtor's avoidance power is moot.

It is clear that a mechanics' lien is a statutory lien, as defined in the Bankruptcy Code. 11 U.S.C. sec. 101(38). The legislative history of the Code makes this explicit. "A statutory lien is only one that arises automatically, and is not based on an agreement to give a lien or on a judicial action. Mechanics', materialmen's, and warehouseman's liens are examples." H.Rept. No. 95–595, 95th Cong. 1st Sess. (1977) 314; S.Rept. No. 95–989, 95th Cong. 2d Sess. (1978) 27, U.S.Code Cong. & Admin.News 1978, pp. 5787, 6271. As a general rule, statutory liens survive the filing of a petition under the Bankruptcy Code so long as the statutory requirements have been strictly complied with.

11 U.S.C. sec. 545 provides that:

> The trustee may avoid the fixing of a statutory lien on property of the debtor to the extent that such lien—(2) is not perfected or enforceable on the date of the filing of the petition against a bona fide purchaser who purchases such property on the date of the filing of the petition, whether or not such purchaser exists; . . .

This expression of the trustee's power to avoid statutory liens is limited by 11 U.S.C. sec. 546(b), which provides that: "(b) The rights and powers of the trustee under section 544, 545, or 549 of this title are subject to any generally applicable law that permits perfection of an interest in property to be effective against an entity that acquires rights in such property before the date of such perfection." The import of this section is that if under applicable law, here the Illinois Mechanics' Lien Act, a later perfection will relate back prior to the bankruptcy filing, the subsequent perfection will be good against the trustee and the lien will not be avoided.

Under Illinois law an inchoate mechanics' lien arises upon the substantial completion of the work contracted for. Upon filing and perfection, the date of perfection relates back to the date upon which the inchoate lien arose. Decatur Bridge Co. v. Standart, 208 Ill.App. 592, 595 (1917). The Illinois Mechanics' Lien Act, Ch. 82, Ill.Rev.Stat., sec. 7 provides, in pertinent part:

> No contractor shall be allowed to enforce such lien against or to the prejudice of any other creditor or incumbrancer or purchaser, unless within four months after completion, . . . he shall either bring suit to enforce his lien therefor or shall file in the office of the recorder of deeds of the county in which the building, erection or other improvement to be charged with the lien is situated, a claim for lien. . . . Such claim for lien may be filed at any time after the contract is made, and as to the owner may be filed at any time

after the contract is made and within two years after the completion
of said contract . . ..

Thus, if a claim for a lien is filed within four months after day of
completion of performance, then the lien will prevail against the
original owner and other creditors, incumbrancers and purchasers.

However, if it is filed after four months but within two years, the
lien will prevail only against the original owner but not third persons.
Therefore, if a claim for lien is filed more than four months after
completion of performance, it cannot prevail against one whom became
a bona fide purchaser prior to its filing.

This view has been strictly adhered to by the courts. Even where a
purchaser has, at the time [he] purchased, actual knowledge that a
claim has been filed against the property, this claim for lien will be
ineffective if it was filed more than four months after completion of
performance. . . .

The mechanics' lien in the instant case was filed outside of the four
month period and would not be good against a bona fide purchaser.
Therefore, pursuant to Illinois law, this lien can be avoided by one
standing in the shoes of such a purchaser.

11 U.S.C. sec. 545 is derived from sections 67b and 67c of the former
law. As explained by George M. Treister,

> [t]he thought is, if a statutory lien is good against a bona fide
> purchaser, then that is a real property interest, but if the state says
> we don't want to give the lienor that much, we will let a BFP cut off
> the statutory lienor's rights, then that is not enough of a property
> interest to be recognized in bankruptcy and will be invalidated as a
> priority. That is how they get at those liens which are not good
> against a BFP through Section 67c.

Plenary Sessions of Regional Bankruptcy Seminars, 1976–1977, From
Presentations by George M. Treister (Federal Judicial Center, December, 1977).

The legislative history of 11 U.S.C. sec. 545 discloses that sections
67b and 67c are to be followed. The Illinois Mechanics' Lien Act, by
virtue of the two periods of limitation set forth—four months and two
years—limits the rights of a lienor versus a bona fide purchaser or one
standing in his shoes. Here the lienor, by its failure to file its claim for
lien within the four month period, has an insufficient property interest
to file a secured claim or to be entitled to what amounts to a priority in
bankruptcy. Therefore, its claim is unsecured. . . .

IN RE HOLT

United States Bankruptcy Court, Western District of Pennsylvania, 1981.
11 B.R. 797.

JOSEPH L. COSETTI, BANKRUPTCY JUDGE.

FACTS

On December 10, 1979 the debtor, Carolyn Holt, filed a petition under Chapter 7 of the Bankruptcy Code. A complaint was filed by the debtor on October 6, 1980 under 11 U.S.C. § 522(f) to avoid a judgment lien against real property of the debtor located at 338 Enright Court, Pittsburgh, PA 15206. The debtor alleges that this lien impairs an exemption to which the debtor is entitled under § 522(d)(1) and (5). On October 10, 1980 the defendant, the Commonwealth of Pennsylvania, Department of Public Welfare (hereinafter "D.P.W.") filed a motion to dismiss the complaint for failure to state a claim upon which relief can be granted. . . .

On April 21, 1980, subsequent to the debtor obtaining her interest in the subject real property, a judgment was recorded against her in the Court of Common Pleas of Allegheny County, Pennsylvania at No. G.D. 75–11092 in the amount of $2,000.00. The debtor has received public assistance of one type or another for several years. As of November 30, 1980 the debtor has received $4,885.90 in cash grants. In order to receive assistance the debtor was required by the D.P.W. to sign a Pa–9 Form. The stated purpose of this form, entitled "Reimbursement Agreement", is to give the D.P.W. a lien on any real property owned by the recipient. The Pa–9 Form also contains a confession of judgment clause. At present the D.P.W. has one lien against the debtor's real property in the amount of $2,000.00.

Schedule B–1 of the debtor's petition listed the market value of the house located at 338 Enright Court, Pittsburgh, Pennsylvania as $24,500.00. A mortgage of $18,000.00 on the real property is in existence as of the time of filing of this petition. The debtor claimed as exempt $6,500.00 of equity in the real property. There was no objection to the debtor's filing of the $6,500.00 exemption.

ISSUES

Is the welfare lien a security interest within the meaning of the Code and not a judicial lien?

Is the lien held by the D.P.W. against the debtor's property a statutory lien not subject to avoidance under 11 U.S.C. § 545, or a judicial lien which can be avoided under 11 U.S.C. § 522(f) to the extent it impairs the debtor's exemptions?

If the D.P.W. lien is a judicial lien, does it impair an exemption of the debtor?

Do considerations of federalism bar the application of § 522(f) under Tenth Amendment considerations?

CONCLUSIONS OF LAW

To determine the status which the D.P.W. lien should be accorded under the Bankruptcy Code, the court must first look to the statutory authorization for this lien and the treatment of the D.P.W. lien in state court.

The D.P.W. lien resulted from the debtor's signing of a Pa–9 Form, "Reimbursement Agreement". The authority for a Pa–9 Form is derived from 62 P.S. § 1974 entitled "Property of Persons Liable for Expenses Incurred for Support and Maintenance." This statute in pertinent part states:

> (a) . . . the real and personal property of any person shall be liable for the expenses of his support and maintenance . . . if such property was owned during the time such expenses were incurred . . . . Any public body or agency may sue the owner of such property for moneys so expended, and any judgment obtained shall be a lien upon the said real estate of such person and shall be collected as other judgments . . . ."

The D.P.W. sought to invoke the remedial provisions of 62 P.S. § 1974 by a "petition and rule" procedure through use of the confession of judgment clause of Form Pa–9. A "petition and rule" is a one party proceeding whereby a party simply files a petition with the court and a ruling or judgment of the court is issued against the other party. A literal reading of 62 P.S. § 1974, which specifically provides "any public body or public agency may sue . . . for moneys so expended," leads to the conclusion that a suit to judgment is required. Perkins v. Yellow Cab Co., 49 Pa.D. & C.2d 297 (1970). The court in *Perkins* said the legislature had intended a more restricted view of the word "sue". The *Perkins* court felt that if the legislature had intended to include "petition and rule" as a means of enforcing the D.P.W. right of action created by 62 P.S. § 1974, the legislature would have so provided. This reasoning is supported by the provisions made by the legislature at § 3 of the Support Law of 1937, 62 P.S. § 1973, specifically providing for "petition and rule" as a means of recovery. Title 62 P.S. § 1973, which provides for the liability of relatives for the support of indigents, was passed by the legislature at the same time as 62 P.S. § 1974. It appears that the legislature was aware of the procedural differences between the two sections and intended to create a unique type of judgment by preventing execution against the home or furnishings during the lifetime of the assisted person, surviving spouse or dependent children. The view by the court in *Perkins*, supra, that the legislature intended to create a right of action specifically requiring a suit to judgment prior to reimbursement, is supported by an earlier decision in Matter of Hoffman, 38 Pa.D. & C.2d 577 (1966). In *Hoffman* a young boy from a family receiving aid was struck by a car and damages were awarded. The state sought to recover the benefits of this tort judgment through the use of 62 P.S. § 1974. The court in *Hoffman* took the view that the claim by the state under 62 P.S. § 1974 must be reduced to judgment.

In the case Comm. Dept. of Public Welfare v. Livingood, 22 Pa. Cmwlth. 530, 349 A.2d 816 (1976), the court held that the D.P.W. must bring a suit by original process in the Court of Common Pleas in order to recover amounts above the ordinary $2,000.00 lien. In *Livingood*, id., the parties did not raise the question of whether the amount covered by the $2,000.00 lien must be brought to judgment in Common Pleas court. For this reason the court does not address the question. In *Livingood,* the D.P.W. brought suit to collect reimbursement money owed to the state after a sheriff's sale by a third party. The court followed the reasoning of *Perkins,* supra, Ryan v. Hockinberry, 42 Pa.D. & C.2d 578 (1967), and Matter of Hoffman, supra, in holding that a petition for a rule to show cause was not a proper procedure in suits for reimbursement under 62 P.S. § 1974. The court in *Livingood,* supra 349 A.2d at 818, adopted the exact language of Judge Cavanaugh's opinion in *Perkins,* rejecting the D.P.W.'s view that it, the D.P.W., could enforce its rights under 62 P.S. § 1974 by petition and rule as well as a suit to judgment.

In *Ryan,* the court reviewed a related section, 62 P.S. § 1975, which did not specifically provide for recovery through the use of petition and rule, and held that a proceeding by a one party petition was not authorized by the statute and therefore not allowed.

In a recent case, Shearer v. Moore, 277 Pa.Super. 70, 419 A.2d 665 (1980), the Pennsylvania Superior Court cites and supports the decision in *Perkins* but lists execution of an "Agreement and Authorization to Pay a Claim" as one of the ways which the state can recover money paid in assistance to a recipient. The Pennsylvania Superior Court stated that the Pa–176K medical assistance reimbursement form (similar to a Pa–9 Form) is merely an affirmation of the statutory liability established by 62 P.S. § 1974. Congleton v. Pa. D.P.W., 48 Pa. Cmwlth. 615, 409 A.2d 1382 (1980). The court cited *Congleton* and stated that the form "does not give the Commonwealth any position other than its rightful one as a common creditor and is not tantamount to legal process." The court did not specifically define what it meant by the use of the term "common creditor".

In the *Congleton* case, id., the court dealt with an attempt by the D.P.W. through the use of a Form Pa–176K to recover benefits due the recipient under a pending Pennsylvania Workman's Compensation claim. Although the validity of the confession of judgment clause was not in issue, the *Congleton* court ruled that "the conditioning of continued eligibility upon the signing of the form (same as in the case of a Pa–9 Form) means that execution of the affirmation is certainly not voluntary."

The only court which allowed the D.P.W. to enforce its claim established by 62 P.S. § 1974 solely by petition and rule was an Orphan's Court. *Garrison's (Minors),* 64 Pa.Dist. & Co.2d 433 (1974). The judge in *Garrison's* reasoned that petition and rule was sufficient because of the special power of the Orphan's Court to exercise the exclusive and mandatory jurisdiction in the administration and distribution of real and personal property of minors' estates, 20 Pa.C.S.A. § 711 (1972).

The Bankruptcy Code defines three types of liens—statutory liens, judicial liens, and security interests. Section 101(27) of the Code defines a judicial lien as a "lien obtained by judgment, levy, sequestration, or other legal or equitable process or proceeding." A statutory lien is defined by 11 U.S.C. § 101(38) as a "lien arising solely by force of a statute on specified circumstances or conditions . . . but does not include security interest or judicial lien whether or not such interest or lien is provided by or dependent on a statute and whether or not such interest or lien is made fully effective by statute." A security interest is defined in 11 U.S.C. § 101(37) as a lien created by agreement. The court in In re Brown, 7 B.R. 479 (M.D.Pa.1980), relying on the legislative history of the Code, H.Rep. No. 95–595, 95th Cong., 1st Sess. 312 (1977); S.Rep. No. 95–989, 95th Cong., 2nd Sess. 25 (1978); U.S.Code Cong. & Adm.News 1978, p. 5787, ruled that "there are three kinds of liens; judicial liens, security interests and statutory liens and these categories are mutually exclusive and exhaustive except in the case of certain common law liens."

The definition of a statutory lien was not substantially changed by enactment of the new Bankruptcy Code. The legislative history of the Code confirms that 11 U.S.C. § 101(38) was to have the same effect as § 1(29a) of the Bankruptcy Act. S.Rep. No. 95–989, 95th Cong., 2nd Sess. 27 (1978); reprinted in 5 U.S.Code Cong. & Adm.News 1979, pp. 5787, 5812 and 5813. Under the old Bankruptcy Act § 1(29a), a statutory lien by definition specifically excluded any lien provided by or dependent upon an agreement to give security whether or not such lien was provided by or dependent on a statute. Congress intended to assure by this section that consensual liens would not be subjected to any of the tests of validity prescribed by § 67(c) which granted special treatment to statutory liens. H.Rep. No. 89–686, 89th Cong., 1st Sess. (1966); 2 U.S.Code Cong. & Adm.News 1966, pp. 2442, 2460.

If a lien arises by force of statute without prior consent between the parties and does not fit the definition of a judicial lien, it will be deemed a statutory lien. After examining the statutory authority for a Pa–9 Form it is clear, based on the Code definition, that the D.P.W.'s lien is not a statutory lien. By its nature the D.P.W. lien is at best a security interest, because it appears to be an agreement (somewhat involuntary) between the parties or it is a judicial lien because of the necessity for use of legal process to bring the lien into existence. For these reasons the D.P.W. lien falls into one or both of the exceptions to a statutory lien as defined by 11 U.S.C. § 101(38). . . .

The D.P.W. lien is not a statutory lien. Using the plain language of the Bankruptcy Code and recent court rulings, D.P.W. does not possess a security interest intended by Congress in enacting the Code. There was no voluntary intent of the debtor to create a security interest in his property. Further, to create a security interest under the Code, the intent of the parties must be clear, the property in which the interest is to be created must be described with some degree of specificity, and one must be able to trace the specific property to the writing evidencing the security agreement. The D.P.W. Pa–9 Form is very general and does not describe specific property. The form states only that "my real and personal property is liable for repayment . . . ." Pennsylvania courts have held that this form constitutes only a general acknowledgment of the duty to reimburse the state. We hold that a lien arising under 62 P.S. § 1974 is a judicial lien and therefore is subject to avoidance under § 522(f)(1) of the Bankruptcy Code. . . .

Notes & Questions

1. *Transforming a Lien into a Consensual Lien.* Suppose the contractor in *Saberman* had made the requisite filing within four months. Suppose also that the contractor's agreement with the owner contained a verbatim reproduction of the language of the Illinois mechanics' lien statute and contained a clause whereby the owner granted the contractor the same rights as are contained in the statute. Would the interest in *Saberman* then be a consensual lien not covered by § 545(2)?

2. *The Role of the Enforcement Mechanism.* In *Saberman,* does the form of enforcement of the lien chosen by the contractor affect the lien's status under § 545(2)? If an Illinois mechanic enforces his lien by judicial proceeding instead of by filing (as permitted by the statute in *Saberman*) within four months of the completion of performance, does the lien become vulnerable in bankruptcy? Is it now a judicial lien instead of a statutory lien?

3. *The Form of the Lien.* Given § 545, are not many mechanics and contractors better off with common law liens than with liens provided expressly by statute? Should their position in bankruptcy turn on whether a state codifies its lien law?

4. *Statutory Liens vs. Judicial Liens.* Should anything in the Bankruptcy Act turn on the difference between a statutory lien and a judicial lien? Are statutory liens vulnerable as preferences? See § 547(c)(6). In the absence of § 547(c)(6), would preference law provide an acceptable method for dealing with statutory liens that become effective only when the debtor is in financial difficulty?

5. *Tax Liens.* Tax liens constitute the most important class of statutory liens. The federal tax lien, discussed in Chapter 8, contains complex, detailed guidance as to its validity against competing interests. Section 7170 of the California Government Code, which is somewhat more manageable, states:

(a) Except as provided in subdivisions (b) and (c), a state tax lien attaches to all property and rights to property whether real or personal, tangible or intangible, including all after-acquired property and rights to property, belonging to the taxpayer and located in this state. A state tax lien attaches to a dwelling notwithstanding the prior recording of a homestead declaration (as defined in Section 704.910 of the Code of Civil Procedure).

(b) A state tax lien is not valid as to real property against the right, title, or interest of any of the following persons where the person's right, title, or interest was acquired or perfected prior to recording of the notice of state tax lien in the office of the county recorder of the county in which the real property is located pursuant to Section 7171:

(1) A successor in interest of the taxpayer without knowledge of the lien.

(2) A holder of a security interest.

(3) A mechanic's lienor.

(4) A judgment lien creditor.

(c) A state tax lien is not valid as to personal property against:

(1) The holder of a security interest in the property whose interest is perfected pursuant to Section 9303 of the Commercial Code prior to the time the notice of the state tax lien is filed with the Secretary of State pursuant to Section 7171.

(2) Any person (other than the taxpayer) who acquires an interest in the property under the law of this state without knowledge of the lien or who perfects an interest in accordance with the law of this state prior to the time that the notice of state tax lien is filed with the Secretary of State pursuant to Section 7171.

(3) A buyer in ordinary course of business who, under Section 9307 of the Commercial Code, would take free of a security interest created by the seller.

(4) Any person (other than the taxpayer) who, notwithstanding the prior filing of the notice of the state tax lien:

(A) Is a holder in due course of a negotiable instrument.

(B) Is a holder to whom a negotiable document of title has been duly negotiated.

(C) Is a bona fide purchaser of a security.

(D) Is a purchaser of chattel paper or an instrument who gives new value and takes possession of the chattel paper or instrument in the ordinary course of business.

(E) Is a holder of a purchase money security interest.

(F) Is a collecting bank holding a security interest in items being collected, accompanying documents and proceeds, pursuant to Section 4208 of the Commercial Code.

(G) Acquires a security interest in a deposit account or in the beneficial interest in a trust or estate.

(H) Acquires any right or interest in letters of credit, advices of credit, or money.

(I) Acquires without actual knowledge of the state tax lien a security interest in or a claim in or under any policy of insurance including unearned premiums.

(J) Acquires any right or interest in property subject to a certificate of title statute of another jurisdiction under the law of which indication of a security interest on the certificate of title is required as a condition of perfection of the security interest.

(5) A judgment lien creditor whose lien was created by the filing of a notice of judgment lien on personal property with the Secretary of State prior to the

time the notice of state tax lien is filed with the Secretary of State pursuant to Section 7171.

To explore the relationship between § 7170 and Bankruptcy Act § 545, consider a debtor who runs a typewriter business and owns a house. Suppose the debtor fails to pay his California state taxes and then files a bankruptcy petition. Does the state have a lien enforceable in bankruptcy against: (a) A typewriter held for sale by the business? (b) A toaster used in the house? Does it matter if the debtor's business sells typewriters on a wholesale or retail basis?

California's State Tax Lien Law was revised in 1980 but there seems to have been no effort to tailor the law to the requirements of the new Bankruptcy Act. See generally Recommendations Relating to Enforcement of Judgments, 15 Cal.L.Revision Comm'n Reports 33 (1980).

6. *§ 546(b).* Note the role of § 546(b) in *Saberman.* To what other situations might it apply?

E. Setoff (§ 553)

JENSEN v. STATE BANK OF ALLISON

United States Court of Appeals, Eighth Circuit, 1975.
518 F.2d 1.

WEBSTER, CIRCUIT JUDGE.

The trustee of the bankruptcy estate of James K. Uhlenhopp appeals from the judgment of the District Court upholding a setoff by the State Bank of Allison against funds of the bankrupt on deposit with the bank in satisfaction of an existing debt to the bank.

Prior to 1970, James K. Uhlenhopp and his wife Judy maintained a checking account at the State Bank of Allison, primarily for their personal use. In May, 1970, Uhlenhopp, who was in the livestock and trucking business, began using the account for business purposes. Shortly thereafter, Uhlenhopp borrowed money from the State Bank of Allison. The loans were evidenced by promissory notes in the amounts of $8,890.62 and $11,217.60 payable October 1, 1970, and December 24, 1970, respectively, and were secured by agreements granting the bank a security interest in the cattle purchased. Each of the notes contained a clause stating that the due dates could be accelerated any time the bank felt insecure. The bank filed financing statements at the local recording office.

On August 19, 1970, the State Bank of Allison learned that the State Bank of Dumont had filed a financing statement which claimed a security interest in Uhlenhopp's property, including after-acquired property. This financing statement had been filed before that of the State Bank of Allison. Deeming itself insecure, the State Bank of Allison accelerated Uhlenhopp's notes to make them payable immediately. It then debited Uhlenhopp's checking account for the full amount of the loans plus interest. Uhlenhopp filed a petition for bankruptcy on September 16, 1970.

Roger A. Jensen, the trustee of Uhlenhopp's estate, brought this action in the District Court to recover the full amount set off from Uhlenhopp's account. The complaint charged that the setoff constituted a voidable preference under § 60 of the Bankruptcy Act, 11 U.S.C. § 96, and, alternatively, was a wrongful conversion under Iowa law.

Following trial of the case, the District Court held that the setoff did not constitute a preference because the trustee had not shown that the bank knew Uhlenhopp was insolvent at the time it debited his account or that he was in fact insolvent at that time. The District Court also found that since the bank had acted within its rights in accelerating the notes and performing the setoff, there was no common law conversion.

The trustee appeals from the dismissal of his complaint, contending that the setoff was a voidable preference and that the bank illegally converted Uhlenhopp's funds. We affirm the judgment of the District Court.

I.

Under the Bankruptcy Act, no voidable preference is ordinarily created when a bank sets off funds in an account of general deposit with it against a debt owed to it by the depositor. Farmers Bank v. Julian, 383 F.2d 314, 324 (8th Cir.), cert. denied, 389 U.S. 1021, 88 S.Ct. 593, 19 L.Ed.2d 662 (1967) wherein we said:

> Section 68(a) of the Bankruptcy Act, 11 U.S.C. § 108 applies and allows a setoff to [a] Bank unless the account has been accepted or built up for the real purpose of permitting the Bank to obtain a preference by way of setoff of the account. A bank account at the time of filing the petition in bankruptcy is a debt due to the bankrupt from the bank, and in the absence of fraud or collusion between the bank and the bankrupt, the bank may set the account off against any indebtedness owed it by the bankrupt. . . . Section 68(a) of the Bankruptcy Act did not create the right of setoff but it 'recognizes this right, and it cannot be taken away by construction because of the possibility that it may be abused.' [sic] as it 'would precipitate bankruptcy and so interfere with the course of business as to produce evils of various and far-reaching consequence'. . . .

> The bank has the right to set off deposits against indebtedness even though the bankrupt is insolvent at the time of setoff and before the petition in bankruptcy is filed. [citations omitted]

See generally 4 J. Moore, Collier on Bankruptcy ¶ 68.15–.19 (1971).

There was no evidence that Uhlenhopp's account had been accepted or built up in order to permit the bank to obtain a preference. The account was one of long-standing. Uhlenhopp began using the account for his livestock business when he began to borrow money from the bank to purchase cattle. The cattle loans were secured by the cattle themselves, and there is nothing in the record to show any kind of build-up in the bank account in order for Uhlenhopp to make a preferential payment to the bank during a period of insolvency. In fact, there is evidence that the bank, without Uhlenhopp's knowledge, deferred posting of some checks drawn against the account in order that there be sufficient funds in the account to cover the setoff. There was "absolutely no evidence of any collusive or prearranged plan of action between [Uhlenhopp] and the Bank to build up this account." See Farmers Bank v. Julian, supra, 383 F.2d at 325.

Accordingly, appellant's contention that the State Bank of Allison's setoff of Uhlenhopp's checking account was a voidable preference must fail.

II.

The claim of conversion presents a closer issue. Iowa law defines a conversion as "any distinct act of dominion or control, wrongfully exerted over the chattels of another in denial of his right thereto." E.g., Goeman v. Live Stock National Bank, 238 Iowa 1088, 29 N.W.2d 528, 531 (1947).

The relationship between a bank and its depositor is that of debtor-creditor. As a general rule there can be no conversion of an ordinary debt. See W. Prosser, Handbook of the Law of Torts § 15, at 82–83 (4th ed. 1971); Restatement (Second) of Torts § 242, comment f (1965). Before applying this principle of law, however, we are bound in this case to consider whether the unseemly conduct of the bank transformed the routine process of setoff into the tortious act of conversion.

The bank gave no notice of its intention to accelerate its notes and to apply the bank account to discharge the debt, which was already secured by purchase money security interests. Instead, stampeded by the thought that it might become embroiled in a dispute with one of its friendly correspondents, the Bank of Allison decided to deem itself insecure and satisfy the notes through Uhlenhopp's bank funds rather than the chattel security. There is no way for us to know to what extent such harsh and unilateral action may have contributed to Uhlenhopp's bankruptcy, which followed in its wake, and that question is not before us.

It is, however, well settled that a bank has a right to set off funds deposited with it in an account of general deposit against a debt owed it by the depositor if the debt is mature or, if the debt is not mature, if the depositor is insolvent. E.g., Olsen v. Harlan National Bank, 162 N.W.2d 755, 759 (Iowa 1968); 9 C.J.S. Banks and Banking § 296 (1938); 10 Am.Jur.2d Banks §§ 666–70 (1963). Here the debt was mature at the time of the setoff if the bank had properly accelerated the due date of Uhlenhopp's loans.

The Iowa statute applicable to acceleration clauses, I.C.A. § 554.1208 (1967), provides:

> A term providing that one party or his successor in interest may accelerate payment or performance or require collateral or addition-

al collateral 'at will' or 'when he deems himself insecure' or in words of similar import shall be construed to mean that he shall have power to do so only if he in good faith believes that the prospect of payment or performance is impaired. The burden of establishing lack of good faith is on the party against whom the power has been exercised.

Good faith is presumed when a creditor accelerates a debt. Sheppard Federal Credit Union v. Palmer, 408 F.2d 1369 (5th Cir. 1969) (applying Texas law). While the bank's judgment in deeming itself insecure upon discovering a prior filed financing statement is clearly open to question, and its heavy-handed treatment of its customer without prior notification is cause for dismay, we cannot say that the District Court's finding of good faith is clearly erroneous. See Fed.R. Civ.P. 52(a).[8]

While notice to the debtor is generally not required before a debt can be accelerated, the holder of an instrument who seeks to accelerate its maturity date must take some positive action to exercise his option to declare payments due under an acceleration clause in the instrument, to avoid waiving his rights to do so. Here the setoff constituted sufficient affirmative action. The debt was therefore mature at the time of the setoff.

The only remaining question is whether the bank was required to exhaust the collateral in which it retained a security interest before performing the setoff. The Iowa courts have not addressed the question, and in view of substantial majority authority to the contrary, we decline to assume that Iowa would adopt the rule proposed by appellant that a bank must first exhaust its collateral before setting off funds it has on deposit. The Washington Court of Appeals recently considered the question in Allied Sheet Metal Fabricators, Inc. v. Peoples National Bank, 10 Wash.App. 530, 518 P.2d 734, cert. denied, 419 U.S. 967, 95 S.Ct. 231, 42 L.Ed.2d 183 (1974):

> Allied argues, however, that the foregoing general rule permitting a setoff in the case of a demand note does not apply until after the bank exhausts its primary collateral security, and Peoples failed to do this. In this regard, Allied relies primarily upon an early California case, McKean v. German-American Sav. Bank, 118 Cal. 334, 50 P. 656 (1897); however, *McKean* states a minority view, and we decline to follow it. The position adopted by the majority of modern jurisdictions is well expressed in Olsen v. Valley Nat'l Bank, 91 Ill.App.2d 365, 371, 234 N.E.2d 547, 550 (1968), as follows:
>
> > A bank should not be deprived of its right of set-off simply because it has the foresight to obtain collateral in exchange for obligations owed to it. The majority rule, including Illinois, is

---

8. The record does not indicate whether the State Bank of Allison had taken those steps required of it under I.C.A. § 554.9312 (1967) to insure that its purchase money security interest in Uhlenhopp's cattle had priority over all other security interests in the cattle.

founded on the rationale that a creditor is able to pursue any one of a number of remedies against a debtor until the debt is satisfied. The minority rule is based upon the rule or statute that there is but one action for the recovery of a debt which is secured by collateral.

Although there appears to be no Washington authority directly in point, we are persuaded that the better reasoned view is that expressed in *Olsen* which recognizes the multiple remedies of a creditor, and therefore we apply that rule to the case at bar.

518 P.2d at 739; accord, Keller v. Commercial Credit Co., 149 Or. 372, 40 P.2d 1018 (1935) (prevailing view is that collateral need not be exhausted before setoff); see Kress v. Central Trust Co., 153 Misc. 397, 275 N.Y.S. 14 (1934), aff'd, 246 App.Div. 76, 283 N.Y.S. 467 (1935), aff'd, 272 N.Y.S. 629, 5 N.E.2d 365 (1936) (in accord with majority rule); Harper v. First State Bank, 3 S.W.2d 552 (Tex.Civ.App.1928) (in accord with majority rule); see Annot. 96 A.L.R. 1240 (1935). No double advantage was gained by the bank's resort to setoff rights; the bank promptly released its security interest in the cattle.

We therefore uphold the conclusion of the District Court that the bank's setoff did not amount to wrongful conversion under Iowa law. The judgment is affirmed.

Notes & Questions

1. *Honoring State Setoff Doctrine.* Bankruptcy law subjects many state statutory liens to scrutiny, including those in *Saberman* and *Holt*, supra. See § 545. Should the same bankruptcy law automatically honor state setoff doctrine in cases like *Jensen*? What role will preference doctrine play in setoff cases under the new act?

2. *Selling Claims.* Debtor has $2,000 on deposit in Bank A. Bank A has lent Debtor $1,000, which is overdue. Debtor owes X $1,000 on an unsecured claim. Bank A and X expect Debtor to go bankrupt and expect that unsecured claims will receive about $.10 on the dollar. May Bank A pay X $500 for X's claim against Debtor? See § 553(a)(2).

3. *The Mechanics of § 553.* Atlas Corp. is a manufacturer with an outstanding one-year term loan with Bank of $1 million, due July 1, 1982. On April 1, 1982 Atlas filed a voluntary petition under Chapter 11 of the Bankruptcy Act. Ninety days before the filing of the petition, Atlas had $75,000 on deposit in its general account with Bank. On April 1, Atlas had $100,000 in its general account and a $50,000 time deposit maturing on August 1, 1982.

  (a) May Bank setoff the $100,000 in Atlas's general account on March 25, 1982? May Bank setoff against the $50,000 time deposit on March 25? May Bank setoff against either deposit on April 2, 1982? See § 362(a)(7). If Bank exercises its right of setoff on March 25, will the trustee be able to recover any portion of the setoff amount? See § 553(b).

(b) Assume that on March 25 Bank expects Atlas to soon file a bankruptcy petition. If the account balances on March 25 are the same as given above for April 1, should Bank consider waiting until *after* bankruptcy to exercise its right of setoff?

(c) May Atlas, as the debtor-in-possession, use the funds in its general account? See §§ 542(b); 506(a); 363(c).

See generally Ahart, Bank Setoff Under the Bankruptcy Reform Act of 1978, 53 Am.Bankr.L.J. 205 (1979); Clark, Bank Exercise of Setoff: Avoiding the Pitfalls, 98 Banking L.J. 196 (1981).

Chapter 15

SPECIAL ASPECTS OF CHAPTER 13

HOUSE REPORT NO. 95-595, 95th CONG., 1st SESS. 118 (1977)

The purpose of chapter 13 is to enable an individual, under court supervision and protection, to develop and perform under a plan for the repayment of his debts over an extended period. In some cases, the plan will call for full repayment. In others, it may offer creditors a percentage of their claims in full settlement. During the repayment period, creditors may not harass the debtor or seek to collect their debts. They must receive payments only under the plan. This protection relieves the debtor from indirect and direct pressures from creditors, and enables him to support himself and his dependents while repaying his creditors at the same time.

The benefit to the debtor of developing a plan of repayment under chapter 13, rather than opting for liquidation under chapter 7, is that it permits the debtor to protect his assets. In a liquidation case, the debtor must surrender his nonexempt assets for liquidation and sale by the trustee. Under chapter 13, the debtor may retain his property by agreeing to repay his creditors. Chapter 13 also protects a debtor's credit standing far better than a straight bankruptcy, because he is viewed by the credit industry as a better risk. In addition, it satisfies many debtors' desire to avoid the stigma attached to straight bankruptcy and to retain the pride attendant on being able to meet one's obligations. The benefit to creditors is self-evident: their losses will be significantly less than if their debtors opt for straight bankruptcy.

Problem

John Debtor is in financial difficulty and is considering filing a bankruptcy petition. On January 31 he seeks your advice as to whether to file a petition and, if you believe he should, your recommendation as to which chapter of the Bankruptcy Act he should file under. Debtor's assets and liabilities are as follows:

Assets

Home ($5,000 protected by state homestead exemption)	$45,000
Personal property exempt under state law	5,000
Other property not exempt ª under state law	2,000

Liabilities

Home mortgage (20 years)	$35,000	
Medium term bank loan (5 years)	15,000	
Tort judgment	20,000	
Child support	500	(per month)
Medical bills	3,500	
Wages owed that were earned by an employee within the last 60 days	500	

Debtor's monthly expenses are as follows:

Miscellaneous	100
Home mortgage	350
Bank loan	500
Taxes (real estate)	100
Food and clothing	150
Child support	500
	$ 1,700

a. For the questionable view that there are no exemptions in Chapter 13, see In re Aycock, 15 B.R. 728 (Bkrtcy.E.D.N.C. 1981). But see In re Hall, 752 F.2d 582 (11th Cir.1985); Baldwin v. Avco Financial Services, 22 B.R. 507 (D.Del. 1982).

Debtor's monthly disposable income is $1,350. He expects to receive a raise every year. Debtor is two months behind on the bank loan and one month behind on his mortgage payments. He wishes to maintain good relations with his doctor as he regularly needs medical attention. On December 31 Debtor paid $5,000 to the doctor (the $3,500 above is the remaining balance due).

What would be the likely outcome for debtor if he filed under Chapter 7 of the Bankruptcy Act? Can you propose a confirmable Chapter 13 plan that might yield results more appealing to Debtor? Keep this problem in mind as you read the cases that follow.

A. Minimum Payments to Creditors

IN RE RIMGALE

United States Court of Appeals, Seventh Circuit, 1982.
669 F.2d 426.

CUMMINGS, CHIEF JUDGE.

This appeal presents for the first time in the Seventh Circuit the need to construe Section 1325 of the Bankruptcy Reform Act, 11 U.S.C. § 1325 (1978). Donald Rimgale, the Chapter 13 debtor, filed a plan that proposed to pay $120 a month for 42 months to various unsecured creditors. The largest of the claims represented a tort judgment owed to Mary Ravenot. Although the judgment debt would not have been dischargeable in a straight Chapter 7 bankruptcy under 11 U.S.C. § 523(a)(4) or (6), it could be discharged under the more generous provisions that obtain once a Chapter 13 plan is successfully completed. 11 U.S.C. § 1328(a). The bankruptcy judge confirmed Rimgale's proposed plan over the objections of Mary Ravenot's representative. On appeal, the district judge reversed. Because we cannot endorse either the district judge's construction of the statute or the bankruptcy judge's cursory inquiry into the debtor's good faith in proposing the plan, we remand for additional proceedings in the bankruptcy court.

I. The Statutory Background

One of Congress' purposes in enacting the Bankruptcy Reform Act of 1978 was to make the old Chapter XIII provisions more accessible and attractive to individual debtors. Liberalized provisions, Congress reasoned, would benefit both debtors and creditors. Debtors would be given more latitude to work out debt composition plans, thus avoiding the stigma of straight backruptcy. Creditors would receive total or substantial repayment under a Chapter 13 plan, but little or nothing in a Chapter 7 liquidation.

To make Chapter 13 work, Congress altered the old Chapter XIII in three important ways. First, it expanded the class of debtors who could take advantage of Chapter 13. Formerly restricted to wage-earner debtors, Chapter 13 was made available to any individual with regular income, whether from wages or other sources.[3] Second, Congress eliminated the requirement that a plan be approved by a majority of unsecured creditors. Concerned that in the past short-sighted and stubborn creditors had blocked feasible plans, Congress provided for creditors to be heard, 11 U.S.C. § 1324, but gave the bankruptcy judge the sole authority to confirm or reject a plan. It also set out the criteria he was to use, 11 U.S.C. § 1325:

3. The effect of this change is to make Chapter 13 available to pensioners, social security recipients, self-employed people, professional people (except stockbrokers and commodity brokers), proprietors of small businesses, and certain farmers. J. Lee, Chapter 13 nee Chapter XIII, 53 Amer.Bankruptcy L.J. 303, 304 (1979).

(a) The court shall confirm a plan if—

(1) the plan complies with the provisions of this chapter and with other applicable provisions of this title;

(2) any fee, charge, or amount required under chapter 123 of title 28, or by the plan, to be paid before confirmation, has been paid;

(3) the plan has been proposed in good faith and not by any means forbidden by law;

(4) the value, as of the effective date of the plan, of property to be distributed under the plan on account of each allowed unsecured claim is not less than the amount that would be paid on such claim if the estate of the debtor were liquidated under chapter 7 of this title on such date;

(5) with respect to each allowed secured claim provided for by the plan—

(A) the holder of such claim has accepted the plan;

(B)(i) the plan provides that the holder of such claim retain the lien securing such claim; and

(ii) the value, as of the effective date of the plan, of property to be distributed under the plan on account of such claim is not less than the allowed amount of such claim; or

(C) the debtor surrenders the property securing such claim to such holder; and

(6) the debtor will be able to make all payments under the plan and to comply with the plan.

Finally, Congress added an incentive for debtors to complete performance under the confirmed plan. 11 U.S.C. § 1328 provides that a debtor who has carried out his plan is entitled to a discharge of virtually all debts provided for in the plan or disallowed.[5] Thus a Chapter 13 debtor may be discharged from a variety of debts that a Chapter 7 bankrupt remains obligated to pay at the conclusion of a liquidation.

The statutory modification of Chapter 13 has had both intended and unintended effects. The number of Chapter 13 cases has increased sharply.[6] Many of them correspond closely to the idealized case Congress had in mind when it wrote the legislation: the debtor, given time and relief from harassment, is able to pay all or most of his debts. Increasingly, however, bankruptcy courts are seeing cases like the one before us, in which debtors propose less substantial, or even nominal, payments under a Chapter 13 plan, in order eventually to take advan-

5. Section 1328(a) exempts from discharge certain long-term indebtedness and alimony and child support payments.

6. The following table is adapted from the 1981 Annual Report of the Director of the Administrative Office of the United States Courts, p. 10.

Filings During the Twelve-Month Periods Ended June 30, 1979 Through 1981

	Chapter XIII	Chapter 13
1979	39,442	
1980	11,322	68,674
1981	56	128,225

tage of Chapter 13's generous discharge provisions. Our task is to determine whether such a plan is permissible under the legislation Congress has drafted. In so doing, we are not free to rewrite the legislation as we think best, but neither are we able to ignore the broad equitable principles that have characteristically animated American bankruptcy law.

II. Rimgale's Chapter 13 Plans

Donald Rimgale filed an original and two amended Chapter 13 plans in the bankruptcy court. Each involved about $6200 of unsecured consumer debt owed to half a dozen creditors, none with enough at stake apparently to file objections to the plan. Each also involved, and offered differing treatments of, a much larger debt owed to Mary Ravenot, the only creditor on whose behalf objections were made.

On May 24, 1979, the Circuit Court of Cook County, Chancery Division, entered a tort judgment against Rimgale and his wife Alice. Alice Rimgale had been employed as a psychiatric nurse at St. Joseph's Hospital in Joliet, Illinois, and had cared for Mary Ravenot, a twenty-six-year-old widow then undergoing psychiatric treatment and since adjudged incompetent. The Rimgales first won Mrs. Ravenot's confidence, then induced her to turn over to them all the proceeds of her husband's life insurance. The judgment against the Rimgales had the following components: (1) compensatory damages of $29,743 and $3,988.39 in prejudgment interest, for which the Rimgales were jointly and severally liable; (2) punitive damages of $5,000 against Donald Rimgale alone; and (3) attorney's fees and costs amounting to $8,857.75, again assessed against Donald Rimgale alone, based on his false pleading and bad faith in the tort litigation.[7] The judge also imposed a constructive trust in Mary Ravenot's favor on real and personal property acquired with the insurance money, including the Rimgales' house in Coal City, Illinois. What part of the judgment debt is secured by the constructive trust is a matter of dispute. Until the filing of the bankruptcy, Mrs. Ravenot had garnished Rimgale's wages in the amount of $264 per month.

Rimgale's first plan, offered on December 18, 1979, listed Mary Ravenot's debt as entirely unsecured, treated both the compensatory damages and the attorney's fees as joint obligations of Donald and Alice Rimgale, and omitted the $5,000 in punitive damages altogether. The plan characterized that portion of the tort debt it listed as "disputed," although the judgment had become final. The plan proposed to make no payments whatsoever to Mary Ravenot. Payments of $110 a month over thirty-six months would, according to the petition, pay 45% of the other unsecured claims.

The first amended plan, filed on April 3, 1980, has been lost and can be only partially reconstructed. It represented that $55 semi-monthly

7. Alice Rimgale never appeared, and a default judgment was entered against her.

payments over thirty-six months would pay one-third of the unsecured claims, but did not change the amount or proposed nonpayment of Mary Ravenot's claim.

The second amended plan, filed on July 10, 1980, attempted to meet the objections of Mrs. Ravenot. It treated her debt as partly secured and partly unsecured. It estimated that she would receive $25,000 from the sale of the Rimgale house,[12] making the unsecured part of her claim $24,799.54. It increased payments under the plan to $120 a month and extended the term of the plan from thirty-six to forty-two months. An estimated 11% of unsecured claims would be paid. Mrs. Ravenot would receive about $2,700. This version of the plan was confirmed by bankruptcy judge Robert Eisen over the objections of Mrs. Ravenot's representative. Judge Eisen also lifted the automatic stay to permit Mrs. Ravenot's lawyers to set in motion the sale of the Coal City house.

III. The Appeal to Judge Decker

Mrs. Ravenot thereupon appealed the confirmation order to the district court. There were three bases for the appeal. First, Mrs. Ravenot argued that she was not receiving at least as much as she would receive in a Chapter 7 liquidation, because her debt could not be discharged under Chapter 7 but would be discharged at the completion of a Chapter 13 plan. The plan therefore did not meet the "best interests" test of Section 1325(a)(4), infra. Second, Mrs. Ravenot contended that the plan had not been proposed in good faith and therefore violated Section 1325(a)(3). Third, Mrs. Ravenot argued that the bankruptcy judge had unduly restricted her arguments against the plan, contrary to the spirit of Section 1324. Judge Decker based his decision for Mrs. Ravenot on the first ground. In re Rimgale, No. 80 C 4862 (N.D.Ill., February 21, 1981). He found that the value of a nondischargeable claim for the whole of the unsecured debt could not easily be quantified. Nonetheless, he assumed that Mrs. Ravenot's objections were a sufficient indication that the claim under Chapter 7 was worth more than the $2,700 she would receive over a forty-two month period under the Chapter 13 plan. Because he found the failure to meet the "best interests" test dispositive, Judge Decker did not reach the good-faith or due process issues.

---

12. In his original petition Rimgale had said his house was worth $48,000 and was mortgaged for $57,384. He did not list the mortgagee, Heritage First National Bank of Lockport, as a partially unsecured creditor. In objecting to the plan, Mrs. Ravenot's attorneys submitted an appraisal of the house showing a market value of $75,000. That figure is evidently the one relied upon in the final version of the plan, although $25,000 overstates the amount Mrs. Ravenot could realize after the mort-gages were satisfied. At oral argument this Court was advised that while the appeal was pending the bankruptcy court had allowed the mortgagee to foreclose on the property and that there were no proceeds, after the foreclosure sale, to transmit to Mrs. Ravenot. It is clear from the foregoing that Mrs. Ravenot's whole claim must be treated henceforth as unsecured, and that the percentage of unsecured claims that the plan would pay must accordingly be revised downward.

IV.　The Appeal to this Court

Donald Rimgale has challenged Judge Decker's interpretation of the statute in this Court. We agree that Judge Decker's analysis cannot stand. The language of the "best interests" test in Section 1325(a)(4) precludes it:

> [T]he value, as of the effective date of the plan, of property to be distributed under the plan on account of each unsecured claim [must] not [be] less than the amount that would be paid on such claim if the estate of the debtor were liquidated under chapter 7 of this title on such date.

What is to be compared is the total of the payments to the creditor, discounted to present value, and the amount the creditor would receive in a straight liquidation. "[T]he amount that would be paid *on such claim* if the estate of the debtor were liquidated" (emphasis added) does not include additional amounts that a creditor may be able to collect *after* a liquidation, if he can keep the judgment alive. Accord, In re Syrus, 12 B.R. 605, 608 (Bkrtcy., D.Kans.1981). If Judge Decker's interpretation were right, any creditor with a nondischargeable debt could block a Chapter 13 plan by insisting that his claim might some day be satisfiable in full. Such a creditor would have a virtual veto over a Chapter 13 plan, while ordinary unsecured creditors have not even a vote. The generous discharge provisions of Chapter 13 would be illusory, subject to abrogation whenever a creditor with the sort of claim they cover objected to the plan. As a *quid pro quo* for not objecting, such a creditor might be able to insist on specific levels of repayment, although the statute itself has no explicit minimum payment requirement. In short, this reading of the "best interests" test undercuts the limiting of creditors' power and the inducement of broad discharges, both integral parts of Congress' revision of Chapter 13.

We cannot accept Rimgale's further argument, however, that Congress intended the confirmation of Chapter 13 plans to be routine if the "best interests" test is met. In eliminating the requirement that a majority of creditors approve a plan, Congress did not also eliminate all scrutiny of plans. Instead it transferred the decision to the bankruptcy judge, aided by the Chapter 13 trustee. It is the bankruptcy court's duty to evaluate the good faith of the plan under Section 1325(a)(3). As the Eighth Circuit has noted,

> "[a] comprehensive definition of good faith is not practical. Broadly speaking, the basic inquiry should be whether or not under the circumstances of the case there has been abuse of the provisions, purpose, or spirit of [the Chapter] in the proposal . . .."

> In re Terry, 630 F.2d 634, 635 (8th Cir. 1980), (quoting 9 Collier on Bankruptcy, ¶ 9.20 at 319 (14th ed. 1978)).

This inquiry imposes a considerable responsibility on bankruptcy judges. And the conduct comprehended under the rubric "good faith" will have to be defined on a case-by-case basis as the courts encounter various problems in the administration of Chapter 13's provisions.

We would emphasize only a few points. The legislative history suggests that Congress intended Chapter 13 for the benefit of debtors who could, given time, satisfy their creditors in full or in substantial measure. Nonetheless, Congress eschewed setting any minimum levels of repayment that a debtor must propose to qualify for Chapter 13 relief. Thus good faith cannot be treated as a license to read into the statute requirements Congress did not enact, e.g., a requirement that a plan pay 70% of unsecured claims to qualify for the discharge benefits. Nor can good faith be defined as the absence of any conduct that would traditionally have barred discharge, without rendering Chapter 13's discharge provisions nugatory. But the opposite extreme, that the good-faith requirement adds nothing to the other criteria for confirmation, is equally unsupportable.

We therefore agree with the analysis of District Judge Ingram in In re Burrell, 6 B.R. 360 (N.D.Cal.1980). He held that a flat 70% repayment requirement was erroneous and remanded to the bankruptcy judge for proceedings on the good-faith issue.

> The correct approach . . . is to treat the issues of substantiality and best effort as elements of good faith. Unless the courts have discretion to consider such factors, the danger exists that Chapter 13 plans could become shams that would emasculate the safeguards that Congress has included in Chapter 7 to prevent debtor abuse of the bankruptcy laws. The courts retain discretion to prevent such abuse, and that discretion can be exercised effectively through a meaningful interpretation of the good faith requirement of § 1325(a) (3). In each case, the bankruptcy court must consider the debtor's entire circumstances to determine whether his plan proposes to make meaningful payments to unsecured creditors. In making that determination, the courts should be mindful of the fact that the unsecured creditors must rely on the court to give meaning to the congressional intent that they receive substantial payments. Within these guidelines, the courts should proceed on a case-by-case basis. 6 B.R. 360, 366.

The following list, by no means exhaustive, is intended to guide the bankruptcy judge's inquiry on remand:

(1) Does the proposed plan state Rimgale's secured and unsecured debts accurately?[18]

(2) Does it state Rimgale's expenses accurately?[19]

---

18. For example, it appears that the first and perhaps subsequent petitions should have listed Rimgale's mortgagee as both a secured and unsecured creditor. There is still dispute about the size of Mary Ravenot's claim (she filed a claim for $51,079.01, but the petition in its final form lists a claim for $49,799.54). Proba-

bly no part of that claim can now be treated as secured, note 12 supra. And no effort has been made to describe what happened to the assets subject to the constructive trust, other than the house.

19. For example, the petitions listed $600 in child support payments. At the

(3) Is the percentage of repayment of unsecured claims correct?[20]

(4) If there are or have been deficiencies in the plan, do the inaccuracies amount to an attempt to mislead the bankruptcy court?[21]

(5) Do the proposed payments indicate "a fundamental fairness in dealing with one's creditors," In re Beaver, 2 B.R. 337, 340 (Bkrtcy.S.D.Cal.1980)?[22]

If the court does undertake to ascertain the good faith of this petition in a more than perfunctory way, Mrs. Ravenot's due process objections will of necessity be overcome.

The judgment of the district court is vacated and the case remanded to the bankruptcy court for further proceedings consistent with this opinion. Costs to appellant.

Notes & Questions

1. *The "Disposable Income" Amendment to § 1325(b).* In 1984, Congress added § 1325(b)(1)(B) and (2) to the confirmation standards for Chapter 13 plans. See also § 1225 (confirmation standard for family farmer plans). A plan cannot be confirmed over an unsecured claimant's objection unless the claimant is to be paid in full or "the plan provides that all of the debtor's projected disposable income to be received in the three-year period" of the plan be applied to payments under the plan. § 1325(b)(1). Section 1325(b)(2) defines "disposable

time of the original petition, no divorce decree had been entered. At the time of the first amended petition, Rimgale was under order to pay $735 per month, but if he had listed that figure his estimated surplus of $210 per month would have dwindled to $75 and confirmation would have been denied under Section 1325(a)(6) ("the debtor will be able to make all payments under the plan and to comply with the plan"). By the time of the second amended petition, one of the Rimgale children had died, and the court had accordingly reduced the payments to $617. That figure is subject to revision as the needs of the Rimgale children change.

20. For $3,960 to pay 45% of unsecured claims, the total of such claims should be $8,800. The original petition listed claims totaling $6,165.61. For $3,960 to pay 33% of unsecured claims, as the first amended petition advertised, such claims should total $12,000. Estimates of percentage repayment under the final plan range from a high of 17% (Rimgale) and 11% (Ravenot) if the Ravenot debt is partially secured, to a low of 9% (Rimgale) and 5% (Ravenot) if it is entirely unsecured. In simple arithmetical terms, the petitions are so defective that they do not permit an informed decision about confirmation.

21. Donald Rimgale was represented in the state tort action and in these bankruptcy proceedings by the same attorney. Under the circumstances one might expect a more careful and knowledgeable preparation of the petition. Furthermore Rimgale, with this attorney acting for him, has a history of making false statements in judicial proceedings, as the Circuit Court's award of attorney's fees and costs attests.

22. In this connection, the bankruptcy court may wish to examine the timing of the bankruptcy filings, the proportion of the total unsecured debt that is represented by the Ravenot judgment, and the equities of classifying together ordinary consumer debt and a judgment debt arising out of intentionally tortious conduct. See In re Sanders, 13 B.R. 320, 322–323 (Bkrtcy.D.Kans.1981) (classification of claims governed by Section 1122, which provides that "a plan may place a claim or an interest in a particular class only if such claim or interest is substantially similar to the other claims or interests of such class"; claims subject to discharge only under Chapter 13 are not "substantially similar" to fully dischargeable claims).

income" to mean income not reasonably necessary for the maintenance
or support of the debtor or a dependent and not reasonably necessary
for the continuation, preservation, and operation of the debtor's business.

How does the amendment change analysis of the "good faith" issue
in *Rimgale?* How should a court analyze a Chapter 13 plan that calls
for no payments to creditors for want of any disposable income?

2. *Advantages of Chapter 13.* In addition to the factors mentioned
in *Rimgale* there are other reasons for a debtor to prefer Chapter 13
over Chapter 7. See, e.g., §§ 1306(b), 1322(b)(3), 1322(b)(9), 1325(a)(5)(B).
Are these differences justifiable? How frequently may a debtor invoke
Chapter 13? See § 1328. How often may a debtor invoke Chapter 7?
See § 727(a)(8), (9).

3. *Disadvantages of Chapter 13.* Are there any disadvantages to
Chapter 13 in addition to the disposable income requirement? See
§ 1322(a)(2). Note the enhanced estate under § 1306. In In re
Koonce, 54 B.R. 643 (Bkrtcy.D.S.C.1985), the debtor won $1.3 million
in a state lottery two years after his Chapter 13 plan was confirmed.
The bankruptcy judge ordered an increase to a 100% dividend to
creditors. See also Education Assistance Corp. v. Zellner, 827 F.2d
1222 (8th Cir.1987) (post-petition lump-sum payment from retirement fund may become property of the estate in Chapter 13).

4. *The Hypothetical Liquidation.* Section 1325(a)(4) requires the
bankruptcy judge to conduct a hypothetical Chapter 7 liquidating
distribution to be sure that each unsecured claimant is receiving in
Chapter 13 at least what the claimant would have received in Chapter
7. To what extent must the hypothetical Chapter 7 distribution reflect
what might actually have happened had the debtor filed under Chapter
7? How does *Rimgale* deal with this issue? See also Education
Assistance Corp. v. Zellner, supra.

In In re Elkind, 11 B.R. 473 (Bkrtcy.D.Colo.1981), a judgment creditor objected to confirmation of a Chapter 13 plan on the ground that
the plan did not provide creditors holding unsecured claims what they
would receive if the debtors' estate were liquidated under Chapter 7.
The creditor alleged that the debtor had made a preferential transfer
which could be set aside by a liquidating trustee, thus increasing the
amount available for distribution to unsecured claimholders. The court
denied confirmation on the basis of § 1325(a)(4).

Does the trustee have the same avoiding powers in Chapter 13 that
he has in Chapter 7? See §§ 1303, 1304; In re Walls, 17 B.R. 701
(Bkrtcy.S.D.W.Va.1982); In re Colandrea, 17 B.R. 568 (Bkrtcy.D.Md.
1982). Does the debtor have any avoiding powers in Chapter 13? See
In re Hall, 26 B.R. 10 (Bkrtcy.M.D.Fla.1982) (yes); In re Walls, supra
(debtor needs trustee's approval to exercise avoiding powers).

5. *Creditor Approval.* Do creditors have any say in whether a
Chapter 13 plan is confirmed? Should they? Is the test of § 1325 an
adequate substitute for creditor approval?

6. *Empirical Data About Debtors' Ability to Repay Debts.* Some of the impetus for the above 1984 Amendment comes from a perception that too many Chapter 13 debtors were proposing zero payment plans, and that many bankruptcy debtors were able to pay more of their debts than the law required. To what extent should the availability of discharge, or the requirement of minimum payments, be shaped by empirical findings about the ability of past debtors to repay? [b]

7. *Involuntary Chapter 13 Plans.* Notice that § 303 does not provide for involuntary Chapter 13 cases. Should it? Consider the following:

> [P]roposals have been made to Congress from time to time that a debtor able to obtain relief under Chapter XIII should be denied relief in straight bankruptcy, and the Commission has received communications expressing support for a change in the Bankruptcy Act to this effect. . . .

> The arguments against the proposal included objections made to the difficulties of achieving any national uniform standard of application by referees throughout the country, as evidenced by the divergence of their viewpoints regarding the virtues of Chapter XIII. Another view expressed by opponents was that fulfillment of a debtor's commitment made pursuant to a Chapter XIII plan requires not merely a debtor's consent but a positive determination by him and his family to live within the constraints imposed by the plan during its entire term and will to persevere with the plan to the end. Imposition of a Chapter XIII plan on an unwilling debtor, it was said, would be almost bound to encourage the debtor to change employment and, if necessary, to move to another area to escape the importuning calls and correspondence of his creditors. Likewise, those petitioning debtors turned away by the court on the ground that they failed to show that relief would not be obtainable under Chapter XIII would be motivated to change jobs and locations to get away from creditors who would threaten garnishment and other means of collecting debts. In states where wage garnishment is an unavailable remedy of creditors, the impact of the proposed legislation would have been minimal. A final argument made in opposition to the proposed legislation was that business debtors are not subject to any limitation on the availability of straight bankruptcy relief, including discharge from debts, and it was pointed out that, quite apart from bankruptcy, business debtors are able to incorpo-

b. A Purdue study about the ability of debtors to repay debts generated one interesting exchange. See Credit Research Center, Krannert School of Management, Purdue University, Monograph No. 23, Consumer Bankruptcy Study Vol. I, Consumers' Right to Bankruptcy: Origins and Effects 88–91 (1982); Sullivan, Warren, and Westbrook, Limiting Access to Bankruptcy Discharge: An Analysis of the Creditors' Data, 1983 Wisc.L.Rev. 1091; Sulli-van, Reply: Limiting Access to Bankruptcy Discharge, 1984 Wisc.L.Rev. 1069. For other debate about the discharge, see Eisenberg, Bankruptcy Law in Perspective, 28 UCLA L.Rev. 953, 977–87 (1981); Harris, A Reply to Theodore Eisenberg's Bankruptcy Law in Perspective, 30 UCLA L.Rev. 327, 351–58 (1982); Eisenberg, Bankruptcy Law in Perspective: A Rejoinder, 30 UCLA L.Rev. 617, 622–26 (1983).

rate and to limit their liability to their investments in corporate assets. To force unwilling wage earners to devote their future earnings to payment of past debts smacked to some of debt peonage, particularly when business debtors could not be subjected to the same kind of regimen under the Bankruptcy Act.

The Commission has considered the arguments made for conditioning the availability of bankruptcy relief, including discharge, on a showing by the debtor that he cannot obtain adequate relief from his condition of financial distress by proposing a plan for payment of his debts out of his future earnings. The Commission has concluded that forced participation by a debtor in a plan requiring contributions out of future income has so little prospect for success that it should not be adopted as a feature of the bankruptcy system.

Commission Report, pt. I, at 158–59. Consider also the following exchange:

Mr. Klee. Is there a distinction between a compulsory chapter XIII, which may have been before this subcommittee, and a discretionary chapter XIII . . . [?]

Mr. Countryman. The proposal which was before this subcommittee was to give the bankruptcy judges discretion to decide whether this man should be forced into chapter XIII. And my recollection at that time was that every bankruptcy judge I talked to . . . was opposed to it. . . .

Mr. Klee. Do you think there are any constitutional limitations, perhaps in the 13th amendment, that would prohibit Congress from legally passing such a provision?

Mr. Countryman. I would be prepared to so argue, and I would also be prepared to argue that it was an invidious discrimination that would violate the due process clause—we do not have any equal protection clause for the Federal Government—to have such a compulsory plan for wage earners only.

Bankruptcy Act Revision: Hearings on H.R. 31 and H.R. 32 Before the Subcomm. on Civil and Constitutional Rights of the House Comm. on the Judiciary, 94th Cong., 1st & 2nd Sess., pt. 1, at 347–48 (1975–76). Can you make persuasive arguments along the lines suggested by Professor Countryman? See In re Noonan, 17 B.R. 793 (Bkrtcy. S.D.N.Y.1982) (taking involuntary servitude argument seriously).

B. Classification of Claims

BARNES v. WHELAN

United States Court of Appeals, District of Columbia Circuit, 1982.
689 F.2d 193.

ROBB, SENIOR CIRCUIT JUDGE: In these consolidated cases the District Court reversed in part decisions of the Bankruptcy Court refusing to confirm Chapter 13 debt adjustment plans filed by appellees Wavalene N. Barnes and Abel Montano. The trustees in bankruptcy appeal, urging us to reinstate the Bankruptcy Court's decisions. Both plans provide that secured creditors or creditors holding cosigned debts receive full payment of the amounts owed them, but that other creditors receive only nominal payments. The central issue on appeal, a controversial question of bankruptcy law undecided in this circuit, is whether the "good faith" requirement for confirmation of personal bankruptcy plans under 11 U.S.C. § 1325(a)(3) bars approval of plans proposing only such nominal payments. We adhere to the traditional meaning of good faith and hold that section 1325(a)(3) does not require any particular level of repayment to unsecured creditors. We also consider the classification of claims, an issue raised by Montano as cross-appellant in No. 81–1825, and hold that Chapter 13 plans may generally classify unsecured debts based on the presence of a co-debtor, but that Montano's plan as presently drafted "unfairly discriminates" between cosigned and non-cosigned debts under 11 U.S.C. § 1322(b)(1). . . .

In February 1980 Montano filed a debt adjustment plan with the United States Bankruptcy Court for the District of Columbia. Montano is employed as a clerk at the World Bank in the District of Columbia and earns a net income of $948 per month. His plan listed expenses of $749 per month for himself, his wife, and one dependent child, leaving an excess of approximately $200 per month available for repayment of his debts. His unsecured indebtedness totalled $31,507, and there were no secured creditors. Montano's plan proposed monthly payments of $200, the full amount available, to be applied as follows: (1) one hundred percent payments to the unsecured creditors with claims guaranteed by cosigners, totalling approximately $7,000; and (2) one percent payments to the remaining unsecured creditors, with claims totalling $24,500. . . .

. . . The Bankruptcy Court . . . issued an opinion denying confirmation of Montano's plan. In re Montano, 4 B.R. 535 (Bkrtcy. D.D.C.1980). The court ruled that in order to satisfy the "good faith" requirement of 11 U.S.C. § 1325(a)(3), the debtor must propose "a plan of meaningful repayment," adding "[t]he court, in determining 'meaningfulness,' will look at each plan on a case-by-case basis, weighing both the interests of creditors and the debtors in light of the rehabilitative goals of Chapter 13." *Montano*, 4 B.R. at 539. The court concluded that Montano's plan, offering one hundred percent repayment to creditors holding cosigned debts and only one percent to all others, "fails to propose meaningful repayment . . .." Id. The Bankruptcy Court also rejected Montano's attempt to treat debts guaranteed by cosigners more favorably than non-cosigned debts, ruling "a plan may classify only on the basis of substantial similarity" between claims, and that the "mere existence of a co-debtor is not legally sufficient to justify separate classification." Id. at 537. The court denied confirmation on both the "good faith" and classification grounds. . . .

The District Court agreed with the Bankruptcy Court that 11 U.S.C. § 1122(a) did not allow separate treatment solely on the basis that certain debts were guaranteed by a cosigner. Id. The District Court ruled that Montano's classification also failed because it discriminated unfairly between unsecured creditors in contravention of 11 U.S.C. § 1322(b)(1). . . .

II. CLASSIFICATION OF DEBTS

Montano's Chapter 13 plan distributes his available monthly income so that creditors holding cosigned debts guaranteed by third parties receive one hundred percent payment, while all other unsecured creditors receive only one percent of their claims. The trustee argues that this arrangement is an improper classification under 11 U.S.C. § 1322(b)(1). That provision states:

> [T]he plan may . . . designate a class or classes of unsecured claims, as provided in section 1122 of this title, but may not discriminate unfairly against any class so designated . . ..

Section 1122, referred to in the language immediately above, reads in full as follows:

> (a) Except as provided in subsection (b) of this section, a plan may place a claim or an interest in a particular class only if such claim or interest is substantially similar to the other claims or interests of such class.

> (b) A plan may designate a separate class of claims consisting only of every unsecured claim that is less than or reduced to an amount that the court approves as reasonable and necessary for administrative convenience.

11 U.S.C. § 1122.

The Bankruptcy Court relied on section 1122(a) in rejecting Montano's plan, holding that cosigned and non-cosigned debts are "substantially similar" and thus may not be separately classified. In re Montano, 4 B.R. at 537. The District Court agreed, adding that a plan which provides one hundred percent payment to creditors with cosigned debts but only one percent to other unsecured creditors unfairly discriminates between classes of creditors within the meaning of section 1322(b)(1). In re Wavalene Barnes, 13 B.R. at 1000.

We think the courts erred in holding that section 1122(a) prohibits classification based on the presence of a codebtor. Section 1122(a) specifies that only claims which are "substantially similar" may be placed in the same class. It does not require that similar claims *must* be grouped together, but merely that any group created must be homogenous. See 5 Collier on Bankruptcy ¶ 1122.03[1][b] at 1122–6 (15th ed.1982); accord, In re Gay, 3 B.R. 336 (Bkrtcy.D.Colo.1980); In re Kovich, 4 B.R. 403 (Bkrtcy.W.D.Mich.1980). Although some courts have held that section 1122(a) prohibits classification based on any criterion other than legal right to the debtor's assets, see, e.g., In re Iacovoni, 2 B.R. 256, 260–61 (Bkrtcy.D.Utah), the plain language of the statute contradicts such a construction. Moreover, section 1122(a) so interpreted would conflict with section 1322(b)(1), which specifically authorizes designation of more than one class of unsecured creditor, each presumably with equal legal rights to the debtor's estate. We therefore hold that section 1122(a) does not prohibit Montano from grouping his unsecured obligations according to whether or not a codebtor is present.

This does not mean Montano's plan should be confirmed. Section 1322(b)(1) states that a plan may not "unfairly discriminate against any class . . .." The critical question is not whether Montano may group cosigned debts apart from non-cosigned, but whether his plan to pay one hundred percent to the first group "unfairly discriminates" against the second, which is to be paid only one percent.

Bankruptcy courts have interpreted unfair discrimination under section 1322(b)(1) in many ways without reaching a consensus. See 5 Collier on Bankruptcy ¶ 1322.01[3][a] (15th ed.1982) (Supp.Nov.1981). Clearly some difference in treatment between classes is permissible, or there would be little point in creating separate classes in the first place. The limits of permissible discrimination, however, are undefined. Montano argues that a plan does not violate section 1322(b)(1) so long as a rational basis exists for the classifications, and each class of unsecured creditor receives more than it would in a Chapter 7 liquidation. (Appellee's Br. at 33). Some bankruptcy courts have applied similar criteria. See, e.g., In re Sutherland, 3 B.R. 420 (Bkrtcy.W.D. Ark.1980). Nonetheless, we cannot agree with Montano's formulation. Section 1322(b)(1) prohibits unfair discrimination, and an inquiry into fairness plainly involves more than the rationality of the debtor's classifications or some minimum amount creditors must receive.

What constitutes fair discrimination will vary from case to case, and we cannot offer a generally applicable definition. The court must examine the amounts proposed for each class in light of the debtor's reasons for classification, and exercise sound discretion. See In re Gay, 3 B.R. 336 (Bkrtcy.D.Colo.1980). Considering the circumstances presented here, we think a ninety-nine percent differential in the amounts paid on cosigned versus non-cosigned debts is unfair. Montano argues that unless cosigned obligations are completely repaid, creditors can proceed against the cosigners, who in turn will put indirect pressure on Montano and interfere with the "fresh start" the Bankruptcy Code is supposed to provide. Filing a Chapter 13 plan, however, does not guarantee unqualified freedom from the pressures of bankruptcy. Nothing in the record suggests Montano will be unable to continue with his plan if cosigned obligations are not paid in full, and Montano raises no other factor that might justify departure from the basic principle that all unsecured creditors should be treated alike. Insulation of Montano from worry does not justify the unequal treatment he proposes.

We hold that Montano's plan "unfairly discriminates" against unsecured creditors holding non-cosigned debts, and therefore violates section 1322(b)(1). As presently drafted the plan may not be confirmed pursuant to section 1325(a)(1), which requires that plans "comply with the provisions of this chapter and with other applicable provisions of this title . . . ." If Montano chooses to modify his plan, the Bankruptcy Court must determine whether any difference in treatment between unsecured creditors is fair considering the circumstances and the debtor's offered justifications. . . .

IN RE SANDERS

United States Bankruptcy Court, District of Kansas, 1981.
13 B.R. 320.

ROBERT B. MORTON, BANKRUPTCY JUDGE.

STATEMENT OF THE CASE

Debtor Thomas Graham Sanders filed a voluntary petition for relief under Chapter 13 of the Bankruptcy Code on March 4, 1981. The debtor's plan proposes to make monthly payments to a creditor outside of the bankruptcy proceedings on a mortgage debt on the debtor's homestead. There are no other secured creditors. There are four unsecured creditors:

John Greenstreet	$ 2,182.52
James R. Schaefer	2,300.00
United American Bank & Trust	68,508.10
Wood Specialists	360.00
	$73,350.62

The plan proposes the above creditors be paid pro rata as funds become available until ten per cent (10%) of each claim has been paid. Debtor requests approval for a payment period in excess of three years, but not more than five years. Two creditors, John D. Greenstreet and United American Bank & Trust Company, object to debtor's plan contending a discharge of the debts owed them was previously denied the debtor.

The denial of discharge was in the framework of prior proceedings initiated by Sanders' voluntary petition for relief with this court on April 23, 1974. Only two creditors, John B. Greenstreet and United American State Bank & Trust Company (now United American Bank & Trust Company) were listed on the debtor's schedules. After extensive discovery and trial, this court determined debtor Sanders was denied a discharge of his debts for failure to satisfactorily explain losses of assets under section 14(c)(7) of the Bankruptcy Act. The decision was affirmed by the Federal District Court for the District of Kansas and an appeal to the Tenth Circuit Court of Appeals was subsequently abandoned by the debtor.

United American Bank & Trust Company (Bank) and John D. Greenstreet, unsecured creditors, object to confirmation of the instant plan, which proposes to pay ten percent (10%) of their respective unsecured claims, because ninety per cent (90%) of their previously determined nondischargeable debts would thereby be discharged.

MEMORANDUM

Section 1325(a) of the Bankruptcy Code sets forth six prerequisites to confirmation of a plan proposed under Chapter 13 of the Code. If these requirements are met, the court is required to confirm the plan. In the instant case Bank argues that debtor's plan fails to meet two of the six requirements. Bank contends (i) a prior denial of discharge prevents the plan from passing the good faith test of section 1325(a)(3) and (ii) the value of property to be distributed to them is less than they would receive if the debtor's estate were liquidated under Chapter 7; therefore, the plan does not satisfy the requirement of section 1325(a) (4).

Pursuant to section 523(a)(9) of the Code, a debt that was scheduled in a prior bankruptcy case in which the debtor was denied a discharge under section 14(c)(7) of the Bankruptcy Act is not dischargeable in a subsequent bankruptcy proceeding. This exception to discharge, however, is not applicable to a discharge granted under section 1328(a) of the Code. The latter states that only debts provided for under section 1322(b)(5) [certain long-term obligations specially provided for under the plan or specified in section 523(a)(5) [alimony, maintenance, and child support] are excepted from discharge. All other debts are dischargeable under a Chapter 13 plan, unless the debtor receives a hardship discharge. This result obtains even though the debts may not be dischargeable in a Chapter 7 proceeding. Under the instant plan, the two objecting creditors would be paid ten per cent of their claims with the corollary that ninety per cent of their debts would be discharged. By contrast, those debts would be entirely nondischargeable in a Chapter 7 liquidation proceeding.

While recognizing that the good faith requirement of section 1325(a) (3) does not explicitly require that relief under Chapter 7 of the Code be available to a debtor before relief under Chapter 13 may be sought, Bank argues that application of the good faith test mandates an examination of all the circumstances surrounding the plan's proposal, including the existence of nondischargeable obligations. This view is consistent with that of other courts.

> [T]he good faith requirement of section 1325(a)(3) should be interpreted as meaning that such plans cannot be confirmed without an inquiry into all of the circumstances involved in each individual case. This inquiry is mandated by the spirit of Chapter 13 as evidenced by its legislative history and the application and interaction of particular provisions of the Bankruptcy Code.

In re Schongalla, 4 B.R. 360, 6 B.C.D. 408, 409 (Bkrtcy.D.Md.1980); see In re Hurd, 4 B.R. 551, 6 B.C.D. 412, 418 (Bkrtcy.W.D.Mich.1980).

This court concludes that the existence of a nondischargeable debt is a factor which the court may consider when determining whether a plan has been proposed in good faith pursuant to Code section 1325(a)(3). The plan in the instant case classifies unsecured nondischargeable debts with other unsecured dischargeable debts and proposes to pay ten per cent to all claimants in that class. Such treatment of unsecured claims appears to conform with section 1322(a)(3) of the Code, which compels the debtor to propose identical treatment of each claim within a particular designated class. Unsecured claims, however, are not required to be classified in the same class. Indeed, section 1322(b)(1) permits a plan to "designate a class *or classes* of unsecured claims, as provided in section 1122 of this title" (emphasis added). Thus, a Chapter 13 debtor is referred to section 1122 for guidance in classifying claims.

Section 1122(a) of the Code provides that "a plan may place a claim or an interest in a particular class only if such claim or interest is substantially similar to the other claims or interests of such class." Section 1322(b)(1), therefore, permits the designation of classes of unsecured claims as authorized under Chapter 11, which restricts membership in a particular class to claims that are *substantially similar*. See 5 Collier on Bankruptcy, paragraph 1322[3][A], at 1322–6–7 (15th ed. 1980). An important distinction exists among the unsecured claims in the instant case which prevents them from being substantially similar: two of the claims are judicially determined nondischargeable debts [2] while the remainder are dischargeable. Consequently, if the debtor were to request relief under Chapter 7 rather than Chapter 13, those two unsecured debts in the former category would be entirely nondischargeable while the remaining unsecured debts could be discharged. That disparity is significant and sufficient to render the claims purportedly in the same class not "substantially similar" in the requisite sense.

The court determines that there are, in effect, two classes of unsecured claims in this case: (1) nondischargeable unsecured claims and, (2) dischargeable unsecured claims. As has been noted, the debtor's plan does not reflect the distinction and attempts to classify in a single class claims that are not substantially similar. In that respect, the plan fails to provide uniform and fair treatment to all claimants and, for that reason, does not meet the "good faith" test of section 1325(a)(3). The objections to the plan and its confirmation are sustained and confirmation of the plan is denied without prejudice to the submittal of an amended plan on or before September 14, 1981.

2. Because this court determined that a discharge should be denied the debtor in a prior bankruptcy proceeding, debts that were scheduled in the prior proceeding are determined to be nondischargeable under section 523(a)(9) of the Code.

Notes & Questions

1. *Why Classify?* Consider the following bases for classifying claims:

　(a) The debtor wishes to protect a codebtor (see § 1322(b)(1)).

　(b) The debtor wishes to distinguish between obligations that would be dischargeable in Chapter 7 and those that would not be.

　(c) The debtor wishes to preserve good relations with a particular creditor or group of creditors.

　(d) A creditor's partially secured status.

Which is a proper basis for classifying claims in Chapter 13? Should the debtor be *required* to treat some unsecured claims differently than other unsecured claims?

2. *Chapter 13 vs. Chapter 7.* Does it make sense to allow classification of claims in Chapter 13 but not to allow classification in Chapter 7? Do whatever reasons that justify classification in Chapter 13 (and Chapter 11) also justify classification in Chapter 7?

Does it make sense to have both a system of statutory priorities in § 507 and to allow the debtor to classify claims? Does it make sense to outlaw preferences and to allow the debtor to classify claims?

3. *Payments "Outside the Plan."* As in *Sanders*, courts sometimes encounter the question of how to deal with Chapter 13 plans that propose to make certain payments "outside the plan." Under Chapter XIII of the Bankruptcy Act of 1898, "secured creditors whose claims are dealt with by the plan" were entitled to vote on the plan. Unless they accepted the plan, it could not be confirmed. The practice developed that secured creditors often were not dealt with by the terms of a plan, but instead were treated "outside the plan" to avoid having to obtain confirmation by the affected secured creditor. The practice of dealing with claims outside a Chapter 13 plan continues under the new act but for different reasons.

In In re Glasper, 28 B.R. 6 (Bkrtcy.App. 9th Cir. 1983), appeal dismissed, 746 F.2d 1485 (9th Cir.1984), the debtor's Chapter 13 plan called for current payments to secured creditors to be made outside the plan and for the payment of arrearages on secured debts to be made through the plan. The court found such a plan not to be authorized by Chapter 13. In In re Foster, 670 F.2d 478 (5th Cir. 1982) the court held, inter alia, that computation of the Chapter 13 trustee's percentage fee, see § 1302(e), may include those payments with respect to which the debtor acts as disbursing agent and which the debtor labels as being outside the plan. Compare In re Bradley, 705 F.2d 1409 (5th Cir.1983) (approving treatment of fully secured claims outside the plan).

See generally Epstein, Chapter 13: Its Operation, Its Statutory Requirements as to Payment to and Classification of Unsecured Claims, and Its Advantages, 20 Washb.L.J. 1 (1980); Vihon, Classification of Unsecured Claims: Squaring A Circle, 55 Am.Bankr.L.J. 143 (1981).

C. The Treatment of Long Term Obligations

IN RE TADDEO

United States Court of Appeals, Second Circuit, 1982.
685 F.2d 24.

LUMBARD, CIRCUIT JUDGE:

Joseph C. and Ellen A. Taddeo live at 6 Ort Court, Sayville, New York. Three years ago they defaulted on their mortgage to Elfriede Di Pierro. Di Pierro accelerated the mortgage, declared its balance due immediately, and initiated foreclosure proceedings. The Taddeos sought refuge under Chapter 13 of the new Bankruptcy Code, staying the foreclosure action under the automatic stay, 11 U.S.C. § [362(a)] (Supp. IV 1980), and proposing to cure the default and reinstate the mortgage under 11 U.S.C. § 1322(b)(5). Di Pierro is listed as the Taddeos' only creditor. She rejected the plan to cure the default, and applied for relief from the automatic stay in order to foreclose. Di Pierro contended that once she accelerated her mortgage, the Taddeos had no way to cure the default under the Bankruptcy Code except to pay the full amount as required by state law. Bankruptcy Judge Parente held that the Taddeos could cure the default and reinstate their mortgage, and denied Di Pierro's motion for relief from the stay. In re Taddeo, 9 B.R. 299 (Bkrtcy.E.D.N.Y.1981). Judge Pratt affirmed, 15 B.R. 273 (Bkrtcy.E.D.N.Y.1981). We affirm. We do not believe that Congress labored for five years over this controversial question only to remit consumer debtors—intended to be primary beneficiaries of the new Code—to the harsher mercies of state law.

Di Pierro originally owned the house at 6 Ort Court. On June 14, 1979, she sold the house to the Taddeos, taking in return a "purchase money second mortgage" to secure a principal balance of $13,000. The property is subject to a first lien held by West Side Federal Savings & Loan Association, which is not involved in this case.[1] Di Pierro's second mortgage was payable over 15 years at 8.5 percent in equal monthly installments of $128.05.

Upon taking occupancy, the Taddeos notified Di Pierro that they had discovered defects in the property.[2] On advice of counsel, the Taddeos said they would withhold mortgage payments, depositing the money instead with their attorney. The Taddeos and Di Pierro corresponded for several months without reaching an agreement. On October 5, 1979, Di Pierro wrote that she was accelerating the mortgage and declaring the entire balance due immediately. The mortgage contained the acceleration clause specifically approved in N.Y. Real Prop. § 258

---

1. The record does not indicate the status of the first lien in the Chapter 13 proceeding.

2. The nature of the alleged defects does not appear in the record.

Schedule M (McKinney 1968), which gives the mortgagee the option to accelerate after a default in mortgage payments.

Di Pierro commenced foreclosure proceedings in state court on October 19, 1979. The Taddeos tendered full payment of their arrears by check on October 31, 1979, but Di Pierro refused to accept payment. The state court granted summary judgment to Di Pierro and ordered a referee to determine the amount owed. After a hearing on June 30, 1980, the referee found the Taddeos liable for $14,153.48 in principal and interest, plus interest subsequent to the award.

Before Di Pierro could obtain final judgment of foreclosure and sale, the Taddeos filed a Chapter 13 bankruptcy petition in the Eastern District on July 10, 1980. The court appointed Harold F. Cullen as interim trustee and Richard McCord as successor trustee. 11 U.S.C. § 1302. The petition listed Di Pierro as the only creditor, and stayed Di Pierro's foreclosure action. The Taddeos filed a plan proposing to pay off arrears on the mortgage in installments of $100 per month. The plan further proposed to restore the mortgage and its original payment schedule, with payments through McCord as trustee to Di Pierro during the 3-year life of the plan and directly to Di Pierro after the plan ended. Di Pierro objected to the plan, and petitioned for relief from the automatic stay so that she could proceed with her foreclosure action. Di Pierro contended that her rights as mortgagee could not be affected by the Chapter 13 plan. Bankruptcy Judge Parente, however, held that the Taddeos could pay their arrearages and reinstate their mortgage under this section notwithstanding Di Pierro's acceleration, analogizing § 1322(b) to 11 U.S.C. § 1124(2), which nullifies acceleration clauses in Chapter 11 corporate reorganizations. Therefore, Bankruptcy Judge Parente denied Di Pierro relief from the automatic stay. District Judge Pratt affirmed on similar reasoning.

Because Di Pierro is the Taddeos' only creditor, continuance of the stay is justified only if the Taddeos' plan can in fact provide for Di Pierro's mortgage. Otherwise, the stay would serve only to delay foreclosure for delay's sake, and would not be justified. Therefore, although the Taddeos' Chapter 13 plan is not before us for approval, the question of whether under the plan the Taddeos can pay arrearages to Di Pierro and thereby cure the default and reinstate the mortgage is squarely presented for decision.

The relevant parts of § 1322(b) read as follows:

(b) . . . the plan may—

. . .

(2) modify the rights of holders of secured claims other than a claim secured only by a security interest in real property that is the debtor's principal residence, or of holders of unsecured claims;

(3) provide for the curing or waiving of any default;

. . .

(5) notwithstanding paragraph (2) of this subsection, provide for the curing of any default within a reasonable time and maintenance of payments while the case is pending on any unsecured claim or secured claim on which the last payment is due after the date on which the final payment under the plan is due;

When Congress empowered Chapter 13 debtors to "cure defaults," we think Congress intended to allow mortgagors to "de-accelerate" their mortgage and reinstate its original payment schedule. We so hold for two reasons. First, we think that the power to cure must comprehend the power to "de-accelerate." This follows from the concept of "curing a default." A default is an event in the debtor-creditor relationship which triggers certain consequences—here, acceleration. Curing a default commonly means taking care of the triggering event and returning to pre-default conditions. The consequences are thus nullified. This is the concept of "cure" used throughout the Bankruptcy Code. Under § 365(b), the trustee may assume executory contracts and unexpired leases only if he cures defaults—but the cure need address only the individual event of default, thereby repealing the contractual consequences. Fogel, Executory Contracts and Unexpired Leases in the Bankruptcy Code, 64 Minn.L.Rev. 341, 356 (1980). See Collier on Bankruptcy § 365.04 at 365–31–32 (L. King 15th Ed. 1981).[5] See also, 11 U.S.C. § 1110(a)(2); 124 Cong.Rec. H 11,102 (Sept. 28, 1978); S 17,419 (Oct. 6, 1978) (trustee may continue in possession of aircraft and ships by curing defaults and making payments in original lease or contract); 11 U.S.C. § 1168(a)(2), H.R.Rept. 595, 95th Cong. 1st Sess. 423 (1977) (trustee may retain rolling stock if he cures default and agrees to make original payments). Such legislative history as there is supports a similar reading of § 1322(b)(5). Both the Bankruptcy Commission's Bill, see § 6–201(2) & (4) and accompanying commentary, and the Bankruptcy Judges' Bill, § 6–301(2), plainly permitted the cure and de-acceleration of residential debt accelerated prior to petition. Although H.R. 6, 95th Cong. 1st Sess. § 1322(b)(1977), which superseded these bills, omitted a proviso contained in § 6–301(2) of the Judges' Bill that made this entirely clear, it is evident that this was done because the clause was regarded as surplusage. H.R. 6 adopted language almost identical to § 6–301(2) of the Commission's Bill, which accomplished just what the Judges' Bill did, albeit in different language. In fact, H.R. 6 went beyond either of its predecessors and permitted the *modification* of debt secured by a debtor's residence. Although the Senate later adopted a prohibition against modification of the rights of holders of secured real estate debt, S. 2266, 95th Cong. 2nd Sess. § 1322(b)(2), which the House accepted insofar as it related to debt secured by a debtor's principal residence, 124 Cong.Rec. H 11106 (September 28, 1978), the cure and maintain powers of paragraph (b)(5) remained unchanged. The history and the policy discussed above compel the conclusion that § 1322(b)(5) was intended to permit the cure

5. The debtor is liable for any damage sustained by the creditor in relying upon acceleration, but is not liable for the acceleration itself. 11 U.S.C. § 365(b)(1)(B).

and de-acceleration of secured long-term residential debt accelerated prior to the filing of a Chapter 13 petition.

Policy considerations strongly support this reading of the statute. Conditioning a debtor's right to cure on its having filed a Chapter 13 petition prior to acceleration would prompt unseemly and wasteful races to the courthouse. Worse, these would be races in which mortgagees possess an unwarranted and likely insurmountable advantage: wage earners seldom will possess the sophistication in bankruptcy matters that financial institutions do, and often will not have retained counsel in time for counsel to do much good. In contrast, permitting debtors in the Taddeos' position to de-accelerate by payment of the arrearages will encourage parties to negotiate in good faith rather than having to fear that the mortgagee will tip the balance irrevocably by accelerating or that the debtor may prevent or at least long postpone this by filing a Chapter 13 petition.

Secondly, we believe that the power to "cure any default" granted in § 1322(b)(3) and (b)(5) is not limited by the ban against "modifying" home mortgages in § 1322(b)(2) because we do not read "curing defaults" under (b)(3) or "curing defaults and maintaining payments" under (b)(5) to be *modifications* of claims.

It is true that § 1322(b)(5)'s preface, "notwithstanding paragraph (2)," seems to treat the power to cure in (b)(5) as a subset of the power to modify set forth in (b)(2), but that superficial reading of the statute must fall in the light of legislative history and legislative purpose. The "notwithstanding" clause was added to § 1322(b)(5) to emphasize that defaults in mortgages could be cured notwithstanding § 1322(b)(2). See 124 Cong.Rec. H.11,106 (Sept. 28, 1978); S.17,423 (Oct. 6, 1978). But the clause was not necessary. The Senate protected home mortgages from *modification* in its last bill, S. 2266, 95th Cong., 2d Sess.; it evinced no intent to protect these mortgages from *cure*. Cf. Hearings on S. 2266 Before the Subcommittee on Improvements in Judicial Machinery of the Senate Committee on the Judiciary, 95th Cong., 1st Sess. 836 (1977) (Statement of Charles A. Horsky, Chairman, National Bankruptcy Conference (S. 2266 "is completely unclear as to whether the plan can provide for the curing of defaults and the making of current payments.")) Indeed, earlier Senate bills along with House bills and the present statute listed the power to cure and the power to modify in different paragraphs, indicating that the power to cure is different from the power to modify. Testimony submitted on behalf of secured creditors distinguished between modifying a claim (by reducing payments due thereon) and curing a default (and maintaining those payments). . . .

Our reading of the statute disposes of Di Pierro's major contentions on appeal. Di Pierro argues that the Taddeos cannot use § 1322(b)(5) to cure their default and maintain payments on her mortgage because (b)(5) applies only to claims whose last payment is due after the last payment under the plan is due. Di Pierro maintains her acceleration of the mortgage makes all payments due *now*. See In re Williams, 11 B.R. 504 (Bkrtcy.S.D.Texas 1981); In re Paglia, 8 B.R. 937 (Bkrtcy.E.D. N.Y.1981). But we hold that the concept of "cure" in § 1322(b)(5) contains the power to de-accelerate. Therefore the application of that section de-accelerates the mortgage and returns it to its 15-year maturity. Alternatively, we hold that the ban on "modification" in § 1322(b) (2) does not limit the Taddeos' exercise of their curative powers under either § 1322(b)(3) or (b)(5). Therefore the Taddeos may first cure their default under (b)(3) and then maintain payments under (b)(5).

Di Pierro also argues that under New York law the Taddeos cannot "cure" an accelerated mortgage without paying the full amount of the claim, and further asserts that the Bankruptcy Code does not empower the Taddeos to override New York law. She asserts that Congress explicitly gave corporate debtors the power to cure defaults without regard to acceleration by passing 11 U.S.C. § 1124(2), and concludes that the absence of similar language in § 1322(b) indicates that Chapter 13 debtors cannot cure defaults unless they also cure acceleration. See In re Williams, 11 B.R. 504 (Bkrtcy.S.D.Tex.1981); In re Paglia, 8 B.R. 937 (Bkrtcy.E.D.N.Y.1981). The bankruptcy court took the opposite tack, reasoning that Congress, having provided corporate debtors with curative powers under § 1124(2), must have intended similar powers to be exercised by consumer debtors under § 1322(b) as consumers are more favored by Chapter 13 than corporate debtors are by Chapter 11.

Both rationales mistake the import of § 1124. That section determines who has the right to vote on a Chapter 11 plan. Those parties with "impaired" claims or interest can vote, and § 1124(1) declares that *any* change in legal, equitable or contractual rights creates impairment. Having defined impairment in the broadest possible terms, Congress carved out a small exception to impairment in § 1124(2) providing that curing a default, even though it inevitably changes a contractual acceleration clause, does not thereby "impair" a creditor's claim. "The holder of a claim or interest who under the plan is restored to his original position, when others receive less or get nothing at all, is fortunate indeed and has no cause to complain." S.Rep.No.989, 95th Cong., 2d Sess. 120 (1978). Section 1124(2) merely takes away the creditor's right to vote in the event of cure; the authority to cure is found in § 1123(a)(5)(G) in plain language similar to § 1322(b). *See* In re Thompson, 17 B.R. 748, 753 (Bkrtcy.W.D.Mich.1982). In short, "curing a default" on Chapter 11 means the same thing as it does in Chapters 7 or 13: the event of default is remedied and the consequences are nullified. A state law to the contrary must fall before the Bankruptcy Code.

Di Pierro argues further that § 1322(b)(5) requires the Taddeos to cure their default "within a reasonable time," and that under New York law that time has passed. But clearly the "reasonable time" requirement refers to time after a Chapter 13 petition is filed. Otherwise Chapter 13 debtors would forfeit their right to cure merely by negotiating with their creditors, or, as in this case, litigating the right of their creditor to declare a default. The bankruptcy courts which have allowed Chapter 13 debtors to cure defaults under § 1322(b)(5) have assumed that "reasonable time" refers to time after the petition was filed. See In re Acevedo, 4 Collier Bankr.Cas.2d (MB) 178, 9 B.R. 852 (Bkrtcy.E.D.N.Y.1981); In re King, 3 Collier Bankr.Cas.2d (MB) 109, 7 B.R. 110 (Bkrtcy.S.D.Cal.1980). We find no support for Di Pierro's contention that state law must govern what constitutes a reasonable time.[6]

Di Pierro's argument reduces in the end to an assertion that because she can accelerate her mortgage under state law, the Taddeos can cure only as provided by state law. This interpretation of § 1322(b) would leave the debtor with fewer rights under the new Bankruptcy Code than under the old Bankruptcy Act of 1898.[7] Defaulting mortgag[ors] would forfeit their right to cure even before the start of foreclosure proceedings, before they have hired lawyers and therefore before they knew anything about their rights under Chapter 13. Such a result would render the remedy in § 1322(b) unavailable to all but a select number of debtors. See In re Thompson, 17 B.R. 748, 752–53 (Bkrtcy. W.D.Mich.1982). Such a result would be totally at odds with the "overriding rehabilitative purpose of Chapter 13." In re Davis, 15 B.R. 22, 24 (Bkrtcy.D.Kan.) aff'd, 16 B.R. 473 (D.Kan.1981).

Affirmed.

. . .

Contra, In re Williams, 11 B.R. 504 (Bkrtcy.S.D.Tex.1981).

Notes & Questions

1. *Prepetition Maturity Date.* Suppose the note had reached its maturity date before the filing of the bankruptcy petition. Could the debtor affect the note and mortgage in bankruptcy? See In re Seidel, 752 F.2d 1382 (9th Cir.1985) (yes). If the debtor cannot, then much turns on the reason the maturity date was reached prior to bankruptcy. Maturity dates reached "naturally" are honored in bankruptcy. Other maturity dates may not be.

2. *Unsecured Claims.* The debtor in *Taddeo* relied on § 1322(b)(5) to deal with a secured creditor. On its face, the section also applies to unsecured claims. Can you think of a situation in which the debtor would want to invoke § 1322(b)(5) against the holder of an unsecured claim? Suppose the debtor attempts to cure because he wants to maintain good relations with a particular creditor. Are plan provisions

6. Events prior to bankruptcy, of course, may influence what constitutes a "reasonable time" to cure defaults after the petition is filed.

7. Under the old Bankruptcy Act, a bankruptcy court could enjoin a mortgagee from foreclosure so long as the injunction did not impair the value of the mortgagee's security and the mortgagee received no less than the payments provided for in the mortgage. Hallenbeck v. Penn Mutual Life Insurance Co., 323 F.2d 566 (4th Cir. 1963); In re Freed & Co., 534 F.2d 1235, 1239 (6th Cir. 1976).

allowed by § 1322(b)(5) subject to the limits on classification of claims that may be embodied in § 1322(b)(1)?

Could the debtor in *Taddeo* have relied on § 1322(b)(3)? How does it differ from § 1322(b)(5)?

3. *Chapter 7 vs. Chapter 13.* The Taddeos only concern was to save their home. They had no other creditors and their Chapter 13 plan contained no other important terms. They could have just as well been in Chapter 7 except for the fact that Chapter 7 contains no provision similar to § 1322(b)(5). Should it? Why should cure of default on secured obligations only be available to Chapter 13 debtors? Cf. Jackson, Bankruptcy, Non-Bankruptcy Entitlements, and the Creditors' Bargain, 91 Yale L.J. 857, 881–87, 898 (1982); Chapter 16, *infra.*

4. *Debts Due After Completion of the Plan.* How does the confirmation standard in § 1325(a)(5) operate in the case of secured debt obligations with respect to which the last payment is due after the final payment under the Chapter 13 plan is due? What is the amount of the claim in the case of such an obligation?

5. *§ 365.* May the debtor deal with long-term obligations through the executory contract provisions contained in § 365? May the trustee? How does § 365's treatment of executory contracts differ from the specialized Chapter 13 provisions? Do these differences make sense?

6. *Interest on Arrearages.* In curing the default under the Chapter 13 plan, must the debtors in *Taddeo* pay interest on the unpaid installment arrearages? In In re Terry, 764 F.2d 1558 (11th Cir.1985), the court held that § 1325(a)(5)(B), requiring present value payments to oversecured creditors, is inapplicable to residential mortgages. Unless the mortgage provides for interest on arrearages, they are not required to be paid under a Chapter 13 plan. In In re Colegrove, 771 F.2d 119 (6th Cir.1985), the court held that a mortgagee is entitled to interest on arrearages regardless of whether the mortgage provides for such interest.

See generally Note, Saving the Family Homestead: Home Mortgages Under Chapter 13, 43 Ohio St.L.J. 905 (1983); Comment, Home Foreclosures Under Chapter 13 of the Bankruptcy Reform Act, 30 UCLA L.Rev. 637 (1983).

D. The Treatment of Secured Claims in Chapter 13

IN RE PETTIT

United States Bankruptcy Court, Southern District of Ohio, 1982.
18 B.R. 832.

R.J. SIDMAN, BANKRUPTCY JUDGE.

William and Bonnie Pettit, joint Chapter 13 debtors, have made an application to this Court for an order avoiding the lien asserted by Bank One of Columbus, NA ("Bank One") against their residential real estate. The lien is in the form of a certificate of judgment filed against the residential real estate of the debtors on October 26, 1977, and according to the proof of claim filed by Bank One is in the amount of $7,696.66. The debtors originally premised their application upon the provisions of § 522(f)(1) of the Bankruptcy Code which state:

"(f) Notwithstanding any waiver of exemptions, the debtor may avoid the fixing of a lien on an interest of the debtor in property to the extent that such lien impairs an exemption to which the debtor would have been entitled under subsection (b) of this section, if such lien is—

(1) a judicial lien . . ."   11 U.S.C. § 522(f)(1).

The debtors claim that the judicial lien of Bank One impairs their exemption in their residential real estate. However, in an additional memorandum in support of this application, the debtors have alternatively requested that the judicial lien of Bank One be cancelled by virtue of certain provisions of § 1327(b) and (c) of the Bankruptcy Code which state:

"(b) Except as otherwise provided in the plan or the order confirming the plan, the confirmation of a plan vests all property of the estate in the debtor.

(c) Except as otherwise provided in the plan or in the order confirming the plan, the property vesting in the debtor under subsection (b) of this section is *free and clear of any claim or interest of any creditor provided for by the plan.*"   11 U.S.C. § 1327(b) and (c) (Emphasis Added).

The debtors' application has been opposed by Bank One. Relevant facts in deciding the present application are found by the Court as follows. The debtors filed a joint petition requesting relief under the provisions of Chapter 13 of the Bankruptcy Code on March 4, 1981. Bank One was a duly listed creditor in the accompanying Chapter 13 statement (although it was listed as "City National Bank", the former name of Bank One) and was duly notified of the filing of the petition. A meeting of creditors under the provisions of § 341 of the Bankruptcy Code was held on April 10, 1981, and the debtors' plan was confirmed by this Court on April 23, 1981. Bank One filed no claim in this case until April 17, 1981, and its subsequent request to be included in the confirmed plan as a secured creditor was denied by Court Order of May 7, 1981, on the grounds that its late filing of its claim could not be excused under the provisions of Rule 13–302(e) of the Bankruptcy Rules. See In re Remy, 8 B.R. 40 (Bkrtcy.S.D.Ohio 1980).

The debtors now seek to take advantage of the fact that Bank One has only an allowed *unsecured* claim in this Chapter 13 case by invoking the provisions of § 1327(c) and having this Court declare that the judicial lien of Bank One is now cancelled by operation of that section.

. . . There is at least one court that appears to have held that the literal language of § 1327(c) of the Bankruptcy Code was not meant by Congress. See Second National Bank of Saginaw v. Honaker (In re

Honaker), 4 B.R. 415, 6 B.C.D. 474 (Bkrtcy.E.D.Mich.1980). Indeed, a respected bankruptcy treatise seems to also so indicate. 5 Collier on Bankruptcy, ¶ 1327.01, p. 1327–5.

However, at least two courts have held that the language of § 1327 directly affects the status of a holder of a secured claim in a confirmed Chapter 13 plan. For instance, the Court in Associates Commercial Corp. v. Brock (In re Brock), 6 B.R. 105, 6 B.C.D. 1065 (Bkrtcy.N.D.Ill. 1980), held that:

> "Section 1327, therefore, virtually renders a secured creditor provided for in a Confirmed Plan impotent." In re Brock, supra, 6 B.R. 105, 6 B.C.D. at 1066.

Also, a bankruptcy court has held that all matters relating to a creditor's interest in the debtor's property, if the debt is provided for by the confirmed plan, are finally determined by the confirmation order, and no subsequent judicial proceeding can reopen those same issues. See Ford Motor Credit Company v. Lewis (In re Lewis), 8 B.R. 132, 7 B.C.D. 105 (Bkrtcy.D.Idaho 1981). Thus, the creditor in the *Lewis* case was prevented from relitigating the question of whether or not the confirmed plan of the Chapter 13 debtor adequately provided for the protection of its interest. Section 1327 of the Bankruptcy Code was cited as support for that position.

This Court hereby finds that the provisions of § 1327(c) as applied in this case operate to exchange the previously held obligation of the Pettits, which was secured by a judicial lien of Bank One on their residential real estate, for an unsecured claim to be paid through the terms of the confirmed Chapter 13 plan. Thus, if the debtors fully comply with the terms of their Chapter 13 plan, the Bank One debt, having been paid as an unsecured claim in the confirmed plan, will be discharged. The rehabilitative purpose of Chapter 13 would be directly frustrated if a creditor in Bank One's posture could, after having been paid in accordance with the provisions of the confirmed Chapter 13 plan, and in accordance with the manner in which its claim was allowed, assert the continued validity of its judicial lien after the conclusion of this case. Bank One could have protected itself in this proceeding by filing a timely proof of claim and insisting on retaining its lien rights. See 11 U.S.C. § 1325(a)(5)(B)(i). It did not. Bank One's only protection at this point in time is the promise of the debtors to pay their creditors under the terms of their confirmed plan, and if such promise is fulfilled, Bank One will have received its proper dividend in this case. It can, under applicable law, expect no more. The Court makes no present finding as to whether the Bank One judicial lien would be subject to a different treatment should the debtors fail to complete their Chapter 13 plan and their case is either dismissed or converted to a Chapter 7 case. The finding that this Court does make is premised upon the debtors' fulfillment of the terms of their confirmed Chapter 13 plan.

Based upon the foregoing, this Court hereby determines that the provisions of § 1327(c) of the Bankruptcy Code operate to avoid Bank One's judicial lien. This Court thus determines that the application of the Pettits is meritorious and it is hereby granted. For the purpose of this Chapter 13 case, Bank One's judicial lien on the debtors' residential real estate is hereby avoided.

Notes & Questions

1. *Effect on Liens.* What should be the effect of a Chapter 13 discharge on liens? Consider the case of a debtor who fulfills a Chapter 13 plan in which he repays each creditor 100% of the creditor's claim. After discharge, may a secured creditor foreclose upon collateral? Or does the lien of the security interest end with the repayment? If so, how can liens survive a discharge under Chapter 7, where the debt underlying a lien does not survive a discharge? See Chapter 13A.

Even if one believes that a debtor who performs a 100% plan should be able to keep property formerly subject to liens, how should the Chapter 13 discharge affect a debtor who pays less than 100%? Is there any justification for treating secured creditors of such a debtor less well than secured creditors of a Chapter 7 debtor?

In Matter of Metz, 820 F.2d 1495 (9th Cir.1987), debtor filed a Chapter 7 proceeding which reduced the mortgage lender's interest to a secured lien against the property. No personal liability on the mortgage remained. Debtor then filed a Chapter 13 proceeding dealing with arrearages owed on the mortgage. The court held that a Chapter 13 petition may include a mortgage claim within a plan even though the underlying obligation of the mortgage was discharged in a prior bankruptcy case. Has the debtor accomplished anything that could not be accomplished in a Chapter 13 proceeding by itself?

2. *Post-Plan Repossession.* After completion of payments under a Chapter 13 plan, may secured creditors with long term obligations (containing terms that extend beyond completion of the plan) repossess any collateral on which they may have liens? Does this depend on whether the debtor continues to make timely payments to them?

3. *The Confirmation Standard.* Section 1325(a)(5) imposes a confirmation standard that must be met with respect to each allowed secured claim provided for by a Chapter 13 plan. If the debtor wishes to retain possession of collateral and the secured party rejects the debtor's Chapter 13 plan, § 1325(a)(5)(B) requires that the secured party retain his lien and that the debtor propose to pay the secured party at least the allowed amount of the secured party's claim.

Note the importance of the discount factor chosen in evaluating proposed installment payments on a secured claim. In Memphis Bank & Trust Co. v. Whitman, 692 F.2d 427, 431 (6th Cir. 1982), the court stated, "we hold that in the absence of special circumstances bankruptcy courts should use the current market rate of interest used for similar loans in the region. . . . The theory of the statute is that the creditor is making a new loan to the debtor in the amount of the current value of the collateral. Under this theory, the most appropriate interest rate is the current market rate for similar loans at the time the new loan is made, not some other unrelated arbitrary rate."

E.　Codebtors

IN RE BURTON

United States Bankruptcy Court, Western District of Virginia, 1980.
4 B.R. 608.

H. CLYDE PEARSON, BANKRUPTCY JUDGE.

The issue here is whether or not First National Exchange Bank of Virginia (Bank) should be granted leave to pursue its claim against a co-debtor of the Chapter 13 Debtor herein.

The facts essentially are as follows: the Debtor filed a petition in this Court seeking relief under Chapter 13 of the Bankruptcy Code of 1978. The plan which has been confirmed provided for the payment of all general creditors 100% of their debts. One of the debts listed in the schedule is that of the Bank upon which a claim has been filed herein. The original debt was in the sum of $3,263.04 made by the Debtor, Brenda M. Burton on September 11, 1979, payable in thirty-two monthly installments of $101.97 commencing October 11, 1979. The Bank at the time the loan was made listed as security for the unsecured note the endorsement of a co-maker, one Joanna H. Myers. The evidence showed in addition to the foregoing, that Joanna H. Myers was a responsible party and a good customer of the Bank. The note in question represented $2,500.00 loan and the remaining portion of the note represented add-on interest and other charges.

The Court set for hearing and heard the evidence upon the Plaintiff's complaint seeking relief from the stay invoked by virtue of 11 U.S.C. § 1301 to be permitted to proceed against the co-maker, Joanna H. Myers.

11 U.S.C. § 1301(a) provides:

"Except as provided in subsections (b) and (c) of this section, after the order for relief under this chapter, a creditor may not act, or commence or continue any civil action, to collect all or any part of a consumer debt of the debtor from any individual that is liable on such debt with the debtor, or that secured such debt, unless—

(1) such individual became liable on or secured such debt in the ordinary course of such individual's business; or

(2) the case is closed, dismissed, or converted to a case under chapter 7 or 11 of this title."

The foregoing section is new to the law of bankruptcy and was written into the Bankruptcy Reform Act of 1978 by Congress in order to eliminate the pressure upon debtors where creditors pursued comakers thereby disrupting the orderly process of a Chapter 13 case. See Bankruptcy Law 5 BK L.Ed. Legislative History, § 82:4.

It is assumed for purposes of this decision, although the evidence did not disclose the facts that this was a consumer debt as provided by 11 U.S.C. § 101(7) and therefore, comes within the purview of 11 U.S.C. § 1301(a). It is also a fact that the consideration representing the debt flowed to the Debtor and not the co-debtor.

The standard which the Court must utilize in consideration of a complaint for relief from the stay is set forth in 11 U.S.C. § 1301(c), which is as follows:

> "On request of a party in interest and after notice and a hearing, the court shall grant relief from the stay provided by subsection (a) of this section with respect to a creditor, to the extent that—
>
> (1) as between the debtor and the individual protected under subsection (a) of this section, such individual received the consideration for the claim held by such creditor;
>
> (2) the plan filed by the debtor proposes not to pay such claim; or
>
> (3) such creditor's interest would be irreparably harmed by such stay."

In accordance with 11 U.S.C. § 1301(c) supra, paragraphs (1) and (2) are excluded from consideration in as much as the debtors received the consideration and propose to pay the claim in full. The crucial issue before the Court is § 1301(c)(3) with respect to irreparable harm which the Bank may suffer if the stay is not lifted. The Court must grant relief from the stay if irreparable harm would result.

The authors of 5 Collier on Bankruptcy ¶ 1301.01[5] (15th ed. 1979) note that the drafters did not indicate who bore the burden of proof on the issue of "irreparable harm":

> Unlike the automatic stay imposed by section 362, no express provision is made for ex parte relief from the automatic stay or *for fixing the burden of proof.* (emphasis added)

Section 362(g) makes it clear upon whom the burden of proof falls unlike Section 1301(c):

> "In any hearing under subsection (d) or (e) of this section concerning relief from the stay of any act under subsection (a) of this section—
>
> (1) the party requesting such relief has the burden of proof on the issue of the debtor's equity in property; and
>
> (2) the party opposing such relief has the burden of proof on all other issues."

The Bank asserted in its complaint that its interest as a creditor would be irreparably harmed should the automatic co-debtor stay continue in effect. While the statute in issue is silent as to the burden of proof, unlike 11 U.S.C. § 362, the common law of evidence indicates that the burden of proof on the issue of irreparable harm rest, quite properly, on the Bank.

Professor Wigmore in his multi-volume treatise on evidence has stated that the term burden of proof is susceptible of two interpretations, one strict and the other incorrectly used. 9 Wigmore on Evidence "Burden of Proof" § 2485 (3rd ed. 1940). The first meaning important for our purposes, is more properly termed the burden of non-persuasion; that is, the ultimate burden of establishing the truth of a given proposition of fact essential to a cause of action. Lilienthol v. U.S., 97 U.S. 237, 24 L.Ed. 901 (1877). Burden of proof in this context means the duty which rests upon the party having the affirmative to establish by a preponderance of the evidence a material proposition essential to the action. 7 M.J. "Evidence" § 29 (1976 Repl.Vol.) The primary test for determining who has the burden of proof is which party to the action will fail if it offers no competent evidence to prove its facts alleged as its basis for relief. Id. Clearly, the Bank in its complaint alleged that its interests would be irreparably harmed. It then becomes incumbent upon the Bank to bring forth such evidence as will prove or persuade the court of its position. Using the test just proposed, the Bank's action would certainly fail if it offered no evidence whatsoever to support its claim. 29 Am.Jur.2d "Evidence" § 127 (1967). In Virginia, the burden of proof by which we mean the burden of persuasion in its technical sense, always rests upon the plaintiff and never shifts as opposed to the burden of producing or going forward with the evidence which shifts throughout the trial. Redford v. Booker, 166 Va. 561, 185 S.E. 879 (1936); Mitchell v. New England Mutual Life Insurance Co., 123 F.2d 246 (4th Cir. 1941). A litigant must always prove his case and the burden is on the plaintiff to sustain the material allegations of its complaint. Mitchell v. Commonwealth, 141 Va. 541, 127 S.E. 368 (1925).

Wigmore notes that whether in the market, the home, or the legal forum, it is the desire to have action taken which is important. Wigmore, supra. In the affairs of life as in the court of law, the penalty for not sustaining the burden of proof—i.e. by non-persuasion of the fact in issue—is that the party to be influenced (the court) will not be in a position to take the desired action to which his persuasion is a prerequisite.

It is sometimes urged that the burden falls upon the one to whose case the fact in issue is essential. Certainly, the Bank is in the position of having to prove the essential facts of its irreparable harm. To do otherwise would place the unfair and inequitable burden of proof upon the defendant Debtor who should not be forced to a showing of no irreparable harm.

Another consideration suggested by Professor Wigmore is that the burden is upon the party who has the peculiar means of knowledge surrounding the fact in issue which would enable him to prove the proposition one way or the other. Wigmore, supra. But, as the author notes:

> This consideration, after all, merely takes its place among other considerations of fairness and experience as a most important one to be kept in mind in apportioning the burden of proof in a specific case.

It becomes then a question more of policy and fairness than a set rule or rules. On the issue of fairness, the Supreme Court in Adams v. U.S., 317 U.S. 269, 281, 63 S.Ct. 236, 242, 87 L.Ed. 268 (1942) stated:

> "It is not asking too much that the burden of showing essential unfairness be sustained by him who claims such injustice and seeks to have the result set aside, and that it be sustained not as a matter of speculation but as a demonstrable reality." (Quoted with approval in Albert v. Commonwealth, 181 Va. 894, 27 S.E.2d 177 (1943)).

We think this rule should apply in the instant case even though *Albert* was a criminal case; the theory is the same. The Bank wants to show that it is unfair if the co-debtor stay pursuant to 11 U.S.C. § 1301 is allowed to remain in effect, thereby foreclosing the Bank's rights under its contract. As the claimant of an essential injustice, the burden of proof on the issue of irreparable harm should properly fall to the plaintiff, the Bank, which seeks relief from the stay.

The only evidence presented which would remotely reflect proof of irreparable harm is most favorable to the Debtor, the Defendant, Brenda M. Burton. That evidence was that Joanna H. Myers was a responsible individual, good customer of the Bank, and acceptable as a co-maker upon this obligation. There is no evidence that the status or character of the co-maker's financial ability has changed from that of a responsible individual.

As is reflected in the foregoing authorities, the burden of showing irreparable harm rests on the Bank. It is assumed that the Congress intended that the burden be proved by positive evidence before the Court is permitted to relieve the stay solely by virtue of irreparable harm being caused. This has not been done and accordingly, it is

Adjudged and Ordered that the prayer of the Complaint be, and the same is hereby denied and the stay of 11 U.S.C. § 1301 against enforcement of this debt against the co-debtor shall remain in full force and effect.

Notes & Questions

1. *Section 362's Automatic Stay.* In addition to providing a stay on some actions against codebtors, the filing of a Chapter 13 petition triggers the automatic stay of § 362. What is the effect of the stay in the following situation? On January 1, D files a Chapter 13 petition. On February 1, C extends credit to D. On February 15, D defaults. May C try to collect the debt from D? May C enforce any judgment

obtained against D? Do these results differ from the results that would obtain if D had filed a Chapter 7 case? What is the effect of § 1306?

2. *Allowed Post-Petition Claims.* How would Chapter 13's treatment of the above case differ if C's claim were one covered by § 1305? See also §§ 1322(b), 1328(d).

Chapter 16

SPECIAL ASPECTS OF REORGANIZATIONS UNDER CHAPTER 11

A. Introduction

It is difficult to draw a line between where the study of general bankruptcy law ends and the detailed study of reorganizations under Chapter 11 begins. Many of the Bankruptcy Act provisions already studied have their primary significance in corporate reorganizations. Questions about the scope of § 362's automatic stay, the trustee's power to accept or reject executory contracts under § 365, and the turnover of property required by § 542 often arise in the context of a reorganization under Chapter 11 and have their greatest economic impact in that context. Although the provisions studied in this Chapter, the internal workings of Chapter 11, also may affect the planning of a wide range of commercial transactions, they are of slightly less general applicability.

1. The Background of Modern Business Reorganization Laws

CLARK, THE INTERDISCIPLINARY STUDY OF LEGAL EVOLUTION, 90 Yale L.J. 1238, 1250–54 (1981)

The history of the law of creditors' remedies against business debtors has at least five distinct phases. Each is characterized by the emergence and widespread use of a legal procedure, or set of legal principles, that significantly improved the efficiency of the debt-enforcement process for the benefit of creditors and, ultimately, of society. This line of legal development is one of primary cost reduction.

Yet, in striking fashion, each of the later four legal inventions (described below) created a need for more numerous or exacting valuation procedures. Consequently, they created new needs and opportunities for cost-reducing legal safeguards against irrationality, inadequate information, fraud, and other abuses in the valuation process. By the mid-twentieth century, this movement had resulted in a hypertrophy of rules, procedures, and litigation relating to questions of valuation. . . .

Consider the five phases. In the beginning, of course, most commercial societies developed legal collection remedies for individual creditors, in part to reduce violence and other externality-producing behavior accompanying self-help. The second step, taken in ancient times by some societies, was the creation of collective procedures for the whole group of creditors to collect from a debtor; that is, liquidation procedures such as those created by early insolvency and bankruptcy laws. Closely entwined with liquidation procedures, in motivating concept and sometimes in practice, were rules voiding preferential transfers. Group collection procedures not only offer the possibility of realizing economies of scale in creditors' efforts to realize on the value of a debtor's assets; they also allow the reduction of many costs created by the disorderly scramble of individual creditors to be first to collect, regardless of any adverse impact on other creditors or on the overall value to be realized on the debtor's assets. Thus, one commentator has argued persuasively that rules about voidable preferences serve the function of preventing an adverse outcome in a situation that is structurally like the Prisoner's Dilemma of game theory, and that those rules therefore eliminate some substantial costs of uncoordinated action.[23] But because the laws naturally make the debtor's insolvency (in one of many possible senses) a major part of the complex of events that lead to application of a collective liquidation procedure or of the rules about preferential transfers, they create a need to determine whether liabilities (however defined) exceed assets (however defined). To answer this question, some method of valuing assets and liabilities must be chosen.

The third phase, which developed much later in history, involved the use of receivers instead of sheriffs. A receivership can best be understood as a deliberately slowed-down liquidation procedure. Receivers are given adequate, flexible periods of time in which to operate the debtor's business while looking for the best buyer or buyers. The more time they have, the better the prices they might get for particular assets of the debtor. Even more important, they might find a person to buy all or most of the business as a going concern and at a price reflecting the true going-concern value, rather than at a distress price caused by forcing a quick sale in an illiquid or otherwise imperfect market for particular kinds of capital goods and businesses. Whenever the going-concern value of an insolvent debtor's business exceeds its piecemeal liquidation value, and the receivership preserves that excess value, there is a net gain for creditors and society. But this efficient procedure creates a new valuation problem, for the receiver or the supervising court must decide whether going-concern value does in fact exceed liquidation value.

The fourth phase of development occurred in the United States when the equity receivership evolved to the point where all or many of the creditors of the insolvent business debtor could themselves act as the buyers of the business—which would be kept as a going concern, if that made sense—using not cash as the means of payment, but their creditor claims, such as notes, bonds, debentures, or the like, usually valued at face value plus accrued interest.[24] The creditors could, in effect, initiate a transformation of their debt holdings into stock, or into

23. Note, Preferential Transfers and the Value of the Insolvent Firm, 87 Yale L.J. 1449, 1451–54 (1978).

24. My simplified account stresses the net result and ignores intermediate steps and complications. For a good introductory discussion of the formal steps that were typically involved, see H. Henn, Law of Corporations 828-29 (2d ed. 1970).

some mixture of new debt and stock, and at the same time exercise their contractual rights of priority among themselves and against the residual claimants (the old shareholders) in a way that was just as definitive as a real liquidation sale to an outside buyer. This procedure made economic sense whenever there were no or few potential outside buyers with accurate and timely information about the true state of affairs and the future prospects of the business, and when the process of searching for and informing outside buyers would itself be very expensive.

On the other hand, the transformed receivership proceeding—transformed because the usual aim was now to effect a smooth rehabilitation of the business rather than a true liquidation or sale—accentuated valuation problems. Not only did it have to be determined whether going-concern value exceeded liquidation value, but some finite value had to be placed on the whole business. Otherwise, there would be no way of telling where, down the contractually created ranks of creditors and preferred shareholders, it was fair to stop issuing shares and other claims in the newly organized entity owning the business. When a liquidation or receivership results in a true sale to outsiders for cash, this problem simply does not exist. After expenses, the liquidator or receiver pays money to the creditors that are contractually most senior (for example, bond holders) until either no money is left or their contractually specified due amounts are paid in full; then he pays money to creditors in the next tier (for example, debenture holders); and he continues in that fashion until the money runs out. By contrast, when the business is not converted to cash or its equivalent, the valuation problem must be faced in order to accomplish a distribution of new tickets. Moreover, the valuation problem is made more difficult by the conflicts of interest that various groups of claimants have with respect to one another. In addition, some groups, such as managers that are also substantial shareholders, may have superior access to information, procedural powers to delay, and other bargaining advantages that are irrelevant to the concept of the receivership and hence felt to be unfair.

The fifth and final phase in the development of corporate debtor-creditor law involved the formal establishment of a bankruptcy reorganization law that offered a more structured version of the transformed equity receivership. In the United States, this occurred most definitively with the passage of the Chandler Act in 1938.[25] The ritual of the self-sale was dropped. All corporations in reorganization would presumptively be subjects of a reorganization plan that would primarily involve a reshuffling of the paper claims against the business assets. Furthermore, such restructuring of debt might be accomplished by a two-thirds majority vote within the classes of debtors, so that a good

25. Chandler Act, Pub.L. No. 75–696, 52 Stat. 840 (1938) (current version at 11 U.S.C. §§ 101–1330 (Supp. III 1979)). Before this Act, Congress had adopted section 77 in 1933 to provide for railroad reorganizations and section 77B in 1934 to cover other corporations. These were replaced by Chapter X of the Chandler Act.

plan might be forced on otherwise obstreperous creditors. These refinements, however, simply increased the need for careful judicial supervision of the valuation process.

It may be wondered why the final two or three phases in the development of creditors' remedies occurred so late in the history of trade and commerce. One explanation might be that lawyers in early times simply failed to think of the legal inventions and their advantages. The hypothesis would be that the timing of legal innovations is basically a random matter, and that it takes time for ingenious persons to happen to be put in contact with situations that admit of improvement, and to see the solutions. An alternative, more idea-oriented explanation is that earlier lawyers were intellectually blinded by the influence of their modes of legal thought. Some general shift in the dominant conceptual frameworks or value systems of leading lawyers was needed before the new procedures could be conceived, taken seriously, and adopted.[26]

Both explanations may well have some validity. But the hypothesis that seems most powerful to me is more economic and institutional: only with the rise of very large business enterprises were there sufficiently frequent and sizable economies of scale in debt-enforcement proceedings to justify the legal innovations in question. Unless the surplus of going-concern value over liquidation value was substantial, as it might be for a large business, or the debtor business was so large and complex that it would have been impossible or quite expensive to find or to create a fair-sized pool of reasonably informed potential outside buyers, the efficiency benefits of a receivership or reorganization proceeding would not exceed the very substantial administrative, negotiating, and legal costs of the proceeding itself.[27] In principle, this hypothesis can be tested against the historical evidence.

Notes & Questions

1. *The Context in which Reorganization Laws are Enacted.* Although the existence of large business enterprises may be a prerequisite to the rise of complex reorganization provisions, a positive theory of their origins might take account of one other factor. Enactment or reliance upon reorganization structures (or any bankruptcy laws) rarely occurs in times of economic prosperity. Their genesis may require both large businesses and substantial widespread economic distress. Does recognition of the economic context in which reorganization provisions arise offer any insights into reorganization laws? Laws born of economic distress can be expected to be heavily oriented towards debtors. Reorganization laws, like other recent bankruptcy laws, provide debtors

---

26. See R. Gordon, Approaches to the Study of Legal Thought and Legal Practice in Late 19th Century America (April 1980) (unpublished paper delivered at a Harvard Law School Seminar on Basic Legal Research).

27. These costs are high in the more advanced proceedings because of the greater need to consider valuation questions.

with substantive rules more favorable than those provided by nonbankruptcy laws.

2. The Effect of the Bankruptcy Reform Act of 1978

J. TROST, G. TREISTER, L. FORMAN, K. KLEE, & R. LEVIN, THE NEW FEDERAL BANKRUPTCY CODE 237–43 (1979)

Under current bankruptcy law [that in effect prior to the Bankruptcy Reform Act of 1978] debtors seeking reorganization rather than liquidation can choose between one of three similar, but yet distinct, reorganization chapters. Individuals and partnerships engaged in business may file under chapter XI, or, if the debtor owns property encumbered by a real estate mortgage, chapter XII. Corporations may file under chapter XI or under chapter X. The basic differences between chapters X and XI are few. Insofar as corporations are concerned, chapter X adds to the reorganization process (1) the substitution of the independent trustee for debtor control in most cases, (2) the absolute priority rule, (3) the active participation of the Securities and Exchange Commission, (4) the requirement of court approval of a plan before solicitation of acceptance of a plan, and (5) the ability to directly deal with stockholders. Notions that chapter X facilitates jurisdiction over subsidiaries or the ability to deal with secured creditors are more imaginary than real. The two most significant differences are with respect to the displacement of management and the absolute priority rule. In chapter XI, the "best interests of creditors" test permits stockholders to retain their interest even though debt is scaled down; and the debtor's management remains in control. In chapter X, the "absolute priority" rule requires that junior interests, whether stockholder or subordinated debt, lose their position unless senior creditors are provided for in full; and the debtor's management is replaced by the independent trustee in almost every case.

Creditors lose an extremely important flexibility in the negotiation process by the current choices of reorganization procedures. Suppose creditors do not want management replaced by an independent trustee, but do want the reorganization plan to adhere to the absolute priority rule. Today, creditors would be required to seek conversion of the proceeding from chapter XI to chapter X; and if successful, management is replaced by a trustee. Or suppose that subordinated debenture holders want management displaced by an independent trustee; they inherit the absolute priority rule and probable loss of their interests.

One of the most significant changes made by the new Bankruptcy Code is in the treatment of business reorganizations. Eliminated is the diverse treatment of public and private corporations first codified in 1938 with the adoption of chapters X and XI. Eliminated are the differences in jurisdiction of the court and powers of the estate between businesses operated in one chapter versus another. Eliminated is the power of the chapter XI debtor to force liquidation if creditors do not agree to his business rescue plan. Controlled is the practice of lawyers trafficking in claims for the purpose of obtaining employment. Eliminated is the fair and equitable rule and its requirement of valuation hearings in every public case and its limitations on the power of creditors to allocate, by majority vote, the going concern values of businesses. Eliminated are the nondischargeable debt threats that hampered many a worthy corporate reorganization. Validated is the pre-bankruptcy solicitation of acceptances to a rescue plan of a public company, and eliminated is the autocratic authority of the Securities & Exchange Commission to decide when to permit pre-filing plans to be approved in bankruptcy without a protracted procedure. And eliminated is the practice of debtors soliciting creditors to accept a substantial reduction in their claims and yet providing only scanty information on which to make that most important business decision.

Replacing our archaic chapters X, XI and XII structure is a single reorganization chapter, chapter 11 of title 11 of the United States Code. Available to all business enterprises, whether individuals, partnerships or corporations, chapter 11 does not distinguish between public and private corporations. Trustees can be appointed in cases large and small, regardless of the form of business entity, whenever the needs of the case require a change in management. Provided the plan is accepted by the requisite majorities, the absolute priority rule is abolished; it is replaced by a simple "more than liquidation" standard to protect the dissenting creditors of accepting classes. Rights of stockholders and secured creditors, as well as priority and non-priority creditors, can be affected in all cases. Adequate disclosure of financial information is required to solicit acceptances to plans in private as well as public enterprises. Procedural delays have been eliminated and no longer should a worthy "patient" succumb to the cost of the financial rehabilitation operation.

3. The Purpose of Chapter 11 Proceedings

(a) *Manville.* On August 26, 1982, Manville Corporation and 20 of its subsidiaries having a net worth of $1.1 billion filed chapter 11 petitions. Manville did not allege that it was insolvent or unable to pay its debts as they became due. The basis for its action is discussed in the following affidavit, filed with the Chapter 11 petition under a local bankruptcy rule. Consider whether Manville should be allowed to invoke Chapter 11.

"Manville is a diversified manufacturing, mining and forest products company which conducts its business through five principal operating subsidiaries. This corporate structure resulted from the 1981 reorganization of Johns–Manville Corporation which was accomplished to promote improved asset management and to increase public awareness of the businesses comprising Manville Corporation. . . .

"Johns-Manville Corporation and various of the other Debtors (collectively 'JM'), were, as of June 30, 1982, defendants or co-defendants in approximately 11,000 asbestos health law suits brought by approximately 15,550 individual plaintiffs in numerous jurisdictions throughout the United States in which the plaintiffs alleged damage to their health particularly due to their exposure to asbestos fiber, either during manufacturing operations in which asbestos fiber was used as a raw material or in the course of handling products containing asbestos.

"The 1982 figures represent an increase over the December 31, 1981 level of 9,300 cases brought by 12,800 plaintiffs and the December 31, 1980 level of 5,087 cases brought by 9,300 plaintiffs.

"During the first half of 1982, JM was the subject of an average of approximately 425 newly-commenced asbestos-related law suits per month instituted by an average of approximately 495 new plaintiffs per month, compared to the 1981 average of 400 new cases and 560 new plaintiffs per month and the 1980 average of 230 new cases and 365 new plaintiffs per month. During the first half of 1982, JM disposed of 698 claims (plaintiffs and potential plaintiffs) at an average cost to JM of $18,690 per claim (excluding defense costs). All disposition cost references exclude legal expenses and court costs. JM disposed of approximately 1,885 claims during 1981 at an average cost per claim of $15,025, while in 1980 470 claims were disposed of at an average cost of $22,710 per claim.

"The cumulative average for all asbestos-related claims disposed of through June 30, 1982 (a total of approximately 3,470 claims) is $16,600 per claim. These disposition costs do not include the verdicts in approximately twenty-three cases which are presently subject to post-trial motions or appeals filed by JM. Including these twenty-three verdicts in historical disposition costs through June 30, 1982 results in an average cost to JM of approximately $20,690 per claim. The current cost for disposition of these cases, including defense expenses, has risen to approximately $40,000.

"JM was, for the first time in 1981, found liable by juries for punitive damages in five separate asbestos-related actions. All of these cases are presently subject to post-trial motions or appeals filed by JM. The average of the punitive damages awarded against JM in these five cases (one of which involved eleven plaintiffs) and five cases decided during the first half of 1982 is approximately $616,000 per case.

"The majority of the foregoing claims upon which these suits are based allege JM and other defendants failed in their duty to warn of the hazards of exposure to and inhalation of asbestos fiber and dust originating from asbestos containing products. JM anticipates an increasing number of such cases both being commenced and proceeding to trial in the future, and thus there continues to be uncertainty as to whether punitive damages will be assessed against JM.

"In early 1981, JM commissioned outside consultants to conduct a study to try to project the future volume of asbestos cases. This study has been completed and indicates that commencement of new asbestos-related litigations may well continue for a number of years.

"Manville Corporation's Board of Directors, and a special committee appointed by the Board to oversee the review of the consultant's report, have concluded that the potential future impact on JM, Manville and various other of the Debtors which are named or potential defendants of pending and future asbestos cases could and probably will exceed Manville's ability to pay and finance the continuing operation of Manville's businesses.

. . .

"It has been estimated that the financial burden of these litigations upon Manville could range from anywhere between $2 billion to many times that amount over the next twenty years. Confronted with such potentially massive liabilities, Manville would have no recourse except to sell, liquidate or otherwise dispose of assets and dismember its businesses in order to continue to pay the costs of disposing of these suits. Not only would a point soon be reached where future successful plaintiffs would be unable to collect the amounts of their judgments or proposed settlements, but all other creditors of Manville would likewise be confronted with the stark realization that they too could not be paid nearly in full.

"Therefore, in order to treat all creditors of Manville even-handedly, whether their claims at the present time be liquidated or unliquidated, contingent or noncontingent, mature or unmatured, Manville has reluctantly, but of necessity, deemed the filing of the within chapter 11 petitions to be an economic imperative. . . .

See generally Note, The Manville Bankruptcy: Treating Mass Tort Claims in Chapter 11 Proceedings, 96 Harv.L.Rev. 1121 (1983).

(b) *Texaco.* On April 12, 1987, Texaco, Inc. filed the largest case in the history of bankruptcy law. Pennzoil prevailed in a Texas state court action alleging that Texaco had induced Getty Oil Co. to breach its contract to sell its shares to Pennzoil. Pennzoil's judgment against Texaco was for more than $8 billion. To stay enforcement of a judgment pending appeal, Texas law required an appellant to post a bond equal to the amount of the judgment. Texaco claimed a net worth well in excess of $8 billion, but was incapable of posting the bond without liquidating assets. It sought relief in federal court from the Texas bonding requirement. The Supreme Court ruled that federal courts should not interfere with the state's enforcement of judgment mechanism and denied relief.[a] Texaco's bankruptcy filing followed.

Should Texaco be able to use bankruptcy law to forestall judgment while it pursues state court appeals? Suppose the state court judgment were final. Should Texaco be able to use bankruptcy law to delay paying the judgment?

B. The Trustee, the Creditors' Committees, and Corporate Governance

The filing of a Chapter 11 petition gives rise to the creation of the creditors' committee. § 1102(a)(1). Many of the important requests in a Chapter 11 case will be made by or passed on by the creditors' committee. It normally will make the initial decision as to whether to ask the court to order liquidation or appointment of a trustee. The committee may hire professionals who may be compensated out of estate assets.[b] §§ 1103(a); 328; 503. The committee may conduct its own investigation of the debtor and will shape or pass judgment upon

---

a. Pennzoil, Co. v. Texaco, Inc., ___ U.S. ___, 107 S.Ct. 1519, 95 L.Ed.2d 1 (1987).

b. For a case holding that members of a creditors' committee may not obtain reim- bursement of *their* costs from the estate, see In re Major Dynamics, 16 B.R. 279 (Bkrtcy.S.D.Cal.1981).

any reorganization plan. Under § 1121(c), it may propose its own plan. Creditors' committees may initiate proceedings to recover preferences, Committee of Unsecured Creditors v. Monsour Medical Center, 5 B.R. 715 (Bkrtcy.W.D.Pa.1980), to prosecute antitrust claims, Liberal Market, Inc. v. Malone & Hyde, Inc., 14 B.R. 685 (Bkrtcy.S.D.Ohio 1981), and to intervene in adversary proceedings. Official Unsecured Creditors' Committee v. Michaels, 689 F.2d 445 (3d Cir. 1982). Because the committee is likely to have substantial influence with the debtor and the court, representation on the committee may be important to a creditor or group of creditors.[c] Given the power of creditors' committees one important decision the United States trustee and bankruptcy courts face is whether to appoint additional committees of creditors or equity security holders. For example, in Texaco's bankruptcy, a committee of industry (oil company) creditors was established separately from the general unsecured creditor's committee.

Assume that you are serving on a creditors' committee and the first question before the committee is whether to seek the appointment of a trustee to run the business. What factors should influence your decision?

IN RE LIBERAL MARKET, INC.

United States Bankruptcy Court, Southern District of Ohio, 1981.
11 B.R. 742

CHARLES A. ANDERSON, BANKRUPTCY JUDGE.

The Liberal Market, Inc. filed a voluntary petition under Chapter 11 of the Bankruptcy Code on 4 February 1981, listing total assets in the amount of $22,551,000.00 and total liabilities in the amount of $29,117,000.00, of which the amount of $8,600,000.00 was delineated as secured.

Prior to filing, a protracted labor dispute had been in process between the Debtor and United Food and Commercial Workers Union, Local 1552 (United), and the Amalgamated Food and Allied Workers, District Union No. 430 (Amalgamated), both of which are affiliated with the United Food and Commercial Workers International Union, AFL–CIO. The Collective Bargaining Agreement had expired on 19 January 1981, and a bitter strike was in process.

Before the strike, 17 super markets in Hamilton, Fairborn, Dayton and Cincinnati, were open for business (several stores having been closed during the previous two years). Two stores were closed shortly before the strike, five were closed after the strike, and eight were in operation after the Chapter 11 case was instituted.

Upon motion filed on 2 March 1981 by a major supplier, Malone & Hyde, Inc., raising the question of adequate protection, and upon

---

c. See generally Meir & Brown, Representing Creditors' Committees Under Chapter 11 of the Bankruptcy Code, 56 Am.Bankr.L.J. 217 (1982).

consent of the Debtor-in-Possession, the operation of the business was ordered terminated by order entered 3 March 1981.

On 3 March 1981, the union filed an application, seeking the appointment of an "Operating Trustee" and "for such other and further relief as [to] this Court may seem just and proper." In pertinent part, it was alleged that the Debtor [in Possession] was continuing payments on unoccupied leased premises, "apparently owned by one of the principal shareholders of the Debtor; and, that Debtor [in Possession] has been selling inventory for as little as one-half its actual value without the permission of the Court."

At a preliminary hearing held on 9 March 1981 on this application, the Creditors' Committee declined to join because of the need for additional time to analyze the business operations. Insufficient evidence as to fraud, dishonesty, incompetence or gross mismanagement by current management, or similar cause for the appointment of a trustee was adduced to justify a finding, although there was a general consensus that the value of the assets would be naturally more enhanced by a going business posture. In behalf of the Unions it was testified that no operating capital could be derived from this source; although, there was testimony that prospects for sale might exist (to sources not disclosed) for the more prosperous locations.

At a continued hearing held on 16 March 1981, the Creditors' Committee joined in support of the motion for appointment of a trustee and filed a memorandum expanding allegations for cause in greater specificity. Summarized, the Committee represented that the "accounting records of the Debtor are likely to be unreliable"; that Debtor "owes its parent corporation and affiliated entities in excess of $7,000,000.00" upon which there had been substantial repayments within the last year; leases of properties from the parent and/or affiliates; the Debtor "shares common officers with its parent and affiliates"; and that the "parent company, two of its affiliates and four of its officers and directors are guarantors" on the debt of the principal secured creditor, Malone and Hyde, Inc. and M & H Financial Corp. Conclusions from this, suggesting dishonesty, conflict of interest and "multiple improprieties", were urged. These allegations were based in great part upon Debtor's own Schedules and Statement of Affairs filed in the case.

In behalf of the Debtor-in-Possession, it was admitted that there is no present intention of devoting any effort to reopen any of the stores; and that a search for buyers is contemplated, as a liquidation of all assets.

DECISION AND ORDER

Based upon the preliminary records before the court and the conclusions urged by the Creditors' Committee, considerable reason exists to appoint a trustee (or examiner, at least).

It must be noted, however, that the allegations of "improprieties" may be a rationalization, which additional facts might mitigate. Because of the need for the urgency in charting a course and the rapidity of hearing schedules, it must be obvious that counsel for the Debtor-in-Possession were seriously hampered in mustering a rebuttal position.

The court feels constrained, therefore, to draw no conclusion at this time as to "cause", as postulated by movants under the provisions of 11 U.S.C. § 1104(a)(1).

However, the question of "the interests of creditors . . . and other interests of the estate" under § 1104(a)(2) must be confronted for several reasons.

In behalf of Debtor it has been urged that assuming that the appointment of a Trustee is clearly in the interests of creditors, Section 1104(a)(2) requires that the appointment be also in the interests of any equity security holders. As urged, "It is clear on the face of the statute that the test to appoint a Trustee . . . is a conjunctive test; a test that finds the appointment of the trustee in the interests of creditors and any equity security holders and other interests of the estate."

This is an interesting reading of the statute. The court can concur in this proposition to the extent that there should be no purpose in appointing a trustee to discriminate unfairly and illegally against the interests of any class, as such. There are other statutory safeguards, nevertheless, to cope with the treatment under a plan of reorganization to be afforded the various types of interests. There is no variation in the confirmation standards after the appointment of a trustee (or an examiner).

11 U.S.C. § 1129 (a)(8) requires that each class either have accepted the plan or remain unimpaired. Also, we again draw attention to the severe inadequacy of assets to meet liabilities if there is to be a liquidation plan. If liquidation occurs, the equity interests are already submerged and valueless. Vestiges of the "absolute priority rule" still arise, and a plan proposed must be fair and equitable to all impaired classes. Under 11 U.S.C. § 1129(b)(2)(C)(ii), the court must confirm a plan despite the dissent of a class of interests if the holders of any interests junior to a dissenting class will not receive or retain any property on the strength of such junior interests.

Hence, the conclusion is inescapable that whenever the appointment of a trustee (or examiner) is in the interests of senior classes, junior classes will not be affected adversely and can only be correspondingly benefitted as senior interests are satisfied. The prime factor for all classes is the maximizing of values.

The first factor involved is the nature of the "reorganization" case as it is now existing. Even though Section 1123(b)(4) permits a plan of reorganization to provide for sale of all or substantially all of the property of the estate, this feature must be read *in pari materia* with

Section 1123(a)(5)(D) which contemplates the sale in the execution of a plan of reorganization.

The second factor of substance is the recommendation of the Creditors' Committee appointed by the Court. It is the Committee which is charged with the responsibility and interposition for the creditors between the Debtor-in-Possession and the judicial process, as fiduciary. The Committee, furthermore, is composed of very busy businessmen who cannot be expected to devote valuable time in actively monitoring all of the day by day intricacies of a liquidating process. In such a case as now *sub judice* the end product is finite—there will be no future potential for the various classes, and no viable business to reorganize.

The estate and the court are confronted with an emergency sitution, the consequences of which very likely will be fatal to the best interests of all interested parties. The fact is not subject to any controversy that the business operations should if possible be reinstituted (and the sooner the better), if a going concern value is to be achieved for the business assets. Every day that the business is closed will directly diminish the feasibility of operating various stores, particularly the more profitable locations because customers will rapidly find other sources of supply.

Debtor's management has unequivocally concluded that no efforts will be made by management to reopen, and no operating capital will be forthcoming from that source. The Creditors' Committee and the unions particularly urge that the business must be operated, although they also have not furnished the source or sources of operating capital.

Since the economic and financial conditions are so desperate and critical, it is obvious that the appointment of a statutory trustee with full powers, authority and duties would be ill-advised, if not foolhardy, because of the consequent, overwhelming drain on assets for the non-productive, administrative expenses of a trustee, especially duplicative of the efforts by Debtor's management to operate the business under the burden of protracted collective bargaining in the labor market for several years. Presumably in the winding down of the business and the liquidation of business assets, submarginal stores would remain closed.

The equity jurisdiction of the bankruptcy court and the functions of the All Writs Statute, 28 U.S.C. § 1651, and 11 U.S.C. § 105 are available to supply interstitial procedural devices in adapting the reorganization vehicle to a viable liquidation vehicle. Furthermore, it may well be rationalized on final analysis that the request for a trustee or "other relief" under such conditions as now exist is in reality a request for conversion to Chapter 7 under 11 U.S.C. § 1112(b).

So as not to thwart the purposes of the Debtor-in-Possession to submit a Plan of reorganization, or other interested parties also to submit a Plan, an interim remedy will be fashioned in order to maintain maximized economic values until more mature business details can be mustered by the parties. The appointment of a trustee and divesting of the title of Debtor on the present condition of the record should, therefore, be forestalled until the expiration of the statutory exclusive time limitations for the Debtor's proposed plan and confirmation, which has not to date been reduced. The appointment of a trustee will continue to be justiciable, upon presentation of more facts by interested parties.

When old case precedents were negated by providing for the liquidation of a business (11 U.S.C. § 1123(b)(4)), certainly such a liquidation is contemplated under Chapter 11 only in connection with a Plan duly confirmed, and not as a substitute to avoid the thrust and expedition of a Chapter 7 Trustee. It is still reasonable to read the spirit of such cases as In re Pure Penn. Petroleum Co., 188 F.2d 851, 2d Cir. (1951), into any scheme of using a "reorganization" process as a subterfuge and overly luxurious administrative vehicle to accomplish a purpose no different from a more expeditious Chapter 7 liquidation. Hence, it is not unreasonable for the court to interpret and conclude in a liquidation Chapter 11 that the mere request to appoint a trustee, for either cause or best interests, may be deemed a request for conversion to a Chapter 7 liquidation. For reasons to be more apparent later, we do not now draw that conclusion.

The court is of the opinion that, short of a conversion, the Debtor should be permitted to exercise its statutory, exclusive right to submit a plan of reorganization and should be permitted to remain in possession, subject to imposed restrictions.

Based upon the record as it now exists, there is not sufficient proof of cause for appointment of a trustee because of fraud, dishonesty, incompetence, or gross mismanagement of the affairs of the debtor by current management, either before or since the commencement of this case. If the stores can be feasibly reopened so as not to lose going concern value, similar cause might well exist on retrospection even before any additional proof has been offered.

This factor alone dictates that the possession and operation of the business by management, which has already concluded that the reopening of business operations is not feasible, should not be countenanced.

The court has a tool available under the terms of 11 U.S.C. § 1106(b), without regard to the equity jurisdiction of a bankruptcy court, to deal with the interests of the various parties now involved. We direct attention to the authority in this statute authorizing an examiner to perform "any other duties of the trustee that the court orders the debtor-in-possession not to perform." Hence, the court may give an examiner additional duties not specifically enumerated as circumstances such as involved *instanter* warrant. See House Report No. 95–595, 95th Cong. 1st Sess. (1977) 404, U.S.Code Cong. & Admin. News 1978, p. 5787. Obviously, operation of the business of Debtor is a function of a trustee conformably to 11 U.S.C. § 1108, which business operation does not even require a court order.

Based upon the foregoing summary analysis, It is

Ordered, Adjudged and Decreed that Ira W. Rubin should be and is hereby appointed as Examiner for and with the following purposes and duties, to-wit:

(1) Except to the extent that the court may order otherwise, investigate the acts, conduct, assets, liabilities, and financial condition of the Debtor, the operation of the Debtor's business and the desirability of the continuance of the business, and any other matter relevant to the case or to the formulation of a plan;

(2) As soon as practicable, file a statement of such investigation, including any fact ascertained pertaining to fraud, dishonesty, incompetence, misconduct, mismanagement, or irregularity in the management of the affairs of the debtor, or to any cause of action available to the estate;

(3) Assume the authority formerly vested in the Debtor-in-Possession to supervise and control the operation of the business, or any part thereof deemed advisable, upon approval of the Creditors' Committee, and as soon as proper financing has been assured.

The Examiner may, at his discretion, draw from the Debtor-in-Possession current management personnel for the implementation of daily business activities.

(4) Recommend as soon as possible whether there should be a conversion of the case to a case under Chapter 7.

Ordered, Adjudged and Decreed, that all of the other statutory rights of a debtor-in-possession, including title and possession of debtor's assets, and the exclusive right to file a Plan of reorganization, shall remain intact and in full force and effect until further order herein.

Ordered, that the chief executive officer, or nominee, of United Food and Commercial Workers Union, Local 1552, and also, of Amalgamated Food and Allied Workers, District Union No. 430, are hereby added as members of the Creditors' Committee heretofore appointed pursuant to 11 U.S.C. § 1102, unless or until a special additional committee of creditors be appointed which includes such labor union executives.

———

See also Official Creditors' Committee v. The Liberal Market, Inc., 13 B.R. 748 (Bkrtcy.S.D.Ohio 1981) (denying appointment of trustee but seeking further information as to whether case should be converted to Chapter 7).

Notes & Questions

1. *Chapter 7 vs. Chapter 11.* Why would a debtor, such as Liberal Market, who believes its business should no longer be operated, invoke Chapter 11 instead of Chapter 7? Compare § 1104 with §§ 701, 702. How should a court respond to this tactic? Do the creditors in *Liberal*

Market have any other remedy? See § 1112. Is Liberal Market a worthier applicant for Chapter 11 relief than Manville Corporation?

2. *Standards Governing Appointment of a Trustee.* The Senate version of the bankruptcy reform bill would have provided for mandatory appointment of a trustee in cases involving "public companies," which the bill defined as companies having more than $5 million in liabilities and more than 1,000 security holders, and would have left the court discretion to appoint a trustee in cases filed by or against nonpublic companies. Senate Report at 115. The House version would have allowed appointment of a trustee only if the protection afforded by the trustee is needed and the costs and expenses of a trustee would not be disproportionately higher than the value of the protection afforded. House Report at 402–03. If a large, publicly held company is in Chapter 11, may the court appoint a trustee because of the diffuse holdings of the security holders and their general need for protection from management?

In Committee of Dalkon Shield Claimants v. A.H. Robins Company, Inc., 828 F.2d 239 (4th Cir.1987), the district court found the debtor, Robins, to be in civil contempt of an order barring Robins from selectively paying off pre-petition debts without prior court approval. Robins made payments on pre-petition claims, including payments to present and past executives and made certain charitable contributions. The district court found that Robins had not only "knowingly, unknowingly, or because of failure to comprehend the Court's order violated a court order, but also [had] taken certain actions prohibited by both the spirit and the letter of the bankruptcy laws." The district court refused to equate the contempt finding with cause for appointment of a trustee under § 1104(a)(1). The court of appeals affirmed.

3. *The Cost of a Trustee.* If a secured party seeks and obtains appointment of a trustee, may it be forced to bear the expenses and fees incurred by the trustee in the event that the reorganization plan fails? See § 506(c). In In re Hotel Associates, Inc., 6 B.R. 108 (Bkrtcy.E.D.Pa. 1980), the secured party did not object to awarding the trustee § 506(c) expenses but was "vehement in its opposition to the granting of an assurance that all administrative costs and expenses which are incurred [in the proposed reorganization] will be honored either by the [secured] asset . . . or th[r]ough the holders of the secured claims." The debtor's sole substantial asset was its interest in the secured party's collateral. The court ordered that the trustee be given the assurance it requested. Compare In re Robertson, 14 B.R. 706 (Bkrtcy. N.D.Ga.1981) (administrative expense of sale does not come ahead of security interest where secured party did not seek trustee's appointment).

4. *Residual Effects of Appointing a Trustee.* A pension fund made a secured loan to a hotel corporation. The debtor defaulted and the pension fund, pursuant to the terms of its mortgage, took possession of the hotel as mortgagee in possession, hired a professional management

service to operate the property, and retained independent accountants
to audit the hotel's books. The evidence showed that the hotel had not
been run properly and that the books had not been properly maintained. Why would the pension fund seek appointment of a trustee
given that it had possession of the property? See § 1121(c)(1); Hotel
Associates, Inc. v. Trustees of Central States Southeast and Southwest
Areas Pension Fund, 3 B.R. 343 (Bkrtcy.E.D.Pa.1980). Does it make
sense to give a party an incentive to seek appointment of a trustee to
enable the party to obtain an early opportunity to file a Chapter 11
plan?

   5. *Examiners.* The *Liberal Market* court refused to appoint a
trustee but did appoint an examiner. What is the difference between
the two? Compare § 1106(b) with § 1108.

C. The Plan and Interim Issues

   The plan is the heart of any Chapter 11 reorganization. It is the
plan that, when confirmed, binds the debtor and the debtor's shareholders and creditors. See § 1141. The plan sets forth the treatment of
claims and interests and the means for fulfilling its goals. § 1123.
Although the standards governing confirmation of plans, studied infra,
shape much of its content, several important issues involving the plan's
content are worth isolating.

IN RE WHITE MOTOR CREDIT CORP.
United States Bankruptcy Court, Northern District of Ohio, 1981.
14 B.R. 584.

MARK SCHLACHET, BANKRUPTCY JUDGE.

   [White Motor Corporation, a manufacturer of heavy trucks and farm
equipment, and its subsidiaries, Gemini and White Motor Credit Corporation ("White Credit"), filed Chapter 11 petitions on September 4,
1980. It listed assets of $598 million and liabilities of $540 million.
The debtor continued to operate the business and its losses mounted.
In June 1981, the White group entered into an agreement to sell
substantially all of its truck manufacturing operations to a subsidiary
of AB Volvo, and sought court approval.]

   This matter arises upon (a) the application of certain debtors (sometimes referred to as a "debtor") for a hearing to consider a sale of
substantially all of the operating assets of White Motor Corporation
("White" or "White Motor") and Gemini Manufacturing Co. ("Gemini"),
and (b) the application relating to such sale filed by the Official
Creditors' Committee of Gemini. Although the scheduling of a hearing
is ordinarily a routine matter, such action herein has most serious
implications and has required hearing time, including substantial testimony and argument, on June 15, July 9 and July 21, 1981.

   7. White's current market penetration is alleged to be 2% as
compared with pre-petition levels in excess of 5%; significant accounts
have lately turned to competitors to fill their needs for diesel trucks,

including fleets thereof; the dealer network has indicated an erosion of confidence in White, while valued employees continue to leave the debtors' employ; losses for 1981 on a "stand-alone" basis are estimated to exceed $40 million with any return to profitability subject to both questionable assumptions and factors (e.g. lower interest rates and general market recovery) over which White has no control.

8. As indicated above, White Motor has incurred significant losses in excess of $33 million since the filing date and management forecasts that such losses will continue.

9. On June 9, 1981, White Motor, Gemini and White Motor International, Inc. entered into an agreement with AB Volvo for the sale of substantially all those debtors' truck manufacturing operations to a subsidiary of AB Volvo. The conditions precedent to the obligations of AB Volvo under this purchase agreement include (a) the entry of an order which unconditionally approves the agreement and the transaction contemplated by it and (b) consummation of the sale no later than August 31, 1981. Accordingly, unless the Volvo transaction is approved by the Court at a time which will permit the closing to take place by August 31, 1981, AB Volvo may withdraw its offer to purchase the truck manufacturing operations of White Motor and its affiliates.

10. As of the date hereof, it does not appear that any other purchaser has come forward with a serious offer to acquire the truck manufacturing operations of White Motor and the related entities.

11. The creditors of White and Gemini include vendors, trade suppliers, holders of public debt, both senior and junior, various lending institutions, employees, pensioners and others. These interests are divergent and indicate varying and opposing preferences as to the future course of debtors' activities.

12. At the hearing held on June 15, 1981, White Motor and Gemini informed the Court that they intended to apply for an order scheduling a hearing to consider the Volvo transaction. At that time, the Indenture Trustee for the subordinated debentureholders of White Motor objected to the proposed application until such time as the Court has determined whether it is appropriate to consider a sale of substantially all of a debtor's assets prior to the filing and/or confirmation of a plan of reorganization. The Court directed all interested parties to address those issues at a hearing scheduled for July 9, 1981.

13. Subsequently, the Official Creditors' Committee of Gemini filed an application with the Court for an order establishing the procedures upon which the Volvo sale might be considered, such procedure to include a determination of whether a plan or plans of reorganization for White Motor and Gemini or their affiliates must be filed or confirmed prior to or concurrent with approval of a sale of substantially all the assets of White Motor and Gemini. As noted above, if such a procedure is established, it is likely that the Volvo agreement will expire before the Court has an opportunity to consider whether such

sale would be in the best interests of creditors of White Motor and affiliated debtors.

14. By order dated May 29, 1981, this Court appointed an Official Committee to represent the interests of equity security holders, which committee has since retained counsel and otherwise functioned as a full participant in these reorganization proceedings. By order dated August 8, 1981, the Court appointed an Official Creditors Committee to represent employees, present and former, which committee has since retained counsel and otherwise functioned as a full participant in these reorganization proceedings. The UAW was appointed to the Official Creditors' Committee of White Motor Corp. and has been active in these proceedings.

15. On April 8, 1981, upon request of Lazard Freres & Co., debtor's investment banker, the Court advised that a transaction with Volvo of the sort now contemplated should be proposed within the context of a plan of reorganization. A similar communication was provided debtor's counsel in May, 1981.

16. Volvo has at all relevant times been indifferent as to the format in which its contemplated asset purchases should be placed before the Court and interested parties.

17. Debtor has had ample opportunity to propose a plan of reorganization premised on the Volvo transaction. This is particularly true in light of 11 U.S.C. § 1129(a)(11), permitting confirmation of a reorganization plan notwithstanding the likelihood of further liquidation or reorganization. See also Section 1127, making liberal provision for plan modification.

18. The Volvo transaction involves a liquidation of all of the assets of Gemini and substantially all of the operating assets of the White Motor Corp.

19. The Official Creditors' Committee of Gemini, subordinated debt equity security holders, and SEC oppose, absent a showing of emergency, consideration of the Volvo transaction in the absence of full compliance by the debtor with subchapter II of Chapter 11 of the Bankruptcy Code.

20. White Credit is a wholly owned subsidiary of White Motor and is a debtor in proceedings before this court. No plan of reorganization has been submitted in said proceeding.

21. Motor has sought and received on eight occasions extensions of the exclusive period within which the debtor alone may propose a plan of reorganization. The period of exclusivity has continued to the present. Thus no other party has had an opportunity to submit a plan of reorganization herein. See 11 U.S.C. § 1121(d).

22. Motor has submitted an extensive "Business Plan", dated July 17, 1981. Such plan does not include specific provision for stand alone interest costs and does not specifically address the implications of

Motor's persistent cash flow problems. It contains the bases for the information contained in paragraphs 7–8 above.

23. Conflicting data, particularly as to the anticipated market share, has been presented to the Court in other proceedings, to wit: on July 30, 1981, U.S.A. Marketing Manager Mr. Mark Obert stated that White expects to enjoy a 5%–6% market share for the fourth quarter, 1981 whereas the business plan suggests a 3.1% market share for the fourth quarter of 1981.

24. The business plan indicates a positive equity, aside from any equity existing by virtue of ownership in White Credit, of up to $100 million in 1987 should the company reorganize on a stand alone basis.

25. It is highly unlikely, under any set of foreseeable conditions or circumstances, that unsecured creditors of White Motor will receive full payment of their pre-petition claims in the near future. A Chapter 7 liquidation of Motor on August 31, 1981 would, absent subordination of major claims and interests, result in the payment of no money in respect of the interest of equity security holders.

PROBLEM

The contemplated sale constitutes a reorganization of White Motor, transforming the manufacturing debtors into what subordinated debt's representative has called a "pot of cash." Debtors seek to accomplish this reorganization under the administrative power of section 363 of the Bankruptcy Code, which section simply permits a sale other than in the ordinary course of business after notice and opportunity for hearing.[1] Such a procedure side-steps the procedural and substantive provisions of Chapter 11 itself, including the disclosure statement (§ 1125), vote (§ 1126) and confirmation standards (§ 1129). There is no acknowledgement or recognition of the sale of all or substantially all of the property of a Chapter 11 debtor outside the provisions of Chapter 11 itself. See, e.g., 11 U.S.C. §§ 1123(a)(5) and (b)(4), 1141(d)(3).

Whether a sale of such scope can be accomplished subject only to section 363 (or its predecessor under the Bankruptcy Act) has never been decided. Similar fact patterns have forged a split of authority. In re D.M. Christian Co., 7 B.R. 561, 7 B.C.D. 87 (Bkrtcy.N.D.W.Va.1980) (rejecting the procedure); contra, In re WFDR, Inc., 10 B.R. 109 (Bkrtcy. N.D.Ga.1981); In re Tele/Resources, Inc., 6 B.R. 628 (Bkrtcy.S.D.N.Y. 1980). Indeed, under the [old] Bankruptcy Act there existed an outright conflict among the circuits. Compare In re Solar Mfg. Corp., 176 F.2d 493 (3rd Cir. 1949), with In re Dania Corporation, 400 F.2d 833 (5th Cir. 1968), cert. denied 393 U.S. 1118, 89 S.Ct. 994, 22 L.Ed.2d 122, reh. denied, 394 U.S. 994, 89 S.Ct. 1455, 22 L.Ed.2d 771 (1969). The

1. It is argued that section 363 is integral to chapter 11. While the statement may be true, it misses the point:

Section 363 is a section of general application in cases under chapters 7, 11 and 13. There are a number of other sec-

tions in the Code of immediate importance in interpreting section 363 or to which reference must be made to understand its application. 2 Collier on Bankruptcy 363–12 (15th ed. 1980).

more restrictive Act authority, i.e., *Solar,* would require an actual emergency, defined perhaps as virtual or near catastrophe. Such emergency would not be found in mere deadlines or eleventh hour pressure imposed by the parties. The liberal view embraced by the Fifth, Seventh and Ninth Circuits permitted such sales in the best interests of the estate merely to avoid erosion of the assets, although in most cases findings of fact indicated severe diminution should the sale not be approved.

The Code's Mandate

In drafting and enacting the Bankruptcy Code, Congress deliberately rejected the suggestion that sales of the scope contemplated by the instant application might be accomplished under section 363(b). The Commission on the Bankruptcy Laws of the United States ("Commission"), charged with the responsibility to study, analyze, evaluate and recommend changes in the bankruptcy laws, submitted in its transmittal to Congress (July 30, 1973) a proposed statute (entitled Bankruptcy Act of 1973) containing the precise provision which debtors and others need in order to sustain their position:

> Sale or Lease of Property. If a lease or sale is not in the ordinary course of business pursuant to section 7–104, the administrator may authorize the sale or lease of property by the trustee or receiver, or by the debtor if there is no trustee or receiver, on such terms and conditions as the administrator may approve. *A sale or lease of all or substantially all of the property of the estate may be authorized by the court if in the best interests of the estate after notice hearing in accordance with Rules of Bankruptcy Procedure.* (emphasis added)

Comm.Rep., pt. II at 239, reprinted in 2 Collier on Bankruptcy (Appendix) (15th ed. 1980). (emphasis added) The explanatory note to the language makes unmistakably clear its relationship to the split of authority identified above, to wit:

> This section is derived from §§ 116(3), 313(2), and 413(2) of the present Act. Property may be sold or leased in the ordinary course of business without additional authorization by the administrator under § 7–104. However, any other sale or lease must be authorized by the administrator. If a debtor, trustee, or receiver believes that a sale or lease of all or substantially all of the property is desirable, such action must be authorized by the court on notice and hearing. There is a split of authority in the case law presently, with some courts allowing this type of sale, but others requiring some showing of emergency. This section makes it clear that a showing of emergency is not necessary.

Clearly, the Commission sought to eliminate the *Solar* requirement that, absent an emergency, virtual liquidations can be accomplished only by way of a plan of reorganization.

The Commission bill was introduced in the House of Representatives on October 9, 1973 as H.R. 10792 by Congressman Donald Edwards, floor manager of the legislation during the entire eight years of its legislative sojourn.   A second bill, containing in section 4–717 the identical language of the last sentence of section 7–205 of the Commission bill, was advanced by the National Conference of Bankruptcy Judges.   It was introduced on September 12, 1974 as H.R. 16643 (the "Judge's bill").   On the Senate side, S. 4026 was the counterpart to the Commission bill.

Matters remained at a standstill until the 94th Congress convened and subjected both proposals to intensive analysis.   The Commission bill was reintroduced as H.R. 31 (S. 236) while the Judge's bill became H.R. 32 (S. 235).   Hearings totalling 56 days were held during 1975–76 in the two Houses.   The Justice Department addressed the legislation orally and in *The Department of Justice Detailed Comments on H.R. 32*[4] which commented specifically on Section 4–717 as follows:

> Sale or lease of 'all or substantially all of the property of the estate' goes beyond the language of the statutes presently applicable.   Sale of so much of the estate's property amounts to a liquidation which should be handled under Chapter V [the liquidation, as opposed to reorganization, chapter] and not in the context of an arrangement or reorganization.   Only in an unusual emergency should such an extensive sale or lease of property be authorized without formal transfer of the case to a liquidation proceeding.

It is difficult to imagine a scenario in which the overruling of *Solar* could be more at issue.

What finally emerged from the Judges bill, Commission bill, hearings and other legislative activity was H.R. 6, the forerunner of the Bankruptcy Code.   Section 363(c) of H.R. 6, identical in relevant aspects to Section 363 of the Bankruptcy Code, granted the trustee or debtor-in-possession administrative power to use, sell or lease property of the estate in the ordinary course of business, without court authorization. This corresponded to sections 7–104 and 4–710 of the Commission and Judges' bills, respectively.   Section 363(b) granted to the trustee or debtor-in-possession authority, after notice and opportunity for hearing, to use, sell or lease property of the estate other than in the [ordinary] course of business.   With procedural differences, e.g., "notice and hearing" rather [than] "on such terms and conditions as the court may approve", such authority corresponded to the first sentence of Sections 7–205 and 4–717 of the Commission and Judges' bills, respectively.

What did not survive the legislative process was the second sentence of sections 7–205 and 4–717 of the two earlier legislative proposals, which provisions had permitted, in the absence of any plan of reorganization, a "sale or lease of all or substantially all of the property of the estate . . . if in the best interests. . . ."   The conscious deletion of the provision is not consistent with its promulgation.

---

4. Hearings on H.R. 31 & H.R. 32, Before the Subcomm. on Civil and Constitutional Rights of the House Comm. on the   Judiciary, 94th Cong., 1st & 2nd Sess., ser. 27, pt. 4 at 2123 (1975–1976).

As a matter of legislative intent, to endow section 363 with the purpose of or a potential for a total reorganization would nullify, at debtor's option, the major protections and standards of chapter 11 of the Code. For example, while section 1129 requires a confirmation hearing as to every liquidating (or other) reorganization plan, section 363 taken together with section 102 requires mere opportunity for hearing. In the instant case, therefore, the Volvo transaction could proceed without any hearing or court order whatever. So manifestly unacceptable a possibility renders further investigation of statutory thrust unnecessary.

It is clear, and the Court holds accordingly, that in a chapter 11 reorganization under the Bankruptcy Code, Section 363(b) does not authorize sale of all or substantially all assets of the estate.

The Emergency Exception

There is an emergency, or at least a crisis, in this case—but one of the debtor's own making. The situation is not one of imminent loss of all assets, but rather, a substantial likelihood of a comparative loss approaching $40 million, according to the debtor's Liquidation Analysis (July 17, 1981), should the sale not proceed. The crisis might have been avoided by firmer Court control and supervision of debtor's activities, or by empowering the examiner with additional functions pursuant to 11 U.S.C. § 1104(c). In any event, it would appear that Congress left the "emergency" exception [intact] and its application is appropriate in this case. 11 U.S.C. § 105.

There are, moreover, other considerations which warrant exceptional treatment of the proposed sale to Volvo. First, White is and has been a first rate if not the leading truck manufacturer in its class VIII classification. Its engineering tradition is second to none. It has, however, suffered over a long period of time from a lack of strong management. While its current chief executive, Wallace Askins, cannot be praised too highly, one man may not be able to, in short order, reinstill the will to survive and accomplish the necessary infusion of dealer confidence.

White's chronic management problems indicate a significant likelihood—particularly under current market conditions over which it has no control—of a less advantageous liquidation should the Volvo agreement not gain approval. In other words, there exists no viable and acceptable alternative to Volvo at this time. No major constituency in this case can cite a strong probability of position enhancement should the Court not consider Volvo prior to August 31st. The potential and probable diminution of assets might well (to those with even a negotiating position) more than offset the anticipated benefits in a stand-alone scenario.

The lack of disclosure and vote cannot at this time be overcome. Nevertheless, it should be noted that the representation enjoyed by employees, pensioners, shareholders and other constituencies herein has been significant if not decisive. Committees have been appointed to represent all substantial interests. These committees have retained professionals, e.g. the equity security holders committee is receiving the assistance of a financial consultant in an effort to identify and assess alternatives to Volvo. All court appointees have been encouraged to co-operate with various interested parties. The SEC and UAW have actively participated in most proceedings and the examiner has proved invaluable as a source of sunshine and enlightenment. Thus, the Volvo transaction has not emerged without the most thorough opportunities for analysis and assessment by all concerned.

Conditional notice of the Volvo proposal has been afforded all creditors, shareholders and other parties in interest. They may appear and be heard.

Thus, while counsel has erroneously disregarded the Court's candid remarks concerning the propriety of a plan format, there has in fact been no purposeful effort by the debtor's management to evade the disclosure requirements of the Code. Indeed, the impact of Volvo on the fate of White Credit (a major subsidiary with a potential dividend to White Motor of $100 million or more) is perhaps the principal justification for the failure to propose a plan in the Motor case. Moreover, based on the present record, the investment banker appears to have performed his tasks well and true; and the examiner has reported that good faith efforts to negotiate a Motor and White Credit plan have been diligently proposed by the debtors and most parties in interest.

The Gemini Problem

The proposed sale of Gemini assets (*i.e.*, the sole source of and manufacturer of cabs for White trucks) presents its own unique problems. Here we have a distinct corporate entity whose assets are commandeered in order to make the Volvo transaction possible. Creditors of Gemini are not told how much Volvo is paying for the assets or what they are worth. Thus, our worst fears emanating from the absence of a reorganization plan are realized.

Specifically, Gemini's creditors are vendors and employees. The lending-institution overlap, which is characteristic of the Motor/Credit relationship, does not exist among Gemini creditors. Hence, a principal justification or reason for failure to file a liquidating plan does not exist. Gemini has other-than-Motor customers. Although Volvo is indifferent as to any allocation to Gemini from gross proceeds, Motor and its creditors have taken no steps to assuage the fears of Gemini creditors emanating from a perceived de facto consolidation of the two firms for purposes of the Volvo transaction.

Thus, a conflict has developed between the two debtors as evidenced by their opposing positions on the sale. While this aspect of the problem should not, in itself, disqualify the transaction, special procedures may be appropriate to assure a fair and expeditious disposition in the Gemini matter. Such procedures must originate with its creditors' committee.   . . .

Procedure

Accordingly, the Court orders as follows:

1. A hearing to consider the proposed sale to Volvo will be held on August 20, 1981, notwithstanding the absence of a plan of reorganization;

2. Upon approval, if any, of the said transaction, Gemini and/or White shall segregate for the benefit of the Gemini estate the sum of $3,500,000, subject to further Order of this Court.

3. In the absence of a plan or plans of reorganization being filed for White Motor, White Credit, Gemini or other affiliates on or before August 31, 1981, the Court may be required to either (a) terminate the exclusive period as to one or more debtors or (b) further empower the examiner(s) to execute the duties contained in 11 U.S.C. § 1106(a)(5).

So Ordered.

JACKSON, BANKRUPTCY, NON–BANKRUPTCY ENTITLEMENTS, AND THE CREDITORS' BARGAIN, 91 Yale L.J. 857, 893–96 (1982)

A reorganization, at least as a start, may be viewed as a *form* of liquidation. The business entity, however, is sold to the creditors themselves rather than to third parties. The drafters of the Bankruptcy Code and almost all commentators have ignored the fact that the Bankruptcy Code's separate system of reorganization is not the only alternative to a piecemeal liquidation of assets. A business may be disposed of ("liquidated") as a *unit* and, if its highest and best use is as a "going concern," it would seem that a properly conceived-of Chapter 7 proceeding would require the entity to be sold (i.e., liquidated) as a unit rather than piecemeal whenever its going concern value exceeds its piecemeal liquidation value.

Reorganization proceedings provide nothing more than a method by which the sale of an enterprise as a going concern may be made to the creditors themselves. This process, like any liquidation procedure, involves two steps. First, the assets of the enterprise are sold. Second, the claims against the debtor are paid out of the proceeds of this sale.

What differs in the situation in which the enterprise is sold to its own claimants is that the valuation of the proceeds out of which the claims against the debtor are to be paid is more difficult. In a straight piecemeal liquidation, either the assets are distributed in kind to secured claimants (thus mimicking their non-bankruptcy rights) or the assets are sold (usually for cash) and the cash is distributed to the parties, principally in the order of their non-bankruptcy entitlements. In a going concern liquidation, the business is sold to a third party, usually for cash and/or marketable securities. In many instances, therefore, the liquidation process will involve simply paying off the claims, in the order of their non-bankruptcy entitlements. The value of the payment for these claims will be easily determinable. In a reorganization, however, the proceeds from the "sale" out of which claims against the debtor will be paid will consist principally of new claims against the same enterprise. This makes the valuation of the payment to the claimants substantially more difficult. It is principally these valuation issues that provide the core of the reorganization chapter's provisions.

The point, however, is that the difficulties associated with a reorganization proceeding are in the valuation of the proceeds received upon the sale of the enterprise. Whether the process be a piecemeal liquidation, a going concern liquidation (i.e., a sale of the entity to a third party), or a reorganization liquidation (i.e., a sale of the entity to the creditors), nothing in the form of the process seems to call for a different standard of *allocation among claims* (the second step) in one type of proceeding than in another.

This suggests that the relevant inquiry in choosing a Chapter 7 liquidation (piecemeal or going concern) or a Chapter 11 reorganization should be at the first step when the decision is made as to which of the three conceptual processes to use. As the creditors' bargain model would suggest, this decision should be made on the basis of which form provides the greatest aggregate dollar-equivalent return from the assets—a determination that should be made without considering the claims outstanding against those assets (this consideration becomes relevant at the payout, but not at the sale, stage).

. . .

In one respect, this account of the similarities between liquidation and reorganization obscures an important difference between them. Normally, in a liquidation under Chapter 7, the assets are sold off and the "debtor" is, effectively, removed from the picture. Third parties are almost certainly involved, as "owners" if not as managers. The essence of a reorganization, however, is that third parties are *not* involved: the debtor is "continued," albeit the "owners" of the debtor may be replaced to some extent. Although it is possible to overstate this distinction, it is plausible to view a reorganized enterprise as a "continuation" of the web of relationships between the debtor and its former owners and creditors while a liquidation, almost by necessity, involves a disruption of those relationships. Liquidations, therefore, may differ from reorganizations in this respect.   . . .

Notes & Questions

1. *Chapter 7 vs. Chapter 11.* On one level *White Motor* raises a question about the relationship between § 363 and the confirmation requirements under Chapter 11. On another level, may the case be viewed as raising questions about the relationship between Chapter 7

and Chapter 11? Is there a difference between a debtor who really "belongs" in Chapter 7 and one who proposes to sell substantially all of its assets while operating under Chapter 11? Why might such a debtor choose Chapter 11 over Chapter 7? Should *White Motor* be converted to Chapter 7?

If White Motors' liquidating plan could have been accomplished under Chapter 7 instead of Chapter 11, does it make sense to have rules in Chapter 11 that differ from the rules governing Chapter 7? See, e.g., § 1124(2). Several courts have approved sale of all of a debtor's assets where "business purpose" dictates such action. E.g., Stephens Indus., Inc. v. McClung, 789 F.2d 386 (6th Cir.1986).

2. *The Scope of the Power to Sell.* In In re Braniff Airways, Inc., 700 F.2d 935 (5th Cir. 1983), Braniff filed a Chapter 11 petition on May 13, 1982. On December 23, 1982, Braniff sought approval of an agreement with PSA which provided for Braniff's transfer of cash, airplanes, and equipment, terminal leases and landing slots to PSA in return for travel scrip, unsecured notes, and a profit participation in PSA's proposed operation. Braniff also sought approval of a "Memorandum of Understanding" as a basis for settling claims with its creditors. The lower courts found the PSA transaction to be authorized by § 363(b) of the Bankruptcy Act. The Court of Appeals found portions of the transaction beyond the scope of § 363.

> Three examples will illustrate our rationale. The PSA Agreement provided that Braniff would pay $2.5 million to PSA in exchange for $7.5 million of scrip entitling the holder to travel on PSA. It further required that the scrip be used only in a future Braniff reorganization and that it be issued only to former Braniff employees or shareholders or, in a limited amount, to unsecured creditors. This provision not only changed the composition of Braniff's assets, the contemplated result under § 363(b), it also had the practical effect of dictating some of the terms of any future reorganization plan. The reorganization plan would have to allocate the scrip according to the terms of the PSA agreement or forfeit a valuable asset. The debtor and the Bankruptcy Court should not be able to short circuit the requirements of Chapter 11 for confirmation of a reorganization of Chapter 11 by establishing the terms of the plan *sub rosa* in connection with a sale of assets.

> Second, under the agreement between Braniff and its creditors, the secured creditors were required to vote a portion of their deficiency claim in favor of any future reorganization plan approved by a majority of the unsecured creditors' committee. Again, such an action is not comprised by the term "use, sell, or lease," and it thwarts the Code's carefully crafted scheme for creditor enfranchisement where plans of reorganization are concerned.

> Third, the PSA transaction also provided for the release of claims by all parties against Braniff, its secured creditors and its officers

and directors. On its face, this requirement is not a "use, sale or lease" and is not authorized by § 363(b).

3. *Chapter 11 vs. Bail-Outs. White Motor* and *Braniff* represent one class of cases in which concern arises over the use of Chapter 11. Are there other cases in which one should be concerned about Chapter 11's nonuse? If Chapter 11 is designed to capture for the benefit of creditors and shareholders the excess of going concern value over liquidation value, should governments "bail out" firms (such as Chrysler and Lockheed) that qualify for relief under Chapter 11? Consider also the case of a utility that has incurred imprudent costs in constructing a power plant. Imprudent costs normally would be disallowed in setting the utility's rates. Should ratemakers allow otherwise disallowable costs to avoid forcing a utility into Chapter 11? See generally Eisenberg, Bankruptcy in the Administrative State, 50 Law & Contemp. Probs. 3 (Spring 1987).

Are there factors present in the case of a large automobile manufacturer that make Chapter 11 less useful than it would be in the case of a large airplane manufacturer? Can Chapter 11 be amended to remedy whatever led to its nonuse in the Chrysler and Lockheed cases? What are the risks of use of Chapter 11 by a regulated utility?

MANVILLE CORPORATION v. THE EQUITY SECURITY HOLDERS COMMITTEE

United States Court of Appeals, Second Circuit, 1986.
801 F.2d 60.

Before OAKES, ALTIMARI, and MAHONEY, CIRCUIT JUDGES.

MAHONEY, CIRCUIT JUDGE:

This action, one segment in a long-running Chapter 11 reorganization proceeding, arose in consequence of the competing interests of creditors, stockholders, and the board of directors in the development of rehabilitation plans for appellee, the Manville Corporation ("Manville"), formerly Johns–Manville Corporation. Appellants are the Equity Security Holders Committee and individual members of that committee (collectively the "Equity Committee"), appointed by the bankruptcy court to represent the interests of stockholders in Manville's reorganization. The Securities and Exchange Commission, although technically an appellee, shares the interests of the Equity Committee in the matter at hand. Manville is aligned for purposes of this appeal with the Committee of Asbèstos Health Related Claimants and/or Creditors (the "Asbestos Health Committee"), which represents the interests of the victims of diseases resulting from exposure to asbestos who have presently existing claims in tort against Manville, and with the Legal Representative, who represents the interests of future claimants who have not yet manifested such diseases.

The instant conflict arises in part because each of the committees representing the various interests in Manville must depend upon the Manville board of directors to advance those interests in the bankruptcy court at this stage of the rehabilitation proceedings. As debtor, Manville had the exclusive right under the Bankruptcy Code to file rehabilitation plans for the first 120 days of reorganization, and the bankruptcy court in these proceedings has granted Manville several extensions prolonging its exclusive filing period. See 11 U.S.C. § 1121(b), (d) (1982 & Supp. III 1986). Therefore, although in theory each of the committees may one day have the opportunity to submit a rehabilitation plan to the bankruptcy court if Manville's own proposals are rejected or if a trustee is appointed to replace the Manville board, see id. § 1121(c), Manville has for three or four years enjoyed the exclusive right, after negotiating with the committees, to file proposed plans. And although any of the committees may decline to accept a plan submitted to the bankruptcy court for confirmation, the power to formulate such plans in the first instance or at least to exercise a voice in their formulation is clearly a desideratum under the program laid down by the Bankruptcy Code, because the bankruptcy court may confirm a plan with or without the acquiescence of all classes of claims. If any impaired class [3] rejects Manville's proposed plan, the court will nevertheless confirm it, upon Manville's request, so long as at least one impaired class has accepted the plan and so long as the court determines that the plan "does not discriminate unfairly" and is "fair and equitable" to each impaired class that has not accepted it. 11 U.S.C. § 1129(b)(1) (1982 & Supp. III 1986).

In order to channel negotiations toward acceptable plans, the various factions interested in Manville's rehabilitation have formed *ad hoc* alliances when the occasion has called for them. The challenge all the committees have faced is to fashion a plan that will preserve Manville's capacity to generate enough revenue to pay existing creditors, to cover its liabilities to present and future tort claimants where liability is certain though its precise extent is unknown, and to satisfy Manville's shareholders. The seemingly strange bedfellows in the instant litigation, Manville and the committees representing present and future tort claimants, have long struggled to devise a reorganization plan acceptable to each. Along the way they have at times been antagonists rather than allies. For example, the Asbestos Health Committee opposed Manville's first proposed plan, sanctioned by the Equity Committee and filed on November 21, 1983. Other disputes, such as the Asbestos Health Committee's initial refusal to represent future tort claimants, which led to litigation over the appointment of the Legal Representative, see In re Johns–Manville Corp., 36 B.R. 743, 749 n. 3 (Bankr.S.D.N.Y.), appeal denied, 39 B.R. 234 (S.D.N.Y.1984), and the Asbestos Health Committee's motion to dismiss Manville's Chapter 11 petition, see In re Johns–Manville Corp., 36 B.R. 727, 729–30 (Bankr. S.D.N.Y.), appeal denied, 39 B.R. 234 (S.D.N.Y.1984), which the Equity

---

3. With certain exceptions, impairment of claims or interests, defined at 11 U.S.C. § 1124 (1982 & Supp. II 1984), occurs when a plan alters the legal, equitable, or contractual rights of the claim or interest holder.

Committee opposed, also diverted the energies of all parties from negotiations that might earlier have led to an acceptable plan.

To their credit, Manville and the Legal Representative finally came to terms in August of 1985, formulating a plan that would earmark billions of dollars for payment to present and future asbestosis victims as well as to others damaged by the asbestos products that Manville once manufactured and sold. They have now received the blessing of the Asbestos Health Committee and apparently of the other creditor committees. Having reconciled their differences, however, they encountered opposition from the Equity Committee immediately following their breakthrough, on the eve of their submission of the plan to the bankruptcy court for confirmation. Under protest, the Equity Committee had been cut out of the negotiations that led to their plan, and if the product of Manville's new understanding with the tort claimants and other creditors is confirmed, equity may be diluted by 90% or more. In re Johns–Manville Corp., 60 B.R. 842, 846 (S.D.N.Y.1986). Displeased with that prospect, which the Equity Committee views as evidence of the Manville board's abdication of its responsibilities to the shareholders, the Equity Committee brought an action in Delaware state court seeking to compel Manville to hold a shareholders' meeting, pursuant to section 211(c) of Delaware's General Corporation Law.[4] The Equity Committee's avowed purpose was to replace Manville directors, so that new directors might reconsider submitting the proposed plan. 60 B.R. at 852 n. 20.

Manville countered with the instant action. At Manville's behest, the bankruptcy court issued an injunction prohibiting the Equity Committee from pursuing the Delaware action on the ground that the holding of a shareholders' meeting would obstruct Manville's reorganization. Denying the Equity Committee's motion for summary judgment, the bankruptcy court granted summary judgment to Manville *sua sponte.* In re Johns–Manville Corp., 52 B.R. 879, 891 (Bankr.S.D. N.Y.1985). The district court affirmed. In re Johns–Manville Corp., 60 B.R. 842 (S.D.N.Y.1986). On appeal, the Equity Committee argues that the district court erred in affirming the decision to enjoin, in affirming the grant of summary judgment to Manville, and in finding that the bankruptcy court had jurisdiction to issue the injunction.

The Injunction and the Grant of Summary Judgment

Turning, then, to the decision to enjoin, we first encounter the well-settled rule that the right to compel a shareholders' meeting for the purpose of electing a new board subsists during reorganization proceedings. See In re Bush Terminal Co., 78 F.2d 662, 664 (2d Cir.1935); In re Saxon Industries, 39 B.R. 49, 50 (Bankr.S.D.N.Y.1984); In re Lionel Corp., 30 B.R. 327, 330 (Bankr.S.D.N.Y.1983). As a consequence of the

4. Del.Code Ann. tit. 8, § 211(c) (1983) provides that upon "a failure to hold the annual meeting . . . for a period of 13 months . . . after its last annual meeting, the Court of Chancery may summarily order a meeting to be held upon the application of any stockholder or director."

shareholders' right to govern their corporation, a prerogative ordinarily uncompromised by reorganization, "a bankruptcy court should not lightly employ its equitable power to block an election of a new board of directors." In re Potter Instrument Co., 593 F.2d 470, 475 (2d Cir.1979). In accordance with this rule, the parties and the lower courts agree that the Equity Committee's right to call a meeting may be impaired only if the Equity Committee is guilty of "clear abuse" in attempting to call one. See In re J.P. Linahan, Inc., 111 F.2d 590, 592 (2d Cir.1940). The Equity Committee's principal argument is that the "clear abuse" standard was not satisfied. In addition, however, the Equity Committee seems to argue that the district court's analysis was incomplete; i.e., the Equity Committee contends that in reviewing the bankruptcy court's decision to issue the injunction, the district court should have required, in addition to a showing of clear abuse, the usual showing of irreparable injury.

An examination of both lower court decisions will clarify the analysis that follows. The bankruptcy court found that "any shareholder meeting and ensuing proxy fight has the potential to derail the entire Manville reorganization with devastating consequences or at least to delay or halt plan negotiations." In re Johns–Manville Corp., 52 B.R. at 888. Reviewing the bankruptcy court's findings, the district court concluded that the Equity Committee intended either to "torpedo" the reorganization or to acquire a bargaining chip in aid of its negotiation power. In re Johns–Manville Corp., 60 B.R. at 852. In either case, the district court reasoned, the bankruptcy court did not err in concluding that the Equity Committee was guilty of clear abuse. Id. at 852–53.

Taking the district court's latter point first, we cannot agree that the Equity Committee's professed desire to arrogate more bargaining power in the negotiation of a plan—in contrast to some secret desire to destroy all prospects for reorganization—may in itself constitute clear abuse. The law of this circuit directs that the shareholders' natural wish to participate in this matter of corporate governance be respected. In re Bush Terminal Co., 78 F.2d 662 (2d Cir.1935), for example, this court reversed an order enjoining a shareholders' meeting to be called for the purpose of advancing a rehabilitation plan more favorable to equity. Expressly upholding the right of a majority shareholder to try to replace board members for that purpose, the court reasoned:

[T]he debtor is given the right to be heard on all questions. Obviously, the stockholders should have the right to be adequately represented in the conduct of the debtor's affairs, especially in such an important matter as the reorganization of the debtor. Such representation can be obtained only by having as directors persons of their choice. . . . [T]he debtor is given the power to propose a plan of reorganization. No reason is advanced why stockholders, if they feel that the present board of directors is not acting in their interest, or has caused an unsatisfactory plan to be filed on behalf of the debtor, should not cause a new board to be elected which will act in conformance with the stockholders' wishes.

Id. at 664.

The court in *In re Bush Terminal Co.* thus clearly intended to protect the right of stockholders to be heard in negotiations leading to a rehabilitation plan. As the court concluded, "If the right of stockholders to elect a board of directors should not be carefully guarded and protected, the statute giving the debtor a right to be heard or to propose a plan of reorganization could not truly be exercised, for the board of directors is the representative of the stockholders." Id. at 665. Under this analysis, the shareholders' mere intention to exercise bargaining power—whether by actually replacing the directors or by "bargaining away" their chip without replacing the board, as the district court suggests they may have wished to do—cannot without more constitute clear abuse. Unless the Equity Committee were to bargain in bad faith—e.g., to demonstrate a willingness to risk rehabilitation altogether in order to win a larger share for equity—its desire to negotiate for a larger share is protected. Moreover, if rehabilitation is placed at risk as a result of the other committees' intransigent unwillingness to negotiate with the Equity Committee, as opposed to their real inability, within some reasonable amount of time, to formulate any confirmable plan more satisfactory to equity, the Equity Committee should not alone bear the consequences of a stalemate by being deemed guilty of clear abuse.[6]

In re Lionel Corp., 30 B.R. 327 (Bankr.S.D.N.Y.1983), buttresses our conclusion that shareholders' desire for leverage is not a basis for denying them an election, so long as leverage means only the improvement of their bargaining position or the assurance of their participation in negotiations. In *In re Lionel Corp.* the bankruptcy court held that the record failed to demonstrate how reorganization would be impeded merely because the shareholders might be successful in their quest to cause the reorganization to "take an entirely different turn." Id. at 330. Surely if the Equity Committee is permitted to elect new directors in order to redirect or alter the course of a reorganization—and the district court here explicitly recognized that the committee is permitted to do that, see In re Johns–Manville Corp., 60 B.R. at 850—the Equity Committee should be permitted, in the district court's words of disapproval, to "use the threat of a new board as a lever vis-a-vis other interested constituencies and vis-a-vis the current Manville board." Id. at 852. The Equity Committee denies that there is evidence tending to

6. We note that if Manville were determined to be insolvent, so that the shareholders lacked equity in the corporation, denial of the right to call a meeting would likely be proper, because the shareholders would no longer be real parties in interest. Although the bankruptcy court discussed the possibility of Manville's insolvency in connection with its treatment of the Equity Committee's request for retention of special counsel and reimbursement of expenses, see In re Johns–Manville Corp., 52 B.R. at 885, an issue that is not a subject of this appeal, the district court did not uphold the determination of clear abuse on that basis, and the parties have not briefed that issue.

show that it meant to use any "threat" as a "lever," but if there is any such evidence, it would suggest only that the Equity Committee might be willing to back away from replacing the directors if it were to find the board more responsive to its interests. For related reasons, we are not persuaded that the Equity Committee's failure to call for a meeting at an earlier stage in the negotiations places its desire for leverage in a different light. If dissatisfaction with the board's representation of shareholders is a legitimate ground for calling a meeting, the Equity Committee did not waive the right to call a meeting by waiting until it became dissatisfied.[7]

Finally, we reject appellees' suggestion that the availability to the Equity Committee of other means with which to oppose Manville's plan robs the Equity Committee of its chosen means. It is true that the Equity Committee could have sought the appointment of a trustee[8] to displace Manville as the sole author of proposed plans and that it may later object to the confirmation of any plan Manville submits to the bankruptcy court. But those correctives provide only imperfect substitutes for a voice in the original formulation of a plan. More to the present point, perhaps, those avenues to shareholder satisfaction cannot be said to be exclusive in light of this circuit's legitimation of the shareholders' right to elect new directors for the frank purpose of advancing a plan they prefer.

In this connection, we must reject Manville's argument that a full inquiry into "clear abuse" would duplicate the confirmation proceedings that will follow submission of its present plan or any other. Unlike the analysis to determine clear abuse, the object of the confirmation proceedings will be to weigh Manville's proposed plan against other possible plans, taking into account the interests of impaired classes that object to Manville's proposals. In contrast, the determination whether the Equity Committee is guilty of clear abuse turns on whether rehabilitation will be seriously threatened, rather than merely delayed, if Manville's present plan is not submitted for confirmation now. See In re Bush Terminal Co., 78 F.2d 662 (2d Cir.1935); In re J.P.

7. We do not suggest, of course, that an equity committee's delay in calling a shareholders' meeting may never contribute to a finding of clear abuse. As the Securities and Exchange Commission pointed out in its brief, an attempt to call a shareholders' meeting after a plan has been submitted to the bankruptcy court and after confirmation hearings have begun would usually be more disruptive to the proceedings than an earlier attempt would be. Such an attempt might also indicate bad faith and a willingness to risk jeopardy to rehabilitation. On the other hand, a rule that required a call before dissatisfaction had crystallized would only encourage preemptive efforts that might otherwise be avoided by negotiation. In this case, the Equity Committee apparently acted promptly upon learning of Manville's proposed plan and is certainly not accountable for any

movement toward confirmation that may have occurred thereafter over its objections.

8. A committee . . . . may move for the appointment of a trustee where current management is not, in the opinion of the committee, negotiating the terms of a plan in good faith. The committee may conclude that the positions taken by the debtor's control group in connection with plan negotiations are not in the best interests of creditors or equity interests. Under such circumstances, the committee may request the appointment of a trustee in order to terminate the control status of current management and to enable the committee to file a plan of reorganization under section 1121(c)(1).

5 Collier on Bankruptcy ¶ 1103.07[7], at 1103–27 to 1103–28 (15th ed. 1986).

Linahan, Inc., 111 F.2d 590 (2d Cir.1940); In re Lionel Corp., 30 B.R. 327 (Bankr.S.D.N.Y.1983). Quite apart from its right to contest confirmation, the Equity Committee has the right to a fair hearing on the latter question and to a decision that recognizes its right to influence its own board.

We now reach the district court's alternative ground for affirming the grant of summary judgment. The bankruptcy court's finding that the proposed stockholders' meeting might jeopardize the reorganization process, "or at least . . . delay or halt plan negotiations," 52 B.R. at 888, a finding reflected in the district court's view that the Equity Committee might have intended to "torpedo" the reorganization, poses an issue more difficult than the question of the stockholders' desire for a voice in negotiations. While delay to rehabilitation would not by itself provide a ground for overriding the shareholders' right to govern Manville—delay being a concomitant of the right to change boards— real jeopardy to reorganization prospects would provide such a ground.

In In re Potter Instrument Co., 593 F.2d 470 (2d Cir.1979), this court upheld the bankruptcy court's refusal, upon a finding of clear abuse, to order a shareholders' meeting to be called for the purpose of electing new directors. We reasoned that "such an election might result in unsatisfactory management and would probably jeopardize both [the debtor's] rehabilitation and the rights of creditors and stockholders— sounding the 'death knell' to the debtor as well as to appellant himself." Id. at 475. In In re Potter Instrument Co., however, the facts were distinct from those considered here, at least on the record before us. Potter, the appellant, had agreed in a consent decree with the Securities and Exchange Commission to limit his management in the debtor and not to vote against any action recommended by a majority of the board of directors. Id. at 474. Attempting to circumvent the agreement, Potter sought to elect new directors who would vote against a proposed plan that would cause the debtor to issue new stock to unsecured creditors and thereby dilute Potter's holdings. The bankruptcy court had found that approval of a plan could probably never be accomplished without issuance of the stock. In addition, the bankruptcy court had noted that it would not be likely to approve control of the debtor by Potter in light of the record before it. Id.

It thus appears that the Equity Committee might distinguish itself from the shareholder in In re Potter Instrument Co., given the opportunity for an evidentiary hearing. The Equity Committee persuasively calls into question whether the bankruptcy court had any basis for concluding here that an election would jeopardize the reorganization process, particularly since the bankruptcy court's articulated basis appears to have been colored by an unsubstantiated suspicion that the Equity Committee affirmatively wished to jeopardize reorganization.[9]

9. In reviewing the bankruptcy court's decision, the district court characterized its findings as follows:

[T]he dim prospects for a successful reorganization following the election of a new board led the bankruptcy court to question the Equity Committee's motivation in seeking a new election. By its own admission, the Equity Committee brought the Delaware action in order to derail the proposed plan. Either the appellants seek to destroy any prospect for

Perhaps Potter was willing to embark on a suicide mission, "sounding the 'death knell' to . . . himself" along with the debtor. But as the Equity Committee argues, the lower courts in this case pointed to no evidence to support any finding that it wished to "torpedo" the reorganization, which the Equity Committee contends would be an irrational goal from its perspective.

The bankruptcy court stated that it relied on "the cumulative record in this case" to distinguish it from In re Lionel Corp., 30 B.R. 327 (Bankr.S.D.N.Y.1983), and In re Saxon Industries, 39 B.R. 49 (Bankr. S.D.N.Y.1984), and to justify application of the *In re Potter Instrument Co.* rationale. See In re Johns–Manville, 52 B.R. at 888. The only evidence the bankruptcy court cited, however, apart from evidence that the Equity Committee meant to influence negotiations in its favor, was the affidavit of G. Earl Parker, a Manville director who might have been replaced if an election had been held. Parroting *In re Potter Instrument Co.*, Parker's affidavit merely concluded that "[t]he consequences flowing from yet another stalemate would place in jeopardy the ability of the Debtors ever to confirm a plan of reorganization or to pay its just debts." 52 B.R. at 888. The district court affirmed on the basis of the Parker affidavit, coupled with the bankruptcy court's "accumulated knowledge" about the case.

The evidence contained in the Parker affidavit, consisting principally in the conclusion quoted above, is insufficient to support the determination of clear abuse underlying the grant of summary judgment. See Rule 56(e), Fed.R.Civ.P. While we agree with the district court that it was proper for the bankruptcy court to consider the record as a whole in determining whether summary judgment was appropriate, see Rule 56(c), Fed.R.Civ.P., without being told which portions of the bankruptcy court's accumulated knowledge it relied on for decision, we cannot agree that no material issues of fact remain to be determined.[10]

a successful reorganization, or they wish to use the threat of a new board as a lever vis-a-vis other interested constituencies and vis-a-vis the current Manville board. Neither the interest in torpedoing the reorganization nor in acquiring a chip to be bargained away are legitimate. Judge Lifland, who was well aware of the dynamics of the Manville bankruptcy, had ample evidence from which to conclude that by either attempting to destroy the prospects for a successful reorganization or by merely attempting to strengthen its bargaining position without changing the current board, the Equity Committee was acting in a clearly abusive manner.

60 B.R. at 852 (footnotes omitted). The bankruptcy court decision itself did not define the Equity Committee's supposed ill motives quite so clearly. At one point, however, the bankruptcy court observed that "[s]ection 105(a) contemplates the

court's use of injunctive relief in precisely those instances where parties are attempting to obstruct the reorganization." 52 B.R. at 889. The bankruptcy court then concluded that "[t]he *carefully timed* Delaware action will have an adverse impact on the Debtor's ability to coalesce with others to formulate an acceptable Chapter 11 plan resulting in irreparable harm and the impeding of the negotiation process." Id. at 890 (emphasis added).

10. In Manville's view, the bankruptcy court did review the facts that led it to find "clear abuse," [adverting] in its opinion to the facts that Manville had been in bankruptcy for three years without any resolution, 52 B.R. at 881; that Manville and committee representatives had engaged in extensive but fruitless negotiations, id.; that Manville did not reach agreement with any other constituency until August 1985, id. at 882; that "[w]ithin two weeks of the announcement of the Principal Ele-

Moreover, as the Equity Committee argues, a finding of clear abuse must be supplemented by a finding of irreparable injury before an injunction may issue. The bankruptcy court seemed to assume that the two inquiries coalesce; after finding clear abuse, it concluded without further analysis that an injunction was necessary to prevent irreparable harm to the reorganization. In re Johns–Manville Corp., 52 B.R. at 891. Cf. In re Lionel Corp., 30 B.R. at 329 (Although the shareholders wished to alter the course of reorganization, "Lionel has failed to demonstrate any irreparable harm, which factor alone requires a denial of an injunction."). In affirming the bankruptcy court, the district court did not discuss the irreparable injury prerequisite for relief.

Although the inquiries into clear abuse and irreparable injury will likely yield the same result in most if not all cases, an articulated analysis of irreparable injury would achieve a better focus and assist the reviewing court. In this connection, it is worth noting that *In re Potter Instrument Co.,* the only authority for a finding of clear abuse in circumstances resembling Manville's, did not deal with injunctive relief at all. There the court merely declined to direct a shareholders' meeting. In any event, on this record any harm to the reorganization was speculative enough that the irreparable injury requirement was not satisfied. . . .

On the record before us we cannot say that either side is entitled to summary judgment in its favor. There may be evidence known to the bankruptcy court but unarticulated in its opinion to support the result it reached. Manville's burden on remand, however, will be altered in accordance with this opinion.

Conclusion

Whether the Equity Committee's call for a shareholders' meeting constitutes clear abuse and whether such a meeting would cause irreparable harm to Manville's reorganization are triable issues of fact. The summary judgment award to Manville is therefore reversed. On remand, the court should undertake a more elaborate inquiry into clear abuse and irreparable harm. Rather than focusing on the Equity Committee's conceded desire to enhance its bargaining position, the court should analyze the real risks to rehabilitation posed by permitting the Equity Committee to call a meeting of shareholders for the purpose of compelling reconsideration of Manville's presently proposed plan. We emphasize, however, that given its greater knowledge about this complex and perhaps fragile reorganization, the bankruptcy court may exercise its legitimate injunctive powers to control the future

ments Agreement, the Equity Committee filed its motion . . . for the purpose of instituting the Delaware Action," id.; and that "no shareholder or director has at any time sought to compel the calling of a shareholder's meeting for the years 1983, 1984 and 1985," id. We do not think that this bare recitation of the events culminating in Manville's plan and the Equity Committee's discontent, when added to the bankruptcy court's stated basis for decision, constitutes a showing that the Equity Committee committed clear abuse.

course of rehabilitation pursuant to appropriate legal standards and evidentiary showings.

OAKES, CIRCUIT JUDGE (dissenting):

I am unclear what the majority intends to accomplish by the reversal and remand, except to compel bankruptcy judges and district courts to make more precise findings in support of their orders. Ordinarily I would support such a limited remand, especially where, as here, the bankruptcy court's reasoning required supplementation by the district court. But here confirmation of a plan in one of the most complicated and difficult bankruptcy reorganizations in history is well under way, and I fear that the court's opinion will not only unnecessarily duplicate, but it will, if not derail, at least delay the confirmation proceedings.

After all, the proposed plan had been in heated, tricky, combative negotiation for some three years prior to the Equity Committee's actions. If the plan is indeed biased, the Equity Committee has ample opportunity to oppose confirmation and to prove discrimination or unfairness to it. See 11 U.S.C. § 1129(b) (1982 & Supp. III 1985).

Under In re Potter Instrument Co., 593 F.2d 470 (2d Cir.1979), the court has a duty to refuse to order a shareholder's meeting upon a showing of clear abuse which "would probably jeopardize both [the debtor's] rehabilitation and the rights of creditors and stockholders. . . ." Id. at 475. To seek a shareholders' meeting at this late date, it seems to me, is just such a clear abuse. The Equity Committee, if it has its way, would set this reorganization back to square one. Apparently satisfied with the Board of Directors for three years following the filing of the bankruptcy petition, the committee waited until the directors finally proposed a plan to object, not only to the plan, but to the directors themselves. In addition to seeking to upset the plan, it is now trying to replace the directors, a result that would require negotiations to recommence from the beginning. In such a complex and lengthy proceeding as this one, the Equity Committee's actions seem to me to be the very essence of abuse. Moreover, the bankruptcy court's determination that a shareholders' meeting would lead to "waste of this estate's resources and thereby jeopardize the reorganization process" and that it "has the potential to derail the entire Manville reorganization with devastating consequences or at least to delay or halt plan negotiations" adequately supports its conclusion of irreparable harm.

But there is an entirely different reason that argues for affirmance. The bankruptcy judge has been living with this reorganization for a long time. He is fully sensitive to the enormity of the problems imposed by billions of dollars of future claims, as well as by billions of dollars of present claims for personal injury, death, and property damage—claims on a scale never before to hit the courts—as well as claims for punitive damages that, given those that have so far been imposed in the tiny fraction of cases that have been decided, are staggering to say the least. I repeat, no more complex reorganization has ever come before any bankruptcy court, and I include the railroad reorganization of recent past as well as of yore. I would here, as seldom elsewhere, defer to the bankruptcy court's discretion.

Yet a third reason calls for no further delay in the name of abstract stockholders' rights. There are innocent injured people, some of whom are survivors of deceased persons, whose recoveries have already been unduly delayed by the reorganization proceedings. Further delay will in many instances be unconscionable.

I would affirm outright and leave the Equity Committee to its usual remedy of objecting to the plan and its fairness in the confirmation proceeding.

Accordingly, I respectfully dissent.

Notes & Questions

1. *Tentative Valuation.* Should the bankruptcy court make a tentative valuation of the shareholders' interests before deciding whether to abrogate their state law rights to elect a board of directors?

2. *The Stakes.* On remand, the bankruptcy court held that the debtor was entitled to an injunction prohibiting the equity holders from calling a shareholders' meeting to elect new directors. 66 B.R. 517 (Bkrtcy.S.D.N.Y.1986). Why are the parties so fearful of a shareholders' meeting? Suppose at the meeting the shareholders elect a board of directors that disavows any plan not highly favorable to shareholders. The other parties to the reorganization then submit a plan that is less favorable to shareholders. A bankruptcy court that is willing to avoid a shareholders' meeting surely would find grounds for approving the non-debtor backed plan.

Or is the concern that those with no actual interest in the debtor (because most of their shares have become worthless) will take over its governance for their own benefit? Against this one might weigh the possibility that current management reached accommodations with non-shareholder interests primarily to benefit current management, and that shareholder interests truly were underrepresented in the proceedings. Is it relevant that the bankruptcy court refused to appoint an official committee to represent the common shareholders, and the district court affirmed? See 68 B.R. 155 (S.D.N.Y.1986), appeal dismissed 824 F.2d 176 (2d Cir.1987).

3. *Who is Delaying Whom?* It took the other parties to the reorganization several years to reach agreement on an acceptable plan. If, during that time, no shareholders' meeting was conducted, should all the blame for the cost of delay in seeking a meeting fall upon the shareholders? Are the shareholders entitled to no voice in a billion dollar business for the duration of lengthy bankruptcy proceedings? Do not the other parties benefit from delays to the extent the delays prevent hostile shareholders from meeting and electing a new board of

directors? When should the equity holders be required to press for a meeting?

4. *Interim Payments.* Consider the claimants who need money during the time the major players are feuding over Manville's future. Should there be interim payments to these claimants in amounts safely below any amounts they might be entitled to in a confirmable reorganization plan?

5. *State Law.* What is the status of state corporate law during the pendency of the bankruptcy proceedings? If a plan proposes to change a corporation's capital structure, must applicable state law provisions be complied with?

Note on Classification of Claims in Chapter 11 Plans

1. *Chapter 13 Reasoning in Chapter 11.* Section 1123(a)(1) authorizes a plan to classify claims. Should the Chapter 13 classification cases, noted in Chapter 15B, be followed in determining permissible classifications under Chapter 11? Are there differences between the two chapters that prevent the Chapter 13 cases from providing useful guidance?

You may wish to defer a final answer to these questions until you gain a fuller sense of the significance of classification in Chapter 11 cases. This requires some knowledge of the confirmation standards, studied infra.

2. *Classifying Similar Claims Separately.* (a) *Small Claims.* A Chapter 11 debtor's plan defines one class of unsecured claims to be "all those unsecured creditors with claims under $10,000" and proposes to pay them in full. The plan proposes to pay other unsecured creditors 50% of the amount of their allowed claims. Does the plan satisfy Chapter 11's requirements as to classification? If so, why allow such disparate treatment?

(b) *Classifying Disfavored Claims Separately.* In In re United States Truck Company, Inc., 800 F.2d 581 (6th Cir.1986), the debtor rejected a collective bargaining agreement with the Teamsters Committee and then sought to classify the union's claim separately from other unsecured claims. The court stated:

> . . . U.S. Truck is using its classification powers to segregate dissenting (impaired) creditors from assenting (impaired) creditors (by putting the dissenters into a class or classes by themselves) and, thus, it is assured that at least one class of impaired creditors will vote for the plan and make it eligible for cramdown considerations by the court. . . .

> . . . The District Court noted three important ways in which the interests of the Teamsters Committee differ substantially from those of other impaired creditors. Because of these differences, the Teamsters Committee has a different stake in the future viability of the reorganized company and has alternative means at its disposal

for protecting its claim. The Teamster's Committee claim is connected with the collective bargaining process. . . .   These differences put the Teamsters Committee's claim in a different posture than the Class XI claims. The Teamsters Committee may choose to reject the plan not because the plan is less than optimal to it as a creditor, but because the Teamsters Committee has a noncreditor interest—e.g., rejection will benefit its members in the ongoing employment relationship. Although the Teamsters Committee certainly is not intimately connected with the debtor, to allow the Committee to vote with the other impaired creditors would be to allow it to prevent a court from considering confirmation of a plan that a significant group of creditors with similar interests have accepted.

800 F.2d at 586–87. If nonbankruptcy law is to guide on the question of classification, what results does it suggest?

(c) *Classifying Favored Claims Separately.* **Matter of Jersey City Medical Center,** 817 F.2d 1055 (3d Cir.1987) (Chapter 9 case in which physicians with claims for indemnity for medical malpractice insurance receive 100%, other unsecured claimants receive 30%).

3. *Public Debt vs. Private Debt.* May a plan classify public unsecured claims differently from private unsecured claims? Why do so?

4. *Conflicts of Interest.* In **In re Martin's Point Limited Partnership,** 12 B.R. 721 (Bkrtcy.N.D.Ga.1981), the plan designated a class of three secured creditors, two of whom voted to accept the plan and one of whom voted to reject the plan. The rejecting creditor asserted that the other members of the class were also equity holders and, therefore, the holders of claims not substantially similar to his claim. The court held that the three creditors could be included in the same class.

Should courts have the power to prevent plans from including in a class claimholders who have interests that may conflict with the interests of other members of their claimholding class? As proposed by the House, § 1126 contained a provision that would have permitted a court "to designate for any class of claims or interests any person that has, with respect to that class, a conflict of interest that is of such nature as would justify exclusion of that person's claim or interest from" the approval requirements set forth in § 1126(c) and (d). House Report at 411. The final bill deleted the section with the comment that, "Section 105 of the bill constitutes sufficient power in the court to designate exclusion of a creditor's claim on the basis of a conflict of interest."

D. Confirmation of Chapter 11 Plans

1. Valuation

Any reasonable effort to carve up the interests in a reorganized entity requires a valuation of the entity. Crucial enterprise valuation issues are expressly built into Chapter 11, which requires that a reorganization plan give each holder of a claim or interest "property of a value, as of the effective date of the plan, that is not less than the amount that such holder would so receive or retain if the debtor were liquidated under chapter 7 of this title on such date . . .." § 1129(a)(7)(A)(ii). Determining what each claimant would have received in a Chapter 7 proceeding requires that the business be valued. See also § 1129(b)(2).

1 J. BONBRIGHT, THE VALUATION OF PROPERTY 233–66 (1937)

The problem here at hand is to value, say, a grocery business rather than either a grocery store or a partnership interest in the business; to value the Pennsylvania Railroad Company's railroad business rather than either its right of way and rolling stock or a 100-share lot of its capital stock. The major question to be discussed is whether this enterprise value should be ascertained by a capitalization of realized or prospective earnings, by an appraisal of the individual assets, by a summation of the market prices of the outstanding security issues, or by some combination of these three appraisals. . . .

Basic Principle That the Value of a Business Depends Solely on Prospective Earnings.

Modern writers in business finance have greatly clarified the problem under review by insisting that, with exceptions later to be noted, the value of an enterprise is dependent *entirely* on prospective earnings. To be sure, the industry which is exploited by this enterprise has a *social* value not measured by the earning power of the exploiting company. Indeed, this social value may be negative despite the prosperity of the company, as in the case of an industry which manufactures harmful drugs. Or it may be positive despite the bankruptcy of the company, as in the case of a railroad performing a necessary service at rates insufficient to pay operating expenses. But an enterprise valuation, like all other valuations of things as *property,* is designed merely to reflect acquisitive values to those persons who are in a position to exploit the business for their own monetary profit. Hence, social value is irrelevant except for its possible bearing on the power of the company to yield an income to its legal or beneficial owners—a bearing far more remote than apologists for the prevailing system of private property are prone to assume.

It follows from this basic principle of enterprise valuation, that the prospective earnings of a company play a role quite different from that played by other data adduced in proof of the value of the property. These other data, such as the original costs of the separate assets, or estimated replacement costs, or current market prices of outstanding security issues, have no significance whatever, save as a clue to the earnings that may fairly be capitalized. The mere fact that the physical assets of a railroad company, or of a steel company, may actually have cost many million dollars to construct, not only fails to determine the present value of the company—it is utterly no influence on this value unless, in some indirect way, it may affect the net earnings. And precisely the same statement applies to estimated replacement costs of the physical assets, no less than to historical costs. It will benefit the owner of an enterprise nothing to possess a company with *costly* assets. What the owner wants is profitableness, not expensiveness. . . .

Bearing of Asset Valuations on an Enterprise Appraisal.

In the valuation of most enterprises, an appraisal of the separate physical assets is of the greatest importance in determining the proper annual deductions for maintenance and depreciation—deductions which the appraiser must make in arriving at the probable net earnings of the company. Even the calculation of some of the other elements of operating expenses, such as annual outlays for insurance and for property taxes, may require an engineering appraisal of the assets. . . .

In concluding this elementary treatment of the relationship between enterprise value and asset values, we must stress the point that the appraiser who takes the latter values into account is by no means necessarily adopting a different theory or concept of value from the appraiser who estimates the value of an enterprise by a capitalization of annual reported earnings. This point needs emphasis, since some writers in business finance have implied that any appraiser or judge who pays the slightest attention to the costs or "physical values" of corporate fixed assets is guilty of an obvious economic fallacy—the fallacy of supposing, in a simple-minded way, that value is determined by cost, whereas in fact value is determined by earning power. This criticism has force with respect to those many cases, such as bankruptcy cases and fire-insurance cases, in which courts have blindly accepted asset-cost valuations in defiance of abundant evidence of chronically impaired earning power. But it does not apply to the sophisticated appraiser who considers asset costs because of their possible indirect bearing on future earning power. Such an appraiser assumes that businessmen do not buy properties because of their cost; but he also assumes that they do not buy properties because of their *already realized* earnings. As a matter of mere logic, therefore, he realizes that there is no more reason to assume that an enterprise is worth its capitalized *reported* earnings than to assume that it is worth what its assets did cost or would now cost. Barring the possibility of liquidation, his eye is entirely on *prospective* earnings, and he is concerned neither with past earnings nor with asset values save as an aid to the forecasting of the future.

The Stock-and-bond Method of Enterprise Appraisal.

Both of the methods of enterprise valuation so far discussed—the capitalized-earnings method and the book-value method—involve an expressed or implied attempt by the appraiser to forecast the future income of the business. A different procedure is involved in the method now to be discussed—the so-called stock-and-bond method. Here the value of an entire business is derived by a summation of the separate market prices of the outstanding securities and of other proprietary and creditor claims against the corporation. Even here, to be sure, the appraiser may assume that the value of the enterprise is determined by prospective earnings. But if he makes this assumption, he relies upon the investors and speculators who compose "the stock market" to do the forecasting.

For practical reasons the stock-and-bond method is applicable generally only to incorporated businesses, and then only to corporations the major securities of which have a readily ascertainable market price. Otherwise, the difficulty of establishing the values of the separate creditor and proprietary interests would be so great that a direct attempt to appraise the business as a whole is clearly more advisable. But under favorable conditions, the charm of this method of appraisal lies in its simplicity of application and in its relative freedom from the influence of the appraiser's personal bias. Assume, for example, the problem of valuing a corporate enterprise with no ownership interests outstanding save $100,000 of bonds quoted at 90 on the market place, and 1,000 shares of common stock quoted at $50 per share. A moment's calculation yields an enterprise value of $140,000—$90,000 for the bondholders' interest plus $50,000 for the stockholders' equity.

To be sure, in any litigated case, controversial issues will arise even when the validity of the stock-and-bond method is agreed upon. The question will be raised whether the securities should be valued strictly at current market prices or at an average of quotations over a considerable period of time. Some of the security issues are likely to have no well-established market price, and an "assumed market value" will be called for. There may also be disputes as to whether short-term debts should be included in the summation of the values of the ownership interests, not to mention allowances for leases, contingent liabilities, etc. Even so, the stock-and-bond method is doubtless the simplest and most expeditious form of enterprise appraisal; and this fact, combined with its relative objectivity, accounts for the favor in which it has been held by some assessors and courts as a basis of tax assessment.

From the standpoint of accuracy, however, the stock-and-bond method has many recognized defects—defects so serious that most appraisal experts are unwilling to approve its use except in situations where a very rough measure of value is deemed adequate, or except for the purpose of checking the inferences derived by a capitalization of earnings or by some alternative method of valuation. . . .

The first defect of the stock-and-bond method lies in an identification of the value of the entire corporate property with only those outstanding legal interests in the property represented by shares of stock and by bonds. Obviously, however, other proprietary and creditor claims should not be ignored. Current liabilities, for however short a term, represent interests in the property no less than funded debt, and they can be omitted only if one artificially restricts the meaning of "the enterprise" to such an interest in the corporation as the stockholders and bondholders enjoy. The value of option warrants, if any are outstanding, must be considered no less than the value of already issued stock. Contingent liabilities, such as guarantees of the bonds of other companies by the company in question, must not be ignored, since they represent a claim against the whole enterprise which tends to detract from the value of the company's own securities.

The second defect of the stock-and-bond method lies in the practical necessity of taking the quoted stock-market prices of the outstanding shares as a measure of the relevant values of these shares. This necessity may lead to error for either of two reasons. In the first place, buyers and sellers of securities are not always intelligent in their evaluation of investment merits. They hardly deserve to be called the persons "in the best position to know." In the second place, security prices are often influenced by speculative and manipulative motives that have little or no bearing on the value of the entire corporate enterprise.

The third defect lies in the assumption that the value of an entire enterprise can be inferred by a summation of the separate values of small amounts of security interests in the enterprise. The lots of stock from which market quotations are generally derived are small lots representing only a minority interest. They do not carry control, and hence their quoted prices are usually determined without reference to the power and perquisites that would be enjoyed by a sole owner of the business. Sometimes, to be sure, the efforts of rival factions to secure control of a corporation will send the quoted market prices of voting stocks to highly inflated levels, quite unjustified by the investment merits of the shares. But in such a period, the control element in the value of an enterprise would be *overstated* by the stock-and-bond method, just as it would be understated, if not completely ignored, in a situation where the interests already in control have no desire to buy up the minority shares. . . .

The Application of the Capitalized-earnings Method: Estimating the Earning Power.

The main object of the preceding discussion has been to explain the apparent conflict between the legal tradition under which realized prospective earnings are considered only as *one element* of enterprise value, and the position of modern financial writers which insists that (with certain definite exceptions) the value of an enterprise is *solely* dependent on its prospective earning power. The conclusion here reached is that the "other elements" which are admitted by courts as evidence of value should be held to have merely a secondary significance, as bearing on the probable future earnings of the company and on the appropriate rate at which these prospective earnings may be capitalized. Exception must be made, however, of assets that are properly valued at their net realization value rather than at their "value to the going concern."

It remains to say something of the technique of estimating and capitalizing the earnings of an enterprise. . . .

Realized Earnings versus Prophesied Earnings.

In the valuation of entire business enterprises or of shareholdings in these enterprises, one of the most sharply contested questions has concerned the relative weight to be given to the earnings actually realized, as shown by the companies' financial statements after proper auditing, and the future earnings as estimated by the witnesses for the two parties to the controversy. Sometimes, indeed, the controversy arises from a denial by one of the parties that prophesied earnings should even be admitted as competent evidence. It is alleged that these prophecies are necessarily too highly speculative to merit consideration; that they are based on guesses as to future business conditions and as to managerial efficiency, the validity of which cannot adequately be checked by cross-examination or by the countervailing testimony of opposing experts. Hence, it is argued, only the realized earnings, whose amount can be approximately established by a careful audit, should be brought to the attention of the tribunal for such weight as it sees fit to give this type of data. . . .

When a court holds that realized earnings are admissible as evidence of present value but that estimated future earnings are inadmissible, its position may be defended only on the ground that the reported earnings are a more reliable test of future earnings than are the estimates of these latter earnings which may be presented by partisan witnesses. In other words, the holding should be based on the belief that future earnings are more likely to approximate past earnings than to approximate what a hired expert *says* that he *thinks* they will be. This is a very reasonable belief; and it often justifies rulings which, on their face, would seem to contradict the principle that present value is based wholly on *anticipated* income. . . .

The Calculation of Realized Net Earnings: Allowance for Depreciation.

Even when an enterprise is valued by a capitalization of reported earnings rather than of prophesied earnings, the question always arises whether the earnings as reflected in the company's periodic reports can be accepted without revision for the purpose of the appraisal. This question is by no means solely concerned with the possibility that the earnings statements may be falsified, or even with the likelihood that they do not conform to "good accounting practice." Accountants well recognize that even the most honestly and carefully prepared report of earnings is, within wide limits, based on opinion estimates rather than on "cold facts"; and they also recognize that a wide variety of accounting procedures, each of them leading to a different statement of the earnings realized during any given year, are all admitted under the heading of "good practice."   . . .

   . . . The point to be emphasized is that the depreciation allowances which the company makes, and properly makes, in its own statement of earnings are likely to differ materially from the deductions which a prospective buyer or seller of the enterprise should make in his attempt to estimate what the enterprise is worth. The purposes for which the company calculates its deduction for depreciation may be very different from the purpose of an appraisal of the enterprise, and this difference may justify a simultaneous allowance, say, of one million dollars for annual depreciation by the company, and of five hundred thousand dollars or of two million dollars by the appraiser.   . . .

   The most obvious need for a recalculation by the appraiser of the company's reported deductions for depreciation arises in those situations where the company follows the orthodox policy of using the original cost of its depreciable assets as the "depreciation basis," despite a marked increase or decrease in current replacement costs. At least with respect to Federal income-tax returns, this basis of calculating annual depreciation is thoroughly sound; and even for other accounting purposes a strong, if not conclusive, case can be made for the original-cost basis of calculation. But where the net earnings are desired solely as an aid to an enterprise valuation, depreciation allowances designed to recapture the original costs of the assets on the dates of their retirements are likely to be very misleading.

   Assume the existence of two business enterprises, identical save for the fact that the fixed assets of enterprise *A* were bought in a period of high prices, whereas those of enterprise *B* were bought in a period of low prices. By hypothesis, the two enterprises have the same prospective earning power and are of equal value. Yet, if both of these companies base their depreciation allowances on the original costs of their fixed assets, the first enterprise will appear to be less profitable than the second. From the standpoint of a prospective purchaser or seller, this appearance is an illusion. The illusion will disappear if the depreciation allowances for the two companies are redetermined by reference to the current replacement costs of their assets.   . . .

The Application of the Capitalized-earnings Method: The Rate of Capitalization.

. . .

Capitalization of Estimated Future Earnings.

   The simplest problem of capitalizing estimated future net earnings arises only in those rare situations where these earnings may be expected to remain stable, year by year, during a specific term of years, or during that indefinitely long period of time which, for appraisal purposes, is the rough equivalent of eternity. Here the prospective flow of earnings is usually valued as one would value an annuity certain or a perpetuity.

But even here, the risk factor is usually much greater than in the case of an annuity—so much so, that its proper treatment becomes critical. In the absence of statistical data such as those embodied in life-insurance mortality tables, whereby the risk of nonreceipt of the anticipated earnings may be expressed mathematically, it has been customary vaguely to allow for the risk factor by the choice of a rate of capitalization higher than the rates fixed by the market place on high-grade bonds. The current yield on these bonds has been taken to approximate the rate of interest on a "riskless investment." If this rate is 4 per cent, the prospective annual earnings of an enterprise with an indefinitely long life expectancy may be capitalized, say, at 10 per cent, or at some higher or lower rate depending on the appraiser's judgment of the riskiness of the business. The differential between the chosen rate of capitalization and the rate of yield on relatively secure bonds is supposed to represent an allowance, not merely for the "actuarial" or "mathematical" risk factor, but also for the "psychological" risk factor. Ordinarily, investors are supposed to demand a premium for successful risk taking; and under this assumption, the rate of capitalization is fixed at a higher amount than would be justified by probability tables, were such tables available.

This attempt by appraisal experts simultaneously to allow for the interest factor and the risk factor by a single, high rate of capitalization, raises actuarial questions that have been given surprisingly little attention by writers in finance. It subjects the risk-factor allowance to a process of compounding, the validity of which may be seriously questioned. To illustrate the point by an artificially simple example, let us assume an enterprise with anticipated stable and continuous net earnings of $100,000 per year. Assume that, if these earnings could be anticipated with that confidence which is the psychological equivalent of certainty, a 4 per cent rate of capitalization would be indicated. But assume, further, that there are nine chances in favor of the exact realization of these anticipated earnings as against one chance in favor of the nonrealization of any net earnings whatsoever. On actuarial principles, and disregarding the "psychological" risk factor, the enterprise should then be valued as a 90 per cent chance of receiving a perpetual income of $100,000 per year and hence as the equivalent of a certainty of receiving $90,000 per year. A 4 per cent capitalization of $90,000 per year would give $2,250,000 as the present value of the enterprise.

This same valuation would be reached by the traditional method only if the appraiser were to capitalize the anticipated net income ($100,000) at 4.44 + per cent. But such a rate would hardly be hit upon except by accident, since it could not be rationally constructed save by going through the mathematical process just indicated. It would seem that the only practical defense of the prevalent practice, whereby both the interest factor and the risk factor are allowed for in a single rate of compound discount, lies in the appraiser's inability to make a more direct estimate of the risk of nonachievement of his prophesied earning power. But such a defense is tantamount to an admission that enterprise valuation, so far from being based on scientific principles, is little more than guesswork, which indeed it is in the present stage of the art of appraisal.

Still assuming that the enterprise whose value must be estimated will have fairly stable annual earnings, so that its probable earning power can be expressed by a single figure (say, $100,000 per year), we have now to take into account the fact that almost never can the appraiser assume that his estimated future earnings will either turn out to be approximately right, or else will be belied by a record of zero earnings. The much greater likelihood is a record of earnings materially higher or lower than the estimates. How may the appraiser take into account this range of expectancies? . . .

We have now to note a further complication in the process of capitalizing anticipated earnings. With most enterprises—those of the decadent type no less than those of the expanding type—any assumption that the future earnings will be stabilized at a fixed amount per year is absurd on its face. This fact would seem to preclude the capitalization of any single estimate of annual earnings and to require the separate discounting of a whole series of estimated earnings. With enterprises of a short life expectancy, such as single-mine ventures, the latter procedure is often adopted. But with enterprises of an indefinite life expectancy, much cruder methods of capitalization are resorted to. As a rule, a purely fictitious "typical" annual earning power is assumed. Where an upward trend is anticipated, the "typical earnings" are set higher than those expected for the next few years, but lower than those expected in the more distant future. Thus the appraiser converts an expected series of unequal earnings into the valuational equivalent of a perpetual annuity. The crudeness of this conversion is apparent.

Still another complication should be mentioned. With an expanding business, the anticipated increase in earnings cannot be credited entirely to the present capital investment. This increase will be attainable only if more funds are invested in the business. But the necessity of investing these funds is a factor adverse to the present value of the enterprise, and it must be allowed for if the appraiser includes the higher anticipated earning power in his estimate of capitalizable earnings.

The problem of making such an allowance could be treated scientifically only by a forecast of the further capital outlays required, year after year, as a means of realizing the estimated increased earning power. The present discounted adverse value of these future outlays could then be deducted from the positive value of the discounted anticipated earnings. But the difficulty of predicting the times and amounts of capital expansion has generally precluded such calculations. Instead, appraisers have made a vague allowance for the possibilities of business expansion by capitalizing at a lower rate than would otherwise be warranted the estimated earnings attainable under the present or immediately prospective capacity of the plant.

From what has been said it is apparent that the determination of a rate at which to capitalize the prospective earnings of a business is a hit-and-miss procedure. Its inaccuracies are generally conceded by the financial writers; but its wild crudeness has seldom been fully exposed even by the experts.

The Rate of Capitalization of Realized Earnings.

. . .

From both a theoretical and a practical standpoint, the choice of a proper rate of capitalization presents even greater difficulties than the determination of the earnings to be capitalized. Some of these difficulties have been noted in the previous section. But they have been given amazingly scant attention in the literature of finance and in the records of the litigated cases, perhaps because their solution has seemed hopeless. In consequence, the legally accepted rates of capitalization have been adopted by an admixture of tradition (such as that in favor of a 6 per cent rate or a 10 per cent rate) and guesswork.

The Relationship Between Present Value Calculations and Valuation.

The preceding excerpt indicates that valuation of a going concern requires estimating future earnings and identifying an appropriate capitalization (or discount) rate. It may be helpful to show how the earnings and capitalization figures enable an appraiser to arrive at a value.

A dollar to be paid in the future is worth less than a dollar paid today. All other things being equal, no one is indifferent to the choice between receiving $100 today and $100 one year from today. This is true because investors are willing to borrow funds at a positive rate of interest. If one receives the $100 today, one can lend it at say 10% and have $110 after one year. If one receives $100 a year from today, one has $100. In arriving at current valuation figures, amounts to be received in the future must be discounted by some factor, usually stated in terms of a rate of interest, if one wishes to arrive at a present value. For example, at a 6% rate of interest, the present (discounted) value of $100 deferred one year is $94. The present value of $100 due in two years is approximately $89. That is, invest $89 now at 6% for two years and, at the end of two years you will have $100.

When one is trying to ascertain the value of a business, the computation is one step more complex. Given an earnings assumption, say $100 per year, and a discount rate, say 6%, how does computing the value of the business relate to the simple discounting process just discussed? To compute the value of a business, assuming one has settled on computing it on the basis of future earnings, one needs to know the present value of a series of future amounts. The series consists of the business's earnings in each future year. If one assumes level earnings in all future years, the problem of arriving at a present value for earnings reduces to the problem of deriving the present value of an annuity, or sequence of future annual payments.

What is the present value of a $100 annuity to be paid at the end of each of X years? This is the same as asking how much must be invested today to yield $100 at the end of each of X years. At a 10% interest rate, the present value of a one year $100 annuity is about $91, a five year annuity is worth $379, and a 50 year annuity is worth $991.

What is the value of an annuity that is to last forever (which corresponds to a company that is assumed to be of perpetual duration)? Again assuming a 10% interest rate, how much money does one need to generate $100 every year? $1,000. So at 10% the present value of an everlasting $100 annuity, also called a perpetuity, is $1,000. Similarly the present value (or capitalized earnings) of a business enterprise that will earn $100 per year in perpetuity, assuming a capitalization rate of 10%, is $1,000.

The capitalized earnings of a business enterprise are its projected future earnings discounted to present value on the assumption that the business will last forever. Note the very small difference in present value between a 50 year $100 annuity and a $100 perpetuity. At any substantial rate of interest, payments due in the distant future have virtually no present value.

Question

How does inflation affect a valuation figure arrived at by capitalizing earnings?

———

See generally V. Brudney & M. Chirelstein, Corporate Finance (3rd ed. 1987); Blum & Katz, Depreciation and Enterprise Valuation, 32 U.Chi.L.Rev. 236 (1965); Note, Inflation and the Concept of Reorganization Value, 34 Vand.L.Rev. 1727 (1981); Roe, Bankruptcy and Debt: A New Model for Corporate Reorganization, 83 Colum.L.Rev. 527 (1983).

2. Absolute Priority

CASE v. LOS ANGELES LUMBER PRODUCTS CO., LIMITED

Supreme Court of the United States, 1939.
308 U.S. 106, 60 S.Ct. 1, 84 L.Ed. 110.

MR. JUSTICE DOUGLAS delivered the opinion of the Court:

These cases present the question of the conditions under which stockholders may participate in a plan of reorganization under § 77B

([June 7,] 1934, 48 Stat. at L. 912, chap. 424) of the Bankruptcy Act where the debtor corporation is insolvent both in the equity and in the bankruptcy sense. . . .

The debtor is a holding company owning all of the outstanding shares of the capital stock (except for certain qualifying shares held by directors) of six subsidiaries. Three of these have no assets of value to the debtor. Two have assets of little value. The debtor's principal asset consists of the stock of Los Angeles Shipbuilding and Drydock Corporation which is engaged in shipbuilding and ship repair work in California. This subsidiary has fixed assets of $430,000 and current assets of approximately $400,000. This subsidiary has only current debts of a small amount, not affected by the plan. The debtor's assets other than the stock of its subsidiaries aggregate less than $10,000.

The debtor's liabilities consist of principal and interest of $3,807,071.88 on first lien mortgage bonds issued in 1924 and maturing in 1944, secured by a trust indenture covering the fixed assets of Los Angeles Shipbuilding and Drydock Corporation (one of the subsidiaries) and the capital stock of all of the subsidiaries. No interest has been paid on these bonds since February 1, 1929. In 1930, as a consequence of the financial embarrassment of the debtor, a so-called voluntary reorganization was effected. To that end, a supplement to this trust indenture was executed, pursuant to a provision therein, with the consent of about 97% of the face value of all the outstanding bonds, which reduced the interest from 7½% to 6% and made the interest payable only if earned. At the same time the old stock of the debtor was wiped out by assessment and new stock issued, divided into Class A and Class B, with equal voting rights. Class A stock was issued to some of the old stockholders who contributed $400,000 new money which was turned over to the Los Angeles Shipbuilding and Drydock Corporation and used by it as working capital. In consideration of this contribution the bondholders who agreed to the modification of the indenture likewise released the stockholders' liability under California law in favor of these contributors. Some Class B stock was issued to bondholders in payment of unpaid interest coupons. At present there are outstanding 57,788 shares of Class A stock and 5,112 shares of Class B stock.

In 1937 the management prepared a plan of reorganization to which over 80% of the bondholders and over 90% of the stock assented. This plan of reorganization, as we shall discuss hereafter, provided for its consummation either on the basis of contract or in a § 77B proceeding, such election to be made by the board of directors. In January 1938 the directors chose the latter course and the debtor corporation filed a petition for reorganization under § 77B of the Bankruptcy Act, with the plan attached and reciting, inter alia, that the required percentage of security holders had consented to it. This plan as filed was later modified by the debtor, as we point out later, in a manner not deemed by us material to the issues here involved. That plan as modified provides for the formation of a new corporation, which will acquire the assets of Los Angeles Shipbuilding and Drydock Corporation, and which will have a capital structure of 1,000,000 shares of authorized $1 par value voting stock. This stock is divided into 811,375 shares of preferred and 188,625 shares of common. The preferred stock will be entitled to a 5% non-cumulative dividend, after which the common stock will be entitled to a similar dividend. Thereafter all shares of both classes will participate equally in dividends. The preferred stock will receive on liquidation a preference to the amount of its par value. Thereupon the common will receive a similar preference. Thereafter all shares of both classes participate equally.

170,000 shares of preferred are reserved for sale to raise money for rehabilitation of the yards. 641,375 shares of the preferred are to be issued to the bondholders, 250 shares to be exchanged for each $1000 bond. The Class A stockholders will receive the 188,625 shares of common stock, without the payment of any subscription or assessment. No provision is made for the old Class B stock. The aggregate par value of the total preferred and common stock to be issued to existing security holders is $830,000—an amount which equals the going concern value of the assets of the enterprise.

The plan was assented to by approximately 92.81% of the face amount of the bonds, 99.75% of the Class A stock, and 90% of the Class B stock. Petitioners own $18,500 face amount of the bonds. They did not consent to the so-called voluntary reorganization in 1930 whereby the trust indenture was amended. And throughout the present § 77B proceedings they appropriately objected that the plan was not fair and equitable to bondholders.

The District Court found that the debtor was insolvent both in the equity sense and in the bankruptcy sense. The latter finding was based upon "appraisal and audit reports." In this connection the court found that the total value of all assets of Los Angeles Shipbuilding and Drydock Corporation was $830,000, those assets constituting practically all of the assets of the debtor and of its various subsidiaries of any value to the estate. Yet in spite of this finding, the court, in the orders now under review, confirmed the plan. And the court approved it despite the fact that the old stockholders, who have no equity in the assets of the enterprise, are given 23% of the assets and voting power in the new company without making any fresh contribution by way of subscription or assessment. The court, however, justified inclusion of the stockholders in the plan (1) because it apparently felt that the relative priorities of the bondholders and stockholders were maintained by virtue of the preferences accorded the stock which the bondholders were to receive and the fact that the stock going to the bondholders carried 77% of the voting power of all the stock presently to be issued under the plan; and (2) because it was able to find that they had furnished the bondholders certain "compensating advantages" or "consideration." This so-called consideration was stated by the District Court in substance as follows:

1. It will be an asset of value to the new company to retain the old stockholders in the business because of "their familiarity with the operation" of the business and their "financial standing and influence in the community;" and because they can provide a "continuity of management."

2. If the bondholders were able to foreclose now and liquidate the debtor's assets, they would receive "substantially less than the present appraised value" of the assets.

3. By reason of the so-called voluntary reorganization in 1930, the bondholders cannot foreclose until 1944, the old stockholders having the right to manage and control the debtor until that time. At least the bondholders cannot now foreclose without "long and protracted litigation" which would be "expensive and of great injury" to the debtor. Hence, the virtual abrogation of the agreement deferring foreclosure until 1944 was "the principal valuable consideration" passing to the bondholders from the old stockholders.

4. Bonding companies are unwilling to assume the risk of becoming surety for the debtor or its principal subsidiary "because of the outstanding bond issue." The government's construction program will provide "valuable opportunities" to the debtor if it is prepared to handle the business. Hence, the value to the bondholders of maintaining the debtor "as a going concern, and of avoiding litigation, is in excess of the value of the stock being issued" to the old stockholders.
. . .

At the outset it should be stated that where a plan is not fair and equitable as a matter of law it cannot be approved by the court even though the percentage of the various classes of security holders required by § 77B(f) for confirmation of the plan has consented. It is clear from a reading of § 77B(f) that the Congress has required both that the required percentages of each class of security holders approve the plan and that the plan be found to be "fair and equitable." The former is not a substitute for the latter. The court is not merely a ministerial register of the vote of the several classes of security holders. All those interested in the estate are entitled to the court's protection. Accordingly the fact that the vast majority of the security holders have approved the plan is not the test of whether the plan is a fair and equitable one. . . .

Hence, in this case the fact that 92.81% in amount of the bonds, 99.75% of the Class A stock, and 90% of the Class B stock have approved the plan is as immaterial on the basic issue of its fairness as is the fact that petitioners own only $18,500 face amount of a large bond issue. . . .

In equity reorganization law the term "fair and equitable" included, inter alia, the rules of law enunciated by this Court in the familiar cases of Chicago, R.I. & P.R. Co. v. Howard, 7 Wall. 392, 19 L.Ed. 117; Louisville Trust Co. v. Louisville, New Albany & Chicago Ry. Co., 174 U.S. 674, 19 S.Ct. 827, 43 L.Ed. 1130; Northern Pacific Railway Co. v.

Boyd, 228 U.S. 482, 33 S.Ct. 554, 57 L.Ed 931; Kansas City Terminal Ry. Co. v. Central Union Trust Co., 271 U.S. 445, 46 S.Ct. 549, 70 L.Ed. 1028. These cases dealt with the precedence to be accorded creditors over stockholders in reorganization plans. In Louisville Trust Co. v. Louisvile, New Albany & Chicago Ry. Co., supra, this Court reaffirmed the "familiar rule" that "the stockholder's interest in the property is subordinate to the rights of creditors; first of secured and then of unsecured creditors." And it went on to say that "any arrangement of the parties by which the subordinate rights and interests of stockholders are attempted to be secured at the expense of the prior rights of either class of creditors, comes within judicial denunciation". 174 U.S. page 684, 19 S.Ct. page 830, 43 L.Ed. 1130. This doctrine is the "fixed principle" according to which Northern Pacific Railway Co. v. Boyd, supra, decided that the character of reorganization plans was to be evaluated. And in the latter case this Court added, "If the value of the road justified the issuance of stock in exchange for old shares, the creditors were entitled to the benefit of that value, whether it was present or prospective, for dividends or only for purposes of control. In either event, it was a right of property out of which the creditors were entitled to be paid before the stockholders could retain it for any purpose whatever." . . . In application of this rule of full or absolute priority this Court recognized certain practical considerations and made it clear that such rule did not "require the impossible and make it necessary to pay an unsecured creditor in cash as a condition of stockholders retaining an interest in the reorganized company. His interest can be preserved by the issuance, on equitable terms, of income bonds or preferred stock." Northern Pacific Railway Co. v. Boyd, supra 228 U.S. page 508, 33 S.Ct. page 561, 57 L.Ed. 931. And this practical aspect of the problem was further amplified in Kansas City Terminal Ry. Co. v. Central Union Trust Co. supra, by the statement that "when necessary, they (creditors) may be protected through other arrangements which distinctly recognize their equitable right to be preferred to stockholders against the full value of all property belonging to the debtor corporation, and afford each of them fair opportunity, measured by the existing circumstances, to avail himself of this right" 271 U.S. pages 454, 455, 46 S.Ct. page 551, 70 L.Ed. 1028. And it also recognized the necessity at times of permitting the inclusion of stockholders on payment of contributions, even though the debtor company was insolvent. As stated in Kansas City Terminal Ry. Co. v. Central Union Trust Co. supra 271 U.S. page 455, 46 S.Ct. page 552, 70 L.Ed. 1028: "Generally, additional funds will be essential to the success of the undertaking, and it may be impossible to obtain them unless stockholders are permitted to contribute and retain an interest sufficiently valuable to move them. In such or similar cases the chancellor may exercise an informed discretion concerning the practical adjustment of the several rights." But even so, payment of cash by the stockholders for new stock did not itself save the plan from the rigors of the "fixed principle" of the Boyd Case, for in that case the decree was struck down

where provision was not made for the unsecured creditor and even though the stockholders paid cash for their new stock. Sales pursuant to such plans were void, even though there was no fraud in the decree. Northern Pacific Railway Co. v. Boyd, supra, 228 U.S. page 504, 33 S.Ct. page 560, 57 L.Ed. 931. As this Court there stated, 228 U.S. page 502, 33 S.Ct. page 559, 57 L.Ed. 931, "There is no difference in principle if the contract of reorganization, instead of being effectuated by private sale, is consummated by a master's deed under a consent decree."
. . .

We come then to the legal question of whether the plan here in issue is fair and equitable within the meaning of that phrase as used in § 77B.

We do not believe it is for the following reasons. Here the court made a finding that the debtor is insolvent not only in the equity sense but also in the bankruptcy sense. Admittedly there are assets not in excess of $900,000, while the claims of the bondholders for principal and interest are approximately $3,800,000. Hence even if all of the assets were turned over to the bondholders they would realize less than 25 per cent on their claims. Yet in spite of this fact they will be required under the plan to surrender to the stockholders 23 per cent of the value of the enterprise.

True, the relative priorities of the bondholders and the old Class A stockholders are maintained by virtue of the priorities accorded the preferred stock which the bondholders are to receive. But this is not compliance with the principle expressed in Kansas City Terminal Ry. Co. v. Central Union Trust Co., supra, that "to the extent of their debts creditors are entitled to priority over stockholders against all the property of an insolvent corporation," for there are not sufficient assets to pay the bondholders the amount of their claims. Nor does this plan recognize the "equitable right" of the bondholders "to be preferred to stockholders against the full value of all property belonging to the debtor corporation," within the meaning of the rule announced in that case, since the full value of that property is not first applied to claims of the bondholders before the stockholders are allowed to participate. Rather it is partially diverted for the benefit of the stockholders even though the bondholders would obtain less than 25% payment if they received it all. Under that theory all classes of security holders could be perpetuated in the new company even though the assets were insufficient to pay—in new bonds or stock—the amount owing senior creditors. Such a result is not tenable.

It is, of course, clear that there are circumstances under which stockholders may participate in a plan of reorganization of an insolvent debtor. This Court, as we have seen, indicated as much in Northern Pacific Railway Co. v. Boyd, supra, and Kansas City Terminal Ry. Co. v. Central Union Trust Co., supra. Especially in the latter case did this Court stress the necessity, at times, of seeking new money "essential to the success of the undertaking" from the old stockholders. Where that necessity exists and the old stockholders make a fresh contribution and receive in return a participation reasonably equivalent to their contribution, no objection can be made." . . .

In view of these considerations we believe that to accord "the creditor his full right of priority against the corporate assets" where the debtor is insolvent, the stockholder's participation must be based on a contribution in money or in money's worth, reasonably equivalent in view of all the circumstances to the participation of the stockholder.

The alleged consideration furnished by the stockholders in this case falls far short of meeting those requirements.'

1. The findings below that participation by the old Class A stockholders will be beneficial to the bondholders because those stockholders have "financial standing and influence in the community" and can provide a "continuity of management" constitute no legal justification for issuance of new stock to them. Such items are illustrative of a host of intangibles which, if recognized as adequate consideration for issuance of stock to valueless junior interests, would serve as easy evasions of the principle of full or absolute priority of Northern Pacific Railway Co. v. Boyd, supra, and related cases. Such items, on facts present here, are not adequate consideration for issuance of the stock in question. On the facts of this case they cannot possibly be translated into money's worth reasonably equivalent to the participation accorded the old stockholders. They have no place in the assets column of the balance sheet of the new company. They reflect merely vague hopes or possibilities. As such, they cannot be the basis for issuance of stock to otherwise valueless interests. The rigorous standards of the absolute or full priority doctrine of the Boyd Case will not permit valueless junior interests to perpetuate their position in an enterprise on such ephemeral grounds.

2. The District Court's further finding that if the bondholders were to foreclose now they would receive "substantially less than the present appraised value" of the assets of the debtor corporation is no support for inclusion of the old stockholders in the plan. The fact that bondholders might fare worse as a result of a foreclosure and liquidation than they would by taking a debtor's plan under § 77B can have no relevant bearing on whether a proposed plan is "fair and equitable" under that section. Submission to coercion is not the application of "fair and equitable" standards. Such a proposition would not only drastically impair the standards of "fair and equitable" as used in § 77B; it would pervert the function of that Act. One of the purposes of § 77B was to avoid the consequences to debtors and creditors of foreclosures, liquidations, and forced sales with their drastic deflationary effects. To hold that in a § 77B reorganization creditors of a hopelessly insolvent debtor may be forced to share the already insufficient assets with stockholders because apart from rehabilitation under that section they would suffer a worse fate, would disregard the standards of "fair and equitable;" and would result in impairment of

the Act to the extent that it restored some of the conditions which the Congress sought to ameliorate by that remedial legislation.

3. The conclusion of the District Court that the virtual abrogation of the agreement deferring foreclosure until 1944 ("the principal valuable consideration" given to the bondholders by the stockholders) justified participation by the stockholders in the plan is likewise erroneous.

What were the rights of the bondholders under the supplemental indenture executed in 1930 we cannot determine. That indenture is not in the abbreviated record before us. The District Court found that for all practical purposes the bondholders could not foreclose until 1944. From the findings below we conclude that that followed as a consequence of making interest payable only if earned. On this record it does not appear whether or not there might be other events of default— such as non-payment of sinking funds—giving bondholders or the trustee the right to foreclose or giving bondholders or the trustee the right to accelerate the maturity of the bonds so that suits could be brought thereon. Hence, we must assume, as the District Court found, that the bondholders and the trustee could not take possession of the property through foreclosure or otherwise until the maturity of the bonds. And as a corollary thereof we likewise assumed that the stockholders, at least so far as the bondholders were involved, could keep their management group in possession and control until that time. And we assume that this right or power on the part of the stockholders to keep possession until 1944 was for them a thing of value, though there is no finding that the old stock had any value, present or prospective.

But we cannot conclude that that right survived the commencement of the proceedings under § 77B. A debtor as well as a creditor who invokes the aid of the Federal courts in reorganization or rehabilitation under § 77B assumes all of the consequences which flow from that jurisdiction. Once the property is in the hands of the court private rights as respects that res are subject to the superior dominion of the court and are to be adjudicated pursuant to the standards prescribed by the Congress. As a result of such proceedings the hand of all executions or levies may be stayed. The court acquires "exclusive jurisdiction of the debtor and its property wherever located for the purposes of this section." The court need not keep the debtor in possession but may substitute for the old management a trustee; or if the old management is retained it operates the business "subject at all times to the control of the judge, and to such limitations, restrictions, terms, and conditions as the judge may from time to time impose and prescribe." Thus, while the property remains in the hands of the court, as it does until dismissal or final decree on confirmation, the debtor, though left in possession by the judge, does not operate it, as it did before the filing of the petition, unfettered and without restraint. The control of the court is then pervasive. Furthermore, stockholders and other junior interests may be excluded from any plan of reorganization if the court finds that the debtor is insolvent. In re 620 Church Street Building Corp., 299 U.S. 24, 57 S.Ct. 88, 81 L.Ed. 16. And on facts such as exist here, these junior interests must be excluded unless they furnish adequate consideration for the interest which they obtain in the new company. And once the jurisdiction of the court has been invoked, whether by the debtor or by a creditor, that petitioner cannot withdraw and oust the court of jurisdiction. He invokes that jurisdiction risking all of the disadvantages which may flow to him as a consequence, as well as gaining all of the benefits. One of those disadvantages from the viewpoint of the debtor and its stockholders is the approval of a plan of reorganization which eliminates them completely. Accordingly, respondent's assertion in this case that the major contribution of these stockholders justifying their inclusion in the plan was the waiver of their right to defer or put off foreclosure until 1944, i.e., to remain in possession, does not stand analysis. The right to remain in unmolested dominion and control over the property was necessarily waived or abandoned on invoking the jurisdiction of the Federal courts in these proceedings. When that jurisdiction attached, the court rather than the stockholders was in control with all of the powers and duties which that entailed under § 77B. Certainly the surrender of a right thus waived is not adequate consideration for the dilution of the bondholders' priorities which this plan would effect.

And there is a further reason why this result necessarily follows, if the will of the Congress as expressed in § 77B is not to be thwarted and if the integrity of such proceedings is to be maintained. As we have said, this plan had its origin in an endeavor on the part of the debtor in 1937 to effect a voluntary reorganization. A plan was proposed by the debtor which was the same as that here involved except for the amount and nature of the stock to be received by the bondholders. That plan contained two methods for its consummation. The first was by means of an amendment to the trust indenture and a recapitalization of the debtor, a method to be followed if the board felt that sufficient approvals had been obtained. The second was by means of § 77B. Over 80% of the bondholders and over 90% of the stock approved the original plan. Thereupon the debtor filed its petition in § 77B. Thereafter, the debtor filed a modification of the plan to which the assents, here relied upon, were obtained. Thus respondent argues that since the plan of reorganization was entered into between the bondholders and the stockholders before institution of the reorganization proceedings under § 77B, the consideration flowing from the stockholders had been furnished and the interests of the bondholders and stockholders in the assets of the debtor had been fixed prior to the filing of the petition. In fact, respondent frankly insists that the stockholders' "right of participation was secured by contract before, and as a condition precedent to, the institution of the 77B proceedings."

But the mere statement of this proposition is its own refutation. If the reorganization court were bound by such conventions of the parties, it would be effectively ousted of important duties which the Act places

on it.   Federal courts acting under § 77B would be required to place
their imprimatur on plans of reorganization which disposed of the
assets of a company not in accord with the standards of "fair and
equitable" but in compliance with agreements which the required
percentages of security holders had previously made.   Such procedure
would deprive scattered and unorganized security holders of the protection which the Congress had provided them under § 77B.   The scope of
the duties and powers of the Court would be delimited by the bargain
which reorganizers had been able to make with security holders before
they asked the intercession of the court in effectuating their plan.
Minorities would have their fate decided not by the court in application
of the law of the land as prescribed in § 77B, but by the forces utilized
by reorganizers in prescribing the conditions precedent on which the
benefits of the statute could be obtained.   No conditions precedent to
enjoyment of the benefits of § 77B can be provided except by the
Congress.   To hold otherwise would be to allow reorganizers to rewrite
it so as to best serve their own ends.

   4.   The holding of the District Court that the value to the bondholders of maintaining the debtor as a going concern and of avoiding
litigation with the old stockholders justifies the inclusion of the latter
in the plan is likewise erroneous.   The conclusion of the District Court
that avoidance of litigation with the stockholders gave validity to their
claim for recognition in the plan involves a misconception of the duties
and responsibilities of the court in these proceedings.   Whatever might
be the strategic or nuisance value of such parties outside of § 77B is
irrelevant to the duties of the court in confirming or disapproving a
plan under that section.   In these proceedings there is no occasion for
the court to yield to such pressures.   If the priorities of creditors which
the law protects are not to be diluted, it is the clear duty of the court to
resist all such assertions.   Of course, this is not to intimate that
compromise of claims is not allowable under § 77B.   There frequently
will be situations involving conflicting claims to specific assets which
may, in the discretion of the court, be more wisely settled by compromise rather than by litigation.   Thus, ambiguities in the wording of two
indentures may make plausible the claim of one class of creditors to an
exclusive or prior right to certain assets as against the other class in
spite of the fact that the latter's claim flows from a first mortgage.
Close questions of interpretations of after-acquired property clauses in
mortgages, preferences in stock certificates, divisional mortgages and
the like will give rise to honest doubts as to which security holders have
first claim to certain assets.   Settlement of such conflicting claims to
the res in the possession of the court is a normal part of the process of
reorganization.   In sanctioning such settlements the court is not bow-
ing to nuisance claims; it is administering the proceedings in an
economical and practical manner.   But that is not the situation here.
As a result of the filing of the petition in this case, the court, not the
stockholders, acquired exclusive dominion and control over the estate.
Hence, any strategic position occupied by the stockholders prior to

these proceedings vanished once the court invoked its jurisdiction. Threats by stockholders of the kind here in question are merely threats to the jurisdiction of the court, which jurisdiction these selfsame stockholders invoked for their benefit when they caused the debtor's petition to be filed. Consequently, these claims of the stockholders are, as we have said, entitled to no more dignity than any claim based upon sheer nuisance value.

In this connection it should be observed that the finding of the court that it was important to admit the stockholders to participation in the plan so as to maintain the debtor as a going concern and thus protect the bondholders was based upon a misconception of its legal powers and duties. For the court assumed that the only alternative to acceptance of this debtor's plan was a dismissal of the proceeding or a liquidation. But this is not true. In the first place, no special perquisites (of consequence here) flow to stockholders by virtue of the fact that the proceedings are instituted by a voluntary rather than an involuntary petition. The criteria for exclusion or inclusion of stockholders in a plan are precisely the same in both situations. In practice it is not infrequent to find proceedings which start with a debtor's petition ending up with plans of reorganization which exclude stockholders. In the second place, failure to accept this plan does not force dismissal or liquidation. Section 77B(c)(8) gives the court explicit powers where "a plan of reorganization is not proposed or accepted within such reasonable period as the judge may fix" either to "extend such period" or to "dismiss the proceeding" or, with exceptions not relevant here, to cause liquidation, such choice to be made "as the interests of the creditors and stockholders may equitably require." Accordingly, dismissal has not infrequently been properly denied. And in this case there has been no showing that a plan which is not only fair and equitable but also meets the other requirements of the Act cannot be adopted nor that all reasonable time for proposal of such alternative plans has expired.

We therefore hold that the plan is not fair and equitable and that the judgment below must be and is reversed.

MR. JUSTICE BUTLER took no part in the consideration or disposition of this case.

Notes & Questions

1. *The Bondholders' Interests.* Is the absolute priority rule of *Case* in the best interests of the bondholders? Do they think it is? What features of the plan that the Court finds not to be "fair and equitable" might appeal to the bondholders? Might they affirmatively want the shareholders to have a continuing interest in the business? Who are likely to be substantial shareholders?

2. *Valuation and Absolute Priority.* Does the absolute priority rule place too much emphasis on the accuracy of the valuation process? In *Case*, suppose the valuation of the business were off by 20%. Would

that make a difference? Suppose in addition that the outstanding debts were only $1 million.

3. *Quality of Securities.* Does the absolute priority rule require that senior creditors receive "better quality" securities than their junior counterparts before a "cram down" (confirmation of a plan over the objection of the senior interests) may be urged? Compare In re Central Railroad Co. of New Jersey, 579 F.2d 804, 812 (3d Cir. 1978) (rejecting, as inconsistent with the absolute priority rule, the use of Conrail securities to pay some administrative claimants when lower priority administrative claimants were receiving cash: "That Conrail's current valuation is speculative and uncertain is enough to indicate that cash is plainly a superior consideration which, if it is to be distributed, must be distributed to claimants with the highest priorities") with In re The Duplan Corp., 9 B.R. 921 (Bkrtcy.S.D.N.Y.1980), affirmed in part and reversed in part, No. 81–5037 (2d Cir. Sept. 8, 1981) (unpublished opinion) (rejecting argument of noteholders that the absolute priority rule entitled them to receive the cash which was going to junior debenture-holders under the plan).

See generally Blum & Kaplan, The Absolute Priority Doctrine in Corporate Reorganizations, 41 U.Chi.L.Rev. 651 (1974).

3. Confirmation Standards Under Chapter 11

(a) *Impairment.* The principal approval requirements for a Chapter 11 plan are contained in § 1129(a)(7) and (8). Note that under § 1129(a)(8), a class either must accept a plan or not be impaired by the plan. (The rules governing when a class is deemed to have accepted a plan are set forth in § 1126(c) and (d).) Even in the absence of the approvals required by § 1129(a)(8)(A), a plan may be confirmed over the objection of an impaired class if the "fair and equitable" test contained in § 1129(b) is satisfied with respect to the dissenting class of claims or interests. Before approval or application of the fair and equitable test may be required, however, § 1129(a)(8) requires that the class be "impaired." See § 1124.

IN RE ROLLING GREEN COUNTRY CLUB
United States Bankruptcy Court, District of Minnesota, 1982.
26 B.R. 729.

KENNETH G. OWENS, BANKRUPTCY JUDGE.

Hearing was held before the undersigned on August 11, 1982 to consider confirmation, or its refusal, of two competing plans of reorganization as submitted respectively by the debtor Rolling Green Country Club and First National Bank of Minneapolis, the holder of security interests in the nature of real estate mortgages on the premises of the debtor. The proponent of each plan has objected to confirmation of the other and the committee of unsecured creditors originally objecting to confirmation of each plan is now an objector only as to the plan of First National Bank of Minneapolis having at hearing withdrawn its objection to the plan of the debtor. The debtor's plan in brief proposes to borrow from one Bruce Hendry $467,444.00 of which $325,000.00 would be available to fund its proposed payment plan. The plan proposes to cure an existing default with respect to the interests of First National Bank of Minneapolis and to pay all other classes of interest in full, except leaving in place for payment on due date November 1, 2001 the holders of bonds, building certificates and transferable certificates. The plan of First National Bank contemplates liquidation of the properties of the debtor through the device of the appointment of a liquidating trustee and provides either for surrender of security, or payment of secured creditors and payment of all other interested parties out of the proceeds of liquidation on an effective date defined to be such date as the proceeds of liquidation in the hands of the trustee become sufficient to effect the required payments.

Neither plan purports to impair any class and neither proponent has made a post-petition solicitation with respect to its plan nor filed and obtained approval of a post-petition disclosure as would otherwise be required by Section 1125 of the Bankruptcy Code, (11 U.S.C. Section 1125). The bank's plan was filed after 120 days after the date of the order for relief, and the court having denied at hearing the debtor's motion to extend its period of exclusivity under Section 1121 of the Code, (11 U.S.C. Section 1121), both plans are timely and to be considerd each on its merits. . . .

PERTINENT FINDINGS OF FACT

1.

The debtor which was formerly known as Brookview Country Club was incorporated in 1947 as a private member-only country club since 1969 located in Hamel, Minnesota. It affords to all its members and their guests the facilities of its clubhouse and appurtenances and to its playing members and their guests the use of its golf course.

2.

The club's facility is encumbered by first and second real estate mortgages securing loans obtained from the First National Bank of Minneapolis. The club has had a long and troubled history of management of that debt. The original principal amount of the debt secured by the first mortgage was $800,000.00 and the second mortgage secures a debt in the original principal amount of $130,000.00. . . .

4.

The principal balance due and owing on the first mortgage at the date of hearing is $605,412.15 and the principal balance owing on the second mortgage is $53,200.64. Interest accrues on the mortgages respectively at the rate of $126.13 per diem and $22.17 per diem.

5.

The present fair market value of the debtor's club premises including the golf course and subject to the mortgages to First Bank is in a range between $1,440,000.00 and $2,000,000.00. The value of the premises is in excess of the total present mortgage debt and the liquidation value of the premises and all other assets of the debtor is in excess of its total listed indebtedness, both secured and unsecured.

6.

First Bank commenced a foreclosure proceeding by advertisement, and a Sheriff's sale was scheduled to be held on January 13, 1982 with respect to the real estate premises subject to its mortgages. On the day prior to the scheduled sale, the debtor on January 12, 1982 filed its voluntary petition for reorganization under Chapter 11 of the Bankruptcy Code in this court and obtained the benefits of the automatic stay provided by Section 362 of the Bankruptcy Code, (11 U.S.C. Section 362).

7.

If First Bank had been permitted to continue its foreclosure proceeding, it would have, on the expiration of the period of redemption, January 13, 1983, a sum having by reason of increased and now prevailing interest rates representing a more valuable investment than the investment presently secured under its mortgages at a lesser rate if the debtor's plan is confirmed, defaults in payments on the mortgages are cured, the expenses of sale and cost of deferment paid and due dates reinstated. The difference in investment value to the bank is $164,651.64 using a discount rate based on opportunity cost of 17.68% with respect to the first mortgage and 17.8% with respect to the second mortgage.

DISCUSSION

OBJECTIONS TO DEBTOR'S PLAN

. . .

The bank's principal contention is that the bank as a claimant separately classified is impaired in that it will not receive payment of the $164,651.64 which it would expect to be able to receive if permitted in effect to re-accelerate its mortgage investment, that it has not accepted the debtor's plan and, the value of its security exceeding its claimed debt, such acceptance is required and, accordingly, the requirements for confirmation found in Section 1129(a)(7), (8) and (10) have not been met. . . .

The bank contends it is impaired because it would be in a better position if permitted to proceed to foreclosure and thus obtain the accelerated fruits of its mortgage, and that the impairment has not been removed by the debtor through compliance in its plan with Section 1124 of the Bankruptcy Code, (11 U.S.C. Section 1124) which provides in relevant part as follows:

"Section 1124. Impairment of claims or interests.

Except as provided in section 1123(a)(4) of this title, a class of claims or interests is impaired under a plan unless, with respect to each claim or interest of such class, the plan—

"(1) leaves unaltered the legal, equitable, and contractual rights to which such claim or interest entitles the holder of such claim or interests;

"(2) notwithstanding any contractual provision or applicable law that entitles the holder of such claim or interest to demand or receive accelerated payment of such claim or interest after the occurrence of a default—

"(A) cures any such default, other than a default of a kind specified in section 365(b)(2) of this title, that occurred before or after the commencement of the case under this title;

"(B) reinstates the maturity of such claim or interest as such maturity existed before such default;

"(C) compensates the holder of such claim or interest for any damages incurred as a result of any reasonable reliance by such holder on such contractual provision or such applicable law; and

"(D) does not otherwise alter the legal, equitable, or contractual rights to which such claim or interest entitles the holder of such claim or interest; or . . ."

If the failure of First Bank to realize the benefits of the acceleration and realization which would have occurred on the anticipated foreclosure of its mortgages constitutes "damages" within the meaning of Section 1124(2)(C) then First Bank as a claimant and as a separate class is impaired for the plan makes no provision for such payment to the bank as a claimant or as a class. . . .

The purpose of the section is to permit the financially embarrassed debtor to retain the security and enjoy the benefits of the original security arrangements. In that the purpose is to protect against the rights lost simply by reason of acceleration. It would seem fruitless indeed if the debtor is required in order to enjoy the benefit of this section to pay the total expected present economic cost of retaining or restoring the maturities provided in the instrument. I conclude accordingly that the term damages does not encompass that result. The damages have a lesser measure intended to protect the security holder from the expenses to which he has been put by reason of the denial of his right of acceleration. That is the extent to which he can reasonably rely on the instrument or on local law and suffer detriment by reason of the effect of this section on such right of acceleration. The security holder simply cannot expect to be held totally harmless from the effects of the application of Section 1124, and any such reliance on the security instrument or local law is not "reasonable" in the context of the title and in the context of the section. The security holder may only reasonably rely on the right of acceleration or foreclosure based on the instrument and local law to the extent of compensation for any expenses he may have incurred, in this case attorneys' fees incident to the foreclosure and reimbursement for the out-of-pocket loss occasioned by the fact that the payments in default have been deferred. That loss is adequately compensated by an appropriate interest allowance. The economic loss of expectation mentioned in the foregoing findings has a speculative basis assuming no decline in the cost of funds over time, and is not "damage" of the type contemplated by this section and need not be compensated.

The plan as amended provides for the payment of such damages "as may be allowed pursuant to 11 U.S.C. Section 1124(2)(C)". I deem that to be a sufficient provision under Section 1124 as reflected in the succeeding findings.

Since the bank is not impaired, there is no necessity for its affirmative acceptance. . . .

Notes & Questions

1. *Reversing Acceleration.* As illustrated by *Rolling Green*, § 1124(2) allows a plan to reverse acceleration of a debt in prebankruptcy default without necessarily obtaining creditor approval. Is the same option available to a debtor in Chapter 7? in Chapter 13? If not, does § 1124 provide debtors with a powerful incentive to prefer Chapter 11 over other bankruptcy proceedings? Is this a wise incentive? In a proceeding seeking relief from the automatic stay, may a Chapter 11 debtor reverse acceleration before filing a plan? See *In re Hewitt*, 16 B.R. 973 (Bkrtcy.D.Alaska 1982) (yes).

Suppose the creditor not only commences foreclosure proceedings but obtains a judgment of foreclosure. May a Chapter 11 plan cure the default and reinstate the debt without impairing the creditor? See *In re Madison Hotel Associates*, 749 F.2d 410 (7th Cir.1984) (yes where order of foreclosure had not been reduced to final judgment under state law). But see *In re Jones*, 32 B.R. 951 (Bkrtcy.D.Utah 1983).

Does the trustee's ability to assume a contract under § 365 provide much the same opportunity as does § 1124? See § 365(c)(2), (e)(3)(B).

2. *Chapter 11 vs. Chapters 7 and 13.* May *individual* business debtors improve their post-bankruptcy interests in secured assets by filing under Chapter 11 and invoking § 1124(2) in their Chapter 11 plans?

3. *Opportunity Costs.* The secured creditor in *Rolling Green* sought compensation for the opportunity to reinvest what was lost as a result of the prohibition on foreclosure. Should this issue be analyzed under the adequate protection standard of § 362? See Chapter 11C. What is

the difference, if any, between the lost opportunity in *Rolling Green* and the opportunity costs that secured creditors seek to have adequately protected under § 362? If "opportunity costs" are not to be taken into account under § 362 might there nevertheless be a case for taking them into account under § 1124(2)?

Impairment Problem

Consider the proposed reorganization of ABC Corp., a public company with $20 million in assets (valued on a "going concern" basis), as described below, and $10 million in secured debt, $9 million in senior unsecured debt, and $2 million in subordinated debt. Its simplified balance sheet might appear as follows:

Before Reorganization (in millions)

Assets		Liabilities	
Cash & accounts receivable	$ 6	Secured debt	$10
Inventory & work in process	8	Senior unsecured debt	9
Machinery, fixtures &		Subordinated debt	2
equipment	6	Shareholder equity	(1)
	$20		$20

Assume that under the reorganization plan, the senior unsecured debtholders agree to accept $5 million in cash (to be raised by new secured loans) in full settlement of amounts owed to them, and the other claims and interests remain unaffected by the plan. From whom must approval of the plan be sought? Are the subordinated debtholders "unimpaired"? Should they be given a vote on the plan?

Now assume that, at the time the Chapter 11 petition was filed, the debtor was six months in arrears on repaying the subordinated debtholders. The Chapter 11 plan provides, in addition to a scaling down of the senior unsecured debt, that the default will be cured and the loans repaid in accordance with their original terms. Must approval be sought from the class of subordinated debtholders?

Suppose ABC decides it is unable to come up with $5 million now for the senior unsecured debtholders and instead proposes a plan under which the senior unsecured debt is to receive a total of $15 million consisting of five annual payments of $3 million each. Must approval be sought from the senior unsecured debt?

May a class be deemed impaired within the meaning of § 1124 when it is receiving more than the value of its interest on the effective date of the plan? Assume ABC's first plan (paying $5 million to senior unsecured debtholders) is to be funded in part by new investors who also are willing to pay the shareholders $1 million for their ownership interests in ABC. Must the shareholders approve the plan? Are their interests impaired by the plan?

See generally Blum & Kaplan, Affecting Rights to Equity Interests Under Chapter XI of the Bankruptcy Act, 1972 Wisc.L.Rev. 978.

(b) *Cram Down Standards*

IN RE LANDMARK AT PLAZA PARK, LIMITED

United States Bankrtuptcy Court, District of New Jersey, 1980.
7 B.R. 653.

RICHARD W. HILL, BANKRUPTCY JUDGE.

This opinion constitutes the Court's findings of fact and conclusions of law with respect to a Chapter 11 confirmation hearing held on debtor's plan of reorganization, as modified. The opinion explains the November 3, 1980, letter decision of the Court.

Debtor, Landmark at Plaza Park, Ltd., is a limited partnership whose only substantial asset is a 200-unit garden apartment complex located in Morrisville, Pennsylvania. City Federal (hereafter City) holds a first mortgage on this property in the face amount of $2,250,000. The mortgage bears an interest rate of 9.5% and is due and payable on October 1, 1986. On October 2, 1980, this Court issued a written decision denying City's request for relief from the automatic stay provisions of Section 362 of the Bankruptcy Code, 11 U.S.C. Section 362, and continuing the stay until the conclusion of the hearing on confirmation of the debtor's plan. This opinion deals with debtor's plan as it affects City, the only objecting class of creditors. As to all other classes of creditors, there is no dispute and the Court is satisfied that the confirmation standards specified in 11 U.S.C. Section 1129 have been met.

. . . [T]he parties have stipulated that for the purpose of the confirmation hearing $2,260,000 is the fair market value of the property. This value was fixed by the Court after lengthy testimony was presented at the Section 362 hearing. . . . City has made an election pursuant to Section 1111(b)(2) of the Code. Thus, its claim in the amount of $2,512,457 will be treated as fully secured.[3]

---

3. Section 506(a) of the Code provides in part that:

(a) An allowed claim of a creditor secured by a lien on property in which the estate has an interest, or that is subject to setoff under section 553 of this title, is a secured claim to the extent of the value of such creditor's interest in the estate's interest in such property, or to the extent of the amount subject to setoff, as the case may be, and is an unsecured claim to the extent that the value of such creditor's interest or the amount so subject to setoff is less than the amount of such allowed claim. Such value shall be determined in light of the purpose of the valuation and of the proposed disposition or use of such property, and in conjunction with any hearing on such disposition or use or on a plan affecting such creditor's interest. 11 U.S.C. Section 506.

Reading this section alone, City would have a secured claim for $2,260,000 and an unsecured claim for $252,457. Section 1111(b)(2), however, provides that, notwithstanding Section 506(a), a creditor in the position of City may elect to be treated as fully secured. Since City has made the election, for purposes of this hearing its claim of $2,512,457 is fully secured.

I. THE PLAN AS MODIFIED

Crucial to an understanding of the Court's decision is a discussion of the plan and how it affects City. Contractually, City is a first mortgagee without recourse. It has possession of the property and is collecting the rents pursuant to a rent assignment agreement. The mortgage has been in default since at least December 1979. City is undersecured and wants to complete its foreclosure action.

The debtor has proposed in substance the following plan:

1. City is to redeliver possession of the property to the debtor.

2. On the 16th month after the effective date of the plan and through the 36th month debtor will commence monthly interest payments at the rate of 12.5% computed on the value of the property–$2,260,000.

3. Debtor will deliver to City a non-recourse note, payable in three years in the face amount of $2,705,820.31, in substitution of all existing liabilities.

4. The existing mortgage will secure the note set forth in paragraph 3, except to the extent that it is inconsistent with or modified by the plan.

5. City is the only member of the class of creditors to which it has been assigned.

The face amount of the note is derived as follows:

a.	Current value of collateral	$2,260,000.00
b.	Unpaid interest: months 1–15 @ 12.5%	353,125.00
c.	Interest on unpaid interest: 21 months @ 15%	92,695.31
	Face amount of note	$2,705,820.31

The debtor's principal theory is that the note will be paid off at the end of 36 months by a combination of refinancing and accumulation of cash from the project, all of which will subsequently be discussed at length. The key to the debtor's plan is a proposal to obtain a new first mortgage in three years in the face amount of $2,400,000.

It is undisputed that pursuant to this plan City is impaired within the meaning of Section 1124 of the Code. City has rejected the plan.

II. THE ISSUES

Confirmation standards under the Code are set forth in Section 1129. Clearly, the debtor has complied with all provisions of that section except for the following subsections: (a)(7)(B); (a)(8); (a)(11); (b)(1); and (b)(2)(A). Actually the list is much shorter. The requirements of (a)(7)(B) are, in effect, carried forward in (b)(1) and (b)(2). Thus if the requirement of subsections (b)(1) and (b)(2) are met (a)(7)(B) will also

There is a slight dispute between City and the debtor as to the amount of the claim. Debtor asserted that the debt was $2,476,449.17 as of November 1, 1980. The difference, however, is immaterial to the outcome of the case.

have been met. Similarly, the requirements of (a)(8) are waived by the specific language of (b)(1) if other requirements of (b)(1) and (b)(2) are met. That leaves at issue the debtor's compliance with subsections (a) (11), (b)(1) and (b)(2). Subsection (a)(11) of Section 1129 is a feasibility requirement and, in a general sense, deals with whether the debtor can and will accomplish what it has proposed. Subsection (b) of Section 1129 is the "cram-down" provision of the Code. It describes those circumstances in which a class of creditors or interests may over its objection be involuntarily subjected to the provisions of a plan. Each of these sections will be discussed at length. The provisions of subsection (b) will be discussed first because certain determinations made there bear on the feasibility determination required by subsection (a)(11).

III. THE REQUIREMENTS OF SECTION 1129(b)(1) and (2)

The provisions of Section 1129(b) specify the circumstances under which a class of creditors or interests may be involuntarily subjected to a plan of reorganization. This "cram-down" provision of the Code provides in part that:

(b)(1) Notwithstanding section 510(a) of this title, if all of the applicable requirements of subsection (a) of this section other than paragraph (8) are met with respect to a plan, the court, on request of the proponent of the plan, shall confirm the plan notwithstanding the requirements of such paragraph if the plan does not discriminate unfairly, and is fair and equitable, with respect to each class of claims or interests that is impaired under, and has not accepted, the plan.

(2) For the purpose of this subsection, the condition that a plan be fair and equitable with respect to class includes the following requirements:

(A) With respect to a class of secured claims, the plan provides—

(i)(I) that the holders of such claims retain the lien securing such claims, whether the property subject to such lien is retained by the debtor or transferred to another entity, to the extent of the allowed amount of such claims; and

(II) that each holder of a claim of such class receive on account of such claim deferred cash payments totaling at least the allowed amount of such claim, of a value, as of the effective date of the plan, of at least the value of such holder's interest in the estate's interest in such property.[4] 11 U.S.C. Section 1129(b).

The concept that a plan is fair and equitable is not fully defined in the Code. Section 1129(b)(2)(A), (B) & (C) states several factors which are included in that requirement but the legislative history accompanying that section makes clear that other factors fundamental to fair and

4. Section 1129(b)(2) is divided into three subparts: Subpart (A) deals with classes of secured claims; Subpart (B) deals with classes of unsecured claims; and Subpart (C) deals with classes of interests. Only Subpart (A) is relevant to this decision.

equitable treatment of a dissenting class were omitted to "avoid complexity." Klee, "All You Ever Wanted To Know About Cram Down Under the New Bankruptcy Code," 53 Amer.Bank.L.J. 133, 142 (1979); 124 Cong.Rec. H 11,103 (daily ed. Sept. 28, 1978) (remarks of Rep. Don Edwards); 124 Cong.Rec. S 17,420 (daily ed. Oct. 6, 1978) (remarks of Sen. DeConcini). Given the present posture of this case the Court is satisfied that the factors set forth in Section 1129(b)(2)(A)(i), dealing with the cram down of a secured creditor, adequately deal with the question of whether the plan, as to City, is fair and equitable, and the Court will limit its consideration to those factors.

To meet the requirements of Section 1129(b)(2)(A)(i) the debtor's plan must do three things. First, it must provide for retention by the creditor of its lien. Second, the total stream of deferred cash payments proposed by the plan must at least total the amount of the secured claim. Third, the total stream of payments must have a value equal to the value of the property. The plan before the Court satisfies the first two requirements, but may not satisfy the third.[5]

The third requirement is found in that portion of Section 1129(b)(2)(A)(i)(II) stating that "each holder of a claim . . . receive . . . deferred cash payments . . . of a value . . . of at least the value of such holder's interest in the estate's interest in such property." This provision requires the Court to determine the present value of the payments to be made under the plan. Here the total stream of payments under the plan is $3,200,195.17.[6] The discounted value of these payments must equal $2,260,000, . . . the value of the property.

The debtor's construct for meeting subsection (b)(2)(A)(i)(II) is simple. It assumes that the value of the property constitutes the principal amount of a loan and purports to repay to City that principal amount together with interest at 12.5% per annum.[7] Thus, the debtor argues that if the interest rate fixed is adequate the discounted value of the principal plus interest must equal the present value of the property. To support the fixing of a 12.5% interest rate debtor presented evidence that at the time of the confirmation hearing certain institutional investors would provide first mortgage loans on similar property at that rate. The testimony also revealed, however, that 12.5% is at the low end of the interest range.

City strongly rejects the present value approach asserted by the debtor. It focuses on the question of whether the stream of payments offered by the debtor could be sold as of the effective date of the plan for a price at least equal to $2,260,000. City presented expert testimo-

5. For purposes of this opinion the allowed amount of the secured claim is $2,512,457. The total stream of payments is $3,200,195.17 consisting of the face amount of the note, $2,705,820.31, plus 21 months interest totaling $494,374.86. Requirement (2) is thus satisfied.

6. See footnote 5, supra.

7. The plan is somewhat oversimplified by this statement because 15 months interest is deferred and the deferred interest itself bears interest at a 15% rate.

ny that attempted to establish two facts: (1) that even assuming that the property was in good condition and under capable management, the only market for debtor's proposed payment stream would be the secondary mortgage market with the purchase price being 50 to 60 percent of the value of the collateral. It is City's contention that regardless of the interest rate offered the value of the payment stream will be less than the value of the property; (2) that with income producing property, a non-recourse note in excess of the value of the property would always be worth less than the value of the property because an investor would always prefer the property to the note. City's expert grudgingly conceded that his opinion of the value of the note would change if he had confidence in management and believed that future income projections would in fact be sufficient to pay off the note. The expert, however, then backtracked and concluded that mortgage loans could not be made in reliance on future income projections.

In the Court's view, City's expert so overstated his position that his opinion on saleability and value cannot be considered. Succinctly stated, the Court is satisfied that a non-recourse note in excess of the value of the property can be worth at least the value of the property if sufficient interest is paid on the note and repayment is sufficiently certain. The question in the present case becomes whether the 12.5% interest rate offered by the debtor is adequate and whether repayment is sufficiently certain.

Conceptually, the modified plan seeks to force City to make a $2,260,000 loan, repayable in three years, with the first 15 months of interest deferred. There is no amortization over the term of the loan. Since there is currently no equity in the property the debtor is asking City to make a 100% loan. The rate of interest on a loan of this type should correspond to the rate of interest which would be charged or obtained by a creditor making a loan to a third party with similar terms, duration, collateral and risk. 5 Collier on Bankruptcy at para. 1129.03 (15th ed. 1980). Although the rate of interest may be identical to the market rate of interest, this will often not be the case because of the particular risk involved. 5 Collier, supra at para. 1129.03.

It appears clear to the Court that the forced loan proposed by the debtor includes terms less favorable to City than would typically be found in the market and that any confirmable plan must compensate City for this deficiency.[9] Testimony presented at the confirmation hearing revealed that institutions such as thrifts, life insurance companies and pension funds would make first mortgage loans on garden apartments with an interest rate ranging from 12.5 to 14 percent. The typical first mortgage loan would have a term of three to ten years,

---

9. In addressing the interest problem a deficiency in the proofs must be noted. The debtor has asserted that a 12.5% rate should be applied. City in effect asserted that regardless of the rate the plan could not be confirmed. The Court has rejected the debtor's rate, but for the purpose of testing the feasibility of the plan has derived a rate. It is not altogether clear that the rate derived by the Court would have been the rate found by the Court if City had presented evidence on the issue.

with amortization calculated on a 25 year payout and a 75% maximum loan to value ratio. Secondary mortgage financing would be available for additional borrowing requirements at five points over the prime rate (which was 14% at the time of the confirmation hearing). For interest rate purposes, therefore, it appears appropriate to treat City as the forced holder of two mortgages: a first mortgage to the extent of 75% of the loan and a second mortgage to the extent of 25% of the loan. The Court believes that the first 75% of the loan should bear an interest rate between 13.5% and 14%, the high end of the range for a typical garden apartment loan. Although the three year term is consistent with that in the marketplace, the deferral of interest and the lack of amortization requires a higher interest rate. The remaining 25% of the loan should bear an interest rate at least consistent with that charged in the commercial secondary mortgage market. Testimony at trial indicated that interest on such mortgages is generally five points over prime. With the prime rate approximately 14% at the time of confirmation, the Court believes that 19% is the minimum interest rate on this portion of the loan. A composite loan rate of 15% is then arrived at, computed as follows:

$$.75(.135) = .1013$$
$$.25(.19) = \underline{.0475}$$
$$.1488$$
$$.75(.14) = .1050$$
$$.25(.19) = \underline{.0475}$$
$$.1525$$

Say 15%

Thus, if a note and interest payments were offered to City by debtor at a 15% rate debtor would appear to meet the requirement that the discounted stream of payments equal the value of the property. Because the 12.5% rate proposed by debtor is below the 15% minimum rate established by the Court the plan as presented does not comply with Section 1129(b)(2)(A)(i)(II) and, therefore, cannot be confirmed. Since the plan could be readily modified, however, the Court must determine whether the plan is feasible if funded at a 15% rate. [The Court then found that the plan would not be feasible within the meaning of § 1129(a)(11).]

Notes & Questions

1. *Cram Down.* Assume that a corporation in Chapter 11 has a going concern value of $2 million, a liquidation value of $1.8 million, and liabilities of $2.2 million, consisting of $1 million in secured debt and $1.2 million in unsecured debt. The corporation proposes to pay the secured creditors according to their original obligations and proposes to pay the unsecured creditors $1 million in cash upon confirmation of the plan in full satisfaction of the amount owed to the unsecured

creditors. The stockholders are unaffected by the plan and maintain control over the company.

(a) Is any class of creditors impaired?

(b) What are the requirements for obtaining approval of a plan by a class? See § 1126.

(c) If an individual member of an approving impaired class rejects the plan, what are his rights? See § 1129(a)(7).

(d) If less than two-thirds of the unsecured creditor class approves of the plan, may the court nevertheless confirm the plan? See § 1129(b)(1).

(e) Is this plan fair and equitable? Does this result differ from the result that would be reached under Case v. Los Angeles Lumber Products?

Now assume that the unsecured creditors are offered $1.5 million to be paid in five $300,000 annual installments. May this plan be confirmed over the objection of the unsecured creditors as a class? May it be confirmed even though a senior class is impaired and a junior class (the shareholders) is participating in the reorganized enterprise? Could such a plan be confirmed under Case v. Los Angeles Lumber Products? What other changes does § 1129 work in the old "fair and equitable" rule?

See generally Klee, All You Ever Wanted to Know About Cram Down Under the New Bankruptcy Code, 53 Am.Bankr.L.J. 133 (1979); Blum, The "Fair and Equitable" Standard For Confirming Reorganizations Under the New Bankruptcy Code, 54 Am.Bankr.L.J. 165 (1980).

2. *Delayed Participation.* Section 7–303(3) of the proposed Bankruptcy Act of 1973 provided that a plan of reorganization

may include, if the plan is based on an estimated valuation which would preclude other participation by any class of creditors, the partners of a partnership debtor, an individual debtor, or equity security holders of the debtor, provisions for delayed participation rights for such a class or classes, holders, partners, or individual conditioned on the court's determination within a period specified in the plan but not later than five years from the date of confirmation that the reorganized debtor or the successor under the plan has attained a financial status that warrants such participation . . ..

Should this proposal have been included in the Code? [c]

3. *Equity's Position.* It is likely that the equity owners of a business debtor will assert an enterprise value in excess of that claimed by the debtor's creditors. Why? Assume a Chapter 11 plan in which the unsecured creditors are given all of a corporation's stock in satisfac-

---

c. Compare Rochelle & Balzersen, Recommendations for Amendments to Chapter X, 46 Am.Bankr.L.J. 93, 99–102 (1972) *with* Brudney, The Bankruptcy Commission's Proposed "Modifications" of the Absolute Priority Rule, 48 Am.Bankr.L.J. 305 (1974) and Note, The Proposed Bankruptcy Act: Changes in the Absolute Priority Rule for Corporate Reorganizations, 87 Harv.L.Rev. 1786 (1974).

tion of their claims. On what grounds may the pre-reorganization shareholders challenge such a plan? Are they impaired within the meaning of § 1124?

4. *New Equity Contributions.* Under § 1129(b)'s fair and equitable standard, confirmation of a plan over the objection of a class of claims may require the elimination of all shareholder interests. If the old shareholder interests contribute new funds to the reorganized enterprise may they retain an ownership interest in the business? See In re Potter Material Service, Inc., 781 F.2d 99 (7th Cir. 1986); In re Landau Boat Co., supra (yes). Is there any limit on the size of the equity interest that may be granted in exchange for the injection of new capital?

In Norwest Bank Worthington v. Ahlers, ___ U.S. ___, 108 S.Ct. 963, ___ L.Ed.2d ___ (1988), the Court of Appeals found that the debtors, farmers, could file a feasible reorganization plan and rejected the creditors' contention the absolute priority rule barred confirmation of any plan which allowed the debtors to retain their equity interest in the farm, which was junior to creditors' unsecured claims. The court held that the absolute priority rule did not bar respondents from retaining their equity interest if they contributed "money or money's worth" to the reorganized enterprise, and that their yearly contributions of labor, experience, and expertise would constitute such a contribution, therefore permitting confirmation of a reorganization plan over creditors' objections. The Supreme Court reversed. Viewed from the time of the plan's approval, the promise of future services was intangible, inalienable, and, in all likelihood, unenforceable. Unlike "money or money's worth," such promises cannot be exchanged in any market for something presently of value to the creditors.

See generally Coogan, Confirmation of a Plan Under the Bankruptcy Code, 32 Case W.Res.L.Rev. 301 (1982).

Notes on the Effect of Confirmation of a Plan

1. *Post-Confirmation Defaults.* Assume that the bankruptcy court confirms a plan under which Creditor is to receive $1,000 a month for one year in satisfaction of Creditor's $20,000 claim for aggravated assault by the Chapter 11 debtor's employees. The debtor fails to make the second monthly payment called for by the plan. May Creditor pursue the debtor for his claim? Would your answer to this question change if the debtor were in Chapter 13 instead of Chapter 11? See § 1141. Could Creditor have pursued the debtor if the debtor were being liquidated under Chapter 7 and Creditor received only $500 in satisfaction of his claim?

2. *Secured Claims.* Suppose a plan is silent as to the treatment of a secured claim. Does the claim survive confirmation of the plan? See § 1141(c).

3. *Chapter 11 vs. Chapter 13.* When might an individual debtor find Chapter 11 more advantageous than Chapter 13? For limitations on an individual's incentives to invoke Chapter 11, see § 1141(d).

4. The Partially Secured Creditor's Election Under Section 1111(b)

Note on the Background of Section 1111(b)

Section 1111(b) contains two strange provisions. Section 1111(b)(2) authorizes a partially secured creditor to elect to treat his claim as fully secured. Section 1111(b)(1)(A) treats a nonrecourse secured claim as a recourse secured claim. Before seeing these provisions in action, it may facilitate understanding them to review the developments that led to their enactment.

In In re Pine Gate Associates, Limited, 2 B.R.Ct.Dec. (CRR) 1478 (Bkrtcy.N.D.Ga.1976), Pine Gate, a limited partnership, filed a petition for a real property arrangement under Chapter XII of the Bankruptcy Act of 1898. Pine Gate owned and operated an apartment project. Secured creditors held a mortgage on the apartment project and the promissory notes evidencing the underlying debts stated that the debtor would not be liable on the notes beyond the value of the property and improvements constituting the apartment project. In other words, neither Pine Gate nor any of the partners were personally liable on the debts owed to the secured creditors. It was a "nonrecourse" loan. The secured creditors disapproved of Pine Gate's plan of arrangement and Pine Gate proposed that the apartment project be appraised and that the creditors be paid the appraised value so that the plan could be confirmed. The secured creditors objected and insisted that Chapter XII required that their debts be paid in full or that the mortgaged property be surrendered to them.

The court rejected the creditors' argument. "[I]f the creditor in lieu of the return of the property receives cash in the appraised value of that property, the creditor receives the 'value of the debt' and the creditor is adequately protected . . . and the plan can be confirmed without the consent of said creditor." Id at 1484. The court also held that the nonrecourse secured creditors were not entitled to vote on Pine Gate's plan as unsecured creditors because they had limited their claims to the value of the security. Id. at 1487.

Pine Gate thus enabled a debtor to "cash out" a dissenting nonrecourse secured creditor by paying that creditor the value of his security. To some, *Pine Gate* gave debtors too powerful a weapon.

[H]ighly leveraged limited partnerships which were established as investment vehicles were able to use the automatic stay against lien enforcement to prevent mortgagees from foreclosing during the Chapter XII case and in many cases successfully avoided the adverse tax consequences to the partners which foreclosure might entail. In addition, the partnership upon confirmation of its plan and the scaling down of its mortgage obligations was able to derive the exclusive benefits of any appreciation in the real estate markets which may not have been anticipated by the court at the time of the court's valuation of the secured creditor's interest in the property.

5 Collier on Bankruptcy ¶ 1111.02, at 1111–18 (L.King ed. 15th ed. 1981). For example, assume that the debt owed to the secured creditors was $1,400,000 and that the property was appraised $1 million. If the debtor's plan of arrangement cashed out the secured creditors for $1 million, they would have no further interest in the property and no further debt. If, after confirmation of the plan, the debtor sold the property for $1,500,000 the debtor would enjoy all the post-confirmation appreciation (or the benefit of an erroneously low appraisal). This result would be avoided if the debtor were forced to turn over the property to the secured creditors, or if the creditors could block confirmation of the debtor's plan.

How does § 1111(b) deal with the problem generated by the old Chapter XII cases like *Pine Gate?* Does it prevent a debtor from cashing out a partially secured lender at an appraised value and then selling the collateral for a greater amount? Or does § 1111(b) merely limit the debtor's chances of obtaining approval of a plan over the objection of a dissenting partially secured creditor?

Is the *Pine Gate* problem any different from the many other valuation problems that attend a bankruptcy law? Should it receive special, complex treatment? If § 1111(b) protects secured lenders from the risk of too low an appraisal of their collateral, should bankruptcy law contain a provision which prevents them from benefiting from too high an appraisal? Suppose a debtor cashes out a secured creditor for $1 million and soon thereafter finds that the property can only be sold for $500,000. Should the secured creditor be required to return the $500,000 difference?

Pine Gate provides part of the genesis of § 1111(b). Its terms were also shaped by a compromise on differences between the House and Senate bankruptcy reform bills over the treatment of dissenting secured creditors in reorganization proceedings. Under § 1129(b) of H.R. 8200, a secured creditor with a nonrecourse claim was entitled to receive payments equal to the value of the collateral but was not entitled to a deficiency claim. Under § 1129(d) of S. 2266, a purchase money lender with a security interest in real property could not be forced to accept less than the full amount of the loan under a reorganization plan. The provision was an express exception to § 506(a) which limits the amount of a secured claim to the value of the collateral. The House version of § 1129(b) was viewed as dealing too harshly with secured creditors and the Senate version would have given the secured lender "veto power over the debtor's reorganization plan and thus to place the lender in a position to force the [debtor] either to abandon the [collateral] or liquidate its assets under chapter 7 of the Code by reason of its inability to confirm a plan without the lender's consent." 5 Collier on Bankruptcy ¶ 1111.02, at 1111–14 (L.King ed. 15th ed. 1981).

On this level, § 1111(b) is the result of two competing visions of how secured creditors ought to be treated.

IN RE GRIFFITHS

United States Bankruptcy Court, District of Kansas, 1983.
27 B.R. 873.

JAMES A. PUSATERI, BANKRUPTCY JUDGE.

In this chapter 11 proceeding, the parties have asked the Court, in a declaratory action, to determine if 11 U.S.C. § 1129(b)(2)(A)(iii) allows the debtors to cram down their plan of reorganization when an electing secured creditor intends to vote to reject the plan.

The issues presented for determination are:

  1. If a recourse, undersecured creditor, in its own class, has made an election under 11 U.S.C. § 1111(b)(2), and rejects the debtor's plan of reorganization, is the creditor receiving the "indubitable equivalent" of its claim, under 11 U.S.C. § 1129(b)(2)(A)(iii) when the debtors propose to surrender to the creditor a portion of the collateral, and pay the creditor a lump sum equal to the highest value of the collateral retained by the debtor. . . .

FINDINGS OF FACT

The debtors are farmers and filed a chapter 11 petition in bankruptcy on August 6, 1982.

The creditor, Union State Bank (USB), has a security interest in personal property of the debtors including machinery, equipment, livestock and stored grain. USB filed an "election" under 11 U.S.C. § 1111(b)(2) in September, 1982.

The debtors intend to treat USB in the plan as follows:

The debtors will return a portion of USB's collateral and pay a lump sum equal to the value of the remaining collateral in total satisfaction of USB's claim. As the disclosure statement indicates:

It is debtors position that this combination of property turnover and payment in lump sum of the fair market value of said property is the "indubitable equivalent" of the creditor's allowed secured claim. This treatment will effectively satisfy Union State Bank's claim and no further payments are contemplated under the Plan.

(First Amended Disclosure Statement, pg. 20).

USB has filed a claim in the amount of $570,670.94. (There appears to be an error on the claim and USB may have intended to file a claim in the amount of $574,670.94. The Court will use the lower figure for the purposes of this opinion.) The total value of the security pledged to USB is less than the amount of the debt and thus, USB is "undersecured."

The debtors also allege the following facts in their reply memorandum which the Court accepts as correct for the purpose of this opinion:

On November 1, 1982, Debtors turned over their commercial cowherd to USB. On November 23, 1982, an adequate protection order was entered whereby Debtors were to pay U.S.B. $500.00 per month for the depreciation to the personal property being retained by Debtors. On December 8, 1982, Debtors turned over to U.S.B. and to Massey Ferguson, certain machinery and equipment and subsequently turned over the Registered Cowherd owned by Debtors. On that date, U.S.B. accepted the payment of $2,000.00, the fair market value of two cows, and Debtors retained two registered cows which are being used in rebuilding Debtors' herd and in the reorganization efforts. Debtors have determined that the personal property still in their possession in which U.S.B. claims an interest, will be beneficial to the rehabilitative efforts they are undergoing and to their Plan of Reorganization. Debtors subsequently proposed to pay U.S.B. more than they would receive if Debtors were to turn over the property. On the notification of U.S.B. that it would not accept such a proposal, its Motion and this Response ensued.

CONCLUSIONS OF LAW

Section 1111(b)(2) states:

If . . . an election is made, then notwithstanding section 506(a) of this title, such claim is a secured claim to the extent that such claim is allowed.

11 U.S.C. § 1111(b)(2). An undersecured creditor, a creditor whose security is worth less than the total amount owed to the creditor, may choose to have its claim treated in two manners: First, it can have a bifurcated claim, with a secured claim to the extent of the value of the collateral, and an unsecured claim for the remainder of the debt owed. 11 U.S.C. § 506(a). Second, the secured creditor can waive its unsecured claim and elect to have its total claim treated as secured. 11 U.S.C. § 1111(b)(2); Klee, All You Ever Wanted to Know About Cram Down Under the New Bankruptcy Code, 53 Am.Bankr.L.J. 133, 153 (1979).

There are two situations in which the election cannot be made. First, if the creditor's interest in the collateral "is of inconsequential value . . . ," the election cannot be made. 11 U.S.C. § 1111(b)(1)(B)(i). Second, if the creditor has recourse against the debtor, such as under K.S.A. § 84-9-504(2) (Supp.1981), and the debtor intends to sell the collateral, such as under 11 U.S.C. § 363(k), the election cannot be made. In the instant case, the collateral has significant value, no sale is in the offing, and therefore the election is not prohibited.

USB is in a class of its own and intends to reject the debtors' plan. The parties agree USB's claim is being impaired. Thus, in order to confirm the plan the debtors will have to seek a cram down on USB. 11 U.S.C. § 1129(b)(1). There are three alternatives to cramming down a class of secured claims. Although not applicable herein, property can be sold, a lien granted on the sale proceeds, and the lien satisfied under one of the remaining two cram down alternatives. 11 U.S.C. § 1129(b) (2)(A)(ii). There can be a cash payment cram down, requiring the debtor to make cash payments of at least the allowed amount of the claim, and the discounted value of these payments must equal at least the value of the collateral. 11 U.S.C. § 1129(b)(2)(A)(i)(II). The debtor does not propose to cram down under this provision.

The debtors choose the third option of giving USB "the indubitable equivalent of such claim . . . ." 11 U.S.C. § 1129(b)(2)(A)(iii). The phrase "indubitable equivalent" is derived from Judge Learned Hand's opinion in In Re Murel Holding Corp., 75 F.2d 941 (2nd Cir. 1935). It includes "abandonment of the collateral" to the secured creditor. 124 Cong.Rec. H 11,104 (daily ed. Sept. 28, 1978) (statement of Rep. Edwards); 124 Cong.Rec. S 17,421 (daily ed. Oct. 6, 1978) (statement of Sen. DeConcini). Indubitable equivalent cash payments must equal at least the secured claim. Payments less than the secured claim are not the indubitable equivalent of the secured claim. Id.

The Court believes there are several reasons the debtors cannot return a portion of the collateral and pay the value of the remaining collateral as the indubitable equivalent of USB's section 1111(b)(2) claim.

First, USB's post-election secured claim is the total amount owed to it, $570,670.94, reduced by the value of any property returned. The debtors must pay the indubitable equivalent of the remaining amount owed, and not simply the indubitable equivalent of the value of the remaining property. The indubitable equivalent of the *claim* must be realized. The post-election claim is something more than the value of the remaining property.

Second, often a creditor will not elect under § 1111(b)(2) because it will

> be reluctant to give up the distribution to unsecured creditors under the plan in exchange for a lien for the full amount of their secured and unsecured claims . . . .. The election to relinquish an unsecured recourse deficiency claim for a larger secured claim will normally be used to prevent a "cash out." Absent the election, a plan could free the collateral by paying the secured creditor the value of the collateral as this would not "impair" the secured creditor.

3 Norton, Bankruptcy Law and Practice § 57.02 at 14–15 (Supp.1982). Thus, creditors may choose to elect in cases where the debtor's plan proposes a minimal or zero payment to unsecured claims. In such a plan, the debtor is proposing to "cash out" the secured creditor by paying the value of the collateral. As Judge Norton indicated, § 1111(b)(2) allows the creditor to decide if it will be cashed out for the value of the collateral. The creditor elects to "prevent a 'cash out.'" See 5 Collier on Bankruptcy ¶ 1111.02[5], at 1111–27 (15th Ed. 1982).

In the instant case, the debtor is essentially proposing to "cash out" USB for the value of the remaining collateral. Section 1111(b)(2) gives USB the ability to prevent the cash out. The Court cannot agree that a cash out payment is the indubitable equivalent of a post election claim that prevented a cash out.

Third, under § 1129(b)(2)(A)(i)(II), payments to the dissenting electing creditor must pass two tests. Under the first test, the total payments must be at least the total allowed claim. When the election has been made, the total amount owed is the allowed claim. Under the second test, those payments must have a present value equal to the value of the collateral. In the instant case, the debtors do not propose to pay the total remaining allowed claim of USB (after credit for returned collateral), but rather only propose to pay the value of the collateral. Thus, under § 1129(b)(2)(A)(i)(II), the first requirement of cash payment cram down would not be satisfied. The Court does not believe § 1129(b)(2)(A)(iii) was intended as an alternative to the cash payment requirements of § 1129(b)(2)(A)(i)(II).

As Collier states:

> On the one hand, section 1111(b), taken in conjunction with sections 1124 and 1129, gives the debtor the power to retain encumbered property essential to the debtor's reorganization and to obtain confirmation of its plan in the face of opposition by a class of creditors whose claims are secured by such property. This preserves the debtor's ability to reorganize.

5 Collier on Bankruptcy ¶ 1111.02[1], at 1111–14 to –15 (15th Ed. 1982). Although a debtor could return all the collateral in satisfaction of the claim, most often,

> the debtor may well want to retain possession of the property particularly if it is essential to the continued operation of the debtor's business. If the plan proposes that the debtor retain the collateral, the plan will have to comply with section 1129(b)(2)(A)(i)
> . . . .

5 Collier on Bankruptcy ¶ 1111.02[5], at 1111–30 (15th Ed. 1982). If all the collateral is not returned, indubitable equivalent in the form proposed by the instant debtors is not available. Id. "Nothing less than the value assured to an electing creditor by section 1129(b)(2)(A)(i) . . . could be crammed down as an "indubitable equivalent." Stein, Section 1111(b): Providing Undersecured Creditors with Postconfirmation Appreciation in the Value of the Collateral, 56 Am.Bankr.L.J. 195, 210 (1982).

Finally, the debtors point out that they could return all the collateral in satisfaction of the post election secured claim. USB agrees. The Court agrees. The debtors argue that there is equitably no difference between returning collateral that could be sold by USB for $x, or just giving USB $x. The argument is alluring, but it has the effect of shifting the power granted under § 1111(b)(2) from the creditor to the debtor. Section 1111(b)(2) gives the creditor the power to decide how it will be treated, and an ability to seek greater payments under a plan calling for zero percent payments to unsecured creditors. Under the debtors' argument, in a cash out plan, the power is always shifted back to the debtor. A debtor could propose zero payments to unsecured creditors under a cash out plan paying nothing to undersecured creditors. If the creditor elects to prevent cash out, the debtor could return anywhere from a small amount of property to a substantial amount of property and pay the value of the remaining property as the indubitable equivalent of returning all the property. The creditor would still be cashed out by receiving only the value of the collateral, and would be powerless to prevent the cash out. Congress intended that § 1111(b)(2) would give the creditor power to prevent cash out. See 5 Collier on Bankruptcy ¶ 1111.02[1] (15th Ed. 1982). A lump sum cash out payment, that removes the impaired electing creditor's power to prevent cash out is not the indubitable equivalent of the electing creditor's claim.

Therefore, the Court holds that the debtors' proposal will not satisfy the provisions of 11 U.S.C. § 1129(b)(2)(A)(iii).   . . .

Notes & Questions

1. *Effect of the Election.* In *Landmark,* supra, and in *Griffiths,* what is the effect of the § 1111(b)(2) election? Why did the creditors make it? Is there ever reason not to make the § 1111(b)(2) election?

Suppose the secured party believes that the collateral will increase in value after the date on which the court valued the collateral, as occurred in the old Chapter XII cases. Should the secured party make the § 1111(b)(2) election?

In *Landmark,* the secured party making the election was "without recourse." Once such a secured party makes the § 1111(b)(2) election, may his claim be any more than the value of the mortgaged property? What does § 1111(b)(1)(A)(i) mean? If it means what it says does it make sense?

See generally, Kaplan, Nonrecourse Undersecured Creditors Under New Chapter 11—The Section 1111(b) Election: Already A Need For Change, 53 Am.Bankr.L.J. 269 (1979).

2. *§ 1111(b)(2) Problem.* Assume that the debtor corporation has assets with a going concern value of $2 million, including real estate worth $600,000. The real estate is subject to a $1 million mortgage. The corporation proposes a plan that pays unsecured creditors 15% of their claims and that leaves its stockholders unaffected. The plan's only additional feature is its provision to pay the mortgage holder $600,000 in four annual installments of $150,000, with the mortgage to remain on the real estate to secure these obligations. Assuming that the secured party does not make the § 1111(b)(2) election, may the plan be confirmed over his objection? See § 1129(b)(2)(A)(i)(II). What

changes would have to be made to be able to cram down the plan despite secured party's objection?

Now assume instead that the secured party makes the § 1111(b)(2) election and that the plan proposes to pay $1 million in four equal annual installments of $250,000, beginning one year after confirmation. May the plan be confirmed over the secured party's objection? What has the secured party sacrificed in making the § 1111(b)(2) election?

3. *Highly Undersecured Creditors.* Does § 1111(b)(2) give away too much to partially secured creditors? Suppose a secured party is owed $1 million and that his collateral is worth only $100,000. By making the § 1111(b) election, may he extract greater payments (even if over an extended period) than he should be able to extract? Did the secured party in *Griffiths* enjoy too much leverage as a result of the election?

Would much of the benefit of § 1111(b) be more simply obtained if we held open the accounting to the secured party until some date in the future when the collateral is sold?

4. *The Timing of the Election.* At what point in a bankruptcy proceeding should a secured creditor be required to make the § 1111(b) election? Rule 3014 of the new Bankruptcy Rules states:

> An election of application of § 1111(b)(2) of the Code by a class of secured creditors in a chapter 9 or 11 case may be made at any time prior to the conclusion of the hearing on the disclosure statement or within such later time as the court may fix. The election shall be in writing and signed unless made at the hearing on the disclosure statement. The election, if made by the majorities required by § 1111(b)(A)(i), shall be binding on all members of the class with respect to the plan.

The Advisory Committee's Note states, in part:

> Generally it is important that the proponent of a plan ascertain the position of the secured creditor class before a plan is proposed. The secured creditor class must know the prospects of its treatment under the plan before it can intelligently determine its rights under § 1111(b). The rule recognizes that there may be negotiations between the proponent of the plan and the secured creditor leading to a representation of desired treatment under § 1111(b). If that treatment is approved by the requisite majorities of the class and culminates in a written, signed statement filed with the court, that statement becomes binding and the class may not thereafter demand different treatment under § 1111(b) with respect to that plan. The proponent of the plan is thus enabled to seek approval of the disclosure statement and transmit the plan for voting in anticipation of confirmation. Only if that plan is not confirmed may the class of secured creditors thereafter change its prior election.

See generally Eisenberg, The Undersecured Creditor in Reorganizations and the Nature of Security, 38 Vand.L.Rev. 931 (1985). Stein,

Section 1111(b): Providing Undersecured Creditors with Postpetition Appreciation, 56 Am.Bankr.L.J. 195 (1982).

5. Disclosure

Many Chapter 11 plans may be viewed as involving the issuance of securities: instead of selling securities and receiving cash, a Chapter 11 debtor often issues stock in exchange for a release from debts. And since Chapter 11 contemplates voting on a plan as a part of the confirmation process, creditors (and interest-holders) are being asked to make an informed decision about a particular plan. Section 1145(a) of the Code provides, generally, that Chapter 11 securities transactions are exempt from the registration requirements of federal and state securities laws, while § 1145(b) sets forth the circumstances under which creditors who receive securities in a Chapter 11 reorganization may resell them without being seemed an "underwriter."[d]

While § 1145 generally may provide an exemption from the registration requirements of federal and state securities laws, the transactions are not exempted from the anti-fraud provisions of the federal securities laws. Sections 12 and 17 of the Securities Act of 1933 and Rule 10b–5, promulgated under the Securities Exchange Act of 1934, apply to a securities transaction even if it is exempt from registration. Section 1125 prescribes the disclosure that must be made in soliciting acceptances of a Chapter 11 plan; § 1125(e) provides a "safe harbor" from these "anti-fraud" securities provisions. See also House Report at 226–31; Note, Disclosure of Adequate Information in a Chapter 11 Reorganization, 94 Harv.L.Rev. 1808 (1981).

Who is authorized to prepare the disclosure statement? May creditors prepare their own statement? Must a disclosure statement reveal any fraudulent conveyances or preferences that emerge in the proceedings?

E. Financing the Plan

IN RE SNOWSHOE COMPANY, INC.

United States Court of Appeals, Fourth Circuit, 1986.
789 F.2d 1085.

Before HALL, PHILLIPS and MURNAGHAN, CIRCUIT JUDGES.

K.K. HALL, CIRCUIT JUDGE:

Shenandoah Federal Savings and Loan Association ("Shenandoah"), the principal creditor in a Chapter 7 bankruptcy proceeding, appeals from two orders of the district court that have been consolidated for purposes of this appeal. The district court permitted the trustee in bankruptcy to obtain additional credit by granting a senior lien on property of the estate pursuant to 11 U.S.C. § 364(d) and to sell certain

---

d. See Orlanski, The Resale of Securities Issued in Reorganization Proceedings and The Bankruptcy Reform Act of 1978, 53 Am.Bankr.L.J. 327 (1979); Corotto, Debtor Relief Proceedings Under the Bankruptcy Act and the Securities Act of 1933: The Registration Requirement and Its Implications, 47 Am.Bankr.L.J. 183 (1973).

obsolete or surplus property free of any existing liens. Shenandoah contends that these actions left its interest in the estate without "adequate protection" as required by 11 U.S.C. § 364(d). We disagree and affirm the decisions below.

I.

The Chapter 7 bankruptcy debtor, the Snowshoe Company ("Snowshoe"), is the principal owner of the Snowshoe Ski Resort located in Pocahontas County, West Virginia. Historically plagued with financial problems, Snowshoe is currently in its fourth bankruptcy proceeding. Only the last two proceedings are relevant to this appeal.

In July of 1982, Snowshoe borrowed $10 million from Shenandoah to finance improvements to the resort, pay off other indebtedness, and contribute to working capital. In August, 1982, Snowshoe borrowed an additional $1.75 million from Shenandoah to fund construction of a conference center at the resort. The loans to Snowshoe were secured by a first lien on Snowshoe's real and personal property, subject only to a prior lien held by Charleston National Bank and certain purchase money liens on equipment and machinery of the resort.

In April, 1984, Shenandoah declared both of its prior loans in default. Facing a foreclosure as a result of the defaults, Snowshoe filed a petition for relief under Chapter 11 of the bankruptcy code listing liabilities of $13,515,545.85.

Several months after the bankruptcy petition was filed, a number of creditors, including Shenandoah, moved for the appointment of a trustee to manage the resort. A hearing was held before Judge John A. Kamlowsky, United States Bankruptcy Court for the Northern District of West Virginia, to determine whether the appointment of a trustee was appropriate.

During the hearing considerable dispute arose concerning the fair market value of the assets of Snowshoe. Various estimates or appraisals were offered ranging from $14.65 million to $31 million. The bankruptcy court concluded that the fair market value of the resort was substantially in excess of $19 million. In support of this conclusion, the court noted that in 1983, John N. Taylor, then Executive Vice-President of Shenandoah, had offered to purchase the resort for $2,000,000 in cash and the assumption of liabilities estimated to be between $15 and $17 million.

The amount actually owed by the debtor to Shenandoah was also contested at the hearing. Snowshoe contended that a substantial portion of its indebtedness to Shenandoah was subject to setoff in an unliquidated amount resulting from alleged fraudulent acts by Shenandoah. A separate action by Snowshoe asserting these claims is currently pending before the district court. The bankruptcy court ultimately determined that the number and seriousness of the issues existing between Shenandoah and Snowshoe required that resolution be sought outside the restraints of a proceeding in bankruptcy. The court, by order dated February 19, 1985, dismissed the Chapter 11 petition *sua sponte*. The order included Judge Kamlowsky's findings on the value of the resort.

Snowshoe then filed a new Chapter 11 petition on March 15, 1985. Judge Kamlowsky subsequently recused himself and on May 24, 1985, Judge Robert Maxwell of the United States District Court for the Northern District of West Virginia, converted the case to proceedings under Chapter 7 of the Bankruptcy Code. Michael L. Bray, appellee in this appeal, was appointed interim trustee.

At the time of his appointment, the trustee was directed by the district court to report whether continued operation of the debtor's business was feasible. On June 17, 1985, the trustee reported that the resort would lose from 50% to 90% of its fair market value if it ceased operations. The trustee further stated that an additional $1.5 to $2 million would be necessary to fund the operation for the coming ski season. Shenandoah did not dispute the trustee's conclusion that the resort's value would suffer a severe diminution if it failed to operate.

The trustee subsequently filed an application to incur debt secured by a senior lien on the property of the estate pursuant to 11 U.S.C. § 364. In support of his application, the trustee asserted that the existing value of the estate provided adequate protection for Shenandoah's interest. He further maintained that, based upon his analysis of the resort's operational history, he believed that the loan would be repaid by March, 1986. Shenandoah opposed the application. After a hearing, the district court concluded, as required by the statute, that the trustee was unable to obtain credit without granting a senior lien and that adequate protection existed to guarantee the existing lienholders the "indubitable equivalent" of their interests. The court, therefore, granted the trustee's application [2] and subsequently granted a second application to sell surplus and obsolete equipment free of any creditor interest.

Shenandoah appeals.

II.

On appeal, Shenandoah contends that (1) the trustee's efforts to obtain additional loans were insufficient to establish that credit was not available without granting the senior lien, and (2) the district court

---

2. Although the district court authorized the trustee to incur debt up to $2 million, the order also incorporated by reference the loan agreement with the lending institution, Community Bank & Trust ("CB & T") of Fairmont, West Virginia. In that agreement, CB & T agreed to lend up to $1.5 million of which $1.39 million was actually obtained by the trustee. Shenandoah's suggestion at oral argument that the portion of Judge Maxwell's order allowing the trustee to obtain additional credit from CB & T without a hearing was an unlimited authorization is highly questionable. It seems clear that any additional credit the trustee would seek from CB & T would be subject to the $2 million limit in the court's order. In any event, the trustee assured this Court at oral argument that not only are no further disbursements from CB & T envisioned but that the repayment process is also substantially in progress.

erred in concluding that adequate protection existed with respect to both the superpriority loan and the sale of surplus property. We see no merit in either of these contentions.

The record clearly indicates that the trustee contacted other financial institutions in the immediate geographic area and was unsuccessful. The statute imposes no duty to seek credit from every possible lender before concluding that such credit is unavailable. This is particularly true when, as the court determined here, time is of the essence in an effort to preserve a vulnerable seasonal enterprise. The district court found that the trustee had demonstrated by a good faith effort that credit was not available without the senior lien. We see no error in that determination.

Our conclusion is not undermined by Shenandoah's suggestion on appeal that it stood ready to lend the additional funds without requiring the senior lien. It is clear from the record that Shenandoah's offer was conditioned upon the trustee's acknowledgement of both the validity of Shenandoah's claimed pre-petition lien and of the amount of its claimed pre-petition debt. Both of these factors are in dispute and, indeed, are the subject of ongoing litigation. We conclude that neither the trustee nor the court was required to consider this conditional offer as an indication that credit was available without the senior lien.

III.

The question of whether Shenandoah's interest in the debtor's property was adequately protected from the consequences of the superpriority loan and the sale of surplus property is a more complex issue but one that we find was also properly resolved by the district court. The Code states in section 361(3) that adequate protection may be provided by assuring a creditor of the "indubitable equivalent" of its interest in the estate. Although there is contrary authority in bankruptcy law,[3] we conclude that a judicial determination of such adequate protection is a question of fact rooted in measurements of value and the credibility of witnesses. See In re Martin, 761 F.2d 472 (8th Cir.1985); In re Ruggiere Chrysler–Plymouth, Inc., 727 F.2d 1017 (11th Cir.1984). Therefore, unless the district court's conclusion was "clearly erroneous," its decision that Shenandoah was adequately protected must be affirmed. Anderson v. Bessemer City, N.C., ___ U.S. ___, 105 S.Ct. 1504, 84 L.Ed.2d 518 (1985).

Shenandoah seeks to avoid this rigorous standard of review by arguing that the district court committed an error of law when it held that adequate protection existed in a supposed equity cushion between the amount of Shenandoah's interest and the value of the estate.[4]

3. See e.g., In re Philadelphia Consumer Discount Co., 37 B.R. 946 (E.D.Penn. 1984), In re Schaller, 27 B.R. 959 (W.D.Wis. 1983).

4. Shenandoah has asserted that the debt owed to it at the time of the hearing was between $13 and $14 million. The district court determined that the resort was worth in excess of $19 million.

Shenandoah contends that in finding this cushion, the court failed to evaluate the estate independently as required by the Code and instead improperly treated the earlier evaluation reached by Judge Kamlowsky as *res judicata*. We disagree.

It is clear from a reading of section 506 of the Bankruptcy Code and its accompanying legislative history that estimates of value made during bankruptcy proceedings are "binding only for the purposes of the specific hearing and . . . [do] not have a *res judicata* effect" in subsequent hearings. Here, we do not find that the district court mechanically applied the valuation determined in the earlier proceeding in order to conclude that an equity cushion existed. The court obviously considered and gave great weight to Judge Kamlowsky's conclusion that the resort was worth substantially in excess of $19 million. Because that conclusion had been reached only five months earlier and was the product of an extensive inquiry, the district court was clearly correct in considering it as continuing evidence of value. The court did not, however, rely solely on Judge Kamlowsky's finding. It also considered a variety of other evidence, including the debtor's schedules listing fair market value of assets at $35 million, financial statements from the two previous years showing assets of approximately $22 to $23 million, the trustee's report of June 17, 1985, that estimated value between $12 to $35 million, and Shenandoah's claim that the assets were worth only $14.65 million.

In February, 1985, Judge Kamlowsky found that the resort was worth substantially in excess of $19 million. In June, 1985, the district court concluded that the resort was *still* worth more than $19 million.[7] We find that the latter conclusion was the product of the independent evaluation required by the Code and not simply an application of *res judicata*. We emphasize that under the facts of this case in which the constraints of passing time weighed heavily, the court was not required to engage in a new battle of appraisers that could have fatally prolonged the proceedings and obviated any need for a new loan by rendering further operation of the resort impossible. We, therefore, hold that an equity cushion was properly determined.

Moreover, at the time that the trustee sought permission to borrow additional funds, he provided the court with detailed fiscal projections to support his contention that a superpriority loan could be repaid in one ski season. Shenandoah's attempt on appeal to characterize those projections as "mere expectations" of the sort rejected by the bankruptcy court in In re St. Petersburg Hotel Associates, Ltd., 44 B.R. 944 (Bankr.M.D.Fla.1984), is not persuasive. In *St. Petersburg,* supra, the *debtor* sought permission to obtain a superpriority loan based on little

---

7. Although two efforts to sell the resort for $19 million by Shenandoah at foreclosure sales in April of 1985 were unavailing, this fact does not invalidate the district court's judgment of value. The limited advertising requirements for a judicial sale under West Virginia law do not demand the level of buyer solicitation required to market an asset of this dimension. Furthermore, the effect on a potential buyer of Shenandoah's inability to sell the resort free of all existing liens cannot be determined.

more than his vaguely anticipated ability to repay within five years. In the present case the loan was sought by an experienced and respected *trustee* who based his belief that the loan would be repaid within one year on a detailed fiscal analysis of the resort's operational profile. Predictions of any variety are never totally reliable but when they are made by a professional operating within his area of competence and supported by data, such predictions are worthy of some deference.[8] We, therefore, believe that the district court was entitled to consider the trustee's economic projections as additional support for its conclusion that Shenandoah's interest was adequately protected and would not be impaired by a superpriority loan.

We are aware that some courts have found that the existence of an equity cushion is sufficient to demonstrate adequate protection while others have held that such a cushion is part of the bargained for consideration and cannot in itself protect the secured creditor. Compare In re Mellor, 734 F.2d 1396, 10 C.B.C.2d 1353 (9th Cir.1984), with In re Alyucan Interstate Corp., 12 B.R. 803 (Bankr.D.Utah 1981). Because we conclude that the district court's determination of adequate protection for the purpose of allowing the superpriority loan was supported by both an equity cushion and the well-reasoned financial analysis of the trustee, we need not decide if an equity cushion alone would constitute sufficient protection.[9]

IV.

In sum, the district court's conclusion that Shenandoah's interest in the bankruptcy estate was adequately protected from the consequences of both the superpriority loan and the sale of surplus equipment is a factual determination in which this Court finds no clear error. For the foregoing reasons, the orders of the district court are affirmed.

Affirmed.

Notes & Questions

1. *The Constitution.* Does issuance of a senior lien to which pre-petition secured parties are subordinated violate the fifth amendment? Recall Louisville Joint Stock Land Bank v. Radford, Chapter 11A. Is § 364(d) constitutional?

8. Information provided by the trustee in response to questions at oral argument strongly suggests that the projected repayment may occur as planned. Of the $1.39 million actually borrowed from CB & T over $400,000 has been repaid. The resort has a $300,000 receivable derived from credit card payments which is to be applied to the loan balance and will earn the right to certain customer deposits as time passes. Additionally, a substantial portion of the income producing season for a ski resort was still ahead at the time this appeal was argued. While it cannot be said with certainty that the trustee's projections will be fully realized, it is clear that they were far more than "mere expectations."

9. With respect to the sale of surplus property, our conclusion that an equity cushion was properly determined fully resolves the issue against Shenandoah, which relies solely on that theory to support its claim of inadequate protection.

In In re Garland Corp., 6 B.R. 456 (Bkrtcy.App. 1st Cir. 1980), the bankruptcy court had authorized the borrowing of operating funds to be secured by theretofore unencumbered assets. The Creditors' Committee, "concerned that the satisfaction of unsecured claims may be delayed, diminished or rendered impossible as a result of the authorization to encumber 'free' assets as security for postpetition operating loans," claimed that the holders of unsecured claims are entitled to adequate protection in advance of fixing liens on unencumbered assets as a means of obtaining postpetition operating loans. Relying on *Louisville Joint Stock Land Bank*, the court stated that "there are no constitutional constraints inhibiting Congress in the exercise of its bankruptcy power from extinguishing the recovery rights of holders of unsecured claims, because an unsecured claim confers no right in specific property of the obligor."

2. *Debtor's Authority to Borrow.* You represent a potential lender to a Chapter 11 debtor. The debtor requests a short term loan to give it enough cash to meet next month's payroll. May the debtor borrow funds while in Chapter 11? Why would anyone lend money to such a debtor? See § 503(b)(1). Should the lender make the loan without express authorization from the court?

3. *Adequate Protection.* What is the relationship between adequate protection under § 364(d) and adequate protection under § 362 (relief from the automatic stay)? Should the creditor in *Snowshoe* be compensated for the additional risk the superpriority lien creates?

4. *Priming a Prime Lien.* May a lender who is given a prime lien certificate under § 364(d) be subordinated to some future lender under § 364(d)? May a § 364(d) lender negotiate for a claim that prohibits prime liens being placed ahead of his "prime" lien?

5. *Cross-Collateralization Clauses.* In In re General Oil Distributors, Inc., 20 B.R. 873 (Bkrtcy.E.D.N.Y.1982), a debtor in dire need of cash proposed to grant a secured lender a security interest in collateral that would secure both new advances of funds and the debtor's prepetition obligations to the lender. The debtor alleged that the lender was fully secured before the filing of the Chapter 11 petition. May the court authorize the granting of a lien on collateral to secure a prepetition claim (a so-called "cross-collateralization" clause)? Compare In re Roblin, Indus., Inc., 52 B.R. 241 (Bkrtcy.W.D.N.Y.1985); In re Vanguard Diversified, Inc., 31 B.R. 364 (Bkrtcy.E.D.N.Y.1983) (authorizing clauses) with In re Monarch Circuit Indus., Inc., 41 B.R. 859 (Bkrtcy.E.D.Pa.1984) (clauses improper); In re Texlon Corp., 596 F.2d 1092 (2d Cir. 1979) (clauses may be invalid).

What is the effect of § 364(e) on this issue? See In re Adams Apple, Inc., 829 F.2d 1484 (9th Cir.1987) (issue moot where no stay issued).

Are cross-collateralization clauses impermissible preferences? How are cross-collateralization clauses different than simply granting an old lender a higher interest rate on newly advanced funds?

Chapter 17

JURISDICTION AND PROCEDURE

A. Jurisdiction

Under the old bankruptcy act, the bankruptcy court only had "summary" jurisdiction. It could adjudicate all administrative matters pertaining to the bankruptcy proceeding, disputes over property in the actual or constructive possession of the debtor, and disputes in which the parties consented to its jurisdiction. Summary jurisdiction contrasted with "plenary" actions, which had to be brought in federal district court or in state court. In such actions (for example, when the trustee sought to enforce a debtor's rights under a contract), the trustee asserted the debtor's rights or defenses in the forum in which such actions would "normally" be brought. The following excerpt summarizes the old summary-plenary distinction.

TREISTER, BANKRUPTCY JURISDICTION: IS IT TOO SUMMARY?, 39 S.Cal.L.Rev. 78, 78–81 (1966)

The term "summary jurisdiction" of a bankruptcy court is unfortunate since it carries misleading implications. One implication is that there must be available a different category of jurisdiction, for example, "general" or "plenary." Yet, summary jurisdiction, is the only type of jurisdiction a bankruptcy court possesses. When it is said that summary jurisdiction is lacking or that a plenary suit is necessary, the result is that the case has to proceed elsewhere. This may be a state forum or perhaps a federal district court; but if it is the latter, the district judge will hear the matter as an ordinary civil action on the regular civil docket. He will not be sitting in his capacity as a bankruptcy court, nor will he refer the case to a referee in bankruptcy, the officer who almost invariably exercises summary jurisdiction as the trial judge.

For present purposes, the types of matters over which a bankruptcy court's summary jurisdiction extends can be roughly classified into two major categories. In the first group are all those proceedings, usually of an administrative nature, which occur during the course of taking the bankrupt estate into possession, liquidating and accounting for it, and deciding which claimants are entitled to share in its distribution. This category also includes those matters internal to the bankruptcy system involving the bankrupt's status and his rights or obligations vis-à-vis the estate.[7] These proceedings, which probably comprise the great

---

7. The first category, sometimes labeled "proceedings in bankruptcy," might be better understood by considering several specific illustrations of what it embraces. For example, summary jurisdiction exists to determine the debtor's status as a bankrupt—*i.e.*, to make or refuse to make an order of adjudication; to pass upon the provability and allowability of claims against the estate; to administer, protect, and supervise the liquidation of the admitted assets of the estate; to pass upon pro-

bulk of the bankruptcy court's work, are for the most part non-adversary, although there are exceptions.[8] The bankruptcy court's jurisdiction over matters in the first category is exclusive.

The second area of summary jurisdiction embraces disputes between a trustee and adverse claimants involving rights to money or property sought to be recovered for the estate or in which the estate claims an interest. These are adversary proceedings almost by definition. Here the existence of summary jurisdiction turns either on possession of the subject matter of the controversy as of the time of the filing of the bankruptcy petition, or upon consent of the adverse party. Possession and consent, however, are tricky concepts. If the bankrupt had demonstrable physical possession of a disputed asset at the date of bankruptcy, there is little difficulty. But according to established decisional law, such possession as will sustain summary jurisdiction may be either actual or constructive. Controversies respecting intangibles often pose a difficult jurisdictional problem since these assets are not capable of possession in any objective sense. Not surprisingly, the authorities show inconsistency in the application of the fiction of constructive possession. Where a disputed asset actually is possessed by an adverse claimant, the bankruptcy court is nevertheless said to have constructive possession if the adverse claimant's asserted rights are "merely colorable," that is to say, a sham or frivolous.

Consent of the adverse party may furnish an alternative basis for summary jurisdiction in those situations where the bankruptcy court has no possession of the *res* or where the trustee seeks an in personam judgment. Moreover, it is not only an actual consent which will suffice. A failure to make timely objection to summary jurisdiction, even when it is improperly invoked, is an implied consent to try the case in the bankruptcy court. And filing a creditor's claim or a reclamation application may result inadvertently in an implied submission to jurisdiction over a counterclaim asserted by the estate. If neither the requisite possession nor consent exists, any cause of action asserted by the trustee must be brought by way of plenary action. As noted above, this means in some court other than the bankruptcy court.

The summary-plenary distinction led to dissatisfaction with the overall jurisdictional scheme for bankruptcy cases. The trustee might

posed compromises of disputes involving the estate or claims against it; to appoint receivers and trustees, and to review their reports and accounts; to authorize the trustee or receiver to employ attorneys, accountants, auctioneers, and others; to fix the allowances or compensation payable out of the estate to the trustee, receiver, and those persons employed by them; to pass upon the bankrupt's right to a discharge in bankruptcy; to determine his right to the exemptions provided for him by the applicable bankruptcy and state laws; and to hold discovery proceeding in which the trustee or creditors may examine the bankrupt or other witnesses under oath concerning any of the debtor's assets, liabilities, or financial transactions.

8. Illustrations of important contests which can develop out of these proceedings are: a trial between an alleged bankrupt and the petitioning creditors over a controverted involuntary petition; a trial on objections to discharge; a trial on objection to creditors' claims filed against the estate.

have to litigate actions relating to the bankruptcy case in several different forums. Without the consent of the defendants, it was not possible to adjudicate all issues arising in a bankruptcy case in a single court. In addition, time and energy were expended on deciding when a case was one within the bankruptcy court's "summary" jurisdiction. Even a simplified statement of the standard—that jurisdiction turned on whether property was in the actual or constructive possession of the debtor—could lead to litigation. Concepts such as possession and constructive possession are not self-defining, particularly when competing claimants assert interests in the same assets. The jurisdictional scheme adopted in the Bankruptcy Reform Act of 1978 was in part a response to these problems.

It enacted a new provision, 28 U.S.C.A. § 1471, to allocate responsibility between the district courts and the bankruptcy courts. The legislative history of § 1471 reads in part as follows:

> Subsection (b) is a significant change from current law. It grants the bankruptcy court original (trial), but not exclusive, jurisdiction of all civil proceedings arising under title 11 or arising under or related to cases under title 11. This is the broadest grant of jurisdiction to dispose of proceedings that arise in bankruptcy cases or under the bankruptcy code. Actions that formerly had to be tried in State court or in Federal district court, at great cost and delay to the estate, may now be tried in the bankruptcy courts. The idea of possession or consent as the sole bases for jurisdiction is eliminated. The bankruptcy court is given in personam jurisdiction as well as in rem jurisdiction to handle everything that arises in a bankruptcy case. . . .

> The phrase "arising under" has a well defined and broad meaning in the jurisdictional context. By a grant of jurisdiction over all proceedings arising under title 11, the bankruptcy courts will be able to hear any matter under which a claim is made under a provision of title 11. . . . Any action by the trustee under an avoiding power would be a proceeding arising under title 11, because the trustee would be claiming based on a right given by one of the sections in subchapter III of chapter 5 of title 11. Many of these claims would also be claims arising under or related to a case under title 11. Indeed, because title 11 . . . only applies once a bankruptcy case is commenced, any proceeding arising under title 11 will be in some way "related to" a case under title 11. In sum, the combination of the three bases for jurisdiction, "arising under title 11," "arising under a case under title 11," and "related to a case under title 11," will leave no doubt as to the scope of the bankruptcy court's jurisdiction over disputes.

House Report at 445–46.

In Northern Pipeline Construction Co. v. Marathon Pipe Line Co., 458 U.S. 50, 102 S.Ct. 2858, 73 L.Ed.2d 598 (1982), the Supreme Court held unconstitutional part of the jurisdictional scheme outlined in

§ 1471. The Court initially stayed its judgment to October 4, 1982 to "afford Congress an opportunity to reconstitute the bankruptcy courts or to adopt other valid means of adjudication, without impairing the interim administration of the bankruptcy laws. The Court later extended the stay to December 24, 1982. 459 U.S. 813, 103 S.Ct. 199, 74 L.Ed.2d 160 (1982).

Congress, however, did not enact legislation responding to *Northern Pipeline* prior to the expiration of the stay. To deal with the possible lapse of bankruptcy court jurisdiction, the Judicial Conference of the United States submitted to each circuit a proposed rule for adoption by the district courts. The rule preserved much of the bankruptcy court's jurisdiction. It was sustained by those circuit courts that considered it but there was doubt about the authority under which the rule was promulgated and about the rule's constitutionality.

A Sketch of the New Jurisdictional Provisions [a]

In Title I of the Bankruptcy Amendments and Federal Judgeship Act of 1984, Congress again reworked the bankruptcy court jurisdictional scheme through amendments to Title 28 of the U.S. Code. Section 151 of Title 28 states that the bankruptcy judges in regular active service shall constitute a unit of the district court to be known as the bankruptcy court for that district. Bankruptcy judges are appointed for fourteen year terms by a majority of the judges of the court of appeals for the circuit in which the bankruptcy court is located. If a majority of the court of appeals judges cannot agree upon an appointment, the chief judge of the court of appeals shall make the appointment. 28 U.S.C.A. § 152.

Section 1334(a) confers upon the district courts original and exclusive jurisdiction of all cases arising under title 11. Under section 1334(b), the district courts have original but not exclusive jurisdiction of all civil proceedings arising under title 11, or arising in or related to cases under title 11.

Section 157 accomplishes much of the division of business between the district court and the bankruptcy courts. Under new section 157(a), each district court may provide that any or all cases under title 11 and any or all proceedings arising under title 11 or arising in or related to a case under title 11 shall be referred to the bankruptcy judges for the district. Under section 157(b)(1), bankruptcy judges may hear and determine all cases under title 11 and all "core proceedings" arising under title 11, or arising in a case under title 11, and referred to a bankruptcy judge under section 157(a). Section 157(b)(2) contains a

a. The 1984 Act has been attacked as violating the Constitution's appointment clause because Congress both created the office of bankruptcy judge and technically appointed persons to fill that office. For a case rejecting the argument, see Matter of Koerner, 800 F.2d 1358 (5th Cir.1986).

For a detailed discussion of the developments preceding the 1984 Act, see Countryman, Scrambling to Define Bankruptcy Jurisdiction: The Chief Justice, The Judicial Conference, and the Legislative Process, 22 Harv.J.Legis. 1 (1985).

lengthy, nonexhaustive list of core proceedings. Under section 157(b)(2)
(B), core proceedings do not include "the liquidation or estimation of
contingent or unliquidated personal injury tort or wrongful death
claims against the estate for purposes of distribution in a case under
title 11." Bankruptcy courts must order that personal injury and
wrongful death claims be tried in the district court in which the
bankruptcy case is pending, or in the district court in the district in
which the claim arose, as determined by the district court in which the
bankruptcy case is pending. 28 U.S.C.A. § 157(b)(5).

If a proceeding is not a core proceeding but is related to a case under
title 11, a bankruptcy judge may nevertheless hear the proceeding. In
such situations, the bankruptcy judge submits proposed findings of fact
and conclusions of law to the district court, and any final order or
judgment is entered by the district judge after considering the bankruptcy judge's proposed findings and conclusions and after reviewing de
novo those matters to which any party has timely and specifically
objected. 28 U.S.C.A. § 157(c)(1). If the parties consent, noncore
proceedings related to a case under title 11 may be referred to a
bankruptcy judge for final disposition, subject only to normal rights of
appeal. 28 U.S.C.A. § 157(c)(2). The bankruptcy judge determines
whether a proceeding is a core proceeding. 28 U.S.C.A. § 157(b)(3).

District courts may withdraw, in whole or in part, any case or
proceeding referred to bankruptcy courts under section 157, on their
own motion or on timely motion of any party, for cause. On a party's
motion the district court must withdraw a proceeding if it determines
that resolution of the proceeding requires consideration of both title 11
and other laws of the United States regulating organizations or activities affecting interstate commerce. 28 U.S.C.A. § 157(d).

In the wake of these changes in bankruptcy jurisdiction, several
important new issues have emerged. Study of the overriding issue, the
constitutionality of the system, may be deferred until one has grasped
the system's internal workings. After studying the issues that arise
under the new system, one is in a position to assess the system under
the standards set forth in *Northern Pipeline.*

1. District Court Jurisdiction

IN RE S.E. HORNSBY & SONS SAND
AND GRAVEL CO., INC.

United States Bankruptcy Court, M.D. Louisiana, 1985.
45 B.R. 988.

WESLEY W. STEEN, BANKRUPTCY JUDGE.

REASONS FOR DENIAL OF MOTION TO ABSTAIN

This opinion is, unfortunately, the first of many that will attempt to
analyze the jurisdictional maze constructed by Congress in 1984.

I. Facts

This bankruptcy case results from, or at least is in large part founded in, difficulties between father, Stanley E. Hornsby (hereinafter "Stanley") and son, Michael E. Hornsby (hereinafter "Michael"). The debtor is S.E. Hornsby & Sons Sand and Gravel Co., Inc. (hereinafter "Debtor"), a Louisiana corporation formed about November 19, 1975. Stanley was the founder of the company; he donated 75% of the stock of the Debtor to his three sons (25% to each) and kept 25%. Two of Stanley's sons sold or attempted to sell their stock (50% of the company) to Michael, the third son. If this sale was effective, Michael now owns 75%, while his father, Stanley, owns 25%. Stanley alleges that the transfer was not validly accomplished because of failure to meet the requirements of stock transfer restrictions contained in the Articles of Incorporation. Some time in early 1983, the Debtor ceased to do business and ceased to have sufficient assets to pay its debts. Stanley petitioned in state court for the involuntary liquidation of the corporation, and, as a result of that petition, Terry Sibley, Certified Public Accountant, Greensburg, Louisiana, was appointed the liquidator by the 21st Judicial District Court, Parish of St. Helena, on July 6, 1983. . . .

On September 7, 1984, an involuntary petition was filed against the Debtor in this Court requesting an order for relief under Chapter 11 of the Bankruptcy Code. Michael was the petitioning creditor. The involuntary petition was served September 10, 1984, on Terry Sibley, liquidator of the Debtor. No answer or other opposition was filed by Mr. Sibley. Therefore, an order for relief under Chapter 11 of Title 11 United States Code, was entered on October 16, 1984. . . .

The schedules confirm that the corporation ceased the active conduct of business on March 30, 1983; that on Stanley's petition the business was placed in involuntary liquidation on July 6, 1983; and that Mr. Sibley was appointed liquidator. The schedules show priority debts of approximately $4,000, an unknown amount of secured debt, and unsecured debt of approximately $140,000. Of this $140,000 unsecured debt, the schedules list approximately $120,000 as being owed to the petitioning creditor (and alleged 75% stockholder), Michael. The schedules show assets of approximately $655,000, of which $355,000 is alleged to be "hard assets" and $300,000 is alleged to be an unliquidated claim against Stanley E. Hornsby for breach of a lease. The schedules list real estate allegedly worth $180,000, consisting of a leasehold interest from Stanley. Thus, if the schedules are to be believed, the assets of the company are approximately $835,000 and the debts are approximately $140,000. The Debtor has little or no liquid assets, however, and the valuation of the other assets is open to serious question.

On November 26, 1984, the trustee filed Adversary No. 84–0154 against Stanley. The adversary action alleges that there was a substantial amount of litigation between the Debtor and Stanley from April 26, 1983, through and including July 6, 1983. It further alleges that in the course of this litigation, Stanley Hornsby obtained possession and sequestration of all of the assets of the Debtor. The complaint seeks an order to require Stanley to turn over to the Debtor any of its assets that are in Stanley's possession or control.

Stanley's attorneys filed a "Motion to Abstain" on November 30, 1984. The essence of his motion is that the Bankruptcy Court cannot decide state law issues and that when a state law issue arises, the Bankruptcy Court must abstain under 28 U.S.C. § 1334(c)(2). The motion and its accompanying memorandum are without foundation and completely misread the law. Stanley's attorneys should have filed a motion for relief from the stay under § 362(d), but even if the correct motion had been filed, mover would not have prevailed for reasons discussed below.

II. The Law

28 U.S.C. § 1334(a) provides that ". . . the district courts shall have original and exclusive jurisdiction of all cases under Title 11." 28 U.S.C. § 1334(b) provides that the district courts shall also have jurisdiction ". . . of all civil proceedings arising under Title 11, or arising in or related to cases under Title 11." [4]

There are three abstention provisions in the law as it was amended by the Bankruptcy Amendments and Federal Judgeship Act of 1984.

First, § 305 of the Bankruptcy Code provides that:

"The court, after notice and a hearing, may dismiss a case under this title, or may suspend all proceedings in a case under this title, at any time if the interests of creditors and the debtor would be better served by such dismissal or suspension."

Second, 28 U.S.C. § 1334(c)(1) provides that:

"Nothing in this section prevents a district court in the interest of justice, or in the interest of comity with State courts or respect for State law, from abstaining from hearing a particular proceeding arising under Title 11 or arising in or related to a case under Title 11."

These two abstention provisions are discretionary. A decision under 11 U.S.C. § 305 to abstain or not to abstain is not reviewable by appeal or otherwise. [5] A decision under 28 U.S.C. § 1334(c)(1) contains no separate provision governing whether it is appealable or not; presuma-

---

4. The text of 28 U.S.C. § 1334(b) is as follows: "Notwithstanding any Act of Congress that confers exclusive jurisdiction on a court or courts other than the district courts, the district courts shall have original but not exclusive jurisdiction of all civil proceedings arising under Title 11, or arising in or related to cases under Title 11."

5. Section 305(c). An unsettled question is whether the absence of appeal rights applies to the Bankruptcy Court decision not to abstain or whether it applies to a district court decision. Can a party appeal a bankruptcy court abstention decision to the district court? If the answer is "no", is that result constitutional? The district court is the appropriate body to

bly a decision to abstain or not to abstain under 28 U.S.C. § 1334(c)(1) would be reviewable on appeal.

The third provision regarding abstention is mandatory. 28 U.S.C. § 1334(c)(2) provides:

"Upon timely motion of a party in a proceeding based upon a State law claim or State law cause of action, related to a case under Title 11 but not arising under Title 11 or arising in a case under Title 11, with respect to which an action could not have been commenced in a court of the United States absent jurisdiction under this section, the district court shall abstain from hearing such proceeding if an action is commenced, and can be timely adjudicated, in a state forum of appropriate jurisdiction."

A decision to abstain under 28 U.S.C. § 1334(c)(2) is not reviewable on appeal "or otherwise." Since this § 1334(c)(2) provision governing appeal denies appeal only if the decision is made to abstain, presumably a decision not to abstain is appealable. . . .

Under this jurisdictional scheme, there is a universe of four categories of cases and proceedings:

A. A case under Title 11;

B. A civil proceeding arising under Title 11;

C. A civil proceeding arising in a case under Title 11;

D. A civil proceeding related to a case under Title 11.

Unfortunately, Congress did not define these categories. We should consider them separately.

Collier does about as well as possible with the definition of a "case under Title 11":

"Obviously, the 'case' referred to in § 1471(a) [the predecessor of § 1334] is the case upon which all of the proceedings which follow the filing of the petition are predicated. The filing of a petition for relief constitutes commencement of the Title 11 case. From that beginning follow all of the proceedings, whether called controversies, suits, actions, or disputes that will occur in the unfolding of the case under the new Bankruptcy Code." [6]

The involuntary petition filed in this case on September 7, 1984, opened the "case." The grant of jurisdiction under 28 U.S.C. § 1334 (formerly under § 1471(a)) is original and exclusive in the district court, and was by district court order referred to the undersigned bankruptcy judge. . . .

The only provision for abstention that applies to Category A cases is § 305 of the Code. 28 U.S.C. § 1334(c)(1) and (2) do not apply to cases under Title 11. Those subsections only apply to abstention under

decide whether an appeal from the bankruptcy court is proper with respect to an abstention decision under § 305. There is simply no authority on point.

[6.] *Collier,* ¶ 3.01.

categories C and D as classed above. Abstention under § 305 will be discussed later.

Category A refers to "cases." It is the bankruptcy case *per se.* Categories B–D refer to "proceedings." The Senate report accompanying S–2266 states that: "As used in this section everything that occurs in a bankruptcy case is a proceeding. Thus, proceeding here is used in its broadest sense, and would encompass what are now called contested matters, adversary proceedings, and plenary actions under current bankruptcy law." The House report is similar: ". . . anything that occurs within a case is a proceeding."

Category B is defined as "proceedings arising under Title 11." As *Collier* puts it:

"What this language seems to mean is that, where a cause of action is one that either is one created by Title 11 or which is concerned with what formerly were called 'administrative' matters in the sense that no adverse third party was involved (e.g. a dispute between the debtor and the trustee regarding a claim to exemptions), then that civil proceeding is one 'arising under Title 11.' " [7]

Category B proceedings would not arise *but for* the Bankruptcy Code. The House Report accompanying HR 8200 cites the following kinds of issues that would be proceedings arising under Title 11:

A. Claims of exemption under the bankruptcy statute;

B. Claims of discrimination against a debtor on account of his filing a bankruptcy proceeding (jurisdiction under 11 U.S.C. § 525);

C. An action by the trustee under an avoiding power of the Bankruptcy Code.[8]

The Senate report which accompanied S–2266 (the Bankruptcy Code as enacted in 1978) states as follows: "The phrase 'arising under Title 11' will enable the bankruptcy court to hear any matter under which a claim is made under a provision of Title 11."

Category C and D proceedings are not differentiated; it would appear that these phrases simply refer to civil disputes that concern the debtor but do not have their foundation in the substantive law of the Bankruptcy Code. . . .

First we deal with abstention in the bankruptcy case. The memorandum in support of Stanley's motion asserts that the Court must abstain under 28 U.S.C. § 1334(c)(2). That section does not apply to a case under Title 11. 28 U.S.C. § 1334(c)(2) only applies to civil proceedings related to a case under Title 11; it does not even apply to proceedings arising under Title 11 or to proceedings arising in a case under Title 11. The memorandum of authorities cites precedent that was decided under 28 U.S.C. § 1334(c)(1), but does not argue that 28 U.S.C. § 1334(c)(1) applies.[9] But 28 U.S.C. § 1334(c)(1) does not apply to

---

7. id.

8. id.

9. Counsel would probably prefer for 28 U.S.C. § 1334(c)(2) to apply since absten-

cases under Title 11, either. Therefore, the cited cases are not sound authority. 28 U.S.C. § 1334(c)(1) only applies to proceedings arising under Title 11 or to proceedings arising in or related to cases under Title 11.

Title 11, § 305 *does* give the Court discretion to abstain from hearing a case under Title 11. Under that section, the Court, after notice and a hearing, *may* dismiss a case under Title 11 if the interest of creditors and the debtor would be better served by such dismissal. There is no allegation in the motion to abstain or in the memorandum of authorities that creditors and the Debtor would be better served by such dismissal.[10] The thrust of Stanley's motion and memorandum is that this Court does not have jurisdiction to hear the case or that the Court should abstain on grounds of respect for state law if it does have jurisdiction. As demonstrated, the Court clearly has jurisdiction; the Court is not required to abstain under 28 U.S.C. § 1334(c)(2) since that section does not apply to a case under Title 11; the Court does not have authority to abstain under 28 U.S.C. § 1334(c)(1) since that section does not apply to cases under Title 11; the Court does not abstain under § 305 of Title 11 since there has been no allegation or assertion (and certainly no proof) that the interests of creditors and the Debtor would be better served by dismissal.

Turn now to the question of whether the Court should abstain in the adversary proceeding. 28 U.S.C. § 1334(c)(2) (mandatory abstention) does not apply. That section only applies to cases that meet the following requirements:

A. A timely motion is made;
B. The proceeding is based upon a state law claim or state law cause of action;
C. The proceeding is related to a case under Title 11;
D. The proceeding does not arise under Title 11;
E. The proceeding does not arise in a case under Title 11;
F. The action could not have been commenced in a court of the United States absent jurisdiction under 28 U.S.C. § 1334; and
G. An action is commenced and can be timely adjudicated in a state forum of appropriate jurisdiction.

28 U.S.C. § 1334(c)(2) does not apply to the adversary proceeding for at least two reasons. First, the proceeding arises under Title 11. The adversary action is based on § 542 of Title 11 and thus arises under Title 11.[11] Regardless, even if this were a proceeding based on a state law claim or cause of action and only related to a case under Title 11,

tion would then be mandatory, not discretionary, as under 28 U.S.C. § 1334(c)(1).

10. In fact, the principal creditor is the one who brought this action. Presumably he believes it to be in his best interests to be in bankruptcy court.

11. Alternatively, the proceeding certainly arises in a case under Title 11 because it seeks the turnover of property allegedly belonging to the Debtor. In either case, one of the requirements of 28 U.S.C. § 1334(c)(2) is not met, and, consequently, that sub-section does not apply.

the final requirement of 28 U.S.C. § 1334(c)(2) would not apply; under that provision, abstention is required only if an action is commenced and can be timely adjudicated in a state forum of appropriate jurisdiction to determine the issues involved. In this case a state law dispute was filed in July of 1983 and had made absolutely no progress through and including the date of the filing of this petition. Even some months subsequent to the filing of the bankruptcy petition the state law liquidator indicated that he had no interest in pursuing the case. The Court can find no evidence to sustain an allegation that an action can be timely adjudicated in a state forum of appropriate jurisdiction. (Assuming such an allegation had been made, which it has not.)

28 U.S.C. § 1334(c)(1) does apply to the adversary proceeding. Under the provisions of that section, the Court may, in its discretion, abstain. The right to abstain may be exercised "in the interests of comity with State courts or respect for State law." The adversary proceeding in this case involves the recovery of property allegedly belonging to the Debtor. 28 U.S.C. § 1334(d) provides that the district court (and the bankruptcy court by delegation) "has *exclusive* jurisdiction of all of the property, wherever located, of the debtor as of the commencement of the case, and of the estate." [Emphasis supplied.] This Court will not abstain from deciding an issue over property within its exclusive jurisdiction when a state court proceeding regarding the same company and property has languished for more than a year in state court with no action whatever. On the contrary, because the property is within the exclusive jurisdiction of this Court, the Court should not abstain in these circumstances.

Finally, the Court will not abstain from hearing the adversary proceeding under the authority of § 305 for the same reasons listed above for determining not to abstain under § 305 with respect to the case under Title 11. . . .

III. Summary

In summary, Bankruptcy Case No. 84–00649, is a case under Title 11, United States Code; the United States District Court has exclusive and original jurisdiction under 28 U.S.C. § 1334(a). The Court declines to abstain under § 305 of the Bankruptcy Code since there has been no allegation that it would be in the best interests of creditors and the Debtor for the Court to do so and since the entire record points to the contrary. The discretionary and mandatory abstention provisions of 28 U.S.C. § 1334(c) do not apply. Under order dated August 2, 1984, the United States District Court for the Middle District of Louisiana referred Case No. 84–00649 to the bankruptcy judge; that referral is proper under 28 U.S.C. § 157(b).

Adversary proceeding 84–0154 is a proceeding that arises under Title 11 U.S.C.; the United States District Court has jurisdiction pursuant to 28 U.S.C. § 1334(b); the mandatory abstention provision of 28 U.S.C. § 1334(c)(2) does not apply since this is a proceeding arising under Title 11 and because it appears that it is not possible to commence an action in state court that can be timely adjudicated. The discretionary abstention provisions of 28 U.S.C. § 1334(c)(1) and of 11 U.S.C. § 305 do apply; however, the Court sees no grounds for abstention and particularly no allegation that abstention would be in the best interests of creditors. More important, 28 U.S.C. § 1334(d) provides that the court is to have exclusive jurisdiction of property of the debtor. The Court does not choose to abstain from deciding an issue concerning property over which it has exclusive jurisdiction. Under order dated August 2, 1984, the United States District Court for the Middle District of Louisiana referred Case No. 84–00649 to the bankruptcy judge; that referral is proper under 28 U.S.C. § 157(b). . . .

Notes & Questions

1. *District Court Jurisdiction.* Consider the basic allocation of bankruptcy business to the district courts. Section 1334(a) and (b), quoted in *Hornsby* reads in full:

(a) Except as provided in subsection (b) of this section, the district courts shall have original and exclusive jurisdiction of all cases under title 11.

(b) Notwithstanding any Act of Congress that confers exclusive jurisdiction on a court or courts other than the district courts, the district courts shall have original but not exclusive jurisdiction of all civil proceedings arising under title 11, or arising in or related to cases under title 11.

What are the differences among civil proceedings "arising under" title 11, civil proceedings "arising in" cases under title 11, and civil proceedings "related to" cases under title 11? Will any case affecting a debtor in bankruptcy not fit one of these descriptions?

2. *Illustration of the "Related to" Standard.* In Pacor, Inc. v. Higgins, 743 F.2d 984 (3d Cir.1984), plaintiffs initially brought suit against Pacor in state court seeking damages allegedly caused by work-related exposure to asbestos supplied by Pacor, a distributor of chemical supplies. In response, Pacor filed a third party complaint impleading Johns–Manville Corporation, which Pacor claimed was the original manufacturer of the asbestos. Johns–Manville later filed a bankruptcy petition in New York, and the state court severed Pacor's action against Manville from plaintiffs' action against Pacor. Pacor sought to remove the state court proceedings to a Pennsylvania bankruptcy court, and to then transfer the proceedings to the` New York bankruptcy court hearing the Manville bankruptcy.

The district court found that the original suit against Pacor was not "related to" the Manville bankruptcy and, therefore, there was no jurisdiction to hear the matter, and remanded the action to state court. The court of appeals affirmed. The district court also found that the Pacor–Manville third party claim was a proceeding "related to" bankruptcy, and remanded that portion of the action to the bankruptcy court for consideration of the transfer of venue motion made by Pacor. With respect to the "related to" standard, the court of appeals stated:

> The usual articulation of the test for determining whether a civil proceeding is related to bankruptcy is whether the outcome of that proceeding could conceivably have any effect on the estate being administered in bankruptcy. . . . Thus, the proceeding need not necessarily be against the debtor or against the debtor's property. An action is related to bankruptcy if the outcome could alter the debtor's rights, liabilities, options, or freedom of action (either positively or negatively) and which in any way impacts upon the handling and administration of the bankrupt estate.
>
> On the other hand, the mere fact that there may be common issues of fact between a civil proceeding and a controversy involving the bankruptcy estate does not bring the matter within the scope of [bankruptcy jurisdiction]. . . . "[J]urisdiction over nonbankruptcy controversies with third parties who are otherwise strangers to the civil proceeding and to the parent bankruptcy does not exist."

743 F.2d at 994 (emphasis deleted).

3. *District Court Abstention.* (a) *General Comity Abstention.* Assume that in *Pacor, supra,* the New York bankruptcy court decides that Manville is a critical party to the plaintiffs' action against Pacor. Should the New York court then invoke § 1334(c)(1) (quoted in *Hornsby*) to order the Pacor–Manville action back to Pennsylvania state court?

(b) *Mandatory Abstention.* Suppose the Manville–Pacor action could not have been brought in federal court for want of a federal question and lack of diversity. What standards determine whether a state court can "timely adjudicate" the action within the meaning of § 1334(c)(2)?

In Acolyte Electric Corp. v. New York, 69 B.R. 155 (Bkrtcy.E.D.N.Y. 1986), the court stated:

> Although several bankruptcy courts have required the movant affirmatively to show that the matter can be timely adjudicated in the state court, [citing *Hornsby*], this would seem to reverse the general rule that the party seeking to litigate in a federal forum must first establish that right. Moreover, the plaintiff in the state court action, who initially invoked the jurisdiction of that forum, would be better positioned to apprise the federal court of any long delay in having the matter adjudicated in the state court.

(c) *Abstention under § 305.* How does § 305 (of Title 11) abstention differ from abstention under § 1334(c)?

Note that abstention by the district court must be distinguished from withdrawal by the district court of proceedings commenced in the bankruptcy court. This issue is discussed infra.

(d) *Overview.* Would it make more sense to have a rule prohibiting the district court from abstaining in any of the above matters except in the case of highly unusual circumstances? Is litigation like *Hornsby* useful? Are we likely to see much more of this kind of litigation?

4. *Article III Subject Matter Limitations.* Assume that the parties in *Hornsby* were residents of the same state, and that the dispute was a common law contract action. In the absence of diversity jurisdiction, would there have been any basis for the assertion of federal jurisdiction of the dispute in this case? If not, should the fact that the dispute arises in a bankruptcy setting make a difference?

The *Hornsby* facts, as altered in the preceding paragraph, raise the question whether federal bankruptcy or district courts may exercise jurisdiction to hear cases that do not fit within the traditional jurisdictional compartments of article III. Could one argue that the case "arises under" federal law within the meaning of article II or within the meaning of the general federal question jurisdictional provision, 28 U.S.C.A. § 1331? If the case does not "arise under" federal law, what is the constitutional authorization for conferring jurisdiction upon any federal court? Does § 1334(c)(2) overcome any constitutional objections that would otherwise exist?

To the extent that the Supreme Court has addressed questions of enhanced federal subject matter jurisdiction in bankruptcy, it seems to have resolved the matter in favor of congressional power. In Williams v. Austrian, 331 U.S. 642, 67 S.Ct. 1443, 91 L.Ed. 1718 (1947), the debtor was in reorganization in the federal district court for the Eastern District of Virginia. The Supreme Court construed the bankruptcy act's jurisdictional provision then in effect to authorize the trustee to bring suit in the federal district court for the Southern District of New York to recover an alleged misappropriation of corporate assets. Justice Frankfurter dissented on the ground that such an enlargement of district court jurisdiction should require express direction from Congress. But even he agreed that Congress *could* authorize such a suit "in a federal district court not the reorganization court, although neither diversity of citizenship nor other ground of federal jurisdiction exists." Id. at 664. See also Schumacher v. Beeler, 293 U.S. 367, 55 S.Ct. 230, 79 L.Ed. 433 (1934) (allowing plenary suit to enjoin the sale of debtor's property); National Mutual Insurance Co. v. Tidewater Transfer Co., Inc., 337 U.S. 582, 594, 69 S.Ct. 1173, 1179, 93 L.Ed. 1556 (1949) (opinion of Jackson, J.) (suggesting that Congress's article I bankruptcy power enables it to require district courts to handle "cases between the trustee and others that, but for the bankruptcy powers, would be beyond their jurisdiction"); Lathrop v. Drake, 91 U.S. 516, 23 L.Ed. 414 (1875) (construing Bankruptcy Act of 1867).

Interesting discussions exist as to when federal jurisdiction is appropriate (or even authorized) in nondiversity cases in which state law provides the source of the cause of action. Some writers view such bankruptcy cases as "arising under" the laws of the United States. See

National Mutual Insurance Co. v. Tidewater Transfer Co., 337 U.S. 582, 604, 69 S.Ct. 1173, 1184, 93 L.Ed. 1556 (1949) (Rutledge, J., concurring); Textile Workers Union v. Lincoln Mills, 353 U.S. 448, 460, 77 S.Ct. 912, 919, 1 L.Ed.2d 972 (1957) (Frankfurter, J., dissenting). Others describe federal jurisdiction in bankruptcy cases raising state law claims as providing a special, "protective" jurisdiction for the national bankruptcy program.

> Congress . . . established and affirmatively enacted [a statute] expressing a national policy [with respect to bankruptcies] . . . . The interests of creditors of an insolvent are an area which Congress has regulated by a complex scheme of legislation. The granting of federal jurisdiction under those circumstances was far from a random extension of the sheltering arm of the central government.
>
> In the net analysis, the function served by the federal judicial "haven" in such cases is not so much the defense of the specific interests concerned, as the protection of the congressional legislative program in the area. And that will be the situation in any area of active national regulation. Regardless of the source of the law applicable to a particular case, an uninformed or hostile attitude on the part of the tribunal deciding cases in such an area might well constitute a significant stumbling block in the way of effectuating federal policy. Even in cases where no specific statutory provision is itself involved, the overall federal policy thus may nonetheless be better protected if all connected litigation is adjudicated by courts well versed in, and receptive to, the national policies established by the legislation. The way the "facts" are viewed, if nothing else, may well be influenced by that awareness of and responsiveness to the congressional plan.

Mishkin, The Federal "Question" in the District Courts, 53 Colum.L. Rev. 157, 195 (1953). Compare Goldberg-Ambrose, The Protective Jurisdiction of the Federal Courts, 30 UCLA L.Rev. 542, 553 (1983) (bankruptcy jurisdiction is not an example of "true" protective jurisdiction).

IN RE WHIPPANY PAPER BOARD, INC.

United States Bankruptcy Court, District of New Jersey, 1981.
15 B.R. 312.

OPINION

Vincent J. Commisa, Bankruptcy Judge.

This matter is before the Court on the motion of the defendant Victory Container Corp. (Victory) to dismiss the instant adversary proceeding for lack of *in personam* jurisdiction over the defendant.

On February 8, 1980 Whippany Paper Board Co. (Whippany) filed a petition for reorganization under Chapter 11 of the Bankruptcy Code. Thereafter on May 2, 1980 Whippany commenced the instant adversary proceeding by filing a complaint in this Court against Victory, alleging that $260,425.79 is due and owing it as a result of accounts stated and accepted between Whippany and Victory.

Victory moves to dismiss this adversary proceeding, contending that the Court lacks *in personam* jurisdiction over it. In its affidavits in support of this motion to dismiss, Victory avers that it is a New York corporation which is neither qualified to do business in New Jersey, nor is subject to qualification. It affirms that it maintains no offices or sales personnel in this state.

The defendant asserts that this Court lacks *in personam* jurisdiction over it by reason of due process limitations on the jurisdiction of this Court. More particularly, Victory maintains that due process requires that the *in personam* jurisdiction of this Court be predicated upon the existence of minimum contacts between the defendant and the State of New Jersey. . . .

The legislative history makes clear that 28 U.S.C. Sec. 1471 [now § 1334] was intended as a comprehensive grant of *in rem* and *in personam* jurisdiction to the bankruptcy courts over all controversies arising out of any bankruptcy or rehabilitation case. In re G. Weeks Securities, Inc., 5 B.R. 220, 224 (B.Ct.D.Tenn.1980), 1 Collier on Bankruptcy, para. 1.03, pp. 1–21 (15th ed. 1980)

> The idea of possession and consent as basis for jurisdiction is eliminated. The adjunct bankruptcy courts will exercise *in personam* jurisdiction as well as *in rem* jurisdiction in order that they may handle everything that arises in a bankruptcy case. . . .

Thus, it is clear that Congress intended to give the Bankruptcy Court the jurisdiction, both *in personam* and *in rem,* in order that the Court may handle everything that may arise in a bankruptcy case, subject, of course, to Constitutional limitations on that authority. The Court notes that Bankruptcy Rule 704(f) authorizes the service of all process, except a subpoena, anywhere in the United States.

As stated above, the defendant contends that due process requires that the *in personam* jurisdiction of this Court is limited by the minimum contacts doctrine enunciated in International Shoe Co. v. Washington, 326 U.S. 310, 66 S.Ct. 154, 90 L.Ed. 95 (1945) and its progeny, most recently World-Wide Volkswagen Corp. v. Woodson, 444 U.S. 286, 100 S.Ct. 559, 62 L.Ed.2d 490 (1980).

The defendant misperceives the scope and purpose of the "minimum contacts" doctrine of *International Shoe*, supra. In Mariash v. Morrill, 496 F.2d 1138 (2d Cir. 1974), the defendants raised the minimum contacts doctrine as a prerequisite to the *in personam* jurisdiction of the District Court in an action alleging violations of the Securities Exchange Act of 1934. The Second Circuit rejected this contention, stating:

> "Appellees respond, however, by arguing that notice and an opportunity to be heard is not sufficient, for "it is still necessary that

defendants have the requisite 'minimal contacts' with *the State* which would exercise its jurisdiction over them.   Hansen [sic] v. Denckla, 357 U.S. 235 [78 S.Ct. 1228, 2 L.Ed.2d 1283] (1958)."   Brief of Appellees at 15 (emphasis added).   Mere statement of this contention reveals its fatal flaw: It is not the State of New York, but the United States "which would exercise its jurisdiction over them [the defendants]."   And plainly where, as here, the defendants reside within the territorial boundaries of the United States, the "minimal contacts," required to justify the federal government's exercise of power over them, are present.   Indeed, the "minimal contacts" principle does not, in our view, seem particularly relevant in evaluating the constitutionality of in personam jurisdiction based on nationwide, but *not* extraterritorial, service of process.   It is only the latter, quite simply, which even raises a question of the forum's power to assert control over the defendant.   . . .

Thus, the "minimum contacts" doctrine of *International Shoe* and its progency, which examines the contacts of the defendant with the forum *state,* has no particular relevance where, as here, jurisdiction is conferred by a federal statute, and not the diversity of citizenship of the parties, and Congress has provided for nationwide service of process.

. . .

The case of W.A. Kraft Corp. v. Terrace on the Park, Inc., 337 F.Supp. 206 (D.N.J.1972) is inapposite.   Therein, the *in personam* jurisdiction of the District Court in a diversity case under the New Jersey "long arm" rule, R.4:4–4(c)(1), was examined in light of the minimum contacts doctrine which, as demonstrated above, has no applicability herein as a constitutional limit on the *in personam* jurisdiction of this Court.   The minimum contacts analysis was employed because the *in personam* jurisdiction of the Federal District Court was, pursuant to F.R.Civ.P. 4(e), (f), limited by the jurisdictional constricts imposed on State courts in the use of long-arm statutes.   In the instant matter, the Court is proceeding under federal question jurisdiction and is possessed of nationwide service of process.   Thus, the constraints imposed by F.R. Civ.P. 4(e), (f) in *Kraft,* supra, are of no import herein.

In re Standard Gas & Electric Co., 119 F.2d 658 (3rd Cir. 1941), is also not on point.   Therein, the trustee brought suit in the District Court of Delaware alleging nineteen causes of action against fifty-six defendants.   Fifty-three of those defendants were not Delaware residents and were served with process outside the territorial limits of Delaware.   As to the service of these defendants, the Court stated:

It will thus be seen that while a reorganization court may issue all necessary process in support of its summary jurisdiction over the debtor's property, it may not without other statutory authority than is afforded by section 77B direct such process to be served upon defendants outside its own district when the suit is a plenary one brought under its diversity of citizenship jurisdiction by adverse claimants for the recovery of an unliquidated claim.   (at 664)

It is obvious that the bankruptcy court therein was proceeding under diversity jurisdiction in a plenary suit. The instant matter is before the Court not as a result of diversity jurisdiction but pursuant to 28 U.S.C. Sec. 1471, which confers on the Bankruptcy Court jurisdiction of all civil proceedings arising in or related to cases under title 11. Thus, the jurisdiction of this Court is not as a result of the diversity of citizenship of the parties, but by virtue of the federal law, bankruptcy, under which the case arises, or is related to same. Moreover, the intention of this Code was to eliminate the summary-plenary distinction which engendered much litigation under the Bankruptcy Act.

Accordingly, this Court finds that it has *in personam* jurisdiction over the defendant and therefore, denies the motion to dismiss plaintiff's complaint for lack of same.

The defendant also asserts that should this Court have *in personam* jurisdiction over the defendant, that defendant's contacts with the State of New Jersey are insufficient to create venue in this state. 28 U.S.C. Sec. 1473 [now § 1409] pertinently provides:

> (a) Except as provided in subsections (b) and (d) of this section, a proceeding arising in or related to a case under title 11 may be commenced in the bankruptcy court in which such case is pending.

> (b) Except as provided in subsection (d) of this section, a trustee in a case under title 11 may commence a proceeding arising in or related to such case to recover a money judgment of or property worth less than $1,000 or a consumer debt of less than $5,000 only in the bankruptcy court for the district in which the defendant resides.[b]

Subsection (d) is not of relevance herein, it is addressed to cases arising after the commencement of the bankruptcy case.

Thus, 28 U.S.C. Sec. 1473(a) clearly provides that venue is proper in this Court, the Court in which the case is pending. Subsection (b) is inapplicable in the instant matter, as the recovery sought herein is substantially in excess of the pecuniary limits therein. The purpose of subsection (b) is to,

> [P]revent unfairness to distant debtors of the estate, when the cost of defending would be greater than the cost of paying the debt owed. H.Rep.No. 595, 95th Cong. 1st Sess. 446 (1977), U.S. Code Cong. & Admin.News 1978, p. 6402.

In drafting the venue statute, Congress obviously considered the cost and practicalities of requiring a defendant to defend in the forum in which the case is pending. Congress elected to exempt from the general applicability of 28 U.S.C. Sec. 1473(a) those defendants with an amount in litigation substantially less than the sum controverted herein.

b. In § 1409, references to the bankruptcy court in the old venue statute have been changed to the district court.

In *In re Cole Associates, supra,* the Bankruptcy Court listed the following factors as relevant to the venue question:

> [T]he relative ease of access to the sources of proof; the availability of compulsory process for the attendance of unwilling witnesses and the cost of obtaining the attendance of willing witnesses; the enforceability of a judgment if obtained; the applicability of a particular state law and the local interest in applying that law through courts within the state; the responsibilities and difficulties of court administration; the relative advantages and obstacles to fair trial; and other practical matters which encourage the efficient and inexpensive trial of the case; the proximity of creditors of every kind to the court; the proximity of the debtor to the court; the proximity of the witnesses necessary to the administration of the estate; the location of the assets; the economic administration of the estate and the necessity for ancillary administration if bankruptcy should result. (7 B.R. at 156–57).

It emphasized that,

> "If one factor could be singled out as having the most logical importance, it would be whether a transfer would promote the efficient and economic administration of an estate." In re United Button Co., 137 F. 668: In re Triton Chemical Corp., 46 F.Supp. 326, 329. (at 157).

The burden of proof lies with the party requesting the change of venue, and that burden must be carried by a preponderance of the evidence. In re Cole Associates, Inc., supra, at 157.

At the outset of its consideration of these factors, the Court observes that the defendant apparently has its offices in New York City. Further, an action has been commenced by the plaintiff herein in the New York courts. That action was removed to the Bankruptcy Court for the Southern District of New York, which the defendant, presumably, prefers as the venue for this matter. The Court observes that the distance and inconveniences involved are not nearly so great as, for example, those of the defendants in In re Cole Associates, Inc., supra, wherein the debtor filed its petition in Utah, and commenced an action in the Bankruptcy Court for that district against defendants located in Wisconsin, Minnesota and New York.

Applying the factors set forth hereinabove, the Court finds that the movant has not carried the requisite burden in its application for a change of venue. The factor having the most logical importance, whether a transfer would promote the efficient and economic administration of the estate, weighs in favor of retaining venue. The bankruptcy case is pending in this Court, the plaintiff in the instant adversary proceeding is litigating similar claims in this Court, the debtor's principal offices are closer to Newark than the Southern District of New York, and finally, the debtor has chosen to litigate this matter in this Court. The defendant herein has not addressed itself to each of the relevant criteria, however, in light of a consideration of the most

important factor, and those factors which are material by virtue of the
unique nature of a bankruptcy proceeding, e.g., the proximity of the
debtor to the Court, the location of the assets and the proximity of the
witnesses necessary to the administration of the estate, the Court finds
that the defendant has not carried its burden and that the venue of this
adversary proceeding should not be transferred.

The defendant asserts that great weight should attach to the fact
that the debtor herein has instituted suit against it in New York, such
suit being removed to the Bankruptcy Court for the Southern District
of New York.   That factor cannot be dispositive when, as here, the
plaintiff-debtor has adversary proceedings pending in this Court, the
bankruptcy case is pending herein, the offices and assets of the debtor
are in closer proximity to this Court and, finally, the burden of proof by
a preponderance of the evidence is on the party requesting a change of
venue.   . . .

Notes & Questions

1.   *The Scope of Personal Jurisdiction in Bankruptcy.*   May a bankruptcy court assert in personam jurisdiction over a party with no
connection to the forum in which the bankruptcy court sits?   Do
whatever considerations support the *International Shoe* line of personal
jurisdiction cases lose all force when the forum becomes federal?   Or do
they become of diminished importance when the federal forum happens
also to be a bankruptcy court?

Rule 7004 of the new Bankruptcy Rules continues to authorize
nationwide service of process in bankruptcy proceedings.   See generally
Fullerton, Constitutional Limits on Nationwide Personal Jurisdiction in
the Federal Courts, 79 Nw.U.L.Rev. 1 (1984).

2.   *Private Contractual Influence on Jurisdiction.*   May the parties
by contract influence the jurisdiction issue in bankruptcy cases?   In
Banque Francaise du Commerce Exterieur v. Rio Grande Trading, Inc.,
17 B.R. 134 (Bkrtcy.S.D.Tex.1981), a French bank issued letters of credit
to companies that supplied crude oil to the debtor.   In return, the
debtor assigned and sold to the bank various accounts receivable.   The
agreement between the bank and the debtor stated "this agreement is
to be governed by and construed in accordance with the laws of France.
All disputes arising in connection with the present agreement shall be
submitted to the exclusive jurisdiction of the Tribunal of Commerce of
Paris."   The court found that it had jurisdiction over a dispute arising
under the agreement.

3.   *Place of Filing; Venue.*   (a) Debtor, a New York corporation
headquartered in New York City, has its major plant in Los Angeles,
California.   Where may Debtor file a bankruptcy petition under Chapter 11?

(b) At the time of the filing, Debtor had a claim for $1 million
against General Maintenance Corp. for breach of a contract in which
General Maintenance agreed to maintain Debtor's Los Angeles plant.

Where may the trustee commence litigation against General Maintenance?

(c) Shortly before bankruptcy, Debtor purchased stock from Smith, its president and a resident of New York City. Smith may have sold the stock for an amount in excess of its fair market value. The sale was made less than a year before the filing of the bankruptcy petition, and was made while Debtor was insolvent. Where may the trustee commence litigation against Smith?

(d) Suppose the events in parts (b) and (c) occurred after the filing of the bankruptcy petition. Where may the trustee commence litigation?

See generally Kennedy, The Bankruptcy Court Under the New Bankruptcy Law: Its Structure, Jurisdiction, Venue, and Procedure, 11 St. Mary's L.J. 251, 302–04 (1979).

4. *Venue.* Compare the Bankruptcy Act's venue provision for cases arising under or related to cases under title 11, 28 U.S.C.A. § 1409, with the general venue provision applicable in federal court. 28 U.S.C.A. § 1391.[c] Are there differences between the two provisions that might influence one's answer to whether the assertion of in personam jurisdiction in *Whippany Paper Board* satisfied constitutional standards?

Compare the function of venue provisions in bankruptcy with the function of venue provisions in other federal proceedings. Are the two sets of venue provisions serving the same goals? Should they?

2. Core Proceedings

Despite the broad grant of jurisdiction to district courts in § 1334, the day-to-day operation of the bankruptcy system remains in the hands of bankruptcy judges. Please read 28 U.S.C.A. § 157.

IN RE MANKIN

United States Court of Appeals, Ninth Circuit, 1987.
823 F.2d 1296.

Before MERRILL, and NOONAN, CIRCUIT JUDGES, and WATERS, SENIOR DISTRICT JUDGE.

LAUGHLIN E. WATERS, SENIOR DISTRICT JUDGE:

This appeal arises from an action filed in a Chapter 7 bankruptcy case by the trustee to avoid, pursuant to 11 U.S.C. § 544(b), an

---

c. Section 1391 states in part:

(a) A civil action wherein jurisdiction is founded only on diversity of citizenship may, except as otherwise provided by law, be brought only in the judicial district where all plaintiffs or all defendants reside, or in which the claim arose.

(b) A civil action wherein jurisdiction is not founded solely on diversity of citizenship may be brought only in the judicial district where all defendants reside,

or in which the claim arose, except as otherwise provided by law.

(c) A corporation may be sued in any judicial district in which it is incorporated or licensed to do business or is doing business, and such judicial district shall be regarded as the residence of such corporation for venue purposes.

(d) An alien may be sued in any district.

alleged fraudulent conveyance made by the Chapter 7 debtor, Roxanne Mankin ("Mankin"). Named as the defendant in the trustee's action is G.B. Munn ("Munn"), the party to whom Mankin made the alleged fraudulent transfer. Two issues have been raised on appeal: (1) whether the trustee's action is a "core proceeding" which Congress intended bankruptcy courts to "hear and determine" pursuant to 28 U.S.C. § 157(b) and, if so, (2) whether exercise of jurisdiction by the bankruptcy court is unconstitutional under the holding of the Supreme Court in Northern Pipeline Construction Co. v. Marathon Pipe Line Co., 458 U.S. 50, 102 S.Ct. 2858, 73 L.Ed.2d 598 (1982).

28 U.S.C. § 157(a) provides that district courts may refer "cases under title 11 or arising in or related to a case under title 11" to bankruptcy judges. Of the cases referred to them pursuant to 157(a), bankruptcy judges are authorized to "hear and determine" "cases under title 11" and "core proceedings" arising under Title 11. 28 U.S.C.A. § 157(b) (West Supp.1987). The "cases under title 11" and "core proceedings" heard and determined by bankruptcy judges pursuant to § 157(a) and (b) are subject to review by a district court "in the same manner as appeals in civil proceedings generally are taken to the courts of appeals from the district courts." 28 U.S.C.A. § 158(c) (West Supp.1987). Non-core proceedings related to cases under Title 11 may also be referred to bankruptcy judges pursuant to 28 U.S.C. § 157(a). However, unless the parties stipulate otherwise, bankruptcy judges are authorized only to "hear" non-core proceedings referred to them and then submit proposed findings of fact and conclusions of law to the district court for *de novo* review. 28 U.S.C.A. § 157(c)(1) (West Supp.1987).

Congress has determined that proceedings to determine, avoid or recover fraudulent conveyances are "core proceedings" which may be referred to bankruptcy judges for determination pursuant to 28 U.S.C. § 157(b). 28 U.S.C.A. § 157(b)(2)(H) (West Supp.1987). There are two separate provisions in Title 11 which authorize a bankruptcy trustee to avoid conveyances: 11 U.S.C. § 544(b) and 11 U.S.C. § 548. Section 548 specifically authorizes the trustee to avoid any transfer of an interest of the debtor that was "made or incurred on or within one year before the date of the filing of the [bankruptcy] petition" if the debtor "made such transfer . . . with actual intent to hinder, delay or defraud [any creditor]." 11 U.S.C.A. § 548(a)(1) (West 1979 & Supp.1987). Section 544(b) gives to the trustee the power to avoid any conveyances which an unsecured creditor could have avoided under applicable state law. *See* 11 U.S.C.A. § 544(b) (West 1979 & Supp.1987). Under California law, unsecured creditors are entitled to set aside fraudulent conveyances made by insolvent debtors. See Cal.Civ.Code §§ 3439–3439.11 (West Supp.1987).

In the present suit, the trustee seeks relief under § 544(b).[1] According to the trustee's complaint, the debtor entered into a written assignment agreement with Munn in which she agreed to transfer to Munn her right to receive profits as a general partner in Capitola Investors, a limited partnership, in exchange for Munn's promise to co-sign and guarantee a loan needed to refinance real property owned by Capitola. The trustee alleges that the transaction was fraudulent in that Munn's promise to co-sign the loan was not fair consideration, the assignment was made while the debtor was insolvent or rendered her insolvent and the assignment was made with intent to hinder, delay or defraud creditors.

The trustee filed his § 544(b) action in the United States Bankruptcy Court for the Northern District of California on February 1, 1985. Munn responded to the complaint by filing a motion to dismiss. In this motion, Munn asserted the same position which he asserts on this appeal: that under the holding of the United States Supreme Court in Northern Pipeline Construction Co. v. Marathon Pipe Line Co., 458 U.S. 50, 102 S.Ct. 2858, 73 L.Ed.2d 598 (1982), adjudication by the bankruptcy court of the trustee's action violates Article III of the Constitution. The bankruptcy court accepted this position and by written order granted Munn's motion to dismiss. This order was filed on May 22, 1985 and entered on May 27, 1985. The trustee then filed a motion for reconsideration which the bankruptcy court denied on July 25, 1985. On August 5, 1985, the trustee filed and served a notice of appeal to the district court from the bankruptcy court's order dismissing the complaint.

In ruling on the trustee's appeal, the district court found that the trustee's action was a "core proceeding" as defined in 28 U.S.C. § 157(b)(2)(H) over which the bankruptcy court had jurisdiction pursuant to 28 U.S.C. § 157(b)(1). The district court also found that the Supreme Court's holding in *Northern Pipeline* did not preclude the bankruptcy court's jurisdiction "because the right of action arises under Title 11." Accordingly, the district court reversed the order of dismissal and remanded the case to the bankruptcy court with instructions to the bankruptcy court to exercise jurisdiction.

The district court's written order was entered on February 14, 1986. Munn noticed an appeal from this order to this court on March 12, 1986. Although the district court's order authorizes further proceed-

---

1. The trustee chose to seek relief under § 544(b) instead of § 548 probably because of the differing limitation periods governing § 548 and § 544(b). While § 548 governs only conveyances made within one year of the filing of a bankruptcy petition, actions to set aside fraudulent conveyances brought pursuant to California law under § 544(b) are subject only to the three year limitations period of California Code of Civil Procedure § 338(4). The conveyance challenged by the trustee was made on October 11, 1982 while the debtor did not file her bankruptcy petition until October 18, 1983. Thus, because the conveyance at issue here was made more than one but less than three years prior to the filing of the Chapter 7 bankruptcy petition by the debtor, the trustee could, and did, seek relief under California law pursuant to § 544(b) but could not seek relief under the federal fraudulent conveyance provision codified in § 548.

ings, we have jurisdiction under 28 U.S.C. § 158(d) to hear the appeal from the district court's order because the bankruptcy court order appealed from was final. *In re Sambo's Restaurants,* 754 F.2d 811, 813–815 (9th Cir.1985).

I. *Statutory Jurisdiction of the Bankruptcy Court*

28 U.S.C. § 157(b)(1) provides for bankruptcy court jurisdiction over core proceedings and 28 U.S.C. § 157(b)(2) lists various types of proceedings deemed by Congress to be core proceedings. Clause (H) of § 157(b)(2) provides that core proceedings include "proceedings to determine, avoid, or recover fraudulent conveyances. . . ." 28 U.S.C.A. § 157(b)(2)(H) (West Supp.1987). A proceeding under 11 U.S.C. § 548, which specifically authorizes a trustee to set aside fraudulent conveyances made within one year of the filing of a bankruptcy petition, is unquestionably the type of proceeding referred to in § 157(b)(2)(H). Whether § 157(b)(2)(H) refers to state fraudulent conveyance actions is, perhaps, somewhat less clear. The right of a trustee to bring state fraudulent conveyance actions is not specifically mentioned in the federal bankruptcy statutes but rather arises from 11 U.S.C. § 544(b), which allows the trustee to set aside a conveyance which an unsecured creditor could have set aside under state law. Munn argues that in order to avoid the constitutional question raised by allowing § 157(b)(2) bankruptcy jurisdiction over state fraudulent conveyance actions, we should construe § 157(b)(2)(H) as referring only to the federal fraudulent conveyance action codified in 11 U.S.C. § 548.

We decline to adopt the construction of § 157(b)(2)(H) suggested by Munn. It is true that "[f]ederal statutes are to be so construed as to avoid serious doubt of their constitutionality." *International Ass'n. of Machinists v. Street,* 367 U.S. 740, 749, 81 S.Ct. 1784, 1790, 6 L.Ed.2d 1141 (1961). By the same token however, "this canon of construction does not give a court the prerogative to ignore the legislative will in order to avoid constitutional adjudication." *Commodity Futures Trading Comm'n. v. Schor,* ___ U.S. ___, 106 S.Ct. 3245, 3252, 92 L.Ed.2d 675 (1986). To construe § 157(b)(2)(H) as being limited to proceedings pursuant to § 548 would be to "ignore the legislative will" underlying the statute. Not only is there nothing in the language of § 157(b)(2)(H) to support Munn's argument, examination of § 157(b)(2)(H)'s context within the Bankruptcy Code, as well as its wording and legislative history, demonstrates that Congress never intended it to be given the restrictive reading that Munn urges.

Section 157(b)(2) does not set categorical limits on the jurisdiction of bankruptcy courts over core proceedings, but rather merely enumerates examples of proceedings falling within a bankruptcy court's core proceeding jurisdiction. That Congress did not intend to limit the bankruptcy courts' jurisdiction over core proceedings by enumerating examples of core proceedings in § 157(b)(2) is apparent from the prefatory language of § 157(b)(2): "Core matters include, *but are not limited to* . . . ." (emphasis added). 28 U.S.C.A. § 157(b)(2) (West Supp.

1987). Thus, in construing a bankruptcy court's jurisdiction over a particular action pursuant to § 157(b)(1), the crucial consideration is not whether the action falls within one of the clauses of § 157(b)(2), but rather whether the action is or is not in fact a core proceeding. As explained later in this opinion, an action by a trustee pursuant to § 544(b) to set aside a fraudulent conveyance is in fact a core proceeding.

Even if the bankruptcy court's § 157(b) jurisdiction over this case did turn on construction of § 157(b)(2)(H), we have found no evidence that Congress intended to restrict § 157(b)(2)(H) to federal fraudulent conveyance proceedings. Not only does § 157(b)(2)(H) not distinguish between state and federal fraudulent conveyance proceedings, the federal law of fraudulent conveyance is essentially identical to the law of fraudulent conveyance adopted by the states. Thus, for purposes of § 157(b)(2)(H), state fraudulent conveyance proceedings are distinguishable from federal fraudulent conveyance proceedings only by the fact that they are of state origin. Congress has explicitly found that this is a distinction which, standing alone, cannot serve as the basis for distinguishing core from non-core proceedings: "A determination that a proceeding is not a core proceeding shall not be made solely on the basis that its resolution may be affected by State law." 28 U.S.C.A. § 157(b)(3) (West Supp.1987). In essence then the explicit provisions of the bankruptcy statutes are contrary to the judicial gloss Munn asks us to place on § 157(b)(2)(H).

Finally, we note that Munn's position would contradict the understanding with which Congress enacted § 157(b). As Representative Kastenmeier explained, "the conference report largely rejects the Senate limitations on the tasks which are to be performed by a bankruptcy judge. The report states that a narrow category of cases are [sic] not to be construed as core proceedings." 130 Cong.Rec. H7492 (daily ed. June 29, 1984). Nothing in the legislative history of § 157(b) suggests that Congress enumerated examples of core proceedings in § 157(b)(2) with anything but a view toward expanding the bankruptcy court's jurisdiction to its constitutional limit. See generally 9 Bankruptcy Service ch. 81:6–8 (Supp.1987) (legislative history of the Bankruptcy Amendments and Federal Judgeship Act of 1984); see also In re Arnold Print Works, Inc., 815 F.2d 165, 168 (1st Cir.1987) (sponsors of 1984 Act "used arguments strongly suggesting that they were pressing the notion [of core proceedings] to its constitutional bounds"). It is inappropriate therefore to construe one of those examples restrictively in order to avoid a test of what the constitutional limit is.[3]

---

3. In re Castlerock Properties, 781 F.2d 159 (9th Cir.1986), does not counsel a different result. There this court held that a bankruptcy court does not have jurisdiction to enter judgment under § 157(b) on a state law counterclaim of a Chapter 11 debtor. In reaching this conclusion, the court commented that a proceeding should not be characterized as "core" if to do so would raise constitutional problems. Id. at 162. In *Castlerock* however the court found that the claim at issue did not fall within any of the specific categories of core proceedings enumerated in 28 U.S.C. § 157(b)(2)(B)–(N) and at most only "arguably" fell within one of the two catchall

II. Constitutionality of Bankruptcy Court's Jurisdiction

Article III of the Constitution provides that judges of courts vested with the "judicial Power of the United States" "shall hold their Offices during good Behavior, and shall, at stated Times, receive for their Services a Compensation, which shall not be diminished during their Continuance in Office." U.S. Const. art. III, § 1. If the requirements of Article III were strictly applied to all cases involving the exercise of federal judicial power, resolution of the constitutional issue in this case would be simple: because the judges of the bankruptcy courts are not guaranteed either lifetime tenure or protection against salary reduction, see 28 U.S.C.A. §§ 152(a)(1), (e), 153(a) (West Supp.1987), their determination of this case would violate Article III. In actuality however resolution of the constitutional issue in this case is not so simple because there have been several instances in which the exercise of federal judicial power by judges without lifetime tenure or protection against salary reduction has been upheld by the Supreme Court under Article III. The trustee argues that this is an instance when a non-Article III officer may exercise federal judicial power. Munn of course argues the contrary.

A. Northern Pipeline and the Subsequent Enactment of the Bankruptcy Amendments and Federal Judgeship Act of 1984

The question of what bankruptcy proceedings can and cannot be committed to the jurisdiction of a non-Article III bankruptcy judge was comprehensively addressed by the United States Supreme Court in Northern Pipeline Construction Co. v. Marathon Pipe Line Co., 458 U.S. 50, 102 S.Ct. 2858, 73 L.Ed.2d 598 (1982). Northern Pipeline involved a state law damages action for breach of contract and warranty filed by a Chapter 11 debtor, Northern Pipeline Construction Company, in a United States Bankruptcy Court. Jurisdiction in the bankruptcy court was premised on § 241(a) of the Bankruptcy Reform Act of 1978 ("1978 Act") which conferred jurisdiction on the bankruptcy court over all "civil proceedings arising under title 11 or arising in or related to cases under title 11." 28 U.S.C. § 1471 (Supp. IV 1976). The defendant, Marathon Pipe Line Company, moved to dismiss the action on the ground that the 1978 Act unconstitutionally conferred Article III judicial power upon judges who lacked life tenure and protection against salary diminution. The Supreme Court agreed with Marathon's position and, in a decision which did not command a majority opinion, affirmed the dismissal of the suit.

provisions of § 157(b)(2). Id. Here on the other hand we find that the claim at issue falls within § 157(b)(2)(H), which is one of the specific provisions of § 157(b)(2). While the principle that constitutional problems are to be avoided in the construction of statutes is apt where a catch-all provision is at issue, more apt in construing a specific provision of a statute is the principle that the will of the legislature underlying the provision is not to be ignored. Moreover, in Castlerock the court concluded that § 157(b) jurisdiction over the claim at issue would in fact be unconstitutional. 781 F.2d at 162. In this case we find that § 157(b) jurisdiction over the claim here at issue is not unconstitutional.

Before finding that the bankruptcy court as constituted under the 1978 Act could not constitutionally exercise the jurisdiction conferred on it by the 1978 Act, the plurality opinion in *Northern Pipeline* first considered when and why the Supreme Court had previously made exceptions to the general rule that federal judicial power is to be exercised only by Article III judges. According to the *Northern Pipeline* plurality, exercise of federal judicial power by a non-Article III officer has been upheld in two types of potentially analogous cases: those involving the adjudication of "public rights" and those in which the non-Article III decision maker acted as an "adjunct" to an Article III court. The plurality concluded that the bankruptcy court jurisdiction at issue violated Article III because it could not be sustained under either the public rights or adjunct court doctrines. However, the concurring opinion did not fully join in the plurality's adjunct court and public rights analysis; a majority of the Justices could only agree that the particular claim before it could not be adjudicated by the bankruptcy court as then constituted. See Thomas v. Union Carbide Agricultural Products, 473 U.S. 568, 584, 105 S.Ct. 3325, 3335, 87 L.Ed.2d 409 (1985) ("The Court's holding [in *Northern Pipeline*] establishes only that Congress may not vest in a non-Article III court the power to adjudicate, render final judgment, and issue binding orders in a traditional contract action arising under state law, without consent of the litigants, and subject only to ordinary appellate review."); accord Commodities Futures Trading Comm'n. v. Schor, ___ U.S. ___, 106 S.Ct. 3245, 3251, 92 L.Ed.2d 675 (1986). Subsequent majority holdings of the Supreme Court have recognized that the adjunct court and public rights doctrines embody valid, if not the exclusive, principles governing the determination of when and under what conditions a particular proceeding may be referred to non-Article III officers for adjudication. See, e.g., Thomas v. Union Carbide Agricultural Products Co., 473 U.S. 568, 588–589, 105 S.Ct. 3325, 3337–38, 87 L.Ed.2d 409 (1985) (majority opinion applying public rights doctrine). We will accordingly consider both the adjunct court and public rights doctrine as explicated by the plurality in *Northern Pipeline* in determining the merit to Munn's argument that the bankruptcy court's jurisdiction over this proceeding violates Article III.

The public rights doctrine derives from a group of cases in which the Supreme Court has upheld the constitutionality of legislative courts and administrative courts. The doctrine, as construed in *Northern Pipeline,* is limited to matters arising "between the Government and persons subject to its authority in connection with the performance of the constitutional functions of the legislative or executive departments" and which "historically could have been determined exclusively by those departments." Northern Pipeline, 458 U.S. at 67–68, 102 S.Ct. at 2869–70, quoting Crowell v. Benson, 285 U.S. 22, 50, 52 S.Ct. 285, 292, 76 L.Ed. 598 (1932) and Ex parte Bakelite Corp., 279 U.S. 438, 458, 49 S.Ct. 411, 416, 73 L.Ed. 789 (1929). As the plurality explained, "[t]he understanding of these cases is that the Framers expected that Congress would be free to commit such matters completely to nonjudicial executive determination, and that as a result there can be no constitutional objection to Congress' employing the less drastic expedient of committing their determination to a legislative court or an administrative agency." 458 U.S. at 68, 102 S.Ct. at 2870. Pursuant to the public rights doctrine, the Supreme Court has, the plurality found, upheld Congress' establishment of summary procedures, outside of Article III courts, to collect a debt due to the government from one of its customs agents, Murray's Lessee v. Hoboken Land & Improvement Co., 59 U.S. (18 How.) 272, 15 L.Ed. 372 (1856), cited in Northern Pipeline, 458 U.S. at 68, 102 S.Ct. at 2870, and has found that the Court of Customs Appeals had been properly constituted by Congress as a legislative court. Ex parte Bakelite, 279 U.S. 438, 49 S.Ct. 411 cited in Northern Pipeline, 458 U.S. at 68–69, 102 S.Ct. at 2870.

In *Northern Pipeline,* Northern Pipeline argued that a discharge in bankruptcy was a public right, similar to such congressionally created benefits as "radio station licenses, pilot licenses, or certificates for common carriers." 458 U.S. at 71, 102 S.Ct. at 2871. However, because the suit at issue in *Northern Pipeline* was between two private parties concerning only their respective liability under the law, the plurality found it could not be viewed as a public rights suit: "[I]t suffices to observe that a matter of public rights must at a minimum arise 'between the government and others.' [Ex parte Bakelite, 279 U.S. at 451, 459, 49 S.Ct. at 413, 416.] In contrast, 'the liability of one individual to another under the law as defined,' Crowell v. Benson, [285 U.S.] at 51 [52 S.Ct. at 292,] is a matter of private rights." Northern Pipeline, 458 U.S. at 69–70, 102 S.Ct. at 2870–71. However, the plurality found that some bankruptcy proceedings *may* fall within the public rights exception: "[T]he restructuring of debtor-creditor relations, which is at the core of the federal bankruptcy power, must be distinguished from the adjudication of state-created private rights, such as the right to recover contract damages that is at issue in this case. The former may well be a 'public right,' but the latter obviously is not." Northern Pipeline, 458 U.S. at 71, 102 S.Ct. at 2871.

The plurality derived the adjunct court exception to Article III from two cases, Crowell v. Benson, 285 U.S. 22, 52 S.Ct. 285, 76 L.Ed. 598 (1932) and United States v. Raddatz, 447 U.S. 667, 100 S.Ct. 2406, 65 L.Ed.2d 424 (1980). At issue in *Crowell* was a congressional scheme which empowered an administrative agency, the United States Employees' Compensation Commission, to make initial factual determinations pursuant to a federal statute requiring employers to compensate their employees for work-related injuries occurring upon the navigable waters of the United States. The Commission's "judicial power" was, however, limited in several ways. One, the federal statute administered by the Commission provided for compensation of injured employees "irrespective of fault" and prescribed a fixed and mandatory schedule of compensation. Crowell, 285 U.S. at 38, 52 S.Ct. at 287, cited in Northern Pipeline, 458 U.S. at 78, 102 S.Ct. at 2875. As a consequence, the Commission was left with the limited role of determining "questions of fact as to the circumstances, nature, extent and consequences of the injuries sustained by the employee for which compensation is to be made." Crowell, 285 U.S. at 54, 52 S.Ct. at 293, cited in Northern Pipeline, 458 U.S. at 78, 102 S.Ct. at 2875. The Court found that in view of these limitations upon the Commission's functions and powers, its determinations were "closely analogous" to those "made, according to familiar practice, by commissioners or assessors." Crowell, 285 U.S. at 54, 52 S.Ct. at 293, cited in Northern Pipeline, 458 U.S. at 78, 102 S.Ct. at 2875. Observing that "there is no requirement that, in order to maintain the essential attributes of the judicial power, all determinations of fact in constitutional courts shall be made by judges," the Court held that the judicial power exercised by the Commission did not violate Article III. Crowell, 285 U.S. at 54, 52 S.Ct. at 293, cited in Northern Pipeline, 458 U.S. at 78, 102 S.Ct. at 2875.

The second case upon which the plurality premised its adjunct court exception to Article III, *United States v. Raddatz,* upheld the practice, authorized by the 1978 Federal Magistrates Act, of referring certain pre-trial criminal motions, including motions to suppress based on alleged violations of constitutional rights, to a magistrate for initial determination. According to the *Northern Pipeline* plurality, the *Raddatz* court found that this practice did not run afoul of Article III because two provisions of the Magistrates Act ensured that ultimate decision making authority respecting the pre-trial motions remained with Article III judges: (1) under the Act, the magistrate's proposed findings and recommendations were subject to *de novo* review by the district court, which was free to rehear the evidence or call for additional evidence; and (2) the Act specified that the magistrates were appointed, and subject to removal, by the district court. Northern Pipeline, 458 U.S. at 79, 102 S.Ct. at 2875.

In reviewing *Crowell* and *Raddatz,* the *Northern Pipeline* plurality found that the two cases established two principles relevant in determining the extent to which Congress may constitutionally vest judicial power in adjuncts to Article III courts. One, the plurality found, when Congress creates a substantive federal right, it possesses substantial discretion to prescribe the manner in which that right may be adjudicated—including the discretion to assign to an adjunct some functions historically performed by judges. This principle, the plurality found, underlies the result in *Crowell:*

> [I]t is clear that when Congress creates a substantive federal right, it possesses substantial discretion to prescribe the manner in which that right may be adjudicated. . . . Thus *Crowell* recognized that Art. III does not require "all determinations of fact [to] be made by judges," [citation omitted]; with respect to congressionally created rights, some factual determinations may be made by a specialized factfinding tribunal designed by Congress, without constitutional bar. . . . [citation omitted].

Northern Pipeline, 458 U.S. at 80–81, 102 S.Ct. at 2876–77.

The second principle the plurality inferred from the cases is that the adjunct must be limited in such a way that "the essential attributes" of judicial power are retained in the Article III court. This principle, the Court found, was embodied in both *Crowell* and *Raddatz:*

> Thus in upholding the adjunct scheme challenged in *Crowell,* the Court emphasized that "the reservation of full authority to the court to deal with matters of law provides for the appropriate exercise of the judicial function in this class of cases." [Citation omitted]. And in refusing to invalidate the Magistrates Act at issue in *Raddatz,* the Court stressed that under the congressional scheme " '[t]he authority—and the responsibility—to make an informed, final determination . . . remains with the judge,' " [citation omitted]; the statute's delegation of power was therefore permissible, since "the ultimate decision is made by the district court," [Citation omitted].

Northern Pipeline, 458 U.S. at 81, 102 S.Ct. at 2877.

In applying the foregoing analysis, the plurality in *Northern Pipeline* found that the first principle—that Congress has greater discretion in prescribing the manner in which rights of its own creation are determined—was of no assistance to Northern Pipeline's position because the lawsuit at issue involved state, and not federally created, rights. "[W]hile *Crowell* certainly endorsed the proposition that Congress possesses broad discretion to assign fact finding functions to an adjunct created to aid in the adjudication of congressionally created rights, *Crowell* does not support the further proposition . . . that Congress possesses the same degree of discretion in assigning traditionally judicial power to adjuncts engaged in the adjudication of rights *not* created by Congress." Northern Pipeline, 458 U.S. at 81–82, 102 S.Ct. at 2876–77. The plurality found this distinction to be of particular constitutional significance because the separation of powers doctrine embodied in Article III is less threatened where the right at issue is congressionally created:

> [The distinction between rights created by Congress and state created rights] seems to us to be necessary in light of the delicate accommodations required by the principle of separation of powers reflected in Art. III. The constitutional system of checks and balances is designed to guard against "encroachment or aggrandizement" by Congress at the expense of the other branches of government. [Citation omitted]. But when Congress creates a statutory right, it clearly has the discretion, in defining that right, to create presumptions, or assign burdens of proof, or prescribe remedies; it may also provide that persons seeking to vindicate that right must do so before particularized tribunals created to perform the specialized adjudicative tasks related to that right. Such provisions . . . are . . . incidental to Congress' power to define the right it has created. No comparable justification exists, however, when the right being adjudicated is not of congressional creation. In such a

situation, substantial inroads into functions that have traditionally been performed by the Judiciary cannot be characterized merely as incidental extensions of Congress' power to define rights it has created. Rather, such inroads suggest unwarranted encroachments upon the judicial power of the United States, which our Constitution reserves for Art. III courts.

Northern Pipeline, 458 U.S. at 83–84, 102 S.Ct. at 2877–78.

The *Northern Pipeline* plurality also found that the delegation of jurisdiction to the bankruptcy judges under the Bankruptcy Reform Act of 1978 was far greater than the delegations approved in *Crowell* and *Raddatz* and that as a consequence the 1978 Act could not be upheld on the ground that Article III judges retained under the Act "the essential attributes" of judicial power. In reaching this conclusion, the plurality emphasized that the subject matter jurisdiction of the bankruptcy courts under the Act encompassed not only traditional matters of bankruptcy, but also "all civil proceedings arising under title 11 or arising in or *related to* cases under title 11." Northern Pipeline, 458 U.S. at 85, 102 S.Ct. at 2878 (emphasis in plurality opinion). The plurality also noted that the Act permitted bankruptcy judges to exercise powers "far greater" than those lodged in the adjunct schemes approved in *Crowell* and *Raddatz* in that the Act permitted bankruptcy judges to issue and enforce orders without resort to the district court and allowed for review of bankruptcy court judgments only under a "clearly erroneous" standard. Id. at 85–86, 102 S.Ct. at 2878–79.

In response to *Northern Pipeline,* Congress enacted the Bankruptcy Amendments and Federal Judgeships Act of 1984 ("1984 Act"). This is the statutory scheme presently in effect and under which the claim here at issue arises. Comparison of the 1984 Act with the 1978 Act, as well as review of the legislative history of the 1984 Act, reveals that in attempting to bring bankruptcy procedures within the limitations of Article III, Congress shaped the 1984 Act with both the public rights and adjunct court doctrines in mind. In apparent response to the distinction made by the *Northern Pipeline* plurality between core bankruptcy proceedings, which "may well be" within the public rights exception, and non-core proceedings, which are not, Congress provided separate procedures in the 1984 Act for adjudication of what are deemed to be "non-core" proceedings. See supra, page 1298. Whereas the 1978 Act conferred broad powers on bankruptcy courts to determine core and non-core proceedings alike, non-core proceedings can, under the 1984 Act, be referred to bankruptcy judges only for recommended findings subject to *de novo* review by a district judge. 28 U.S.C.A. § 157(c)(1), (2) (West Supp.1987). Core proceedings on the other hand are treated no differently than matters referred to bankruptcy judges under the 1978 Act: the decision of the bankruptcy judge is reviewable by an Article III judge only by an appeal governed by the same rules applicable to appeals taken to the courts of appeals from the district courts. 28 U.S.C.A. §§ 157(b)(1), 158(a), (c) (West Supp.1987). Thus, because Congress has deemed an action by the trustee to set aside fraudulent conveyances as a "core proceeding," 28 U.S.C.A. § 157(b)(2) (H) (West Supp.1987), the role of the bankruptcy judge in adjudicating the claim at issue here is essentially the same as it would have been under the 1978 Act.

The analysis in *Northern Pipeline* with respect to the adjunct court doctrine finds expression in the portion of the 1984 Act concerning the appointment of the bankruptcy judges. Under the 1978 Act the bankruptcy judges were appointed by the President, with the advice and consent of the Senate, while under the 1978 Act the bankruptcy judges are appointed by the appropriate court of appeals upon recommendation of the Judicial Conference. 28 U.S.C.A. § 152(a) (West Supp.1987). As noted by the plurality in *Northern Pipeline*, in *Raddatz* the Supreme Court found that referral of pre-trial motions to magistrates under the Magistrates Act of 1978 was constitutional in part because the magistrates were appointed under the Magistrates Act by Article III judges.

B. *Analysis*

There are several distinctions between this case and *Northern Pipeline* which are relevant to the consideration of whether the bankruptcy jurisdiction at issue in this case comes within either the public rights or adjunct court doctrines described in *Northern Pipeline*. One, this case arises under a different statutory scheme [than] that which was in effect at the time of *Northern Pipeline*. This is obviously a relevant distinction because, as discussed above, Congress enacted the present statutory scheme for the specific purpose of curing the constitutional problems of the scheme under which *Northern Pipeline* arose. Perhaps more importantly however, the nature of the claim at issue here is significantly different from the nature of the claim at issue in *Northern Pipeline*. The claim at issue here has been deemed by Congress to involve "core" issues concerning the restructuring of debtor-creditor relations while the claim at issue in *Northern Pipeline* was in the bankruptcy court merely because it was "related to" a case arising under Title 11. In addition, while it is state law that provides the rule of decision in both this case and *Northern Pipeline*, as will be discussed in greater detail below, the claim in this case has a relation to federal law which the claim at issue in *Northern Pipeline* did not have.

Despite the distinctions between this case and *Northern Pipeline*, *Northern Pipeline* unquestionably provides an important frame of reference for determining whether the manner prescribed by Congress for adjudicating the bankruptcy proceeding at issue here is acceptable under Article III. However, in determining the constitutional significance of the distinctions between this case and *Northern Pipeline*, we need not decide if this case neatly falls within the *Northern Pipeline* plurality's definitions of either the public rights or the adjunct court doctrines. Although the plurality in *Northern Pipeline* gave separate and alternative application to the public rights doctrine and the adjunct court doctrine when determining whether the bankruptcy jurisdiction there at issue violated Article III, this categorical approach to applying Article III doctrines did not then and does not now command the support of a majority of the Justices. See Northern Pipeline, 458 U.S. at 91, 102 S.Ct. at 2882 (Rehnquist, J., concurring) ("[It is not necessary to] decide whether these cases in fact support a general proposition and three tidy exceptions, as the plurality believes. . . ."); see also Thomas v. Union Carbide Agricultural Products Co., 473 U.S. 568, 584–586, 105 S.Ct. 3325, 3335–36, 87 L.Ed.2d 409 (1985). As the Supreme Court has noted, "practical attention to substance rather than doctrinaire reliance on formal categories should inform application of Article III." Thomas v. Union Carbide Agricultural Products Co., 473 U.S. at 586–587, 105 S.Ct. at 3336. Accordingly, in determining the amount of judicial involvement required by Article III in this case, our primary concern is not mechanical application of the public rights or adjunct court doctrines, but is rather the determination of whether the rationales underlying those doctrines are applicable in this case to a sufficient degree to satisfy Article III.

Munn argues that the power to set aside fraudulent conveyances is not at the core of the federal bankruptcy power in that *Northern Pipeline* "establishes that actions to bring property into the estate are not . . . integral to the restructuring of debtor-creditor relations." However, Munn's characterizations of the holding of *Northern Pipeline* and the trustee's suit are misleading. It is true that the trustee is, like the debtor in *Northern Pipeline,* seeking to bring property into the estate. However, the trustee here, unlike the debtor in *Northern Pipeline,* is acting pursuant to his duty under federal bankruptcy law to gather property into the estate on the behalf of creditors of the debtor to facilitate the restructuring of creditor-debtor relations. The suit at issue in *Northern Pipeline* on the other hand was not inherently connected to the debtor's bankruptcy. That suit sought to gather assets into the estate; it did not do so on behalf of creditors nor did it seek to determine or adjust any of the debtor's relations with its creditors.[4] In short, the right at issue here, unlike the right at issue in *Northern Pipeline,* directly relates to the restructuring of debtor-creditor relations and is not merely an action to bring property into the estate. Munn fails to offer, and we do not see, any compelling reason why the congressional determination that this type of suit is a core proceeding should be upset.

Of course the fact that this suit has properly been designated as a core proceeding would not justify the bankruptcy court's jurisdiction over the matter if we were to find that, contrary to the suggestion of the plurality in *Northern Pipeline,* the restructuring of debtor-creditor relations is not a public right. As noted above, the public rights

---

4. Moreover, the contract suit in *Northern Pipeline* could have been brought whether or not the plaintiff was bankrupt. A fraudulent conveyance, though, can only exist if the conveyor is insolvent or about to become insolvent, and thus is inextrica-bly tied to the bankruptcy scheme. See In re Kaiser, 722 F.2d 1574, 1582 (2d Cir. 1983). If a conveyor enjoys good financial health, a conveyance cannot harm its creditors, who would thus have no cause of action to recover transfer.

doctrine, as construed by the *Northern Pipeline* plurality, is limited to matters arising "between the Government and persons subject to its authority in connection with the performance of the constitutional functions of the legislative or executive departments" and which "historically could have been determined by those departments." Northern Pipeline, 458 U.S. at 67–68, 102 S.Ct. at 2869–70, quoting Crowell v. Benson, 285 U.S. 22, 50, 52 S.Ct. 285, 292, 76 L.Ed. 598 (1932) and Ex parte Bakelite Corp., 279 U.S. 438, 458, 49 S.Ct. 411, 416, 73 L.Ed. 789 (1929).

While the Supreme Court now recognizes that the presence of the government as a party of record is not an absolute requirement of the public rights doctrine, Union Carbide, 473 U.S. at 586, 598, 105 S.Ct. at 3337 (majority and concurring opinions), the rights determined in connection with the granting of a discharge in bankruptcy do not fit easily within the *Northern Pipeline* plurality's definition of the public rights doctrine. The administration of a bankrupt's estate has never been committed exclusively to the legislative or executive branches and we would have great difficulty in concluding that it "could have been." Unlike such congressionally created benefits as radio station licenses, pilot licenses or certificates for common carriers, the grant of a discharge in bankruptcy directly alters and often abrogates pre-existing, legally cognizable property rights. It would be foreign to our constitutional system to allow the type of property rights ordinarily possessed by creditors to be determined exclusively by the legislative or executive branches of government. See International Union v. Keystone Consolidated Industries, 793 F.2d 810, 817 (7th Cir.), cert. denied, ___ U.S. ___, 107 S.Ct. 403, 93 L.Ed.2d 356 (1986) (employer's entitlement to waiver of ERISA funding requirements which would abrogate rights in collective bargaining agreement cannot be determined by non-Article III agency).

Nevertheless, we believe the rationale underlying the public rights doctrine has at least some applicability to the proceeding at issue here. The public rights doctrine in large part simply constitutionalizes the historical understanding of what need and need not be committed to Article III officers for determination. See Commodity Futures Trading Comm'n. v. Schor, ___ U.S. ___, 106 S.Ct. 3245, 3258, 3259, 92 L.Ed.2d 675 (1986) (Article III requirements more strictly applied where matters traditionally tried in Article III courts are at issue); In re Arnold Print Works, Inc., 815 F.2d 165, 169 (1st Cir.1987). While, as indicated above, it has always been understood that the property rights of creditors cannot be committed exclusively to the political branches for determination, by the same token it has always been understood that bankruptcy proceedings need not be solely determined by Article III officers. Arnold, 815 F.2d at 169. Given the historical understanding of how bankruptcy proceedings are to be determined, we find that adjudication of core bankruptcy proceedings requires less Article III supervision then does adjudication of claims merely "related to" a bankruptcy proceeding. Thus, the fact that Congress has properly designated the claim at issue here as a core proceeding militates in favor of upholding the manner Congress has prescribed for the adjudication of the claim.

We also find that the first principle inferred by the *Northern Pipeline* plurality from *Crowell*—that Congress has greater discretion in prescribing the manner in which a right of its own creation is determined than it has with respect to rights not of its own making—has application in this case. As related above, in *Northern Pipeline* the plurality found that this principle was not applicable in the case before it because the claim at issue arose from state law. Insofar as the claim at issue here undeniably implicates state law, it is arguable that in this case we too should conclude that a principle concerning determination of congressionally created rights is inapplicable. However, for the reasons set forth below, we believe that the relation the claim at issue here has to federal law is sufficient to entitle Congress to greater discretion in determining how the claim is to be adjudicated than it is allowed with respect to a purely state claim.

Ordinarily of course, creditors' rights, like the creditor's right at issue here, arise from state law. However, the power of the states to create creditors' rights is subordinate to the power of Congress, conferred by Article I, § 8, clause 4 of the Constitution, to establish uniform bankruptcy laws. Congress can, and often has, exercised its bankruptcy power to modify, or even abrogate, creditors' rights in the independent federal interest of providing an equitable restructuring or liquidation of a bankrupt's estate. This case involves an instance in which Congress has exercised its bankruptcy power by assuming control of the private, state-created right of creditors to set aside a fraudulent conveyance and vesting that right in the trustee. Thus, even though the right here initially arises from state law, because it pertains to a debtor under the protection of the federal bankruptcy laws, the right is as dependent for its existence on federal law as it is on state law. Indeed the right that is at issue here belongs to the trustee pursuant to federal law, not to a specific creditor under state law.

It is nonetheless arguable that the fact that a creditor's right is subject to the federal bankruptcy power does not mean that that right is actually created by Congress. However, even if this were true, it would not dissuade us from concluding that Congress should have greater discretion in determining the manner of adjudication of the right at issue here than it would have of a purely state based claim. When determining whether a right is of state or federal origin where the issue is if the right must be adjudicated by an Article III judge, the crucial consideration is not which sovereign created the right, but rather whether Congress utilized the right for federal purposes. Where, as was the case in *Northern Pipeline,* Congress authorizes a federal officer to determine a state right which is not directly related to a federal constitutional concern, federalism concerns give rise to the need, arguably recognized in *Northern Pipeline,* to ensure that the state right is adjudicated in accord with the policies the state sought to effectuate in creating the right. See Geras v. Lafayette Display Fixtures, Inc., 742 F.2d 1037, 1052 (7th Cir.1984) (dissenting opinion); but see Commodity Futures Trading Comm'n. v. Schor, ___ U.S. ___, 106 S.Ct. 3245, 3261, 92 L.Ed.2d 675 (1986). When, on the other hand, Congress utilizes state law for federal purposes, the paramount concern is federal, not state, policy, even though Congress has chosen state law as a guideline for effectuating federal policy. As a consequence, when Congress utilizes a state law right for the purpose of effectuating federal policy, there is no reason why it should not be allowed at least some of the additional discretion in determining the manner in which the right is adjudicated that it is allowed with respect to "purely" federal rights.

Here it is clear that Congress conferred the right on the trustee to set aside conveyances which could be set aside under state law for the purpose of restructuring debtor-creditor relations pursuant to the federal bankruptcy power.[5] While the rule of decision is supplied by state law, the concern in applying the rule is to effectuate the policy of federal bankruptcy law. The fact that Congress has chosen to look to state law in defining the trustee's rights does not markedly lessen Congress' discretion in determining how those rights are determined.

Finally, we find it relevant that this case arises under a scheme in which the non-Article III decision-maker is appointed by Article III judges whereas *Northern Pipeline* arose under a scheme in which the non-Article III decision maker was appointed by the President. The purpose of the lifetime tenure/no salary diminution requirement of Article III is in part to ensure that federal judges are independent of political pressure from the other branches of government. Where the non-Article III officer is appointed by Article III judges, there is less threat that exercise of "judicial power" will be unduly influenced by the executive or legislative branches. Northern Pipeline Construction Co. v. Marathon Pipe Line Co., 458 U.S. 50, 79 n. 30, 102 S.Ct. 2858, 2875 n. 30, 73 L.Ed.2d 598 (1982) (plurality opinion); Pacemaker Diagnostic Clinic of America v. Instromedix, 725 F.2d 537, 543 (9th Cir.), cert. denied, 469 U.S. 824, 105 S.Ct. 100, 83 L.Ed.2d 45 (1984).

Viewing together all the factors present in this case relevant to the determination of what Article III requires, we are satisfied that the manner prescribed by Congress for adjudication of the right at issue here does not violate Article III. Congress has found, and we agree, that this proceeding falls within the core of the federal bankruptcy power. We are not inclined to upset the historically-based presumption that Con-

---

5. It is noteworthy that there is evidence that Congress utilized state law in the 1984 Act with the understanding that it was not preserving state rights but was rather expounding federal rights. "State law rights arising in core bankruptcy proceedings are functionally equivalent to congressionally created rights, because Congress has the power to modify State law rights in bankruptcy proceedings. . . . Indeed, the very purpose of bankruptcy is to modify the rights of the debtors and creditors, and the bankruptcy code authorizes the bankruptcy court to abrogate or modify State-created rights in many ways." 130 Cong.Rec. H1110 (daily ed. March 20, 1984) (statement of Rep. Kastenmeier).

gress has substantial discretion in determining how core bankruptcy proceedings are to be adjudicated. The fact that the rule of decision in this case is provided by state law does not take away from the fact that this proceeding relates directly to the restructuring of the relationships between a debtor and its creditors which is at the core of the federal bankruptcy power. We also believe that although the right at issue here derives from state law, Congress has utilized the right to effectuate federal policy and that therefore Congress should be allowed some of the additional discretion in determining the manner in which the right is determined that it is allowed with respect to purely federal rights. Finally, we find it significant that Congress has provided for a substantial degree of separation of power by placing control over the employment of bankruptcy judges exclusively in the hands of Article III judges. The provision concerning the appointment of the bankruptcy judges ensures compliance with Article III to the extent that the right at issue here might not be considered a congressionally created public right.

C. *Conclusion*

The jurisdiction of the bankruptcy court pursuant to 28 U.S.C. § 157(b) does not in this case violate Article III. Accordingly, the order of the district court reversing the bankruptcy court's order of dismissal is Affirmed and this case is Remanded to the bankruptcy court for further proceedings.

Notes & Questions

1. *Purer State Law Claim.* Suppose state fraudulent conveyance law had provisions that allowed attacks on transfers that could not be made under Bankruptcy Act § 548. Would a trustee's action relying on state law and § 544(b) be a core proceeding? Could it constitutionally be treated as one?

Suppose a Chapter 11 debtor brings a state law contract claim against a defendant seeking money that the defendant allegedly owed the debtor before the debtor went bankrupt? May the contract law claim be heard by the bankruptcy court as a core proceeding? See In re Arnold Print Works, Inc., 815 F.2d 165 (1st Cir.1987) (part of effort to liquidate assets is core proceeding).

2. *Difference Between Appellate and De Novo Review.* As a practical matter, is it likely to make a difference whether a proceeding is a core proceeding or not a core proceeding? Will district judges handle appeals from bankruptcy court decisions in core proceedings substantially differently than how they handle the partial *de novo* review mandated in the case of noncore proceedings?

3. *Withdrawal Mechanism of § 157(d).* Delay often is a useful tactic in bankruptcy (and other) proceedings. Consider possible stalling tactics in light of § 157(d). May a debtor repeatedly request withdrawal of adversary proceedings to the district court and litigate the propriety of the withdrawal?

May the defendants in *Mankin* now move in district court for an order of withdrawal? What should count as "cause shown" for such an order within the meaning of § 157(d)? How should the district court's response to such a motion be influenced by the bankruptcy court's determination that these are core proceedings?

Mandatory Withdrawal of Interstate Commerce Cases. Under the second sentence of § 157(d), the district court must withdraw proceedings that require consideration of both the Bankruptcy Act and "other laws of the United States regulating organizations or activities affecting interstate commerce."

4. *Bring Back the Good Old Days?* We have returned to a bifurcated system, but one arguably more complex than any that preceded the 1978 Act. The distinction is no longer between plenary and summary jurisdiction. There are instead two separate distinctions. One divides the world of cases into those in which the district court should abstain and those in which it should not. The other relevant distinction is between "core proceedings" and other proceedings. Do §§ 1334 and 157(b) contain sufficiently detailed guidance to foreclose most litigation over whether a district court should hear a case and, if so, how much of the case should be referred to the bankruptcy court?

5. *Northern Pipeline and Delegation to Bankruptcy Judges.* Suppose bankruptcy judges and litigants routinely leave all matters pertaining to bankruptcy cases to bankruptcy judges. Does the actual manner in which the bankruptcy courts operate affect the *Raddatz* - like branch of *Northern Pipeline?* What options does *Northern Pipeline* leave open to Congress in designing the bankruptcy system?

Note on the United States Trustee System

The provisions at issue in *Northern Pipeline* were enacted out of concern over the cumbersome jurisdictional structure of the old bankruptcy act. There also was concern over perceptions about the basic fairness of the system. Under prior bankruptcy law, the bankruptcy judge or referee often served both as administrator of a case and adjudicator of disputes that arose during the case.

A more substantial factor relates to the effect of the referee's involvement in administering an estate on his ability to act judicially in resolving any controversies which arise. . . . After a referee has read the debtor's petition, schedules, and statement of affairs, and has examined him and others at the first meeting of creditors, it is obviously difficult to resolve questions arising in a proceeding to determine whether the debtor ought to be discharged or even whether a particular debt is dischargeable, without being influenced by information and impressions gained during his previous contact with the debtor and the papers in the case. When the referee has appointed, or approved the appointment of, a trustee to take charge of the property of the estate, has supervised and perhaps instructed the trustee in the performance of his duties, and has approved the trustee's choice of counsel and the initiation of an action, the referee may not appear to the trustee's adversary as one fitting the model of judicial objectivity. The problem is aggravated in metropolitan centers where there is sufficient concentration of bankruptcy business for a specialized bankruptcy bar to develop. Members of the specialized bar are a valuable source of knowledgeable and capable trustees on whom the referee is able to draw when creditors do not elect a trustee. The involvement of the referee in the administration of estates entails numerous conferences and communications that are informal and *ex parte*. The responsibility resting on a conscientious referee under the present Act is thus conducive to the development of what appears to attorneys who are not included among the specialists, to their clients, and to the public generally, as an unseemly and continuing relationship between the referee and the members of the specialist bar. He is thus vulnerable to being linked by imputation to the so-called "bankruptcy ring," which is the opprobrious label frequently given to the specialized bankruptcy bar in a community.

Without undertaking to determine whether the criticisms of referees for permitting their relationships with the bankruptcy bar to become too close are justified, the Commission believes that making an individual responsible for conduct of both administrative and judicial aspects of a bankruptcy case is incompatible with the proper performance of the judicial function. Even if a paragon of integrity were sitting on the bench and could keep his mind and feelings insulated from influences which arise from his previous official connections with the case before him and with one of the parties to it, he probably could not dispel the appearance of a relationship which might compromise his judicial objectivity. The Commission accordingly recommends that the bankruptcy judges be removed from the administration of bankrupt estates and be restricted to the performance of essentially judicial functions, that is, primarily to the resolution of disputes or issues involving adversary parties and matters appropriate for judicial determination.

Commission Report, pt. I, at 93–94. In response to this problem, Congress enacted a new supplementary system of bankruptcy administration. Under the new system the Attorney General appoints a United States trustee for each region, and one or more assistant United States trustees for a region when the public interest so requires. 28 U.S.C. §§ 581(a), 582. These federal officials appoint trustees for bankruptcy cases, appoint creditors' committees, serve as trustees, monitor and comment on plans filed under Chapters 11, 12, and 13, and generally relieve judges of the burden of appointing persons who may later be litigating before them. 28 U.S.C. § 586.[c]

c. In the 1978 act Congress enacted a five-year pilot United States trustee program in selected districts. 11 U.S.C.A. § 1501 (now repealed). The 1984 amendments extended the program to September 1986, and the 1986 amendments made the program permanent and applicable to all districts.

3. The Special Case of Personal Injury Claims

In re WHITE MOTOR CREDIT; CITIBANK, N.A. v. WHITE MOTOR CORPORATION

United States Court of Appeals, 6th Circuit, 1985.
761 F.2d 270.

Before MERRITT and KENNEDY, CIRCUIT JUDGES, and PRATT, DISTRICT JUDGE.

MERRITT, CIRCUIT JUDGE.

In this large Chapter 11 reorganization proceeding, the procedural history of which we have described in more detail in earlier opinions, see White Motor Corporation v. Citibank, 704 F.2d 254 (6th Cir.1983), approximately 160 separate, unliquidated and contingent products liability personal injury cases have been filed in various state and federal courts against the debtor, White Motor Corp., a truck manufacturer. The issues before us now relate to the procedures that should be followed in liquidating the contingent tort claims filed in this Chapter 11 proceeding in light of congressional enactment of the Bankruptcy Amendments and Federal Judgeship Act of 1984, Pub.L. No. 98–353, 98 Stat. 333 (1984).

In an earlier opinion dealing in part with these tort cases, White Motor, supra, an opinion published prior to the adoption of the 1984 Bankruptcy Act, we instructed the District Court under the law at that time that the unliquidated tort claims could be liquidated by trial in the District Court or in the Bankruptcy Court or before a Special Master or "in the courts where they were pending initially." Id. at 265. After a hearing in which these four alternatives were considered, the District Court ordered that the claims should be individually liquidated through adjudication in the various state and federal courts in which they are pending. The claims, once liquidated, are to be paid from insurance and a reserve compensation fund established by the plan of arrangement confirmed by the Bankruptcy Court.

The principal issue before us arises from the debtor White Motor's contention on appeal that section 104(a) of the 1984 Act, 28 U.S.C. § 157(b)(5), prevents the District Court from leaving these tort cases in other courts for adjudication. Section 157(b)(5) says that "personal injury tort and wrongful death claims shall be tried in the district court in which the bankruptcy case is pending, or in the district court in which the claim arose, as determined by the district court in which the bankruptcy case in pending."

When read in isolation, section 157(b)(5) seems to support the debtor's contention that the tort claims may not be liquidated in other courts, as the District Court has ordered; but a reading of the entire law in light of its purpose and history leads to the opposite conclusion.

The new Act has a number of conflicting provisions and is confusing to say the least. It divides bankruptcy matters into "cases," "proceedings arising under" bankruptcy, "proceedings arising in" bankruptcy, "proceedings related to" bankruptcy and "core proceedings." No category of cases other than "core proceedings" is defined in any way, and there is no House or Senate report of any kind and no conference report.

There are five sets of sections in the new legislation relating to the subject of "abstention" or the reference of claims and cases brought by or against the debtor to other courts for liquidation through adjudication:

1. The first mention of abstention is in 28 U.S.C. § 1334(c)(1). Section 1334(c)(1), which authorizes reference to other courts in the discretion of the district court having jurisdiction over a bankruptcy case of all "proceedings arising under," "arising in" or "related to" bankruptcy.[1]

2. The second pertinent section, 28 U.S.C. § 1334(c)(2), makes it mandatory for the court to abstain in "causes of action" which are "related to" but do not "arise under" or "arise in" bankruptcy if the action in question could not have been brought in the federal court in the absence of bankruptcy jurisdiction, and if a state court can "timely adjudicate" the case. But personal injury cases are not subject to this mandatory abstention provision. 28 U.S.C. §§ 157(b)(2) and (4), defining the so-called core proceedings, which may be heard by bankruptcy judges, say that although "personal injury tort" and "wrongful death" claims are "non-core" proceedings outside the jurisdiction of bankruptcy judges, such cases "shall not be subject to the mandatory abstention provisions of section 1334(c)(2)." No provision of the new law speaks to the issue of whether such tort cases are subject to the discretionary abstention provisions of 28 U.S.C. § 1334(c)(1).

3. 28 U.S.C. § 157(b)(5) is quoted above.

4. 28 U.S.C. § 1411(a) provides that in a "personal injury or wrongful death tort claim" the bankruptcy laws do not affect any rights to trial by jury that an individual has under applicable non-bankruptcy law.

5. Section 122 of the 1984 Bankruptcy Act, Pub.L. No. 98–353, § 102, 98 Stat. 333, 346 (1984), makes all the provisions of the 1984 Bankruptcy Act applicable to pending cases, except the mandatory abstention provision and the jury trial provision for tort cases.

The apparent conflict between sections 157(b)(5) and 1334(c)(1) of title 28—the first of which requires tort cases to be tried in federal courts and the second of which allows them to be referred to the courts in which they are pending—came out of the Conference Committee as a compromise after the House and the Senate passed differing bankruptcy bills. The only specific explanation of these compromise provisions

1. 28 U.S.C. § 1334(c)(1) provides in full:

Nothing in this section prevents a district court in the interest of justice, or in the interest of comity with State courts or respect for State law, from abstaining from hearing a particular proceeding arising under title 11 or arising in or related to a case under title 11.

is found in the remarks by one of the conferees, Senator Dole, in the Senate debate on the Conference report prior to its adoption by the Senate:

> As most of my colleagues are aware, the Senate conferees dif-
> fered over whether to retain the abstention language found in the
> original Senate bill. The majority of the Senate conferees—this
> Senator included—felt that the Senate language was too broad, in
> that it prohibited the Bankruptcy Courts or the district courts from
> considering any case that was based upon a State law claim.
> Mandatory abstention in favor of State courts in those cases was
> required. The House provision on abstention was, however, limited
> to Marathon type proceedings and the party seeking abstention
> would have been required to show that the cause could be timely
> adjudicated in the State courts before abstention would have been
> required. The Senate conferees reached a fair compromise on this
> issue. The result of the Conference discussion was a provision that
> preserved the integrity of bankruptcy jurisdiction while allowing
> abstention for personal injury cases where they can be timely
> adjudicated in State courts. In addition, where abstention does not
> occur, those cases will be handled by the district court where
> bankruptcy has been filed or, if that court finds it appropriate,
> where the claim arose. 130 Cong.Rec. S8889 (daily ed. June 29,
> 1984)

Although able counsel for the parties did not bring to our attention or in any way refer to the last two sentences of Senator Dole's remarks, we believe they are significant. In his view, the Act "allows abstention for personal injury cases" and only "where abstention does not occur" will the requirement for adjudication in a district court take effect. These two sentences indicate clearly that the conferees contemplated that in liquidating tort cases in bankruptcy, the district court would first decide whether it should leave the cases with respect to which claims have been filed in the bankruptcy court in the courts in which they are pending and then, if it decides against this course, the district court must try the cases itself or send them to the federal court for the district in which they arose. These sentences from Senator Dole's remarks, plus the fact that section 157(b)(4) of title 28 removes tort cases from mandatory abstention under section 1334(c)(2) but does not remove discretionary abstention under section 1334(c)(1), convinces us that the district court has the authority to leave tort cases in the courts in which they are pending for liquidation there.

The debtor has pointed to no persuasive reason in principle or policy which argues against this construction. For many years, under both the Bankruptcy Act of 1898 and the Bankruptcy Act of 1978, the Bankruptcy Courts have had the authority to lift the automatic stay in such tort cases, as in other cases, and let the cases go forward in their home courts. Our construction works no change in traditional bank-ruptcy principles. It allows the court to leave the liquidation of individual claims to other courts without undermining complete relief of the debtor.

The statute authorizes abstention in the interest of justice or comity. These requirements are more than adequately met in the circumstances. Since there are other defendants in many of the tort cases against White Motor—defendants who cannot be transferred out of the jurisdiction they are now in—the cases will have to be tried twice in different courts if the district court decides to liquidate the individual cases. This is a strong reason for leaving the cases where they are.

In addition, plaintiffs and defendants might be faced with inconsistent rulings and verdicts and multiple res judicata problems. Moreover, United Mine Workers v. Gibbs, 383 U.S. 715 (1966), a pendent jurisdiction case which discusses somewhat similar issues concerning the exercise of federal jurisdiction, emphasizes that federal courts should be hesitant to exercise jurisdiction when "state issues substantially predominate, whether in terms of proof, of the scope of the issues raised, or of the comprehensiveness of the remedy sought." 383 U.S. at 726. In these products liability cases, state issues clearly predominate.

Finally, in large bankruptcy cases with hundreds or even thousands of tort litigants beating on the door of one federal judge, judicial health and survival, or at least judicial economy and expeditiousness, may depend on the court's authority to refer cases to other courts. Since the 1984 Bankruptcy Act prevents reference of these tort cases to bankruptcy courts, as in the past, it makes good sense to give the district courts wide latitude in referring the cases through abstention to other courts. Accordingly, this aspect of the judgment of the District Court below is affirmed. Since these cases are to be tried in the courts in which they are now pending, they will be tried according to the forms, procedures and rights of that jurisdiction including forms, procedures and rights respecting trial by jury.

White argues that even if the Bankruptcy Court may abstain and permit state courts to liquidate contingent disputed tort personal injury and death claims, it may not do so after a plan of reorganization is approved, which triggers the permanent statutory injunction of section 524(a) and the discharge of debts that arose before the date of confirmation by reason of section 1141(d)(1)(A)(i). Unlike section 362(a), which expressly provides that the automatic stay of pending cases may be lifted to permit such cases to proceed, section 524(a) is silent as to any exception. However, a modification or temporary lifting of the permanent injunction is necessary for consummation of the plan. Sections 1141–1143 give the court broad powers to consummate the plan. Section 524 must be read in conjunction with the overall purposes of the Code. Congress must have contemplated that plans would be confirmed before all contingent claims can be liquidated in various courts.

The District Court appears to have contemplated that to the extent the liquidated claims are covered by insurance, they could be paid as each one is liquidated. Since the insurance companies are not parties to this proceeding, the District Court's authority is limited to permitting the claimants to proceed against the insurance companies without waiting to find out what percentage they will be able to claim from the reserve fund, which can only be determined after all claims are liquidated. Were it not for the fact that all parties are in agreement that the insurance coverage is adequate to cover all filed claims, it would be necessary to liquidate all claims before any insurance money was paid out; otherwise, some claimants would receive an unequal portion of the insurance assets of the debtor. . . .

Permissive abstention requires the reorganization court in exercising its discretion to maintain ongoing supervision over these state court cases to ensure that disposition of no claim is unduly delayed because of the forum in which it is pending. Wholesale abstention as to all claims as a class could otherwise constitute an abuse of discretion, since it would not satisfy the "interests of justice" criterion of the statute.

The judgment of the District Court on the abstention issues is affirmed. The case is remanded to the District Court for further proceedings consistent with this opinion. Each party will bear its own appellate costs.

Notes & Questions

1. *The Importance of Insurance.* In *White Motor,* there was insurance and a reserve compensation fund to pay the claims, once liquidated. Would it make sense to leave the cases in state court if there were no such fund? If there were doubts as to its sufficiency to cover all claims? How can there ever not be such doubts? In A.H. Robins Co., Inc. v. Piccinin, 788 F.2d 994 (4th Cir.1986), cert. denied ___ U.S. ___, 107 S.Ct. 251, 93 L.Ed.2d 177 (1986), the district court entered an order fixing the venue for the trial of personal injury tort claims against the debtor in the bankruptcy court, noting that nothing in *White Motor Credit* was inconsistent with such a result.

2. *Venue for Purposes of Estimation.* In *In re UNR Industries, Inc.,* 45 B.R. 322 (N.D.Ill.1984), the Official Creditor's Committee of Asbestos–Related Plaintiffs moved for an order allowing 17,000 asbestos claims to proceed to trial against the debtor. The court found that § 157(b)(5) requires that the claims be tried in district court. It then discussed the question of when the trials should begin:

III. MUST TRIALS BEGIN NOW?

The second, and crucial, question is when the trials commanded by § 157(b)(5) are to take place. In its reply brief the Committee argues § 157(b)(5) specifies that estimation of such claims are not core proceedings and therefore the bankruptcy court has no power to estimate those claims. Since those claims obviously *must* be estimated if the bankruptcy proceedings are to go forward, the Committee concludes that the trials mandated by § 157(b)(5) must have been meant to serve as the estimation method for those claims and therefore those trials should begin immediately.

In response, UNR points out that § 157(c)(1) allows the bankruptcy judge to in effect act as a magistrate for non-core proceedings. However, to conclude that § 157(c)(1) authorizes the bankruptcy judges to act as a magistrate with respect to these asbestos claims for all purposes would render § 157(b)(5) a nullity, which as already noted is a result to be avoided. Therefore, the Committee is correct that § 157(b)(5) must take effect at *some* point before final distribution of the asbestos claims.

In choosing the beginning of the estimation process as that point, however, the Committee has overlooked the express terms of § 157(b)(2)(B). That section does not exclude from the definition of core proceedings estimation of personal injury and wrongful death claims for *all* purposes, but only "for purposes of distribution." Estimation of such claims for other purposes, such as "confirming a plan" (§ 157(b)(2)(B)), apparently remains a core proceeding for the bankruptcy judge. It is therefore not necessary to order trials now so that these claims can be valued; the presently proceeding study by Towers, Perrin, Foster & Crosby can, in both the statutory and empirical senses, fulfill that function.

The Committee also offers several policy reasons why the trials should begin now. Estimating these asbestos claims would require at least a hearing, asserts the Committee, and therefore allowing the bankruptcy judge to estimate the claims will not be any more efficient than ordering district court trials. This contention both understates the time and expense of trials and overstates the time and expense of the estimation process. Even should Judge Toles decide the Towers study is insufficient to accurately estimate asbestos claims and that some sort of hearing is necessary, there is no reason to believe 17,000 hearings must be held to get an accurate enough picture of the debtor's liability to asbestos victims.

The Committee also argues that trials should begin now so that when distribution time comes these plaintiffs can collect their due immediately rather than waiting until a trial can be had and concluded. This Court is certainly sympathetic to the plight of asbestos victims, but is persuaded that ordering the parties to trial makes no sense until there is at least some indication of the debtor's financial health and some reason to believe that the time and expense of trials will not simply deplete the estate and leave these plaintiffs and the other creditors with empty judgments.

The Committee's final argument is that it would be unfair to allow the bankruptcy court to estimate these claims for purposes of developing a plan because that court may undervalue the claims "so that the trials to which such plaintiffs are entitled would serve only as a measure of their pro-rata share of a pie which is much too small." Committee's Reply Brief at 22. Contrary to the Committee's implication, this Court has the utmost confidence in the bankruptcy court's ability to accurately estimate the asbestos claims. Moreover, in this regard the asbestos claimants stand in the same position as any creditor with an unliquidated claim. Though problems of accuracy in estimation may be greater when personal injury and wrongful death claims are involved, nothing in the Act indicates such claims are to be treated differently from other unliquidated claims for purposes other than distribution.

In light of *UNR,* is there now a class of "quasi-core" proceedings, generated by certain tort (and perhaps other?) claims, in which the estimation of the claim is a core proceeding to be conducted in the bankruptcy court, and the adjudication of the claim is a non-core proceeding that must be tried in the district court? See also A.H. Robins Co., Inc., supra, 788 F.2d at 1012–13; In re Johns–Manville Corp., 45 B.R. 823, 825–26 (S.D.N.Y.1984).

What happens if the jury in the district court believes that the damages should exceed the amount estimated by the bankruptcy court?

3. *Timing of Commencement of an Action.* Does it matter in *UNR* whether an asbestos claimant had commenced a lawsuit prior to the filing of the debtor's bankruptcy petition? As to those claimants who had commenced suit, would the considerations that prevailed in *White Motor* apply to support remanding such claimants to their suspended state court tort actions?

4. *Proceeding in State Court and the Federal Concept of Claim.* Recall the question whether tort claims that have not manifested themselves by the date of bankruptcy should be treated as "claims" for bankruptcy purposes. Given *White Motor's* green light for state court adjudication of tort claims, how will such contingent claims be handled if, under state law, there was no cause of action on the date of the petition?

B. Removal, Transfer, Appeal

BEAULIEU v. AMATEX CORP.
United States Bankruptcy Court, District of Maine, 1983.
28 B.R. 171.

FREDERICK A. JOHNSON, BANKRUPTCY JUDGE.

This proceeding involves two consolidated asbestos civil actions, which were removed to this court from state court by a codefendant.

By complaint dated May 15, 1980, the plaintiff commenced an action in the Cumberland County Superior Court against Johns-Manville Sales Corporation and eleven other defendants. Beaulieu v. Amatex Corp., Civ. No. 80–612 (Cumb.Cty.Super.Ct.). By complaint dated July 23, 1980, the plaintiff commenced another action against Crane Packing Company and six other defendants. Beaulieu v. Anchor Packing Co., Civ. No. 80–866 (Cumb.Cty.Super.Ct.). The actions were consolidated by order of the Superior Court dated November 19, 1981.

The consolidated superior court actions are based upon the illness and ultimate death of Stephen A. Beaulieu, Jr., the plaintiff's husband. The plaintiff alleges that her husband's death was caused by his inhalation and/or ingestion of asbestos dust and fibres from products manufactured, fabricated, distributed, or supplied by the defendants, while he was employed at S.D. Warren Paper Company in Westbrook, Maine.

On July 29, 1982, Unarco Industries, Inc., one of the defendants in the consolidated actions, filed for relief under chapter 11 of the Bankruptcy Code in the northern district of Illinois. On August 26, 1982, Johns-Manville Sales Corporation, another defendant, filed for chapter 11 relief in the southern district of New York. On September 10, 1982, the Superior Court ordered a temporary stay of the consolidated actions.

On September 27, 1982, John Crane-Houdaille, Inc., also known as Crane Packing Company, a codefendant in one of the consolidated superior court actions, removed the actions to this court pursuant to 28 U.S.C.A. § 1478(a) (Supp.1982) [now § 1452]. On the same date, Crane moved, pursuant to 28 U.S.C.A. § 1475 (Supp.1982) [now § 1412], to transfer the proceeding to the Bankruptcy Court for the Southern District of New York. On October 27, 1982, the plaintiff, acting pursuant to 28 U.S.C.A. § [1452(b)], moved to remand the cases to the Cumberland County Superior Court.

After notice, hearings were held on both motions before this court. Meanwhile, a third codefendant, Amatex Corporation, also filed for chapter 11 relief in the Bankruptcy Court for the Eastern District of Pennsylvania.

The filing of chapter 11 petitions by Johns-Manville, Unarco, and Amatex created extremely difficult problems for the codefendants in this proceeding and in thousands of similar proceedings pending in various jurisdictions throughout the United States. The magnitude of the problem was clearly expressed by an officer of Johns-Manville:

> Johns-Manville Corporation and various [affiliates] were, as of June 30, 1982, defendants or co-defendants in approximately 11,000 asbestos health law suits brought by approximately 15,550 individual plaintiffs in numerous jurisdictions throughout the United States in which the plaintiffs alleged damage to their health particularly due to their exposure to asbestos fibre . . . .[1]

Crane argues that transfer of the proceeding to the Bankruptcy Court for the Southern District of New York is the only procedure that is fair to all parties. It argues that if the proceeding is remanded to state court and Johns-Manville is severed from the proceeding, it may be forced to pay the entire amount of any judgment recovered by the plaintiff and will then have to file its claim for contribution or indemni-

1. Affidavit under Local Rule XI-2, In re Johns-Manville Corp., No. 82–B. 11656 (Bankr.S.D.N.Y. filed Aug. 26, 1982).

ty in the New York bankruptcy court. It argues that this is unfair and
will waste time, money, and human resources. The plaintiff, on the
other hand, urges that the proceeding be remanded to state court so
that she may be afforded her day in court.

The court concludes that the proceeding must be remanded to the
Cumberland County Superior Court.

The issue is whether this proceeding should be remanded to state
court "on any equitable ground," as provided for by section [1452(b)],[3] or
whether it should be transferred to the Bankruptcy Court for the
Southern District of New York "in the interest of justice [or] for the
convenience of the parties" as provided for by section [1412].[4]

THE MOTION TO TRANSFER

Because section [1412] contains a more familiar test, we will deal
with it first. This section of title 28 is derived from Bankruptcy Rules
116 and 782.[5] H.R.Rep. No. 595, 95th Cong., 1st Sess. 447, reprinted in
1978 U.S.Code Cong. & Ad.News 5787, 5963, 6403. The relevant
language of section [1412] is nearly identical to Rule 782.[6] Cases
interpreting that rule and 28 U.S.C.A. § 1404(a) (1976)[7] are useful in
interpreting the section.

It is not possible to catalogue the circumstances which will justify or
require either the grant or denial of transfer. Gulf Oil Corp. v. Gilbert,
330 U.S. 501, 67 S.Ct. 839, 91 L.Ed. 1055 (1947). The cases decided
under Rule 782 and section 1404(a), however, suggest many factors to
be considered: (1) plaintiff's choice of forum; (2) relative ease of access
to proof; (3) availability of compulsory process for attendance of unwilling witnesses; (4) cost of obtaining attendance of willing witnesses; (5)
practical matters which may tend to expedite the proceeding with
maximum ease and minimum expense; (6) responsibilities and difficulties of court administration; (7) desirability of a determination of local
law by local courts; (8) residence of potential witnesses; (9) location of
documents and records; (10) place where challenged conduct occurred;
(11) related actions; (12) relative condition of court calendars; (13)

possibility of a view of the premises if appropriate; and (14) factors of public interest. Several of the above factors, of course, are not of critical importance to this proceeding. We will discuss those factors that are important.

The plaintiff's choice of forum is an important factor. The United States Supreme Court has stated that "unless the balance is strongly in favor of the defendant, the plaintiff's choice of forum should rarely be disturbed." Gulf Oil Corp., 330 U.S. at 508, 67 S.Ct. at 843.

The relative ease of access to proof is another factor which weighs in the plaintiff's favor here. The plaintiff's deceased husband was born, worked, lived his life, became ill, and died in the local area. His medical records, employment records, and other vital records are here, together with most of the witnesses who may be needed to verify and interpret them.

The expense of obtaining attendance of plaintiff's witnesses and the inconvenience to them will obviously be less if the proceeding is tried in the local area. The plaintiff's witnesses reside in Maine. Most of Crane's witnesses are company officials and experts and there is no demonstrable evidence that it would be less convenient or more costly to have them attend trial in Maine rather than in New York.

Of critical importance is the fact that the alleged wrongful conduct occurred while Mr. Beaulieu was employed with S.D. Warren Paper Company in Westbrook, Maine. Finally, the plaintiff's cause of action is based upon Maine statutes and should be tried in a Maine court. In fact, nearly all of the factors which have been considered by courts in considering transfer motions favor denial of Crane's motion to transfer.

The court is not unmindful of the dilemma faced by Crane and the other codefendants in this proceeding. Most of Crane's arguments focus upon the hardship and injustice imposed upon it and the other non-debtor codefendants by Johns-Manville's filing for relief in bankruptcy court. It falls short, however, of demonstrating how transfer of the case to the Bankruptcy Court for the Southern District of New York will solve the dilemma, or to phrase it in the words of section 1475, of demonstrating that such transfer is in "the interest of justice and for the convenience of the parties." While it may be true that the Bankruptcy Court for the Southern District of New York is the "only court with unquestionable jurisdiction over all the parties," as Crane asserts,[9] it does not necessarily follow that transfer of this proceeding (and perhaps thousands like it) will assist Judge Lifland [10] in devising a remedy to accommodate all of the competing interests, as Crane suggests, and certainly not in time to prevent an injustice to this and other plaintiffs who are entitled to their day in court. Judge Lifland, in a recent decision, refused to broaden the automatic stay of 11 U.S.C.A.

9. It should be observed that two of Crane's codefendants, Unarco and Amatex, have filed chapter 11 petitions in the northern district of Illinois and the eastern district of Pennsylvania, respectively.

10. Burton R. Lifland is the bankruptcy judge who is handling the Johns-Manville chapter 11 case in the southern district of New York.

§ 362(a) (1979) to include nondebtor codefendants, such as Crane, in pending asbestos litigation throughout the country. GAF Corp. v. Johns-Manville Corp. (In re Johns-Manville Corp.), 26 B.R. 405, 9 B.C.D. 1403 (Bkrtcy.S.D.N.Y.1983). In that proceeding, Judge Lifland rejected many of the arguments made by Crane here, as does this court.

The interest of justice requires that this plaintiff have her day in court; the proceeding has been pending for nearly three years; much discovery has been completed under the aegis of the Superior Court; and many of the plaintiff's witnesses are co-workers of her deceased husband who may become unavailable to testify. While the court recognizes the hardships Crane faces, upon balance, the expense, inconvenience, and delay which would inevitably occur if the proceeding were transferred would impose a far greater hardship on this plaintiff.

The motion to transfer must be denied.

THE MOTION TO REMAND

For the reasons stated above, and for the further reason that the Cumberland County Superior Court is better able to respond to this proceeding, which involves three state statutes, 1 Collier on Bankruptcy ¶ 3.01[f[iii] (L. King 15th ed. 1982), the proceeding should be remanded to that court.

Crane argues that this court should transfer the proceeding to the Bankruptcy Court for the Southern District of New York and that Judge Lifland should rule on the plaintiff's motion to remand. It is sufficient to point out that section [1452(b)] requires that this court, "to which such claim or cause of action is removed," act on plaintiff's motion.

This court makes no finding on the issue of whether Johns-Manville, Unarco, or Amatex are indispensible parties within the meaning and intent of Rule 19(b) of the Maine Rules of Civil Procedure, Bankruptcy Rule 719(c), or Rule 19(b) of the Federal Rules of Civil Procedure. That is an issue for the state court after remand.

This proceeding is a related proceeding as defined by Local Rule 41(d)(3).[11] These findings and conclusions, together with a proposed order, will be submitted to the United States District Judge pursuant to subsection (d)(3)(B) of the Rule for his review as required by subsection (e)(2).

ON MOTION TO TRANSFER

GIGNOUX, CHIEF JUDGE.

The motion of John Crane, Houdaille, Inc. (a/k/a Crane Packing Company) to transfer this proceeding to the Bankruptcy Court for the

---

11. The emergency rule, adopted pursuant to a resolution of the Judicial Conference, to "permit the bankruptcy system to continue without disruption . . .," effective December 25, 1982.

Southern District of New York was heard, after notice by Frederick A. Johnson, Bankruptcy Judge, and a decision having been rendered,

It is Ordered that the motion to transfer is Denied.

ON MOTION TO REMAND

The plaintiff's motion to remand this proceeding to the Cumberland County Superior Court was heard, after notice, by Frederick A. Johnson, Bankruptcy Judge, and a decision having been duly rendered,

It is Ordered that the plaintiff's motion is Granted and that the proceeding be remanded to the Cumberland County Superior Court from which it was removed.

It is further Ordered that the clerk of this court mail a certified copy of this order of remand, by certified mail, to the clerk of the Cumberland County Superior Court and that court may thereupon proceed with the proceeding. Local Bankruptcy Rule 7005(j).

Notes & Questions

1. *Who Should Be Able to Remove?* Note that § 1452(a) authorizes a "party" to remove a case from state court to federal court. Should a plaintiff be entitled to removal? Under what circumstances might a plaintiff seek removal?

In evaluating a request for remand under § 1452(b), what factors should a federal court take into account? Should it be governed by the same factors that influence a district court in cases removed under 28 U.S.C.A. § 1441?[e]

2. *Interdistrict Transfers.* In evaluating a § 1412 request to transfer a case from one district court to another district court, what factors should a court take into account? Should it be governed by the same factors that courts consider in evaluating transfer motions under 28 U.S.C.A. § 1404?

Would it make sense for the court in *Beaulieu* to allow removal of the civil action from state court to the Maine bankruptcy court and to deny transfer of the action from the Maine bankruptcy court to a

---

e. Section 1441 states in part:

(a) Except as otherwise expressly provided by Act of Congress, any civil action brought in a State court of which the district courts of the United States have original jurisdiction, may be removed by the defendant or the defendants, to the district court of the United States for the district and division embracing the place where such action is pending.

(b) Any civil action of which the district courts have original jurisdiction founded on a claim or right arising under the Constitution, treaties or laws of the United States shall be removable without regard to the citizenship or resi-

dence of the parties. Any other such action shall be removable only if none of the parties in interest properly joined and served as defendants is a citizen of the State in which such action is brought.

(c) Whenever a separate and independent claim or cause of action, which would be removable if sued upon alone, is joined with one or more otherwise non-removable claims or causes of action, the entire case may be removed and the district court may determine all issues therein, or, in its discretion, may remand all matters not otherwise within its original jurisdiction.

bankruptcy court in which a defendant's bankruptcy proceeding was pending?

Note on Appeals in Bankruptcy Cases

The district courts have jurisdiction to hear appeals from bankruptcy judges in cases referred under section 157. 28 U.S.C.A. § 158(a). If the district judges approve, the judicial council of a circuit may establish bankruptcy appellate panels, consisting of three bankruptcy judges, to hear, upon the consent of the parties, appeals that would otherwise go to the district courts. 28 U.S.C.A. § 158(b). The courts of appeals have jurisdiction of appeals from the appellate decisions of the district courts and the bankruptcy appellate panels. 28 U.S.C.A. § 158(d).

Because of technical flaws in the 1984 Act, there is some confusion about whether the courts of appeals have jurisdiction to hear direct appeals from decisions of bankruptcy judges. See Hubbard v. Fleet Mortgage Co., 810 F.2d 778 (8th Cir.1987); In re General Coffee Corp., 758 F.2d 1406 (11th Cir.1985) (finding no jurisdiction).

C. Jury Trial

KATCHEN v. LANDY
Supreme Court of the United States, 1966.
382 U.S. 323, 86 S.Ct. 467, 15 L.Ed.2d 391.

MR. JUSTICE WHITE delivered the opinion of the Court.

The disputed issue here is whether a bankruptcy court has summary jurisdiction to order the surrender of voidable preferences asserted and proved by the trustee in response to a claim filed by the creditor who received the preferences. The Court of Appeals held that the bankruptcy court had such summary jurisdiction. 336 F.2d 535. We affirm.

The corporate bankrupt began business on April 21, 1960, and borrowed $50,000 from two local banks. Petitioner, then an officer of the company, was an accommodation maker on the two corporate notes delivered to the banks. After the corporate bankrupt in this case suffered a disastrous fire, its funds and collections were placed in a "trust account" under the sole control of petitioner. From this account petitioner made two payments on one of the company notes on which he was an accommodation maker and one payment on the other. Bankruptcy followed within four months of these payments. Petitioner filed two claims in the proceeding, one for rent due him from the bankrupt and one for a payment on one of the notes made from his personal funds. The trustee responded with a petition asserting that the payments from the trust fund to the banks were voidable preferences and demanding judgment for the amount of the preferences . . .. Petitioner's objection to the summary jurisdiction of the referee was overruled, and judgment was rendered for the trustee . . .. Petitioner's claims were to be allowed only when and if the judgment was satisfied. The District Court sustained the referee. A divided Court of Appeals, sitting *en banc*, . . . affirmed the judgment for the amount of the voidable preferences . . .. We granted certiorari on the creditor's petition because of the diversity of views among the Courts of Appeals on the issue involved and the importance of the question in the administration of the bankruptcy laws. 380 U.S. 971, 85 S.Ct. 1328, 14 L.Ed.2d 268.

The crux of the dispute here concerns the mode of procedure for trying out the preference issue. The bankruptcy courts are expressly invested by statute with original jurisdiction to conduct proceedings under the Bankruptcy Act.[2] These courts are essentially courts of equity, and they characteristically proceed in summary fashion to deal with the assets of the bankrupt they are administering. The bankruptcy courts "have summary jurisdiction to adjudicate controversies relating to property over which they have actual or constructive possession." They also deal in a summary way with "matters of an administrative character, including questions between the bankrupt and his creditors, which are presented in the ordinary course of the administration of the bankrupt's estate." Taylor v. Voss, 271 U.S. 176, 181, 46 S.Ct. 461, 463, 70 L.Ed. 889; U. S. Fidelity & Guaranty Co. v. Bray, 225 U.S. 205, 218, 32 S.Ct. 620, 625, 56 L.Ed. 1055. This is elementary bankruptcy law which petitioner does not dispute.

But petitioner points out that if a creditor who has received a preference does not file a claim in the bankruptcy proceeding and holds the property he received under a substantial adverse claim, so that the property may not be deemed within the actual or constructive possession of the bankruptcy court, the trustee may recover the preference only by a plenary action under § 60 of the Act, 11 U.S.C. § 96 (1964 ed.), see Taubel-Scott-Kitzmiller Co. v. Fox, 264 U.S. 426, 44 S.Ct. 396; and in a plenary action in the federal courts the creditor could demand a jury trial, Schoenthal v. Irving Trust Co., 287 U.S. 92, 94–95, 53 S.Ct. 50, 51, 77 L.Ed. 185; Adams v. Champion, 294 U.S. 231, 234, 55 S.Ct. 399, 400, 79 L.Ed. 880; compare Buffum v. Peter Barceloux Co., 289 U.S. 227, 235–236, 53 S.Ct. 539, 542, 77 L.Ed. 1140. Petitioner contends the situation is the same when the creditor files a claim and the trustee not only objects to allowance of the claim but also demands surrender of the preference. This is so, petitioner argues, because the Bankruptcy Act does not confer summary jurisdiction on a bankruptcy court to order preferences surrendered and because, if it does, petitioner's rights under the Seventh Amendment of the Constitution are violated. We agree with neither contention. . . .

Our examination of the structure and purpose of the Bankruptcy Act and the provisions dealing with allowance of claims therefore leads us to conclude, and we so hold, that the Act does confer summary

2. Bankruptcy Act § 2a, 11 U.S.C.A § 11(a) (1964 ed.), provides:

"(a) The courts of the United States hereinbefore defined as courts of bankruptcy are created courts of bankruptcy and are invested, within their respective territorial limits as now established or as they may be hereafter changed, with such jurisdiction at law and in equity as will enable them to exercise original jurisdiction in proceedings under this title . . . .."

jurisdiction to compel a claimant to surrender preferences that under § 57g would require disallowance of the claim.   . . .

Petitioner contends, however, that this reading of the statute violates his Seventh Amendment right to a jury trial. But although petitioner might be entitled to a jury trial on the issue of preference if he presented no claim in the bankruptcy proceeding and awaited a federal plenary action by the trustee, Schoenthal v. Irving Trust Co., 287 U.S. 92, 53 S.Ct. 50, when the same issue arises as part of the process of allowance and disallowance of claims, it is triable in equity. The Bankruptcy Act, passed pursuant to the power given to Congress by Art. I, § 8, of the Constitution to establish uniform laws on the subject of bankruptcy, converts the creditor's legal claim into an equitable claim to a pro rata share of the *res*, Gardner v. State of New Jersey, 329 U.S. 565, 573–574, 67 S.Ct. 467, 471–472, a share which can neither be determined nor allowed until the creditor disgorges the alleged voidable preference he has already received. See Alexander v. Hillman, 296 U.S. 222, 242, 56 S.Ct. 204, 211, 80 L.Ed. 192. As bankruptcy courts have summary jurisdiction to adjudicate controversies relating to property over which they have actual or constructive possession, Thompson v. Magnolia Petroleum Co., 309 U.S. 478, 481, 60 S.Ct. 628, 629; Cline v. Kaplan, 323 U.S. 97, 98–99, 65 S.Ct. 155, 156; May v. Henderson, 268 U.S. 111, 115–116, 45 S.Ct. 456, 458; and as the proceedings of bankruptcy courts are inherently proceedings in equity, Local Loan Co. v. Hunt, 292 U.S. 234, 240, 54 S.Ct. 695, 697; Pepper v. Litton, 308 U.S. 295, 304, 60 S.Ct. 238, 244; there is no Seventh Amendment right to a jury trial for determination of objections to claims, including § 57g objections. As this Court has previously said in answering the argument that disputed claims must be tried before a jury:

> "But those who use this argument lose sight of the fundamental principle that the right of trial by jury, considered as an absolute right, does not extend to cases of equity jurisdiction. If it be conceded or clearly shown that a case belongs to this class, the trial of questions involved in it belongs to the court itself, no matter what may be its importance or complexity.
>
> .   .   .
>
> "So, in cases of bankruptcy, many incidental questions arise in the course of administering the bankrupt estate, which would ordinarily be pure cases at law, and in respect of their facts triable by jury, but, as belonging to the bankruptcy proceedings, they become cases over which the bankruptcy court, which acts as a court of equity, exercises exclusive control. Thus a claim of debt or damages against the bankrupt is investigated by chancery methods."

Barton v. Barbour, 104 U.S. 126, 133–134, 26 L.Ed. 672.   . . .

Petitioner's final reliance is on the doctrine of Beacon Theatres v. Westover, 359 U.S. 500, 79 S.Ct. 948, 3 L.Ed.2d 988, and Dairy Queen v. Wood, 369 U.S. 469, 82 S.Ct. 894, 8 L.Ed.2d 44 that "where both legal and equitable issues are presented in a single case, 'only under the most imperative circumstances, circumstances which in view of the flexible procedures of the Federal Rules we cannot now anticipate, can the right to a jury trial of legal issues be lost through prior determination of equitable claims.'"   369 U.S., at 472–473, 82 S.Ct., at 897.

The argument here is that the same issues—whether the creditor has received a preference and, if so, its amount—may be presented either as equitable issues in the bankruptcy court or as legal issues in a plenary suit and that the bankruptcy court should stay its own proceedings and direct the bankruptcy trustee to commence a plenary suit so as to preserve petitioner's right to a jury trial.   Unquestionably the bankruptcy court would have power to give such an instruction to the trustee, Thompson v. Magnolia Petroleum Co., 309 U.S. 478, 483–484, 60 S.Ct. 628, 630–631; see Bankruptcy Act § 2a(7), 11 U.S.C. § 11(a)(7) (1964 ed.), and some lower courts have required such a procedure, B. F. Avery & Sons Co. v. Davis, 192 F.2d 255 (C.A.5th Cir. 1951), cert. denied, 342 U.S. 945, 72 S.Ct. 559; Triangle Electric Co. v. Foutch, 40 F.2d 353 (C.A.8th Cir. 1930); see Katchen v. Landy, 336 F.2d 535, 543 (C.A.10th Cir. 1964) (Phillips, J., dissenting in part).   Nevertheless we think this argument must be rejected.

At the outset, we note that the *Dairy Queen* doctrine, if applicable at all, is applicable whether or not the trustee seeks affirmative relief. For, as we have said, determination of the preference issues in the equitable proceeding would in any case render unnecessary a trial in the plenary action because of the *res judicata* effect to which that determination would be entitled.   Thus petitioner's argument would require that in every case where a § 57g objection is interposed and a jury trial is demanded the proceedings on allowance of claims must be suspended and a plenary suit initiated, with all the delay and expense that course would entail.   Such a result is not consistent with the equitable purposes of the Bankruptcy Act nor with the rule of *Beacon Theatres* and *Dairy Queen*, which is itself an equitable doctrine, Beacon Theatres v. Westover, 359 U.S., at 509–510, 79 S.Ct., at 955–957.   In neither *Beacon Theatres* nor *Dairy Queen* was there involved a specific statutory scheme contemplating the prompt trial of a disputed claim without the intervention of a jury.   We think Congress intended the trustee's § 57g objection to be summarily determined; and to say that because the trustee could bring an independent suit against the creditor to recover his voidable preference, he is not entitled to have his statutory objection to the claim tried in the bankruptcy court in the normal manner is to dismember a scheme which Congress has prescribed.   See Alexander v. Hillman, 296 U.S. 222, 243, 56 S.Ct. 204, 211. Both *Beacon Theatres* and *Dairy Queen* recognize that there might be situations in which the Court could proceed to resolve the equitable claim first even though the results might be dispositive of the issues involved in the legal claim.   To implement congressional intent, we think it essential to hold that the bankruptcy court may summarily adjudicate the § 57g objection; and, as we have held above, the power to adjudicate the objection carries with it the power to order surrender of the preference.

Affirmed.

MR. JUSTICE BLACK and MR. JUSTICE DOUGLAS dissent for the reasons stated in the dissenting opinion of Judge Phillips in the Court of Appeals.

AMERICAN UNIVERSAL INSURANCE COMPANY v. PUGH

United States Court of Appeals, Ninth Circuit, 1987.
821 F.2d 1352.

Before ANDERSON, TANG and NOONAN, CIRCUIT JUDGES.

J. BLAINE ANDERSON, CIRCUIT JUDGE:

American Universal Insurance Company ("American") appeals from the district court's affirmance of the bankruptcy court's denial of its request for a jury trial. Joe and Joan Pugh (the "Pughs") cross-appeal from the district court's reversal of an award of attorney's fees in their favor by the bankruptcy court.

I. MAIN APPEAL

A. Facts

The Pughs operated a commercial fishing business. In November, 1982, they filed a petition for Chapter 11 bankruptcy. In June, 1983, the Pughs purchased from American a marine insurance policy in the amount of $400,000 covering one of their vessels. Four months later, the vessel sank. American paid the policy limits.

In February, 1984, American commenced an adversary proceeding in the Pughs' pending consolidated bankruptcy cases claiming that the Pughs had intentionally caused the sinking of the vessel in order to defraud American. American's complaint and amended complaint prayed for money had and received from American and to impose a constructive trust on the proceeds in the Pughs' possession.

In March, 1984, American timely filed a request for a jury trial in the adversary proceeding before the bankruptcy court. In May, 1984, the bankruptcy court, after a hearing, entered its memorandum opinion and order denying American's request for a jury trial. A motion for leave to appeal was denied. The adversary proceeding was tried to the court. In September, 1984, the bankruptcy court entered its judgment dismissing the action on its merits.

American filed a notice of appeal with the district court. In May, 1986, the district court affirmed the bankruptcy court and ruled that American was not entitled to a jury trial before the bankruptcy court. 72 B.R. 174 (Bkrtcy.D.Or.1986). American timely appealed to this court. We affirm.

B. Discussion

The single issue raised by American in its appeal is whether it was entitled to a jury trial in the adversary proceeding before the bankruptcy court.

In order to understand the problem and confusion of whether a bankruptcy court is empowered to determine the right to jury trial and empowered to conduct a jury trial, a cursory examination of the recent history of jury trials in bankruptcy courts is appropriate:

> In an attempt to resolve, among other things, the problems of summary and plenary jurisdiction, the Bankruptcy Reform Act of 1978 [§ 1480(a)] abolished those jurisdictional distinctions and authorized the bankruptcy court to conduct jury trials in cases and proceedings. [§ 1480(a)] did not enlarge or diminish the right to jury trial but only allowed a bankruptcy court to hear jury trials.

> On June 28, 1982, the Supreme Court held in Northern Pipeline Construction Company v. Marathon Pipe Line Co. (Marathon) 458 U.S. 50, [102 S.Ct. 2858, 73 L.Ed.2d 598] (1982) that the granting of Article III powers to the bankruptcy courts was an unconstitutional delegation of Article III powers. . . .

> The Emergency Rule of Reference promulgated by the Judicial Conference and adopted by the District Courts as a local rule, in response to *Marathon,* prohibited bankruptcy judges from conducting jury trials. No interpretative comments accompanied this rule nor were any reasons for this prohibition made apparent.

> On August 1, 1983, the new Bankruptcy Rules of Procedure became effective. The Bankruptcy Rules were recommended by the Judicial Conference of the United States and prescribed by the Supreme Court of the United States pursuant to Section 2075, Title 28, United States Code and therefore are accorded the force and effect of law. To add to the confusion over the issue of jury trials, Bankruptcy Rule 9015 sets forth detailed provisions for Bankruptcy Judges conducting Jury Trials. Rule 9015(b)(3) expressly vests the Bankruptcy Court with the power in Code cases to "determine whether there is a right to trial by jury of the issues for which a jury trial is demanded. . . ." [T]he bankruptcy courts have determined the issue of the right to jury trial under the Code and even while under the auspices of the Emergency Rule. See, e.g., Periera v. Checkmate Communications Co., 21 B.R. 402, 403 (D.E.D.N.Y. 1982); In re Newman, 14 B.R. 1014 (Bankr.S.D.N.Y.1981); Busey v. Fleming, 8 B.R. 746, 7 B.C.D. 252 (Bankr.N.D.Ga.1980).

> . . .

> The Bankruptcy Amendments and Federal Judgeship Act of 1984 was enacted July 10, 1984. There is no prohibition under the Amendments against jury trials being conducted by the bankruptcy court. The Amendments are silent on the right of the debtor, trustee, or creditors to jury trials in cases and proceedings. Title 28

U.S.C. § 1411(a) states "[T]his chapter and Title 11 do not affect any right to trial by jury that an individual has under applicable non-bankruptcy law with regard to a personal injury or wrongful death tort claim."

In re Rodgers & Sons, Inc., 48 B.R. 683, 685 (Bkrtcy.E.D.Okla.1985) (Footnotes omitted).

Prior to the passage of the Bankruptcy Amendments and Federal Judgeship Act of 1984 ("the Amendments"), the starting place for analysis of the right of a jury trial in bankruptcy court was § 1480(a), contained in the Bankruptcy Reform Act of 1978. There is some uncertainty over the fate of § 1480 since the Amendments failed to specifically repeal that section of the Reform Act. Various courts have held that § 1480 did not survive the Act of 1984; either it never became effective or it was repealed. Hauytin v. Grynberg, 52 B.R. 657, 660 (Bkrtcy.D.Colo.1985); In re Bokum Resources Corp., 49 B.R. 854, 867 (Bkrtcy.D.N.M.1985); In re O'Bannon, 49 B.R. 763, 766 (Bkrtcy. M.D.La.1985). Regardless, after *Marathon* was decided on June 28, 1982, § 1480 was in doubt.

The Bankruptcy Amendments and Federal Judgeship Act of 1984 provided that it would "not affect any right to trial by jury that an individual has under applicable nonbankruptcy law with regard to a personal injury or wrongful tort claim." 28 U.S.C. § 1411(a). This provision, however, did not apply to "cases" under the Bankruptcy Title that were pending on July 10, 1984 "or to proceedings arising in or related to such cases." Pub.L. 98–353 § 122. The Pughs filed their bankruptcy petition on November 2, 1982. American's proceeding against the Pughs does not fall within § 1411, both by reason of the nature of American's suit and by reason of the exception as to cases pending on July 10, 1984.

American requested a jury trial in March of 1984, after *Marathon* had placed § 1480 in doubt. As a consequence, the only rule, act, statute, or other controlling authority in effect at the times relevant to this case was Bankruptcy Rule 9015. The question, then, is whether under the provisions of this rule, the bankruptcy court erred in denying American's request for a jury trial.

At the outset, it is important to emphasize that there is a distinction between the power of a bankruptcy court to *conduct* a jury trial and the power of that court to determine whether there is a *right* to a jury trial. Much of the controversy, and most of the arguments raised by the Pughs, go to the power of the bankruptcy courts to *conduct* a jury trial. Because we find below that American is not entitled to a jury trial, we need not address this issue.

A bankruptcy court is an appropriate tribunal for determining whether there is a right to a trial by jury of issues for which a jury trial is demanded. B.R. 9015(b)(3); In re Energy Resources Co., Inc., 49 B.R. 278, 281 (Bkrtcy.D.Mass.1985). In deciding whether a litigant has the right to a jury trial in a bankruptcy proceeding, some courts continue to analyze whether the action in question would have been a summary proceeding (requiring no jury trial) or a plenary proceeding (requiring a jury trial). In re Energy Resources, 49 B.R. at 281; In re Portage Associates, 16 B.R. 445, 447 (Bkrtcy.N.D.Ohio 1982). This distinction was established under § 1480(a). The recent trend has been to abandon this summary/plenary distinction in favor of deciding whether a litigant is entitled to a jury trial based on the nature of the cause of action (i.e., is the cause of action one of law or equity?). In re Energy Resources, 49 B.R. at 281; In re Hinkley, 58 B.R. 339, 345 (Bkrtcy.S.D. Texas 1986); Hauytin, 52 B.R. at 660; In re Country Junction, Inc., 41 B.R. 425, 431 (Bkrtcy.W.D.Texas 1984), aff'd, 798 F.2d 1410 (5th Cir. 1986) (analyzing right to jury trial under both tests); In re First Intern. Services Corp., 37 B.R. 856, 859–60 (Bkrtcy.D.Conn.1984) (both tests used). We find the trend toward the law/equity test persuasive and hereby adopt that test.[2]

Under the law/equity test, the determination of entitlement to a jury trial depends on the nature of the issue to be tried rather than the character of the overall action. Hauytin, 52 B.R. at 661. Generally, three factors are applied in determining whether the nature of the claim is legal or equitable: "first, the pre-merger custom [of the separate law and equity courts] with reference to such questions; second, the remedy sought; and, third, the practical abilities and limitations of juries." Id. (quoting Ross v. Bernhard, 396 U.S. 531, 538 n. 10, 90 S.Ct. 733, 738 n. 10, 24 L.Ed.2d 729 (1970)).

Prior to the merger of law and equity, there were no bankruptcy courts, so there is no pre-merger custom to examine. However, " 'the proceedings of bankruptcy courts are inherently proceedings in equity.' " In re Country Junction, 41 B.R. at 429 (quoting Katchen v. Landy, 382 U.S. 323, 336–37, 86 S.Ct. 467, 476–77, 15 L.Ed.2d 391 (1966)).

American's amended complaint prayed for money had and received by the Pughs, for the imposition of a constructive trust upon all funds received, and for an accounting. The imposition of a constructive trust is purely an equitable remedy and equitable remedies are not triable of right by a jury. In re First Financial Group of Texas, Inc., 11 B.R. 67, 70 (Bkrtcy.S.D.Texas 1981). Moreover, an accounting is an equitable remedy. In re Energy Resources, 49 B.R. at 282.

American argues that because it is asking for monetary relief in the amount of $400,000, the remedy it requests is legal. Where monetary relief must necessarily be a part of the equitable remedy, the case remains equitable in nature. Whitlock v. Hause, 694 F.2d at 863; In re Energy Resources, 49 B.R. at 287. Even though American's complaint seeks monetary relief, the action is nonetheless equitable in nature because, "where a plaintiff seeks to recover monies alleged to be

2. Even if we were to decide this case under the summary/plenary test, American would not prevail. American's action is a summary action because it involves property (insurance proceeds) actually or constructively in the possession of the bankrupt. See Whitlock v. Hause, 694 F.2d 861, 862 (1st Cir.1982).

wrongfully withheld, the basis for such an action is wholly equitable."
In re Energy Resources, 49 B.R. at 282. For example, "where a cause of
action seeking monetary relief is integral to the equitable relief sought,
such as the imposition of a constructive trust . . . the action lies in
equity with no right of jury trial." Matter of Paula Saker & Co., 37
B.R. 802, 808 (Bkrtcy.S.D.N.Y.1984). In the case at bar, American is
not asking for $400,000 in damages. Rather, it is asking for the return
of money wrongfully received and held and it asks the court to accomplish this through an equitable constructive trust. American's action is
one in equity in which it is not entitled to a jury trial. The district
court did not err in affirming the bankruptcy court's denial of American's request for a jury trial. . . .

Notes & Questions

1. *Katchen v. Landy and the New Bankruptcy Law.* Assume the
trustee is seeking to recover as a preference property transferred by the
debtor to a creditor. The property is in the possession of the creditor
and the creditor has no claim against the debtor. Where may the
trustee's action against the creditor be brought? Is the creditor entitled to a jury trial?

2. *The Shift from § 1480 to § 1411.* Section 1480(a), the provision
technically at issue in *American Universal*, states:

(a) Except as provided in subsection (b) of this section, this chapter
and title 11 do not affect any right to trial by jury, in a case under
title 11 or in a proceeding arising in or related to a case under title
11, that is provided by any statute in effect on September 30, 1979.

Subsection (b) deals with the right to trial by jury in an involuntary
case under 11 U.S.C.A. § 303. Does the shift in phrasing from
§ 1480(a) to § 1411(a) affect the scope of the right to trial by jury in
bankruptcy cases?

3. *Property Not in the Possession of the Debtor.* Suppose American
had not paid the Pughs' insurance claim and that the Pughs were suing
American for breach of the insurance contract. Would American or
the Pughs be entitled to a jury trial under the equity test? under the
summary/plenary test? Is a jury trial required whenever a debtor
seeks to enforce contractual rights? Is the *American Universal* court
correct to ignore *Katchen v. Landy?*

INDEX

955

958

INDEX
References are to Pages

CONSTITUTIONAL LIMITATIONS—Cont'd
Repossession, 67–75.

CONSUMER GOODS
After-acquired property, 46, 75.
Classification, 29.
Filing after interstate move, 171.
Sale by consumer, 78.

CONSUMERS
See also Consumer Goods; Fair Credit
Reporting Act; Fair Debt Collection
Practices Act.
Special protection upon default, 75.
Structure of protective legislation, 256–
258.
Wage garnishment,
See Wages.

CONTINGENT CLAIMS, 597

CONTRACTS
See Executory Contracts.

**CONVERSION OF BANKRUPTCY PRO-
CEEDINGS**, 455

CORE PROCEEDINGS, 915–932, 940

CRAM DOWN, 866, 872–879

CREDIT REPORTING
See Fair Credit Reporting Act.

CREDIT SALE, 133–148

CREDITORS' COMMITTEES, 814–815

CURE, 792–798

CUSTODIAN, 509

DEBT COLLECTION
Enforcement of judgments, 345–406.
Fair Credit Reporting Act, 218–244.
Fair Debt Collection Practices Act, 244–
258.
Fraudulent Conveyances,
See Fraudulent Conveyances.
Provisional remedies, 259–279.

DEBT POOLING, 435–436

DEBTOR
Definition, 12, 116–119.
Discriminatory treatment of, 677–686.
Meaning in purchase money transaction,
116–119.

DEFAULT
Acceleration, 599–601.
Commercially reasonable sale, 67–75.
Constitutionality of remedies, 74.
Cure in Chapter 13, pp. 792–798.
Deficiency judgment, 67–75.

DEFAULT—Cont'd
Events of, form, 22–23.
Improper procedure by secured party, 67–
75.
Levy as, 381.
Notice of sale, 67–75.
Redemption of collateral, 647–652.
Repossession of collateral, 67–75.
Retention of collateral, 67–75.
Reversing acceleration, 792–798, 866–870.
Sale of collateral, 67–75.
Waiver, 23.

DEPOSIT ACCOUNTS
As proceeds, 42–46, 147, 745–750.
Perfection of security interest, 209–217.
Setoff, 217.

DESCRIPTION OF COLLATERAL, 24–28

DISCHARGE
Alimony and child support, 675.
Assignment for the benefit of creditors,
451–452.
Chapter 7, pp. 644–675.
Chapter 11, pp. 879.
Chapter 13, pp. 644, 798–801.
Claims dischargeable, 657–663.
Credit binges, 664.
Discrimination, 677–686.
Effect on liens, 644–657, 798–802.
Exceptions to, 493–502, 663–675.
Fraud or defalcation, 666–675.
Fraudulent or reckless misrepresentation,
664–665.
Fraudulent transfer, 493–502.
Reaffirmation, 675–677.
Relation to doctrine of impossibility, 634–
637, 643.
Relation to priority, 674.
Taxes, 664.
Trusts, 666–675.
Waivability, 637–643.
Written misrepresentations, 664–665.

DISCOUNT RATE, 801–802, 851–855, 877–
878

DISCRIMINATION
See also Classification.
Chapter 13, pp. 784–792.
Discharge debtor, 677–686.

DISPOSABLE INCOME, 781–782

DISPUTED CLAIMS, 462–467

DISTRIBUTION IN BANKRUPTCY
Claims,
See Claims in Bankruptcy.
Priority,
See Priority in Bankruptcy.

DISTRICT COURTS, 898–932

†

0–88277–643–6